Tolley's
Value Added Tax
1999–2000

First Edition

by
Robert Wareham BSc (Econ) FCA
and
Alan Dolton MA (Oxon)

Tolley Publishing

A part of Reed Elsevier (UK) Limited

Published by Tolley
2 Addiscombe Road
Croydon CR9 5AF England
0181–686 9141

Printed in Great Britain by The Bath Press, Bath

ISBN 0 75450 113–2

About This Book

Value added tax commenced in the United Kingdom on 1 April 1973. Since that date a mass of legislation, Orders, Regulations, law cases and explanatory notices and leaflets support a system which has become increasingly complex. Tolley's Value Added Tax seeks to aid practitioners and traders by being their first point of reference on this tax.

This edition includes the current law and practice of value added tax up to 31 December 1998. Relevant statutory instruments, tribunal, and court cases, C & E notices, leaflets, business briefs and news releases are also covered.

Chapters in this book are in alphabetical order for ease of reference to a particular subject and cross-references, an index and a table of statutes provide further ways of quickly finding the matter required.

Comments on this annual publication and suggestions for improvements are always welcomed.

TOLLEY PUBLISHING

Contents

Abbreviations and References

Court cases. Citation where appropriate is of Simon's Tax Cases and is preceded by the Court and year of the decision (if different from the citation).

Tribunals cases. Citation is either by reference to a Value Added Tax Tribunal Report (VATTR) (e.g. *(1980) VATTR 42*) or Value Added Tax and Duties Report (VATDR) published by H.M. Stationery Office or the number assigned to the decision by the VAT Tribunals Headquarters (e.g. *(6575)*). In all tribunal cases only the appellant or applicant is named.

OTHER TOLLEY PUBLICATIONS

Retention of Tolley's. Subscribers should preserve each year's edition of Tolley's VAT because the necessity of including considerable new material each year involves the omission of older out-of-date material.

Tolley's VAT Cases 1999 contains summaries of over 3,000 VAT tribunal decisions and court decisions from 1973 to 1 January 1999. The summaries are in chapters arranged alphabetically by subject, with index and tables for quick reference to the matter required. £81.95.

Tolley's VAT Planning 1998/99 published in November 1998 highlights the major financial drawbacks that can result by underestimating the importance of VAT and gives practical advice on achieving the optimum tax position. £56.95.

Tolley's Practical VAT is an eight page, monthly newsletter containing news, articles and items of practical use to all involved with VAT. By subscription only.

Tolley's Income Tax 1998/99 is a comprehensive detailed guide to income tax with relevant case law to the date of Royal Assent of the Finance Act 1998. £54.95.

Tolley's Corporation Tax 1998/99 is the companion publication to Tolley's Income Tax and sets out the application of the taxing statutes to the income and chargeable gains of companies to the date of Royal Assent of the Finance Act 1998. £54.95.

Tolley's Capital Gains Tax 1998/99 is a detailed guide to the statutes and case law to the date of Royal Assent of the Finance Act 1998. In the same alphabetical format as Tolley's Income Tax and Tolley's Corporation Tax. £54.95.

Tolley's Inheritance Tax 1998/99 is a detailed guide to the inheritance tax provisions to the date of Royal Assent of the Finance Act 1998. £54.95.

Tolley's Tax Computations 1998/99 contains copious worked examples covering income tax, corporation tax, capital gains tax, inheritance tax and value added tax. £44.95.

BUTTERWORTHS PUBLICATIONS

De Voil Indirect Tax Service contains text of all relevant statutes, statutory instruments, EC Directives and Regulations, C & E notices and leaflets and press releases, together with a commentary cross-referenced to source material and case digests. Looseleaf updated monthly. POA.

1   Introduction and General Principles

1.1   VAT LEGISLATION AND INTERPRETATION

Value added tax (VAT) was introduced in the UK on 1 April 1973 by the *Finance Act 1972*. Successive Finance Acts have made amendments to the law which has also been consolidated, first by the *Value Added Tax Act 1983* (*VATA 1983*) and subsequently by the *Value Added Tax Act 1994* (*VATA 1994*) with effect from 1 September 1994.

The Acts provide the framework of the tax but much of the detail is to be found in statutory instruments, either in the form of *Orders* made by the Treasury or *Regulations* made by Customs and Excise (C & E).

1.2   European Community legislation

The overriding law on VAT throughout the European Community (EC) is in the EC *Directives*, notably the *6th VAT Directive*. The form and method of compliance is left to individual EC countries but, where any of the provisions are mandatory, EC law takes precedence if there are any inconsistencies with national law. See EUROPEAN COMMUNITY LEGISLATION (22) for further details.

1.3   Interpretation of the law by C & E

C & E issue explanatory notices on VAT, together with VAT notes, news releases and business briefs. These explain how C & E interpret the law. **With certain exceptions, these are not part of the law and this should be borne in mind where the text indicates a notice or leaflet, etc. as source material.**

If a taxable person disagrees with the interpretation, he has a right of appeal, in certain cases, to a VAT tribunal. See APPEALS (5).

1.4   GENERAL PRINCIPLES OF VAT

VAT is a tax on consumer expenditure and is collected on business transactions and imports.

The basic principle is to charge VAT at each stage in the supply of standard-rated goods and services (output tax). If the customer is registered for VAT and uses the supplies for business purposes, he will receive credit for this VAT (input tax). The broad effect is that businesses are not affected and VAT is actually borne by the final consumer.

1.5   Scope of VAT

A transaction is within the scope of UK VAT if all the following conditions are met.

- *It is a supply of goods or services.* The term 'supply' is not defined in the legislation but is broadly interpreted. See 64.2 SUPPLY for the meaning of supply and 64.3 and 64.4 SUPPLY for supplies of goods and services respectively. Certain transactions, although supplies, are regarded as supplies of neither goods nor services and are outside the scope of UK VAT. See 64.5 SUPPLY.

- *It takes place in the UK.*

- *It is made by a taxable person.* A taxable person is an individual, firm or company, etc. which is registered for VAT or which is required to register for VAT but has failed to do so. See 1.13 below.

1

1.6 Introduction and General Principles

- *It is made in the course or furtherance of any business carried on by that person.* See 8.1 to 8.3 BUSINESS for the interpretation of 'business'.

A transaction which does not meet all of the above conditions is outside the scope of UK VAT.

1.6 Place of supply

To be within the charge to UK VAT, a supply must be made in the UK. Supplies made outside the UK are outside the scope of UK VAT (although they may be liable to VAT in another country).

Separate rules apply for determining the place of supply of goods and services. See 64.8 and 64.18 SUPPLY for the place of supply of goods and services respectively.

1.7 Time of supply (tax point)

The time at which a supply of goods is treated as taking place is called the tax point. VAT must normally be accounted for in the prescribed accounting period (see 1.18 below) in which the tax point occurs and at the rate of VAT (see 1.11 below) in force at that time. Small businesses can, however, account for VAT on the basis of cash paid and received (see 1.21 below).

Basic tax point. The basic tax point for a supply of goods is the date the goods are removed i.e. sent to, or taken by, the customer. If the goods are not removed, it is the date they are made available for his use.

The basic tax point for a supply of services is the date the services are performed.

Actual tax points. In the case of both goods and services, where a VAT invoice is raised or payment is made *before* the basic tax point, there is an earlier actual tax point at the time the invoice is issued or payment received, whichever occurs first.

There is also generally an actual tax point where a VAT invoice is issued within 14 days *after* the basic tax point. This overrides the basic tax point but not the actual tax point created by the issue of an invoice or payment before the basic tax point.

There are also special provisions for particular supplies of goods and services.

For further details see 64.32–64.58 SUPPLY.

1.8 Value of supply

The value of a supply is the value on which VAT is due. The amount of VAT is then the value multiplied by the VAT rate (see 1.11 below).

The value of a supply normally depends upon what is given in exchange for the supply, i.e. the consideration. If this is wholly in money, the value will be based on that amount. If not, the value is the monetary equivalent of the consideration.

There are special rules relating to discounts offered, transactions between connected persons and values expressed in foreign currencies. Imports (see 1.14 below) and acquisitions from other EC countries (see 1.16 below) also have their own valuation rules.

See VALUATION (69) for further details.

1.9 Output tax

Output tax is the VAT due on taxable supplies and is normally the liability of the person making the supply. In addition to straightforward business transactions, output tax may also be due on business gifts and private use of own goods and services.

A particular supply may be complicated by being a mixed supply where a single inclusive price is charged for a number of separate supplies. Where these supplies are taxable at different rates, a fair and justifiable apportionment of the total price must be made. See OUTPUT TAX (47) for further details.

Special schemes for retailers. Traders registered for VAT normally issue an invoice for each sale made in order to have the necessary records to calculate output tax. As this may be difficult or impossible where goods are sold directly to the public, special schemes are available for use by retailers only. See RETAIL SCHEMES (60) for further details.

Second-hand goods. There are special provisions for second-hand goods. Subject to certain conditions being satisfied, under the Margin Scheme VAT is only chargeable on the amount by which the selling price of a particular item exceeds the price paid when it was obtained. The scheme extends to almost the full range of second-hand goods. There is also a Global Accounting Scheme which is a simplified scheme for VAT on low value, bulk volume second-hand goods. Under this scheme, VAT is accounted for on the difference between the total purchases and sales of eligible goods in each VAT period rather than on an item by item basis. See SECOND-HAND GOODS (61) for further details.

Flat-rate scheme for farmers. Farmers who are certified under the scheme do not have to account for VAT on sales of goods and services within designated activities but are not able to recover input tax incurred on purchases. To compensate for this, farmers in the scheme may charge (and retain) a fixed flat-rate addition of 4% on top of the sale price. The customer can recover the addition as if it were VAT. See 63.15 to 63.20 SPECIAL SCHEMES for further details.

1.10   Input tax

A taxable person is entitled to reclaim input tax suffered on goods and services supplied to him, imports from outside the EC (see 1.14 below) and acquisition of goods from other EC countries (see 1.16 below) provided that the input tax relates to

- standard-rated or zero-rated business supplies made by him; or

- supplies made by him which are outside the scope of UK VAT but which would have been standard-rated or zero-rated if made in the UK; or

- certain supplies by him of exempt insurance and financial services to persons belonging outside the EC.

VAT cannot be recovered on goods and services which are not used for business purposes (e.g. for private use). Where goods are used partly for business and partly for non-business purposes, the VAT incurred is normally apportioned.

VAT incurred on a number of items is non-deductible. These include motor cars (with certain exceptions), business entertainment, goods sold under one of the second-hand schemes and certain articles installed in buildings by builders.

Special rules also apply to input tax incurred before registration for VAT and after deregistration.

See INPUT TAX (35) for further details.

1.11   VAT rates

There are currently two main rates of VAT, a standard rate of 17½% and a zero rate. See ZERO-RATED SUPPLIES (72) and supporting chapters for goods and services which are currently zero-rated.

1.12   Introduction and General Principles

The effect of a supply being zero-rated is as follows.

* The amount of VAT on the supply is nil but it is still a taxable supply.

* As a taxable supply, it must be taken into account in determining whether registration is required (see 1.13 below).

* Input tax may be reclaimed subject to the same rules as for standard-rated supplies.

* Where a supply could be either zero-rated or exempt (see 1.12 below), zero-rating takes priority.

A reduced rate of 5% applies to VAT on fuel and power for domestic and certain other qualifying uses. See FUEL AND POWER (29).

1.12   Exempt supplies

Certain supplies are exempt from VAT. See EXEMPT SUPPLIES (24) and supporting chapters. This means that no VAT is chargeable but, unlike zero-rated supplies, related input tax is not recoverable.

Where a person makes both taxable supplies and exempt supplies, he is partially exempt and may or may not be able to recover all his input tax. All input tax directly attributable to taxable supplies can be reclaimed but none of the input tax directly attributable to exempt supplies (subject to a *de minimis* limit). Special rules then apply to work out how much input tax can be reclaimed on general overheads, etc. See PARTIAL EXEMPTION (49).

1.13   Registration

Where a person is in business and making taxable supplies, the value of these supplies is his taxable turnover. If, at the end of any month,

* taxable turnover in the year then ended has exceeded a specified limit, or

* there are reasonable grounds for believing that the value of taxable supplies in the next 30 days will exceed a specified limit,

that person normally becomes a taxable person and must notify C & E of his liability to register for VAT. There are financial penalties for failing to do so. Where, however, only zero-rated supplies are made, C & E have a discretion to exempt a person from registration.

Even if taxable turnover is below the specified limit, a person who makes taxable business supplies can request voluntary registration.

A person who is registered for VAT ceases to be liable to be registered and can apply to be deregistered if the VAT-exclusive value of supplies in the next twelve months will not exceed a specified limit.

See 59.1 to 59.10 REGISTRATION for further details including how to apply for registration and deregistration.

See also

* 8.5 BUSINESS for anti-avoidance measures to combat business splitting and the conditions for the separation of a previously single business into independent parts for registration purposes;

* 31.1 to 31.5 GROUPS OF COMPANIES for group registration;

* 48.1 to 48.4 OVERSEAS TRADERS for registration by overseas traders; and

- 59.30 REGISTRATION for divisional registration by companies.

Even where there is no liability to register for VAT in respect of UK supplies of goods or services, a liability may arise in respect of

- 'distance selling' to non-taxable persons in the UK by suppliers in other EC countries (see 59.11 to 59.17 REGISTRATION); or

- acquisitions of goods in the UK from other EC countries (see 59.18 to 59.25 REGISTRATION).

1.14   Imports

Unless special relief applies, VAT is charged and payable on the importation of goods into the UK from outside the EC. The rate of VAT is the same as if the goods had been supplied in the UK.

Unless the goods are placed under customs or excise warehousing or certain customs arrangements (e.g. free zones, inward processing relief or Community Transit arrangements) any VAT due must normally either be paid at the time of importation or deferred with any duty if the importer or his agent are approved for deferment. VAT paid on the importation of goods can be claimed as input tax, subject to the normal rules.

See IMPORTS (34) for further details.

1.15   Exports

Provided various conditions are met, goods exported outside the EC are zero-rated. See EXPORTS (25) for further details.

1.16   Transactions with other EC countries

The concepts of 'imports' and 'exports' of goods apply only to transactions with countries outside the EC. For intra-EC movements of goods, the terms 'acquisitions' and 'supplies' are used. It is no longer necessary to make an import declaration on an acquisition of goods in the UK from another EC country or to pay VAT at the frontier.

Supplies of goods to a customer registered for VAT in another EC country can be zero-rated provided certain conditions are met. These include obtaining the customer's VAT registration number and showing it on the VAT invoice. The customer then accounts for VAT at the appropriate rate on the goods in the EC country of destination. If the conditions cannot be met, VAT must be charged in the country of origin at the rate applicable to the goods in that country.

VAT must also be charged on supplies of goods to non-registered customers in other EC countries. Where, however, the supplier is also responsible for the delivery of the goods, once the value of such 'distance' sales to any particular EC country exceeds an annual threshold set by that country, the supplier is automatically liable to register for VAT in that other country. VAT on any further sales is then due in the EC country of destination.

Special rules apply to transfers of own goods between EC countries, goods installed or assembled at the customer's premises, new means of transport and goods subject to excise duty purchased by non-taxable persons. There are also special rules for 'triangulation' i.e. where a chain of supplies of goods involves three parties and, instead of goods physically passing from one party to the next, they are delivered from the first party to the last party in the chain.

1.17 Introduction and General Principles

See EUROPEAN COMMUNITY: SINGLE MARKET (23) for further details. Note that the rules are only intended to be transitional until a system for taxing trade between EC countries in the country of origin can be decided on.

1.17 Invoices

A registered taxable person must issue a VAT invoice where he makes a standard-rated supply to another taxable person in the UK or a standard or zero-rated supply to a person in another EC country.

See INVOICES (40) for further details including the particulars required to be shown on the invoice and special invoices which may be issued by retailers and cash and carry wholesalers.

1.18 Returns and payment of VAT

Every taxable person must keep a VAT account summarising the output tax and input tax for each prescribed accounting period. See 57.12 RECORDS. A prescribed accounting period is normally three months but a one-month period is also allowed, particularly where input tax is likely to exceed output tax on a regular basis.

The information in the VAT account, plus certain statistical information, must then be shown on a VAT return for that period. The return must be sent to C & E, and any VAT due to C & E paid, no later than one month after the end of the period. The due date for payment will normally be extended by seven days where payment is made by credit transfer. Certain large VAT payers must make monthly payments on account.

See ACCOUNTING PERIODS AND RETURNS (2) and 51.1 to 51.4 PAYMENT OF VAT for further details.

Annual accounting. Smaller businesses with turnover below an annual limit (currently £300,000) may apply to join the annual accounting scheme. This allows them to complete one VAT return each year. Depending upon the level of turnover, quarterly or monthly interim payments on account are required (based on an estimate of the amount of VAT due) although some smaller businesses are exempt from this requirement. The annual VAT return must be completed and sent to C & E, with any balancing payment, within two months of the end of the annual VAT accounting period. See 63.9 to 63.14 SPECIAL SCHEMES for further details.

1.19 Records

Every taxable person must keep such records as C & E require. Specifically, these include business and accounting records, the VAT account (see 1.18 above), copies of all VAT invoices and credit notes issued and received, and documentation relating to imports, exports, acquisitions of goods from other EC countries and goods dispatched to other EC countries. All such records must be kept for six years unless C & E agree to a shorter period.

See RECORDS (57) for further details.

1.20 Bad debts

VAT is normally due by reference to the tax point (see 1.7 above). The supplier must therefore account to C & E for the VAT even if the debt, including the VAT, is not paid. By way of relief, VAT can be reclaimed where a debt has been written off and six months has elapsed from the date payment is due. See BAD DEBT RELIEF (7).

The problem of VAT on bad debts can also be removed by using the cash accounting system (see 1.21 below).

1.21   Cash accounting

Provided turnover is below an annual limit (currently £350,000), a taxable person may, subject to conditions, account for and pay VAT on the basis of cash or other consideration paid and received. The main advantages of the scheme are automatic bad debt relief and the deferral of the time for payment of VAT where extended credit is given. See 63.2 to 63.8 SPECIAL SCHEMES for further details.

1.22   Assessments

C & E are given powers to raise an assessment where VAT returns have not been made or it appears to them that returns are incomplete or incorrect. The assessment must normally be made within two years from the end of the return period in question or, if later, within one year of the facts on which the assessment is based coming to their knowledge. An assessment cannot be raised more than three years after the end of the return period except in cases of fraud when the period is extended to 20 years. Where the taxable person has died, an assessment cannot be made more than three years after death or relate to a period more than three years before death.

See ASSESSMENTS (6) for further details.

1.23   Interest and penalties

Interest is chargeable in certain circumstances where VAT has been underdeclared or overclaimed. See 51.5 PAYMENT OF VAT. On the other hand, repayment supplement is due where C & E do not make a repayment on time and interest can be paid to the taxpayer where VAT has been overpaid or underclaimed as a result of error by C & E. See 51.10 and 51.11 PAYMENT OF VAT.

There is an extensive range of criminal and civil penalties including the following.

Offence	Maximum penalty
Criminal	
Fraudulent evasion of VAT	Unlimited fine or 7 years imprisonment
Producing false documents	Unlimited fine or 7 years imprisonment
Civil	
Evasion of VAT	Amount of VAT evaded
Misdeclaration or neglect	15% of the VAT which would have been lost
Repeated misdeclarations	15% of the VAT which would have been lost
Failure to register	15% of the VAT which would have been due
Failure to keep records	£500
Default surcharge	15% of the unpaid VAT

See PENALTIES (52) for further details of these and other penalties. Liability for certain civil penalties can be avoided where there is reasonable excuse for conduct and can be mitigated by C & E or a VAT tribunal.

1.24   Appeals

An appeal against a decision of C & E on certain matters may be made to a VAT and Duties tribunal and from there, on a point of law, to the High Court (Court of Session in Scotland) and continued up to the House of Lords under normal procedure. The matters on which an appeal to a tribunal may be made are restricted and certain conditions must be complied with. Notably, unless C & E agree otherwise, the appellant must have made all the returns he is required to make and paid over the VAT due according to those returns. Notice of the appeal must be served within 30 days of the disputed decision.

See APPEALS (5) for further details.

2   Accounting Periods and Returns

Cross-references. See 51 PAYMENT OF VAT ; 52 PENALTIES ; 57 RECORDS ; 63.9 SPECIAL SCHEMES for annual VAT returns.

De Voil Indirect Tax Service. See V5.101–108.

The contents of this chapter are as follows.

2.1   MAKING RETURNS

A taxable person must account for and pay VAT by reference to prescribed accounting periods. For this purpose, he must make a return to C & E, not later than the last day of the month following the end of the return period, showing the amount of VAT payable by or to him and containing full information in respect of other matters specified in the return. [*VATA 1994, s 25(1); SI 1995/2518, Reg 25(1)*].

2.2   ACCOUNTING PERIODS

Subject to the exceptions below, returns must be completed for three-monthly periods ending on the dates notified in the certificate of registration (or otherwise). [*SI 1995/2518, Reg 25(1)*].

In order to spread the flow of returns over the year, taxable persons are allocated to one of the three groups of prescribed accounting periods ('VAT periods') as follows.

• Three month periods ending on 30 June, 30 September, 31 December and 31 March.

• Three month periods ending on 31 July, 31 October, 31 January and 30 April.

• Three month periods ending on 31 August, 30 November, 28 February and 31 May.

(C & E Notice 700, para 9.4).

A taxable person who was, or is, required to be registered (but has not done so) will, unless C & E otherwise allow, be allocated to the first group.

Exceptions.

(*a*) **Annual returns.** See 63.9 SPECIAL SCHEMES.

(*b*) **Monthly returns.** C & E may allow or direct a person to complete returns for periods of one month and to submit these within one month of the period to which they relate. [*SI 1995/2518, Reg 25(1)(a)*]. If repayments are expected to be received (e.g. because most of the outputs are zero-rated) this method of accounting is advantageous. Where monthly VAT returns are prepared and the business changes from receiving repayments to making payment of VAT, it may have to change to three-monthly VAT periods. (C & E Notice 700, para 9.4).

2.3 Accounting Periods and Returns

(c) **The first return period** commences on the effective date on which the taxable person was, or should have been, registered. [*SI 1995/2518, Reg 25(1)(b)*].

(d) **C & E may vary the length of any period** or the date on which any return is to be submitted. This applies whether or not the varied period has ended. [*SI 1995/2518, Reg 25(1)(c)*]. There is no appeal against their decision to the VAT tribunal under *VATA 1994, s 83(a)* (*Punchwell Ltd, [1981] VATTR 93 (1085); Selected Growers Ltd (10)*).

In particular:

- Application may be made to the VAT office (quoting registration number and dates) to have VAT periods corresponding with the financial year of the business.

- Where there is a new registration either because of a transfer of a going concern or a change in circumstances of a registered business (see 59.29 and 59.7 REGISTRATION respectively) application can be made to retain the VAT periods of the previous registration.

- Special consideration will also be given, **where accounting systems are not based on calendar months,** to arrangements for VAT periods to fit in with the particular system. For example, quarterly VAT periods ending within 14 days of the end of the standard period *or* monthly VAT periods ending within 7 days of the end of the calendar month (14 days for a four-weekly accounting cycle) are acceptable.

- Any other arrangement will be specially considered.

(C & E Notice 700, para 9.4).

(e) **Where control of the assets of any registered person passes** to a trustee in bankruptcy, administrative receiver, liquidator or person otherwise acting in a representative capacity, the current prescribed accounting period in which the date of the receiving order, appointment of administrative receiver or provisional liquidator or winding up order etc. (the '*relevant date*') occurs is divided into two periods. The first period ends on the day prior to the relevant date and the appropriate return must be submitted by the last day of the following month. The second period commences on the relevant date and ends (and all subsequent periods end) on the normal last day for the prescribed accounting periods. [*SI 1995/2518, Reg 25(3)*].

(f) **Final return.** Any person who

- ceases to be liable to be registered, or

- ceases to be entitled to be registered under *VATA 1994, 1 Sch 9* (see 59.2 REGISTRATION) or *VATA 1994, 1 Sch 10* (overseas traders not making taxable supplies in the UK, see 48.4 OVERSEAS TRADERS)

must submit a final return on Form VAT 193 *unless* the registration is allocated to the purchaser on the transfer of a business as a going concern (see 59.29 REGISTRATION). Unless C & E allow otherwise, the return must contain full information of the matters specified in the form and a declaration, signed by the taxpayer, that the return is true and complete. The return must be furnished by a person who was or is registered within one month of the effective date for cancellation of registration and by any other person within one month of the date on which he ceases to be liable to be registered. [*SI 1995/2518, Reg 25(4)*].

2.3 VAT RETURNS

The prescribed forms are

- Form VAT 193 in the circumstances under 2.2(f) above; and
- Form VAT 100 for use in all other cases.

2.4   **ESTIMATED RETURNS**

Where C & E are satisfied that a person is not able to account for the exact amount of output tax chargeable or claim the exact amount of input tax to be deducted in any prescribed accounting period, that person may estimate a part of his output tax or input tax for that period provided

- the estimate is adjusted and exactly accounted for in the next prescribed accounting period; or

- if the exact amount is still not known and C & E are satisfied that it could not with due diligence be ascertained, the estimate is adjusted in the next but one prescribed accounting period.

[SI 1995/2518, Regs 28, 29(3)].

Permission for estimated returns must be obtained in advance. If the estimated return is submitted, and the VAT shown paid, by the due date, the taxpayer will not be in default for the purposes of the default surcharge provisions (see 52.15 PENALTIES). Permission will still be considered after the due date has passed, but it will not affect any default which has already been recorded. (C & E Notice 700, para 9.6(d)).

Local authorities. See 43.5 LOCAL AUTHORITIES AND STATUTORY BODIES for special estimation schemes for local authorities.

De Voil Indirect Tax Service. See V3.505.

2.5   **COMPLETION OF RETURN FORM 100**

The procedure outlined in 2.6 to 2.16 below should be adopted for the completion of return Form 100. [SI 1995/2518, Reg 39].

(C & E Leaflet 700/12/95).

2.6   **Box 1**

Enter the total VAT due on sales and other outputs for the prescribed accounting period for which the return is submitted.

In addition to VAT on sales and other taxable business income in the period, VAT is also due on the following.

- Supplies to staff
- Sales of business assets
- Road fuel used for private motoring (including scale charges)
- Hire or loan of goods to another person
- Postal imports (other than Datapost) with a value of £2,000 or less
- Imported services on which VAT must be accounted for under the 'reverse charge' procedure (see 39.4 INTERNATIONAL SERVICES)
- Purchases of gold subject to the special accounting scheme (see 30.4 GOLD AND PRECIOUS METALS)
- Gifts of goods costing more than £15 (excluding VAT)

- The full value of goods sold where something has been taken in part exchange
- Goods taken out of the business for own use
- Self-supplies
- Supplies of goods to unregistered customers in other EC countries

Any VAT on credit notes issued to customers during the period should be deducted. If for this or any other reason a minus figure needs to be entered in Box 1, it should be shown in brackets.

Errors in output tax in earlier periods may be entered provided the net effect of all earlier errors in input tax and output tax discovered in the period of the return does not exceed £2,000 (see 57.11 RECORDS).

For sales under the cash accounting scheme (see 63.2 SPECIAL SCHEMES) this box should be completed on the basis of payments received and *not* invoices issued.

2.7 Box 2

Enter VAT due on acquisitions from other EC countries (see 23.3 EUROPEAN COMMUNITY: SINGLE MARKET). Errors in VAT on acquisitions in earlier periods may be entered provided the net effect of all earlier errors in input tax and output tax discovered in the period of the return does not exceed £2,000 (see 57.11 RECORDS). If for any reason a minus figure needs to be entered in Box 2, it should be shown in brackets.

2.8 Box 3

Insert total of Boxes 1 and 2 i.e. total output tax.

2.9 Box 4

Enter VAT reclaimed in the period on purchases and other inputs, i.e. the aggregate of all entries in the VAT allowable portion of the VAT account (see 57.12 RECORDS) for the prescribed accounting period for which the return is furnished. This includes VAT on imports and removals from C & E warehouse or from a free zone, and VAT deductible on acquisitions of goods from other EC countries and services under the 'reverse charge' procedure. It excludes VAT on the following.

- Motor cars (other than taxis, driving school and self-drive hire cars or cars where there is no use for private motoring)
- Business entertainment
- Goods bought under one of the schemes for SECOND-HAND GOODS (61)
- Purchases for purely private or personal use
- Purchases for non-business activities
- Accommodation for directors of limited companies

Any VAT on credit notes issued by suppliers during the period should be deducted.

Errors in input tax in earlier periods may be entered provided the net effect of all earlier errors in input tax and output tax discovered in the period of the return does not exceed £2,000 (see 57.11 RECORDS).

For purchases under the cash accounting scheme (see 63.2 SPECIAL SCHEMES) this box should be completed on the basis of payments made and *not* invoices received.

Also use this box to claim VAT under the special rules for BAD DEBT RELIEF (7) or any adjustment under the CAPITAL GOODS SCHEME (10).

2.10   **Box 5**

Insert difference between Box 3 and Box 4. If less than £1, no payment should be sent (and no repayment will be made) but the return should still be sent.

2.11   **Box 6**

Insert value of total outputs including

- standard-rated supplies (including road fuel scale charges)
- supplies to VAT-registered traders in other EC countries
- supplies to non-VAT registered or private individuals in other EC countries (distance sales)
- supplies which are outside the scope of VAT under the place of supply rules (see 64.7–64.38 SUPPLY)
- any own goods transferred to other EC countries
- sales to customers in other EC countries on a sale or return basis
- deposits for which an invoice has been issued
- zero-rated supplies, including exports
- exempt supplies
- any other business income
- 'reverse charge' transactions
- purchases under the special accounting scheme for gold (see 30.4 GOLD AND PRECIOUS METALS)

Any amount entered in Box 8 below must also be entered in Box 6.

If the cash accounting scheme is used (see 63.2 SPECIAL SCHEMES), figures should be based on payments received and *not* invoices issued.

2.12   **Box 7**

Insert value of total inputs (including imports, acquisitions and 'reverse charge' transactions) and other business expenses. Any amount entered in Box 9 must also be entered in Box 7.

If the cash accounting scheme is used (see 63.2 SPECIAL SCHEMES), figures should be based on payments made and *not* invoices received.

2.13   **Boxes 6 and 7**

The following should be left out.

- VAT itself
- Wages and salaries, PAYE and NIC
- Money put into or taken out of the business by the trader
- Loans, dividends and gifts of money

- Insurance claims

- Stock Exchange dealings (unless a financial institution)

- MOT certificates

- Motor vehicle licence duty

- Local authority rates

- Income which is outside the scope of VAT because it is not consideration for a supply

Figures should be net of any credits received but cash discounts should not be taken off. If accounts are kept net of cash discounts a reasonable amount should be added back for any discounts given or received.

2.14 Box 8

Insert total value of supplies of *goods* (and related services) to other EC countries, including

- supplies of goods to VAT-registered persons in other EC countries

- transfers of own goods from the UK to other EC countries (see 23.23 EUROPEAN COMMUNITY: SINGLE MARKET)

- consignment stocks transferred from the UK to other EC countries (see 23.23 EUROPEAN COMMUNITY: SINGLE MARKET)

- goods supplied to VAT registered customers in other EC countries on a call-off basis (see 23.29 EUROPEAN COMMUNITY: SINGLE MARKET)

- goods supplied to customers in other EC countries on sale or return, approval or similar basis (see 23.30 EUROPEAN COMMUNITY: SINGLE MARKET)

- goods dispatched from the UK for installation or assembly in other EC countries (see 23.28 EUROPEAN COMMUNITY: SINGLE MARKET)

- distance sales to unregistered customers in other EC countries where on or above the distance selling threshold for that country (or the seller has voluntarily registered in that country) (see 23.18 EUROPEAN COMMUNITY: SINGLE MARKET)

- supplies of new means of transport to unregistered customers in other EC countries (see 23.32 EUROPEAN COMMUNITY: SINGLE MARKET)

Separate supplies of services to other EC countries should only be included in Box 6.

The value to be included is the invoice (or contract) price, including related services such as commission, packing, transport and insurance costs charged by the supplier to the purchaser or customer. The supply or receipt of other services should not be included.

2.15 Box 9

Insert the total value of acquisitions of *goods* from other EC countries, including any goods removed to the UK from another EC country even if no actual purchase takes place (e.g. goods transferred between divisions of the same company) or the person invoiced is located outside the EC. Included are supplies of goods installed or assembled in the UK which have been despatched from another EC country.

The value to be included is the invoice (or contract) price, including related services such as commission, packing, transport and insurance costs charged by the supplier to the purchaser or customer. The supply or receipt of other services should not be included.

2.16   Declaration

The return must contain full information in respect of the matters specified in the return and a declaration, signed by the taxpayer, that the return is true and complete. [*SI 1995/2518, Reg 25(1)*]. This declaration must be unqualified (*DK Wright and Associates Ltd, [1975] VATTR 168 (203)*).

2.17   INCORRECT AND INCOMPLETE RETURNS OR FAILURE TO MAKE A RETURN

Any error in accounting for VAT or in the return generally must be corrected as required by C & E. [*SI 1995/2518, Reg 35*]. See 57.11 RECORDS.

The consequences of incorrect returns or failure to make a return are as follows.

- C & E may assess the amount of VAT due to the best of their judgment (see 6.1 ASSESSMENTS). C & E have indicated that incomplete or incorrect returns will be returned for correction. Traders classified as 'payment traders' will be assessed and the notice of assessment will accompany the rejected return with an error-return notice. For traders classified as 'repayment traders' the period will remain open until an acceptable return is received. Repayments will not be made until the error has been corrected.

- A VAT tribunal cannot normally entertain an appeal unless the appellant has made all the returns he is required to make and paid the amounts shown (see 5.4 APPEALS).

- Criminal or civil penalties may be incurred for failure to comply with the necessary requirements. See 52 PENALTIES and particularly 52.10 for penalties for misdeclaration or neglect resulting from understatements or overclaims and 52.15 for default surcharge for failure to submit returns on time or pay the VAT due.

2.18   RETURNS BY PERSONS SELLING UNDER A POWER OF SALE

Where a business is carried on by a taxable person and goods forming part of the business are sold by another person under any power exercisable by him in satisfaction of a debt owed by the taxable person, the goods are deemed to be supplied by the taxable person in the course or furtherance of his business. Land forming part of the assets of the business is treated as if it were goods and any sale includes a reference to a grant or assignment of any interest in, right over or licence to occupy the land concerned.

The auctioneer (on a sale by auction) or the person selling the goods must, *whether or not registered*, within 21 days of the sale, send the VAT and a statement on Form VAT 833 to VAT Central Unit at Southend-on-Sea showing

- his name, address and registration number (if registered);

- the name, address and registration number of the taxable person;

- the date of sale;

- the description and quantity of goods sold at each rate of VAT; and

- the sales proceeds and the VAT charged at each rate.

The auctioneer or person selling the goods must also send a copy of the statement to the taxable person within the same time limit. Both parties must then exclude the VAT chargeable from their normal returns, if any. [*VATA 1994, 4 Sch 7, 9, 11 Sch 2(12); SI 1995/2518, Reg 27*].

The auctioneer etc. must also issue a VAT invoice but giving the name, address and VAT registration number of the supplier. He need not be registered to issue it and should not ask the supplier for a VAT invoice.

This procedure does not normally apply to liquidators, administrative receivers or trustees in bankruptcy (see 36.1 INSOLVENCY), who continue to account for VAT in the normal way.

(C & E Notice 700, para 7.3).

De Voil Indirect Tax Service. See V5.142.

2.19   **EC SALES LISTS**

C & E have powers to require taxable persons to submit statements containing particulars of transactions involving the movement of goods between EC countries. [*VATA 1994, 11 Sch 2(3)*]. These statements are known as EC sales lists (ESLs).

Subject to the exceptions in 2.25 below or as C & E allow, every taxable person who has in any particular quarter made a supply of, dispatched, transported or transferred goods to a person who was registered in another EC country must submit an ESL within 42 days of the end of the quarter.

C & E may allow a taxable person to submit ESLs for monthly periods in which case the ESL must be submitted within 42 days of the end of the calendar quarter in which the month occurs.

Branch and group registration. Application may be made to the VAT office for separate branches in a company to send in separate ESLs. This also applies to individual companies or divisions within a group registration. Divisions of a company registered separately for VAT *must* send in separate ESLs. (C & E Notice 725, para 14.9).

Penalties. See 52.18 and 52.19 PENALTIES respectively for inaccuracies in, and failure to submit, ESLs.

Nil returns. If no such supply, etc. is made during a return period, there is no need to submit a return and a penalty will not be imposed. (C & E Notice 725, para 14.6).

[*SI 1995/2518, Regs 21, 22(1); SI 1996/210*].

De Voil Indirect Tax Service. See V5.271.

2.20   **Information to be disclosed**

Unless C & E allow otherwise, the ESL must contain the following information.

(*a*) The name, address and VAT registration number of the taxable person. The prefix GB must be shown before the VAT registration number. (This is pre-printed on Form VAT 101.)

(*b*) The date of submission of the ESL and the last day of the period to which the ESL refers.

(*c*) A two-letter prefix code identifying the customer's country and the VAT registration number of each person acquiring, or deemed to have acquired, goods in the period. The codes are

Austria—AT
Belgium—BE

Denmark—DK
Finland—FI
France—FR
Germany—DE
Greece—EL
Ireland—IE
Italy—IT
Luxembourg—LU
Netherlands—NL
Portugal—PT
Spain—ES
Sweden—SE

Where the VAT registration number in another EC country contains alphabetical as well as numerical characters, alphabetical characters should be underlined to reduce the possibility of misinterpretation (VAT Notes 2/97).

(*d*) The 'total value' of the goods supplied in the period to each person in (*c*) above. Do not include on the ESL supplies to non-registered customers or to registered customers where their VAT number is not known (and the supply has therefore been taxed). Negative amounts due to credit notes should be enclosed in brackets.

'*Total value*' means the consideration for the supply including costs of any freight transport services and ancillary transport services charged by the supplier of the goods to the customer.

If goods are supplied free of charge, there is a deemed supply of goods which must be included in the EC sales list at the cost of the goods to the supplier.

(*e*) In the indicator column, enter '2' if an intermediary in a triangular transaction (see 2.22 below) and leave the column blank in any other case.

[*SI 1995/2518, Regs 21, 22(3); SI 1996/210*].

For general guidance on the completion of an ESL, see VAT Information Sheet 1/96 *Filling in Your EC Sales List.*

2.21   *Goods sent for processing*

Any transactions involving goods sent for processing in another EC country are to be ignored on the ESL. [*SI 1995/2518, Regs 21, 22(4); SI 1996/210*].

2.22   *Triangulation*

Where the intermediate supplier in a triangular transaction within the EC (see 23.22 EUROPEAN COMMUNITY: SINGLE MARKET) is registered in the UK, his ESL must state for such transactions the information under 2.20(*a*)–(*c*) above and the total value of the goods supplied by him. In each case, the figure '2' should be inserted in the indicator box on form VAT 101 to show that the information describes triangular trade. Such triangular transactions must be reported separately on the ESL on a different line from the total of normal direct supplies to each EC customer. [*SI 1995/2518, Reg 22(5)*]. (VAT Information Sheet 1/96).

2.23   **Method of sending**

Form VAT 101. C & E automatically send a Form VAT 101 for use as an ESL where they have identified a registered person as being required to submit a return. Continuation sheets (Form VAT 101A) are available from VAT offices.

Electronic data interchange, etc. A registered person may apply to send in the ESL by electronic data interchange, magnetic tape or diskette. Information on this is available from

HM Customs and Excise
Tariff and Statistical Office Helpdesk
21 Victoria Avenue
Southend-on-Sea
SS2 6AL

Tel: 01702 367248

Plain paper returns. With prior consent of C & E, a return can be submitted on own A4 computer paper of at least 80g/m² weight provided, *inter alia*, that the format and layout is very like that of Form VAT 101 and 101A, the printing is of letter quality and on one side of the paper only, the type face is not less than 12 point, and there are no more than 15 double-spaced lines of data to a page. Applications to use this method, including a sample plain paper return, should be made to

HM Customs and Excise
ESL Unit (Plain Paper Section)
3rd Floor SW
Queens Dock
Liverpool
L74 4AA

(C & E Notice 725, para 14.7).

2.24 **Correction of errors**

C & E must be informed of certain errors or omissions on an ESL. These comprise all errors which exceed the greater of £100 and 2% of the declared total value of supplies to a customer; any incorrect VAT registration number; and any incorrect statement that supplies were part of a triangular transaction. Errors must be disclosed by completion of a form VAT 101B obtainable from any VAT office. This form must be used whatever method is used to send in the ESL. (C & E Notice 725, para 14.8).

2.25 **Exceptions**

C & E may vary the requirements to prepare ESLs in the following circumstances.

(*a*) **Persons with low turnover.** Where a taxable person satisfies C & E that

   (i) *either* at the end of any month the value of his taxable supplies in the period of one year then ending is less than the 'relevant figure' *or* at any time there are reasonable grounds for believing that the value of his taxable supplies in the period of one year beginning at that or any later time will not exceed the relevant figure, *and*

   (ii) *either* at the end of any month the value of his supplies to persons registered in other EC countries in the period of one year then ending is less than £11,000 *or* at any time there are reasonable grounds for believing that the value of his supplies to such persons in the period of one year beginning at that or any later time will not exceed £11,000, *and*

   (iii) the supplies do not include new means of transport (see 23.31 EUROPEAN COMMUNITY: SINGLE MARKET)

   C & E may allow him to submit an annual ESL containing only the information required by 2.20(*a*)–(*c*) above (i.e. an annual list of VAT registration numbers of EC customers but no details of values). The ESL must be submitted within 42 days of the end of the year to which it relates.

'*Relevant figure*' is the compulsory VAT registration threshold (see 59.3 REGISTRATION) plus £25,500.

(*b*) **Persons preparing annual VAT returns, etc.** Where C & E have allowed a taxable person to prepare VAT returns for periods longer than three months (i.e. normally annual returns but including any other non-standard return period) and the taxable person satisfies C & E that

    (i) *either* at the end of any month the value of his taxable supplies in the period of one year then ending is less than £145,000 *or* at any time there are reasonable grounds for believing that the value of his taxable supplies in the period of one year beginning at that or any later time will not exceed £145,000, *and*

    (ii) either of the conditions in (*a*)(ii) above is satisfied, *and*

    (iii) the supplies do not include new means of transport (see 23.31 EUROPEAN COMMUNITY: SINGLE MARKET)

    C & E may allow him to submit an ESL for the same period as his VAT return. The return must be submitted within 42 days of the end of the return period.

[*SI 1995/2158, Regs 1, 22(1)(2)*].

2.26 Final statements

Any person who ceases to be registered for VAT under *VATA 1994, 1 Sch* must submit a final ESL *unless* the registration is allocated to the purchaser on the transfer of a business as a going concern (see 59.29 REGISTRATION). Unless C & E allow otherwise, the ESL must contain full information normally required and be submitted within 42 days of the date from which the VAT registration is cancelled. [*SI 1995/2158, Reg 23*].

2.27 INTRASTAT

Intrastat is a system for collecting statistics on the trade in goods between EC countries. The statistics are collected from two sources.

•   *The VAT return.* All VAT-registered businesses must complete Boxes 8 and 9 on the VAT return showing details of goods supplied to ('dispatches') and acquired from ('arrivals') other EC countries.

•   *Supplementary declarations.* VAT-registered businesses with a value of dispatches or arrivals exceeding a threshold must make Supplementary Declarations each month. Separate thresholds for dispatches and arrivals are set for each calendar year. Where a registered person's dispatches or arrivals in the previous calendar year exceeded the threshold for the current year, monthly Supplementary Declarations must be made for the full year. Additionally if the cumulative total of dispatches or arrivals in the current calendar year from 1 January exceeds the threshold for the current year, Supplementary Declarations must be made for the rest of the year, commencing with the month in which the threshold is reached. The level of thresholds have been set as follows.

	Dispatches	Acquisitions
1996	£160,000	£160,000
1997	£195,000	£195,000
1998	£225,000	£225,000
1999	£230,000	£230,000

[*SI 1995/2946; SI 1996/2968; SI 1997/2864; SI 1998/2973*].

2.27   Accounting Periods and Returns

Depending upon the particular values of the trade, Supplementary Declarations may be required for dispatches or acquisitions or both.

See *SI 1992/2790*, as amended, for the requirement to keep and maintain records, access by C & E to the recorded information, and criminal penalties for failing to furnish Supplementary Declarations.

Fuller details, including arrangements for providing Supplementary Declarations, the information required and rules for declaring goods are given in C & E Notice 60.

De Voil Indirect Tax Service. See V5.276.

3   Administration

De Voil Indirect Tax Service. See V1.216–219, 224.

3.1   VAT is 'under the care and management of the Commissioners' (i.e. the Commissioners of Customs and Excise). [*VATA 1994, s 96(1), 11 Sch 1*].

3.2   **VAT OFFICES**

VAT offices deal with the administration of VAT in their area but not the issue of return forms or the receipt of VAT which is dealt with by VAT Central Unit.

The addresses and phone numbers of VAT offices are listed in 3.9 below. They are generally open each weekday from 10.00 to 16.00.

All VAT offices are linked to the central VAT computer. Any queries about VAT payments and repayments should be made at the VAT office, not the VAT Central Unit.

3.3   **VAT CENTRAL UNIT**

The Central Unit at Alexander House, 21 Victoria Avenue, Southend-on-Sea SS99 1AA (there is a special postcode for completed return forms) keeps registration records, despatches return forms and reminders, receives completed forms and VAT payments, and repays VAT.

3.4   **ORDERS AND REGULATIONS**

Much of the detailed legislation on VAT is in the form of orders, regulations and rules made by statutory instrument by the Treasury or C & E and may be annulled by resolution of the House of Commons.

Certain Treasury orders must be positively approved by the House of Commons (see *VATA 1994, s 97(4)*). Any such order not approved within 28 days from the date it was made (excluding time when Parliament is dissolved or prorogued or during which it is adjourned for more than four days) ceases to have effect at the end of that 28 day period. This is without prejudice to anything previously done under the order or to the making of a new order.

[*VATA 1994, s 97; FA 1995, s 21; FA 1996, s 33, 41 Sch*].

3.5   **PUBLICATIONS**

C & E issue

- **Notices** and (formerly) **leaflets,** which are numbered booklets explaining various aspects of VAT. A list of those currently in issue is given under 16.1 CUSTOMS AND EXCISE: EXPLANATORY NOTICES ETC.

- **VAT Notes** to bring to the notice of all registered persons details of information available from VAT offices. They are sent out with VAT return forms.

- **News releases** and **business briefs** are issued as informative news items. They are numbered and dated.

- **VAT information sheets** on items of particular interest.

Most of the Notices and Leaflets are available from VAT enquiry offices.

3.6 Administration

3.6 PUBLICITY BY C & E OF CHANGES IN INTERPRETATION OF VAT LAW

C & E apply what they consider to be the correct interpretation of the law relating to VAT. Where interpretation changes, the change will be applied as quickly as possible. Publicity for any change will include consultation with relevant trade bodies and representative organisations, issue of a News Release or Business Brief, coverage in VAT Notes and, in due course, updating of any relevant Notice or Leaflet.

If, despite taking all reasonable steps to keep informed about changes, a person is not aware of a change

- where, as a result, VAT is overcharged, C & E will normally agree to the change being applied retrospectively with an adjustment of the VAT due (provided any repayment does not unjustly enrich the claimant); and

- where, as a result, VAT is undercharged, C & E will normally require any extra VAT only from the date when it was reasonable for the person to have known about the change. This would normally be no later than the date of receipt of VAT Notes referring to the change.

(C & E Business Brief 14/94, 6 July 1994).

3.7 MAKING ENQUIRIES

Registered persons can visit, telephone or write to their VAT enquiry office. General questions may be answered over the telephone but it is preferable to put any detailed questions in writing.

A registered person can get a written decision from his enquiry office on a particular transaction that has occurred or is due to occur shortly. He must supply the following information.

- Business name, address and VAT registration number.

- All the relevant facts and copies of any relevant documents, together with any other information considered relevant (e.g. court or tribunal decisions).

- The nature of the decision required.

- The use to be made of the decision (e.g. whether it will be passed on to other businesses or trade associations so that C & E can consider any general application of the decision).

Provided this information is given, C & E regard themselves as bound by the decision until

(*a*) developments such as court or tribunal rulings subsequently change the VAT position (in which case the taxpayer will only be asked to pay an extra VAT from the date he is advised of the new position by C & E or from such earlier date as he could reasonably be expected to know of the change); or

(*b*) they publish information which would clearly change the position.

Tax advisers should address queries about specific client's affairs to the client's VAT office. Factual queries which are not specific to a particular client should be addressed to the tax adviser's own enquiry office. Approach should only be made to C & E Headquarters if enquiries are being made on behalf of an entire industry or if lobbying or otherwise acting as a member of a representative or consultative body concerned with the effect of present or proposed legislation.

(C & E Notice 700/51/95).

3.8   MAKING COMPLAINTS ABOUT C & E

The following remedies are available to a person who has a complaint against C & E.

(a) **Complaint to the VAT office**. If a person thinks that a C & E officer has

- exceeded his powers without a satisfactory explanation, or

- acted improperly in any other way

he should write to the Collector in charge of the VAT office setting out full details. If the complaint is not within the responsibility of the Collector, the complaint will be passed to the appropriate senior official elsewhere in C & E for investigation.

Alternatively a professional adviser or trade association may lodge the complaint on the person's behalf. In such a case, the representative must also forward written agreement from the complainant that C & E may disclose any matters relating to his VAT affairs which are relevant to answering the complaint.

See also C & E Notice 1000 *Complaints and putting things right* available from VAT offices.

(b) **Complaint to the independent Adjudicator**. The Adjudicator for the Inland Revenue also deals with unresolved complaints about C & E. The adjudicator will consider (amongst other things) complaints about delay, rudeness, mistakes, harassment during a VAT investigation, application of extra-statutory concessions, requests for time to pay and refusal of information under the Open Government provisions. The adjudicator will not examine cases which are appealable to a VAT tribunal nor intervene once a matter is before the criminal courts.

The address of the adjudicator is

The Adjudicator's Office
Haymarket House
28 Haymarket
London SW1Y 4SP

Tel: 0171 930 2292
Fax: 0171 930 2298

(c) **Complaint to a Member of Parliament**. A person can complain to his local MP. If appropriate, the MP can deal with the complaint

- personally (e.g. by direct correspondence with C & E or by asking a Parliamentary question); or

- with the person's consent, by forwarding the complaint to the Parliamentary Commissioner for Administration (PCA) normally known as the 'Ombudsman'.

The PCA can only act on written complaints forwarded by an MP alleging maladministration and has no power to enforce a remedy.

(d) **Appeal to a VAT tribunal**. An appeal to a VAT tribunal can only be made against a decision of C & E falling within one of the categories in *VATA 1994, s 83* (see 5.3 APPEALS). Although some of these categories relate to administrative decisions, in general a VAT tribunal does not have supervisory jurisdiction over administrative decisions taken by C & E. Tribunals do have jurisdiction to hear appeals against decisions which, although not falling within *VATA 1994, s 83*, result in a decision (e.g. an assessment) which does. [*VATA 1994, s 84(10)*].

(e) **Judicial review**. Where a tribunal does not have power to review an administrative decision, a taxpayer can apply to the High Court for a judicial review. Appeals are heard by the Queen's Bench Division.

3.9 Administration

VAT OFFICES

Listed below are the addresses and telephone and fax numbers of VAT offices. The numbers in brackets are the VAT office official reference numbers. These are included so that the office may be traced from the official reference and do not form part of the address.

Boundaries are subject to change from time to time so it is wise to telephone the selected office before writing or calling in person to ensure that it is indeed the one responsible for the business concerned.

Aberdeen (001)
Customs House
28 Guild Street
Aberdeen AB11 6GY
Tel: 01224 844844
Fax: 01224 844600
(*All general enquiries to 0345 442266*)

Bedford (076)
Greylaw House
8 Goldington Road
Bedford
MK40 3NL
Tel: 01234 270066
Fax: 01234 269978

Belfast (007)
Business Advice Unit
Custom House
Custom House Square
Belfast BT1 3ET
Tel: 01232 562600
Fax: 01232 562971/2
(*All general enquiries to 0345 125730*)

Birmingham (051)
2 Broadway
Broad Street
Fiveways
Birmingham B15 1BG
Tel: 0121 697 4000
Fax: 0121 697 4002

Blackburn (020)
Chaucers Walk
Furthergate Industrial
Estate
Blackburn
Lancs BB1 3AF
Tel: 01254 347544
Fax: 01254 347599

Bradford (013)
87 Manningham Lane
Bradford
West Yorkshire
BD1 3DD
Tel: 0113 230 4466
Fax: 0113 288 3453

Brighton (073)
Martello House
315 Portland Road
Hove
East Sussex BN3 5SZ
Tel: 01273 430011
Fax: 01273 431425

Bristol (030)
Froomsgate House
Rupert Street
Bristol BS1 2QP
Tel: 0117 900 2000
Fax: 0117 900 2006

Cambridge (103)
Lockton House
Clarendon Road
Cambridge CB2 2BH
Tel: 01223 357124
Fax: 01223 356750
(*All general enquiries to 08450 199399*)

Canterbury (078)
Clarkson House
Rhodaus Town
Canterbury
Kent CT1 2RR
Tel: 01227 769461
Fax: 01277 783635
(*All general enquiries to 08450 199199*)

Cardiff (035)
Portcullis House
21 Cowbridge Rd East
Cardiff CF1 9SS
Tel: 01222 386000
Fax: 01222 386444

Carlisle
Stocklund House
Castle Street
Carlisle
Cumbria CA3 8SY
Tel: 0191 201 1719
Fax: 01228 810496

Cheadle (021)
Boundary House
Cheadle Point
Cheadle
Cheshire SK8 2JZ
Tel: 0161 912 7999
Fax 0161 912 6299

Chester (023)
Eden House
Lakeside
Chester Business Park
Wrexham Road
Chester CH4 9QY
Tel: 01244 684200
Fax: 01244 684217
(*All general enquiries to Cardiff*)

Chesterfield (269)
Dents Chambers
New Square
Chesterfield S40 1AJ
Tel: 01246 501000
Fax: 01246 551531

Colchester (060)
Northgate House
St Peters Street
Colchester CO1 1HT
Tel: 01206 733000
Fax: 01206 767486
(*All general enquires
to 08450 199299*)

Coleraine (004)
Mill House
24 Railway Road
Coleraine
Co Londonderry
BT52 1PH
Tel: 01265 44803
Fax: 01265 44979

Colwyn Bay (059)
Government Buildings
Dinerth Road
Colwyn Bay
Conway LL28 4UL
Tel: 01492 544261
Fax: 01492 549128
(*All general enquiries
to Cardiff*)

Coventry (052)
Park Court
Warwick Road
Coventry CV3 6QH
Tel: 01203 234400
Fax: 01203 234490

Croydon (088)
AMP House
Dingwall Road
Croydon CR9 3RQ
Tel: 0181 680 1700
Fax: 0181 760 9945
(*All general enquiries
to 0171 202 4087*)

Derby (041)
Gower House
Gower Street
Derby DE1 1NQ
Tel: 01332 362121
Fax: 01332 372122

Doncaster (014)
Weston House
92–98 Cleveland Street
Doncaster
South Yorks DN1 3LG
Tel: 01302 791180
Fax: 01302 791101

Douglas
PO Box 6
Custom House
North Quay
Douglas
Isle of Man IM99 1AG
Tel: 01624 648130
Fax: 01624 661725

Droitwich (053)
Block B
Government Buildings
Worcester Road
Droitwich
Worcs WR9 8BT
Tel: 01905 855600
Fax: 01905 776752

Dundee (064)
Caledonian House
Greenmarket
Dundee DD1 1HD
Tel: 01382 200822
Fax: 01382 313247
(*All general enquiries
to 0345 442266*)

Edinburgh (063)
44 York Place
Edinburgh EH1 3JW
Tel: 0131 469 2000
Fax: 0131 469 7321
(*All general enquiries
to 0345 442266*)

Enniskillen
8 High Street
Enniskillen
BT74 4EH
Tel: 01365 324821
Fax: 01365 322246

Exeter (031)
Rensdale House
Bonhay Road
Exeter EX4 3DA
Tel: 01392 315000
Fax: 01392 413178

Finchley (092)
Berkeley House
304 Regents Park Rd
London N3 2JY
Tel: 0171 865 3100
Fax: 0181 346 9154

Glasgow (003)
Portcullis House
21 India Street
Glasgow G2 4PZ
Tel: 0141 221 3828
Fax: 0141 308 3402
(*All general enquiries
to 0345 442266*)

Gloucester (038)
Block B
Elmbridge Court
Cheltenham Road
Gloucester GL3 1JX
Tel: 01452 306522
Fax: 01452 302258
(*All general enquiries
to Bristol*)

Greenock (006)
Custom House
Custom House Quay
Greenock PA15 1EQ
Tel: 01475 726331
Fax: 01475 881455

Grimsby (042)
Imperial House
77 Victoria Street
Grimsby
South Humberside
DN31 1DB
Tel: 01472 245900
Fax: 01472 245929

3.9 Administration

Halifax (015)
Unit OP 140
Dean Clough Industrial
Park
Dean Clough
Halifax
West Yorks HX3 5AX
Tel: 01422 864200
Fax: 01422 864211

Harlow (084)
12th Floor
Terminus House
The High
Harlow
Essex CM20 1TX
Tel: 01279 429591
Fax: 01279 451867
(*All general enquiries
to 08450 199399*)

Hastings
Ashdown House
Sedlescombe Road
North
St Leonards-on-Sea
East Sussex TN34 1AE
Tel: 01424 436413
Fax: 01424 453255
(*All general enquiries
to 08450 199299*)

Hull (016)
Customs House
King George Dock
Hull HU9 5PW
Tel: 01482 785800
Fax: 01482 785971
(*All general enquiries
to Newcastle*)

Ipswich (061)
Haven House
17 Lower Brook Street
Ipswich
Suffolk IP4 1DN
Tel: 01473 235700
Fax: 01473 235924
(*All general enquiries
to 08450 199399*)

Kettering
Unit 1420
Montagu Court
Venture Park
Kettering Parkway
Kettering
Northants NN15 6XR
Tel: 01536 516263
Fax: 01536 485346

Leeds (017)
Peter Bennett House
Redvers Close
West Park Ring Road
Leeds LS16 6RQ
Tel: 0113 230 4444
Fax: 0113 288 3309
(*All general enquiries
to Newcastle*)

Leicester (043)
Citygate House
St Margarets Way
Leicester LE1 3DA
Tel: 0116 256 1750
Fax: 0116 256 1701

Lincoln
7th Floor
Wigford House
Brayford Wharf East
Lincoln LN5 7AY
Tel: 01522 513166
Fax: 01522 567435

Lisburn (008)
All correspondence to
Belfast office

Liverpool (024)
1st Floor
Queens Dock
Liverpool L74 4AA
Tel: 0151 703 8000
Fax: 0151 703 1201

London (City) (104)
Thomas Paine House
Angel Square
Torrens Street
London EC1V 1TA
Tel: 0171 865 3100
Fax: 0171 865 3171

**London (South
Bank)** (105)
Dorset House
Stamford Street
London SE1 9PY
Tel: 0171 928 3344
Fax 0171 202 4131
(*All general enquiries
to 0171 202 4087*)

Londonderry
Customs House
Queens Quay
Londonderry
BT48 7AR
Tel: 01504 261937
Fax: 01504 263869

Luton (069)
Jansel House
Hitchin Road
Luton LU2 7XJ
Tel: 01582 444100
Fax: 01582 444190

Maidenhead (081)
Bell Tower House
Bell Street
Maidenhead SL6 1BU
Tel: 01628 425000
Fax: 01628 425099

Maidstone (079)
Concord House
10–12 London Road
Maidstone
Kent ME16 8HL
Tel: 01622 765181
Fax: 01622 673962
(*All general enquiries
to 08450 199299*)

Manchester
Customs House
Furness Quay
Salford M5 2XX
Tel: 0161 912 7999
Fax: 0161 912 6499

Middlesborough
6th Flr Church House
Grange Road
Middlesborough
Cleveland TS1 2LP
Tel: 01642 218191
Fax: 01642 245950

Milton Keynes
Bowbank House
200 Silbury Boulevard
Milton Keynes
MK9 1NL
Tel: 01234 270066
Fax: 01908 691621

**Newcastle under
Lyme** (055)
Blackburn House
The Midway
Newcastle-under-Lyme
ST5 1UT
Tel: 01782 711101
Fax: 01782 712428

**Newcastle upon
Tyne** (012)
Dobson House
Regent Centre
Gosforth
Newcastle-upon-Tyne
NE3 3PS
Tel: 0191 201 1700
Fax: 0191 201 1742

Northampton (045)
Princess House
Cliftonville Road
Northampton
NN1 5AE
Tel: 01604 731400
Fax: 01604 731456

Norwich (062)
Rosebury Court
St Andrews Business
Park
Central Avenue
Norwich NR7 0BR
Tel: 01603 704100
Fax: 01603 704101
(*All general enquiries
to 08450 199399*)

Nottingham (044)
Bowman House
100–102 Talbot Street
Nottingham NG1 5NF
Tel: 0115 971 2100
Fax: 0115 948 3487

Oxford (075)
2nd Floor
Littlegate House
St Ebb's Street
Oxford OX1 1QA
Tel: 01865 386000
Fax: 01865 386111

Peterborough (046)
Ashurst
Southgate Park
Bakewell Road
Orton Southgate
Peterborough PE2 6YR
Tel: 01733 370007
Fax: 01733 370032

Plymouth (032)
Crownhill Court
Tailyour Road
Crownhill
Plymouth PL6 5BZ
Tel: 01752 777123
Fax: 01752 765828

Poole (071)
St Johns House
1–9 Serpentine Road
Poole
Dorset BH15 2AQ
Tel: 01202 361720
Fax 01202 361759

Portsmouth (070)
Wingfield House
316 Commercial Road
Portsmouth PO1 4TG
Tel: 01705 852400
Fax: 01705 852499

Reading (077)
Eldon Court
75 London Road
Reading
Berks RG1 5BS
Tel: 0118 964 4211
Fax: 0118 964 4208

Redhill (082)
Warwick House
67 Station Road
Redhill RH1 1QU
Tel: 01737 734500
Fax: 01737 734600
(*All general enquiries
to 08450 199299*)

Romford (097)
Chaucer House
28 Western Road
Romford
Essex RM1 3JT
Tel: 01708 758700
Fax: 01708 758908
(*All general enquiries
to 0171 202 4087*)

3.9 Administration

Salford
Customs House
Furness Quay
Salford M5 2XX
Tel: 0161 912 6444
Fax: 0161 912 7099

Sheffield (018)
Regent Court
30 Regent Street
Sheffield S1 4DA
Tel: 0114 282 3000
Fax: 0114 282 3020

Shrewsbury (056)
Mayfield House
Mayfield Drive
London Road
Shrewsbury
SY2 6PE
Tel: 01743 235656
Fax: 01743 368283
(*All general enquiries
to Cardiff*)

South Lakes
Kentmere House
Blackhall Road
Kendal
Cumbria
LA9 4BT
Tel: 01539 797905
Fax: 01539 797911

Southampton (072)
Roebuck House
26 Bedford Place
Southampton
SO15 2DB
Tel: 01703 330330
Fax: 01703 827907

Southend-on-Sea(099)
9th Floor
Maitland House
Warrior Square
Southend-on-Sea
SS1 2FG
Tel: 01702 367720
Fax: 01702 367701
(*All general enquiries
to 08450 199399*)

Staines (101)
14 Thames Street
Staines
Middlesex TW18 4UD
Tel: 01784 895600
Fax: 01784 895722

Swansea (037)
Oldway House
Rutland Place
Swansea SA1 3NF
Tel: 01792 350100
Fax: 01792 648583
(*All general enquiries
to Cardiff*)

Taunton (033)
Brendon House
35–36 High Street
Taunton
Somerset TA1 3DR
Tel: 01823 324314
Fax: 01823 332199
(*All general enquiries
to Bristol*)

Uxbridge (090)
1 Park Road
Uxbridge
Middlesex UB8 1RW
Tel: 01895 842200
Fax: 01895 814305

Wakefield
22-29 The Springs
Wakefield
West Yorkshire
WF1 1QA
Tel: 01924 299786
Fax: 01924 299787

Washington (019)
Coniston House
District 1
Washington
Tyne & Wear
NE38 7RN
Tel: 0191 201 2500
Fax: 0191 415 5321

Wembley (091)
Valiant House
365 High Road
Wembley
Middlesex HA9 6AY
Tel: 0181 903 7811
Fax: 0181 903 1135

Whitby
Custom House
1 Old Market Place
Whitby
North Yorkshire
YO21 3BT
Tel: 01947 821449
Fax: 01947 820 830

Wigan (029)
Lingate House
102 Chapel Lane
Wigan
Lancs WN3 4BJ
Tel: 01942 756610
Fax: 01942 756659

Woking (083)
Bradfield House
Bradfield Close
York Road
Woking
Surrey GU22 7RD
Tel: 01483 254800
Fax 01483 254847

Wolverhampton
Deansgate
62–70 Tettenhall Rd
Wolverhampton
WV1 4TZ
Tel: 01902 771921
Fax: 01902 317002

Workington
Venture House
Regents Court
Guard Street
Workington
Cumbria
CA14 4EW
Tel: 01900 604611
Fax: 01900 604044

York
Prudential House
28-40 Blossom St
York
North Yorkshire
YO24 1GY
Tel: 01904 620421
Fax: 01904 626291

3.10   OTHER USEFUL C & E ADDRESSES

Solicitor's Office
HM Customs and Excise
New Kings Beam House
22 Upper Ground
London SE1 9PJ
Tel: 0171 620 1313
Fax: 0171 865 5022

VAT Central Unit
HM Customs and Excise
Alexander House
21 Victoria Avenue
Southend-on-Sea
SS99 1AA
Tel: 01702 348944
Fax: 01702 366687

4 Agents

Cross-references. See 11.6, 11.7 and 11.8 CATERING for catering in factories, hospitals and schools respectively supplied by agents.

De Voil Indirect Tax Service. See V3.221.

The contents of this chapter are as follows.

4.1 MEANING OF AGENT

There is no definition of 'agent' in the legislation. An agent is someone who acts for, or represents, someone else (the principal) in arranging supplies of goods and services. Supplies arranged by an agent are made by or to the principal represented. The principal cannot avoid any liability to account for VAT on supplies, or to pay VAT on purchases, by using an agent. However, whether or not a person is an agent for another person depends upon the actual arrangement between them and not simply upon the trading titles adopted. For example, 'motor agents and distributors' usually trade as principals and travel agents and employment agencies are not usually agents in all their activities. Solicitors and architects are normally principals but may occasionally arrange supplies as agents for their clients.

An agent/principal relationship exists if both parties agree that it does *and* the agent has agreed with the principal *to act on his behalf* in relation to the particular transaction concerned. The agreement may be written, oral or merely inferred from their general relationship and the way their business is conducted. Whatever form this relationship takes, the following conditions must be satisfied.

(*a*) It must always be clearly established between the agent and principal, and acceptable to C & E, that the agent is arranging transactions for the principal, rather than trading on his own account.

(*b*) The agent must never be the owner of the goods or use any of the services bought or sold for the principal.

(*c*) The agent must not alter the nature or value of any of the supplies made between the principal and third parties.

(C & E Notice 700, para 10.1).

In *C & E Commrs v Johnson QB, [1980] STC 624* Woolf J took agency as the 'relationship which exists between two persons, one of whom expressly or impliedly consents that the other should represent him or act on his behalf and the other of whom similarly consents to represent the former or so to act'.

Whether acting as agent or principal — case law. For decisions in specific cases as to whether a person was acting as agent or principal see *JK Hill & Co v C & E Commrs QB, [1988] STC 424* (sales of craft pottery); *C & E Commrs v Paget and Another QB, [1989] STC 773, Flashlight Photography Ltd (9088)* and *H Tempest Ltd [1975] VATTR 161 (201)* (school photographs—see also 20.11 EDUCATION); *C & E Commrs v Music & Video Exchange Ltd QB, [1992] STC 220* (second-hand musical equipment); *Bagshawe (JNS) and Walker (CAE) (1762)* (art dealers); *National Bus Company (2530)* (refreshments sold by hostesses on buses); *Dr R Nader (t/a Try Us) (4927)* (meals delivered by taxi); *Prontobikes Ltd (13213)* (motorcycle courier service); *Cornhill Management Ltd [1991] VATTR 1 (5444)* (company investing money deposited by clients); *LS & A International Ltd (3717)* (purchases of paper); *Jocelyn Feilding Fine Arts Ltd [1978] VATTR 164 (652)* (auctioneers); *Leapmagic Ltd (6441)* (hostesses at night club); and *Ivychain Ltd (5627)* (service washes at launderette). For a fuller list, see Tolley's VAT Cases.

4.2   AGENTS AND VAT

An agent will usually be involved in at least two separate supplies at any one time and it is important to distinguish between them.

• The supply of own services to the principal for which the agent charges a fee or commission. The normal VAT rules apply to such services.

• The supply made between the principal and the third party.

The VAT liability on the supply of agent's services will not necessarily be the same as the liability of the supply between the principal and the third party.

(C & E Notice 700, para 10.2).

Registration. In determining whether an agent is liable to be registered for VAT, turnover included the value of services to the principal and the value of any supplies which the agent is treated as making through acting in his own name (see under 4.4 below). (C & E Notice 700, para 10.6).

4.3   Agents acting in the name of their principals

An agent may only take a minor role in a transaction and simply introduce the principal to potential clients or suppliers. Alternatively, the agent may be more closely involved and receive/deliver goods, make/receive payment and possibly hold stocks of goods on behalf of the principal. However, provided that the invoicing for the supply is between the principal and the customer, the only VAT supply made by the agent is the provision of services to the principal. (C & E Notice 700, para 10.3).

4.4   Agents acting in their own name

An agent may be empowered by a principal to enter into contracts with a third party on behalf of the principal. In such cases, particularly where the principal wishes to remain unnamed or undisclosed, the agent may receive and issue invoices in his own name for the supplies concerned. In such circumstances, although in commercial terms the

4.5 Agents

transaction remains between the principal and third party, for VAT purposes special rules apply as set out below. (C & E Notice 700, para 10.4).

Goods. Where an agent acts in his own name in relation to a supply and either

(*a*) goods are imported from outside the EC by a taxable person who supplies them as agent for a non-taxable person, or

(*b*) goods are acquired from another EC country by a non-taxable person and a taxable person acts as agent in relation to the acquisition, and then supplies the goods as agent for that non-taxable person, or

(*c*) where neither (*a*) nor (*b*) above applies in relation to a supply, goods are supplied through an agent

then the goods *must* be treated, as the case may be, as imported and supplied by the agent, acquired and supplied by the agent or supplied to and by the agent as principal. For these purposes, a person who is not resident in the UK and whose place (or principal place) of business is outside the UK may be treated as being a non-taxable person if as a result he will not be required to be registered under *VATA 1994*.

[*VATA 1994, s 47(1)(2)(2A); FA 1995, s 23*].

Services. Where an agent arranges a supply of taxable services and both the agent and supplier are registered for VAT, the agent *may* treat himself as both receiving and supplying the services. If so, the agent will be regarded as acting in his own name. [*VATA 1994, s 47(3); FA 1995, s 23*]. (C & E Notice 700, para 10.4).

Accounting for VAT. Where an agent acts in his own name, he should reclaim input tax and must account for output tax. As the nature or value of the supply is unchanged the amount of input and output tax will be the same unless the liability of the supplies is different. For example, the agent may zero-rate the supply by him for exportation provided he holds valid proof of exports (see 25.24 EXPORTS). The deemed supply to and by the agent are simultaneous and he cannot reclaim the input tax on the supply to him in one period but defer the time when he is required to account for output tax to a later period in which he invoices the supply made by him (*Metropolitan Borough of Wirral v C & E Commrs QB, [1995] STC 597*).

Second-hand goods. Where any supplies by an agent acting in his own name are eligible goods under one of the second-hand goods schemes, the agent may be able to include the value of services to the principal (i.e. commission, etc.) in calculating the VAT due. All the conditions of the scheme must be satisfied. See SECOND-HAND GOODS (61) for full details.

Supplies for travellers. The above arrangements cannot be used for supplies which are for the benefit of travellers (e.g. supplies of accommodation or passenger transport). (C & E Notice 700, para 10.4).

De Voil Indirect Tax Service. See V3.423.

4.5 **Invoices for supplies made through a selling agent not using a margin scheme**

Where an agent is registered for VAT and is acting in his own name, the procedure outlined in 4.4 above must be used. If the principal is registered for VAT either the principal must issue a VAT invoice to the agent or the agent can use the self-billing procedure (see 40.2 INVOICES). The agent must account for output tax on his onward supply to his customer and, if the customer is registered, issue a VAT invoice to him. The agent must account for VAT on the value of his own supply of services (e.g. commission) in arranging the supply on behalf of the principal.

Where an agent is acting in the name of his principal, the procedures depend upon whether or not the principal is registered for VAT.

- If the principal is registered for VAT, the principal must issue the invoice made out to the customer. This can be issued direct to the customer or can be passed to the agent for onward transmission. If the agent is VAT-registered, he need only account for VAT on services to the principal.

- If the principal is not registered for VAT, no VAT is due on the supply arranged by the agent.

A registered agent must account for output tax on his supply of services to the principal. The agent must also have evidence that he is arranging the supply on behalf of the principal and the supply should be readily distinguishable in his records from supplies on which VAT is charged. The evidence may be a standing agreement between agent and principal or a signed declaration from the principal giving his name and address and confirming that he is not a registered person making a supply in the course of business. (C & E Notice 700, para 10.7(A)).

4.6   Invoices for supplies obtained through a buying agent not using a margin scheme

Where an agent is registered for VAT and is acting in his own name, the procedure outlined in 4.4 above must be used. If the supplier is registered for VAT, the supplier must issue a VAT invoice to the agent who may reclaim the VAT as input tax. The agent must account for output tax on his onward supply to the buyer and, if the buyer is registered, issue a VAT invoice to him. The principal (the buyer) should be able to know the price paid by his agent in obtaining the supply. The agent must also account for output tax on the value of his own supply of services (e.g. commission) in arranging the supply on behalf of the principal.

Where an agent is acting in the name of his principal, the procedures depend upon whether or not the supplier is registered for VAT.

- If the supplier is registered, the supplier should issue the VAT invoice made out to the principal. This can be issued direct to the principal or can be passed to the agent for onward transmission. If the agent is VAT-registered, he need only account for VAT on services to the principal.

- If the supplier is not registered for VAT, no VAT is due on the supply arranged by the agent. A registered agent must account for output tax on his supply of services to the principal.

(C & E Notice 700, para 10.7(B)).

4.7   DISBURSEMENTS

Where a supplier incurs incidental costs (e.g. travelling expenses, postage, telephone) in the course of making the supply and charges these items separately on the invoice to the client, such costs must be included in the value when VAT is calculated. See *Rowe & Maw v C & E Commrs QB, [1975] STC 340* (travelling expenses billed by solicitors to client), *Shuttleworth & Co, [1994] VATTR 355 (12805)* (bank transfer fees re-charged to client) and *National Transit Insurance Co Ltd v C & E Commrs QB 1974, [1975] STC 35* (fee for handling insurance claim). However, where amounts are paid to third parties as agent of a client, such payments may be treated as disbursements if all the following conditions are satisfied.

(*a*)   The agent acted for his client when paying the third party.

4.8 Agents

(b) The client actually received and used the goods or services provided by the third party. This condition usually prevents the agent's own travelling expenses, telephone bills, postage etc. being treated as disbursements for VAT purposes.

(c) The client was responsible for paying the third party.

(d) The client authorised the agent to make the payment on his behalf.

(e) The client knew that the goods or services would be provided by a third party.

(f) The agent's outlay must be separately itemised when invoicing the client.

(g) The agent must recover only the exact amount he paid to the third party.

(h) The goods or services paid for must be clearly additional to the supplies made to the client.

If a payment qualifies as a disbursement, it can be treated in either of the following ways.

- The disbursement can be passed on to the client as a VAT-inclusive amount (if taxable) and excluded when calculating any VAT due on the main supply to the client. The agent cannot reclaim VAT on the supply (since no goods or services have been supplied to him). Unless the VAT invoice for the disbursement is addressed directly to the client, the client is also prevented from reclaiming input tax as he does not hold a valid invoice. Generally, therefore, it is only advantageous to treat a disbursement in this way if no VAT is chargeable on the supply by the third party or the client is not entitled to reclaim the VAT.

  If an agent does treat a payment as a disbursement in this way, he must keep evidence to enable him to show that he was entitled to exclude the payment from the value of his supply to his client. He must also be able to show that he did not reclaim input tax on the supply by the third party.

- The goods or services can be treated as supplied to and by the agent under 4.4 above. The agent can then reclaim the related input tax (subject to the normal rules) and charge VAT on the onward supply if appropriate.

Solicitor's search fees. Fees paid by a solicitor for a personal search of official records (e.g. a Land Registry search) in order to extract information needed to advise a client cannot be treated as disbursements. However, where a solicitor pays a fee for a postal search, this may be treated as a disbursement as the solicitor is merely obtaining a document on behalf of the client. See also 4.20 below.

(C & E Notice 700, para 10.8).

Counsel's fees. A concessionary treatment has been agreed with C & E for counsel's fees. The agent (usually a solicitor or accountant) may treat the counsel's advice as supplied directly to the client and the settlement of the fees as a disbursement. Counsel's VAT invoice may be amended by adding the name and address of the client to it and inserting 'per' before the agent's own name and address. The fee note from counsel will then be recognised as a valid VAT invoice in the hands of the client. Where the agent considers that the services of counsel, if supplied directly to the client, would be outside the scope of UK VAT, he may certify the counsel's fee note to this effect and pay the counsel only the net of VAT fee. (Tax Faculty of the ICAEW Guidance Notes 15/94, paras 23–26).

4.8   VAT REPRESENTATIVES AND AGENTS FOR OVERSEAS PRINCIPALS

C & E may *direct* a person who

(a) is a taxable person or, without being a taxable person, makes taxable supplies or acquires goods in the UK from one or more other EC countries, (*b*)   does not have any business establishment or other fixed establishment in the UK, and

(*c*)   in the case of an individual, does not have his usual place of residence in the UK

to appoint a VAT representative to act on his behalf for VAT purposes in the UK. A person is treated as having been directed to appoint a VAT representative if C & E have served notice of the direction on him or have taken all such other steps as appear to them to be reasonable for bringing the direction to his attention.

A person who has not been required by C & E to appoint a VAT representative but who satisfies the conditions in (*a*) to (*c*) above may nevertheless appoint a VAT representative with the agreement of C & E.

[*VATA 1994, s 48(1)(2)(8)*].

4.9   Effect of appointment

Subject to below, any person appointed as a VAT representative

*   is entitled to act on his principal's behalf for all purposes relating to VAT;

*   must ensure (if necessary by acting on his behalf) that his principal complies with, and discharges, all his obligations and liabilities relating to VAT; and

*   is jointly and severally liable with his principal for complying with UK VAT law.

A VAT representative is not, by virtue of the above, guilty of any offence committed by his principal unless he has consented to it or connived in its commission, its commission is attributable to any neglect on his part, or the offence is a contravention by the VAT representative of an obligation which, under those provisions, is imposed on both him and his principal.

[*VATA 1994, s 48(3)(5)*].

4.10   Failure to appoint a VAT representative

Where a person fails to appoint a VAT representative when directed to do so, C & E may require him to provide such security, or further security, as they think appropriate for the payment of any VAT which is or may become due from him. A person is treated as having been required to provide security if C & E have served notice of the requirement on him or have taken all such other steps as appear to them to be reasonable for bringing the requirement to his attention. Where any such security has been required and is not lodged, it can be recovered by distraint on goods (in Scotland through diligence) as if it were VAT due. See 17.3 and 17.4 CUSTOMS AND EXCISE: POWERS. There may also be a liability to a criminal penalty under 52.6 PENALTIES. [*VATA 1994, s 48(7)(7A)(8), 11 Sch 5(10); FA 1997, s 53(6)*].

4.11   Notification of appointment and changes

Any person appointed as a VAT representative of another must register for UK VAT on his behalf on Forms VAT 1 and VAT 1TR within 30 days. Evidence of the appointment must also be sent. If either the representative or the principal is a partnership, Form VAT 2 must also be completed. C & E must then register the name of the VAT representative against that of his principal in the register kept for the purposes of *VATA 1994*. A VAT representative can act for more than one principal at the same time but will be separately registered for each. These registrations are entirely separate from the VAT representative's own registration (if any).

4.12   Agents

Once appointed, the VAT representative must, within 30 days, notify C & E in writing of any changes in the name, constitution or ownership of his business or of his ceasing to act as his principal's VAT representative or of any other event which would require a change in the register. The date of cessation is the date of notification although where another person has been appointed as a VAT representative, C & E may treat the date of cessation as the date of appointment of that other person. A person also ceases to be a VAT representative with effect from the date he dies or becomes insolvent or incapacitated.

[*SI 1995/2518, Reg 10*]. (C & E Notice 725, paras 8.9–8.11).

4.12   Records to be kept

A VAT representative must set up and maintain a separate VAT account for each principal represented and keep enough documents to show how the VAT account is built up. He is also required to make any Intrastat Supplementary Declarations where the level of EC trade is above the appropriate threshold (see 2.27 ACCOUNTING PERIODS AND RETURNS).

The principal, because he is making taxable supplies in the UK, must keep all the RECORDS (57) required to be kept under UK law.

(C & E Notice 725, para 8.12).

4.13   EMPLOYMENT AGENCIES/BUREAUX

The agency will normally act in one of the following ways.

* The agency acts as a principal, supplying its own staff to the client. The staff may be employees of the agency or may be self-employed and engaged by the agency. In either case the worker's services are provided to the agency who in turn makes a supply to the client. The agency must account for VAT on the full charge to the client.

 From a date yet to be fixed, the government have announced new rules governing the conduct of employment bureaux. Under normal circumstances *any* temporary workers supplied by an employment bureau will have a contractual relationship with the bureau supplying them (either being an employee of the bureau under a contract of service or self-employed and engaged by the agency under a contract for services). In either case, the bureau will be acting as a principal for VAT purposes and VAT will be due on the full amount received from the client, including salary and associated costs in relation to the temporary worker. Until these new arrangements are in place, the staff hire concession which allows employment bureau hiring out staff not to charge VAT on salary costs if the client pays the staff direct (see 44.4 MANAGEMENT SERVICES AND SUPPLIES OF STAFF for details) will continue to apply. (C & E Business Brief 20/98, 28 September 1998).

* The agency, acting as an agent for the client, finds workers who enter into a direct contractual relationship with the client. This is similar to an introductory service and the agency must account for VAT on its agency charges to the client.

* The agency acts as an intermediary agent for both the client and the worker and supplies its agency service to both parties. In this case, VAT must be accounted for on the agency charges made to both parties.

The actions of the parties and all the relevant documentation must reflect the chosen method of operation.

(C & E Leaflet 700/34/94, para 12).

4.14   ESTATE AGENTS

The arrangement of the sale, purchase or lease of a client's property is a single supply of services to the client and cannot be broken down into the various items making up the service. If the property is in the UK or Isle of Man, the supply is standard-rated. If the property is situated outside the UK, the supply is treated as taking place where the land is situated and is therefore outside the scope of UK VAT. [*SI 1992/3121, Art 5*]. If the supply of services relates to land in another EC country, however, a liability to account for VAT on the services might arise in that country.

Where a purchaser is not found but a payment is received to cover out-of-pocket expenses, VAT must be accounted for at the standard rate on the payment received.

Where more than one estate agent is involved in the sale of a property because one estate agent (A) seeks the assistance of another (B), if the vendor is required to make the whole payment to A, that payment is consideration for A's taxable supply to the vendor. If A passes some of that payment to B, it is the consideration for the taxable supply of services from B to A.

Printed matter. The cost of buying or producing and distributing printed matter (e.g. pamphlets, leaflets, catalogues) are expenses incurred in the course of making the single supply of services to the client and cannot be treated as the separate supply of zero-rated printed matter even if itemised on the invoice. Charges for bought-in printed matter are not disbursements for VAT purposes.

Other items. Separate charges for maps, photographs, registration fees, notice boards, newspaper advertising, hire of rooms and travelling expenses are part of the overall charge and taxable as part of that supply. On the other hand, payments made to third parties as agent for the client may be treated as disbursements (see 4.7 above).

(C & E Leaflet 700/28/94).

See *C & E Commrs v Redrow Group plc CA, [1997] STC 1053* for disallowance of a claim to input tax by a builder where it paid the fees of estate agents instructed in the sale of the existing house of a purchaser of one of its new houses.

De Voil Indirect Tax Service. See V6.139.

4.15   AGENCIES SUPPLYING NURSING STAFF

Agencies supplying nurses and nursing auxiliaries may be acting as agent or as principal. The contractual relationships between the parties may be relevant but the true construction of the contractual documents might not always determine the nature of the supply for VAT purposes. Where this is so, the nature of the supplies for VAT purposes (i.e. whether supplied as agent or principal) becomes one of fact for a tribunal to decide rather than of law for the court to consider (*C & E Commrs v Reed Personnel Services Ltd QB, [1995] STC 588*).

C & E require evidence that an agreement exists before it can be accepted for VAT purposes that a person is acting as an agent. Such evidence is likely to be contained in the published terms of trading (e.g. brochures). If an agency claims to be the agent of the worker, it would be expected that the conditions of the worker's membership of the agency would include a statement to that effect. Similarly, where an agency claims to be the agent of the client, it would be expected that the agreement with the client includes a statement to that effect. If a worker is an employee of an agency (i.e. under contract of service) the agency will always be a principal in the supply of that worker's services to the client. Deduction of income tax and National Insurance from wages does not, however, necessarily mean that the worker is an employee. Similarly, the method of invoicing (i.e. whether this shows the total amount due as a single figure or the various component parts making up the total — nursing care, national insurance, commission) does not indicate whether the relationship is one of agency or principal.

Nurses' agencies may only supply registered or enrolled nurses and midwives.

- *If acting as agent*, the commission, fee or charge for providing services to the client is standard-rated. The nurse's services in carrying out nursing care are exempt. Payments by the agency to the nurses are disbursements made on behalf of the client and do not form part of the agency's outputs.

- *If acting as principal*, a single supply is being made and the whole charge to the client is exempt.

See *Allied Medicare Nursing Services Ltd (5485)* and *British Nursing Co-Operation Ltd (8816)*.

Employment agencies. Where employment agencies supply registered or enrolled nurses and midwives, the same rules apply as for nurses' agencies above. Where, however, they supply nursing auxiliaries:

- *If acting as agent*, the commission, fee or charge for providing services to the client is standard-rated. The nurse's services in carrying out nursing care are exempt if carried out in a hospital or other similar approved institution but standard-rated if carried out elsewhere. (The distinction is, however, unimportant unless the particular nurse's earnings exceed the VAT registration threshold.) Payments by the agency to the nurses are disbursements made on behalf of the client and do not form part of the agency's outputs.

- *If acting as principal*, a single supply is being made which is exempt from VAT if the services are carried out in a hospital or other approved institution and standard-rated if carried out elsewhere.

(C & E Leaflet 710/2/83).

4.16   **THEATRICAL AGENTS**

Where a theatrical agent acts as an agent in the strict sense of that word and introduces artists to venues for a commission, the normal provisions apply. It is, however, a common practice for some artists to contract their services to a theatrical agent for an agreed period and fee. This arrangement is usually referred to as a Nett Act or Nett Deal. In such a case, the agent is acting as principal and, if registered for VAT, must account for VAT on the total charge to the venue whether or not the act is registered. There is also a taxable supply of services to the agent by the artist (assuming he is registered for VAT purposes).

(C & E Leaflet 710/1/91).

4.17   **TRAVEL AGENTS**

The following provisions explain how a travel agent should account for VAT when arranging travel services as an agent or intermediary. The provisions do not cover

- supplies by tour operators buying in and reselling travel facilities in their own right (for which see 66 TOUR OPERATORS' MARGIN SCHEME); or

- supplies by travel agents who are acting in the capacity of a principal.

A travel agent may act as an agent for some travel sales and as a principal for others. For any particular transaction, a person will normally be regarded as a travel agent if

- he has some documentary evidence from the principal confirming his status as an agent;

- there are clear statements included in the terms and conditions of the contract with the customer that the service he is arranging is supplied by a named principal; and

- he is not taking any significant commercial risk in relation to the service he is arranging.

Once it is established that a travel agent is acting as an agent, it is then necessary to determine whether the place of supply is in the UK and, if so, whether the supply is standard-rated, zero-rated or exempt. For a detailed consideration of the place of supply of services generally, see 64.18–64.31 SUPPLY.

The more common supplies by travel agents are considered below.

(*a*) **Insurance and financial services**. If a travel agent makes arrangements for the supply of insurance or makes a charge for exchanging currency or travellers' cheques, the place of supply of his services is

  (i) where the customer belongs if the customer belongs

  - outside the EC; or

  - in another EC country and receives the supply of services for business purposes; and

  (ii) where the travel agent belongs in all other cases.

Any charges for exchanging currency are exempt under *VATA 1994, 9 Sch Group 5, Item 1*. See 27.3 FINANCE.

The supply of arranging travel insurance in the UK is exempt if supplied

- in isolation of any travel; or

- in relation to a supply of travel on which no UK VAT is payable; or

- in relation to a sale of travel services which bears UK VAT provided that the travel agent notifies the traveller, in writing, of the price of the insurance as due under the contract of insurance *and* any fee related to that insurance charged over and above the premium.

See 37.11 INSURANCE.

(*b*) **Other travel facilities**. If a travel agent makes a charge for arranging any other travel facilities not falling within (*a*) above, the place of supply is

  (i) for services in the EC for a principal who is registered for VAT in the EC, the country where the principal is registered;

  (ii) for services outside the EC or for a principal who is not registered for VAT in the EC, the country where the supply being arranged is made and for this purpose

  - designated travel services are made where the tour operator belongs;

  - passenger transport is supplied in the country or countries where it takes place;

  - accommodation is supplied in the country where it is situated;

  - tuition (e.g. on educational holidays) and live entertainment are supplied where performed; and

  - car hire is normally supplied where the supplier belongs (but see also 64.30 SUPPLY).

If the place of supply of arranging any such travel services is outside the UK, there is no liability to UK VAT. If the place of supply is another EC country, the travel agent may be liable to register and account for VAT there, although if the *principal* is registered for VAT in a different EC country, the principal is responsible for accounting for VAT under the 'reverse charge' procedure.

Arranging passenger transport. Zero-rating applies to a travel agent's services of making arrangements for supplies of passenger transport which are themselves zero-rated under *VATA 1994, 8 Sch Group 8, item 4.* This includes making arrangements for scheduled flights, international journeys and most UK transport in vehicles with carrying capacity of twelve or more persons. The travel agent's customer might be the supplier of the passenger transport, the purchaser or both.

The services of a sub-agent (i.e. an agent acting for another agent) and the making of arrangements for designated travel services under the TOUR OPERATORS' MARGIN SCHEME (66) are standard-rated.

See 68.14 to 68.23 TRANSPORT AND FREIGHT for a more detailed consideration of passenger transport and 68.30 TRANSPORT AND FREIGHT for services of agents in providing transport generally.

Examples of zero-rated supplies

- Sales of tickets as agent for an airline ('seat-only' sales) unless a pleasure flight or a domestic flight in an aircraft with a carrying capacity of less than twelve people when standard-rated

- Sales of tickets for zero-rated passenger transport as agent for a ferry operator or rail operator

- Sale of tickets for international flights ('seat-only' sales) as agent for a non-EC tour operator

- Arranging a zero-rated cruise as the agent of a cruise operator

Examples of standard-rated supplies

- Sales of tickets for any transport as agent for a tour operator who has bought in the transport

- Arranging package holidays as agent for a tour operator

- Arranging a cruise as agent of a tour operator who has bought in the cruise

- Sale of tickets for any flight on behalf of another agent

- Arranging taxi transfers as agent for a taxi firm

(C & E Notice 709/6/97).

4.18   AUCTIONEERS

The rules in 4.2–4.7 above apply to auctioneers if they offer goods for sale as agents of the seller. If an auctioneer issues an invoice for goods in his own name, the goods are treated as supplied to the auctioneer by the vendor and by the auctioneer to the buyer. The auctioneer is liable to account for VAT on the supply of the goods as well as on the commission charged to the seller and, if applicable, on any fee charged to the buyer (the 'buyer's premium'). However, where an auctioneer arranges supplies of second-hand goods, works of art or collectors' items, he may be able to use the special accounting scheme for auctioneers. This scheme allows auctioneers to calculate their VAT on a margin basis. The margin on such sales is normally equal to the commission and associated charges and the amount of output tax due is largely unchanged in comparison to supplies by auctioneers made before that date. See 61.53 SECOND-HAND GOODS for further details.

(C & E Notice 700, para 10.5).

See 2.18 ACCOUNTING PERIODS AND RETURNS where an auctioneer arranges sales of goods in satisfaction of a debt (e.g. under a court order) of a registered person and the goods sold are part of the debtor's business assets. The procedures outlined above for agents must not be followed.

De Voil Indirect Tax Service. See V6.107–107C.

4.19   **DEBT COLLECTION AGENCIES**

The following VAT treatment applies with effect from 1 April 1998 to debt collectors who act as agents.

(*a*)   **Court fees.** Amounts paid by collectors to solicitors in respect of court fees may be treated as disbursements on behalf of the creditor. Any amount recovered from debtors in respect of such fees and retained by collectors may then be regarded as reimbursement of the amount disbursed and outside the scope of VAT.

(*b*)   **Legal fees.** Two options are open to collectors in respect of VAT charged by solicitors for their services.

●   Collectors may choose not to recover the VAT as input tax and treat the charges as disbursements under 4.7 above. If so, where the agreement with the creditor provides that the collector bears the cost of solicitors' services but may retain, as reimbursement of his costs, any amounts recovered from the debtor in respect of solicitors' scale charges awarded by the court, such amounts may be treated as outside the scope of VAT.

●   Collectors may choose to recover the VAT as input tax, subject to the normal rules, but recharge the legal fees, plus VAT, to the creditor under *VATA 1994, s 47(3)* (see 4.4 above). The scale charges retained represent payment of the fees recharged.

If a debt collector considers that he is acting as a principal, any VAT charged to him by a solicitor is recoverable as input tax, subject to the normal rules. However, any amounts recovered by the collector from the debtor in respect of court fees and/or solicitors' scale charges and retained represents consideration for the collector's supply of services to the creditor. Output tax must be accounted for on all such amounts in the normal way. This treatment does not apply if the collector has received an equitable or legal assignment of the debts, whether in whole or in part. Such an assignment is an exempt supply of services to the collector and the collection of the debts is outside the scope of VAT.

(C & E Notice 700, para 10.12).

4.20   **SEARCH AGENCIES**

With effect from 1 February 1998, C & E regard the fiche or document obtained from a source such as Companies House as a piece of information rather than a tangible object. The recharge of a search fee to the customer for the provision of a fiche or document may be treated as a disbursement under 4.7 above provided

●   the information is passed on without analysis or comment; or

●   the agency carries out a process on the fiche or document (e.g. conversion of a fiche to hard copy or provision of typewritten extracts) but does not use the data to inform an opinion or report.

4.21 Agents

Where the agency analyses, comments on, or produces a report on a fiche or document, or otherwise uses the information obtained on a search to make a report, the search fee is not a disbursement but a component part of the cost of providing the service to the customer, and is taxable at the standard rate.

(C & E Notice 700, para 10.11).

4.21 'PARTY PLAN' AND 'DIRECT' SELLING

See 69.4 VALUATION for supplies of goods made to non-taxable persons for retail sale.

See also *Churchway Crafts Ltd (No 1) (782)* and *(No 2) (1186)* ; *C & E Commrs v Pippa-Dee Parties Ltd QB, [1981] STC 495* and *Younger (1173)*. For a discussion of the nature of the distributor/dealer relationship, see *P & R Potter CA 1984, [1985] STC 145* where the relationship was found to be that of principal to principal and VAT payable on the recommended retail price. See also *Betterware Products Ltd v C & E Commrs QB, [1985] STC 648*.

For the VAT position of any incentive gifts to encourage individuals to act as agents for mail order concerns, see 47.4 OUTPUT TAX and *GUS Merchandise Corporation Ltd v C & E Commrs CA, [1981] STC 569*.

5   Appeals

Cross-references. See 6.8 ASSESSMENTS for correction of assessments on appeal by tribunals; 8.9 BUSINESS for appeals regarding registration of two or more persons as one taxable person; 31.5 GROUPS OF COMPANIES; 35.12 INPUT TAX for appeals in respect of input tax; 52.20 PENALTIES for mitigation of penalties by a tribunal on appeal.

De Voil Indirect Tax Service. See V5.4.

The contents of this chapter are as follows.

5.1   RECONSIDERATIONS

When a person disagrees with a decision made by C & E, he may ask his VAT office to reconsider it. This is an informal process of looking again at the decision and will be carried out internally by C & E but by an officer independent of the officer who made the original decision. The role of the review officer is not to defend the appealed decision but rather to consider the appellant's case objectively and attempt to resolve the dispute. The officer will be seeking to avoid a formal appeal except in cases of genuine disagreement and has considerable scope for negotiation and compromise. This may mean overturning or varying the original decision.

A person should ask C & E to reconsider a decision if he can provide further information or there are facts which he thinks have not been fully taken into account. Asking for a reconsideration does not deny the right of an appeal to a VAT tribunal and C & E will discuss or review a case at any time, even though an appeal may have already been lodged with the VAT tribunal. C & E aim to complete a reconsideration within six weeks of the request.

Although a reconsideration can be requested at any time, a notice of appeal to VAT tribunal must normally be served within 30 days of date of the disputed decision (see 5.5 below). If a reconsideration is requested within the 30-day time limit for an appeal, and the reconsideration then exhausts that 30-day period, C & E can

(*a*)   confirm the original decision, in which case the trader has a further 21 days from the date of confirmation to lodge an appeal with a VAT tribunal; or

(*b*)   send a revised decision, in which case he has a further 30 days from the date of that decision to lodge an appeal.

In any case, the trader should ask C & E to extend the time limit for appealing against the decision in case agreement cannot be reached.

If a reconsideration is requested after the 30-day time limit for an appeal, C & E have no equivalent powers to grant an extension of time and the trader must apply to the tribunal for an extension (see 5.5 below).

(C & E Notice 700, paras 13.1; 13.3; C & E Manual V1-29, Chapter 1, Chapter 2 section 1).

5.2   **APPEALS — INTRODUCTION**

An appeal against a decision of C & E on certain matters may be made to a VAT tribunal and from there, *on a point of law only*, to the High Court (Court of Session in Scotland) and continued up to the House of Lords under normal procedure. The matters on which an appeal to a tribunal may be made are restricted and certain conditions must be complied with.

Legal aid is not available for appeals to tribunals. However, a potential appellant may be able to obtain advice on an appeal or application under the Legal Aid 'Green Form' scheme. Advice can be obtained at all Legal Aid area offices (addresses available at any solicitors or Citizens Advice Bureau).

Constitution. The functions of the VAT tribunals are carried out by a President, a panel of chairmen and a panel of other members. The responsibility for administering the VAT tribunals rests with the Lord Chancellor in relation to England, Wales and Northern Ireland and, for Scotland, with the Secretary of State for Scotland whose responsibilities are discharged by the Scottish Courts Administration.

The tribunals operate under the supervision of the Council on Tribunals whose offices are at St Dunstan's House, Fetter Lane, London EC4A 1HD. They are statutory bodies independent of the Commissioners with headquarters in London at 15/19 Bedford Avenue, London WC1B 3AS (Tel: (0171) 631 4242).

[*VATA 1994, 12 Sch 1-7*].

Procedural rules. The Lord Chancellor after consultation with the Lord Advocate may make rules with respect to the procedure to be followed on appeals to, and in other proceedings before, tribunals and such rules may include provisions for

• limiting the time within which appeals may be brought, see 5.5 below;

• enabling hearings to be held in private, see 5.16 below;

• parties to the proceedings to be represented by such persons as may be determined, see 5.16 below;

• requiring persons to attend and give evidence, see 5.14 below;

• discovery and for requiring persons to produce documents, see 5.11 below;

• the payment of expenses and allowances to persons attending as witnesses or producing documents, see 5.14 below;

• the award and recovery of costs, see 5.18 below; and

• authorising the administration of oaths to witnesses, see 5.16 below.

[*VATA 1994, 12 Sch 9*].

Penalties. A person who fails to comply with a direction or summons issued by a VAT tribunal is liable to a penalty not exceeding £1,000. The penalty may be awarded summarily by the tribunal notwithstanding that no proceedings for its recovery have been commenced. Appeal lies to the High Court (Court of Session in Scotland) which court may confirm or reverse the decision of the tribunal and reduce or increase the penalty. Any penalty so awarded is recoverable as VAT due from the person liable. [*VATA 1994, 12 Sch 10*].

De Voil Indirect Tax Service. See V1.241; V5.391.

5.3 **MATTERS OF APPEAL**

An appeal to a tribunal against a decision of C & E may only be made on the following matters.

(*a*) The registration or cancellation of registration of any person.

(*b*) The VAT chargeable on the supply of any goods or services, on the acquisition of goods from another EC country or, subject to (ii) below, on the importation of goods from a place outside the EC. A tribunal has no jurisdiction in relation to future supplies (*Allied Windows (S Wales) Ltd v C & E Commrs QB, April 1983 (unreported); Odhams Leisure Group Ltd v C & E Commrs QB, [1992] STC 332*).

(*c*) The amount of any input tax which may be credited to a person.

(*d*) Any claim for a refund by virtue of regulations made under *VATA 1994, s 13(5)* (acquisitions of goods from another EC country where VAT has also been paid in that other country).

(*da*) A decision by C & E under *VATA 1994, s 18A* on the approval of a person as a fiscal warehousekeeper or the withdrawal of such approval or the fiscal warehouse status from any premises. See 70.13 WAREHOUSED GOODS AND FREE ZONES.

(*e*) The proportion of input tax allowable under *VATA 1994, s 26*.

(*f*) A claim by a taxable person under *VATA 1994, s 27* (goods imported for another person for private purposes, see 35.8 INPUT TAX).

(*fa*) A decision by C & E that an election under *SI 1993/2001, Art 12A* (right to elect under the payments on account provisions to pay actual liability for the preceding month rather than the predetermined amount) shall cease to have effect. See 51.4 PAYMENT OF VAT.

(*g*) The amount of any refunds under *VATA 1994, s 35* (construction of certain buildings otherwise than in the course of a business by 'do-it-yourself' builders, see 42.53 LAND AND BUILDINGS).

(*h*) A claim for a refund under *VATA 1994, s 36* or earlier provisions (see BAD DEBT RELIEF (7)).

(*j*) The amount of any refunds under *VATA 1994, s 40* (supplies of new means of transport to other EC countries by non-taxable persons, see 23.34 EUROPEAN COMMUNITY: SINGLE MARKET).

(*k*) Any refusal of an application under *VATA 1994, s 43* (applications re group treatment, see 31.3 GROUPS OF COMPANIES).

(*l*) The requirement of any security under *VATA 1994, s 48(7)* or *11 Sch 4(2)* (for the payment of VAT due or which may become due, see 17.1 CUSTOMS AND EXCISE: POWERS).

(*m*) Any refusal or cancellation of certification under *VATA 1994, s 54* or any refusal to cancel such certification (flat-rate scheme for farmers, see 63.15 SPECIAL SCHEMES).

(*n*) Any liability to a penalty or surcharge under *VATA 1994, ss 59–69* (see 52.9–52.15, 52.18 and 52.19 PENALTIES). See also 52.20 PENALTIES for mitigation by the tribunal.

5.3 Appeals

(*o*) A decision of C & E under *VATA 1994, s 61* (liability of a director where the conduct of a company gives rise to a penalty for VAT evasion, see 52.9 PENALTIES).

(*p*) The making or amount of an assessment under *VATA 1994, s 73(1)(2)* for any period for which the appellant has made a return or under *VATA 1994, s 73(7)(7A)(7B) or 75* (see 6.1(*b*)-(*g*) ASSESSMENTS).

(*q*) The amount of any penalty, interest or surcharge specified in an assessment under *VATA 1994, s 76* (see 6.3 ASSESSMENTS). See also 52.20 PENALTIES for mitigation by the tribunal.

(*r*) The making of an assessment, on the basis set out in *VATA 1994, s 77(4)*, outside the normal time limit where it is believed that VAT may have been lost through fraud, conduct involving dishonesty, failure to notify liability to be registered or unauthorised issue of VAT invoices. See 6.4 ASSESSMENTS.

(*s*) Any liability of C & E to pay interest under *VATA 1994, s 78* or the amount of the interest payable (see 51.11 PAYMENT OF VAT).

(*sa*) An assessment under *VATA 1994, s 78A* (interest overpayments) or the amount of such an assessment (see 6.5 ASSESSMENTS).

(*t*) A claim under *VATA 1994, s 80* (refund of VAT overpaid by taxpayer, see 51.7 PAYMENT OF VAT), an assessment under *VATA 1994, s 80(4A)* (repayment to C & E of overpaid refund, see 6.5 ASSESSMENTS) or the amount of such an assessment.

(*ta*) An assessment under *VATA 1994, s 80B(1)* (recovery by C & E under the unjust enrichment provisions of refunds made to a taxpayer) or the amount of such an assessment (see 6.5 ASSESSMENTS).

(*u*) Any direction or supplementary direction under *VATA 1994, 1 Sch 2* (registration of two or more persons as one taxable person, see 8.5 BUSINESS).

(*v*) Any direction under *VATA 1994, 6 Sch 1 or 2* or under *VATA 1983, 4 Sch 2* (VAT on transactions between connected persons and supplies of goods to non-taxable persons for retail sale and, see 69.3 and 69.4 VALUATION).

(*w*) Any direction under *VATA 1994, 7 Sch 1* (VAT on acquisitions of goods between connected persons to be charged on the open market value, see 69.9 VALUATION).

(*wa*) Any direction or assessment under *VATA 1994, 9A Sch* (anti-avoidance provisions for groups, see 31.5 GROUPS OF COMPANIES).

(*x*) Any refusal to permit the value of supplies to be determined by a method described in a C & E Notice published under *VATA 1994, 11 Sch 2(6)* (see 60.1 RETAIL SCHEMES).

(*y*) Any refusal of authorisation or termination of authorisation in connection with the scheme under *VATA 1994, 11 Sch 2(7)* (cash accounting scheme, see 63.2 SPECIAL SCHEMES).

(*z*) Any requirement imposed by C & E in a particular case under *VATA 1994, 11 Sch 3(2)(b)* (production of VAT invoices by computer, see 40.13 INVOICES).

[*VATA 1994, s 83; FA 1996, s 31(3), 3 Sch 12; FA 1997, ss 45(2)(5), 46(3)(4), 47(7)(9); SI 1997/2542*].

No appeal lies to a tribunal on

(i) any matter which is outside (*a*) to (*z*) above (subject to below); or

(ii) any decision which C & E can be required to review under *FA 1994, s 14* (decisions relating to customs duty or the Community Customs Code or made under *CEMA*

1979) unless no request for a review has been made or the decision relates only to whether or not zero-rating applies to the importation of the goods in question and/or the rate of VAT charged on the goods.

[*VATA 1994, s 84(9)*].

Where an appeal is against a decision of C & E which depended upon a prior decision taken by them in relation to the appellant, the fact that the prior decision was not within (*a*) to (*z*) above (e.g. the exercise of a discretion by C & E) does not prevent the tribunal from allowing the appeal on the grounds that it would have allowed an appeal against the prior decision. [*VATA 1994, s 84(10)*]. This follows the decision in *JH Corbitt (Numismatists) Ltd HL, [1980] STC 231.*

Extra-statutory concessions. In *RW Shepherd, [1994] VATTR 47 (11753)*, the tribunal held that C & E were bound to have regard to the terms of their concessions and while the tribunal could not interfere with those terms, it was entitled to consider whether those terms had been complied with. A similar conclusion was reached in *British Teleflower Service Ltd, [1995] VATDR 356(13756)*. However, it has been held in *Dr BN Purdue (13430)* and subsequently in *C & E Commrs v Arnold, QB [1996] STC 1271* that a tribunal has no jurisdiction in relation to non-statutory arrangements or concessions which are a matter for the Commissioners. In *Arnold*, Hidden J, disapproving of the decision in *British Teleflower Service Ltd*, held that the provisions of *VATA 1994, s 84(10)* (see above) only applied to a case where there were two separate decisions (as had been the case in *JH Corbitt (Numismatists) Ltd*) and did not apply in the present case where there had only been one decision.

De Voil Indirect Tax Service. See V5.404–406.

5.4   **CONDITIONS OF APPEAL**

No appeal will be entertained unless the following conditions are satisfied.

  (i) The appellant has made all the returns which he is required to make. No appeal may be entertained for an accounting period (even if valid for that period by a return having been submitted in respect of it) as long as default continues in respect of the return of any other accounting period (*Shaft Sports Ltd, [1983] VATTR 180 (1450)*).

 (ii) The appellant has paid the amounts shown in those returns as payable by him. See *R v VAT Tribunal (ex p Minster Associates) QB, [1988] STC 386* and *R v C & E Commrs, ex p Menzies QB 1988, [1989] STC 40*.

(iii) In the case of an appeal on matters under 5.3(*b*), (*n*), (*p*), (*q*) or (*sa*) above,

  • the amount which C & E have determined to be payable as VAT (or, in the case of 5.3(*sa*) have notified by assessment) has been paid or deposited with them; or

  • on being satisfied that the appellant would otherwise suffer hardship, C & E agree, or the tribunal decides, that the appeal be entertained notwithstanding non-payment (see 5.21 below). For the powers of the tribunal where an assessment covers several prescribed accounting periods, see *Don Pasquale (a firm) v C & E Commrs CA, [1990] STC 556*. Note that if the hardship application is granted but, subsequently, the appeal is lost, default interest on the amount of the disputed VAT may be payable. Conversely, if the hardship application is lost but, subsequently, the appeal is won, C & E are liable to pay interest on any amount of disputed VAT paid or deposited with them which is repayable (see 51.11 PAYMENT OF VAT).

5.5   Appeals

[*VATA 1994, s 84(2)(3); FA 1995, s 31; FA 1997, s 45(3)(5)*].

(iv) The appellant has a sufficient interest in maintaining the appeal. (See *Williams and Glyn's Bank Ltd, [1974] VATTR 262 (118)*). The appellant is not required to be a taxable person accountable for the VAT in dispute (e.g. he may be an unregistered recipient of taxable supplies) but where he is the recipient of a supply, he should wherever possible seek the consent of the supplier to the appeal being brought jointly (*Processed Vegetable Growers Association Ltd, [1973] VATTR 87 (25)*). For other cases where a tribunal allowed an appeal by the recipient of a supply, see *Dr Cameron, [1973] VATTR 177 (41); Gilbourne, [1974] VATTR 209 (109)* ; and *Beckley (JR) (114)*.

C & E may however waive the requirements of (i) and (ii) above which are to protect them from frivolous and delaying appeals (*Stilwell Darby & Co Ltd, [1973] VATTR 145 (35); Gittins, t/a Robinsons Ironmongery, [1974] VATTR 109 (87)*).

Where C & E have obtained a final judgment against the applicant for VAT on an assessment, the tribunal has no jurisdiction to entertain an appeal unless the applicant first procures the High Court judgment against him to be set aside (*Digwa (TS), [1978] VATTR 119 (612)*).

De Voil Indirect Tax Service. See V5.402; V5.421–423.

5.5   TIME LIMIT FOR APPEALS

A notice of appeal must be served at the appropriate tribunal centre within 30 days after the date of the document containing the disputed decision of C & E. If, during the 30 days, C & E so notify the appellant by letter, his time to appeal is extended until the expiration of 21 days after a date set out in that letter or to be set out in a further letter. [*SI 1986/590, Rule 4*].

A tribunal may of its own motion, or on application of either party, extend the time limit for doing anything in relation to the appeal. [*SI 1986/590, Rule 19(1)*]. If the time limit has expired, any notice of appeal to the tribunal should be served together with a Notice of Application for an extension of time setting out the reason for the delay.

An extension has been allowed where the appellant was mistakenly under the impression that the matter was being handled by his accountants (*Hallam (WR) (683)*) and where the appeal was delayed through the illness of a partner (*Hornby (WW & JH) (155)*). Application was refused, although within the discretion of the tribunal, where to admit it would be to enable the applicant to recover VAT paid voluntarily under a mistake of law (*Kyffin (R), [1978] VATTR 175 (617)*). In *WJ Price, [1978] VATTR 115 (559)* an extension was allowed where, although no real excuse for delay existed, there was evidence that the taxpayer intended to appeal, but this decision was not followed in *Wan & Wan (14829)* on the grounds that the earlier tribunal's reasoning was inconsistent with subsequent decisions of the Court of Appeal including that in *Norwich & Peterborough Building Society v Steed, CA [1991] 1 WLR 449; [1991] 2 All ER 880*.

5.6   MAKING AN APPEAL

The following standard forms for use in connection with appeals (and applications) to a tribunal are available from any tribunal office or VAT office.

Form Trib 1	Notice of Appeal
Form Trib 2	List of Documents (see 5.11 below)
Form Trib 3/3a	Witness Statement and Continuation (see 5.14 below)
Form Trib 4	Notice of Objection (to Witness Statement)

Form Trib 5   Notice of Application (see 5.21 below)
Form Trib 6   Notice of Application for an appeal to be heard without payment or deposit of VAT (see 5.21 below)

It is not essential to use the printed forms but any notice or document served must contain all information required to be set out by *SI 1986/590* (see below).

Contents and serving of notice of appeal. The notice of appeal, signed by or on behalf of the appellant, must

* state the name and address of the appellant;

* state the date (if any) with effect from which the appellant was registered for VAT and the nature of his business;

* state the address of C & E office from which the disputed decision was sent;

* state the date of the document containing the disputed decision and the address to which it was sent; and

* have attached a document containing the disputed decision and the grounds for the appeal, including in a Category 2 appeal (see 5.9 below), particulars of the excuse relied upon.

The grounds must be stated in sufficient detail to enable C & E to appreciate the case to be presented to the tribunal by the appellant. It must have attached a copy of any letter from C & E extending the time limit for appeal against the disputed decision and any further letter notifying the appellant of a date from which his time to appeal runs. [*SI 1986/590, Rule 3; SI 1994/2617*].

When completed, the notice of appeal should be handed, or sent by post or fax, to the 'proper officer' at the 'appropriate tribunal centre'. The '*proper officer*' is a member of the administrative staff of the tribunals appointed for the purpose. The '*appropriate tribunal centre*' is normally that centre for the area covering the address to which C & E's decision was sent. Application may be made (on *Form Trib 5*) to the appropriate tribunal centre for the transfer of an appeal to another tribunal centre. [*SI 1986/590, Rules 2, 15, 31; SI 1991/186, Rule 23; SI 1997/255*]. See 5.23 below for addresses of VAT tribunal centres and VAT offices covered.

The notice of appeal must be acknowledged and a copy will be sent to C & E. The acknowledgement and copy must state the date of service and date of notification to C & E. It will also show the tribunal reference number to be quoted in future correspondence. [*SI 1986/590, Rule 5; SI 1991/186, Rule 4*].

Representatives of the appellant may be authorised to receive acknowledgement of service of appeal and other documents will be sent to that person. [*SI 1986/590, Rule 32; SI 1991/186, Rule 24*].

One or more partners in a firm may appeal in the name of the firm, unless a tribunal directs otherwise, but with the same consequences as would have ensued if brought in the individual names of the partners. [*SI 1986/590, Rule 12; SI 1994/2617*].

On the death or bankruptcy of an appellant, if his liability or interest passes to another person (the 'successor'), the tribunal may direct, on the application of C & E or the successor, that the successor is substituted for the original appellant. Written consent is required from the successor. Where this is not received within two months of being requested by the tribunal, the tribunal may, of its own motion or on application by C & E, and after having given written notice to the successor, dismiss the appeal. It may similarly dismiss any appeal where it is satisfied that there is no person interested in it in succession to the original appellant. [*SI 1986/590, Rule 13; SI 1994/2617*].

5.7 Appeals

Withdrawal of an appeal. A person may withdraw an appeal at any time by notice in writing, signed by him or on his behalf, to the proper officer at the appropriate tribunal centre. The withdrawal of an appeal does not prevent a party from applying for an award of costs or interest (see 5.18 and 5.19 below) or a tribunal from making such award as it thinks fit. [*SI 1986/590, Rule 16; SI 1994/2617; SI 1997/255*]. If he notifies C & E, whether orally or in writing, that he does not wish to proceed with the appeal, then unless C & E object in writing to the withdrawal of the appeal within 30 days of notification, the provisions relating to settling appeals by agreement (see 5.8 below) are treated as having effect as if, at the date of notification, the appellant and C & E had come to an agreement that the decision under appeal should be upheld without variation. [*VATA 1994, s 85(4)*]. If an appellant wishes to withdraw his appeal after a date has been set for a hearing, he should notify the tribunal centre immediately. C & E may ask for costs if they attend a mutually agreed hearing where the appellant fails to appear.

De Voil Indirect Tax Service. See V5.411; V5.461; V5.462.

5.7   **REJECTION AND AMENDMENT OF AN APPEAL**

Where C & E contend that

(*a*)   no appeal lies to the tribunal (see 5.3 above); or

(*b*)   an appeal cannot be entertained because the conditions of appeal have not been satisfied (see 5.4 above)

they must serve a notice to that effect at the appropriate tribunal centre (with copy to the appellant) containing the grounds for such contention. A copy of the disputed decision must also be sent unless previously served. In the case of Category 2 appeals (see 5.9 below) the hearing of C & E's application can immediately precede the hearing of the substantive appeal. [*SI 1986/590, Rule 6*].

The tribunal must strike out an appeal where (*a*) above applies and dismiss an appeal where (*b*) above applies. The tribunal may dismiss an appeal for want of prosecution where the appellant (or the person to whom his interest has been assigned etc.) has been guilty of inordinate and inexcusable delay. No appeal can be struck out or dismissed without a hearing unless the parties have settled the appeal by agreement (see 5.8 below). [*SI 1986/590, Rule 18*].

The tribunal may, at any time, either on its own motion or on the application of any party, direct that a notice or document (but not a tribunal decision) be amended on such terms as it thinks fit. [*SI 1986/590, Rule 14*].

De Voil Indirect Tax Service. See V5.412.

5.8   **SETTLING APPEALS BY AGREEMENT**

Where a person has given notice of appeal but before the appeal is determined by a tribunal he comes to an agreement with C & E, the agreement is binding as if a tribunal had determined the appeal in accordance with the terms of the agreement (including any terms as to costs). This applies whether the decision under appeal is treated as upheld without variation, varied in a particular manner or discharged or cancelled. The agreement need not be in writing but, in the case of verbal agreement, the fact that agreement was reached and the terms of that agreement must be confirmed in writing by either party. The time of the agreement is then treated as the date of giving that notice of confirmation. The appellant may, however, within 30 days of the agreement, give written notice to C & E that he desires to repudiate or resile from the agreement. A person may act through an agent in all matters relating to settling appeals by agreement. [*VATA 1994, s 85(1)–(3)(5)*]. Where C & E and the taxpayer reach a compounding agreement, the dispute between the parties is resolved and any assessments raised effectively treated as discharged. Any outstanding appeal must be treated as having been settled by agreement (*Cummings (C) (14870)*).

Where the parties have agreed on the terms of any decision or direction to be given by a tribunal, a tribunal may give such decision or direction without a hearing. [*SI 1986/590, Rule 17*].

5.9   **PREPARATION FOR THE HEARING**

There are three different categories of appeal to the tribunals and procedure varies accordingly.

Category 1. Evasion penalty appeal. This is an appeal against

- a liability for a penalty under *VATA 1994, ss 60* or *61* (see 52.9 PENALTIES) assessed on the grounds that the taxpayer (or a director or similar person) has been guilty of dishonest conduct, or

- the amount of such a penalty.

Category 2. Mitigation appeals and reasonable excuse appeals. A '*mitigation appeal*' is an appeal to a tribunal to reduce the amount of a penalty assessed under 52.9 to 52.12 PENALTIES.

A '*reasonable excuse*' appeal is either

- an appeal against any liability to, or the amount of, one of the penalties in 52.10 to 52.14 or 52.17 to 52.19 PENALTIES on the grounds that there is a reasonable excuse for the conduct which gave rise to the penalty; or

- an appeal against a liability to, or the amount of, a default surcharge (see 52.15 PENALTIES) on the grounds that *either* the return or VAT was sent at such a time or in such a manner that it would be reasonable to expect that it would be received by C & E within the time limit *or* there is a reasonable excuse for the return or the VAT not having been so despatched.

If the appellant is both appealing against the liability to a penalty or surcharge and also seeking a discharge of the penalty or surcharge on the grounds of reasonable excuse, the appeal falls within Category 3 below.

Category 3. Other appeals. These are all other appeals not falling within Categories 1 and 2. They include all appeals against decisions of C & E with respect to assessments for VAT (as distinct from penalties, interest or surcharges) and the amounts of any such assessments. If the appeal is against both an assessment and for an accompanying penalty for dishonest conduct, the appeal falls within Category 1 above.

[*SI 1986/590, Rule 2; SI 1994/2617; SI 1997/255*].

5.10   **Statement of case**

Unless the tribunal otherwise directs, C & E must, within 42 days of the date of notification to them of the notice of appeal for Category 1 appeals (30 days for Category 3 appeals), serve at the appropriate tribunal centre a statement of case setting out the matters and facts on which they rely (including full particulars of the alleged dishonesty in a Category 1 appeal and the relevant statutory provision). Where C & E have made an application under *Rule 6* (see 5.7 above) which has been withdrawn or dismissed, the period runs from the date of notification of withdrawal or dismissal, if later. A copy of the disputed decision must be attached unless previously served by either party. If C & E are late in serving their statement of case and apply for an extension of time, this will normally be granted where there is no obvious injustice to the appellant. The period during which the documents should have been, but were not, served may be ignored in calculating interest on any VAT which may ultimately be due (*Dormer Builders (London) Ltd, [1986] VATTR 69 (2044)*).

No statement of case is required in a Category 2 appeal as particulars are set out in the Notice of Appeal (see 5.6 above).

A copy of the statement of case will be sent to the appellant by the tribunal centre. In a Category 1 appeal, the appellant must, within 42 days of the notification to him of the case stated by C & E, make out and send to the tribunal centre a defence setting out, in numbered paragraphs, the facts and the matters upon which he seeks to rely in the proceedings. At the hearing, C & E will not be required to prove or bring evidence of any matter or fact admitted in the defence. Following notification to them of the defence, C & E then have a further 21 days to serve a reply to the defence. They must reply where it is necessary to set out specifically any matter or fact

* showing illegality;

* which they allege makes the defence not maintainable;

* which might otherwise take the appellant by surprise; or

* which raises any issue of fact not arising out of the statement of case.

In a Category 1 appeal, the burden of proof falls on C & E although they are not required to prove any matter or fact admitted by the appellant in his defence.

[*SI 1986/590, Rules 2,7,8,10(3); SI 1991/186, Rules 3,5,6; SI 1994/2617; SI 1997/255*].

Where C & E wish to contend that the amount of an assessment is less than it ought to have been, their statement of case must indicate the amount of the alleged deficiency and the method of calculation. [*SI 1986/590, Rule 8A; SI 1997/255*].

The tribunal may at any time direct a party to the appeal to serve further particulars of his case with at least 14 days' notice. [*SI 1986/590, Rule 9*].

All documents must be acknowledged to the server and copies sent to the other party by the tribunal centre. [*SI 1986/590, Rule 10(3)*].

De Voil Indirect Tax Service. See V5.412; V5.415.

5.11   **Disclosure, inspection and production of documents**

Each party to a Category 1 or Category 3 appeal and each party to an application for a '*hardship direction*' (i.e. a direction that an appeal be entertained without payment or deposit of VAT, see 5.21 below) must serve at the appropriate tribunal centre a list of the documents he proposes to produce. In a Category 1 appeal, this must be done within 36 days of the date of notification of defence; in a Category 3 appeal, it must be done within 30 days of the date of notification of notice of the appeal (or, if later, the date of notification of withdrawal or dismissal of an application by C & E under *Rule 6*, see 5.7 above); and in a hardship direction it must be done within 30 days of the notification of the application. The tribunal may also, on application of one party, direct the other party to serve a list (verified by affidavit if so ordered) of documents which have been or are in the possession of the other party relating to any question in issue in the appeal. If a party wishes to claim that any document in such a list is privileged from production in the appeal, the claim and grounds therefor must be made in the list.

Copies of any lists must be sent by the tribunal centre to the other party who may inspect and take copies of them (unless privileged) at a time mutually agreed or as directed by the tribunal.

Documents listed must be available for production at the hearing (unless privileged). [*SI 1986/590, Rule 20; SI 1991/186, Rules 12, 13; SI 1994/2617*].

In practice, C & E will supply copies of their listed documents on written request and it simplifies matters if the appellant gives the same facilities to them.

De Voil Indirect Tax Service. See V5.413; V5.419.

5.12   **Witness statements**

Each party may within a specified time limit serve at the tribunal centre a witness statement (signed by the witness) containing evidence proposed to be given by any person at the hearing. Unless the other party gives notice of objection to such witness statement within 14 days of its notification to him, the statement will be admitted as evidence at the hearing without the witness giving oral evidence. The time limit is

* in a Category 1 appeal, within 21 days after the last date for the service of C & E's reply to the appellant's defence (i.e. within 42 days of the date of service of the appellant's defence);

* in a Category 2 appeal, within 21 days after the date of the notification of the notice of appeal; and

* in a Category 3 appeal, within 21 days after the date of notification of C & E's statement of case.

A copy of each witness statement or any objection must be sent to the other party by the tribunal centre. [*SI 1986/590, Rule 21; SI 1991/186, Rule 14; SI 1994/2617; SI 1997/255*]. If notice of objection is given the statement cannot be read or used at the hearing. However, the witness may give oral evidence. Standard *Forms Trib 3/3a* and *Trib 4* may be used for the witness statement and the notice of objection respectively. See 5.6 above.

De Voil Indirect Tax Service. See V5.414; V5.457.

5.13   **Affidavits and depositions made in other legal procedures**

These are admissible as evidence of any fact stated therein which would have been admissible by oral evidence of the person making them but who is dead, outside the UK, medically unfit to attend as a witness or, despite reasonable diligence, cannot be traced. Notice of intention to use such a document must be served within 21 days of the date of notification of the notice of appeal or application. Any party objecting to its use must serve a notice of application for directions with regard to it within 21 days of notification of its intended use. [*SI 1986/590, Rule 21A; SI 1991/186, Rule 15*].

De Voil Indirect Tax Service. See V5.457.

5.14   **Witness summonses and summonses to third parties**

Each party may apply to a tribunal to issue a summons to a witness in the UK to attend a hearing. He may also apply for the issue of a summons to a third party in the UK requiring him either to produce documents necessary for the hearing for inspection or copying at a specified time and place or to post such documents to the applicant. If a summons is issued, the party must serve the summons not less than four days before the date on which the attendance of the witness or third party, or posting of the document, is required. Notice is served by showing the original and leaving a copy of the summons with the witness or third party. Where the witness or third party is a company, the summons must be served by sending a copy by post, or leaving it at, the registered or principal office of the company in the UK or Isle of Man. Reasonable expenses must be tendered at the time the summons is served. No person can be required to attend and give evidence, or to produce any document, which he could not be compelled to give or produce by a court of law. [*SI 1986/590, Rule 22; SI 1991/186, Rule 16; SI 1994/2617*]. Failure to comply with a summons renders a person liable to a penalty not exceeding £1,000. [*VATA 1994, 12 Sch 10*]. A person on whom a summons is served may apply to the tribunal to have it set aside (see 5.21 below).

De Voil Indirect Tax Service. See V5.419.

5.15   **NOTICE AND LOCATION OF A HEARING**

Notice of a hearing of an appeal or application must be sent to each party by the tribunal centre not less than 14 days before the hearing. [*SI 1986/590, Reg 23; SI 1997/255*]. Hearings take place at tribunal centres in London, Manchester and Edinburgh (see 5.23 below). The tribunal also arranges to hear appeals in Belfast, Birmingham, Newcastle, Leeds, Cardiff, Bristol, on the Isle of Man and, exceptionally, in other places.

Postponement. If the appellant wishes any hearing to be postponed for any good reason (such as illness or non-availability of a witness) he or his representative should immediately notify the appropriate tribunal centre by telephone. A written application for the postponement, stating the reasons why it is sought, should be served at that centre as soon as practicable. A postponement is entirely a matter for the discretion of the tribunal. In cases of illness, the tribunal may require a medical certificate. The appellant should offer, or be prepared to accept, an alternative hearing date.

De Voil Indirect Tax Service. See V5.441; V5.443.

5.16   **PROCEDURE AT THE HEARING**

An appeal is usually heard by a chairman sitting alone (where it appears that only a question of law is involved) or with one or two other members (where questions of fact may be in issue). [*VATA 1994, 12 Sch 5*]. It is heard in public unless a tribunal directs otherwise on application by a party to the appeal. [*SI 1986/590, Rule 24*]. An application for a private appeal may be made in advance by serving *Form Trib 5* (Notice of Application) at the appropriate tribunal centre or may be made at the hearing without notice. A direction will only be made in exceptional circumstances, e.g. where the disclosure of confidential information would harm the appellant's business or his competitive position (*Consortium International Ltd (824)*). Where the appeal is held in private, expert witnesses from both sides may attend throughout (*R v Manchester VAT Tribunal (ex p C & E) QB 1982 (unreported)*).

Representatives. The appellant or applicant may conduct his own case or be represented by any person he appoints. C & E may be represented by any person they appoint. [*SI 1986/590, Rule 25*].

Failure to appear at a hearing by both parties will lead to dismissal of the case by the tribunal but the tribunal may reinstate the hearing on application, within 14 days after its written decision or direction, by either party or any person interested. If one party fails to appear, the tribunal may proceed in his absence but may set aside any decision if the absent party or other person interested makes an application to have the case reinstated within 14 days after the written decision. However, where the applicant does not attend the hearing of that application, he is not entitled to apply to have a decision or direction of the tribunal on the hearing of that application set aside. [*SI 1986/590, Rule 26; SI*

1991/186, Rule 17; SI 1994/2617]. Applications should be made on *Form Trib 5* (see 5.6 above) and should give the reasons for non-attendance on the hearing date.

At the hearing, a tribunal may regulate its own proceedings as it sees fit but must allow each party or his representative to address the tribunal, give evidence, call and cross-examine witnesses. Normally the case for the appellant will be presented first followed by that of C & E. The representative of C & E (normally a member of their Solicitor's office) will then address the tribunal. Finally the appellant or his representative has a right of reply. The tribunal will, whenever appropriate, help an appellant in putting forward his case.

Evidence may consist of oral evidence of witnesses, production of documents, statements read contained in witness statements (see 5.12 above) and any other evidence admitted by the tribunal. The tribunal will not refuse evidence on the grounds only that it would be inadmissible in a court of law. See *Bord (7946)*. It may require witnesses to give evidence on oath. [*SI 1986/590, Rules 27, 28; SI 1994/2617*]. Hearsay evidence may be introduced if not objected to by the other party or excluded by the chairman (*Wayne Farley Ltd and Another v C & E Commrs QB, [1986] STC 487*).

In a Category 1 appeal the burden of proof lies upon C & E. [*VATA 1994, s 60(7)*]. Their representative is obliged, therefore, to begin the hearing. Otherwise the onus of adducing evidence and satisfying the tribunal the assessment is wrong lies on the appellant (*Tynewydd Labour Working Men's Club and Institute Ltd v C & E Commrs QB, [1979] STC 570; Grunwick Processing Laboratories Ltd v C & E Commrs CA, [1987] STC 357*).

De Voil Indirect Tax Service. See V5.446–448; V5.451; V5.452; V5.456.

5.17   DECISION OF THE TRIBUNAL

The tribunal may reserve its decision or announce it at the conclusion of the meeting. A written document containing all findings of facts and reasons for the decision must be recorded and sent to each party unless, in a Category 2 appeal, the Chairman announces his decision and the parties present agree the decision need not be recorded in writing. The Chairman or the Registrar may correct any clerical mistake or other error in the document and send a corrected copy to each party. Where the decision follows a failure to attend the hearing, the person in default must be informed, with the copy of the decision, of his right to apply for reinstatement of the appeal. [*SI 1986/590, Rule 30; SI 1991/186, Rules 19–22; SI 1994/2617*].

Although in practice tribunals normally follow previous tribunal decisions, they are not obliged to do so.

Casting vote. Where the tribunal chairman is sitting with one other lay member, and they form different opinions as to the decision, the chairman has a casting vote so that his conclusion determines the outcome of the appeal. [*VATA 1994, 12 Sch 5(2)*]. See also *Rahman (t/a Khayman Restaurant) (14918)*.

De Voil Indirect Tax Service. See V5.469.

5.18   Costs

Award by tribunal. A tribunal may direct one party to pay to the other party a sum it may specify on account of that party's costs of appeal. It may also direct such costs to be determined on a taxation by a Taxing Master of the Supreme Court or a district judge of the High Court (in Scotland by the Auditor of the Court of Session and in Northern Ireland by the Taxing Master of the Supreme Court of Northern Ireland). Any sum awarded is recoverable as a civil debt. [*SI 1986/590, Rule 29; SI 1991/186, Rule 18; SI*

1994/2617]. Where either party wishes to obtain a direction for the payment by the other party of a sum on account of costs, he should, at the hearing, indicate the amount considered appropriate and tender evidence in support of such contention. A direction for the payment of costs is in the discretion of the tribunal but normally a wholly successful party will not be directed to make any payment. Costs allowed include reasonable barristers', solicitors' and accountants' fees and costs and expenses of employees attending hearings. For a consideration of what is 'reasonable' and not excessive, see *VSP Marketing Ltd (No 3, [1995] VATDR 328 (13587)*.

A tribunal may make an award of costs to C & E even though no application for costs has been made (*Houston Stewart (9526)*). The tribunal has frequently awarded costs to C & E where appellants have abandoned appeals at the last moment or failed to attend to pursue their appeals or applications without reasonable explanation. See, for example, *Santi (954)*. Where the parties have reached a compromise, the compromise agreement should also provide for any costs and a tribunal will not continue the appeal purely in relation to an award of costs (*The Cadogan Club Ltd (548)*).

Where an appeal relates to two or more distinct issues or assessments which could have been heard separately, an appellant may be awarded costs in respect of a successful appeal on one assessment even if overall VAT is due to C & E (*EA Kilburn (4866)*).

The tribunal's power to award costs is confined to those costs recoverable at common law. As these are recoverable by way of indemnity only, where there is no liability on the appellant to pay his costs there is no basis for an award of costs. See *C & E Commrs v Vaz QB 1994, [1995] STC 14* where there was an agreement to limit fees to the amount, if any, recovered by way of an award of costs so that, without such an award, no fees were payable.

The *Litigant in Person (Costs and Expenses) Act 1975* does not apply to VAT tribunals (*C & E Commrs v Ross and Others QB, [1990] STC 353*). Costs can only therefore be awarded to such a person on the common law basis that a litigant in person is entitled only to out-of-pocket expenses and not costs in respect of time spent preparing for the hearing. See also *Nader (t/a Try Us) v C & E Commrs CA, [1993] STC 806* where the court rejected claims for loss of business income. In *G A Boyd Building Services Ltd, [1993] VATTR 26 (9788)* a limited company was held not to be a litigant in person because it must be represented by one of its officers or a third party. Time spent by a director in preparing for the company's case was therefore taken into account in determining costs. In *Rupert Page Developments Ltd (9823)* the tribunal held that there was no logical distinction between a company and a litigant in person for these purposes so that the company was not entitled to claim costs in respect of time expended by its chairman, only out-of-pocket expenses. This contention was in turn rejected in *Alpha International Coal Ltd (11441)* where the company was represented by its company secretary (a certified accountant) who was not a shareholder.

C & E policy with regard to seeking costs. C & E have concluded that, as a general rule, they will continue their policy of not seeking costs against unsuccessful appellants; however they will ask for costs in certain cases so as to provide protection for public funds and the general body of taxpayers. For instance, they will seek costs at those exceptional tribunal hearings of substantial and complex cases where large sums are involved and which are comparable with High Court cases, unless the appeal involves an important point of law requiring clarification. See, for example, *University of Reading, [1998] VATDR 27 (15387)*. C & E will also consider seeking costs where the appellant has misused the tribunal procedure e.g. in frivolous or vexatious cases, where he has failed to appear or to be represented at a mutually arranged hearing without sufficient explanation, or where he has first produced at a hearing relevant evidence which ought properly to have been disclosed at an earlier stage and which could have saved public funds had it been produced timeously. Appeals against penalties under *VATA 1994, s 60* on the grounds that a person has evaded VAT and his conduct has involved dishonesty are comparable with High Court cases. Where such an appeal is unsuccessful, C & E will normally seek an award of costs. (Hansard 24 July 1986, cols 459, 460; C & E Press Notice 1132, 5 August 1986).

De Voil Indirect Tax Service. See V5.481–485.

5.19   **Award of interest**

Where a tribunal decides that any VAT paid or deposited should be repaid to the appellant or any amount of input tax should be paid to him, it must direct that the amount is repaid with interest at such rate as it may specify. [*VATA 1994, s 84(8)*]. See also 51.13 PAYMENT OF VAT.

De Voil Indirect Tax Service. See V5.487–489.

5.20   **Enforcement of decisions**

Where, as a result of the tribunal's decision, any amount of VAT due or recoverable from any person or any costs are awarded to C & E, then the decision may

*   in England and Wales be registered by C & E under the rules of court and enforced by the High Court as if due to C & E in pursuance of a judgment or order of the High Court;

*   in Scotland be recorded for execution in the Books of Council and Session and enforced accordingly; and

*   in Northern Ireland be enforced by the Enforcement of Judgments Office under *Judgments Enforcement (Northern Ireland) Order 1981, Art 2(2)*.

[*VATA 1994, s 87*].

For this purpose, on request in writing within one year of the date on which the decision is released, the outcome of the appeal and any award of costs or interest must be recorded in a written direction signed by the Chairman or Registrar. [*SI 1986/590, Rule 30; SI 1991/186, Rule 19*]. This will enable a decision to be registered at less administrative cost.

5.21   **APPLICATION FOR A DIRECTION**

An application to a tribunal, made otherwise than at a hearing, for the issue of a witness summons or a direction (including a hardship direction or a direction setting aside a witness summons) is made by notice served at the appropriate tribunal centre. The notice must

*   state the name and address of the applicant;

*   state the direction sought or details of the witness summons sought to be issued or set aside;

*   set out, or have a document attached, containing the grounds for the application; and

*   if served by an intending appellant

    (i)   state the address of C & E from which the disputed decision was sent, the date of the decision and the address to which it was sent;

    (ii) set out shortly the disputed decision or attach a copy of the document containing it; and

(iii) have attached a copy of any letter from C & E extending the time limit for appeal or notifying the date from which the time limit runs.

A notice of application for a hardship direction must be served at the appropriate tribunal centre within the period for the service of a notice of appeal (see 5.5 above).

The tribunal centre must acknowledge the application and send a copy of it, together with any attachments, to the other party, stating the date of service and date of notification of the notice of application. That other party must then, within 14 days of the date of notification, indicate whether or not he consents to the application and, if not, his reasons.

[*SI 1986/590, Rule 11; SI 1991/186, Rules 7–9*].

An application may be made and direction given regarding

- the hearing of an appeal without payment or deposit of VAT;

- leave to make assessments;

- the issue of a witness summons (see 5.14 above);

- the setting aside of the issue of a witness summons;

- the granting of an extension of time (e.g. the time for the service of a notice of appeal or application for relief from payment or deposit of VAT);

- the right to inspect and take copies of any document in the list of documents of C & E (see 5.11 above);

- the postponement or adjournment of a hearing;

- the substitution of a person interested for an appellant or an applicant who has died or become bankrupt (see 5.6 above);

- the transfer of an appeal or an application to another tribunal centre;

- the reinstatement of an appeal which has been dismissed following a failure to attend at a hearing or a refusal or failure to comply with a direction of a tribunal; or

- the furnishing to C & E of details of an actual supply or importation on which VAT may be chargeable.

Withdrawal of application. A person may withdraw his application at any time by notice in writing, signed by him or on his behalf, to the proper officer at the appropriate tribunal centre. This does not prevent him from applying for an award of costs (see 5.18 above) or a tribunal from making such award as it thinks fit. [*SI 1986/590, Rule 16; SI 1997/255*].

Agreement by the parties. Where the parties to an application have agreed upon the terms, a tribunal may make a direction in accordance with those terms without a hearing. [*SI 1986/590, Rule 17*].

Preparation for the hearing. The provisions relating to *disclosure, inspection and production of documents* and *witness summonses* (but not witness statements) apply to hearings of applications as they do to appeals.

Notice of hearing must be sent to each party by the tribunal centre not less than 14 days before the hearing although, unless the tribunal otherwise directs, an application made at a hearing will be heard forthwith and no notice is sent to the parties. [*SI 1986/590, Rule 23; SI 1997/255*].

Procedure at hearings of applications. The provisions relating to appeals (see 5.16 above) also apply to applications except that all applications made otherwise than at or subsequent to the hearing of an appeal take place in private. [*SI 1986/590, Rule 24(2)*]. The announcement of the decision (see 5.17 above) and provisions relating to an award of costs (see 5.18 above) also apply to applications.

Power to extend time. A tribunal may on the application of any party, or of its own motion or without reference to any party, extend the time limit for doing anything in relation to the application upon such terms as it thinks fit. [*SI 1986/590, Rule 19(1)–(3); SI 1994/2617*].

Failure to comply with any direction of the tribunal. The tribunal may allow or dismiss the appeal. The tribunal may, however, waive any breach or non-observance of the rules or any direction as it thinks fit. [*SI 1986/590, Rule 19(4)(5); SI 1991/186, Rule 11*].

De Voil Indirect Tax Service. See V5.431; V5.435.

5.22   **FURTHER APPEALS AGAINST A TRIBUNAL DECISION**

Appeals to the High Court. If any party to proceedings before the tribunal is dissatisfied on a *point of law* with a decision of the tribunal, he may either appeal therefrom to the High Court or require the tribunal to state and sign a case for the opinion of the High Court. In Scotland, the appeal lies to the Court of Session, in Northern Ireland to the High Court of Justice of Northern Ireland and in the Isle of Man to the Staff of Government Division. Written application should be made to the appropriate tribunal centre for any documents required in connection with such an appeal. [*Tribunal and Inquiries Act 1992, s 11*].

The decision of the tribunal on a question of fact is final. The leading case on the question of the distinction between fact and law is *Edwards v Bairstow & Harrison HL 1955, 36 TC 207*.

There is a further appeal from the High Court to the Court of Appeal and the House of Lords. The Court of Appeal may, in certain circumstances, be 'leap-frogged'.

Appeals direct to the Court of Appeal. If any party to proceedings before the tribunal is dissatisfied on a *point of law* with a decision of the tribunal, he may appeal direct to the Court of Appeal provided the parties consent and the tribunal endorses its decision with a certificate that the decision involves a point of law relating wholly or mainly to the construction of an Act, statutory instrument or EC Treaty or Instrument which has been fully argued before it and considered by it.

The party wishing to appeal must apply to the tribunal for the certificate at the conclusion of the hearing or within 21 days after the date on which the tribunal's decision is released.

[*VATA 1994, s 86; SI 1986/590, Reg 30A; SI 1986/2288; SI 1986/2290; SI 1994/1978; SI 1994/2617*].

Costs. The general rule in appeal courts is that the losing party risks having to pay the other side's costs. However, C & E may consider waiving their claim in particular where they are appealing against an adverse decision. Influential factors include the risk of financial hardship to the other party and whether the case is one of significant interest to taxpayers as a whole, turning on a point of law in need of clarification. If C & E do come to such an arrangement, they would expect to do so in advance of the hearing and following an approach by the taxpayer. (Hansard 12 March 1980, Vol 980, col 572).

De Voil Indirect Tax Service. See V5.476.

5.23 Appeals

5.23 **ADDRESSES OF VAT TRIBUNAL CENTRES**

London
The London Tribunal Centre
15/19 Bedford Avenue
London W1B 3AS

Tel: (0171) 631 4242
Fax No: (0171) 436 4150/4151

Manchester
The Manchester Tribunal Centre
Warwickgate House, Warwick Road,
Manchester M16 0GP

Tel: (0161) 872 6471
Fax No: (0161) 876 4479

Edinburgh
The Edinburgh Tribunal Centre
44 Palmerston Place
Edinburgh EH12 5BJ

Tel: (0131) 226 3551
Fax No: (0131) 220 6817

6 Assessments

Cross-references. See 5 APPEALS; 31.5 GROUPS OF COMPANIES; 51 PAYMENT OF TAX.

De Voil Indirect Tax Service. See V5.131–140.

The contents of this chapter are as follows.

6.1 ASSESSMENTS OF VAT DUE

VAT is normally paid (without any assessment being made) on the submission of a return for a prescribed accounting period.

However, subject to the time limits in 6.2 below, C & E are given power to raise assessments where the following circumstances apply.

(a) *Returns have not been made.* Assessments will generally be based on centrally stored data concerning the trader's business and VAT history and will normally be withdrawn if an acceptable return is made and the VAT declared on it paid.

(b) *Documents have not been kept* and facilities have not been afforded to verify returns.

(c) *It appears to C & E that the returns are incomplete or incorrect.* This will most frequently happen following control visits by C & E officers.

(d) *Incorrect VAT credits,* i.e. where for any prescribed accounting period an amount has been paid or credited to any person as either a repayment or refund of VAT or as being due as a VAT credit and the amount ought not to have been paid or credited. This is further extended to cover an amount which would not have been so paid or credited had the facts been known or been as they later turn out to be (e.g. where bad debt relief has been claimed and subsequently the debt, or part, has been repaid without the VAT element being paid to C & E). C & E may assess the amount as being VAT due for the period in question. An amount which has been paid to any person as a VAT credit and which is not due because his registration has been cancelled by C & E may be assessed even though his registration has been cancelled.

(e) *Failure to account for goods,* i.e. where goods have, in the course or furtherance of a business, been supplied to a taxable person, acquired or obtained by him from another EC country or imported by him from a place outside the EC and he is unable to prove to C & E that the goods

  • have been, or are available to be, supplied by him;

  • have been exported or otherwise removed from the UK without being exported or so removed by way of supply; or

  • have been lost or destroyed.

(f) *A fiscal warehousekeeper has failed to pay VAT required under VATA 1994, s 18E on any missing or deficient goods or it appears to C & E that goods have been removed from a warehouse or fiscal warehouse without payment of the VAT required under VATA 1994, s 18(4) or 18D.*

6.1 Assessments

(g) *Goods subject to excise duty or new means of transport* have been acquired in the UK from another EC country by a person who at that time was not a taxable person and

   (i) no notification of that acquisition has been given to C & E by the person required to give it;

   (ii) C & E are not satisfied that the particulars in a notification are accurate or complete; or

   (iii) there has been a failure to supply C & E with the information necessary to verify the particulars contained in the notification.

See 23.9 and 23.35 EUROPEAN COMMUNITY: SINGLE MARKET for general provisions relating to such acquisition of dutiable goods and new means of transport respectively.

Any amount assessed and notified under these provisions is deemed to be an amount of VAT due and, if the person fails to pay, enforcement action can be taken to recover the debt.

(h) *VAT has been lost as a result of conduct involving dishonesty* within *VATA 1994, s 60* (see 52.9 PENALTIES), conduct for which a person has been convicted of fraud, or registration irregularities or unauthorised issue of VAT invoices under *VATA 1994, s 67* (see 52.12 PENALTIES).

An amount assessed and notified to a person under any of the above provisions is, subject to appeal, deemed to be an amount of VAT due and is recoverable unless the assessment is subsequently withdrawn or reduced.

Where a person is assessed under either of (a) to (c) *and* (d) above for the same prescribed accounting period, assessments may be combined and notified to the person in one assessment.

[*VATA 1994, ss 73(1)–(4)(7)(7A)(7B)(9), 75(1)(3), 77(4); FA 1996, 3 Sch 10, 11*].

C & E may raise a single or 'global' assessment covering more than one accounting period (*SJ Grange Ltd v C & E Commrs CA 1978, [1979] STC 183*). This power may be necessary where it is impossible or impracticable to identify the specific accounting periods for which the VAT claimed is due but is not restricted to such cases. It is a question of fact (important for time limit purposes) whether there is one global assessment or a number of separate assessments notified together. The Form on which C & E notify assessments is clearly intended to be used for either a single or a number of assessments and the fact therefore that demands for multiple accounting periods are included on the same form does not necessarily constitute a single global assessment (*C & E Commrs v Le Rififi Ltd CA 1994, [1995] STC 103* not following the earlier decision in *Don Pasquale (a firm) v C & E Commrs CA, [1990] STC 556*).

The assessment, to be valid, must show the period covered not just the end of that period (*RE Bell, [1979] VATTR 115 (761)*) although the information need not necessarily be on the assessment itself. See *House (PJ) (t/a P & J Autos) v C & E Commrs CA 1995, [1996] STC 154* where the dates covered by the assessment were left blank but the period assessed was indicated by accompanying schedules. A notice of assessment issued 'without prejudice' is not invalid (*McCafferty (483)*).

Where an assessment has been made as a result of a person's failure to submit a return for a prescribed accounting period and, although the VAT assessed has been paid, no proper return has been made for that period, if C & E find it necessary to raise assessments for later periods due to the failure to submit returns by that person or a representative of his (see 6.9 below) then C & E may raise the later assessments for amounts greater than that which they would otherwise consider to be appropriate. [*VATA 1994, s 73(8)*].

Subject to the foregoing, assessments under (*a*) to (*c*) and (*e*) to (*g*) above must be made to the best of C & E's judgment. [*VATA 1994, ss 73(1)(7)(7A)(7B), 75(1); FA 1996, 3 Sch 10*]. C & E must exercise their powers honestly and bona fide and there must be material before them on which to make their judgment. Although their decisions must be reasonable and not arbitrary, they are under no obligation to do the work of a taxpayer by carrying out exhaustive investigations but if they do make investigations, they must take into account material disclosed by them (*Van Boeckel v C & E Commrs QB 1980, [1981] STC 290*). The function of the tribunal is supervisory. An assessment should only be held to fail the 'best judgment' test if made dishonestly, vindictively or capriciously, where it is a spurious estimate or guess in which all the elements of judgment are missing, or where it is wholly unreasonable. Short of such a finding there is no justification for setting aside an assessment. In the normal case, the important issue is the amount of the assessment (*MH Rahman (t/a Khayam Restaurant) v C & E Commrs QB, [1998] STC 826*) and once the tribunal has accepted that C & E were entitled to make that assessment, the amount is for the tribunal to decide (*Murat v C & E Commrs, QB [1998] STC 923*). The function of the tribunal is to decide what information C & E relied upon to make the assessment and then make a value judgment as to how they arrived at the assessment. It is not a function of the tribunal to engage in a process that looks afresh at all the evidence before it (*Georgiou and another (t/a Mario's Chippery) v C & E Commrs QB, [1995] STC 1101*). See also *Seto v C & E Commrs CS 1980, [1981] STC 698*. An assessment must be considered as a whole and if it is not made to the best of C & E's judgment, then it is wholly invalid and void and cannot be corrected by any subsequent amendment to it or treated as partly valid. See *Barber (JH), [1992] VATTR 144 (7727)* where an assessment partly covered a period for which a previous assessment had already been raised.

Once an assessment has been raised, it is not open to C & E to seek to treat that assessment, on fresh evidence, as an assessment for some other purpose. In *Ridgeons Bulk Ltd v C & E Commrs QB, [1994] STC 427*, C & E initially raised an assessment for overclaimed input tax but subsequently, when that could not be supported, sought to treat the assessment as one for undeclared output tax for a different amount. The court held that the correct procedure would have been to issue a further assessment under 6.6 below (which was not possible as the time limit had expired).

De Voil Indirect Tax Service. See V5.132; V5.133; V5.139; V5.239; V5.261; V5.267.

6.2   Time limits

The time limits for assessments under 6.1 above in respect of any prescribed accounting period are as follows.

(*a*)   Under 6.1(*a*)–(*d*), subject to the provisions relating to death below, an assessment for any prescribed accounting period cannot be made after the later of

    (i) two years after the end of the prescribed accounting period; or

    (ii) one year after evidence of fact, sufficient in the opinion of C & E to justify the making of an assessment, comes to their knowledge

but in any case not more than three years (six years before 18 July 1996) after the end of the prescribed accounting period. See 6.6 below for further assessments.

Where a single global assessment is made because it is not possible to identify a specific period for which VAT is due, the time limit in (i) above runs from the end of the *first* prescribed accounting period it covers (*International Language Centres Ltd (No 2) QB, [1983] STC 394*). Where a global assessment is raised out of time on this basis, it is a nullity *ab initio* even if the taxpayer failed to lodge an appeal against it in due time with a VAT tribunal (*Lord Advocate v Shanks (t/a Shanks &*

6.2 Assessments

Co), CS [1992] STC 928]. See however 6.1 above for the different interpretation of what constitutes a global assessment following the decision in *C & E Commrs v Le Rififi Ltd CA 1994, [1995] STC 103.*

A tribunal considering the possible application of (ii) above must decide what were the facts which, in the opinion of the officer making the assessment on behalf of C & E, justified the making of the assessment and then decide when the last of these facts came to the knowledge of the officer. The period of one year then runs from that date (*Heyfordian Travel Ltd, [1979] VATTR 139 (774)*). 'Evidence of facts' means what it says; the words do not encompass constructive knowledge (*Spillane v C & E Commrs QB 1989, [1990] STC 212*). This was confirmed in *C & E Commrs v Post Office QB, [1995] STC 749* where it was held that the relevant date was not when any error should have been discovered but when evidence of facts actually came to the knowledge of C & E. Nothing in the statutory provisions encompasses constructive knowledge. There is no obligation on C & E to be alert to discover a mistake (*FC Milnes (Bradford) Ltd (478)*). Following the rule in *J H Corbitt (Numismatists) Ltd*, the Court is prevented from substituting its opinion for that of C & E and therefore it can only interfere if there is material to show that an officer's failure to make an earlier assessment was perverse (*Cumbrae Properties (1963) Ltd QB, [1981] STC 799*).

Where returns which are clearly incorrect are in the hands of C & E, assessments are out of date if made outside the two year period in (i) above and no evidence of new facts have come to C & E's attention to bring the case within (ii) above (*Lord t/a Lords Electrical and Fancy Goods (320)*).

For the purposes of 6.1(*d*) above, where an incorrect VAT credit is claimed in a later prescribed accounting period than the period of actual payment, the two year time limit in (i) above runs from the end of period of claim and not the period of payment (*C & E Commrs v The Croydon Hotel & Leisure Co Ltd, CA [1996] STC 1105*).

(*b*) Under 6.1(*e*)(*f*) above, subject to the provisions relating to death below, an assessment cannot be made more than three years (six years before 18 July 1996) after the end of the prescribed accounting period or importation or acquisition concerned.

(*c*) Under 6.1(*g*) above, subject to the provisions relating to death below, an assessment cannot be made after the later of

(i) two years after the time of notification to C & E of the acquisition of the goods in question; or

(ii) one year after evidence of fact, sufficient in the opinion of C & E to justify the making of an assessment, comes to their knowledge

but in any case not more than three years (six years before 18 July 1996) after the end of the prescribed accounting period. See 6.6 below for further assessments.

(*d*) Under 6.1(*h*) above, subject to the provisions relating to death below, an assessment cannot be made more than 20 years after the end of the relevant period or two years after the VAT due for the relevant period has been finally determined.

Death. Where the taxable person has died, any assessment cannot be made more than three years after death. In addition, for assessments within 6.1(*h*) above, the 20 year time limit above is reduced to three years (six years before 18 July 1996) but any assessment which, from the point of view of time limits, could have been made immediately after death may be made at any time within three years after it.

[*VATA 1994, ss 73(6), 75(2), 77(1)(4)(5); FA 1997, s 47(10)*].

De Voil Indirect Tax Service. See V5.136.

6.3   **ASSESSMENTS OF PENALTIES, INTEREST AND SURCHARGES**

C & E may assess and notify any amount due by way of

(*a*)   default surcharge under *VATA 1994, ss 59, 59A* (see 52.15 and 52.16 PENALTIES),

(*b*)   penalty under *VATA 1994, ss 60–69* (see 52.9 to 52.14, 52.18 and 52.19 PENALTIES), or

(*c*)   interest under *VATA 1994, s 74* (see 51.5 PAYMENT OF VAT)

except that a penalty under 52.14(*b*)(v)–(ix) PENALTIES can only be assessed if, within the two years preceding the date of the assessment, C & E have issued a written warning of the consequences of a continuing failure to comply with the relevant requirement.

Unless the assessment is withdrawn or reduced, the amount is recoverable as if it were VAT due. The fact that the conduct giving rise to any penalty may have ceased before an assessment is made does not affect the powers of C & E to make an assessment.

Combining assessments. Where for a particular accounting period a person is assessed for VAT due under 6.1(*a*)–(*g*) as well as surcharge, penalty or interest under these provisions, C & E may combine the assessments but the amount of the penalty, interest or surcharge should be shown separately.

Allocation of VAT between periods. Where any penalty etc. must be calculated by reference to VAT which was paid late and that VAT (or the supply giving rise to it) cannot be readily attributed to one or more prescribed accounting periods, C & E are empowered to allocate the VAT due to such period or periods as they determine to the best of their judgment.

Penalties, interest accruing on daily basis. Where a penalty or interest accrues on a daily basis, the assessment must specify a date (not later than the date of the notice) to which the penalty or interest is calculated. If the penalty or interest continues to accrue after that date, a further assessment or assessments may be made in respect of amounts so accruing. C & E, however, may notify the person liable of a period during which he may remedy the failure or default which caused the penalty or pay the amount on which interest was charged. If the person meets this requirement, no further penalty or interest accrues after the date specified in the assessment.

[*VATA 1994, s 76; FA 1996, s 35(7), 3 Sch 11*].

De Voil Indirect Tax Service. See V5.132.

6.4   **Time limits**

An assessment for any relevant period under 6.3 above cannot be made after the following times or, where there is an alternative, the *earlier* of such times.

(*a*)   Where VAT has been lost as a result of conduct falling within *VATA 1994, s 60(1)* (VAT evasion: conduct involving dishonesty, see 52.9 PENALTIES) or conduct for which a person has been convicted of fraud

•   20 years after the end of the relevant period; or

•   two years after the VAT due for the relevant period has been finally determined.

(*b*)   Where VAT has been lost in circumstances giving rise to a penalty under *VATA 1994, s 67* (registration irregularities and unauthorised issue of VAT invoices, see 52.12 PENALTIES) 20 years after the event giving rise to the penalty.

(c) For assessments under *VATA 1994, s 59* (default surcharge, see 52.15 PENALTIES), *VATA 1994, s 63* (misdeclaration, see 52.10 PENALTIES) or *VATA 1994, s 74* (interest on VAT, see 51.5 PAYMENT OF VAT)

- three years (six years before 18 July 1996) after the end of the relevant period; or

- two years after the VAT due for the relevant period has finally been determined.

(d) For assessments under *VATA 1994, s 62* (incorrect certificates of zero-rating, see 52.17 PENALTIES), *VATA 1994, s 64* (repeated misdeclaration, see 52.11 PENALTIES), *VATA 1994, s 68* (breaches of walking possession agreements, see 52.13 PENALTIES) or *VATA 1994, s 69* (breaches of regulatory provisions, see 52.14 PENALTIES) three years (six years before 18 July 1996) after the event giving rise to the penalty.

(e) For assessments under *VATA 1994, s 65* (inaccuracies in EC sales statements, see 52.18 PENALTIES) or *VATA 1994, s 66* (failure to submit EC sales statements, see 52.19 PENALTIES)

- three years (six years before 18 July 1996) after the event giving rise to the penalty; or

- two years after the time when sufficient information came to the knowledge of C & E to indicate that, as the case may be, the statement had a material inaccuracy or there had been a default in the submission of a sales statement.

Death. Where the taxable person has died, any assessment under (*a*)–(*e*) above cannot be made more than three years after death. In addition, for assessments within (*a*) or (*b*) above, the 20 year time limit is reduced to three years (six years before 18 July 1996) but any assessment which, from the point of view of time limits, could have been made immediately after death may be made at any time within three years after it.

[*VATA 1994, s 77(1)–(5); FA 1997, s 47(10)*].

De Voil Indirect Tax Service. See V5.136.

6.5   **ASSESSMENTS FOR OVERPAID INTEREST AND REPAYMENTS**

Where

(a) after 17 July 1996, C & E have paid interest under *VATA 1994, s 78* (see 51.11 PAYMENT OF VAT) to any person who was not entitled to it, or

(b) after 17 July 1996, C & E have made a repayment under *VATA 1994, s 80* (see 51.7 PAYMENT OF VAT) in excess of their repayment liability at that time, or

(c) any person is liable under *VATA 1994, s 80A* to pay to C & E any VAT previously repaid by C & E to them on the understanding that it would be reimbursed to customers (see 51.7 PAYMENT OF VAT)

C & E may assess the amount paid under (*a*) or (*b*) (but not before 4 December 1996) or due under (*c*) to the best of their judgement and notify the person accordingly. For these purposes, the repayment liability under (*b*) above may be reduced by provisions which are enacted after a repayment has been made but which are deemed to come into force from a date earlier than the repayment.

Unless the assessment is withdrawn or reduced, the amount is recoverable as if it were VAT due.

Time limits. Any such assessment cannot be made more than two years after evidence of facts, sufficient in the opinion of C & E to justify the making of an assessment, comes to their knowledge.

Interest. The provisions of *VATA 1994, s 74* (interest payable on VAT, see 51.5 PAYMENT OF VAT) apply to such an assessment except that in the calculation of the period of interest, interest runs from the date the assessment is notified until the date of payment.

C & E may assess and notify any amount due by way of interest on a recovery assessment but (without prejudice to the power to make assessments for interest for later periods) the assessment is restricted to interest for a period of no more than two years ending with the time when the assessment to interest is made. The assessment must specify a date (not later than the date of the notice) to which the interest is calculated. If the interest continues to accrue after that date, a further assessment or assessments may be made in respect of the amounts so accruing. C & E, however, may notify the person liable of a period during which he may pay the underlying assessment and, if the person meets this requirement, no further interest accrues after the date specified in the assessment.

Further assessments. See 6.6(*b*) below.

Notification of an assessment to a personal representative, trustee in bankruptcy, interim or permanent trustee, receiver, liquidator or person otherwise acting in a representative capacity is treated as notification to the person on whose behalf he acts.

[*VATA 1994, ss 78A, 80(4A)-(4C), 80B; FA 1997, ss 45(1)(4), 46(2)(4), 47(6)(9)*].

Transitional provisions for set-offs by taxpayer after 17 July 1996 and before 4 December 1996. Where

(i) at any time before 4 December 1996, a taxpayer became liable to pay VAT, penalties, interest or surcharge to C & E (the '*relevant sum*'), and

(ii) at any time after 17 July 1996 and before 4 December 1996 the taxpayer sets off an amount against the relevant sum in respect of an overpayment by him which, because of the three-year time limit applying with effect from 17 July 1996, can no longer be set off

C & E may, to the best of their judgement, raise an assessment to recover any residual VAT which remains unpaid as a result. The taxpayer's liability under such an assessment is limited to the amount previously set off which is no longer allowed to be set off. Similar provisions as to *Time limits, Interest, Further assessments* and *Notification of an assessment* apply as above. An appeal may be made against the assessment or the amount of it.

[*FA 1997, s 49*].

6.6   **FURTHER ASSESSMENTS**

C & E may make further assessments in the following circumstances.

(*a*)   Where, after an assessment has been made under 6.1(*a*)–(*d*) or (*g*) above, further 'evidence of facts', sufficient in the opinion of C & E to justify the making of an assessment, comes to their knowledge. [*VATA 1994, ss 73(6), 75(2)*]. The further assessment must also be within the time limit (see 6.2 above). Contents of nil returns submitted by a taxpayer do not amount to 'evidence of facts' justifying a further assessment (*Parekh & another v C & E Commrs QB, [1984] STC 284*). In that case, Woolf J also observed that, where the two-year time limit for an assessment has elapsed. C & E should only be allowed to make a further assessment in relation to the VAT due based on the evidence which has come to their

6.7 Assessments

knowledge since the earlier assessment. Where, however, the two-year period has not elapsed, C & E are not prevented from withdrawing the earlier assessment and replacing it by another.

(*b*) If, otherwise than in circumstances falling within (*a*) above, it appears to C & E that the amount which ought to have been assessed under any of the provisions of 6.1, 6.3 or 6.5 above exceeds the amount which was so assessed, then a supplementary assessment of the amount of the excess may be made and notified to the person concerned under the same provisions and within the same time limits as the original assessment. [*VATA 1994, ss 77(6), 78A(6); FA 1997, s 45(1)*]. Note that there is no requirement for further evidence as in (*a*) above.

De Voil Indirect Tax Service. See V5.134.

6.7   **NOTIFICATION OF ASSESSMENTS**

Where C & E intend raising a VAT assessment, they may first send a letter to the taxpayer detailing the intended calculations. This will enable the taxpayer to query the computation before the assessment is actually raised.

Subsequently, C & E must formally notify the taxpayer by way of assessment of the amount of VAT due [*VATA 1994, s 73(1)*] but there is no express provision as to the manner in which this is to be done.

Any notice for VAT purposes can be served on a person by sending it by post in a letter addressed to him or his VAT representative (see 4.8 AGENTS) at the last or usual residence or place of business of that person or representative. [*VATA 1994, s 98*]. See 50.5 PARTNERSHIPS for the special provisions for serving notice on partners and 6.9 below for service on representatives.

An assessment which is incorrectly notified (e.g. by being sent to the taxpayer's solicitors without authority) is not invalid but simply unenforceable until properly notified to the taxpayer (*Grunwick Processing Laboratories Ltd v C & E Commrs QB, [1986] STC 441*).

De Voil Indirect Tax Service. See V5.137; V5.138.

6.8   **CORRECTIONS OF ASSESSMENTS BY TRIBUNALS**

Where on an appeal against a decision within 6.1(*b*)–(*e*) above it is found that the amount specified in the assessment is less than it ought to have been, the tribunal may give a direction specifying the correct amount. The appellant is deemed to have been notified of the revised amount. [*VATA 1994, s 84(5)*]. A tribunal may exercise its power to increase an assessment in order to correct arithmetical errors or where C & E have argued at the hearing that the assessment should be increased. A tribunal does not have a free-standing power to increase an assessment entirely of its own initiative. Furthermore, if a tribunal was contemplating increasing an assessment, the appellant should be given a fair opportunity (by adjournment, if necessary) to consider the position (*Elias Gale Racing v C & E Commrs, [1998] STI 1711*).

A tribunal may reduce or discharge an assessment on appeal. See 5 APPEALS.

6.9   **ASSESSMENTS ON, AND NOTIFICATION TO, REPRESENTATIVES**

Where a person required to make a return as a personal representative, trustee in bankruptcy, receiver, liquidator or otherwise in a representative capacity fails to make that return or makes a return which appears to C & E to be incomplete or incorrect, assessments (including assessments of penalties, interest or surcharges) may be made by C & E on that person in his representative position and a notification to him is treated as also notifying the person for whom he acts. [*VATA 1994, ss 73(5)(10), 76(10); FA 1997, s 45(6)*].

Similar provisions apply to assessments on, and notifications to, such persons in respect of acquisitions of goods subject to excise duty or new means of transport under 6.1(*g*) above. [*VATA 1994, s 75(4)*].

7 Bad Debt Relief

Cross-references. See 47.10 OUTPUT TAX for loss of goods; 59.29 REGISTRATION where transfer of registration with a business as a going concern.

De Voil Indirect Tax Service. See V5.156; V5.157.

The contents of this chapter are as follows.

7.1 INTRODUCTION

A supplier has to account to C & E for output tax even if the debt, including the VAT, is not paid. The VAT paid to C & E cannot subsequently be reclaimed by issuing a credit note for the unpaid amount (*Peter Cripwell & Associates (660); Temple Gothard & Co (702)*). However, relief for VAT on bad debts is claimable under certain conditions.

Relief depends upon the supply being written off as a bad debt in the books of the claimant and a period of six months having elapsed since the date payment becomes due. For full details see 7.2 to 7.8 below.

Appeals. Where a claim to bad debt relief is refused, an appeal may be made to a VAT tribunal. [*VATA 1994, s 83(h)*]. See 5.3(*h*) APPEALS.

Cash accounting scheme. Subject to conditions, including an annual turnover limit, taxable persons may account for and pay VAT by reference to the time when the consideration for the supply is received. See 63.2 SPECIAL SCHEMES. The adoption of such a scheme removes the problem of VAT on bad debts from the supplier.

Retail schemes. Where a retail scheme is used, bad debt relief may be available under the normal provisions described in this chapter. However, as most retailers do not issue VAT invoices, they must negotiate with C & E how the requirements of the scheme can be met.

Where such a claim is made, any refund must be accounted for outside the retail scheme. If, after claiming a refund, payment is received for the supplies, any repayment of relief to C & E must also be dealt with outside the scheme.

Factored debts. Where debts are factored, bad debt relief is not available where the assignment of the debt is absolute (i.e. where there is no provision for the reassignment of the debt in the contract). Where there is such provision, bad debt relief is available, subject to the normal conditions, once the debt has been reassigned. Any payment from the factor to the business for the purchase of the debts is consideration for an exempt supply of finance and is disregarded for the purposes of bad debt relief. (C & E Manual V1-22, Chapter 2 para 2.8).

7.2 CONDITIONS FOR RELIEF

A person is entitled, on making a claim, to a refund of VAT by reference to '*the outstanding amount*' where the following conditions are satisfied.

(*a*) He has supplied goods or services and has accounted for and paid the VAT on the supply.

Before 31 July 1998, the legislation required the goods or services to be supplied for a consideration in money. However, following the decision in *Goldsmiths (Jewellers) Ltd v C & E Commrs, CJEC [1997] STC 1073* that UK legislation could not discriminate between those transactions for a consideration in money and those for which the consideration was in kind (barter transactions), C & E extended relief to barter transactions on an administration basis pending the change in legislation. Provided other conditions for claiming relief are satisfied, retrospective claims can be made for bad debt relief on barter transactions on supplies between 1 October 1978 (when bad debt relief was first introduced) and 31 March 1989 under the 'old' scheme and 1 April 1989 and 28 February 1997 under the 'new' scheme. Claims in respect of supplies on or after 1 March 1997 should be made on the VAT return in the normal way. (C & E Business Brief 21/97, 3 October 1997).

Only the actual supplier can claim. The one exception to this rule is where, after 30 April 1997, a business has been transferred as a going concern and the transferee takes on the transferor's VAT registration number. In such a case, the transferee acquires the transferor's entitlement to any bad debt relief (whether or not existing at the time of the transfer). (C & E Notice 700/18/97, para 2.8).

(*b*) The whole or part of the consideration for the relevant supply has been written off in his accounts as a bad debt. *With effect from 17 December 1996*, this is to be taken as done when an entry is made in the 'refunds for bad debts account' which must be kept (see 7.3 below).

(*c*) Six months must have elapsed from

- the date of supply; and,

- with effect from 17 December 1996, the time when the consideration became due and payable to (or to the order of) the supplier.

(*d*) The value of the supply is equal to or less than its open market value.

(*e*) *In the case of a supply of goods made on or before 19 March 1997*, the property in the goods must have passed to the person to whom they were supplied or to a person deriving title from, through or under that person. No relief, for example, could be claimed under a contract with a clause which reserved title until the goods had been paid for (a 'Romalpa' clause). However, where goods were supplied under such a contract and the goods had not been passed on, with good title, to a third party, relief could be claimed provided the claimant formally gave up his rights under the clause. See 27.21 FINANCE.

(*f*) No claim for a refund has been made in relation to the supply under the earlier provisions for bad debt relief for supplies made before 27 July 1990.

(*g*) *With effect from 1 May 1997*, where the customer is a taxable person, the claimant must, not before but within seven days from the date of making the claim, give written notice to the customer of

- the date of issue of the notice;

- the date of the claim;

- the date and number of any VAT invoice issued in relation to each relevant supply;

- the amount of consideration for each relevant supply which the claimant has written off as a bad debt; and

- the amount of the claim (except where the claim is for a supply accounted for under a margin scheme).

A suggested format of the notice is shown below (although a notice may form part of the supplier's existing bad debt recovery procedures).

To: XYZ Ltd

Notification of a claim for VAT bad debt relief

I hereby notify you of a claim for VAT bad debt relief in respect of the following supply/supplies made to you for which payment has not been received.

Date of this notice:	25 August 1997
Invoice date:	10 January 1997
Invoice No:	5/97
Total amount due	£117.50
Bad debt relief claimed	£17.50
Date of claim:	21 August 1997

You are now required to repay any VAT claimed on these supplies to Customs and Excise until such time as payment is made.

This notification has been issued to comply with the VAT Regulations 1995 (as amended). Payment including VAT in respect of the supplies remains due and should be made forthwith.

(C & E Notice 700/18/97, para 2.4, Appendix A).

(*h*)   In respect of claims made on or after 1 May 1997, the claim must be made within three years and six months from the later of

- the date on which the consideration (or part) which has been written off as a bad debt becomes due and payable to, or to the order of, the person who made the relevant supply; and

- the date of supply

unless the later of those dates fell before 1 May 1997. A person entitled to a refund who has not made a claim within that period is regarded as having ceased to be so entitled.

'*The outstanding amount*' means the consideration for the supply written off in the accounts as a bad debt *less* any part of that consideration received before the time of the claim. Where a supplier has insured its debts, any payment by the insurers does not affect entitlement to relief. However, where a supplier receives payment, in full or part, from a guarantor or other person (e.g. a director of a debtor company) entitlement to relief is reduced by the amount paid. Similarly, where the debtor is insured for the costs of the supply (e.g. when a garage repairs a damaged car) any payment received directly from the debtor's insurers must be taken into account. (C & E Manual V1-22, Chapter 2 para 2.6). Where, under a voluntary arrangement, creditors receive shares in full satisfaction of outstanding debts, there is no longer an '*outstanding amount*' and bad debt relief cannot be claimed (*AEG (UK) Ltd, [1993] VATTR 379 (11428)*).

The normal provisions as to the time of supply of goods or services apply. See 64.32 *et seq* SUPPLY.

[*VATA 1994, s 36(1)-(4); FA 1997, s 39(1); FA 1998, s 23; SI 1995/2518, Regs 6(3), 165A, 166A, 172(1A)(2); SI 1996/2960; SI 1997/1086, Regs 3, 10, 12, 14*].

7.3   PROCEDURE FOR CLAIMING RELIEF

If all the conditions in 7.2 above are satisfied, a claim may be made for refund of the VAT on the bad debt.

Evidence required. Unless C & E allow otherwise, before submitting his claim the claimant must hold the following in respect of every relevant supply.

- A copy of any VAT invoice provided or, where there was no obligation to provide a VAT invoice, a document showing the time and nature of the supply, purchaser and consideration.

- Records, or any other document, showing that VAT has been accounted for and paid on the supply and that the consideration has been written off in his accounts as a bad debt. [*SI 1995/2518, Reg 167*].

Records required. Unless C & E allow otherwise, the claimant must keep the following records in respect of each claim made.

(*a*)   In respect of each relevant supply for that claim

- the amount of the VAT chargeable;

- the prescribed accounting period in which the VAT chargeable was accounted for and paid to C & E;

- the date and number of any invoice issued or, where there is no such invoice, such information as is necessary to identify the time, nature and purchaser; and

- any payment received for the supply.

(*b*)   The amount outstanding to which the claim relates.

(*c*)   The amount of the claim.

(*d*)   The prescribed accounting period in which the claim is made.

(*e*)   A copy of the notice to the customer required under 7.2(*g*) above.

Any records created under (*a*) to (*d*) above must be kept in a single account to be known as the '*refunds for bad debts account*'. [*SI 1995/2518, Reg 168; SI 1997/1086, Reg 13*].

Preservation of evidence and documents. Unless C & E allow otherwise, the claimant must preserve the documents, invoices and records required above for a period of four years from the date of making the claim. He must also produce them, on demand, for inspection by an authorised person and permit him to remove them at a reasonable time and for a reasonable period. [*SI 1995/2518, Reg 169*].

Making a claim. The claim is made by including the correct amount of the refund in Box 4 on Form 100 on the return for the prescribed accounting period in which entitlement to the claim arises or, subject to 7.2(*h*) above, any later return.

If at the time the claimant becomes entitled to a refund he is no longer required to make returns, he should write to his VAT office giving former VAT registration number; name and address of the debtor(s); amount of refund claimed; copies of supporting evidence (e.g. invoices); proof that the debt has remained unpaid for six months from the date payment became due and payable or, if later, the time of supply; and proof that he possesses a separate bad debt ledger. [*SI 1995/2518, Reg 166; SI 1997/1086, Reg 11*]. (C & E Notice 700/18/97, para 2.10).

Annual returns. By concession, pending the introduction of the necessary legislation, C & E allow a business which accounts for VAT by using annual returns to claim bad debt relief on debts over six months old in the same return as VAT on the debt is accounted for. (C & E Business Brief 9/97, 27 March 1997).

Groups of companies. In the case of a group registration (see 31 GROUPS OF COMPANIES) each member must keep its own separate bad debts records for debts written off. The representative member of the group claims any refund on behalf of each member while

7.4   Bad Debt Relief

they are in the VAT group. Where a member leaves a group, any VAT bad debt relief on supplies made by that company when it was a group member, but which cannot be claimed until after it has left the group, is due to that company (and not the representative member of the group). (C & E Notice 700/18/97, para 2.11). See also *Triad Timber Components Ltd, [1993] VATTR 384 (10694)* and *Proto Glazing Ltd (13410)*.

7.4   AMOUNT OF THE CLAIM

The amount of relief claimable will normally be the amount of VAT charged on the supply or supplies in respect of which the bad debt has arisen and will be readily ascertained. However, special rules apply where the claimant owes money to, or holds a security enforceable against, the purchaser (see 7.5 below) or part payment has been received (see 7.6 below).

7.5   Mutual supplies etc.

Where the claimant owes an amount of money to the purchaser which can be set off, the consideration written off in the accounts must be reduced by the amount so owed. Similarly where he holds a security which is enforceable against the purchaser, the consideration written off must be reduced by the value of the security. [*SI 1995/2518, Reg 172(3)(4)*].

Example

A bad debt has arisen in respect of a supply for which the claimant has charged £705 (£600 + VAT). The claimant also owes £235 (£200 + VAT) to the debtor.

The amount of the debt for relief purposes is £705 – £235 = £470

The amount of the bad debt relief is

£470 × 7/47= £70

7.6   Part payment

Where the claimant has made more than one supply (whether taxable or not) to the purchaser and a payment is received in relation to those supplies, then in calculating any VAT due on the outstanding debt (net of any set-offs or enforceable securities under 7.5 above) the payment is attributed to earliest supplies first. Supplies made on the same day are aggregated and treated as one. The payment is then rateably apportioned. Any supply to which the purchaser has allocated a payment in full must be excluded from the calculation. [*SI 1995/2518, Reg 170*].

Example 1

The claimant has made the following supplies to the purchaser.

Date of supply	Supply	VAT exclusive £	VAT £	VAT inclusive £
30.6.98	1	1,000	Zero-rated	1,000
28.7.98	2	1,000	175	1,175
25.8.98	3	2,000	350	2,350
29.9.98	4	350	Exempt	350
27.10.98	5	800	140	940
24.11.98	6	2,600	455	3,055
		£7,750	£1,120	£8,870

A payment of £3,300 has been received.

The amount of the bad debt is £8,870 – £3,300 = £5,570

Working from the earliest supply, the payment relates to supplies 1, 2 and part of 3 i.e.

Supply	VAT inclusive £	VAT £
1	1,000	–
2	1,175	175
3	1,125	Part of £350
Amount of payment	£3,300	

VAT included in supplies 1 and 2 is £175. The proportion of VAT included in supply 3 which has been paid is

$$\frac{\text{That part of 3 included in payment}}{\text{VAT-inclusive amount of supply 3}} \times \text{VAT on supply 3}$$

$$= \frac{1,125}{2,350} \times £350 = \underline{£167.55}$$

The total VAT paid is £175 + £167.55 = £342.55

The total bad debt relief claim is £1,120 – £342.55 = £777.45

Example 2

The figures are as in Example 1 above except that supplies 1, 2 and 3 were all made on the same day.

The VAT-inclusive amount of the debt (as above) is £5,570. The proportion of VAT in supplies 1, 2 and 3 to which the payment relates is

$$\frac{\text{Payment} \times \text{VAT in supplies 1, 2 and 3}}{\text{Total VAT-inclusive value of supplies 1, 2 and 3}} = \frac{3,300}{4,525} \times £525 = \underline{£382.87}$$

The bad debt relief claim is £737.13 (£1,120 – £382.87).

In *Enderby Transport Ltd (1607)* the customer paid the full price for the goods (£10,200) but not the VAT (£816). The tribunal held that as the amount of the debt outstanding was £816, the VAT element of this was £106.43 (3/23 rds) and bad debt relief should be restricted to this amount. In *Palmer (t/a R & K Engineering) (11739)* the tribunal allowed full bad debt relief where, following registration with retrospective effect, an invoice was raised charging VAT on supplies originally invoiced (and paid) without VAT and the customer went into receivership without paying the VAT. The tribunal did however comment that C & E had been dilatory in dealing with registration and the position might be different where late registration is due to the trader's own default.

7.7   **Second-hand goods and tour operators' margin scheme**

From 1 May 1997 bad debt relief may be claimed in respect of supplies made under the margin schemes for SECOND-HAND GOODS (61) or the TOUR OPERATORS' MARGIN SCHEME (66) as follows.

- If the debt is equal to or less than the profit margin, bad debt relief may be claimed on the VAT fraction of the debt.

- If the debt is greater than the profit margin, bad debt relief is limited to the VAT fraction of the profit margin (i.e. the amount of VAT which the supplier has paid to C & E).

7.8 Bad Debt Relief

[*SI 1995/2518, Regs 172A, 172B; SI 1997/1086, Reg 15*]. (C & E Business Brief 9/97, 27 March 1997).

Example

Second-hand goods purchased for £400 are sold for £500 (i.e. the profit margin is £100). If the customer pays only (*a*) £450; and (*b*) £350, bad debt relief is calculated as follows.

(*a*) The debt is £50 which is less than the profit margin of £100. Bad debt relief can be claimed on

$$7/47 \times £50 = £7.45$$

(*b*) The debt is £150 which is greater than the profit margin. Bad debt relief can be claimed on

$$7/47 \times £100 = £14.89$$

7.8 REPAYMENT OF REFUND

Repayment of VAT refunded by C & E is required where

(*a*) a payment for the relevant supply is subsequently received;

(*b*) a payment is, under 7.6 above, treated as attributed to the relevant supply; or

(*c*) the claimant fails to comply with the requirements of 7.3 or 7.6 above.

Under (*a*) and (*b*) above the amount of the repayment is

$$\frac{\text{Amount of payment received or attributed}}{\text{Amount of outstanding consideration}} \times \text{Amount of refund}$$

Under (*c*) above repayment must be made of the full amount of the refund obtained from C & E by the claim to which the failure to comply relates.

The repayment is made by including the appropriate amount in Box 1 on the Form VAT 100 for the prescribed accounting period in which the payment is received under (*a*) or (*b*) or as designated by C & E under (*c*). If at that time the claimant is no longer required to make returns, the repayment must still be made and the supplier should contact the local VAT office. [*SI 1995/2518, Reg 171*].

A refund does not have to be repaid if the supplier is insured for the VAT-inclusive amount of the debt and is repaid by the insurer. (C & E Notice 700/18/97, para 2.15).

7.9 REPAYMENT OF INPUT TAX BY PURCHASER

In respect of supplies made after 26 November 1996, where

- a valid claim to VAT bad debt relief has been made under the provisions in 7.1 to 7.7 above; and

- the purchaser has claimed deduction of the whole or part of the VAT on the relevant supply as input tax

then, from the date of the claim, the purchaser is taken not to be entitled to credit for input tax in respect of the VAT which has been refunded to the supplier on the claim.

The supplier must notify the purchaser of the claim (see 7.2(*g*) above) and the purchaser must make a negative entry in Box 4 of his return for the prescribed accounting period in which the supplier claims bad debt relief. The amount of that negative entry is calculated by the formula

$$\frac{\text{Amount of the VAT claim by the supplier}}{\text{VAT on the relevant supply}} \times \text{Input tax claimed}$$

Such an entry is not treated as a voluntary disclosure of an error for the purposes of *SI 1995/2518, Reg 34* (see 57.11 RECORDS).

Where, after 30 April 1997, a business has been transferred as a going concern and the transferee takes on the transferor's VAT registration number, the transferee takes over the transferor's obligation to make any repayments of input tax under these provisions.

Insolvency. By concession, an insolvency practitioner need not repay input tax under the above provisions where, after an 'insolvency procedure' has been commenced, the practitioner receives notice of a claim to VAT bad debt relief from a supplier in respect of pre-insolvency transactions provided

- C & E have been properly notified of the insolvency (see 36.2 INSOLVENCY); and

- the application of the concession does not give rise to tax avoidance.

The concession applies whether or not the business of the insolvent person is carried on.

The '*insolvency procedures*' to which the concession applies are bankruptcies, compulsory liquidations, creditors' and members' voluntary liquidations, administrative receiverships, administration orders, individual and company voluntary arrangements, Scottish trust deeds and deeds of arrangement, partnership voluntary arrangements and liquidations, partnership administration orders, sequestrations, county court administration orders, schemes of arrangement, and deceased persons' administration orders.

The effective date for the application of the concession is the relevant date of the insolvency and the date of the insolvency meeting if applicable (or, in the case of an administration order, the date of that order). The concession only applies to a provisional liquidation if it is followed by a permanent liquidation although, in such a case, the concession takes effect from the date of the provisional liquidation.

If an insolvency arrangement fails, the requirement to account for clawback is reinstated.

(C & E Business Brief 5/98, 10 February 1998).

Restoration of entitlement to input tax. Where

- the purchaser has made a negative entry in a VAT return under the above provisions (the 'input tax repayment') and has paid any VAT due in respect of that period, and

- the supplier has made a repayment of any bad debt refund to C & E under 7.8 above,

the purchaser can make a positive entry in Box 4 of his VAT return for the prescribed accounting period in which the repayment is made. The amount of that positive entry is calculated by the formula

$$\frac{\text{Amount of the VAT repaid by the supplier}}{\text{Total amount of the claim}} \times \text{Input tax repayment}$$

Such an entry is not treated as a voluntary disclosure of an error for the purposes of *SI 1995/2518, Reg 34* (see 57.11 RECORDS).

[*VATA 1994, s 36(4A); FA 1997, s 39(2)(3); SI 1985/2518, Regs 6(3), 172C–172E; SI 1997/1086, Regs 3, 16*].

7.10   **SALE OF PROPERTY UNDER A POWER OF SALE — RECOVERY OF VAT ON COSTS INCURRED BY MORTGAGE LENDERS**

Where a property is repossessed by the lender, although the sale of the property is a supply by the borrower, C & E accept that the lender may be treated as agent of the

7.10   Bad Debt Relief

borrower in relation to certain costs of sale. This applies whether or not the mortgage deed specifies such a relationship. As an agent, the lender may treat these costs incurred as supplies made to him and by him under *VATA 1994, s 47(3)*. Where the proceeds of sale are insufficient to cover all or part of the costs of sale, the lender can therefore recover any unpaid VAT under the bad debt provisions. For these purposes, the order of attribution of the sale proceeds follows the normal rules under the bad debt relief regulations (i.e. allocate to the earliest supply, the mortgage, first) rather than those under *Law of Property Act 1925, s 105* (which requires proceeds to be first allocated to the selling costs). The arrangements apply to VAT on the following costs.

(*a*)   Costs relating directly to the sale of the property which would ordinarily have been incurred by the borrower had he arranged the sale himself (e.g. legal and estate agency fees for professional services connected with the sale).

(*b*)   *Law of Property Act* (LPA) receiver's charges relating specifically to the sale of the property and any costs incurred by the receiver in respect of the sale, but only where the proceeds of sale received by the lender have been reduced by the VAT element of the charges (and not where the LPA receiver recovers the VAT incurred on behalf of a VAT-registered borrower and this is reflected in the proceeds passed to the lender).

(*c*)   Build-out costs (i.e. expenses incurred on completion of a partly-completed building or major refurbishment of the property before sale) but only where

  (i) the sale of the building by the borrower is the subject of a taxable supply or the transfer of a going concern for VAT purposes; or

  (ii) the property is the subject of a taxable let and output tax on the rents has been accounted for to C & E.

The arrangement does not apply if the proceeds of sale or rent received by lenders reflect any input tax on build-out costs recovered by the borrower.

(*d*)   Repair and maintenance expenses.

(*e*)   A lender's own in-house estate agency or solicitor's services to the borrower provided output tax has been accounted for on the supply under normal rules.

The arrangement does not cover any costs incurred in relation to letting (other than those within (*c*) above). Nor does it cover costs incurred on services provided to, and used by, the lender as principal even if charged to the borrower under the mortgage deed (e.g. legal fees associated with taking possession; locksmith's fees for securing the property; and costs incurred in pursuing claims against a valuer for negligence).

(C & E Business Brief 24/94, 8 December 1994).

8 Business

Cross-reference. See 71.6 WORKS OF ART for sales of antiques etc. from stately homes.

De Voil Indirect Tax Service. See V2.2.

The contents of this chapter are as follows.

8.1–8.4	General meaning of business
8.5–8.9	Disaggregation of business activities
8.10–8.15	Transfer of a business as a going concern

8.1 GENERAL MEANING OF 'BUSINESS'

EC legislation. The *EC 6th Directive* adopts the term 'economic activity' rather than business. See 22.6 EUROPEAN COMMUNITY LEGISLATION. Unless a decision of the CJEC provides otherwise, the meaning of economic activity is not materially different from the meaning of 'business' in the UK legislation.

UK legislation. The proper identification of an activity as a 'business' activity is fundamental to the operation of VAT. Output tax must be charged on any taxable supply of goods or services made in the UK by a taxable person *in the course or furtherance of any business* carried on by him. [*VATA 1994, s 4(1)*]. Similarly, input tax must relate to supplies of goods and services to a taxable person (and, where relevant, acquisitions and importations of goods by him) used or to be used *for the purpose of any business* carried on or to be carried on by him. [*VATA 1994, s 24(1)*].

Despite the importance of the meaning of *'business'*, it is not comprehensively defined in UK (or EC) legislation. *VATA 1994, s 94* gives the following guidance as to what the term encompasses and excludes. If a particular activity is not covered, then it is necessary to apply the 'business test' developed by the Courts (see 8.2 below).

(*a*) It includes any trade, profession or vocation.

(*b*) The following (without prejudice to the generality of anything else in *VATA 1994*) are deemed to be the carrying on of a business.

> (i) The provision by a club, association or organisation (for a subscription or other consideration) of the facilities or advantages available to its members (but see (*c*) below). See also 14.1 CLUBS AND ASSOCIATIONS.

> (ii) The admission, for a consideration, of persons to any premises (see *The Eric Taylor Testimonial Match Committee [1975] VATTR 8 (139)*).

(*c*) A body which has objects which are in the public domain and are of a political, religious, philanthropic, philosophical or patriotic nature is not to be treated as carrying on a business only because its members subscribe to it (see (*b*)(i) above) if a subscription obtains no facility or advantage for the subscriber other than the right to participate in its management or receive reports on its activities. See also 14.10 CLUBS AND ASSOCIATIONS.

(*d*) Where a person accepts any office in the course or furtherance of a trade, profession or vocation, services supplied by him as holder of that office are treated as supplied in the course or furtherance of that trade, profession or vocation. See 8.4(*k*) below, 44.8 MANAGEMENT SERVICES AND SUPPLIES OF STAFF and 50.6 PARTNERSHIPS.

(*e*) Anything done in connection with the termination or intended termination of a business is treated as being done in the course or furtherance of that business.

8.2 Business

(*f*) The disposition of a business as a going concern, or of its assets or liabilities (whether or not in connection with its reorganisation or winding up) is a supply made in the course or furtherance of the business (but see 8.10 below).

De Voil Indirect Tax Service. See V2.202.

8.2   The business test

When considering whether an activity is to be treated as a business, if it is not one of the deemed businesses under 8.1 above then the 'business test' must be applied. This test is derived from decisions of the VAT tribunals and Courts.

The following principles, as summarised in *C & E Commrs v Lord Fisher QB, [1981] STC 238* are a guide as to whether an activity is a business although the absence of one common attribute of ordinary businesses (e.g. the pursuit of profit) does not necessarily mean that the activity is not a business and the criteria are not therefore conclusive in every case.

(*a*) By providing in *VATA 1994, s 94* (see 8.1 above) that business *includes* any trade, profession or vocation, it is clear that a wide meaning of 'business' is intended.

(*b*) In determining whether any particular activity constitutes a business it is necessary to consider the whole of that activity.

(*c*) A business activity can generally be identified from the answers to the following criteria (as laid down in *C & E Commrs v Morrison's Academy Boarding Houses Association CS 1977, [1978] STC 1*).

(i) Is the activity a 'serious undertaking earnestly pursued' or a 'serious occupation not necessarily confined to commercial or profit making undertakings'?

(ii) Is the activity an occupation or function actively pursued with reasonable or recognisable continuity?

A one-off supply or a series of infrequent, unconnected supplies is not normally a business activity in its own right although it is important to consider the nature of the activity. For example, occasional sales by small speculative builders and property developers are business activities.

(iii) Does the activity have a certain measure of substance as measured by the quarterly or annual value of taxable supplies made?

(iv) Is the activity conducted in a regular manner and on sound and recognised business principles?

(v) Is the activity predominantly concerned with the making of taxable supplies to consumers for a consideration?

This is perhaps the most important point to establish, bearing in mind that 'consideration' need not necessarily be monetary. If a trader is carrying on an activity which does not involve the making of any supplies for a consideration and there is no intention in the future of doing so, then the activity is unlikely to be regarded as business even if all the other criteria are met.

In *C & E Commrs v The Apple and Pear Development Council HL, [1988] STC 221* the Council's principal activity was to advertise English apples and pears, which activity was financed by a statutory levy on growers. The CJEC ruled that the levy was not consideration because there was no direct link between the payments and the benefits of individual growers (*CJEC, [1988] STC 221*) on which basis the House of Lords concluded that the activity was not 'business' in the VAT sense. Similarly, a charity raising funds in a 'business-like' manner from its activities was held not to be running a business unless taxable supplies, made for a consideration, formed the basis of the fund raising (*C & E Commrs v Royal Exchange Theatre Trust QB, [1979] STC 278*).

Where an activity is just beginning and no supplies are being made at the time but there is a clear intention to do so at some time in the future, then the activity may qualify as a business. See *Rompelman v Minister van Financien, CJEC [1985] 3 CMLR 202; [1985] ECR 655* and *Merseyside Cablevision Ltd, [1987] VATTR 134 (2419)*.

(vi) Are the taxable supplies of a kind which are commonly made by those who seek to profit by them?

If a person is carrying on an activity and it is not clear whether it amounts to a business, it is more likely to be regarded as such if others are carrying on the same type of activity and are clearly doing so on a commercial basis. See *Church of Scientology of California (No 1) v C & E Commrs CA 1980, [1981] STC 65* where courses in the study of its beliefs provided by the Church, some of which competed with those offered by trained psychologists and psychiatrists, were found to be business activities.

(*d*) Whether the activity is pursued for profit or some other private purpose or motive is not decisive in determining whether the activity is a business.

(*e*) If all or a sufficient number of the above criteria are satisfied in sufficient measure to override any contra-indications which might be seen in the facts, then as a matter of law the activity must be held to be a business.

The carrying on, by a regulatory authority, of a statutory licensing activity to protect the public interest is not a business activity even though carried on for a consideration. See *Institute of Chartered Accountants in England and Wales v C & E Commrs, CA [1997] STC 1155* in respect of the Institute's authorisation to issue licences to auditors, insolvency practitioners and persons carrying on investment business.

See the chapter *Business* in *Tolley's VAT Cases* for tribunal and court decisions involving the general meaning of 'business'.

De Voil Indirect Tax Service. See V2.202–V2.209.

8.3 **Business and non-business activities**

Businesses with more than one activity. Where a taxable person undertakes distinct and separate activities, some of these may be business and others non-business. The business test must be applied to each activity. See, for example, *Rainheath Ltd (1249)* (yacht purchased by a farming business); *DA Walker [1976] VATTR 10 (240)* (accountant with furnished letting income); and *RW & AAW Williamson [1978] VATTR 90 (555)* (retail partnership also renting out lock-up garages).

Hobbies. Activities of pleasure and social enjoyment, though organised in a business-like way, do not amount to a 'business' if no taxable supplies are made for a consideration (*C & E Commrs v Lord Fisher QB, [1981] STC 238*).

Traders may sometimes have hobbies that involve the making of taxable supplies (e.g. repairing cars or selling stamps). These supplies are not automatically made in the course or furtherance of business and the business test must be applied. Hobbies which involve a registered trader making minimal supplies are unlikely to be seen as business. However, a hobby may develop to such an extent that it becomes a business. See, for example, *Haydon-Baillie, [1986] VATTR 79 (2072)*.

8.4   Business

Disposal of private assets. This is normally a non-business activity. Where, however, the assets are disposed of through the trader's own business the disposal may occasionally be treated as business. See, for example, *Mittu (1275)* where a jeweller sold items of jewellery belonging to his wife through the business and paid the proceeds into the business account.

When deciding if a sale is private or business the following questions should be considered.

● Are the goods of a type normally sold through the business?

● Was the sale dependent upon the contacts and reputation of the business?

● How were the receipts dealt with and accounted for?

The independent disposal of private assets merely to raise funds for a business is non-business and outside the scope of VAT. See *RWK Stirling, [1985] VATTR 232 (1963)*.

(C & E Manual V1-6, Chapter 2 paras 4.1- 4.3).

8.4   **Particular problem areas**

(*a*)   **Bloodstock**.

(i) **Breeders**. VAT registration is required (or allowed voluntarily) where a business exists of breeding horses for sale. For breeding to be regarded as a business, C & E require to be satisfied that

● the breeding is carried on predominantly for sale; and

● the activity has, over a period of years, a realistic expectation of a profit commensurate with the financial outlay.

When applying the general business test (see 8.2 above) C & E will bear in mind factors such as the number and quality of the brood mares owned and whether the stated intentions of the breeder are in fact carried out. However, in practice it is unlikely that a 'non-business' view will be taken if any breeding activity is carried out on a relatively large scale (even if the breeder retains and races a large proportion of the horses rather than selling them).

Following the introduction of the Registration Scheme for racehorse owners (see 63.21 SPECIAL SCHEMES) C & E accept that, where breeders engage in racing activities with the intention of enhancing the value of their stock and/or general standing of the business, those activities are regarded as being by way of business. The input tax incurred on the purchase and racing expenses of both fillies and colts may be deducted in full subject to the normal rules. Gelding cannot form part of a breeder's activities and consequently input tax cannot be deducted through the breeding account.

There is no liability to output tax when the breeding stock is transferred to training but output tax is due on the full amount realised on the sale of stock.

Breeders who race their own personal horses cannot claim input tax deduction through the breeding account but may qualify to do so under the Registration Scheme for racehorse owners (see 63.21 SPECIAL SCHEMES).

(ii) **Trainers**. VAT registration is required (or allowed voluntarily) where a business exists of providing training services to owners. C & E accept that a trainer who has an unrestricted licence to train horses owned by other unconnected persons is making business supplies of training. If horses owned by the trainer's relatives are trained as part of such an activity, this can also be accepted as business provided that a commercial charge is made for the service.

C & E accept that where horses are both owned and trained by a trainer, the related costs are regarded as being business expenditure for VAT purposes provided

- the number of such horses is not disproportionate to the main activity; and

- the majority of the horses are available for sale.

Trainers who own horses which are raced for personal enjoyment and are not for sale, cannot claim input tax deduction through the training account but may qualify to do so under the Registration Scheme for racehorse owners (see 63.21 SPECIAL SCHEMES).

(iii) **Dealers.** VAT registration is required (or allowed voluntarily) for persons engaged in the purchase and sale of horses on a commercial basis. Factors which C & E take into account when deciding whether a dealing activity can be treated as a business include

- the scale of the buying and selling in the previous few years;

- the average length of time each horse is in the dealer's ownership;

- whether the trader makes an overall profit on the activity;

- whether the trader acts in a commercial manner; and

- if the trader also acts as a purchasing or selling agent charging commission (a good indication that the activity is a business).

C & E accept that where dealers engage in racing activities with the intention of enhancing the value of their stock and/or general standing of the business, those activities are regarded as being by way of business. The input tax incurred on purchase and racing expenses of fillies, colts and geldings can be deducted in full subject to the normal rules.

Dealers who race their own personal horses cannot claim input tax deduction through the dealing account but may qualify to do so under the Registration Scheme for racehorse owners (see 63.21 SPECIAL SCHEMES).

(C & E Manual V1-6, Chapter 3 section 1).

De Voil Indirect Tax Service. See V6.113–116A.

(*b*)   **Boats.** Where a boat owner independently pursues the activity of letting boats to the public, the basic test in 8.2 above must be applied to determine whether a business is being carried on. The supply on hire of a single boat may amount to a business if actively and continuously carried on throughout the season. See, for example, *C R King and Partners (Holdings) Ltd (6695)*. Following the decision in *Lennartz v Finanzamt Munchen CJEC, [1995] STC 514* a business may also exist where the predominant use of the boat is for non-business purposes (although in such a case the non-business use must be treated as a taxable supply of services).

Use of boat hire companies as principals. Frequently, however, a boat owner enters into an agreement with a boat hire company (normally in business on its own account) which lets out the boat(s) as principal on behalf of the owner. In such cases, the terms of the agreement between a boat owner and a boat hire company, and in particular the extent of control and management of the boat(s) retained by the owner, will be important in determining whether the boat owner is in business.

8.4 Business

The long-term supply of a boat by the owner to a boat hire company is a single supply of letting for the period of the agreement. Such an isolated supply is not normally regarded as a business activity (*Coleman (KG), [1976] VATTR 24 (242)*). This applies equally to two boats or where a partnership/company is set up for the specific purpose of letting out on hire one or two boats via a boat company. Even in such circumstances, it may still be possible to satisfy the business test. Factors which will be taken into account include

- the scale of the activity;

- whether the owner, in addition to letting to the hire company, also lets out direct to the public for part of the year (although where such activity is minimal – as a rule of thumb no more than three weeks in a twelve month period – this may not satisfy the test of being seriously pursued); and

- whether the boat owner has other VAT business activities and the letting on hire can be regarded as forming part of the overall business.

Where three or more boats are let on hire to a boat hire company, the scale of the activity is more likely to be considered sufficient to allow the owner to be regarded as carrying on a trade (subject to the extent to which they are exploited to make taxable supplies).

Use of boat hire companies as agents. A boat owner may satisfy the business test by hiring out a boat to the public through the agency of a boat hire company.

(C & E Manual V1-6, Chapter 3 section 2).

(c) **Light aircraft.** Similar guidance applies as for boats under (*b*) above. See also *Three H Aircraft Hire QB 1978, [1979] STC 653.*

(d) **Broadcasting.** The broadcasting activity of the BBC is not considered to be a business activity because it is carried out as part of its duties as a public authority. Other activities of the BBC (e.g. sale of videos, books and programmes overseas) are business activities.

ITV companies are commercial organisations and are not providing broadcasting under a statutory obligation. Their broadcasting activities (as well as sales of programmes overseas, videos, etc.) are therefore business.

ITN has a right to broadcast news services on the ITV network. It is financed by a levy imposed on the ITV companies and this is not considered to be a supply in the course of business.

Many overseas state broadcasters have representative offices in the UK, often for the provision of news services to the overseas parent body. Such a broadcaster may have a combination of business and non-business activities. It is likely to be in business if it undertakes an activity for a consideration (e.g. commercial advertising or pay per view). This applies regardless of whether the activity is undertaken because of its statutory obligations. However, activities undertaken for no consideration are not business activities.

(C & E Manual V1-6, Chapter 3 section 3).

(e) **Building and construction.** One of the criteria to be established under the business test is whether the activity is carried out on a regular and consistent basis since a one-off supply or a series of infrequent, unconnected supplies is not normally regarded as a business activity. See, however, *David Wickens Properties Ltd, [1982] VATTR 143 (1284)* where the tribunal decided that, where property is concerned, the infrequency of supplies did not necessarily prevent an activity from being treated as a business.

Where a sole proprietor builds a house on his own land for his own occupation, C & E regard this as a business activity provided the builder has already built at least one other house for sale on the open market to an unconnected person.

(C & E Manual V1-6, Chapter 3 section 4).

(*f*)   **Charities.** See 12.4 CHARITIES.

(*g*)   **Clubs and associations.** See 14.1 CLUBS AND ASSOCIATIONS.

(*h*)   **Education.** See 20.2 EDUCATION.

(*i*)   **Local authorities** (see 43.4 LOCAL AUTHORITIES AND STATUTORY BODIES) and **government departments and health authorities** (see 43.6 LOCAL AUTHORITIES AND STATUTORY BODIES).

(*j*)   **Shooting rights.** See 58.16 RECREATION AND SPORT.

(*k*)   **Office holders.** Under *VATA 1994, s 94(4)* where a person in the course or furtherance of a trade, profession or vocation accepts any office, services supplied by him as the holder of that office are treated as supplied in the course or furtherance of the trade, profession or vocation. Both public and private office holders can be affected. The appointments will generally be held for an indefinite period (often on a part-time basis). Payment is normally in the form of fees and expenses or an annual retainer. The status of the office holder is not affected by fees being described as a salary.

The provisions only apply to persons such as solicitors, accountants and other practising consultants in business to provide professional services and who continue to supply their services and skills in the course of their duties as office holders. C & E do not regard the provisions as applying to the following categories of office holders whose services as such are treated as outside the scope of VAT.

- Persons who can demonstrate that their appointment to an office was offered and accepted in writing before their business consultancy began. See *Gardner (JJ), [1989] VATTR 132 (3687)*.

- Persons appointed on grounds of their personal merit, occupational expertise or experience, or standing in the community as distinct from professional expertise as solicitors, etc. as above.

- Persons who do not otherwise provide professional services.

- Persons who practice their profession solely as partners in a firm providing professional services and who accept the appointment in a purely private capacity.

- Persons who are genuinely retired from active professional business and who supply their professional services solely as office holders.

- Persons whose status is that of an employee or who by virtue of their conditions of appointment as office holders are effectively employees (e.g. they have conditioned hours of work, leave and sick leave entitlement, superannuation benefits, etc.)

See also 44.8 MANAGEMENT SERVICES AND SUPPLIES OF STAFF for directors or employees or a company, sole traders and partners as office holders.

(C & E Manual V1-6, Chapter 3 section 10 which also see for special rules applying to ecclesiastical legal appointments, judicial appointments, Legal Aid Committee members, Notaries Public and Commissioners for Oaths and services provided in connection with debt recovery).

(*l*) **Works of art – disposals from stately homes**. See 71.6 WORKS OF ART ETC.

(*m*) **Grant-funded bodies**. Some traders receive grants (e.g. from central government, local authorities or the national lottery) to support their activities. Although such grants are normally outside the scope of VAT, in some circumstances they can be seen as direct or third party consideration for a supply.

The receipt of outside the scope income does not automatically mean that an activity is non-business. Each grant-funded activity should be looked at separately and the business test applied.

• If an activity involves the making of no taxable supplies for consideration and is entirely funded by outside the scope income, it is non-business (and no VAT relating to it can be treated as input tax).

• If an activity involves the making of some taxable supplies and the receipt of some outside the scope income, then the treatment depends upon the application of the business test. The receipt of money to act as a subsidy for a loss-making commercial activity need not result in input tax restriction. However, in many cases the outside the scope income is indicative of the existence of a non-business activity and an apportionment is needed.

(C & E Manual V1-6, Chapter 3 section 12 para 12.1).

8.5   **DISAGGREGATION OF BUSINESS ACTIVITIES**

EC legislation. See 22.6 EUROPEAN COMMUNITY LEGISLATION.

The following provisions are designed to prevent the maintenance or creation of any 'artificial' separation of business activities carried on by two or more persons from resulting in the avoidance of VAT. With effect from 19 March 1997, in determining whether any separation of business activities is '*artificial*', consideration must be given to the extent to which the different persons carrying on those activities are closely bound to one another by financial, economic and organisational links.

C & E may make a direction under which the persons specified therein become treated as a single taxable person carrying on the activities of a business described in the direction. That taxable person is then liable to be registered under *VATA 1994, 1 Sch* with effect from the date of the direction or such later day as is specified. The direction must be served on each person named in it.

If, immediately before the direction (or any supplementary direction below) any person named therein is already registered in respect of taxable supplies made by him, he ceases to be liable to be registered from the date of the direction or, if later, the date with effect from which the single taxable person concerned became liable to be registered.

Supplementary directions. C & E may subsequently make and serve a supplementary direction adding a further person's name to those detailed in the earlier direction where that person appears to C & E to be making taxable supplies in the course of the activities of the business previously specified. The name is added from the date on which he began making those taxable supplies or, if later, the date with effect from which the single taxable person referred to in the earlier direction became liable to be registered under *VATA 1994, 1 Sch*.

[*VATA 1994, 1 Sch 1A, 2(1)(3)–(5); FA 1997, s 31(1)(2)(4)*].

De Voil Indirect Tax Service. See V2.123.

8.6   **Preconditions for making a direction**

Before making a direction naming any person C & E must be satisfied that (*a*) he is making or has made taxable supplies;

(*b*) the activities in the course of which he makes or made those supplies form only part of certain activities, the other activities being carried on concurrently or previously (or both) by one or more other persons; and

(*c*) if all the taxable supplies of the business described in the direction were taken into account, a person carrying on that business would at the time of the direction be liable to be registered under the normal registration rules.

In respect of directions made before 19 March 1997, C & E also had to be satisfied that the main reason (or one of the main reasons) for the person concerned carrying on the activities in (*b*) in the way he did was to avoid liability to be registered (whether that liability would be his, another person's or that of two or more persons jointly).

[*VATA 1994, 1 Sch 2(2); FA 1997, s 31(2)(4)*].

8.7   **C & E policy**

Artificial separation. In deciding whether or not to make a direction, C & E will be concerned with separations which are devices contrived to circumvent the normal VAT registration rules. Whether any particular separation is artificial will, in most cases, depend upon the facts. The following are examples of where C & E would at least make further enquiries.

• Separate entities supply registered and unregistered customers.

• The same equipment/premises is used by different entities on a regular basis. This may occur, for example, in launderettes, food take-aways or mobile catering equipment.

• Splitting up of what is usually a single supply, e.g. bed and breakfast and the livery trade.

• Artificially separated businesses which maintain the appearance of a single business, e.g. bar sales and catering in a public house (although the relationship between the parties is important here as truly franchised 'shop within a shop' arrangements will not normally be considered artificial).

• One person has a controlling influence in a number of entities which all make the same type of supply in diverse locations.

Financial, economic and organisational links. Again these will depend upon the specific circumstances but the following examples illustrate the types of factors indicative of the necessary links.

(*a*) *Financial links*

• Financial support given by one part to another.

• One part would not be financially viable without support from another.

• Common financial interest in the proceeds of the business.

(*b*) *Economic links*

• Seeking to realise the same economic objective.

• The activities of one part benefit the other part.

• Supplying the same circle of customers.

8.8 Business

(c)   *Organisational links*

* Common management.

* Common employees.

* Common premises.

* Common equipment.

(C & E Notice 700/61/97, paras 1.5, 1.6).

| 8.8 | **Effect of a direction** |

The effects of a direction on the *'constituent members'* (i.e. all those named in the direction and any supplementary direction) are as follows.

(*a*)   The taxable person carrying on the specified business is registrable in such name as the persons named in the direction jointly nominate in writing within 14 days of the direction. Otherwise the taxable person is registrable in such name as may be specified in the direction.

(*b*)   Any supply of goods or services by or to one of the constituent members in the course of the specified business is treated as a supply by or to the taxable person.

(*c*)   Any acquisition of goods from another EC country by one of the constituent members in the course of the specified business is treated as an acquisition by the taxable person.

(*d*)   Each of the constituent members is jointly and severally liable for any VAT due from the taxable person.

(*e*)   Without prejudice to (*d*) above, any failure by a taxable person to comply with any VAT requirement is treated as a failure by each of the constituent members severally.

(*f*)   Subject to (*a*)–(*e*) above, the constituent members are treated as a partnership carrying on the specified business and any question as to the scope of that business at any time is determined accordingly.

C & E may subsequently give notice that one of the constituent members is no longer to be regarded as such for the purposes of (*d*) or (*e*) above. He then ceases to have any liability for those purposes after a date specified in the notice and, from the same date, ceases to be regarded as a member of the partnership referred to in (*f*) above.

[*VATA 1994, 1 Sch 2(6)–(8)*].

| 8.9 | **Appeals** |

An appeal may be made against a direction or supplementary direction but the tribunal cannot allow the appeal unless it considers that C & E could not reasonably have been satisfied that there were grounds for making that direction or supplementary direction. [*VATA 1994, s 84(7); FA 1997, s 31(3)*].

For cases where C & E's direction was upheld, see *Chamberlain v C & E Commrs QB,[1989] STC 505* (associated companies operating launderettes); *Osman v C & E Commrs QB, [1989] STC 596* (husband and wife acting as tax consultants from the same office); *TSD & Mrs M E Williams (2445)* (married couple carrying on business as a café and bread shop from the same premises); *MJ & P Summers (3498)* (health studio operated by married couple and son); *P & RJ Jervis* (catering at a public house); *West End Health and Fitness Club (4070)* (company operating a fitness club and a director and his wife operating a beauty salon in partnership from the same premises); *Old Farm Service Station Ltd & L Williams (4261)* (company operating a service station and a director's son running a video club at the same premises); *Allerton Motors (9427)* (car sales and car washing at same premises); *EM, PG & CP Evans (10532)* (fairground amusement operators); and *A & S Essex (t/a Essex Associates) (15072)* (married couple providing computer programming services via a partnership and supplying computer hardware via a limited company).

For cases where the appellants were successful, see *D & Mrs LM Horsman (5401)* (farming and pony trekking carried on by married couple); *P, C & J Allen (12209)* (where, to avoid inheritance tax, a husband, who ran a bookselling business and three launderettes, took his wife into partnership in the bookselling business, transferred one of the launderettes to her and took his son into partnership in another of the launderettes); and *I Reayner, J Colegate & A Reayner (15396)* (dry-cleaning businesses operated from separate premises by a mother, her son and his common law wife).

8.10   **TRANSFER OF A BUSINESS AS A GOING CONCERN ('TOGC')**

EC legislation. See 22.7 EUROPEAN COMMUNITY LEGISLATION.

In certain circumstances, the sale of a business or part of a business is not treated as a supply for VAT purposes. The sales affected are those where a business is sold as a going concern or where the sale is of part of a business capable of separate operation. The transfer may be to a person with no previous interest in the business or may simply be a change in legal identity (e.g. a sole proprietor forming a limited company or taking someone into partnership). There is no TOGC merely because of a sale of shares in a company or a change in the constitution of a partnership. (C & E Notice 700/9/96, para 1.2).

The provisions have two main purposes.

* To help businesses by improving their cash flow and avoiding the need to separately value assets which have been sold as a whole.

* To protect the revenue by removing a charge to VAT and entitlement to input tax where the output tax may not be paid to Customs (e.g. 'Phoenix' businesses).

Where the conditions in 8.11 below are met, the transfer is not a taxable supply and VAT must not be charged on the assets transferred (except, in certain circumstances as indicated in 8.12 below, on the land and buildings used in the business). The vendor should cancel any VAT invoice issued and provide the purchaser with a refund of the VAT charged. Normally this will be by issue of a credit note or similar document. (C & E Notice 700/9/96, para 2.1). Any VAT incorrectly charged, if shown on a VAT invoice and not cancelled, is recoverable by C & E from the transferor, see 17.2 CUSTOMS AND EXCISE: POWERS.

If VAT is charged when it should not be, the purchaser has no right to deduct the 'VAT' as input tax even if he has paid the amount to the vendor in good faith. However, where C & E are wholly satisfied that the amount of 'VAT' has been both declared and paid to them by the seller, they may allow the purchaser to recover it as if it were input tax. (C & E Manual V1-10, Chapter 2 para 3.2).

De Voil Indirect Tax Service. See V2.226; V3.116.

8.11   **Conditions for transfer not to be a taxable supply**

The supply by a person of the assets of his business to a person to whom he transfers that business (or part thereof) as a going concern is neither a supply of goods nor a supply of services provided all the following conditions are satisfied.

8.11 Business

(a) The assets are to be used by the transferee in carrying on the same kind of business, whether or not as part of an existing business, as that carried on by the transferor in relation to the whole or part transferred. [*SI 1995/1268, Art 5(1)*].

The same kind of business has been held to be carried on where a public house was subsequently aimed at different clientele and sold different beer (*G Draper (Marlow) Ltd (2079)*) and where an Indian restaurant became an Italian restaurant (*Tahmassebi (t/a Sale Pepe) (13177)*). There is not necessarily a different kind of business because the seller made supplies to wholesalers and the purchaser sells to retail customers. See, for example, *Village Collection Interiors Ltd (6146)*.

If the new owner is to use the assets to carry on a different kind of business, VAT must be charged in the normal way.

It is implied that the transferor had to have been carrying on the business, or part of the business, transferred. See *Kwik Save Group plc, [1994] VATTR 457 (12749)* where a holding company carrying on the business of food retailers purchased foodstores (not a taxable supply) and then transferred them to a subsidiary which carried on a similar business but without itself in the meantime having traded at those foodstores (a taxable supply).

(b) In a case in which the transferor is a taxable person (i.e. registered or liable to be registered for VAT), the transferee must already be a taxable person or immediately become, as a result of the transfer, a taxable person (or Isle of Man equivalent). [*SI 1995/1268, Art 5(1)*]. In determining whether the transferee is a taxable person, the turnover of the seller must also be taken into account. See 59.3 REGISTRATION.

(c) In relation to a part transfer, that part is capable of separate operation. [*SI 1995/1268, Art 5(1)*]. It does not matter whether it will, in fact, be operated separately from any other business the new owner carries on.

(d) The effect of the transfer must be to put the new owner in possession of a business which can be operated as such. A sale of capital assets is not in itself a TOGC but if the effect is to put the purchaser in possession of a business, then it is such a transfer even if the assets are transferred on different dates. (C & E Notice 700/9/96, para 2.2).

(e) The business, or part, transferred must be a 'going concern' at the time of transfer. This does not necessarily imply that the business is commercially viable. It may have been scaled down due to financial difficulties or in anticipation of sale or be trading under a liquidator or administrative receiver. See, for example, *Baltic Leasing (2088)* and *C & E Commrs v Dearwood Ltd QB, [1986] STC 327*.

In order for a business to be regarded as 'dead', C & E would normally expect such evidence as all employees having been made redundant, orders no longer being accepted/sought, supplies ceasing, etc. The effect of a break in trading before sale will depend upon the kind of business involved. For example, a seasonal business which has been closed during what is normally the closed season may still be a going concern because it is advertising for customers, accepting bookings, etc.

(C & E Notice 700/9/96, para 2.2; C & E Manual V1-10, Chapter 2 para 2.6).

In *JMA Spijkers v Gevroeders Benedik Abattoir CV CJEC, [1986] 2 CMLR 296* it was held that there could be a TOGC even if there had been a cessation of trading before the date on which the transfer took place provided the wherewithal to carry on the business, such as plant, building and employees, were available and were transferred.

(f) There must not be a series of immediately consecutive transfers of the business. Where A sells its assets to B who immediately sells those assets to C, B has not carried on the business. As a result, B can neither receive nor make an onward supply of the assets under the special provisions. In relation to property transactions, such immediate transfers often occur where A contracts to sell property to B, and B sells on to C with both contracts being completed by a single transfer from A to C. There is an exception to this for the transfer of a property rental business in Scotland where, subject to the provisions relating to land and buildings in 8.13 below, the disposition of the *dominium utile* may be seen to be direct from A to C. (C & E Notice 700/9/96, para 2.2).

(*g*) There should be no significant break in the normal trading pattern before or immediately after the transfer. A short period of closure which does not significantly disrupt the existing trading pattern, e.g. for redecoration, will be ignored. (C & E Notice 700/9/96, para 2.2).

In deciding whether a transaction amounts to a TOGC, regard must be had to its substance rather than its form, and consideration must be given to the whole of the circumstances, weighing the factors which point in one direction against those which point in another. In the end, the vital consideration is whether the effect of the transaction was to put the transferee in possession of a going concern, the activities of which he could carry on without interruption. Many factors may be relevant to this decision though few will be conclusive in themselves. Thus, if the transferee carries on the business in the same manner as before, this will point to the existence of a transfer, but the converse is not necessarily true, because the transfer may be complete even though the transferee does not choose to avail himself of all the rights which he acquires thereunder. Similarly an express assignment of goodwill is strong evidence of a transfer of a business, but the absence of such an assignment is not conclusive the other way. The absence of the assignment of premises, stock or outstanding contracts will likewise not be conclusive, if the particular circumstances of the transferee enable him to carry on substantially the same business as before. (*Kenmir Ltd v Frizzell QB, [1968] 1 All ER 414*).

C & E officers are advised to take to following into account when determining whether there has been a TOGC although is not possible to say that the presence or absence of a particular factor means that a transaction is or is not such a transfer.

- *Goodwill.* Whilst its absence from any transfer does not imply that no TOGC has taken place, its presence normally gives a very good indication that it has. This is so even if the contract for sale attributes only a nominal value to goodwill. See, for example, *Quadrant Stationers (1599)*.

- *Whether the business name has been transferred.*

- *Customer lists, knowledge of customers and common directors.* The sale of a list of previous or potential customers is a good indication of a TOGC. However, a transfer of a customer list alone is not likely to be the transfer of a business, even in the case of a service business whose only real asset of worth it may be.

- *Transfer of contracts and work in progress.* If a purchaser takes over contracts with suppliers, buys work in progress or takes over obligations under contracts with customers, this is a good indication that he is to carry on the business of the seller.

- *Stock.* The transfer of stock to a single purchaser can indicate a TOGC; the sale of a small proportion of stock is less likely to, unless the effect is to put the purchaser in possession of an identifiable business.

- *Plant and equipment.* The transfer of the equipment needed to carry on the business is an indication that there is a TOGC. However, if it is not transferred, the transaction can still be a TOGC, especially if the purchaser already owns similar equipment.

8.12 Business

- *Premises.* The transfer of premises is significant for two reasons. First, some businesses are so closely linked to the premises from which they are run that, if they are not transferred, it is unlikely or even impossible that the business has been transferred (e.g. a property letting business, theatre, bowling alley). Secondly, goodwill often attaches to the premises (e.g. in retail businesses where the location of the premises is significant) so that their transfer is a good indication of a TOGC.

- *Staff.* If the new business takes over the contracts of existing staff, or even re-employ staff made redundant, this will suggest a TOGC.

- *Restrictive covenants.* The presence of a restrictive covenant in the contract of sale (e.g. preventing the seller from trading in the same business in the same area) is a good indicator that a TOGC has taken place.

- *The contract of sale and other documentation* although statements in the contract that a transaction is, or is not, a TOGC are not conclusive. See also *C & E Commrs v Padglade Ltd QB, [1995] STC 602.*

- *Consensus* between the vendor and purchaser.

- *Advertisements.* The way in which a sale is advertised is an indication of the vendor's intentions. C & E may also look at any advertisements issued announcing the purchase. Phrases such as 'Under new management' will indicate the same type of business is being carried on and there has been a TOGC.

(C & E Manual V1-10, Chapter 2 para 2.5).

For cases held to fall within the special provisions (so that VAT charged was not recoverable by the purchaser) see *E & E Phillips (1130), Advance Business Technology Ltd (1488), C & E Commrs v Dearwood Ltd QB, [1986] STC 327* and *Electragate (13752).* For cases held not to fall within the special provisions (so that VAT was chargeable by the vendor and recoverable by the purchaser), see *Eric Ladbroke (Holbeach) Ltd (1557), Computech Developments Ltd (9798)* and *E J Caunt (t/a Edward James Confectionery) (1561).*

8.12 Land and buildings

Where the assets transferred include

- land or buildings, the supply of which would be exempt under *VATA 1994, 9 Sch Group 1* but for an election which the *transferor* has made to waive exemption (see 42.20 LAND AND BUILDINGS), or

- new and uncompleted buildings liable to VAT at the standard rate under 42.4 LAND AND BUILDINGS

the transfer of the premises is a taxable supply unless the *transferee* has made an election to waive exemption in relation to the land and buildings concerned and given written notification of the election to C & E. The election must be in effect on the date upon which the grant would have been treated as having been made or, if there is more than one such date, the earliest of them. (Where a deposit which would otherwise create a tax point is paid, the election must therefore be in effect at the time of payment of that deposit.) The purchaser must also have notified C & E of the election no later than that date.

Where the transferee has not made such an election, the transfer of the land and buildings is a supply and VAT is due at the standard rate.

[VATA 1994, s 5(3); SI 1995/1268, Art 5(2)(3)]. (C & E Manual V1-10, Chapter 2 para 5.3).

8.13   **Transfer of a property rental business**

C & E give the following examples of circumstances concerning the transfer of land and buildings where there may be a transfer of a business of property rental as a going concern. Provided the conditions in 8.12 above relating to land and buildings and the general conditions in 8.11 above are satisfied, the supply of the assets can then be ignored for VAT purposes.

Examples where a business can be transferred as a going concern.

1.   Where the freehold property is owned and is sold with the benefit of an existing lease (or where a leasehold interest is owned and assigned with the benefit of a sub-lease), even if the property is only partly tenanted.

2.   Where a building is owned which is being let but is sold during an initial rent-free period.

3.   Where a lease has been granted in respect of a building but the tenants are not yet in occupation.

4.   Where a property is owned and tenants have been found but the property is transferred to a third party with the benefit of a prospective tenancy before a lease agreement has been signed.

5.   Where a property developer sells a site as a package (to a single buyer) which is a mixture of let and unlet, finished and unfinished properties, and the sale of the site would otherwise have been standard-rated, provided the purchaser elects to waive exemption for the *whole* site.

6.   Where a property is owned by a member of a VAT group and a tenant who is a member of the landlord's VAT group is one of a number of tenants of the property. The presence of a tenant or tenants outside the group means that the whole transaction can still be treated as a TOGC.

There is not a transfer of a going concern in the following circumstances.

1.   Where a property developer sells a property which he has built and which

- he has allowed someone to occupy temporarily (without any right to occupy after the proposed sale); or

- he is 'actively marketing' in search of a tenant.

This is because a property rental business is not being carried on.

2.   Where a freehold property is owned and a lease is granted, or where a headlease is owned and a sub-lease granted (because there is no transfer of a business, just the creation of a new asset).

3.   Where a property is sold and a lease previously granted is surrendered immediately before the sale (because the property rental business ceases when the lease is surrendered).

4.   Where a property is sold to an existing tenant who leases the whole premises from the seller (because the tenant cannot carry on the same business of property rental).

5.   With effect from 1 January 1999 (unless a deposit or other part-payment of the purchase price was made before that date), where the purchaser of the property rental business is a member of the same VAT group as the existing tenant. This is because the property rental business ceases after the transfer because the tenant and new landlord effectively become one taxable person.

6.   With effect from 1 January 1999 (unless a deposit or other part-payment of the purchase price was made before that date), where a member of a VAT group sells a

property, which is being rented to another member of the group, to a third party. This is because C & E believe that no business exists which is making relevant taxable supplies capable of a transfer as a going concern.

(C & E Notice 700/9/96, para 2.4, Appendix B; C & E Business Brief 26/98, 18 December 1998).

Nominee transferee. Strictly, a transfer of a going concern cannot occur where the transferee is a nominee for a beneficial owner because the beneficial owner will be the person carrying on the business, not the nominee. However, where the legal title in land is to be held by a nominee for a *named* beneficial owner, that beneficial owner (and not the nominee) may optionally, for the purposes of establishing the transfer of a property letting business as a going concern, be considered to be the transferee. The transferor, nominee and beneficial owner must agree to this optional treatment in writing. Examples of where a nominee might hold property for a beneficial owner are where the legal title is held on trust for a partnership, unincorporated association or pension fund. (C & E Notice 700/9/96, para 2.4, Appendix D). The Appendix contains an example format that the parties can use to record their agreement.

The option does not need to apply to transactions where the nominee is the transferor of the legal title. In these cases, *VATA 1994, 10 Sch 8* deems the beneficial owner to be the transferor. See 42.17 LAND AND BUILDINGS.

8.14 Other assets

Unidentifiable goodwill. The sale of unidentifiable goodwill (i.e. the difference between the value of a business as a whole and the sum of the values of its identifiable assets) is treated as a taxable supply unless brought outside the scope of VAT by satisfying the provisions in 8.11 above. Sales of goodwill which can be specifically identified as an asset of the business (e.g. the use of a trade mark, sole right to trade in a particular area, lists of customers etc.) are taxable supplies of services. (C & E Press Notice 790, 10 December 1982).

8.15 Miscellaneous aspects

Registration. See 59.3 REGISTRATION for circumstances where the transferee is liable to be registered at the time the business is transferred. See also 59.29 REGISTRATION for the re-allocation of the transferor's registration number.

Deduction of related input tax. Although a transfer of a going concern is not a supply for VAT purposes, this does not prevent the deduction of input tax on related expenses. There is, however, a distinction between the extent to which the transferor and the transferee can deduct that input tax. For the position of the transferee following the decision in *C & E Commrs v UBAF Bank Ltd*, see 49.8 PARTIAL EXEMPTION. In the case of the transferor, since the sale of the business as a going concern is not a supply, the input tax incurred on the costs of selling the business cannot be attributed to a supply by the transferor. These costs are therefore treated as a general business expense and the input tax is residual input tax to be apportioned as necessary by the transferor's agreed partial exemption method. (C & E Notice 700/9/96, para 2.5).

Retention of records. The previous owner of the business must transfer any records he was obliged to keep to the new owner unless, exceptionally, he applies to the VAT office for permission to retain them. Business records generally have to be kept for six years. [*VATA 1994, s 49(1)(b)*]. (C & E Notice 700/9/96, para 5.1).

Supplies to partly-exempt VAT groups. On certain transfers of businesses to partly-exempt VAT groups, the chargeable assets transferred are treated as being supplied to and by the representative member of the group at the open market value. See 31.7 GROUPS OF COMPANIES.

Capital goods scheme. Where a business is sold as a going concern and the assets transferred include land or buildings or a civil engineering work worth £250,000 or more and/or computer equipment worth £50,000 or more, the new owner takes over responsibility for applying the capital goods scheme. See 10.7 CAPITAL GOODS.

Anti-avoidance provisions — subsequent free supply. Where goods or services are transferred as part of a TOGC and the transferor (or any previous owner) has deducted input tax on those goods or services, output tax is chargeable on any subsequent free supply of those goods or services by the transferee. See 47.4 and 47.5 OUTPUT TAX.

9 Business Entertainment

De Voil Indirect Tax Service. See V3.446.

9.1 **SUPPLIES TO A TAXABLE PERSON**

VAT charged on any goods or services supplied to a taxable person, or on any goods acquired or imported by him, is excluded from any credit where the goods or services in question are used or to be used for the purpose of 'business entertainment' [*SI 1992/3222, Art 5(1)*].

'*Business entertainment*' means entertainment (including hospitality of any kind) provided by a taxable person in connection with a business carried on by him, but does not include the provision of any such entertainment for either or both

- employees of the taxable person; or

- if the taxable person is a company, its directors or persons engaged in the management of the company

unless the provision of entertainment for such persons is incidental to its provision for others. [*SI 1992/3222, Art 5(3)*].

9.2 **General scope**

Following on from the definition in 9.1 above, C & E regard business entertainment as including

- provision of food and drink;

- provision of accommodation (hotels, etc.);

- provision of theatre and concert tickets;

- entry to sporting events and facilities;

- entry to clubs, nightclubs, etc; and

- use of capital goods such as yachts and aircraft for the purpose of entertaining.

Where the cost of providing hospitality is passed on as part of the overall charge for a taxable supply, VAT incurred in providing the hospitality cannot be reclaimed.

(C & E Notice 700/65/96, paras 1, 13; C & E Manual V1-13, Chapter 2A para 12.3).

See *C & E Commrs v Shaklee International and Another CA, [1981] STC 776* for the provision of food and accommodation for self-employed agents undergoing training; *BMW (GB) Ltd v C & E Commrs QB, [1997] STC 824* for hospitality provided to dealers and potential customers at 'track days' where vehicles could be test driven; *Medicare Research Ltd (1045)* for refreshments and hospitality provided at business discussion meetings in the course of making taxable supplies; *Webster Communications International Ltd, [1997] VATDR 173 (14753)* for meals and refreshments provided at sponsored conferences to delegates nominated by the sponsor and attending free of charge; *Wilsons Transport Ltd (1468)* for launching parties; *Polash Tandoori Restaurant (10903)* for free drinks supplied to customers; and *William Matthew Mechanical Services Ltd, [1982] VATTR 63 (1210)* for subscription for theatre seats used to extend hospitality and entertainment to clients. However, if the entertainment is not given gratuitously but is provided under a contractual obligation, it does not fall within the scope of the provision. See *Celtic Football and Athletic Club Ltd v C & E Commrs CS, [1983] STC 470* and *C & E Commrs v Kilroy Television Company Ltd QB, [1997] STC 901.*

9.3   Employees

For business entertainment purposes, C & E regard *'employee'* as including

* a director of a company or anyone engaged in the management of the company;

* anyone casually or temporarily employed at sporting and similar events, see 9.6 below; and

* a self-employed person who works to the direction of a single 'employer', uses tools provided by that 'employer' and is paid on a fixed rate basis being unassociated with the trading profits of the business

but it does not include pensioners and other former employees, job applicants, shareholders (unless employees in their own right) and families of employees.

Staff entertainment. Following the decision in *Ernst & Young, [1997] VATDR 183 (15100)* C & E accept that where a business provides entertainment to its employees in order to maintain and improve staff relations, it does so wholly for business purposes and any VAT incurred is input tax and recoverable (subject to the normal rules). Where the entertainment has no discernible business purpose and no connection with business activities, any VAT incurred is not input tax. In the case of a partnership, any entertainment provided solely for the partners is not for business purposes. Previously, as a rule of thumb, C & E treated only 50% of the VAT incurred on entertainment of employees as input tax to reflect the personal benefit derived (although, depending on the circumstances, the percentage could be lower or higher). Businesses which have apportioned tax incurred on this basis and can show that the expenditure qualifies for full input tax deduction on the revised basis, can claim the additional VAT (subject to the three year cap). (C & E Business Brief 25/97, 10 November 1997).

Employees acting as hosts. Where employees take part in any business entertainment provided for persons who are not employees, none of the VAT can be reclaimed.

Subsistence expenses. Where meals etc. are provided away from the place of work on a business trip, the VAT incurred on the employee's meal can be claimed as input tax under the subsistence rules (see 35.13 INPUT TAX) provided that any entertainment is secondary to the main purpose of the trip. If the business trip is made solely for the purpose of business entertainment, then the provisions under *Staff entertainment* or *Employees acting as hosts* above apply as appropriate.

(C & E Notice 700/65/96, paras 2–5).

Staff parties with guests. In *KPMG (No 2), [1997] VATDR 192 (14962)* an accountancy firm organised dinner dances for its employees, each of whom was entitled to bring one guest. It was held that the related input tax should be apportioned on the basis that the proportion of the expenditure attributable to the guests constituted business entertainment. The entertainment of the non-employees could not be treated as incidental to the entertainment of the employees (in contrast to the specific provision made in the converse case, see 9.1 above). This decision came after the decision in *Thorn EMI plc v C & E Commrs CA [1995] STC 674 (* see 9.4 below) that input tax relating to business entertainment can be apportioned. The decision in *KPMG(No 2)* was distinguished in *Ernst & Young (15100)* where a charge of £15 per head was made for guests. The tribunal held that the crucial characteristic of 'entertainment' in the phrase 'business entertainment' was that it was provided free of charge. Although the £15

97

charge was considerably less than the cost of the party, it was not so small as to say the meal was provided free of charge.

9.4   **Apportionment between business entertainment and other use**

In *Thorn EMI plc v C & E Commrs CA, [1995] STC 674*, C & E sought to exclude credit for all input tax on hospitality chalets constructed to receive customers at shows although accepting that the chalets were used partly for business purposes. It was held, upholding the decision in the High Court and reversing the decision in *C & E Commrs v Plant Repair & Services (South Wales) Ltd QB, [1994] STC 232*, that C & E's approach was unreasonable. Applying the general principle in *EC 6th Directive, Art 17*, apportionment should be allowed.

Consumable goods. Some goods may be used for a variety of purposes, e.g. food and drink may be used for trading stock or subsistence meals for employees (VAT fully recoverable) or business entertainment (VAT not recoverable). Where possible, stocks to be used for entertaining should be kept separately. If, however, it has not been decided how the goods will be used at the time of purchase, a record must be kept of goods used for entertainment so the input tax recoverable can be calculated at the end of each VAT period. This record forms part of the VAT records and must be available for inspection by visiting VAT officers. (C & E Notice 700/65/96, para 7).

Capital goods. Where a capital asset, such as a yacht or private aircraft, is used solely for business entertainment, the VAT incurred is not recoverable. If it is used for both business entertainment and other business purposes, the input tax must be apportioned. (C & E Notice 700/65/96, para 8).

9.5   **Exclusions**

There are a number of circumstances where business entertaining is apparently provided but the associated input tax may be recovered.

- **Entertainment of members of clubs, associations, etc**. without specific charge and which is available to all subscribing members or all such members within a particular category. This is considered to be part of the benefits received in return for payment of the appropriate membership subscription. VAT incurred on the cost of entertainment of non-members cannot be reclaimed as input tax. Non-members include a member's family not specifically covered by membership subscription, members of other clubs, visiting teams, etc.

- **Free drinks to customers at restaurants, etc.** The amounts paid by customers for meals are considered to be inclusive of any drinks, etc. given 'freely'.

- **Meals provided to delayed air passengers** are normally supplied direct from the caterer to the passengers and therefore the VAT on such meals is not the input tax of the airline even if it pays for all or part of the meal (see *British Airways plc v C & E Commrs, QB [1996] STC 1127*). If, exceptionally, such meals were to be supplied to the airline, the input tax would be subject to the business entertainment block with the sole exception of meals provided to passengers who are denied boarding due to overbooking. Passengers delayed for other reasons (e.g. bad weather, industrial action, etc.) are not legally or contractually entitled to compensation and therefore the meals are free hospitality.

- **Accommodation provided to delayed air passengers**. There is a long-standing agreement that airlines that book accommodation for their delayed passengers may treat the VAT incurred as deductible input tax. Although the validity of this arrangement is not free from doubt, C & E have decided not to disturb it pending consideration of the EC Commission's proposals for an input tax restriction upon expenditure on accommodation.

- **Free wine or beer tasting events** for trade customers or journalists which allow sampling but not drinking, or a free glass of whisky following a tour of the distillery, etc.

- **Free meals provided to coach drivers** at motorway service stations. These are considered to be business gifts on which output tax may be due. See 47.4 OUTPUT TAX and *C & E Commrs v Westmorland Motorway Services Ltd CA, [1998] STC 431.*

- **Entertainment provided by local authorities at civic functions.** This is not business entertainment because the function is a non-business activity.

- **Entertainment of a non-personal nature provided freely by stores, etc.** to members of the general public, e.g. hiring circus performers, musicians, or other entertainers to attract custom or advertise a trader's premises. This does not apply to promotional events where customers attend by invitation, e.g. where a motor dealer invites customers to the launch of a new car and incurs VAT on providing them with free hospitality.

(C & E Manual V1-13, Chapter 2A para 12.10).

9.6   **Miscellaneous provisions**

Subsistence for helpers at shows, sporting events, etc. Such helpers (e.g. stewards and others) who are essential to the running of the event but are not full-time employees of the organisers can be treated in the same way as full-time employees and input tax may be recovered on their subsistence expenses. The business entertainment provisions do apply to VIPs, journalists and others not involved in actively running the event.

Seminars etc. for persons who are not employees. Where it is clear from the promotional literature that the cost of the seminar etc. includes meals and/or accommodation, input tax can be reclaimed. Where no charge is made, VAT on meals etc. provided for persons who are not employees cannot be reclaimed. Input tax on any separately itemised charges for hire of a room, equipment etc. can normally be reclaimed as can VAT on subsistence expenses for employees who are involved in running the activity.

Entertainment provided to be used by another person. Where meals are supplied to another person who uses them for business entertainment (e.g. where a promotion is arranged on behalf of a client and the promotion includes a dinner for potential customers) any VAT incurred on the dinner can be recovered. This is because the guests are being entertained by the client. The invoice to the client must separately identify any charge made for the entertainment from other charges made (e.g. promotional fees) and output tax must be accounted for. The business entertainment provisions then apply to the client.

(C & E Notice 700/65/96, paras 9, 10, 12).

Amateur sports persons. Amateur players are, by definition, not employees and input tax on business entertainment provided for them is therefore blocked. Where the entertainment is provided by a club out of players' subscriptions to it, input tax may be reclaimed under the provisions above for entertainment of members of clubs. Where, however, certain bodies choose, from affiliated clubs, individual amateur sports persons to represent their country or county, the persons selected are not full subscribing members of the representative body and therefore the provisions applying to clubs above cannot apply. By concession C & E have agreed that input tax necessarily incurred on the provision of accommodation and meals for team members selected by such representative bodies, and committee members of that body, may be deductible as input tax. The concession does not cover alcoholic drinks and tobacco. (C & E Notice 48, ESC 2.10).

9.7 SUPPLIES BY A TAXABLE PERSON

Following the decision in *EC Commission v Italian Republic, CJEC [1997] STC 1062*, where, as a result of 9.1 above, no input tax has been claimed by a taxable person on a supply, acquisition or importation of any goods or on a supply of any services, the disposal of such goods or services should be treated as exempt, regardless of whether they are sold at a profit or loss. C & E are considering changes which may be necessary to UK legislation to implement this decision. In the meantime, a taxable person may choose either to exempt the supply or continue to apply the existing legislation outlined below which taxes any profit margin. Treating the supply as exempt may affect any partial exemption computation. Claims for refund of overpaid VAT (subject to the three year cap) can be submitted where VAT has been accounted for on the margin. Such claims must take into account any partial exemption implications of treating disposals as exempt.

Under existing UK legislation, VAT must be charged on a supply of the goods (other than on hire) or services in question as if made for a consideration equal to the excess of

(*a*) the consideration for which the goods and services are supplied by the taxable person, over

(*b*) the 'relevant amount'.

Where (*b*) is greater than (*a*), the supply is treated as outside the scope of VAT.

The '*relevant amount*' is the consideration for the supply to him. Where the goods in question had been acquired from another EC country or imported from outside the EC, the relevant amount is the value of the acquisition or the value of the goods for importation purposes (as the case may be) plus, in each case, the VAT chargeable. [*SI 1992/3222, Art 5(2)(4)*].

Note that the above provisions only apply where *no* input tax has been claimed (e.g. where a capital asset, such as a yacht or private aircraft, is used solely for entertaining). Where, however, the asset was used for both entertaining and business purposes, on resale VAT must be accounted for on the full selling price. (C & E Notice 700/65/96, para 8).

10   Capital Goods Scheme

Cross-references. See 38.1 INTERACTION WITH OTHER TAXES for the effect on capital allowances where adjustments are made to input tax deduction under the capital goods scheme.

De Voil Indirect Tax Service. See V3.470–476.

10.1   ADJUSTMENTS TO THE DEDUCTION OF INPUT TAX ON CAPITAL ITEMS ('THE CAPITAL GOODS SCHEME')

The capital goods scheme applies to certain items of computer equipment, land and buildings and civil engineering works which are used for non-taxable purposes. The provisions do not apply to any such capital items acquired or brought into use before 1 April 1990.

When a capital asset is acquired, the normal rules for claiming input tax apply. If the asset is used wholly in making taxable supplies, input tax is recoverable in full; if used wholly in making exempt supplies, none of the input tax is recoverable; and if used for making taxable and exempt supplies, a proportion of the input tax may be claimed under the partial exemption rules. Where subsequently in a period of adjustment (see 10.3 below) there is a change in the extent of taxable use, an input tax adjustment has to be made. If taxable use increases, a further amount of input tax can be claimed and, if it decreases, some of the input tax already claimed must be repaid.

10.2   CAPITAL ITEMS WITHIN THE SCHEME

Capital items to which the provisions apply are any items of the following descriptions which the owner uses in the course or furtherance of a business carried on by him, and for the purpose of that business, otherwise than solely for the purpose of selling that item (i.e. items purchased for resale, such as stock-in-trade, are not covered by the scheme). All values are VAT-exclusive.

(*a*)   A computer, or an item of computer equipment, worth £50,000 or more supplied to, or acquired or imported by, the owner. Any delivery or installation costs should be included unless invoiced separately. If imported, the value for VAT at importation (including import duty) should be taken. In practice the scheme will mainly cover minicomputers and mainframe computers as the £50,000 limit applies to individual items of computer equipment, not complete systems. *Excluded* are computer software and computerised equipment e.g. a computerised telephone exchange or lift system (unless installed as a fixture in a new building covered under (*b*) to (*e*) below). (C & E Leaflet 706/2/90, paras 3, 6).

(*b*)   Land, a building or part of a building or, after 2 July 1997, a civil engineering work or part of a civil engineering work where the value of the interest supplied to the owner, by a taxable supply other than a zero-rated supply, is £250,000 or more. When determining whether the value of the supply is £250,000 or more, any part of that value consisting of rent (including charges reserved as rent) is excluded provided that, after 2 July 1997, it is neither payable nor paid more than twelve months in advance nor invoiced for a period in excess of twelve months.

Not included is the freehold of a piece of bare land purchased for possible future development e.g. acquired for a 'land bank' and not used before development or sale. (C & E Leaflet 706/2/90, para 4).

(*c*)   A building or part of a building where the owner's interest in, right over or licence to occupy it

(i) is treated as self-supplied to him under the provisions in 42.26 LAND AND BUILDINGS (change of use of residential or charitable buildings); or

(ii) was, on or before 1 March 1997, treated as self-supplied to him under the provisions in 42.27 *et seq.* LAND AND BUILDINGS (developer's self-supply charge).

In each case, the value of the supply, as determined under the respective provisions, must be £250,000 or more. See also *R & R Pension Fund QB, [1996] STC 889.*

(*d*) A building not falling, or capable of falling, within (*c*) above constructed by the owner and first brought into use by him after 31 March 1990 where the aggregate of

- the value of taxable grants relating to the land on which the building is constructed made to the owner after that date, and

- the value of all the taxable supplies of goods and services, other than any that are zero-rated, made or to be made to him for, or in connection with, the construction of the building after that date

is £250,000 or more.

(*e*) A building which the owner alters, or an extension or an annex which he constructs, where additional floor area is created in the altered building, extension or annex, of 10% or more of the original floor area before the work was carried out. The value of all taxable supplies of goods and services, other than any that are zero-rated, made or to be made to the owner after 31 March 1990 for, or in connection with, the alteration etc. must be £250,000 or more.

(*f*) A civil engineering work constructed by the owner and first brought into use by him after 2 July 1997 where the aggregate of

- the value of taxable grants relating to the land on which the civil engineering work is constructed made to the owner after that date, and

- the value of all the taxable supplies of goods and services, other than any that are zero-rated, made or to be made to him for, or in connection with, the construction of the civil engineering work after that date

is £250,000 or more.

(*g*) A building which the owner refurbishes or fits out where the value of capital expenditure on the taxable supplies of services and of goods affixed to the building, other than any that are zero-rated, made or to be made to the owner for, or in connection with, the refurbishment or fitting out in question after 2 July 1997 is £250,000 or more.

[*SI 1995/2518, Regs 112, 113; SI 1997/1614, Reg 10*].

When considering whether expenditure constitutes 'capital expenditure' normally, the accounting treatment adopted by the owner can be accepted for VAT purposes. If the expenditure is treated as a cost in calculating the owner's profit and loss, the expenditure will not be capital expenditure. If, on the other hand, the expenditure is added to the cost of assets for accounting purposes, it will be capital expenditure. Subject to this, the costs under (*d*) and (*e*) include all those involved in making the building ready for occupation e.g. professional and managerial services, demolition and site clearance, building and civil engineering contractors' services, materials used in the construction, security, equipment hire, haulage, landscaping, fitting out etc. (C & E Leaflet 706/2/90, para 6; C & E Manual V1-15, Chapter 2 para 10.9).

10.3   THE PERIOD OF ADJUSTMENT

The period of adjustment consists of five successive intervals for

(i) computers etc. under 10.2(*a*) above, and

(ii) land, buildings and civil engineering works under 10.2(*b*) above where the interest has less than ten years to run at the time it is supplied to the owner (e.g. an eight-year lease).

For all other land and buildings not within (ii) above the period of adjustment consists of ten successive intervals.

[*SI 1995/2518, Reg 114(3); SI 1997/1614, Reg 11*].

10.4   **First interval**

Subject to the special case below and the rules in 10.6 and 10.7 below, the first interval commences, as the case may be,

• where the owner is a registered person when he imports, acquires or is supplied with the item as a capital item or when he appropriates an item to use as a capital item, the date of importation, acquisition, supply or appropriation,

• where the capital item falls within 10.2(*c*)(i) above, on the date of the self-supply under those provisions,

• where the capital item falls within 10.2(*c*)(ii) above, on the date that the owner first uses the building or, if later 1 April 1990, and

• where the capital item falls within 10.2(*d*)-(*g*) above, on the date that the owner first uses the building, altered building, extension, annex, civil engineering work or building which has been refurbished or fitted out

and runs to the end of the day before the commencement of the tax year following that date i.e. it normally runs to the following 31 March, 30 April or 31 May depending upon his prescribed accounting periods, see 49.9 PARTIAL EXEMPTION.

Where the owner is not registered when he first uses an item as a capital item

• if he subsequently becomes a registered person, the first interval commences on his effective date of registration and ends on 31 March, 30 April or 31 May depending upon the prescribed accounting period allocated to him; and

• if he is subsequently treated as a member of a group for VAT purposes (see 31 GROUPS OF COMPANIES), the first interval corresponds with, or is that part still remaining of, the then current tax year of the group.

[*SI 1995/2518, Reg 114(4); SI 1997/1614, Reg 11*].

Special case — extended first interval. After 2 July 1997, where

• the extent to which a capital item is used in making taxable supplies does not change between what would otherwise have been the first interval above and the first subsequent interval under 10.5 below, and

• the length of the two intervals taken together does not exceed twelve months

the first interval applicable to the capital item ends on what otherwise would have been the end of the first subsequent interval i.e. the two periods are combined to become the first interval.

[*SI 1995/2518, Reg 114(5A); SI 1997/1614, Reg 11*].

10.5   **Subsequent intervals**

Subject to the rules in 10.6 and 10.7 below, each subsequent interval corresponds with a longer period applicable to the owner or, if no longer period applies, a tax year. In either

10.6 Capital Goods Scheme

case this will normally run to the following 31 March, 30 April or 31 May depending upon the owner's prescribed accounting periods, but see 49.9 PARTIAL EXEMPTION for exceptions. [*SI 1995/2518, Reg 114(5); SI 1997/1614, Reg 11*].

10.6 Groups of companies

Provisions applying after 2 July 1997. On the first occasion during a period of adjustment that the owner of a capital item

(*a*) being a registered person subsequently becomes a member of a group of companies for VAT purposes (see 31 GROUPS OF COMPANIES), or

(*b*) being a member of a group for VAT purposes ceases to be a member of that group (whether or not he immediately becomes a member of another such group)

the interval then applying ends on the day before the owner becomes a member of the group or the day the owner ceases to be a member of the group (as the case may be). Each subsequent interval (if any) applicable to the capital item ends on the successive anniversaries of that day.

[*SI 1995/2518, Reg 114(5A); SI 1997/1614, Reg 11*].

Provisions applying before 3 July 1997. On any occasion during a period of adjustment where (*a*) or (*b*) above applied, the interval then applying ended on the day before the owner became a member of the group or the day the owner ceased to be a member of the group (as the case may be).

Where (*a*) applied, each subsequent interval (if any) ended on the last day of a longer period applicable to the group or, if no longer period applied, the last day of a tax year of that group.

Where (*b*) above applied

- if the owner immediately became a member of a second VAT group, subsequent intervals (if any) ended on the last day of a longer period applicable to the second group or, if no longer period applied, the last day of a tax year of that group; and

- otherwise, the next interval (if any) ran to the following 31 March, 30 April or 31 May depending upon the prescribed accounting periods allocated to the owner when registered alone. Each subsequent interval (if any) corresponded with a longer period applying to the owner or, if no longer period applied, a tax year of the owner.

Longer periods and tax years both normally ran to the following 31 March, 30 April or 31 May depending upon the owner's prescribed accounting periods, but see 49.9 PARTIAL EXEMPTION for exceptions.

[*SI 1995 No 2518, Reg 114(6) revoked by SI 1997/1614, Reg 11*].

10.7 Transfers of businesses as going concerns

Where the owner of a capital item transfers it during the period of adjustment in the course of the transfer of his business or part of his business as a going concern (the item therefore not being treated as supplied)

(*a*) *if the new owner takes over the registration number of the original owner*, the interval applying at the time of the transfer does not end at that time but on the last day of the longer period applying to the new owner immediately after the transfer or, if no longer period then applies, on the last day of his tax year following the day of transfer; and (*b*) *if the new owner does not take over the registration number of the original owner*, the interval then applying ends on the day before the owner transfers the business or part. Each subsequent interval (if any) applicable to the capital item ends on the successive anniversaries of that day. *Before 3 July 1997*, each subsequent interval (if any) ended on the last day of a longer period applying to the new owner or, if no longer period applied, the last day of a tax year of the new owner.

[*SI 1995/2518, Reg 114(5A)(7); SI 1997/1614, Reg 11*].

Longer periods and tax years both normally run to the following 31 March, 30 April or 31 May depending upon the owner's prescribed accounting periods, but see 49.9 PARTIAL EXEMPTION for exceptions.

As the new owner takes over responsibility for applying the capital goods scheme, in order to make the necessary calculations (see 10.8 below) he will need to know for each relevant capital item

- the date of acquisition and number of remaining intervals in the period of adjustment;

- the total input tax incurred; and

- the percentage of that input tax which was claimed on the item in the first interval.

(C & E Leaflet 706/2/90, para 21).

10.8   **Method of adjustment**

Where the extent to which a capital item is used in the second or later interval is greater or less than it was used in the first interval, an adjustment is required calculated by the formula

$$\frac{\text{'Total input tax on the capital item'}}{A} \times \text{'the adjustment \%'}$$

where

A = 5 or 10 depending on the number of intervals in the period of adjustment (see 10.3 above)

'*Total input tax on the capital item*' means

- for a capital item within 10.2(*a*) or (*b*) above, VAT charged on the supply, acquisition or importation. Any VAT charged on rent (including charges reserved as rent) is excluded unless, after 2 July 1997, it is payable or paid more than twelve months in advance or invoiced for a period in excess of twelve months;

- for a capital item within 10.2(*c*) above, the VAT charged on the supply which the owner is treated as making to himself; and

- for a capital item under 10.2(*d*)-(*g*) above, the aggregate of the VAT charged on the supplies described, other than VAT charged on rent (if any)

and includes any VAT treated as input tax under the rules relating to pre-registration or pre-incorporation input tax (see 35.10 INPUT TAX).

'*The adjustment %*' is the difference (if any) between the extent, expressed as a percentage, to which the capital item is used (or regarded as being used) in making taxable supplies in the first interval and the extent to which it is so used or treated in the subsequent interval in question. Where the owner of a building within these provisions grants or assigns a tenancy or lease in the whole or part of the building and the premium (or if no premium is payable the first payment of rent) is zero-rated, any subsequent

10.8 Capital Goods Scheme

exempt supply arising from the grant (e.g. rent) is disregarded in determining the extent to which the building is used in making taxable supplies.

The percentage is

- where the item is used wholly for making taxable supplies — 100%
- where it is used wholly for making exempt supplies — 0%
- where it is used for making both taxable and exempt supplies — normally the claimable percentage of non-attributable input tax following the partial exemption annual adjustment for the respective year (see 49.9 PARTIAL EXEMPTION) (although C & E may allow, or direct, the use of another method). Where the standard method is used (see 49.6 PARTIAL EXEMPTION) the same percentage applies to the whole of the non-attributable input tax. If a special method is used (see 49.7 PARTIAL EXEMPTION) involving different calculations for different parts of the business, the percentage to be used is that which applies to the part of the business in which the capital item is used.

Where, after 2 July 1997, 10.6(*a*) or (*b*) above or 10.7(*b*) above applies, subsequent intervals do not necessarily correspond with the annual adjustment period for partial exemption purposes and the attribution of total input tax is determined by such method as is agreed with C & E.

Where during an interval the use of a capital asset changes from one of these categories to another (or different percentages are calculated in different parts of the business and the item moves from one part of the business to another) the percentage of taxable use for the interval overall must be calculated taking into account the number of days of use in each category during the interval.

Example

A partly exempt business purchases a computer for £100,000 (plus £17,500 VAT). For the first three intervals and for 120 days in the fourth interval it is used for making taxable and exempt supplies. The percentages of taxable use are as follows.

Interval 1	48%
Interval 2	51%
Interval 3	43%
Interval 4 (first 120 days)	45%

For the remainder of the period of adjustment the equipment is leased to another company.

Interval 1
Initial input tax claim = £17,500 × 48% = £8,400

Interval 2
Additional input tax claimed from C & E

$$\frac{17,500}{5} \times (51-48)\% = £105$$

Interval 3
Input tax repayable to C & E

$$\frac{17,500}{5} \times (48-43)\% = £175$$

106

Interval 4
Adjustment % for the interval

$$\frac{(120 \times 45\%) + (245 \times 100\%)}{365} = 81.92\%$$

Additional input tax claimed from C & E

$$\frac{17,500}{5} \times (81.92 - 48)\% = £1,187.20$$

Interval 5
Additional input tax claimed from C & E

$$\frac{17,500}{5} \times (100 - 48)\% = £1,820$$

[*SI 1995/2518, Regs 115(1)(2)(5), 116; SI 1995/3147; SI 1997/1614, Regs 12, 13*].
(C & E Leaflet 706/2/90, paras 11–13).

10.9   Sale of assets and deregistration

Where, during an interval other than the last interval, the owner of a capital item either

- supplies it, or

- is deemed to supply it on ceasing to be a taxable person (see 59.27 REGISTRATION), or

- would have been deemed to supply it on ceasing to be a taxable person but for the fact that VAT on the deemed supply would not have been more than £250 (whether by virtue of its value or because it is zero-rated or exempt),

then

(*a*)   if that supply is a taxable supply, the owner is treated as having used the capital item for each of the remaining *complete* intervals wholly in the making of taxable supplies; and

(*b*)   if that supply is an exempt supply, he is treated as not using the capital item for each of the remaining *complete* intervals in making any taxable supplies.

For the interval in which the capital item is sold, the 'change of use' adjustment compared to the first interval is calculated in the normal way *as if the item had been in use for the whole of that interval*. This applies whether it was sold on the first or last day of the interval.

For the remaining complete intervals in the period of adjustment, the recovery percentage will be 100% where (*a*) above applies or 0% where (*b*) above applies, but this is subject to the following two provisos.

(1)   The aggregate of the amounts which may be deducted in respect of the remaining complete intervals cannot exceed the output tax chargeable on the supply of the capital item.

(2)   After 2 July 1997, a 'disposal test' applies. Where the total amount of input tax deducted or deductible by the owner as a result of

- the initial deduction;

- any normal adjustments made in intervals up to and including the interval of supply or deemed supply; and

- any adjustment which would otherwise have been made for remaining complete intervals exceeds the output tax chargeable on the supply of the capital item, *unless C & E allow otherwise* the owner must pay to C & E, or as the case may be may deduct, such an amount as results in the total input tax deducted or deductible being equal to the output tax chargeable on the supply of the capital item.

The 'disposal test' is an anti-avoidance measure to ensure that partly exempt businesses such as banks, insurance companies, educational establishments, sports clubs and providers of private health-care do not obtain an unjustified tax advantage, for example by making a substantial exempt supply of a long lease of a property followed immediately by the taxable disposal of the freehold for low consideration. C & E do not intend that the disposal test should be applied to *bona fide* commercial transactions. Given the policy objective, the disposal test will not be applied

- to sales of computer equipment;

- where the owner disposes of an item at a loss due to the market conditions;

- where the value of the item is reduced for other legitimate reasons (e.g. accepting a low price for a quick sale);

- where the amount of output tax on disposal is less than the total input tax only because of a reduction in the VAT rate; and

- where the item is used only for taxable (including zero-rated) purposes throughout the adjustment period (which includes the final disposal).

Where there is an unjustified tax advantage, a business must calculate the net tax advantage (i.e. the overall benefit derived from the avoidance device, normally the amount of input tax that would still be subject to adjustment under the scheme were it not for the sale of the capital item less any output tax due on the sale) and then work out how much of the net tax advantage is unjustified. Normally this could be achieved by using the ratio that the value of the final taxable sale bears to the value of both the exempt supply and the final taxable sale. (C & E Business Brief 30/97, 19 December 1997).

If an asset is sold without ever having been used, C & E do not regard it as a capital item for the purposes of the scheme.

Example

The facts are the same as in the example in 10.8 above except that the computer is sold in interval 4 for £10,000, the current market value.

Intervals 1 to 3 No change

Interval 4
Input tax repayable to C & E

$$\frac{17,500}{5} \times (48-45)\% = £105$$

Interval 5
Additional input tax claimed from C & E

$$\frac{17,500}{5} \times (100-48)\% = £1,820$$

but restricted under proviso (1) above to £10,000 × 17.5% = £1,750

A final adjustment of £1,645 (£1,750 – £105) should be made in respect of interval 4.

[*SI 1995/2518, Reg 115(3)(3A)(3B); SI 1997/1614, Reg 12*]. (C & E Leaflet 706/2/90, paras 17–19).

10.10   **Lost, stolen, destroyed or expired assets**

If, during the period of adjustment, a capital item is

● irretrievably lost or stolen or is totally destroyed, or

● an interest in land or buildings which expires

no further adjustment is made in respect of the remaining *complete* intervals applicable to it. The normal 'change of use' adjustment is made for the period of loss, etc. as if the item had been used for the whole period.

[*SI 1995/2518, Reg 115(4)*]. (C & E Leaflet 706/2/90, para 20).

10.11   **Capital items temporarily not used**

Once the period of adjustment has started, if a capital item is not used for a while (e.g. a computer is overhauled) it is treated as being used during that period for the same purpose as it was previously used. (C & E Leaflet 706/2/90, para 9).

10.12   **Returns**

Where an adjustment under 10.8 to 10.11 above is required, the taxable person must include the adjustment in his return for the second prescribed accounting period following the interval to which the adjustment relates or in which the supply as a result of sale, or deemed supply as a result of deregistration, takes place (i.e. the period after the one in which the partial exemption annual adjustment is made). The adjustment should be included in Box 4 of the VAT return.

Where an interval has come to an end because

● the owner of the capital asset has ceased to be a member of a group, or

● the owner (who remains a taxable person) has transferred part of his business as a going concern,

the adjustment for that interval must be included in the return for the group or transferor for the second prescribed accounting period after the annual adjustment period for partial exemption purposes in which the interval in question fell.

C & E may allow the necessary adjustment to be made in a later return but, with effect from 1 May 1997, only if it is a return for a prescribed accounting period commencing within three years of the end of the period when the adjustment should have been made.

[*SI 1995/2518, Reg 115(6)-(8); SI 1997/1086, Reg 8; SI 1997/1614, Reg 12*]. (C & E Leaflet 706/2/90, para 14).

11 Catering

De Voil Indirect Tax Service. See V4.227; V6.121–122A.

Note. The provisions in this chapter deal with the VAT liability of food and drink supplied in the course of any catering business. The rules do not apply to food or drink supplied as groceries, for which see 28 FOOD. Where overnight accommodation is also provided, see 33 HOTELS AND HOLIDAY ACCOMMODATION.

11.1 SUPPLIES IN THE COURSE OF CATERING

A supply of food and drink in the course of 'catering' is standard-rated. [*VATA 1994, 8 Sch Group 1(a)*].

The word 'catering' is not defined in the legislation but includes everything which would be regarded as catering if the word was given its ordinary everyday meaning. In *C & E Commrs v Cope QB, [1981] STC 532* it was taken to mean the provision of food incidental to some other activity, usually of a sporting, business, entertainment or social character, thus covering food supplied at football matches, race meetings, wedding receptions, exhibitions and theatres, etc.

The catering in these situations may take place at the caterer's premises or where the event is held but also includes any meals, snacks, etc. delivered to customers for a function or similar event (unless the food or drink requires further preparatory work such as thawing, cooking or re-heating before consumption which is zero-rated).

Where the supply can be identified as catering in its everyday meaning, it is *per se* standard-rated and it is not necessary to consider the problems relating to 'premises' and 'hot take-away food' (see (*a*) and (*b*) below). This point was clarified in *Cope* above.

C & E consider the following questions as pointers to help in clarifying whether a supply is one of catering.

- Is the supply linked to an event, function or social occasion?
- Does the trader by his trading name or advertising indicate that he is a caterer?
- Is there a menu?
- Does the supply require some preparation of the food?
- Is the food presented in a way to make it different from food sold in a supermarket or grocer's shop?
- Is the supply to the final consumer or a person receiving it on behalf of the final consumer?
- Is the food, whether hot or cold, supplied for immediate consumption?
- Is there provision of tables and chairs, cutlery, plates, napkins, or condiments etc?
- Is there an element of service provided to the customer? This could vary from a full waiter/waitress service to simply laying out sandwiches on a platter.
- If the food is delivered, is there only minimal preparation required by the customer?
- If an invoice is raised is it on a per person basis rather than per item?

The list is not exhaustive but if the answers are 'yes' to most of these questions then C & E are likely to regard the supply as being in the course of catering. If the answer to any question is 'no' (e.g. there is no menu or no invoice has been raised), the supply may still be in the course of catering depending on the facts of the individual case, particularly if it is linked to an occasion.

(C & E Manual V1-7, Chapter 1 Part C, section 2.1; C & E Leaflet 709/2/91, para 4).

In *Out to Lunch (a firm) (13031)* it was held that the supply of sandwich platters comprising sandwiches, fruit, cakes, etc. available for take-away or delivery from the shop was not in the course of catering even though described as 'for meetings'. Compare, however, *Wendy's Kitchen (15531)* and *PJ & LJ Lawson (t/a Country Fayre) (14903)* where on the evidence, including advertising material, 'finger buffets' supplied to local offices were held to be supplies in the course of catering. See also *Safeway Stores plc QB 1996, [1997] STC 163* for 'party trays' of food sold from delicatessen counters. For a general consideration of delivered cold meals, etc., see *C Chasney Ltd, [1989] VATTR 152 (4136)*.

Delivered food such as milk, bread and other groceries are zero-rated unless they are certain goods which are always standard-rated (see 28.3-28.13 FOOD). (A charge for delivery may be taxable, see 47.8 OUTPUT TAX.) If food which a customer has provided is cooked or prepared (e.g. for a dinner party) this is standard-rated. (C & E Leaflet 709/2/91, paras 2, 4).

Although, as stated above, there is no definition of 'catering' in the legislation, catering does specifically include the following.

(*a*) **Food and drink for consumption on the premises.** Any supply of food and drink for consumption on the premises on which it is supplied is standard-rated. [*VATA 1994, 8 Sch Group 1, Note 3(a)*]. 'Premises' are widely defined. See 11.2 below. This applies not only to complete meals but also to snacks, sandwiches, hot dogs, hamburgers, teas, coffees, etc. (C & E Leaflet 709/2/91, para 3).

(*b*) **Hot take-away food.** Any supply of 'hot food' for consumption off the premises on which it is supplied. See 11.2 below for premises.

'*Hot food*' means food which, or any part of which, has been heated for the purpose of enabling it to be consumed at a temperature above the ambient air temperature and which is, at the time of supply, above that temperature. [*VATA 1994, 8 Sch Group 1, Note 3(b)*].

Included in standard-rating when sold hot are fish and chips; chicken etc. and chips; chips sold on their own; Chinese, Indian, Greek, Italian and similar take-away meals and dishes; baked potatoes with hot or cold filling; hot dogs and hamburgers; pies, sausage rolls, pasties and similar items (but see below if sold freshly baked); toasted sandwiches; cups of tea, coffee etc.; cups of soup; and roasted chestnuts. If an item of hot food has an ingredient which is cold (e.g. a chip butty or a hot dog) the whole supply is standard-rated (see *Marshall (t/a Harry Ramsbottom's) (13766)*). Any minor items for which no charge is made (e.g. salt, pepper, vinegar or sauce) should be ignored.

Freshly baked products. These are standard-rated if sold for consumption while hot. Some products which may be eaten while still hot are also bought like other grocery items for consumption later, either cold or after re-heating. Examples include pies, sausage rolls, cooked chickens and croissants. If such items are sold freshly baked or cooked, liability will depend on the way in which they are sold. If food is sold while still warm only because it is freshly baked and not to be eaten while still hot, it is zero-rated. Any food sold specifically for consumption while still hot, including

● where the business has an established hot take-away trade any hot food sold as part of that trade,

● any food advertised as 'hot take-away food', and

11.1 Catering

- any food sold with napkins, forks, etc. to enable it to be eaten before it cools is standard-rated.

(C & E Leaflet 709/2/91, para 5, 7).

Indicators that the purpose is to supply hot take-away food include

- food is thrown away once cold,
- food is microwaved (or otherwise heated) by the trader on request,
- food spoils on re-heating,
- use of heat-retentive containers, and
- trader reheats or replaces food on complaint that it is too cold.

Indicators that the purpose is not to supply hot take-away food include

- it is made clear to the customer that they should reheat the food and instructions are given,
- food is kept at a minimum temperature for hygiene reasons and is too cold to eat at the time of sale,
- lack of heat-retentive containers, and
- food is not re-heated.

(C & E Manual V1-7, Chapter 1 Part C, section 3.2).

In *John Pimblett & Sons Ltd v C & E Commrs CA 1987, [1988] STC 358* it was held that for supplies of freshly baked pies to be taxed as hot take-away food, it had to be shown that the predominant subjective purpose of the seller in heating the food was to enable it to be consumed while still hot. If the seller's predominant purpose was to assure customers that it had been freshly baked, the food was not standard-rated, even though some customers consumed the food while still hot.

In *The Lewis's Group Ltd (4931)* it was held that the supply of hot freshly-roasted chickens from the food department was not a supply in the course of catering because it was not the supplier's predominant purpose, in heating the chicken, to enable customers to eat it at any particular temperature. However, in *Malik (t/a Hotline Foods) v C & E Commrs QB, [1998] STC 537* the court dismissed the appellant's contentions that standard-rating only applied where the food had been heated as opposed to cooked and that, if the only heating which occurred was part of the cooking process, the predominant purpose of that heating was to make the food edible and not so that it could be consumed above the ambient air temperature.

Mixed supplies of standard-rated and zero-rated supplies sold at a special inclusive price may be apportioned to calculate the tax value of each supply (see 47.3 OUTPUT TAX). This includes, for example, a hamburger and milk shake; baked potato with separately packaged coleslaw or salad; or a meal consisting of hot and cold dishes supplied in separate containers.

Vending machines. Supplies of hot food and drink are standard-rated as are certain other items which are always standard-rated (see 28.3–28.13 FOOD). Other supplies are standard-rated if the food and drink is to be consumed on the premises where the machine is placed (see 11.2 below). (C & E Leaflet 709/2/91, para 8). See also 47.15 OUTPUT TAX for hiring of vending machines.

Packed lunches. Where the supply of packed lunches is incidental or ancillary to an event/function (e.g. for coach parties, race meetings etc.) C & E consider the supplies to be in the course of catering and therefore standard-rated.

Where there is no link to an event/function and consumption is off the supplier's premises the supply will normally be of zero-rated cold foodstuffs unless comprising items which are always standard-rated (see 28.3-28.13 FOOD). This includes packed lunches provided by hotels and similar establishments for which a separate charge is made. However, where the supply by the hotel consists of accommodation and meals at an inclusive price (e.g. full board, half board, or bed and breakfast) this should be treated as a single standard-rated supply even if any of the meals are taken as packed lunches. (C & E Manual V1-7, Chapter 1 Part C, section 4.6).

Supplies to customers for resale. A supply in the course of catering is, for VAT purposes, to be taken as a supply to the final consumer or to a person receiving it on behalf of the final consumer. Where a trader supplies prepared cold food and drink to a customer who then sells it in the course of catering, the first supply is not regarded as being made in the course of catering. Examples are bulk supplies of sandwiches, salads and prepared meals requiring cooking or re-heating.

However, it should be borne in mind that

- some items are always standard-rated (see 28.3-28.13 FOOD);

- if food is prepared on the premises where it is to be eaten then the supply is regarded as being in the course of catering and standard-rated (see (*a*) above); and

- if the food is supplied hot to be eaten while still hot then the supply is in the course of catering and standard-rated (see (*b*) above).

(C & E Manual V1-7, Chapter 1 Part C, section 4.11).

Catering on aircraft, ships, etc. Where the catering is an adjunct to the supply of the transport and no separate charge is made for it, the consideration for the ticket need not be apportioned. The catering is treated as part of the supply of the passenger transport (*British Airways plc v C & E Commrs CA, [1990] STC 643*). Otherwise the catering is a separate supply of services (rather than a supply of goods). The place of supply is where the supplier has his established place of business. See *Faaborg-Gelting Linien A/S v Finanzamt Flensburg, CJEC [1996] STC 774* where meals provided on board Danish ferries travelling between Denmark and Germany were held to be taxable in Denmark only and not partly in Germany.

11.2 Premises

As a consequence of 11.1(*a*) and (*b*) above, standard-rating applies to

- hot and cold food and drink supplied for consumption on the premises; and

- hot food for consumption off the premises.

It is clearly important therefore to determine what is meant by 'premises' in relation to the supply of catering. The correct interpretation of 'premises' has been debated in many court and tribunal decisions and its application can still cause problems.

C & E's view is that the wording ensures that all meals supplied in premises such as restaurants, cafés and canteens are, as Parliament intended, excluded from zero-rating. Additionally, however, they regard standard-rating as applying to meals and snacks supplied and consumed on the same premises but where the food outlet is part of larger premises existing to serve another function. It includes, therefore, the whole of an enclosed site, a factory, a single occupancy building, or a sports ground. These are relatively straightforward because, in each case, the boundary of the premises could objectively be determined. In many cases, however, the boundary of the premises is less clear. C & E's treatment of common examples of premises is set out below. It should be borne in mind that it is the actual circumstances rather than the generic description

11.2 Catering

which will be the deciding factor and in some cases it is necessary to consider whether there is catering *per se* (see 11.1 above).

Agricultural shows and markets	'Closed' shows are one set of premises. In 'open' shows only the catering outlet and facilities for consumption are premises
Airports, amusement parks, bus and railway stations	Areas with restriction of access to the public are premises. In areas with no restriction of access only the catering outlet and facilities for consumption are premises
Building sites	The whole of the site is one set of premises
Clubs	The building and its curtilage are the premises. See *Ivy Café Ltd (288)*
Coaches, trains, ships and aircraft	All are premises but supplies may be incidental to the main supply
Exhibition halls	The whole of the exhibition hall is one set of premises
Factories	The whole factory site is one set of premises
Film and TV location sets	This is normally catering *per se*
Football grounds and sports stadia	The whole ground including its adjacent car parks is premises. See *C & E Commrs v Cope QB, [1981] STC 532* and *Bristol City Football Supporters Club, [1975] VATTR 93 (164)*
Holiday camps, caravan parks and camping sites	The open grounds of a site are to be treated as if they were a public space. However, food supplied for consumption in any building in which it is supplied is standard-rated
Hospitals	A single site is usually premises. See *Ashby Catering Ltd* (4220)
Hotels, hostels, motels and the like	Each establishment is one set of premises
Industrial estates	Each unit rather than the estate is a set of premises
Markets and covered shopping areas	Unless there is a discrete area for consumption these are treated as public open spaces. See *Armstrong (M), [1984] VATTR 53 (1609)* and *Crownlion (Seafood) Ltd, [1985] VATTR 188 (1924)*
Military bases	The whole base is one set of premises. However, residential areas such as married quarters are not part of the same premises
Mobile outlets in public open spaces	Only the outlet and facilities like counter, tables and chairs are treated as premises. See *Fresh Sea Foods (Barry) Ltd, [1991] VATTR 388 (6658)* and *Skilton and Gregory (11723)*

Motorway service areas	Catering outlets and associated facilities are treated as premises. The rest of the service area is a public open space
Office buildings Single occupancy	The whole building is one set of premises. See *Bergonzi (t/a Beppi's Buffet Service) (12122)*
Multiple occupancy	The part occupied by each individual tenant is premises. See *R v C & E (ex p Sims (t/a Supersonic Snacks)) QB, [1988] STC 210*
Piers	One set of premises if there is restricted access
Public buildings	Where the building has single occupancy e.g. a museum or library the building and its curtilage form one set of premises. Where there is multiple occupancy e.g. a county hall which incorporates some retail outlets each outlet is separate premises
Public car parks	No premises — this is a public open space
Restaurants, cafés, pubs and similar outlets	The whole outlet, including any forecourt or garden, is premises
Schools and colleges	Are mostly one set of premises. See, however, *St Benedict Trading Ltd, [1994] VATTR 376 (12915)*. Supplies may be incidental and therefore exempt or non-business
Showgrounds	Areas with restricted public access are premises. Where there is no restriction only the food outlet and facilities for consumption are premises. But in connection with events consider catering *per se*

The grounds surrounding an office, factory, café or public house are also treated as part of those premises where the grounds are not a public thoroughfare.

Sales in premises other than from a fixed outlet. Following the decision in *Zeldaline Ltd, [1989] VATTR 191 (4388)* C & E now accept that where a sandwich seller enters a building to sell sandwiches, etc. it is not a supply in the course of catering. More generally, where a trader's business is selling to individuals from baskets, a mobile van or mobile trolley, and sales are made on what might be called a casual and roving basis, if the trader

(a)   does not have any verbal or written agreement with any of the occupiers, over and above the permission of reception staff, to enter the premises; and

(b)   is not bound by any contractual agreement to supply the occupants

it is likely that the situation is similar to the *Zeldaline* case and it is not one of catering.

(C & E Manual V1-7, Chapter 1 Part C, section 3.5, 3.6; C & E Notice 709/2/91, paras 3, 6).

11.3 Catering

11.3 Accounting for VAT

Current provisions. If each sale can be recorded as it takes place, the normal method of accounting can be used. This applies whether sales are only standard-rated or a mixture of standard-rated and zero-rated.

If each sale cannot be recorded as it takes place, then the Point of Sale scheme must normally be used (see 60.14 RETAIL SCHEMES) unless the catering adaptation described below can be used. (It is not normally possible to use the Apportionment or Direct Calculation schemes. These assume that goods bought at one rate of VAT will be sold at the same rate and food bought at the zero-rate often becomes standard-rated when supplied in the course of catering.)

Catering adaptation. A caterer may use a special catering adaptation to account for VAT provided

- he can satisfy C & E that it is impracticable to keep records to operate the Point of Sale scheme;

- he has reasonable grounds for believing that the VAT-exclusive value of standard-rated and zero-rated catering supplies will not exceed £1 million in the next twelve months; and

- the use of the catering adaptation produces a fair and reasonable result in any period.

If the conditions (which have the force of law) are met, he must notify the VAT office that he intends to operate the catering adaptation and may then begin to operate it as soon as acknowledgement of the letter is received.

To calculate output tax for each VAT period

Step 1	Add up daily gross takings	A
Step 2	Calculate the percentage of total supplies of catering made at the standard rate (see below)	B%
Step 3	Apply the percentage at Step 2 to the daily gross takings in Step 1	
Step 4	To calculate output tax, multiply the total at Step 3 by the VAT fraction	

In algebraic form, output tax is

$$A \times \frac{B}{100} \times V$$

See 60.8 and 60.9 RETAIL SCHEMES for general rules applying to the calculation of daily gross takings. Service charges (but not tips) and the value of any meals or drinks given in exchange for an identifiable benefit to the business (see 11.4 below) should be included. It is not necessary to include the cost of food or drink used for free meals for family and staff but the full cost of any standard-rated items of food taken out of business stock for own or family use should be included (see 11.4 below).

The percentage of total supplies of catering made at the standard rate must be based on a sample of actual sales for a representative period. The period depends on the nature of the business but C & E must be satisfied that it takes account of hourly, daily and seasonal fluctuations. Details of the sample, including dates and times, must be retained and a new calculation must be carried out in each tax period.

If the conditions of the adaptation are not complied with, C & E may assess for any undeclared VAT and/or refuse use of the adaptation for future periods.

(C & E Notice 709/2/91, paras 11-15; C & E Notice 727, Appendix C).

Old retail scheme calculations. If each sale could be recorded as it took place, the normal method of accounting could be used. This applied whether sales were only standard-rated or a mixture of standard and zero-rated.

If each sale could not be recorded as it took place,

- where only standard-rated supplies were made, Scheme A could be used (see 60.23 RETAIL SCHEMES); and

- where both standard and zero-rated supplies were made, either Scheme F (see 60.32 RETAIL SCHEMES) or the special method described below could be used.

Special method. Where a caterer who made both standard-rated and zero-rated supplies was unable to keep a record of each sale as it took place *and* could satisfy C & E that such a record was impracticable, he could estimate the proportion of gross takings which related to standard-rated supplies and advise the VAT office. The estimate had to be arrived at by recording transactions for a selected period (which was representative of trading) and had to be regularly updated, e.g. if the pattern of trade changed or there was a change in the VAT liability on certain items of food and drink. The VAT office also had to be advised of any change. If not satisfied with any further estimate, C & E could determine the proportion to be used. [*SI 1995/2518, Reg 73 revoked by SI 1997/2437*].

The output tax was then calculated as follows

Output tax = $(T + P) \times V$

where

T = that part of the 'gross takings' for the period estimated to represent the value of standard-rated supplies.

P = total cost, including VAT, of standard-rated goods used by the supplier or his family in the period.

V = VAT fraction.

Other retail supplies. Where other retail non-catering supplies are made, it may be possible to run separate retail schemes for each part of the business provided separate books are kept. See 60.4 RETAIL SCHEMES.

Catering staff wages concession. Where a catering contractor

(*a*) acts as an agent of its client and not as a principal,

(*b*) pays the wages of its own staff who are employed solely to serve that particular client, and

(*c*) clearly identifies their wages in profit and loss accounts and/or invoices to that client,

then the contractor may treat such wages as disbursements and need not charge VAT on them. VAT is chargeable on the remainder of the management charge to the client. C & E have reviewed the continuance of this concession and, although it has no statutory basis, have decided not to withdraw it for the time being. (C & E Manual V1-7, Chapter 1 Part C, section 4.2).

De Voil Indirect Tax Service. See V3.554.

11.4 **Free supplies of catering**

Catering for employees or family. Where employees are provided with food or drink free of charge (including supplies from vending machines), the consideration for the supply is taken to be nil (and no VAT is chargeable). Where there is any consideration, in cash or otherwise (e.g. deduction from wages) the supply, valued at the amount of the payment or deduction, is standard-rated. *[VATA 1994, 6 Sch 10(1)(2)]*. C & E accept that where employees are paid a minimum wage under a *Wages Order* for an industry and that *Order* allows for appropriate reductions to be made for catering and accommodation, these calculations are steps in arriving at the amount of the weekly wage to be paid and are not monetary consideration on which the employer is liable to VAT (*RW & MJ Goodfellow, [1986] VATTR 119 (2107)*, and C & E Press Notice 1137, 20 August 1986).

Where the proprietor of a restaurant, cafe or other catering establishment provides meals for himself or his family, these are not regarded as catering and VAT need not be accounted for on them. But VAT must be accounted for on the full cost of any standard-rated items which are taken out of business stock for own or family use. See 28.3–28.13 FOOD for standard-rated items of food. (C & E Leaflet 709/2/91, para 17).

Catering for customers and friends. Free meals or drink provided for customers or friends are regarded as business entertainment and any input tax incurred in the provision of the meal or the purchase of the drink is non-deductible. See also 9 BUSINESS ENTERTAINMENT. Where meals or drinks are given in exchange for an identifiable benefit to the business (e.g. coach drivers or group organisers in return for bringing a party to the establishment) any VAT incurred can be deducted but output tax must also be accounted for. (C & E Leaflet 709/2/91, para 18). Output tax should be calculated on the cost of the goods purchased or, if this cannot be established, on the cost of producing the goods.

11.5   Service charges and tips

Service charges are standard-rated but any tips given freely are outside the scope of VAT. (C & E Notice 700, para 3.18; C & E Leaflet 709/2/91, para 16).

11.6   CATERING IN FACTORIES ETC.

See 11.1 and 11.2 above for the general provisions applying to all supplies in the course of catering, including those made in factories, etc., and for the interpretation of premises for the purpose of take-away food.

(*a*)   **Catering provided by the owners of the catering facilities.** Such persons are acting as principals and must account for VAT under the rules explained in 11.1 and 11.2 above. All normal rules about deductibility of input tax etc. apply.

(*b*)   **Catering provided by catering contractors acting as principals.** Such persons must account for VAT at the standard rate on fees for services to the client, which fees should cover all services provided, and any subsidy received e.g. to balance a profit and loss account. Otherwise, VAT must be accounted for under the rules in 11.1 and 11.2 above for meals etc. supplied and the VAT charged on supplies is deductible subject to normal rules.

(*c*)   **Catering provided by catering contractors acting as agents (known as managing agents).** Such persons are not liable for VAT on meals, the VAT is the responsibility of the principal. Similarly, VAT on food etc. paid for by the managing agent but invoiced to the principal can only be deducted by that principal. Such receipts and payments should be included on any periodic statement of account to the principal on a VAT-inclusive basis. Any surplus paid over or deficit reimbursed is then outside the scope of VAT. Food etc. invoiced to the managing agent should be re-invoiced to the principal. The agent must account for any VAT on the recharge and can deduct input VAT on the supplier's invoice subject to the normal rules. Provided a VAT invoice is issued for such food etc., the receipts and payments may be included on any periodic statement of account to the principal on a VAT-inclusive basis. Where, however, the normal practice is to issue a single document to serve as both a VAT invoice and statement of account, the dual purpose of the document must be clearly shown and the VAT invoice details should be kept separate from the other information. VAT must be accounted for at the standard rate on the fee charged for running the canteen.

(d) **Catering provided by catering contractors acting both as principals and agents.** Where prepared food and drink is supplied to the owner of the catering facilities and the food is also served to the users of the canteen etc. on the owner's behalf, VAT must be accounted for on the supplies of food and drink and the fee for services to the owner. The caterer can reclaim VAT on supplies of food invoiced to him and the owner can reclaim VAT on the fees, in each case subject to the normal rules. The owner must account for VAT on the supplies of catering under the rules in 11.1 and 11.2 above.

(C & E Leaflet 709/1/87, paras 1–7).

11.7   CATERING IN HOSPITALS ETC.

(a) **Catering provided by the hospital, nursing home, clinic etc.** Care, including the supply of meals and non-alcoholic refreshment directly to the patients, is exempt if provided in a hospital or other statutorily registered institution (see 32.10 HEALTH AND WATER UTILITIES). The supply may be made by the institution itself or an outside caterer. Catering for staff and visitors is standard-rated.

(b) **Catering provided by catering contractors acting as principals.** The procedure in 11.6(b) above applies. VAT must be accounted for on the supplies even if the institution's supplies are exempt.

(c) **Catering provided by catering contractors acting as agents.** The procedure in 11.6(c) above applies but where the services of the institution are exempt, the liability of the supply of catering supplied by the institution is as under (a) above.

(d) **Catering provided by catering contractors acting both as principals and agents.** The procedure in 11.6(d) above applies but where the services of the institution are exempt, the liability of the supply of catering by the institution is as under (a) above.

(C & E Leaflet 709/1/87, paras 8–11).

11.8   CATERING IN SCHOOLS, UNIVERSITIES AND COLLEGES

(a) **Catering provided by schools etc.** Catering supplied to pupils and students in a non-local authority school, etc. is exempt as incidental to the provision of education provided the provision of the education itself is exempt (see 20.7 EDUCATION) *and* the catering is provided by the institution. Catering for staff and visitors is standard-rated and either VAT must be accounted for at the point of sale or a method of apportionment must be agreed with the VAT office. *Before 31 August 1997*, by concession, where catering for staff and visitors was provided in a refectory mainly used by students and it was not possible to identify clearly supplies to staff and visitors, all catering could be regarded as exempt.

Where supplies of catering are exempt, items of food (other than alcoholic drinks) which are normally standard-rated (see 28.3–28.13 FOOD) are exempt if supplied as part of a meal in dining accommodation by schools etc.

The provision of education in schools by a local authority is a non-business activity. Catering supplied by a local authority to its own pupils is regarded as incidental to the provision of that education and likewise, therefore, a non-business activity.

(b) **Catering provided by catering contractors acting as principals.** The provisions in 11.6(b) above apply. Even if the educational institution's services are exempt, VAT must be accounted for on all supplies.

(c) **Catering provided by catering contractors acting as agents.** The procedure in 11.6(c) above applies but where the services of the institution are exempt, the liability of catering supplied by the institution to students, staff etc. will be as under (a) above.

(d) **Catering provided by catering contractors acting both as principals and agents.** The procedure in 11.6(d) above applies but where the services of the institution are exempt, the liability of catering supplied by the institution to students, staff, etc. is as set out in (a) above.

(C & E Leaflet, 709/1/87, paras 12–15).

11.9 FRANCHISED CATERING IN CLUBS

It is common for clubs to have their catering undertaken by a franchised caterer, often the club steward or their spouse acting as a self-employed person (who may, or may not, be VAT registered).

Generally, C & E consider VAT incurred by the club on goods and services in connection with catering (e.g. fuel and kitchen equipment) is the club's input tax because the catering is part of the facilities and advantages to subscribing members. However, the precise extent to which the club may recover input tax depends upon the nature of the supplies made by the club.

Where the club simply rents the kitchen premises to the caterer, it makes an exempt supply (subject to the option to tax the rents) and the normal partial exemption rules apply.

Where the club does not rent any part of the premises to the caterer but simply enters into a franchise agreement setting out what is to be provided, the agreement normally makes the club responsible for providing heat, light, and kitchen equipment.

- If the club makes a taxable charge to the franchisee for the right to use its facilities, the club may recover the input tax incurred on the overheads and will have no liability to output tax on any deemed non-business use.

- If the club makes no charge for the use of its facilities, the treatment is as follows.

    (a) *Gas and electricity* used by the caterer is not used for a business purpose by the club. The simplest way to deal with these supplies of goods is to agree some reasonable apportionment of input tax between the proportion of fuel used by the caterer and the remainder used by the club. (Strictly, as goods are involved, the club could follow the *Lennartz* approach (see 35.7 INPUT TAX) and claim all input tax but this would give the same VAT result as output tax would then have to be accounted for on supplies to the caterer each VAT period.)

    (b) *Kitchen equipment* (cookers, microwaves). As the club pays for and owns such items (which may be used by a number of successive caterers) C & E accept that the equipment is bought for the purposes of the club's business. VAT incurred is input tax and deductible by the club. Output tax is however due from the club under *VATA 1994, 4 Sch 5* for each VAT period during which the goods are used by the caterer. See 47.5 OUTPUT TAX.

    (c) *Building services.* As the building is an asset of the club and used by the members, C & E consider that VAT incurred on building works is input tax and deductible. Strictly the provisions of *SI 1993/1507* (services put to non-business use, see 47.5 OUTPUT TAX) could apply in respect of VAT incurred on building repairs and maintenance to areas of a club's premises used only by the caterer but such sums would usually be so small as to be *de minimis*. If a club builds an extension to house a kitchen for use by the caterer, then the club should account for output tax under *SI 1993/1507* but note that once output tax paid under those provisions equals the input tax incurred, there is no further VAT due.

(C & E Manual V1-13, Chapter 2A para 18.6).

12 Charities

Cross-references. See 29 FUEL AND POWER for reduced rate on supplies to charities for non-business use.

De Voil Indirect Tax Service. See V6.123–126A.

12.1 CHARITY, CHARITABLE PURPOSES — GENERAL PRINCIPLES

The term 'charity' has no precise meaning in law. Under the *Recreational Charities Act 1958, s 1* the provision, in the interest of social welfare, of facilities for recreation or other leisure time occupation, is deemed to be charitable (subject to the principle that, unless the trust is for the relief of poverty (*Dingle v Turner HL, [1972] 1 All ER 878*), a trust or institution to be charitable must be for the public benefit).

In England and Wales, most charities are registered with the Charity Commission under the *Charities Act 1993* (which is not the same as registration for VAT purposes) but certain charities (e.g. universities, churches and other places of worship and certain small charities with annual income below £1,000) are exempt from such registration. They are still, however, charities. Charities in Scotland and Northern Ireland are not required to register with the Charity Commission.

Subject to the above, what is a charity rests largely on judicial interpretation. A leading case is *Special Commrs v Pemsel HL, [1891] 3 TC 53* in which Lord Macnaghten laid down that 'charity' should be given its technical meaning under English law and comprises 'four principal divisions; trusts for the relief of poverty, trusts for the advancement of education, trusts for the advancement of religion and trusts beneficial to the community and not falling under any of the previous heads. The trusts last referred to are not the less charitable . . . because incidentally they affect the rich as well as the poor'. Included are trusts for the relief of sickness and infirmity, nature conservation trusts and trusts for support of the arts.

There is no distinction for VAT purposes between those charities registered with the Charity Commission and those that are not. However, unregistered charities claiming VAT relief may need to demonstrate that they have 'charitable status'. This may be achieved from their written 'objects' or by the recognition of their charitable status by the Inland Revenue. (C & E Notice 701/1/95, para 2). For guidelines issued by C & E to establish charitable status, see C & E VAT Manual Part 9, Chapter 2, paras 3.1–3.13.

12.2 CHARITIES AND VAT

Since the introduction of VAT, the law has provided a range of special reliefs which cover many supplies to and by charities. Zero-rating applies to some supplies to charities and there are some exemptions, zero-rating and other concessions for business supplies by charities. However, there is no general relief from VAT for goods supplied to charities and in general the normal VAT rules apply to business supplies made by charities.

Trading activities. Charity law restricts the activities in which a charity can engage to those relating to its charitable objects. In addition, 'trading' activities of charities are exempt from corporation tax only to the extent that they are in pursuit of the organisations charitable objectives. As a result, many charities establish trading subsidiaries which engage in a wide range of commercial ventures to raise money for the parent charity. Although profits of these subsidiaries can be passed to the charity free of corporation tax, it is important to remember that the trading subsidiaries are not charities and, although some VAT reliefs are available (e.g. sale of donated goods and fund-raising events) many of the VAT reliefs are only available to the parent charity itself.

Business activities. It is important not to confuse the term 'trading' as frequently used by a charity to describe its non-charitable commercial fund-raising activities with 'business' as used for VAT purposes. Although trading activities will invariably be business activities, 'business' for VAT purposes can have a much wider application and include some or all of the charity's primary or charitable activities. See 12.4 below for further consideration of business and non-business activities.

One-off extra-statutory concessions. These are only available in extremely limited circumstances and cannot be used as a means of extending reliefs. This would too easily set a precedent and other charities would demand similar relief. Individual ESCs have been allowed only in special and unique cases where a relief clearly exists for the goods or services but, because of the particular circumstances or the way in which the charity organised the matter, the supply did not qualify for relief. Any claims for concessional treatment should be made to the VAT office who will refer the matter to the VAT Policy Directorate, Charities Branch. (C & E Manual V1-9, Chapter 1 para 9).

12.3   REGISTRATION

For VAT registration purposes, a charity only need take account of its income from taxable business activities. Where that income exceeds the limit for registration, the charity must register for VAT. It may also apply for voluntary registration if taxable supplies are made below the registration limit. See 59 REGISTRATION generally for the limits and how to apply for registration.

Charities with branches. Where branches or sections are part of a main charity, it is the combined taxable income of the whole charity which decides whether the charity is liable to be registered for VAT.

Sections or branches often have varying degrees of independence making it difficult to decide whether a separate entity exists for VAT purposes. A separately incorporated company set up by a charity as its trading arm could be a separate entity for VAT purposes. Other signs of separation are full legal and financial responsibility held by a branch for its own affairs and vested in its own committee.

Where there is true separation, registration is only required based on the taxable income of that branch, etc. See, however, 8.5 BUSINESS for C & E powers following a disaggregation of business activities to avoid VAT.

Any proceeds from the activities of the separate entity passed over to the charity can be treated as donations provided they are not the consideration for services given by the charity.

Individuals and unincorporated associations of persons engaging in fund-raising activities. The above provisions also apply where such persons engage in fund-raising activities on their own account in aid of charity i.e. they are not required to register if they have full legal and financial responsibility for their activities and the taxable turnover does not exceed the registration limits.

(C & E Notice 701/1/95, paras 13, 14).

12.4   BUSINESS AND NON-BUSINESS ACTIVITIES

It is important for a charity to determine whether any particular activity is a 'business' or a 'non-business' activity. This applies both when considering registration (if there is no

12.4 Charities

business activity a charity cannot be registered and therefore cannot recover any input tax) and after registration. Whether an activity is business or not can determine the VAT rate on certain purchases made by the charity for use in that activity (e.g. new buildings).

If registered, a charity must account for VAT on all taxable supplies it makes by way of business. Income from any non-business activities affects the amount of VAT reclaimable as input tax (see 35.7 INPUT TAX).

'*Business*' has a wide meaning for VAT purposes and may mean that charitable activities are deemed to be business even though they are performed for the benefit of the community. Normally an activity is a business activity if it is concerned with the making of supplies for a consideration, has a degree of frequency or scale and is continued over a reasonable period. The position is not affected if the amount charged for the supply does no more than cover the cost to the charity of making the supply nor if the charge made is less than cost (but see non-business supplies of welfare services below). A single activity may nevertheless be business (e.g. an annual concert for which an admission fee is charged). See 8.1 to 8.3 BUSINESS for a fuller consideration of the meaning of 'business'.

The following is a guide to the business and non-business position of some of the more common activities of charities.

Activities which are non-business

- *Donations and other voluntary contributions* from the public (e.g. proceeds of flag-days, house to house collections) where all the donor receives is a flag or similar emblem.

- *Voluntary services performed free of charge* e.g. first aid at public functions, rescue at sea, rites of worship (weddings, etc. conducted by churches and other religious bodies). Where recipients of these activities make a contribution towards the work of the charity (e.g. church offertories) the payment may be treated as a donation above provided it is freely given.

- *Free supply of goods.* This is normally non-business (but see below for export of goods outside the EC).

- *Grants* unless they are payments in return for the provision of services.

- *Legacies.* The receipt of a legacy or bequest is non-business.

- *Meals on Wheels.* Where these are delivered by a charity as the agent of a local authority they form part of the non-business activities of the local authority. See also 12.9 below.

- *Share dealings.* The acquisition or disposal of shares and other securities by a charity is not a business activity. Any VAT incurred in connection with such acquisition or disposal, or the management of the investments, cannot be treated as input tax. See *National Society for the Prevention of Cruelty to Children, [1992] VATTR 417 (9325)* where the tribunal held that the charity's investment activities, although having a turnover in excess of £7 million, did not amount to a business as the charity was not predominantly concerned with those supplies. See also *The Wellcome Trust Ltd v C & E, CJEC [1996] STC 945.*

- *Dividends* received on shares are outside the scope of VAT and are regarded as part of the charity's non-business income.

- *Interest* received from banks, building societies and other financial institutions.

Business activities

- *Admissions* (see 12.10 below).

- *Sales of bought-in goods.*

- *Sales of donated and bequeathed goods* (see 12.6 below).

- *Hiring out charity-run buildings.*

- *Exports of goods outside the EC* (see 12.6 below).

Activities which can be business or non-business

- *Production of charity brochures.* All sums received from advertisers for advertisements in brochures, programmes, annual reports, etc. can, by concession, be treated as non-business provided at least 50% of the total number of advertisements are clearly from private individuals. An example of a private advertisement is one that says 'Good wishes from John Smith' or 'Space donated by John Smith' but not 'Good wishes from John Smith, Grocer, 49 High Street'. The selling of advertising space to commercial organisations is regarded as business even if the advertisements make no specific reference to trading activities.

  If private advertising is less than 50%, income from all advertisements is business (and standard-rated) unless the supply is to another charity (see 54.28 PRINTED MATTER, ETC.) or the brochure is supplied as part of a fund-raising event (see 12.9 below).

- *Welfare services.* By concession, supplies of 'welfare services' and related goods by charities at significantly 'below cost' to distressed people for the relief of distress may be regarded as a non-business activity. See 12.9 below for the definition of '*welfare services*'. The recipient of the supply must be the person who is in need of the welfare (and not, for example, a local authority providing the welfare services).

  '*Below cost*' means subsidised by at least 15%. Cost should be calculated to include all out-of-pocket expenses incurred by the charity but to exclude capital expenditure, depreciation charges and the creation of financial reserves. No value should be placed on unpaid volunteer labour or donated goods used.

  There must be a deliberate policy to subsidise the welfare services by at least 15% i.e. the subsidy should not be achieved as a result of circumstance or unintentionally. The service subsidy must be available both to people who can and cannot afford to pay the full rate and must not be applied conditionally (e.g. only during cold weather or only to persons in certain areas or of a certain age).

  Subject to the above concession, supplies of welfare services and related goods are business supplies which are exempt from VAT if made 'otherwise than for a profit' (see 12.9 below).

  Supplies of food and drink by charities from trolleys, canteens or shops are business but exempt when connected with the welfare of those in hospital, prison etc. (see 12.9 below).

- *Catering.* Catering ancillary to welfare services is an exempt business supply (see above). Catering supplied to staff and members of the public is standard-rated, as are supplies of excisable goods (e.g. tobacco and alcohol).

  Catering is only regarded as non-business when it forms part of a non-business supply of welfare (see above).

- *Sponsorship.* If the sponsor receives nothing in return for his contribution, the donation is non-business and outside the scope of VAT. If the contribution is made on condition that the company's name is advertised or promoted or the company receives some benefit (e.g. free tickets, free advertising space in a charity event programme), it is the consideration for a business supply and standard-rated. See 58.18 RECREATION AND SPORT.

12.4 Charities

If the supply is made in connection with a fund-raising event, the supply will be business but exempt. See 12.9 below.

- *Secondment of staff.* In general, the total payment for the secondment or loan of staff, even if supplied at or below cost, is a standard-rated supply of services. By concession, it has been agreed with the National Council of Social Services that where staff are seconded from one charity or non-profit-making voluntary organisation to another on the basis of salary reimbursement, the supply can be treated as non-business and outside the scope of VAT provided

  (i) the employee seconded has been engaged only in the non-business activities of the lending charity and will only be engaged in such activities of the borrowing organisation; and

  (ii) the consideration for the supply of the employee's services does not exceed 'normal remuneration' (calculated *pro rata* for part-time secondments). '*Normal remuneration*' means the total cost incurred by the lending charity, i.e. salary, NIC, pension costs, etc.

- *Membership subscriptions* are business income and standard-rated unless, in the case of a charity, members are entitled to nothing more than the right to participate in management or receive reports on the charity's activities. See 14.1 and 14.10 CLUBS AND ASSOCIATIONS. See also 14.2 CLUBS AND ASSOCIATIONS for apportionment of subscriptions to reflect zero-rating relief available if literature is supplied as one of the benefits of membership.

Activities which are partly business and partly non-business

- *Affinity credit card schemes.* These are schemes whereby a charity endorses a credit card and recommends its use to its members or supporters. The financial institution which issues the card makes payments to the charity each time a card is issued and used. Typically, a charity (and its trading subsidiary) will supply the card issuer with the following services.

  (*a*) Access to the charity's membership or mailing lists and/or mailing of the card issuer's promotional literature to members.

  (*b*) Endorsement of the card and marketing it to members/supporters.

  (*c*) The right to use the charity's name and logo on the card and promotional literature.

  There should be two separate agreements. One agreement should provide for the services under (*a*) and (*b*) above (standard-rated supplies) and should preferably be between the charity's trading subsidiary and the card issuer. The second agreement for services under (*c*) above (outside the scope supplies) must be between the charity and the card issuer. If so, C & E accept that only part (at least 20%) of any initial payment on the issue of each new card can be treated as the consideration for standard-rated business supplies. The remaining 80% or less of the initial payment, and all subsequent turnover based payments based on usage of the card, are outside the scope of VAT. If a charity seeks to allocate less than 20% of the initial payment to the taxable supply, C & E would not accept that this represents a realistic valuation of the services provided.

- *Fund-raising activities.* Fund-raising is a composite term which covers a wide range of activity which must be judged to be business or non-business under normal rules. Some events may be business but qualify for exemption (see 12.9 below). Raising funds by asking for donations is always a non-business activity.

(C & E Notice 701/1/95, paras 4–11; C & E Manual V1-9, Chapter 2 paras 2.9–2.17, 2.19, 2.23, Chapter 3 Table 3).

12.5   **STANDARD-RATED SUPPLIES BY CHARITIES**

Where charities engage in business activities as a means of fund-raising, VAT must be accounted for at the standard rate in the normal way unless the supplies can be zero-rated under 12.6 below or are exempt under 12.9 below.

12.6   **ZERO-RATED SUPPLIES BY CHARITIES**

Certain supplies by charities are zero-rated not because of the charitable status of the supplier but because they are covered by general application. See 72.1 ZERO-RATED SUPPLIES. In addition, the following zero-rating provisions apply specifically to charities.

(*a*)   **Sale of donated goods.** Zero-rating applies to

   (i)   the supply by a charity of any goods which have been donated for sale; and

   (ii) the supply of donated goods by a taxable person who has covenanted by deed to give all the profits of that supply to a charity. This extends the relief to charities' trading companies where charities hive off their trading activities to a subsidiary.

For supplies made after 25 November 1996, zero-rating only applies if

(A)   the supply is a sale of goods donated to that charity or taxable person;

(B)   the sale takes place as a result of the goods being made available for purchase by the general public (whether in a shop or elsewhere such as a charity auction); and

(C)   no arrangements relating to the goods have been entered into by each of the parties to the sale before the goods were made available to the general public.

By concession, zero-rating also applies where (A) above applies but the goods, although of a kind made available for purchase by the general public under (B) above, are by reason of their poor quality not fit to be so made available. This concession will benefit many charities, particularly those selling scrap clothing to rag merchants or those who are prevented under safety legislation from selling certain goods to the public (e.g. second-hand electrical goods and toys). (C & E Business Brief 13/97, 16 June 1997).

For supplies made before 26 November 1996, only condition (A) applied.

[*VATA 1994, 8 Sch Group 15, Item 1 and Note (1); FA 1997, s 33*].

The relief is not restricted to second-hand goods but the goods must have been 'donated for sale'. For example, relief does not apply where goods are

•   donated to a charity for its own use and subsequently sold;

•   donated as raffle prizes; or

•   donated and used to make other goods for sale (e.g. a painting donated and used to make prints for resale).

(C & E Manual V1-9, Chapter 2 para 4.10).

Where the goods have not been donated (e.g. bought in goods such as Christmas cards and stationery) the supplies are normally standard-rated (unless sold as part of a one-off fund-raising event, see 12.9 below).

Following legal advice, C & E have decided that buildings and land are not covered by the above provisions because they are not 'goods which have been donated for sale'. In most cases, where dwellings or land are bequeathed to a charity, the property in question would not have been a business asset of the deceased person or the charity. Any supply of the property would normally be outside the scope of VAT and the charity would not be able to claim input tax deduction on expenses in connection with the sale. (C & E Business Brief 12/92, 29 July 1992).

(*b*) **Export of any goods by a charity** is zero-rated. [*VATA 1994, 8 Sch Group 15, Item 3*]. Proof of export is required. See 25.24 EXPORTS.

The export is treated as a supply made by the charity in the UK and in the course or furtherance of a business carried on by the charity. [*VATA 1994, s 30(5); FA 1995, s 28*]. This enables a charity to reclaim any VAT paid on the purchase of the goods and any overheads of exporting them (or to register for VAT in order to do so) where the VAT would not otherwise be deductible (e.g. where the goods are given away overseas as part of a non-business activity such as relief aid).

De Voil Indirect Tax Service. See V4.266.

12.7 ZERO-RATED SUPPLIES TO OR FOR CHARITIES

The following supplies to charities are zero-rated.

(*a*) The supply to the Royal National Institute for the Blind, the National Listening Library or other similar charity of

(i) magnetic tape specially adapted for the recording and reproduction of speech for the blind or severely handicapped;

(ii) apparatus designed or specially adapted for the making on magnetic tape, by way of transfer of recorded speech from another magnetic tape, of a recording as in (vi) below;

(iii) apparatus designed or specially adapted for transfer to magnetic tapes of a recording made by apparatus within (ii) above;

(iv) apparatus for rewinding magnetic tape described in (vi) below;

(v) apparatus designed or specially adapted for the reproduction from recorded magnetic tape of speech for the blind or severely handicapped which is not available for use otherwise than by them;

(vi) magnetic tape on which has been recorded speech for the blind or severely handicapped, such recording being suitable for reproduction only in the apparatus mentioned in (v) above;

(vii) apparatus solely for the making on a magnetic tape of a sound recording which is for use by the blind or severely handicapped;

(viii) parts and accessories (other than a magnetic tape for use with apparatus in (vii) above) for goods comprised in (i) to (vii) above; and

(ix) the supply of a service of repair or maintenance of any goods within (i) to (viii) above.

Included is the letting on hire of eligible goods under (i) to (vii) above. [*VATA 1994, 8 Sch Group 4, Item 1*].

(*b*) Wireless receiving sets or apparatus solely for the making and reproduction of sound recording on a magnetic tape permanently contained on a cassette. In each case, the goods must be solely for gratuitous loan to the blind. Included is the letting on hire of eligible goods. [*VATA 1994, 8 Sch Group 4, Item 2*].

(c)   Certain goods to be made available to persons with disabilities and services of adapting, repairing and installing goods for such persons. See 32.16 to 32.19 HEALTH AND WATER UTILITIES.

(d)   Donation of any goods for sale or export by a charity or by a taxable person within 12.6(a)(ii) above. [*VATA 1994, 8 Sch Group 15, Item 2*]. A taxable person who donates business goods to a charity for sale or export can therefore zero-rate the supply. Goods donated for the charity's own use do not qualify; nor does bequeathed property unless bequeathed specifically for sale or export by the charity.

(e)   Lifeboats, including repairs and maintenance and spares and accessories, supplied to a charity providing rescue and assistance at sea. See 68.13 TRANSPORT AND FREIGHT.

(f)   The supply to a charity for the purposes of raising money for, or making known the objects or reason for the objects of, the charity, of the following.

(i) The broadcast on television or radio, or screening in a cinema, of an advertisement. [*VATA 1994, 8 Sch Group 15, Item 8(a)*]. Relief is confined to the cost of broadcasting or screening the advert and does not extend to the cost of making the advert. (C & E Notice 701/1/95, para 16(c)). Advertisements displayed on the Internet or on repeating loop systems (e.g. in post offices) are not included. (C & E Manual V1-9, Chapter 2 para 10.6).

(ii) The publication of an advertisement in any newspaper, journal, poster, programme, annual, leaflet, brochure, pamphlet, periodical or similar publication. [*VATA 1994, 8 Sch Group 15, Item 8(b)*]. See 54.28 PRINTED MATTER for further details.

The charity must provide the supplier with a declaration that the advertisement is for a qualifying purpose. See C & E Notice 701/1/95, Annex H for the suggested form of the declaration required.

(g)   The supply to a charity

(i) providing care or medical or surgical treatment for human beings or animals; or

(ii) engaging in medical or veterinary research

of a 'medicinal product' where the supply is solely for use by the charity in such care, treatment or research.

'*Medicinal product*' means any 'substance' or article (not being an instrument, apparatus or appliance) which is for use wholly or mainly in either or both of the following ways, viz. by being 'administered' to one or more human beings or animals for 'medicinal purposes' or as an 'ingredient' in the preparation of a substance or article to be so administered.

'*Substance*' means any natural or artificial substance, whether in solid or liquid form or in the form of a vapour or gas.

'*Administer*' means administering whether orally, by injection or by introduction into the body in any other way, or by external application, whether by direct contact with the body or not and includes both administering a substance in its existing state or after it has been dissolved, diluted or mixed with some other substance used as a vehicle.

Use for '*medicinal purpose*' includes use for treating or preventing of disease; diagnosing disease or ascertaining physiological condition; contraception; inducing anaesthesia; or otherwise bringing about some alteration in the physical or physiological state of the patient or animal.

'Ingredient', in relation to the manufacture or preparation of a substance, includes anything which is the sole active ingredient of that substance as manufactured or prepared.

[*VATA 1994, 8 Sch Group 15, Item 9; Medicines Act 1968, ss 130(2)(9), 132*].

C & E use the following guidelines.

- *Medical and veterinary research* should be given its technical meaning i.e. it is restricted to activities which are directed towards opening up new areas of knowledge or understanding, or initial development of new techniques, rather than towards mere quantitative additions to human knowledge.

- *Medical or veterinary treatment* includes the administration of medicines, physiotherapy and surgery.

(C & E Manual V1-9, Chapter 2 para 9.16).

(*h*) The supply to a charity of a 'substance' directly used for synthesis or testing in the course of medical or veterinary research. See (*g*) above for *'substance'*. [*VATA 1994, 8 Sch Group 15, Item 10*].

(*j*) The grant by a person constructing a building of a major interest in it provided the building is intended solely for use for a relevant residential purpose or use for a relevant charitable purpose. See 42.48 LAND AND BUILDINGS.

(*k*) Supplies to a charity of services in the course of construction of a new building intended solely for use for a relevant residential purpose or use for a relevant charitable purpose. See 42.31 LAND AND BUILDINGS.

Proof of zero-rating. Zero-rating of items under (*a*), (*b*), (*e*), (*g*) and (*h*) above may depend on the *use* rather than the nature of the item. The charity must, therefore, give the supplier a certified declaration that the goods are to be used for the specified purpose. Declaration forms are not supplied by C & E but appropriate wording for items (*a*) and (*b*), item (*e*) and items (*g*) and (*h*) above are included in C & E Notice 701/1/95, Annexes F, G and I respectively. These can be reproduced in any convenient way, e.g. by incorporating them in any order form. It is the supplier's responsibility to take reasonable steps to satisfy himself that the charity is entitled to zero-rating and the declaration is correct. Where, however, despite taking all reasonable steps, nonetheless the supplier fails to identify the inaccuracy and in good faith makes the supplies concerned at the zero rate, C & E will not seek to recover the VAT due from the supplier. (C & E Notice 48, ESC 2.11).

Importation. Imports by charities of any goods within (*a*), (*b*), (*e*), (*g*) and (*h*) above can be zero-rated under the same conditions as supplies made to them in the UK. The appropriate declaration (see under *Proof of zero-rating* above) must be presented with the customs entry form.

De Voil Indirect Tax Service. See V4.262.

12.8 **Charity-funded equipment for medical and veterinary uses**

The following supplies are zero-rated.

(*a*) 'Relevant goods' supplied *for donation* to a nominated 'eligible body' where the funds for the purchase (or the letting or hire) are provided by a charity or from voluntary contributions. Where the donee of the goods is not a charity, it must not have contributed, wholly or in part, to the purchase or hiring of the goods.

(b)   'Relevant goods' supplied to an 'eligible body' where that body pays for them (or hires them) with funds provided by a charity or from voluntary contributions. Where the eligible body is not a charity, it must not have contributed, wholly or in part, to the purchase or hiring of the goods.

(c)   'Relevant goods' supplied to an 'eligible body' which is a charitable institution providing 'care' or medical or surgical treatment for 'handicapped' persons. For supplies made after 25 November 1996, either

(i)   such care or treatment must be provided in a 'relevant establishment' where the majority of those receiving that care or treatment are handicapped; or

(ii)   the charitable institution must provide 'medical care' to handicapped persons in their own homes and the relevant goods must fall within (1) below (or be parts or accessories for use in or with relevant goods within (1) below).

The additional requirements for supplies after 25 November 1996 follow the tribunal decision in *Help The Aged (14180)* where the tribunal held that, to qualify for zero-rating, it was only essential that the charity's objects included the provision of care for the handicapped and that the charity actually provided some such care to a minimal number of disabled persons.

C & E will be flexible when applying the 'majority' test under (i) above. They will accept that the majority of people provided for are handicapped if this is the normal and consistent pattern for the relevant establishment, and will not refuse claims for zero-rating simply because an establishment falls slightly below this level temporarily. This pattern should be evident from the relevant establishment's own records. If those records show that, over an extended period of time, 51% or more of the people receiving care or treatment are handicapped, the body will be eligible. (VAT Information Sheet 8/98, para 2.3).

(d)   The repair and maintenance of 'relevant goods' provided they are owned by an 'eligible body' and the services are paid for by a charity or from voluntary contributions. It does not matter how the goods themselves were bought in the first place. Spare parts etc. supplied in connection with the repairs and maintenance are also relieved. If the owner or hirer of the goods repaired or maintained is not a charity, it must not have contributed, wholly or in part, to the cost of the repairs or spares.

(e)   By concession, 'relevant goods' supplied to a charity

(i)   whose sole purpose and function is to provide a range of care services to meet the personal needs of handicapped people (of which transport might form a part); or

(ii)   which provides transport services predominantly to handicapped people.

In theory, any relevant goods can be supplied at the zero rate under this concession. In practice, the type of relevant goods which are most likely to be purchased by these charities (and which were the basis of discussion between C & E and the representative bodies) are motor vehicles adapted for use by handicapped passengers (with space for at least one wheelchair user) or a motor vehicle to transport mainly blind, deaf, mentally impaired or terminally sick persons. Boats that are designed or permanently adapted for use by handicapped people are also eligible for zero-rating.

It is the responsibility of the purchasing charity to prove that it is entitled to buy the relevant goods at the zero-rate. To avoid charities having to keep detailed records simply to prove eligibility, C & E will use records and documentation already kept by the charity for non-VAT purposes, for example

- its charitable aims and objectives;

- its publicity and advertising material;

- any documents issued for the purpose of obtaining funds from a third party such as a local authority;

- evidence of its day-to-day operations; and

- any other relevant evidence.

When a charity claims zero-rating on an adapted motor vehicle (or any other relevant goods), it must issue a certificate to the supplier claiming eligibility for zero-rating and, where required, it must attach documentary evidence (as outlined above) to support the claim. (Some documents, particularly funding documents or aims and objectives, are lengthy. A charity need not provide the whole document, but it should provide the parts which will enable it to make the declaration for relief.) The charity should make up two sets of the documents listed above, one set for itself and one to present to *each* supplier. This means the charity in reality has to search for and collate the information only once. It can then be retained by the charity for any future supplies. A charity need only provide the supporting evidence once to each supplier unless there have been relevant changes to its operation.

(C & E Business Brief 13/97, 16 June 1997; VAT Information Sheet 8/98, paras 3.1, 3.3-3.5). See Annexes B to E of the VAT Information Sheet for examples of documents which might be produced by charities intending to purchase an adapted motor vehicle.

Relevant goods. These comprise the following.

(1) Medical, scientific, computer, video, sterilising, laboratory or refrigeration 'equipment' 'for use in' medical or veterinary research, training, diagnosis or treatment (including 'parts' and 'accessories').

'Equipment' means *articles* designed for a specific purpose. Disposable items (e.g. syringes) which may be designed to be used once only are still articles for the purpose of this relief. They should be distinguished from 'consumables' which are not covered. Goods which are not articles (e.g. liquids, powders, pellets, granules or other bulk materials) are not equipment. (C & E Notice 701/6/97, para 5.2).

'For use in'. The equipment only qualifies for relief if purchased for use in medical or veterinary research, etc. Where equipment is to be used partly for a qualifying use and partly for a non-qualifying use, it is only eligible for relief if mainly for qualifying use. This means that substantial, real and continuing qualifying use is to be the main initiating factor behind the purchase. (C & E Notice 701/6/97, para 6.1).

'Parts' means integral components without which the equipment is incomplete. (C & E Notice 701/6/97, para 5.3).

'Accessories' means optional extras which can be used to improve the operation of the equipment or enable it to be used, or be used to better effect, in particular circumstances. This would include, for example, a printer for use with a computer or a rack for holding test tubes. It does not include articles which have independent uses (e.g. televisions) or articles which are accessories to accessories. (C & E Notice 701/6/97, para 5.3).

C & E have indicated the following guidelines.

Medical equipment means items designed for use in the diagnosis or treatment of patients. *Eligible* are anaesthetic apparatus; aprons (lead lined for X-ray protection);

bandages; bedpans; highly specialised beds (e.g. net suspension beds, medical water beds); catheters; medical clamps; dental chairs, drills, mirrors and spittoons; drip poles; endoscopes; electro-cardiographs; eye test charts; adjustable examination couches; first aid kits (supplied as pre-packaged units); forceps; surgical gloves; heart pacemakers; hypodermic needles; identification bracelets for patients; kidney bowls; mattresses specially designed for the relief/prevention of pressure sores; medicine measures (graduated); operating lights; patient trolleys and stretchers; specialised physiotherapy equipment (other than gymnasium equipment); orthopaedic pillows specially designed and used for neck or spinal injuries; radiography equipment; resuscitation equipment; scalpels; sphygmomanometers; splints; stethoscopes; surgical gloves, gowns and masks; suture needles; swabs; clinical thermometers; tongue depressors; wound dressings; X-ray films and plates; medical X-ray machines and X-ray viewers. *Not eligible* are alarm bracelets; aprons (not lead lined); blankets; cotton wool; disinfectants; drugs trolleys; first aid dummies; gloves (other than surgical); gymnasium equipment; hearing aids; nurse call systems; occupational therapy materials; overbed tables; pagers; pillows (other than specially designed orthopaedic pillows as above); resuscitation dummies; screens; towels; training aids; and uniforms.

Scientific equipment means equipment which performs a scientific function *not* equipment which works on a scientific principle. It covers precision measuring, analytical and weighing equipment. *Eligible* are barometers; centrifuges; microscopes; non-clinical thermometers; weighing machines; and non-medical X-ray machines.

Computer equipment means computer hardware and includes 'normalised' (off-the-shelf) computer programmes. See (7) below for more restricted relief for custom-made software. *Eligible* are computer disks and tapes, keyboards, mouses, printers, screens, screen filters and servers. *Not eligible* is computer stationery; and machinery or other equipment which is operated by computer or which has computerised components.

Video equipment covers video recording and playback equipment. *Eligible* are video cameras, tapes, players and monitors.

Sterilising equipment covers specialised equipment using steam or other high temperature processes. *Eligible* are autoclaves and bedpan washers with sterilising steam cycles. *Not eligible* are microwave ovens and other cooking appliances even if they can be used to sterilise; and sterilising solutions.

Laboratory equipment covers goods *designed* for use in a laboratory (therefore as long as the goods qualify within this category there is no requirement that they must be *used* in a laboratory). *Eligible* are specialised sinks and catchpots; Bunsen burners; centrifuges; fume cupboards; laboratory benches and glassware; microscopes; pipettes; and test tubes. *Not eligible* are ordinary cupboards, lockers, seats and furniture even if supplied for laboratory use; and laboratory animals.

Refrigeration equipment includes all cooling and freezing equipment whether of an industrial type, special design for specific purpose or the common domestic fridge. *Eligible* are deep freezer and ice-making machines.

Ineligible equipment. Relief does not apply to equipment used for general biology studies, environmental research or research into animal husbandry or food production methods, administrative record-keeping, entertainment, general comfort and security. Examples of ineligible equipment include air conditioners; security and smoke alarms; still cameras; catering equipment; cleaning equipment; closed circuit television systems; curtains; fuel; lockers; overhead projecting units; stationery; tape recorders; television sets; waste disposal bags, boxes, jars and sacks; and waste disposal machinery.

12.8 Charities

(C & E Notice 701/6/97, paras 5.3, 6,4, Appendix F).

Medical and veterinary research means original research into disease and injury of human beings or animals. (C & E Notice 701/6/97, para 6.3).

Medical or veterinary training covers training doctors, nurses, surgeons (including dental surgeons) and other professionals involved in diagnosis or treatment. The overall programme of training must include the physical application by the students of theoretical knowledge. The teaching of subjects such as biology and zoology where there is no practical medical involvement with patients is not regarded as training. (C & E Notice 701/6/97, para 6.3).

Medical or veterinary diagnosis and treatment means the diagnosis and treatment of a physical or mental abnormality by a medical or paramedical practitioner or a veterinary surgeon. (C & E Notice 701/6/97, para 6.3).

(2) 'Ambulances' (including 'parts' and 'accessories'). '*Ambulance*' denotes a vehicle of the emergency kind used for transporting sick and injured people or animals. It includes specially equipped airborne or water craft. The vehicle must have

- the front and both sides permanently fitted with signs indicating that the vehicle is an ambulance;

- adequate door space for the loading of a patient on a stretcher;

- seating at the rear of the driver or pilot in the ambulance compartment for at least one attendant; and

- at least one stretcher measuring 2.28 metres (for human patients) with handles extended, together with permanent fittings to hold it in position. Any reasonable alternative for lifting and carrying animals will be acceptable.

'*Parts*' means integral components without which the ambulance is incomplete. '*Accessories*' means optional extras which can be used to improve the operation of the ambulance or enable it to be used, or be used to better effect, in particular circumstances.

(C & E Notice 701/6/97, para 5.3).

(3) Goods of a kind described in *VATA 1994, 8 Sch Group 12, Item 2* (medical and surgical appliances — see 32.17(*a*) HEALTH AND WATER UTILITIES).

(4) Motor vehicles (other than vehicles with more than 50 seats) designed or substantially and permanently adapted for the safe carriage of a 'handicapped' person in a wheelchair provided that vehicles with 17 to 26 seats have provision for at least two handicapped persons; 27 to 36 seats at least three such persons; 37 to 46 at least four such persons; and 47 or more seats at least five such persons. There must be either a fitted electrically or hydraulically operated lift or, in the case of a vehicle with less than 17 seats, a fitted ramp to provide access for a passenger in a wheelchair.

(5) Motor vehicles with more than six but fewer than 51 seats for use by an eligible body providing care for blind, deaf, mentally handicapped or terminally sick persons mainly to transport such persons;

(6) Telecommunication, aural, visual, light enhancing or heat detecting equipment (not being equipment ordinarily supplied for private or recreational use) solely for use for the purpose of rescue or first aid services undertaken by a charitable institution providing such services. *Eligible* are image intensifiers, heat seekers and similar specialist equipment used to locate casualties and flares used to illuminate large areas for search purposes. Two-way radios may be allowed relief provided

they are pre-calibrated to the emergency frequency. *Not eligible* are general items such as mobile phones and pagers, binoculars, torches, search lights and loudhailers. (C & E Notice 701/6/97, para 5.3).

(7) For the purposes of (*b*) and (*c*) above only, computer services by way of the provision of computer software solely for use in medical research, diagnosis or treatment.

Installation. If the normal selling price of the eligible goods includes an amount for fixing or connecting to mains services and/or testing the equipment on site, the whole supply can be included in the relief. Any building work (e.g. removal of walls or reinforcing floors) is standard-rated even if carried out by the supplier. (C & E Notice 701/6/97, para 5.4).

Relevant establishment means either of the following.

•   A day centre other than one that exists primarily to provide social or recreational activities. It must concentrate on providing some form of care or treatment to those attending. Examples of centres which would qualify include physiotherapy centres for disabled children or charitable establishments which run daily rehabilitation or training classes for disabled adults.

•   An institution which is approved, licensed or registered under the relevant social legislation or which is exempt from those obligations by that legislation. This includes the wide range of residential care institutions, such as nursing homes for disabled adults or residential homes for disabled children.

(C & E VAT Information Sheet 8/98, para 2.2).

Handicapped means chronically sick or disabled. Generally, chronic sickness is of a severe and long-term nature, and a disability implies a permanent condition which significantly restricts normal activities. Temporary disability caused by illness or injury and frailty by reason of age are not included. (C & E Notice 701/6/97, para 3.5).

Eligible body means any of the following.

•   A Health Authority or Special Health Authority in England and Wales.

•   A Health Board in Scotland.

•   A Health and Social Services Board in Northern Ireland.

•   A 'hospital' or 'research institution' whose activities are 'not carried on for profit'.

    A '*hospital*' is an institution which has diagnostic facilities, provides a range of medical treatments and has in-patient facilities.

    '*Research institution*' includes a university where post-graduates carry out research projects.

    '*Not carried on for profit*' means that the hospital or research establishment

    (i)   does not intend to make a surplus;

    (ii) is precluded by its constitution from distributing any profits; and

    (iii) is only allowed to use any surplus to further its objectives.

    (C & E Notice 701/6/97, paras 3.1-3.3).

•   A charitable institution (including a charitable hospice, see C & E Notice 701/6/97, para 3.1) providing 'care' or medical or surgical treatment for handicapped persons. For supplies made after 25 November 1996, either

(a)   the relevant goods must be for use in a 'relevant establishment' in which the charity provides care or treatment to persons the majority of whom are handicapped; or

(b)   the charity must provide 'medical care' to handicapped persons in their own homes and the relevant goods must be medical equipment and its parts or accessories used in, or in connection with, that care.

C & E will be flexible when applying the 'majority' test under (a) above. They will accept that the majority of people provided for are handicapped if this is the normal and consistent pattern for the relevant establishment, and will not refuse claims for zero-rating simply because an establishment falls slightly below this level temporarily. This pattern should be evident from the relevant establishment's own records. If those records show that, over an extended period of time, 51% or more of the people receiving care or treatment are handicapped, the body will be eligible. (VAT Information Sheet 8/98, para 2.3).

- The Common Services Agency for the Scottish Health Service, the Northern Ireland Central Services Agency for Health and Social Services, or the Isle of Man Health Services Board.

- A charitable institution providing rescue or first-aid services.

- A National Health Service trust established under *National Health Service and Community Care Act 1990, Part I* or *National Health Service (Scotland) Act 1978.*

Excluded are clinics, general practitioners' surgeries and non-charitable nursing homes. (C & E Notice 701/6/97, para 3.1).

[*VATA 1994, 8 Sch Group 15, Items 4-7; Health Authorities Act 1995, s 127; FA 1997, s 34*].

Care means some form of continuing personal contact in looking after, helping or supervising people. It includes

- helping with personal needs (e.g. bathing, dressing, feeding);

- the type of care provided by residential homes; and

- supervision (where the person supervising has responsibility for those being supervised) such as provided in day care centres to people who are vulnerable and might come to harm if left alone.

Catering or transport services and services performed remotely from the beneficiary (e.g. laundry) are not 'care' in this sense.

(C & E Notice 701/6/97, para 3.4).

Medical care refers to the sort of care a nurse would carry out or supervise, e.g. washing, getting people out of bed, administering drugs, etc. It does not cover supplies of basic domestic help services, e.g. cooking, cleaning, shopping or laundry. (VAT Information Sheet 8/98, para 2.9).

Evidence of eligibility. It is the supplier's responsibility to ensure that VAT is applied at the correct rate. Examples of certificates that could be obtained from the customer are reproduced in the Supplement to C & E Notice 701/6/97. If a certificate is not obtained, the same information must be provided to the supplier in order that the supply can be zero-rated. The certificate or other evidence must be retained for production to C & E if required.

Even where evidence has been obtained, the supplier must still take steps to check any apparent inconsistency and confirm the validity of any declaration. However, if after having taken all reasonable steps to check the validity of a declaration a supplier, in good faith, makes a supply at the zero-rate, C & E will not seek to recover the VAT due from him.

(C & E Notice 701/6/97, paras 9.1-9.4).

Imports. Goods that meet all the conditions for zero-rating when purchased in the UK can be zero-rated on importation. Declarations (in the forms given in the Supplement to C & E Notice 701/6/97) must be lodged with C & E at the port of entry. Special provisions apply to the importation of computer software. See 34.32 IMPORTS. (C & E Notice 701/6/97, para 8.1).

Acquisitions from other EC countries. Where a VAT-registered eligible body acquires goods from another EC country, the normal rules for acquisitions apply. If the supply meets all the conditions for relief, no VAT is due. Certificates do not need to be obtained from the overseas supplier but evidence that the supply is correctly zero-rated should be retained for production to C & E if required.

Where an eligible body is not VAT-registered, any goods acquired from another EC country are subject to VAT at the rate in force in that country. The UK relief for charity funded equipment does not apply.

(C & E Notice 701/6/97, para 8.2).

Supplies to eligible bodies in other EC countries. There is no requirement in the legislation that the eligible body must be within the UK (apart from the specific UK Health Boards, etc.). Qualifying hospitals and research and charitable institutions in other EC countries that are not VAT-registered in their own country may therefore purchase goods under this relief. The supplier should obtain evidence of relief before zero-rating the supply.

If the hospital, etc. is VAT-registered in its own country or is outside the EC, the supply of goods can be zero-rated under the normal rules. (C & E Notice 701/6/97, para 8.3).

De Voil Indirect Tax Service. See V4.266.

12.9   EXEMPT SUPPLIES BY CHARITIES

Certain supplies by charities are exempt from VAT not because of the charitable status of the supplier but because they are covered by general application. See 24 EXEMPT SUPPLIES. In addition, the following exemptions apply specifically to charities.

(*a*)   **Fund-raising events.** The supply of goods and services by a charity in connection with a 'fund-raising event' organised for charitable purposes by a 'charity' (or jointly by more than one charity) is exempt.

'*Fund-raising event*' means a fete, ball, bazaar, gala show, performance or similar event, which is separate from and not forming any part of a series or regular run of like or similar events.

'*Charity*' includes a body corporate, wholly owned by a charity, whose profits (from whatever source) are payable to the charity.

[*VATA 1994, 9 Sch Group 12, Item 1*].

The exemption applies to all admission charges, the sale of commemorative brochures, the sale of advertising space in those brochures and other items sold by the charity at the event e.g. tee shirts, auctioned goods, etc. It also includes sponsorship payments directly connected with the qualifying event.

Apart from the events mentioned above, exemption covers dinner dances, discos, film premieres, theatre first nights and concerts which normally take place during a single day. Exceptionally, C & E allow dinners alone which are clearly for fund-raising purposes and which are budgeted on the basis of raising substantial funds and not just an incidental profit. School open days, competitions and flower shows are not included. An event exceeding one day may qualify for exemption provided it is organised as a single organic whole and the activities for each day differ significantly in character and not simply in minor detail. See *Reading Cricket and Hockey Club (13656)* where the tribunal held that, on the fact, a three day real ale and jazz festival, planned as a single event, fell within the exemption even though tickets were sold separately for each evening. However where an event is held over a number of days and each of the days closely resemble one another, then it is unlikely to qualify for relief on the basis that what is provided could be either a series or regular run of like or similar events.

The restriction to 'one-off' events is to prevent charities gaining an unfair advantage over the activities of commercial organisations. Charities can hold a number of the same type of events in a year and, provided they are reasonably spread apart, they can all benefit from exemption. (Low key events, e.g. coffee mornings and jumble sales, can be held on the same premises and at any frequency and still come within the exemption because the risk of distortion of trade is less.) A regular annual concert can qualify for exemption. However, events must stand alone to qualify for exemption and the relief does not extend to a series of events for which season tickets can be purchased or for which a lesser amount (or no payment at all) is required for second and subsequent events.

Similar events organised in different parts of the country by a national charity can be allowed within the exemption even if taking place in the same week provided the venues are reasonably far apart.

Where a qualifying event is organised for a charity by a company or club, any income passed over to the charity is covered by the exemption but any part of the gross income retained to cover expenses is the consideration for agency services and subject to VAT.

(C & E Notice 701/1/95, paras 27–36; C & E Manual V1-9, Chapter 2, paras 6.4, 6.5).

See 12.10 below for admission charges where a fund-raising event does not qualify for exemption under these provisions.

See *Northern Ireland Council for Voluntary Action, [1991] VATTR 32 (5451)* where the tribunal held that, although a week of fund-raising activities including several performances of a play could be described as a single fund-raising event, the restriction on the scope of the exemption under *VATA 1994, 9 Sch Group 12* for a series of similar events was permissible and did not breach *EC 6th Directive, Art 13A(1)(o)*.

(*b*) **Welfare services.** The supply, 'otherwise than for a profit', by a charity of 'welfare services' and of goods supplied in connection therewith is exempt.

'*Welfare services*' means services directly connected with

(i) the provision of 'care', treatment or instruction designed to promote the physical or mental welfare of elderly, sick, distressed or disabled persons;

(ii) the 'protection of children and young persons'; or

(iii) the provision of 'spiritual welfare' by a religious institution as part of a course of instruction or a retreat, not being a course or retreat designed primarily to provide recreation or a holiday.

Excluded is the supply of accommodation or catering unless ancillary to the provision of care, treatment or instruction.

[*VATA 1994, 9 Sch Group 7, Item 9*].

The supply of catering to elderly people in sheltered housing accommodation was held to be ancillary in *Viewpoint Housing Association Ltd (13148)* and the supply of hotel accommodation and catering to cancer patients and their families was held to be ancillary in *Trustees for the Macmillan Cancer Trust (15603)*.

'Otherwise than for a profit'. Following the decision in *C & E Commrs v Bell Concord Educational Trust Ltd CA 1988, [1989] STC 264*, C & E accept that supplies are made 'otherwise than for a profit' if they are made by charities in circumstances where any surpluses are applied solely to the furtherance of the activity which generated the surplus. Where, however, a charity pursues more than one activity, the welfare services will not be supplied otherwise than for a profit if surpluses from welfare services are applied to the maintenance or furtherance of the other activities, even though charitable.

'Welfare' is usually defined as financial and other assistance given to people in need. This definition draws out the three main strands of any welfare service, namely that the services will be

- of help and benefit to the recipient;

- given rather than sold (although in practice a nominal charge may be made provided not sufficient to allow the service to be operated on a commercial basis); and

- provided to people in need.

'Care'. C & E regard care as meaning some form of continuing personal contact in looking after, helping or supervising people. They originally took the view that 'care' meant personal care such as bathing, dressing or feeding and excluded services such as cleaning, cooking and shopping. However, in *Watford & District Old People's Housing Association Ltd (t/a Watford Help In The Home Service) (15660)* the tribunal held that domestic help services such as cleaning, cooking and shopping could constitute 'care' when supplied to 'people for whom there is either current or imminent substantial risk to the health and welfare of the person, and who have major difficulty in safely carrying out some key daily living tasks'. The tribunal stressed the significance of the high level of recipients' needs which had been identified by Social Services assessments. C & E now accept that domestic help can constitute care for the purposes of VAT exemption under these circumstances and are consulting interested parties with a view to announcing a revised interpretation of the law. Once this has been agreed, claims for repayments can be made, subject to the three-year cap and, where VAT on costs has been passed on to private individuals, subject to the unjust enrichment provisions. Protective claims can be submitted during the consultation period to protect the position with regard to the three-year time limit. Taxpayers may, if they wish, apply the wider exemption during the consultation period but, if they do so, may be liable to default interest (but not misdeclaration penalty) where any services are confirmed to be taxable. (C & E Business Brief 24/98, 2 December 1998).

The *'protection of children and young persons'* under (ii) above is not limited to protection from physical harm but also includes

- services designed to improve the well-being of the young; and

- the protection of the young from malign influences.

'Spiritual welfare'. In determining whether a supply qualifies as spiritual welfare, it is necessary to look behind the supply to, for example, the way in which it is

advertised and the objects and purpose of the organisation making the supply. Spiritual counselling and retreats leading a group in the exploration of their spiritual needs and development would normally qualify. Conferences, courses and retreats where spiritual welfare is only an incidental benefit should not be treated as exempt. As with welfare services, the recipient of spiritual welfare must be a person in need of such and not someone who merely wishes to expand their knowledge of spiritual matters.

Meals on Wheels. This service is often run by a charity on behalf of a local authority. Any charge made to the recipient for the meals is not consideration paid to the charity but is part of the local authority's non-business income. If the charity makes a charge to the local authority for providing the service, this is the taxable supply of a delivery service and not a welfare supply by the charity.

(C & E Notice 701/1/95, para 10(*b*)). (C & E Manual V1-9, Chapter 2 paras 5.2, 5.4–5.6, Chapter 3 Appendix F).

See 12.4 above for welfare services supplied consistently below cost.

The making of exempt supplies may also mean that the charity is unable to recover all its input tax under the PARTIAL EXEMPTION (49) rules.

De Voil Indirect Tax Service. See V4.171.

12.10   **ADMISSION CHARGES**

Admission charges by charities to entertainments, functions etc. not covered by the exemption for fund-raising events under 12.9 above are subject to VAT but it is still open to a charity to set a basic minimum charge (standard-rated) and to invite those attending to supplement this with a voluntary donation. The extra contribution will be outside the scope of VAT provided

(*a*)   it is clearly stated on all publicity material, including tickets, that anyone paying the minimum charge will be admitted without further payment;

(*b*)   the extra payment does not give any particular benefit (e.g. better seats);

(*c*)   the extent of further contributions is ultimately left to the ticket holders to decide, even if the organiser indicates a desired level of donation;

(*d*)   for film or theatre performances, concerts, sporting fixtures, etc. the minimum charge is not less than the usual price of the particular seats at a normal commercial event of the same type; and

(*e*)   for dances, dinners and similar functions, the minimum total sum upon which the organisers will be liable to VAT will not be less than their total costs incurred in arranging the event.

If the publicity material for the event suggests that those paying a recommended extra amount are more likely to be admitted than those paying the basic ticket price, then the extra amount becomes part of the consideration for the supply of services and subject to VAT at the standard rate.

(C & E Notice 701/1/95, para 37).

An admission fee of £20 plus a 'minimum voluntary contribution' of £30 has been held to fail the above test, implying that the £30 donation was compulsory (*Glasgow's Miles Better Mid Summer 5th Anniversary Ball (4460)*).

For admission charges to entertainment, cultural activities and sporting events generally, see 58.6 RECREATION AND SPORT.

12.11   RELIEF FOR IMPORTATIONS

No VAT is payable on the importation of the following goods from outside the EC.

(*a*)   Basic necessities (i.e. food, medicines, clothing, blankets, orthopaedic equipment and crutches, required to meet a person's immediate needs) obtained without charge for distribution free of charge to the needy by a 'relevant organisation'. *Excluded* are alcoholic beverages, tobacco products, coffee, tea and motor vehicles other than ambulances.

(*b*)   Goods donated by a person established outside the EC to a 'relevant organisation' for use to raise funds at occasional charity events for the benefit of the needy. There must be no commercial intent on the part of the donor. *Excluded* are alcoholic beverages etc. as in (*a*) above.

(*c*)   Equipment and office material donated by a person established outside the EC to a 'relevant organisation' for meeting its operating needs and carrying out its charitable aims. There must be no commercial intent on the part of the donor. *Excluded* are alcoholic beverages etc. as in (*a*) above.

(*d*)   Goods imported by a 'relevant organisation' for distribution or loan, free of charge, to victims of, or for meeting its operating needs in the relief of, a disaster affecting the territory of one or more EC countries. This relief only applies where the Commission of the European Communities has made a decision authorising the importation of the goods.

(*e*)   Articles donated to and imported by an approved organisation principally engaged in the education of, or the provision of assistance to, blind or other physically or mentally handicapped persons for loan, hiring out or transfer other than on a profit-making basis (and whether for consideration or free of charge) to such persons and specially designed for their education, employment or social advancement. There must be no commercial intent on the part of the donor.

(*f*)   Spare parts, components or accessories for any article within (*e*) above, including tools for its maintenance, checking, calibration or repair. The goods must be imported with an article within (*e*) above to which they relate or, if imported subsequently, must be identifiable as being intended for such an article.

'*Relevant organisation*' means a State organisation or other approved charitable or philanthropic organisation.

The above reliefs are conditional on

(i)   the goods being put to the use or purpose specified; and

(ii)   unless specifically allowed above, the goods not being lent, hired out or transferred unless to an organisation which would itself be entitled to the relief if importing the goods on that date. In the latter case, prior notification in writing must be received from C & E and the goods must be used solely in accordance with the relieving provisions.

Where any condition ceases to be satisfied and written notice of this fact is given to C & E, VAT becomes payable as if the goods had been imported on that date and VAT is calculated accordingly. The VAT must not, however, exceed the VAT relieved in the first place.

[*SI 1984/746, Art 6(1), 7, 8, 2 Sch Group 6; SI 1992/3120*].

See also Notice 317 *Imports by charities.*

12.12   Charities

12.12   NEW BUILDING PROJECTS ON A SELF-BUILD OR SELF-HELP BASIS

Refunds of VAT may be available to a charity involved in a self-build project of a building intended solely for use for a relevant charitable purpose. See 42.52 LAND AND BUILDINGS.

13   Clothing and Footwear

De Voil Indirect Tax Service. See V4.287.

13.1   The supply of goods within 13.2 and 13.5 below is zero-rated. Also included is the supply of an undivided share of the property in the goods or the possession of the goods (e.g. on hire or loan) and the use of such business goods for private or non-business purposes.

13.2   **YOUNG CHILDREN'S CLOTHING AND FOOTWEAR**

Articles designed as clothing (including hats and other headgear) or footwear for young children and not suitable for older persons are zero-rated. Clothing (other than headgear, gloves, footwear, buttons, belts and buckles) made wholly or partly of 'fur skin' is excluded (and therefore standard-rated). Fur skin may be used for trimming unless it has an area greater than one-fifth of the area of the outside material or, in the case of a new garment, represents a cost to the manufacturer greater than the cost of the other components.

'Fur skin' means any skin with fur, hair or wool attached except

●   rabbit skin;

●   woolled sheep or lamb skin; and

●   the skin, if neither tanned nor dressed, of bovine cattle (including buffalo), equine animals, goats or kids (other than Yemen, Mongolian and Tibetan goats or kids), swine (including peccary), chamois, gazelles, deer or dogs.

[*VATA 1994, 8 Sch Group 16, Item 1*].

Clothing includes items such as hats, caps, braces, garters and scarves but does not include haberdashery items and accessories sold separately (e.g. fastenings such as buckles, buttons and zips; shoe laces and stick-on soles; badges; collars, cuffs and other sew-on or iron-on items; hat decorations; or ear or hand muffs).

Footwear includes boots, shoes, sandals and slippers even if designed for special purposes, e.g. roller-skating boots and football boots.

(C & E Notice 714, paras 3, 15).

Whether an item is clothing or not is a question of fact in which the purpose for which it was intended to be used is not conclusive. Clothing must be given its ordinary meaning (*British Vita Co Ltd (332)*). For a consideration of the phrase 'articles designed as clothing' see *C & E Commrs v Ali Baba Tex Ltd QB, [1992] STC 590*.

13.3   **Conditions for zero-rating**

An item of clothing or footwear can be zero-rated provided *either* of the following conditions are met.

(*a*)   It is clearly suitable only for young children. There is often an overlap between body measurements of young children and small adults. It has been agreed that only clothing and footwear sizes up to those suitable for 13 year olds as determined by the British Standards Institution can be zero-rated. Details of the maximum measurements of clothing and sizes of footwear are given in C & E Notice 714A. Garments are always standard-rated if they are labelled, or otherwise 'held out for sale' for body sizes exceeding those of the average 13 year old, which are

13.4　Clothing and Footwear

> Height:　　158 cm (62 inches)
> Chest:　　84 cm (33 inches)
> Waist:　　71 cm (28 inches)
> Hips:　　86 cm (34 inches)

(*b*) It is 'held out for sale' specifically for young children and does not exceed the maximum measurement of clothing or size of footwear in C & E Notice 714A.

'*Held out for sale*' means the way in which it is packaged, labelled, displayed, invoiced or advertised, including in any promotional literature, catalogue or price list.

Manufacturers must be able to demonstrate that an article of clothing has been designed for a young child and must identify the article accordingly in any promotional literature and on invoices.

Wholesalers and distributors must similarly identify the article as being for young children on invoices and price lists. Any catalogue should preferably have a separate children's section and an identical garment in the same size range should not appear in both the adult and children's sections.

Retail sales. Goods sold cannot necessarily be zero-rated because they were zero-rated on purchase e.g. any goods sold in a shop or department catering exclusively for customers aged 14 or over must be standard-rated. In order to zero rate clothing and footwear for young children, retailers must

- make it clear in any catalogue, advertisement, etc. that it is intended for children; and *either*

- sell it from a shop or separate department catering exclusively for children; *or*

- keep it apart from adult sizes by selling it from separate shelves, display units etc. described as 'boys', 'girls' or 'children's'.

(C & E Notice 714, paras 2, 4, 5).

13.4　Specific items

Babies' clothing. Articles which can be zero-rated include bonnets, bootees and matinee jackets; hooded rain covers for push-chairs provided suitable for wear as a rain cape when out of the push-chair; nappies and nappy liners (disposable or of terry or gauze) not exceeding 30 inches on the longest side; white or pastel shaded square shawls measuring 42–54 inches; padded sleeping garments similar to sleeping bags shaped at the neck and armhole provided they have sleeves and/or legs; and towelling bathrobes provided they have hoods or sleeves.

Hats and headgear. Hats and headgear which are clearly only suitable for babies and young children (e.g. babies' bonnets, school hats and cub scout hats) can be zero-rated even though they could physically be worn by an older person. See *Charles Owen & Co (Bow) Ltd, [1993] VATTR 514 (11267)*. Hats which, by design, are also suitable for older persons may only be zero-rated if they are too small for older persons to wear except that

- cycle helmets may be zero-rated up to a maximum size of 59 cm in circumference provided they are designed and marketed specifically for young children; and

- riding hats may be zero-rated up to and including size 6¾ inches (jockey skulls up to size 1) even if they are not held out for sale specifically for young children.

Standard-rated items include alice bands, hair ribbons and slides, 'scrunchies', sports and other headbands, sun visors and ear muffs. Novelty, party and play hats made out of material such as paper or plastic are regarded as toys and standard-rated.

School uniform. Garments, irrespective of size, may be zero-rated if they bear a prominent logo or badge identifying them as part of the official uniform of schools or youth organisations catering exclusively for children under 14 years of age. Unidentified items, such as plain shirts, trousers, blouses and skirts and unbadged blazers, and all uniform items for schools or organisations with pupils or members 14 years and older, remain subject to the normal criteria for zero-rating.

Making up. Making up ('cut, make and trim') young children's clothing from cloth owned by another person is zero-rated. Other processes may also be eligible for zero-rating if, after the work is finished, the processed article clearly becomes a child's garment which is itself normally zero-rated. This is because such work is treated as a supply of services and zero-rated under *VATA 1994, s 30(2A)* as the application of a process to another person's goods which produces goods which are themselves zero-rated. Simply altering a garment (e.g. hemming) is standard-rated.

One-size garments and stretch garments. Articles sold in one size only and suitable for adults and children must be standard-rated. This also applies to garments made from stretch material although some such garments (e.g. leotards and swimming costumes) can be zero-rated if within the maximum measurements set out in C & E Notice 714A and clearly held out for sale for young children.

Mixed supplies (e.g. children's play outfits comprising a cowboy suit and gun) must be apportioned between the zero-rated and standard-rated components. See 47.3 OUTPUT TAX. However, if the standard-rated component or components

- cost no more than 20% of the total cost of the combined supply (excluding VAT); and

- cost no more than £1 (excluding VAT)

by concession the whole supply can be zero-rated.

Unisex footwear can only be zero-rated up to the maximum size for girls' footwear as set out in Notice 714A.

Packaged kits. Packaged kits for making garments which would themselves be zero-rated can be zero-rated provided the material is already cut to the pattern or the pattern is indelibly marked on the material.

(C & E Notice 714, paras 7–12, 14, 16, 19).

13.5   **PROTECTIVE BOOTS AND HELMETS**

Supplies of the following are zero-rated.

(*a*) Protective boots (not shoes) and helmets for industrial use. The supply must not be to persons for use by their employees.

(*b*) Protective helmets for wear by a person driving or riding a motor bicycle.

The articles concerned must

- be manufactured to standards approved by the British Standards Institution and bear a mark of compliance; or

- meet safety standards set by *EC Council Directive 89/686/EEC* (whether under UK law or that of another EC country) and bear an identifying mark to that effect.

For these purposes, 'supply' includes sale, hire or loan, and supply of a part interest.

[*VATA 1994, 8 Sch Group 16, Items 2 and 3*].

13.5 Clothing and Footwear

Boots and helmets under (*a*) above must bear the 'CE' mark and at least a year of affixation (e.g. CE95). Boots must have a protective toe cap. Protective helmets under (*b*) above are specifically excluded from the scope of the 'CE' mark and must bear the British Standard 'Kitemark'.

Zero-rating covers accessories (e.g. visors and ear protectors) fitted as an integral part of an approved helmet. Zero-rating does not cover accessories supplied as optional extras or cycling helmets or protective riding hats (but see under 13.4 above for such headwear for young children).

Supplies from a manufacturer to a wholesaler who in turn supplies them to a retailer, and supplies from an employer to an employee, can be zero-rated subject to the above conditions. But otherwise, before zero-rating a supply within (*a*) above, the supplier should ascertain that the customer is not an employer purchasing the boots etc. for use by employees (e.g. by considering the customer's trading style, the quantity ordered and whether the nature of the contract indicates a trade order).

(C & E Notice 701/23/95). See also that notice for the difference between a boot and a shoe, definition of 'protective' and 'industrial use', current British and European standards which must be met, and how boots and helmets must be marked.

14   Clubs and Associations

Cross-references. See 9.6 BUSINESS ENTERTAINMENT for free entertainment of members; 11.9 CATERING for franchised catering in clubs; and 20.11 EDUCATION for the provision of youth club facilities.

De Voil Indirect Tax Service. See V6.127–129.

14.1   INTRODUCTION

Under *EC 6th Directive, Art 13A*, countries must exempt certain activities in the public interest. Those relating to clubs and associations are covered by *Art 13A(l)* (see 22.17(*l*) EUROPEAN COMMUNITY LEGISLATION). The provisions have been incorporated into UK legislation in three ways.

Firstly, under *VATA 1994, s 94(3)*, if certain organisations with objects in the public domain provide their members with no more than the minimal benefits of the right to participate in management or receive reports of activities, the provision of membership supplies is not treated as a business activity. See 14.10 below.

Secondly, under *VATA 1994, 9 Sch Group 9*, if the organisation is a trade union, professional or representative body, supplies to members referable to its aims and available without payment other than a membership subscription are exempt. See 14.7 below.

Subject to the above, if a 'club, association or organisation' provides facilities or advantages to its members in return for a 'subscription or other consideration', it is deemed to be carrying on a business activity. [*VATA 1994, s 94(2)(a)*]. Such a body must therefore register for VAT (subject to the registration limit) and account for VAT on its subscription income (but see 14.2 below for apportionment of subscriptions).

Meaning of 'club, association or organisation'. There is no definition of 'club or association' in the legislation but for an organisation to be accepted as such for the purposes of *VATA 1994, s 94(2)(a)* C & E expect that it will have most, if not all, of the following characteristics.

• The organisation should be a body membership of which is voluntary.

• The organisation and administration of the body should be governed by written rules or articles.

• A committee or secretariat, elected by members (in the case of a members' club) should have responsibility for the running of the club's affairs.

• In the case of a members' club, the amount of the subscription will be determined by agreement within the club.

• The club will have an aim of promoting a type of activity or pursuit.

• Payment of a subscription or other type of consideration will be compulsory for the provision of facilities.

C & E also regard the provisions as extending to companies and associations where the membership is composed of other organisations.

'Subscription or other consideration' . The term 'subscription' is not defined but should be given its everyday meaning i.e. a payment that gives a person membership of a body, entitling them to take part in the body's activities and receive the benefits that the body supplies. Subscriptions will generally be paid periodically to secure membership for a set time but a 'one-off' payment (e.g. for lifetime membership) is still capable of being regarded as a subscription. 'Other consideration' may be monetary or non-monetary. Monetary consideration not only includes levies and joining fees but also cases where a member pays for a package of a share or debenture plus membership supplies. In such cases, the total paid must be apportioned to reflect the values of the exempt security and the standard-rated membership supplies. Non-monetary consideration cases are those where, for example, the act of making a loan or purchasing a share or debenture is a necessary requirement for membership benefits to be supplied. The implications of these other forms of consideration are considered in more detail in 14.5 below.

(C & E Manual V1-6, Chapter 3 section 6, paras 3.2, 3.3).

Particular types of clubs and associations. The provisions of *VATA 1994, s 94(2)(a)* have been held to be applicable in *C & E Commrs v British Field Sports Society CA, [1998] STC 315* (campaigning against stag and deer hunting), *Eastbourne Town Radio Cars Association v C & E Commrs CA, [1998] STC 669* (association of taxi-drivers) and *Manor Forstal Residents Society Ltd, [1976] VATTR 63 (245)* (association of local residents); and not applicable in *New Ash Green Village Association, [1976] VATTR 63 (245)* (village development association), *Notts Fire Service Messing Club, [1977] VATTR 1 (348)* (canteen at fire station) and *Friends of the Ironbridge Gorge Museum, [1991] VATTR 97 (5639)* (fund-raising association for a museum).

See C & E Manual V1-6, Chapter 3 section 6, paras 4.1-4.37 for further guidance on

- Agricultural co-operatives
- Buying organisations
- City livery companies ('Worshipful companies')
- Football clubs
- Hunt committees and masters of foxhounds
- The Lawn Tennis Associations
- Masonic lodges and clubs
- The National Trust
- Political parties
- The Rotary Organisation
- Round Tables
- The Royal British Legion
- Wildlife trusts
- Wimbledon debentures

De Voil Indirect Tax Service. See V2.211.

14.2   **APPORTIONMENT OF SUBSCRIPTIONS**

Subscriptions are normally wholly standard-rated. See, however, 14.10 below for subscriptions to certain organisations which are 'non-business' and outside the scope of VAT and 58.9 RECREATION AND SPORT for certain membership subscription of non-profit making bodies providing sport and physical education services.

Zero-rated or exempt supplies. Where some of the membership benefits supplied are identifiable supplies of zero-rated or exempt goods and services, subscriptions may be apportioned so that the part which relates to zero-rated or exempt supplies is relieved of VAT. Any joining fees can be apportioned in the same proportions as ordinary membership subscriptions. This also applies to life membership fees unless life members receive special benefits not available to ordinary members. Subscriptions cannot be apportioned on account of an association, etc. *receiving* zero-rated or exempt supplies from a third party. See 54.13 PRINTED MATTER, ETC. for apportionment where books or magazines are supplied.

There are no specific rules for making apportionment but see 47.3 OUTPUT TAX for general guidance. C & E generally accept apportionment of the total subscription income to reflect the relative cost to the association of providing various supplies to members. There is no objection to calculations for the current financial period being based on the accounts for the previous financial year, providing the method is adopted consistently. Other methods will be considered if submitted in writing to C & E. They do not consider apportionment justified if the value of zero-rated or exempt supplies is trivial compared with the value of membership benefits as a whole represented by the annual subscription.

(C & E Leaflet 701/5/90, para 4).

See *C & E Commrs v The Automobile Assn QB, [1974] STC 192* where the proportion of the subscription reasonably attributable to the supply of the Members' Handbook and a magazine was zero-rated.

When apportioning subscriptions, only facilities and advantages that are supplied to members in return for the subscriptions should be taken into account. Items free to members and non-members, and items available to both members and non-members at the same price, should be ignored. Additionally, following the decision in *Friends of the Ironbridge Gorge Museum [1991] VATTR 97 (5639)* that *VATA 1994, s 94(2)(a)* does not apply to bodies if their members only receive benefits from another body, it seems that such benefits should also be disregarded when an apportionment is made. (C & E Manual V1-6, Chapter 3 section 6, Annex para 12).

Overseas subscriptions. Overseas subscriptions will normally follow the same VAT liability as subscriptions paid by UK members. However, if the subscriptions relate almost entirely to the provision of information or consultancy services, associations may be able to justify such subscriptions being outside the scope of UK VAT where the recipients *either* belong in another EC country and use the supply for business purposes *or* belong outside the EC. [*SI 1992/3121, Art 16*]. See 64.26 SUPPLY. (C & E Leaflet 701/5/90, para 5).

14.3   REGISTRATION

A club, etc. may be registered in the name of that club and in determining whether goods and services are supplied to or by it, or whether goods are acquired by it from another EC country, no account is taken of any change in its members. C & E are empowered to make provisions to determine what persons are responsible for carrying out the requirements of the VAT legislation where a club, etc. is managed by its members or a committee. Under these powers C & E have regulated that the necessary requirements are the joint and several responsibility of

- every member holding office as president, chairman, treasurer, secretary or any similar office; or in default of any thereof,

- every member holding office as a member of a committee; or in default of any thereof,

- every member.

[*VATA 1994, s 46(2)(3); SI 1995/2518, Reg 8*].

For the requirements relating to registration see 59 REGISTRATION. Even if a club, etc. is not required to register under the general requirements based on taxable supplies in the UK, it may be liable to register for VAT where it makes certain acquisitions of goods from other EC countries in excess of an annual threshold. See 59.18 REGISTRATION.

14.4 Clubs and Associations

14.4 Clubs in sections and multi-tiered bodies

Two common situations arise in practice.

- An 'umbrella' organisation may have separate sections, each providing a different activity for its members (e.g. a sports association may have different sections for different sports). Members may pay subscriptions solely to the parent organisation, solely to the section, or part to each.

- A body may be organised at national, regional and local levels. A member's subscription paid at local level may be transferred in part to the regional or national level as part of an affiliation fee.

Registration. Generally, such bodies will be regarded as separate registrable entities if the branches or sections can demonstrate that they are both constitutionally and financially independent of the parent body.

Accounting for VAT on subscription income. Where there are several registrable entities within the overall organisation, the VAT liability of each will depend upon

- the nature of the subscriptions;

- the final destination of the subscriptions (e.g. moneys received from subscriptions collected at one level may be retained, passed up to a higher level or returned to a lower level as a grant or subsidy); and

- what supplies are made by each tier and to whom (e.g. supplies may be made by one tier to another above or below as distinct from its own members).

This will determine whether the various tiers are receiving money in their own right or as agents for different tiers and whether the income received from members or other parts of the organisation constitutes consideration for taxable supplies made or is outside the scope of VAT.

Where part of the subscription collected at local level is passed upwards to a national/regional tier which qualifies for treatment under *VATA 1994, s 94(3)* (see 14.10 below), that part is outside the scope of VAT provided

- the local clubs and national/regional tiers of the organisation are separately registrable for VAT;

- the national/regional tier qualifies for treatment under *VATA 1994, s 94(3)* in that no supplies are made to the lower tiers or individual members (or, if there are such supplies, they are covered by the minimal rights criteria laid down); and

- the lower tier merely remits the payment to the higher tier and does not add it to local funds or otherwise apply it to the making of supplies to members locally.

See also *Rotary International [1991] VATTR 177 (5946)*.

(C & E Manual V1-6, Chapter 3 section 6, para 3.13).

14.5 COMMON RECEIPTS OTHER THAN SUBSCRIPTIONS

The following is a list of some of the more common supplies of goods and services made by clubs and associations with an indication of the VAT liability.

Admission charges. See 58.6 RECREATION AND SPORT.

Amusement machines and games of skill are standard-rated. See 58.3 RECREATION AND SPORT.

Bar sales, catering and teas. Food and drink is always standard-rated if it is supplied by way of catering. Hot food and drink and food and drink for consumption on the premises are included. See 11 CATERING. The argument that there is no 'supply' because, in law, drinks obtained by members are not sold to them has been dismissed. (*Carlton Lodge Club v C & E Commrs QB, [1974] STC 507*).

Bingo. See 58.2 RECREATION AND SPORT.

Competition entry fees are normally standard-rated but may be exempt in the case of certain competitions in sport or physical recreation. (See 58.5 RECREATION AND SPORT.)

Court fees, green fees etc. are normally standard-rated. When payments are linked to the operation of lighting e.g. squash courts or snooker tables, the full amount payable by players is standard-rated as the charge is for the right to use the facilities and does not relate to the supply of electricity. See *St Annes-on-Sea Lawn Tennis Club Ltd, [1977] VATTR 229 (434)*. See however 58.7 to 58.13 RECREATION AND SPORT for exemption of fees in certain cases.

Discos, dances, socials etc. VAT must be accounted for on the gross taxable supplies (e.g. admission, catering) and not on the net amounts after band, floor shows etc. expenses are paid.

Donations are outside the scope of VAT if entirely voluntary and the donor received nothing in return.

Fixture cards are standard-rated if any portion for completion occupies more than 25% of total area, otherwise they are generally zero-rated. See also 54.20 PRINTED MATTER, ETC.

Gaming machine takings. VAT is due on the total amount put into the machine by players less amounts returned as winnings. See 58.3 RECREATION AND SPORT.

Hire of pitches for football etc. are normally standard-rated but may be exempt. See 58.8 RECREATION AND SPORT.

Insurance supplied with goods or other services. See 37.11 INSURANCE.

Interest (banks etc.) is exempt. See 27.8 FINANCE.

'Joining' fees (e.g. an initial fee in addition to the annual subscription) has the same liability as the subscriptions. See *The Royal Scottish Automobile Club (257)*.

Jumble sales. Sale of goods and services follow the normal liabilities. See above for admission charges.

Levies. These are normally demanded from existing members when a body requires additional funds. Where a levy is raised and members' benefits remain unaltered, the levy retains the same liability as the existing subscription. However, where there is a change to the continuing benefits (e.g. a zero-rated benefit is introduced when all previous benefits were standard-rated) the subscription from that time will need to be apportioned to reflect the new liabilities (see 14.2 above) and the levy will follow the liability of the newly-apportioned subscription. Similarly, where a levy is used to fund a one-off supply, the liability of the levy would be determined by the liability of that supply, irrespective of the subscription's liability.

Lotteries. See 58.4 RECREATION AND SPORT.

Loans from members. Clubs often raise capital to finance the renewal or development of facilities by means of loans from members.

14.5 Clubs and Associations

Compulsory interest-free loans. Such a loan constitutes non-monetary consideration from the members. The value of the loan is

L × I × V

where

L = the total loan capital standing to the credit of existing members on the first day of the month in which the subscriptions were due (or the first day of the club's financial year if more convenient)

I = the base lending rate in force at that date

V = the VAT fraction (currently 7/47ths)

Compulsory loans with minimal interest. If interest charged is commercially unrealistic, the same calculation should be performed as above except that I is the difference between the base lending rate and the interest actually paid. If the difference between the two rates is negligible, no calculation is necessary.

Compulsory 'permanent' loans. These require members to lend a specified sum which is only repaid on cessation of membership. No interest is payable during membership but on cessation the ex-member receives a sum in excess of that originally lent (perhaps based on inflation). The same calculation should be performed as above except that, before applying the VAT fraction, the total of 'excess' payments to outgoing members in the preceding year should be deducted from L × I.

Compulsory loans which become voluntary donations. At the end of the specified loan period, members may decide that the club can retain the money permanently. Provided this is done voluntarily, the loan can be regarded as having been converted into an outside the scope donation and the club will no longer be required to account for notional interest.

Voluntary interest-free loans. C & E's policy has been to treat such loans according to whether lenders receive any preferential treatment.

● Where no benefits are received, no VAT is due.

● Where subscriptions are reduced or waived, members are treated as having received the rights of membership but for a non-monetary consideration. The value is determined by reference to the subscriptions paid by members who have not made loans. However, where the majority of members have made loans, the subscription cannot be regarded as the normal monetary equivalent and the notional interest calculation should be used instead.

● Where subscriptions are not reduced but additional advantages are offered, the notional interest calculation as above should be used if the advantages are not available to anyone else. Otherwise, the value of the loan is determined by how much others pay for the additional advantages.

Interest free loans with compulsory and voluntary elements. Each element of the loan should be valued separately as above.

See also *Exeter Golf and Country Club Ltd v C & E Commrs CA, [1981] STC 211* and *Dyrham Park Country Club Ltd [1978] VATTR 244 (700)*.

Match and training fees are taxable at the standard rate on full gross receipts before deduction of expenses (e.g. referees, catering).

Prizes in cash and the award of challenge cups and other perpetual trophies remaining the property of the club are outside the scope of VAT. Prizes of goods are regarded as gifts and VAT must be accounted for on the full value if the cost exceeds £15. Otherwise no VAT is due.

Shares and debentures. These are used by clubs to raise extra finance from members or prospective members. It is necessary to consider:

* Whether or not there is a single supply (and, if so, whether it is of an exempt security or standard-rated subscriptions).

* If there is a mixed supply, can either element be disregarded on minimal grounds.

* Whether the standard-rated benefits are only being granted as an inducement to persuade people to acquire the exempt supply. C & E's policy is to reject this argument but see *Hinckley Golf Club Ltd, [1992] VATTR 259 (9527)* where the tribunal held that the offer of free membership to certain shareholders was simply an inducement to invest and the only supply to those shareholders was an exempt supply of shares in consideration for the purchase price of those shares.

Where any part of the consideration for a share or debenture is to be treated as an additional payment for the advantages of membership, it should be treated as a levy or, for non-monetary consideration, as an interest-free loan (see above).

Sponsorship rights are taxable at the standard rate on money received from the sponsor and payments made by the sponsor to third parties in respect of expenses and prizes. See 58.18 RECREATION AND SPORT.

Telephone coin boxes. See 47.12 OUTPUT TAX.

(C & E Leaflet 701/5/90 Annex; C & E Manual V1-6, Chapter 3 section 6, paras 3.4, 3.5 and Annex paras 5-8).

14.6   **NON-BUSINESS ACTIVITIES**

If an association etc. has subscriptions which are wholly outside the scope of VAT (see 14.10 below) then the servicing of the membership (e.g. arrangement of the annual general meeting) is a non-business activity for VAT.

Any association, whether or not its provision of membership benefits is a business activity, may have non-business activities i.e. activities not predominantly concerned with the making of supplies for a consideration (e.g. free admission to premises or free literature for non-members and spreading political beliefs or lobbying for a cause). See 8 BUSINESS generally for what constitutes a business for VAT purposes. Any VAT incurred for the purpose of non-business activities is not input tax and cannot be deducted. If the association has both business and non-business activities, VAT incurred must be apportioned. See 35.7 INPUT TAX.

(C & E Leaflet 701/5/90, para 6).

14.7   **TRADE UNIONS, PROFESSIONAL BODIES AND LEARNED SOCIETIES**

The provision of facilities and advantages to members of clubs, associations and other organisations is normally standard-rated (see 14.1 above) but their provision by certain professional, learned or representational associations can be exempt. See 22.17(*l*) and (*o*) EUROPEAN COMMUNITY LEGISLATION for the provisions of the *EC 6th Directive*.

The eligible organisations are those 'non-profit making' bodies falling into one of the following categories.

(*a*)   **Trade unions and other organisations** whose main objectives are to negotiate the terms and conditions of employment of their members.

'*Trade union*' is an organisation (whether permanent or temporary) which consists wholly or mainly of

- workers of one or more descriptions; or

- constituent or affiliated organisations; or

- representatives of such constituent or affiliated organisations. The principal purposes of the organisation must include the regulation of relations between workers and employers or employers' associations.

[*VATA 1994, 9 Sch Group 9, Item 1(a); Trade Union and Labour (Consolidation) Act 1992, s 1*].

EC 6th Directive, Art 13(A)(l) (in English translation) refers to 'organisations with aims of a . . . trade-union . . . nature'. The CJEC has held this to mean 'an organisation whose main aim is to defend the collective interests of its members—whether they are workers, employers, independent professionals or traders carrying on a particular economic activity—and to represent them vis-à-vis the appropriate third parties, including the public authorities' provided those objects were put into practice. (*Institute of the Motor Industry v C & E Commrs, CJEC [1998] STC 1219*).

(*b*) **Professional associations,** membership of which are 'wholly or mainly' restricted to individuals who have or are seeking a qualification appropriate to the practice of the profession concerned. [*VATA 1994, 9 Sch Group 9, Item 1(b)*].

Membership of the association should be obligatory, or at least customary, for those pursuing a career in that profession.

'*Wholly or mainly*'. C & E regard any association with a membership comprising of 75% or more individuals as satisfying this criterion. Professional firms which have partnership status can be regarded as individuals.

The qualifications held or sought must relate to what is a recognised profession. They should be obligatory or customary to enable the profession to be undertaken and should be awarded by the association of which the holder is a member.

'Profession' is not defined but C & E regard it as restricted to those occupations which would be generally understood to be professions. Indications which point towards this are

- the status of the occupation and those engaged in it;

- whether or not persons within the occupation require a qualification;

- whether the persons within the occupation are governed by a code of conduct;

- a distinctive and broad base of knowledge from which a person may subsequently diversify into more specialised areas;

- the association's aims and objectives; and

- the actual activities carried out by it.

However, these are not fixed criteria and some occupations which are not currently regarded as professions may acquire that status in the future.

(C & E Notice 701/33/97, para 2.4).

Bookmaking (*The Bookmakers' Protection Association (Southern Area) Ltd, [1979] VATTR 215 (849)*), driving a taxi-cab (*City Cabs (Edinburgh) Ltd (928)*) and the practice of reflexology (*The Association of Reflexologists (13078)*) have been held not to be professions but the teaching of dance has been so held (*Allied Dancing Association Ltd, [1993] VATTR 405 (10777)*). See also *Institute of Leisure and Amenity Management v C & E Commrs QB, [1988] STC 602*. For a fuller list of associations which have been held to fall within or, as the case may be, outside these provisions, see the chapter *Trade Unions and Professional Bodies* in Tolley's VAT Cases.

(c) **Learned societies**, i.e. any association, the 'primary purpose' of which is the advancement of a particular 'branch of knowledge' or the fostering of professional expertise, connected with the past or present professions or employments of its members. Membership must be restricted 'wholly or mainly' to individuals whose present or previous professions or employments are directly connected with the purposes of the association. [*VATA 1994, 9 Sch Group 9, Item 1(c)*].

'*Primary purpose*'. An association can have only one primary purpose (although it does not have to be the sole purpose) which should be clear from

- the objects and objectives set out in the memorandum and articles of association or constitution;

- the powers and actual activities of the association;

- what the association itself and the members consider its primary purpose to be.

The '*branch of knowledge*' must be a recognised branch of science or the arts and should therefore be more academic than practical in content. Normally it would be included in a degree course or equivalent. Knowledge relating to the confined area of a specific job does not constitute a branch of knowledge.

See (b) above for a consideration of 'profession'. Professional expertise is construed accordingly.

'*Wholly or mainly*' is regarded as 75% or more.

(C & E Notice 701/33/97, para 2.5).

See *Royal Photographic Society [1978] VATTR 191 (647)* (where lack of the restriction on membership disqualified the Society from exemption) and *Institute of Leisure and Amenity Management v C & E Commrs QB, [1988] STC 602*.

(d) **Representational trade associations**, i.e. any association, the 'primary purpose' of which is to make representations to the Government on legislation and other public matters which affect the business or professional interests of its members. Membership must be restricted 'wholly or mainly' to individuals or corporate bodies whose business or professional interests are directly connected with its aims. [*VATA 1994, 9 Sch Group 9, Item 1(d)*].

See (c) above for the primary purpose test. The representations should be to the UK government.

'*Wholly or mainly*' is regarded as 75% or more.

(C & E Notice 701/33/97, para 2.6).

(e) An organisation or association, the membership of which consists wholly or mainly of constituent or affiliated associations which as individual associations would be within (a) to (d) above. [*VATA 1994, 9 Sch Group 9, Note (3)*].

'*Non-profit making*'. A body whose constitution, articles of association, etc. bars it from distributing surpluses of income over expenditure to members, shareholders or any other party (other than in the event of liquidation or cessation of activities) is normally accepted as non-profit making for these purposes. Another factor in judging whether an organisation is non-profit making is the objects for which it has been established as distinct from its financial policy. Although an organisation may generate income surpluses from various activities, it will not be refused recognition as a non-profit making organisation simply because these surpluses subsidise other activities. (C & E Notice 701/33/97, para 2.2).

De Voil Indirect Tax Service. See V4.156; V6.173-174A.

14.8 Clubs and Associations

14.8   **Exempt supplies**

Supplies of services, and related goods, by a non-profit-making body within 14.7(*a*)-(*d*) above to its members are exempt provided

- they are made available without payment (other than a membership subscription); and

- they relate only to the aims of the organisation.

[*VATA 1994, 9 Sch Group 9, Item 1*].

Exemption does not apply to

(*a*)   supplies that do not relate to the body's aims as set out in its rules, articles of association, constitution, etc. (although see 14.9 below for provision of hospitality to members);

(*b*)   the supply of any right of admission to any premises, event or performance (e.g. for a conference) for which non-members have to pay [*VATA 1994, 9 Sch Group 9, Note (1)*];

(*c*)   any supplies which are not provided automatically as part of the membership benefits and for which an additional sum is charged; and

(*d*)   supplies to non-members.

Supplies within (*a*)-(*d*) above are taxable unless exempt under any other provision. These might include training under *VATA 1994, 9 Sch Group 6* (see 20.6 EDUCATION), one-off fund-raising events within 14.11 below, and sporting services under *VATA 1994, 9 Sch Group 10* (see 58.9 RECREATION AND SPORT).

Where any clearly identifiable zero-rated benefits (such as a year book) are provided in return for members' subscriptions, such supplies can be treated as zero-rated and any related input tax can be recovered, subject to the normal rules.

Value of exempt supply. The value of the exempt supply is normally the full amount of the subscriptions. Where, however, subscriptions also cover taxable supplies (including zero-rated supplies) the subscriptions must be apportioned. See 47.3 OUTPUT TAX.

Discounted admission charges and exclusive right of attendance. With effect from July 1997, where subscriptions are apportioned and

- subscription benefits include a right to a discount on admission charges, or an exclusive right of attendance, to a taxable event such as a conference, seminar or dinner (but not a social event such as a Christmas meal or dance);

- a separate charge is made to members for admission to the event concerned; and

- the event is linked to the aims of the organisation and is self-financing (i.e. not subsidised from subscription income)

those rights are treated as part of the exempt element of the subscription. Previously, C & E had treated such rights as standard-rated. Repayment claims may be made for periods before July 1997 (subject to the three-year cap). All payments for admission additional to the subscription are standard-rated.

(C & E Notice 701/33/97, paras 3.2-3.7; VAT Information Sheet 5/97, July 1997).

14.9   **Other supplies**

Registration fees. In certain professions, persons cannot practice unless they are registered with a statutory body and have paid fees which are prescribed by law. Such registration fees are normally outside the scope of VAT because, in carrying out these statutory functions, the organisation is not supplying a service in the course of its business. Where, however, there is no such statutory requirement, the liability is as follows.

- *Registration in return for a subscription payment.* Where no additional fee is charged and the member is automatically registered on payment of the subscription, the service of registration is standard-rated unless referable to the aims of the association in which case it qualifies for exemption under 14.8 above.

- *Registration for a separate fee.* As the registration is in return for a payment 'other than a membership subscription' it cannot qualify for exemption under 14.8 above and is standard-rated.

If the registration is accompanied by other clearly identifiable supplies of goods or services, the fee must be apportioned accordingly.

Collection charges for union subscriptions. Charges raised by employers for deducting union subscriptions from employees' pay are exempt under *VATA 1994, 9 Sch Group 5*. See 27.10 FINANCE.

Provision of hospitality. Where meals, hotel accommodation, etc. are provided to members without charge, then unless directly connected with the organisation's aims (e.g. at the annual conference), the supply is standard-rated and the subscription must be apportioned. Such hospitality is not business entertainment (because the membership in general is paying for it in the subscription) and input tax incurred can therefore be deducted, subject to the normal rules. The business entertaining provisions do apply to free hospitality to non-members and input tax cannot be deducted.

The provision of hospitality for a charge to members or non-members is standard-rated.

(C & E Notice 701/33/97, paras 3.8–3.10).

14.10   **ORGANISATIONS OF A POLITICAL, RELIGIOUS, PHILANTHROPIC, PHILOSOPHICAL OR PATRIOTIC NATURE**

Where a body has objects which are in the public domain and are of a political, religious, philanthropic, philosophical or patriotic nature, it is not to be treated as carrying on a business only because its members subscribe to it if a subscription obtains no facility or advantage for the subscriber other than the right to participate in its management or receive reports on its activities. [*VATA 1994, s 94(3)*]. The subscription income of any such association is regarded as 'non-business' and outside the scope of VAT. A working men's club has been held to be outside the exception (*Southchurch Workingmen's Clubs and Institute Ltd (613)*).

'*Public domain*'. To benefit from this 'non-business' treatment, the body must be in the '*public domain*'. This covers bodies that benefit, or are of concern to, the general public or a substantial part thereof. The essential requirement is that the aims of the body must be directed outside the particular organisation and beyond the members themselves to the general community. See also *The English-Speaking Union of the Commonwealth, [1980] VATTR 184 (1023)*.

'*Right to participate in management*' covers all those participatory activities that are a necessary part of running the organisation (e.g. the right to attend and vote at annual general or extraordinary meetings) but not the right to attend meetings or events that are not connected with the management of the body.

'*Right to receive reports*' covers those reports that arise from the management activities (e.g. annual accounts and annual general meeting reports). Reports that are a 'bare summary' of the body's activities for the past period are also allowed but not any literature that goes beyond this (e.g. containing letters, general information items, stories or competitions).

(C & E Manual V1-6, Chapter 3 section 6, paras 2.2, 2.4).

Other facilities available to members cannot be ignored on *de minimis* grounds. See, for example, *The English-Speaking Union of the Commonwealth* above where the only additional advantages available to members over non-members were a journal published every few months issue free (15p to non-members) and the ability to obtain contacts and introduction to other members.

Where the body supplies any other benefits to members, it falls within the 'deemed business' provision in *VATA 1994, s 94(2)(a)* (see 14.1 above) and its subscriptions are liable to VAT in the ordinary way (see 14.2 above).

Fund-raising events. See 14.11 below.

14.11   **FUND-RAISING EVENTS BY NON-PROFIT MAKING BODIES**

The supply of goods and services by

- any non-profit making body within 14.7(*a*)–(*e*) above or 14.10 above,

- any non-profit making body established for the principal purpose of providing facilities for participating in sport or physical education, or

- any body which is an eligible body for the purposes of *VATA 1994, 9 Sch Group 13, Item 2* (see 58.6 RECREATION AND SPORT)

in connection with a 'fund-raising event' organised exclusively for its own benefit is exempt.

[*VATA 1994, 9 Sch Group 12, Item 2 and Note 3; SI 1996/1256*].

The provisions also apply to fund-raising events organised for charitable purposes by a charity. See 12.9 CHARITIES for further details of qualifying events etc. which apply equally to events organised by the above bodies.

15   Confidentiality of Information

15.1   DISCLOSURE OF INFORMATION BY C & E

C & E are authorised to disclose information to the following.

- **Inland Revenue.** C & E are authorised to disclose information to the Commissioners of Inland Revenue (or an authorised officer of the Commissioners) to assist them in the performance of their duties. Information may also be disclosed for the purposes of any proceedings connected with the duties performed. [*FA 1972, s 127*]. In practice, exchanges of information take place at local level with particular emphasis on combating large cases of suspected tax evasion. (C & E News Release 12/88, 8 March 1988).

- **DSS.** With effect from 2 July 1997, C & E may disclose information to the DSS for the purposes of preventing, detecting, investigating and prosecuting offences relating to social security and for maintaining and improving the accuracy of social security information. [*Social Security Administration (Fraud) Act 1997, s 1; SI 1997/1577*].

- **Office for National Statistics or the Departments of Trade and Industry.** For statistical purposes, C & E are authorised to disclose VAT registration numbers allocated to persons and reference numbers for members of a group; the names, trading styles and addresses of persons so registered or of members of groups and status and trade classifications of businesses; and actual or estimated value of supplies. The information disclosed may be further disclosed only to another government department for similar purposes. Otherwise it may only be disclosed with the consent of the registered person or in such a form that individual particulars cannot be identified. [*VATA 1994, s 91; SI 1996/273*].

- **Isle of Man Customs and Excise** may be given information for the purpose of facilitating the proper administration of common duties and the enforcement of prohibitions or restrictions on imports or exports between the IOM and the UK. [*IMA 1979, s 10*].

- **Tax Authorities of other EC countries** provided they observe rules of confidentiality not less strict than in the UK and use the information for tax purposes or to facilitate legal proceedings for failure to observe the tax laws of the receiving country. [*FA 1978, s 77; FA 1980, s 17(2)(3); FA 1990, s 125(5)*]. Under *EC Council Directives Nos 77/799/EEC* and *79/1070/EEC* information may be exchanged (i) on the request of an EC country (although the other country need not comply if the requesting country has not exhausted its own usual sources of information) [*Article 2*]; (ii) regularly in certain determined categories of cases [*Article 3*]; and (iii) spontaneously where there may be a loss of tax in the other EC country [*Article 4*].

De Voil Indirect Tax Service. See V1.221.

15.2   Penalties for disclosure of information

A person who discloses any information which he holds or has held in the exercise of 'tax functions' is guilty of an offence if it is information about any matters relevant, for the purposes of those functions, to tax or duty in the case of any identifiable person.

'*Tax functions*' means, *inter alia*, functions relating to tax or duty of C & E and its officers and persons carrying out the administration work of any VAT tribunal, together with any other person providing, or employed in the provision of, services to any such officer or person.

The provisions do not apply to any disclosure of information with 'lawful authority'; with the consent of any person in whose case the information is about a matter relevant to tax or duty; or which has been lawfully made available to the public before the disclosure is made. A disclosure of information is made with '*lawful authority*' if, and only if, it is made

(*a*) by a Crown servant in accordance with his official duty,

(*b*) by any other person for the purposes of the function in the exercise of which he holds the information and without contravening any restriction duly imposed by the '*person responsible*' i.e. the Commissioners,

(*c*) to, or in accordance with an authorisation duly given by, the person responsible,

(*d*) in pursuance of any enactment or of any order of a court, or

(*e*) in connection with the institution of, or otherwise for the purposes of, any proceedings relating to any matter within the general responsibility of C & E.

It is a defence for a person charged under these provisions to prove that, at the time of the alleged offence, he believed that he had lawful authority to make the disclosure and had no reasonable cause to believe otherwise *or* he believed that the information had previously been lawfully made available to the public and had no reasonable cause to believe otherwise.

A person guilty of an offence under these provisions is liable, on conviction on indictment, to imprisonment for a term not exceeding two years or a fine or both, and on summary conviction, to imprisonment for a term not exceeding six months or a fine not exceeding the statutory maximum or both.

A prosecution for an offence under these provisions is instituted by the Commissioners or by or with the consent of the Director of Public Prosecutions (or NI equivalent).

Similar provisions apply to the Board of Inland Revenue.

[*FA 1989, s 182*].

15.3   DISCLOSURE OF INFORMATION TO C & E

The following are authorised to disclose information to C & E.

- **Inland Revenue.** The Inland Revenue are authorised to disclose information to the Commissioners (or an authorised officer of the Commissioners) to assist them in the performance of their duties. Information may also be disclosed for the purposes of any proceedings connected with the duties performed. [*FA 1972, s 127*]. In practice, exchanges of information take place at local level with particular emphasis on combating large cases of suspected tax evasion. (C & E News Release 12/88, 8 March 1988).

- **DSS.** With effect from 2 July 1997, the DSS are authorised to pass information to the Commissioners (or any person by whom services are being provided to the Commissioners) for use in the prevention, detection, investigation or prosecution of offences which it is the function of C & E to prevent, etc. The information may also be used in connection with the assessment or determination of non-criminal penalties and to check the accuracy of information held by C & E. [*FA 1997, s 110; SI 1997/1603*].

15.4   CORRESPONDENCE, ETC. BETWEEN BUSINESSES AND THEIR TAX ADVISERS

Information relating to goods and services, etc. C & E need access to information relating to goods and services and to their supply, acquisition or importation, to enable them to check the amounts of VAT payable or recoverable by a business and to ensure that liabilities are correctly accounted for. They have statutory powers of access in this respect.

Confidential advice by tax advisers. As part of their services to clients, tax advisers communicate with clients or other tax advisers to give or obtain opinions or advise about client's past and future affairs. Such communications may include notes of meetings and telephone calls, internal memoranda, letters and faxes. C & E will not normally request a tax adviser or trader to produce such a communication relating to confidential opinions or advice. Auditors' working papers and management letters also fall into this category unless containing information relating to goods and services, etc.

Mixed information. Where a document (e.g. working papers or a management letter) contains both information relating to goods and services (e.g. details about the origins of figures in accounts, returns and other information submitted to C & E, or the relationship of those figures with the books and records of the business) and confidential advice, C & E will normally accept an extract from the document. This should be supported by a written statement from the tax adviser or auditor that in his opinion C & E do not have the power to see the other part or parts of the document.

(C & E Leaflet 700/47/93).

16 Customs and Excise: Explanatory Notices, Etc.

16.1   C & E publish Notices and Information Sheets on VAT. (In the past, they have also published Leaflets associated with Notices but as these are updated and replaced, they are redesignated as Notices.)

Current issues of Notices, Leaflets and Information Sheets are listed below, together with a table of references to where they are covered in the text.

NOTICE AND LEAFLETS

48   **Extra-statutory concessions (1997)**
            See 26 EXTRA-STATUTORY CONCESSIONS for full listing.
700   **The VAT guide (1996 with Updates 1 to 3)**

para 3.1	69.2, 69.5, 69.6
para 3.2	47.3
para 3.3	47.6
para 3.4	47.8
para 3.5	27.19
para 3.7	64.4
para 3.10	47.4
para 3.13	47.5
para 3.14	47.10
para 3.16	47.12
para 3.17	33.4
para 3.18	11.5
para 4.6	35.7
paras 4.7, 4.8	35.13
para 4.9	35.10
para 5.1	64.37, 64.39, 64.49, 64.50
para.5.2	64.26
para 5.4	27.19, 64.57
para 6.1	40.12
para 6.3	40.4
paras 6.5, 6.6	40.7
para 6.7	40.8
paras 6.8, 6.9	40.2
para 6.10	40.11
para 6.11	40.13
para 6.12	40.14
paras 7.1, 7.2	40.15
para 7.3	2.18
para 8.1	57.1, 57.3, 57.4, 57.13
para 8.3	57.1
para 8.4	57.5
para 8.5	57.6
para 8.6	57.7
para 8.7	57.8
para 8.8	57.9
para 8.9	57.10
para 9.4	2.2
para 9.6	2.4, 52.15

16.1 Customs and Excise: Explanatory Notices, Etc.

16.1   Customs and Excise: Explanatory Notices, Etc.

16.1 Customs and Excise: Explanatory Notices, Etc.

16.1 Customs and Excise: Explanatory Notices, Etc.

16.1   Customs and Excise: Explanatory Notices, Etc.

16.1 Customs and Excise: Explanatory Notices, Etc.

16.1 Customs and Excise: Explanatory Notices, Etc.

16.1 Customs and Excise: Explanatory Notices, Etc.

17 Customs and Excise: Powers

Cross-references. See 6.1 ASSESSMENTS for powers of C & E to raise assessments and to assess an over-repayment and 6.3 for assessments of penalties, interest and surcharges; 8.5 BUSINESS for powers to make a direction treating two or more persons as one taxable person; 15.1 CONFIDENTIALITY OF INFORMATION for the power to disclose or exchange information with other authorities and government departments; 31.5 GROUPS OF COMPANIES for powers re groups; 51.6 PAYMENT OF VAT for power to withhold a repayment of VAT due where returns are outstanding; 52.2–52.4 PENALTIES for powers of arrest; 52.20 PENALTIES for power of mitigation; 57.1 RECORDS for the power to require records to be kept; and 59.10 REGISTRATION for powers to enforce compulsory deregistration.

17.1 POWER TO REQUIRE SECURITY AND PRODUCTION OF EVIDENCE

C & E may require a taxable person to

(*a*) produce documents relating to VAT (e.g. invoices) supplied to him as a condition of allowing or repaying any input tax;

(*b*) give such security as appears appropriate to them as a condition of making any VAT credit; and

(*c*) give security, or further security, of such amount and in such manner as they determine, against the payment of any VAT due, or which may become due

  (i) as a condition of his supplying goods or services under a taxable supply; or

  (ii) because he has failed to appoint a VAT representative when required to do so (see 4.8 AGENTS).

[*VATA 1994, s 48(7), 11 Sch 4*].

C & E may issue a notice of requirement to give security where persons concerned in the business are connected with past failures to pay VAT due, have failed to comply with VAT obligations on more than one occasion or have been prosecuted or penalised for a VAT offence. They may also require security where the business is run by disqualified directors or undischarged bankrupts. The amount of the security is normally based on the estimated VAT liability for six months (four months if monthly returns are made) but may also include any outstanding VAT due. There is no rule to prevent security being required in excess of estimated liabilities (*Labelwise Ltd (1499)*). Security must normally be provided by cash or banker's draft or by guarantee from an approved financial institution and should be sent to C & E within 30 days of the date of the notice. It will be held until C & E consider the risk to the collection of VAT no longer applies.

(C & E Notice 700/52/96).

Although an appeal may be made against the security demanded under (*c*) above (see 5.3(*l*) APPEALS), any person who supplies taxable goods or services without giving the security demanded, is liable to a penalty. See 52.6 PENALTIES.

In *Mr Wishmore Ltd v C & E Commrs QB, [1988] STC 723*, Farquarson J held that the jurisdiction of the tribunal was supervisory rather than appellate. The tribunal could only interfere if the decision of C & E was one which no reasonable body could have come to. The tribunal was not concerned with standards of proof and should not proceed on the basis of possible loss of revenue. It should restrict itself to considering whether the appellant had established whether the decision of C & E was unreasonable and whether it took into account irrelevant considerations or ignored relevant ones. The decision in *Mr Wishmore Ltd* has been applied in a very large number of subsequent cases. In *C & E*

Commrs v Peachtree Enterprises Ltd QB, [1994] STC 747 Dyson J confirmed the supervisory role of the tribunal and observed that 'in exercising its supervisory jurisdiction the tribunal must limit itself to considering facts and matter which existed at the time the challenge to the decision was taken' and should not, for example, take into account the fact that the person concerned had subsequently made all returns and paid the VAT due on time.

Where it is shown that C & E failed to take additional information into account, an appeal against the requirement to give security may still be dismissed if, had the additional material been taken into account, the decision would *inevitably* have been the same (*C & E Commrs v John Dee Ltd CA, [1995] STC 941*).

A tribunal has no jurisdiction to hear an appeal against the requirement to give security under (*b*) above. See *Strangewood Ltd (No 2) [1988] VATTR 35 (2599)*.

De Voil Indirect Tax Service. See V5.186.

17.2   RECOVERY OF VAT

Where an invoice shows a supply of goods or services with VAT chargeable on it, the person issuing the invoice is liable for the amount of VAT shown (or the amount of VAT included if not shown separately) whether or not

(*a*)   the invoice has been correctly prepared as required by the legislation (see 40 INVOICES);

(*b*)   the supply actually takes, or has taken, place;

(*c*)   the amount shown as VAT, or any amount of VAT, is or was chargeable on the supply; or

(*d*)   the person issuing the invoice is a taxable person.

[*VATA 1994, 11 Sch 5(1)–(3)*].

If any of the conditions in (*b*)–(*d*) above are not met, the sum recoverable is not VAT due under *VATA 1994* but is a debt due to the Crown. The practical effect of this is that normal assessment procedures cannot be used. The recovery of the incorrectly shown VAT is effected by means of a formal demand letter.

Penalties for unauthorised issue of invoices (see 52.12 PENALTIES) and interest on late paid VAT (see 51.5 PAYMENT OF VAT) may also be due.

Concessionary reliefs. Where the amount shown on an invoice is not actually VAT, the person issuing the invoice has no legal entitlement to treat the VAT incurred on his own related purchases as input tax. Equally, the person receiving the invoice has no legal entitlement to claim the VAT shown on the invoice as input tax. However, by concession, C & E may allow

- VAT incurred on purchases directly related to the invoiced supplies to be treated as input tax and deducted from the amount due provided

    (i)   a supply has taken place;

    (ii)   there is satisfactory evidence of the VAT incurred;

    (iii)   there is positive evidence of costing the supply on the VAT-exclusive cost of the trader's purchases;

    (iv)   the input tax does not exceed the amount recoverable from the supplier under *VATA 1994, 11 Sch 5* above; and

    (v)   the claim does not include VAT on capital goods or petrol; and

- the customer, if he acted in good faith, to retain the amount of input tax deducted.

(C & E Notice 48, ESC 2.9; C & E Manual V1-24, section 2.43).

Partnerships. See also 50.4 PARTNERSHIPS for recovery of VAT from individual partners.

VAT due to other EC countries. The provisions of *Council Directives 76/308/EEC and 79/1071/EEC* have been enacted in the UK as *FA 1977, s 11* and *FA 1980, s 17(1)*. C & E may recover a sum owed as undisputed VAT to a tax authority in another EC country as if it were a debt due to the Crown. Proceedings may be stayed in the UK if the defendant satisfies the court that proceedings are either pending or about to be instituted in the EC country concerned but this stay will be removed if no effort is made to promulgate proceedings there. If the defendant shows that a final decision has been given in his favour in the other EC country, that is sufficient defence in any UK proceedings.

De Voil Indirect Tax Service. See V1.222; V5.171.

17.3   DISTRESS (NOT SCOTLAND)

Where, following a written demand, a person neglects or refuses to pay any VAT due (or any amount recoverable as if it were VAT) a C & E officer may levy distress on that person's goods and chattels. He may also direct, by warrant, any authorised person to levy such distress in which case distress must be levied by or under the direction of, and in the presence of, that authorised person.

Goods and chattels subject to levy. Distress may be levied on any goods and chattels located in any place (including on the public highway) except for the following.

- Any of the under-mentioned goods and chattels which are located in a dwelling house and which are reasonably required for domestic needs of any person residing in that house:

  Beds and bedding; household linen; chairs and settees; tables; food; lights and lighting fittings; heating appliances; curtains; floor coverings; furniture, equipment and utensils for cooking, storing or eating food; refrigerators; articles used for cleaning, mending or pressing clothes; articles used for cleaning the home; furniture used for storing clothing, bedding, household linen, articles for cleaning the home and utensils for cooking or eating food; articles used for safety in the home; toys for the use of a child within the household; and medical aids and medical equipment;

- Any of the under-mentioned goods and chattels which are located in premises used for any profession, trade or business:

  Fire-fighting equipment for use on the premises; and medical aids and medical equipment for use on the premises.

Perishable goods which cannot be restored to the debtor in the same condition as when distress is levied are exempt from distress (*Morley v Pincombe, ExD 1848, 2 ExD 101*). Tools of the trade are only exempt from distress for rent and not for tax (*MacGregor v Clamp & Sons KB, [1914] 1 KB 288*).

Time limits. Where the VAT is due under *VATA 1994, s 73(9)* (see 6.1(*a*)-(*f*) ASSESSMENTS) distress cannot be levied during the period in which an appeal against the assessment can be raised (i.e. 30 days from the date of the assessment or such longer period as C & E allow for an appeal against it). The fact that distress has been correctly levied does not prevent a late appeal being entertained by a VAT tribunal (*PJ Davies, [1979] VATTR 162 (791)*).

A levy of distress must commence between 8 a.m. and 8 p.m. but may continue outside that period until the levying is complete. Where, however, a business is carried on partly or wholly outside these hours, a levy of distress may commence at any time during its business hours.

Costs. The owner of the goods and chattels is liable to pay the C & E officer or authorised person for costs in connection with the levying of distress, including scale charges for levying distress and taking possession of the goods, reasonable costs for appraising, removing and storing goods and advertising their sale, and scale charges for selling the goods based on the sum realised. An authorised person can retain costs out of the net proceeds but only after accounting for the VAT due to C & E. If there is any dispute with regard to costs, the amount must be taxed by a county court judge.

Sale. The goods and chattels taken must be kept for five days to allow the person in default time to settle the outstanding VAT and costs. Otherwise, the goods, etc. may be sold. Any surplus remaining, after retaining the VAT due and costs, must be restored to the owner of the goods.

[FA 1997, s 51; SI 1997/1431].

Before 1 July 1997, broadly similar provisions applied, the main differences being that only C & E officers of certain rank could levy distress and there were no regulations on goods subject to levy, times of day for levying distress or scale costs. [*VATA 1994, 11 Sch 5(4); FA 1997, 18 Sch; SI 1995/2518, Reg 212; SI 1996/2098; SI 1997/1433*].

De Voil Indirect Tax Service. See V5.173.

17.4   DILIGENCE (SCOTLAND)

Where any VAT (or any sum recoverable as if it were VAT) is due and has not been paid, the sheriff, on an application by C & E accompanied by a certificate by them, must grant a summary warrant in a form prescribed by Act of Sederunt authorising the recovery of the amount remaining due and unpaid by means of

- a poinding and sale in accordance with *Debtors (Scotland) Act 1987, 5 Sch* ;

- an earnings arrestment; or

- an arrestment and action of forthcoming or sale.

The certificate issued by C & E must state that none of the persons specified in the application has paid the VAT or other sum due from him; state that payment of the amount due from each such person has been demanded from him; and specify the amount due from and unpaid by each such person.

No fee must be charged by the sheriff to the debtor for collecting, and accounting to C & E for, sums paid to him by the debtor. Subject to this and without prejudice to *Debtors (Scotland) Act 1987, 5 Sch 25–34* (expenses of poinding and sale) the sheriff officer's fees, together with the outlays necessarily incurred, in connection with the execution of a summary warrant are chargeable against the debtor.

Both the application to the sheriff and the certificate may be made on behalf of C & E by a Collector or an officer of rank not below that of Job Band 7 (as defined). Such person is also authorised to do any of the acts which C & E are entitled to do as a creditor during the course of the poinding or sale (other than the exercise of the power under *Debtors (Scotland) Act 1987, 5 Sch 18(3)*).

[FA 1997, s 52, 18 Sch; SI 1995/2518, Reg 213; SI 1996/2098; SI 1997/1432].

De Voil Indirect Tax Service. See V5.173.

17.5   Customs and Excise: Powers

17.5   FURNISHING OF INFORMATION AND PRODUCTION OF DOCUMENTS

Furnishing of information. In order to maintain their records, C & E have powers to make regulations requiring taxable persons to notify them of any changes in personal or business circumstances. In addition, every person

(*a*)   who is concerned (in whatever capacity) in the supply of goods or services in the course or furtherance of a business, or

(*b*)   to whom a supply within (*a*) above is made, or

(*c*)   who is concerned (in whatever capacity) in the acquisition of goods from another EC country, or

(*d*)   who is concerned (in whatever capacity) in the importation of goods from a place outside the EC in the course or furtherance of business

must furnish C & E, within such time and in such form as they may reasonably require, such information relating to the goods or services or to the supply, acquisition or importation as C & E may reasonably specify.

[*VATA 1994, 11 Sch 7(1)(2)*].

The above does not entitle C & E to send an officer to put oral questions to a taxable person and demand oral answers on the spot (*C & E Commrs v Harz & Power HL 1966, [1967] 1 All ER 177*). See also *EMI Records Ltd v Spillane and Others CD, [1986] STC 374*.

Production of documents. In addition, any person who is connected (in whatever capacity) with the activities in (*a*)–(*d*) above must, upon demand by a person acting under the authority of C & E (an '*authorised person*') produce for inspection by that person any 'document' relating to the goods or services or to the supply, acquisition or importation. The document must be produced at the principal place of business (or at such other place as may be reasonably required) at such time as may be reasonably required. The authorised person also has power to require the production of the documents concerned from any other person who appears to be in possession of them (but without prejudice to any right of lien). He may take copies or make extracts of any document and may, at a reasonable time and for a reasonable period, remove any document, giving a receipt if requested. Where any document removed is reasonably required for the proper conduct of the business, a copy must be provided free of charge as soon as practicable. If any documents removed are lost or damaged, reasonable compensation must be paid. [*VATA 1994, 11 Sch 7(2)(3)(5)–(8)*].

'*Document*' means anything in which information of any description is recorded and '*copy*', in relation to a document, means anything onto which information recorded has been copied, by whatever means and whether directly or indirectly. [*VATA 1996, s 96(1); Civil Evidence Act 1995, 1 Sch 20*]. Any profit and loss account or balance sheet, relating to the business in the course of which the goods or services are supplied or the goods are imported, is included. In the case of an acquisition from another EC country, any profit and loss account or balance sheet relating to any business or other activity of the person by whom the goods are acquired is included. [*VATA 1994, 11 Sch 7(4)*].

C & E will generally examine the documents at the person's place of business and will only remove them when it is absolutely necessary, normally only with the agreement of the trader, etc. concerned.

De Voil Indirect Tax Service. See V5.234; V5.235.

17.6   **POWER TO TAKE SAMPLES**

A person acting under the authority of C & E may at any time, if he deems necessary on the grounds of fraud or mistake, take samples from the goods in the possession of

- any person who supplies goods or acquires them from another EC country, or

- a fiscal warehousekeeper

in order to determine how the goods, or the materials of which they are made, should be treated for VAT purposes. Any sample may be disposed of and accounted for as C & E may direct but where it is not returned in a reasonable time (not defined) and in good condition, C & E must pay compensation of the cost of the sample or any greater amount as they determine. [*VATA 1994, 11 Sch 8; FA 1996, 3 Sch 16*].

De Voil Indirect Tax Service. See V5.240.

17.7   **OPENING OF GAMING MACHINES**

A person acting under the authority of C & E may at any reasonable time require a person supplying services by means of gaming machines (or any person acting on his behalf) to open any gaming machine and to carry out any other operation which may be necessary in order to ascertain the value of taxable supplies. [*VATA 1994, 11 Sch 9*]. See 58.3 RECREATION AND SPORT for the definition of 'gaming machine'.

De Voil Indirect Tax Service. See V5.238.

17.8   **ENTRY AND SEARCH OF PREMISES AND PERSONS**

A person acting under the authority of C & E (an '*authorised person*') may at any reasonable time

(*a*)   enter premises used in connection with the carrying on of a business;

(*b*)   enter and inspect any premises and any goods found on them if he has reasonable cause to believe those premises are used as a fiscal warehouse or in connection with

   (i)   the supply of goods under taxable supplies, or

   (ii)   the acquisition of goods under taxable acquisitions from other EC countries

and that goods to be so supplied or acquired are on those premises.

[*VATA 1994, 11 Sch 10(1)(2); FA 1996, 3 Sch 17*].

Officers are invariably authorised in writing and instructed to produce the authority on request. Entry will normally be by prior appointment, e.g. under (*a*) for an audit visit (see 17.11 below). There is no requirement that the supplier is registered for VAT purposes. See 52.7 PENALTIES for obstruction of officers in the performance of their duties under *CEMA 1979, s 16*.

Use of warrants. A justice of the peace (justice in Scotland) may issue a written *warrant* authorising entry and search of premises, if necessary by force, if satisfied, on information under oath, that there are reasonable grounds for suspecting a 'fraud offence' which appears to be of a serious nature has been, is being or is about to be, committed or that evidence of such an offence is to be found there. The entry and search must be carried out within one month of the issue of the warrant. Any persons entering the premises under the authority of the warrant may, where there are reasonable grounds, seize and remove documents, etc. required as evidence in proceedings and search any person on the premises who may be in possession of documents, etc. No woman or girl may be searched except by a woman.

'*Fraud offence*' means any offence within *VATA 1994, s 72(1)–(8)*. See 52.2–52.4 PENALTIES.

Search warrants may specify the maximum number of authorised persons who may carry out the search and the times at which it may be exercised and may provide that a constable in uniform should be present. A copy of the warrant must be supplied to the occupier or person in charge of the premises or, failing this, must be left in a prominent place.

[*VATA 1994, 11 Sch 10(3)–(6); Criminal Procedure (Consequential Provisions) (Scotland) Act 1995, 4 Sch 91*].

See also 17.9 below for procedure where documents are removed.

For matters relating to issues of warrants generally, see *CIR and Another v Rossminster Ltd and Others HL 1979, 52 TC 106, [1980] STC 42*.

De Voil Indirect Tax Service. See V5.231–233.

17.9 ORDER FOR ACCESS TO RECORDED INFORMATION

On application, a justice of the peace (justice in Scotland) may make an order permitting a person acting under the authority of C & E (an '*authorised person*') to have access to, copy or make extracts from, or remove recorded information reasonably required. Where the recorded information consists of computer data, the information must be visible and legible and, if required, in a form which can be removed. The justice must be satisfied that there are reasonable grounds for believing that a VAT offence has, is being, or is about to be committed and that the information in the possession of the person named in the order may be required as evidence. The order must be acted upon within seven days of issue (or such longer period as the order specifies).

For the conditions for making an order, see *R v Epsom Justices (ex p Bell and Another) QB 1988, [1989] STC 169* and *R v City of London Magistrates (ex p Asif and Others) QB, [1996] STC 611*.

Procedure where documents are removed. Where an authorised person removes any documents under 17.8 above or recorded information under the above provisions, he must, on request and within a reasonable time, provide a record of what has been removed. The officer in overall charge of the investigation (i.e. the person whose name is endorsed on the order) must, on request, allow access to such documents etc. and allow them to be copied or photographed unless he has reasonable grounds for believing that to do so would prejudice any investigation or criminal proceedings. Where a person acting on behalf of C & E has failed to comply with these requirements, an application may be made to a magistrate's court (sheriff in Scotland and court of summary jurisdiction in Northern Ireland) which may order that person to comply.

[*VATA 1994, 11 Sch 11–13; Criminal Procedure (Consequential Provisions) (Scotland) Act 1995, 4 Sch 91*].

De Voil Indirect Tax Service. See V5.236.

17.10 POWER TO INSPECT COMPUTERS

Any provision of any Act which requires a person, in connection with an 'assigned matter', to

(*a*) produce, furnish or deliver any document (or cause any document to be produced, etc.); or

(*b*) permit C & E to inspect, copy or make extracts from, or remove any document

has effect as if any reference to a document were a reference to anything in which information of any description is recorded and any reference to a copy of a document were a reference to anything onto which information recorded in a document has been copied, by whatever means and whether directly or indirectly.

In connection with any assigned matter, a person authorised by C & E is entitled, at any reasonable time, to have access to, and to inspect and check the operation of, any computer and any associated apparatus or material which is, or has been, in use in connection with any document required to be produced, etc. under (a) above or made available under (b) above. The authorised person may also require the person by whom, or on whose behalf, the computer is used, or any person concerned in the operation of the computer, to give such assistance as is necessary.

Any person who obstructs an authorised person or who fails to assist him without reasonable excuse within a reasonable time, is liable, on summary conviction, to a penalty of level 4 on the standard scale laid down in *Criminal Justice Act 1982, s 75*.

'*Assigned matter*' means any matter in relation to which C & E are for the time being required in pursuance of any enactment to perform any duties.

[*FA 1985, s 10; Civil Evidence Act 1995, 1 Sch 11*].

De Voil Indirect Tax Service. See V5.237.

17.11   **AUDIT VISITS BY VAT OFFICERS**

A C & E officer will examine the business records, methods and premises and give guidance. C & E emphasise that it is the taxpayer's responsibility to account for VAT correctly. It cannot be assumed that this is so simply because a C & E officer does not find any errors. The interval between visits will vary depending on the size and complexity of the business and past compliance. Businesses which send in late or incorrect declarations and payments are visited more often. For a small business, a visit may only take a few hours; for a large or complex business it can last two or more days. A visit will normally take place at the main place of business. If records are kept elsewhere, C & E should be informed when the appointment is made. The person in charge of VAT affairs should be present. A professional adviser can also be there.

Before the visit, C & E will

• confirm who they will want to see;

• agree a mutually convenient appointment date and time;

• advise the name and contact number of the officer conducting the visit;

• indicate the records and relevant periods required;

• indicate the likely length of the visit;

• give the business the opportunity to indicate any matters of concern so that the officer can be better prepared; and

• give the business the option to have the above details confirmed in writing.

If it is necessary to postpone a visit, C & E should be given as much notice as possible.

On occasions, C & E will call without an appointment.

During a visit, C & E will

• identify themselves by name on arrival, and if requested, produce an identity card;

• explain the main purpose of the visit;

- discuss the various aspects of the business at the outset so as to keep claims on staff's time to a minimum (although new points may arise as they look at the records);

- examine the records of the business and, where appropriate, inspect the premises and goods thereon;

- where appropriate, take details of supplies made to/by the business to check the correct VAT treatment in the records of the business's suppliers/customers. (Occasionally, this will be the main purpose for the visit but C & E will explain this at the time they make the appointment.);

- deal with your VAT affairs confidentially;

- advise of overpayments as well as underpayments;

- where possible, endeavour to resolve matters during the visit.

At the end of the visit, C & E will

- review the main work done;

- explain any areas of concern in relation to that work, discuss them and agree any future action that needs to be taken; and

- illustrate as fully as possible the size and the reason for any adjustment to the VAT payable, describe how the adjustment will be made, agree the adjustment whenever possible, and inform the business of how it may seek review or appeal of the decision if it disagrees.

After the visit, C & E will

- where requested, or where they feel it is necessary, put in writing a summary of the visit, any rulings, agreements or recommendations; and

- where matters are unresolved, give the business a reasonable time within which to provide further information or comment.

(C & E Notice 700, para 14.2; C & E Notice 989).

De Voil Indirect Tax Service. See V5.221–224.

17.12   **ESTOPPEL**

Where, following a control visit or otherwise, a C & E officer makes representations which are later shown to be incorrect, a taxpayer may seek to claim that the doctrine of estoppel should be applied. This doctrine prevents a person from acting inconsistently with a representation which he has made to another party, in reliance upon which that other party has acted to his detriment. The representation may be by words, conduct or silence, but it must be a representation of existing fact and not a representation of law or of intention.

The position of C & E in relation to estoppel has not been considered by the courts in a VAT appeal. The appeal in *GUS Merchandise Corporation Ltd* below went to the courts but the estoppel position, considered by the tribunal, was not raised there.

It has been held that there is no question of estoppel against C & E (*Cupboard Love Ltd (267)*), the Crown (*T Wood (6992)*) or the mandatory provisions of a taxing statute (*Medlam (545)*). More specifically, there is no claim if the element of detriment or prejudice is lacking e.g. where on advice VAT has been incorrectly calculated but the taxpayer has had the benefit of the cash he should have accounted for at the time and there is no evidence that he has charged lower prices because of the advice (*Ribbans (346)*). It has also been held that an inspection of a trader's records and a general assurance that they are in order is insufficient to form the basis of an estoppel (*GUS Merchandise Corporation Ltd, [1978] VATTR 28 (553)*).

In Scotland, the equivalent of estoppel is a plea of personal bar. It has been held that such a plea, at all events in matters of taxation, does not operate against the Crown, following *Lord Advocate v Meiklam, (1860) 22 D 1427* and other authorities (*Milne and Mackintosh t/a Jack and Jill, [1981] VATTR 61 (1063)*).

C & E's practice where taxpayer misled by a VAT officer. C & E have indicated that where an officer, with the full facts before him, has given a clear and unequivocal ruling on VAT in writing, or it is established that an officer knowing the full facts has misled a trader to his detriment, they will only raise an assessment based on the correct ruling from the date the error was brought to the attention of the registered person concerned (*Hansard, 21 July 1978, col 426*) (C & E Notice 48, ESC 2.5). This practice is not, however, binding and should not be relied upon in all cases. It is not clear whether a tribunal has the jurisdiction to hear an appeal on whether circumstances fall within the statement of practice although a tribunal has found that a taxpayer was misled to such an extent that the statement was operative (*C & G Developments Ltd (2384)*).

De Voil Indirect Tax Service. See V1.236; V1.237.

17.13   EVIDENCE BY CERTIFICATE ETC.

A certificate of C & E of any of the following is sufficient evidence of that fact until proved to the contrary.

- A person was, or was not, at any date, registered.

- Any return required has not been made or had not been made at any date.

- Any EC sales list (see 2.19 ACCOUNTING PERIODS AND RETURNS) has not been submitted or had not been submitted by any given date.

- Notification of liability on an acquisition of exciseable goods or a new means of transport (see 23.9 and 23.35 EUROPEAN COMMUNITY: SINGLE MARKET) has not been given or had not been given by any date.

- Any VAT shown as due in any return or assessment has not been paid.

- A person was or was not, at any date, taxable in another EC country.

- Any VAT payable under the law of another EC country has or has not been paid.

A photograph of any document furnished to C & E, certified by them, is admissible in any civil or criminal proceeding to the same extent as the document itself.

Any document purporting to be a certificate under the above provisions is deemed to be such a certificate until the contrary is proved.

[*VATA 1994, s 92(5), 11 Sch 14*].

18 Customs and Excise: Standard Forms

De Voil Indirect Tax Service. See V16.1.

18.1 The following is a list of the more common standard forms issued by C & E for VAT use as indicated.

VAT 1	Application for registration (see 59.5 REGISTRATION)
VAT 1A	Application for VAT registration – distance selling (see 59.13 REGISTRATION)
VAT 1B	Application for VAT registration – acquisitions (see 59.20 REGISTRATION)
VAT 2	Notification of liability to be registered (partners' details, see 59.5 REGISTRATION)
VAT 4	Certificate of registration for VAT (see 59.5 REGISTRATION)
VAT 20	Welsh version of VAT 1 (see 59.5 REGISTRATION)
VAT 50	Application for corporate bodies to be treated as members of a group for VAT (see 31.3 GROUPS OF COMPANIES)
VAT 51	List of corporate bodies to be included in a group registration (see 31.3 GROUPS OF COMPANIES)
VAT 56	Application to change representative member of a group registration (see 31.3 GROUPS OF COMPANIES)
VAT 58	Group registration: advice of change in subsidiary member details
VAT 65	Refund: application by a taxable person not established in the country for a refund of VAT
VAT 65A	Application by a business person not established in the Community for refund of VAT
VAT 66	Certificate of status of taxable person
VAT 66A	Certificate of status of business person
VAT 68	Transfer of a business as a going concern – re-allocation of a VAT registration number (see 59.29 REGISTRATION)
VAT 98	Flat rate scheme for agriculture: application for certification (see 63.17 SPECIAL SCHEMES)
VAT 100	Tax return (see 2.5 ACCOUNTING PERIODS AND RETURNS)
VAT 101	EC sales list (see 2.23 ACCOUNTING PERIODS AND RETURNS)
VAT 101B	Correction of errors on EC sales list (see 2.24 ACCOUNTING PERIODS AND RETURNS)
VAT 110	Welsh version of VAT 100
VAT 126	Claim for refund of VAT under Sec 20 (local authorities and similar bodies) (see 43.5 LOCAL AUTHORITIES AND STATUTORY BODIES)
VAT 193	Final VAT return (see 2.3 ACCOUNTING PERIODS AND RETURNS)

VAT 195	Final demand for VAT
VAT 197	Welsh version of VAT 193
VAT 291	Civil penalty due (see 52.12 PENALTIES)
VAT 407	VAT refunds for visitors to the UK (see 25.12 EXPORTS)
VAT 410	Personal export of new motor vehicle (see 25.18 EXPORTS)
VAT 411	New means of transport for removal from the UK to another EC country (see 23.32 EUROPEAN COMMUNITY: SINGLE MARKET)
VAT 426	Insolvent Traders: Claims for input tax after deregistration (see 36.13 INSOLVENCY)
VAT 431	VAT refunds for DIY builders (see 42.53 LAND AND BUILDINGS)
VAT 435	VAT refunds for UK residents going abroad and crews of ships and aircraft (see 25.15 EXPORTS)
VAT 436	VAT-free purchases of sailaway boats (see 25.19 EXPORTS)
VAT 600	Application to join annual accounting scheme (see 63.10 SPECIAL SCHEMES)
VAT 652	Voluntary disclosure of errors on VAT returns (see 57.11 RECORDS)
VAT 769	Notification of insolvency details (see 36.2 INSOLVENCY)
VAT 811	Application by barristers for deferment of payment of VAT due on outstanding professional fees (see 64.58 SUPPLY)

See also 5.6 APPEALS for standard forms for use in connection with appeals and applications to VAT tribunals.

19 Death

19.1 VAT CONSEQUENCES OF DEATH

Assets passing to personal representative. Where the control of a deceased person's assets passes to a personal representative, that person must comply with the requirements of C & E but any liability to VAT is limited to the assets over which he has control. [*SI 1995/2518, Reg 30*].

Carrying on a business. Where a taxable person dies, C & E may, from the date of death until some other person is registered in respect of the taxable supplies made (or intended to be made) by a business, treat any person carrying on the business as a taxable person. The person carrying on the business must, within 21 days of commencing to do so, inform C & E in writing of the date of death and the fact that the business is being continued. [*VATA 1994, s 46(4); SI 1995/2518, Reg 9*].

Appeals to VAT tribunals. Where a person who is in the course of applying or appealing to a VAT tribunal dies and his liability or interest passes to another person (the 'successor'), the tribunal may direct, on the application of C & E or the successor, that the successor is substituted for the original applicant or appellant. Written consent is required from the successor. Where this is not received within two months of being requested by the tribunal, the tribunal may, of its own motion or on application by C & E, and after having given written notice to the successor, dismiss the application or appeal. It may similarly dismiss any application or appeal where it is satisfied that there is no person interested in it in succession to the original applicant or appellant. [*SI 1986/590, Rule 13; SI 1994/2617*].

19.2 VAT RELIEFS

Relief from VAT is given under the circumstances in 19.3 to 19.6 below.

19.3 Foreign legacies

A person who has become entitled as legatee to property situated outside the VAT territory of the EC (see 21.2 EUROPEAN COMMUNITY: GENERAL) may import into the UK, without payment of VAT or duty,

- household effects; and

- any personal property for personal use or meeting household needs including household pets and riding animals, cycles, motor vehicles and their trailers, caravans, pleasure boats and private aircraft.

Excluded are

- any goods which, by their nature or quantity, indicate that they are being imported for commercial purposes;

- alcoholic beverages and tobacco products;

- any motor road vehicle designed for or capable of carrying either more than nine persons including the driver or goods;

- any special purpose vehicle or mobile workshop;

- articles (other than portable instruments of the applied or liberal arts) used in the exercise of a profession or trade before his death by the person from whom the legatee has acquired them;

- stocks of raw materials and finished or semi-finished products; and
- livestock and agricultural products exceeding the quantities for normal family requirements.

The legatee must either be

(*a*) 'normally resident' in the UK or Isle of Man; or

(*b*) a 'secondary resident' who is not normally resident outside the VAT territory of the EC; or

(*c*) a body incorporated in the UK or Isle of Man, carrying on a non-profit making activity.

A person is '*normally resident*' in the country where he usually lives for a period (or periods) amounting to at least 185 days in a twelve month period because of his 'occupational ties' and/or 'personal ties'. Where he has occupational ties in one country and personal ties in another country he is treated as being normally resident in the latter country provided *either* his stay in the former is in order to carry out a task of definite duration *or* he returns regularly to the country where he has personal ties. Notwithstanding this, a UK citizen whose personal ties are in the UK but whose occupational ties are outside the VAT territory of the EC may for the purposes of this relief be treated as normally resident in the country of his occupational ties provided that he has lived there for a period or periods amounting to at least 185 days in a twelve month period.

'*Occupational ties*' do not include attendance by a pupil or student at a school, college or university.

'*Personal ties*' means family or social ties to which a person devotes most of his time not devoted to occupational ties.

A '*secondary resident*' is a person who, without being normally resident in the UK or Isle of Man, has a home there which he owns or is renting for at least twelve months.

Unless C & E allow otherwise, the property must be imported not later than two years after the date of entitlement as legatee is finally determined. At the time of importation etc., the person must produce the property to the proper officer for examination and furnish proof of his entitlement as legatee. See 19.4 below.

[*Customs and Excise Duties (General Reliefs) Act 1979, s 7; FA 1984, s 14; SI 1992/3193, Arts 2, 3, 8, 21*].

19.4   *Claiming relief*

Claims and enquiries should be made at VAT offices. The evidence required to establish the claim will normally include

- a certified copy of the will etc.;
- if the goods are not precisely specified in the will etc. (e.g. where they formed part of the residue) a declaration by the person winding up the estate that the goods formed part of that estate; and
- a declaration signed by the beneficiary or a solicitor acting for him.

See C & E Notice 368 for the importation procedures and documentation.

Release of goods. If C & E are satisfied, goods will be released without payment of duty or VAT. If the required documents and evidence are not immediately available, the goods can be released against a deposit to cover the VAT and duty. If the evidence is produced

19.5 Death

later, the deposit may be recovered. Duty and VAT may also be assessed if a postal packet is not properly marked. The goods will then only be delivered by the Post Office on payment of the charges. The addressee should pay the charges which will be refunded on submission to C & E of satisfactory documentation.

(C & E Notice 368).

Note. The fact that relief may be granted does not relieve the importer from compliance with requirements arising out of any relevant import prohibition or restriction e.g. quarantine and firearm licensing requirements.

19.5 Relief for imports re funerals, war graves

The following goods are relieved from VAT on importation from a country outside the EC.

- Goods imported by an approved organisation for use in the construction, upkeep or ornamentation of cemeteries, tombs and memorials in the EC which commemorate war victims of other countries.

- Coffins or urns containing human remains, together with accompanying flowers, wreaths or other ornamental objects.

- Flowers, wreaths or other ornamental objects imported without commercial intent by a person resident outside the EC for use at a funeral or to decorate a grave.

[*SI 1984/746, Art 2, 2 Sch Group 11; SI 1992/3120*].

19.6 American war graves

In order to place inland purchases on the same footing as imported goods, VAT is remitted on the supply of goods and services to the American Battle Monuments Commission for the maintenance of the American Military Cemetery and Memorial at Maddingley, Cambridge and Brookwood, Surrey. (C & E Notice 48, ESC 1.5).

19.7 BURIAL AND CREMATION

The disposal of the remains of the dead, and the making of arrangements for or in connection with the disposal of the remains of the dead, are exempt supplies. [*VATA 1994, 9 Sch Group 8*].

Supplies by undertakers.

Providing a funeral. The effect of *VATA 1994, 9 Sch Group 8* is that

(*a*) the supply of services of embalming and the digging and preparation of graves are always exempt supplies;

(*b*) if an undertaker supplies a coffin and the carriage of the deceased to the burial ground or crematorium, then that supply is exempt, together with

- the cover and fittings for the coffin;

- the casket or urn;

- a shroud or robe;

- use of a chapel of rest;

- provision of bearers;

- transport of mourners; and

- bell tolling and music at the funeral service; and

(c) if an undertaker is involved in arrangements which are directly connected to the disposal of the corpse, the supply is exempt even if a coffin is not provided (e.g. where a corpse is brought from a different part of the UK by another undertaker or repatriated from abroad).

If an undertaker sub-contracts services to a third party, the subcontractor's supplies to the undertaker are exempt if they amount to the supply of an exempt funeral.

Providing other services. The supply of goods or services not falling within (a) above by an undertaker who is not involved in the disposal of the body is standard-rated (e.g. the sale of a coffin to the bereaved or the hire of additional limousines to another undertaker).

The hire or letting out of a room or hall for a funeral reception is normally exempt unless the option to tax has been exercised (see 42.20 LAND AND BUILDINGS). The letting of a room in a hotel or similar establishment where catering is also provided is standard-rated (see 33.1 HOTELS AND HOLIDAY ACCOMMODATION).

Non-essential supplies are normally standard-rated. These include flowers, wreaths, commemorative items, announcement cards, newspaper announcements and refreshments.

Cemeteries and crematoria. Exempt supplies include

- burial or cremation in a cemetery or crematorium;

- the digging, preparation and refilling (but not the brick-lining) of a grave; and

- the supply of an urn or casket in connection with a particular funeral.

See also 19.8 below.

Any charge to a monumental mason for the right to operate in the cemetery or crematorium (e.g. the right to operate a showroom or to erect, work on or repair monuments) is standard-rated.

Commemoration of the dead. A monumental mason must standard-rate any supplies made in connection with the commemoration of the dead. This includes the supply, repair and maintenance of memorials, headstones, plaques, commemorative trees, memorial seats, etc. The inscription of memorials and the making of entries in a book of remembrance are also standard-rated.

Any charges for removing and re-fixing a gravestone or memorial (including incidental cleaning) to enable a further burial to take place is exempt, but VAT must be charged for adding another inscription to the gravestone, etc.

Single price packages. Where exempt supplies (including those relating to land under 19.8 below) and standard-rated commemorative items are provided as a single price package, a suitable apportionment must be made for VAT purposes (see 47.3 OUTPUT TAX).

Transport of corpses within the UK. Transport of a corpse as part of the supply of a funeral in the UK is exempt. The transport of a corpse to a university or other eligible body which supplies exempt research, and subsequently from the university, etc. to the place of burial or cremation, is also exempt. Other services (e.g. removal of a corpse from the scene of an accident to a mortuary) are standard-rated.

International transport of corpses. The transport of a corpse between the UK and a place outside the EC is zero-rated to the extent that it takes place in the UK and otherwise outside the scope of UK VAT. The transport of a corpse from the UK to another EC country is standard-rated unless the customer is registered for VAT in

19.8   Death

another EC country, in which case there is no need to charge VAT and the customer must account for the VAT due in the other EC country under the 'reverse charge' procedure.

Exhumation and reburial. Exhumation is standard-rated. The subsequent service of reburial is exempt unless carried out as part of a contract for the single supply of exhumation and reburial, in which case it is standard-rated.

Fees and certificates. Fees payable to

- churches and clergy in connection with funerals, and

- Registrars for certified copies of death certificates

are outside the scope of VAT.

Fees charged by a doctor for a certificate issued before a corpse can be cremated are exempt.

Disbursements. For the treatment of disbursements generally, see 4.7 AGENTS.

Funerals for pets are standard-rated.

(C & E Notice 701/32/97).

De Voil Indirect Tax Service. See V4.151.

19.8   Grants re land

The grant or an interest in, right over or licence to occupy land is exempt under *VATA 1994, 9 Sch Group 1*. This includes the right to a grave space, the right to construct a burial vault and the right to place an urn in a niche at a crematorium. (C & E Notice 701/32/97, para 2). The grantor has the option to tax any such supply at the standard rate (see 42.20 LAND AND BUILDINGS).

20   Education

Cross-references. See 22.17 EUROPEAN COMMUNITY LEGISLATION for the provisions of the *EC 6th Directive* ; 29.10 FUEL AND POWER for supplies of fuel and power to charitable schools; 32.10 HEALTH AND WATER UTILITIES for supplies by registered nurseries and playgroups.

De Voil Indirect Tax Service. See V4.141; V6.133; V6.134.

20.1   **EXEMPT SUPPLIES**

VAT exemption for education, research and training is largely dependent on

- whether the body is in business for VAT purposes (see 20.2 below); and
- if so, whether it is an eligible body (see 20.3 below).

Having established that the activities are business

(*a*)   supplies of education and vocational training by an eligible body are exempt (see 20.4 and 20.6 below respectively);

(*b*)   supplies of research by an eligible body to an eligible body are exempt (see 20.5 below); and

(*c*)   supplies of certain goods and services related to exempt supplies within (*a*) and (*b*) above are also exempt (see 20.7 below);

Exemption may also apply to private tuition (see 20.8 below) and examination services (see 20.9 below).

20.2   **Business**

For VAT purposes, business has a wide meaning and includes any continuing activity which is mainly concerned with making supplies to other persons for any form of payment or consideration. For a general consideration of the meaning of business, see 8.1 to 8.3 BUSINESS.

As regards education, where this is provided for payment in any form, monetary or otherwise, there is a supply for VAT purposes which will normally be in the course or furtherance of business. If there is no payment, the education is not a supply and is a non-business activity.

Education is normally funded in one of three ways.

- *By making a charge*, in which case it is a business activity whoever pays the charge (e.g. a student, an employer or a local authority) and whether charges raised are sufficient to meet full costs or are subsidised (e.g. by central government grant, bursaries or scholarships).

  Establishments which require payment and are therefore in business include

  - independent fee paying schools, including non-maintained special schools
  - universities
  - institutions teaching English as a foreign language

- *By direct funding from local or central government.* Education funded in this way is not a business activity and the supply is outside the scope of VAT. This will normally apply to
  - local authority schools

- voluntary aided schools
- voluntary controlled schools
- special agreement schools
- county schools
- grant-maintained schools
- grant-maintained (integrated) schools (Northern Ireland)
- self governing schools (Scotland)
- city technology colleges

● *By a combination of government grants and charges.* In such a case, there is a supply for VAT purposes but the government funding is an 'outside the scope' contribution to a business activity. Examples of institutions which may require payment include

- sixth form colleges
- tertiary colleges
- colleges of further education

These institutions generally provide education for no charge (non-business) but charge for students who are over the age of 19 or foreign nationals (business).

(C & E Notice 701/30/97, paras 2.1–2.5).

20.3 Eligible bodies

An *'eligible body'* for the purposes of providing exempt education comprises any of the following.

(a) A school within the meaning of *Education Act 1996, Education (Scotland) Act 1980, Education and Libraries (Northern Ireland) Order 1986 (SI 1986/594)* or *Education Reform (Northern Ireland) Order 1989 (SI 1989/2406)* which is

(i) provisionally or finally registered (or deemed to be registered) as a school within the meaning of that legislation in a register of independent schools;

(ii) a school in respect of which grants are made by the Secretary of State to the proprietor or managers;

(iii) a community, foundation or voluntary school within the meaning of the *School Standards and Framework Act 1998*, a special school within the meaning of *Education Act 1996, s 337* or a maintained school within the meaning of *Education and Libraries (Northern Ireland) Order 1986*;

(iv) a public school within the meaning of *Education (Scotland) Act 1980, s 135(1)*;

(v) a self-governing school within the meaning of *Self-Governing Schools (Scotland) Act 1989*; or

(vi) a grant-maintained integrated school within the meaning of *Education Reform (Northern Ireland) Order 1989, Art 65.*

Many of the types of school included above (notably grant-maintained and local authority maintained schools and their equivalents in Scotland and NI) do not generally make a charge for the education they provide and this education is, for the most part, non-business and outside the scope of VAT (see above). However, under limited circumstances, they can make a charge (e.g. music tuition or mature students filling sixth form places) and, because they are eligible bodies, such charges are exempt.

Schools not covered by (i)–(vi) above may be covered by the eligible body criteria in (e) below.

(b) A UK university, and any college, institution, school or hall of such a university. *Not included* are subsidiary companies that universities and colleges set up to pursue commercial business.

(c) An institution

(i) falling within *Further and Higher Education Act 1992, s 91(3)(a)* or *(b)* or *91(5)(b)* or *(c)*;

(ii) which is a designated institution as defined in *Further and Higher Education (Scotland) Act 1992, s 44(2)*;

(iii) managed by a board of management as defined in *Further and Higher Education (Scotland) Act 1992, s 36(1)*; or

(iv) to which grants are paid by the Department of Education for Northern Ireland under *Education and Libraries (Northern Ireland) Order 1986, Art 66(2)*.

This includes all further education colleges or organisations defined or designated as such under the various *Education Acts* (including the Workers' Educational Association (WEA)), together with higher educational institutions defined in the *Education Acts* but not covered by (b) above.

(d) A government department or local authority (or a body which acts for public purposes and not for its own profit and performs functions similar to those of a government department or local authority). *Included* are executive agencies and Health Authorities.

(e) A body which

(i) is precluded from distributing and does not distribute any profit it makes; and

(ii) applies any profits made from exempt supplies of education, research or vocational training to the continuance or improvement of such supplies.

Most such bodies will be charities, professional bodies or companies limited by guarantee. However, provided they satisfy the conditions in (i) and (ii) above, *ad hoc* groups organising specific conferences or training events are eligible. The UK campuses of foreign universities are also eligible bodies but non-profit making organisations that belong overseas do not qualify as eligible.

(f) A body not falling within (a)–(e) above which provides the teaching of English as a foreign language (see 20.10 below).

[*VATA 1994, 9 Sch Group 6, Note 1; SI 1994/2969; Education Act 1996*].

Eligible bodies do not include bodies such as tutorial colleges, computer training organisations, secretarial schools and correspondence colleges which operate with a view to making and distributing a profit.

(C & E Notice 701/30/97, paras 3.2, 3.3, 3.5-3.8).

20.4   **Education**

The provision of 'education' by an 'eligible body' is exempt. [*VATA 1994, 9 Sch Group 6, Item 1(a)*]. See 20.3 above for '*eligible body*'.

20.5 Education

'*Education*' is not defined in the legislation. C & E regard education as meaning 'a course, class or lesson of instruction or study in any subject, whether or not normally taught in schools, colleges or universities and regardless of where and when it takes place. Education includes lectures, educational seminars, conferences and symposia, together with holiday, sporting and recreational courses. It also includes the provision of distance teaching and associated materials, if the student is subject to assessment by the teaching institution.' Any separate charge for registration is part of the supply of education.

In the sports sector, education includes classes that are led and directed (e.g. instruction in the use of equipment and 'warming-up' techniques in a multigym, particularly on enrolment) rather than merely supervised.

(C & E Notice 701/30/97, para 3.11).

See 20.10 below for the teaching of English as a foreign language.

20.5 Research

The provision of research supplied *by* an 'eligible body' *to* an eligible body is exempt. [*VATA 1994, 9 Sch Group 6, Item 1(b)*]. See 20.3 above for '*eligible body*'. See also 20.12 below for supplies between local authorities.

'*Research*' is not defined in the legislation. C & E regard research as meaning 'original investigation undertaken in order to gain knowledge and understanding . . . It is the intention at the beginning of a project which will determine whether a supply qualifies as research. If the intention is to progress understanding, the supply is one of research. By contrast, the mere confirmation of existing understanding is not research.' The fact that a project may have commercial application does not prevent it from being research.

The following are examples of work which C & E do not regard as being research.

- Management consultancy and business efficiency advice.

- Collection and recording of statistics, without accompanying collation, analysis and interpretation.

- Market research and opinion polling.

- Writing computer programs.

- Routine testing and analysis of materials, components and processes.

Some of these activities may, however, qualify if supplied as part of a research project (e.g. devising a specialist software program before it is possible to carry out the main tasks of the project).

(C & E Notice 701/30/97, para 3.12).

If either of the parties to a supply of research is not an eligible body (e.g. a commercial organisation) the supply will normally be standard-rated (but see below). Note, however, that the recipient of the supply does not have to be involved in the field of education, research or vocational training. If the recipient is a non-profit making body satisfying the criteria in 20.3(*e*)(i) above, but making no supplies of education etc., the criteria of 20.3(*e*)(ii) above have no relevance and it is an eligible body. Supplies of research to that body are exempt. The supplier must determine the status of the customer and if not satisfied that the customer is an eligible body must standard-rate the supply.

Supplies to overseas bodies. Where a supply of research falls within *VATA 1994, 5 Sch 3* (see 64.27(*c*) SUPPLY) then if the recipient either

- belongs outside the EC, or

- belongs in another EC country and the services are supplied for business purposes

the place of supply of the services is where the recipient belongs and hence the supply is outside the scope of UK VAT. See 64.26 SUPPLY.

20.6   Vocational training

The following supplies of 'vocational training' are exempt.

(a)   The provision of vocational training by an 'eligible body'. [*VATA 1994, 9 Sch Group 6, Item 1(c)*]. See 20.3 above for '*eligible body*'.

(b)   The provision of vocational training to the extent that the consideration payable is ultimately a charge to funds provided pursuant to arrangements made under *Employment and Training Act 1973, s 2, Employment and Training Act (Northern Ireland) 1950, s 1A* or *Enterprises and New Towns (Scotland) Act 1990, s 2*. Included is the supply of any goods or services essential to the vocational training provided directly to the trainee by the person providing the training. [*VATA 1994, 9 Sch Group 6, Item 5 and Note 5; SI 1994/2969*].

This provides exemption for supplies of vocational training under government approved vocational training schemes by suppliers who are not eligible bodies. The exemption extends to all subcontractors' supplies of vocational training to the extent that these services are ultimately funded by a Training and Enterprise Council (TEC), Local Enterprise Company (LEC), Chamber of Commerce, Training and Enterprise (CCTE), the Further Education Funding Council (FEFC), or the European Social Fund (ESF) under a scheme approved by the Department for Education and Employment.

Government approved schemes usually provide vocational training to young and unemployed people (e.g. Youth Training, Modern Apprenticeships, Work-based Training, etc.) but also cover other forms of training (e.g. training workplace assessors in connection with National Vocation Qualifications and training aimed at providing additional skills to Health and Safety and First Aid Officers for use in the workplace).

Where any funding from a TEC, etc. must be passed on to trainees or students (e.g. statutory living allowances and travel and lodging expenses) this is outside the scope of VAT and does not form part of the supply of vocational training.

Where the contract to supply vocational training is with a further education college, the supplier must find out what proportion of the payment by the college derives from FEFC funds. If the college pays for a particular training course using both FEFC funds and money available to it from other sources (e.g. trainees or their employers may pay part from their own resources) then the part of the supply financed from those other resources is only exempt if the supplier is an eligible body (so that the supply is exempt under (a) above). Otherwise the supply must be apportioned between the exempt and standard-rated elements. In determining the proportions, the college may opt to apply a global formula rather than perform a separate calculation each time it buys in a supply of vocational training, i.e. it may express its annual FEFC allocation as a percentage of its total income for the year and apply this percentage to each purchase of vocational training made in the subsequent year in order to arrive at the proportion that qualifies for exemption.

(C & E Notice 701/30/97, paras 3.4, 8.1-8.7; C & E Business Brief 13/96, 1 July 1996).

'*Vocational training*' means training, re-training or the provision of work experience for

- any trade, profession or employment; or

- any voluntary work connected with education, health, safety or welfare or with the carrying out of activities of a charitable nature.

[*VATA 1994, 9 Sch Group 6, Note 3*].

Vocational training includes courses, conferences, lectures, workshops and seminars designed to prepare those attending for future employment or to add to their knowledge in order to improve their performance in their current work. Not included are services such as counselling, business advice and consultancy, which are designed to improve the working practices and efficiency of an organisation as a whole rather than to enhance the ability of individuals (although such services might qualify for exemption if provided as part of a comprehensive training package). (C & E Notice 701/30/97, para 3.13).

20.7   **Related goods and services**

Exemption also applies to the supply of any goods or services (other than examination services within 20.9 below) which are 'closely related' to an exempt supply within 20.4, 20.5 or 20.6(*a*) above (the 'principal supply') provided

(*a*)   the supply is made by or to the 'eligible body' making the principal supply;

(*b*)   the goods or services are for the direct use of the pupil, student or trainee (as the case may be) receiving the principal supply; and

(*c*)   where the supply is to the eligible body making the principal supply, it is made by another eligible body.

The above provisions do not apply to goods or services supplied to pupils by *commercial providers* of English as a foreign language which remain taxable. See 20.10 below.

[*VATA 1994, 9 Sch Group 6, Item 4 and Note 2*].

See 20.3 above for '*eligible body*'.

'*Closely related*' limits the provisions to goods and services that are necessary for delivering the education to the pupil, student or trainee. Accommodation, catering, transport and school and field trips can be treated as closely related but not

- supplies to staff (including tutors on summer schools) and to other non-students;

- sales of goods from school shops, campus shops and student bars;

- sales from vending machines;

- sales of goods that are not needed for regular use in class;

- separately charged laundry and other personal services;

- sales of school uniforms and sports clothing;

- admission charges (other than for taking part in sports activities), e.g. admissions to plays, concerts, dances, sporting venues, exhibitions, museums, zoos;

- administration and management services; and

- commission for allowing sales by outside organisations at an educational establishment.

Supplies of goods and services which are not closely related to education are taxable unless relief is available elsewhere.

For whether catering is incidental to education, see *International Bible Students Association v C & E Commrs QB, [1987] STC 412* and for hot and cold food supplied by a shop within a school, see *St Benedict Trading Ltd, [1994] VATTR 376 (12915)*. See 11.8 CATERING where a contract for supplies of catering is made.

It should be noted that the provisions only apply where the supplies are closely related to a principal supply which is an *exempt* supply. Where the principal supply of education is not supplied in the course or furtherance of business and therefore outside the scope of VAT (e.g. supplies by a grant-maintained school), any goods or services supplied by the school to its pupils, etc. are not exempt, even though they might be closely related to the education. However, where they are closely related and are sold to pupils, etc. at or below cost, they are non-business and are thus outside the scope of VAT. Equally, the exemption does not apply to closely linked goods and services supplied by an eligible body to another eligible body providing the education, etc. if the latter body is not providing education in the course or furtherance of a business.

Supplies of closely related goods and services by an eligible body to other eligible bodies. As a result of the above provisions, the VAT position can be summarised as follows.

(1)   If the supplier is a commercial provider of English as a foreign language, supplies are standard-rated (see 20.10 below).

(2)   Where (1) above does not apply

(*a*)   if the supplies are directly to pupils of an educational institution or LEA

- supplies by an education institution or LEA are exempt; and

- supplies by other eligible bodies are standard-rated;

(*b*)   if the supplies are not directly to pupils of an education institution or LEA

- supplies to a body supplying education by way of business (charging fees) are exempt; and

- supplies to other eligible bodies are standard-rated.

(C & E Notice 701/30/97, paras 6.1–6.5, Appendix C).

20.8   **Private tuition**

The supply of private tuition is an exempt supply provided it is

(*a*)   in a subject ordinarily taught in a school or university; and

(*b*)   given by an individual teacher acting independently of an employer.

[*VATA 1994, 9 Sch Group 6, Item 2*].

A reasonable test for 'ordinarily' is whether the subject is taught in a number of schools and/or universities on a regular basis. Subject to satisfying this test, tuition in subjects of a recreational or sporting nature are included, whether or not on a one-to-one basis.

Teachers working under a franchise agreement authorising them to use teaching methods of another person or organisation, or to use their name or trading style, can still be regarded as providing private tuition, provided all other conditions are satisfied.

The restriction in (*b*) above means that private tuition provided by an employee of another person or an employer who engages others to carry out the instruction is not included. Such supplies are therefore standard-rated unless the person qualifies as an eligible body (see 20.3 above).

(C & E Notice 701/35/97, para 4.1).

20.9 Education

C & E originally took the view that the use of the words 'by an individual teacher' in (*b*) above excluded private tuition supplied by a partner. However, following the tribunal decision in *C & E Clarke; A & H Clarke (15201)* they accept that exemption for private tuition applies to partnerships where all partners are jointly responsible for giving the instruction as individual teachers and on their own behalf. They do not accept a supply as exempt private tuition if one or more of the partners takes no part in giving instruction or if the partnership employs or engages anyone else to provide any form of tuition on its behalf. Exemption is not ruled out merely because the partnership employs others for *non-teaching* purposes. (C & E Business Brief 1/98, 7 January 1998).

20.9 **Examination services**

The provision of 'examination services'

(*a*) by or to an 'eligible body', or

(*b*) to a person receiving education or vocational training which is

(i) exempt under 20.4, 20.6 or 20.8 above, or

(ii) provided otherwise than in the course or furtherance of a business

is an exempt supply.

'*Examination services*' include

- the setting and marking of examinations;

- the setting of educational or training standards;

- the making of assessments; and

- other services provided with a view to ensuring educational and training standards are maintained.

[*VATA 1994, 9 Sch Group 6, Item 3 and Note 4*].

See 20.3 above for '*eligible body*'.

Examples of activities treated as examination services are services connected with GCSE and GCE examinations and National Curriculum tests, National Vocational Qualification (NVQ) assessments, course accreditation services, validation, certification, and registration of candidates. Not included are purely secretarial or advertising services (unless provided as part of a broader package).

Included under (*b*) above is the supply of examination services *directly* to pupils of independent fee paying schools, local authority schools or grant-maintained schools; students of further education colleges; trainees of government approved training schemes; and employees receiving in-house training from their employers. Examination boards normally provide GCSE and GCE examinations direct to school pupils. Schools can usually treat as disbursements the payments they receive from and on behalf of pupils for these examinations. See 4.7 AGENTS for the treatment of disbursements.

School inspections, in principle, fall within the scope of the exemption for examination services. Any supplies made direct to a school or local authority are exempt but, for the time being and until further notice, supplies under contract to the Office for Standards in Education (OFSTED) may continue to be standard-rated.

(C & E Notice 701/30/97, paras 5.1–5.3).

20.10 **English as a foreign language (EFL)**

Exemption applies to tuition in EFL by *any* body (see 20.3(*f*) above). Where, however, the body does not also qualify as an eligible body under another category within

20.3(*a*)-(*e*) above, exemption does not extend to any other supplies which the body makes apart from the 'teaching of English as a foreign language'. [*VATA 1994, 9 Sch Group 6, Note 2; SI 1994 No 2969*].

Exemption does not therefore extend to other education, research or vocational training (e.g. training in the teaching of EFL) supplied by a commercial provider of EFL who is not within 20.3(*a*)-(*e*) above. Similarly, any closely related goods or services supplied by such a body in conjunction with EFL are outside the exemption as they are not the 'teaching' of English as a foreign language. As a result

- for *commercial providers* of EFL, exemption does not cover supplies of catering and accommodation; course books and other educational materials; sightseeing visits (whether or not accompanied by a teacher); sporting, recreational and other social events; and transport to and from airports, etc. Where a single charge is made for tuition and other goods and services by a commercial provider, the cost of the course should therefore be apportioned, based on the value of the different components; and

- supplies of EFL by eligible bodies within 20.3(*a*)-(*e*) above are exempt, together with supplies of closely related goods and services within 20.7 above.

(C & E Notice 701/30/97, paras 7.1–7.5).

See also *C & E Commrs v Pilgrims Language Courses Ltd (and cross appeals) QB, [1998] STC 784*.

20.11   Youth clubs

The provision of facilities is exempt if supplied by

- a 'youth club' or an association of youth clubs to its members; or

- an association of youth clubs to members of a youth club which is a member of that association.

A *'youth club'* is a club established to promote the social, physical, educational or spiritual development of its members and which satisfies the requirements of 20.3(*e*)(i) and (ii) above. The members of the club must be mainly under 21 years of age.

[*VATA 1994, 9 Sch Group 6, Item 6 and Note 6*].

'Mainly under 21' means that 51% or more of the members must be aged 20 years or less.

To qualify for exemption a youth club would be expected to show evidence of having its own constitution and be able to produce its own accounts showing that none of its income is used to subsidise any outside activity. Youth sections of organisations such as sports clubs, cultural societies and environmental groups are not regarded as youth clubs unless separately constituted, etc. See also *Haggs Castle Golf Club (13653)*.

Exemption covers any facilities which members receive in return for their subscriptions or, if the facilities are directly related to the club's ordinary activities, for an additional payment. *Not included* are

- activities which do not constitute normal supplies by a youth club to its members (e.g. sales of food and drink, purely recreational holidays); and

- supplies which are not made to members (e.g. supplies to clubs which are not members of the association or by youth clubs to an association of youth clubs).

(C & E Notice 701/35/95).

20.12 EDUCATION SUPPLIED BY LOCAL AUTHORITIES

Local authorities are eligible bodies (see 20.3(*d*) above). Also a number of the different types of 'schools' under 20.3(*a*) above are local authority maintained schools (or the equivalent in Scotland and Northern Ireland). Although they generally provide free education, they are included because they are able to provide fee-paying education in their own right.

Any education or vocational training provided by local authorities for no charge or which they provide under a statutory obligation is a non-business activity. All other educational or vocational training courses provided for any form of charge or payment are generally exempt business supplies, irrespective of any subsidy they may receive.

Any research provided by a local authority is exempt if provided to another eligible body. Otherwise it is standard-rated. However, the supply of research to another local authority may still be treated as being non-business under *Local Authorities (Goods and Services) Act 1970*.

Adult education. The *Further and Higher Education Act 1992* transferred certain responsibilities for further education from local authorities to Further Education Funding Councils. It allows local authorities to provide adult education but it does not oblige them to do so.

Where local authorities are not under a statutory obligation to provide adult education, the provision of courses is a business activity carried out in direct competition with other suppliers of further education. Any charge for such a course, whether subsidised or not, is an exempt supply of education.

(C & E Notice 701/30/97, para 3.9; C & E Business Brief 14/95, 3 July 1995).

20.13 SCHOOL PHOTOGRAPHERS

Sales of photographs by the photographer directly to parents. The photographer must account for VAT on the final selling price of the photographs to the parents. The position of the school depends upon whether it acts for the LEA or for the governing body in supplying the use of its facilities to the photographer.

(*a*) *LEA schools.* In the case of

- LEA maintained schools (including 'voluntary controlled' schools) in England and Wales,

- public schools in Scotland (as defined in *Education (Scotland) Act 1980, s 135*), and

- 'controlled' schools in Northern Ireland,

the school (normally in the person of the head teacher) may act an agent for the LEA when contracting with the photographer. If so, the LEA must account for VAT on the commission or discount the school receives. This will almost always be the case for schools without governing bodies.

Alternatively, following the tribunal decision in *Lancashire County Council, [1996] VATDR 550 (14655)* C & E accept that, where the governing body has full control of receipts paid into the 'unofficial' school funds, the school (normally in the person of the head teacher) may act as agent for the governing body. The governing body must account for VAT on the supply of the facilities to the photographer where its taxable turnover (including income from the photographer) exceeds the VAT registration threshold or where it has voluntarily registered. Before the *Lancashire*

County Council decision, C & E took the view that the facilities were supplied by the LEA rather than the school and that the LEA had to account for VAT on this income.

To decide the correct VAT treatment of the discount or commission they give, school photographers should confirm which situation applies for each contract they enter into.

(b)   *Grant-maintained and similar schools.* In the case of

- voluntary aided, special agreement, grant-maintained and grant-maintained special schools in England and Wales,

- self-governing schools in Scotland, and

- voluntary-maintained, voluntary grammar and grant-maintained integrated schools in Northern Ireland

where the head teacher is an employee of the governing body of the school and is acting on its behalf, the governing body must account for VAT on the supply of the facilities to the photographer where its taxable turnover (including income from the photographer) exceeds the VAT registration threshold or where it has voluntarily registered.

(c)   *Independent schools.* The school must account for VAT on the supply of the facilities to the photographer where its taxable turnover (including income from the photographer) exceeds the VAT registration threshold or where it has voluntarily registered.

Sales of photographs by the photographer to LEA's, schools and other bodies. Where the contractual arrangements provide that the supply of photographs is to the LEA, school or other body,

- *if the LEA, etc. is registered for VAT*, the photographer must account for VAT on the price actually charged. The LEA, etc. can recover the VAT as input tax subject to the normal rules and must account for output tax on the full value of the supply to the parents or pupils.

- *if the LEA, etc. is not registered for VAT*, C & E may issue a Notice of Direction under *VATA 1994, 6 Sch 2* requiring the photographer to account for VAT on the final selling price charged by the unregistered school to the parents or pupils. Where no such Notice of Direction has been issued, the photographer should account for VAT on the amount actually charged to the unregistered school or other organisation.

(C & E Notice 701/46/96; C & E Business Brief 11/97, 9 May 1997; C & E Business Brief 21/97, 3 October 1997).

21 European Community: General

21.1 EUROPEAN COMMUNITY INSTITUTIONS

The three European Communities are the European Coal and Steel Community ('ECSC'), the European Community ('EC') (previously the European Economic Community but renamed by the Maastricht Treaty) and the European Atomic Energy Community ('EAEC' or 'Euratom').

The EEC is the body principally concerned with VAT. It was set up by *The First Treaty of Rome* ('*EEC Treaty*') with effect from 1 January 1958 and was entered into initially by Belgium, Federal Republic of Germany, France, Italy, Luxembourg and The Netherlands (who were also the initial members of ECSC and EAEC). By *The Treaty of Accession*, the UK, Ireland and Denmark entered the Communities with effect from 1 January 1973. The relevant UK legislation is *European Communities Act 1972*. Greece joined with effect from 1 January 1981, Spain and Portugal with effect from 1 January 1986 and Austria, Finland and Sweden with effect from 1 January 1995.

The *EEC Treaty* is widely drafted and there is an emphasis on provisions for the free movement of persons, goods, services and capital as well as powers for the implementation of common policies in many areas of economic and social life. It provides for a *Council of Ministers* which is composed of representatives of the governments of the member countries and effectively has the power to make decisions.

The *European Commission* is the executive constitution of the EEC and also formulates the policy acted upon by the Council.

The *European Parliament* has, primarily, only supervisory and consultative powers.

The *European Court of Justice* is empowered to ensure that in the interpretation and application of the *EEC Treaty* the law is observed. In this connection it is the ultimate court of appeal.

All the above bodies are common to both ECSC and EAEC.

The *European Council*, consisting of Heads of State of the member countries, is not recognised as such by the *EEC Treaty*, although this body has become an important focus of attention because of its obvious importance.

De Voil Indirect Tax Service. See V1.201; V1.244; V1.245; V1.252.

21.2 VAT TERRITORY OF THE EC

The VAT territory of the EC consists of

Austria

Belgium

Denmark (not the Faroe Islands and Greenland)

Finland (not the Aland Islands)

France (including Monaco but not including Martinique, French Guyana, Guadeloupe, Reunion and St Pierre and Miquelon)

Germany (not Busingen and the Isle of Heligoland but including Jungholz and Mittelberg)

Greece (not Mount Athos (Agion Poros))

The Republic of Ireland

Italy (not the communes of Livigno and Campione d'Italia and the Italian waters of Lake Lugano)

Luxembourg

Netherlands

Portugal (including the Azores and Madeira)

Spain (including the Balearic Islands but not Canary Islands, Ceuta and Melilla)

Sweden

United Kingdom (including the Isle of Man but not the Channel Islands or Gibraltar)

[*VATA 1994, s 93; SI 1995/2518, Regs 136, 137, 139*]

De Voil Indirect Tax Service. See V1.206.

21.3   **CUSTOMS TERRITORY OF THE EC**

The customs territory of the EC consists of the VAT territory (see 21.2 above) plus

Andorra

The Aland Islands

Channel Islands

San Marino

The Canary Islands

The overseas departments of the French Republic (Guadeloupe, Martinique, Reunion and French Guyana)

Mount Athos (Agion Poros)

21.4   **EXCISE TERRITORY OF THE EC**

The excise territory of the EC consists of the VAT territory (see 21.2 above) plus

San Marino

21.5   **TRADE STATISTICS TERRITORY OF THE EC**

The trade statistics territory of the EC consists of the VAT territory (see 21.2 above) plus

San Marino

Mount Athos

For trade statistics purposes, both the Isle of Man and the Channel Islands are part of the UK. Trade between them and other EC countries is included in the Intrastat system but trade between them and the UK is excluded.

21.6   **TRADE WITH TERRITORIES WITH WHICH THE EC HAS SPECIAL RELATIONS**

The following rules apply.

• For trade with such territories outside the VAT, customs, excise *and* trade statistics territories (see 21.2 to 21.5 above), the same procedures apply as before the

21.7 European Community: General

introduction of the single market. Such territories are treated in the same way as any other non-EC country.

- For trade with the Azores, the Balearic Islands, Madeira and Monaco (which are within the VAT, customs, excise *and* trade statistics territories, see 21.2 to 21.5 above), the same procedures apply as for trade with other EC countries. This also applies to trade between the Isle of Man and EC countries other than the UK.

- Where goods are imported into the EC from any of the additional territories within the Customs territory (see 21.3 above), there is no liability to customs duty but VAT may be payable. (There are special schemes for goods such as cut flowers which enter the UK from the Channel Islands.) Excise duty may also be payable but not on goods imported from San Marino (which is inside the Excise territory).

- Trade statistics are collected for trade between Andorra, the Canary Islands, French Guyana, Guadaloupe, Martinique, Reunion and the EC (and for trade between the Channel Islands and EC countries except the UK). The same procedures for reporting statistics on trade with these territories apply as before the introduction of the single market.

21.7 AUSTRIA

What is VAT called. Mehrwertsteuer (Mwst)

Address for general information on VAT system. Finanzamt Graz-Stadt, Referat fürausländische Unternehmer, Conrad von Hötzendorfstrasse 14-18, 8018 GRAZ (Tel: (00 43) 316 8810)

VAT registration numbers. An Austrian VAT registration number consists of the letter 'U' followed immediately by eight digits, all in one block (e.g. U12345678).

Registration. There is no minimum threshold for registration. A business required to register for VAT in Austria, but which has no permanent residence or establishment there, must appoint a fiscal representative in that country. To register for VAT, application must be made to the local tax office for the area where the business or tax representative is based.

VAT returns. Monthly VAT returns are normally required and must be submitted, with payment, by the 15th day of the second month after the period end.

21.8 BELGIUM

Customs/fiscal authority. (French): Ministère des Finances, Administration des Douanes et Accises, Cité Administrative de l'Etat, Tour Finances – Boîte 37, Boulevard du Jardin Botanique 50, 1010 Bruxelles. (Dutch): Ministerie van Financiën, Administratie voor Douane en Accijnzen, Gebouwen van Staatsadministratie, Financietoren – Bus 37, Kruidtuinlaan 50, 1010 Brussel

Address for general information on VAT system. (French): Bureau Central de la TVA pour les Assujettis Etrangers, Rue d'Orley 15, 1000 Bruxelles. (Dutch): Centraal BTW Kantoor voor Buitenlandse Belastingplichtigen, Van Orleystraat 15, 1000 Brussel (Tel: (00 32) 2 218 3860)

What is VAT called. (French): Taxe sur la Valeur Ajoutèe (TVA). (Dutch): Belasting over de Toegevoegde Waarde (BTW)

VAT registration numbers. A Belgian VAT registration number (numèro TVA (N° TVA) or BTW–Nummer (BTW-Nr)) consists of nine digits (e.g. 123456789).

Registration. If the business has a permanent establishment in Belgium, application for a VAT registration number must be made to the VAT inspectorate in whose area the main establishment of the business is located. Otherwise before any taxable supplies are made, it is necessary to register for VAT and appoint a local VAT representative who must (a) live and be established in Belgium; (b) be legally competent to conclude contracts for the business; (c) be solvent and in a position to pay for the sums for which he or she is jointly or severally liable with the business; and (d) have explicitly agreed to represent the business.

The name of the VAT representative must be submitted with the registration application to the address for general information above. Form 604A should be used to notify the authorities of the start of business activities in Belgium and Form 800 to notify them of the appointment of a VAT representative. The representative should submit Form 801.

There is no minimum threshold for registration.

VAT returns. A return normally covers a calendar quarter although monthly returns must be submitted if annual turnover exceeds a specified limit or there is no entitlement to deduct input tax. There is also an annual accounting scheme where turnover is below a specified limit.

Returns must be submitted with payment by the 20th day (or next working day) of the month following the period covered. There are some extensions for holiday periods. Where quarterly returns are submitted, monthly payments on account must be made of one third the VAT due for the previous quarter.

An annual statement listing supplies and VAT charged to businesses registered in Belgium must also be submitted.

EC sales lists must be submitted for calendar quarters by the 20th day of the following month.

(C & E Single Market Information Sheet SM3).

21.9   **DENMARK**

Customs/fiscal authority. Skatteministeriet, Told-og Skattestyrelsen, Amaliegade 44, 1256 København K

Address for general information on VAT system. Skatteministeriet, Told-og Skattestyrelsen, Hermodsgade 8, 200 KØBENHAVEN (Tel: (00 45) 35 87 73 00)

What is VAT called. Omsaetningafgift

VAT registration numbers. A Danish VAT registration number (varemodtagers moms-nr (SE-nr)) consists of eight digits (e.g. 12345678).

Registration. If the business has a permanent establishment in Denmark, it must apply for registration (not later than eight days before it starts to trade) to the Danish Embassy in the country where the business is based or to a regional Customs and Tax office in Denmark. Otherwise a local VAT representative (a person or enterprise whose place of business is Denmark) must be appointed to register on behalf of the business. The business and the VAT representative will be jointly liable for VAT due to the Danish authorities.

There is a minimum annual threshold below which businesses do not have to register.

VAT returns. A return normally covers a calendar quarter and must be submitted, with payment, within ten days of the end of the month following the quarter. Repayment businesses and bad payers must submit monthly or weekly returns. Forestry, farming, fishing and similar businesses must submit six-monthly returns which are due within two months and 20 days of the end of the period. Payment is then due in two instalments: the first within five months and ten days of the end of the six-month period and the second within eight months and ten days of the end of that period.

EC sales lists normally cover calendar quarters although annual lists may be submitted where annual turnover and EC supplies are below specified limits. Lists must be submitted within ten days of the end of the month following the period covered. Businesses involved in agriculture or fisheries can prepare six-monthly lists and submit them within two months and 20 days of the end of the period covered.

(C & E Single Market Information Sheet SM3).

21.10   **FINLAND**

Customs/fiscal authority. The National Board of Taxes, Haapaniemenkatu, PO Box 325, 00531 Helsinki

Address for general information on VAT system. Uudenmaan Lääninverovirasto, Rejusterö intitoimisto, PL 8, 00052 VEROTUS (Tel: (00 358) 973 1142)

What is VAT called. Arvonlisavero (ALV)

VAT registration numbers. A Finnish VAT registration number consists of eight digits (e.g. 12345678).

Registration. There is a minimum annual threshold for registration. A business required to register for VAT in Finland, but which has no business premises there, must appoint a fiscal representative based in that country and approved by the tax office.

VAT returns. Monthly VAT returns are required and must be submitted within one month and 25 days of the period end.

21.11   **FRANCE**

Customs/fiscal authority. Direction Générale des Douanes et Droits Indirects, Ministère du Budget, 23 bis rue de l'Université, 75700 Paris 07 SP

Address for general information on VAT system. Direction Générale des Impôts, Bureau des Relations Publiques, 86–92 alle de Bercy, 75012 Paris (Tel: (00 33) 1 40 04 11 203)

What is VAT called. Taxe sur la Valeur Ajoutée (TVA)

VAT registration numbers. A French VAT registration number (numéro d'identification) always consists of 11 characters, normally 11 digits but in some cases (mostly local authorities and government departments) the first, second or first and second characters are alpha characters. All alpha characters except I and O are valid.

Registration. A business with a permanent establishment in France must apply for registration (within 15 days of becoming liable to VAT) by submitting a *déclaration d'existence* and a *déclaration d'identification* to register with the Centre de Formalité des Entreprises which covers the type of activity in which the business is engaged. Otherwise a local VAT representative (a trader established in France and known to the French tax authorities) must be appointed. The representative's name and address must appear on invoices.

There is a minimum annual threshold below which businesses do not have to register.

VAT returns. A return normally covers a month although where annual turnover is less than certain specified amounts (depending on the nature of the business) the business may be liable to a flat-rate scheme requiring annual returns or may be able to submit quarterly returns under a simplified scheme. In any case, the return must be submitted, with payment, by the end of the month following the period covered (although the exact deadline will depend on the VAT registration number).

EC sales lists (which are combined with Supplementary Declaration information) cover calendar months and include details of acquisitions as well as supplies. Lists must be submitted within ten working days of the end of the month covered.

(C & E Single Market Information Sheet SM3).

21.12 GERMANY

Customs/fiscal authority. Bundesministerium der Finanzen, Graurheindorfer-straße 108, 53225 Bonn 3

Address for general information on VAT system. Finanzamt Saarbrücken, 2-4, Am Stadtgraben, 66111 SAARBRÜCKEN (Tel: (00 49) 681 30000)

What is VAT called. Mehrwertsteuer (Mwst)

VAT registration numbers. A German VAT registration number (Umsatzsteuer-Identifikationsnummer (USt-IdNr) consists of nine digits (e.g. 123456789).

Registration. If the business has a principal establishment in Germany, it must apply for registration at the district tax office for that establishment. Otherwise application must be made in writing to Bundesamt für Finanzen, Außenstelle, Industriestraße 6, 66738 Saarlouis. No provision has been made in Germany for the appointment of VAT representatives.

There is a minimum annual threshold below which businesses do not have to register.

VAT returns. A preliminary return normally covers a calendar month. Where annual payment of VAT (excluding VAT on acquisitions) is below specified limits, either quarterly preliminary returns or no preliminary returns at all are required. Preliminary returns, with payment, must be submitted within ten days of the end of the period covered. *All* businesses must however submit an annual final VAT return within five months of the end of the year covered and pay any VAT due within four weeks of the end of that year.

EC sales lists normally cover a calendar quarter although annual lists may be submitted if total annual trade and EC supplies of goods are below specified limits. Lists must be submitted within ten days of the end of the period covered.

(C & E Single Market Information Sheet SM3).

21.13 GREECE

Customs/fiscal authority for VAT. Ministry of Finance, 14th Directorate of VAT and Indirect Taxes, Sina 2-4, 10672 Athens (Tel: (00 30) 1 36 472 03)

What is VAT called. Arithmos Forologikou Mitroou FPA

VAT registration numbers. A Greek VAT registration number consists of nine digits commencing with a zero (e.g. 012345678). Before 1 January 1999, it consisted of eight digits without the initial zero.

Registration. The Greek fiscal authorities must be contacted at the local tax office for the business's head office in Greece or for the VAT representative.

If the business has a permanent establishment in Greece, a statement of commencing trade must be submitted to the Public Finance Office covering the business. Otherwise, before making taxable supplies in Greece, a local tax representative must be appointed. A copy of the power of attorney, authenticated by the Greek Embassy (Commercial Section), 1A Holland Park, London W11 3TP, must be lodged with the head of the Public Finance Office in Greece which deals with the VAT representative's income tax. The representative can be any citizen able to enter into legal transactions, i.e. he or she must be (*a*) over 18 years old; (*b*) not judicially or legally barred; (*c*) considered solvent to discharge the obligations he or she undertakes; and (*d*) resident in Greece. The Greek tax authorities may ask for a guarantee that the representative fulfils these requirements.

There is a minimum annual threshold for goods and a separate threshold for services below which businesses do not have to register.

VAT returns. Unless annual supplies of goods or services are below specified limits, preliminary VAT returns must be submitted, depending upon the level of turnover, covering either one calendar month (within 25 days of the end of the month), two calendar months (within 20 days of the end of the two months covered) or a calendar quarter (within 15 days of the end of the quarter). *All* businesses must also submit an annual final VAT return within one month and 25 days of the end of the year covered (or, where monthly returns are submitted, within ten days of finalising the balance sheet). Any VAT due must be paid by the same deadlines.

With preliminary returns, 25% of the VAT due must also be paid in advance and this is then added to the input VAT for the next period.

EC sales lists cover a calendar quarter and must be submitted by the 25th day of the month following the quarter covered.

(C & E Single Market Information Sheet SM3).

21.14 **IRELAND**

Customs/fiscal authority. Office of the Revenue Commissioners, Dublin Castle, Dublin 2

Address for general information on VAT system. Taxes Central Registration Office, Arus Brugha, 9/15 Upper O'Connell Street, Dublin 1 (Tel: (00 353) 1 8746821)

What is VAT called. Value added tax (VAT)

VAT registration numbers. An Irish VAT registration number consists of eight characters including one or two alpha characters either last or second and last (e.g. 1234567A or 1A34567A).

Registration. If a business has a permanent establishment in Ireland, when it becomes liable for registration it must submit Form VAT1 to the local Inspector of Taxes of that establishment. Otherwise, the form must be submitted to Inspector of Taxes, Dublin VAT District, 4 Claremont Road, Sandymount, Dublin 4. There is no obligation to appoint a local representative.

There is a minimum annual threshold for goods and a separate threshold for services below which businesses do not have to register. However, there is no minimum threshold for businesses without a permanent establishment in Ireland which make supplies there.

VAT returns. A return normally covers two calendar months although repayment businesses may submit monthly returns and small businesses may submit annual returns under a special scheme. Returns must be submitted by the 19th day of the month following the period covered. Payment is normally due with the return but if VAT liability for the year to 30 June exceeds a specified limit, an advance payment of VAT must be made in December each year. Unless an annual VAT return is completed, an Annual Return of Trading must also be submitted.

EC sales lists normally cover a calendar quarter although more frequent lists may be submitted on request. Lists must be submitted by the end of the month following the period covered.

(C & E Single Market Information Sheet SM3).

21.15   **ITALY**

Customs/fiscal authority. Ministero delle Finanze, Dipartmento delle Dogane e delle imposte indirette, Capo delle Circoscrizioine reggente 11, Roma

Address for general information on VAT system. Ministero delle Finanze, Centro Informativo Tasse, Via Mario Carucci 99, 00143 Roma (Tel: (00 39) 6 502 53172)

What is VAT called. Imposta sul Valore Aggiunto (IVA)

VAT registration numbers. An Italian VAT registration number (codice IVA or numero di partita IVA (P.IVA) consists of eleven digits (e.g. 12345678901).

Registration. If a business has a permanent establishment in Italy, it must apply to the local VAT office responsible for the area in which it is situated. Otherwise, a local VAT representative (an Italian citizen resident in Italy) must be appointed within 30 days of the business becoming liable for VAT. The appointment of the representative must be validated by a notary or by registered letter and proof sent to the representative's district tax office. Customers must also be notified of the appointment before supplies are made to them.

There is no minimum threshold for registration.

VAT returns. A return covers a year and must be submitted within two months and five days of the end of that year. VAT due must normally be paid on the 20th day of every month although, if annual supplies of goods or services are less than specified limits, quarterly payments may be made within one month and five days of the end of the quarter covered. In the latter case, interest must also be paid on the VAT due.

EC sales lists. Depending upon the level of turnover, lists (which are combined with Supplementary Declaration information) cover a month (for submission by the 15th working day of the month following the month covered) or a quarter or a year (for submission by the end of the month following the period covered). Details of acquisitions as well as supplies must be included.

(C & E Single Market Information Sheet SM3).

21.16   **LUXEMBOURG**

Customs/fiscal authority. Administration des Douanes, Boîte Postale 26, 2010 Luxembourg

Address for general information on VAT system. Bureau d'Imposition X, Administration de l'Enregistrement et des Domaines, 9B Boulevard Prince Henri, BP 31, 2010 Luxembourg (Tel: (00 352) 4490 5451)

What is VAT called. Taxe sul la Valeur Ajoutée (TVA)

VAT registration numbers. A Luxembourg VAT registration number (numéro d'identification) for EC trade purposes consists of eight digits (e.g. 12345678). The eleven digit number which businesses registered for VAT in Luxembourg also have is for use for trade within Luxembourg only.

Registration. Application must first be made to the Service du Répertoire Général to be included on the National Register of Natural and Legal Persons. Foreign businesses who supply services in Luxembourg must apply to the Ministère des Classes Moyennes, Service des Autorisations d'Etablissement, 6 Avenue Emile Reuter, 2937 Luxembourg to obtain a licence to do business. Within 15 days of becoming liable for VAT, a declaration relating to commencement of taxable economic activity must be submitted to the address above for general information on VAT. That office must also be notified of any substantial changes in business activities.

If the business has no permanent address in Luxembourg, it can be required to appoint a VAT representative (a Luxembourg resident) who can be held jointly and severally responsible for VAT obligations. Alternatively, the business may be required to lodge a security of banker's guarantee.

There is a minimum annual threshold below which businesses do not have to register.

VAT returns. A VAT return normally covers a month although businesses with turnovers below specified limits may prepare quarterly or annual returns. Returns must be submitted, and the VAT paid, by the 14th day of the month following the period covered (two months following the period covered for annual returns). Where monthly or quarterly returns are prepared, a recapitulative annual return must also be submitted by 30 April.

EC sales lists normally cover calendar quarters although annual lists may be prepared where annual turnover and value of EC supplies of goods are below specified limits. Lists must be submitted by the 15th day of the month following the period covered.

(C & E Single Market Information Sheet SM3).

21.17   NETHERLANDS

Customs/fiscal authority. Directoraat-Generaal der Belastingen, Ministerie van Financiën, Korte Voorhout 7, Postadres Postbus 20201, 2500 EE 'S-Gravenhage

Address for general information on VAT system. Belasting dienst Particulieren, Ondernemingen Buitenland, Postbus 2865, 6401 D J Heerlen (Tel: (00 31) 45 573 6666)

What is VAT called. Belasting over de Toegevoegde Waarde (BTW)

VAT registration numbers. A Dutch VAT registration number (Omzetbelasting-nummer (OB nummer)) consists of nine digits followed by a three character suffix in the range B01–B99 (e.g. 123456789 B01).

Registration. If a business has a permanent establishment in the Netherlands, application must be made at the local tax office for the area in which the establishment is located. Otherwise, as soon as liability for VAT arises, a business must register at the VAT office at Heerlen (Eenheid Belastingdienst Particulieren/Ondernemingen Buitenland, Postbus 2865, 6401 DJ Heerlen. It is not obligatory to appoint a local VAT representative (except for distance sales purposes). Any representative must obtain a licence by making a written declaration to the Dutch authorities, accompanied by a declaration from the business that he or she is authorised to act as the VAT representative.

There is no minimum threshold for registration but, depending on the amount of VAT due, graduated VAT relief following registration is available on application for small businesses who are sole proprietors or partnerships.

VAT returns. A VAT return normally covers a calendar quarter although if the annual payment of VAT is above a specified limit monthly returns must be submitted. Small businesses may prepare annual returns. The return, and VAT due, must be submitted within one month of the end of the period covered.

EC sales lists normally cover calendar quarters although businesses with annual turnover and EC trade below specified limits may apply to submit annual returns and/or have the period for their ESLs aligned with their VAT returns. Lists must be submitted within one month of the end of the period covered.

(C & E Single Market Information Sheet SM3).

21.18   PORTUGAL

Customs/fiscal authority. Ministério das Finanças, Direcçâo-geral das Alfândegas, Rua das Alfândegas, 1194 Lisboa Codex

Address for general information on VAT system. Serviço de Administraçao do IVA, Avenida Joao XXI 76, 1000 Lisboa (Tel: (00 351) 793 6673)

What is VAT called. Imposto sobre o Valor Acrescentado (IVA)

VAT registration numbers. A Portuguese VAT number (numero de identifiaçao fiscal (NIPC)) consists of nine digits (e.g. 123456789).

Registration. A Portuguese VAT registration number must be obtained from Registro Nacional de Pessoas Colectivas, Praça Silvestre Pinheiro Ferreira 1-C, 1500 Lisboa. If the business has a permanent establishment in Portugal, a declaration of commencement of activities must be submitted to the office of the third Lisbon tax district (Bairro Fiscal). Otherwise a local VAT representative must be appointed by means of a power of attorney through a notary public or Portuguese diplomatic or consular official. The business must then register with the local tax office for the head office, principal establishment or home of the local tax representative.

There is a minimum annual threshold below which businesses do not have to register.

VAT returns. A return normally covers a calendar quarter and must be submitted, with the VAT due, by the end of the second month following the end of the quarter covered. If annual turnover is more than a specified limit, monthly returns are required which must be submitted, with the VAT due, within 15 days of the end of the month following the month covered.

An annual statement of acquisitions and supplies of goods and services must also be submitted.

EC sales lists are annexed to the VAT return and must be submitted at the same time.

(C & E Single Market Information Sheet SM3).

21.19   SPAIN

Customs/fiscal authority. Dirección General de Aduanas e Impuestos Especiales, Ministerio de Economía y Hacienda, c/Guzmán el Bueno 137, 28003 Madrid. Tele 00 34 1 554 3200

Address for general information on VAT system. Subdirección de Assistencia Tributaria, Agencia Estatal de la Admistracion Tributaria, C/Infanta Mercedes No 37, 28071 Madrid (Tel: (00 34) 1 583 8976)

What is VAT called. Impuesto sobre el Valor Añadido (IVA)

VAT registration numbers. A Spanish VAT registration number (numero de identificacion fiscal (NIF)) consists of nine characters including one or two alpha characters either first, last or first and last (e.g. A12345678 or A1234567B).

Registration. All taxable persons must identify themselves for VAT purposes by submitting a declaration (Form 036) specifying the VAT scheme under which they will pay VAT. If the business has a permanent establishment in Spain, application for a VAT registration number must be made to the branch or office of the AEAT for the area in which the establishment is located. Otherwise the business must register by applying through a local VAT representative to the AEAT branch or office responsible for one of the areas in Spain where the business will be operating.

There is no minimum threshold for registration.

VAT returns. A return normally covers a calendar quarter although businesses with annual turnover above a specified limit must submit annual returns. Businesses operating special simplified schemes for calculation of VAT due submit special returns. Returns must be submitted, and payment made, by the 20th day of the month following the period covered. Special rules apply for returns covering July, August and the last VAT period of the year.

An annual statement (Form 390) must also be submitted with the last return for the year.

EC sales lists normally cover a calendar quarter although annual lists may be submitted where annual supplies and EC supplies of goods are below specified limits. Lists must be submitted by the 20th day of the month following the period covered. The list for the final quarter of the year is due by 31 January. Lists include details of acquisitions as well as supplies.

(C & E Single Market Information Sheet SM3).

21.20   **SWEDEN**

Address for general information on VAT system. Skattemyndigheten i, Stockholms Län, Länsskattekontoret, 10661 Stockholm, Sweden (Tel: (00 46) 87142000)

What is VAT called. Mervärdeskatt (MOMS)

VAT registration numbers. A Swedish VAT registration number consists of 12 digits (e.g. 123451234501). From 1 January 1998, any number which does not end in the digits 01 is invalid.

Registration. Application should be made to the local tax office for the area in which the main business activity is carried out or, where the business has a representative in Sweden, the local tax office for the region in which the representative is located.

There is no minimum threshold for registration. A business required to register for VAT in Sweden, but which has no permanent place of business there, must appoint a fiscal representative resident in that country and approved by the tax authorities.

VAT returns. A return normally covers a two-month period and must be submitted, with payment, within five days of the end of the second month following the return period. Where annual turnover is less than a specified limit, a return need only be filed once a year.

21.21   **REFUND OF VAT TO PERSONS ESTABLISHED IN OTHER EC COUNTRIES**

Under the *EC 8th Directive*, a taxable person may recover certain VAT suffered in another EC country provided he is not already registered in that country (in which case that country's domestic VAT legislation would apply). See 22.49 EUROPEAN COMMUNITY LEGISLATION for a summary of the provisions of the *8th Directive*. The taxable person must comply with the following conditions.

(*a*) He must complete a claim form and send it to the competent authority in the country where the VAT was incurred.

A form printed in any of the EC official languages may be used to apply for a refund in any EC country. A standard design is used throughout the Community. The English version, Form VAT 65, is available from any VAT office. The form, however, must be completed in block letters *in the language of the country to which it is to be sent.*

Original copies of invoices, import documentation, etc. must be sent with the completed form.

(*b*) In order to prove his eligibility to the refund, he must obtain a certificate of status from the competent authority in the country in which he is registered and send it to the competent authority in the other EC country with the claim form.

A separate certificate of status must therefore be sent to each country for which a refund is claimed but once a competent authority holds a certificate, a further certificate need not be produced for a period of one year from the date of issue.

A certificate of status for a UK-registered taxable person (Form VAT 66) is obtained from the VAT office shown on the certificate of registration. In making requests for certificates, a taxable person should be sure to ask for sufficient information to be included to enable the relevant competent authority to be satisfied with the claim, e.g. a company's trading style as well as the name of the legal entity. Group status certificates should show the names of group members involved or likely to be involved in claims as well as the name of the representative member. (C & E Notice 723, para 1.8).

De Voil Indirect Tax Service. See V5.151.

21.22 **Applications to other EC countries by UK taxable persons**

The domestic VAT legislation of EC countries other than the UK is outside the scope of this book. As such provisions will have a significant bearing on the making of an application for recovery of VAT suffered, professional advice may need to be sought. See 21.23 to 21.36 below for details of where to obtain forms, non-refundable VAT and minimum claims in different EC countries. Further information on use of agents, method of repayment and appeals against rejection of claims etc. is summarised in C & E Notice 723, paras 1.11–1.24.

VAT is not refundable if it would be disallowed for credit if incurred by a person registered in the EC country. VAT incurred on the following supplies is not refunded by any EC country.

● Dispatches of goods (but these will be zero-rated provided the supplier has the necessary evidence).

● Goods and services (e.g. hotel accommodation) which have been bought for resale and which are for the direct benefit of travellers. (C & E Notice 723, para 1.3).

Flat-rate scheme for farmers. Where a VAT-registered person in the UK acquires goods or services from a farmer in another EC country who charges the flat-rate addition (see 63.15 SPECIAL SCHEMES for the equivalent scheme for UK farmers), the addition must be reclaimed from the VAT authority in the supplier's country (not C & E via the VAT return). (C & E Leaflet 700/46/93, para 19).

21.23   *Austria*

Forms and information are obtainable from

Finanzamt Graz-Stadt

Referat für ausländische Unternehmer
Conrad von Hötzendorfstrasse 14-18
8018 GRAZ
Austria

Tel: (00 43) 316 8810
Fax: (00 43) 316 81 76 08

Non-refundable VAT. In addition to the supplies listed in 21.22 above, refunds cannot be claimed on entertainment expenses, car hire and petrol.

Minimum claim. If for three months, claim must be for at least Sch 5,000. If for a year, claim must be for at least Sch 500.

21.24   *Belgium*

Forms and other information are obtainable from

(French):
Bureau Central de TVA pour assujettis etrangers
Service de Remboursement TVA
Boulevard Bisschoffsheim 38, 38A
B–1000 BRUXELLES

Tel: (00 32) 2 218 29 05
Fax: (00 32) 2 219 27 91

(Dutch):
Centraal BTW kantoor voor buitenlandse belasting-plichtigen
Dienst Terugbetaling BTW
Bisschoffsheimlaan 38, 38A
1000 BRUSSEL

Tel: (00 32) 2 218 29 05
Fax: (00 32) 2 219 27 91

The form must be completed in French or Dutch.

Non-refundable VAT. In addition to the supplies listed in 21.22 above, refunds cannot be claimed on manufactured tobacco; alcoholic drinks (unless intended for resale or to be provided as part of a supply of services); accommodation and food and drink for on-the-spot consumption (unless the cost is incurred by staff supplying goods or services away from business premises or a taxable person who supplies it on for a consideration); and entertaining expenses.

Minimum claim. If for less than one year, claim must be for at least BF9000 unless it is for the final period of the year. No claim can be for less than BF1000.

21.25   *Denmark*

Forms and other information are obtainable from

Told–og Skatteregion Sønderborg
Hilmar Finsens Gade 18
6400 SØNDERBORG
Denmark

Tel: (00 45) 74 12 73 00
Fax: (00 45) 74 42 28 09

The form must be completed in Danish.

Non-refundable VAT. In addition to the supplies listed in 21.22 above, refunds cannot be claimed on entertainment expenses, hotel expenses and car rental.

Minimum claim. If for less than one year, claim must be for at least DKr 1500 unless it is for the final period of the year. No claim can be for less than DKr 200.

21.26   *Finland*

Forms and other information are obtainable from

Uudenmaan lääninverovirasto
Arvonlisäverotoimisto
PL 5
00521 VEROTUS

Tel: (00 358) 973 114327
Fax: (00 358) 973 114395 or 114399

Non-refundable VAT. In addition to the supplies listed in 21.22 above, refunds cannot be claimed on business entertainment; car hire, fuel and car repairs; and motor cycles, caravans, private aircraft and related supplies.

Minimum claim. If for three months, claim must be for at least FIM 1200. If for a year, claim must be for at least FIM 150.

21.27   *France*

Forms and other information are obtainable from

Direction Générale des Impôts
Centre des Non-Résidents
9, Rue d'Uzès
75084 PARIS Cedex 02

Tel: (00 33) 14 236 02 33
Fax: (00 33) 14 236 16 84

The form must be completed in French.

Non-refundable VAT. In addition to the supplies listed in 21.22 above, refunds cannot be claimed on housing, hotel accommodation, lodging, entertainment and restaurant expenses; passenger transport and any incidental activities; motor fuel (except diesel fuel); goods and services supplied free or at much less than the normal price; and services relating to non-deductible goods such as repairs to cars. Only a proportion of the VAT on motor diesel fuel can be reclaimed and it must be used solely for business purposes.

Minimum claim. If for less than one year, claim must be for at least FFrs 1400 unless it is for the final period of the year. No claim can be for less than FFrs 170.

21.28   *Germany*

Forms and other information are obtainable from

Bundesamt für Finanzen
Friedhofstrasse 1
53225 BONN
Germany

Tel: (00 49) 228 406 403
Fax: (00 49) 228 406 661

The form must be completed in German.

Non-refundable VAT. There are no other non-refundable supplies other than those listed in 21.22 above but

● full details must be provided for business entertainment claims; and

● claims for subsistence expenses must be below the specified limit (currently DM 64 a day).

Minimum claim. If for less than one year, claim must be for at least DM 400 unless it is for the final period of the year. No claim can be for less than DM 50.

21.29   *Greece*

Forms and other information are available from

Ministry of Finance
14th Directorate of VAT and Indirect Taxes
Sina 2–4
10672 ATHENS
Greece

Tel: (00 30) 1 364 72 03
Fax: (00 30) 1 364 54 13

Forms must be completed in Greek.

Non-refundable VAT. In addition to the supplies listed in 21.22 above, refunds cannot be claimed on non-business supplies; food; drink and tobacco products; hotel and other accommodation; entertainment, hospitality or amusements; acquisition, leasing or hire, modification, repair or maintenance of passenger motor vehicles, pleasure boats and private aircraft; and transport of taxable persons or of members of their staff.

Minimum claim. If for less than one year, claim must be for at least 46,000 Drachmar unless it is for the final period of the year. No claim can be for less than 6,000 Drachmar.

21.30   *Republic of Ireland*

Forms and other information are obtainable from

The Revenue Commissioners
VAT Repayment Section
Government Buildings
ENNIS
County Clare
Republic of Ireland

Tel: (00 353) 65 41200
Fax: (00 353) 65 40394

The form must be completed in English.

Non-refundable VAT. In addition to the supplies listed in 21.22 above, refunds cannot be claimed on food and drink; hotel and other accommodation; personal services; entertainment expenses; purchase and hire of passenger motor vehicles; petrol; goods or services used for the purpose of an exempt activity; and goods for supply in the Republic of Ireland or for hiring out for use there.

Minimum claim. If for less than one year, claim must be for at least IR £155 unless it is for the final period of the year. No claim can be for less than IR £19.40.

21.31   *Italy*

Forms and other information are obtainable from

2° Ufficio I.V.A. di Roma
IV Reparto Rimborsi
Via Canton n.10
00144 ROMA
Italy

Tel: (00 39) 6 520 90 222
Fax: (00 39) 6 520 39 07

Italy has a history of delaying VAT refunds and currently delays of up to four years are being experienced. In order to speed up the refund, payments of any claims not properly completed or submitted late (after 30 June of the calendar year following that to which the claim relates) will be rejected. In particular, forms will be rejected if (*a*) not completed in Italian (although the form itself may be in any official language); (*b*) not signed; or (*c*) requests for refunds are to be credited to a foreign account in lire not in the name of the applicant.

Non-refundable VAT. In addition to the supplies listed in 21.22 above, refunds cannot be claimed on hotel accommodation; food and drink; travel; the acquisition or hire of passenger motor vehicles, aeroplanes, pleasure boats and motorcycles; petrol diesel or other fuels for such transport; and luxury goods such as furs, sparkling wines and oriental carpets.

Minimum claim. If for less than one year, claim must be for at least LIT 398,000 unless it is for the final period of the year. No claim can be for less than LIT 50,000.

21.32   *Luxembourg*

Forms and other information are obtainable from

Administration de l'Enregistrement et des Domaines
Bureau d'Imposition XI
17 Ave Guillaume
BP 31
2010 LUXEMBOURG

Tel: (00 352) 44 90 51 (switchboard)
Tel: (00 352) 44 90 54 55 (Bureau XI)
Fax: (00 352) 25 07 96 (Bureau X1)

Forms must be completed in French.

Non-refundable VAT. In addition to the supplies listed in 21.22 above, refunds cannot be claimed on recreation or entertainment expenses.

Minimum claim. If for less than one year, claim must be for at least Lfrs 9000 unless it is for the final period of the year. No claim can be for less than Lfrs 1100.

21.33   *Netherlands*

Forms and other information are obtainable from

Belastingdienst Particulieren/Ondernemingen
Postbus 2865
6401 DJ HEERLEN

Tel: (00 31) 45 573 66 66
Fax: (00 31) 45 574 28 00

The form must be completed in Dutch.

Non-refundable VAT. In addition to supplies listed in 21.22 above, refunds cannot be claimed on food and drink for on-the-spot consumption in hotels, restaurants and similar establishments supplied to persons staying only a short time; goods and services used to maintain a certain status, such as luxuries, amusements or entertainment; goods or services to be used as business or other gifts to people who would not be able to deduct all or most of the turnover tax on them if it had been charged to them; and goods or services to be used to make supplies to staff of housing, wages in kind, sport and recreational facilities, private transport and any other supplies for their personal use, except for food and drink.

Minimum claim. If for less than one year, claim must be for at least FL 470 unless it is for the final period of the year. No claim can be for less than FL 60.

21.34   *Portugal*

Forms and other information are available from

Direcçâo-Geral das Contribuiçôes e Impostos
Direccáo de Serviços de Reembolsos do. IVA
Avenida Joâo XXI
Apartado 8220
1802 LISBOA Codex

Tel: (00 351) 1 795 01 02
Fax: (00 351) 1 793 81 13

Forms must be completed in Portuguese.

Non-refundable VAT. In addition to the supplies listed in 21.22 above, refunds cannot be claimed on the supply, manufacture, importation or hire of a private vehicle; the purchase of petrol (gas oil is allowed at 50% of the VAT paid); transport, business trips, tolls; accommodation, food, drinks, tobacco or entertainment; and amusements or luxuries.

Minimum claim. If for less than one year, claim must be for at least 32,000 Escudos unless it is for the final period of the year. No claim can be for less than 4,000 Escudos.

21.35   *Spain*

Forms and other information are obtainable from

Delegación Especial de Madrid de la Agencia Estatal de Administración Tributaria
Dependencia Regional de Gestión
Sección de Regimenes Especiales
C/. Guzmán el Bueno, 139, Planta 1a
28071 MADRID

Tel: (00 34) 1 582 67 39
Fax: (00 34) 1 582 67 57

The form must be completed in Spanish.

Non-refundable VAT. In addition to the supplies listed in 21.22 above, VAT cannot be reclaimed on accommodation, meals and travel expenses (unless deductible for personal or corporate income tax purposes); entertainment expenses; and car hire and fuel (unless used exclusively for business activities).

Minimum claim. If for less than one year, claim must be for at least Ptas 25,000 unless it is for the final period of the year. No claim can be for less than Ptas 3,000.

21.36   *Sweden*

Forms and information are obtainable from

Särskilda Skattekontoret
77183 LUDVIKA
Sweden

Tel: (00 46) 240 870 00
Fax: (00 46) 240 103 40

Non-refundable VAT. In addition to the supplies listed in 21.22 above, VAT cannot be reclaimed on entertainment expenses; transport (unless used exclusively for business activities); and car hire (50% of VAT can be recovered if used exclusively for business).

Minimum claim. If for three months, claim must be for at least SEK 2,000. If a year, claim must be for at least SEK 950.

21.37   **Applications to the UK by persons established in other EC countries**

Persons to whom the regulations apply. The regulations apply to a person carrying on business in an EC country other than the UK but do not apply to such a person if in the period of claim

(*a*)   he was established in the UK; or

(*b*)   he made supplies in the UK of goods and services other than

   (i)   transport of freight outside the UK or to or from a place outside the UK (and ancillary services); and

   (ii) services where the VAT on the supply is payable solely by the person to whom they are supplied under the reverse charge provisions (see 39.4 INTERNATIONAL SERVICES); and

   (iii) goods where the VAT on the supply is payable solely by the persons to whom they are supplied under *VATA 1994, s 14* (see 23.22 and 23.28 EUROPEAN COMMUNITY: SINGLE MARKET).

For these purposes a person is treated as established in a country if he has a business establishment there or he has no business establishment anywhere but his usual place of residence is there. The usual place of residence of a company is where it is legally constituted. A person carrying on business through a branch or agency in any country is treated as having a business establishment there.

Method of claiming. Claim forms are obtainable from any VAT office or

HM Customs and Excise
8th/13th Directive
Custom House
PO Box 34
LONDONDERRY
BT48 7AE
Northern Ireland

Tel: 44 1504 37 27 27
Fax: 44 1504 37 25 20

Forms must be completed in English and must be sent to the above address, together with the supporting documentation and, if appropriate, a certificate of status.

Non-refundable VAT. Refunds cannot be claimed on VAT incurred on

- a supply (or part of a supply) which is not used for the purpose of the business;

- a supply or importation of goods or a supply of services used (or intended to be used) by the claimant for the purpose of any supply by him in the UK;

- a supply or importation of goods which the claimant has removed (or intends to remove) to another EC country or which he has exported (or intends to export) outside the EC;

- a supply or importation where input tax recovery is restricted in the UK (e.g. most motor cars, business entertainment, and second-hand goods for which no VAT invoice is issued);

- goods and services which have been bought for resale and which are for the direct benefit of travellers, e.g. hotel accommodation bought in by tour operators, travel agents, etc. to make up package holidays.

Minimum claim and time limit. The claim must be made not later than six months after the end of the calendar year in which the VAT claimed was charged and must be for a period of not less than three months and not more than one year.

If the claim is for less than a year, it must be for at least £130 unless it is for the final part of the calendar year. No claim can be for less than £16.

Methods of repayment. Payments will normally be made either to a UK bank or by payable order in sterling directly to the claimant or his appointed agent. Payments cannot be made by payable order or credit transfer to overseas banks. Where a claimant does not have a UK bank account, his own bank should present the payable order to a UK clearing bank which will then pay the amount shown in the appropriate currency.

Agents. If the claimant appoints an agent to act on his behalf, the agent must submit a power of attorney or letter of authority stating that they can make claims and accept monies on the claimant's behalf. The following is an example of the format of a letter of authority acceptable to C & E.

'I [name and address of claimant] hereby appoint [name and address of agent] to act on my behalf in connection with any claims I make to Her Britannic Majesty's Commissioners of Customs and Excise under the Value Added Tax Regulations 1995, Part XX as from time to time amended or replaced. Any repayment of VAT to which I am entitled pursuant to such claim made on my behalf by my above named agent shall be paid to [name and address of payee].

Date..............................Signed..............................[by the claimant]'

Appeals. An appeal may be made to an independent VAT tribunal against a refusal by C & E to allow all or part of a repayment. A Notice of Appeal must be served at the London VAT Tribunal Centre within 30 days of the date of the letter notifying the refusal. Alternatively, the applicant may first ask C & E to review their decision and extend the time for service of a Notice of Appeal. If the decision is maintained and such an extension is granted the applicant then has 21 days from the date of the letter upholding the decision to serve a Notice of Appeal.

Importations. The above provisions also allow repayment of VAT charged on the importation of goods into the UK from places outside the EC but only if no other relief is available.

[*VATA 1994, s 39; SI 1995/2518, Regs 173–184*]. See also C & E Notice 723, para 1.25.

Isle of Man. Applications for refunds of VAT incurred in the Isle of Man should be made to the UK competent authority.

22   European Community Legislation

De Voil Indirect Tax Service. See V1.301–328.

The contents of this chapter are as follows.

22.1   LEGAL INSTRUMENTS OF THE EC

Statements of the European Council and European Commission are graded under the *EEC Treaty* as follows.

• **Regulations** are binding in their entirety and have general effect to all EC countries. They are directly applicable in the legal systems of EC countries.

• **Directives** are binding as to result and their general effect is specific to named EC countries. The form and methods of compliance are left to the addressees.

• **Decisions** are binding in their entirety and are specific to an EC country, commercial enterprise or private individual.

• **Recommendations and Opinions** are not binding and are directed to specific subjects on which the Council's or Commission's advice has been sought.

De Voil Indirect Tax Service. See V1.253–255; V1.258.

22.2   EC LEGISLATION AS PART OF UK LEGISLATION

EC law is made effective for UK legislation. [*European Communities Act 1972, s 2*]. The basis for VAT as the common EC turnover tax derives from *EEC Treaty, Arts 3(g)(h), 99* and Council and Commission statements thereunder. The effects of EC law as regards UK VAT legislation can be summarised as follows.

(*a*)   **Direct effect.** Although *EEC Treaty, Article 189* does not specifically allow for direct effect in an EC country, the Court of Justice has held 'wherever the provisions of a directive appear. . . to be unconditional and sufficiently precise, those provisions may. . . be relied upon as against any national provision which is incompatible with the directive insofar as the provisions define rights which individuals are able to assert against the state' (*Becker v Finanzamt Münster-Innenstadt, CJEC [1982] ECR 53; [1982] 1 CMLR 499*). See also *Staatssecretaris van Financien v Cooperatieve Vereninging Cooperatieve Aardappelenbewaarplaats GA, CJEC [1981] ECR 445; [1981] 3 CMLR 337* which case was considered in *UFD Ltd, [1981] VATTR 199 (1172)* in which it was said 'in all appeals involving issues of liability, the tribunal should consider the relevant provisions of the Council directives to ensure that the provisions of the UK legislation are consistent therewith'. See also *Yoga for Health Foundation v C & E Commrs QB, [1984] STC 630* where exemption from VAT was allowed for certain welfare services under *EC 6th Directive* although there was no corresponding provision in the UK legislation.

22.3   European Community Legislation

(b)   **Primacy of EC Directives over national legislation.** A national court which is called upon, within the limits of its jurisdiction, to apply provisions of Community law, is under a duty to give full effect to those provisions, if necessary refusing of its own motion to apply any conflicting provision of national legislation, even if adopted subsequently, and it is not necessary for the court to request or await the prior setting aside of such provisions by legislative or other constitutional means (*Amministrazione delle Finanze dello Stato v Simmenthal SpA, CJEC [1978] ECR 629; [1978] 3 CMLR 263*).

In *EC Commission v United Kingdom, CJEC [1988] STC 456* the CJEC ruled that the UK had contravened the provisions of *EC 6th Directive* by zero-rating certain supplies of sewerage and water, news services, supplies of fuel and power and the construction of commercial buildings. In the earlier decision *EC Commission v United Kingdom, [1988] STC 251* the CJEC had similarly ruled in relation to the exempting of supplies of spectacles, contact lenses and hearing aids. As a result of each decision, the UK law was amended.

In *Direct Cosmetics v C & E Commrs, CJEC [1985] STC 479* it was held that an amendment to UK legislation, which had been previously enacted under the derogation powers in *EC 6th Directive, Art 27* (see 22.30 below), was itself a 'special measure' requiring derogation to be authorised by the European Commission. As this had not been obtained, the whole provisions failed and could not be relied on against the taxpayer.

(c)   **Interpretation of UK law.** If the domestic VAT legislation of the UK is unclear or ambiguous, tribunals are 'entitled to have regard to the provisions of the *Sixth Directive* in order to assist in resolving any ambiguity in the construction of the provisions under consideration' (*English-Speaking Union of the Commonwealth, [1980] VATTR 184 (1023)*). If EC law appears unclear it may be interpreted by referring to the legislative history ('*travaux preparatoires*') but such evidence has been held to be admissible only by reference to tests in *Fothergill v Monarch Airlines Ltd, [1981] AC 251 (The Open University, [1982] VATTR 29 (1196))*. This decision is open to doubt. See, for example, *EC Commission v The Kingdom of Belgium, CJEC [1984] ECR 1861* where the Belgium government used minutes of a Council meeting held prior to the adoption of the *EC 6th Directive* in evidence.

Judgments in the European Court of Justice also have supremacy over domestic decisions even if the proceedings commenced in another EC country.

For further consideration of the effect of Community law, including inconsistencies between UK domestic law and Community law and reference to Community law in VAT tribunal decisions, see the chapter on *European Community Law* in *Tolley's VAT Planning*.

De Voil Indirect Tax Service. See V1.261; V1.262.

22.3   VAT HARMONISATION DIRECTIVES

A directive must be read as a whole. The preamble, which sets out the purpose of the legislation, is an essential part of it. Moreover, as distinct from UK law, it is acceptable when determining the purpose of the legislation to consider the discussions, decisions, etc. ('*travaux preparatoires*') which led to the legislation being drafted in its final form.

The principal directives issued by the EC Council on the harmonisation of legislation of EC countries concerning turnover taxes, and which are still current and relevant in the UK, are as follows.

- *1st Directive. [67/227/EEC]*. This provides for a common VAT system to be operated by EC countries.

- *6th Directive. [77/388/EEC]*. This is the so-called 'harmonisation directive' and clarifies many of the definitions of basic terms used in the legislation of individual EC countries. See 22.4 *et seq* below.

- *7th Directive. [94/5/EEC]*. This provides for special arrangements applicable to second-hand goods, works of art, collectors' items and antiques. See SECOND-HAND GOODS (61).

- *8th Directive. [79/1072/EEC]*. This provides for the refund of VAT suffered by Community traders in those EC countries where they do not have a business establishment. See 22.49 below.

- *10th Directive. [84/386/EEC]*. This amends and clarifies the provisions of the *6th Directive* in connection with the hiring out of moveable tangible property.

- *13th Directive. [86/560/EEC]*. This provides for refund of VAT to taxable persons not established in the EC. See 22.50 below.

- *17th Directive. [85/362/EEC]*. This introduces the exemption from VAT on certain temporary importations from other EC countries or from outside the EC. The provisions ceased to have effect after 31 December 1992.

- *18th Directive. [89/465/EEC]*. This abolishes a number of derogations provided for in *6th Directive*.

A number of subsidiary directives have also been made.

De Voil Indirect Tax Service. See V1.256; V1.257.

22.4   **SIXTH DIRECTIVE**

Many of the *Articles* of the *EC 6th Directive* are similar to the provisions of the *VATA 1994*. Where they are unconditional and precise (e.g. as evidenced by the use of the word 'must' in the text below) their wording takes preference to that in the *VATA 1994*. Where *Articles* are discretionary (e.g. as evidenced by the use of the words 'countries may' in the text below) the UK may apply the provisions or not as it wishes. However, where they are applied, the provisions once adopted must be applied precisely.

22.5   **Scope**

VAT applies to

- the supply of goods or services (see 22.7 and 22.8 below) effected for consideration within the territory of the country by a taxable person (see 22.6 below) acting as such; and

- the 'importation of goods'.

'Importation of goods' means

(i) the entry of goods into the EC which do not satisfy the conditions laid down in *Articles 9* and *10* of the *Treaty establishing the EEC* or, where the goods are covered by the *Treaty establishing the European Coal and Steel Community*, are not in free circulation; and

(ii) the entry into the Community of goods from a 'third territory', other than goods covered by (i) above. *'Third territory'* means any territory other than those defined as the territory of an EC country in 21.2 EUROPEAN COMMUNITY: GENERAL.

[*EC 6th Directive, Arts 2, 7(1)*].

The principle of fiscal neutrality precludes a generalised differentiation between lawful and unlawful transactions except where, because of the special characteristics of certain products, all competition between a lawful economic sector and an unlawful sector is precluded. Thus the illegal sale of drugs is not a supply for VAT purposes (*Mol v Inspecteur der InVoerrechten Accijinzen, CJEC 1988, [1989] BVC 205*) but the supply of counterfeit perfume is. See *R v Goodwin and Unstead CA, [1997] STC 22, CJEC, [1998] STC 699*. The prohibition on such products stems from the fact that they infringe intellectual property rights and is conditional not absolute (as in the case of drugs and counterfeit money). There is scope for competition between counterfeit perfumes and perfumes which are traded lawfully and although supply of the former is unlawful, such perfume is not liable to seizure in the hands of the final customer. The unlawful operation of a form of roulette was similarly held to be a supply for VAT purposes in *Fischer v Finanzamt Donaueschingen, CJEC [1998] STC 708*. However, although the unlawful playing of a game of chance is a supply, it is not taxable where the corresponding activity is exempt when carried on lawfully by a licensed casino.

In *Tolsma v Inspecteur der Omzetbelasting Leeuwarden, CJEC [1994] STC 509* an individual who played a barrel organ on the public highway and invited donations from the public was held not to be supplying services for a consideration. There was no agreement between the parties and also 'no necessary link between the musical service and the payment to which it gave rise'.

22.6   **Taxable persons**

Taxable person means any person who 'independently' carries out in any place any 'economic activity' whatever the purpose or result of that activity.

'*Economic activity*' comprises all activities of producers, traders and persons supplying services including mining and agricultural activities and activities of professions. Included is the exploitation of tangible and intangible property for the purposes of obtaining income on a continuing basis.

In *Rompelman v Minister van Financien, CJEC [1985] 3 CMLR 202; [1985] ECR 655* the acquisition of a future right of joint ownership in property under construction with a view to letting that property in due course was held to be an economic activity although objective evidence (e.g. proposed contracts, planning permission) that arrangements have been made to begin making taxable supplies should be produced. The first investment expenditure incurred for the purpose of a business can be regarded as an economic activity even if it does not give rise to any taxable transactions. See *Intercommunale voor Zeewaterontzilting (in liquidation) v Belgian State CJEC, [1996] STC 569* where VAT was held to be deductible on a profitability study although, as a result of the study, the company did not move to the operational phase. See also *WM van Tiem v Staatssecretaris van Financien, CJEC 1990, [1993] STC 91*.

The holding of shares does not amount to an economic activity if the shareholder is not involved in the management of the companies whose shares it holds. Neither is it the exploitation of assets for the purposes of obtaining income because any dividend received arises from the ownership of the shares, not from an economic activity (*Polysar Investments Netherlands BV v Inspecteur der Invoerrechten en Accijnzen, Arnhem, CJEC [1993] STC 222*). See also *Harnas & Helm CV v Staatssecretaris van Financien, CJEC [1997] STC 364*. The purchase and sale of shares by trustees in the course of the management of a charitable trust does not amount to an economic activity (*The Wellcome Trust Ltd v C & E Commrs, CJEC [1996] STC 945*).

See 8.1 BUSINESS for the meaning of 'business' under UK legislation.

The use of the word '*independently*' excludes employed and other persons from VAT in so far as they are bound to an employer by a contract of employment or by any other legal ties creating the relationship of employer and employee as regards working conditions, remuneration and employer's liability.

Countries may also treat as taxable persons anyone who carries out, on an occasional basis, a transaction relating to an economic activity and in particular

- the supply before first occupation of buildings (or part) and the land on which they stand. Countries may apply criteria other than first occupation e.g. the period elapsing between the date of completion of the building and the date of first supply (not exceeding five years) or the period elapsing between the date of first occupation and the date of subsequent supply (not exceeding two years); and

- the supply of building land.

Single taxable person. Each country may treat different persons established in their territory as a single taxable person where those persons, although legally independent, are closely bound to one another by financial, economic and organisational links. See 8.5 BUSINESS for UK provisions.

Local authorities etc. States, regional and local government authorities and other bodies governed by public law are not considered taxable persons in respect of the activities or transactions in which they engage as public authorities unless treatment as non-taxable persons would lead to significant distortions of competition. In any case, provided they are not carried out on such a small scale as to be negligible, these bodies are considered taxable persons in relation to the activities of telecommunications; the supply of water, gas, electricity and steam; the transport of goods; port and airport services; passenger transport; supply of new goods manufactured for sale; agricultural intervention agencies; the running of trade fairs and exhibitions; warehousing; the activities of commercial publicity bodies and travel agents; the running of staff shops, cooperatives and industrial canteens and similar institutions; and public radio and television bodies of a commercial nature. For a general consideration of these provisions see *Ufficio Distrettuale delle Imposte Dirette di Fiorenzuola d'Arda v Comune di Carpaneto Piacentino* and *Ufficio Provinciale Imposta sul Valore Aggiunto di Piacenza v Comune di Rivergaro and Others, CJEC 1989, [1991] STC 205*.

Countries may also treat activities of these bodies which are exempt under 22.17 to 22.19 and 22.31 below as activities they engage in as public authorities. This applies even if the body acted in a similar manner to a private trader (*Finanzamt Augsburg-Stadt v Marktgemeinde Welden, CJEC [1997] STC 531*).

[*EC 6th Directive, Art 4*].

See 43 LOCAL AUTHORITIES AND STATUTORY BODIES for UK provisions.

De Voil Indirect Tax Service. See V2.101; V2.108; V2.201.

22.7   **Supply of goods**

Supply of goods means the transfer of the right to dispose of 'tangible property'.

'*Tangible property*' includes electric current, gas, heat, refrigeration and the like. Countries may consider it to include certain interests in moveable property; rights *in rem* giving the holder a right of user over immovable property (see *WM van Tiem v Staatssecretaris van Financien, CJEC 1990, [1993] STC 91*); and shares etc. giving the holder *de jure* or *de facto* rights of ownership or possession over immovable property.

A supply of goods includes

(*a*) the transfer, by order made by or in the name of a public authority or in pursuance of the law, of the ownership of property against payment of compensation;

(*b*) the actual handing over of goods under a contract for the hire of goods for a certain period or for the sale of goods on deferred terms, where the contract provides that in the normal course of events ownership must pass at the latest upon payment of the final instalment;

(*c*) the transfer of goods pursuant to a contract under which commission is payable on purchase or sale;

(*d*) the application by a taxable person of business assets for his private use or that of his staff;

(*e*) the disposal of business assets free of charge;

(*f*) the application of business assets other than for business purposes;

and, at the consideration of the country, may include

(*g*) the handing over of certain works of construction;

(*h*) the application by a taxable person for the purposes of his business of goods produced, constructed, extracted, processed, purchased or imported in the course of the business, where the VAT on the goods would not be wholly deductible had the goods been acquired from another taxable person; and

(j) the application of goods for a non-taxable transaction or the retention of goods by a taxable person or his successors where VAT was wholly or partly deductible on acquisition or upon application under (*h*) above.

Under (*d*) to (*f*) above, the supply is only treated as a supply of goods for a consideration if VAT on the goods in question or the component parts thereof was wholly deductible and the supply is not the giving of samples or the making of gifts of small value for the purposes of the business.

See 64.3 SUPPLY for UK provisions.

Transfers of businesses etc. In the event of a transfer of all the assets (or part thereof) countries may consider that no supply of goods takes place. In that event the recipient must be treated as the successor to the transferor. Countries may take the necessary measures to prevent distortion of competition where the recipient is not wholly liable to VAT. See 8.10 BUSINESS for UK provisions.

[*EC 6th Directive, Art 5*].

22.8   Supply of services

Supply of services means any transaction which does not constitute a supply of goods (see 22.7 above). Included is

(*a*) the assignment of intangible property;

(*b*) an obligation to refrain from an act or to tolerate an act or situation;

(*c*) the performance of services in pursuance of an order by or in the name of a public authority or in pursuance of the law;

(*d*) the use of business assets for the private use of the taxable person or his staff or generally for non-business purposes where VAT on such goods is wholly or partly deductible;

(e) the supply of services carried out free of charge by the taxable person for his own private use or that of his staff or generally for non-business purposes.

Countries may derogate from the provisions of (d) and (e) above provided that this does not lead to distortion of competition.

Where a taxable person acting in his own name but on behalf of another person takes part in the supply of services, he must be considered to have received and supplied the services himself.

Self-supply of services. To prevent distortion of competition, countries may treat the supply by a taxable person of services for the purposes of his undertaking as a supply of services for a consideration provided the VAT on the service would not have been wholly deductible had it been supplied by another taxable person.

[*EC 6th Directive, Art 6*].

See 64.4 SUPPLY for the UK provisions.

22.9   **Place of supply of goods**

The place of supply of goods is deemed to be as follows. See, however, 22.36 below for transitional provisions applying to trade between EC countries until a definitive VAT system, based on the principle of taxation of goods in the EC country of origin, can be decided upon.

(a) *In the case of goods dispatched or transported*, the place where the goods are at the time when dispatch or transport to the person to whom they are supplied begins. Where the goods are installed or assembled by or on behalf of the supplier, the place of supply is deemed to be the place where the goods are installed or assembled. If this is a different EC country to that of the supplier, the country within which the installation or assembly is carried out must take necessary steps to avoid double taxation in that country.

By way of derogation, where the place of departure of the consignment or transport of the goods is in a country outside the EC, the place of supply by the importer and the place of any subsequent supplies is deemed to be within the EC country of import of the goods.

(b) *In the case of goods not dispatched or transported*, the place where the goods are when the supply takes place.

(c) *In the case of goods supplied on board ships, aircraft or trains during the part of a transport of passengers effected in the EC* at the point of the departure of the transport of passengers.

[*EC 6th Directive, Art 8*].

Imports. The place of supply of imports is the EC country within the territory of which the goods are when they enter the EC except that where goods are, on entry into the EC, placed under one of the arrangements referred to in 22.22(b)(i)–(iv) below, under arrangements for temporary importation with total exemption from import duty or under external transit arrangements, the place of import is the EC country within the territory of which they cease to be covered by those arrangements.

See 64.8 SUPPLY for the UK provisions.

22.10   **Place of supply of services**

General rule. Subject to below, services are deemed to be supplied in the place where the supplier has established his business or has a fixed establishment from which the service is supplied or, in the absence of any such place of business or establishment, the place where he has his permanent address or usually resides. See, however, 22.39 below for transitional provisions applying to services rendered by intermediaries until a definitive VAT system, based on the principle of taxation of services in the EC country of origin, can be decided upon.

The general rule above is overridden in the following circumstances.

(*a*)   The place of supply of services connected with immovable property, including the services of estate agents and experts, and services for preparing and co-ordinating construction services (e.g. architects and on-site supervisors) is the place where the property is situated.

(*b*)   The place of supply of transport services is where the transport takes place, having regard to the distance covered. See, however, 22.37 below for transitional provisions applying until a definitive VAT system, based on the principle of taxation of services in the EC country of origin, can be decided upon.

(*c*)   The place of supply of services relating to

(i)   cultural, artistic, sporting, scientific, educational, entertainment or similar activities, including the activities of the organisers of such activities, and where appropriate the supply of ancillary services,

(ii)   ancillary transport activities such as loading, unloading, handling, and similar activities, and

(iii)   valuation of, and work on, moveable tangible property,

is the place where those services are physically carried out.

See, however, 22.38 and 22.39 below for transitional provisions applying to services under (ii) and (iii) above respectively until a definitive VAT system, based on the principle of taxation of services in the EC country of origin, can be decided upon.

(*d*)   The place where the following services are supplied when performed for customers established outside the EC, or for taxable persons established in the EC but not in the same country as the supplier, is the place where the customer has established his business or has a fixed establishment to which the service is supplied or, in the absence of such a place, the place where he has a permanent address or usually resides. The services in question are

(i)   transfers and assignments of copyrights, patents, licences, trade marks and similar rights;

(ii)   advertising services (see *EC Commission v France, Luxembourg, Spain, CJEC 1993, [1997] STC 684*);

(iii)   services of consultants, engineers, consultancy bureaux, lawyers, accountants and other similar services, as well as data processing and the supply of information;

(iv)   obligations to refrain from pursuing or exercising, in whole or in part, a business activity or a right within this list;

(v)   banking, financial and insurance transactions including reinsurance, with the exception of the hire of safes;

(vi)   the supply of staff;

(vii)   the services of agents who act in the name and for the account of another, when they procure for their principals the services referred to within this list; and

(viii)   the hiring out of moveable tangible property with the exception of all forms of transport.

In order to avoid double taxation, non-taxation or the distortion of competition, a country may, in relation to services under (*d*) above or the hiring out of forms of transport, treat the place of supply of services

(i) which would otherwise be within that country as being outside the EC where the effective use and enjoyment of the services takes place outside the EC; and

(ii) which would otherwise be outside the EC as being within that country where the effective use and enjoyment of the services takes place within that country.

[*EC 6th Directive, Art 9*].

See 64.18 SUPPLY for the UK provisions.

22.11   **Time of supply**

A chargeable event occurs and VAT becomes chargeable when goods are delivered or services performed. Deliveries of goods (other than those in 22.7(*c*) above) and supplies of services which give rise to successive statements of account or payments are regarded as being completed at the time when the periods, to which such statements of account or payments pertain, expire. However, where a payment is made on account before the goods are delivered or the services performed, VAT becomes chargeable on receipt of the payment and on the amount received.

By way of derogation from the above, countries may provide that VAT becomes chargeable, for certain transactions or for certain categories of taxable person, either

(*a*)   no later than the issue of the invoice; or

(*b*)   no later than receipt of the price; or

(*c*)   where an invoice is not issued, or is issued late, within a specified period from the date of the chargeable event.

See 64.32 SUPPLY for the UK provisions.

Imported goods. The chargeable event occurs and the VAT becomes chargeable when the goods are imported. Where, on entry, goods are placed under

• one of the arrangements referred to in 22.22(*b*) below, or

• arrangements for temporary importation with total exemption from import duty, or

• external transit arrangements

the chargeable event occurs and the VAT becomes chargeable only when the goods cease to be covered by those arrangements.

Where, however, imported goods are subject to customs duties or agricultural levies or similar charges, the chargeable event occurs and the VAT becomes chargeable at the same time.

See 34.2 IMPORTS for the UK provisions.

[*EC 6th Directive, Art 10*].

22.12   **Taxable amount: supplies within a country**

Subject to the exceptions below, the taxable amount in respect of supplies of goods or services is everything which constitutes the consideration which has been or will be obtained by the supplier from the purchaser, the customer or a third party for such supplies, including subsidies directly linked to the price of the supplies. The exceptions are as follows.

- In respect of supplies within 22.7(*d*)(*e*)(*f*) *(h)* and (*j*) above, the taxable amount is the purchase price of the goods or of similar goods or, in the absence of a purchase price, the cost price, determined at the time of supply.

- In respect of supplies within 22.8(*d*) and (*e*) above, the full cost to the taxable person of providing the services.

- In respect of the self-supply of services under 22.8 above, the open market value of the services supplied.

Included in the taxable amount are

(*a*) taxes duties, levies and charges, excluding VAT itself;

(*b*) incidental expenses e.g. commission, packing, transport and insurance costs charged by the supplier;

but excluded are

(*c*) price reductions by way of discount for early payment;

(*d*) price discounts and rebates allowed to the customer and accounted for at the time of supply; and

(*e*) the amounts received by a taxable person from his purchaser or customer as repayment for expenses paid out in the name and for the account of the latter and which are entered in his books in a suspense account. The taxable person must furnish proof of the actual amount of this expenditure and cannot deduct any VAT which may have been charged on these transactions.

[*EC 6th Directive, Art 11*].

See 69 VALUATION for UK provisions.

22.13 Taxable amount: imports

The taxable amount is the value for customs purposes as determined in accordance with EC provisions in force.

The taxable amount includes taxes etc. as in 22.12(*a*) above due outside the importing EC country and those due by reason of importation, excluding the VAT to be levied; and incidental expenses as in 22.12(*b*) above incurred up to the 'first place of destination' within the territory of the importing country. It must not include 22.12(*c*) and (*d*) above.

'*First place of destination*' is the place mentioned on the consignment note etc. or, in the absence of any such indication, the place of first transfer of cargo in the importing EC country.

The incidental expenses referred to above must also be included in the taxable amount where they result from transport to another place of destination within the territory of the community provided that place is known when the chargeable event occurs.

Where goods have been temporarily exported from the EC and are re-imported after having undergone repair, processing or adaptation, or after having been made up or reworked, outside the EC, countries must take steps to ensure that the treatment of goods for VAT purposes is the same as that which would have applied to the goods in question had the operations been carried out within the territory of the country.

[*EC 6th Directive, Art 11*].

See 69.7 VALUATION for UK provisions.

22.14   Miscellaneous provisions

(*a*)   In case of *cancellation, refusal or total or partial non-payment*, or where the price is reduced after the supply takes place, the taxable amount must be reduced accordingly under conditions determined by each EC country although, in the case of total or partial non-payment, countries may derogate from this rule.

(*b*)   Where information for determining the taxable amount is expressed in *foreign currency*,

- for importations, the exchange rate must be determined in accordance with EC provisions governing the calculation of the value for customs purposes (see *EC Council Regulation 1224/80/EEC*); and

- the exchange rate applicable for transactions other than importations is the latest selling rate recorded, at the time the VAT becomes chargeable, on the most representative exchange market or markets of the EC country concerned.

See 69.6 VALUATION for the UK provisions.

(*c*)   As regards *returnable packing costs*, countries may either

- exclude them from the taxable amount and take the necessary measures to see that this amount is adjusted if the packing is not returned; or

- include them in the taxable amount and take the necessary measures to see that this amount is adjusted where the packaging is returned.

[*EC 6th Directive, Art 11*].

22.15   Rates

The rate applicable to taxable transactions is that in force at the time of the chargeable event. However, where a payment is made on account before the goods are delivered or the EC country has derogated under 22.11(*a*) to (*c*) above, the rate to be used is that in force when the VAT becomes chargeable.

Importation of goods. The rate applicable on the importation of goods is that applied to the supply of like goods within the country at the time the VAT on the importation becomes chargeable.

Standard rate. A standard rate of VAT must be applied which, until 31 December 1998, cannot be less than 15%.

Reduced rates. Countries may also apply either one or two reduced rates. These cannot be less than 5% and can only be applied to goods or services listed in *Annex H*. These include foodstuffs, water supplies, pharmaceutical products and medical equipment, aids for the handicapped, passenger transport, books and printed matter, admissions to shows and sporting events and use of sporting facilities, housing supplies as part of a social policy, holiday accommodation, certain charitable supplies, undertakers' and cremation services, and medical and dental care. Countries may also apply a reduced rate to supplies of natural gas and electricity (provided that no risk of distortion of competition exists) and imports of works of art, collectors' items and antiques.

During a transitional period until a definite VAT system is decided upon, exemptions with refund of VAT paid at the preceding stage (i.e. zero-rating in the UK) may be maintained provided they were in force on 1 January 1991 and were in accordance with Community law.

[*EC 6th Directive, Arts 12, 28(2)*].

22.16   Exemptions

EC countries must exempt certain activities under conditions that they lay down for the purpose of ensuring the correct and straightforward application of such exemptions and of preventing any possible evasion, avoidance or abuse. These are divided into exemptions for certain activities in the public interest (see 22.17 below), other exemptions (see 22.18 below), exemptions on importation (see 22.20 below) and exemption of exports and like transactions and international transport (see 22.21 below).

22.17   *Exemptions for certain activities in the public interest*

The following activities should be exempt.

(*a*)   The supply by the public postal service of services other than passenger transport and telecommunications services, and the supply of goods incidental thereto.

(*b*)   Hospital and medical care and closely related activities undertaken by bodies governed by public law or, under social conditions comparable to those applicable to bodies governed by public law, by hospitals, centres for medical treatment or diagnosis and other duly recognised establishments of a similar nature.

(*c*)   The provision of medical care in the exercise of the medical or paramedical professions as defined by the country concerned.

(*d*)   Supplies of human organs, blood and milk.

(*e*)   Services supplied by dental technicians in their professional capacity and dental prostheses supplied by dentists and dental technicians.

(*f*)   Services supplied by independent groups of persons whose activities are exempt from or not subject to VAT, for the purpose of rendering their members the services directly necessary for the exercise of their activity, where these groups merely claim from their members exact reimbursement of their share of joint expenses, provided that such exemption is not likely to produce distortion of competition.

(*g*)   The supply of services and of goods closely linked to welfare and social security work, including those supplied by old people's homes, by bodies governed by public law or by other organisations recognised as charitable by the country concerned. See *The Lord Mayor and Citizens of the City of Westminster, [1989] VATTR 71 (3367)* where the Council ran a hostel for single and homeless men.

(*h*)   The supply of services and of goods closely linked to the protection of children and young persons by bodies governed by public law or by other organisations recognised as charitable by the country concerned.

(*i*)   Children's or young people's education, school or university education, vocational training or retraining, including the supply of services and of goods closely related thereto, provided by bodies governed by public law having such as their aim or by other organisations defined by the country concerned as having similar objects.

(*j*)   Tuition given privately by teachers and covering school or university education.

(*k*)   Certain supplies of staff by religious or philosophical institutions for the purposes of (*b*), (*g*), (*h*) or (*i*) above and with a view to spiritual welfare.

(*l*)   Supply of services and goods closely linked thereto for the benefit of their members in return for a subscription fixed in accordance with their rules by non-profit-making organisations with aims of a political, trade union, religious, patriotic, philosophical, philanthropic or civic nature, provided that this exemption is not likely to cause distortion of competition.

(*m*) Certain services closely linked to sport or physical education supplied by non-profit-making organisations to persons taking part in sport or physical education.

(*n*) Certain cultural services and goods closely linked thereto supplied by bodies governed by public law or by other cultural bodies recognised by the country concerned.

(*o*) The supply of services and goods by organisations whose activities are exempt under (*b*), (*g*), (*h*), (*i*), (*l*), (*m*) and (*n*) above in connection with fund-raising events organised exclusively for their own benefit provided that exemption is not likely to cause distortion of competition. Countries may introduce any necessary restrictions in particular as regards the number of events or the amount of receipts which give entitlement to exemption.

(*p*) The supply of transport services for sick or injured persons in vehicles specially designed for the purpose by duly authorised bodies.

(*q*) Activities of public radio and television bodies other than those of a commercial nature.

The supply of goods and services under (*b*), (*g*), (*h*), (*i*), (*l*), (*m*) and (*n*) above is not exempt if

- it is not essential to the transaction exempted; or

- its basic purpose is to obtain additional income for the organisation by carrying out transactions which are in direct competition with those of commercial enterprises liable for VAT.

Countries may make the granting to bodies other than those governed by public law of exemption under (*b*), (*g*), (*h*), (*i*), (*l*), (*m*) and (*n*) above subject to one or more of the following conditions.

(i) They do not systematically aim to make profit. Any profits arising must not be distributed but assigned to the continuance or improvement of the services supplied.

(ii) They must be managed and administered on an essentially voluntary basis by persons who have no direct or indirect interest in the results of the activities concerned.

(iii) They charge prices approved by the public authorities or which do not exceed such approved prices or, in respect of those services not subject to approval, prices lower than those charged for similar services by commercial enterprises subject to VAT.

(iv) Exemption of the service concerned must not be likely to create distortions of competition such as to place at a disadvantage commercial enterprises liable to VAT.

[*EC 6th Directive, Art 13A*].

22.18   *Other exemptions*

The following activities should be exempt.

(*a*) Insurance and reinsurance transactions, including related services performed by insurance brokers and agents.

(*b*) The leasing or letting of immovable property other than

- the provision of accommodation in the hotel or similar sectors, including holiday camps and camping sites;

- the letting of premises and sites for parking vehicles;

- letting of permanently installed equipment and machinery; and

- hire of safes.

(*c*)   The granting and the negotiation of credit and the management of credit by the person granting it.

(*d*)   The negotiation of, or any dealings in, credit guarantees or any other security for money and the management of credit guarantees by the person who is granting the credit.

(*e*)   Transactions, including negotiations, concerning deposit and current accounts, payments, transfers, debts, cheques and other negotiable instruments, but excluding debt collecting and factoring.

(*f*)   Transactions, including negotiations, concerning currency, bank notes and coins used as legal tender, with the exception of collectors' items.

(*g*)   Transactions, including negotiations but excluding management and safekeeping, in shares, interests in companies or associations, debentures and other securities, excluding

- documents establishing title to goods;

- rights *in rem* giving the holder thereof a right of user over immovable property; and

- shares or interests equivalent to shares giving the holder thereof *de jure* or *de facto* rights of ownership or possession over immovable property or part thereof.

(*h*)   Management of special investment funds as defined by countries.

(*i*)   The supply at face value of postage stamps valid for use for postal services within the territory of the country, fiscal stamps and similar stamps.

(*j*)   Betting, lottery and other forms of gambling, subject to conditions and limitations laid down by each country.

(*k*)   The supply of buildings or parts thereof, and of land on which they stand, other than the supply before first occupation.

(*l*)   The supply of land which has not been built on other than building land as defined by each country.

(*m*)   Supplies of goods

- used wholly for an activity exempted under (*a*) to (*l*) above or under 22.17 above or by an EC country under a derogation when these goods have not given rise to the right to deduction; or

- on the acquisition or production of which VAT did not become deductible.

[*EC 6th Directive, Art 13B*].

For a consideration of the scope of (*e*) and (*f*) above see *Sparekassernes Datacenter (SDC) v Skatteministeriet, CJEC [1997] STC 932.*

22.19   *Options*

Countries may allow taxpayers a right of option to tax in cases of

- letting and leasing of immovable property; and

• the transactions under 22.18(*c*)–(*g*), (*k*) and (*l*) above.

[*EC 6th Directive, Art 13C*].

22.20   *Exemptions on importation*

Countries must exempt the following.

(*a*)   Final importation of goods of which the supply by a taxable person would in all circumstances be exempted within the country.

(*b*)   Final importation of goods qualifying for exemption from customs duties other than as provided for in the Common Customs Tariff. Countries have the option of not granting exemption if this might have a serious effect on conditions of competition.

(*c*)   Reimportation by the person who exported them of goods in the same state as which they were exported, where they qualify for exemption from customs duties.

(*d*)   Importation of goods under diplomatic and consular arrangements etc. which qualify for exemption from customs duties; by international organisations; and into the territory of EC countries which are parties of the North Atlantic Treaty by the armed forces of other states which are parties to the treaty.

(*e*)   Importation into ports by sea fishing undertakings of their catches, unprocessed (except for preservation) but before being supplied.

(*f*)   The supply of services in connection with the importation of goods where those services are included in the taxable amount (see 22.13 above).

(*g*)   Importations of gold by central banks.

[*EC 6th Directive, Art 14*].

22.21   *Exemption of exports from the EC and like transactions and international transport*

Countries must exempt the following.

(*a*)   The supply of goods dispatched or transported to a destination outside the EC

(i)   by or on behalf of the vendor, or

(ii)   by or on behalf of a purchaser not established in the country (except for goods transported by the purchaser himself for equipping, fuelling, etc. pleasure boats and private aircraft or any other means of transport for private use). In the case of a supply of goods to be carried in the personal luggage of travellers, this exemption applies on condition that the traveller does not hold an EC passport; the goods are transported to a destination outside the EC before the end of the third month following that in which the supply takes place; and the total value of the supply (including VAT) is more than the equivalent of ECU 175 in national currency (countries may exempt supplies with lower values).

(*b*)   The supply of services consisting of work on moveable property acquired or imported for the purpose of undergoing such work in the EC and dispatched or transported out of the EC by the person providing the services *or* by his customer if established outside the country *or* on behalf of either of them.

(*c*)   The supply of goods for the fuelling and provisioning of vessels

(i)   used for navigation at sea and carrying passengers for reward or used for the purposes of commercial, industrial or fishing activities;

(ii) used for rescue or assistance at sea;

(iii) of war leaving the country and bound for foreign ports or anchorages.

(*d*) The supply, modification, repair, maintenance, chartering and hiring of sea-going vessels within (*c*)(i) and (ii) above or aircraft used by airlines operating for reward chiefly on international routes and the supply, hiring, repair and maintenance of equipment (including fishing equipment) incorporated or used therein.

(*e*) The supply of goods for the fuelling and provisioning of aircraft within (*d*) above.

(*f*) The supply of services other than those referred to in (*d*) above to meet the direct needs of sea-going vessels or aircraft referred to in (*d*) above or of their cargoes.

(*g*) Supplies of goods and services

(i) under diplomatic and consular arrangements, etc;

(ii) to international organisations;

(iii) effected within an EC country which is a party to the North Atlantic Treaty and intended for use by the forces of other states which are party to the treaty or the civilian staff accompanying them, or for supplying their messes and canteens when such forces take part in the common defence effort; and

(iv) to another EC country and intended for the forces of any EC country which is a party to the North Atlantic Treaty, other than the country of destination itself, for the use of those forces, etc. as under (iii) above.

(*h*) Supplies of gold to Central Banks.

(*i*) Goods supplied to approved bodies which export them from the EC as part of their humanitarian, charitable or teaching activities outside the EC.

(*j*) The supply of services including transport and ancillary operations (but excluding the supply of services exempted under 22.17 to 22.19 above) where these are directly linked with

(i) the export of goods;

(ii) the import of goods placed under one of the arrangements in 22.22(*b*)(i)–(iv) below under arrangements for temporary importation with total exemption from import duty or under external transit arrangements; or

(iii) the import of goods intended to be placed under warehousing arrangements other than customs.

(*k*) Services supplied by brokers and other intermediaries, acting in the name and for the account of another person, where they form part of transactions within this *Article* or of transactions carried out outside the EC. This exemption does not apply to travel agents who supply in the name and for the account of the traveller services which are supplied in other EC countries.

[*EC 6th Directive, Art 15*].

22.22   *Special exemptions linked to international goods traffic*

Countries may take special measures designed to relieve the following transactions from VAT, provided that they are not aimed at final use or consumption and that the amount of VAT charged at entry for home use corresponds to the VAT which should have been charged had the transaction been taxed on import or within the country.

(*a*)   imports of goods which are intended to be placed under warehousing arrangements other than customs;

(*b*) supplies of goods which are intended to be

(i) produced to customs and, where applicable, placed in temporary storage;

(ii) placed in a free zone or in a free warehouse;

(iii) placed under customs warehousing arrangements or inward processing arrangements;

(iv) admitted into territorial waters either to be incorporated in, or for the purposes of repair of, drilling or production platforms or for the fuelling and provisioning of such platforms;

(v) placed under warehousing arrangements other than customs;

(*c*) supplies of services relating to supplies of goods under (*b*) above;

(*d*) supplies of goods and services carried out in the places listed in (*b*) and still subject to one of the arrangements specified therein; and

(*e*) supplies of goods

(i) still subject to arrangements for temporary importation with total exemption from import duty or to external transit arrangements; or

(ii) imported from a territory within 21.2 EUROPEAN COMMUNITY: GENERAL and still subject to the internal Community transit procedure under 22.32 below.

Re-exportations. Countries may also opt to exempt imports for, and supplies of goods to, a taxable person intending to export them as they are or after processing, as well as supplies of services linked with the export business, up to a maximum equal to the value of his exports during the preceding 12 months. See, however, 22.44 below for transitional provisions applying after 31 December 1992.

[*EC 6th Directive, Art 16*].

22.23 Deductions

The right to deduct input tax arises when the deductible VAT becomes chargeable.

Where goods and services are used for the purposes of his taxable transactions, a taxable person is entitled to deduct from the VAT which he is liable to pay

(*a*) VAT due or paid in respect of goods or services supplied or to be supplied to him by another taxable person;

(*b*) VAT due or paid in respect of imported goods; and

(*c*) VAT due under 22.7(*h*) above or the self-supply rules under 22.8 above.

Included is VAT in so far as the goods and services are used for the purposes of

(i) transactions relating to economic activities carried out in another country which would be eligible for deduction if carried out in that country;

(ii) transactions within 22.20(*f*), 22.21 and 22.22(*b*) to (*d*) and re-exportations; and

(iii) any of the transactions exempted under 22.18(*a*)(*c*)–(*g*) when the customer is established outside the EC or when the transactions are directly linked with goods intended to be exported to a country outside the EC.

See 35.1–35.3 INPUT TAX for the UK provisions.

Where goods and services are used by the taxable person both for transactions covered by (*a*) and (*b*) above and for transactions in respect of which VAT is not deductible, the proportion deductible is given by the fraction

$$\frac{A}{B}$$

where

A = the total amount, exclusive of VAT, of turnover per year attributable to transactions in respect of which VAT is deductible; and

B = the total amount, exclusive of VAT, of turnover per year attributable to all transactions.

The proportions must be determined on an annual basis, fixed as a percentage and rounded up to a figure not exceeding the next unit. By derogation, EC countries may exclude supplies of capital goods, incidental transactions within 22.18(*c*)–(*h*) and incidental real estate and financial transactions.

Countries may, however, authorise or compel the taxable person to determine a proportion for each sector of his business and keep separate accounts for each sector or to make deductions on the basis of the use of the goods and services. Countries may also provide that where non-deductible VAT is insignificant it is treated as nil.

See 49 PARTIAL EXEMPTION for the UK provisions.

[*EC 6th Directive, Arts 17, 19*].

22.24 *Adjustments of deductions*

The initial deduction must be adjusted, according to the procedures laid down by the EC country where, for example, that deduction was higher or lower than that to which the taxable person was entitled or after the return is made changes occur in the factors used to determine the amount to be deducted. [*EC 6th Directive, Art 20*].

22.25 *Capital goods*

In the case of capital goods, adjustments must be spread over five years including that in which the goods were acquired or manufactured. By derogation the period may commence from the time the goods are first used. The annual adjustment must be made only in respect of one-fifth of the VAT imposed on the goods and must be made on the basis of the variations in the deduction entitlement in subsequent years in relation to that for the year in which the goods were acquired or manufactured.

In the case of immovable property, the adjustment period may be extended to up to 20 years.

Where capital goods are supplied during the period of adjustment, they are treated as if they had still been applied for business use by the taxable person until the expiry of the period of adjustment. Such business activities are presumed to be fully taxed in cases where the supply of the goods is taxed and fully exempt where the supply is exempt. The adjustment is made only once for the whole period of adjustment still to be covered.

[*EC 6th Directive, Art 20*].

See CAPITAL GOODS SCHEME (10) for UK provisions.

22.26 *Exercising the right to deduct*

To exercise his right to deduct, the taxable person must

(*a*) in respect of deductions under 22.23(*a*) hold a proper VAT invoice;

(*b*) in respect of deductions under 22.23(*b*) hold an import document specifying him as consignee or importer and stating or permitting the calculation of the amount of VAT due;

(*c*) in respect of deductions under 22.23(*c*) comply with the formalities laid down by each EC country; and

(*d*) when he is required to pay VAT as a customer or purchaser under 22.27(*a*)–(*c*) below, comply with the formalities laid down by the EC country.

He then effects the deduction by subtracting from the total amount of VAT due for a given tax period the total amount of the VAT in respect of which, in the same VAT period, the right to deduct has arisen.

Countries may require that, for taxable persons who carry out occasional transactions, the right to deduct can be exercised only at the time of the supply.

Where for a given VAT period the amount of authorised deductions exceeds the amount of VAT due, the EC country may either make a refund or carry the excess forward to the following period according to conditions which they determine.

[*EC 6th Directive, Art 18*].

22.27 Persons liable to pay the VAT

Under the internal system, the person liable to pay the VAT is as follows.

(*a*) The taxable person carrying out the taxable supply of goods or of services other than one of the supplies of services within (*b*) below. Countries may provide that where the taxable transaction is carried out by a person established outside the territory of the country, the VAT is payable by another person (e.g. a VAT representative). They may also provide that someone other than the taxable person is jointly and severally liable for payment.

(*b*) The customer for services within 22.10(*d*) above (and, during a transitional period until a definite VAT system can be agreed upon, 22.37, 22.38 or 22.39 below) carried out by a taxable person established abroad. Countries may require the supplier of the services to be jointly and severally liable for payment.

(*c*) Any person who mentions VAT on an invoice or other document serving as an invoice.

(*d*) During a transitional period until a definite VAT system can be agreed upon, any person effecting a taxable intra-Community acquisition of goods. Countries may provide that where such an acquisition is effected by a taxable person established abroad, the VAT is payable by another person (e.g. a VAT representative). They may also provide that someone other than the person effecting the intra-Community acquisition is jointly and severally liable for payment.

On importation, the person liable is the person designated or accepted as being liable by the EC country into which the goods are imported.

[*EC 6th Directive, Arts 21, 28g*].

22.28 Obligations of taxable persons and EC countries

Taxable persons and EC countries have the following obligations. Many of the obligations arise only during a transitional period until a definitive VAT system, based on the principle of taxation of services in the EC country of origin, can be decided upon.

(*a*) Every taxable person must state when his activity as a taxable person commences, changes or ceases.

During the transitional period

- without prejudice to the above, every taxable person within 22.34(*a*)(i)–(iii) below must state that he is effecting intra-Community acquisitions of goods when the conditions for application of the derogation are not fulfilled; and

- with certain exceptions, EC countries must take measures to identify, by means of an individual number, every taxable person who effects supplies of goods and services, or intra-Community acquisitions, within the territory of the country and every taxable person within 22.34(*a*)(i)–(iii) below or who exercises the option for the derogation not to apply.

(*b*) Every taxable person must keep accounts in sufficient detail for VAT to be applied and inspected by the tax authority.

(*c*) Every taxable person must issue an invoice in respect of

(i) goods and services supplied by him to another taxable person or, during the transitional period, to a non-taxable legal person,

(ii) during the transitional period, supplies of goods within 22.36 below and goods supplied under the conditions within 22.40(*a*) below, and

(iii) payments on account made to him before any supply of goods within (i) or (ii) above or made to him by another taxable person or by a non-taxable legal person before the provision of services is completed

and must keep copies thereof. The invoice must clearly state the price exclusive of VAT and the relevant VAT at each rate as well as any exemptions.

During the transitional period, the invoice must also show

- for transactions falling within 22.37 to 22.39 below, the number by which the taxable person is identified in the territory of the country and the number by which the customer is identified and under which the service has been rendered to him;

- for transactions falling within 22.40(*a*) below, the number by which the taxable person is identified in the territory of the country and the number by which the person acquiring the goods is identified in another EC country; and

- in the case of the supply of a new means of transport, the necessary particulars to show that the vehicle, etc. falls within those provisions.

Countries must lay down the criteria for deciding whether a document may be considered an invoice.

(*d*) Every taxable person must submit a return within an interval after the end of the VAT period (not more than two months) to be determined by each EC country. The return must set out

(i) all information needed to calculate the VAT that has become chargeable and the deduction to be made;

(ii) where appropriate, the total value of transactions relative to the VAT and deductions within (i) above and the value of any exempt transactions;

(iii) during the transitional period, the total value, less VAT, of supplies of goods within 22.40(*a*) below on which VAT has become chargeable in the period;

(iv) during the transitional period, the total value, less VAT, of the supplies of installed or assembled goods and goods within 22.36 above effected within the territory of another EC country for which VAT has become chargeable in the return period where the place of departure of the dispatch or transport of the goods is situated in the territory of the country;

(v) during the transitional period, the total value, less VAT, of intra-Community acquisitions within 22.34(a) below effected within the territory of the country on which VAT has become chargeable; and

(vi) during the transitional period, the total value, less VAT, of supplies as in (iv) above effected within the territory of the country where the place of departure of the dispatch or transport of the goods is situated in the territory of another EC country.

Every taxable person must pay the net amount of VAT when submitting the return although countries may fix a different date or may demand an interim payment.

(e) Countries may require a taxable person to submit a statement, including all the particulars within (d) above, concerning all transactions carried out in the preceding year.

(f) During the transitional period, every taxable person identified for VAT purposes must submit a recapitulative statement for every quarter of the acquirers identified for VAT purposes to whom he has supplied goods under the conditions in 22.40(a) and (d) below. The statement must show

(i) the VAT registration number of the taxable person;

(ii) the VAT registration number of his customer in another EC country, together with a country identifier; and

(iii) the aggregate value of goods and associated services supplied to that customer.

The Council may authorise a country to allow any taxable person to file such recapitulative statements annually where his supplies do not exceed specified limits and a taxable person who already prepares annual VAT returns to prepare the recapitulative statement for the same period where his supplies do not exceed a (higher) specified limit.

(g) During the transitional period, where supplies of new means of transport are effected under the conditions in 22.40(b) below by a taxable person identified for VAT purposes to a purchaser not identified for VAT purposes (or by a person regarded as a taxable person for these purposes under 22.40 above), countries must take the measures necessary to ensure that the vendor supplies all the necessary information to the tax authorities.

(h) Countries may impose other obligations which they deem necessary for the correct collection of VAT and the prevention of evasion, subject to the requirement of equal treatment for domestic transactions and transactions carried out between member states.

[EC 6th Directive, Arts 22, 28h].

Imports. Countries must lay down the detailed rules for the making of the declarations and payments and may provide that VAT need not be paid at the time of importation. [EC 6th Directive, Art 23].

22.29   Special schemes

(a) **Small undertakings.** Countries may apply simplified procedures to small undertakings for charging and collecting VAT and may grant an exemption from VAT to taxable persons whose annual turnover is below a certain limit.

(*b*) **Common flat-rate scheme for farmers.** Countries may apply such a scheme to farmers where the application of the normal VAT scheme, or the simplified rules for small undertakings above, would give rise to difficulties. See 63.15 SPECIAL SCHEMES for UK provisions.

(*c*) **Special schemes for travel agents.** Where a travel agent (including a tour operator) deals with customers in his own name and uses supplies and services of other taxable persons in the provision of travel services, all transactions performed by him in respect of a journey are treated as a single service supplied by him to the traveller. The supply is taxable in the EC country in which the travel agent has established his business or has a fixed establishment from which he has provided the services. The taxable amount, and the price exclusive of VAT under 22.28(*c*) above, is the travel agent's margin, i.e. the difference between the total amount to be paid by the traveller, exclusive of VAT, and the actual cost to the travel agent of supplies and services provided by other taxable persons where these transactions are for the direct benefit of the traveller. See *Independent Coach Travel (Wholesaling) Ltd, [1993] VATTR 357 (11037)* where the tribunal held that 'customers' should be construed as a reference to 'travellers' and that these provisions only apply to travel agents dealing with travellers and not those who act as wholesalers making supplies to retailers.

Where transactions carried out by other taxable persons on behalf of the travel agent are performed outside the EC, the travel agent's services are treated as an exempt intermediary transaction under 22.21(*k*) above.

VAT charged to the travel agent by other taxable persons on the transactions which are for the direct benefit of the traveller is not eligible for deduction or refund in the EC.

The above provisions do not apply to travel agents who are acting only as intermediaries and accounting for VAT under 22.12(*e*) above.

The fact that the travel agent provides accommodation only, and not transport, does not exclude such a service from the ambit of these provisions (*Beheersmaatschappij Van Ginkel Waddinxveen BV and Others v Inspecteur der Omzetbelasting, Utrecht, CJEC 1992, [1996] STC 825*).

See TOUR OPERATORS' MARGIN SCHEME (66) for UK provisions.

(*d*) **Second-hand goods, works of art, collectors' items and antiques.** All countries must apply special arrangements for taxing the profit margin made by a taxable dealer in respect of supplies by him of second-hand goods, works of art, collectors' items and antiques where those goods were supplied to him by

• a non-taxable person;

• another taxable person in so far as the supply of goods by that other person is exempt under 22.18(*m*) above;

• another taxable person in so far as the supply of goods by that other person qualifies for exemption under (*a*) above and involves capital assets; or

• another taxable dealer in so far as the supply of goods by that other dealer was subject to VAT under these special arrangements.

The taxable amount is the profit margin (i.e. the difference between the selling price and the buying price) made by the taxable dealer, less the VAT relating to it.

Countries must also allow taxable dealers to opt to use the scheme for supplies of works of art, collectors' items and antiques which they have imported and works of art supplied by their creators (or their successors in title).

Where supplies are made under the scheme, any input tax incurred on the purchase of the goods cannot be deducted.

To simplify the procedure for charging VAT, countries may provide that, for certain transactions or certain categories of dealer, the taxable amount of supplies of goods under the scheme is to be determined for each VAT period as a whole (rather than for each individual transaction).

Countries may make special arrangements for sales by public auctions.

See SECOND-HAND GOODS (61) for UK provisions.

(e) **Special scheme for investment gold.** From 1 January 2000, all countries must exempt the supply, acquisition and importation of 'investment gold', including investment gold represented by certificates for allocated or unallocated gold or traded on gold accounts and including, in particular, gold loans and swaps, involving a right of ownership or claim in respect of investment gold, as well as transactions concerning investment gold involving futures and forward contracts leading to a transfer of right of ownership or claim in respect of investment gold. Countries must also exempt services of agents acting in the supply of investment gold for their principals.

'*Investment gold*' comprises bars and wafers of very high purity as traded in the bullion markets and gold coins the value of which primarily reflects their gold price. Such coins are not, for these purposes, considered to be bought for numismatic interest. Each country must before 1 July each year inform the EC Commission of coins meeting the specified criteria which are traded in that country.

Option to tax. Countries must allow taxable persons who produce investment gold, or transform any gold into investment gold, a right to opt to tax supplies of investment gold to another taxable person. They may also allow taxable persons who supply gold for industrial use to opt to tax the supply to another taxable person of investment gold in the form of bars and wafers (but not coins). Where the supplier has exercised such an option, a country may allow any agent acting for that supplier to opt to tax his services. It may also designate the purchaser as the person liable to pay the tax under the reverse charge procedure.

Transactions on the regulated gold bullion market. An EC country may disapply the exemption for investment gold in respect of specific transactions, other than intra-EC supplies or exports, concerning investment gold taking place in that country

(a)   between taxable persons who are members of a regulated bullion market; and

(b)   where the transaction is between a member of a regulated bullion market and another taxable person who is not such a member.

Under such circumstances, the transactions are taxable.

Input tax. Taxable persons are entitled to deduct VAT due or paid in respect of

• investment gold supplied to them by a person who has exercised the option to tax as above or under the procedure for regulated bullion markets as above,

• the supply to them, or intra-EC acquisition or importation by them, of gold other than investment gold which is subsequently transformed by them (or on their behalf) into investment gold, and

• services supplied to them consisting of change of form, weight or purity of gold including investment gold, if their subsequent supply of the gold is exempt under these provisions.

Taxable persons who produce investment gold, or transform any gold into investment gold, are entitled to deduct VAT due or paid in respect of supplies, intra-EC acquisitions, importations or services linked to the production or transformation of that gold as if their subsequent supply of the gold exempted under these provisions were taxable.

[*EC 6th Directive, Arts 24-26(b)*].

22.30   **Derogations**

The Council may authorise any EC country to introduce special measures for derogation from the provisions of the *6th Directive* in order to simplify the procedure for charging VAT (without affecting the amount of VAT due at the final consumption stage except to a negligible extent) or to prevent certain types of tax evasion or avoidance. In addition countries were allowed to retain special measures which were in force on 1 January 1977 provided that they notified the Commission of them before 1 January 1978 (when the *6th Directive* was implemented).

The derogations granted to the UK government are in connection with the following.

● Special RETAIL SCHEMES (60).

● Trading stamps. The special provisions relating to trading stamps were repealed with effect from 1 June 1996.

● Exemption from registration where, although taxable supplies exceed the registration limit, all supplies are, or would be, zero-rated if the taxable person was registered. See 59.6 REGISTRATION.

● Valuation for VAT purposes where certain companies, for example in the field of cosmetics, sell products to individuals who are outside the tax net for resale to the final customer. See 22.2(*b*) above and 69.4 VALUATION.

● Operation of UK TERMINAL MARKETS (65).

● Long stays in hotels. See 33.2 HOTELS AND HOLIDAY ACCOMMODATION.

● Treatment of goods in warehouse.

● Voluntary accounting scheme for transactions in GOLD (30).

● Fuel expenditure for company cars. See 45.16 MOTOR CARS.

● Cash accounting scheme. See 63.2 SPECIAL SCHEMES.

● Transfer of assets to a partly exempt group. See 31.7 GROUPS OF COMPANIES.

● Direction to use open market value for exempt supplies to connected persons (see 69.3 VALUATION) and acquisitions of goods from connected persons (see 69.9 VALUATION).

● Taxation of self-supplies of land and buildings to be based on open market value. This derogation has not been introduced.

● Preparation of annual EC sales lists by persons with low turnover and by persons who prepare annual VAT returns. See 2.25 ACCOUNTING PERIODS AND RETURNS.

● Valuation of, and work carried out on, goods in the UK for VAT-registered customers in other EC countries. This derogation became redundant after 31 December 1995.

● Transport services directly linked to an intra-Community transport of goods. See 68.26 TRANSPORT AND FREIGHT.

- Restricting to 50% the right of the hirer or lessee to deduct input tax on car hire or leasing transactions where the car is used for private purposes and waiving VAT payable on the private use of the car in question. See 45.11 MOTOR CARS.

- The place of supply of telecommunications services. See 64.28 SUPPLY.

[*EC 6th Directive, Art 27*].

22.31   Transitional provisions

For a transitional period, countries are allowed to

- continue to tax certain items set out in *Annex E* to the *Directive* which are otherwise exempted under the provisions of 22.17, 22.18 and 22.21 above; and

- continue to exempt certain items set out in *Annex F* to the *Directive* which are otherwise taxable.

The *18th Directive* phased out most of these provisions over the period from 1 January 1990 to 1 January 1993.

[*EC 6th Directive, Art 28*].

22.32   Trade with countries in the customs territory of the EC

Goods entering the Community from, or as the case may be dispatched from the Community to, a territory which forms part of the customs territory of the Community but which is considered a third country for VAT purposes (see 21.3 EUROPEAN COMMUNITY: GENERAL) are subject to special provisions. The formalities relating to the entry into the Community/(export from the Community) of such goods are the same as those in force for the import of goods into/(export of goods from) the customs territory of the Community.

[*EC 6th Directive, Art 33a*].

22.33   SIXTH DIRECTIVE — TRANSITIONAL ARRANGEMENTS FOR THE TAXATION OF TRADE BETWEEN EC COUNTRIES

The transitional arrangements in 22.34 to 22.48 below came into force on 1 January 1993 and modify or extend the provisions in 22.5 to 22.32 above. They will apply until a definitive system, based upon the taxation of goods and services in the EC country of origin, can be decided on and enter into force. [*EC 6th Directive, Art 28l*].

22.34   Scope

(*a*) **Intra-Community acquisitions of goods.** Subject to the derogation below, 'intra-Community acquisitions of goods' for a consideration within the territory of a country by a taxable person or a non-taxable legal person are subject to VAT where the vendor is a registered taxable person who is not covered by the arrangements for installed or assembled goods (see 22.9(*a*) above) or the derogation in 22.36 below.

By way of derogation, VAT is not chargeable on intra-Community acquisitions of goods (other than new means of transport and products subject to excise duty) effected by

(i) a taxable person eligible for a flat-rate scheme for farmers (see 22.29 above),

(ii) a taxable person who only supplies goods or services that are not deductible, or

(iii) a non-taxable legal person

253

for a total amount not exceeding, during the current calendar year, a threshold to be determined by each EC country (but which must not be less than the national equivalent of 10,000 ECUs). To qualify in any calendar year, the total of intra-Community acquisitions effected by that person in the previous calendar year must not have exceeded the threshold set by that country.

Intra-Community acquisitions of goods includes the use by a taxable person for the purposes of his undertaking in an EC country of goods dispatched from another EC country where they were produced, purchased, acquired or imported by him within the framework of his undertaking.

(*b*)   **Intra-Community acquisitions of new means of transport.** Such acquisitions (as defined) are subject to VAT when effected for a consideration within the country by taxable persons, non-taxable legal persons qualifying for the derogation in (*a*) above or any other non-taxable person.

(*c*)   **Intra-Community acquisitions of goods subject to excise duty.** Such goods are subject to VAT when effected for a consideration within the country by taxable persons or non-taxable legal persons qualifying for the derogation in (*a*) above.

'*Intra-Community acquisitions of goods*' means acquisition of the right to dispose as owner of movable tangible property dispatched or transported to the person acquiring the goods to an EC country other than that from which the goods are dispatched or transported.

Where goods acquired by a non-taxable legal person are dispatched or transported from a country outside the EC and imported by that person into an EC country other than the country of arrival of the goods, the goods are deemed to have been dispatched, etc. from the EC country of import.

A person who from time to time supplies a new means of transport under the conditions laid down in 22.40 below must be regarded as a taxable person. EC countries must lay down detailed rules allowing the taxable person the right of deduction of the VAT, at the time of supply, included in the purchase, acquisition or importation price not exceeding the VAT for which he would be liable if the supply were not exempt.

Goods effected for a consideration include the transfer by a taxable person of goods from his undertaking to another EC country (subject to exceptions).

[*EC 6th Directive, Art 28a*].

22.35   **Place of intra-Community acquisition of goods**

Subject to below, the place of the intra-Community acquisition of goods is deemed to be the place where the goods are at the time when dispatch or transport to the person acquiring them ends.

Without prejudice to the above, the place of intra-Community acquisition of goods within 22.34(*a*) above is deemed to be within the EC country which issued the VAT identification number under which the person acquiring the goods made the acquisition (unless the person acquiring the goods establishes that that acquisition has been subject to VAT in accordance with the above general rule).

[*EC 6th Directive, Art 28b(A)*].

22.36   **Place of supply of goods**

Derogation. Subject to the exception below, by way of derogation from 22.9(*a*), the place of supply of goods dispatched or transported from an EC country other than that of arrival of the dispatch or transport is deemed to be the place where the goods are when dispatch or transport to the purchaser ends provided

(*a*) the supply is effected for a taxable person eligible for the derogation under 22.34(*a*) above, a non-taxable legal person eligible for the same derogation or for any other non-taxable person; and

(*b*) the supply is of goods other than new means of transport and other than goods supplied after assembly or installation by or on behalf of the supplier.

Where the goods thus supplied are dispatched or transported from a country outside the EC and imported by the supplier into an EC country other than that of arrival of the goods, they are to be regarded as having been dispatched or transported from the EC country of import.

Exception to the derogation. Where the supply is of goods other than products subject to excise duty, the above provisions do not apply to supplies of goods dispatched or transported to the same EC country of arrival where

- the total value of such supplies, less VAT, does not in one calendar year exceed the equivalent of 100,000 ECUs; and

- the total value, less VAT, of supplies of goods other than products subject to excise duty effected under those provisions in the previous calendar year did not exceed the equivalent of 100,000 ECUs.

Countries have the option of restricting the figure of 100,000 ECUs above to 35,000 ECUs if it would otherwise lead to the distortion of conditions of competition.

Countries within the territory of which the goods are at the time of departure of the dispatch or transport must grant those taxable persons who effect supplies of goods eligible for the exception the right to choose that the place of such supplies shall be determined under the derogation above.

[*EC 6th Directive, Art 28b(B)*].

22.37   **Place of supply of services in the intra-Community transport of goods**

By way of derogation from 22.10(*b*) above, the place of supply of services in the 'intra-Community transport of goods' is to be determined as follows.

(*a*) Subject to (*b*) below, the place of supply of services in the intra-Community transport of goods is the place of departure.

(*b*) The place of supply of such services rendered to customers identified for VAT purposes in a country other than that of the departure of the transport is deemed to be within the EC country which issued the customer with the VAT identification number under which the service was rendered to him.

(*c*) Countries need not apply VAT to that part of the transport corresponding to journeys made over waters which do not form part of the territories of the EC.

The '*intra-Community transport of goods*' means transport where the place of departure and place of arrival are in two different EC countries. The transport of goods where the place of departure and arrival are in the same country is treated as intra-Community transport of goods where such transport is closely linked to transport of goods where the place of departure and arrival are in different EC countries.

[*EC 6th Directive, Art 28b(C)*].

22.38 **Place of supply of services ancillary to the intra-Community transport of goods**

By way of derogation from 22.10(c)(ii) above, the place of supply of services involving activities ancillary to the intra-Community transport of goods, rendered to customers identified for VAT purposes in an EC country other than that within which the services are physically performed, is deemed to be within the EC country which issued the customer with the VAT identification number under which the service was rendered to him.

[*EC 6th Directive, Art 29b(D)*].

22.39 **Place of supply of services — other provisions**

Services rendered by intermediaries. By way of derogation from the general rule in 22.10 above, the place of supply of services rendered by intermediaries acting in the name and for the account of other persons is, subject to below,

(*a*) where the services form part of the supply of services in the intra-Community transport of goods, the place of departure of the goods;

(*b*) where the services form part of the supply of services the purpose of which is activities ancillary to the intra-Community transport of goods, the place where the ancillary services are physically performed; and

(*c*) where such services form part of a transaction not falling within (*a*) or (*b*) above or 22.10(*d*) above, the place where those transactions are carried out.

Where, however, the customer for whom the services under (*a*) to (*c*) above are rendered by the intermediary is identified for VAT purposes in an EC country other than the place of supply under those provisions, the place of supply is deemed to be within the EC country which issued the customer with the VAT identification number under which the services were rendered to him by the intermediary.

[*EC 6th Directive, Art 28b(E)*].

Valuation of or work on movable tangible property. By way of derogation from 22.10(*c*)(iii) above, the place of supply of services involving valuations or work on movable tangible property, provided to customers identified for VAT purposes in an EC country other than that in which the services are physically carried out, is deemed to be within the EC country which issued the customer with the VAT identification number under which the service was carried out for him. This derogation does not apply where the goods are not dispatched or transported out of the EC country where the services were physically carried out.

[*EC 6th Directive, Art 28c(F)*].

22.40 **Exempt supplies of goods**

Without prejudice to other EC provisions and subject to such conditions as they stipulate, countries must exempt the following supplies.

(*a*) Supplies of goods (as defined in 22.7 above) dispatched or transported out of the territory but within the EC, effected for another taxable person or a non-taxable legal person in an EC country other than that of the departure of the dispatch or transport of the goods except for

● supplies of goods by taxable persons exempt from registration; and

- supplies of goods effected for taxable persons or non-taxable legal persons who qualify for derogation under 22.34(*a*) above.

(*b*) Supplies of new means of transport, dispatched or transported to the purchaser out of the territory but within the EC, effected for taxable persons, non-taxable legal persons who qualify for the derogation under 22.34(*a*) above or any other non-taxable person.

(*c*) Supplies of goods subject to excise duty dispatched or transported to the purchaser outside the territory but inside the Community and effected for taxable persons or non-taxable legal persons who qualify for the derogation under 22.34(*a*) above. This does not, however, apply to supplies of goods subject to excise duty effected by taxable persons who benefit from the exemption from VAT set out in *Art 24* (special schemes for small undertakings).

(*d*) The transfer, under certain circumstances, by a taxable person of goods from his undertaking to another EC country (deemed to be a supply of goods under 22.34 above) if such a supply would qualify for exemption under (*a*)–(*c*) above if carried out for another taxable person.

[*EC 6th Directive, Art 28c(A)*].

22.41 Exempt intra-Community acquisitions of goods

Without prejudice to other Community provisions and subject to such conditions as they stipulate, countries must exempt the intra-Community acquisition of goods

(*a*) the supply of which by taxable persons would in all circumstances be exempt within the territory of the country;

(*b*) the importation of which in all circumstances would be exempt under 22.20 above; and

(*c*) where, under 22.23(i)–(iii) above, the person acquiring the goods would in all circumstances be entitled to full reimbursement of the VAT due under 22.34(*a*) above.

[*EC 6th Directive, Art 28c(B)*].

22.42 Exempt transport services

Countries must exempt the supply of intra-Community transport services involved in the dispatch or transport of goods to and from the Azores and Madeira as well as the dispatch or transport of goods between those islands. [*EC 6th Directive, Art 28c(C)*].

22.43 Exempt importation of goods

Where goods dispatched or transported from a country outside the EC are imported into an EC country other than that of arrival of the dispatch or transport, countries must exempt such imports where the supply of such goods by the importer is exempt under 22.40 above. [*EC 6th Directive, Art 28c(D)*].

22.44 Other exemptions

Where countries adopt the special measures under 22.22 above, they must take necessary measures to ensure that intra-Community acquisitions of goods intended to be placed under one of the arrangements, etc. under 22.22(*b*) above benefit from the same provisions as supplies of goods effected within the territory of the country under the same conditions.

The provisions in 22.22 above under the heading *Re-exportation* are extended to intra-Community acquisitions of goods made by a taxable person. The goods must be exported outside the Community.

[*EC 6th Directive, Art 28c(E)*].

22.45   Chargeable event and chargeability of VAT

The chargeable event occurs when the intra-Community acquisition of goods is effected i.e. when the supply of similar goods is regarded as being effected within the territory of the country.

VAT becomes chargeable on intra-Community acquisitions of goods, and supplies of goods effected under the conditions in 22.40 above, on the 15th day of the month following that during which the chargeable event occurs or on the issue of the invoice (or document serving as an invoice) if earlier.

[*EC 6th Directive, Art 28d*].

22.46   Taxable amount and rate applicable

For intra-Community acquisitions of goods, the taxable amount must be established on the same basis as those used under 22.12 above to determine the taxable amount for supply of the same goods within the territory of the country. The rate of VAT is that in force when the VAT becomes chargeable on the supply of like goods within the territory of the country. [*EC 6th Directive, Art 28e*].

22.47   Right of deduction

The right to deduct input tax is extended to cover VAT due on intra-Community acquisitions under 22.34(*a*) above and goods or services used for the purposes of transactions which are exempt under 22.40 above.

To exercise the right to deduct VAT on intra-Community acquisitions, the taxable person must keep records of all the information needed for the amount of that VAT to be calculated and hold a proper invoice.

[*EC 6th Directive, Art 28f*].

22.48   Tax-free shops

Until 30 June 1999, countries may exempt supplies by tax-free shops in airports and ports of goods to be carried away by travellers taking intra-Community flights or sea crossings to EC countries (including in-flight and on-board sales) subject to a limit of ECU 90 per person per journey.

They must also allow the right of a deduction or refund input tax in so far as the goods or services are used for the purposes of such supplies.

[*EC 6th Directive, Art 28k*].

22.49   EIGHTH DIRECTIVE: REFUNDS OF VAT TO PERSONS ESTABLISHED IN OTHER EC COUNTRIES

The *8th Directive* enables a taxable person to recover VAT suffered in another EC country provided he is not already registered in that country (in which case that countrry's domestic VAT legislation would apply).

The taxable person must not be established in the relevant country (but must be established elsewhere in the EC) and must not make supplies of goods or services therein except of transport (and related) services carried out in connection with the international carriage of goods and services where the VAT on the supply is accounted for solely by the person to whom they are supplied. [*EC 8th Directive, Articles 1, 2*]. These may differ slightly between EC countries but broadly correspond to those listed in *VATA 1994, 5 Sch* (see 64.27 SUPPLY). Recovery only extends to VAT on business supplies and to qualify the taxable person must

(*a*)   submit to the competent authority of the relevant country a prescribed application form *completed in block capitals in the language of that country* attaching originals of invoices or import documents (but see *Société Générale des Grandes Sources d'Eaux Minérales Françaises v Bundesamt für Finanzen, CJEC [1998] STC 981* where it was held that a country *could* accept duplicate or photocopied invoices where the originals had been lost through no fault of the taxpayer and there was no risk of a further application for a refund. Moreover, if that country accepted internal claims for input tax in similar circumstances, the principle of non-discrimination in the preamble to the *8th Directive* required it to extend the same possibility to persons established in other EC countries);

(*b*)   produce a certificate of status (valid for one year) issued by the official authority of the country in which he is registered stating that he is a taxable person (see *Debouche v Inspecteur der Invoerrechten en Accijnzen, CJEC [1996] STC 1406*);

(*c*)   give a written declaration that no goods or services have been supplied in the EC country (except as above); and

(*d*)   undertake to repay any sum recovered in error.

[*EC 8th Directive, Articles 3, 4*].

VAT is not refundable if it would be disallowed for credit if incurred by a person registered in the EC country. Similarly, exempt supplies of goods are outside the provisions. However, the country must not impose any condition as to recoverability outside the *Directive's* provisions otherwise than to justify an application. [*EC 8th Directive, Articles 5, 6*].

Applications must relate to invoiced supplies or imports made during a period of not less than three months or not more than one calendar year. Applications may, however, relate to a period of less than three months where the period represents the remainder of a calendar year. An application may relate to invoices etc. not covered by previous applications although applicable to charges incurred during the calendar year in question, but applications must otherwise be submitted within six months of the end of the calendar year in which the VAT became chargeable. Provision is made for the exclusion of small claims, the prevention of invoices being used more than once and the return of documents to the claimant within one month. A decision whether or not to grant an application must be made by the relevant authority within six months of submission. Payment must be made within the same period either in the relevant country or in the country in which the applicant is registered, in which case any bank charges must be borne by the applicant. Refusal to grant an application must give grounds for the decision and appeals must be allowed to be made on the same basis as domestic cases. A competent authority is given powers to reclaim amounts paid under fraudulent applications for a period of two years from the date of the fraudulent application. [*EC 8th Directive, Article 7*].

See 21.22–21.36 and 21.37 EUROPEAN COMMUNITY: GENERAL for applications to other EC countries by UK taxable persons and applications to the UK by persons established in other EC countries respectively.

22.50 THIRTEENTH DIRECTIVE: REFUNDS OF VAT TO PERSONS ESTABLISHED OUTSIDE THE EC

The *13th Directive* requires each EC country to introduce a scheme to enable a taxable person established outside the EC to recover VAT suffered in that country provided he is not already registered there.

The taxable person must not make supplies of goods or services in the particular EC country other than

*   supplies of transport (and related) services carried out in connection with the international carriage of goods; or

*   services where the VAT on the supply is accounted for solely by the person to whom they are supplied.

Countries may make the refunds conditional upon the granting of comparable advantages regarding turnover tax by the territory where the taxable person is established. [*EC 13th Directive, Articles 1, 2*].

Administrative arrangements and conditions for submitting applications, time limits and periods covered, minimum amounts claimable and methods of repayment are left to the individual countries. Refunds cannot be granted on terms more favourable than those applied to EC taxable persons. Countries may provide for the exclusion of certain expenditure. [*EC 13th Directive, Articles 3, 4*].

See 48.5 OVERSEAS TRADERS below for the scheme introduced in the UK.

23   European Community: Single Market

Cross-references. See 2.19 ACCOUNTING PERIODS AND RETURNS for EC sales statements; 2.27 ACCOUNTING PERIODS AND RETURNS for Intrastat; 21.2 EUROPEAN COMMUNITY: GENERAL for the VAT territory of the EC; 40.5 INVOICES for particulars required on VAT invoices issued to persons in other EC countries; 57 RECORDS generally; 59.11 *et seq* REGISTRATION for the liability to register in the UK in respect of distance sales from another EC country; 59.18 *et seq* REGISTRATION for the liability to register in the UK in respect of acquisitions from other EC countries; 64.8 SUPPLY for the place of supply of goods; 68.26 and 68.28 TRANSPORT AND FREIGHT for special provisions applying to intra-EC freight transport and ancillary services; 69.8–69.12 VALUATION for the valuation rules applying to acquisitions from other EC countries; 70 WAREHOUSED GOODS AND FREE ZONES for movement of goods in warehouse and free zones to and from EC countries.

The contents of this chapter are as follows.

23.1   INTRODUCTION

With the completion of the Single Market on 1 January 1993, and the removal of fiscal frontier controls between EC countries, fundamental changes took place in the way VAT is charged and accounted for on goods moving within the EC. See 21.2 EUROPEAN COMMUNITY: GENERAL for a list of the territories which make up the VAT territories of the EC. The concepts of 'imports' and 'exports' of goods apply only to transactions with countries outside the EC. For intra-EC movements of goods, the concept of 'acquisitions' is introduced to replace 'imports' and 'exports' are referred to as goods removed, dispatched or transported to EC destinations.

The rules are complex and, in any case, are only intended to be transitional until a definitive system for the taxation of trade between EC countries is introduced based on the principal of taxing goods and services in the EC country of origin.

De Voil Indirect Tax Service. See V1.306.

23.2   MOVEMENTS OF GOODS BETWEEN EC COUNTRIES: GENERAL PROVISIONS

Deemed supply. Unless specifically overridden by other provisions, there is deemed to be a supply of goods where goods forming part of the assets of any business are removed from any EC country, by or under the directions of the person carrying on the business, and taken to another EC country in the course or furtherance of the business. This applies whether or not the removal is, or is in connection with, a transaction for a consideration. [*VATA 1994, 4 Sch 6(1)*]. The supply is treated as taking place in the EC country from which the goods are dispatched. [*VATA 1994, s 7(7)*].

There is no deemed supply under the above provisions where

(a)   the goods are removed from an EC country in the course of their removal from one part of that country to another part of the same country; or

(b)   the goods have been removed from a place outside the EC for entry into the territory of the EC and are removed from an EC country before the time when any EC customs duty on their entry into the EC would be incurred. See 34.20 IMPORTS.

[*VATA 1994, 4 Sch 6(2)*].

Charging VAT. Subject to special rules in the cases listed below, a VAT registered trader in one EC country need not charge VAT on dispatch of goods to a registered trader in another EC country. The customer then has to account for the VAT on the goods concerned at the rate in force in the EC country to which they are delivered. Where, on the other hand, goods are supplied to customers in other EC countries who are not registered for VAT, VAT is normally charged and accounted for by the supplier in the EC country from which the goods are dispatched.

See 23.3 *et seq* below for acquisitions of goods in the UK from other EC countries and 23.11 *et seq* below for supplies from the UK to other EC countries.

Special rules apply to the following.

•   Certain transfers of own goods between EC countries. See 23.23–23.27 below.

•   Goods installed or assembled at a customer's premises. See 23.28 below.

•   Distance sales (i.e. sales to non-taxable persons in another EC country where the supplier is responsible for delivery) above certain limits. See 23.10 below for distance selling to the UK and 23.18 for distance selling from the UK.

•   Acquisitions by non-VAT registered businesses and non-taxable organisations in excess of an annual threshold. See 59.18 REGISTRATION for the liability to register for VAT in the UK where there is no liability to be registered in respect of supplies in the UK.

•   Goods subject to excise duty purchased by non-taxable persons. See 23.9 below for acquisitions in the UK and 23.17 below for supplies to other EC countries.

•   New means of transport. See 23.31 *et seq* below.

•   Supplies to diplomats, international organisations, NATO forces and other entitled persons and bodies in other EC countries which may in certain circumstances be relieved from VAT. See 23.21(c) below.

De Voil Indirect Tax Service. See V3.213.

23.3   **ACQUISITIONS OF GOODS IN THE UK FROM OTHER EC COUNTRIES**

It is no longer necessary to make an import declaration on an acquisition of goods from another EC country (with certain exceptions) or pay VAT at the frontier. Instead, where a person registered for VAT in the UK receives goods from another EC country supplied by a business registered for VAT in that country, he must account for VAT in the UK on the acquisition of the goods. The rate of VAT due is that applicable to the supply of the same goods in the UK. No VAT will therefore be due on the acquisition of goods which are zero-rated in the UK. The VAT must be accounted for on the VAT return for the period in which the tax point occurs and, subject to the normal rules, the taxable person may recover the VAT as input tax on the same VAT return.

These provisions are considered in more detail in 23.4 to 23.10 below.

De Voil Indirect Tax Service. See V3.361; V3.362; V3.389.

23.4   **Meaning of 'acquisition of goods from another EC country'**

An '*acquisition of goods from another EC country*' is any acquisition of goods under a transaction where both of the following conditions are satisfied.

(*a*)   The transaction is, or is treated for the purposes of *VATA 1994* as, a supply of goods.

(*b*)   The transaction involves (but need not be restricted to) the movement of goods from another EC country.

For these purposes, it is immaterial whether the removal (i.e. transportation) of the goods is undertaken by or on behalf of the supplier, the customer or some other person.

Where the person with the property in the goods does not change in consequence of anything treated as a supply under *VATA 1994*, that supply is to be treated as a transaction under which there is an acquisition of goods by the person making it. The transfer of a person's own goods to another EC country therefore leads to an acquisition of goods by him in that country. See 23.23 below.

The Treasury may provide, by order, that any acquisition of goods is not to be treated as an acquisition of goods from another member state. See 30.1 GOLD AND PRECIOUS METALS for gold supplied to a Central Bank in the UK.

[*VATA 1994, s 11*].

De Voil Indirect Tax Service. See V3.363.

23.5   **Scope of VAT on acquisitions**

Subject to zero-rating below, VAT is due in the UK on any acquisition from another EC country where the following conditions are satisfied.

(*a*)   The acquisition is a 'taxable acquisition'.

(*b*)   The acquisition takes place in the UK. See 23.6 below.

(*c*)   The acquisition is not the result of a taxable supply in the UK (see, for example, 23.28 below for installed and assembled goods).

(*d*)   Either

   (i)   the person making the acquisition is a '*taxable person*' i.e. a person who is, or is required to be, registered; or

   (ii)   the goods are subject to excise duty (see 23.9 below); or

   (iii)   the goods are a new means of transport (see 23.31 below).

A '*taxable acquisition*' is an acquisition (other than an 'exempt acquisition') where the goods are acquired by

   (i)   a person in the course or furtherance of a business carried on by him, or

   (ii)   a person in the course or furtherance of any activities carried on, otherwise than by way of business, by any body corporate or by any club, association, organisation or other unincorporated body

where the supplier is a taxable person in another EC country at the time of the transaction and is acting in the course or furtherance of a business carried on by him.

The acquisition of a new means of transport (see 23.31 below) from another EC country is always a taxable acquisition.

An '*exempt acquisition*' is one under which the goods are acquired in pursuance of an exempt supply.

See 59.18 REGISTRATION for the requirement to register by persons within (ii) above who make acquisitions above an annual threshold and who would not otherwise be liable for registration in respect of supplies made.

Liability for VAT. The VAT on any acquisition is a liability of the person who acquires the goods and, subject to provisions about accounting and payment, becomes due at the time of acquisition (see 23.7 below).

[*VATA 1994, ss 1(3), 3(1), 10, 31(1)*].

Zero-rating. Where the goods acquired fall within *VATA 1994, 8 Sch*, no VAT is chargeable on their acquisition, except as otherwise provided in that *Schedule.* [*VATA 1994, s 30(3)*].

De Voil Indirect Tax Service. See V3.366–371.

23.6   **Place of acquisition**

An acquisition of goods is a taxable supply in the EC country in which it takes place.

Subject to below, the following provisions apply for determining whether goods acquired from another EC country are acquired in the UK.

(*a*)   Goods are treated as acquired in the UK if the transaction involves their removal to the UK and does not involve their removal from the UK (i.e. the transport of the goods ends in the UK). Subject to the following, the goods are otherwise to be treated as acquired outside the UK.

(*b*)   Goods are treated as acquired in the UK where a person uses a UK VAT registration number in order to acquire the goods. This applies whether or not the goods are to be transported to the UK.

The above is subject to the special provisions applying to warehoused goods (see 70.6 WAREHOUSED GOODS AND FREE ZONES).

[*VATA 1994, s 13; FA 1996, 3 Sch 4*].

Under the above rules, VAT on acquisitions will, in most cases, be due only in the country where the goods are received. For example, if a UK taxable person acquires goods from a supplier in Germany for delivery to the UK and quotes his VAT registration number, the place of supply is the UK under both (*a*) and (*b*) above. If, however, the UK taxable person quotes his UK VAT registration number to his supplier but the goods are not to be received in the UK and are delivered to France, there is an acquisition in France under (*a*) above *and* an acquisition in the UK under (*b*) above. In circumstances such as these

● the taxable person will be liable to account for acquisition VAT in the UK unless he can demonstrate that VAT has already been paid in the EC country to which the goods were sent; and

● if he has accounted for acquisition VAT in the UK and is later required to pay VAT on the acquisition in the EC country of destination of the goods, he may obtain a refund of the VAT paid in the UK. This will only be necessary, however, if the taxable person has not claimed full input tax credit.

(C & E Notice 725, para 2.3).

De Voil Indirect Tax Service. See V3.376; V3.377.

23.7   **Time of acquisition**

Subject to below, the time of acquisition of goods from another EC country (which is the same time as the corresponding supply of goods in the EC country of dispatch, see 23.16 below) is the earlier of

(a)   the 15th day of the month following that in which the first removal of the goods occurred; and

(b)   the date of issue of an invoice containing such details as C & E require. For this purpose, the invoice is one which is issued by the supplier under the provisions of the law of the EC country where the goods were supplied corresponding to the provisions in *SI 1995/2518, Regs 13, 14* relating to invoices for supplies in the UK. See 40 INVOICES.

Note that, unlike the rules for supplies in the UK, part or full payment for the goods does not create a tax point for acquisitions. However, the receipt of a payment on account does make the supplier liable to raise an invoice which will in turn trigger a tax point under (b) above.

C & E may, by regulations, make provision for the time at which an acquisition is treated as taking place where the whole or part of any consideration is determined or payable periodically, or from time to time, or at the end of a period. Under these powers, where any water, gas or any form of power, heat, refrigeration or ventilation within 64.46 SUPPLY is acquired from another EC country on such terms, the goods are treated as separately and successively acquired on each occasion that the supplier issues an invoice within (b) above.

See also 70.6 WAREHOUSED GOODS AND FREE ZONES for special rules for warehoused goods.

[*VATA 1994, s 12; FA 1996 3 Sch 3; SI 1995/2518, Regs 83, 87*].

De Voil Indirect Tax Service. See V3.388.

23.8   **Recording and accounting for VAT due on acquisitions**

In addition to the normal VAT records, a registered person who acquires goods from a trader registered for VAT in another EC country must

(a)   keep records of the goods acquired and hold commercial documentation, such as supplier's invoices;

(b)   calculate the VAT due on the acquisition of these goods and enter it on the 'VAT payable' side of his VAT account;

(c)   subject to the normal rules for allowable input tax, deduct the VAT due on the acquisition as input tax on the 'VAT allowable' side of the VAT account; and

(d)   include the VAT due under (b) above in Box 2 of the VAT return for the VAT period in which the time of acquisition occurs (see 23.7 above) and the input tax under (c) above in Box 4 on the same return. The invoice or contract value must be included in Boxes 7 and 9.

See 69.8–69.12 VALUATION for the valuation rules applying to acquisitions from other EC countries. Where the time of acquisition of any goods from another EC country is determined under 23.7(b) above by reference to the issue of an invoice, VAT must be accounted for and paid in respect of the acquisition only on so much of its value as is shown on the invoice. [*SI 1995/2518, Reg 26*].

23.9 **Acquisition of goods subject to excise duty**

All taxable acquisitions (i.e. acquisitions for business purposes and acquisitions for non-business purposes by clubs, organisations etc., see 23.5 above) of exciseable goods are taxed in the EC country of destination.

Where the person who acquires the exciseable goods from a supplier in another EC country is a UK VAT-registered person, he must account for VAT in the same way as for any other acquisition.

Where, however, the person making the taxable acquisition is not registered for UK VAT (because his turnover is under the registration limit or because his activities are not business activities) VAT cannot be accounted for by means of a VAT return. In order to avoid the need to register all persons making such acquisitions, C & E are empowered to introduce a special mechanism to collect the VAT due.

Under these provisions, the person acquiring such goods must notify C & E of the acquisition at the time of the acquisition or the arrival of the goods in the UK, whichever is the later. The notification must be in writing in English and contain the following particulars.

● The name and current address of the person acquiring the goods.

● The time of acquisition.

● The date when the goods arrived in the UK.

● The value of the goods including any excise duty payable.

● The VAT due on the acquisition.

The notification must include a signed declaration that all the information given is true and complete.

The VAT due is payable at the time of notification and, in any event, not later than the last date on which the person is required to make such notification as above. Where the person required to make the notification dies or becomes incapacitated, the liability to notify passes to the personal representative, trustee in bankruptcy, liquidator etc., as does the liability to pay the VAT (although only to the extent of assets passing to that person).

[*VATA 1994, 11 Sch 2(4)(5)(8); SI 1995/2518, Regs 31(3), 36*].

Note that the above provisions for acquisitions by non-registered persons are only necessary where the person acquiring the goods arranges for the delivery of the goods. Otherwise the distance selling provisions in 23.10 below apply.

De Voil Indirect Tax Service. See V5.126.

23.10 **Distance selling to the UK from other EC countries**

Distance selling occurs when a supplier in one EC country supplies goods, and is responsible for their delivery, to any person in another EC country who is not registered for VAT. This may include not only private individuals but public bodies, charities and businesses too small to register or with activities that are entirely exempt.

VAT on such distance sales to non-VAT registered customers in the UK from another EC country are normally subject to VAT in that other country. However, once the value of distance sales in the UK exceeds an annual threshold

● the supplier is automatically liable to register for VAT in the UK (see 59.11 REGISTRATION);

- the UK becomes the place of supply (see 64.11 SUPPLY); and
- VAT on any further sales is taxed in the UK.

The supplier may, if he wishes, opt to make the UK the place of supply before reaching the annual threshold. See 59.14 REGISTRATION.

Goods subject to excise duty. Distance sales of such goods to non–VAT registered customers in the UK are always taxed (for excise duty and VAT purposes) in the UK whatever the level of sales and the EC supplier is required to register in the UK.

VAT returns. For distance sales to the UK over the distance selling threshold (or where the seller has voluntarily registered in the UK), output tax must be included in Box 1 and the invoice or contract amount in Box 6.

23.11   SUPPLIES OF GOODS FROM THE UK TO OTHER EC COUNTRIES

Supplies of goods to other EC countries can be zero–rated provided the following conditions are satisfied.

(*a*)   The supply involves the removal of the goods from the UK.

(*b*)   The goods are acquired by a customer who is registered for VAT in another EC country.

(*c*)   The supplier obtains his customer's VAT registration number and shows this on his VAT invoice. See 23.12 below for checking a customer's VAT registration number and 40.1 and 40.5 INVOICES for the obligation to provide a VAT invoice and the particulars to be included thereon.

(*d*)   Within three months of the time of supply (see 23.16 below) the supplier obtains and keeps valid commercial documentary evidence that the goods have been removed from the UK. See 23.13–23.15 below for evidence of removal.

(*e*)   The goods must not be second–hand goods or works of art, etc. which the supplier has opted to tax on the profit margin. See 61.12 SECOND-HAND GOODS.

[*VATA 1994, s 30(8); SI 1995/2518, Reg 134*]. (C & E Notice 703, para 8.4 which has the force of law).

If all the above conditions cannot be met (which includes all supplies to non–registered customers in other EC countries), the supply cannot be zero–rated (unless the goods in any case fall to be zero–rated under *VATA 1994, 8 Sch*). VAT must then be accounted for at the standard–rate on the goods in the UK.

VAT returns. Where the supply is zero–rated, the invoice or contract value must be included in Boxes 6 and 8. Where the zero–rating conditions are not fulfilled, the VAT due must be entered in Box 1 and the invoice or contract value in Box 6 for the period in which the three months time limit expires.

EC sales list. Where the supply is zero–rated, the customer's VAT number and invoice or contract value must be shown on the ESL. Where the zero–rating conditions are not fulfilled, no entries are required.

Subsequent receipt of a VAT registration number. Where VAT is charged to a customer in another EC country because a valid VAT registration number is not known at the time of raising the invoice, a credit note may be issued if the customer subsequently produces such a number provided he was registered with the number at the time of supply and the other conditions for zero–rating are complied with. In such a case, the VAT-exclusive value of the supply must be entered on the EC sales list at the time of issuing the credit note (as this will not have been recorded at the time of the original sale).

Effect of failure to comply with conditions. Where the supply of any goods has been zero-rated under the above provisions and either any of the above conditions is not complied with or the goods are found in the UK after the date of alleged removal, the goods are liable to *forfeiture*. Any VAT which would have been due but for zero-rating is payable forthwith by the person to whom the goods were supplied or by any other person in whose possession the goods are found in the UK. C & E may waive payment of the VAT in whole or in part. [*CEMA 1979, 4 Sch 12; VATA 1994, s 30(10)*].

De Voil Indirect Tax Service. See V4.341–366.

23.12   **Checking VAT registration numbers**

C & E recommend that UK suppliers write to all of their customers in other EC countries asking for their VAT registration numbers which have been allocated for intra-EC trade, keeping a record of these and retaining the accompanying letter or advice.

Where a supplier has a doubt as to whether a particular registration number is valid, he should contact his VAT office which can normally check and confirm whether this is the case and whether the number is correctly associated with a specific name or address.

A supplier will not be liable to account for VAT where a registration number obtained from a customer and quoted on an invoice subsequently turns out to be false provided all reasonable steps have been taken to ensure that the customer is registered for VAT in the EC country of acquisition and all other conditions for zero-rating have been complied with. C & E do not regard reasonable steps as having been taken if a VAT number is used

- which does not conform to the published format for the customer's country (see 21.7 to 21.20 EUROPEAN COMMUNITY: GENERAL);

- after C & E advise that it is invalid; or

- which is known not to belong to the customer.

(C & E Notice 703, paras 8.5, 8.6; C & E Notice 725, para 2.2(b)).

23.13   **Evidence of removal, dispatch or transport**

No single document is specifically required to support zero-rating. Instead, C & E will allow zero-rating provided the supplier holds clear documentary evidence that the goods have been removed from the UK. For this purpose, any combination of the following may be used.

- Commercial transport documents from the carrier responsible for removing the goods from the UK.

- Customer's order.

- Inter-company correspondence.

- Copy sales invoice.

- Advice note.

- Packing list.

- Details of insurance or freight charges.

- Evidence of payment.

- Evidence of receipt of goods abroad.

- Any other documents relevant to the removal of the goods in question which you would normally obtain in the course of intra-EC business.

Goods delivered personally by the supplier. In addition to the examples of acceptable documentary evidence listed above, travel tickets can be used to demonstrate that an intra-EC journey took place for the purpose of removing the goods from the UK. (C & E Notice 703, paras 8.7, 8.8).

23.14   *Goods collected in the UK by the customer*

If the EC customer collects or arranges the collection of the goods and their removal from the UK, the supplier should confirm how the goods are to be removed from the UK and what proof of removal will be sent. The supplier should also consider taking a deposit from the customer equal to the amount of VAT in case satisfactory evidence of removal is not received.

In addition to the examples of acceptable documentary evidence listed in 23.13 above, the supplier must also obtain from the customer:

- a written order showing name, address and VAT number of the acquirer and the address where the goods are to be delivered; and

- a signature for the goods and the registration number of the vehicle that is to carry the goods out of the UK (if going by road).

If the goods are removed in a container, the supplier should also consider recording its identification number. (C & E Notice 703, para 8.9).

23.15   *Irish Land Boundary*

Commercial evidence of removal of goods from Northern Ireland forms the basis for zero-rating supplies to VAT-registered customers in the Republic of Ireland as follows.

- Removals by road by independent carriers — carrier's invoice or consignment note supported by evidence that the goods have been delivered (e.g. a receipted copy of the consignment note).

- Removals by rail — consignor's copy of the consignment note signed by the railway official accepting the goods for delivery.

- Removals by own transport — in addition to the normal commercial records in 23.13 above, the internal transport instructions for delivery plus a copy of the delivery note showing a name, address and VAT registration number for the customer in the Republic of Ireland, signed to confirm receipt of the goods.

- Goods collected by the customer — in addition to the normal commercial records in 23.13 above, a written order from the customer showing his name, address and VAT registration number *and* the address where the goods are to be delivered in the Republic of Ireland as well as the registration number of the vehicle carrying the goods. The customer must also sign for the goods.

(C & E Notice 703, para 8.10).

23.16   Time of supply

Zero-rated supplies to taxable persons in another EC country. Where a supply of goods involves

- the removal of the goods from the UK, and

- their acquisition in another EC country by a person who is liable for VAT on the acquisition under the provisions of that country corresponding to those in 23.3 above,

the time of supply is the earlier of the 15th day of the month following that in which the goods are removed or the date of the issue of a VAT invoice or other prescribed invoice in respect of the supply.

The tax point should be used as the reference date for including these supplies on the VAT return and EC sales list.

Supplies to non-taxable persons in another EC country. These are taxable in the UK and the tax point is determined under the normal rules. See 64.32 *et seq.* SUPPLY.

[*VATA 1994, s 6(7)(8)*].

23.17   **Supplies of exciseable goods to other EC countries**

VAT registered customers. Supplies of exciseable goods to a VAT registered customer in another EC country where the supplies are used for business purposes are taxable on the customer in that country. The customer will account for the VAT on his tax return as an acquisition.

Non-registered persons for non-private purposes. There are special arrangements for supplies of exciseable goods to non-registered persons in other EC countries when the purchases are made for *non-private* purposes. This applies to purchases by businesses which are below the registration threshold in their country or by non-registered legal persons (associations and unincorporated bodies, etc.) whose activities are not business activities for VAT purposes. Such supplies can be zero-rated provided the following conditions are met.

(a)   All goods must travel with an accompanying document to indicate the status of the goods.

- If the goods are moving under authorised duty suspension arrangements (e.g. from an excise warehouse), the consignor must complete an Administrative Accompanying Document (AAD). In these cases there must be a guarantee to cover all excise duty liabilities during the movement.

- If UK excise duty has already been paid on the goods, they should travel with a Simplified Administrative Accompanying Document (SAAD). The customer must also provide evidence that the excise duty in the EC country of destination has been paid or secured to the satisfaction of the fiscal authorities there, *before* the supplier despatches the goods.

(*b*)   The goods are removed from the UK to a destination in another EC country by or on behalf of the customer. (If the supplier arranges for the delivery to a non-VAT registered person in another EC country, he is liable to register in that country under the distance selling arrangements, see 23.18 below.)

(*c*)   Within 15 days of the end of the month in which the goods are removed, the supplier obtains and keeps copy 1 of the AAD and a receipted copy 3 of the AAD certified by the consignee or fiscal authority of the EC country of destination.

(*d*)   The movement of the goods must be completed, and the receipt issued, within four months of the time of supply.

(*e*)   The goods must not be second-hand goods or works of art, etc. which the supplier has opted to tax on the profit margin. See 61.12 SECOND-HAND GOODS.

The customer then pays the VAT in the EC country of destination.

[*SI 1995/2518, Reg 135*]. (C & E Notice 725, para 2.2).

De Voil Indirect Tax Service. See V4.352.

23.18   **Distance selling from the UK to other EC countries**

Distance selling occurs when a taxable person in one EC country supplies and delivers goods to a non-taxable person in another EC country. This may include not only private individuals but public bodies, charities and businesses too small to register or with activities that are entirely exempt.

VAT on such distance sales from the UK to non-VAT registered customers in another EC country are normally subject to UK VAT. However, once the value of distance sales to any particular EC country exceeds an annual threshold set by that country for distance selling,

- the supplier is automatically liable to register for VAT in that country;

- that country becomes the place of supply (see 64.12 SUPPLY); and

- VAT on any further sales is taxed in the EC country of destination of the goods.

Each EC country has the option of applying a distance selling threshold of either 35,000 ECU (about £25,000) or 100,000 ECU (about £71,000) per calendar year which is set in its own currency. The UK, together with Austria, France, Germany, Luxembourg and the Netherlands have indicated that they intend to adopt a threshold of 100,000 ECU. Belgium, Denmark, Finland, Greece, Ireland, Italy, Portugal, Spain and Sweden have indicated that they intend to adopt a threshold of 35,000 ECU.

Goods subject to excise duty. Distance sales of such goods to non-VAT registered customers in another EC country are always taxed (for excise duty and VAT purposes) in the country of destination whatever the level of sales and a UK supplier is required to register in that country.

Compulsory registration. UK traders who are required to register for VAT in another EC country must notify the tax authority in that country, allowing sufficient time to become registered by the appropriate date in accordance with the rules of that country.

Tax representatives. It may be possible (or obligatory) for the seller to appoint a tax representative to act on his behalf in the other EC country.

Voluntary registration. A UK trader may, if he wishes, opt to make the EC country of destination the place of supply of goods and register in that country before reaching the distance selling threshold as above. If he does so, he must notify his VAT office not less than 30 days before the date of the first supply to which the option relates. The notification must be in writing and contain the name of the country or countries involved. He must also, within 30 days of the first supply after the option, provide C & E with documentary evidence that he has notified the tax authority in the other EC country that he intends to account for VAT there (i.e. the application for, or certification of, registration in that country). Where such an option has been exercised, it may not be withdrawn from a date earlier than

- 1 January which is, or next follows, the second anniversary of the date of the first supply following the option (i.e. until at least two full *calendar* years have elapsed); and

- 30 days after the receipt by C & E of notification of withdrawal.

Subject to this, the original option may be withdrawn (and the place of supply moved back to the UK) by giving further written notification to C & E not later than 30 days before the date of the first supply he intends to make after the cancellation. [*SI 1995/2518, Reg 98*].

VAT groups. UK VAT groups are not recognised outside the UK and each individual group member must consider separately whether registration is required in another EC country or whether to register voluntarily there.

(C & E Notice 725, paras 4.1–4.6).

VAT returns. For distance sales from the UK below the distance selling threshold for another EC country, output tax must be included in Box 1 and the invoice or contract amount in Box 6. For distance sales from the UK over the distance selling threshold for that country (or where the trader has adopted voluntary registration there), the invoice or contract value should be included in Boxes 6 and 8.

EC sales lists. No entries are required on ESLs for distance sales.

23.19   **Goods accidentally lost, destroyed or stolen in transit**

VAT must be accounted for on goods sent to other EC countries which have been accidentally lost, destroyed or stolen *en route* as follows.

• **If lost, etc. before supplied, no VAT is due.**

• **If lost, etc. in transit and the supplier is responsible for transport,**

   (i) if the supplier has valid proof of removal from the UK *and* the VAT registration number of the customer, zero-rating may stand; and

   (ii) where (i) does not apply, VAT is due in the UK unless the supplier holds evidence of loss, etc. (e.g. an insurance claim, police investigation, etc.).

• **If lost, etc. in transit and the customer is responsible for transport,**

   (i) if the supplier has valid proof of removal from the UK *and* the VAT registration number of the customer, zero-rating may stand but as an acquisition has taken place in the EC country where the goods have disappeared, the customer is liable to account for the goods in that country; and

   (ii) if the goods are lost etc. in the UK, VAT is due in the UK (because the goods have been delivered in, but not removed from, the UK) unless the customer has provided evidence of loss, etc. (e.g. an insurance claim, police investigation, etc.).

(C & E Notice 725, para 2.2).

23.20   **Tax free shops**

Before 1 July 1999, the supply of the following goods is zero-rated.

(*a*)   The supply by a person in the course of carrying on business in a 'tax free shop' to a traveller making a 'relevant journey' of

   (i) goods (other than tobacco products, alcoholic beverages and perfumes) up to £75 in aggregate, or

   (ii) tobacco products, alcoholic beverages and perfumes up to certain quantities (e.g. 200 cigarettes, one litre of spirits and 60 ml of perfume) provided that the goods are to be carried in the traveller's personal luggage.

(*b*)   The supply of any goods within (*a*)(i) or (ii) above to a traveller on board a ship or aircraft making a relevant journey by a person who supplies the traveller's air or sea transport (or by any other person authorised by that person).

The provisions do not apply to the supply of tobacco products or alcoholic beverages to persons under 17 years of age.

'*Tax free shop*' means any shop approved by C & E within an airport or port or in the vicinity of the Channel Tunnel terminal.

'*Relevant journey*' means a journey by air or sea from the UK to a place in another EC country where the traveller is to disembark. For the purposes of (*a*) above, this includes a journey by a Channel Tunnel shuttle train.

[*VATA 1994, 8 Sch Group 14; SI 1995/3041*]. (C & E News Release 76/93, 24 December 1993).

With effect from 1 July 1999, VAT and duty-free sales to travellers on 'intra-EC journeys' are abolished. Goods supplied on board ferries and aircraft are subject to VAT at the rate applicable in the EC country of departure (irrespective of whether the goods are actually sold in the territorial waters of the country of departure or arrival or in international waters). Thus a ferry operator working between England and Belgium must register and account for UK VAT on sales during journeys from England to Belgium and register and account for Belgian VAT for journeys from Belgium to England.

'*Intra-EC journeys*' are those commencing in one EC country and ending in another even if the ferry/aircraft crosses international waters/airspace.

Goods loaded on board during an intermediate call in a third country or on the high seas. If a ferry or aircraft travelling between two EC countries (e.g. Sweden and Finland) makes an intermediate call in a non-EC country (e.g. Estonia) or in a territory outside the EC fiscal territory (e.g. the Aland Islands) the rules applicable to travellers to and from non-EC countries continue to apply provided the passengers have the opportunity to disembark and make purchases in that country or territory.

If untaxed third country goods are loaded on to a ferry travelling between two EC ports while the ferry is outside EC territorial waters, those goods are subject to the same VAT (and duties) as are applicable to all imports from outside the EC. In such circumstances, VAT (and duties) would be payable by both the passenger who has bought these products and the ferry operator.

Goods sold or supplied free for immediate consumption on board ferries and aircraft continue to be free of VAT and duty provided the national legislation of the individual EC country grants such exemption for stores on board ferries and aircraft.

Sales at shops in airports and the Channel Tunnel terminals to persons travelling within the EC are subject to VAT and duties at rates applicable to other retail sales in the EC country where they are situated.

(EC News Release, 2 October 1998).

De Voil Indirect Tax Service. See V4.285.

23.21   Miscellaneous

Note. The arrangements in (*a*)–(*c*) below are subject to change.

23.21 European Community: Single Market

(*a*) **Export houses before 1 April 1999.** The arrangements under 25.6 EXPORTS also apply to supplies of goods to export houses for trade to EC destinations. The export house must obtain the customer's VAT registration number. The export house (but not the supplier) must also include details of the supply on its VAT return and EC Sales list. (C & E Notice 725, para 10.1; C & E Notice 48, ESC 3.2)

(*b*) **Ships and aircraft stores.** The arrangements under 25.3 EXPORTS continue to apply to all ships, etc. leaving the UK. There is no need to obtain the VAT registration number of the customer if goods are supplied as stores at UK airports and ports. The goods do not have to be entered on the EC sales lists. Additionally, UK suppliers can zero-rate the supply of stores, etc. to other EC countries for loading on a ship or aircraft on a non-private journey to *any* destination provided the supplier

   (i) receives a written statement from the agent or master when placing the order that the supply is exempt under *EC 6th Directive, Art 15.4–15.7* (see 22.21(*c*)–(*e*) EUROPEAN COMMUNITY LEGISLATION);

   (ii) makes a similar statement on the delivery note and sales invoice; and

   (iii) within one month of the supply, obtains and holds commercial evidence that the goods have been removed from the UK and delivered directly to the vessel or aircraft, and a receipt for the goods from a responsible person.

(C & E Notice 725, para 10.6).

(*c*) **Diplomats, international organisations, NATO forces, etc. in other EC countries.** Supplies to diplomatic missions, international organisations, visiting NATO forces and their personnel based in other EC countries may be zero-rated under *EC 6th Directive, Art 15(10)*. The scope of the relief and the restrictions and conditions attached are determined by the host authority for the entitled person or body.

In order to qualify for zero-rating

   (i) the goods (or services) must be for either the personal use of entitled persons or the official use of entitled bodies;

   (ii) the supplier must obtain documentation from the customer, as laid down by their host authority, claiming exemption under *Art 15(10)*;

   (iii) any goods supplied must be removed from the UK; and

   (iv) the supplier must obtain and keep proof of the removal of the goods within three months of the supply.

In general, transactions zero-rated under *Art 15(10)* are not regarded as distance sales and do not count towards the distance selling threshold. However, in the case of supplies to customers based in Germany, the supplier should check with the German authorities if registration in Germany is required. Entries on EC sales lists are not required for these supplies.

These arrangements cover all goods except for new means of transport which are dealt with under the rules in 23.31 *et seq* below.

(C & E Notice 703, para 8.11; C & E Notice 725, para 2.8; C & E Notice 48, ESC 3.3).

(*d*) **Tools for the manufacture of goods for export.** Provided the supply of the main goods meets the conditions in 23.11 above, zero-rating also applies to the supply of jigs, patterns, templates, dies, moulds, punches and similar tools that are used in the UK for the manufacture of the goods and which form an integral part of the contract (or series of contracts) to supply those goods to a VAT-registered person in another EC country. (C & E Leaflet 701/22/95, para 3).

(*e*)   **Freight containers**. The removal of a container to another EC country can be zero-rated provided

(i)   the supplier obtains the customer's VAT registration number and shows this on the VAT invoice;

(ii)   the container is sent from the UK to a destination in another EC country; and

(iii)   within three months of the date of supply, the supplier obtains and keeps valid commercial evidence that the container has been removed from the UK.

Where the customer collects or arranges collection of the container, the supplier should confirm with the customer how the container is to be removed and what evidence of this will be available.

If the customer is not registered for VAT, or all the above conditions are not met, the supply is standard-rated.

(C & E Notice 703/1/95, para 4 which has the force of law).

Leasing or hiring of containers. Where a container is leased/hired to a customer in business in another EC country, the supply is treated as made in that other country and the supplier will normally have to account for VAT there under the 'reverse charge' procedure.

Temporary movements of containers. The temporary movement of a container from the UK to another EC country (whether involved in transporting goods or where the container is on lease/hire) is not treated as a removal from the UK with acquisition in the destination country. See 23.24 below. Details of the movement must be entered in a register of temporary movements. See 23.27 below.

(C & E Notice 703/1/95, paras 4, 7).

23.22   **TRIANGULATION**

General background. This is the term used to describe a chain of supplies of goods involving three or more parties where, instead of the goods physically passing from one party to the next, they are delivered directly from the first party to the last party in the chain. This may occur, for example, when goods are moved directly from a supplier in one EC country to the final customer in another EC country on the instruction of an intermediate party located in yet another EC country.

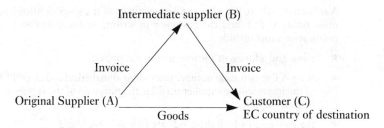

Under the normal VAT arrangements for movement of goods between EC countries, the intermediate supplier B may have a potential liability to register for VAT in the country of destination of the goods to account for VAT on their acquisition (see 23.6(*a*) above) and the onward supply of the goods there. To avoid imposing this additional burden, all EC countries have agreed to a simplified procedure which means that businesses registered for VAT in one EC country may no longer be required to register for VAT in another EC country purely as a result of these triangular transactions. Instead, B can opt to have his customer C in the country of destination of the goods account for the VAT due there on his behalf provided B is not registered or otherwise required to be registered in that country and C is registered there. If B does so opt, C must account for the VAT on the supply of goods made to him (i.e. the simplification procedure is compulsory if B so opts) and the acquisition of the goods by B is disregarded both in his own country and the country of destination. The initial supplier A must treat his transaction in the same way as any other intra-EC supply i.e. he may zero–rate the supply subject to the usual conditions and should record the supply on an EC sales list in the normal way.

Intermediate suppliers from outside the EC may also use the simplification procedure provided they are registered for VAT in one EC country (otherwise they will not be able to comply with the requirement to issue a VAT invoice to their customer and include the supply on an EC sales list).

Detailed UK provisions. UK provisions specifically cover the two positions where either the customer C or the intermediate supplier B is registered in the UK.

(*a*) **Customers registered in the UK.** Where

- the original supplier A makes a supply of goods to an intermediate supplier B who 'belongs in another EC country';

- that supply involves the removal of the goods from another EC country and their removal to the UK but does not involve the removal of goods from the UK;

- both that supply and the removal of the goods to the UK are for the purposes of a supply by B to a customer C who is registered under *VATA 1994* ;

- neither of those supplies involves the removal of the goods from an EC country in which B is taxable at the time of the removal without also involving the previous removal of the goods to that country; and

- there would be a taxable acquisition by C if the supply to him involved the removal of goods from another EC country to the United Kingdom,

then, provided B complies with requirements laid down by C & E, the supply by A to B is disregarded for the purposes of *VATA 1994*, and the supply by B to C is treated, other than for the purposes of *3 Sch* (registration in respect of acquisitions from another EC country), as a taxable acquisition. The taxable acquisition is treated as taking place on the date of the issue of the invoice for the transaction. [*VATA 1994, s 14(1)(3)(4)*].

Notification. Where B wishes to take advantage of the simplification provisions, he must notify C & E and the customer in writing of his intention to do so. The notification must include

- name and address of the intermediate supplier;

- the VAT registration number (including alphabetical code, see 40.5 INVOICES) of the intermediate supplier used for the purposes of the supply to him by the original supplier;

- the date upon which the goods are first delivered; and

- the name, address and VAT registration number of the customer to whom the goods are supplied (and who will account for the VAT).

Notification to C & E must be direct to LVO 050, Custom House, 28 Guild Street, Aberdeen, AB9 2DY.

The notification must be made no later than the provision of the first invoice in relation to the supply (see below). It must be made separately in relation to each customer to whom it is intended to make supplies under these provisions but, once made in relation to the first supply to any customer, is deemed to apply to all subsequent supplies to that customer as long as the intermediate supplier continues to belong in another EC country.

[*SI 1995/2518, Reg 11*].

Invoices. The intermediate supplier B must issue an invoice to the customer C which complies with the requirements of the EC country that issued the VAT registration number used for the purposes of the supply to him by the original supplier. It must bear the legend 'VAT: EC ARTICLE 28 SIMPLIFICATION INVOICE'. The invoice must be provided no later than 15 days after, and must relate to a supply of at least the same extent as would have been required under, the normal time of supply rules if these provisions had not applied. Such an invoice is then treated as if it were an invoice for the purposes of 23.7(*b*) above. [*SI 1995/2518, Reg 18*].

EC sales list. The intermediate supplier B must record the supply on his EC sales list in the country where he is registered.

Records. The UK customer C must account for the VAT on the goods supplied to him as an acquisition. He must record the VAT on the goods on the VAT payable side of his VAT account and include the VAT in Box 2 of his VAT return for the tax period in which the tax point occurs (i.e. the date of issue of the appropriate invoice by the supplier). He must include the net value of the acquisition in Box 9 of his return. He can also deduct this VAT as input tax on the same return (subject to the normal rules). He must enter the VAT on the VAT deductible side of his VAT account, include the VAT in Box 4 of his VAT return and include the net value in Box 7 of his VAT return. No VAT is due on goods which are zero-rated in the UK.

C must send in Supplementary Declarations for goods on which he accounts for VAT under these simplification arrangements.

(*b*) **Intermediate suppliers registered in the UK.** Where in a triangular transaction similar to that outlined in (*a*) above, B is registered in the UK and the goods are removed to another EC country, the supply to him of those goods and the supply by him of those goods to C are both disregarded for the purposes of *VATA 1994* but without prejudice to the power of C & E to require production of records and accounts and furnishing of information. [*VATA 1994, s 14(6)*].

In such circumstances, B can use his UK VAT registration number to secure zero-rating of the goods from the original supplier A in the EC country of despatch of the goods. If B wishes to use the simplification procedure to meet his obligations in the EC country of destination, he is not required to account for acquisition VAT there provided he issues C with a VAT invoice containing all the details normally required for intra-EC supplies (see 40.5 INVOICES) and the invoice bears the legend 'VAT: EC ARTICLE 28 SIMPLIFICATION INVOICE'.

B should not give details of triangular transactions involving either A or C on his VAT return or statistical returns.

EC sales lists. B must report triangular transactions separately on his EC sales lists. The total of these transactions for each customer, with the figure 2 entered in the indicator box to show that the information describes triangular trade, must appear on a different line from the total of normal direct supplies to each EC customer.

(C & E Notice 725, para 3.3).

For the purposes of (*a*) and (*b*) above, a person '*belongs in another EC country*' if

(i) he has no business establishment or other fixed establishment in the UK and does not have his usual place of residence in the UK;

(ii) he is neither registered nor required to be registered under *VATA 1994* (ignoring supplies disregarded under these provisions);

(iii) he does not have, and is not for the time being required to appoint, a VAT representative; and

(iv) he is taxable in another EC country.

[*VATA 1994, s 14(5); SI 1995/2518, Reg 17*].

Multiple chain transactions. The simplification procedure outlined above cannot be used by all intermediate suppliers in a chain of transactions involving more than three parties. Only one of the intermediate suppliers can opt to have their customer account for the VAT on his behalf. Other intermediaries still have an obligation to register in either the EC country of despatch or arrival of the goods.

De Voil Indirect Tax Service. See V3.380.

23.23   TRANSFER OF OWN GOODS TO ANOTHER EC COUNTRY

Subject to the exceptions in 23.24–23.26 below, the transfer of goods within the same legal entity from one EC country to another (e.g. between branches of the same company) is deemed to be a supply of goods for VAT purposes under the general provisions of *VATA 1994, 4 Sch 6* (see 23.2 above) and is liable to VAT under the normal arrangements for intra-EC supplies. Where a taxable person transfers own goods from the UK to another EC country in the course of his business (e.g. to sell them on from that country or to use them there), he is liable to account for VAT in that EC country on the acquisition of the goods. He may need to register for VAT there both in order to meet his obligations there and to use an overseas VAT registration number to support zero-rating of the deemed supply when the goods leave the UK. Otherwise he must account for VAT in the UK on the transfer. Similarly, where a taxable person transfers own goods from another EC country to the UK in the course of business VAT must be accounted for on the acquisition of the goods under the normal rules. (C & E Notice 725, para 2.4).

VAT returns. Where own goods are transferred from the UK to another EC country, the value based on the cost of the goods must be included in Boxes 6 and 8. Where own goods are transferred from another EC country to the UK, acquisition tax (for positive rated goods) must be included in Box 2, input tax (subject to the normal rules) included in Box 4 and the value of goods based on cost included in Boxes 7 and 9.

EC sales lists. Where own goods are transferred from the UK to another EC country, their value based on cost must be shown on the ESL.

Consignment stocks. Where a trader transfers goods to another EC country to create a stock under his own control from which supplies will be subsequently made by him (or on his behalf) in that country, the movement of goods from the UK is treated as a supply under the above arrangements. Similarly if a trader brings goods to the UK in these circumstances, he will be liable to account for VAT on the acquisition of the goods and on his subsequent supply in the UK. (C & E Notice 725, para 2.8). The requirements relating to VAT returns and EC sales lists are as above.

23.24   Temporary movements of own goods to other EC countries

The following temporary movements of own goods between EC countries are not treated as supplies for VAT purposes and no VAT is due in the prescribed accounting period in which the removal takes place. No entries are therefore necessary on the VAT return or EC sales list.

(a) Where

(i) the owner is established in the EC country of dispatch but not that of arrival;

(ii) the goods are removed for the sole purpose of being used by the owner in the course of a supply of services to be made by him;

(iii) at the time of their removal there is a legally binding obligation to make that supply of services (i.e. a specific contract to fulfil); and

(iv) the owner intends to remove the goods back to the EC country of dispatch when he has ceased to use them in making the supply.

This could apply, for example, to tools and equipment and goods intended for loan, hire or leasing.

The removal back to the EC country of dispatch under (iv) is also not treated as a supply for VAT purposes.

(b) Where goods are removed to another EC country and

(i) temporary importation relief would have been given if the goods had been imported from outside the EC; and

(ii) the owner intends to export the goods outside the EC or remove them to an EC country other than the country to which the goods have been removed, in either case not later than two years after the day upon which the goods were removed.

The export or removal under (ii) is also not treated as a supply for VAT purposes.

It is a condition for the temporary movements of goods under (a) and (b) above not to be treated as a supply of goods that the relevant intention of the owner under (a)(iv) or, as the case may be, (b)(ii) above is fulfilled. Where it is not, the original movement of goods must be belatedly treated as a deemed intra-EC supply and acquisition and the owner must account for VAT in the prescribed accounting period in which the condition is not complied with. This would occur under (b)(ii) above where, for example, the goods are sold in the EC country to which they are removed or remain there for more than two years.

[SI 1992/3111, Arts 4(f)(g)(h), 5; SI 1995/2518, Reg 42].

Although the above transfers are not treated as supplies for VAT purposes, commercial documentary evidence should be held to prove that the goods have left the UK and have later returned. (C & E Notice 725, para 2.5).

See 23.27 below for the requirement to keep a register of such movements of goods.

23.25 **Goods sent to another EC country for treatment, processing, valuation or repair work, etc.**

A supply of goods is not treated as taking place in the following circumstances.

(a) Where the owner, who is registered in the EC country of dispatch but not of arrival,

(i) sends the goods to another person in another EC country for treatment or processing; and

(ii) intends that the goods produced will be returned to him in the EC country of dispatch upon completion.

It is a condition for the dispatch of the goods not to be treated as a supply of goods that the intention of the owner under (ii) above is fulfilled. Where it is not, the original movement of goods must be belatedly treated as a deemed intra-EC supply and acquisition and the owner must account for VAT in the prescribed accounting period in which the condition is not complied with.

(*b*) Where the owner sends the goods to another person in another EC country who is to value or carry out work on them and the supply made by that person is or will be a supply of services treated as having been made in that EC country. This covers movement of goods between EC countries for repair or minor alteration.

The return of the goods to the original EC country is also not treated as a supply of goods.

[*SI 1991/3111, Arts 4(d)(e)(h)(i), 5; SI 1995/2518, Reg 42*].

See 23.27 below for the requirement to keep a register of movement of the goods.

23.26   *VAT treatment of the work carried out on the goods*

Special place of supply rules apply to the services of treatment, processing, valuation or repair work, etc. under 23.25 above. See 64.25 SUPPLY for full details. The effect of these rules is as follows.

(a) *UK supplier providing such services to a customer registered for VAT in another EC country.* If a UK supplier performs these services in the EC to a customer registered for VAT in another EC country, the place of supply is where the service is physically performed. However, if the customer is VAT registered in an EC country which is different to the one in which the service is performed,

- if the goods subsequently leave the country in which the service was performed, the place of supply moves to the customer's country, the UK supplier should not charge UK VAT and the customer is required to account for VAT under the 'reverse charge' procedure in his own country; and

- if the goods do not subsequently leave the country in which the service was performed, the place of supply stays in the place of physical performance and the UK supplier may be liable to register for VAT in that country and account for any VAT due.

(*b*) *UK supplier providing such services to a customer not registered for VAT in any EC country.* If a UK supplier performs these services within the EC for a customer who is not VAT-registered in the EC, the place of supply of the service is the country where the service is physically performed. The supplier may be liable to register for VAT in that country and account for any VAT due.

(*c*) *UK supplier providing such services to a customer registered for VAT in the UK.* If a UK supplier performs these services in the UK for a UK VAT-registered customer, the place of supply is the UK whether or not the goods subsequently leave the UK. The supplier must account for any UK VAT.

If the supplier performs the services in an EC country other than the UK for a UK VAT-registered customer,

- if the goods subsequently leave the country where the services are physically performed, the place of supply is the UK and the supplier must account for any UK VAT; and

- if the goods do not subsequently leave the country where the service are physically performed, the place of supply remains in that country and the supplier may be liable to register for VAT and account for any VAT due there. The UK VAT-registered customer may be eligible to make a claim for a refund of the overseas VAT under the *EC 8th Directive* refund procedure.

(d) *UK supplier providing such services outside the EC.* If a UK supplier physically performs these services outside the EC, the supply is outside the scope of UK and EC VAT. This applies irrespective of the location and VAT registration status of the customer.

(e) *UK customer sending goods to another EC country.* Where such services are performed in the EC for a UK VAT-registered customer

- by a supplier who is established outside the UK (including outside the EC), and

- the goods do not remain in the country where the work has been performed,

the place of supply is the UK and the UK customer must account for any UK VAT due under the 'reverse charge' procedure. The 'reverse charge' procedure only applies if VAT would be charged when the service is performed in the UK for a VAT-registered customer in the UK.

The place of supply is in the EC country of physical performance if either the goods are not subsequently removed from that country (in which case a UK VAT-registered customer may be eligible to make a claim under the *EC 8th Directive*) or the supply is received by a non-VAT registered person.

(C & E Notice 725, para 2.6).

23.27 Register of temporary movement of goods to and from other EC countries

Every taxable person must keep and maintain a register of

- goods dispatched temporarily to another EC country under the circumstances in 23.24–23.26 above; and

- goods received temporarily from other EC countries for processing under 23.25 above

where the goods are to be returned within a period of two years of their first date of removal or receipt.

The register must contain the following information.

- The date of removal of goods to another EC country and the date of receipt of the goods when they are returned from that or another EC country.

- The date of receipt of goods from another EC country and the date of removal of the goods when they are returned to that or another EC country.

- A description of the goods sufficient to identify them.

- a description of any process, work or other operation carried out on the goods either in the UK or in another EC country.

- The consideration for the supply of the goods and for any processing, work or other operation carried out on the goods.

The register need not be in any particular format but the information set out above must be easily available for all goods temporarily moved to and from the UK.

[*SI 1995/2518, Reg 33*]. (C & E Notice 725, para 13.8).

De Voil Indirect Tax Service. See V5.212.

23.28   INSTALLED AND ASSEMBLED GOODS

General rule. The movement of goods between EC countries for the purpose of a supply of installed or assembled goods is not treated as a supply and acquisition under the normal rules for the transfer of own goods. [*SI 1992/3111, Art 4(a)*]. Instead, where the supply of goods involves their installation or assembly, they are treated as supplied where they are installed or assembled. [*VATA 1994, s 7(3)*].

If, therefore, a UK supplier supplies goods which he is to install or assemble in another EC country, his supply takes place in that country and is liable for VAT there. He may, therefore, need to register there in order to account for the VAT due. There is no need to show the movement of goods on an EC sales list but the value should be included in Box 6 and Box 8 on the VAT return.

Similarly, if a person supplies goods from another EC country to be installed or assembled in the UK, the supply is liable to UK VAT and the supplier may have to register in the UK. If he is registered in the UK, he must include output tax in Box 1 of his VAT return and the invoice or contract value in Box 6.

Simplification procedure. To avoid imposing the burden on the supplier of installed or assembled goods of having to register in another EC country, a simplified procedure has been agreed by some countries. Instead of registering in that other EC country, the supplier can opt to have his customer account for the VAT due there on his behalf provided the customer is registered in that EC country. If the supplier so opts, the customer *must* account for the VAT (i.e. the simplification procedure is compulsory if the supplier opts).

Installation or assembly in the UK. Where

(*a*)   a person belonging in another EC country makes a supply of goods to a person registered under *VATA 1994* and the supply involves their installation or assembly at a place in the UK to which they are removed; and

(*b*)   there would be a taxable acquisition by the registered person if that supply were treated as not being a taxable supply in the UK (under the general rule above) but as involving the removal of the goods from another EC country to the UK,

then, provided the supplier complies with requirements laid down by C & E, the supply is treated, other than for the purposes of *3 Sch* (registration in respect of acquisitions from another EC country), as a taxable acquisition. the taxable acquisition is treated as taking place on the date of the issue of the invoice for the transaction.

For these purposes, a person is treated as '*belonging in another EC country*' if

•   he has no business establishment or other fixed establishment in the UK and does not have his usual place of residence in the UK;

•   he is neither registered nor required to be registered under *VATA 1994* (ignoring supplies disregarded under these provisions);

•   he does not have, and is not for the time being required to appoint, a VAT representative; and

•   he is taxable in another EC country.

[*VATA 1994, s 14(2)–(5)*].

Notification. If the supplier wishes to take advantage of the simplification provisions and avoid registering for VAT in the UK, he must notify C & E and the registered person in writing of his intention to do so. The notification must include

•   name and address of the person belonging in another EC country;

- the VAT registration number (including alphabetical code, see 40.5 INVOICES) by which that person is identified for VAT in the EC country in which he belongs;

- the date upon which the installation or assembly of the goods commences; and

- the name, address and VAT registration number of the registered person to whom the goods are supplied (and who will account for the VAT).

Notification to C & E must be direct to LVO 050, Custom House, 28 Guild Street, Aberdeen, AB9 2DY.

The notification must be made no later than the provision of the first invoice in relation to the supply (see below). It must be made separately in relation to each registered person to whom it is intended to make supplies under these provisions but, once made in relation to the first supply to any registered person, is deemed to apply to all subsequent supplies to that registered person as long as the person making the supply continues to belong in another EC country.

[*SI 1995/2518, Reg 12*].

Invoices. The supplier belonging in the other EC country must issue an invoice to the registered person which complies with the requirements of that other country and bears the legend 'SECTION 14(2) VATA INVOICE'. The invoice must be provided no later than 15 days after, and must relate to a supply of at least the same extent as would have been required under, the normal time of supply rules if these provisions had not applied. Such an invoice is then treated as if it were an invoice for the purposes of 23.7(*b*) above. [*SI 1995/2518, Reg 19*].

EC sales list. The supplier must record the supply on his EC sales list in the EC country where he is registered.

Records. The UK customer must record the VAT on the VAT payable side of his VAT account, include the VAT in Box 2 of his VAT return and include the net value of the supply in Box 9 of his return. He can also deduct this VAT as input tax on the same return (subject to the normal rules). He must enter the VAT on the VAT deductible side of his VAT account, include the VAT in Box 4 of his VAT return and include the net value in Box 7 of his VAT return. No VAT is due on goods which are zero-rated in the UK.

Installation or assembly by UK supplier in another EC country. Not all EC countries have simplified procedures for supplies of installed or assembled goods. UK businesses supplying such goods in another EC country should make enquiries with the appropriate fiscal authority. In the absence of simplification arrangements, the business may be required to register for VAT in that country although it may be possible to appoint a VAT representative to account for VAT there on its behalf.

De Voil Indirect Tax Service. See V3.381.

23.29   **'CALL-OFF' STOCKS**

Where a UK supplier provides goods to another EC country so that the customer can maintain a stock for 'call-off' (i.e. use and payment as needed), the supply in the UK can be treated under the normal arrangements for intra-EC movements. The goods can therefore be zero-rated when sent from the UK subject to the normal requirements.

If a UK trader receives 'call-off' stocks in the UK from a supplier in another EC country, he must account for VAT on the acquisition on the basis of the movement of the goods even though title may not pass until he calls-off the goods. This arrangement only applies when the goods are intended for use solely by the UK customer (whether in the business or to make onward supplies to own customers). Stocks sent to the UK by an EC supplier for, or for call-off by, more than one customer they should be treated as consignment stock, as should call-off goods delivered to storage facilities operated by the supplier rather than the customer (see 23.23 above).

(C & E Notice 725, para 2.8).

23.30 GOODS SOLD ON SALE OR RETURN, APPROVAL OR SIMILAR TERMS

Goods supplied to a customer in another EC country on such terms are treated as intra-EC transfers of own goods under 23.23 above, i.e. a deemed supply and acquisition. If and when the goods are eventually adopted by the customer, there is a domestic supply of goods within that country.

If goods are supplied from another EC country to a UK customer on sale or return or similar terms, the supplier is liable to account for VAT on his acquisition of those goods in the UK. He must also account for VAT on any subsequent supply in the UK under the normal rules for sale or return goods in the UK (see 64.43 SUPPLY).

(C & E Notice 725, para 2.8).

23.31 NEW MEANS OF TRANSPORT

The following are regarded as new means of transport (NMT) for the purposes of 23.32–23.36 below, provided that, in each case, it is intended for the transport of persons or goods.

(*a*) Any ship, including a hovercraft, exceeding 7.5 metres in length provided that three months or less have elapsed since its first entry into service or, since that time, it has travelled under its own power for 100 hours or less. A ship is treated as having first entered into service

- when it is delivered from its manufacturer to its first purchaser or owner or is first made available to that person (whichever is the earlier); or

- if applicable, when its manufacturer first takes it into use for demonstration purposes.

(*b*) Any aircraft the take-off weight of which exceeds 1,550 kilograms provided that three months or less have elapsed since its first entry into service or, since that time, it has travelled under its own power for 40 hours or less. An aircraft is treated as having first entered into service

- when it is delivered from its manufacturer to its first purchaser or owner or is first made available to that person (whichever is the earlier); or

- if applicable, when its manufacturer first takes it into use for demonstration purposes.

(*c*) Any motorised land vehicle which

- has an engine with a displacement or a cylinder capacity exceeding 48 cc; or

- is constructed or adapted to be electrically propelled using more than 7.2 kilowatts

provided that six months or less have elapsed since its first entry into service or, since that time, it has travelled under its own power for 6,000 kilometres or less. A motorised land vehicle is treated as having first entered into service

(i) on its first registration for road use in the EC country of its manufacturer or when a liability to register for road use is first incurred there (whichever is the earlier); or

(ii) where (i) does not apply, its removal by its first purchaser or owner, its first delivery or its being made available to its first purchaser (whichever is the earlier); or

(iii) if applicable, when its manufacturer first takes it into use for demonstration purposes.

Where the time of first entry into use under (*a*)–(*c*) above cannot be established to the satisfaction of C & E, a means of transport is to be treated as having first entered into service on the issue of an invoice relating to its first supply.

[*VATA 1994, s 95; SI 1994/3128; SI 1995/2518, Reg 147*].

De Voil Indirect Tax Service. See V1.282.

23.32   **Supplies of new means of transport by persons registered in the UK to non-registered persons in other EC countries**

A supplier who is registered for VAT in the UK should zero-rate the supply of a NMT to a non-registered person from another EC country provided

(*a*)   the means of transport qualifies as 'new' under 23.31 above;

(*b*)   the purchaser (or his authorised chauffeur, pilot or skipper) personally takes delivery of the NMT and removes it from the UK to the EC country of destination within two months of the date of supply; and

(*c*)   the supplier and the customer make a joint declaration on Form VAT 411.

Copies of Form VAT 411 are obtainable from VAT offices and Excise Advice Centres. It comprises an original (or top sheet) and three copies. When the form has been fully completed, the supplier must send the original to

HM Customs and Excise
Central Processing Unit
Postal Depot
Charlton Green
Dover
Kent CT16 1EH

within six weeks of the end of the calendar quarter in which the supply is made.

The first copy of Form VAT 411 should be given to the customer. The second copy is retained by the supplier and the third copy attached to any application for registration for road use (see below).

Using a new vehicle on UK roads. If any new unregistered vehicle is to be used in the UK before its removal to another EC country, it must be licensed, insured and registered before delivery. The supplier will obtain the registration number (a special 'VAT-free' series which allows the vehicle to be identified as tax free whilst it remains in the UK prior to removal) by presenting the third copy of the completed Form VAT 411, attached to the application for registration, to one of the following Vehicle Registration Offices.

Birmingham	St Martins House, 10 The Bullring, Birmingham B5 5DP Tel: 0121 643 2261
Bristol	Northleigh House, Lime Kiln Close, Stoke Gifford, Bristol BS12 6SR Tel: 01272 315511

Chelmsford	2nd Floor, Parkway House, 49 Baddow Road, Chelmsford CM2 0XJ Tel: 01245 281111
Coventry	Greyfriars House, Greyfriars Lane, Coventry CV1 Tel: 01203 256427
Hull	Kingston House, Myton Street, Hull HU1 3PE Tel: 01482 223685
Leeds	24a Union Street, Leeds LS2 7JR Tel: 01532 443035
London Central	1 Zoar Street, London SE1 0SY Tel: 0171 928 3163
Luton	2 Dunstable Road, Luton LU1 1EB Tel: 01582 412143
Northampton	Wootton Hall Park, Northampton NN4 9BG Tel: 01604 762131
Northern Ireland	Vehicle Licensing Central Office, County Hall, Castlerock Road, Coleraine, Co Londonderry BT51 3H5 Tel: 01265 44133
Norwich	Rouen House, Rouen Road, Norwich NR1 1UP Tel: 01603 616411
Oxford	Ground Floor, 3 Cambridge Terrace, Oxford OX1 1RW Tel: 01865 724056
Stoke	London House, 4th Floor, Hide Street, Stoke ST4 1EL Tel: 01782 747421
Taunton	Brendon House, High Street, Taunton TA1 3DT Tel: 01823 254404

Failure to remove the NMT from the UK within the time allowed. If, in exceptional circumstances, the customer is unable to remove the NMT from the UK, he must inform C & E Central Processing Unit at the above address immediately in writing and within the two-month period. C & E will then calculate the VAT due and issue a demand for immediate payment. If the NMT is not removed from the UK within the two-month period and C & E have not been informed, the vehicle may be liable to forfeiture.

[*SI 1995/2518, Regs 22(6), 155*]. (C & E Notice 725, paras 7.5–7.8; C & E Notice 728, paras 5–8, 20, 21).

The customer must pay any taxes due on the NMT in the EC country of destination under the laws of that state.

De Voil Indirect Tax Service. See V5.272.

23.33   **Supplies of new means of transport by persons registered in the UK to persons registered in other EC countries**

A supplier who is registered for VAT in the UK should zero-rate the supply of a NMT to a VAT-registered person from another EC country provided

(*a*)   the means of transport qualifies as 'new' under 23.31 above;

(*b*)   the customer's VAT registration number (with two digit code prefix) is shown on the invoice;

(*c*)   the NMT is dispatched or transported from the UK to another EC country within two months of the date of issue of the invoice for supply; and

(*d*)   the supplier holds valid commercial documentary evidence that the NMT has been removed from the UK (see 23.13 above).

The customer must account for any VAT due on the acquisition in the EC country of destination under the laws of that country.

Using a new vehicle on UK roads. If any new unregistered vehicle is to be used in the UK before its removal to another EC country, it must be licensed, registered and insured against third-party liabilities before delivery. The supplier and the customer must complete and sign a declaration on Form VAT 411A obtainable from VAT offices. This form must be sent or produced to one of the Vehicle Registration Offices listed in 23.32 above.

The VRO will issue a special registration number which identifies the vehicle as having 'tax free' status and as intended for removal from the UK to another EC country.

Failure to remove the NMT from the UK within the time allowed. If, in exceptional circumstances, the customer is unable to remove the NMT from the UK, he must inform C & E Central Processing Unit at the above address immediately in writing and within the two-month period. C & E will then calculate the VAT due and issue a demand for immediate payment. If the NMT is not removed from the UK within the two-month period and C & E have not been informed, the vehicle is liable to forfeiture and may be seized.

(C & E Notice 725, paras 7.4, 7.9).

23.34   **Supplies by non-registered persons: recovery of VAT**

Where a non-taxable person supplies a NMT which involves its removal to another EC country, C & E must, on a claim, refund to him the VAT which he paid on the supply to him (or acquisition or importation by him, as the case may be) but not exceeding the amount of VAT which would have been payable on the supply by him involving removal if it had been a taxable supply by a taxable person and had not been zero-rated. [*VATA 1994, s 40*].

The claim must be in writing and be made no earlier than one month, and no later than 14 days, before the making of the supply by virtue of which the claim arises. It must include a signed declaration that all the information entered in, or accompanying it, is true and complete and must be sent to Customs Central Processing Unit at the address in 23.32 above. It must contain the following information.

• The name, current address and telephone number of the claimant.

• The place where the NMT is kept and the times when it may be inspected. (C & E may need to inspect the NMT before it is sold to confirm its eligibility for refund.)

• The name and address of the person who supplied the NMT to the claimant.

• The price paid by the claimant for the supply of the NMT to him, excluding VAT.

• The amount of any VAT on that supply.

• The amount of any VAT paid by the claimant on the acquisition or importation of the NMT by him.

• The name and address of the proposed purchaser, the EC country to which the NMT is to be removed and the date of the proposed purchase.

• The price to be paid by the proposed purchaser.

• A full description of the NMT including, as the case may be, its mileage or hours of use since first entry into service (see 23.31 above).

• Necessary details of the ship's length, aircraft's weight or motorised land vehicle's power (as the case may be) to establish that it qualifies under 23.31 above.

• The amount of the refund being claimed.

The claim must initially be accompanied by the following.

• Proof of original purchase (normally the invoice or documentary evidence of its importation or acquisition from another EC country).

• Evidence that the VAT has been paid on the original purchase.

The claim is subsequently completed by the submission, in due course, of the sales invoice (or similar document) identifying the NMT and showing the price paid by the claimant's customer, together with documentary evidence that it has been removed to another EC country.

[*SI 1995/2518, Regs 146, 149–154*]. (C & E Notice 728, paras 17, 18).

De Voil Indirect Tax Service. V5.154.

23.35   **Acquisitions by non-registered persons in the UK from other EC countries**

An acquisition of a NMT is taxed in the EC country of destination. In order to avoid the need to register persons making such acquisitions in the UK who would not otherwise be liable to be registered, C & E are empowered to introduce a special mechanism to collect the VAT due. [*VATA 1994, 11 Sch 2(4)(5)*].

Under these powers, where a non-taxable person makes a taxable acquisition of a NMT in the UK, he must notify C & E within seven days of its acquisition or its arrival in the UK, whichever is the later.

The notification should be in English and should be sent by post to C & E Central Processing Unit at the address in 23.32 above. The form in Notice 728, Appendix D should be detached and used for this purpose. It includes a signed declaration that all the information entered in it is true and complete. C & E will also need to see the original purchase invoice, any foreign registration documents held, and any documents relating to the transport of the NMT and its arrival in the UK.

Payment of VAT. C & E will calculate the VAT due on the acquisition and send a written demand which must be paid within 30 days of issue. See 69.12 VALUATION for the conversion of foreign currencies into sterling.

[*SI 1995/2518 Reg 148*]. (C & E Notice 728, paras 9–14).

Records. The person acquiring the NMT must keep his copy of the purchase invoice and proof that he has paid the VAT for six years. If the NMT is sold within this period, these records should be passed on to the new owner so that he can demonstrate its VAT status. [*VATA 1994, 11 Sch 6(1); SI 1995/2518, Reg 31(3)*]. (C & E Notice 728, para 15).

Penalties. The provisions of *VATA 1994, s 67* (failure to notify) are extended to impose a penalty where an unregistered person fails to notify an acquisition of a new means of transport. See 52.12 PENALTIES.

De Voil Indirect Tax Service. See V5.127.

23.36   **Acquisitions by persons registered in the UK from another EC country**

Where a VAT-registered person in the UK acquires a NMT free of VAT from a person in another EC country, he should account for the VAT due on his normal VAT return for the period in which he acquires the NMT. (C & E Notice 725, para 7.10).

23.37   **SALES AND PURCHASES OF SECOND-HAND GOODS**

The liability of sales and purchase of second-hand goods within the EC is as follows.

• **Sale by UK-registered person to a person registered in another EC country.**

Such a sale under the Margin Scheme is taxable in the UK with no further liability to pay VAT on acquisition in another EC country. If the sale is excluded from the Margin Scheme, it may be zero-rated subject to the normal conditions but the customer will not be able to include the goods in a second-hand scheme in his own country.

• **Sale by UK-registered person to a private individual in another EC country.** Such a sale is taxable in the UK. VAT is calculated on the margin for eligible goods sold under one of the schemes for SECOND-HAND GOODS (61).

• **Acquisition by UK-registered person from a person registered in another EC country.** Such an acquisition from a seller who deals with the goods under a second-hand scheme is subject to VAT in the other EC country with no liability to acquisition VAT on entry into the UK. Eligible goods may be sold under one of the schemes for SECOND-HAND GOODS (61) as the invoice will not show VAT as a separate item. If the sale is not dealt with under a second-hand scheme in the other EC country it will be zero-rated subject to the normal conditions and the UK buyer must account for any VAT due on the acquisition. The UK buyer cannot deal with the goods under the Margin Scheme (with the exception of motor cars on which the acquisition VAT cannot be reclaimed, which may be sold under the Margin Scheme).

• **Acquisition by UK-registered person from a private individual in another EC country.** No VAT is due when the goods are brought into the UK and the goods can therefore be sold under one of the special schemes for SECOND-HAND GOODS (61).

- **Acquisition by a private individual in the UK from a registered person in another EC country.** Such an acquisition is subject to VAT in the other EC country.

23.38   GOODS OBTAINED IN THE EC BY TRAVELLERS RETURNING TO THE UK VIA A NON-EC COUNTRY

Where travellers return to the UK through non-EC countries (including the Channel Islands) carrying goods purchased for their personal use duty and VAT paid in another EC country, no further duty will be payable in the UK on production, if requested, of evidence of payment of that duty and VAT (e.g. an invoice). (C & E News Release 57/93, 20 August 1993).

24 Exempt Supplies

24.1 A supply of goods or services is an exempt supply if it is of a description for the time being specified as such under various Group headings in *VATA 1994, 9 Sch. [VATA 1994, s 31(1)]*. A person who makes exempt supplies but no taxable supplies is not a taxable person and cannot be registered. *[VATA 1994, ss 3(1) 4(2)]*. Output tax is not chargeable on exempt supplies or recoverable on related input tax. Where both exempt and taxable supplies are made, the rules as to PARTIAL EXEMPTION (49) are applied and only part of the input tax may be reclaimable.

The general categories of exemption are

Group 1	Land (see 42.2 LAND AND BUILDINGS)
Group 2	Insurance (see 37 INSURANCE)
Group 3	Postal services (see 24.2 below)
Group 4	Betting, gaming and lotteries (see 58.1-58.4 RECREATION AND SPORT)
Group 5	Finance (see 27 FINANCE)
Group 6	Education (see 20 EDUCATION)
Group 7	Health and welfare (see 32.1 HEALTH AND WATER UTILITIES ; 12.9 CHARITIES ; 43.7 LOCAL AUTHORITIES AND STATUTORY BODIES and 24.3 below)
Group 8	Burial and cremation (see 19.7 DEATH)
Group 9	Trade unions and professional bodies (see 14.7 CLUBS AND ASSOCIATIONS)
Group 10	Sport, sports competitions and physical education (see 58.5 and 58.9 RECREATION AND SPORT)
Group 11	Works of art, etc. — certain disposals exempted from capital taxes (see 71.1 WORKS OF ART ETC.)
Group 12	Fund-raising events by charities and other qualifying bodies (see 12.9 CHARITIES and 14.11 CLUBS AND ASSOCIATIONS).
Group 13	Cultural services, etc. — admission to museums, exhibitions, zoos and performances of a cultural nature supplied by public bodies and eligible bodies (see 58.6 RECREATION AND SPORT).

[VATA 1994, 9 Sch].

The descriptions of the Groups above are for ease of reference only and do not affect the interpretation or the description of items within them. *[VATA 1994, s 96(10)]*. The Treasury may vary the Groups (and notes contained therein which form an integral part) by adding, deleting or amending any description of supply for the time being specified. The *Schedule* may also be varied so as to describe a supply of goods by reference to the use which has been made of them or to other matters unrelated to the characteristics of the goods themselves. *[VATA 1994, ss 31(2), 96(9)]*.

Where a supply of goods falls within one of the above Groups but is also covered by the provisions relating to ZERO-RATED SUPPLIES (72), the latter take priority. *[VATA 1994, s 30(1)]*.

De Voil Indirect Tax Service. See V4.101–103.

24.2 **POSTAL SERVICES**

EC legislation. See 22.17(*a*) and 22.18(*i*) EUROPEAN COMMUNITY LEGISLATION.

UK legislation. The following are exempt from VAT.

24.3 Exempt Supplies

- The conveyance *by the Post Office* of any postal packets i.e. letters, postcards, reply postcards, newspapers, printed packets, sample packets, parcels and every packet or article transmissible by post (but not telegrams).

- The supply *by the Post Office* of any services (except the letting on hire of goods) in connection with the conveyance of postal packets.

[*VATA 1994, 9 Sch Group 3*].

The cost of postage charged by a supplier in addition to the cost of goods is not within the exemption, see 47.8 OUTPUT TAX.

Stamps. Unused current or valid UK and Isle of Man postage stamps are not chargeable with VAT if supplied at or below face value. *First day covers* are taxable at the standard rate on their full value whether supplied by the Post Office Philatelic Bureau or stamp dealers. For stamps generally, see 58.19 RECREATION AND SPORT.

De Voil Indirect Tax Service. See V4.126.

24.3   RELIGIOUS COMMUNITIES

The supply, otherwise than for a profit, of goods and services incidental to the provision of spiritual welfare by a religious community is exempt when supplied to a resident member of that community in return for a subscription or other consideration paid as a condition of membership. [*VATA 1994, 9 Sch Group 7, Item 10*]. See 12.9 CHARITIES for the interpretation of '*otherwise than for a profit*' and '*spiritual welfare*'.

24.4   SALE OF GOODS ON WHICH NO INPUT TAX CREDIT WAS PERMITTED

If at the time goods are purchased they are to be used exclusively for making exempt supplies, any input tax incurred is not recoverable under *VATA 1994, s 26*. On disposal of such goods, C & E practice has been to treat sales as being exempt by administrative concession. Following the decision in *EC Commission v Italian Republic, CJEC [1997] STC 1062*, this practice has been confirmed and C & E are considering introducing amendments to UK legislation to make the exemption statutory. Businesses which have disposed of such goods and not taken advantage of the concession may claim refunds of overpaid VAT (subject to the three year cap). (C & E Business Brief 23/97, 13 October 1997).

25   Exports

De Voil Indirect Tax Service. See V4.301–334.

General notes

(*a*)   **The single market.** The provisions of this chapter apply to goods which are exported outside the EC. **For the provisions relating to supplies of goods from the UK to other EC countries, see 23.11** EUROPEAN COMMUNITY: SINGLE MARKET .

(*b*)   **The Isle of Man,** although not part of the UK, is treated as part of the UK for VAT purposes. All references in this chapter to the UK apply equally to the Isle of Man. Under no circumstances can goods sent to the Isle of Man be treated as exports and VAT must be charged at the appropriate rate.

(*c*)   **The Channel Islands** are part of the EC for customs purposes but *outside* the EC for VAT purposes. Supplies of goods sent to the Channel Islands are therefore regarded as exports.

The contents of this chapter are as follows.

25.1   CONDITIONS FOR ZERO-RATING

An export of goods from the UK is the despatch or transport of goods to a destination outside the EC. In a series of transactions leading to an export, only the final supply (the supply to the overseas person) can be zero-rated unless the transaction is covered by the export house arrangements (see 25.6 below).

To zero-rate supplies for export, the 'exporter' must comply with all the following conditions (which have the force of law).

(*a*)   The exporter must not supply the goods to a UK VAT-registered trader other than an export house (see 25.6 below).

(*b*)   The exporter must ensure that the goods are exported from the UK within specified time limits.

•   'Direct exports' must be exported within three months of the time of supply.

•   'Indirect exports' must be exported within one month of the time of supply.

25.1 Exports

The time of supply in most cases is the earlier of

- the date on which the goods are sent to the customer or the customer takes them away, and

- the date full payment is received for the goods. (Any deposit received is a part payment and has the same VAT liability as the final supply. However, only the final payment creates a time of supply point for these purposes.)

For both direct and indirect exports, if the goods are not exported within the time limit, the supply must not be zero-rated. If, however, the goods are subsequently exported and valid evidence of export is held, the supply may then be zero-rated and the VAT account adjusted for the period in which the evidence is obtained.

'*Direct exports*' are where the complete export transaction is under the control of the UK owner or supplier. The goods may be exported in own baggage or transport or by rail, post or courier service. Alternatively, they may be exported by a person acting on behalf of the UK owner or supplier, for example a shipping line, airline or freight forwarder (but not by a person acting on behalf of the overseas person). In any case, a person acting on behalf of the UK owner or supplier is usually responsible for the physical export of the goods.

'*Indirect exports*' are where the goods are exported by someone other than their UK owner or supplier (e.g. an overseas person or a freight forwarder acting on his behalf).

(c) The exporter must obtain and keep valid commercial or official evidence of export. See 25.12 *et seq.* below for proof of export. The time limits for obtaining this evidence are

- for direct exports, three months from the time of supply; and

- for indirect exports, one month from the date of export.

(d) The exporter must not deliver or post the goods to a UK person or a UK customer at a UK address even if it is claimed that they are for subsequent export. (Goods may be delivered to an overseas person in the UK for export within one month of supply as indirect exports under (b) above.)

(e) The exporter must not allow the goods to be collected by or on behalf of a UK person or a UK customer even if it is claimed that they are for subsequent export. The exporter may, however, deliver the goods to an independent freight forwarder, a shipping line or airline for immediate export on behalf of a non-VAT registered UK customer, or on behalf of an export house (see 25.6 below) provided valid commercial evidence of exportation is obtained from the carrier. See 25.10 below for details of deliveries made to another UK trader for consolidation, processing or incorporation prior to export. (Goods may be collected by an overseas person in the UK for export within one month of supply as indirect exports under (b) above.)

(f) The exporter must not allow the goods to be used in the UK in the period between supply and export (except where specifically authorised by C & E in a Notice).

(g) The exporter must keep records of the export transaction (see 25.28 below).

(h) The exporter must comply with the conditions specified in the legislation and in C & E Notice 703 which for this purpose has the force of law. As to whether the conditions laid down by C & E are reasonable or complied with, see *Henry Moss of London Ltd and Another v C & E Commrs CA 1980, [1981] STC 139.*

The '*exporter*' is the person who, for VAT purposes, supplies the goods directly to an overseas person or, where there is no such supply (see 25.23 below), is the owner of the goods exported.

(C & E Notice 703, paras 1.8, 1.9, 1.11–1.13, 1.17, 2.2, 4.2).

Effect of failure to comply with conditions. Where the supply of any goods has been zero-rated as an export and either

- any of the above conditions (or any other specific conditions relating to a particular type of export) is not complied with, or

- the goods are found in the UK after the date of alleged exportation,

the goods are liable to *forfeiture*. Any VAT which would have been due but for zero-rating is payable forthwith by the person to whom the goods were supplied or by any other person in whose possession the goods are found in the UK. C & E may waive payment of the VAT in whole or part. [*CEMA 1979, 4 Sch 12; VATA 1994, s 30(10)*].

Appointment of an agent. An exporter or overseas customer can appoint a freight forwarder, shipping company, airline or other person to handle the export transaction and produce the necessary declarations to customs on his behalf. In such circumstances the exporter must provide the agent with full information on the goods (e.g. copy invoices, packing lists and technical details) so that the agent can complete the export declaration and transport documents. The agent must then take reasonable steps to ensure that the goods are as described by the exporter, ensure the customs formalities are complied with and the goods exported within the time limits, keep records of each export transaction, obtain and provide valid evidence of export and send it to the exporter once the goods have been exported, and notify C & E if the export is aborted after lodgement of the export documentation. If the agent fails to fulfil its obligations, the exporter is responsible for accounting for any VAT which becomes chargeable. (C & E Notice 703, para 2.5, 2.6).

De Voil Indirect Tax Service. See V4.305, V4.307, V4.309.

25.2   CATEGORIES OF ZERO-RATED EXPORTS

Subject to meeting the general conditions in 25.1 above and any specific conditions in the appropriate paragraph of this chapter, the following categories of exports are zero-rated.

- **Direct exports.** [*VATA 1994, s 30(6)*]. See 25.1(*b*) above.

- **Stores for ships, aircraft, etc.** [*VATA 1994, s 30(6)*]. See 25.3 below.

- **Certain supplies in connection with the management of defence projects.** [*VATA 1994, 8 Sch Group 13, Item 2*]. See 25.4 below.

- **Tools for the manufacture of goods for export.** [*VATA 1994, 8 Sch Group 13, Item 3*]. See 25.5 below.

- **Goods exported by a charity** (whatever the nature of the goods). [*VATA 1994, 8 Sch Group 15, Item 3*]. See 12.6 CHARITIES.

- **Supplies to export houses.** [*SI 1995/2518, Reg 127*]. See 25.6 below.

- **Exports of freight containers.** [*SI 1995/2518, Reg 128*]. See 25.7 below.

- **Supplies to overseas persons.** [*SI 1995/2518, Reg 129*]. See 25.8 to 25.10 below.

- **Supplies to persons departing from the EC – retail export scheme.** [*SI 1995/2518, Regs 130, 131*]. See 25.11 to 25.15 below.

- **Exports of motor vehicles.** [*SI 1995/2518, Regs 132, 133*]. See 25.16 to 25.18 below.

- **Sailaway boats supplied for export.** See 25.19 below.

- **Supplies to the FCO and other government departments.** See 25.20 below.

25.3 Exports

- Supplies to regimental shops. See 25.21 below.

- Supplies intended for continental shelf installations. See 25.22 below.

- Supplies at tax-free shops. Where goods which are liable to VAT are supplied to persons leaving on flights to destinations outside the EC at tax-free shops approved by C & E, the supplier may be regarded as the exporter and zero-rate the supply of those goods which are exported. See C & E Notice 48, ESC 4.1.

25.3 **Stores for use in ships, aircraft or hovercraft**

Stores are goods for use in a ship, aircraft or hovercraft and include

- fuel;

- goods for running repairs or maintenance (e.g. lubricants, spare and replacement parts);

- goods for general use on board by the crew; and

- goods for sale by retail to persons carried on voyages or flights.

A VAT-registered shipping line or airline operator can choose one of the following options for supplies made to it.

- It can have all supplies, including those intended for stores, charged to VAT at the standard rate where appropriate. If so, input tax can be deducted subject to the normal rules and the subsequent transfer to the ship or aircraft is a non-supply.

- It can have supplies of stores made direct to foreign-going craft. Such supplies can then be zero-rated provided the following conditions are met.

  (i) The goods are for use as stores on a voyage or flight which is to be made for a non-private purpose and the person to whom the goods are to be supplied declares this in writing.

  (ii) The stores are to be shipped from the UK within one month of supply.

  (iii) The supplier obtains and keeps a written order or confirmation given by the master or duly authorised agent. This must contain a declaration that the goods are solely for use as stores on a named ship or aircraft that is entitled to duty-free stores for the voyage or flight in question i.e. to an eventual destination outside the UK. Aircraft making through international flights are eligible to receive VAT-free stores even if the aircraft makes one or more stops in the UK in the course of such a flight.

  (iv) The goods must be sent either direct to the ship or aircraft *or* through freight forwarders for consolidation and delivery direct to the ship or aircraft *or* addressed and delivered to the master c/o the shipping company or agent.

  (v) The supplier must obtain and keep a receipt confirming delivery of the goods on board, signed by the master or other responsible officer.

  (vi) Where supplies are made direct from a bonded warehouse not operated or owned by the supplier to an eligible vessel or aircraft, the supplier must hold a signed and dated certificate of export from the warehousekeeper. The advice note issued by the warehousekeeper normally serves this purpose.

Goods for sale. These provisions also apply to goods supplied for sale in ships' shops and on board aircraft even though there may be no taxable supply at the time of shipment (e.g. transfer of own goods, supply on sale or return terms). Where goods have been shipped on a foreign-going ship or aircraft, any later sale of the goods is a supply outside the UK and there is no further liability to VAT unless they are re-landed (see below). VAT is charged on goods sold on board a vessel on a coastwise journey or aircraft on an internal flight.

Relanded stores. Stores supplied under the above provisions and re-landed are treated as IMPORTS (34).

Marine fuel. By concession, commercial vessels engaged on voyages within home waters (i.e. those during which the vessel is at all times either at sea or within the limits of a port) may receive certain types of fuel VAT-free. The supplier can zero-rate the supply provided

(*a*) a written declaration is obtained from the person to whom the marine fuel is supplied that the goods are for use as stores on a non-private voyage;

(*b*) a written order or confirmation is obtained from the master, owner or duly authorised agent of the vessel declaring that the fuel is solely for use on a named ship;

(*c*) the fuel is sent direct to the ship or addressed and delivered to the master of a named vessel c/o the shipping agent or line; and

(*d*) a receipt confirming delivery of the fuel on board, signed by the master or other responsible officer, is held.

Such VAT relief extends only to those types of fuel such as fuel oil, kerosene or gas oil which were zero-rated before 1 July 1990. It does not cover petrol, derv or lubricating oil.

Mess and canteen stores. Goods can be zero-rated where supplied for use as mess and canteen stores on HM ships about to leave for a foreign port or a voyage outside UK territorial waters of more than 15 days' duration. The goods must be ordered for the general use on board by the ship's company. Orders must be certified by the Commanding Officer and goods delivered direct to the ship. A receipt must be obtained and kept.

Duty-free goods supplied on sale or return to messes in HM ships cannot be zero-rated when sent out to the ship. The taxable supply occurs only when the goods are adopted, i.e.

• when the customer pays for the goods or otherwise indicates his wish to keep them; or

• at the end of twelve months or any shorter period agreed for the goods to be bought or returned.

The supplier is responsible for ensuring that the messes inform him promptly of when the adoption of the goods took place. If adoption occurs when the vessel is in UK territorial waters, the supply is taxable; if outside, there is no supply for VAT purposes. Commanders of HM ships will provide suppliers with this information.

[*VATA 1994, s 30(6)*]. (C & E Notice 703, para 7.1–7.8; C & E Notice 48, ESC 4.2).

De Voil Indirect Tax Service. See V4.321; V4.322.

25.4   **International collaboration defence arrangements (ICDAs)**

The supply to, or by, an 'overseas authority', 'overseas body' or 'overseas trader', charged with the management of any defence project which is the subject of an 'international collaboration arrangement' (or under direct contract with any government or government-sponsored international body participating in defence projects under such an arrangement) of goods or services made for the purpose of fulfilling contracts is zero-rated. The zero-rating only applies to a limited number of projects and traders who are concerned with them are notified individually by C & E.

'*Overseas authority*' means any country other than the UK or any part of, or place in, such a country or the government of such a country, part or place.

'*Overseas body*' means a body established outside the UK.

'*Overseas trader*' means a person who carries on a business and has a principal place of business outside the UK.

An '*international collaboration arrangement*' is any arrangement made between the UK government and the government of one or more other countries (or any government-sponsored international body, e.g. NATO) for collaboration in a joint project of research, development or production. The arrangement must specifically provide for participating governments to relieve the cost of the project from taxation.

[*VATA 1994, 8 Sch Group 13, Item 2*].

Under an ICDA, the responsibility for project definition, direction, control and funding rests with the participating governments (with the Ministry of Defence (MOD) representing the UK). The participants usually use a single body as a project management organisation (PMO). This may be an agency of one of the governments (e.g. the MOD Procurement Executive) or a multi-national body which may be set up specifically for the purpose (e.g. the NATO Multi-Role Combat Aircraft Management Agency). A PMO is funded by the participants and acts as contracting authority to procure the work required. It will be responsible to the participants and will employ one or more prime contractors which it will pay with funds provided by the participants. Any UK PMO will be registered for VAT. Participants' funding of the PMO is consideration for supplies by the PMO to the extent that the supplies come within the scope of UK VAT. Prime contractors will be appointed by the PMO (or the individual participants if there is not a PMO) from different countries to carry out specific technical responsibilities. Each prime contractor may engage first level sub-contractors who may in turn engage second level sub-contractors and so on. Zero-rating under *VATA 1994, 8 Sch Group 13, Item 2* cannot apply below the first level of transactions between a prime contractor and a first level sub-contractor.

The agreement reached by the different governments involved in the project is recorded in a Memorandum of Understanding (MOU). This document determines whether the project is approved as an ICDA for the purposes of *Item 2*. If so, the MOD will notify C & E and give details of the participants, PMO (if any) and prime contractor(s) for the individual projects. Zero-rating then applies to any supply by or to any of these bodies where one or other of them belongs overseas and the supply is in a chain that leads to the delivery to the participants of services or equipment in accordance with the objectives of the arrangement.

All supplies made in the UK between the MOD and UK contractors follow the normal VAT rules as relief under *Item 2* applies only to supplies made to or by an overseas body charged with the management of an ICDA. Goods forming part of an ICDA may be delivered from one participating contractor to another within the UK for process or assembly.

Following discussions with the MOD, C & E accept that relief under *Item 2* includes the supply of the finished product (i.e. the final supply) of a collaborative project.

Own variant products from ICDAs which, whilst researched, developed or produced jointly, include features specific to the requirements of an individual country, qualify for relief under *Item 2* provided they are funded by the ICDA.

(C & E Manual V1-7, Chapter 13 sections 3.1, 3.2, 4.1, 4.3, 4.5, 4.6). See C & E Manual V1-7 Chapter 13 generally for further information including a list of ICDAs involving the UK at 1 April 1997 as quoted in Hansard on 19 February 1998).

De Voil Indirect Tax Service. See V4.283.

25.5   **Tools for the manufacture of goods for export**

The supply to an 'overseas authority', 'overseas body' or 'overseas trader' of jigs, patterns, templates, dies, moulds, punches and similar machine tools used in the UK solely for the manufacture of goods for export is zero-rated. The overseas authority etc. must not be

- a taxable person,

- another EC country,

- any part of or place in another EC country,

- the government of any such country, part or place,

- a body established in another EC country, or

- a person who carries on business, or has a place of business, in another EC country,

otherwise the supply is taxable in the normal way.

[*VATA 1994, 8 Sch Group 13, Item 3*].

Normal proof of export must be obtained and retained, together with a signed statement (or similar definite evidence) from the customer that he is not registered or required to be registered for VAT. (C & E Leaflet 701/22/95, paras 1 and 2).

25.6   **Supplies to export houses before 1 April 1999**

An 'export house' is any person registered for VAT in the UK who, in the course of business in the UK, arranges or finances the export of goods from the UK to a place outside the EC. Both the supplier and the export house can zero-rate the supply of the same goods for export (i.e. exceptionally zero-rating is allowed one stage back from the actual export). The supplier can zero-rate a supply of goods to an export house provided

(*a*)   the export house is registered for VAT in the UK;

(*b*)   when the goods leave the supplier's premises they are not collected by or delivered to the export house anywhere in the UK but sent

(i)   direct to a port, airport or inland clearance depot for 'immediate' shipment; or

(ii)   to an independent export packer or freight forwarder who will deliver the goods direct to a port, airport or inland clearance depot for immediate shipment; and

(*c*)   both the supplier and export house, within one month of the time of supply, obtain and keep satisfactory proof of export.

For these purposes '*immediate*' means within seven to ten days or on the next available ship or aircraft provided that this occurs within one month of the time of supply.

If the conditions are not satisfied, the supply to the export house must be standard-rated (even if the goods are subsequently exported by the export house and evidence of export is obtained).

25.7 Exports

If the export house arranges the export, it must send a certified copy of the evidence of export to the supplier (and vice versa). In each case this must be sent within one month of the time of supply.

[*SI 1995/2518, Regs 117(3), 127*]. (C & E Notice 703, para 4.7).

Supplies after 31 March 1999. The above provisions are withdrawn with effect from 1 April 1999. From that date supplies to export houses are treated in the same way as any other supplies made to UK customers. Export houses can zero-rate supplies to overseas customers as exports subject to the normal conditions. (VAT Information Sheet 2/98, June 1998).

De Voil Indirect Tax Service. See V4.324.

25.7   **Freight containers supplied for export**

Subject to such conditions as C & E impose, the supply of a 'container' is zero-rated where C & E are satisfied that it is to be exported.

For these purposes, a '*container*' is defined as an article of transport equipment (lift-van, movable tank or similar structure)

*   fully or partially enclosed to constitute a compartment for goods;

*   of a permanent character strong enough for repeated use;

*   designed to facilitate the carriage of goods, by one or more modes of transport, without intermediate reloading;

*   designed for ready handling and to be easy to fill and empty; and

*   having an internal volume of one cubic metre or more.

It includes accessories and equipment as appropriate but excludes vehicles, spares for vehicles and packaging.

[*SI 1995/2518, Regs 117(2), 128*].

Although not strictly within the definition, 'flats' or 'Lancashire flats' (i.e. bases without head and tail boards having a floor area of a 20 ft or 40 ft container) are included as are air transport containers whatever their internal volume. Pallets, road vehicles and trailers including tanks on wheels are not included. (C & E Notice 703, para 6.5; C & E Notice 703/1/95, para 2).

Direct export. The supply of a container for direct export may be zero-rated provided the container is actually exported and the normal conditions for export are complied with. (C & E Notice 703/1/95, para 3).

Indirect export. The supply of a container for indirect export may be zero-rated provided the supplier obtains a written undertaking from the customer that

(*a*) the container will be exported from the EC;

(*b*) the container will not be used in the EC except for

   (i) a single domestic journey before export (on which inland freight may be carried) on a reasonably direct route between the point of supply and the place where the container is to be loaded with the export cargo or exported; and

   (ii) international movement of goods (which may include a journey within the UK for the purpose of loading or unloading the goods);

(*c*) the customer will keep records sufficient to satisfy C & E that

(i) the container has not been used in the EC (except as allowed under (*b*) above); and

(ii) the container has either been exported or has been sold/leased to someone else who has given a similar written undertaking.

If the container is subsequently used in the UK other than within the exact terms of the undertaking, the container is liable to be seized by C & E and the VAT which would have been charged on the supply if standard-rated is due immediately from the customer or any other person in possession of the container.

(C & E Notice 703/1/95, paras 5, 6 which have the force of law).

Lease or hire of containers. *Where the supplier and the customer both belong in the UK*, the supply is treated as made in the UK. If the customer is to export the container, the leasing/hiring may be zero-rated provided the supplier obtains a written undertaking from the customer as for indirect exports above.

Where the supplier belongs in the UK but the customer belongs outside the EC, the supply is treated as being made in the customer's country and no UK VAT is due.

Incidental charges which under the terms of the lease agreement are charged to the lessee are regarded as part of the consideration for the leasing of the container and have the same VAT liability. Included are repair, delivery, regulator and handling charges, extra rental and any charge for the option to terminate the lease at an earlier date.

(C & E Notice 703/1/95, paras 7, 8).

De Voil Indirect Tax Service. See V4.323.

25.8   **Supplies to overseas persons**

Where C & E are satisfied that 'goods' intended for export have been supplied to an 'overseas person' who is not a taxable person, the supply is zero-rated. Supplies to a member of the crew of any ship or aircraft departing from the UK are excluded (but see 25.14 below). For export of motor vehicles generally, see 25.16 to 25.18 below.

'*Overseas person*' is

● a person not resident in the UK;

● a trader who has no business establishment in the UK from which taxable supplies are made; or

● an overseas authority (i.e. any country other than the UK or any part or place in such a country or the government of any such country, part or place). This includes goods ordered through embassies, High Commissions and purchasing agents of foreign governments in the UK.

[*SI 1995/2518, Reg 117(4)–(7), 129; SI 1996/210*].

C & E require that

(*a*) the supplier clearly identifies the transaction in his records including evidence that the supply has been made to an overseas person (e.g. the official order for the goods showing their name and address);

(*b*) the goods are exported within one month of the time of supply;

(*c*) valid proof of export is obtained within one month of the date of export; and (*d*) the goods are not used for any purpose between the time of leaving the supplier's premises and exportation (either for their normal purpose or for any other purpose including display, exhibition or copying).

(C & E Notice 703, paras 4.3, 6.17).

De Voil Indirect Tax Service. See V4.326–328.

25.9 *Work carried out on goods owned by overseas persons*

Work carried out on goods owned by an 'overseas person' (see 25.8 above) can normally be zero-rated within the following categories. The provisions do not apply to goods owned by persons resident in the EC, even though they are kept permanently abroad.

- *Goods temporarily imported for specific work to be carried out before re-export.* Any work on such goods (including motor vehicles and light aircraft) may be zero-rated provided evidence is obtained that the customer is an overseas person and that the goods are subsequently re-exported.

- *Goods obtained in the UK.* The supply of work on goods obtained in the UK by an overseas person for export may, with the exception below, be zero-rated provided evidence is obtained that the customer is an overseas person and that the goods are exported. These provisions do not apply to work carried out on

  (i) a motor vehicle supplied by the same person unless the vehicle is supplied as a direct export; or

  (ii) a motor vehicle obtained by an overseas person from a third person unless it has been specifically obtained in the UK for the purpose of refurbishment or restoration before export.

- *Repairs to vehicles, etc. during a visit by an overseas person.* If an overseas person visits the UK with a motor vehicle, boat or light aircraft and during the visit requires repair work to it, the repair work itself cannot be zero-rated but parts and equipment fitted in the course of supplying those repairs may be zero-rated

  (i) if supplied for the purposes of the overseas person's business, provided the conditions in 25.1(*a*)(*b*)(*d*)(*e*) above are satisfied; or

  (ii) if supplied for private use, under the Retail Export Scheme (see 25.11 to 25.15 below).

(C & E Notice 703, para 4.6).

25.10 *Supplies to overseas persons for export after consolidation, processing or incorporation*

Goods supplied for export to an overseas person but delivered to a third person in the UK who is also making a taxable supply to that overseas person are zero-rated provided

(*a*) the goods are only being delivered and not supplied to the third person in the UK;

(*b*) no use is made of the goods other than for processing or incorporation into other goods, or consolidation with other goods, for export;

(*c*) the goods are exported from the EC within six months of the time of supply and proof of export from the actual exporter is obtained within one month of export;

(*d*) the supplier's records show the

- name and address of the overseas person,

- invoice number and date,

- description, quantity and value of goods,

- name and address of the third person in the UK to whom the goods were delivered,

- date by which the goods must be exported and proof of export obtained, and

- date of actual exportation.

(C & E Notice 703, para 4.4).

25.11 **Retail export scheme**

The retail export scheme allows (i.e. it is not obligatory) a registered trader to zero-rate the supply of goods (but not services) to certain entitled persons. A leaflet entitled *Traveller's Guide to the Retail Export Scheme* is available from VAT enquiry offices explaining how the scheme works, a copy of which may be usefully given to customers using the scheme.

To use the scheme, the following conditions (which have the force of law) must be met.

(*a*) The customer must be an '*overseas visitor*' i.e. someone who has not been in the EC for more than 365 days in the two years before the date he buys the goods and who intends to leave the EC with the goods within three months of the date of purchase for a final destination outside the EC.

(*b*) The customer must make the purchase in person.

(*c*) The goods must be eligible for the scheme. Any *standard-rated goods* can be sold under the scheme except for the following.

- Motor vehicles (see 25.16 below).

- Sailaway boats (see 25.19 below).

- Goods over £600 in value exported for the customer's business purposes.

- Goods for consumption in the EC. (No refunds will be made on consumable items (e.g. perfume) which are wholly or partly consumed in the EC.)

- Goods requiring an export licence with the exception of antiques. Antiques can be sold under the scheme even if they do require an export licence. Where an export licence is required for an antique, this must be produced to Customs on departure from the UK. Further advice can be obtained from

  The Department of Trade and Industry
  Export Control Organisation
  Kingsgate House
  66–74 Victoria Street
  London SW1E 6SW

- Unmounted gemstones.

- Bullion over 125g (2.75 troy or 10 Tolas).

Zero-rated goods sold to a customer must not be shown on the VAT refund form.

(*d*) The goods must be exported from the EC within three months of the end of the month of purchase. This time limit cannot be extended. Goods exported after the time limit must not be zero-rated or the VAT refunded even if the VAT refund document has been certified in error by UK or other EC Customs.

(*e*) The customer must send evidence of export to the retailer. It must be certified by UK or other EC Customs on an approved VAT refund document and the retailer must retain the evidence.

25.12 Exports

A retailer is not obliged to use the scheme for all lines sold and can fix a minimum sales level.

[*SI 1995/2518, Regs 117(8), 131; SI 1995/3147*]. (C & E Notice 704, paras 1.1–1.3, 1.7–1.9, 1.17).

De Voil Indirect Tax Service. See V4.331.

25.12   *Procedure*

At the time of sale, the retailer must establish that the customer is entitled to use the scheme by qualifying as an overseas visitor and, if so, agree how the refund will be paid. He must give the customer a document with which the customer can claim a refund after the goods have been exported. This VAT refund document can be either of the following.

(*a*)   Form VAT 407 in which case it can either be

- Form VAT 407 (1993 print) issued by C & E and available free of charge from VAT offices;

- the retailer's own version of Form 407 provided it is approved beforehand by C & E; or

- a refund company's approved version of Form VAT 407 provided it is approved beforehand by C & E. (Refund companies are not retailers but companies which administer refund arrangements on behalf of retailers.)

The goods must be described on the form in enough detail for them to be clearly identified (e.g. by including manufacturer, serial number, etc.) and the invoice number, date and total value should be shown. Any unused lines should be crossed through. The form and declarations must be completed in full and signed by both the retailer (or responsible person in the business) and the customer.

(*b*)   A sales invoice approved by the VAT office. It must be at least A5 size (15 cm by 21 cm) and preferably A4.

The invoice should be clearly marked 'Retail Export Scheme' and provide spaces for the retailer's and customer's declarations, including details of the customer's passport number, date of arrival in the EC, intended date of departure from the EC and a box (at least 5 cm by 3.5 cm) for official certification by export officers at the customer's port or airport of departure from the EC. It must also show the following details.

- An identifying serial number and date.

- The retailer's name, address and VAT registration number.

- The date of sale.

- The customer's name and address.

- A description which clearly identifies the goods, and for each description the quantity of goods, the rate and amount of VAT (but see 25.13 below for goods sold under the second-hand scheme); and the amount payable inclusive of VAT, expressed in sterling.

- The amount of VAT included in the total price.

- The amount of any administration charge (see below).

- The net refund due.

As a protection against fraud, it is advisable to show either the VAT, VAT-inclusive price or net refund due in words as well as figures.

When the VAT refund document is completed, it should be handed over to the customer with an envelope addressed to the retailer or the refund company as the case may be.

If the customer is intending to carry some goods in hand baggage and other goods in hold baggage, it is recommended that separate VAT refund documents should be issued. This is particularly essential where the customer is leaving the UK on a through flight via another EC country as goods in hold baggage must be declared on departure from the UK and the goods in hand baggage must be declared in the country of final departure from the EC.

Administrative or handling charges. If an administrative or handling charge is to be deducted from the refund due, the amount and net refund must be shown on the VAT refund document. The charge is a consideration for the supply of services to the customer in connection with the export of specific goods to a destination outside the EC and is zero-rated under *VATA 1994, 8 Sch Group 7, Item 2(a)*.

Charging VAT. Any sale under the scheme must be treated as standard-rated until the VAT refund form, certified by the UK or other EC Customs Export officer, is received. Only then can the sale be zero-rated in the records. It is, therefore, in the interests of the retailer to refund the VAT only when valid evidence of export is received. Where it is not, VAT must be accounted for even if not charged to the customer at the point of sale.

Action required by customer. Customers must always carry higher value goods (e.g. jewellery, furs, cameras, expensive watches, silverware and small antiques) in their hand baggage. They must produce the VAT refund document and all the goods to Customs at the port or airport of departure from the EC. If satisfied, Customs will then certify the VAT refund document and return it to the customer. The customer must then send it back to the retailer or refund company in the envelope provided.

Receipt of evidence. On receipt of certified evidence, the retailer or refund company should make the refund to the customer by the agreed method. If the documents are sent back uncertified, the retailer must cancel and return the documents to the customer advising that a refund cannot be made.

Loss of VAT refund documents. If the customer loses the VAT refund document before leaving the EC, the retailer may provide a duplicate clearly marked as such. If the document is lost after certification, a duplicate may only be issued where a photocopy of the certified original is produced. The duplicate and photocopy must then be sent to the export officer who certified the original document for certification of the duplicate. Only then should the refund be made.

(C & E Notice 704, paras 1.10, 1.11, 1.15, 2.2–2.4, 2.7–2.9).

25.13   *Accounting for VAT*

Suppliers also using a special retail scheme. See 60.9 RETAIL SCHEMES.

Other retailers. Other retailers must keep a record of all sales under the Retail Export Scheme. If a properly certified VAT refund document has not been received within one month of the intended export date, VAT must be accounted for on the sale at the standard-rate. If the evidence arrives after VAT has been accounted for, the VAT can still be refunded. The transaction should then be treated as a credit in the VAT records.

Sales by auctioneers. If an auctioneer sells goods on behalf of a retailer to someone entitled to use the Retail Export Scheme, the sale can be zero-rated provided that a VAT refund document is completed and certified by Customs. The auctioneer will usually arrange export from the EC and produce the goods and VAT refund documents to Customs. The auctioneer will also pass on the certified VAT refund document to the retailer once the goods are shipped abroad.

If the auctioneer is registered for VAT and sells goods in his own name to someone who is entitled to use the scheme then, for VAT purposes, he is treated as both receiving and making a supply of goods and can zero-rate the sale and refund the VAT provided he has a certified VAT refund document.

Second-hand goods. If a sale is made under the scheme for second-hand goods schemes and the retailer does not wish to disclose the amount of VAT charged, the VAT refund document should be adapted as follows.

- Head the document 'Second-hand goods – this document is adapted in accordance with Notice 704, paragraph 1.13'.

- Leave the VAT box (or space for the VAT total) blank.

- Enter the VAT-exclusive prices, and delete from the price column on the VAT refund document the reference to 'including' (VAT) and insert 'excluding'.

(C & E Notice 704, paras 1.12–1.14).

25.14 *Supplies to ships' crew etc. and entitled EC residents going abroad for at least one year*

The retail export scheme also allows a registered trader to zero-rate the supply of goods to

- *an 'entitled EC resident'* i.e. a person who has been resident in the EC for at least 365 days in the two years before the date of purchase of the goods and who is going outside the EC for a continuous period of at least 12 months. Included is an overseas student or worker who has lived in the EC for more than one year; or

- a *member of the crew of a ship or aircraft* who

  (i) has not been in the EC for more than 365 days in the two years before the date of purchase of the goods; and

  (ii) is going to a final destination outside the EC.

See 25.11(*b*)–(*e*) above for conditions for using the scheme. The goods must be delivered direct to the ship or aircraft, or to an independent freight forwarder for export, and the customer must not take possession of them before he departs from the EC. Note that although the scheme includes export by aircraft, in practice airlines find it impractical to make the necessary arrangements.

[*SI 1995/2518, Reg 130*]. (C & E Notice 704, paras 1.1, 1.2, 1.4, 1.5, 1.7–1.9, 1.17).

25.15 *Procedure for supplies to ships' crew etc. and entitled EC residents going abroad for at least one year*

At the time of sale, the retailer must establish that the customer is entitled to use the scheme, by qualifying as an entitled EC resident or as the member of a ship's crew, and, if so, agree how the refund will be paid. He must give his customer a document with which the customer can claim a refund after the goods have been exported. The same provisions apply to this refund document as in 25.12(*a*) and (*b*) above but substituting 'Form VAT 435' or 'Form VAT 407'.

Administrative or handling charges and *Charging VAT*. The same provisions apply as under 25.12 above.

Export procedure. The completed VAT refund document must be put in an envelope, attached to the package of goods sold, and clearly marked 'VAT refund document for production to Customs before shipment'. The package should then be sent, either direct or through a freight forwarder, to the shipping company concerned at the port of departure with instructions that it must be produced to the Customs officer controlling shipment no later than the customer's time of embarkation. Once the VAT refund document has been certified, the freight forwarder or shipping company must return the document to the retailer and, with the agreement of the Customs officer, pass the package to the ship's purser or other responsible officer.

If the goods cannot be exported on the same ship as the customer, they can be exported as unaccompanied baggage or as freight. The package should be clearly marked 'For export as unaccompanied baggage on .... (ship's name) from .... (port) on .... (date)'. An envelope marked 'VAT refund document for production to Customs before shipment' should be attached. Arrangements should then be made through the shipper or agent for the VAT refund document and goods to be produced to Customs at export from the EC.

Receipt of evidence. On receipt of certified evidence, the refund should be made to the customer by the agreed method. If the documents are sent back uncertified, the retailer must cancel and return the documents to the customer advising that a refund cannot be made.

Accounting for VAT. The same procedures should be followed as in 25.13 above.

(C & E Notice 704, paras 1.10–1.14, 3.2–3.6, 3.8, 3.9).

25.16   **Motor vehicles**

Direct exports. Any motor vehicle, new or second-hand, supplied for direct export may be zero–rated provided it is exported from the EC and the conditions in 25.1(*b*) above are satisfied. Evidence of exportation must be obtained and retained.

Indirect exports. The supply of a new or second-hand motor vehicle can be zero–rated under the conditions in 25.17 below. A new motor vehicle can also be zero–rated under the Personal Export Scheme in 25.18 below.

De Voil Indirect Tax Service. See V4.334.

25.17   *Vehicles delivered in the UK for subsequent export by or on behalf of the purchaser*

The supply to an overseas person (see 25.8 above) of any motor vehicle new or second-hand) can be zero–rated provided

(*a*)   the supplier keeps a separate record of the transaction, including evidence that the buyer was an overseas customer;

(*b*)   the vehicle is not subsequently hired before it is exported from the EC;

(*c*)   the vehicle is not subsequently used except for the trip to the place of departure from the EC;

(*d*)   the vehicle is exported within one month of the time of supply; and

(*e*)   the supplier obtains proof of export within one month of the date of export.

(C & E Notice 703, para 6.3).

25.18   *New vehicles delivered in the UK for temporary use and subsequent export by the purchaser (the 'Personal Export Scheme')*

The Personal Export Scheme allows new motor vehicles (including motor cycles and motor caravans but not pedal cycles and trailer caravans) to be purchased free of VAT provided all the following conditions (which have the force of law) are met. (Note that it is not possible to get a refund of VAT on a motor vehicle purchased VAT-paid even if it is later exported and would have qualified under the scheme.)

(*a*)   The vehicle must be purchased from a VAT-registered trader who operates the Personal Export Scheme.

(b)   The purchaser must personally take delivery of the vehicle in the UK.

(c)   The purchaser must export the vehicle within

- twelve months of the date of delivery if he is an 'overseas visitor'; or

- six months of the date of delivery in any other case.

An '*overseas visitor*' for these purposes is a person who has not been in the EC for more than 365 days in the last two years immediately before the date of application or 1,095 days in the six years immediately before that date.

The final date for exportation is shown in the registration document. Shipping arrangements must be made in good time to ensure that the vehicle is exported by that date.

(d)   The purchaser must intend to leave, and remain outside the EC with the vehicle for a period of at least six consecutive months.

(e)   The vehicle may be used in the UK in the period before exportation but only

- by the purchaser and his or her spouse; or

- if the purchaser is still in the EC, by another person who intends to leave the EC and has the purchaser's permission to use it.

The vehicle may also be driven for the purchaser by a chauffeur.

(f)   The purchaser must not attempt to dispose of the vehicle in the UK by hire, pledge as security, sale, gift or any other means.

(g)   If the purchaser changes his plans before the vehicle is removed from the UK and can no longer comply with (c) or (d) above, he must notify C & E immediately and pay the full amount of VAT. If the vehicle is in another EC country, the purchaser should contact the fiscal authorities of that country (in which case any taxes due are payable to that fiscal authority).

If any of the above conditions are broken, the vehicle is liable to forfeiture and may be seized. VAT is payable on the value of vehicle when new. Even if the vehicle cannot be exported for unavoidable reasons (e.g. theft or accident write-off) the VAT must still be paid. It should also be noted that it can be very difficult to import motor vehicles into some countries and it is advisable to check with the embassy for that country before ordering a vehicle under the scheme.

Procedure. Application may be made up to 15 months before the intended departure date by an overseas visitor or nine months before that date by any other person. If satisfied that the prospective purchaser is entitled to use the scheme, the trader must give him a copy of Notice 705 and ask him to complete Form VAT 410 (both obtainable from VAT offices). Completed applications must be serially numbered by the trader in the top right hand corner (each separate franchise at the same location requires a separate series of numbers) and submitted, at least two weeks before date of delivery of the vehicle, to

HM Customs and Excise
Third Country Transport Unit
Central Processing Unit
Parcel Post Depot
Charlton Green
Dover
Kent CT16 1EH

Tel: 01304 224606
Fax: 01304 215786

If the order for the vehicle is cancelled before delivery, the trader must immediately notify the TCTU, quoting name of applicant, make/model of vehicle and serial number on application form.

To register the vehicle, the trader must complete an application form (V55) headed 'PERSONAL EXPORT (VAT FREE) VEHICLE', attach it to the VRO copy of Form VAT 410, and send it to the VRO in Bristol, Birmingham, Chelmsford, Coventry, Leeds, London Central, Luton, Northampton, Norwich, Oxford or Stoke-on-Trent (see 23.32 EUROPEAN COMMUNITY: SINGLE MARKET for addresses). A pink registration book (VX 302) and a special tax disc will be issued. The trader must complete the details required on pages 5 and 8 of the pink registration book before the vehicle is delivered, showing the amount of VAT remitted, the date of delivery, and the final date for export (see (c) above).

The trader must supply and invoice a VAT-free vehicle direct to the applicant. Factory fitted extras can only be supplied VAT-free if they are included on the invoice for the supply of the vehicle.

Records. In addition to the normal VAT records and his copy of the Form VAT 410, the trader must keep for each vehicle supplied under the scheme a separate record of

- date of delivery;

- applicant's name and UK address;

- particulars of the vehicle including type, chassis number and registration number;

- amount of VAT remitted on the delivery price (including any accessories or extras and any delivery charges less any discount allowed); and

- a certificate of receipt of the vehicle, detailing chassis number and registration number, which must be signed and dated by the applicant.

Temporary visits abroad. Temporary visits abroad may be made with the vehicle to a country outside the EC provided it is declared to Customs at the place of reimportation when brought back to the EC and the vehicle registration document is shown to the official. Note, however, that if the vehicle has been used in the EC for more than three months, it may not be possible to re-import it VAT-free. See C & E Notice 3 *Bringing your belongings and private motor vehicle to the UK from outside the European Community* for further information.

Temporary visits may also be made with the vehicle to another EC country. The vehicle can be brought back into the UK without any Customs formalities provided it is brought back before the date for exportation shown in the registration document and the purchaser still intends to leave the EC with the vehicle by that date. The purchaser is advised to check with the relevant VAT authority of the EC country in case, since the vehicle has been supplied free of VAT, any Customs requirements must be complied with on entry.

Reimportation. If the vehicle is brought back into the UK after the date shown for export, taxes must be paid on importation unless the person is eligible for relief from VAT and duty (see C & E Notice 3 *Bringing your belongings and private motor vehicle to the UK from outside the European Community*). Where the purchaser is not eligible for relief, the VAT due is that which was not charged on purchase (as shown on the registration document) unless either the vehicle is imported three months or more after the final exportation date shown in the registration document or the purchaser can show that he and the vehicle have remained outside the EC for at least six consecutive months. In those cases, the VAT payable will be based on the value of the vehicle at the time of reimportation. The vehicle must also be registered and licensed on return to the UK unless the vehicle is not to be used or kept on the public roads.

[*SI 1995/2518, Regs 117(8), 132, 133*]. (C & E Notice 705; C & E Notice 705A).

25.19 Exports

25.19 Sailaway boats supplied for export

Under the conditions outlined below (which have the force of law), it is possible to zero-rate the supply of a boat which is to be exported outside the EC under its own power. The scheme cannot be used for boats supplied for export on a trailer or for parts or accessories supplied for export. It is only possible to zero-rate a sale once satisfactory evidence has been received that the boat has been exported in the time allowed. It is advisable, therefore, to arrange for a deposit of the VAT involved on the sale and to refund this when evidence is received. It is recommended that a deposit should *always* be taken on boats sold to EC residents or emigrants. If satisfactory evidence is not received, the sale must be standard-rated, even if VAT was not charged at the point of sale.

The scheme may be used for the supply of a boat to a 'non-EC resident' or a 'non-EC trader' visiting the EC or to an EC resident (including a UK resident) for export to a destination outside the EC. The supplier must

(*a*) check whether the customer is a non-EC resident, non-EC trader or an EC resident;

(*b*) ensure that the customer intends to export the boat under its own power from the EC within six months of the 'date of delivery' in the case of a non-EC resident, one month of that date in the case of a non-EC trader, or two months of that date in the case of an EC resident;

(*c*) in the case of a customer who is an EC resident, ensure that he intends to keep the boat outside the EC for a continuous period of at least twelve months;

(*d*) ensure that Form VAT 436 is fully completed by the customer;

(*e*) complete the supplier's declaration when the boat is delivered to the customer;

(*f*) ensure that the customer knows he must not dispose or attempt to dispose of the boat in the UK or other EC country by hire, pledge as security (other than as part of the financing arrangements for the purchase of the boat itself), sale, gift or any other means;

(*g*) keep a separate record of the sale (the sales invoice must clearly show that the supply of the boat was made under the Sailaway Boat Scheme); and

(*h*) agree how any refund of VAT will be paid.

A '*non-EC resident*' is a person visiting the EC who normally lives outside the EC and has not been in the EC for more than 365 days in the two years immediately before the date of purchase of the boat.

A '*non-EC trader*' is a person visiting the EC who is in business outside the VAT territory of the EC and has no business establishment in the EC from which taxable supplies are made.

'*Date of delivery*' is normally the date the boat leaves the supplier's premises.

Accounting for VAT. The sale can only be zero-rated if satisfactory evidence is held that the boat has been exported. If this is not received within one month of the time allowed for export, VAT must be accounted for at the standard rate. If evidence is later received, the supply can be zero-rated provided the actual export was within the time limit. The transaction should then be treated as a credit in the VAT records.

Forms. The forms to be used are Form 88 (SAD) copies 1 to 3, Form VAT 436 (the application and declaration) and Form C1331 (to advise departure from the UK). The use of these forms varies according to whether a boat departs to a destination outside the EC directly from the UK or via another EC country.

Reimportation. If the original or subsequent owner of a boat which was supplied free of VAT under the scheme imports it back into the EC, the importation must be declared to Customs in the EC country of arrival. VAT will then be payable unless some other relief is available (e.g. non-EC residents may qualify for temporary importation relief for pleasure sailing or repair or refit).

The Channel Islands are outside the EC VAT area and therefore qualify as a final destination for boats bought under the scheme. EC residents who register VAT-free boats there cannot claim VAT-free temporary importation of such boats into an EC country and must pay the VAT on these importations. Private persons resident in the Channel Islands are entitled to temporarily import their boats into the VAT territory of the EC for their own personal use for up to six months in any period of twelve months without payment of VAT.

(C & E Leaflet 703/2/93, Parts 1, 2, 4; C & E Notice 48, ESC 3.1).

See C & E Leaflet 703/2/93, Part 4 for the different documentation and export procedures required depending upon whether the boat is delivered

- directly to the customer outside the EC;

- to a customer leaving the UK directly for a final destination outside the EC; or

- to a customer calling into another EC country before finally exporting the boat from the EC.

25.20   **Supplies to the FCO and other government departments**

Foreign and Commonwealth Office (FCO). Goods ordered by British Embassies, High Commissions (see 25.8 above) and diplomats abroad which are delivered to FCO for export via diplomatic channels can be zero-rated provided a certificate of receipt for the goods is obtained from the FCO within one month of the time of supply of the goods. The certificate may be on a copy of the sales invoice or itemised list and must be retained. The supply of goods ordered by and delivered to the FCO for general distribution cannot be zero-rated.

Ministry of Defence (MOD). The MOD is registered for VAT in the UK and all supplies to them or to any military establishment in the UK on their behalf should include VAT at the appropriate rate. Direct exports to overseas military and similar installations may be zero-rated provided the supplier arranges export and holds valid proof of export.

Other government departments. The supply of goods to other government departments can only be zero-rated if supplied by direct export to an overseas destination. Goods for export delivered to government departments in the UK must not be zero-rated even if the goods are ordered for or by an overseas establishment.

(C & E Notice 703, paras 6.13-6.15).

25.21   **Supplies to regimental shops**

Supplies to regimental shops are normally taxable. However, where the regiment (or equivalent military unit) is about to be posted to a location outside the UK, supplies of goods to a regimental shop can be zero-rated provided the following conditions are satisfied.

(*a*)   Each written order received from the President of the Regimental Institute (PRI) states that the regiment is about to take up an overseas posting and that the goods ordered will be exported from the UK.

25.22 Exports

(*b*) The goods are delivered to the PRI ready packed for shipment no more than 48 hours before the regiment is due to depart for the overseas posting.

(*c*) The goods are exported outside the UK.

(*d*) The supplier retains a certificate of receipt signed by the PRI which clearly identifies the goods, gives full shipment details and states the date on which they were exported from the UK.

The PRI will keep a full record of such transactions for reference purposes for a period of not less than six years.

(C & E Notice 703, para 6.16).

25.22 **Supplies intended for continental shelf installations**

The following provisions apply to the export of goods to structures such as oil rigs, dwelling units, accommodation platforms and similar oil or gas exploration/exploitation structures. It also applies to mobile floating structures such as drill ships, tankers, jack-up rigs, semi-submersible rigs and Floating Production Storage and Offloading (FPSO) vessels which are often stationed at fixed locations.

Exports to installations outside EC territorial waters

- *Goods supplied and exported by a supplier to an installation which he does not own.* Such supplies are zero-rated as direct exports provided proof of export is obtained within three months of the supply.

- *Goods sent to an installation owned by the supplier or goods sent to replenish own stocks on an installation not owned by the supplier.* This is a transfer of own goods and not a taxable supply (see 25.23 below). Valid proof of export must still be held to demonstrate how the goods have been disposed of.

Goods supplied for sale on installations situated outside UK territorial waters. Such supplies can be zero-rated provided

(*a*) a written order for the goods is obtained from a responsible person on the installation to which the goods are to be sent;

(*b*) the goods are supplied either direct to the installation or through an agent for consolidation followed by direct delivery to the installation; and

(*c*) a receipt for the goods, signed by a responsible person on the installation, is obtained within one month of the time of supply.

Goods supplied and delivered within the UK (including territorial waters). If such goods are

- supplied to an overseas person (see 25.8 above) for export by that person as an indirect export and the necessary conditions in 25.1(*b*) above are met, or

- supplied to an overseas person but delivered to a third person in the UK for processing, etc. and subsequent export and the conditions in 25.10 above are met,

the supply can be zero-rated.

Otherwise, VAT must be charged at the standard rate (unless the goods are zero-rated in their own right). This includes

- goods delivered to the quayside where they may be consolidated with goods from other suppliers, or the customer's own goods, before loading on to a vessel which will deliver them outside UK territorial waters; and

- goods delivered to the quayside, or loaded on board a vessel, or delivered to a customer's premises for subsequent export by the customer.

(C & E Notice 703, para 6.9).

25.23   EXPORTS WHERE THERE IS NO TAXABLE SUPPLY

There is no need to account for VAT in the following circumstances.

(a)   The supply and export of goods which the supplier is to install outside the EC for his customer.

(b)   The transfer of own goods to a place outside the EC by a person making taxable supplies in the UK. Proof of export is still required so that the owner can show C & E how he has disposed of the goods. Any related input tax can be deducted subject to the normal rules but the value of the goods transferred should not be included in Box 6 of the VAT return.

(c)   The temporary export of goods outside the EC for exhibition and return.

(d)   The export of goods on sale or return.

(C & E Notice 703, paras 1.14, 4.5).

25.24   PROOF OF EXPORT

A supplier must ensure that he has proof of export readily available for C & E. This must be obtained within the appropriate time limit (see 25.1(c) above) and retained for six years.

Proof of export consists of

- official evidence – normally a Single Administrative Document (SAD) (Form C88) stamped by C & E; or

- commercial evidence (see below).

The documents obtained as proof of export, whether official or commercial, must clearly identify the exporter, the customer, the goods (including an accurate value) and the export destination. In both cases, this evidence should be supported by other documentation associated with the supply, such as the customer's order, sales contract, inter-company correspondence, copy export invoice, advice note, consignment note, packing list, insurance and freight charges, evidence of payment, and evidence of receipt of goods abroad.

Commercial evidence. Commercial export evidence is of two types.

- *Primary evidence* issued by shipping lines, airlines and railway companies in the form of authenticated sea waybills, air waybills and PIM/PIEX International Consignment Notes for individual consignments, vehicles and containers, or Master air waybills or bills of lading for individual or groupage shipments.

- *Secondary evidence* issued by freight forwarders and other carriers who export goods for a number of exporters by sea, air, road or rail. The freight forwarder, etc. will obtain primary evidence as above and then issue to the exporters secondary evidence of export in the form of authenticated house air or sea waybills, CMR notes and similar documents, or certificates of shipment based on the primary evidence of export.

Air and sea freight. If goods are exported by air, the supplier should obtain a copy of the authenticated master or house air waybill endorsed with the flight prefix and number, and the date and place of departure.

If goods are exported by sea, the supplier should keep one of the copies of the shipped bill of lading or sea waybill (certifying actual shipment) or, where a shipping company does not issue these, a certificate of shipment given by a responsible official of that company.

Commercial certificates of shipment for groupage or consolidation transactions. Commercial certificates of shipment are usually produced by packers and consolidators involved in road, rail and sea groupage consignments when they themselves receive only a single authenticated transport document from the carrier. The commercial certificate of shipment is an important document which should be sent to the exporter as soon as the goods have been exported from the UK. Although the certificate of shipment can be in any format, it must be an original and will usually contain

- the name and address of the issuing company;
- a unique reference number or issuer's file reference;
- the name of the exporter (and VAT number, if known);
- the place, port or airport of loading;
- the place, port or airport of shipment;
- the name of the export vessel or the aircraft flight prefix and number;
- the date of sailing or flight;
- the customer's name;
- the destination of the goods;
- a full description of the goods exported (including quantity, weight and value);
- the number of packages;
- the exporter's invoice number and date if known;
- the bill of lading or air waybill number (if applicable); and
- the identifying number of the vehicle, container or railway wagon.

The certificate must be authenticated by an official of the issuing company unless it is computer produced on a once-only basis as a by-product of the issuing company's accounting system.
(C & E Notice 703, paras 5.1-5.6).

Photocopy export evidence. Photocopy certificates of shipment are not normally acceptable as evidence of export, nor are photocopy bills of lading (unless authenticated by the shipping line), sea waybills or air waybills. Photocopies authenticated by either the originator, or intermediary recipient of the original document, may exceptionally be used as supporting documents in certain circumstances. (C & E Notice 703, para 5.8).

Lost or mislaid export evidence. If an exporter has lost or mislaid the official or commercial evidence of export supplied by the shippers or freight forwarders, duplicate evidence of export may be issued. The replacement evidence of export must be clearly marked 'DUPLICATE EVIDENCE OF EXPORT' and be authenticated and dated by an official of the issuing company. (C & E Notice 703, para 5.9).

Other export procedures. See also C & E Notice 703 for proof of export under the following procedures.

Merchandise in Baggage (MIB)   Para 5.7
Road vehicle via a 'roll-on roll-off' ferry   Para 5.10
Groupage or consolidation transactions   Para 5.11
By post   Para 5.12
By courier and fast parcel services   Para 5.13
By rail   Para 5.14
Through packers   Para 5.15
Through Approved Depositories   Para 5.16
Liquid and natural petroleum gases   Para 6.7
From Customs and/or Excise (fiscal) warehouses   Para 6.10

De Voil Indirect Tax Service. See V4.306.

25.25   **Exports through auctioneers**

Auctioneers not acting in their own name. A supplier who sells goods through auctioneers who

- are not acting in their own name; and

- export the goods

may zero-rate the supply provided a certificate of export is obtained from the auctioneers in the following form within one month of the date of the auction. The auctioneer must hold valid evidence of export for the goods.

For goods exported direct by the auctioneer as air or sea freight

I (insert full name) certify that the article(s) detailed below and sold as Lot No(s) . . . . at auction by me on (insert date of sale) has/have been exported from the United Kingdom on the undermentioned vessel/aircraft:

Description of article(s)   Lot No   Value

Name of export vessel, or aircraft flight prefix and number
Port or airport of loading
Date of sailing or departure
Destination
Bill of lading or air waybill number (where appropriate)
Identifying number of container or railway wagon (if used)

.... (Signature of auctioneer)
.... (Date)

For goods exported direct by the auctioneer by parcel post or courier service

I (insert full name) certify that the article(s) detailed below and sold as Lot No(s) . . . . at auction by me on (insert date of sale) has/have been exported from the United Kingdom by post/courier service:

Description of article(s)   Lot No   Value

Place of posting
Method of posting (parcel/letter etc.)
Date of posting
Destination
Certificate(s) of posting numbers held by me

.... (Signature)
.... (Date)

25.26 Exports

Auctioneers acting in their own name. If a supplier sells goods through auctioneers who act in their own name, the goods are treated as being supplied to the auctioneer and must not be zero-rated by the supplier as an export. The auctioneer will be able to zero-rate the onward supply subject to the normal rules.

(C & E Notice 703, para 5.17, Appendices F and G).

25.26 Exports to the Channel Islands

Although Community law requires the use of the SAD (Form C88) for exports to the Channel Islands, where goods are not dutiable or restricted a simplified pre-shipment advice may be used. It may be a copy of an approved standard commercial document or a partly completed SAD (see Customs Notice 275 *Export Procedures* for further details). At south coast ferry ports a combined Consignment Note and Customs Declaration (CNCD) with a supporting itemised schedule of goods exported replaces the SAD and sea waybill for manifested freight.

Evidence of export for goods sent to the Channel Islands is

- goods shipped directly by the south coast ferry companies – an authenticated copy of the CNCD;

- goods carried as Merchandise in Baggage – a customs' certified copy 3 of the SAD (Form C88);

- goods shipped by air – an authenticated master air waybill or house air waybill;

- goods shipped through a freight forwarder – a certificate of shipment issued by the freight forwarder or an authenticated copy of the CNCD;

- goods shipped through a fast parcel or courier service – a receipted copy of the export declaration.

(C & E Notice 703, para 6.18).

25.27 Exports via EC countries

Where goods are exported outside the EC but via other EC countries, official or commercial documentary evidence is required that the goods have left the EC.

Official evidence of export will normally be copy 3 of the export SAD (Form C88) endorsed at the customs office of exit from the EC. The office of exit will vary depending on the type of transport used and the nature of the supply.

Commercial evidence of export will consist of the normal documentation for the type of transport concerned.

Full details of the different procedures involved are given in Customs Notice 275 *Export Procedures*.

Where goods subject to excise duty are moving under duty suspension arrangements, the customs office of exit from the Community will certify the accompanying document (an 'attestation' in EC terms) and return it to the consignor as evidence of exportation from the EC. The standard time limits for obtaining the evidence of export apply.

(C & E Notice 703, para 6.19).

25.28 RECORDS AND RETURNS

Where goods are exported or supplied as ships' stores, the normal rules for record keeping still apply (see 57 RECORDS). The records must provide a clear link with the evidence of export required (see 25.24 above). In addition to the normal requirement, the rules set out below must be followed.

Direct exports can be zero-rated in the records at the time of supply to the customer.

Where, however, the goods have not been exported or evidence of export is not obtained within three months of the time of supply, and the supply would normally be standard-rated in the UK, VAT must be accounted for on the taxable proportion of the invoiced amount or consideration received (i.e. for a VAT rate of 17.5% the VAT element would be calculated at 7/47). This VAT must be included in Box 1 of the VAT return for the period in which the three month time limit expires.

If the goods are subsequently exported and/or evidence of export is obtained, the supply can then be zero-rated and the VAT account adjusted for the period in which the evidence is obtained.

Retail schemes. See 60.9 RETAIL SCHEMES for treatment of direct exports where a retail scheme is used.

Indirect exports. A special record of these transactions must be kept.

If evidence of export is obtained within the time allowed, the supply can be zero-rated and any deposit of VAT taken can be refunded to the customer.

If the goods have not been exported within one month of the time of supply or evidence of export is not obtained within one month of the date of export, and the supply would normally be standard-rated in the UK, VAT must be accounted for on the taxable proportion of the invoiced amount or consideration received (i.e. for a VAT rate of 17.5% the VAT element would be calculated at 7/47). This VAT must be included in Box 1 of the VAT return for the period in which the one month time limit expires.

If the goods are subsequently exported and/or evidence of export is obtained, the supply can then be zero-rated and the VAT account adjusted for the period in which the evidence is obtained. (This is provided that the goods have been supplied to an overseas person (see 25.8 above) and have not been used in the UK prior to export.)

For goods supplied to an overseas person for export after consolidation, processing or incorporation (see 25.10 above) the same rules apply but the time limit for the goods to be exported is within six months of the time of supply and evidence of export must be obtained within one month of the date of export.

Retail schemes. Where a retail scheme is used, indirect exports should be treated as if they were direct exports and the rules in 60.9 RETAIL SCHEMES followed except that the time limits for obtaining evidence of export is one month rather than three months.

(C & E Notice 703, paras 9.1–9.3).

26   Extra-Statutory Concessions

26.1   EXTRA-STATUTORY CONCESSIONS

The following is a summary of all VAT concessions in force at 1 July 1997 as published by Customs and Excise in Notice 48. All necessary conditions must be satisfied before a concession can be used. Further details are available from C & E enquiry offices.

Part 1 International field

1.1 Visiting forces, NATO and US and Canadian government expenditure. Duty (including all import and excise duties) are remitted or refunded on

(*a*)   goods and services imported by or supplied to visiting forces and their instrumentalities, for the official use of the force, or their instrumentalities;

(*b*)   goods and services imported by or supplied to NATO military headquarters, organisations or agencies, for their official use;

(*c*)   US and Canadian government expenditure on mutual defence or mutual aid contracts; and

(*d*)   temporary importations of equipment required by contractors for fulfilling NATO infrastructure contracts or in connection with the provision and maintenance of US forces defence facilities in the UK.

1.2 UK-manufactured alcoholic liquor and tobacco products purchased by diplomats. VAT (and duty) are remitted on alcoholic liquor and tobacco products of UK manufacture imported by, or supplied to, diplomatic representatives of foreign states in the UK who are entitled to similar privileges in respect of imported products of foreign manufacture under *Diplomatic Privileges Act 1964*.

1.3 United States Air Force. Relief from VAT (and/or excise duty) is allowed, in accordance with certain conditions agreed with the US Air Force, on

(*a*)   charges for admission to air shows and open days; and

(*b*)   goods sold by US forces organisations during air shows and open days to persons not entitled to receive/consume them unless customs charges have been paid.

1.4 Gifts by US forces. VAT (and duty) are remitted on gifts (whether imported or purchased in the UK) from US forces to charitable organisations.

1.5 American war graves. See 19.6 DEATH.

Part 2 Concessions designed to remove inequities or anomalies in administration

2.1 Purchases of road fuel. *VATA 1994, s 56* requires payment of a scale charge if road fuel purchased by a business is used for private journeys. However, where input tax is not claimed on *any* road fuel used by the business, whether for business or private journeys, the VAT scale charge will not apply. See 45.16 MOTOR CARS.

2.2 Group supplies using an overseas member: anticipation of legislative changes. With effect from 26 November 1996, a charge to VAT arises where supplies of a type within *VATA 1994, 5 Sch* are purchased by an overseas group member and used for making supplies within *5 Sch* to a UK group member.

(*a*)   For supplies made between 26 November 1996 and 19 March 1997, no charge to VAT was triggered where an overseas member of a VAT group was supplied with services within *VATA 1994, 5 Sch* which were exempt from VAT because they fell within *VATA 1994, 9 Sch.* See 31.6 GROUPS OF COMPANIES. (This concession was made statutory for supplies made after 19 March 1997 by *FA 1997, s 41.*)

(*b*) The amount of the VAT charge is calculated by reference to the value of the supply by the overseas member to the UK member but may be reduced to the value of the 5 *Sch* services purchased by the overseas member provided certain conditions are met. See 31.6 GROUPS OF COMPANIES.

This concession cannot be used for tax avoidance purposes.

2.3 Group supplies using an overseas member: transitional relief. With effect from 26 November 1996, a charge to VAT arises where supplies of a type within *VATA 1994, 5 Sch* are purchased by an overseas group member and used for making supplies within *5 Sch* to a UK group member. Where the UK group member paid for any services within these provisions on or after 26 March 1996 but the services were performed to any extent before that date, the group may account for VAT only on that proportion of the services which were performed on or after 26 November 1996. The concession does not apply to telecommunications services and cannot be used for tax avoidance purposes. See 31.6 GROUPS OF COMPANIES.

2.4 Misunderstanding by a VAT trader. Where certain conditions are fulfilled, VAT undercharged by a registered trader as a result of a *bona fide* misunderstanding may be remitted. See 47.1 OUTPUT TAX.

2.5 Misdirection. If a C & E officer, with the full facts before him, has given a clear and unequivocal ruling on VAT in writing or, knowing the full facts, has misled a registered person to his detriment, any assessment of VAT due will be based on the correct ruling from the date the error was brought to the registered person's attention. See 17.12 CUSTOMS AND EXCISE: POWERS.

2.6 Coin-operated machines. As an accounting convenience, operators may delay accounting for VAT until the takings are removed from the machine. See 58.3 RECREATION AND SPORT and 64.56 SUPPLY.

2.7 VAT on minor promotional items supplied in linked supply schemes. These are schemes in which a minor article is linked with a main article and sold at a single price. Provided the cost of the minor article is within certain limits, it can be treated as taxable at the same rate as the main article. See 67.10 TRADING STAMP AND PROMOTION SCHEMES.

2.8 Use of margin scheme for vehicle sales when incomplete records have been kept. Where a dealer has the required information on the purchase or sale of a car but not both, subject to conditions VAT may be accounted for on the purchase price or half the selling price. See 61.35 SECOND-HAND GOODS.

2.9 Recoveries of VAT under *VATA 1994, 11 Sch 5* (VAT charged by unregistered persons). Where an amount is shown or represented as VAT on an invoice issued by a person who is neither registered nor required to be registered for VAT at the time the invoice is issued, C & E may require that person to pay an equivalent amount to them. By concession, the person may be permitted to deduct any VAT incurred on supplies to him that were directly attributable to the invoiced supplies. Also by concession, if the recipient of the supplies is a taxable person C & E may allow the recipient to treat the amount shown or represented as VAT as input tax. See 17.2 CUSTOMS AND EXCISE: POWERS.

2.10 VAT on necessary meals and accommodation provided by recognised representative sporting bodies to amateur sports persons chosen to

represent that body in a competition. In such circumstances, the input tax incurred may be deductible as input tax and not treated as business entertainment. See 9.6 BUSINESS ENTERTAINMENT.

2.11 Incorrect customer declaration. Where a customer provides an incorrect declaration claiming eligibility for zero-rating under *VATA 1994* and the supplier, despite having taken all reasonable steps to check the validity of the declaration, fails to identify the inaccuracy and, in good faith, zero-rates the supply, C & E will not seek to recover the VAT due from the supplier. See 12.7 CHARITIES, 29.2 FUEL AND POWER, 32.19 HEALTH AND WATER UTILITIES and 42.51 LAND AND BUILDINGS.

2.12 Buses with special facilities for carrying disabled persons. Where a vehicle has less than twelve seats because it is equipped with facilities for carrying persons in wheelchairs, it can be treated, for VAT purposes, as if it had at least twelve seats. See 32.17(*l*) HEALTH AND WATER UTILITIES, 45.1 MOTOR CARS and 68.16 TRANSPORT AND FREIGHT.

2.13 Group treatment following redefinition of 'subsidiary'. From 1 November 1990, some subsidiaries which are registered as part of a group for VAT purposes may cease to be eligible for group treatment under *CA 1985*. Such groupings will be allowed to continue for VAT purposes. (*Note.* This concession has been cancelled with effect from 1 January 1998.) See 31.2 GROUPS OF COMPANIES.

2.14 Repayment of import VAT to shipping agents and freight forwarders. Under certain conditions, import VAT may be repaid directly to shipping agents and freight forwarders where importers go into insolvency or receivership leaving the agents unable to recover VAT paid on their behalf. See 34.8 IMPORTS.

2.15 Zero-rating of certain supplies of free zone goods. From 1 August 1991, the supply of goods subject to import VAT which are free zone goods in the UK may be zero-rated on condition that there is an agreement between the supplier and the customer that the customer will clear the goods for removal from the zone and will take responsibility for payment of the import VAT. See 70.23 WAREHOUSED GOODS AND FREE ZONES.

2.16 Property converted into domestic accommodation. The restriction on the option to tax applying to buildings intended for use as domestic accommodation does not apply where a grant is made to a person who intends to convert a non-residential building into domestic accommodation. (*Note.* This concession was made statutory by *FA 1997, s 36* with effect from 19 March 1997.) See 42.22 LAND AND BUILDINGS.

2.17 Printed matter published in instalments. Individual component parts of loose-leaf books may be zero-rated. See 54.18 PRINTED MATTER, ETC.

2.18 Connection to gas and electricity mains supply. The first time connection to the gas or electricity mains supply of a qualifying building, residential caravan or houseboat may be zero-rated. See 29.7 FUEL AND POWER.

2.19 *VAT (Buildings and Land) Order 1994*: fully taxable person. For the purposes of *VATA 1994, 10 Sch 3(8A)* a person may be treated as a fully taxable person if, at the end of the prescribed accounting period in which the grant is made, he is entitled to recover 80% of the VAT incurred (or would be so entitled if not for other supplies falling within *VATA 1994, 9 Sch Group 1*). See 42.22 LAND AND BUILDINGS.

2.20 *VAT (Buildings and Land) Order 1994*: small self-administered pension schemes. For the purposes of *VATA 1994, 10 Sch 3(8A)* a small self-administered pension scheme may be treated as a fully taxable person. See 42.22 LAND AND BUILDINGS.

2.21 Zero-rating of supplies of training for foreign governments. From 1 October 1993, zero-rating applies to training services supplied to a foreign government in furtherance of its sovereign activities. See 39.6 INTERNATIONAL SERVICES.

2.22 Exemption of all domestic service charges. From 1 April 1994, all mandatory service charges paid by occupants of residential property towards the upkeep of the property and the provision of caretakers are exempt. See 42.16 LAND AND BUILDINGS.

2.23 Developer's self-supply on 1 March 1997. No charge arose on 1 March 1997 provided certain conditions were met. See 42.27 LAND AND BUILDINGS.

Part 3 Facilitation of exports

3.1   Sailaway boats. Where a boat is supplied to a UK resident who intends to export it under its own power within two months of delivery and keep the boat outside the VAT territory of the EC for a continuous period of at least twelve months, the supplier may, subject to conditions, zero-rate the supply of the boat. See 25.19 EXPORTS.

3.2   Export houses. The provisions under which goods supplied to export houses for export outside the UK are zero-rated (see 25.6 EXPORTS) continue to apply concessionally to goods removed to another EC country. See 23.21 EUROPEAN COMMUNITY: SINGLE MARKET.

3.3   Supplies to diplomat missions, international organisations, NATO forces, etc. in other EC countries. Subject to certain conditions, a VAT-registered trader can zero-rate supplies of goods to entitled persons and bodies resident or situated in other EC countries. See 23.21 EUROPEAN COMMUNITY: SINGLE MARKET.

Part 4 Non-commercial transactions

4.1   VAT on goods supplied at duty-free and tax-free shops. Where goods liable to VAT are supplied to intending passengers at duty-free and tax-free shops approved by C & E, the supplier may be regarded as the exporter and zero-rate the supply of those goods which are exported. See 25.2 EXPORTS.

4.2   Marine fuel. Certain supplies of marine fuel may be received free of VAT. See 25.3 EXPORTS and 29.5 FUEL AND POWER.

4.3   Personal reliefs for goods permanently imported from third countries. Property purchased by diplomats, members of certain international organisations and NATO forces which otherwise qualifies for relief on the transfer of normal residence from outside the EC will not be refused relief solely because C & E cannot satisfy themselves that the goods have borne all duties and taxes normally applicable in their country of origin. See 34.22 IMPORTS.

4.4   Personal reliefs for goods permanently imported from third countries. Property purchased outside the EC by UK forces which otherwise qualifies for relief on the transfer of normal residence from outside the EC will not be refused relief solely because C & E cannot satisfy themselves that the goods have borne all duties and taxes normally applicable in their country of origin. See 34.22 IMPORTS.

4.5   Personal reliefs for goods permanently imported from third countries. Property purchased under a UK export scheme by members of the UK diplomatic service, members of UK forces and members of International Organisations and which otherwise qualifies for relief on the transfer of normal residence from outside the EC will not be refused relief solely because C & E cannot satisfy themselves that the goods have borne all duties and taxes normally applicable in their country of origin. See 34.22 IMPORTS.

4.6 Personal reliefs for goods permanently imported from third countries. Personal belongings otherwise qualifying for relief on the transfer of normal residence from outside the EC may still be granted relief from VAT on importation if failing to qualify only because they have not been possessed and used for the specified period. See 34.22 IMPORTS.

4.7 Personal reliefs for goods permanently imported from third countries. Personal belongings otherwise qualifying for relief on the transfer of normal residence from outside the EC may still be granted relief from VAT on importation if failing to qualify only because the property is declared for relief outside the specific periods. See 34.22 IMPORTS.

De Voil Indirect Tax Service. See V1.264.

26.2 AGREEMENTS WITH TRADE BODIES

C & E have entered into a number of agreements with trade bodies which permit their members to use procedures to meet their obligation under VAT law and which take into account their individual circumstances.

The agreements apply only to areas where C & E can exercise discretion and they convey no direct financial advantage or relief from the legal requirements. Some of the agreements might usefully be applied to other traders but note that any special method based on these arrangements can only be adopted with the approval of the local VAT office.

Agreements entered into at the time of publication are as follows. For full details, see C & E Notice 700/57/95.

- Association of British Insurers (engineering insurance business).

- London Bullion Market Association (supplies of bullion).

- Brewers' Society (deduction of input tax in respect of brewers' tenanted estate).

- Building Societies Association (partial exemption).

- Association of British Factors and Discounters (partial exemption).

- Finance Houses Association Ltd (partial exemption).

- Association of British Insurers (recovery of input tax incurred in the UK in connection with supplies by branches outside the EC).

- Association of Investment Trust Companies (partial exemption).

- British Printing Industries Federation (apportionment of subsidy publishing supplies).

- Marine, aviation and transport underwriters who are members of an unnamed insurance traders association (claims-related input tax and associated imported services).

- Association of British Insurers, Lloyds' of London, the Institute of London Underwriters and the British Insurance and Investment Association (coding supplies of marine, aviation and transport insurance services).

- National Caravan Council Limited and the British Holiday and Home Park Association Limited (method of valuing removable contents sold with zero-rated caravans).

- Association of Unit Trust and Investment Managers (VAT liability of charges made in connection with personal equity plans).

- British Bankers' Association (VAT liability of electronic banking/cash management services).

- British Vehicle Rental and Leasing Association (car leasing and repairs and maintenance services).

- Society of Motor Manufacturers and Traders (output tax on the self-supply of a motor vehicle).

- Opticians' professional bodies (apportioning selling prices of spectacles—withdrawn from 1 January 1998).

27 Finance

Cross-reference. See 22.18 EUROPEAN COMMUNITY LEGISLATION for the provisions of the *EC 6th Directive*.

De Voil Indirect Tax Service. See V4.136; V6.147–152.

The contents of this chapter are as follows.

27.1 PLACE OF SUPPLY OF FINANCIAL SERVICES

Special place of supply rules apply to services falling within *VATA 1994, 5 Sch 1–8*. This includes financial services (*5 Sch 5*) and services rendered by one person to another in procuring such services for the other (*5 Sch 8*).

The place of supply of such services is treated as being

(*a*) where the recipient belongs if

- he belongs outside the EC; or

- he belongs in an EC country other than that of the supplier and the services are supplied to him for his business purposes; and

(*b*) where the *supplier* belongs in all other cases, i.e. where the recipient

- belongs in the UK or Isle of Man; or

- belongs in an EC country but not in the same country as the supplier and receives the supply other than for business purposes.

[*VATA 1994, s 7(10)(11); SI 1992/3121, Art 16*].

See 64.19 SUPPLY for the place of belonging. For the countries making up the EC, see 21.2 EUROPEAN COMMUNITY: GENERAL.

In the case of a UK supplier, supplies within (*a*) above are outside the scope of UK VAT and supplies within (*b*) above are exempt or taxable in the UK (depending on the nature of the supply).

Special rule for sales of securities. When (and only when) the identity (and hence the place of belonging) of a purchaser of securities is not known to a UK supplier, the supplier may either treat the supply as taking place in the UK or may determine the place of supply as follows.

(i) If the place of the *transaction* is known

- a sale transacted in the UK is treated as made to a person belonging in the UK (i.e. within (*b*) above);

- a sale transacted elsewhere in the EC is treated as made to a taxable person belonging in another EC country (i.e. within (*a*) above); and

- a sale transacted outside the EC is treated as made to a person belonging outside the EC (i.e. with (*a*) above).

(ii) If the place where a sale is transacted is not known, this can be deemed to be where the security is listed.

(iii) If the security is not listed or is listed on both an EC and non-EC exchange, then a sale can be deemed to be transacted where the final broker belongs.

This rule can also be used to determine the place of supply of a broker's services where he is unable to determine where the purchaser belongs.

(C & E Notice 741, Appendix E)

27.2 INPUT TAX RECOVERY IN RESPECT OF FINANCIAL SERVICES

Subject to the normal rules, input tax may be recovered which relates to

- taxable supplies of financial services (i.e. supplies with a place of supply in the UK other than exempt supplies);

- supplies of financial services with a place of supply outside the UK which would be taxable if made in the UK;

- supplies of financial services which

    (i) are supplied to a person who belongs outside the EC; or

    (ii) are directly linked to the export of goods to a place outside the EC; or

    (iii) consist of making the arrangements for supply of services within (i) or (ii) above

    where the supply is exempt or would have been exempt if made in the UK.

[*VATA 1994, s 26(1)(2); SI 1992/3123*].

27.3 FINANCIAL DEALINGS IN MONEY AND SECURITIES FOR MONEY

The following supplies of financial services in the UK are exempt from VAT.

(*a*) The issue, transfer or receipt of, or any dealings with, 'money', and any security for money or any note or order for the payment of money.

(*b*) The making of arrangements for, or the underwriting of, any transaction within, (*a*) above.

(*c*) The operation of any current deposit or savings account. This covers charges made by a bank or similar organisation.

'*Money*' includes currencies other than sterling.

Excluded from (*a*) above are all services falling within 27.11(*a*) below (which are exempt under those provisions) and excluded generally is the supply of coins or banknotes (whether legal tender or not) as collectors' pieces or investment articles.

[*VATA 1994, s 96(1), 9 Sch Group 5, Items 1, 5, 8 and Notes 1 and 2*].

See 27.4 below for dealings with money, 27.5 below for securities for money and 27.10 below for brokerage services within (*b*) above.

27.4 Dealing with money

A '*dealing with money*' includes the exchange of legal tender for an equivalent amount in different denominations or a different currency e.g. the normal domestic transactions of banks and bureaux de change as well as foreign currency dealings. The services of sorting and counting money and giving change are also exempt as dealing with money.

The exemption does not apply to

- dealings with banknotes and coins supplied as collectors' pieces, investment articles or items of numismatic interest (e.g. proof coins, maundy money) whether or not the items are legal tender and whether or not they are sold for more than their face value. Such supplies are taxable on the full selling price. See however 61.3 SECOND-HAND GOODS for the use of the second-hand scheme for supplies of collectors' pieces;

- dealings in precious metal coin whether legal tender or not. See 30.3 GOLD AND PRECIOUS METALS ;

- the issue or reissue, by the bank of issue, of Bank of England, Scottish and Northern Irish bank notes (zero-rated under *VATA 1994, 8 Sch Group 11*);

- certain money flows which are not the consideration for any supply and are outside the scope of VAT, e.g. payment and receipt of dividends, receipt of pension contributions and the payment of pensions out of a pension fund.

(C & E Leaflet 701/29/92, paras 2, 7).

Foreign exchange transactions. Where a person, as a principal, deals with money and charges a commission or fee for his services, the consideration for the supply is that commission or fee and is exempt. Following the decision in *C & E Commrs v First National Bank of Chicago, CJEC [1998] STC 850* C & E accept that, with effect from 14 July 1998, where no specific commission or fee is charged on particular transactions (e.g. where services are paid for by the spread between the bid and offer rates), those transactions are nevertheless supplies for VAT purposes, the consideration being 'the net result of the transactions of the supplier of the service over a given period of time', i.e. the net profit on the transactions. Any changes to the partial exemption method used must be agreed with C & E. In most cases it will be appropriate to isolate the input tax incurred on foreign exchange transactions and deal with VAT separately within the method used. Businesses may apply the decision in *First National Bank of Chicago* from an earlier date. For claims for VAT refunds relating directly to this decision, C & E have confirmed that the three-year time limit applies to claims arising after 13 October 1995 and, concessionally, claims for the period from October 1992 to October 1995 can be submitted up to 2 December 1999. (C & E Business Brief 16/98, 28 July 1998; C & E Business Brief 24/98, 2 December 1998).

Dealing with money connotes financial transactions or operations and not simple handling of money, e.g. the transport of cash between branches of a bank by a security firm (*Williams & Glyn's Bank Ltd, [1974] VATTR 262 (118)*) even if involving the re-stocking of cash dispensing machines and reporting any discrepancies (*Nationwide Anglia Building Society, [1994] VATTR 30 (11826)*). C & E consider that it also applies to replenishing automated teller machines at supermarkets, etc. and VAT must be accounted for on such services at the standard rate. (C & E Business Brief 25/94, 16 December 1994). A trade association acting as a clearing house for its members (by monthly settlement of amounts due to supplier on their behalf) has been held to be dealing with money (*British Hardware Federation, [1975] VATTR 172 (216)*).

The *assignment of a debt* is also exempt. The exempt output is the total amount for which the debt is assigned. (C & E Leaflet 701/29/92, para 3).

27.5   **Securities for money**

'*Securities for money*' include bills of exchange, trading coupons, eurocurrency paper, instruments and paper negotiable for cash, local authority bills and certain promissory notes and commercial paper. Not included are certain securities or secondary securities within 27.11 below.

Where securities for money are dealt with as a principal, any consideration for the supply is exempt. C & E accept that the consideration for the supply by the drawer of the security is the price paid. This treatment also applies to any subsequent sale of the security, except at redemption when it is outside the scope of VAT. (C & E Business Brief 25/95, 20 November 1995).

The issue as securities for money, and for a consideration, of guarantees, bonds, other forms of indemnity and other commercial undertakings is exempt provided the guarantee, etc. is secondary to a primary contract and is

• a contract of security issued by a guarantor; or

• a surety obliging the guarantor to indemnify a party to the primary contract for any loss arising from the failure or default of the other party to fulfil his obligations under that contract.

Exemption does not apply to warranties and contracts for the supply, repair, servicing or maintenance of goods (even if described as guarantees).

(C & E Leaflet 701/29/92, paras 4, 5).

27.6   **Miscellaneous**

Compensation for dishonoured cheques, etc. Any compensation sought from customers to cover bank charges incurred through failure to honour cheques or make direct debit payments is not the consideration for a supply and outside the scope of VAT.

Financial futures and options. For details of the VAT position of trading in financial futures contracts and options on the London Financial Futures and Options Exchange (LIFFE), see C & E Leaflet 701/43/93.

Interest rate and currency swaps. During the term of an interest rate swap, there is a continuous supply of services. The party who has the higher rate of interest to repay on any settlement date pays the net difference between the two interest charges to the other party. The party who receives money makes a supply which is exempt under 27.3(*a*) above. The paying party is regarded as making a supply for no consideration.

Similar treatment applies to currency swaps. The counterparties make periodic exchanges of interest in the different currencies. The difference between the exchange rates determines the consideration and the supply in the same way as the difference between interest rates affects the outcome of interest rate swaps.

Travellers' cheques. The issue or encashment of travellers' cheques is exempt under 27.3(*a*) above. Unissued, unsigned travellers' cheques are neither securities for money nor notes for the payment of money and their supply to the issuer is standard-rated on their value as stationery.

(C & E Leaflet 701/29/92, paras 6, 9, 17).

Electronic banking/cash management services. C & E and the British Bankers' Association have agreed that the liability of electronic banking services should be determined by examining the status of the individual services provided. In principle, services which would have been treated as exempt if provided by the bank by conventional means should be treated as exempt where provided in the framework of electronic banking services. See C & E Notice 700/57/95 for full details.

27.7 Finance

Outsourcing of financial services. In *Sparekassernes Datacenter (SDC) v Skatteministeriet CJEC, [1997] STC 932* a company (SDC) carried out a variety of operations on behalf of Danish savings banks, including processing payments or transfers by electronic means between the banks' clients and between banks. SDC had no contractual relationship with the banks' clients. The CJEC held that to qualify for exemption a service did not have to be supplied by a person who stood in a direct legal relationship with the bank's final customer. Subcontracted services could be exempt provided they qualified for exemption in their own right.

27.7 PROVISION OF CREDIT

The making of loans and the granting of credit in the UK is an exempt supply. See 27.8 below. Exemption also extends to instalment credit supplied under hire purchase, conditional sale or credit sale agreements. See 27.9 below.

27.8 Loans, deposits and granting credit

The following supplies of financial services in the UK are exempt from VAT.

(a) The making of any advance or the granting of any credit. Included is the supply of credit by a person, in connection with the supply of goods or services by him, for which a separate charge is made and disclosed to the recipient of the supply.

(b) The making of arrangements for any transaction within (a) above.

[*VATA 1994, 9 Sch Group 5, Items 2, 5 and Note (3)*].

See 27.10 below for brokerage services within (b) above.

The value of the exempt supply is the gross interest or other sum received by the person making the loan or granting credit. Interest received on money deposited (e.g. with a bank or building society) is consideration for the supply of an advance and exempt. (C & E Leaflet 701/29/92, para 8).

Commission received from a bank by a company which encouraged its members to use a credit card issued by the bank was held to be exempt under (b) above (*C & E Commrs v Civil Service Motoring Association CA 1997, [1998] STC 111*). For the treatment of interest received by solicitors on bank and building society accounts see *Hedges and Mercer, [1976] VATTR 146 (271)*.

The expression 'the granting of credit' is wide enough to encompass credit provided by a supplier of goods in the form of deferment of payment for the goods. The wording does not require exemption to be confined to credit granted by banks and financial institutions. However, where payment is only deferred until delivery of the goods or services, interest is not a reward for credit but part of the taxable consideration for the supply (*Muys en De Winters's Bouw-en Aannemingsbedrijf BV v Staatssecretaris van Financiën, CJEC 1993, [1997] STC 665*).

Credit and charge card companies. Any supply by a person carrying on a credit card, charge card or similar card operation is exempt when made in connection with that operation to a person who accepts the card used in the operation when presented to him in payment for goods or services. [*VATA 1994, 9 Sch Group 5, Note (4)*]. Exempt under this provision are the charges made to retailers by Access, Visa, American Express, Diner's Club, Connect and Switch, together with any third party operating an 'in-house' scheme for a particular retailer or other outlet. The consideration for these supplies usually takes the form of a discount on the amount reimbursed to the retailer, etc. See *C & E Commrs v Diners Club Ltd and Another CA, [1989] STC 395*. Annual membership charges made by the issuing organisations or charges made for the issue of a card are also exempt. (C & E Leaflet 701/29/92, para 10).

Fuel cards. Whether use of a fuel card results in

(i) a supply from the retailer to the card issuer (so that the card issuer makes standard-rated supplies of goods to the cardholder), or

(ii) a supply from the retailer directly to the cardholder (so that the card issuer makes an exempt supply of financial services to the cardholder)

depends on the precise terms of the contractual arrangements between the parties. Previously, as a result of the uncertainty following the decision in *The Harpur Group Ltd, [1994] VATTR 180 (12001)*, C & E accepted that all such agreements were for the supply of standard-rated goods by the card issuer. (C & E Business Brief 25/94, 16 December 1994).

Check trading companies. Charges made by check trading companies to participating retailers are similarly treated as exempt. (C & E Press Notice 1045, 21 October 1985). (Check trading is a means of buying goods on credit whereby a check trading company sells a trading check for a specified amount to a customer who pays for the check on credit terms over a period of time. The customer then uses the check to purchase goods from the participating retailer.)

Late payment penalties, imposed because a customer does not pay by the due date, are not consideration for a supply and are outside the scope of VAT. Where, however the terms of the contract provide for the opportunity to postpone payment for a charge which represents interest that charge is the consideration for granting credit under (*a*) above. (C & E Leaflet 701/29/92, para 13).

27.9   **Instalment credit**

The following supplies of financial services in the UK are exempt from VAT.

(*a*)   The provision of the facility of instalment credit in a hire purchase, conditional sale or credit sale agreement for which a separate charge is made and disclosed to the recipient of the goods.

(*b*)   The provision of administrative arrangements and documentation and the transfer of title to the goods in connection with the supply within (*a*) above if the total consideration therefor is specified in the agreement and does not exceed £10.

(*c*)   The making of arrangements for any transaction within (*a*) or (*b*) above.

[*VATA 1994, 9 Sch Group 5, Items 3–5*].

Option fees paid under a hire purchase agreement are included under (*b*) above. (C & E Leaflet 701/29/92, para 12).

The value of the exempt supply is the interest paid with each repayment or the fee for the administrative arrangements, etc.

See 27.10 below for brokerage services within (*c*) above. See also 27.19 to 27.22 below for hire purchase, conditional sale and credit sale agreements generally.

27.10   **BROKERAGE SERVICES**

The intermediary services of mortgage and money brokers in making arrangements for any advance of money, or granting any credit, are exempt. To qualify for exemption, the intermediary must actively participate in arranging a specific supply which is clearly envisaged at the time the intermediary's services are supplied. These arrangements may include assistance with the completion of, and checking, forms and submission to the lender. The mere introduction of a client to a broker or lender, without processing the loan application, is not making arrangements and not therefore exempt.

Where the lender subcontracts the administration of the loan to an independent third party, the latter's services *before* the loan is granted (e.g. vetting applicants, obtaining legal advice and arranging completion of forms) are exempt but not any services supplied *after* the loan has been granted (e.g. monitoring and recording interest payments and chasing late payment). General administration services not linked to the granting of a specific loan are also taxable.

The services of accepting receipts paid by borrowers and passing the money to the lender are exempt. However, where positive action is taken on the lender's behalf to monitor repayments, chase late payers, notify revised rates, etc. such services are taxable. (C & E Leaflet 701/29/92, para 14).

Deductions from pay. Charges made by an employer for the deduction from pay of insurance premiums, mortgage repayments and union subscriptions etc. are exempt. Any charges made, however, for deductions from pay in compliance with an Attachment of Earnings Order are regarded as a token reimbursement of expenses incurred in carrying out a statutory duty and outside the scope of VAT. (C & E Leaflet 701/29/92, para 15).

27.11 SECURITIES AND RELATED SERVICES

The following supplies of financial services in the UK are exempt from VAT.

(*a*) The issue, transfer or receipt of, or any dealing with, any security or secondary security being

- shares, stock, bonds, notes (other than promissory notes), debentures, debenture stock or shares in an oil royalty; or

- any document relating to money, in any currency, which has been deposited with the issuer or some other person, being a document which recognises an obligation to pay a stated amount to bearer or to order, with or without interest, and being a document by the delivery of which, with or without endorsement, the right to receive that stated amount, with or without interest, is transferable; or

- any bill, note or other obligation of the Treasury or of a Government in any part of the world, being a document by the delivery of which, with or without endorsement, title is transferable, and not being an obligation which is or has been legal tender in any part of the world; or

- any letter of allotment or rights, any warrant conferring an option to acquire a security included in this item, any renounceable or scrip certificates, rights coupons, coupons representing dividends or interest on such a security, bond mandates or other documents conferring or containing evidence of title to or rights in respect of such a security; or

- units or other documents conferring rights under any trust established for the purpose, or having the effect of providing, for persons having funds available for investment, facilities for the participation by them as beneficiaries under the trust, in any profits or income arising from the acquisition, holding, management or disposal of any property whatsoever.

(*b*) The making of arrangements for, or the underwriting of, *any transaction* within (*a*) above. Included is the introduction to a person affecting such transactions of a person seeking to acquire or dispose of securities within (*a*) above.

(c) The management of an 'authorised unit trust scheme' or of a 'trust based scheme' by the 'operator' of the scheme. (See *FSA 1986, s 207(1)* and *SI 1989/28, Reg 2(1)(b)* for the meanings of terms.)

C & E policy had been to extend this exemption to services provided by a third party to the operator. However, this relaxation was withdrawn with effect from 24 March 1997 subject to a gradual relief for contracts existing at that date. (C & E News Release 12/97, 13 March 1997).

(d) The services of the 'authorised corporate director' of an open-ended investment company so far as they consist in managing the company's scheme property. The *'authorised corporate director'* is the director of the company (or equivalently designated person) who has responsibility for the management of, and is managing, the company's scheme property i.e. the property subject to the collective investment scheme constituted by the company. See *FSA 1986, s 75* for 'open-ended investment company' and 'collective investment company'.

Exemption does not extend to sub-contracted supplies to the authorised corporate director or other supplies made by the open-ended investment company itself. (C & E News Release 12/97, 13 March 1997).

[*VATA 1994, 9 Sch Group 5, Items 6, 7, 9, 10 and Notes (5)-(10); SI 1997/510*].

In broad terms, the above provisions give exemption from VAT to

• the supply of securities (see 27.12 below);

• broking services for transactions in securities (see 27.13 below);

• underwriting services for the issue of securities (see 27.14 below);

• corporate financing services which involve negotiation of the issue, disposal or acquisition of securities (see 27.15 below);

• dealings in units in unit trusts, and the management of authorised unit trusts and open-ended investment companies (see 27.17 below);

• introductory services (see 27.18 below);

• nominee services and global custody arrangements (see 27.18 below); and

• dealing system services (see 27.18 below).

However, a number of other services involving securities are not exempt including

• PEP management (see 27.16 below);

• investment and portfolio management (see 27.18 below);

• registrar services (see 27.18 below);

• safe custody services (see 27.18 below); and

• valuation, advisory and research services (see 27.18 below).

(C & E Notice 701/44/98, para 1.2).

International transactions. See 27.1 above for the place of supply of services within these provisions, including the special rule for the place of supply of securities sold where the identity of the purchaser is not known. The place of supply affects both the VAT liability of a financial service and whether the supplier can reclaim related input tax. See 27.2 above.

27.12 Finance

27.12 Securities transactions by principals

Business transactions in the securities listed in 27.11(*a*) above give rise to exempt supplies when there is consideration for the sale, transfer or holding of such securities by a person on a principal basis. An exempt supply of securities may arise in many different situations, e.g. trading in securities for profit or investment; capital-raising operations by companies, governments and other organisations; and share placings and rights issues to existing investors.

The value of the exempt supply is the total consideration received for the security. The proceeds from a redemption of stock at maturity does not give rise to any exempt output.

Interest and dividends. The gross interest earned from holding an interest-bearing security is part of the measure of the exempt supply. However, any dividend received on holding a security is outside the scope of VAT as it is not consideration for any supply of goods or services by the holder of the securities.

(C & E Notice 701/44/98, para 2.1).

27.13 'Making of arrangements' and broking services

The making of arrangements for the issue, transfer, receipt of, or any dealing with securities is exempt if made in the UK (see 27.11(*b*) above). Therefore, a person who acts as an intermediary or negotiates a trade in securities between a buyer and seller can exempt the supply of services. The exemption covers

- any stock or share broking services (see below); and

- arranging issues or placements of securities whether as offers for sale, rights issues, cash offers, vendor placings or bids with underwritten cash alternatives, including the service of co-ordinating an issue when a number of participants are involved in the share or other placing. But see 27.15 below which covers corporate finance services.

Exemption does not apply to professional services supplied in connection with share issues, acquisitions or disposals, which do not secure the connection between buyer and seller. Accountancy services, tax and legal advice, supplying a draft prospectus, or preparing advice on a take-over bid are therefore all taxable.

Broking services. Where a broker acts as an 'execution only' broker, buying or selling securities on client's instructions, but does not offer advice on securities, his supply is exempt. Where a broker acts as an advisory broker, arranging transactions and offering investment advice to the client,

- if the advice is made as a separate supply and for an identifiable charge it is taxable; but

- if his contract with the client is for arranging transactions in securities, and he raises charges only in relation to transactions executed, with advice being simply incidental to that service, a single exempt supply is made for VAT purposes.

Where a broker arranging a securities transaction splits the contract note to show as separate items the basic charge for broking services and any compliance or regulatory charges made to cover the cost of meeting regulatory requirements, the additional charges are still part of the consideration for his exempt broking service. This does not however apply to any statutory levies (e.g. stamp duty) which are a liability of the client. These are outside the scope of VAT.

International transactions. The services of arranging a sale or disposal of securities in the UK is exempt. However, the VAT position is also affected by the place of belonging of the recipient of the brokerage services and, sometimes, by the place of belonging of the buyer of securities. The following table summarises the liability of supplies of brokerage in the most common transactions.

Commission charged to supplier belonging in	VAT	Sells to	Commission charged to recipient belonging in	VAT
UK or other EC (private)	E		UK or other EC (private)	E
UK or other EC (private)	E		Other EC (business)	OS
UK or other EC (private)	E(R)		Non-EC	OS(R)
Other EC (business)	OS		UK or other EC (private)	E
Other EC (business)	OS		Other EC (business)	OS
Other EC (business)	OS(R)		Non-EC	OS(R)
Non-EC	OS(R)		UK or other EC (private)	E
Non-EC	OS(R)		Other EC (business)	OS
Non-EC	OS(R)		Non-EC	OS(R)

E   = Exempt
E(R) = Exempt but with refund of related input tax
OS   = Outside the scope of UK VAT with no refund of related input tax
OS(R) = Outside the scope of UK VAT with refund of related input tax

(C & E Notice 701/44/98, para 2.3, Appendix D).

27.14   **Underwriting services**

Where, for a fee, an underwriter's services provide that

- a securities issue or sale will be subscribed for or purchased; and

- the issuer will receive a certain amount of capital,

that supply is exempt under 27.11(*b*) above.

Alternatively, an underwriter may underwrite an issue by agreeing to purchase the whole block of securities offered by the issuer, instead of guaranteeing that buyers will be found. In this case, exemption applies under 27.11(*a*) above. There is an exempt supply of securities by the issuer to the underwriter and, normally, a subsequent exempt supply of securities by the underwriter.

Where an underwriter's charge for services is adjusted to reflect the entitlement to purchase his allotted securities at a special price, the value of the discount must be regarded as part of the consideration for his exempt supply of underwriting services. The supply by the issuer of the right to acquire the securities at a special price is exempt under 27.11(*a*) above, the value being the discount allowed. However, where an underwriter is obliged to buy further securities which remain unsold and the underwriting agreement allows him to buy these unsold securities at a price lower than the offer price, this reduction is not regarded as consideration for the underwriting service and is outside the scope of UK VAT.

Sub-underwriters. Exemption also applies to the supply made by a sub-underwriter who agrees to underwrite a proportion of the issue or sale. Depending upon the contractual arrangements, a sub-underwriter's client may be the underwriter or the issuer. Where the underwriting has international aspects, this will affect the VAT position. For example, if a sub-underwriter's supply is to a lead underwriter belonging in the UK, the supply is exempt with no input tax recovery (even though the issuer belongs outside the EC). If, on the other hand, the sub-underwriter's supply was to the issuer belonging outside the EC, the supply would be outside the scope of UK VAT (see

27.15 Finance

27.1 above) with input tax credit (see 27.2 above), even though the lead underwriter belongs in the UK.

(C & E Notice 701/44/98, para 2.6).

27.15 Corporate finance services

In any corporate finance arrangement which involves investment advice or management, it is necessary to determine to what extent the activity comprises or includes a supply which involves effecting a transaction in securities. Every contract for a capital raising operation, share placement, merger or acquisition deal, which involves a transaction in securities will have its own features, each of which must be taken into account in determining the appropriate VAT treatment.

In the course of a corporate finance transaction involving a supply of securities, a number of different parties participate in the supply of services to either of the principals to the securities deal. The exemption for the 'making of arrangements' does not apply to all these parties. Corporate financing is often a two stage process. First, the sponsor seeks information from a variety of professional sources and, having obtained it, prepares a prospectus. Services performed in this first stage (e.g. reporting accountants) are generally taxable. Services performed during the second stage, the actual transaction in securities, may qualify for exemption.

Exemption applies only to the services provided by the party (or occasionally parties) who actually negotiates or co-ordinates all of the components of the transaction and concludes it. Typically this might include

- bringing together sellers/issuers and purchasers/investors;

- carrying out/co-ordinating the necessary negotiations essential to the conclusion of the whole deal;

- instructing/organising and co-ordinating the work of other parties involved, such as lawyers and accountants;

- carrying out the necessary consultations with appropriate regulatory authorities; and

- acting as the central point of contact and execution between the party intending to effect a transaction in securities and their other advisers.

Other specialist services (e.g. legal advisers or document printers) are taxable, even if supplied in connection with the second stage.

Services to a target company. Where services are provided to a company to enable it to defend itself against a hostile take-over bid, such services are wholly taxable if the defence does not involve making of arrangements for the issue of shares or for raising capital as part of the defence. If the defence involves both advice on resisting the hostile bid and making of arrangements (e.g. where the defence strategy involves a de-merger or sale of a subsidiary), it may be that services of a taxable and exempt nature are involved.

(C & E Notice 701/44/98, para 2.5).

27.16 Personal equity plans (PEPs)

The services of a PEP manager are essentially investment management (see 27.18 below). Where a plan contract provides for a periodic fee to the manager, and the client is not expected to meet the cost of transaction charges separately, the manager makes a single taxable supply of management services. The exemption under 27.11(c) or (d) above can only apply if the PEP is entirely based on authorised unit trusts or on open-ended investment companies respectively.

Any charges by a PEP manager for dealing in securities on a client's behalf, and which the client is expected to bear, is an exempt supply of broking services.

See C & E Notice 701/44/98, Appendix C for full details of the VAT liability of a wide range of services provided by PEP managers, based on an agreement reached between C & E and the Association of Unit Trust and Investment Funds. See also *Ivory & Sime Trustlink v C & E Commrs CS, [1998] STC 597* concerning initial charges for managed personal equity plans.

(C & E Notice 701/44/98, para 2.10).

27.17 **Unit trusts and open-ended investment companies**

Unit trusts. Where a company manages a trust, it acts as the trustee's agent in the purchase and sale of the securities which make up the units, but sells the units to investors and buys them back as principal. The management company derives its income partly from the margin on its dealings in units (the difference between the buying bid and selling offer prices) and partly from a periodic management charge, calculated as a percentage of the value of the deposited property of the fund.

Units in a unit trust are securities for the purposes of 27.11(*a*) above and their sale by the manager of the trust is exempt. The value of the exempt supply is the total price paid for the units by the investor. A unit trust itself will hold and deal in securities within 27.11(*a*) above and the sale of these underlying securities is an exempt supply by the trust.

The management of a unit trust by the operator of the trust is an exempt supply provided the trust is authorised under *FSA 1986* (see 27.11(*c*) above). Exemption does not apply for any share registration services performed for the trustees if these services are separately identified and paid for. If the unit trust is not authorised under *FSA 1986*, the supply of management services is standard-rated.

PEPs based on unit trusts. See C & E Notice 701/44/98, Appendix C for full details of the VAT liability of a wide range of services provided by PEP managers, based on an agreement reached between C & E and the Association of Unit Trust and Investment Funds. See also *Ivory & Sime Trustlink v C & E Commrs CS, [1998] STC 597* concerning initial charges for managed PEPs.

(C & E Notice 701/44/98, para 2.8).

Open-ended investment companies. Supplies of shares in an OEIC are covered by 27.11(*a*) above and their issue by the company is exempt. The authorised corporate director (ACD) of the OEIC (similar to the manager of an authorised unit trust) sells shares in the OEIC on its own account. These shares may have been issued by the company to the ACD or the ACD may have redeemed them from a previous shareholder. In addition, the ACD may arrange for the company to issue shares direct to the purchaser. The sale of shares is exempt under 27.11(*a*) above.

The OEIC holds and deals in securities within 27.11(*a*) above and the sale of these underlying securities is an exempt supply by the OEIC.

The investment management of an OEIC by its ACD is exempt under 27.11(*d*) above. Where there is a single contract between the ACD and the OEIC for the administration of the OEIC and for its investment management (even if this is effected by the ACD sub-contracting the service or by the OEIC contracting directly with a third party) there is a single exempt supply of investment management. Sub-contracted supplies and supplies by third parties to the OEIC itself do not benefit from the exemption. (C & E Notice 701/44/98, para 2.9).

27.18   Miscellaneous

Dealing systems and data services. The supply of a dealing system which allows

- a user to insert bid and offer quotes for securities,

- another user to insert acceptance, and

- for the system to match buy and sell deals,

is exempt as a transfer or dealing with any security. Electronic data services which simply provide subscribers with a message facility or an information service (e.g. on share price movements or financial news) are taxable. (C & E Notice 701/44/98, para 2.13).

Financial futures and options. For details of the VAT position of trading in financial futures contracts and options on the London Financial Futures and Options Exchange (LIFFE), see C & E Leaflet 701/43/93.

Introductory services. The service of introducing clients who wish to buy or sell securities to a person effecting transactions in securities is exempt (even if the intended securities transaction later falls through). Commission received from a broker in these circumstances is consideration for an exempt supply. (C & E Notice 701/44/98, para 2.4).

Investment/portfolio management. The management of a client's holding of securities is taxable. Even though services described as portfolio, fund or asset management involve the purchase or sale of securities for a client, the exemption under 27.11(*b*) above for the making of arrangements does not apply. The purpose and substance of the service is to make available the professional skill needed to acquire, hold and dispose of securities in the way that best meets the investment needs of a client. Any exempt broking or dealing charges incurred are cost components of the taxable service provided in return for the periodic fee for services.

In other investment management situations, it may be that the arrangements between manager and client involve both management services and broking services. This depends on the charge for the broking service being treated as a disbursement or as payment for an exempt supply made to the client. In either case the contract and what is actually being supplied and the payment structure must all be consistent with the tax treatment claimed for the situation.

(C & E Notice 701/44/98, para 2.7).

Nominee services. The services of acting as nominal holder of securities on behalf of the beneficial owner are exempt. (C & E Notice 701/44/98, para 2.11).

Safe custody services. The provision of the purely physical service of safekeeping (safe deposit facilities) is standard-rated irrespective of where the recipient belongs (because such services are expressly excluded from services within *VATA 1994, 5 Sch 5* and therefore the place of supply is, under the basic rule, where the supplier belongs) and irrespective of whether the securities are stored in the UK, at an overseas branch of the business or elsewhere.

Where a specific site is hired to a client (rather than the service of secure storage within premises generally), the supply is in the UK if the site is in the UK, but outside the scope of UK VAT if the site is an overseas branch of the business or elsewhere. There may, however, be a liability to account for VAT in another EC country if the place of supply is elsewhere in the EC.

Safe custody services sometimes involve a package of services including physical safekeeping, collection of dividends/interest on securities held, dealing with scrip/rights issues, and payment against the delivery or receipt of stock. In such a case, the supply of the whole service, including the physical service of safekeeping, is exempt. (C & E Notice 701/44/98, para 2.12).

Share registers. The supply of share registration services is taxable. Such services may cover

- operating a company's share register;
- designating certificates;
- attending shareholders' meetings;
- processing proxy forms;
- registering grants of probate; and
- administering share option and dividend schemes.

Statutory fees charged for inspection of the register and for production of lists of shareholders in accordance with companies' legislation are outside the scope of UK VAT.

(C & E Notice 701/44/98, para 2.15).

Stock-lending. In a stock-lending transaction, a 'lender' transfers to a 'borrower' all the dividends, rights and legal title to securities. The borrower agrees to return to the lender an equivalent number of the same securities as those which were originally received.

For VAT purposes, there are exempt supplies under 27.11(*a*) above in both directions. The exempt value of the supply by the lender is the open market value of the securities transferred to the borrower, plus any interest received or other payment in lieu of interest. The exempt value of the later supply by the borrower to the lender is the open market value of the equivalent securities, plus any fee charged for depositing a cash collateral.

(C & E Notice 701/44/98, para 2.2).

Valuation, research and advisory services. The supply of services of

- valuing a client's holding of securities,
- assessing the direct tax liabilities of a holding,
- investment analysis,
- market sector research,
- share consultancy, or
- general financial or investment advice

are taxable if supplied separately from any other specialist service offered, e.g. a broking service under 27.13 above.

(C & E Notice 701/44/98, para 2.14).

27.19 **HIRE PURCHASE ETC.**

If the possession of goods is transferred under agreements which expressly contemplate that the property also will pass at some time in the future (determined by, or ascertainable from, the agreements but in any case not later than when the goods are fully paid for) a supply of goods takes place. [*VATA 1994, 4 Sch 1(2)(b)*].

The above covers sales by means of

(*a*) **hire purchase agreements** i.e. agreements (other than conditional sale agreements) under which goods are hired for periodic payments and where the hirer has the option to purchase;

(*b*) **conditional sale agreements** i.e. agreements for the sale of goods where the price is payable by instalments and the goods remain the property of the seller until the full price is paid or another condition is met by the customer;

(*c*) **credit sale agreements** i.e. agreements for the sale of goods which immediately become the property of the customer but where the price is payable by instalments.

VAT is due on the full value of the *goods* at the time of supply (see 64.32 SUPPLY).

Supplies not involving finance companies. If an agreement is made to supply goods under (*a*) to (*c*) above without involving a finance company, any credit charge disclosed separately to the customer in writing (see 27.9(*a*) above) is the consideration for a separate exempt supply of credit or credit facilities. The consideration for the taxable supply of the goods is then the cash price stated in the agreement. If there is no exempt supply, the consideration for the supply of the goods is the full amount paid by the customer.

Option fees etc. are also exempt if not exceeding £10 (see 27.9(*b*) above).

Finance companies. If the finance company becomes the owner of goods (e.g. when a purchase is financed by a hire-purchase agreement) the supply of goods is by the supplier to the finance company, not the customer, and is taxable. The finance company in turn, makes a supply of goods and a supply of credit. The supply of credit is exempt if the credit charge is disclosed to the customer in writing.

If the finance company does not become owner of the goods (e.g. when a purchase is financed by a loan agreement) the supply of goods is to the customer, not the finance company, even though the company may make the payment direct to the supplier. The supply is taxable and VAT is due on the selling price to the customer even if a lesser amount is received from the finance company. The finance company, in a separate transaction, makes a supply of credit facilities to the customer.

(C & E Notice 700, para 3.5).

The tax point for the exempt supply of the *services* is treated as taking place each time a payment is received unless the VAT office has approved a written application for an earlier date to be used. For administrative reasons, application is often made to treat the supply of goods and exempt services as taking place together. (C & E Notice 700, para 5.4(*k*)).

27.20   **Transfers of agreements**

(*a*) **By the owner**. If the owner of the goods assigns his rights, interests and ownership under a hire-purchase or conditional sale agreement to

 • *a bank or finance company* (for example under a block discounting arrangement) the transfer is outside the scope of VAT. [*SI 1995/1268, Art 5(4)*]. Neither the owner nor the assignee if he later takes possession of the goods can use the concession in 27.21 below; or

 • *a dealer* (for example under a recourse agreement) the transfer is a single supply of goods and is taxable in the normal way. Although the owner has not repossessed the goods, he can use the concession in 27.21 below if all the other conditions are met. The dealer cannot use the concession even if he subsequently takes possession of the goods.

(*b*)   **By the customer.** If a customer buys goods under a hire purchase or conditional sale agreement and subsequently transfers his rights and obligations to another customer, he is making a standard-rated supply of services to the new customer. There is no supply for VAT purposes from the owner to the new customer. VAT must be accounted for on the open market value of the supply i.e. the total amount payable by the new customer to the owner to complete the agreement plus any amount he pays to the original customer to secure the transfer. The owner cannot use the concession in 27.21 below if he subsequently repossesses the goods from the new customer. Where, however, the transfer forms part of a transfer of a business as a going concern (see 8.10 BUSINESS) the supply of services representing the transfer of rights and obligations under the HP agreement can be ignored for VAT purposes (Tolley's Practical VAT 1990, p 30). See also *Phillip Drakard Trading Ltd v C & E Commrs QB, [1992] STC 568.*

(C & E Leaflet 700/5/85, para 6).

27.21   **Repossession of goods**

Where goods are supplied under a hire purchase or conditional sale agreement, including a reservation of title (Romalpa) agreement, all VAT due under the agreement is payable at the outset. See 27.19 above. If the goods are subsequently repossessed or returned, there is no supply to the owner for VAT purposes. On repossession of goods not fully paid for, the supplier cannot issue a credit note for the amount invoiced and substitute a new invoice for hire charges for the period of use (*Mannesmann Demag Hamilton Ltd, [1983] VATTR 156 (1437)*).

For supplies made after 19 March 1997, the supplier can claim BAD DEBT RELIEF (7) on the unpaid amount.

For supplies made on or before 19 March 1997, bad debt relief could not be claimed as one of the conditions for that relief was that the property in the goods must have passed from the supplier to the customer. However, by concession, the owner could reduce both the original value of the sale in the VAT account and his liability to account for output tax provided the following conditions were met (C & E Notice 748, ESC 8, now withdrawn).

For agreements with VAT registered customers

● The customer expressly agreed to the reduction in the original valuation.

● The goods were repossessed or returned under the terms of the agreement. If the goods could not be repossessed (e.g. because they had been lost) this condition could not be met.

● There were unpaid instalments due from the customer for which the owner made no claim and for which he issued a credit note to the customer to cover the full amount.

● The owner kept a record of the credit allowed.

● The resale of the goods would be a taxable supply.

● The owner had satisfactory evidence from the customer that he had accepted the credit note.

For agreements with non-registered customers

- The goods were repossessed or returned under the terms of the agreement. If the goods could not be repossessed (e.g. because they had been lost) this condition could not be met.

- There were unpaid instalments due from the customer for which the owner made no claim.

- The resale of the goods would be a taxable supply.

- The owner kept documentary evidence to show the nature of the adjustment and the reason for it.

The amount of the credit note was the total price shown on the original agreement less

(*a*) any payment received for the supply;

(*b*) any amounts claimed from the customer or anyone else for the goods (e.g. damages for restoring the goods to a saleable condition or amounts claimed in a receivership or liquidation); and

(*c*) any exempt credit charges under the agreement (see 27.19 above).

The VAT credited to the customer was found by applying the VAT fraction (7/47ths) to this amount.

(C & E Leaflet 700/5/85, paras 1–4).

27.22 **SALE OF REPOSSESSED ASSETS**

The sale of goods by a person (including a finance company) who repossessed them under the terms of a finance agreement or by an insurer or mortgagee who has taken possession of them in settlement of a claim under a policy of insurance or terms of mortgage is a supply and VAT must normally be paid on the full selling price. However, sales of

(i) boats and aircraft by a mortgagee after he has taken possession of them under the terms of a marine or aircraft mortgage, or

(ii) works of art, antiques and collectors' items, and second-hand goods by a person who has repossessed them under the terms of a finance agreement or by an insurer in settlement of a claim under an insurance policy

are outside the scope of VAT if the following conditions are met.

(*a*) The goods so disposed are in the same condition at the time of disposal as when they were repossessed or taken into possession.

(*b*) For goods other than motor cars

(i) if the goods had been supplied in the UK by the person from whom they were obtained, that supply would not have been chargeable with VAT or would have been chargeable on less than full value;

(ii) if the goods have been imported into the UK, they must have borne VAT which has neither been reclaimed nor refunded; and

(iii) the goods must not have been reimported having previously been exported from the UK free of VAT by reason of zero-rating.

(c) In the case of motor cars the VAT on any previous supply acquisition or importation must have been wholly excluded from credit.

[*SI 1992/3122, Art 4; SI 1995/1268, Art 4; SI 1995/1269; SI 1995/1385; SI 1995/1667*].

Where the above conditions are not satisfied, VAT is chargeable on the full amount realised on the sale (not the original cost of the asset, see *Darlington Finance Ltd, [1982] VATTR 233 (1337)*). Although the property is repossessed and sold by the lender/insurer, the sale of the asset is still a supply by the borrower/insured. The lender must, however, account for any VAT due on the sale direct to C & E. See 2.18 ACCOUNTING PERIODS AND RETURNS.

De Voil Indirect Tax Service. See V3.117.

28 Food

Cross-references. See also CATERING (11) for supplies in the course of catering and take-away food; 47.6 OUTPUT TAX for packaging of food products.

De Voil Indirect Tax Service. See V4.221; V4.226.

The contents of this chapter are as follows.

28.1 ZERO-RATING GENERALLY

The supply of food (including drink) comprised in the following *General items*, is zero-rated.

1. Food of a kind used for human consumption (see 28.2 to 28.14 below).

2. Animal feeding stuffs (see 28.15 and 28.19 below).

3. Seeds or other means of propagation of plants within 1. or 2. above (see 28.20 below).

4. Live animals of a kind generally used as, or yielding or producing, food for human consumption (see 28.21 to 28.23 below).

There are however a number of *Excepted items* (which are standard-rated) and *Overriding items* (which are zero-rated because they override the *Excepted items*).

Catering. Specifically excluded from zero-rating is any supply in the course of catering which includes

- any supply of food for consumption on the premises where it is supplied; and

- any supply of hot food for consumption off those premises.

See 11 CATERING for full details.

[*VATA 1994, 8 Sch Group 1, General Items 1-4*].

In applying zero-rating, the law is primarily concerned with the nature of the product itself rather than with its end use. For example the sale of fish, such as mackerel, fit for human consumption is covered by *General Item 1* above (and not covered by any of the *Excepted items*) and can therefore be zero-rated. No consideration need be given to the use to which it will be put even, for example, if it is sold as bait. Similarly salt of a culinary type is zero-rated because it is of a kind used for human consumption even though it may be put to other uses. However, in some cases, the wording of the law requires a distinction to be made. For example, some products can be used both as animal feeding stuffs (zero-rated) and as pet food (standard-rated). It then becomes important to determine how a product is '*held out for sale*', i.e. the way in which it is packaged, labelled, displayed or advertised. (C & E Manual V1-7, Chapter 1 Part A, para 1.6).

28.2 FOOD FOR HUMAN CONSUMPTION

The supply of food of a kind used for human consumption is zero-rated. Food includes drink. [*VATA 1994, 8 Sch Group 1, General Item 1*].

Meaning of 'food'. The law does not include a definition of 'food' and the word should therefore be given its ordinary and everyday meaning (applying *Brutus v Cozens, [1972] 2 All ER 1297*).

A product is considered to be 'food' if the average person would consider it so. C & E regard the term as including products eaten as part of a meal or snack. However, many products are sold in a form in which they are not fit to be consumed without some preparation by the user and the words 'of a kind used for' are included to reflect this fact (*C & E Commrs v Macphie & Co (Glenbervie) Ltd CS, [1992] STC 886*). Products, therefore, like flour which, although not eaten by themselves, are generally recognised as food ingredients are included. 'Food' would not normally include

- medicines and medicated preparations consisting of a drug or medicine added to normal food and held out for sale as medicines (but see 32.14 HEALTH AND WATER UTILITIES for zero-rating of certain medicines),

- dietary supplements (see 28.11 below), or

- food additives and similar products (see 28.12 below)

which, although edible, are not generally regarded as 'food'.

Palatability and other matters may be taken into account (*Marfleet Refining Co Ltd, [1974] VATTR 289 (129)*) and also nutritive value (*Soni, [1980] VATTR 9 (897)*).

Waste and contaminated food products (including used cooking oil) are not allowed zero-rating because, although they could be described as 'food', they are not 'of a kind used for human consumption'. (They may, however, qualify for zero-rating as animal feeding stuffs, see 28.15 below.)

(C & E Notice 701/14/97, para 1.2).

Exceptions. Food of a kind used for human consumption is generally zero-rated under *General Item 1* above. There are, however, a number of categories of *Excepted items* (including ice cream and similar products, confectionery, alcoholic and other beverages, crisps, roasted and salted nuts) which are standard-rated and *Overriding items* (including tea and coffee) which override the *Excepted items* and remain zero-rated.

For a consideration of food for human consumption generally, see 28.3 to 28.14 below.

Catering. For food supplied in the course of catering and take-away food generally, see CATERING (11).

28.3   Basic foodstuffs

All supplies of unprocessed foodstuffs such as raw meat and fish, vegetables and fruit, nuts and pulses and fresh culinary herbs are zero-rated provided they are of a quality fit for human consumption. This applies whether the produce is supplied direct to the public or for use as ingredients in the manufacture of processed foods. (If not fit for human consumption, it may still be eligible for zero-rating as animal feeding stuffs, see 28.15 below.)

Meat and poultry. Zero-rating applies whether sold as a complete carcass or butchered and extends to more exotic meats such as ostrich, crocodile, kangaroo, horsemeat, etc. (The rules are different for sale of live animals where zero-rating only applies if the animal is of a species generally used for consumption in the UK so that, for example, the sale of a live horse is standard-rated, see 28.21 below).

Fish. The same rules apply as for meat above. Provided the species is one generally used for human consumption in the UK, it is zero-rated whether supplied live, whole or filleted.

28.4   Food

Vegetables, fruit and culinary herbs are zero-rated when sold unprocessed provided they are fit for human consumption (e.g. ornamental cabbages are standard-rated). See 28.20 below for supplies of growing plants and seeds. Zero-rating only applies to culinary herbs not medicinal ones. See 28.12 below for a list of herbs accepted by C & E as culinary.

Fruit and vegetable pulps are zero-rated but most juices and juice concentrates are standard-rated as beverages (see 28.8 below).

Cereals (wheat, barley, maize, etc.) of a kind fit for human consumption are zero-rated whether supplied as a growing crop, in bulk, or cleaned and packaged for retail sale. (Cereals unfit for human consumption may be eligible for zero-rating as animal feeding stuffs, see 28.15 below.)

See 28.14 below for processing other people's cereal crop.

Nuts and pulses. Raw and unprocessed nuts and pulses fit for human consumption are zero-rated, as are nuts roasted or salted in their shells. This applies whether they are sold in bulk or in small retail packs. Nuts which are shelled and either roasted or salted are standard-rated (see 28.9 below).

Bakery products. *Bread and bread products* (e.g. rolls, baps, pitta bread) are zero-rated unless supplied as part of a hot take-away meal (e.g. a bun containing a hot hamburger). For hot take-away food, see 11 CATERING. *Cakes* and *biscuits* (other than chocolate covered biscuits) are normally zero-rated (see 28.6 below) but other confectionery is normally standard-rated (see 28.5 below).

Freshly baked products. Many bakery products (e.g. pies, pasties and other savouries) are baked on the premises and sold while hot. See 11.1 CATERING for the distinction between freshly baked food (zero-rated) and hot take-away food (standard-rated).

Processed food. *Canned* and *frozen foods* take the liability of the equivalent unprocessed product. Ice creams, etc. are standard-rated (see 28.4 below).

Ready meals. Sales of convenience foods and prepared meals which require further preparation (e.g. reheating) at home are zero-rated; but where premises and/or facilities for eating the food are provided or hot take-away food is supplied, there could be a supply of standard-rated catering. See 11 CATERING.

Sandwiches supplied pre-packed as part of a general range of prepared grocery items are usually zero-rated. However, if supplied as part of a buffet or party service, or if premises are provided for their consumption, there could be a supply of standard-rated catering. See 11 CATERING.

(C & E Notice 701/14/97, paras 2.2-2.5).

28.4   **Ice cream, etc.**

The supply of ice cream, ice lollies, frozen yoghurt, water ices and similar frozen products, and prepared mixes and powders for making such products, are standard-rated. [*VATA 1994, 8 Sch Group 1, Excepted Item 1*]. Yoghurt unsuitable for immediate consumption when frozen is zero-rated. [*VATA 1994, 8 Sch Group 1, Overriding Item 1*].

Standard-rated items include

- sorbets and granitas

- ice cream gateaux and cakes, including arctic rolls

- fruit syrups sold in plastic tubes for home freezing as ice lollies

Zero-rated items include

- products which are supplied frozen but which have to be cooked (e.g. baked alaska) or thawed completely (cream gateaux, mousse) before eating

- desserts which can be eaten either straight from the freezer or left to thaw (unless primarily designed for eating while frozen and made substantially of ice cream or any of the other excepted items)

- toppings, sauces and syrups for serving with ice cream (unless sold on the ice cream)

Wafers, cones, etc. sold complete with ice cream are standard-rated as part of that ice cream. If sold separately, they are treated as biscuits (see 28.6 below).

(C & E Notice 701/14/97, para 2.6).

28.5   **Confectionery**

'Confectionery' is standard-rated. '*Confectionery*' includes chocolates; sweets; biscuits wholly or partly covered with chocolate or with some product similar in taste and appearance; drained, glacé or crystallised fruits (but not drained cherries or candied peel which are zero-rated); and any item of sweetened prepared food which is normally eaten with the fingers. [*VATA 1994, 8 Sch Group 1, Excepted Item 2; Overriding Items 2 and 3* and *Note (5)*].

Such items must be both sweetened *and* have some sweetness in the taste. Standard-rating applies to products falling within the general definition of confectionery even if intended to meet special nutritional needs (e.g. chocolate for diabetics and slimmers' meal replacements in biscuit form with a chocolate or similar coating).

Standard-rated items include

- chocolates, chocolate bars (including those containing nuts, fruit, toffee, biscuit or any other ingredient), liqueur chocolates

- boiled sweets, lollipops and candyfloss

- fruit pastilles and gums and similar jelly sweets

- liquorice sweets

- turkish delight

- sweets made from marzipan or marzipan substitute

- sherbet

- marshmallows, 'snowballs', fondants and similar confectionery

- chewing and bubble gum

- nuts or fruit with a coating, e.g. of chocolate, yoghurt or sugar

- crystallised or sugared ginger (but ginger preserved in syrup, drained ginger or dusted ginger can be zero-rated as long as not held out for sale as confectionery)

- compressed fruit bars, consisting mainly of fruit and nuts, with added sweetening matter

- bars consisting mainly of sesame seeds and sugar or other sweetening matter (but halva is zero-rated unless coated with chocolate or chocolate substitute or held out for sale as confectionery)

- marrons glacé

28.6 Food

- sweetened popcorn (*C & E Commrs v Clark's Cereal Products Ltd QB 1965, [1968] 3 All ER 778* – a purchase tax case)

- sweetened dried fruit, e.g. banana chips, pineapple and papaya (unless sold as suitable for confectionery/snacking *and* home cooking (see 28.12 below) when zero-rated irrespective of bag size)

- cereal bars, whether or not coated with chocolate (except for bars qualifying as cakes)

- florentines

- coconut ice

Zero-rated items include

- Angelica, 'glacé' cherries, and cocktail or maraschino cherries

- cakes (see 28.6 below)

- biscuits not covered with chocolate or a similar product (see 28.6 below)

- chocolate spread

- liquid chocolate icing

- toffee apples (*Candy Maid Confections Ltd & Others v C & E Commrs ChD, [1968] 3 All ER 773* – a purchase tax case)

- traditional Indian and Pakistani delicacies, e.g. barfis, halvas, jelabi, laddoos (but not petha which is crystallised fruit)

- traditional Japanese delicacies

See 28.6 below for edible and inedible cake decorations and 28.13 below for mixtures and assortments.

(C & E Notice 701/14/97, paras 2.5, 2.7).

28.6   **Cakes and biscuits**

Cakes and biscuits (other than biscuits wholly or partly covered with chocolate or some product similar in taste and appearance) are zero-rated. [*VATA 1994, 8 Sch Group 1, Excepted Item 2*].

Cakes include (whether or not they are covered with chocolate)

- sponges and fruitcakes

- meringues

- slab gingerbread (gingerbread men are treated as biscuits)

- flapjacks (but not flapjack-type products containing cereals other than oats, which are confectionery, see 28.5 above)

- marshmallow teacakes (despite the fact that they comprise a combination of chocolate coated biscuit and marshmallow, both of which are regarded as standard-rated confectionery) but not 'snowballs' which are confectionery, see 28.5 above

- 'crunch cakes' consisting of corn flakes or other breakfast cereal products coated in chocolate or carob and pressed into flat cakes

- caramel or 'millionaire's' shortcake (*Marks & Spencer plc (4510)*)

- lebkuchen

- jaffa cakes (see (*United Biscuits (UK) Ltd (6344)*))

Cakes provided as part of a supply of catering are standard-rated as part of that supply. See 11 CATERING. However, if a commemorative cake is provided to a caterer or individual, the supply can be zero-rated provided the supplier

- takes no further part in the provision of catering; and

- does not take the cake to the premises to set it up/supervise its disposal.

Cake decorations. *Inedible* cake decorations are standard-rated where sold on their own. If supplied as part of a cake, an inedible decoration can be zero-rated unless it is clearly a separate item its own right (e.g. a toy with a child's birthday cake intended to be used after the cake is eaten).

Edible cake decorations are zero-rated when sold as part of a cake. They are also zero-rated when sold separately unless standard-rated as confectionery (see 28.5 above) or roasted nuts (see 28.9 below).

Zero-rated decorations include

- chocolate couverture

- chocolate chips

- hundreds and thousands, vermicelli and sugar strands

- chocolate leaves, scrolls, etc, jelly shapes, and sugar flowers, leaves, etc. (provided designed specifically for cake decorations)

- royal icing

- toasted coconut and toasted almonds held out specifically for baking use

- cherries used in baking ('glacé')

Standard-rated cake decorations include

- chocolate buttons

- chocolate flakes (except where supplied within the bakery and ice cream industries when they may be zero-rated if sold in packs of 144 or more and clearly labelled 'for use as cake decorations only: not for retail sale')

- any other items sold in the same form as confectionery

Biscuits. Biscuits covered or partly covered in chocolate (or some other product similar in taste and appearance) are standard-rated. Other biscuits are zero-rated.

Standard-rated biscuits include

- chocolate shortbread

- gingerbread men decorated with chocolate (unless only dots for eyes)

- ice cream wafers partly covered in chocolate, e.g. chocolate oysters (but see *Marcantonio Foods Ltd (15486)* for waffle cones)

Zero-rated biscuits include

- chocolate chip biscuits where the chips are either included in the dough or pressed into the surface before cooking

- bourbon and other biscuits whether the chocolate or similar product only forms a sandwich layer

See also *C & E Commrs v Ferrero UK Ltd, CA [1997] STC 746.*

28.7 Food

Mixtures and assortments. See 28.13 below.

(C & E Notice 701/14/97, para 2.5).

28.7 Alcoholic drinks

Beverages chargeable with any excise duty specifically charged on spirits, beer, wine or made-wine and preparations thereof are standard-rated. [*VATA 1994, 8 Sch Group 1, Excepted Item 3*].

All supplies of drinks containing alcohol are standard-rated, whether sold for consumption on or off the premises. This includes

- beer, cider and perry (including black beer and shandy)
- wine (including made-wine and fermented communion wine)
- spirits and liqueurs

Food products, other than beverages, containing alcohol follow the normal liability rules, e.g. fruit preserved in alcohol is zero-rated as any other preserved fruit and rum babas are zero-rated as cakes.

(C & E Notice 701/14/97, para 2.8).

28.8 Non-alcoholic drinks

Supplies of 'beverages' not within 28.7 above (including fruit juices and bottled waters) and syrups, concentrates, essences, powders, crystals or other products for the preparation of beverages are standard-rated, subject to the following overriding exceptions which are zero-rated.

(*a*) Tea, maté, herbal teas and similar products, and preparations and extractions thereof.

(*b*) Cocoa, coffee and chicory and other roasted coffee substitutes, and preparations and extractions thereof.

(*c*) Milk and preparations and extracts thereof.

(*d*) Preparations and extracts of meat, yeast or eggs.

[*VATA 1994, 8 Sch Group 1, Excepted Item 4, Overriding Items 4–7*].

'*Beverage*' must be given its ordinary meaning and covers drinks and liquids that are commonly consumed. Liquids that are commonly consumed are those that are characteristically taken to increase bodily liquid levels, to slake thirst and to fortify or give pleasure (*Bioconcepts Ltd (11287)*). C & E have accepted this definition.

Following the tribunal decision in *McCormick (UK) plc (15202)* C & E accept that mulling spices, whiskey todd mixtures, spiced cider mixtures, etc. are not 'products for the preparation of beverages' and are zero-rated.

Standard-rated beverages include

- carbonated drinks such as lemonade, cola and mixers such as tonic and soda
- fruit cordials and squashes
- mineral, table and spa waters held out for sale as beverages
- alcohol-free beer and wines
- fruit and vegetable juices (but lemon juice for culinary use is not a beverage)

348

- ginger, glucose, honey, peppermint and barley water drinks

- flavourings for milk shakes (except preparations and extracts of cocoa or coffee, which are zero-rated)

- purgative and laxative 'teas', such as senna, and similar medicinal teas

- soft drinks containing tea as only one of several ingredients, e.g. fruit flavoured 'iced tea', see *Snapple Beverage Corporation (13690)*

C & E state that zero-rating does not apply to medicinal herbal teas but see *Dr X Hua (13811)* where the tribunal held that herbal teas sold at a homeopathic clinic were substantially the same as herbal teas sold commercially and the fact that they were prescribed by a doctor did not prevent them from being zero-rated.

Khat (or Chat) is standard-rated from 1 February 1998 as C & E no longer regard it as a food product. (VAT Notes 4/97).

Drinks which are not beverages. Some drinks do not fall within the definition of 'beverage'. Such drinks, and mixes, etc. for making them, can therefore be zero-rated. These include

- plain soya or rice milk (unflavoured and unsweetened)

- coconut milk

- meal replacement drinks for slimmers or invalids

- unfermented fruit juice specifically for sacramental purposes (see 28.11 below)

- angostura bitters

(C & E Notice 701/14/97, para 2.8).

28.9   **Savoury snacks**

The following are standard-rated.

- Potato crisps, sticks or puffs and similar products made from potato, potato flour or potato starch when packaged for human consumption without further preparation.

- Savoury food products made by swelling cereals or cereal products when packaged for human consumption without further preparation.

- Salted or roasted nuts other than nuts in shell.

[*VATA 1994, 8 Sch Group 1, Excepted Item 5*].

'Without further preparation' effectively means that the items are sold in retail packs for eating out of the packet with the fingers. *Excepted Item 5* does therefore not cover products which would otherwise meet the descriptions within it but which are sold for use in cooking or products which need other preparation before being ready to eat (e.g. breakfast cereals). (C & E Manual V1-7, Chapter 1 Part B, section 6.2).

Standard-rated products include

- savoury popcorn (but not 'microwave' popcorn)

- snack-sized prawn crackers

- mini rice cakes (but not regular rice cakes intended for consumption with cheese or other toppings)

- 'light' extruded products where air is introduced under pressure into the cereal flour or starch paste during manufacture to produce an expanded, aerated product

28.10 Food

Zero-rated products include

- tortilla chips

- corn chips

- bagel chips

- breadsticks, mini-garlic breads and other bread-based snacks

- twiglets

- cocktail cheese savouries

- Japanese rice crackers

- 'microwave' popcorn

- toasted coconut, almonds and chopped nuts held out for sale in retail packs specifically for home baking

(C & E Notice 701/14/97, para 2.9).

See 28.13 below for mixtures containing standard and zero-rated items (e.g. Bombay mix).

28.10 **Ingredients for domestic beer and wine making**

Goods otherwise qualifying as food for human consumption, animal feeding stuffs (see 28.15 below) or seeds (see 28.20 below) but which are canned, bottled, packaged or prepared for use in domestic

- brewing of beer,

- making of cider or perry, or

- production of wine or made-wine

are standard-rated. [*VATA 1994, 8 Sch Group 1, Excepted Item 7*].

Included are

- kits for home-brewing, wine-making, etc.

- retail packs of hopped malt extract, malted barley, roasted barley and hops

- special wine and brewer's yeast

- grape concentrates

- retail packs of foods which are specialised to home wine-making, e.g. dried elderberries or sloes

Any general food product that is held out for sale specifically for home wine making or brewing must also be standard-rated. In this context, goods are held out for sale for home brewing and wine making if

(*a*) sold in a retail outlet (or department or section of a general outlet) specialising in home brewing and wine making;

(*b*) labelled, advertised or otherwise displayed as materials for home brewing or wine making; or

(*c*) provide or packaged with any brewing or wine making recipes or instructions for using them in the making or beer or wine.

(C & E Notice 701/14/97, para 2.8).

28.11   **Specialised products**

The liability of such products depends upon whether they fall within the normal meaning of 'food' (see 28.2 above). If they do, then they are treated under the normal rules and are zero-rated unless falling within one of the *Excepted items*.

(*a*) **Food supplements**. Dietary supplements of a kind not normally purchased and used as food are standard-rated. This includes

  • vitamin and mineral supplements of all kinds

  • royal jelly products but not regular products such as honey which have royal jelly added (see *Grosvenor Commodities Ltd (7221)*)

  • tablets, pills and capsules containing, for example, wheatgerm, iron, calcium, fibre, yeast, garlic, pollen, propolis, seaweed, evening primrose, guarana or other similar herbal preparations, and powders of these other than garlic and yeast. See *Nature's Balance Ltd (12295)* and *Hunter Ridgeley Ltd (13662)* for algae tablets and *National Safety Associates of America (UK) Ltd (14241)* for fruit and vegetable tablets. A high protein powder marketed as a dietary supplement and intended to be mixed with water and drunk was held to qualify as food in *Arthro Vite Ltd (14836)*

  • charcoal biscuits

  • cod liver oil and other fish oils held out for sale as dietary supplements (see *Marfleet Refining Co Ltd (129)*)

  • elixirs and tonics, including mixtures of cider vinegar and honey sold as a dietary supplement

  • malt extract with cod liver oil (but the supply of plain malt extract, with or without added vitamins, is zero-rated unless held out for sale for home brewing, etc.)

(*b*) **Invalid foods**. These products, including parenteral products given intravenously, can be zero-rated (subject to the normal rules) provided they are designed to meet the nutritional needs of the consumer and not to provide treatment for any medical condition. Foods intended to build patients up which are sold in liquid form are zero-rated as food since they fall outside the definition of a beverage (see 28.8 above).

(*c*) **Diabetic and hypoallergenic products**. Specialised foods designed for diabetics or allergy sufferers are zero-rated (e.g. sugar-free preserves or gluten-free flour and cakes) unless falling within any of the *Excepted items* (e.g. sugar-free confectionery or gluten-free chocolate biscuits) in which case they are standard-rated.

(*d*) **Slimmers' foods**. Low calorie foods for slimmers are treated in the same way as their mainstream food equivalent. Slimmers' meal replacement products (including drinks) are zero-rated unless in the form of confectionery (see 28.5 above).

Appetite suppressants in whatever form are not food and must be standard-rated. Genuine slimmers' food products containing appetite suppressants (e.g. soups containing cellulose) can be zero-rated provided the product is obviously food and is meant to take the place of a 'normal' food equivalent in the slimmers' daily food intake.

(*e*) **Sports products**. With effect from 1 December 1997, following a review by C & E

  • *beverages* (and powders for making beverages) to supplement normal protein and carbohydrate intake with the aim of building up muscle bulk or improving athletic performance and products aimed at rehydrating athletes are standard-rated unless covered by one of the *Overriding exceptions* (e.g. preparations of milk, meat or egg). See 28.8 above;

- *tablets* are standard-rated with the exception of glucose, dextrose and Horlicks tablets which are zero-rated; and

- items made wholly or mainly from *creatine* are standard-rated unless it is clear that the main benefit of the product is not the creatine but carbohydrate, protein or fat when it is zero-rated unless falling within one of the *Excepted items*.

Where, from 1 December 1997, liability for energy foods changed from standard-rated to zero-rated, repayment claims may be made (subject to the three year cap and unjust enrichment). C & E do not intend to recover VAT where liability changes from zero-rated to standard-rated. (VAT Notes 3/97).

See 28.5 above for cereal/fruit bars.

(*f*)   **Food and drink for religious and sacramental use.** Religious laws requiring certain foods to be prepared in particular ways (e.g. kosher or halal) does not affect the liability of the final product. However, by concession, zero-rating has been agreed for the following food products which have exclusive sacramental use.

- Communion wafers used in the celebration of the Christian Communion, Mass or Eucharist

- Unfermented communion wine (fermented wine is standard-rated)

- Unfermented grape juice for use at the Jewish seder or kaddish provided it is marked prominently in English 'for sacramental use only'

(C & E Notice 701/14/97, para 2.10).

28.12   **Ingredients and additives**

Home cooking. Most ingredients used in home cooking and baking (e.g. flour and sugar) are clearly foodstuffs in their own right. As a general principle, products sold for use as an ingredient in home cooking or baking can be zero-rated if

- it has some measurable nutritional content;

- it is used solely or predominantly, in the particular form in which it is supplied, in the manufacture of food; and

- it does not fall within any *Excepted item*.

Pre-mixes. Prepared cake, soup, sauce and other mixes sold for making up in the home kitchen are zero-rated except for mixes for ice creams and similar frozen products within 28.4 above.

Cooking oils. Maize (corn) oil, rapeseed oil, groundnut (arachis) oil, olive oil (including olive oil BP), almond oil (but not bitter almond oil), sesame seed oil, sunflower seed oil, palm kernel oil, walnut oil, soya oil and blends of any of these oils can be zero-rated provided

- they are of a type suitable for culinary use; and

- they do not contain any substance, such as perfume, that would make them unsuitable for culinary use.

If they meet these conditions, such oils may be zero-rated even if held out for sale for other purposes (e.g. massage or cosmetic oils).

Linseed oil and essential oils are always standard-rated. Waste and used oils for recycling are ineligible for relief as 'food for human consumption' but may be eligible for relief as animal feeding stuffs (see 28.15 below).

Starch and gelatine are zero-rated if edible but standard-rated if inedible or unsuitable for human consumption (e.g. starch for stiffening collars and 'photographic' gelatine).

Salt for culinary use is zero-rated. This includes fine salt (undried vacuum and pure dried vacuum), dendritic salt, and rock and sea salt in retail packs for culinary use (12.5 kilo packs or less). Non-culinary salt is standard-rated. This includes compacted, granular and soiled salt, and salt of any type specifically held out for use in dishwashers or for other non-food use.

Sweeteners. Natural products used as sweeteners (e.g. sugar and honey) are food products in their own right and zero-rated. Artificial sweeteners (e.g. saccharin, aspartame and sorbitol) can also be zero-rated whether supplied in tablet or powder form.

Sweetened dried fruit sold as suitable for home baking *and* snacking can be zero-rated irrespective of the bag size. If sold purely as confectionery, it is standard-rated under 28.5 above. (C & E Business Brief 11 September 1998).

Herbs and spices. Certain herbs and spices can be zero-rated whether supplied fresh or dry and even if held out for sale for therapeutic rather than culinary use. These are angelica, anise, basil, bay leaves, borage, chillies (fresh, dried or powdered), chives, cinnamon (dried or ground), cloves, coriander, cumin, curry leaves, curry powder, dill (seed or leaf), fennel (root, seed or leaf), garlic (fresh, dried or powdered but garlic capsules sold as a food supplement are standard-rated), ginger (fresh or dried root or ground but crystallised ginger is standard-rated as confectionery), liquorice root, lovage, mace, marjoram, mint, mixed herbs, nutmeg (whole or powdered) oregano, paprika, parsley, pepper, poppy seeds, rosemary, saffron, sage, tarragon, thyme and turmeric.

Herbs taken solely for their therapeutic or medical qualities are standard-rated.

Other flavourings and flavour enhancers. Zero-rating applies to

- natural flavouring essences (e.g. vanilla, peppermint and culinary rosewater)

- synthetic flavourings if designed specifically for food use

- flavouring mixes (e.g. dusting powders or blended seasonings) whether made or natural or synthetic components

- mixes for marinating meat, fish or poultry before cooking

- mulling spices, whiskey todd mixtures, spiced cider mixtures, etc. (see *McCormick (UK) plc (15202)*)

Unflavoured brining mixes (wet or dry) and flavour enhancers (e.g. monosodium glutamate) which do not contribute flavour themselves are standard-rated.

Other additives. By concession, zero-rating applies to baking powder, cream of tartar and rennet. Pectin is zero-rated if supplied in retail packs for culinary use.

Bicarbonate of soda is always standard-rated, as are saltpetre and other single chemicals that may be sold for use in the brining or other processing of meats or fish.

(C & E Notice 701/14/97, para 2.3)

Commercial food manufacture. Many substances are used in the preparation of commercially produced foodstuffs which would not be used in the domestic kitchen. The distinction between standard and zero-rated products is largely the distinction between zero-rated ingredients (which are included for their nutritional content and are food products in their own right) and standard-rated additives (which are included for other than strictly nutritional reasons and are not themselves food).

Ingredients. Most ingredients in commercial food production are the same as those used in home cooking and baking and clearly foodstuffs in their own right. As a general principle, any edible product supplied for incorporation as ingredients in foodstuffs be zero-rated if

(a)   it has some measurable nutritional content (even if its nutritional contribution to the finished food is tiny);

(b)   it is used solely or predominantly, in the particular form in which it is supplied, in the manufacture of food; and

(c)   it is essential to the making of that particular food.

Products which do not meet these criteria are standard-rated as food additives with the exception of flavourings (natural and synthetic) which may be zero-rated provided they meet the criteria in (b) and (c) above. This includes commercial premixes, dusting mixes, marinades and sausage skins (see *Devro Ltd (7570)*).

Additives. Products supplied for incorporation in foodstuffs which do not meet the requirements in (a)-(c) above are treated as additives and standard-rated. They are generally included for commercial reasons (e.g. to prolong shelf life) and do not fall within the everyday meaning of the word 'food' (see 28.2 above). This includes

- preservatives including unflavoured wet and dry brine mixes and cures for curing or salting meats

- anti-oxidants including vitamins A and E

- vitamin supplements (including those required by law to fortify flour before it can be put on the market)

- stabilisers and thickening agents (e.g. agar, carageenan, guar gum, gum arabic, gum tragacanth and xanthan gum, but not corn starch)

- fillers and bulking agents other than flour and starch

- colourants other than naturally-derived colourings which are also culinary spices in their own right (e.g. caramel, cocoa, saffron, turmeric and cochineal)

- flavour enhancers (e.g. monosodium glutamate), ribonucleotides and hydrolysed vegetable protein

- flour improvers and bleaching agents

Some commercial additives are accepted for VAT purposes as food in their own right. These are

- food grade, naturally derived emulsifiers and stabilisers (e.g. lecithin) specifically tailored and mixed for food purposes which are essential to the production of that food and cannot be used for any other purpose

- artificial sweeteners and artificial flavourings

(C & E Notice 701/14/97, paras 3.1-3.3).

28.13   **Mixed supplies and assortments**

There is a mixed supply if standard and zero-rated food items, or zero-rated food items and standard-rated non-food items) are supplied together for a single price. Examples of mixed supplies containing foodstuffs include

- food hampers

- special gift or presentation packs containing linked items (e.g. coffee supplied with a mug, tea with a pack of chocolate biscuits)

- linked goods promotions

- food supplied in or with re-usable storage containers

Normally, the total price must be apportioned in order to arrive at the output tax due. See 47.3 OUTPUT TAX for the general rules on the treatment of mixed supplies and various methods of apportionment.

Linked goods concession. Where, however, a *minor* standard-rated item is supplied with a main zero-rated item, the supply can be treated as a single supply of the main zero-rated item provided the standard-rated item

- is not charged at a separate price;

- costs no more than 20% of the total cost of the supply; and

- costs no more than £1 (excluding VAT).

Once these conditions have been met, the linked goods are treated as a single zero-rated supply throughout the distribution chain. A wholesaler or retailer receiving goods already linked, and who is unsure whether the conditions have been met, should refer to the supplier's supporting documentation and, if still in doubt, check with the supplier.

Mixtures and assortments Some food contains mixtures which are both zero-rated and standard-rated when supplied separately. Generally, the tax value of each part must be ascertained to calculate VAT due. See 47.3 OUTPUT TAX. However, the following products, containing only small quantities of standard-rated items, may, by concession, be treated as a single zero-rated supply.

- Assortments of biscuits where the weight of standard-rated chocolate biscuits (see 28.6 above) does not exceed 15% of total net weight.

- Fruit and nut mixes (including Bombay and similar savoury mixes) where the weight of standard-rated items (e.g. sweetened fruit, chocolate pieces or roasted nuts) does not exceed 25% of total net weight.

- Petits fours where the net weight of chocolate biscuits and sweets does not exceed 15% of total net weight (25% where sweets only are included).

The concession only applies to mixtures and assortments supplied in a single pack, not to 'variety' selections of individual packs.

If any of the above assortments fail to meet the conditions, they can still be treated as a single zero-rated supply if they satisfy the linked goods concession above.

(C & E Notice 701/14/97, paras 4.1, 4.2; C & E Notice 48, ESC 2.7).

For mixtures involving food packaging (e.g. containers, storage jars), see 47.4 OUTPUT TAX.

28.14   Food processing

Any work done on another person's goods is a supply of services. The supply of a treatment or process to another person's goods can be zero-rated, if by doing so, zero-rated goods are produced. [*VATA 1994, s 30(2A); FA 1996, s 29(2)(5)*]. Processing which results in the production of a new zero-rated food product may therefore be zero-rated. Processing which does not result in the production of a new food product, or which results in the production of a standard-rated food product, is a standard-rated supply.

Zero-rated processes include

- drying, cleaning and coating seed or grain to make it marketable as seed for sowing
- milling grain into flour, meal or semolina
- refining crude oil into edible oil; processing used or contaminated oil into edible oil
- cooking, canning or otherwise preserving fruit and vegetables
- drying fruit
- roasting and/or grinding coffee beans
- grinding granulated sugar into caster or icing sugar
- processing of liquid milk into dried milk
- butchering carcasses; boning and jointing meat
- brining or curing pork into ham
- processing meat into sausages
- smoking trout and salmon
- kneading blocks of frozen butter, adding salt and water and packing

Standard-rated processing includes

- cleaning and conditioning grain
- drying grain
- harvesting crops
- malting barley
- slaughtering animals (without further processing of the carcasses)
- blending tea
- maturing cheese or any other product (effectively a process of storage during which a natural change occurs)
- smoking herrings to make kippers
- smoking cod or haddock
- shelling shrimps, prawns or other shellfish; skinning fish
- sorting, grading or packaging any product
- pasteurisation
- sterilisation
- roasting or salting peanuts or other nuts
- supervision of foodstuffs to ensure that manufactured and prepared foods meet religious dietary regulations

(C & E Notice 701/14/97, paras 5.1–5.3).

28.15   **ANIMAL FEEDING STUFFS**

The supply of 'animal' feeding stuffs is zero-rated. '*Animal*' includes bird, fish, crustacean and mollusc. [*VATA 1994, 8 Sch Group 1, General Item 2*].

Most commodities recognised as animal feeds are included unless 'held out for sale' (see 28.1 above) for other purposes such as bedding, packaging, thatching, fertiliser or pet food (see 28.19 below).

Zero-rated items (subject to the above) include the following.

- Cereal and cereal by-products including bran, sharps and similar residues

- Compound feeds consisting of a number of different ingredients (including major minerals, trace elements, vitamins and other additives), mixed and blended in appropriate proportions to provide properly balanced diets for all types of livestock at every stage of growth and development

- Feed blocks

- Forage crops

- Ground oyster shell

- Hay and straw unless held out for sale for non-feed purposes (e.g. bedding). In the case of straw holding out for sale for non-food use includes supplies to customers known to be market gardeners or other horticultural concerns and industrial packers or other non-agricultural businesses

- Molasses

- Oils and fats (including tallow) suitable for use in animal feeding stuffs unless *either* they require further processing before becoming suitable for inclusion in animal feeds *or* are held out for sale for non-feed purposes. Waste oil from fish and chip shops, etc. normally requires processing and is therefore standard-rated

- Oilseed residue (except castor oil)

- Peanuts

- Protein concentrates, i.e. products specifically designed for further mixing (at an inclusion rate of 5% or more) with planned proportions of cereals and other feeding stuffs. They consist of appropriate blends of animal or vegetable protein (or both), plus other essential nutrients, e.g. vitamins, minerals, etc.

- Rabbit food

- Specialised diets formulated for laboratory animals

- Specialised diets formulated for racing greyhounds. To be zero-rated (as opposed to standard-rated as pet food) (i) the product must be a complete feed providing all the required elements for a balanced diet for a dog without having to be mixed with any other food (apart from water); (ii) the product must be specifically held out for sale for racing greyhounds; and (iii) the supplier must be able to demonstrate that the product is designed specifically to meet the nutritional requirements of racing greyhounds (for a retailer, this information will normally be provided to him by the manufacturer on the packaging or in the accompanying literature)

- Straights, i.e. single feeding stuffs of animal or vegetable origin which may have undergone some form of processing. Examples include wheat, barley, flaked maize, field beans, groundnut cake and meal, soya bean meal, fish meal, meat meal and meat and bone meal.

- Supplements, i.e. products designed for adding to other feed in a proportion of less than 5% of the whole (see also protein concentrates above) to supply planned proportions of vitamins, trace minerals, one or more non-nutrient additives and other special ingredients. Normally, the active ingredients are combined with an inert 'carrier' (e.g. cereal) to make for easier mixing by the purchaser. They may be supplied to manufacturers or to farmers for making feed on the farm. Their liability will depend on whether they are for medicinal or nutritional purposes (see 28.18 below for the borderline), but most are nutritional and so zero-rated. Zero-rated nutritional supplements (whether intended to be added to normal feed or given separately, e.g. in pill or capsule form) include grit (soluble and insoluble) for poultry and game; and mineral blocks, mixes and licks. Supplements designed for pet species, and held out for sale for pets, are standard-rated.

Standard-rated items include the following.

- Additives (i.e. substances added to either compound feeds or protein concentrates – see above – in the course of manufacture for some specific purpose other than as a direct source of nourishment) supplied on their own. This would include antibiotics and other medicinal products, anti-oxidants, colouring agents, binders, flavourings, etc. Once additives have been incorporated into a feed, the liability of the final product will depend on its nature (see 28.18 below) although normally, it will still be primarily a feeding compound and so zero-rated.

- Bait (e.g. lugworms, maggots) except for fish of a kind and quality suitable for human consumption which may be zero-rated

- Castor oil seed residue

- Single chemicals and minerals, other than salt (even when fed direct to animals)

- Thatching material (e.g. Norfolk reed, wheat reed or straw reed)

- Urea (unless specifically held out for sale for animal feeding purposes)

(C & E Notice 701/15/95, paras 3, 4, 7-9, 17; C & E Manual V1-7, Chapter 1 Part D, para 2.3).

28.16   **Grazing rights and keeping of animals**

Grazing rights. The grant of grazing rights (i.e. the right to allow someone else's animals to graze on your land, also known as grass keep letting) is both the grant of a licence to occupy land and the supply of animal feeding stuffs, i.e. grass. C & E accept that the supply of animal feed takes precedence over the supply of a licence to occupy, and the supply is zero-rated. In some parts of the country, while the contract is ostensibly for grazing only, it is the custom to provide an element of oversight as well. If this oversight extends to more than a 'seen daily' or 'seen twice daily' routine, the supply may be of the keep of animals rather than grazing.

Keep of animals. Where an element of 'care' is provided (other than a minimal 'seen daily' or 'seen twice daily' routine) the whole consideration (including any animal food or grazing rights) is standard-rated as a supply of the keep of animals. 'Care' includes turning the animals out to graze; feeding; mucking out; spreading straw and other bedding; exercising; and taking any responsibility for the animals' welfare on behalf of the owner. Where occasional services are provided in cases of emergency (e.g. veterinary and farriery services) C & E only regard these as 'care' if it was understood between the parties that it was landowner's actual responsibility to arrange the services. See *S & J Marczak (t/a Suzanne's Riding School) (13141)*.

D-I-Y livery. This is an arrangement whereby there is a genuine supply of grazing rights or other feed together with a separate supply of stabling. Provided

- the animals' owner has exclusive use of all or an identifiable part of the stabling for his animals, and

- no element of care is supplied (see above)

the arrangement consists of separate supplies of feed (zero-rated) and stabling (an exempt supply of rights over land, unless the supplier opts to tax). See *Fidler (RW & JR) (t/a Holt Farm Partners) (12892)*. If any element of care is present, there is a single standard-rated supply of the keep of animals.

(C & E Notice 701/15/95, para 10; C & E Manual V1-7, Chapter 1 Part D, para 2.4).

28.17   **Products which may be used both as animal feed and for other purposes**

Many products sold as animal feed ingredients have other uses. In deciding the VAT liability of these products, it is necessary to determine whether the trader is supplying the product as zero-rated animal feed or some other standard-rated supply.

- Where products are produced in different grades for feed and non-feed use, regulations require all products sold for animal feed to be accompanied by a 'statutory declaration' identifying the product and giving details of its composition and purpose. In most cases, therefore, identification of animal feed will not be difficult.

- Organic products (e.g. blood, bonemeal, fishmeal and other meat and fish by-products) which may be used either as animal feeding stuffs (usually as an ingredient in a compound feed) or as a fertiliser similarly require a form of statutory declaration when used for fertiliser.

- Where there is no physical difference between feed and non-feed products, liability will depend on how the product is 'held out for sale' (see 28.1 above).

Silage enhancers are products, usually derived from molasses or other sugars, which are added to silage to increase fermentation and absorb and retain the liquid effluent which would otherwise escape during the process and be lost. Most silage enhancers, including all bacterial products, are not fed directly to animals and therefore standard-rated. Non-bacterial products which are marketed as having an alternative direct-feed use may be zero-rated.

(C & E Manual V1-7, Chapter 1 Part D, para 2.5).

28.18   **The borderline between feed and medicine**

Medicines are often administered to farm animals in feed. The products may be provided as medicines to be added by the farmer, or pre-mixed into a specialised feed, e.g. a normal compound feed may include an anti-parasitic compound.

Medicines. Purely medicinal products are always standard-rated. They can normally be readily identified by the packaging or accompanying documentation which will carry dosage instructions and identify the condition the product is intended to cure or guard against.

Feed products containing medicines. Feeds containing medicines may be zero-rated or standard-rated according to whether they are used primarily as a feed (i.e. taken for purposes of nutrition) or a medicine (taken to cure or prevent a specific medical condition). C & E's policy is to follow that of MAFF and class a product as 'medicinal' (and therefore standard-rated) if it requires a MAFF-issued product licence or marketing authorisation.

Growth promoters (i.e. antibiotics for incorporation into animal feed to prevent a low-level infection retarding normal development) are standard-rated. Feed containing growth promoters should be judged according to the principles of feed products containing medicines above.

Probiotics increase the efficiency of the digestive tract, improving the animal's resistance to disease and countering the detrimental effects of stress. They are not considered to be medicinal products by MAFF but equally, as they are not a source of direct nourishment in their own right, they are not considered to be foodstuffs and are standard-rated for VAT purposes.

Vitamin supplements are regarded as essential ingredients of manufactured feed. included for nutritional rather than therapeutic reasons. They are therefore zero-rated for VAT purposes both as single vitamins and supplement mixtures. (Compare the VAT treatment of vitamin supplements for humans which are not considered to be 'food of a kind used for human consumption' and are standard-rated.)

(C & E Manual V1-7, Chapter 1 Part D, para 2.6).

28.19   **Pet food**

The following items are standard-rated.

(a)   **Pet food which is canned, 'packaged' or 'prepared'.** [*VATA 1994, 8 Sch Group 1, Excepted Item 6*].

Meaning of 'pet'. There is no definition of 'pet' in *VATA 1994*. In *Popes Lane Pet Food Supplies [1986] VATTR 221 (2186)* the tribunal suggested that a pet was 'an animal (tamed if it was originally wild) which is kept primarily as an object of affection [including] an animal kept primarily for ornament.' On this basis, C & E regard the following animal species as 'pet species' in that the great majority of that species are kept and reared as objects of affection.

- Cage birds.

- Cats.

- Dogs (except racing greyhounds) — but see below.

- Ferrets.

- Goldfish, aquarium fish and pond fish.

- Guinea pigs.

- Hamsters, gerbils, rats and mice (except rats and mice bred specifically for the laboratory).

Other species (including most farm animals) can be as clearly identified as 'non-pets'.

Between these extremes are species which C & E regard as 'mixed' species, i.e. animals which are sometimes kept as pets, and sometimes as food or working animals, or simply left in the wild. Included are rabbits and most of the 'exotics'. Tribunals have also treated dogs as within this category distinguishing between pet dogs and working dogs (e.g. sheep dogs, police dogs, guard dogs, gun dogs and packs of hounds). See *Popes Lane Pet Food Supplies* above, *LJ & H Norgate (t/a Dog's Dinner) (5241)* and *Peters & Riddles (t/a Mill Lane Farm Shop) (12937)*.

Pet food is any product that is supplied for consumption by pet animals which would include both 'pet species' and individual pets of 'non-pet' or 'mixed' species (see above). Animal foods products are not necessarily pet food because they are sold in pet shops or because a company name or trading name refers to pets. For VAT purposes, pet food is animal feed which is

(i)   'held out for sale' as pet food (see 28.1 above);

(ii) formulated specially for a 'pet species' of animal; or

(iii) otherwise specialised for the pet food market by undergoing any one of certain processes. These are the addition of colouring, flavouring, preservative, binder or gelling agents; the mixing or blending of ingredients to meet the specific nutritional requirements of a pet species within (ii) above; the cooking of meats and meat products; and the mixing or blending of four or more meat and/or fish products.

Having established that a product is a pet food, is it then necessary to decide whether it is canned, packaged *or* prepared before it is ruled standard-rated.

'*Packaged*' means pre-packed for retail sale in a sealed bag, carton or other container. Putting a loose product in a plain paper or polythene bags at the point of sale (whether after purchase by the customer or in anticipation of sales) is not considered packaging. See *B Beresford (9673)*.

'*Prepared*' includes any processing of mixing or blending different ingredients; washing or polishing; cooking; mincing, dicing and similar processes (but see below); and the inclusion of additives.

Meat products for dogs and cats. As tribunals have decided that not all dogs are pets (see above), such meat products cannot be classed as pet food simply because they are for feeding to dogs. C & E regard supplies of fresh, frozen or chilled meat and fish (including offal) for dogs and cats, whether or not packaged, as zero-rated (even if minced or diced) provided it has not undergone any further preparation and it is not held out for sale as pet food. See *Popes Lane Pet Food Supplies* and *LJ & H Norgate (t/a Dog's Dinner)* above and *Normans Riding Poultry Farm Ltd, [1989] VATTR 124 (3276)*.

Food for fish. The VAT liability of food for fish follows the normal rules, according to whether the fish species involved is a 'pet', 'non-pet' or 'mixed' species (see above). Dry compounded diets blended specifically for pet fish (usually in granular or flake form) are therefore standard-rated, while those blended for farmed fish are zero-rated. Live food (other than Artemia) is supplied virtually exclusively for ornamentals, and is therefore pet food. However, it is only standard-rated if 'canned, packaged or prepared' which, given the nature of the product, is unlikely. Live Artemia are fed to farmed fish, in the early stages of rearing, as well as to pet fish, and therefore are not considered to be 'pet food'. Frozen or freeze-dried Artemia, daphnia etc are 'prepared' pet food and standard-rated.

Day-old chicks, rats, mice, etc. sold as food for 'exotics'. Because exotic species (e.g. snakes) are not 'pet' species (see above), such food is treated in the same way as any other food for a 'mixed' species, i.e. zero-rated unless they are specifically held out for sale as pet food *and* canned, packaged or prepared. The initial killing of the creatures does not constitute 'preparation' for VAT purposes. See 28.21 below for sales of live animals.

(*b*) **Wild bird food.** Packaged foods (not being pet food) for birds other than poultry (see 28.22 below) and game is standard-rated. [*VATA 1994, 8 Sch Group 1, Excepted Item 6*].

Food which is either mixed specifically for feeding to wild birds, or is held out for sale for feeding to wild birds, is standard-rated if it is packaged. In this context C & E regard 'packaged' as meaning supplied in a sealed retail pack. The dividing line between retail packs and wholesale packs is set at 25 kilos. Sealed packs of wild bird feed of less than 25 kilos in weight are assumed to be for retail sale and classed as 'packaged' for VAT purposes (and therefore standard-rated). Packs of 25 kilos and above are assumed to be for breaking down and repackaging in smaller quantities by a retailer and not 'packaged' for VAT purposes (and therefore zero-rated).

28.20 Food

Food for poultry and game is zero-rated. Cage birds are treated as a 'pet species' (see (*a*) above) and food for such birds is therefore treated as pet food.

(*c*)   **Biscuits and meal for cats and dogs.** [*VATA 1994, 8 Sch Group 1, Excepted Item 6*]. Biscuits and meal for cats and dogs is standard-rated whether or not for pet animals and whether or not sold packaged or loose. Included are rusks and similar cooked or baked cereal based products.

(C & E Notice 701/15/95, paras 11–19; C & E Manual V1-7, Chapter 1 Part D, paras 3.3–3.7, 4.1, 4.2). See Annex B of the Notice for lists of items which may be sold by pet shop retailers and their potential VAT liabilities.

28.20   **SEEDS AND PLANTS**

Plants grown as food for human consumption or animal feeding stuffs are zero-rated under *VATA 1994, 8 Sch Group 1, General Items 1 and 2.* See 28.2 *et seq.* and 28.15 *et seq.* above. Any crop that generally produces items that are not fed to humans or animals (i.e. for 'industrial' purposes) is always standard-rated.

Seeds or other means of propagation (spores, rhizomes, etc.) of plants used for human consumption or animal feeding stuffs are also zero-rated. [*VATA 1994, 8 Sch Group 1, General Item 3*]. But see 28.19 above for seeds held out for sale as pet food or food for wild birds.

Examples of zero-rated plants and seeds

- Seeds, crowns, spores, tubers and bulbs of edible vegetables and fruit.

- Vegetable seedlings.

- All grass seeds (whether used for agricultural purposes or amenity purposes) and other herbage seeds. Pre-germinated grass seed is standard-rated as it is used almost exclusively for amenity purposes (C & E Business Brief 12/95, 19 June 1995).

- Mushroom spawn.

- Cucumber and tomato 'rootstock'.

- Plants, bushes and trees normally used in this country for the production of edible fruit (including nuts). (Strictly the law zero rates only plants which *themselves* are food of a kind used for human consumption but C & E extend this to plants *producing* food because it was considered reasonable and sensible to do so.)

  C & E regard the *definitive* list of fruit-producing plants which may be zero-rated as almond (not 'flowering almond'), apple, apricot, blackberry, blackcurrant, blueberry, boysenberry, bullace, cherry (not 'flowering cherry'), citrus trees (other than ornamental varieties), cobnut, common quince (not chaenomeles), cowberry, crab (only fruiting varieties), cranberry, damson, fig, filbert, gages, gooseberry, grapevines, hazel, huckleberry, loganberry, medlar, mulberry, nectarine, peach, pear, plum (not 'flowering plum'), raspberry, redcurrant, strawberry, sweet chestnut, tayberry, walnut, whitecurrant, wineberry and worcesterberry.

- Seeds and plants producing culinary herbs (but not bay trees).

- Oilseed rape ('OO' varieties and, when sold off the farm, HEAR varieties.) The supply of pressed oil for industrial use from HEAR varieties is standard-rated although the residual meal produced is zero-rated when supplied for use as animal feed.

Examples of standard-rated plants and seeds

- Seeds, tubers, bulbs, corms, crowns, rhizomes, cuttings, etc. of flowers (but see below for flowers for human consumption).

- Ornamental nursery stock including trees, shrubs, herbaceous plants, alpines (including bay trees) and ornamental brassicas.

- Cut flowers.

- Turf.

- Pot plants.

- Plants, seeds and fruit of a kind used for the production of perfumes, pharmaceutical products, insecticides, fungicides, etc.

- Canary seed, millet seed.

- Rootstock, whether for ornamental or food plants (but not cucumber and tomato 'rootstock').

- Norfolk reed grown for thatching.

Herbs. Plants of species which are generally accepted as reared primarily for culinary use are zero-rated irrespective of how they are held out for sale. These comprise angelica, anise, anise hyssop, basil, borage, caraway, cardamom, cardoon, celery wild, celery wild alpine, chervil, chicory, chives, coriander, cumin, curry leaf, dandelion, dill, fennel, fenugreek, garlic, ginger, good king henry, horseradish, lemon grass, liquorice, lovage, marjoram, mint, onion, orache, oregano, parsley, pennyroyal, rocket, rosemary, saffron, sage, salad burnet, savory, skirret, sorrel, tarragon, thyme and watercress.

Plants which, although not species supplied predominantly as culinary herbs, do have recognised culinary uses, may be zero-rated provided

(*a*)   they have been raised according to the conditions required by *Food and Environment Protection Act 1985* (evidence of which may be required);

(*b*)   they have been held out for sale as culinary herbs; and

(*c*)   they are supplied in individual pots (not bedding strips) of a size less than two litres.

These comprise alecost, alexanders, allspice, asafoetida, bay (provided not exceeding 50 cm in height and not clipped, etc. to specialise them as ornamental), bergamot, bistort, catmint, chamomile, comfrey, clove pink, clover, cowslip, curry plant, elder, feverfew, hop, hyssop, juniper, landcress, lavender, lemon balm, lemon verbena, marigold (pot), melilot, nasturtium (salad), pelargonium (scented), purslane, rue, sweet cecily, tansy, violet (sweet) and woodruff.

Herbs supplied for medical rather than culinary use are not eligible for zero-rating.

Flowers for human consumption. Certain seed varieties can be zero-rated provided they are held out for sale as food of a kind used for human consumption. These comprise bergamot, clove pink, lavender, nasturtium, pelargonium, pink, poppy, pot marigold, sunflower and violet. In this context, seeds would be so held out for sale if marked as edible in a catalogue (or, if no catalogue is produced, in information at the point of sale) and food-based information is available on the seed packet and can be supplied on customer's request.

Plant-growing kits including growing medium, fertilizer and container, etc. are normally standard-rated unless

(i)   the standard-rated element (e.g. growing medium, fertiliser and pot) accounts for less than 10% of the total cost; or

(ii) the supply comprises a planting medium (e.g. small peat cubes) as a means of simplifying planting, impregnated with edible vegetable or fruit seeds

in which case the supply is zero-rated.

In the case of *mushroom growing kits*, VAT treatment depends upon the container. If supplied in a non-reusable container, the whole supply is zero-rated (the container being regarded as normal and necessary packaging). If supplied in a plastic bucket or similar reusable container, the supply must be apportioned and VAT accounted for on the container and any other packaging costs. The spawn and the growing medium are both zero-rated.

Seeds/growing kits sold with books. Where a zero-rated book on a generalised gardening theme is sold with a standard-rated packet of seeds or plant-growing kit, the selling price must normally be apportioned. However, by concession, if the minor article (the standard-rated seeds)

- is not charged separately to the customer,

- costs the supplier no more than 20% of the total cost of the combined supply (excluding VAT), and

- costs the supplier no more than £1 (excluding VAT) if included with the goods intended for retail sale or £5 (excluding VAT) otherwise,

the supplier may account for VAT on the seeds at the same rate as the book. An apportionment is not permitted where the 'book' element is merely a specialised instruction leaflet. In such a case, the liability follows that of the seeds.

Seeds that undergo a treatment or process. With effect from 1 January 1996, the application of a treatment or process to another person's goods (so as to produce new goods) is a supply of services, the liability of which follows that of the resulting goods. The drying, cleaning and dressing of zero-rated seeds is therefore a zero-rated supply of services. The rolling and grinding of the same seed is also zero-rated. The supply of seeds coated with insecticides and/or fertiliser is a single supply, the supply being essentially one of seeds and follows the liability of the particular seed.

The drying only of grain is not a treatment or a process producing new goods and is therefore a standard-rated supply of services.

(C & E Leaflet 701/38/93; C & E Manual V1-7, Chapter 1 Part E, paras 2.1, 2.2, 3.1, 4.1, 6.2, 6.4, 6.6).

28.21   **LIVE ANIMALS**

Live animals of a kind generally used as, or yielding or producing, food for human consumption are zero-rated. This includes birds, fish, crustacea and molluscs. [*VATA 1994, 8 Sch Group 1, General Item 4*].

Examples of zero-rated animals are cattle, pigs, sheep, goats, deer, rabbits, hares, ostriches, guinea fowl, game birds, bees, lobsters, crabs, shrimps, prawns, oysters, mussels and whelks. See 28.22 below for poultry and 28.23 below for fish.

All other species and breeds are standard-rated even if occasionally eaten e.g. horses, ornamental fish and poultry, and racing pigeons. (C & E Notice 701/37/94, para 2).

Insemination. The hire of an animal for insemination purposes is zero-rated provided the supply of the animal itself is zero-rated. The hire of a bull is therefore zero-rated but the hire of a horse is standard-rated. Supplies of semen are standard-rated. (C & E Notice 701/37/94, para 5).

28.22   **Poultry**

The following are zero-rated.

(*a*)   Chicken, domestic fowl including those used for the production of eggs and flesh.

(*b*)   Ducks (Aylesbury, Campbell, Indian Runner, Muscovy, Peking).

(*c*)   Geese (Brecon Buff, Chinese Commercial, Embden, Roman, Toulouse).

(*d*)   Turkeys (Beltsville White, British White, Broadbreasted White, Bronze, Norfolk Stock).

Derivatives and crosses of poultry in (*b*) to (*d*) are also zero-rated. All breeds which are essentially ornamental are standard-rated even if suitable for human consumption. (C & E Notice 701/37/94, para 3).

28.23   **Fish**

Coarse fish (e.g. bream, pike, perch) usually supplied to angling clubs for stocking recreational waters; fish for aquaria; and fish eggs (unless supplied as roe suitable for human consumption) are standard-rated. Freshwater fish commonly recognised as food for human consumption (e.g. salmon, trout, eels) are zero-rated even when sold to angling clubs. (C & E Notice 701/37/94, para 4). Koi carp are standard-rated (*JR Chalmers (1433)*).

28.24   **ABATTOIRS**

The following provisions apply whether the supplies are made by the operator of an abattoir or by an independent person working in an abattoir.

The **killing and dressing** of someone else's animals is zero-rated if the carcass is of a kind which is zero-rated. Goods produced in an abattoir are standard-rated if

(a)   held out for sale for a non-feeding purpose, e g. blood for fertiliser (normally recognisable by declaration of nitrogen/phosphoric acid content);

(b)   used solely for a non-feeding purpose, e.g. hair, horns, hoofs, manure;

(c)   held out for sale as pet food *and* packaged or prepared (see 28.19 above);

(d)   they have undergone some further preparation beyond mincing and dicing, which would specialise the products to the pet food market (28.19 above); or

(e)   are used exclusively in the preparation of pharmaceutical products, e.g. gall bags, glands, ovaries, placenta.

Greaves supplied in pieces of a size suitable for feeding to pets are also standard-rated.

Meat and offal which is suitable for human consumption or for use as an animal feeding stuff is zero-rated provided it does not fall within (*a*)–(*e*) above. See *Popes Lane Pet Food Supplies Ltd, [1986] VATTR 221 (2186)*. Where zero and standard-rated goods are delivered from the same carcass to the owner of the animal, the whole supply is zero-rated if the standard-rated products are incidentals (e.g. the hide is returned with the meat). VAT must be accounted for at the standard rate on the supply of standard-rated products to any person other than the owner.

The **slaughtering** of animals without further preparation of the carcasses is a standard-rated service (see *Darlington Borough Council, [1980] VATTR 120 (961)*).

Other services. A toll which covers slaughter (or killing and dressing) and other related services, is the charge for a single supply, which is standard or zero-rated as explained above. Supplies of services not included in the toll are chargeable at the appropriate rate. Cold storage is normally standard-rated unless it is supplied for domestic use or the non-business use of a charity. Supplies of lairage, stallage, standing, pennage etc. are standard-rated but if specific stalls, pens etc. are allocated for the exclusive use of a customer, the supply is exempt (subject to the option to tax being exercised, see 42.20 LAND AND BUILDINGS).

Meat and Livestock Commission charges. The Meat and Livestock Commission levy is the consideration for a supply of services and subject to VAT at the standard rate. A slaughterer can treat the VAT on the 50% of the general levy which is absorbed by him as deductible input tax, subject to the normal rules. In respect of the remaining 50% of the general levy and 100% of the promotion levy which is due from the producers but paid by the slaughterer on their behalf and subsequently recovered from them, the producers can recover the VAT charged by the Commission subject to the normal rules. The slaughterer should treat himself as an undisclosed agent, deducting the input tax on the charges from the Commission but charging and accounting for an equal amount of output tax in the same VAT period.

The Commission's charge for classifying pig carcasses is standard-rated. Where the slaughterer passes on all or part of that charge to his customer, he must account for output tax, even if it is shown separately on the invoice.

(C & E Leaflet 701/40/91; C & E Notice 701/15/95, para 5). See the Annex to Leaflet 701/40 for a list of goods liable at zero rate (unless put up for sale for a non-feeding purpose) and standard rate.

The preparation and certification of meat as 'kosher' is zero-rated (*The London Board for Shechita, [1974] VATTR 24 (52)*).

29 Fuel and Power

Cross-reference. See 25.3 EXPORTS for stores for use in ships, aircraft and hovercraft; 32.21 HEALTH AND WATER UTILITIES for supplies of hot water and steam; 64.46 SUPPLY for the time of supply rules.

De Voil Indirect Tax Service. See V1.126.

29.1 INTRODUCTION AND RATES OF VAT

The supply of any form of power, heat, refrigeration or ventilation is a supply of goods (and not a supply of services). [*VATA 1994, 4 Sch 3*]. The rates of VAT on such supplies are as follows.

1.9.97 onwards	5% for 'qualifying use'
	17½% for all other supplies
1.4.94–31.8.97	8% for 'qualifying use'
	17½% for all other supplies
1.7.90–31.3.94	Zero–rated for 'qualifying use'
	17½% for all other supplies
Before 1.7.90	Zero–rated for all supplies

The lower rate applying from 1 April 1994 also applies to acquisitions from other EC countries and importations from outside the EC.

[*VATA 1994, s 2(1A)–(1C); FA 1995, s 21*].

29.2 QUALIFYING USE

'*Qualifying use*' means domestic use or use by a charity otherwise than in the course or furtherance of a business.

The following supplies are always supplies for domestic use.

(*a*) A supply of not more than one tonne of coal or coke held out for sale as domestic fuel.

(*b*) A supply of wood, peat or charcoal not intended for sale by the recipient.

(*c*) A supply to a person at any premises of '*piped gas*' (i.e. gas within 29.4 below, or petroleum gas in a gaseous state, provided through pipes) where the gas, together with any other piped gas provided to him at the premises by the same supplier, was not provided at a rate exceeding 150 therms a month or if the supplier charges for gas by reference to the number of kilowatt hours supplied, 4397 kilowatt hours a month. (This limit applies whether the bill is based on a meter reading or on an estimate.)

(*d*) A supply of petroleum gas in a liquid state where the gas is supplied in cylinders the net weight of each of which is less than 50 kilogrammes and either the number of cylinders supplied is 20 or fewer or the gas is not intended for sale by the recipient.

(*e*) A supply of petroleum gas in a liquid state otherwise than in cylinders, to a person at any premises at which he is not able to store more than two tonnes of such gas.

(*f*) A supply of not more than 2,300 litres of fuel oil, gas oil or kerosene.

(*g*) A supply of electricity to a person at any premises where the electricity, together with any other electricity provided to him at the premises by the same supplier, was not provided at a rate exceeding 1,000 kilowatt hours a month. (This limit applies whether the bill is based on a meter reading or on an estimate.)

A supply for the purposes of (*a*)–(*g*) above is the amount delivered. It must be supported by evidence such as a delivery note, the amount shown on an invoice or amounts shown on a separately itemised composite invoice. Where the supplier is claiming to have made a number of separate supplies each within the limit (rather than one supply exceeding the limit) this must be reflected in the contract with the customer or by the existence of separate delivery notes. (C & E Notice 701/19/95, para 4).

Supplies not within (*a*)–(*g*) above are supplies for domestic use if, and only if, the goods supplied are supplied for use in

(i) a building, or part of a building, which consists of a dwelling or a number of dwellings or which is used for a 'relevant residential purpose';

(ii) self-catering holiday accommodation (including any accommodation advertised or held out as such);

(iii) a caravan; or

(iv) a 'houseboat' i.e. a boat or other floating decked structure designed or adapted for use solely as a place of permanent habitation and not having means of, or capable of being readily adapted for, self-propulsion.

Use for a '*relevant residential purpose*' means use as a home or other institution providing residential accommodation either for children or with personal care for persons in need of such care by reason of old age, disablement, past or present dependence on alcohol or drugs or past or present mental disorder; a hospice; residential accommodation for students or school pupils or members of any of the armed forces; a monastery, nunnery or similar establishment; or an institution which is the sole or main residence of at least 90% of its residents. *Excluded* is use as a hospital, a prison or similar institution or an hotel or inn or similar establishment.

[*VATA 1994, A1 Sch 1(2), 2, 3; FA 1995, s 21*].

Buildings forming a set of premises with one of those under (i)–(iv) above (e.g. a garage with a house) are regarded as the same residential unit. This can also apply to a subsidiary building situated a short distance away (e.g. a garage in a block located away from the house). Corridors, lifts, hallways and stairways in a residential unit are also treated as part of the domestic premises. (C & E Notice 701/19/95, para 2).

Part qualifying use. Where a supply of fuel or power is partly for qualifying use and partly not, then provided at least 60% is supplied for qualifying use, the whole supply is to be treated as a supply for qualifying use. In any other case, an apportionment must be made. [*VATA 1994, A1 Sch 1(3); FA 1995, s 21*]. For supplies of fuel and power to managed licensed premises where part of the premises are set aside as private residential accommodation, C & E have agreed a 90:10 split between commercial and domestic use respectively with Grand Metropolitan Retailing. (C & E Manual V1-7, Chapter 5 section 4.7).

Certificates. If in doubt about the liability of the supply under (i)–(iv) above, the supplier should get a certificate from the customer declaring what percentage of the fuel or power supplied for use on those premises is for qualifying use. A certificate is not required if the supply falls within (*a*)–(*g*) above. There is no official form of certificate but C & E have issued the following example and any other form must contain the same information.

'Certificate to supplier in respect of premises qualifying for lower rate supplies of fuel and power

1. Address of qualifying premises.

2. Name of business or organisation (if applicable) and VAT registration number if registered.

3. Percentage used for qualifying use.

4. Full name of signatory and (where appropriate) status held.

I certify that the information given above is correct and complete. I undertake to inform [name of supplier] if there is any significant change in the circumstances. I understand that any incorrect statement may make me liable to a financial penalty under Value Added Tax Act 1994, as amended.'

Signed   Dated

If any supply is incorrectly charged at the lower rate, the supplier may have to pay any VAT undercharged unless he holds a valid certificate *and* has good reason to believe that the fuel or power supplied to the customer is for qualifying use. It is the supplier's responsibility to take reasonable steps to satisfy himself that the customer is entitled to zero-rating and the declaration is correct. Where, however, despite taking all reasonable steps, the supplier fails to identify the inaccuracy and in good faith makes the supplies concerned at the zero rate, C & E will not seek to recover the VAT due from the supplier. (C & E Notice 48, ESC 2.11).

(C & E Notice 701/19/95, para 3, Annex D).

29.3   **SOLID FUELS**

Supplies of coal, coke and other solid substances are taxable at the lower rate provided they are held out for sale solely as fuel and are supplied for qualifying use (see 29.2 above). Included are combustible materials put up for sale for kindling fires but not matches. [*VATA 1994, A1 Sch 1, 4; FA 1995, s 21*]. All other supplies of solid fuels are standard-rated.

To be taxable at the lower rate, the fuel must be offered in a form and at a price that is compatible with it being sold as fuel.

Lower-rated supplies. Provided the conditions for qualifying use are met, the lower rate can be applied to the following solid fuels.

*   Coal (including anthracite and lignite)
*   Coal dust
*   Coal briquettes
*   Coke (e.g. Coalite, Thermabrite, Coalite Nuts, Beacon Beans, Sunbrite small nuts, Blazeglow)
*   Pulverised coal
*   Smokeless fuel
*   Wood logs
*   Other firewood (including offcuts, chips, shavings, scrap or damaged wood and compresses or agglutinated sawdust)
*   Barbecue fuels
*   Briquettes of straw and recycled waste or other combustible materials
*   Charcoal

29.4 Fuel and Power

- Firelighters
- Peat blocks, sods or briquettes
- Solid methaldehyde (solid meths)

Standard-rated supplies. The following items are always standard-rated.

- Any product not consumed in the lighting process (e.g. pumice blocks, pottery, etc. soaked in paraffin, gas pokers, electric hot-air igniters)
- Artists' charcoal
- Binding agents used to convert coal dust or sawdust in blocks
- Coke for use in the manufacture of electrodes
- 'DIY' offcuts and remnants
- Filtration charcoal or coke
- Forestry thinnings for fencing or staking
- Laboratory charcoal blocks
- Peat for use in horticulture or as cattle litter
- Sawdust, chips or shavings for pet litter
- Standing trees
- Wood for pulping

(C & E Notice 701/19/95, para 5).

Barbecue food flavour enhancers (e.g. hickory chips) which are absorbed into the food by burning are not fuel (or food for human consumption) and are standard-rated. (VAT Notes 1992 No 1).

29.4   GASES

Coal gas, water gas, producer gas and similar gases and petroleum gases, and other gaseous hydrocarbons, whether in a gaseous or liquid state, are taxable at the lower rate provided they are supplied for qualifying use (see 29.2 above). Excluded is any road fuel gas (within the meaning of the *Hydrocarbon Oil Duties Act 1979*) on which excise duty has been or is chargeable. [*VATA 1994, A1 Sch 1, 4; FA 1995, s 21*].

Lower-rated supplies. Provided the conditions for qualifying use are met, the lower rate can be applied to liquefied petroleum gas (e.g. propane or butane), acetylene, butylene, methylene, methane, natural gas and propylene. Minor impurities in a hydrocarbon gas can be ignored but otherwise any such gas that does not consist entirely of carbon and hydrogen is standard-rated.

Standard-rated supplies. Supplies of all other gases (e.g. carbon dioxide, hydrogen, oxygen, ammonia, chloride, nitrogen and refrigeration and aerosol gases) are standard-rated although certain gases for medical care (e.g. anaesthetics and oxygen) may be zero-rated under *VATA 1994, 8 Sch Group 12* or exempt under *VATA 1994, 9 Sch Group 7.*

(C & E Notice 701/19/95, para 6).

Gas sold in cylinders and similar containers

Disposable cartridges. When gas is supplied in disposable cartridges at an inclusive price covering both gas and cartridge, the supply is standard-rated throughout the supply chain until the point of final sale. A supply of disposable cartridges at the point of final sale is taxable at the lower rate.

Charged refillable cylinders. On the first sale of a refillable cylinder containing gas taxable at the lower rate, the price must be apportioned and VAT accounted for on the standard-rated cylinder which becomes the property of the buyer. (The price of the cylinder should be taken as the difference between the VAT-exclusive price of the filled cylinder and the charge for refilling a customer's own cylinder.)

When a filled container is exchanged for an empty one of the same size owned by the customer, the refill charge is treated as being wholly for the supply of gas and any nominal charge for inspection and maintenance can be ignored.

Rented cylinders. On the first supply of gas in a rented cylinder, VAT must be accounted for at the standard rate on the hire charge. When an empty cylinder is exchanged for a full one of the same size, any refill charge, including any nominal charge for inspection or maintenance, can be taxed at the lower rate (subject to qualifying use of the gas). Any charge made for a lost or damaged cylinder (such as the loss of a deposit) is outside the scope of VAT. But if a separate charge is made for the retention of a cylinder this is standard-rated.

Bulk storage tanks installed on customers' premises normally remain the property of the supplier. Charges for gas consumed are at the lower rate (subject to qualifying use) but any charge specifically for repair, maintenance etc. of equipment is standard-rated.

(C & E Notice 701/19/95, para 7). See *Calor Gas Ltd, [1973] VATTR 205 (47)*.

Gases used as road fuel. Supplies of gases for use as road fuel are standard-rated. VAT is due on the total value including the excise duty chargeable. (C & E Notice 701/19/95, para 6).

See also 29.7 below.

29.5   **OILS**

'Fuel oil', 'gas oil' and 'kerosene' are taxable at the lower rate provided they are supplied for qualifying use (see 29.2 above). Excluded is hydrocarbon oil on which a duty of excise has been or is to be charged without relief from, or rebate of, such duty by virtue of the provisions of the *Hydrocarbon Oil Duties Act 1979*. All other supplies of oil are standard-rated.

'*Fuel oil*' means heavy oil containing in solution an amount of asphaltenes of not less than 0.5 per cent or which contains less than 0.5 per cent but not less than 0.1 per cent of asphaltenes and has a closed flash point not exceeding 150C.

'*Gas oil*' means 'heavy oil' of which not more than 50 per cent by volume distils at a temperature not exceeding 240C and of which more than 50 per cent by volume distils at a temperature not exceeding 340C.

'*Kerosene*' means heavy oil of which more than 50 per cent by volume distils at a temperature not exceeding 240C.

'*Heavy oil*' has the same meaning as in the *Hydrocarbon Oil Duties Act 1979*.

Fuel oil, gas oil and kerosene chargeable with excise duty at a full (unrebated) rate, together with other heavy hydrocarbon oils, light hydrocarbon oils, lubricating oils and lubricants, are standard-rated.

[VATA 1994, A1 Sch 1, 4; FA 1995, s 21].

371

The effect of the above is that fuel oil, gas oil or kerosene (which includes paraffin) within the above definitions are taxed at the lower rate provided they are supplied for qualifying use, are not supplied as road fuel and are either chargeable with excise duty at a rebated rate or are relieved from excise duty.

Standard-rated supplies include any heavy oil for use as road fuel; aviation spirit; avgas; creosote; crude oil; derv; kerosene, paint thinners or white spirit unless meeting the specification for lower rate oils; liquid lighter fuel; recycled oil; waste oil; bitumen; black varnish; coal tar; lubricating oils and gases; methylated spirit; other articles which contain hydrocarbon oil but are not themselves wholly hydrocarbon oil; petrol substitutes; and petrol and other light oils (e.g. benzene, toluene and naphtha). (C & E Notice 701/19/95, para 9).

Marine fuel. Vessels may receive as stores fuel oil, kerosene or marked gas oil (but not petrol, unmarked gas oil, e.g. derv, or lubricating oil) free of VAT if they are entitled, for the voyage in question, to use

- heavy oil free of excise duty under the terms of Notice 263 (Voyages in home waters – duty relief for heavy oil); or

- hydrocarbon oil free of excise duty under the terms of Notice 248 (Hydrocarbon oil used on fishing boats: repayment of excise duty).

(C & E Notice 48, ESC 4.2).

29.6   **ELECTRICITY, HEAT AND AIR CONDITIONING**

Supplies of electricity, heat and air conditioning are taxable at the lower rate provided they are supplied for qualifying use (see 29.2 above). [*VATA 1994, A1 Sch 1; FA 1995, s 21*]. All other supplies of electricity, etc. are standard-rated.

See also 29.7 below.

Where electricity is supplied through the use of a mobile generator, the liability of the supply depends upon whether the supplier is supplying the electricity or hiring out the machine.

- If the supplier operates the equipment and charges for power supplied for a qualifying use, the total charge is at the lower rate.

- If the supplier charges for the hire of the generator to the customer, the supply is standard-rated.

(C & E Notice 701/19/95, para 16).

Batteries. Supplies of batteries on hire, recharging of batteries or exchanging charged batteries for discharged ones are standard-rated. (C & E Notice 701/19/95, para 17).

Heating contracts. If a contractor agrees to provide both fuel and staff required to operate and maintain the customer's heating system, the supply is taxable at the lower rate (subject to qualifying use of the heat). But repairs and maintenance etc. alone can only be so taxable where they are covered by an overall contract for the supply of heat and are directly related to and essential for maintaining the supply. (C & E Notice 701/19/95, para 18).

Refrigeration. Supplies of refrigeration (including quick freezing) for a qualifying use are taxable at the lower rate. Any charge for a separate supply of weighing, sorting or similar handling services is normally standard-rated but where a single overall charge is made for refrigeration which includes such handling, the whole charge is at the lower rate (subject to qualifying use). Cold storage is not automatically a supply of refrigeration. It may constitute a licence to occupy land in which case the supply is exempt (subject to the option to tax). See 42.2 LAND AND BUILDINGS. Where storage is supplied with no specific right over land, the supply is normally standard-rated. Certain storage and handling services relating to goods carried in ships and aircraft and imports and exports are zero-rated (see 68.9 TRANSPORT AND FREIGHT). (C & E Notice 701/19/95, para 19).

29.7   **CHARGES MADE BY FUEL AND POWER SUPPLIERS**

Lower rate supplies. Certain charges made to customers by a fuel and power supplier for the supply of fuel or power for a qualifying use (see 29.2 above) are taxable at the lower rate.

To qualify for charge at the lower rate, the supply must be made by a person who supplies and invoices the fuel or power to the consumer, inseparable from a supply of fuel or power to that consumer, and supplied and charged to that consumer. Examples of lower rate supplies include the following.

- Standing charges

- Rental charges for meters (including secondary meters used by landlords)

- Disconnection and re-connection of the supply and special meter readings at the instigation of the supplier

- Installation of a check meter

- Installation tests and re-tests where required by the supplier to protect their equipment

- Removal of damaged coins, etc. from meters

- Repair, maintenance or replacement of equipment and gas pipes or electric cables belonging to the supplier up to and including the consumer's meter

- Replacing a credit meter with a pre-payment meter under the supplier's code of practice, or replacing or resiting by a supplier of his meter at his own instigation

- Maximum demand and minimum guarantee charges

- Installation or replacement of lines and switchgear belonging to the electricity supplier

- Replacement of main fuses and provisions of earthing terminals

- Installation by a supplier of liquefied petroleum gas of a bulk gas tank regarded as essential to the supply of liquefied petroleum gas

Standard-rated supplies. The following supplies are always standard-rated.

- Repairs, maintenance and replacement of pipes not belonging to the fuel or power supplier

- Servicing contracts

- Sale of meters to industrial and commercial consumers for their own use

- Altering coin mechanisms of secondary meters

- Services in connection with tests carried out, for example, at the request of estate agents or prospective purchasers of premises

- Replacement of meters not under the supplier's code of practice and resiting meters at the request of the consumer

- Diverting mains, etc. to meet local authority requirements
- Raising or lowering an overhead power line in connection with the movement of abnormal loads
- Supply, repair and maintenance of public lighting circuits to local authorities
- Temporary floodlighting, emergency or decorative lighting
- Charges for playing games such as squash, tennis, snooker collected by means of coin-operated meters

Outside the scope. The following charges are outside the scope of VAT.

- Replacement by the gas or electricity supplier of dangerous, obsolete or inefficient appliances or parts, after the meter, under statutory contractual obligation
- Charges by a gas or electricity supplier for repairs to its property following damage

Zero-rating. Certain supplies of civil engineering services in the course of the construction of qualifying buildings or an approved alteration to a protected building may be zero-rated under *VATA 1994, 8 Sch Group 5 or 6*. See 42.31 to 42.34 LAND AND BUILDINGS. This would include civil engineering services necessary for the first time connection of fuel or power to the building. In addition, by concession, customer contribution to a first time connection to the gas or electricity mains supply which would have been zero-rated before 1 April 1994 may continue to be zero-rated after that date provided it is the connection to the mains of

- a building, or part of a building, which consists of a dwelling or number of dwellings;
- a building, or part of a building, used solely for a relevant residential purpose (see 42.1 LAND AND BUILDINGS);
- a residential caravan (i.e. a caravan on a site in respect of which there is no covenant, statutory planning consent or similar permission precluding occupation throughout the year);
- a houseboat; or
- a building, or part of a building, used by a charity for its non-business activities

and provided that the person receiving the supply does not do so for the purposes of any business carried on by him. (C & E Notice 48, ESC 2.18).

Part-qualifying use. Where charges are made in connection with fuel or power with part qualifying use, the liability of the charges follows that of the fuel or power (see 29.2 above). However, where the supply of fuel or power is taxed at the lower rate because of domestic use within 29.2(*a*)–(*g*) above, any charges which *specifically* relate to that supply (e.g. the standing charge) are similarly taxed.

Supplies by persons who are not the fuel or power suppliers cannot be taxed at the lower rate whether the fuel or power supplier or consumer is invoiced. Where, however, the supplies are connected with the first-time installation of the fuel and power into a qualifying building, the supply may be zero-rated as above.

(C & E Notice 701/19/95, Annex E).

29.8   **SUPPLIES OF FUEL AND POWER TO AND BY LANDLORDS, ETC.**

Supplies to a landlord, managing agent, residents association or caravan park owner are taxable at the lower rate provided the fuel or power is used for qualifying purposes. (C & E Notice 701/19/95, para 12). All other supplies of fuel and power to landlords, etc. are standard-rated.

Supplies by a landlord. Where a tenant of rented accommodation has a *coin-operated* gas or electricity meter, money placed in the meter is the consideration for a supply taxable at the lower rate when made for a qualifying use. This applies whether the supply is at cost or a mark-up.

If a *secondary credit meter* is used, the charges for gas or electricity supplied by the landlord are taxable at the lower rate when made for a qualifying use. This also applies if the quantity of gas or electricity supplied to each tenant for a qualifying use can be identified.

For unmetered supplies, C & E's policy is that the supply of heat, etc. forms an integral part of the main supply which is usually one of accommodation. For domestic tenants, this supply is

• a non-business supply and outside the scope of VAT if made by a local authority; and

• normally exempt if made by other landlords.

Where a tenant has the option of taking any services as additional services for an identifiable consideration, these form a separate single supply which takes its own VAT liability. See, however, *Suffolk Heritage Housing Association Ltd (13713)* where the tribunal held that the association's long-standing practice of recovering heating costs as a separate charge from the rent should be treated as a separate supply for VAT purposes. C & E have appealed against this decision to the High Court.

(C & E Notice 701/19/95, para 13; C & E Business Brief 2/96, 9 February 1996).

29.9   FACILITIES REQUIRING FUEL AND POWER

The use of washing machines, hot showers and all other facilities (including those for playing sport) which depend on temporary power or light and which are charged for by meter are *not* supplies of fuel and power. They are supplies of the particular facility concerned and liable to VAT at the appropriate rate. (C & E Notice 701/19/95, para 15). See *Mander Laundries Ltd, [1973] VATTR 136 (31)* and *St Annes-on-Sea Lawn Tennis Club Ltd, (1977) VATTR 229 (434)*.

See also *Showtry Ltd (10028)* where the supply of fuel for use in hired agricultural machinery was held to be part of a composite standard-rated supply under the hire contract.

29.10   FUEL AND POWER SUPPLIED TO CHARITABLE SCHOOLS

Fuel and power supplied for use by a charity otherwise than in the course or furtherance of a business is taxable at the lower rate. See 29.2 above. Schools which are treated as charities and which do not charge fees are not in business and therefore any supply of fuel or power to them is at the lower rate. These include voluntary aided schools, grant-maintained schools, schools which have opted out of the local authority control, and city technology colleges.

Independent schools and other schools which are charities but which charge fees to their pupils are in business for VAT purposes and supplies of fuel and power to them are generally standard-rated. The exception is that the lower rate applies to supplies of fuel and power for any separate residential accommodation for students or school pupils.

(C & E Notice 701/19/95, para 21).

30   Gold and Precious Metals

Cross-reference. See 65 TERMINAL MARKETS for zero-rating of certain transactions in gold on the London Gold Market.

De Voil Indirect Tax Service. See V4.277.

30.1   GOLD

Zero-rating. Zero-rating applies to the supply of gold (including gold coins) held in the UK by

- a Central Bank to either another Central Bank or a member of the London Gold Market; and

- a member of the London Gold Market to a Central Bank.

Included is the granting of a right to acquire gold and the supply of a part interest in gold. [*VATA 1994, 8 Sch Group 10*].

Importations. VAT is not payable on the importation of gold (including gold coin) from outside the EC by a Central Bank. [*SI 1992/3124*]. Importation of gold by other persons is chargeable to VAT at the standard rate. But see 71.3 WORKS OF ART ETC. for relief from VAT on the importation of gold coins over 100 years old under the special scheme for antiques, etc.

Acquisitions. Where gold is supplied to a Central Bank by a supplier in another EC country and the transaction involves the removal of the gold from that or some other EC country to the UK, the taking possession of the gold by the Central Bank concerned is not treated as an acquisition of goods from another EC country. [*SI 1992/3132*]. Consequently, VAT does not become chargeable on the receipt of such gold by the Central Bank concerned. Acquisitions of gold by other persons are subject to the normal rules. See 23.3 EUROPEAN COMMUNITY: SINGLE MARKET.

Exports and removals. The supply of gold which is physically exported by the supplier to a place outside the EC is zero-rated under the normal rules for exports.

Similarly the supply of gold which is physically removed from the UK and acquired by a taxable person in another EC country is zero-rated provided certain conditions are met. See 23.11 EUROPEAN COMMUNITY: SINGLE MARKET.

For the liability of sales to overseas customers where the gold is not physically removed from the UK, see 30.2 below.

30.2   Liability of particular transactions in gold

A supply of gold which is not zero-rated under 30.1 above and is not eligible for relief under the provisions relating to TERMINAL MARKETS (65) (e.g. gold coins supplied by members of the London Gold Market to non-members and all supplies by other traders) will generally fall into one of the following categories.

(*a*)   '**Allocated gold**'. The supply of allocated gold held

(i)   outside the UK is outside the scope of UK VAT; and

(ii)   in the UK is standard-rated even if the supplier is an overseas trader (unless zero-rated because the goods are physically exported under the normal rules for the export of goods).

'*Allocated gold*' is gold or gold coins set apart and designated as belonging to or reserved for specific persons or purposes. If gold etc. is delivered, it is of necessity allocated.

(*b*) **'Unallocated gold' supplied by UK traders.** The supply is

   (i) standard-rated if made to a trader or person who belongs in the UK;

   (ii) outside the scope of UK VAT (but with input tax credit) if made to a trader or person who belongs outside the EC;

   (iii) outside the scope of UK VAT (but with input tax credit) if made for the purposes of his business to a trader who belongs in another EC country; and

   (iv) standard-rated if made to a person in another EC country not fulfilling the conditions in (iii).

This is because, under (ii) and (iii) above, the place of supply of services is treated as made where the recipient belongs under *SI 1992/3121, Art 16* but under (i) and (iv) is made where the supplier belongs under the general rule for place of supply of services.

(*c*) **Unallocated gold—supplies received from traders who belong overseas.** Such a supply to a person who belongs in the UK is

   (i) standard-rated as the importation or acquisition of a financial service if received by a taxable person (see 39.4(*a*) INTERNATIONAL SERVICES and 64.27(*e*) SUPPLY); and

   (ii) outside the scope of UK VAT if received by a private or non-taxable person.

'*Unallocated gold*' is gold or gold coins forming an unidentifiable part of a large stock held by a supplier. The sale of unallocated gold gives the buyer the right to call for delivery, but not ownership of a specific parcel of gold.

See 21.2 EUROPEAN COMMUNITY: GENERAL for the VAT territory of the EC.

(C & E Leaflet 701/21/93, paras 4, 10).

30.3 Gold coins

Supplies of gold coins, whether legal tender or not, are taxable at the standard rate unless

(*a*) eligible for relief under 30.1 above; or

(*b*) eligible for relief under the provisions relating to TERMINAL MARKETS (65); or

(*c*) outside the scope of VAT under 30.2 above.

Where gold coins are over 100 years old or collectors' pieces they may be dealt with under the special scheme for antiques etc. (see 61.3 SECOND-HAND GOODS).

(C & E Leaflet 701/21/93, para 7).

30.4 Accounting and payment system for gold

Transactions between registered traders. In relation to 'supplies of gold', where

(*a*) the seller and buyer are both registered for VAT or liable to be registered as a consequence of the transaction (see below),

(*b*) the supply by the seller is by way of business, and

(*c*) the buyer is making the purchase in connection with any business carried on by him,

the buyer must account for and pay the output tax on the supply on the seller's behalf and his obligations to do so can be enforced as if he were the supplier.

In determining liability for registration under (*a*) above for the purposes of *VATA 1994, 1 Sch*, a standard-rated supply of gold (but not a zero-rated supply) is treated as a taxable supply by the buyer in the course or furtherance of his business (as well as a taxable supply by the seller). The supply by the buyer cannot be disregarded on the grounds that it is a supply of capital assets for his business.

The time of supply of all goods covered by the scheme is the date of delivery of the goods or when they are made available for removal by the buyer.

'*Supplies of gold*' within the scheme are as follows.

(i) Supplies of fine gold of a purity of 995 parts per thousand or greater. *Excluded* are supplies of dental gold, gold slugs and gold targets.

(ii) Supplies of gold grain of any purity (before 29 November 1995, the scheme only applied to supplies of fine gold grain).

(iii) Supplies of gold coins of any purity.

(iv) Supplies of goods containing gold where the price paid (apart from the VAT) does not exceed, or exceeds by only a negligible amount, the 'open market value' of the gold contained in the goods. This includes supplies of scrap (including live scrap) and sweepings. *Excluded* are supplies of part manufactured or finished jewellery and gold compounds and semi-manufactured carated products (except gold grain).

(v) Any supply of services consisting of the application to another person's goods of a treatment or process which produces goods, a supply of which would fall within (i) above.

The '*open market value*' of the gold is, in effect, the 'fix price' of the gold. This is the price set twice a day in London by members of the London Bullion Market Association.

The seller must issue a VAT invoice to the buyer showing all the information normally required on a VAT invoice (see 40.4 INVOICES) including the date of supply and a description sufficient to identify the goods. This description must include the weight and purity of the gold; the number of individual items where possible; and (apart from gold coins) the fix price of the gold on the day of delivery. The invoice must be endorsed with words such as

'£. . . output tax on this supply of gold to be accounted for to Customs and Excise by the buyer.'

The buyer pays the seller only for the VAT-exclusive price of the gold. He must declare the VAT due to C & E on his VAT return by entering VAT due on his purchases in Box 1. On the same return he may deduct as input tax the amount of the VAT shown on the seller's invoice (subject to the usual rules).

Antique items containing gold may fall outside the scheme (because the value of the goods substantially exceeds the open market value of the gold in them or because VAT due on the supply of the item may be treated under the second-hand scheme). However, antique gold coins cannot be sold under the second-hand scheme if they were purchased under the special accounting and payment scheme.

[*VATA 1994, s 55; FA 1996, ss 29(3)(5), 32*]. (C & E Leaflet 701/21/93, paras 11–18).

Other transactions. VAT on non-business supplies of gold is charged and collected by the seller in the normal way.

See TERMINAL MARKETS (65) for the arrangements for zero-rated supplies on the London Gold Market.

De Voil Indirect Tax Service. See V5.143.

30.5   **Manufactured gold jewellery**

For a consideration of the basis of the valuation of a supply for VAT purposes where gold jewellery is made for customers wholly or partly by refashioning gold supplied by the customer, see *C & E Commrs v Sai Jewellers QB, [1996] STC 269.*

30.6   **OTHER PRECIOUS METALS**

The provisions in 30.2(*b*) and (*c*) above relating to supplies of unallocated gold also apply to supplies of unallocated silver, platinum, palladium, rhodium, ruthenium, osmium and iridium. (C & E Business Brief 20/94, 18 November 1994).

31 Groups of Companies

Cross-references. See 7.3 BAD DEBT RELIEF; 23.18 EUROPEAN COMMUNITY: SINGLE MARKET for distance selling from the UK by VAT groups; 42.20 LAND AND BUILDINGS for election to waive exemption.

31.1 VAT GROUP TREATMENT

EC legislation allows countries to treat independent legal persons as a single taxable person provided such legal persons are closely bound to one another by financial, economic and organisational links and are established within the confines of the particular country. [*EC 6th Directive, Art 4(4)*].

UK legislation applicable to the registration of groups of companies is considered in 31.2 to 31.4 below. It should be noted that the term 'group' in this context is used for VAT purposes only.

VAT group registration reduces the burden on businesses by allowing two or more associated companies to account for VAT as a single taxable person. It may be administratively convenient where a group accounting function is centralised. Also, because supplies between group members are normally disregarded for VAT purposes, VAT invoices need not be issued for such supplies. On the other hand, because a single VAT return is submitted for the whole group, there may be practical problems in gathering together the information necessary to complete the return on time.

31.2 Eligibility for group treatment

Two or more 'bodies corporate' are eligible to be treated as members of a group if

(*a*) one of them controls each of the others, or

(*b*) one person (whether a body corporate or an individual) controls all of them, or

(*c*) two or more individuals carrying on a business in partnership control all of them

and each of the bodies is 'resident in the UK' or has an 'established place of business' in the UK. [*VATA 1994, s 43(3)*].

A '*body corporate*' is a form of corporation where a number of persons are united and consolidated together so as to be considered as one person in law. There are several ways in which a body might be incorporated. *Companies Act 1985* provides five ways in which a body may be incorporated (public limited companies limited by shares or by guarantee with a share capital; private companies limited by shares; private companies limited by guarantee with a share capital; private companies limited by guarantee; and unlimited companies). In addition bodies may also be incorporated by Act of Parliament or by Royal Charter. (C & E Notice 700/2/97, para 1.11).

A corporate body registered for VAT in the names of its divisions (see 59.30 REGISTRATION) cannot have one of its divisions included in a VAT group registration. Similarly, a company which is a member of a VAT group will not be allowed to register one of its divisions separately outside the group while it remains in the group. (C & E Notice 700/2/97, para 1.10).

'*Resident in the UK*' is not defined, but UK for this purpose will include the Isle of Man. In order for a company to be considered resident some part of the actual control and management of the company must be carried out in the UK by some part of its superior and directing authority. This would be satisfied if at least one director with full voting rights is UK resident and regularly attends board meetings. (C & E Notice 700/2/97, para 1.12).

A company has an *'established place of business'* in the UK if it has a specific or identifiable place at which it carries on business and there is some visible sign or physical indication that the company has a connection with the particular premises. The place of business must be intended to be permanent. A company is not generally considered to have an established place of business in the UK merely because it has a 'brass plate' residence there or it carries on business through a UK agent or it has a UK subsidiary or one or more of the directors regularly stays in a specific hotel in the UK. (C & E Notice 700/2/97, para 1.12).

Control of a company by another company exists if it is 'empowered by statute' to control the company's activities or if it is the company's 'holding company' within the meaning of the *Companies Act 1985*. An individual, or individuals, is taken to control a company, if he or they, were he or they a company, would be the company's holding company as above. [*VATA 1994, s 43(8)*].

'Empowered by statute' means empowered by a provision contained in an Act of Parliament (*British Airways Board: British Airways Pension Fund Trustees Ltd (846)*).

A company is a *'subsidiary'* of another company, its *'holding company'*, if

(i) that other company holds a majority of the voting rights in it; or

(ii) that other company is a member of it and has the right to appoint or remove a majority of its board of directors; or

(iii) that other company is a member of it and controls alone, pursuant to an agreement with other shareholders or members, a majority of the voting rights in it; or

(iv) it is a subsidiary of a company which is itself a subsidiary of that other company. [*CA 1985, s 736; CA 1989, s 144*].

Until 31 December 1997, a subsidiary company which was part of a VAT group before 2 November 1990 (when the revised definition of 'subsidiary company' *CA 1985, s 736* took effect) and which did not satisfy the revised definition above was allowed to remain within the VAT group. (C & E Notice 48, ESC 2.13). The concession was withdrawn with effect from 1 January 1998. (C & E News Release 13, 26 November 1996).

C & E have no discretion to accept group registration where the above requirements are not met (*E Du Vergier & Co Ltd, [1973] VATTR 11 (4)*).

De Voil Indirect Tax Service. See V2.104.

31.3 **Application for group treatment**

An application to be treated as members of a group on behalf of two or more eligible companies is made to C & E who will so treat them from the beginning of a prescribed accounting period, one of the companies being treated as the 'representative member' (see 31.4 below). Applications in respect of the companies involved must be made by one of those companies or by the person controlling them.

Where group treatment is already in effect further application may be made, so that from the beginning of a prescribed accounting period

(*a*) a further eligible company may be included as a group member; or

(*b*) an existing group member is excluded from group treatment; or

(*c*) another group member is substituted for the existing representative member; or (*d*) the companies forming the group no longer continue to do so.

Any application regarding group treatment must be made not less than 90 days before the date from which it is to take effect 'or such later time as C & E may allow'.

C & E may refuse an application to form a group for VAT purposes, or an application under (*a*)–(*d*) above, if it appears necessary to do so for the protection of the revenue but they cannot refuse an application under (*b*) or (*d*) above if it appears to have been made because a company or companies have ceased to be eligible for group treatment through lack of control. Applications for group treatment may be refused where

- the proposed group members have poor compliance records which might pose a threat to C & E's ability to collect VAT;

- C & E have reason to believe that the applicants intend to use the grouping facilities to operate a VAT avoidance scheme; or

- group treatment would create a distortion in the VAT liability of the group's supplies (e.g. where exempt supplies would become taxable with consequent increase in input tax recovery or where entitlement to recover previously irrecoverable input tax is increased)

but these are only broad examples and should not be taken as an exhaustive list. (C & E Business Brief 31/97, 22 December 1997).

An appeal may be made against a refusal of an application. See 5.3(*k*) APPEALS.

Where a company is treated as a group member on the basis of control of it by another person and it appears to C & E that the company has ceased to be so controlled, they are obliged, by notice to that other person, to terminate the group treatment from such date as may be specified in the notice.

[*VATA 1994, s 43(4)–(7); FA 1995, s 25*].

The words '*or at such later time as C & E may allow*' permit retrospective group registration but only within the discretion of C & E and not a tribunal (*C & E Commrs v Save and Prosper Group Ltd QB 1978, [1979] STC 205*). C & E will generally only allow retrospective applications for group treatment in circumstances arising from the actions of, or lack of actions by, a C & E officer. However, with effect from 26 November 1996, companies applying to leave one group and join another are allowed to backdate their move by up to 30 days before the date of application or, if later, to the beginning of the current prescribed accounting period of the company or the group being joined (whichever is the later). (C & E Notice 700/2/97, para 1.16; C & E News Release 13, 26 November 1996).

Applications for group treatment are made in practice by the proposed representative member applying on Forms VAT 50 and VAT 51 to the VAT office. At the same time Form VAT 1 must be completed by the representative member in respect of its own activities, not those of the group as a whole. Application is made similarly to include another company in the group (Forms VAT 50 and VAT 51), to change the representative member (Form VAT 56) or, by written notice, to exclude an existing member or to terminate the group treatment. Existing VAT registration numbers already held will be cancelled in respect of new members forming a group. The group itself will be allocated a registration number which will identify the group as a taxable person and this number will remain unchanged even if the membership is varied or the representative member changes. On the termination of the group treatment the group registration number is cancelled but any existing member still liable to be registered will be allocated a new number. (C & E Notice 700/2/97, paras 14, 15, 17).

De Voil Indirect Tax Service. See V2.104; V2.114.

31.4   Consequences of group treatment

Group treatment creates a single taxable person (*C & E Commrs v Kingfisher plc QB, [1994] STC 63*). One of the companies applying for group treatment is nominated as the representative member (see 31.3 above) and the registration is then made in the name of that member who is responsible for completing VAT returns and paying/reclaiming VAT on behalf of the group.

The following consequences then apply.

(*a*)   Any business carried on by a member of the group is treated as though carried on by the representative member.

(*b*)   Subject to the anti-avoidance provisions in 31.5 below and the provisions relating to groups supplies using an overseas member in 31.6 below, any supply of goods or services by a member of the group to another member of the group is disregarded for VAT purposes.

(*c*)   Any supply not disregarded under (*b*) above which is a supply of goods (including SELF-SUPPLY (62)) or services (including deemed supply) by or to a group member is treated as a supply by or to the representative member.

(*d*)   Any VAT paid or payable by a group member on the acquisition of goods from EC country or on the importation of goods from outside the EC is treated as paid or payable by the representative member and the goods are treated as having been acquired or imported by the representative member.

All members of the group are jointly and severally liable for any VAT due from the representative member. If the representative member is unable to meet a debt of the group, each member will be held liable for the amount of the debt. A former member is also liable for VAT due during its period of membership.

Assessments can be validly raised on the representative member where relating to earlier periods when it was not the representative member and even if it was not a member of the group at that time (*Thorn plc, [1998] VATDR 80 (15283)*). Also, under the anti-avoidance provisions in 31.5 below, current members of a VAT group may be held liable for assessments relating to periods when they were not members of the group. For liability of members when the representative member goes into liquidation, see 36.14 INSOLVENCY, and where a corporate pension trustee is a member, see 53.3 PENSION SCHEMES.

[*VATA 1994, s 43(1)(2); FA 1995, s 25*].

Only the representative member has *locus standi* to bring an appeal (*Davis Advertising Service Ltd, [1973] VATTR 16 (5)*).

It follows from the above that extreme care should be taken in initially planning the structure of a group and consequently the carrying out of the accounting necessary to put the group treatment into effect. Special regard must usually be made to prospective members who make a proportion of exempt supplies in order to ensure the group as a whole does not suffer the loss of input tax through the PARTIAL EXEMPTION (49) rules. As the group is a single taxable person, the partial exemption *de minimis* limit, the limit for voluntary disclosures of errors in past VAT returns and the VAT payment on account scheme apply to the whole group.

Special provisions also apply under the capital goods scheme when a VAT group is formed or disbanded or there is a change in membership. See CAPITAL GOODS (10).

(C & E Notice 700/2/97, paras 1.2, 1.3, 1.5, 1.7).

31.5 Groups of Companies

'Special status' companies. The VAT liability of certain supplies, acquisitions and importations is dependent on the status of the person by or to whom the supply, etc. is made (e.g. education, insurance and certain supplies involving charities). Following the decision in *C & E Commrs v Kingfisher plc* above that a VAT group is a single taxable person, it had been argued that where such a special status person was the representative member of a VAT group, its status was automatically passed on to the other members of the group. Although C & E did not accept this interpretation, for the avoidance of doubt in relation to a supply, acquisition or importation taking place after 26 November 1996 the representative member of a group is treated as if it had the status of the group member who, but for the provisions in (*c*) or (*d*) above, would have made or received the supply, etc. in question. This does not apply, however, to the extent that what is material for the purpose of the relevant supply, etc. is whether a person is a taxable person. [*VATA 1994, s 43(1AA)(1AB); FA 1997, s 40(1)(3)*].

De Voil Indirect Tax Service. See V2.114.

31.5 Anti-avoidance provisions

With effect from 29 April 1996, but in relation to events occurring after 28 November 1995, *FA 1996, s 31, 4 Sch* inserts a new *VATA 1994, 9A Sch* which enables C & E to direct that

- separately registered companies eligible to be treated as members of a VAT group are to be treated as grouped from a specified date;

- a company within a group is removed from that group from a specified date; or

- a supply within a VAT group initially treated as a disregarded supply is to be subjected to VAT.

The provisions are designed for use only against certain categories of avoidance scheme which rely on the existence of the group registration provisions in *VATA 1994, s 43*. Features common to such avoidance schemes are that input tax deduction is taken against standard-rated supplies, but output tax does not fall on the full value of those supplies because they are treated to some extent as being made between members of the same VAT group and so are disregarded for VAT. The simplest means of bringing the disregard into play is by moving a company into or out of a VAT group at a critical moment. But a similar result could be secured by entering into some other transaction, such as the transfer of assets or the assignment of an agreement to or from a group member.

The detailed provisions are outlined below. C & E have issued a Statement of Practice (SP) dated June 1996 setting out how they will seek to apply the provisions. Extracts are included in the text where appropriate.

Power to give directions. C & E may give a direction if certain conditions are met. [*VATA 1994, 9A Sch 1(1)*]. Taken together, the conditions require that a relevant event causes a situation where standard-rated supplies, which have given rise to an input tax credit by any person, are not taxed on their full value, so leading to a tax advantage. The conditions are as follows.

(*a*) A 'relevant event' has occurred, i.e. a company has either

   (i) joined or ceased to be a member of a group, or

   (ii) entered into any 'transaction'

after that date. [*VATA 1994, 9A Sch 1(2), 4(2)*].

The word '*transaction*' is capable of a very wide meaning but, in the context of this provision, the key to its interpretation is that a relevant event occurs when a taxpayer *enters into* a transaction. Generally, C & E will take this to mean when the taxpayer enters into a contract or other disposition, such as a gift. For example, C & E will regard entering into a lease or the assignment, variation or surrender of a lease as a transaction which might potentially bring a company within the provisions. The performance of obligations under the lease (e.g. carrying out repairs or paying rent) would not normally be caught unless, exceptionally, such obligation constituted the entering into of a separate contract. (SP, para 3.5).

(*b*) There has been (or will or may be) a taxable supply on which VAT has been (or will or may be) charged otherwise than by reference to its full value due to the supply in question being disregarded under 31.4(*b*) above. [*VATA 1994, 9A Sch 1(3)(a)(9)*]. Supplies which, although not disregarded under 31.4(*b*) above, are less than full value for other reasons are not covered. C & E could not, for example, compulsorily group the parties to a lease and leaseback agreement under arrangements that had nothing to do with the operation of an intra-group disregard. (SP, para 3.6).

(*c*) At least part of the supply in (*b*) above is not (or would not be) zero-rated. [*VATA 1994, 9A Sch 1(3)(b)*].

(*d*) The charging of VAT on the supply in (*b*) above otherwise than by reference to full value gives rise (or would give rise) to a tax advantage because a person has become entitled to

  (i) credit for input tax as attributable to that supply (or part of it); or

  (ii) a repayment of VAT under the provisions in 21.37 EUROPEAN COMMUNITY: GENERAL or 48.5 OVERSEAS TRADERS (refunds of VAT to persons in business abroad).

[*VATA 1994, 9A Sch 1(3)(c)(4)(5)*].

It is not essential that the right to credit or repayment should be that of the supplier of the undercharged supply. The legislation specifically provides that the condition is also fulfilled where the supplier acquires the goods and/or services VAT free under the provisions relating to the transfer of a business as a going concern, and the transferor (or some previous owner) of the business has been entitled to an input tax credit. [*VATA 1994, 9A Sch 1(6)(7)*].

(*e*) The requirements in (*b*)-(*d*) above would not be fulfilled apart from the occurrence of the relevant event.

(*f*) Where the relevant event is a transaction within (*a*)(ii) above, the supply on which VAT is undercharged must not be the only supply by reference to which the case falls within (*a*)-(*e*) above.

To pre-empt avoidance of the provisions, in determining whether the input tax credit is used to make an undercharged supply, separate rights to goods or services (including options or priorities in connection with goods or services), and the goods or services themselves are treated as a single supply. [*VATA 1994, 9A Sch 1(8)(10)*].

C & E must not give a direction if satisfied that the main purpose, or each of the main purposes, of the relevant event was a genuine commercial purpose unconnected with the consequences in (*b*)-(*d*) above. [*VATA 1994, 9A Sch 2*]. This recognises the fact that, in the vast majority of cases, businesses are moved into and out of groups for reasons which have no avoidance motive whatsoever. However, it is important to realise that where, in additional to acceptable commercial purpose, C & E also identify other main purposes indicating VAT avoidance, they will seek to use their powers to nullify that advantage. (SP, paras 3.11-3.13, Annexes 1-3).

31.5 Groups of Companies

Form of directions. A direction may take the following forms.

(i) That a supply of goods or services, in whole or part, from one company to another does not fall within 31.4(*b*) above (where it otherwise would).

(ii) That for such periods as may be described in the directions a company is not to be treated as a member of a group (where it otherwise would). To the extent that the direction applies to VAT periods after the direction is issued, *all* supplies between that company and other group members are treated as taxable supplies. For events prior to the issue of the direction, see under the heading *Assessments* below.

(iii) That for such periods as may be described in the directions, a company is to be treated as a member of a group (where it otherwise would not). Such a direction may also identify the company which is assumed to be the representative member of the group for those periods.

Subject to the time limits below, the periods under (ii) or (iii) above may comprise times before the giving of the direction or times afterwards or both.

Where a direction requires any assumptions to be made, *VATA 1994* has effect from the date of the direction in accordance with those assumptions. (For periods before the date of the direction, the assumptions are given effect by C & E raising an assessment for unpaid VAT, see below.)

The fact that C & E have accepted or refused an application for a company to join a group does not prejudice their powers to make a direction to the opposite effect.

[*VATA 1994, 9A Sch 3(1)-(6)(8)*].

Withdrawal of direction. C & E may withdraw a direction at any time by notice in writing to the person to whom it was given. [*VATA 1994, 9A Sch 3(7)*].

Time limits. A direction cannot be given more than six years after the later of

• the occurrence of the relevant event; and

• the time when the entitlement to input tax under (*d*)(i) or (*d*)(ii) above arose.

However, where a direction is appropriate, it can require assumptions to be made about transactions made before either of those times without any limit. [*VATA 1994, 9A Sch 4(1)(3)*].

C & E will not, however, seek application of any direction from a date earlier than that required to nullify the tax advantage derived from the relevant event. Usually, this will be the first day of the prescribed accounting period in which the scheme commences or the relevant event occurs (whichever is earlier). (SP, para 3.18).

Method of giving directions. A direction relating to a supply under (i) above may be given to the person who made the supply and a direction relating to a company under (ii) or (iii) above may be given to that company. In either case, the direction may also be given to the representative member of the group. Any direction must be in writing and must specify the relevant event by reference to which it is given. [*VATA 1994, 9A Sch 5*].

Assessments. Where a direction is given and there is an amount of unpaid VAT for which a 'relevant person' would have been liable based on the assumptions specified in the direction, C & E may, to the best of their judgment, assess the amount of unpaid VAT as VAT due from a relevant person and notify their assessment to that person. The assessment may be incorporated in the direction. See 6.1 ASSESSMENTS for interpretation of 'to the best of C & E's judgment'. Where, however, C & E are satisfied that the actual revenue loss is less than the unpaid VAT the amount assessed must not exceed the revenue loss (calculated to the best of their judgement). [*VATA 1994, 9A Sch 6(1)-(5)*].

'*Relevant person*' means the person to whom the direction is given, the representative member of the group to which that person was treated as being a member, or any company which, under the direction, is treated as being the representative member of such a group. [*VATA 1994, 9A Sch 6(11)*].

Calculation of VAT charge.

- Where a direction is made under (i) above, VAT will become payable according to its value (adjusted as appropriate to take account of any direction issued under *VATA 1994, 6 Sch 1* — supplies between connected persons, see 69.3 VALUATION). A credit will be allowed for that part of the VAT which would have been deductible according to the partial exemption method of the VAT group registration.

- Where a direction is made under (ii) above, in relation to events prior to the issue of the direction, only those transactions relevant to the tax advantage will be affected. Input tax that would have been deductible on the basis of the assumptions in the direction can be taken into account in appropriate cases. All other supplies made by the parties involved will be unaffected so there will be no need for any retrospective VAT accounting adjustment in their regard.

- Where a direction is made under (iii) above, the purpose of the direction will normally be to enable C & E to recoup any excess claim to input tax. In such cases, the amount of VAT to be charged will be the amount of input tax recovered less the amount which would otherwise have been recoverable in accordance with the partial exemption method of the appropriate VAT group registration. A credit will also be allowed in connection with any output tax charged between the parties which would not have been due according to the assumptions specified in the directive.

(SP, paras 3.18, 5.1-5.3).

The amount assessed and notified to a person is, subject to appeal, deemed to be an amount of VAT due and is recoverable, from that person or the representative member of the group, unless the assessment is subsequently withdrawn or reduced. To the extent that more than one person is liable for the same unpaid VAT under any assessment, they are each jointly and severally liable for the full amount. [*VATA 1994, 9A Sch 6(7)(8)*].

Time limit. An assessment under these provisions cannot be made more than one year after the date of the direction or in the case of any direction which has been withdrawn. [*VATA 1994, 9A Sch 6(6)*].

Supplementary assessments. Where it appears to C & E that the amount which ought to have been assessed exceeds the amount actually assessed, a supplementary assessment of the amount of the excess may be made and notified under the same provisions and within the same time limit as the original assessment. [*VATA 1994, 9A Sch 6(9)*].

Interest payable. The provisions of *VATA 1994, s 74* on interest (see 51.5 PAYMENT OF VAT) also apply to assessments under the above provisions, except that interest runs from the date on which the assessment is notified rather than the reckonable date. The period for interest is confined to the two years ending with the time when the assessment to interest is made. [*VATA 1994, 9A Sch 6(9)(10)*].

Appeals against directions by C & E. An appeal may be made against a direction by C & E under the above provisions. See 5.3(*wa*) APPEALS. The tribunal must allow the appeal if satisfied that

- the conditions for making the direction were not fulfilled; or

- the main purpose, or each of the main purposes, of the relevant event was a genuine commercial purpose unconnected with the consequences in (*b*) above.

31.6   Groups of Companies

[*VATA 1994, s 84(7A); FA 1996, s 31*].

Following correction of a tax advantage to the satisfaction of C & E, they will consider any subsequent application to join or leave a group subject to their normal powers of discretion. (SP, para 3.20).

Transitional provisions. Where a relevant event occurs after 28 November 1995 and before 29 April 1996, C & E will not use the powers under *VATA 1994, 9A Sch* if an assessment under *VATA 1994, s 43(1A)* (see below) could be raised to correct the mischief from an avoidance scheme. (SP, para 5.4).

Earlier provisions. Following the tribunal decision in *Thorn Materials Supply Ltd* and *Thorn Resources Ltd (12914)* (which decision was subsequently overturned by the Court of Appeal, see *[1996] STC 1490* and the House of Lords, see *[1998] STC 725*), the consequences in 31.4(*b*) above did not apply in relation to supplies made after 28 February 1995 (or before that date if both the relevant bodies were still group members on that date), unless both the member making the supply and the member supplied continued to be members of that group until

- in the case of a supply of goods, a time after the removal of the goods in pursuance of the supply (where the goods are not to be removed, a time after the goods are to be made available to the member supplied); or

- in the case of a supply of services, a time after the services have been performed.

These provisions ceased to have effect in relation to supplies on or after 29 April 1996 from which date the transactions are covered by the more general anti-avoidance provisions outlined above.

[*VATA 1994, s 43(1A); FA 1995, s 25; FA 1996, 4 Sch*].

De Voil Indirect Tax Service. See V2.105.

31.6   Group supplies using an overseas member

In relation to supplies made after 25 November 1996, a supply between a member of a VAT group ('*the supplier*') and another member of the group ('*the UK member*') is not disregarded under 31.4(*b*) above if the following conditions are satisfied.

(*a*)   If there were no group, the supply would be a supply of services falling within *VATA 1995, 5 Sch* to a person belonging in the UK.

(*b*)   Those services are not within any of the descriptions specified in *VATA 1994, 9 Sch* (exempt supplies).

(*c*)   The supplier has been supplied (whether or not by a person belonging in the UK) with any services falling within *VATA 1994, 5 Sch 1–8* (see 64.27 SUPPLY) which are not within any of the descriptions specified in *VATA 1994, 9 Sch* (exempt supplies). (The exclusion of exempt supplies applies by statute for supplies made after 19 March 1997 and by concession for supplies made from 26 November 1996 to 19 March 1997, see C & E Notice 48, ESC 2.2.)

(*d*)   The supplier belonged outside the UK when it was supplied with the services in (*c*) above.

(*e*)   Those services have been used by the supplier for making the onward supply to the UK member.

The provisions apply even if the bought-in supply only forms a cost component of the onward supply to the UK group member but generally C & E will treat bought-in supplies as *de minimis* if their value is less than 5% of the value of the onward supply. However, C & E will not apply this rule rigidly (e.g. where they suspect that supplies or values have been manipulated to meet the 5% test or where, despite the fact that the 5% test is not met, the charge would be insignificant). The extent to which VAT on the charge could be recovered under the group's partial exemption method, along with the amount of the charge in the context of the group's size, will also be considered when deciding whether a potential charge is *de minimis*. (C & E Business Brief 11/97, 9 May 1997).

Where the condition are met, the following consequences apply.

(1) The supply is treated as a taxable supply in the UK by the representative member to itself.

(2) Except as allowed by C & E, the deemed supply by the representative member cannot be taken into account when determining its allowable input tax.

(3) The deemed supply is treated as a supply between connected persons for the purposes of any direction by C & E as to open market value under *VATA 1994, 6 Sch 1* (see 69.3 VALUATION).

(4) Subject to (3) above, the deemed supply has the normal value rules for supplies subject to the reverse charge (see 39.4 INTERNATIONAL SERVICES), i.e. it is calculated on the value of the supply by the overseas member to the UK member. However, by concession, the value may be reduced to the value of the services *purchased* by the overseas group member where

(i) evidence of this valuation can be produced in the UK;

(ii) those services have not been undervalued; and

(iii) the concession is not used for tax avoidance purposes.

(C & E Notice 48, ESC 2.2).

Under (i) above, where a service is bought in by an overseas group member for the exclusive use of a UK group member, copies of invoices from the external supplier are acceptable evidence. Alternatively, businesses may be able to agree with their VAT office that different evidence is adequate (e.g. evidence that the overseas group member buys in services and applies a fixed mark-up would normally be satisfactory evidence that the value of the bought-in service was equal to the value of the onward supply less the mark-up). Where services are not bought in for exclusive use or mark-ups vary, a fair and reasonable value must be calculated. C & E have indicated that, in most cases, the evidence required to support the reduced value consists of a summary statement of the overseas member's costs; an outline of the basis on which the overseas member calculates its charge; and a record of the method for reducing the charge to an amount based on the bought-in supplies. (C & E Business Brief 11/97, 9 May 1997).

(5) The supply has the normal time of supply rules for supplies subject to the reverse charge (see 39.4 INTERNATIONAL SERVICES). However, by concession, as a transitional relief, where the UK group member paid for the services in question on or after 26 November 1996 but the services were performed to any extent before that date, the group may account for VAT only on that proportion of the services which were performed on or after 26 November 1996. The concession does not apply to telecommunications services and cannot be used for the purposes of tax avoidance. (C & E Notice 48, ESC 2.3).

Transfers of going concerns. Where a business or part of a business is transferred as a going concern and is treated as neither a supply of goods nor services under 8.10 BUSINESS (or would be so treated if made in the UK), if the transferor satisfied conditions (*c*) and (*d*) above before the transfer and the services in question are used by the transferee to make the supply within (*e*) above, the services are deemed to have been supplied to the transferee at a time when the transferee belonged outside the UK (so that the above conditions are deemed to have been met). The conditions are also deemed to be met in cases involving successive business transfers.

[*VATA 1994, s 43(2A)-(2E); FA 1997, s 41*].

Interim payments. Where interim payments are made in respect of supplies subject to these provisions, VAT must be accounted for on each payment. If the group cannot calculate the reduced value of the charge by the time it has to account for VAT, it should account for VAT from month to month on a best estimate, making an appropriate adjustment at the end of the year.

Misdeclaration penalties. Failure to comply with the provisions may incur a misdeclaration penalty, subject to normal rules. See 52.10 PENALTIES. However, C & E have indicated such a penalty will only be assessed before 1 January 1998 in exceptional circumstances.

(C & E Business Brief 11/97, 9 May 1997).

De Voil Indirect Tax Service. See V2.105.

31.7   **ACQUISITION OF A BUSINESS AS A GOING CONCERN BY A PARTLY EXEMPT VAT GROUP**

Where a business, or part of a business, carried on by a taxable person is transferred as a going concern to any member of a VAT group and the transfer of any 'chargeable assets' involved is treated as neither a supply of goods nor a supply of services (see 8.10 BUSINESS), then, subject to below, the chargeable assets are treated (at the time of the transfer) as being supplied to the representative member of the group for the purpose of its business and supplied by that member in the course or furtherance of its business. The supply is at the 'open market value' of the chargeable assets.

Assets are '*chargeable assets*' if their supply in the UK by a taxable person in the course or furtherance of his business would be a taxable supply (and not a zero-rated supply).

'*Open market value*' is the price that would be paid on a sale (on which no VAT was payable) between a buyer and seller who are not in such a relationship as to affect the price.

The above provisions do not apply if

(*a*)   the representative member is entitled to credit for the whole of the input tax on supplies to it and acquisitions and importations by it during the prescribed accounting period in which the assets are transferred *and* any longer accounting period over which input tax is attributed under the partial exemption provisions;

(*b*)   C & E are satisfied that the assets were assets of the taxable person transferring them more than three years before the day on which they are transferred; or

(*c*)   the chargeable assets consist of certain computers, computer equipment, land or buildings covered by the capital goods scheme (see 10.2 CAPITAL GOODS).

A supply treated as made by the representative member under these provisions is not taken into account when determining the allowance of input tax for the group under the partial exemption provisions.

C & E may reduce the VAT chargeable under these provisions if they are satisfied that the person transferring the chargeable assets has not received credit for the full amount of input tax arising on the supply to him, or acquisition or importation by him, of the chargeable assets.

[*VATA 1994, s 44*].

VAT is not due on goodwill (e.g. unidentified goodwill, use of a trademark or trading name, the sole right to trade in a particular area, etc.).

If the transferor of the assets is unconnected with the VAT group the consideration paid for the chargeable assets will normally be accepted as the open market value. But if both chargeable and non-chargeable assets are transferred, the total consideration must be fairly apportioned.

(C & E Notice 700/9/96, paras 4.1–4.3).

31.8   **SURRENDER OF CORPORATION TAX LOSSES**

Under *ICTA 1988, s 402*, companies within a *corporation tax* group may surrender the benefit of corporation tax losses from one to another under certain circumstances. The company receiving the benefit usually makes a payment for the use of the losses. See Tolley's Corporation Tax. Where the two companies involved are also within the same VAT group the surrender has no VAT effect following 31.4 above. Where the two companies are not in the same VAT group C & E have stated that group relief payments in themselves do not usually give rise to taxable supplies (CCAB Statement TR 344 June 1979). See, however, 44.3 MANAGEMENT SERVICES AND SUPPLIES OF STAFF.

31.9   **SUPPLIES THROUGH SUBSIDIARY COMPANIES WITHOUT ASSETS**

Companies acting as principals who make supplies through the agency of subsidiary companies without assets ('shell companies') must account for VAT by either

(*a*)   treating the supplies as made by the principal company to the shell company and by the shell company to the customer. Invoices must be issued by the principal company to the shell company, possibly in the form of a monthly invoicing procedure;

(*b*)   applying, where eligible, for a group registration to include both the principal and the shell companies (see 31.2–31.4 above); or

(*c*)   the principal company invoicing supplies directly to the customer.

The same principle applies if the principal company is receiving supplies through a shell company. If method (*c*) is adopted, the shell company may cease to make any taxable supplies and may no longer be liable to be registered. (C & E Press Notice 768, 12 October 1982).

31.10   **DEDUCTION OF INPUT TAX BY HOLDING COMPANIES**

The basic functions of a holding company are to acquire and hold shares in subsidiaries from which it may receive dividends; defend itself and its subsidiaries from takeovers; and make disposals. From time to time it may invest, deposit or lend money, and issue or sell shares. Some of these activities are outside the scope of VAT while others are exempt. A holding company which has no other activities is not eligible to register for VAT and is not able to recover any VAT on its purchases.

Holding companies are liable to register for VAT where they have taxable trading activities, supply management services to subsidiaries or are included in a VAT group with trading subsidiaries.

31.10   Groups of Companies

Subject to below, deduction of input tax for holding companies is calculated on the following basis.

- Input tax on supplies to the holding company must be attributed to taxable, exempt or other non-taxable outputs to the greatest possible extent, and the normal rules applied.

- Any residual input tax which cannot be directly attributed will be accepted as a general overhead of the taxable person.

- The amount of the residual input tax which can be recovered will be determined in accordance with the partial exemption rules.

Most costs related to acquisitions and defence against takeovers fall into the 'overhead' category.

However, where a VAT-registered holding company is not

- an active trading company in its own right, or

- grouped with active trading subsidiaries making taxable supplies outside the group, or

- providing genuine management services to separate trading subsidiaries,

it will not be able to recover input tax on costs incurred in acquiring another company, disposing of a subsidiary, restructuring the group or any subsidiary, or holding investments. This is because C & E do not regard such costs as relating to any taxable supply. This change follows the decision in *Polysar Investments Netherlands BV v Inspecteur der Invoerrechten en Accijnzen, CJEC [1993] STC 222* which held that the basic activities of a holding company are not business activities and there is no right to deduct the VAT incurred in carrying out such activities.

(C & E News Release 59/93, 10 September 1993).

See also *BLP Group plc v C & E Commrs, CJEC [1995] STC 424* where input tax on professional fees incurred in connection with the disposal of shares in a subsidiary company to pay debts was held as being not recoverable as relating to the exempt sale of shares (rather than recoverable as relating to the payment of debts derived from taxable transactions effected by the company).

Dividends received by a holding company from subsidiaries where there is no involvement in the management are to be excluded from total income in making any proportionate calculations (*Satam SA v Minister Responsible for the Budget, CJEC 1993, [1997] STC 226*).

32   Health and Water Utilities

Cross-references. See 4.15 AGENTS for services provided by nursing agencies; 29 FUEL AND POWER.

De Voil Indirect Tax Service. See V4.146; V6.157–158A.

The contents of this chapter are as follows.

PART I HEALTH

32.1   EXEMPT SUPPLIES

EC legislation. See 22.17(*b*)–(*e*), (*g*), (*k*), (*o*) and (*p*) EUROPEAN COMMUNITY LEGISLATION and *Barkworth v C & E Commrs QB, [1988] STC 771.*

UK legislation. Supplies within 32.2 to 32.13 below are exempt. Exemption under 32.2 to 32.9 is limited to the medical services of the professional discipline for which the person is statutorily registered. It includes expert evidence given in court and advice to audiences about their own or their families' health. Not included is general advice to factory management etc. about health matters, and lecturing to medical students, first aid staff, police etc. (C & E Leaflet 701/31/92, para 4).

32.2   Doctors

The supply of services by a person registered or enrolled on the register of medical practitioners or the register of medical practitioners with limited registration is exempt. *Excluded* is the letting on hire of goods except where the letting is in connection with a supply of other services comprised in the exemption. [*VATA 1994, 9 Sch Group 7, Item 1(a) and Note 1*]. See 32.1 above for limitations on the services which are exempt.

Included are supplies of goods which are a minor and inseparable part of the service of medical care, such as the application of bandages and dressings or the injection of drugs.

See 32.14 below for dispensing of drugs by a doctor.

Deputising services to doctors. The provision of a deputy for a person registered in the register of medical practitioners or the register of medical practitioners with limited registration is also exempt. [*VATA 1994, 9 Sch Group 7, Item 5*].

A telephone answering service available separately is not included but might be exempt if directly supervised by a doctor. (C & E Leaflet 701/31/92, para 3(*k*)).

Visiting EC practitioners. Included in the above exemption is the supply of services in an urgent case as mentioned in the *Medical Act 1983, s 18(3)* by a person who is not registered in the visiting EC practitioners list in the register of medical practitioners at the time he performs the services but who is entitled to be registered in accordance with that *section. [VATA 1994, 9 Sch Group 7, Note 4].*

Registration of general practitioners. C & E are prepared to accept that GPs are not employees of the NHS but independent contractors in respect of their NHS work. Accordingly, they make exempt supplies of professional services to the NHS. (C & E News Release 44/93, 19 March 1993; C & E Business Brief 8/96, 17 May 1996).

Medico-legal services. With effect from 20 January 1997, certain medico-legal services provided by doctors to third parties are standard-rated (previously exempt although doctors could treat such services as taxable before that date if they wished). Taxable services are those in the medico-legal field where the doctor plays an integral role in the legal work and which are usually carried out to satisfy the needs of third parties (e.g. insurers and solicitors). They cover

- arbitration, mediation and conciliation services;

- investigating the validity of claims against parties such as insurers;

- considering medical reports and other evidence in order to resolve disputes; and

- work (other than just medical reports) for lawyers and insurers in preparing reports for the resolution of disputes following personal injury.

Exemption continues to apply to

- services provided by doctors arising out of the normal doctor/patient relationship; and

- services which, although they may be for the information needs of third parties, are predominantly medical and not legal (e.g. medical reports for employers and life assurance policies and the provision of expert medical advice).

(C & E Business Brief 26/96, 19 December 1996).

32.3   Opticians

The supply of services by persons registered in either of the registers of ophthalmic opticians or the register of dispensing opticians kept under the *Opticians Act 1989* or either of the lists under *section 9* of that *Act* of bodies corporate carrying on business as ophthalmic opticians or as dispensing opticians is exempt. *Excluded* is the letting on hire of goods except where the letting is in connection with a supply of other services comprised in the exemption.

[VATA 1994, 9 Sch Group 7, Item 1(b) and Note 1].

See 32.1 above for limitations on the services which are exempt.

Included is the ophthalmic examination of a patient's eyes and checks to see whether the patient is medically fit to wear contact lenses. Any charge made for professional advice is also exempt but services which do not amount to care or treatment (e.g. repairs, repolishing contact lenses) are standard-rated.

Subject to below, supplies of spectacles, contact lenses and other appliances designed to correct or relieve a sight defect are standard-rated unless the goods are either

- supplied in hospital, in which case they are exempt (see 32.10 below); or

- certain specialised appliances designed solely for use by the handicapped (e.g. artificial eyes and certain low vision aids), in which case they are zero-rated (see 32.17(*a*)(vii) below).

Supplies of ancillary goods (e.g. cases, cleaning solution) are standard-rated. (C & E Leaflet 701/31/92, para 3(b)).

However, in *C & E Commrs v Leightons Ltd QB, [1995] STC 458*, the court upheld the earlier decision of the tribunal that the price paid for spectacles includes two separate supplies – a standard-rated supply of goods (the spectacles) and an exempt supply of opticians' services. Claims for repayment of VAT (with interest) may be made. For claims lodged before 4 August 1997, C & E will repay agreed claims in full back-dated to 1 September 1988 (when sales of spectacles became standard-rated, previously having been exempt). Any claims not lodged by that date are subject to the three-year time limit on repayments generally. With effect from the beginning of the first VAT accounting period starting on or after 1 January 1998, there are no set method of apportionment of spectacle sales between exempt and standard-rated elements (previous agreed methods as set out in C & E Business Briefs 8/95, 19/95 and 3/96 and C & E Notice 700/57/95 being withdrawn from that date). If practicable, opticians should calculate VAT by separating the standard-rated and exempt elements at the point of sale. If this is not possible, an individual method must be agreed with C & E which gives a fair and reasonable valuation of VAT payable without placing an undue burden on the optician. For a *suggested* method based on full cost apportionment, see C & E Notice 700/57/95 and VAT Information Sheets 3/97 and 10/98.

32.4   **Supplementary professions and osteopaths**

The supply of services by persons on the following registers is exempt.

(*a*)   Any register kept under the *Professions Supplementary to Medicines Act 1960*. Professions covered include chiropodists, dieticians, laboratory technicians, occupational therapists, orthoptists, physiotherapists, radiographers and remedial gymnasts. (C & E Leaflet 701/31/92, para 3(*c*)).

(*b*)   With effect from 12 June 1998, the register of osteopaths maintained in accordance with the provisions of the *Osteopaths Act 1993*. By concession, exemption can be applied with effect from 9 May 1998 (the date the register was opened) provided the osteopath was on the register at the earlier date. (C & E Business Brief 13/98, 9 June 1998).

Excluded from exemption under (*a*) or (*b*) above is the letting on hire of goods except where this is in connection with a supply of other services comprised in the exemption. [*VATA 1994, 9 Sch Group 7, Items 1(c)(ca) and Note 1; SI 1998/1294*].

See 32.1 above for limitations on the services which are exempt. In any case, exemption does not apply to

- services by a person who practices a profession otherwise falling within (*a*) or (*b*) above but whose name is not on the appropriate register;

- services of a medical nature but where there is no statutory medical register (e.g. chiropractors, psychoanalysts, herbalists, acupuncturists and masseurs); or

- services of health farms, hydros, clubs and the like.

(C & E Leaflet 701/31/92, para 4).

32.5   **Nurses, midwives and health visitors**

The supply of services by a person registered or enrolled in the register of qualified nurses, midwives and health visitors kept under the *Nurses, Midwives and Health Visitors*

32.6   Health and Water Utilities

Act 1979, s 10 is exempt. *Excluded* is the letting on hire of goods except where the letting is in connection with a supply of other services comprised in the exemption. [*VATA 1994, 9 Sch Group 7, Item 1(d) and Note 1*]. See 32.1 above for limitations on the services which are exempt.

32.6   Hearing aid dispensers

A supply of services by a person registered in the register of dispensers of hearing aids or the register of persons employing such dispensers maintained under the *Hearing Aid Council Act 1968, s 2* is exempt. *Excluded* is the letting on hire of goods except where the letting is in connection with a supply of other services comprised in the exemption. [*VATA 1994, 9 Sch Group 7, Item 1(e) and Note 1*]. See 32.1 above for limitations on the services which are exempt.

Hearing aids designed for the auditory training of deaf children are zero-rated (see 32.17(*a*)(vii) below). Otherwise supplies of hearing aids and their repair, batteries, accessories and spare parts are standard-rated. (C & E Leaflet 701/31/92, para 3(*f*)).

32.7   Dentists etc.

The supply of any services or dental prostheses (e.g. false teeth, bridges, crowns) by

(*a*) a person registered in the dentist's register,

(*b*) a person enrolled in any roll of dental auxiliaries having effect under *Dentists Act 1984, s 45*, or

(*c*) a dental technician

is exempt. [*VATA 1994, 9 Sch Group 7, Item 2*].

The exemption extends to any services supplied by dentists provided they are acting in their professional capacity (e.g. professional advice on dental matters). Supplies within (*c*) above are exempt, irrespective of whether the supply is made directly to the patient or to a dentist.

Exemption also covers the supply of consumables used or administered in the course of treatment. It does not, however, cover the sale of other goods (e.g. toothpaste and oral hygiene products).

Supplies between dentists. A dental practice is often comprised of a number of dentists operating out of the same premises. There are a number of possible arrangements under which practitioners may co-operate in dental practice.

- *Employer/employee relationship.* The employee is usually referred to as an 'assistant'. Any goods or services provided by the employer to an employee solely for the purposes of the employee's employment is not a supply for VAT purposes.

- *Partnership.* For VAT purposes, a partnership is a single business. Supplies of goods or services between dentists within the partnership are disregarded. VAT is only concerned with supplies made by the partnership to others.

- *Associateship agreements.* A dentist (or a number of dentists in partnership) may own a dental practice and then make facilities available for other dentists to practice ('associate dentists'). Each associate is self-employed and is an independent separate 'business' for VAT purposes. Associate dentists generally have their own patients and supply their services as independent practitioners. The practice usually makes supplies of goods and services to the associate dentists (e.g. use of a fully-equipped surgery, materials and consumables necessary in the provision of treatment, the services of a chair-side assistant, the introduction of patients, laboratory services, and the use of reception, accounting and other common services). The practice may also provide professional help and guidance to the associates. In return the associate dentists undertake to pay to the practice a percentage of their fee income. In most cases, the practice collects and receives fees (from the patient or the NHS) as agent for the associates, deducts the agreed percentage and passes the balance to the associates.

Supplies of services (use of facilities, equipment, staff etc.) and dental prostheses by a practice to associates to enable them to carry out dentistry within that practice can be regarded as exempt. Supplies of goods for sale apart from dental prostheses (e.g. toothpaste, oral hygiene products) are taxable supplies. The sale of dental equipment to an associate is also a taxable supply. However, supplies of parts and consumables for dental equipment used by the associates but owned by the practice are included in the practice's exempt supply of facilities.

Exemption will only apply to supplies which allow the associates to perform dentistry. For example, the supply of staff only will not be covered by the exemption.

Supplies made by a dentist who has ceased to practise are not covered by the exemption. (Supplies made by practice owners who do not practice dentistry in their own practice are covered by the exemption as long as they practice elsewhere, for example, in a dental hospital.)

- *Expense sharing agreements.* Expense sharing arrangements typically involve a number of independent dentists who agree to share the expenses of operating common premises, support staff etc. Each remains an independent practitioner. There is no partnership and no practice/associate relationship.

  The VAT implications of such arrangements depend on the facts and the wording of individual agreements. Typically, the parties agree to bear certain shares of the common expenses of the practice (e.g. insurance, lighting and heating, staff and other office expenses). Where one dentist pays for the supplies and recharges the other dentists their agreed share, there is a supply for VAT purposes. To the extent that the amounts paid are the consideration for supplies of dental facilities to enable the recipient to carry out dentistry on the premises, then the supply is exempt. To the extent that taxable goods are supplied (e.g. sale of equipment by one dentist to another) these are taxable supplies. Where, however, the agreement provides for common ownership of goods, any payment from one of the parties in respect of their share in the items commonly owned is not the consideration for the supply of goods and VAT does not apply.

(VAT Information Sheet 5/96, May 1996).

32.8   Supervised services

Supplies of services made by a person who is not registered or enrolled in any of the registers or rolls specified in 32.2 to 32.5 or 32.7(*a*) or (*b*) above is exempt where the services are wholly performed or directly supervised by a person who is so registered or enrolled. [*VATA 1994, 9 Sch Group 7, Note 2*].

See 32.1 above for limitations on the services which are exempt.

Supervision does not necessarily require the supervisor to continually observe the unqualified person or necessarily be on the same premises provided there is a check as often as the circumstances require and a system for that person to contact the supervisor. Supervision is 'direct' if carried out on a one-to-one basis without an intermediary. (*Elder Home Care Ltd (11185)*). See also *M G Parkinson (6017)*. Services by a chiropractor to patients referred by a surgeon or other registered medical practitioner are not regarded as directly supervised even though the practitioner has a continuing responsibility for the patient and receives reports on the patient from the chiropractor (*Pittam (C) (13268)*).

C & E originally interpreted 'direct supervision' as requiring a substantial degree of physical presence. However, following an internal review and consultation with representative bodies, C & E accept that, if all the following conditions are met, services supplied qualify for VAT exemption even though those services have not been supplied directly by qualified staff.

(*a*)   The supervisor must

(i)   be an appropriately registered person;

(ii)   see the client at the outset of treatment and at the outset of any new treatment required thereafter;

(iii)   be readily available for the whole of the time that the unqualified staff are working, and be able to take appropriate action in an emergency;

(iv)   decide the treatment to be provided by the unqualified staff; and

(v)   be able to demonstrate that they monitor the services of the unqualified staff.

(*b*)   Supervision cannot take place via a third party (i.e. the supervisor must always be in a direct relationship with the unqualified staff).

(*c*)   The presence of the appropriately qualified supervisor must be required at appropriate times during the process and he or she must be responsible, contractually, for supervising the unqualified staff. See, however, *A J Land (t/a Crown Optical Centre (15547)* where the tribunal held that, although a contract may be valuable evidence of responsibility, it was not essential and supervision could be an implicit term of the relationship.

C & E will not accept that direct supervision exists where a supervisor is introduced primarily to gain VAT exemption and in practice carries out little or no supervision.

(*d*)   The services performed by the unqualified staff must require supervision. C & E will not accept exemption for services performed by unqualified staff for which no supervision is required and will not accept that services which are not broadly of a medical or caring nature can gain exemption simply by the use of a qualified individual in a supervisory or managerial role.

(*e*)   The ratio of registered professionals to unqualified staff must be such that it enables requirement (*a*)(iii) above to be fulfilled.

The supervisor need not always be the same individual (e.g. a number of registered professionals working within an establishment can supervise different unqualified staff as demand dictates; a registered locum may be brought in to cover periods of holiday or similar; or a team of supervisors, all of whom are qualified as above, can rotate the supervision of particular staff amongst themselves to fit in with their other commitments).

There are special guidelines for the optical and homecare sectors, details of which are available from C & E.

(C & E News Release 23/96, 11 April 1996).

32.9   **Pharmaceutical chemists**

The supply of any services (but not the letting on hire of goods) by a person registered in the register of pharmaceutical chemists kept under the *Pharmacy Act 1954* or the

Pharmacy (Northern Ireland) Order 1976 is exempt. With effect from 1 January 1997, exemption is extended to supplies of services made by a person who is not so registered (e.g. a company or partnership) but where the services are performed by a person who is so registered. Such exemption had been applied previously by concession. [*VATA 1994, 9 Sch Group 7, Item 3 and Notes 2A and 3; SI 1996/2949*]. See 32.1 above for limitations on the services which are exempt.

Included are analytical medical services (e.g. pregnancy testing), acting as a locum in the dispensary of a pharmacist, and services covered by NHS payments which are designed to secure the maintenance of pharmaceutical services (e.g. basic practice allowance, rota service payments, additional remuneration to essential small pharmacies, collection and delivery charges).

Excluded are activities as trading chemists.

(C & E Leaflet 701/31/92, para 3(h)).

For dispensing of drugs by registered pharmacists, see 32.14 below.

32.10   **Hospitals etc.**

The provision of 'care' or medical or surgical treatment and, in connection with it, the supply of any goods, in any hospital or other institution approved, licensed, registered or exempted from registration by a public general Act of Parliament (or equivalent NI legislation) is exempt. [*VATA 1994, 9 Sch Group 7, Item 4*].

Examples of institutions covered are NHS hospitals (but the provision of care, treatment and medical goods by them to patients is generally treated as outside the scope of VAT); registered or approved nursing homes or mental nursing homes; registered residential homes for the elderly or disabled or persons with alcohol or drug dependency or mental disorder; registered voluntary homes for children; voluntary controlled or assisted community homes exempted from registration; approved probation and bail hostels; and registered nurseries and playgroups.

C & E maintain that the supply of care by all providers is exempt regardless of their status provided they are registered under the relevant legislation. (C & E Business Brief 1/97, 24 January 1997). The *EC 6th Directive, Art 13A(1)(b)* confines the exemption to 'bodies governed by public law'. In *Kaul (t/a Alpha Care Services), [1996] VATDR 360 (14028)* the tribunal held that this should be interpreted as limiting exemption to activities carried out by companies, bodies and other 'legal' persons and not by individuals or 'natural' persons. Subsequently, the tribunal in *J & M Gregg (14937)* referred to the CJEC the question of whether a two-person partnership was excluded from exemption. Although the court has yet to rule, the Advocate-General has given his opinion that a partnership was not excluded from exemption. An entity which has the necessary infrastructure to carry on independently an activity in the area of hospital and medical care and which is duly recognised under national law should be regarded as falling within *EC 6th Directive, Art 13A(1)(b)*.

Included is accommodation, catering, medical and nursing services, and drugs (see below), appliances etc. supplied in connection with the latter. The supply may be made by, or direct to, the institution, or by another body such as a charity catering to patients in hospitals, or by a firm supplying nursing services (see 4.15 AGENTS). *Excluded* are supplies made outside the institution.

Item 4 above exempts the supply of medical care, including the supply of drugs to a patient in hospital. *Before 1 January 1998*, the supply of drugs to a patient in hospital could, if separately itemised, be treated as separate supplies so as to qualify for zero-rating under *VATA 1994, 8 Sch Group 12, Item 1* (see 32.14 below). Similarly, any prostheses (e.g. hip joint replacements, heart pacemakers and valve replacements) supplied could be zero-rated under 32.17(*a*)(i) below when supplied to a disabled person (*C & E Commrs v Wellington Private Hospital; British United Provident Association Ltd v C & E Commrs (and cross-appeal) CA, [1997] STC 445*).

'Care' covers medical treatment, protection, control and guidance of the individual, provided it involves some personal and continuing contact between the person supplying the service and the patient. It includes the provision of light refreshments (other than alcoholic drinks) to patients in the inpatients' wards, the outpatients' department or the casualty department of a hospital from hospital trolleys, canteens or shops (but not supplies to visitors or staff). It is not essential that the person providing the care should be medically qualified.

(C & E Leaflet 701/31/92, para 3(j) and Annex B).

The provision of accommodation and catering to a parent of a child patient is a supply of care to the patient (*Nuffield Nursing Homes Trust, [1989] VATTR 62 (3227)*).

32.11 Human blood, organs and tissue

The supply of human blood (and products for therapeutic purposes derived from it) and human (including foetal) organs or tissue for diagnostic or therapeutic purposes or medical research is exempt. [*VATA 1994, 9 Sch Group 7, Items 6–8*]. The importation of these items is also exempt from VAT. [*SI 1983/499; SI 1984/746, 2 Sch Group 5, Items 4–6*]. See C & E Notice 369.

Recombinant factor VIII (as opposed to plasma-derived human factor VIII) is outside the exemption as it is not derived from human blood. (HC Written Answer, Vol 267 col 837, 30 November 1995; *Baxter Healthcare Ltd (14670)*).

32.12 Transport of sick and injured

The supply of transport services for sick or injured persons in vehicles specially designed for that purpose is exempt. [*VATA 1994, 9 Sch Group 7, Item 11*]. *Included* are airborne and waterborne ambulances. International passenger transport remains zero-rated. (C & E Leaflet 701/31/92, para 3(m)).

32.13 Services linked to welfare and social work

The supply, otherwise than for a profit, by a charity or public body of welfare services and goods supplied in connection therewith is exempt. See 12.9 CHARITIES and 43.7 LOCAL AUTHORITIES AND STATUTORY BODIES.

EC 6th Directive, Art 13A directs countries to exempt 'the supply of services and goods closely linked to welfare and social security works'. In *Yoga for Health Foundation v C & E Commrs QB, [1984] STC 630*, it was held that the word 'welfare' was not confined to services connected with the relief of poverty or provision of purely material benefits.

32.14 DISPENSING OF DRUGS, ETC.

The supply of goods can be zero-rated in the following circumstances.

(*a*) **Pharmacists.** The supply of any 'qualifying goods' dispensed to an individual for his 'personal use' where the dispensing is by a registered pharmacist (as defined) on the prescription of a person registered in the register of medical practitioners, the register of medical practitioners with limited registration or the dentists' register.

'*Qualifying goods*' means any goods designed or adapted for use in connection with any medical or surgical treatment. This definition allows zero-rating for goods such as those listed in the Drug Tariff (e.g. drugs and chemical reagents, catheters, chiropody appliances, contraceptive devices, hosiery, pessaries, trusses, etc.) but prevents zero-rating for supplies of other goods which are not so designed or adapted, such as overbed tables. Specifically excluded from zero-rating are hearing aids, dentures, spectacles and contact lenses.

'*Personal use*' does not include any use by the individual in question while being provided with medical or surgical treatment or any form of care as an in-patient or resident of, or whilst attending, a hospital or nursing home.

Included is the supply of services of letting on hire of the goods and goods prescribed by a visiting EC practitioner, entitled to be but not registered in the visiting EC practitioners list in the register of medical practitioners, in an urgent case within *Medical Act 1983, s 18(3)*. Goods so prescribed which are acquired in the UK from another EC country or imported from a place outside the EC are not zero-rated on acquisition or importation.

Before 1 January 1998, zero-rating applied to the supply of *any* goods dispensed by a registered pharmacist on the prescription of a person registered in the register of medical practitioners, the register of medical practitioners with limited registration or the dentists' register. The supply of drugs to a patient in hospital could therefore, if separately itemised, be treated as a separate supply qualifying for zero-rating under these provisions rather than being exempt under 32.10 above. (*C & E Commrs v Wellington Private Hospital; British United Provident Association Ltd v C & E Commrs (and cross-appeals) CA, [1997] STC 445*).

[*VATA 1994, 8 Sch Group 12, Item 1 and Notes 1, 2, 2A, 5, 5A and 5I; SI 1997/2744*].

Zero-rating applies equally to goods dispensed on NHS and privately and covers both the prescription payments and those received from the NHS (to cover cost of goods, containers and service element in dispensing).

Not included are goods supplied without prescription and other payments from the NHS e.g. rota service and rural dispensing payments (which are exempt, see 32.9 above).

(C & E Leaflet 701/31/92, para 2).

(*b*)   **Doctors**. The supply of any 'qualifying goods' (before 1 January 1998, any goods) by a person registered in the register of medical practitioners or the register of medical practitioners with limited registration in accordance with a requirement or authorisation under NHS regulations. (Under such regulations doctors can be required or authorised by the NHS to provide pharmacy services where, because of distance or inadequacy of means of communication, patients would have serious difficulty in obtaining drugs from a pharmacist.)

See under (*a*) above for '*qualifying goods*'.

Included is the supply of services of letting on hire of the goods. Goods so prescribed which are acquired in the UK from another EC country or imported from a place outside the EC are not zero-rated on acquisition or importation.

[*VATA 1994, 8 Sch Group 12, Item 1A and Notes 1 and 5; SI 1995/652; SI 1997/2744*].

GPs providing NHS pharmacy services may therefore register for VAT and reclaim the VAT on their purchases of drugs and a proportion of overheads relating to the NHS pharmacy services. Alternatively, if their zero-rated supplies exceed the registration threshold but they do not wish to register, they should apply for exemption from registration (see 59.6 REGISTRATION). (VAT Information Sheet 6/95, 1 April 1995; C & E Business Brief 18/95, 6 September 1995).

Private prescriptions. The dispensing of goods on private prescription (e.g. drugs, vitamin supplements and homeopathic preparations) by a doctor is always standard-rated. (C & E Leaflet 701/31/92, para 3(*a*)).

De Voil Indirect Tax Service. See V4.281.

32.15 IMPORTATIONS

The following importations are free of VAT.

(*a*) Animals specially prepared for laboratory use and sent free of charge to a 'relevant establishment'.

(*b*) Biological or chemical substances sent from outside the EC to a 'relevant establishment'.

(*c*) Reagents for use in blood type grouping (or the detection of blood grouping incompatibilities) or in determining human tissue types, by approved institutions or laboratories exclusively for non-commercial medical or scientific purposes.

(*d*) Pharmaceutical products by or on behalf of persons or animals for their use while visiting the UK to participate in an international sporting event.

(*e*) Samples of reference substances approved by the WHO for the quality control of materials used in the manufacture of medicinal products provided the samples are addressed to consignees authorised to receive them free of VAT.

'*Relevant establishment*' is a public establishment, or a department of such, principally engaged in education or scientific research *or* a private establishment so engaged, which is approved by the Department of Trade and Industry or, in the case of (*a*) above, by the Home Office.

[*SI 1984/746, 2 Sch Group 5, Items 1–3, 7–10; SI 1988/2212, Art 5; SI 1992/3120*]. See C & E Notices 365 and 366.

PART II RELIEFS FOR PEOPLE WITH DISABILITIES

32.16 INTRODUCTION

Certain supplies of specialised goods and services may be zero-rated when needed by '*handicapped persons*' defined as the chronically sick or disabled [*VATA 1994, 8 Sch Group 12, Note 3*]. See *Tempur Pedic (UK) Ltd (13744)* for a consideration of the meaning of the words 'chronically sick'. In particular, 'chronic' implies lasting a long time rather than the colloquial meaning of very bad or acute. 'Disabled' includes mental disability and may include those who are blind or partially sighted or suffer from acute hearing loss. (C & E Manual V1-7, Chapter 12 sections 3.4, 3.5). Persons who are frail simply because of old age are not considered to be handicapped (*Help the Aged QB, [1997] STC 406*). Tribunals have also held that a person was not chronically sick or disabled where suffering from a slipped disc (*Aquakraft Ltd (2215)*), neck and back pain (*Posturite (UK) Ltd (7848)*) or asthma (*GD Searle & Co Ltd (13439)*).

In this and the following paragraphs, 'disabled' is used to include the chronically sick.

In most cases, zero-rating applies only to supplies made <u>directly to disabled persons</u>; in other cases it applies only to supplies to charities providing care or other facilities for disabled persons; and in some cases it applies to supplies to either disabled persons or charities. See 32.17 below for further details. In all cases, the customer must give the supplier an eligibility declaration before the supplier can zero-rate the supply. See 32.19 below.

For zero-rating to apply, it is essential that both the goods or services *and* the recipient qualify. The relief is not intended to cover all supplies of goods and services to disabled persons (or charities providing facilities for the disabled), nor does it mean that eligible goods and services can be zero-rated when supplied to people who are not disabled. For example, supplies to a nursing home would not be zero-rated under these provisions even if all the residents were chronically sick or disabled. See *KA Conray (1916)*.

It is the supplier's responsibility to account for VAT correctly and ensure that the intended supply can be zero-rated under these provisions. Where appropriate, written confirmation that goods are designed solely for disabled persons should be obtained from the manufacturer/designer. The supplier cannot take the decision to zero-rate if the manufacturer has made no such claim. (C & E Notice 701/7/94, para 31).

32.17   ZERO-RATED SUPPLIES TO DISABLED PERSONS AND CHARITIES

The following supplies are zero-rated.

(*a*) **Supplies of goods.** The supply (including the letting on hire) to

- a disabled person for 'domestic or personal use', or

- a charity for making available, by sale or otherwise, to specific disabled persons for domestic or personal use

of any of the goods within (i)-(ix) below. See, however, after (ix) below for exclusions applying with effect from 1 January 1998.

(i) *Medical or surgical appliances designed solely for the relief of a 'severe abnormality' or 'severe injury'.*

Excluded are hearing aids (unless designed for auditory training of deaf children, see (vii) below); dentures (but these are usually exempt under 32.7 above); and spectacles and contact lenses (but see (vii) below for certain low vision aids).

Included are clothing, footwear and wigs; and renal haemodialysis units, oxygen concentrators, artificial respirators and other similar apparatus.

The words 'severe abnormality' and 'severe injury' are not defined but among the disabilities falling within this category are amputation, spinal injuries, rheumatoid or severe osteo arthritis, severe disfigurement, congenital deformities, organic nervous diseases, mental disorders and blindness. (C & E Notice 701/7/94, para 5).

(ii) *Electrically or mechanically adjustable beds designed for invalids.* See *Back in Health Ltd (10003)* and *Niagara Holdings Ltd (11400)*.

(iii) *Commode chairs and stools, devices incorporating a bidet jet and warm air drier and frames or other devices for sitting over or rising from sanitary appliances.*

(iv) *Chair or stair lifts designed for use in connection with invalid wheelchairs.* It is not necessary for the lift to carry the person sitting in a wheelchair. (C & E Notice 707/7/94, para 6). (The supply and installation of a lift can also be zero-rated in certain circumstances under (*h*) below.)

(v) *Hoists and lifters designed for use by invalids.*

(vi) *Motor vehicles designed or substantially and permanently adapted for the carriage of a disabled person in a wheelchair or on a stretcher and of no more than five other persons.*

In the case of a vehicle designed or adapted for carrying a disabled person in a wheelchair, the vehicle must provide the necessary space and facilities for a disabled person to be transported whilst sitting in reasonable comfort in the wheelchair (see also *Oliver (JG) (10579)*). It must also have a permanent fitted hoist or ramp to enable a person to embark and disembark from the vehicle while sitting in the wheel chair, and suitable clamps to secure the wheelchair.

In the case of a vehicle for carrying a disabled person on a stretcher, the vehicle must be designed or adapted to provide adequate means of access to, and space within the vehicle for, the stretcher and suitable fixtures to secure it.

The person buying the vehicle should ensure that the conversion is carried out before the vehicle is supplied. Provided one payment is then made to cover the cost of the vehicle and the conversion, the supplier can zero-rate the whole transaction even where he arranges for a third party to carry out the conversion. If, however, he supplies a standard production vehicle and subsequently arranges for the conversion, only the charge for conversion can be zero-rated and VAT is due at the standard rate on the supply of the vehicle itself.

The VAT office may wish to inspect any new vehicle which a supplier intends to zero-rate to check that all the conditions for relief have been met and the supplier should contact the VAT office before delivering the vehicle.

(C & E Notice 701/7/94, para 8).

The Scott-Track Venturer has been accepted by C & E as eligible for zero-rating. (Hansard, 15 February 1996, Vol 569, Col 720).

See also (*k*) below for the letting of vehicles under the Motability scheme.

(vii) *Equipment and appliances not within (i) to (vi) above 'designed solely for use by a disabled person'.* *Specifically included* are invalid wheelchairs and carriages (other than mechanically propelled vehicles intended or adapted for use on roads) and hearing aids designed for the auditory training of deaf children.

In determining whether goods are 'designed solely for use by a disabled person' tribunals have considered both the subjective intention of the designer (see, for example, *Tempur Pedic (UK) Ltd (13744)*), the manufacturer's or importer's advertising literature, and the objective facts of how and to whom the goods were marketed. General purpose goods are not eligible. However, an article designed solely for the disabled remains eligible even if suitable for use by other people (although if an item is sold in significant numbers to able-bodied people, it is likely that the item has not been designed solely for use by the disabled). VAT offices have been asked not to accept requests for liability rulings from retailers. Retailers should refer queries to the manufacturer or importer who should obtain a ruling from their VAT office. (C & E Notice 701/7/94, para 10).

Air-conditioning and similar general purpose equipment is not included. (C & E Manual V1-7, Chapter 12 Annex C). Oxygen concentrators, artificial respirators and similar apparatus specifically designed for providing artificial ventilation for patients are included under (i) above. See also *Simmons (6622)*.

Asthma, hay fever and allergy products. With effect from 26 August 1996 supplies of all vacuum cleaners, air purification products and similar allergy relief products are standard-rated irrespective of to whom they are supplied. Previously C & E had accepted that such items could be zero-rated under *Group 12, Item 2(g).* (C & E Business Briefs 16/96, 30 July 1996; 17/96, 27 August 1996; and 20/97, 24 September 1997; C & E Manual V1-7, Chapter 12 Annex C). See also *GD Searle and Co Ltd (13439).*

Carpets are not included. See *The David Lewis Centre QB, [1995] STC 485.*

Computer equipment. There is no relief for general purpose computer equipment but specialist items (e.g. speech synthesisers and braille embossers) do qualify for zero-rating. From 1 August 1996, traders supplying disabled persons with complete packages of computer equipment containing specialist items can use a composite rate of VAT based on supplies of such packages over a recent period. (The arrangements do not apply to replacement units or upgrading items.) In calculating the composite rate, C & E is prepared to allow the cost of a central processor which has been adapted to allow the running of the specialist items, and installation and training costs, towards the value of the zero-rated portion.

Example

Z Ltd supplies five different qualifying packages of computer equipment in a representative period of three months. In package A, the zero-rated element is £1,500 at sales value and the standard-rated element is £500 plus £87.50 VAT. The total cost of the package is £2,087.50 of which £87.50 is VAT. The composite rate is the rate which needs to be applied to the total VAT-exclusive sale value (£2,000) to ensure the correct VAT is declared, i.e.

$$\frac{87.50}{2,000} \times 100 = 4.375\% \text{ rounded up to } 4.4\%$$

The composite rates and value of sales for each of the five packages offered in the representative period are as follows.

Package	Composite rate	Sales value	VAT
A	4.4%	500,000	22,000
B	6%	200,000	12,000
C	3%	100,000	3,000
D	3.8%	100,000	3,800
E	4.1%	100,000	4,100
		£1,000,000	£44,900

The overall composite rate is

$$\frac{44,900}{1,000,000} \times 100 = 4.49\% \text{ rounded up to } 4.5\%$$

Z Ltd can apply a composite rate of 4.5% to all sales of qualifying packages. The overall composite rate should be recalculated every twelve months. (C & E Manual V1-7, Chapter 12 Annex C).

Golf buggies are not included (see *Foxer Industries (13817)*).

Hearing aids. Hearing aids are specifically excluded (see (i) above) but zero-rating can be applied to auditory training aids for deaf children (elaborate systems used by teachers and parents to give deaf children with a little residual hearing at least the possibility of acquiring adequate speech).

Other specialised aids designed for people with severely defective hearing but which are not 'hearing aids' (e.g. TV hearing aids, tinnitus maskers and induction loop equipment) are also eligible for zero-rating. (C & E Manual V1-7, Chapter 12 Annex C).

Hydrotherapy pools. See *The David Lewis Centre (10860)* and *Boys' and Girls' Welfare Society (15274)*. Following these decisions, C & E now accept that a hydrotherapy pool qualifies for zero-rating provided it is sited indoors; has a uniform or a very gradual change in depth of water; has water heated to at least 32 degrees centigrade; has fixed means of access to the pool either by way of ramps, shallow rising steps with railings or a fixed hoist; and incorporates safety features to prevent accidents. (C & E Manual V1-7, Chapter 12 Annex C).

Kitchens. Kitchen furniture fitted into a kitchen during the construction of a new dwelling may be zero-rated under *VATA 1994, 8 Sch Group 5, Item 4* (see 42.37 LAND AND BUILDINGS). For existing kitchens, items must be solely designed for disabled persons (e.g. specially adapted taps with long handles). See also *Softley Ltd (t/a Softley Kitchens), (15034)* where it was held that certain items of kitchen equipment could be zero-rated when made to the individual specifications of a disabled person.

Low vision aids. Spectacles and contact lenses are specifically excluded (see (i) above) but zero-rating can be applied, for example to custom-made spectacle-mounted low visions aids and closed circuit video magnification systems capable of magnifying text and images. (C & E Manual V1-7, Chapter 12 Annex C).

Spa baths are unlikely to qualify (see *Aquakraft Ltd (2215)*).

TENS machines. Transcutaneous electric nerve stimulators machines can be zero-rated under this provision. (C & E Business Brief 4/94, 21 February 1994; C & E Manual V1-7, Chapter 12 Annex C).

(viii) *Parts and accessories designed solely for use in or with goods described in (i) to (vii) above.*

(ix) *Boats designed or substantially and permanently adapted for use by disabled persons.*

To qualify for relief, the boat must include all or most of the following features: a ramp for wheelchairs; lifts and level non-cambered surfaces to accommodate wheelchair movements; specialised washing/toilet facilities accessible for use by disabled persons; handrails; wheelchair clamps; galley area; sleeping area and steering facilities specialised for use by disabled persons. (C & E Notice 701/7/94, para 9).

Although (viii) above does not refer to parts and accessories for boats within this item, C & E consider this to be a drafting error and allow zero-rating where a person supplies parts and accessories which meet all the other criteria of (viii) above even when they are supplied for use in a boat which qualifies for relief under this item. (C & E Manual V1-7, Chapter 12 section 4.34A).

Exclusions. Zero-rating under the above provisions is restricted in the following circumstances.

(1)   With effect from 1 January 1988, in respect of

(A)   supplies to a disabled person by a Health Authority, Health Board, NHS trust or other 'relevant institution' (other than the supply of a wheelchair or invalid carriage or any parts or accessories designed solely for use therein), and

(B) supplies to a disabled person by any other person not within (A) above of medical or surgical appliances within (i) above, parts and accessories thereto, and incontinence products and wound dressings

'*domestic or personal use*' does not include any use by the disabled person in question while being provided with medical or surgical treatment or any form of care as an in-patient or resident of, or whilst attending, a '*relevant institution*', i.e. any institution providing such care or treatment which is approved, licensed or registered (or which is specifically exempt from any such requirement).

Supplies to charities are not affected by this restriction.

(2) With effect from 1 January 1998, zero-rating does not apply to

(A) a supply made in accordance with an agreement, arrangement or understanding to which a Health Authority, Health Board, NHS trust or other relevant institution is or has been a party otherwise than as the supplier, or

(B) a supply where all or any part of the consideration has been provided (directly or indirectly) by a Health Authority, Health Board, NHS trust or other relevant institution but in the case of a supply of an invalid wheelchair or invalid carriage to a disabled person only if a Health Authority, Health Board or NHS trust has provided *all* of the consideration or another 'relevant institution' is involved.

For the above purposes, references to an invalid wheelchair and invalid carriage do not include references to any mechanically propelled vehicle intended or adapted for use on roads.

[*VATA 1994, 8 Sch Group 12, Item 2 and Notes 4, 5, 5B–5I; SI 1997/2744*].

The effect of the above provisions is that it removes the ability of institutions such as private hospitals, nursing homes and residential homes to recover VAT charged on the purchase of supplies for disabled persons which are used in their supply to in-patients and residents. It also prevents them and the NHS making arrangements for third parties to make VAT-free supplies, such as incontinence products and wound dressings, on the institution's behalf to patients who live in their own homes and for which the institution pays. Instead, such supplies are supplied by the institution as part of its VAT-free care. Supplies of incontinence products, etc. direct to the disabled person by independent suppliers and for which the disabled person pays are not affected. (VAT Information Sheet 6/97).

Before 1 January 1998, following the decision in *British United Provident Association Ltd v C & E Commrs (and cross-appeal), CA [1997] STC 445*, any prostheses (e.g. hip joint replacements, heart pacemakers and valve replacements) supplied and fitted in a hospital, if itemised separately, were not an integral part of an exempt composite supply of medical care under *VATA 1994, 9 Sch Group 7, Item 4* (see 32.10 above) and could be zero-rated under (*a*)(i) above when supplied to a disabled person.

(*b*) **'Talking books' for the blind.** 'Talking books' for the blind and severely handicapped when supplied to the Royal National Institute for the Blind, the National Listening Library and other similar charities. Included is certain apparatus and tapes designed or specially adapted for such use and non-specialist sound recording equipment. Also zero-rated are wireless receiving sets and non-specialist sound recording equipment supplied to a charity for free loan to the blind. See 12.7(*a*) and (*b*) CHARITIES for full details.

(c) **Adaptation of goods.** The supply

- to a disabled person of services of adapting goods to suit his or her condition, and

- to a charity of services of adapting goods to suit the condition of a handicapped person to whom the goods are to be made available, by sale or otherwise, by the charity,

together with a supply of goods in connection with the supply of those services.

Where goods are adapted prior to supply, an apportionment must be made to determine the supply of services of adaptation (zero-rated) and the supply of the goods in their original state (probably standard-rated).

[*VATA 1994, 8 Sch Group 12, Items 3, 4, 6 and Note 8*].

(d) **Repair and maintenance.** The supply to a handicapped person or charity of a service of repair or maintenance of any goods supplied under (a) above or (h) or (j) below, together with a supply of any goods in connection with those services. [*VATA 1994, 8 Sch Group 12, Items 5 and 6*].

(e) **Installation of goods.** The supply to a disabled person or to a charity of services necessarily performed in the installation of equipment or appliances (including parts and accessories therefor) within (a) above and supplied as described therein. [*VATA 1994, 8 Sch Group 12, Item 7*].

(f) **Ramps, doorways and passages.** The supply

- to a disabled person of a service of constructing ramps or widening doorways or passages for the purposes of facilitating that person's entry to or movement within his or her private residence, and

- to a charity of such services for the purpose of facilitating a disabled person's entry to or movement within *any* building (not just a private residence),

together with a supply of goods in connection with the supply of those services.

[*VATA 1994, 8 Sch Group 12, Items 8, 9 and 13*].

Preparatory work and necessary restoration work (e.g. when widening a doorway, removal of bricks and mortar and restoration of the immediate decor) can also be zero-rated provided the supply is made to the disabled person or charity concerned, as the case may be.

The services of an architect are not covered.

(C & E Notice 701/7/94, paras 20, 27).

Supplies to disabled persons. Where, strictly, the supply should be to the disabled persons, zero-rating will normally still be permitted if

- the disabled person is a minor or a dependent relative living with the householder so that the supply may technically be to the householder;

- a relative commissions work before a disabled person moves into the residence and the disabled person subsequently dies before moving in; or

- a local authority takes over a grant assigned to a disabled person and carries out the work (but not if the local authority commissions and pays for the work and the disabled person is merely a passive recipient).

(C & E Manual V1-7, Chapter 12 section 5.10).

(g) **Bathrooms, washrooms and lavatories.** The supply

- to a disabled person of a service of providing, extending or adapting a bathroom, washroom or lavatory in that person's private residence where such provision, etc. is necessary by reason of his or her condition,

- to a charity of a service of providing, extending or adapting a bathroom, washroom or lavatory for use by disabled persons in a residential home where such provision, etc. is necessary by reason of the condition of the disabled persons, and

- to a charity of a service of providing, extending or adapting a washroom or lavatory for use by disabled persons in a building (or part of a building) used principally by a charity for charitable purposes (e.g. a church hall, day centre or village hall) where such provision, etc. is necessary to facilitate the use of the washroom or lavatory by disabled persons,

together with a supply of goods in connection with the supply of those services.

[*VATA 1994, 8 Sch Group 12, Items 10–13*].

Preparatory work and necessary restoration work (e.g. ground levelling, work for the provision of water, gas, electricity and drainage as necessary, and restoration of the immediate decor) can also be zero-rated provided the supply is made to the disabled person or charity concerned, as the case may be. The services of an architect are not covered.

Where economy and feasibility dictate that a bathroom, washroom or lavatory has to be constructed or extended in a space occupied by an existing room (e.g. a bedroom or kitchen), the restoration of that room to its original size can be regarded a part of the work essential to the provision of the bathroom, etc. and can be zero-rated provided the supply is also made to the disabled person. Where the provision, extension or adaptation of a bathroom, washroom or lavatory includes the construction of an adjoining new bedroom/day room, the supply should be apportioned between the zero-rated and standard-rated parts.

(C & E Notice 701/7/94, paras 20, 27).

See also (f) above under the heading *Supplies to disabled persons* which equally applies to bathrooms, washrooms and lavatories.

(h) **Lifts.** The supply

- to a disabled person of services necessarily performed in the installation of a lift for the purpose of facilitating his or her movement between floors within that person's own private residence, and

- to a charity providing a permanent or temporary residence or day centre for disabled persons of services necessarily performed in the installation of a lift for the purpose of facilitating movement of disabled persons between floors in that building,

together with a supply of goods in connection with the supply of those services.

[*VATA 1994, 8 Sch Group 12, Items 16–18*].

Preparatory work and necessary restoration work can also be zero-rated provided the supply is made to the disabled person or charity concerned, as the case may be. The services of an architect are not covered. (C & E Notice 701/7/94, paras 20, 27).

See also (a)(iv) above.

(*j*)   **Emergency alarm systems**. The supply to

- a disabled person for his or her domestic or personal use, or

- a charity for making available to disabled persons, by sale or otherwise, for domestic or their personal use

of an alarm system designed to be capable of operation by a disabled person, and to enable him or her to alert directly a 'specified person or a control centre'.

Zero–rating also applies to the supply of services necessarily performed by a control centre in receiving and responding to calls from such an alarm system.

'*Specified person or control centre*' is a person or centre who or which is appointed to receive directly calls activated by the alarm system; and who or which retains information about the disabled person to assist that person in the event of illness, injury or similar emergency.

[*VATA 1994, 8 Sch Group 12, Items 19, 20 and Note 9*].

The specified person may be a relative, friend or neighbour.

Not included is the installation of ordinary telephone lines, telephones, internal communication systems, and intruder alarm systems which activate bells, lights or sirens.

(C & E Notice 701/7/94, para 7).

(*k*)   **Letting on hire of motor vehicles (Motability scheme)**. The letting on hire of *any* motor vehicle (i.e. whether or not specially designed/adapted for a disabled person) to a disabled person in receipt of a disability living allowance by virtue of entitlement to the mobility component or of mobility supplement (as defined) provided

- the lessor's business consists predominantly of the provision of motor vehicles to such persons;

- the vehicle is unused at the commencement of the period of letting;

- the letting is for a period of not less than three years; and

- the consideration for the letting consists wholly or partly of sums paid to the lessor, directly by the DSS or Ministry of Defence on behalf of the lessee, in respect of mobility allowance or mobility supplement to which the lessee is entitled.

The sale of the motor vehicle following the period of letting is also zero–rated provided the sale constitutes the first supply after the period of letting.

[*VATA 1994, 8 Sch Group 12, Items 14 and 15 and Notes 6 and 7*].

In practice, only vehicles leased under the Motability scheme meet the above conditions. Further information on the scheme is available from Motability, Castlewood House, 77 New Oxford Street, London WC1A 1PP.

See also (*c*) above for letting on hire of other vehicles.

(*l*)   **Transport services**. The provision of transport services is zero–rated as passenger transport provided that the vehicle is designed or adapted to carry twelve or more passengers. [*VATA 1994, 8 Sch Group 8, Item 4*]. This applies whether or not the transport service is for disabled persons.

Where the vehicle has a carrying capacity of fewer than 12 passengers, VAT must normally be charged at the standard rate on the transport services provided.

However, by concession, where the capacity is fewer than twelve solely because the vehicle has been equipped with facilities for persons in wheelchairs, the supply of transport services may be zero-rated, regardless of to whom the supply is made. The supplier is not required to obtain any declaration from the person receiving the supply. (C & E Notice 48, ESC 2.12; C & E Notice 701/7/94, Annex A).

De Voil Indirect Tax Service. See V4.281.

32.18	**IMPORTED GOODS AND ACQUISITIONS FROM OTHER EC COUNTRIES**

Imports into the UK. Where goods are imported from outside the EC by a disabled person for domestic or his personal use, or by a charity for making available to disabled persons (by sale or otherwise), they can be relieved of the VAT due on importation under the same conditions as for a supply of goods in the UK under 32.17 above. [*VATA 1994, 8 Sch Group 12, Note 1*]. The disabled person or charity (as the case may be) must sign a declaration and make sure that it is lodged with the import entry declaration made to C & E at the port or airport of importation. (C & E Notice 701/7/94, para 32).

Acquisitions from other EC countries. VAT-registered traders acquiring goods from other EC countries are not normally required to pay VAT at the place of importation but account for any VAT due (and, subject to the normal rules, claim it back as input tax) on their next VAT return. A *VAT-registered charity* which acquires from another EC country qualifying goods within 32.17 above for disabled persons can account for VAT at the zero-rate on the VAT return.

Disabled persons and non-registered charities do not have this facility.

- If they acquire goods in another EC country and bring them, or arrange for them to be brought, to the UK, VAT is chargeable on the goods at the rate prevailing in that country. Any VAT payable cannot be refunded in the UK by C & E.

- If they acquire goods in another EC country but the supplier arranges delivery, special 'distance selling' rules apply (see 23.10 EUROPEAN COMMUNITY: SINGLE MARKET) and the VAT treatment will depend upon whether the supply is treated as taking place in that other EC country or the UK.

(C & E Notice 701/7/94, para 33).

32.19	**CERTIFICATION BY DISABLED PERSON OR CHARITY**

The goods and services in 32.17 above can only be zero-rated if the disabled person or charity gives the supplier a certified declaration which the supplier keeps for production to C & E if requested. Without such a declaration, the supplier becomes liable for VAT.

Obtaining a certificate does not in itself justify zero-rating. It is still the responsibility of the supplier to take reasonable steps to satisfy himself that the customer is entitled to zero-rating and the declaration is correct. C & E will not, however, seek to recover VAT due from a supplier where a customer provided an incorrect declaration and the supplier, having taken all reasonable steps to check the validity of the declaration, fails to identify the inaccuracy and, in good faith, makes the supply at the zero-rate. (C & E Notice 48, ESC 2.11).

Declaration forms are not supplied by C & E but appropriate wording for

- goods and services supplied to an individual;

- goods and services supplied to a charity;

- a specialised vehicle supplied to an individual;

- a specialised vehicle supplied to a charity;

- importation of goods by an individual; and

- importation of goods by a charity

are included in C & E Notice 701/7/94, Annexes D, E, F, G, H and J respectively. The declarations reproduced must include all the wording appropriate to the particular relief as set out in the Annex. The declaration must be separate from, or clearly distinguished on, any order form or invoice, so that the customer does not automatically have to sign a declaration in circumstances where VAT relief is not properly available.

Where a disabled person is unable to sign a declaration, the signature of a parent, guardian or doctor is acceptable. It is similarly accepted that goods are supplied to a disabled person when supplied to a parent, spouse, guardian or trustee acting on that person's behalf.

(C & E Notice 701/7/94, para 31).

PART III WATER UTILITIES

32.20   SEWERAGE SERVICES

The following supplies are zero-rated.

(*a*) **Services of reception, disposal or treatment of foul water or sewage in bulk**. [*VATA 1994, 8 Sch Group 2, Item 1(a)*].

Included is the provision of sewerage services

- against payment of an unmeasured charge, standing charge or other availability charge; and

- for which a specific charge is made (e.g. the reception into the sewerage system and treatment of effluent charged for by reference to volume and nature, and domestic sewerage services charged for by volume).

Not included (and consequently standard-rated) are the cleaning, etc. of sewers and drains; and the removal of industrial and farm waste not discharged into the sewer.

(C & E Leaflet 701/16/92, para 2).

(*b*) **Services of emptying of cesspools, septic tanks or similar receptacles**. Zero-rating does not apply if the cesspools etc. are used in connection with the carrying on in the course of a business of a 'relevant industrial activity'.

'*Relevant industrial activity*' means any activity described in any of Divisions 1 to 5 of the 1980 edition of the publication prepared by the Central Statistical Office and known as the Standard Industrial Classification.

[*VATA 1994, 8 Sch Group 2, Item 1(b)*].

The activities within divisions 1 to 5 are as follows.

1. Energy and water supply industries.

2. Extraction of minerals and ores other than fuels; manufacture of metals, mineral products and chemicals.

3. Metal goods, engineering and vehicle industries.

4. Other manufacturing industries.

5. Construction.

If the predominant activity of the organisation is an industrial customer within 1 to 5 above, standard-rating applies to supplies for offices etc. which support the industrial activity. Different companies within a group or organisation should be classified separately. Where properties are used for both domestic and business purposes, a 'predominant use' test should be applied and the whole supply either standard or zero-rated. (C & E Leaflet 701/16/92, para 1). With effect from 28 July 1998, any business whose predominant activity falls within 1 to 5 above but which has a separate, non-industrial VAT exempt activity can receive supplies *for that activity* at the zero-rate. The exempt business activity must be capable of standing alone and C & E would usually expect it to operate from separate premises which are capable of being separately invoiced (i.e. they do not envisage that there should be any apportionment of invoices). The supplier should be given evidence that the business is entitled to zero-rating – simply a certificate or declaration by the customer will usually serve this purpose. (C & E Business Brief 16/98, 28 July 1998).

De Voil Indirect Tax Service. See V4.271.

32.21   WATER

Supply of goods. The supply of water insofar as it is not otherwise a supply of goods is to be treated as a supply of goods (and not services). [*SI 1989/1114*].

Zero-rating. The supply of water is zero-rated unless

(*a*)   the water is used in connection with the carrying on, in the course of a business, of a '*relevant industrial activity*' (see 32.20(*b*) above);

(*b*)   the water is distilled water, deionized water or water of similar purity;

(*c*)   the water is comprised in any of the excepted items in *VATA 1994, 8 Sch Group 1* (see 28.8 FOOD); or

(*d*)   for supplies, acquisitions or imports after 26 June 1996, the water has been heated so that it is supplied at a temperature higher than that at which it was before it was heated.

[*VATA 1994, 8 Sch Group 2, Item 2; SI 1996/1661*].

Included (except when made to an industrial customer) are supplies of water and ice; the provision of water against payment of an unmeasured charge, standing charge or other availability charge; charges for the abstraction of water by licence; specific charges for the supply of water by hosepipes, swimming pools, sprinklers and sprinkler licence fees; disconnection and reconnection charges through non-payment of bills; and opening and closing stopcocks at the behest of the water supplier.

Not included (and consequently standard-rated) are mineral, table and spa waters in bottles or similar containers held out for sale as a beverage.

For the purposes of (*d*) above, water naturally heated by geo-thermal energy (the earth's natural heat) is not treated as 'heated water' but where water has been deliberately heated (e.g. by pumping down cold water which returns to the surface heated) and is supplied heated, it is heated water for those purposes and excluded from zero-rating. (C & E Manual V1-7, Chapter 2 para 5).

The supply of sterile water is always zero-rated whatever the status of the customer. This even applies to water which is both sterile and distilled or deionised, except where additives alter the nature of the product.

(C & E Leaflet 701/16/92, para 3).

Water-related supplies. Always standard-rated are fluoridation charges; pressure testing of fire sprinkler systems; installation and repair of fire hydrants; hire of stand-pipes and water bowsers (irrespective of the liability of the water supplied); disconnection and reconnection of water supplies, testing private pipework and opening and closing stopcocks at the consumer's request; and rewashering ball valves and taps. (C & E Leaflet 701/16/92, para 5).

Connected civil engineering work. Certain supplies by water companies may be of a civil engineering nature and qualify for zero-rating. See 42.31-42.34 LAND AND BUILDINGS. *Water Act 1989* makes provision for raising an infrastructure charge on water and sewerage services. This charge is standard-rated. (C & E Leaflet 701/16/92, para 4).

Water meters. Always standard-rated are the supply of a water meter without installation; meter survey fees; meter-testing fees at the request of the customer; special meter-reading charges; and separate charges for maintenance of meters. The supply *and* installation of a water meter is normally standard-rated but may be zero-rated when

- the installation is carried out at the same time as that of a communication pipe or other civil engineering work in the course of construction of a qualifying building;

- it is carried out in the course of an approved alteration to a listed building for which listed building consent is required and obtained; or

- the supply is made to a non-industrial customer at the request of the water supplier.

(C & E Leaflet 701/16/92, para 6).

Water, supplied as part of an overall service e.g. in a launderette, is not a separate supply and is standard-rated (*Mander Laundries Ltd, [1973] VATTR 136 (31)*).

De Voil Indirect Tax Service. See V4.271.

33   Hotels and Holiday Accommodation

Cross-reference. See 66 TOUR OPERATORS' MARGIN SCHEME.

De Voil Indirect Tax Service. See V4.113.

33.1   HOTELS, INNS AND BOARDING HOUSES

Supplies of accommodation. The provision in a hotel, inn, boarding house or 'similar establishment' of

(*a*)   sleeping accommodation;

(*b*)   accommodation in rooms which are provided in conjunction therewith (e.g. private bathrooms and sitting-rooms in suites); and

(*c*)   accommodation for the purpose of a supply of catering

is standard-rated.

'*Similar establishment*' includes premises in which there is provided furnished sleeping accommodation (with or without board or facilities for the preparation of food) and which are used by or held out as being suitable for use by visitors or travellers.

[*VATA 1994, 9 Sch Group 1, Item 1(d)*].

Accommodation in motels, guest houses, bed and breakfast establishments, private residential clubs and hostels is included. Furnished sleeping accommodation in any other premises (e.g. service flats) which are used by or held out as being suitable for use by visitors, travellers or others for whom the accommodation is not permanent is also standard-rated. In most cases such establishments will provide one or more meals, possibly at an inclusive price, but board, or the facilities for the preparation of food, is *not* necessary for an establishment to be regarded as a hotel, etc. (C & E Leaflet 709/3/93, para 2). See, however, *International Student House (14420)* where fees for accommodation provided by a charity for overseas students were held to be exempt because the charity was providing the accommodation to help overseas students and improve international relations rather than for gain. The buildings were not therefore 'similar establishments'.

Rooms used for catering. Where rooms are supplied in a hotel, etc. for the purpose of a supply of catering *by the hotel*, the supply is standard-rated under (*c*) above whatever the length of the let. If the rooms are let without catering (or the catering is supplied by another person) the letting of the room is normally exempt. Similarly, the grant of a concession to operate a kitchen, restaurant or kiosk facilities for the preparation of food or drink within a hotel, etc. is normally exempt because there is no supply of catering to the concessionaire. (C & E Leaflet 709/3/93, para 3).

Other accommodation and services. Other supplies of accommodation or rooms in a hotel, etc. (e.g. letting of conference rooms, halls, shops and display cases) are generally exempt, subject to any option to tax under 42.20 LAND AND BUILDINGS. Any goods or services provided in conjunction with accommodation (e.g. catering, car parking, use of equipment) and any extras charged for separately (e.g. telephone calls) are standard-rated. Any services charge is standard-rated but tips freely given over and above the total charge are outside the scope of VAT. (C & E Leaflet 709/3/93, para 4).

33.2   Stays over four weeks

For the first four weeks of any stay VAT is due on the full amount payable in the normal way.

33.2 Hotels and Holiday Accommodation

Where accommodation within 33.1 above is provided to an *individual* for a period exceeding four weeks, from the 29th day of the stay (or letting) VAT is only due on

(*a*) meals, drinks and service charges; and

(*b*) facilities provided apart from the right to occupy the accommodation (i.e. the value of the accommodation is excluded from the VAT calculation).

The value of the facilities subject to VAT under (*b*) above must not be less than 20% of the total amount due for those facilities and the accommodation. Throughout the period the accommodation must be provided *for the use of the individual* either alone or with one or more other persons who occupy the accommodation with him but not either directly or indirectly at their own expense.

[*VATA 1994, 6 Sch 9*].

The rules do not apply to bookings by companies where the accommodation is used by a succession of short-term occupants and each stay is less than four weeks at a time.

Example

Weekly terms for accommodation, facilities and meals are £235 (£200 plus £35 VAT) of which £94 (£80 + £14 VAT) represents the charge for meals. For the first 4 weeks, the VAT charge is the full £35 but thereafter a reduced VAT value may be calculated in one of the following ways. The proportion for meals has been taken to be 40% but this will not always be so.

(*a*) *If charges are expressed in VAT-exclusive terms*

	£	£
Total VAT-exclusive weekly charge	200.00	
VAT-exclusive charge for meals	80.00	14.00
	£120.00	
VAT-exclusive value of facilities (20% minimum)	24.00	4.20
VAT due		£18.20

Weekly terms are therefore £200.00 + £18.20 VAT.

(*b*) *If charges are expressed in VAT-inclusive terms and the total amount charged to the guest is reduced to take account of the reduced element of VAT*

VAT is as under (a) above but the calculation is

	£	£
Total VAT-inclusive charge	235.00	
VAT-inclusive charge for meals	94.00	14.00
VAT-inclusive charge for facilities and accommodation	141.00	
VAT included 7/47 × £141	£121.00	
Balance (exclusive of VAT)	£120.00	
VAT-exclusive value of facilities (20% minimum)	24.00	4.20
VAT due		£18.20

The weekly terms are £200 + £18.20 VAT.

(c) *If charges are expressed in VAT-inclusive terms but the total amount charged to the guest is not reduced to take account of the reduced element of VAT*

	£	£
Total VAT inclusive charge	235.00	
VAT-inclusive charge for meals	94.00	14.00
VAT-inclusive charge for facilities and accommodation	141.00	
VAT included 7/207* × £141	4.76	4.76
VAT-exclusive charge for facilities and accommodation	£136.24	
Total VAT		£18.76

The weekly terms are not reduced (i.e. £235 including £18.76 VAT).

$$*\quad \frac{17.5 \times \text{facilities element \%}}{100 + (17.5 \times \text{facilities element \%})} = 7/207 \text{ where facilities element is 20\%}$$

Although VAT is only due on the reduced amount, the full VAT-exclusive amount (£200.00 in (*a*) and (*b*) and £216.24 in (*c*)) must be included in Box 6 of the VAT return. This is because the accommodation element of the total charge continues to be the consideration for a standard-rated supply even though the value for the purposes of calculating the VAT becomes nil after the first four weeks.

Taxable turnover. Where the reduced rate rules for stays longer than four weeks are used, taxable turnover for registration purposes is the full value of meals, accommodation and facilities supplied to all customers *less* the value of the accommodation provided to customers after the initial four week period (subject to a maximum of 80% of the value of facilities and accommodation provided after the initial four week period).

Breaks in stays. Normally, the reduced value rules above cannot be used unless the guest stays for a continuous period of more than four weeks. For example, stays of three weeks in every month are subject to VAT in full. Similarly, if a guest stays for five weeks, is away for a week and then returns for five weeks, each stay is treated separately and the reduced value basis can only be used for the fifth week of each stay. There are two exceptions to this. A period of absence is not treated as ending a stay if the guest

- is a long-term resident and leaves for an occasional weekend or holiday; or

- is a student who leaves during the vacation but returns to the same accommodation for the next term; or

- pays a retaining fee.

In such cases, the stay is treated as continuous and VAT need only be charged in full for the first four weeks of the overall stay. A guest need not necessarily occupy the same room for his stay to be treated as continuous.

If a retaining fee is paid for a period of absence during the first four weeks of a stay, VAT is due on it at the standard rate. If paid for a period of absence after that period, then the reduced value rules above apply. Provided the fee is no more than the amount treated as payment for accommodation, no VAT is due. Otherwise the fee must be treated as payment for both accommodation and facilities using the rules outlined above.

(C & E Leaflet 709/3/93, para 5).

33.3   **Accommodation and catering supplied by employers to employees**

The value of accommodation and catering in a hotel etc. supplied to its employees is to be taken to be nil unless made for a consideration wholly or partly in money in which case the value is determined without regard to any consideration other than money. [*VATA 1994, 6 Sch 10(1)(b)*]. Any payments (e.g. in cash or by a deduction from wages not provided for in the contract of employment) are treated as VAT inclusive. The reduced value provisions in 33.2 above may apply to accommodation. Where employees are paid a minimum wage under a *Wages Order* for an industry and that *Order* allows for appropriate reductions to be made for catering and accommodation, these calculations are steps in arriving at the amount of the weekly wage to be paid and are *not* monetary consideration on which the employer is liable to VAT (*RW & MJ Goodfellow, [1986] VATTR 119 (2107)*). (C & E Leaflet 709/3/93, para 6).

33.4   Deposits, cancellation charges and booking fees

Most deposits are advance payments on which VAT must be accounted for in the return period in which they are received.

If a cancellation charge is made when a customer cancels a booking, no VAT is due on the charge (because it is not a payment in respect of a supply). If the customer has to forfeit a deposit, any VAT accounted for on the deposit can be reclaimed.

The provision of a guarantee or insurance against customers paying cancellation charges is standard-rated. However, if

- the taxable person is permitted to carry on insurance business under *Insurance Companies Act 1982, s 2*, or

- he arranges as an agent for insurance to be provided to his customer by a permitted insurer and, under the policy, it is the individual customer's risk which is insured,

the insurance charge made is exempt.

Any commission received from a permitted person for arranging a supply of insurance is also exempt.

Booking fees charged by a person supplying accommodation are treated as deposits above. Booking fees charged by agents who arrange a supply on behalf of someone else are the consideration for a taxable supply and VAT is due whether or not the accommodation is taken up.

(C & E Notice 700, para 3.17; C & E Leaflet 709/3/93, paras 7, 8).

Charges levied on customers who make 'guaranteed reservations' of hotel accommodation but do not take up that accommodation are subject to VAT (*C & E Commrs v Bass plc QB 1992, [1993] STC 42*).

33.5   HOLIDAY ACCOMMODATION ETC. IN THE UK

The grant of any interest in or right over or licence to occupy 'holiday accommodation' is standard-rated. *Included* is

- the grant of an interest in, or in any part of, a building designed as a dwelling or number of dwellings or the site of such a building if

  (i) the interest granted is such that the grantee is not entitled to reside in the building, or part, throughout the year; or

  (ii) residence there throughout the year, or the use of the building or part as the grantee's principal private residence, is prevented by the terms of a covenant, statutory planning consent or similar permission; and

- any supply made pursuant to a tenancy, lease or licence under which the grantee is or has been permitted to erect and occupy holiday accommodation.

Excluded (and therefore exempt) is the grant of the fee simple, or a tenancy, lease or licence to the extent it is granted for consideration in the form of a premium, in a building or part which is not a 'new building'. A *'new building'* is one completed less than three years before the grant.

'*Holiday accommodation*' includes any accommodation in a building, hut (including a beach hut or chalet), caravan, houseboat or tent which is 'advertised or held out as' holiday accommodation or as suitable for holiday or leisure use, but excludes any accommodation within 33.1 above.

See 42.1 LAND AND BUILDINGS for the meaning of '*interest in or right over*' and '*licence to occupy*'.

[*VATA 1994, 9 Sch Group 1, Item 1(e), Notes 11–13*].

The effect of the above is that the sale or lease of a house, flat or other accommodation is generally standard-rated as holiday accommodation if the property is new and the purchaser cannot reside there throughout the year or use it as his principal private residence. VAT must be accounted for on the initial charge and on any periodic charges such as ground rent and service or other charges. If the accommodation is no longer new, any payment for the freehold or premium under the lease is exempt but any periodic charges, including rent and service charges, are standard-rated. However, following the tribunal decision in *Ashworth (Mrs B), [1994] VATTR 275 (12924)*, the sale or lease of a flat or house which can be used as a person's principal private residence but which cannot be occupied throughout the year due to a time-related restriction on occupancy (in *Ashworth* the lessees were unable to occupy the property for the month of February each year) is exempt provided the development on which the property is situated is not a holiday development and is not advertised or held out as such. This also applies to any periodic charges such as rent and service charges.

The provision of a site for holiday accommodation under a tenancy, lease or licence is standard-rated even if the person to whom the site is provided is responsible for erecting the accommodation on it. (C & E Leaflet 709/3/93, paras 11, 12).

'*Advertised or held out as*' is regarded by C & E to include accommodation

• where it is advertised, or allowed to be advertised,

  (i) for holiday or leisure use;

  (ii) in a specialist publication involving tourism, holidays or leisure activities; or

  (iii) by a body promoting such activities;

• where the terms or conditions on which it is let indicate that it is for holiday accommodation; or

• supplied during the holiday season only.

Residential accommodation is not included merely because it is situated in a holiday resort.

(C & E Leaflet 709/3/93, para 10).

See *RW and B Sheppard [1977] VATTR 272 (481)* for a case concerning short letting of furnished flats treated as holiday accommodation in which the above tests were considered.

Even where a property has been 'held out' as holiday accommodation, where there is no causative nexus between the publication of the advertisement of holiday accommodation and the letting of the whole building for some different purpose, there is no provision of holiday accommodation. See *Cooper and Chapman (Builders) Ltd v C & E Commrs QB 1992, [1993] STC 1.*

Options to purchase interests or rights. The grant of any right to call for or to be granted an interest or right which would be standard-rated under the provisions above is also standard-rated. *Included* is an equitable right, a right under an option or right of pre-emption and, in relation to Scotland, a personal right. [*VATA 1994, 9 Sch Group 1, Item 1(n)*].

Value for VAT purposes. VAT is payable on the full amount due for the holiday accommodation, including incidental services, irrespective of the length of the stay. (See 33.2 above for long stay arrangements in hotels, etc.) (C & E Leaflet 709/3/93, para 17).

Deposits, cancellation charges and booking fees. See 33.4 above.

33.6   Off-season letting

Holiday accommodation advertised or offered at lower rates during the off-season may be treated as *residential* accommodation provided it is let for that purpose and for more than four weeks and the property is situated where holiday trade is clearly seasonal e.g. not in London. In such cases the whole of the let, including the first four weeks, is an exempt supply. The 'season' in such resorts would normally be expected to be at least from Easter to the end of September. (C & E Leaflet 709/3/93, para 13). See, however, 42.20 LAND AND BUILDINGS for the option to tax such lettings.

33.7   Time-share and multi-ownership schemes

A supply of holiday accommodation in a house, flat, chalet, etc. under a time-share or multi-ownership scheme is standard rated if the initial supply is of 'new' accommodation and exempt if it is no longer new. A property is *'new'* if completed less than three years before the grant. Any additional maintenance and periodic charges are standard-rated in all cases. These liability rules apply however the supply is effected e.g. by lease or licence, through membership of a time-share club or through shares in a company set up for that purpose. (C & E Leaflet 709/3/93, para 14).

See *American Real Estate (Scotland) Ltd, [1980] VATTR 80 (947).* Time-shares etc. cannot be zero-rated as tenancies for a term certain exceeding 21 years (or Scottish equivalent) within the definition of 'major interest'. [*VATA 1994, 8 Sch Group 5, Item 1 and Note 13; SI 1995/280*]. See also *Cottage Holiday Associates Ltd v C & E Commrs QB 1982, [1983] STC 278* and *Mr & Mrs Cretney [1983] VATTR 271 (1503)* where an option to purchase freehold reversion was also offered.

For time-sharing of a yacht based abroad, see *Oathplan Ltd, [1982] VATTR 195 (1299).*

33.8   Construction of holiday accommodation

A builder can zero-rate the supply of services in the course of construction of a dwelling even though it will be used to supply holiday accommodation. The word 'dwelling' takes on its normal everyday meaning. (C & E Leaflet 709/3/93, para 19).

33.9   Caravans and camping

Holiday accommodation provided in any type of caravan already sited on a pitch is standard-rated. (The provision of *other* accommodation in such a caravan is exempt.) The hire for holiday purposes, or any other use, of

- caravans suitable for use as trailers drawn by motor vehicles having an unladen weight of less than 2,030 kilogrammes; and

- caravan units designed to be mounted and carried on, and demounted from, motor vehicles

is standard-rated.

[*VATA 1994, 8 Sch Group 9, Item 3; 9 Sch Group 1, Item 1(e)*]. (C & E Leaflet 709/3/93, para 15).

Caravan pitches. See 42.8 LAND AND BUILDINGS for caravan pitches.

Camping. The provision of holiday accommodation in a tent is standard-rated. [*VATA 1994, 9 Sch Group 1, Item (e)*]. Any associated facilities are also standard-rated. See 42.8 LAND AND BUILDINGS for tent pitches.

34 Imports

Cross-references. See 12.11 CHARITIES for relief for importations; 19.3 DEATH for imported legacies; 39.4 INTERNATIONAL SERVICES for imported services; 54.30 PRINTED MATTER, ETC. for imported printing matter; 69.7 VALUATION for valuation of imports; 70 WAREHOUSED GOODS AND FREE ZONES; 71.3, 71.4 and 71.5 WORKS OF ART ETC. for importations and reimportations.

De Voil Indirect Tax Service. See V3.301–357.

The contents of this chapter are as follows.

34.1 GENERAL NOTES

The single market. The provisions of this chapter apply to importations of goods from outside the EC. **For the provisions relating to acquisitions of goods from other EC countries, see 23.3** EUROPEAN COMMUNITY: SINGLE MARKET.

The Isle of Man, although not part of the UK, is treated as part of the UK for VAT purposes. VAT is chargeable in the Isle of Man under Manx law which generally parallels UK legislation. Goods removed from the Isle of Man to the UK are not normally treated as imports provided any VAT has been accounted for in the Isle of Man or, if the goods were relieved of VAT in the Isle of Man, the conditions of that relief have not been broken. However, where goods are removed from the Isle of Man into the UK and were charged to VAT in the Isle of Man at a different rate to that applicable in the UK (or were relieved from VAT subject to a condition which was not subsequently complied with) the difference in the tax will be charged in the UK. [*SI 1982/1067, Art 3*]. (C & E Notice 702, para 1.5).

The Channel Islands are part of the Customs territory of the EC but not part of the VAT territory. Any goods received from the Channel Islands are therefore regarded as imports. (C & E Notice 702, para 1.6).

Trader's Unique Reference Number (TURN). Any VAT-registered person who imports goods from outside the EC needs a TURN. Without this, it may not be possible to get the evidence needed to reclaim the VAT paid on imports. TURNs are obtained by writing (stating full name, address and VAT registration number) to

TURN Team T & SO 6
Room 904, Portcullis House
Victoria Avenue
Southend-on-Sea SS2 6AL

Tel 01702-366425/27

De Voil Indirect Tax Service. See V3.302.

34.2 THE CHARGE TO VAT

VAT is charged and payable on the importation of goods into the UK (which for VAT purposes includes the territorial sea of the UK i.e. waters within twelve nautical miles of the coastline) as if it were a duty of customs. The rate of VAT is the same as if the goods had been supplied in the UK (whether or not the person importing the goods is registered for VAT). The VAT is chargeable in addition to any customs and/or excise duty or other charges due and is calculated on the value which includes such charges. See 69.7 VALUATION.

CEMA 1979 and other UK legislation relating to customs or excise duties charged on importation into the UK and any Community legislation relating to customs duties charged on goods entering the EC, apply in modified form so as to relate to VAT on importations.

Goods are treated as imported from a place outside the EC where

(*a*) they arrive in the UK directly from outside the EC and are entered for home use in the UK (or customs duty otherwise becomes payable on them); or

(*b*) they have been placed, in another EC country or in the UK, under one of the customs arrangements listed below and are entered for removal to home use in the UK (or customs duty otherwise becomes payable on them).

[*VATA 1994, ss 1(1)(4), 2(1), 15, 16, 96(11)*].

The customs arrangements referred to in (*b*) above are as follows.

  (i) Temporary storage (not strictly a customs arrangement but all goods arriving from outside the EC have the status of goods in temporary storage until they are entered and cleared for home use or another procedure).

  (ii) Free zones.

  (iii) Customs warehousing.

  (iv) Inward processing relief (duty suspension system).

  (v) Temporary importation (including means of transport) with total relief from customs duty.

  (vi) External Community Transit (T1) arrangements.

  (vii) Internal Community Transit (T2) arrangements (applies to some trade with special territories inside the EC customs area but outside the EC for VAT purposes).

(viii) Goods admitted into territorial waters in order to be incorporated into drilling or production platforms for purposes of the construction, repair, maintenance or alteration or fitting-out of such platforms, or to link such drilling or production platforms to the mainland.

  (ix) Goods admitted into territorial waters for the fuelling and provisioning of drilling or production platforms.

(C & E Notice 702, para 1.3, Appendix B).

VAT is also payable on imported goods removed from C & E warehouses and free zones. See 70 WAREHOUSED GOODS AND FREE ZONES.

The time of importation of any goods is

- where brought by sea, when the ship carrying them comes within the limits of a port;

- where brought by air, when the aircraft carrying them lands in the UK or when the goods are unloaded in the UK, whichever is the earlier;

- where brought by land, when the goods are brought across the boundary into Northern Ireland;

- where brought by pipeline, when the goods are brought within the limits of a port or brought across the boundary into Northern Ireland.

[*CEMA 1979, s 5(2)(6)*].

In short, the time of importation for VAT purposes is the moment when customs duty is due on the goods.

Supplies between the time of arrival in the UK and before delivery of import entry. If imported goods are supplied between the time of their arrival in the UK and the time when an import entry is delivered to Customs, the supply can be zero-rated provided, by arrangement, the purchaser is required to make the import entry. [*VATA 1994, 8 Sch Group 13, Item 1*].

De Voil Indirect Tax Service. See V3.302; V3.312; V3.313.

34.3   IMPORT ENTRY PROCEDURE

All goods imported into the UK must be declared to Customs using the Single Administrative Document (SAD Form C88). Goods may be subject to examination and documentary checks are carried out on import entries so that Customs can satisfy themselves that

- all documents required for VAT purposes are present;

- the value declared for VAT and the amount of VAT declared as due are correct;

- the rate of VAT applicable at the time of acceptance of the entry is correctly stated; and

- importers are eligible for any VAT relief claimed.

The import declaration must normally be accompanied by a declaration of value of Form C105, C105A, C105B or C109 as appropriate.

Unless the goods are placed under excise warehousing or one of the customs arrangements listed in 34.2 (i)–(ix) above, any VAT due must normally either be paid at the time of importation or be deferred with any duty if the importer or his agent are approved for deferment.

Bulked entry. Bulked entry allows a person making the entry to make a single entry where goods are consigned to several importers, or a single importer receives goods imported in the same vessel or aircraft from several suppliers. To use this facility where goods are consigned to several importers, the person making the entry must have prior approval of C & E at the place of importation. Single importers do not need prior approval. An agent making bulked entry on behalf of several consignees must pay the VAT or, if deferring payment, use his own deferment account.

Amendment of entries. Where amendment of an entry is made after the goods have been cleared out of official charge and this results in less VAT being payable than was originally declared and paid, the higher amount of VAT should generally be reclaimed in the normal way. Exceptionally, the procedure for reclaiming VAT overpaid in 34.6 below can be used. Where amendment of an entry after clearance results in more VAT being payable, a completed Form C18 must be submitted together with the additional amount of VAT due. The additional payment will appear on the import VAT certificate as evidence for input tax deduction (see 34.11 below).

Postal imports

- *Consignments (other than Datapost packets) not exceeding £2,000.* A VAT-registered person importing goods for business purposes does not have to pay VAT immediately on importation. Instead, he may account for the VAT due in Box 1 of the VAT return covering the period of importation. Input tax deduction can be claimed on the same return (subject to the normal rules). A customs declaration must accompany the goods showing the consignee's VAT registration number and the nature, quantity and value of the goods. If the VAT number is not clearly shown, VAT may be charged. A cash refund will not be made so the charge label, postal wrapper and any customs declaration attached to the package must be kept to support the claim to input tax. [*SI 1995/2518, Reg 122*].

- *Datapost packets not exceeding £2,000 in value.* For such imports, the Post Office require payment of the VAT when the package is delivered. The charge label attached must be kept to support any claim to input tax. It is not possible to defer payment of import charges.

- *Consignments over £2,000 in value.* For these imports, an entry (which will be sent to the consignee) must be made and returned to C & E together with an invoice or other acceptable evidence of value. VAT and other charges due at importation are payable immediately unless the consignee is approved to use the deferment scheme. After payment, C & E send the consignee a copy of the entry to support any claim to input tax.

Period entry. This is a scheme which allows authorised importers, who use computers for accounting and stock control purposes, to provide C & E with the required import information on a periodic post-import basis in the form of supplementary declarations on computer media. Authorised importers obtain clearance of their goods either by making a simplified declaration on a SAD or, if they are also authorised for Local Import Control (LIC), by an input to their computer system. Duty and VAT are paid using the deferment system.

Simplified procedure for import clearance (SPIC). SPIC is a simplified procedure for declaring and clearing certain low value goods instead of completing a SAD. The SPIC entry (Form C1451) allows up to six different consignments to be shown on separate lines on the form. Customs charges can be deferred against the deferment number of either the importer or the person making the declaration on each line of the form. These imports appear on the import VAT certificate (the normal evidence for input tax deduction).

Goods received from outside the EC and consigned to another EC country. Where a person receives goods from outside the EC and consigns them to a destination in another EC country, he must normally either

(*a*) put the goods in free circulation in the UK, paying any customs duty and/or import VAT due; or

(*b*) place the goods under the external Community Transit (T1) arrangements, in which case any duty and/or VAT is payable in the EC country of destination.

See, however, 34.20 below for VAT relief for goods imported and put into free circulation in the UK in the course of a zero-rated supply of those goods to a taxable person in another EC country.

(C & E Notice 702, paras 4.1–4.7).

De Voil Indirect Tax Service. See V3.318.

34.4 Imports

34.4 PAYMENT OF VAT

Payment of VAT on imported goods is due at the time of importation (or removal from warehouse) unless the importer or his agent is approved for deferment. [*CEMA 1979, ss 43(1), 44(1), 45, 93(1)(2); VATA 1994, s 38*].

De Voil Indirect Tax Service. See V5.115–122.

34.5 Deferment of VAT

A registered trader approved by C & E may defer paying charges due on importation or removal of goods from a customs or an excise warehouse or from a free zone. An agent who enters goods for an importer or owner may also use the scheme. The charges which can be deferred under these circumstances are VAT; customs duties; excise duties (including tobacco products duty); levies imposed under the Common Agricultural Policy (CAP) of the EC; positive Monetary Compensatory Amounts under the CAP; and anti-dumping or countervailing duties imposed by the EC. VAT and excise duty can be deferred where payable on the following home-produced or home-manufactured goods on removal from excise warehouse, viz. spirits (including perfume and composite goods); wine and made-wine fortified or rendered sparkling in the warehouse; cider and perry; and hydrocarbon oils. Deposits for any of the above charges may also be deferred.

Period of deferment. Except for excise duties, charges deferred during a calendar month ('*the accounting period*') must be paid as a lump sum on the 15th of the next month or, if that is not a 'working day', on the next working day *after* it. For excise duty, the accounting period runs from the 15th of one month to the 14th of the next month and payment must be made on the 29th of the latter month (28th February in non-leap years) or, if that is not a working day, on the working day *before* it. '*Working day*' is any day on which the Bank of England in London is open for business.

Payment. Payment is made by the Bank Giro system of direct debit. No other method of payment is accepted although special arrangements will be made if an emergency prevents C & E collecting by direct debit.

Guarantees. A guarantee on Form C1201 (obtainable from local C & E offices) is required from an approved bank or insurance company. The guarantor agrees to cover all amounts deferred up to an overall maximum amount in each calendar month (the '*deferment limit*') which must be enough to cover all deferable liabilities. The guarantee can be varied by replacement with a bigger or smaller amount or by giving a supplementary guarantee to cover extra liabilities in peak periods. Any supplementary guarantee must also be given on Form C1201 and must run to the last day of a calendar month. Both replacement and supplementary guarantees must run from the first day of a calendar month and must be received before the starting date.

Approval. Application forms for deferral are available from HM Customs and Excise, ASD 8D, Central Deferment Office, 10th Floor South East, Alexander House, 21 Victoria Avenue, Southend-on-Sea, Essex SS99 1AA (Tel: (01702) 367425/431/450). A set of forms comprises

Form C1200   Application form
Form C1201   The guarantee
Form C1202   Direct debit mandate
Form C1207N   Agents' authority (see below)

If satisfied with the application, C & E will issue a Certificate of Approval showing a *deferment approval number* (DAN). This must be quoted on each request for deferment and any correspondence with C & E (including correspondence from the guarantor).

Approval covers the importer etc., to the limit of his guarantee, for deferment of all eligible charges and can be used at any port, airport, warehouse etc. in the UK. Companies which are members of the same group registration for VAT can apply for group approval.

The Deferment Section must be notified immediately of any change of name, address or VAT registration number or of ceasing to trade. A new direct debit mandate on Form C1202 must be sent at least 10 days before the next payment is due if a bank account is transferred to another bank.

Approval can be revoked at any time for reasonable cause. The direct debit mandate must not be cancelled until all deferred payments have been made.

Procedure. At importation, deferment is requested on the import entry by putting the deferment approval number and the correct payment code in the boxes provided. Charges may be deferred against the importer's account or an agent's account (see below). Deferment cannot be requested on importations for which no entry is required (unless an entry is made for them) or on postal importations (except those with a value exceeding £2,000 and entered on Form C88A).

On removal from customs warehouse, deferment is requested on the entry (warrant) for removal. This applies also under scheduling or other approved simplified arrangements where the entry is presented after the removal of the goods. Charges due on deficiencies in warehouse or in transit cannot be deferred.

On removal from free zone, deferment is requested on the entry presented when the goods are removed from the zone.

If deferment is requested, it must be for the total of all the deferable charges on the entry. It is, however, possible to defer VAT against the importer's account and other charges against an agent's account (see below). Deferment can be refused if the guarantee limit for the calendar month has been exceeded or if the amount of the guarantee left is insufficient to fully cover the deferment requested.

Where, after having allowed deferment, it is found that more or less was payable on the entry, C & E will normally adjust the deferment account accordingly. Where this is not possible, if more was payable, the balance is payable immediately and if less was payable, the amount overdeclared will be repaid on, or as soon as possible after, the direct debit day on which it is paid. However, repayments of VAT are not normally made to VAT registered traders who are expected to recover the amount on their next VAT return.

Agents. An agent making an entry can request deferment against his principal's approval number provided he is authorised to do so. This can be done on Form C1207N (standing authority allowing the agent to use the number whenever or wherever entering goods and obtainable with the deferment application) or Form C1207S ('one-off' authority in respect of a specific consignment or removal of goods and obtainable from local C & E offices).

In emergencies (e.g. when goods are diverted to another port at short notice) C & E will accept a telex worded as follows as authority to an agent.

To HM Customs and Excise at (insert name of port/airport)

1. I am/we are (insert name of business)

2. My/our telephone number is (insert number)

3. I/we hereby authorise (insert name of agent) to use my/our deferment approval number (insert number) when requesting deferment of the charges on the goods imported by me/us on the attached entry.

Alternatively a facsimile copy of a completed Form C1207S signed by a responsible officer, or a statement on headed paper using the telex wording above and signed by a responsible person, is acceptable. The telex or facsimile must be sent to the agent to present with the entry.

If an agent appoints a sub-agent (e.g. because he has no office at a particular port) the sub-agent can request deferment against his own approval number or the importer's number if authorised under the above procedure. He cannot request deferment against the other agent's number.

An agent making a bulked entry of goods consigned to several importers may use his own account to defer the charges payable but cannot defer the charges against individual importer's accounts.

Statements. Periodic statements are sent at approximately weekly intervals summarising details of deferments at each accounting centre and showing the total amount deferred so far in that particular month. Any queries should be taken up immediately with the accounting centre concerned. 'Nil' statements are not normally sent.

Reclaiming VAT. Deferment statements cannot be used as evidence for input tax deduction. See 34.11 below for evidence required.

[*SI 1976/1223; SI 1978/1725*]. See also C & E Notice 101.

De Voil Indirect Tax Service. See V3.306.

34.6   **Reclaiming VAT overpaid**

General. Import VAT can only be reclaimed as input tax by a VAT-registered importer. However, amounts overpaid as import VAT (e.g. because of misclassification) are generally repayable to the person who paid the amount to C & E, subject to certain conditions.

Repayments to VAT-registered traders. A VAT-registered trader who has overpaid import VAT can apply for the payment to be adjusted. The importer or his agent must complete Form C285 and the importer must support the request with the signed written declaration:

'I am expecting direct repayment/partial repayment to be made, and no claim to input tax deduction has been or will be made by me on the basis of the document as originally issued.'

If the request is accepted, C & E will make the repayment. Any such repayment will be processed through the duty adjustment system. VAT repayments are not given special priority, and consideration should therefore be given as to whether the money could be recovered more quickly through the normal input tax deduction system.

A claim for immediate repayment may also be made if VAT has been wrongly charged because an incorrect Deferment Approval Number (DAN) has been quoted or keyed. Any claim should be submitted to the relevant Entry Processing Unit.

Repayments to agents. See 34.8 below for the normal rules. However, an agent who has overpaid import VAT (e.g. because goods have been misclassified) may be able to reclaim the amount overpaid if he can provide evidence that he has not been, and will not be, reimbursed by his importer.

(C & E Notice 702, para 2.6).

34.7   **Goods lost or destroyed before clearance**

In such an event, application can be made to Customs at the place where the import entry was presented for repayment or remission of the VAT due using Form C285 (see above under *Reclaiming VAT overpaid*). (C & E Notice 702, para 2.9).

34.8   **Repayment of import VAT to shipping and forwarding agents by C & E if the importer fails to pay him**

If an importer fails to pay a shipping or forwarding agent any VAT paid by the agent on his behalf, in normal circumstances the agent's only recourse is to the importer. However, by concession, if an importer becomes insolvent without reimbursing the agent for VAT paid or deferred, C & E will repay the import VAT to the agent provided all the following conditions are satisfied.

(*a*)   Either

   •   the importer has gone into liquidation; or

   •   an administrator or administrative receiver has been appointed who certifies that in his opinion the assets of the insolvent importer are insufficient to cover payment of *any* dividend to the unsecured creditors.

(*b*)   The interval between the date of import entry for the goods and the date of insolvency is no more than six months.

(*c*)   The agent entered the goods in accordance with instructions from the importer.

(*d*)   The goods have been re-exported from the UK in the same state as they were imported and, during the time they were in the UK, the goods were under the control of the agent and were not used.

(*e*)   The agent must write to the Entry Processing Unit (EPU) where the goods were entered and VAT paid enclosing

   •   evidence that the input tax has been paid to C & E;

   •   a certificate from the liquidator, etc. that the VAT has not been, and will not be, reclaimed as input tax;

   •   confirmation from the liquidator, etc. of (*b*) above;

   •   a declaration that he will not recover the relevant VAT in whole or in part from the insolvency; and

   •   evidence to satisfy C & E of (*c*) above.

(C & E Notice 702, para 2.5; C & E Notice 48, ESC 2.14).

De Voil Indirect Tax Service. See V5.160.

34.9   **Unregistered persons**

Where goods are imported for business purposes, the same procedures apply for entry of goods on importation and payment or deferment of VAT as for registered traders except that an unregistered person does not require an import VAT certificate (C79) and is not entitled to claim import VAT and does not therefore receive a copy of the import VAT certificate. He may reclaim VAT paid on imported goods only when VAT was overpaid (by using Form C285) or the goods were not in accordance with contract (see 34.19 below). See also 34.24 below for relief for re-importations by unregistered persons. (C & E Notice 702, para 6.1).

34.10 Imports

34.10 INPUT TAX DEDUCTION

VAT paid on the importation of goods can be claimed as input tax subject to the normal rules.

34.11 Evidence for input tax deduction

The normal evidence of the payment of import VAT is the Import VAT Certificate (Form C79) which is issued monthly. This certificate is sent, normally around the 12th day of the following month, to the VAT-registered person whose VAT registration number, plus a three digit suffix, is shown on the import entry. The whole number is known as the Trader Unique Reference Number (TURN). The date when the VAT shown on the certificate may be treated as input tax is normally the accounting date alongside each item, not the date when the certificate is issued.

The certificate may be copied for internal purposes and a copy is allowed as an accounting document for input tax deduction provided the original is made available for inspection by the control officer on demand.

If a monthly certificate is lost, replacements can be obtained (for up to six years) from HM Customs and Excise, VAT Central Unit, Section 4B, 1st Floor Alexander House, Victoria Avenue, Southend-on-Sea, SS99 1AU. Applications should be in writing quoting VAT registration number and the month(s) for which replacement is required.

There are still, however, some types of importation which do not appear on Form C79. The following list summarises the various methods of import procedures and the acceptable evidence of payment.

Import procedure	*Evidence for input tax deduction*
Air/maritime imports	
Single Administration Document (SAD) – manually processed	Monthly VAT certificate
SAD – trader input/computer processed	Monthly VAT certificate
SAD – Customs input/computer processed	Monthly VAT certificate
Bulked entries (see below) – SAD	Customs authenticated invoices
Registered consignees	Customs authenticated invoices
Period entry (see below) – SAD (simplified)	Trader produced computer schedule PE 33 (not authenticated by Customs) VAT adjustment schedule
Period entry – Adjustment schedules only	Monthly VAT certificate
Transit Shed Register – imports not exceeding £600 (non DTI)	Customs authenticated commercial invoice or locally produced forms certified by Customs. The concession allowing use of copies of agents' disbursement invoices in certain circumstances will continue
Simplified Procedure for Import Clearance (SPIC) – imports not exceeding £600 – Form C1451	Monthly VAT certificates

Postal imports

Exceeding £2,000 – SAD

Not exceeding £2,000 – Customs declaration (Form CI (Green Label) or Form C2/CP3)

Authenticated copy 8 SAD

No input tax evidence issued

Post entry correction

Monthly VAT certificates

Removals from warehouse

Customs warehouse

Excise or C & E warehouse

Hydrocarbon oils

Monthly VAT certificates

Monthly VAT certificates

Monthly VAT certificates

(C & E Leaflet 702/6/91).

34.12 Shipping and forwarding agents

Where a shipping or forwarding agent acts for an importer and pays the VAT on his behalf (or defers it under his own deferment guarantee), this is only a commercial arrangement. The agent cannot claim the VAT as input tax as the goods are not imported for the purpose of his business. Only the importer has the legal right to reclaim the VAT paid on the imported goods as input tax, subject to the normal rules. (C & E Notice 702, para 2.4). See, however, 34.8 above for concessional repayment of import VAT to agents in certain cases where the importer fails to pay him.

34.13 Goods lost or destroyed after clearance

In such an event, the VAT paid can be deducted as input tax (subject to the normal rules) provided the goods were to be used for business purposes. There is no need to account for output tax unless the goods were supplied to someone else before the loss or destruction. (C & E Notice 702, para 2.9).

34.14 RELIEFS FROM CHARGE

No VAT is charged on the following imports.

1. Capital goods and equipment imported by a person for the purposes of a business he has ceased to carry on abroad. See 34.15 below.

2. Certain imports by charities. See 12.11 CHARITIES.

3. Decorations and awards. See 34.16 below.

4. Donated medical equipment for charities. See 12.8 CHARITIES.

5. Exhibition goods. See 34.17 below.

6. Funerals, war graves, etc. See 19.5 DEATH.

7. Goods for testing. See 34.18 below.

8. Certain goods for disabled persons. See 32.18 HEALTH AND WATER UTILITIES.

9. Goods not in accordance with contract. See 34.19 below.

10. Goods imported for sale to another EC country. See 34.20 below.

11. Animals and biological or chemical substances for research; blood and human organs, etc. See 32.15 HEALTH AND WATER UTILITIES.

12. Inherited goods. See 19.3 DEATH.

13. Miscellaneous items. See 34.21 below.

14. Personal property permanently imported. See 34.22 below.

15. Printed matter. See 54.30 PRINTED MATTER, ETC. and 34.23 below.

16. Reimported goods. See 34.24 below.

17. Small non-commercial consignments. See 34.25 below.

18. Temporary importations. See 34.30 below.

19. Fuel and certain other essential items necessary for transport. See 34.26 below.

20. Travellers' allowances. See 34.27 below.

21. United Nations produced visual and auditory materials of an educational, scientific or cultural character within certain limits. [*SI 1984/746, Art 4, 1 Sch; SI 1987/2108*]. See Notice 370.

22. Goods imported by visiting forces and diplomats. See 34.28 below.

23. Certain aircraft ground and security equipment. See 34.29 below.

24. Works of art and collectors' pieces. See 71.3, 71.4 and 71.5 WORKS OF ART ETC.

25. Zero-rated goods under *VATA 1994, 8 Sch* (with some exceptions). See 72.1 ZERO-RATED SUPPLIES. [*VATA 1994, s 30(3)*].

34.15 Capital goods and equipment transferred from abroad

No VAT is charged on 'capital goods and equipment' imported from a country outside the EC by a person for the purposes of a business he has ceased to carry on outside the EC and which he has notified C & E is to be carried on by him in the EC and concerned exclusively with making taxable supplies. This does not apply if such business is to be merged with, or absorbed by, another business already carried on there.

The goods must

(*a*) have been used in the business for at least twelve months before it ceased to be carried on outside the EC;

(*b*) be imported within twelve months of the business ceasing to be carried on outside the EC (or any longer period allowed); and

(*c*) be appropriate both to the nature and size of the business to be carried on in the EC.

'*Capital goods and equipment*' includes livestock not in possession of a dealer but not food for human consumption or animal feeding stuffs, fuel, stocks of raw materials or finished or semi-finished products or any motor vehicle ineligible for deduction of input tax (see 45.3 MOTOR CARS).

[*SI 1984/746, 2 Sch Group 1; SI 1992/3120*].

34.16 Decorations and awards

No VAT is charged on the following imports.

• Any honorary decoration conferred by a government or Head of State outside the EC on a person resident in the EC and imported on his behalf.

• Any cup, medal or similar article of an essentially symbolic nature, intended as a tribute to activities in the arts, sciences, sport or public service, or in recognition of merit at a particular event. It must be donated by an authority or person established outside the EC for the purpose of being presented in the EC or awarded outside the EC to a person resident in the EC and imported on his behalf.

- Awards, trophies and souvenirs of a symbolic nature and of limited value intended for free distribution at business conferences or similar international events to persons normally resident in a country other than the UK.

The awards etc. must not be of a commercial character. [*SI 1984/746, 2 Sch Group 8, Items 5, 6, 9; SI 1988/2212, Art 7; SI 1992/3120*].

Not eligible are items in any way involved with a commercial operation (e.g. items donated by a commercial sponsor) or items such as watches, cameras, cars, long service awards given by employers and prizes won in minor competitions such as deck or card games.

VAT relief may be claimed by the recipient or the person who is to present the award etc. Evidence that relief is due will be required e.g. a certificate relating to the award etc., press publicity or a letter from the donor. A written declaration may be asked for on Form C920. (C & E Notice 364).

34.17 Exhibition goods

No VAT is charged on the following imports.

- Goods to be distributed free of charge at an 'event' as small representative samples (as defined) for use or consumption by the public (excluding fuels, alcoholic beverages and tobacco products).

- Goods imported solely for the purpose of being demonstrated at, or used in the demonstration of any machine or apparatus displayed at, an event (excluding fuels, alcoholic beverages and tobacco products).

- Paints, varnishes, wallpaper and other low value materials to be used in the fitting out or decoration of a temporary stand at an event.

- Catalogues, prospectuses, price lists, calendars, photographs and other printed matter or articles advertising goods displayed at an event, supplied without charge for distribution free of charge to the public at such event.

'*Event*' comprises

- any trade, industrial, agricultural or craft exhibition, fair or similar show or display which is not organised for private purposes in a shop etc. with a view to the sale of the goods displayed;

- any meeting of representatives of international organisations and ceremonies of an official or commemorative character; and

- exhibitions and meetings primarily for charitable purposes or to promote friendship between peoples, religious knowledge or worship or any branch of learning, art, sport, trade union activity or tourism.

In all cases, the value and quantity of the goods etc. must be appropriate to the nature of the event, number of visitors and extent of the exhibitor's participation. Where relief has been afforded for goods for demonstration or use, the goods must be consumed, destroyed or rendered incapable of being used again for the same purpose either in the course of or as a result of such demonstration or use.

[*SI 1984/746, Art 6(2), 2 Sch Group 3, Items 4–8*].

See also 34.23 below and C & E Notice 200.

34.18 Imports

34.18 Goods for testing, etc.

No VAT is charged on goods imported for examination, analysis or testing to determine their composition, quality or their technical characteristics, to provide information or for industrial or commercial research. The quantities imported should not exceed the amounts necessary for their purpose and examination must be completed within such time as C & E require. Any goods not completely used up or destroyed by the testing and any products resulting from the testing, must be destroyed or rendered commercially worthless or exported. Goods are not eligible where the examination etc. itself constitutes a sales promotion. [*SI 1984/746, Art 6(3), 2 Sch Group 4*]. The testing must normally be completed within twelve months of the date of entry although extension may be given on written application before the time limit expires. See C & E Notice 374.

34.19 Goods not in accordance with contract

Repayment of VAT can be claimed provided the goods

(*a*) were imported in pursuance of a contract;

(*b*) were not in accordance with contract because they were of the wrong description, quality, state or condition or were damaged in transit;

(*c*) have not been used; and

(*d*) are, with the consent of the seller, either returned by the importer to the seller or destroyed by the importer.

Repayment cannot be allowed on goods imported on approval, sale or return etc; received in excess of the number ordered; received after an agreed delivery date; remaining unsold; subject to licensing when a licence is not issued; or when the importer made a mistake in his order.

Most registered traders can reclaim as input tax the whole of the VAT due on imported goods. As no VAT arises when goods are destroyed or returned abroad by the importer, no further relief is necessary. A partly exempt person whose method of apportionment does not allow him to recover all the relevant input tax should consult his VAT office. A non-registered person or a taxable person importing goods for non-business purposes should follow the procedure for claiming relief explained in C & E Notice 266.

34.20 Goods imported for sale to another EC country

Subject to such conditions as C & E impose, the VAT charged on the importation of goods from a place outside the EC is not payable where

(*a*) the goods are imported by a taxable person;

(*b*) he imports the goods in the course of an onward zero-rated supply of the goods by him to a taxable person in another EC country;

(*c*) C & E are satisfied that he intends to remove the goods to another EC country and he does in fact so remove the goods within one month of the date of importation (i.e. the date the goods enter free circulation). C & E may approve a longer period.

C & E may require the deposit of security up to the value of the VAT chargeable on the importation.

[*SI 1995/2518, Reg 123*].

In the above circumstances, no import VAT is due in the UK or the EC country of destination but VAT on the supply/acquisition is accounted for by the purchaser in the EC country of destination. In order to claim the relief, the goods must be imported specifically in order to make a taxable supply to an EC customer. Relief does not apply if goods are merely imported with a view to sale to an EC customer.

See also C & E Leaflet 702/7/93, including how to complete the import SAD.

34.21   Miscellaneous

No VAT is charged on the following imports.

- Materials relating to trademarks, patterns or designs and supporting documents and applications for patents imported for submission to competent bodies to deal with protection of copyright or industrial or commercial patent rights.

- Objects imported for submission as evidence, or for a like purpose, to a court or other official body in the EC.

- Photographs, slides and stereotype mats for photographs sent to press agencies and publishers of newspapers or magazines.

- Recorded media, including punched cards, sound recordings and microfilm, sent free of charge for the transmission of information.

- Goods (other than alcoholic beverages or tobacco products) sent on an occasional basis as a gift of friendship or goodwill between bodies, public authorities or groups carrying on an activity in the public interest. The goods must not be of a commercial character. The provision does not apply where relief is available under the rules relating to personal property permanently imported (see 34.22 below).

- Any consignment of goods (other than alcoholic beverages, tobacco products, perfumes or toilet waters) not exceeding £18 in value.

[*SI 1984/746, 2 Sch Group 8, Items 1–4, 7, 8; SI 1987/155; SI 1988/2212, Art 7; SI 1990/2548; SI 1992/3120; SI 1995/3222*].

34.22   Personal property permanently imported

Certain 'property' may be imported without VAT liability by persons who intend to become 'normally resident' in the UK.

'*Property*' means any personal property intended for personal or household use, including household effects, provisions and pets; riding animals, cycles, motor vehicles, caravans, pleasure boats and private aircraft; but excluding any goods imported for a commercial purpose.

'*Normally resident*' in a country is where a person usually lives

(*a*)   for a period, or aggregate of periods, of at least 185 days in a period of twelve months;

(*b*)   because of his 'occupational ties'; and

(*c*)   because of his 'personal ties'.

Where a person has occupational ties and personal ties in different countries, he will be treated as normally resident in the country where he has personal ties provided the stay in the country where he has occupational ties is to carry out a task of a definite duration or regular returns are made to the country with personal ties. However, a UK citizen with personal ties in the UK but with occupational ties abroad may have relief as if personal ties are ignored provided that he satisfies the condition in (*a*) above in the country with occupational ties. '*Occupational ties*' do not include attendance by a pupil or student at a school, college or university. '*Personal ties*' mean family or social ties to which a person devotes most of his time not devoted to occupational ties.

See also *Rigsadvokaten v N C Ryborg, CJEC [1993] STC 680.*

Conditions for relief. Relief will only be given if the goods are declared for relief to the proper officer. Where any goods are declared before the date on which a person becomes normally resident in the UK or, if he intends to become so resident on the occasion of his marriage, before such marriage has taken place, relief is subject to such security as C & E require being furnished.

Where relief is given, the goods must not, subject to exceptions, be lent, hired-out, given as security or transferred in the UK within a period of twelve months of the relief being given unless so authorised by C & E who may then require payment of the VAT.

Where any conditions are not complied with (including the intention of becoming normally resident and the use to which the goods are put) the VAT becomes payable forthwith (unless C & E see fit to waive payment or part) and the goods are liable to forfeiture.

[*SI 1992/3193, Arts 2, 3, 6–10*].

Transfer of normal residence from outside the EC. No VAT is chargeable on property (as defined above, but excluding alcoholic beverages, tobacco products, any motor vehicle capable of carrying more than nine persons, any special purpose vehicle and articles for use in a trade or profession other than portable instruments of the arts) imported by a person intending to become normally resident in the UK after being normally resident outside the EC for a continuous period of at least twelve months. The property must have been in his possession and used by him at least six months before its importation and must be declared for relief within the period from six months before becoming normally resident in the UK to twelve months after. Before relief is given, C & E must be satisfied that the property has borne (and not been exempted from, or had refunded, because of exportation) all duties and taxes normally applicable in their country of origin or exportation. [*SI 1992/3193, Arts 11, 12*]. By concession,

- relief may still be granted where personal belongings fail to qualify only because they have not been possessed and used for the specified period or have been declared for relief outside the specified time limit; and

- property (including motor vehicles) purchased

    (i) by diplomats, members of certain international organisations and NATO forces,

    (ii) by UK forces (or civilian staff accompanying them) outside the EC, and

    (iii) under a UK export scheme by members of the UK diplomatic service, members of UK forces and members of certain international organisations

which otherwise qualifies for relief will not be refused relief solely because C & E cannot satisfy themselves that the goods have borne all duties and taxes normally applicable in their country of origin.

(C & E Notice 48, ESCs 4.3–4.7).

Also relief is given on property (limited to household effects and trousseaux) imported by a person intending to become normally resident in the UK on the occasion of his marriage provided declaration for relief is made within the period from two months before the wedding to four months after. Any wedding gift up to £800 given by a person normally resident abroad is also included. [*SI 1992/3193, Arts 13–15*].

Transfer of normal residence from another EC country. Goods transferred from other EC countries are not treated as imports and therefore special relief is not necessary.

Pupils and students. No VAT is chargeable on scholastic equipment (i.e. household effects representing the normal furnishings for the room of the pupil etc., clothing, uniforms, and articles or instruments normally used by pupils etc. for their studies, including calculators and typewriters) imported by a pupil etc. normally resident outside the EC who has been accepted to attend a full-time course at a school, college or university in the UK provided the equipment belongs to him and is intended for his use during his studies. [*SI 1992/3193, Art 16*].

Honorary decorations, awards and goodwill gifts. No VAT is chargeable when

- a person normally resident in the UK imports

    (i) any honorary decoration confirmed on him by a government outside the EC; or

    (ii) any cup, medal or similar article of an essentially symbolic nature awarded to him outside the EC as a tribute to his activities in the arts, sciences, sport or public service or in recognition of merit at a particular event;

- a person normally resident in the UK, returning from an official visit outside the EC, imports goods not intended for a commercial purpose given to him on his visit by the host authorities; or

- a person normally resident outside the EC paying an official visit to the UK imports goods not intended for a commercial purpose which are in the nature of an occasional gift he intends to offer to the host authorities during his visit.

Imports of tobacco products and alcoholic beverages are excluded. The conditions for relief above do not apply. [*SI 1992/3193, Arts 17–20*].

34.23   **Promotion of trade**

No VAT is charged on the following imports.

- Articles of no intrinsic value sent free of charge by suppliers of goods and services for the sole purpose of advertising.

- Samples of negligible value of a kind and in quantities capable of being used solely for soliciting orders for goods of the same kind. Where C & E require, the goods must be rendered permanently unusable, except as samples, by being torn, perforated, clearly and indelibly marked, or by any other process.

- Printed advertising matter, including catalogues, price lists, directions for use or brochures, which relates to goods for sale or hire by a person established outside the EC or to transport, commercial insurance or banking services offered by a person established in a third country. The material must clearly display the name of the person established outside the EC by whom the goods or services are offered. Subject to below, relief does not apply to consignments containing two or more copies of different documents or two or more copies of the same document (unless the total gross weight of the consignment does not exceed one kilogram). Any goods which are the subject of a grouped consignment from the same consignor to the same consignee are also excluded. The restrictions on relief do not apply in the case of imported printed matter intended for free distribution and relating to either goods for sale or hire or to services offered by a person established elsewhere in the EC.

[*SI 1984/746, 2 Sch Group 3, Items 1–3; SI 1988/2212, Art 4*].

See also 34.17 above.

34.24 **Reimported goods**

Where the importer is not a taxable person or, if he is, the goods are not imported in the course of his business, no VAT is payable if the goods

(*a*) were last exported from the EC by him or on his behalf;

(*b*) were supplied, acquired or imported into the EC before export and VAT or other tax due was paid at that time and not refunded *or* the goods are imported by the person who made them;

(*c*) were not exported free of VAT because of zero-rating provisions in *VATA 1994, s 30(6)–(8)* or equivalent provisions elsewhere in the EC;

(*d*) were not subject to process or repair outside the EC other than necessary running repairs which did not increase their value; and

(*e*) were at the time of exportation intended to be reimported *or* have been returned for repair or replacement or after rejection by a customer outside the EC or because it was not possible to deliver them *or* were in private use and possession in the EC before they were exported.

[*SI 1995/2518, Reg 124*]. See also C & E Notice 236.

Where the importer is a taxable person importing the goods in the course of his business, no VAT is payable if

(*a*) the goods were last exported from the EC by him or on his behalf;

(*b*) the goods were not subject to process or repair outside the EC other than necessary running repairs which did not increase their value;

(*c*) the goods were either

  (i) owned by him at exportation and have remained his property; or

  (ii) returned from the continental shelf; or

  (iii) owned by him at exportation and have been returned after rejection by, or failure of delivery to, a customer outside the EC; and

(*d*) where the goods were supplied or acquired in or imported into the EC before their export, any VAT chargeable on that supply, acquisition or importation has been paid and not refunded.

[*SI 1995/2518, Reg 125*].

Goods reimported after exportation for treatment or process. Subject to any conditions which C & E may impose, VAT chargeable on the importation of goods which have been temporarily exported outside the EC and are reimported after repair, process or adaptation there is payable as if such treatment etc. had been carried out in the UK. C & E must be satisfied that at the time of exportation the goods were intended to be reimported after completion of the treatment and the ownership in the goods was not transferred to any other person at exportation or at any time the goods were abroad. [*SI 1995/2518, Reg 126*]. The effect of this is that goods so reimported bear VAT only on the value of the process etc. plus any freight and insurance if not already included plus any customs or excise duty or other import charges payable in the UK. No VAT is due on reimportation if the process has been carried out for no charge (e.g. because the goods were under warranty or guarantee) or where the goods processed are zero-rated in the UK. (C & E Notice 702, para 5.3).

34.25 **Small non-commercial consignments**

No VAT is charged on the importation of small non-commercial consignments which are not part of larger consignments provided

(a)   the value does not exceed £36 and the consignment is of an occasional nature;

(b)   it is consigned by one private individual to another;

(c)   it is not imported for any consideration; and

(d)   it is intended solely for personal use of the consignee or of his family and not for any commercial purpose.

Tobacco products, alcoholic beverages, perfumes and toilet waters contained in any consignment must be below permitted quantities (as defined) otherwise no relief is given for any goods within that description. Goods contained in the baggage, or carried with, a person entering the UK are not included in the exemption.

[SI 1986/939; SI 1991/2535; SI 1992/3118].

34.26   **Transport**

No VAT is charged on the following imports.

- Fuel contained in the standard tanks (as defined) of a vehicle or of a 'special container', for use exclusively by such vehicles or such special container.

- Fuel, not exceeding ten litres for each vehicle, contained in portable tanks carried by a vehicle, for use exclusively by such vehicle. This does not apply to a special purpose vehicle or one which, by its construction and equipment, is designed for and capable of transporting goods or more than nine persons including the driver.

- Lubricants contained in a vehicle, for use exclusively by such vehicle and necessary for its normal operation during the journey.

- Litter, fodder and feedingstuffs contained in any means of transport carrying animals, for the use of such animals during their journey.

- Disposable packings used for the stowage and protection of goods during the transportation to the UK and where the cost is included in the consideration for the goods transported.

'*Special container*' means any container fitted with specially designed apparatus for refrigeration, oxygenation, thermal insulation and other systems.

[SI 1984/746, 2 Sch Group 10; SI 1988/2212, Art 8].

34.27   **Travellers' allowances**

A person who has travelled from a third country is relieved from payment of VAT and excise duty on goods of value up to certain specified limits which he has obtained in a third country and are contained in his personal luggage. The goods must not be imported or used for commercial purposes otherwise they are liable to forfeiture. The limits are as follows.

- Goods (other than tobacco products, alcoholic beverages and perfumes) up to £145 in aggregate; or

- Tobacco products, alcoholic beverages and perfumes up to certain quantities (e.g. 200 cigarettes, one litre of spirits, two litres of wine, 60ml of perfume and 250ml of toilet water).

[SI 1994/955; SI 1995/3044].

34.28   **Visiting forces and diplomats**

Conditions for relief. Where relief is given as below, the goods must not be lent, hired-out, given as security or transferred in the UK without the prior authorisation of

C & E who may then require the payment of VAT. The goods must be used exclusively by the entitled person or a member of his family forming part of his household. Where any conditions are not complied with, the VAT becomes payable forthwith (unless C & E sanction non-compliance in writing) and the goods are liable to forfeiture. Any VAT due is the liability of the entitled person or any person in possession of the goods at that time.

Visiting forces and headquarters. No VAT is chargeable on

(*a*) the purchase of a motor vehicle manufactured in an EC country (other than the UK) or a member of EFTA, or

(*b*) the importation, acquisition from another EC country or removal from warehouse of any goods

by an entitled person (as defined and who must not be a UK national or a permanent resident of the UK) or the gift by dispatch from abroad to an entitled person of goods (other than tobacco products and alcoholic beverages).

In the case of a motor vehicle, no relief is available if the entitled person has previously been afforded relief in respect of any other motor vehicle unless he has disposed of all such vehicles (or all but one if his spouse is present in the UK) and paid any duty or tax required by C & E under the conditions for relief above.

Under (*a*) above it is a condition of the relief that the entitled person delivers five copies of Form C & E 941A each signed by the entitled person and his commanding officer. Two copies are to be delivered to the visiting forces, two copies to the proper officer and one copy to the supplier of the motor car.

Where a motor vehicle is imported or acquired under (*b*) above, it is a condition of relief that the entitled person delivers four copies of Form C941 each signed by the entitled person and his commanding officer. One copy is to be delivered to the visiting forces, and three copies to the proper officer.

Diplomats. No VAT is chargeable on the supply to an entitled person (as defined and who must not be a UK national or a permanent resident of the UK) of tobacco products or alcoholic drinks removed from warehouse or a motor vehicle manufactured in a country (other than the UK) which is an EC country or a member of EFTA.

In the case of a motor vehicle, no relief is available if the entitled person has previously been afforded relief in respect of any other motor vehicle unless he has disposed of all such vehicles (or all but one if his spouse is present in the UK) and paid any duty or tax required by C & E under the conditions for relief above. It is a condition of the relief that the entitled person gives the supplier of the vehicle a completed Form C428. This must be signed by the entitled person, the head of the mission or body of which he is a member, an authorised person at the Foreign and Commonwealth Office and the supplier.

[*SI 1992/3156*].

34.29 **Aircraft ground and security equipment**

By concession, no VAT or duty is chargeable on the importation of the following ground and security equipment for aircraft by an airline of another contracting state of the Convention on International Civil Aviation (Chicago Convention).

- All repair and maintenance material for airframes, engines and instruments; specialised aircraft repair kits; starter batteries and carts; maintenance platforms and steps; test equipment for aircraft, aircraft engines and aircraft instruments; aircraft engine heaters and coolers; ground radio equipment.

- Passenger-handling equipment: passenger-loading steps; specialised passenger-weighing devices; specialised catering equipment.

- Cargo-loading equipment: vehicles for moving or loading baggage, cargo, equipment and supplies; specialised cargo-loading devices; specialised cargo-weighing devices.

- Component parts for incorporation into ground equipment including the items listed above.

- Security equipment: weapon-detecting devices; explosives-detecting devices; intrusion detecting devices.

- Component parts for incorporation into security equipment.

Claims for relief under this concession should be addressed to the Customs Entry Processing Unit where the goods are to be cleared.

(C & E Business Brief 18/97, 22 August 1997).

34.30   **GOODS IMPORTED UNDER CUSTOMS SUSPENSIVE ARRANGEMENTS**

Goods received from outside the EC and placed under one of the customs arrangements listed in 34.2(i)–(ix) above with relief from customs duty do not constitute imports for VAT purposes unless and until the goods are removed from those arrangements. The importer will then normally have to pay import VAT when he removes the goods for home use in the UK. Whilst under those arrangements, the goods are subject to the provisions of *EC Council Regulation 3599/82* concerning temporary importation reliefs from customs duty applied to VAT by *VATA 1994, s 16(1)*. Goods can be moved from one arrangement to another without the payment of import VAT.

Persons who temporarily import goods may either

- take advantage of the above provisions, pay no VAT at the time of importation but deposit any security required by C & E for VAT (and duty) which would become due if the conditions for temporary importation are not met; or

- if they are taxable persons importing the goods for business purposes, pay the VAT at the time of temporary importation (or defer it under the provisions relating to deferment of VAT, see 34.5 above) and reclaim the VAT paid as input tax subject to the normal rules. If this is done, there is no limit on the length of time that the goods may be held in the UK before re-exportation (although the relevant controls and time limits for any duty remain).

Supplies of goods under temporary importation relief. Although import VAT is suspended while goods are held under temporary import arrangements, supplies of such goods are chargeable with VAT in the normal way. This is subject to the following exceptions.

Supplies to persons established outside the EC. Where goods held under temporary import arrangements are supplied, that supply is treated as neither a supply of goods nor a supply of services provided that the goods remain eligible for temporary importation arrangements and the supply is to a person established outside the EC. [*SI 1992/3130*].

Second hand goods and works of art. Where

- second-hand goods are imported with a view to their sale by auction, or

- 'works of art' are imported for exhibition with a view to possible sale,

any sale by auction of the second-hand goods or works of art at a time when the goods are still subject to temporary importation arrangements with total exemption from import duty is treated as neither a supply of goods nor a supply of services. The provision of any services relating to the transfer of ownership is similarly treated.

'*Works of art*' means painting, drawing and pastels executed by hand but not consisting of manufactured articles that have been hand-painted or hand-decorated; collages and similar decorative plaques; original engravings, lithographs and other prints; and original sculptures and statuary, in any material.

[*SI 1995/958*]. (C & E News Release 20/95, 5 April 1995).

34.31 **Temporary importations—special arrangements**

Goods imported for processing or repair. For goods imported for inward processing relief (IPR) under the duty suspension system, it is not necessary to pay import VAT at the time of entry provided that the goods enter free circulation in the UK. These arrangements extend to goods subject to VAT only. It is also possible to remove goods from a customs warehousing regime to IPR suspension without payment of import VAT. For goods entered for IPR under the drawback system, import VAT must be paid at the time of entry.

Temporary imported road transport for business use. A vehicle temporarily imported from outside the EC for business use can enter the EC with no customs documentation and be relieved of duty and VAT if it meets the following conditions.

(i) It is imported and used by a person established outside the EC (or an authorised person acting on their behalf).

(ii) It is registered (or belongs to a person established) outside the EC.

(iii) It is only used for a transport operation which begins or ends outside the EC.

(iv) It is not used for private purposes, hired-out, leased or lent to any person established in the EC.

(v) It is not used to pick up and set down goods or persons within the EC.

See C & E Notice 115 for further details.

Containers and pallets. Containers and pallets temporarily imported and re-imported into the EC may enter with little or no Customs documentation and be relieved of duty and VAT. The owner or operator must have a representative with an address in the EC and supply on request details of the movement of containers and pallets to any Customs officer.

For full details see C & E Notices 306 (Containers) and 307 (Pallets).

34.32 **IMPORTING COMPUTER SOFTWARE**

'**Normalised' software** comprises mass-produced items which are freely available to all customers in a standard form and usable by them independently to carry out the same applications or functions. Included are personal and home computer software, games packages, etc. and standard packages adapted at the suppliers' instigation to include security or similar devices.

Importation of normalised items are regarded as the importation of goods made up of the '*carrier medium*' (magnetic tapes, disks, diskettes, compact disks, 'read only' CD videos, etc.) and services comprising the data, program and/or instructions.

If the goods and services cannot be identified separately, the whole importation may be treated as the importation of goods.

If the goods and services can be identified separately, a UK taxable person may pay VAT on importation only on the carrier medium. The supply of services falls within *VATA 1994, 5 Sch 3* and VAT on these must be accounted for under the 'reverse charge' procedure. See 39.4 INTERNATIONAL SERVICES.

'**Specific' software** products are

- items made to customers' special requirements (either as unique programs or adaptations from standard programs);

- inter-company information data and accounts;

- enhancement and updates of existing specific programs; and

- enhancements and updates of existing normalised programs supplied under contractual obligation to customers who have bought the original program.

The importation of a specific item of software is made up of an importation of goods (the carrier medium (see above) and a supply of services (the data and/or instructions) but to simplify import procedures, the carrier medium is treated as an accessory to the data and the importation is treated as a supply of services. No import VAT is charged on the carrier medium at importation.

The supply of services falls within *VATA 1994, 5 Sch 3* and a UK business must account for VAT on the supply under the 'reverse charge' procedure. See 39.4 INTERNATIONAL SERVICES.

(C & E Notice 702/4/94).

35   Input Tax

Cross-references. See 9 BUSINESS ENTERTAINMENT for disallowed input tax; 10 CAPITAL GOODS SCHEME; 21.22 EUROPEAN COMMUNITY: GENERAL for recovery of input tax suffered in another EC country; 31.10 GROUPS OF COMPANIES for recovery of input tax by holding companies; 34 IMPORTS; 42.52 LAND AND BUILDINGS for refund of VAT to do-it-yourself housebuilders; 43.5 LOCAL AUTHORITIES AND STATUTORY BODIES for refund of input tax for non-business purposes; 45 MOTOR CARS for disallowed input tax on cars, accessories and petrol etc.; 49 PARTIAL EXEMPTION for restriction on recovery of input tax where exempt supplies are made; 53.2 PENSION SCHEMES.

The contents of this chapter are as follows.

35.1   INTRODUCTION

EC legislation. See 22.23 EUROPEAN COMMUNITY LEGISLATION for the provisions of the *EC Sixth Directive*.

UK legislation. Input tax, in relation to a taxable person, comprises VAT

(*a*)   on goods and services supplied to him;

(*b*)   on the acquisition of any goods by him from another EC country; and

(*c*)   paid or payable by him on the importation of goods from outside the EC

provided the goods or services are used, or to be used, for the purpose of business carried on, or to be carried on, by him.

[*VATA 1994, s 24(1)*].

VAT paid does not, however, become input tax simply because it has been incurred. It becomes input tax when it satisfies various criteria in 35.2 below arising out of the above definition and other legal requirements.

35.2   CRITERIA FOR VAT INCURRED TO BE TREATED AS DEDUCTIBLE INPUT TAX

Before any VAT paid can be deducted as input tax, a number of criteria must be met.

(*a*)   The recipient of the supply, or the person acquiring or importing the goods, must be a taxable person (i.e. registered or required to be registered under *VATA 1994*) at the time the VAT was incurred. See, however, 35.10 and 35.11 below for pre-registration and post-deregistration VAT.

(b)   The VAT must relate to an actual supply, acquisition or importation. Where payments are made in advance but the goods are never physically supplied, input tax cannot be reclaimed as no supply has taken place. See *Weldons (West One) Ltd (984)*, *Theotrue Holdings Ltd (1358)* and *C & E Commrs v Pennystar Ltd QB 1995, [1996] STC 163*.

(c)   The amount to be claimed is the VAT properly chargeable and not the VAT actually charged where this is different. See *Podium Investments Ltd, [1977] VATTR 121 (314)* and *Genius Holding BV v Staatssecretaris van Financien, CJEC 1989, [1991] STC 239*. This gives rise to a number of consequences.

   (i)   If the supplier is not a taxable person but shows VAT on the invoice, the VAT is not input tax and there is no automatic right of deduction. However, by concession, C & E may allow a claim in these circumstances where they are satisfied that

   • the recipient of the supply is neither involved in nor has close knowledge of the supplier's business;

   • it was reasonable for the recipient to consider that he had been lawfully charged VAT; and

   • the claim is made in respect of goods and services genuinely supplied at the stated value.

   (ii)   If the supplier is a taxable person but has failed to register for VAT, any VAT charged is recoverable as input tax (subject to meeting the other conditions for recovery) even though there can be no valid VAT invoice because, *inter alia*, the supplier has no registration number (see *Ellen Garage (Oldham) Ltd, [1994] VATTR 392 (12407)*).

   (iii)   VAT wrongly charged on a supply, etc. which is outside the scope of VAT, exempt or zero-rated is not input tax. See *Da Conti International Ltd (6215)*.

(d)   The goods or services on which the VAT was charged must have been supplied to, or acquired or imported by, the person seeking to claim the input tax. See 35.4 below.

(e)   The supplies must have been incurred for the purpose of the business. See 35.6 below.

(f)   The supplies received must not be subject to input tax restriction either in the form of a Treasury 'blocking order' or otherwise. See 35.8 below.

(g)   The supplies must normally be received in the accounting period in which the claim is to be made. See 35.9 below.

(h)   The person seeking to claim input tax must hold a valid invoice or other document. See 57.7 RECORDS.

   See, however, *Croydon Hotel & Leisure Co Ltd, [1997] VATDR 254 (14920)* where it was held that a person is entitled to reclaim input tax even where a VAT invoice has not been issued, the right to deduct not being limited to cases were output tax has been paid but extending to cases where it is payable. In that case, the tribunal held that a payment of £2 million by the company was VAT-inclusive even though an earlier tribunal (*Holiday Inns (UK) Ltd, [1993] VATTR 321 (10609)*) had (incorrectly in the second tribunal's opinion) held that in the hands of the recipient the payment did not represent consideration for a taxable supply.

(C & E Notice 48, ESC 2.9; C & E Manual V1-13, Chapter 1 para 1, Chapter 2 paras 2.2, 2.3, Chapter 3 Table 1).

De Voil Indirect Tax Service. See V3.402; V3.406; V3.407.

35.3 Input Tax

35.3 AMOUNT OF ALLOWABLE INPUT TAX

The amount of allowable input tax is so much of the input tax on supplies, acquisitions and importations in the period as is allowable as being attributable to the following supplies made, or to be made, by the taxable person in the course or furtherance of his business.

(*a*) '*Taxable supplies*', i.e. supplies of goods or services made in the UK other than exempt supplies.

(*b*) Supplies outside the UK which would be taxable supplies if made in the UK.

(*c*) Supplies of services which

(i) are supplied to a person who belongs outside the EC, or

(ii) are directly linked to the export of goods to a place outside the EC, or

(iii) consist of the making of arrangements for a supply of services within (i) or (ii) above

provided that the supply is exempt (or would have been exempt if made in the UK) by virtue of *VATA 1994, 9 Sch Group 2* (insurance) or *VATA 1994, 9 Sch Group 5, Items 1–7* (finance).

C & E must make regulations for securing a fair and reasonable attribution of input tax to the supplies within (*a*) to (*c*) above.

[*VATA 1994, ss 4(2), 26; SI 1992/3123*].

See 22.23 EUROPEAN COMMUNITY LEGISLATION for the provisions of the *EC Sixth Directive*.

The effect of the above is that VAT cannot be reclaimed on goods and services which are not used for business purposes (see 35.6 below) and, where exempt supplies are made, it may not be possible to recover all input tax incurred. See PARTIAL EXEMPTION (49).

If input tax can be reclaimed in full, the amount to reclaim is normally that shown on the VAT invoice received from the supplier (but see 35.2(*c*) above where VAT is incorrectly charged). In the case of a less detailed tax invoice (see 40.7 INVOICES) which does not show VAT separately, input tax is found by applying the VAT fraction (see 47.2 OUTPUT TAX) to the total amount charged.

No taxable supplies. Where a person has made no taxable supplies in the period concerned or any previous period, any refunds of input tax are subject to such conditions as C & E think fit to impose, including conditions as to repayment in specified circumstances. [*VATA 1994, s 25(6)*]. This could arise, for example, where a person has recently registered and is incurring expenditure but has yet to make any supplies. See, however, *D A Rompelman v Minister van Financien, CJEC [1985] 3 CMLR 202* for when input tax credit becomes deductible.

De Voil Indirect Tax Service. See V3.417; V3.418.

35.4 WHO CAN CLAIM INPUT TAX

Subject to 35.5 below, for an input tax claim to be valid, the claim must be made by the person to whom the supply was made. This is a fundamental principle and overrides the question of who may have paid for the supply or who may have possession of the relevant invoice or other evidence.

Where a third party pays for goods or services which are supplied to another person, the third party does not have the right to deduct input tax. This applies whether the payment was made due to a legal requirement or is simply a normal commercial practice. Examples of where this is likely to occur include

• payment of legal costs awarded against the unsuccessful party in litigation;

• payment of a landlord's costs by a tenant for the drawing up of a lease (see 42.15 LAND AND BUILDINGS); and

• payment by a business of the costs of a viability study undertaken by a bank in respect of the business's activities (see 36.11 INSOLVENCY).

For a consideration of whether a supply has been made to a taxable person, even though it is physically delivered to a third party (e.g. in a tripartite arrangement) see *Leesportefeuille 'Intiem' CV v Staatssecretaris van Financien, CJEC [1989] 2 CMLR 856* (petrol supplied to employees) and *C & E Commrs v Redrow Group plc CA, [1997] STC 1053* (estate agents' fees for sales of existing homes paid for by builder on purchase of one of its new houses). See also the Input Tax chapter in Tolley's VAT Cases under the heading *Whether supplies made to the appellant.*

(C & E Manual V1-13, Chapter 2 paras 3.1, 3.2).

35.5   **Supplies to employees**

The Treasury may, by order, provide that goods or services of any specified description supplied to a person who is not a taxable person are to be treated as supplied to another (taxable) person. *[VATA 1994, s 24(4)]*. This power has been used to make specific provision for fuel bought by employees to be treated as having been supplied to the business. See 45.15 MOTOR CARS.

More generally, C & E accept that, in certain circumstances, a supply which is *prima facie* to an employee, can be treated as made to the employer provided the employer meets the full cost and the supply is legitimately financed by the employer for the purposes of the business. Examples include

• subsistence costs (see 35.13 below);

• removal expenses arising from company relocations or transfer of staff (see 35.13 below); and

• sundry items such as small tools, materials, etc. purchased 'on site'.

This treatment does not apply to business perks (e.g. membership of a club, hotel accommodation or a holiday which the business provides free to an employee by way of reward or motivation) where the services are supplied to the employee (which is normally the case). Where, exceptionally, the services are supplied to the employer, the perks are a legitimate business expense. In such cases, the VAT incurred is deductible as input tax but the business is making those services available for private or non-business use and a supply of services also takes place. See 47.5 OUTPUT TAX.

Self-employed labourers and contractors. In addition to supplies to employees, C & E accept that VAT can be treated as input tax where a business reimburses subsistence, road fuel and other motoring costs incurred by self-employed persons working for the business where the following conditions are met.

• The individual is 'employed' on the same basis as an employee, i.e. is paid on a fixed rate basis, being unassociated with the trading profits of the business.

• The individual incurs the expenditure only in respect of 'employment' by the business. Where the individual represents a number of firms at the same time (e.g. a self-employed salesman) any subsistence does not relate to one 'employer' and none of those firms can treat the VAT incurred as input tax.

- The individual receives no payment from the end customer.

- The business reimburses the individual at cost, including VAT, dealing with the expense in the normal business accounts.

The above treatment also applies to actors, extras and other casual workers engaged in film, TV or similar productions.

Where the self-employed individual is VAT-registered, the VAT should normally be treated as incurred by the individual for the purpose of their business although, exceptionally, C & E may allow recovery by the 'employer' if satisfied that the individual has not recovered VAT under their own registration.

If a self-employed labourer or contractor buys tools or materials to use for a specific job for a business, C & E may accept that the VAT incurred is input tax of the business provided additionally, in the case of tools, they become the property of the business and, in the case of materials, they are incorporated into and become a cost component of the supply by the business to the end customer.

(C & E Manual V1-13, Chapter 2 paras 3.4, 3.5, 5.16).

Commercial and agricultural premises leased in the name of a partner or director. It is common for a landlord to grant a lease to a partner (rather than to the partnership of which he is a member) or a director (rather than the incorporated company) as it is easier for the landlord to take effective action should the rent not be paid. In such circumstances, C & E accept that the partnership/company is entitled to treat the VAT as input tax provided

- the individual is not VAT-registered in his own right and simply passes the rent invoice over to the business for payment to the landlord; and

- the business uses the whole of the premises for the purposes of its business and shows the expenditure in full in its accounts.

(C & E Manual V1-13, Chapter 2 para 3.7).

35.6   **USE FOR BUSINESS PURPOSES**

There is no definition of whether goods or services have been supplied for the 'purposes of the business'. Where the connection between the expenditure and the business is not clear, the following tests can be applied.

(*a*) Determine the intention of the person at the time of incurring the expenditure. This is a subjective test and where there is no obvious association between the business and the expenditure concerned, the court should approach any assertion that it is for the business with circumspection and care (*Ian Flockton Developments Ltd v C & E Commrs QB, [1987] STC 394*).

(*b*) Establish whether or not there is a clear connection between the actual or intended use of the goods or services and the activities business. This is an objective test of the use to which the goods or services are put.

Expenditure, even if for the benefit of the business, is not necessarily for the purpose of the business. See, for example, *C & E Commrs v Rosner QB 1993, [1994] STC 228* and *Wallman Foods Ltd (1411)* where VAT on legal costs incurred in defending a sole trader/director against criminal charges was held to be non-deductible under this principle. Compare, however, *P & O European Ferries (Dover) Ltd, [1992] VATTR 221 (7846)* where VAT on legal costs in defending the company and certain of its employees charged with manslaughter following the sinking of a ferry was held to be deductible as it had clearly been incurred for the purpose of the business even though it also had the effect of benefiting individual employees.

Where goods or services supplied are not used for business purposes, any VAT suffered is not input tax and cannot be reclaimed. This includes

- expenditure related to domestic accommodation (see 35.13 below);
- pursuit of personal interests such as sporting and leisure activities (see also 35.13 below);
- expenditure for the benefit of company directors, proprietors, etc;
- supplies to a business used in connection with a non-business activity (see 35.7 below for apportionment where used for both a business and non-business activity);
- supplies for another person's business; and
- supplies to another person, even if the taxable person pays for them (see 35.4 above).

(C & E Manual V1-13, Chapter 2 paras 4.2, 4.3).

There have been a large number of court and tribunal cases concerned with whether supplies are used for the purpose of the business, in particular in relation to legal costs, premises costs of sole traders and partnerships, sporting activities (horse racing, show jumping, powerboat racing, motor racing and rallying, yachting, etc.) and personalised number plates. See the chapter Input Tax in Tolley's VAT Cases under the heading *Whether supplies used for the purposes of the business.*

35.7   **Goods and services only partly used for business purposes**

Where

- goods or services supplied to a taxable person,
- goods acquired by a taxable person from another EC country, or
- goods imported by a taxable person from a place outside the EC

are used or to be used *partly* for the purposes of a business carried on or to be carried on and partly for other purposes, VAT paid must be apportioned so that only so much as is referable to business purposes is counted as input tax. [*VATA 1994, s 24(5)*]. See, however, under the heading *The Lennartz approach* below for an alternative treatment to apportionment for goods (but not services).

Apportionment for private use. Common examples of partly business goods and services are telephone, light and heat, repairs and maintenance, etc. for example where a business is conducted from home or the taxpayer lives above a shop.

Example

VAT of £100 is paid on an item and one quarter of its use is for business purposes.

Input tax is £100 × 1/4 = £25

Apportionment for non-business use. Where income is received from non-business activities (e.g. by charities), any VAT paid on purchases cannot be deducted. However, where other taxable supplies are made, an apportionment falls to be made (see *Whitechapel Art Gallery v C & E Commrs QB, [1986] STC 156*). The following procedure may be adopted.

35.7 Input Tax

- Identify as far as possible VAT on purchases wholly attributable to either a business or a non-business use. Any VAT on purchases used wholly for a non-business use is not input tax.

- Apportion the VAT on the remaining purchases (i.e. those with both business and non-business use and those where it is not possible to identify the use).

There is no special method of apportionment but the method used must be fair and reasonable. The following is an example of how VAT could be apportioned on the basis of income received.

Example

A taxable person pays £1,000 VAT on purchases which are used for both business and non-business purposes. Income from business activities (taxable and exempt supplies) amounts to £20,000 per year. Total income from all sources, including business activities, grants and donations, amounts to £50,000 per year. Input tax is calculated as follows.

$$\text{Proportion which is business income} \; \frac{£20,000}{£50,000} = \frac{2}{5}$$

$$\text{VAT to be provisionally treated as input tax} \; £1,000 \times \frac{2}{5} = \underline{£400}$$

At the end of each VAT period, the provisional input tax can be reclaimed, subject to the normal rules. At the end of each VAT year, an adjustment is made by applying the same calculation to total figures for the year. Where quarterly returns are made, the VAT year ends on 31 March, 30 April or 31 May depending on the VAT periods allocated. Where monthly returns are made, the VAT year ends on 31 March.

If the above procedure is not suitable, another formula can be used if it is agreed with C & E. Where a revised method is agreed, it is not possible to make a retrospective claim for earlier periods. Although the income-based method of apportionment outlined above was criticised in the *Whitechapel Art Gallery* case on the grounds that grants and donations received should not be included in the calculation, that method is an acceptable method of apportionment and its adoption, even if disadvantageous, does not constitute an 'error' which may be subsequently corrected (*Victoria & Albert Museum Trustees v C & E Commrs QB, [1996] STC 1013*).

The Lennartz approach. The provisions of *VATA 1994, s 24(5)* above as they apply to goods (but not services) were called into question by the ruling in *Lennartz v Finanzamt Munchen III, CJEC 1991, [1995] STC 514*. The Court ruled that where goods are acquired solely for a private or non-business purpose, VAT incurred is not recoverable, even if the goods in question are later put to a deductible business use (because the right to deduct VAT arises, and is exercisable, at the time when the VAT is incurred). If, however, a taxable person acquires goods and used them partly for business purposes and partly for private or non-business purposes, he has a right to total and immediate input tax deduction (unless the goods are subject to input tax restriction under 35.8 below). Where the goods are later used for private or non-business purposes, that use is to be treated as a taxable supply of services and VAT must be accounted for under *VATA 1994, 4 Sch 5(4)* (see 47.5 OUTPUT TAX) in each VAT period in which private or non-business use of the asset occurs. Records must be kept showing how the relevant asset has been used.

Businesses may either apportion input tax as above or apply the *Lennartz* ruling and take an immediate full input tax credit.

Partial exemption. Where exempt supplies are made, this may also affect the amount of input tax reclaimable. In such a case, the apportionment of VAT incurred between business and non-business use must be made before any apportionment of input tax because of partial exemption.

(C & E Notice 700, para 4.6, Appendix F; C & E Business Brief 4/92, 10 February 1992).

Change in use of goods and services. See 47.5 OUTPUT TAX for the possibility of a taxable supply where goods or services on which input tax has been claimed on the basis that they were obtained for wholly business purposes are subsequently put to private or non-business use.

De Voil Indirect Tax Service. See V3.408; V3.409.

35.8   **NON-DEDUCTIBLE INPUT TAX**

Input tax cannot usually be reclaimed on the following.

- Goods to be sold under one of the margin schemes for SECOND-HAND GOODS (61).
- Goods or services to be used for the purpose of BUSINESS ENTERTAINMENT (9).
- Motor cars other than taxis unless purchased for one of the qualifying uses (see 45.3 MOTOR CARS).
- Certain accessories installed in motor cars (see 45.13 MOTOR CARS).
- Purchases which fall within the TOUR OPERATORS' MARGIN SCHEME (66).
- Certain articles to be installed in new dwellings (see 42.50 LAND AND BUILDINGS).
- Assets acquired under the transfer of a business as a going concern (see 8.10 BUSINESS).
- Domestic accommodation for its directors or proprietors (see 35.13) below).
- Goods imported by a taxable person where

    (i) at the time of importation the goods belong wholly or partly to another person, and

    (ii) the purposes for which they are to be used include private purposes either of himself or of the other person.

    In such a case, the VAT due on import is not available for deduction as input tax, but a separate claim for repayment may be made to C & E if a double charge to VAT would arise. The repayment of VAT to the taxable person will be made only to the extent necessary to avoid a double charge and C & E will have regard to the circumstances of the importation and, as far as appears relevant, things done with, or occurring in relation to, the goods at any subsequent time.

    [*VATA 1994, s 27*].

De Voil Indirect Tax Service. See V3.416; V5.153.

35.9   **WHEN TO CLAIM INPUT TAX**

A '*taxable person*' (i.e. a person who is, or is required to be, registered under *VATA 1994*) is entitled, at the end of each VAT period, to credit for so much of his input tax as is allowable. [*VATA 1994, ss 3(1), 25(2)*].

Input tax should be claimed on the VAT return for the period in which the VAT became chargeable, i.e. the period covering

- for supplies of goods and services, the supplier's tax point;

- for goods acquired from another EC country, the date of acquisition;

- for imported goods, the date of the importation; and

- for goods removed from a customs and/or excise warehouse, the date of removal.

If a business does not deduct VAT in the proper period due to an error, it is entitled to correct that error and recover the tax in a later period. In all other circumstances where a trader does not, or cannot, deduct the VAT in the proper period (e.g. because the necessary evidence is not received in time or lost), recovery is subject to C & E's discretion. However, with effect from 1 May 1997, VAT cannot in any case be reclaimed more than three years after the date by which the return for the period in which the VAT was chargeable is required to be made.

[*SI 1995/2518, Regs 29(1)(1A), 34, 35; SI 1997/1086, Reg 4*].

Cash accounting. Certain small businesses are allowed to account for VAT on the basis of cash paid and received. See 63.2 SPECIAL SCHEMES. Where the cash accounting scheme is used, a taxable person must not reclaim input tax until the necessary evidence is received and the supply has been paid for.

Claims for early payment. C & E may authorise a claim for early payment of input tax (i.e. before the end of the normal VAT period) but only in cases where serious delay has occurred as a result of C & E's action (e.g. such as undue delay in processing an application for registration). All such requests must be submitted in writing. (C & E Manual V1-13, Chapter 2 para 7.15).

35.10   **Pre-registration VAT**

Although VAT incurred before registration is not input tax, it can be treated as such subject to certain conditions. The VAT should be claimed on the first VAT return required to be made following registration. C & E may allow the claim to be made on a later return but, with effect from 1 May 1997, cannot allow a claim to be made more than three years after the date the first return was required. Any claim must be supported by invoices and other evidence as C & E require.

VAT on goods. C & E may allow a taxable person to treat as input tax any VAT on goods supplied to him before the date on which he was (or was required to be) registered or paid by him on the acquisition or importation of goods before that date provided the following conditions are satisfied.

- The goods are for the purpose of a business which either was carried on or was to be carried on by him at the time of the supply or payment.

- The goods have not been supplied *by* or (unless C & E otherwise allow) consumed by the taxable person before the date with effect from which he was (or was required to be) registered (see *Schemepanel Trading Co Ltd v C & E Commrs QB, [1996] STC 871*). C & E deem this condition to be satisfied if the goods have been used to make other goods which are still held at that date. (C & E Notice 700, para 4.9(*a*)).

- With effect from 1 May 1997, the goods must not have been supplied to, or imported or acquired by, the taxable person more than three years before the date with effect from which he was (or was required to be) registered. Under transitional arrangements, this did not apply to a person who was registered before 1 May 1997 and who had not made his first return by that date.

- All the normal rules allow the input tax to be reclaimed.

- A stock account is compiled (and preserved for such a period as C & E require) showing separately quantities purchased, quantities used in the making of other goods, date of purchase and date and manner of subsequent disposals of both such quantities.

VAT on services. C & E may allow a taxable person to treat as input tax any VAT on services supplied to him before the date on which he was (or was required to be) registered provided the following conditions are satisfied.

• The services are for the purpose of a business which either was carried on or was to be carried on by him at the time of such supply.

• The services have not been supplied *by* the taxable person before the date with effect from which he was (or was required to be) registered.

• The services have not been performed on

(i) goods which have been supplied *by* or (unless C & E otherwise allow) consumed by the taxable person before the date with effect from which he was (or was required to be) registered (e.g. repairs to a machine sold before registration); or

(ii) with effect from 1 May 1997, goods which have been supplied to, or imported or acquired by, the taxable person more than three years before that date. Under transitional arrangements, this did not apply to a person who was registered before 1 May 1997 and who had not made his first return by that date.

• The services have not been supplied to the taxable person more than six months before the date with effect from which he was, or was required to be, registered. There is no discretion to allow VAT recovery on services received more than six months before registration. The only way that this can be done is by backdating the registration.

• All the normal rules allow the input tax to be reclaimed.

• A list showing the description, date of purchase and date of disposal (if any) of the services is compiled and preserved for such period as C & E require.

VAT on supplies before incorporation. C & E may allow a body corporate (including a company, charity or association) to treat as input tax any VAT on goods obtained for it before its incorporation, or on the supply of services before that time for its benefit or in connection with its incorporation, provided the following conditions are satisfied.

• The person to whom the supply was made or who paid VAT on the importation or acquisition

(i) became a member, officer or employee of the body and was reimbursed (or has received an undertaking to be reimbursed) by the body for the whole amount of the price paid for the goods or services;

(ii) was not at the time of supply, acquisition or importation a taxable person; and

(iii) imported, acquired or was supplied with the goods or received the services for the purpose of a business to be carried on by the body and has not used them for any purpose other than such business.

• The conditions for recovery of input tax on goods or, as the case may be, services as detailed above are satisfied. In the case of pre-incorporation supplies, the references in those conditions to supplies, etc. of goods and services to and by the taxable person before registration are to be taken as references to such supplies to and by the person who obtained the supplies for the company before registration.

[*SI 1995 No 2518, Reg 111(1)-(4); SI 1997/1086, Reg 7*].

35.11 Input Tax

Partial exemption. The provisions in *Reg 111* above do not specify how pre-registration VAT of a partly exempt business should be treated. C & E take the view that it is only allowable to the extent that, at the time the VAT was incurred, the relevant goods and services were used, or to be used, to make taxable supplies, i.e. they apply direct attribution. This approach was upheld by the tribunal in *T Douros (t/a Olympic Financial Services) (12454)* and *GN Byrd (t/a GN Byrd and Co) (12675)*. (C & E Manual V1-13, Chapter 2 para 7.5).

VAT groups. If an unregistered company joins a VAT group, the representative member may recover VAT incurred by the new member prior to its entry into the group subject to the normal rules above. (C & E Manual V1-13, Chapter 2 para 7.10).

De Voil Indirect Tax Service. See V3.431; V3.432.

35.11 Post-deregistration VAT

As a general rule, input tax cannot be claimed on supplies received after the date of deregistration. However, on a claim, C & E may refund to a person any VAT on *services* supplied to him after the date from which he ceased to be (or to be required to be) registered and which relate to taxable supplies of the business carried on by him before deregistration. With effect from 1 May 1997, no such claim can be made more than three years after the date on which the supply of services was made (unless the person ceased to be registered, or ceased to be required to be registered, before 1 May 1997 and the supply was made before that date). [*SI 1995/2518, Reg 111(5)-(7); SI 1997/1086, Reg 7*].

This covers, for example, solicitors' and accountants' services which cannot be claimed on the final returns as the invoices are not received in time. It does not include VAT incurred in disposing of business premises after deregistration where the supply is exempt but if such a disposal is a possibility, C & E can be requested to delay cancellation of registration for up to six months. Claims should be made as soon as possible after cancellation of registration on Form VAT 427. The relevant invoices must be submitted. (C & E Notice 700/11/98, para 9).

Insolvencies. For the procedure for claiming post-deregistration input tax in insolvencies, see 36.13 INSOLVENCY.

Partial exemption. Where the business made exempt supplies whilst registered for VAT, direct attribution of VAT must be used when submitting the claim. There is no *de minimis* limit following deregistration so that no VAT incurred which relates to the making of exempt supplies can be claimed. With regard to non-attributable input tax, the recoverable proportion applicable immediately prior to deregistration should be used. (C & E Manual V1-13, Chapter 2 para 7.9).

VAT groups. If a member leaves a VAT group and does not register in its own right, the representative member may recover VAT incurred by the departed company after the date of its leaving, subject to the normal rules above. (C & E Manual V1-13, Chapter 2 para 7.10).

De Voil Indirect Tax Service. See V5.165.

35.12 APPEALS IN RESPECT OF INPUT TAX

An appeal may be made to a VAT tribunal in connection with the amount of input tax that may be credited and the proportion of input tax allowable under *VATA 1994, s 26*. See 5.3(*c*)(*e*) APPEALS.

Luxuries, amusements and entertainment. In any appeal relating to input tax where (*a*)   the appeal relates, in whole or in part, to a determination by C & E

    (i)   as to the purposes for which any goods or services were, or were to be, used by any person, or

    (ii)   as to whether and to what extent input tax was attributable to matters other than the making of supplies within 35.3(*a*)–(*c*) above, and

(*b*)   the input tax for which, following the determination, there is no entitlement to credit relates to a supply, acquisition or importation or something in the nature of a luxury, amusement or entertainment,

the tribunal cannot allow the appeal so far as it relates to that determination unless it considers that it was unreasonable to make that determination. In reaching this conclusion, the tribunal may take into consideration information brought to their attention which could not have been made available to C & E at the time.

[*VATA 1994, s 84(4)(11)*].

The effect of the above provisions is that in cases involving expenditure on luxuries, amusements and entertainment, a tribunal cannot apply a decision of its own to the case but is restricted to considering whether C & E's decision was reasonable. Even though it might not have arrived at the same decision, the tribunal must uphold C & E's decision unless it considers that they acted unreasonably.

The provisions have no effect on expenditure which is genuinely used for business purposes, such as

- goods and services which are stock in trade of a business or which are specifically purchased for making taxable supplies;

- goods or services purchased for genuine advertising purposes, e.g. advertising at sporting events or sponsorship where the clear intention is to obtain benefit from the advertising; and

- subsistence expenses.

In considering any claim for input tax recovery, C & E will take into account the nature of the goods or services; how they related to the taxpayer's business activity; whether they are of a kind suitable for private use; whether the cost is out of proportion to the claimed business aims; the taxpayer's intention at the time of supply and the actual use to which the goods or services were put.

(C & E Leaflet 700/55/93).

35.13   TREATMENT OF INPUT TAX IN PARTICULAR CASES

(1)   **Accountancy fees.** Accountancy fees of a sole trader or a partnership normally relate to a number of services, e.g. general accountancy advice, VAT advice and income tax advice. Although it is arguable that income tax is the responsibility of the sole trader or partner as an individual and is not strictly a business matter, to avoid lengthy disputes, C & E's policy is that such fees should usually be allowable in full, subject to the normal rules. The only exception to this treatment is where the accountant's fees clearly relate to taxation matters which are not related to the VAT-registered business (e.g. significant costs relating to inheritance tax).

The position is similar in the case of companies paying corporation tax. The exception in this case would cover, for example, advice relating to a director's inheritance tax liabilities.

(C & E Manual V1-13, Chapter 2A para 15.10).

(2) **Barristers in chambers**. Barristers may share chambers, office equipment and services, etc. and periodically apportion costs between them on an agreed basis. Invoices for the supply of common goods or services may be made out to the head of chambers, a nominated member or the barristers' clerk (if the clerk is not a registered person).

Three special accounting methods have been agreed. The choice of method is up to the barristers, but whichever method is chosen the conditions relating to it must be complied with.

Method 1

The nominated member to whom invoices are addressed treats the full amount of VAT as input tax. Output tax is accounted for on the shares charged out to all the other members of chambers. Registered members are entitled to deduct the VAT charged as input tax. By concession, VAT invoices need not be issued by the nominated member. Each member's record must be cross-referenced to

- output tax charged by the nominated member;

- the input tax deducted by other members; and

- the original VAT invoice.

The records of all members of chambers must be available during a visit to any one of them.

Method 2

The nominated member to whom invoices are addressed does not charge output tax on the member's contributions. The input tax is apportioned so that registered members may deduct it on the basis of their own contributions. Records must be kept of the apportionment of input tax between the members of chambers. Each member's records should cross-reference the input tax deducted to the VAT invoice to ensure that no more than the total VAT stated on the invoice has been deducted. The records of all members of chambers must be available during a visit to any one of them.

Method 3

The nominated member to whom invoices are addressed deducts the whole amount of input tax but also pays an equal amount into the common fund. This method may only be used when all members of chambers are registered for VAT.

(C & E Manual V1-13, Chapter 2, para 8.13).

(3) **Capital goods**. See 10 CAPITAL GOODS SCHEME for possible adjustment in subsequent years to the initial input tax recovery on certain items of computer equipment, land and buildings and civil engineering works used for non-taxable purposes.

(4) **Churches and cathedrals**. Cathedrals and churches exist primarily for non-business purposes but frequently derive significant income from their status as tourist attractions. Informal agreement has been reached between C & E and The Churches Main Committee on the recovery of input tax which is not directly attributable to a business or non-business activity, notably repairs and maintenance, etc. to the cathedral or church itself and all associated buildings within its curtilage except domestic accommodation. A cathedral or church is allocated to one of the following bands for rate of recovery of input tax.

- Band A (90%) — to apply where there are significant admission charges to all main areas (e.g. St Paul's Cathedral, Ely Cathedral).

- Band B (65%) — to apply where there is no admission charge into the Cathedral, but there are high numbers of visitors and significant taxable income (e.g. from admission charges to other areas such as crypt, museum, tower, etc; lettings for concerts etc.).

- Band C (45%) — to apply where is no admission charge into the Cathedral, insignificant taxable income from admission charges for other areas, but a reasonable number of visitors generating income from other sources (e.g. the book/souvenir shop).

- Band D (25%) — to apply where there are no admission charges or only a few small charges and small numbers of visitors and little taxable income.

Where any exempt supplies are made, a separate partial exemption calculation must be made based on the total of input tax attributable to business activities and the proportion of residual input tax as calculated above.

Domestic accommodation is outside the banding system. C & E consider input tax recovery to be dependent upon the occupants' terms of employment and duties and whether they are engaged on business or non-business activities. For persons engaged by the Church for religious purposes C & E consider none of the tax is input tax. For lay persons engaged on some business activities an apportionment of VAT may be agreed. See *The Dean and Chapter of Hereford Cathedral (11737)*, concerning VAT incurred on renovation work to accommodation lived in by vergers. On the facts, the tribunal allowed 50% of the VAT to be treated as input tax although each case will need to be decided on its own merits.

(C & E Manual V1-13, Chapter 2A paras 17.2-17.7).

(5) **Clothing.** Subject to the special cases below, the provision of clothing is normally a personal responsibility. VAT on clothing purchased 'to cultivate a professional image' in order to attract business was disallowed in *BJ Brown (6552)* as was VAT on suits worn while working in *JK Hill and SJ Mansell (t/a JK Hill & Co) (2379)*. VAT on a fur coat purchased by an author was held to be partly input tax in *RA Sisson (1056)* although an appeal in such a case would now be restricted under 35.12 above. The following special cases are recognised.

(a) *Uniforms and protective clothing.* VAT incurred by a business person on uniforms or protective clothing worn by the proprietors or their employees in the performance of their duties is input tax.

(b) *Employees.* Perks are an accepted business expense therefore if employers decide to provide their employees with clothing (not falling within (a) above) the VAT incurred is input tax. However, a supply of goods has also taken place and the normal business gifts rules apply. See 47.4 OUTPUT TAX.

(c) *Barristers.* The wig, gown and bands that a barrister is required to wear in court are considered to be a uniform and the VAT incurred is input tax. It is also a court requirement that barristers wear dark clothing. For example, male barristers may wear striped trousers, a black jacket and a waistcoat with a white wing-collar, and for a female barrister a dark (black, navy or grey) suit and a white blouse. If barristers claim that this clothing would not have been purchased if they did not have to attend court, the VAT may be deducted as input tax. See also *EM Alexander (251)*.

(d) *Entertainers.* The VAT on clothing used solely as stage costumes is input tax. Ordinary clothing worn by an entertainer or TV personality will usually be worn privately as well, in which case C & E regard the provisions of 35.7 above for part business/private use as applying. See, however, *J Pearce (7860)* where the tribunal allowed full input tax recovery on clothing such as dress suits worn by a actor where it had not been worn privately. See also *JM Collie (6144)* where input tax was allowed in full on a wig purchased by a professional musician to maintain his image.

(C & E Manual V1-13, Chapter 2A para 18.3).

(6) **Domestic accommodation.** As a general principle, the provision of domestic accommodation is regarded as a personal rather than a business responsibility and in most cases the VAT incurred is not input tax. However, the fact that a business is operated from home does not prevent VAT that is genuinely incurred for business purposes being deducted as input tax.

(*a*) **Sole proprietors and partners.** If a sole proprietor or partner carries on a business from home and uses a particular room or area specifically for business (e.g. an office or workshop), VAT incurred on costs which can be identified specifically to that area can be treated wholly as input tax. This would apply mainly to fixtures and fittings and decorating costs. VAT on any items used purely for domestic purposes (e.g. a bedroom suite) is not deductible. Where expenditure relates to both domestic and business use (e.g. fuel and power, security systems and general maintenance), the procedure in 35.7 above should be followed. (C & E Manual V1-13, Chapter 2A para 14.3). See also under (*d*) below for farmhouses.

(*b*) **Directors.** Where a company purchases, acquires or imports goods or services which are used or to be used in connection with the provision of domestic accommodation by the company for a 'director' of the company or a person connected with a director of the company, those goods and services are not treated as used or to be used for the company's business and any input tax is not recoverable.

'*Director*' means

- where the company is managed by a board of directors or similar body, a member of that board or body;

- where it is managed by a single director or similar person, that director or person; and

- where it is managed by the members, a member of the company.

A person is connected with a director if that person is the director's wife or husband, or is a relative (or the wife or husband of a relative) of the director or of the director's wife or husband.

[*VATA 1994, s 24(3)(7)*].

The provisions cover repairs, maintenance, refurbishments, furnishing and legal and estate agents' fees. They apply whether or not the accommodation is a main residence, whether or not it is provided for a consideration and even if the business owns the accommodation.

Where a domestic room or rooms is put to business use C & E may agree to an apportionment using an objective test of the extent to which the room is put to business use.

(C & E Notice 700, para 4.8; C & E Manual V1-13, Chapter 2A, paras 14.6, 14.7).

For apportionment on the purchase of time share accommodation used by the directors for business and domestic purposes, see *Suregrove Ltd (10740)*. See also *Giffenbond Ltd (13481)* for apportionment where a garage was constructed at a director's home on land transferred to the company.

(c) **Employees**. Where a business has to provide domestic accommodation to its employees in order to facilitate the running of the business, the expenditure is regarded as having been incurred wholly for a business purpose. The most frequent instances of employers providing accommodation for staff are in the farming and hotel industries where it is essential to have staff available at all times of the day and where there is very little or no suitable accommodation available within reasonable distance of the business premises.

If an employer pays for

- goods which become the property of its employees
- the domestic fuel and power of its employees, or
- the private telephone calls of employees

the VAT incurred is treated as the employer's input tax, but the business must account for output tax as a supply of goods or services as appropriate (see 47.5 OUTPUT TAX).

(C & E Manual V1-13, Chapter 2A para 14.4).

(d) **Repairs, renovations, etc. to farmhouses**. The following guidelines have been agreed with the National Farmers Union as regards input tax claims by sole proprietors and partnerships. Where the occupant of the farmhouse is a director of a limited company, or a person connected with the director of the company, the provisions under (a) above apply. The guidelines do not give an automatic entitlement to recover VAT and businesses should continue to consider their own particular circumstances, and use the guidelines to assess the proportion of input tax that is claimable.

- Where VAT is incurred on repairs, maintenance and renovations, 70% of that VAT may be recovered as input tax provided the farm is a normal working farm and the VAT-registered person is actively engaged full-time in running it. Where farming is not a full-time occupation and business for the VAT-registered person (i.e. income is received from either full-time employment or other sources) input tax claimable is likely to be between 10%-30% on the grounds that the dominant purpose is a personal one.

- Where the building work is more associated with an alteration (e.g. building an extension) the amount that may be recovered will depend on the purpose for the construction. If the dominant purpose is a business one then 70% can be claimed. If the dominant purpose is a personal one C & E would expect the claim to be 40% or less, and in some cases, depending on the facts, none of the VAT incurred would be recoverable.

(C & E Business Brief 18/96, 27 August 1996 which also see for retrospective claims).

De Voil Indirect Tax Service. See V3.410; V3.450.

(7) **Entertainment**. See 9.1–9.6 BUSINESS ENTERTAINMENT.

(8) **Holding companies**. See 31.10 GROUPS OF COMPANIES.

(9) **Imports**. See 34.10–34.13 IMPORTS.

(10) **Insurance claims**. See 37.7 INSURANCE.

(11) **Land and buildings**. See 42.25 LAND AND BUILDINGS for input tax recovery where the option to tax has been exercised; 42.50 LAND AND BUILDINGS for deduction of input tax by developers; and 42.52 LAND AND BUILDINGS for deduction of input tax by do-it-yourself housebuilders.

(12) **Legal costs**. For VAT on legal costs to be recoverable as input tax, the legal services should be supplied for the purpose of the business rather than for the trader, directors or employees in a personal capacity. The extent to which the substance of an action does relate to the activities of a business is a matter of judgement.

Criminal cases. VAT on legal costs has been disallowed in *Wallman Foods Ltd (1411)* (handling stolen property); *Britwood Toys Ltd (2263)* (successfully defending a charge of corruption in relation to acquisition of stock); *LHA Ltd (11911)* (personal assault); *C & E Commrs v Rosner QB 1993, [1994] STC 228* (conspiracy to defraud); and *RN Scott (2302)* (motoring offences). VAT has been held to be deductible in *P & O European Ferries (Dover) Ltd, [1992] VATTR 221 (7846)* (employees charged with manslaughter). In *SR Brooks (12754)* VAT on legal costs of successfully defending charges in connection with evasion of Customs duties on gold transactions was held to be allowable although the tribunal indicated that this might not have been the case if the defendant had been charged with a smuggling offence.

Civil cases. VAT in legal costs has been disallowed in *JG & MV Potton (2882)* (freeholder's costs paid by lessees in a breach of covenant case); *Ingram (t/a Ingram & Co) (4605)*, *C Mills (4864)*, *B Stone (12442)* and *K Lister (13044)* (partnership disputes); *Brucegate Ltd (4903)* and *Ash Fibre Processors Ltd (12201)* (transfer of share capital); *Morgan Automation Ltd (5539)* (director's dispute with previous company); and *HD Marks (11381)* and *P Oldfield (12233)* (action against former employer).

'Party and party' costs. Where the court orders one party to an action to pay costs to the other party, this sum is not consideration for any kind of supply. There is no liability for output tax on the part of the recipient nor any entitlement to recover input tax on the part of the paying party. (C & E Manual V1-13, Chapter 2A para 15.6).

Debt collection agencies. See 4.19 AGENTS.

(13) **Local authorities**. See 43.5 LOCAL AUTHORITIES AND STATUTORY BODIES.

(14) **Motor cars and motoring expenses**. See in particular 45.3 MOTOR CARS for purchases of cars, 45.7 MOTOR CARS for car dealers, 45.11 MOTOR CARS for leasing or hiring motor cars, 45.12 MOTOR CARS for repairs and maintenance, 45.13 MOTOR CARS for accessories and 45.14 and 45.15 MOTOR CARS for motor fuel.

(15) **Pension schemes**. See 53.2 PENSION SCHEMES for input tax deductible by employers.

(16) **Removal expenses**. Where a business reimburses employees (including new employees) for removal expenses, they can treat VAT incurred as input tax if relating to

● estate agents' and solicitors' fees;

● storage and removal of household and personal effects; and

● services such as plumbing in washing machines or altering curtains.

Where a proportion of the costs are reimbursed, a similar proportion of the input tax can be claimed. It does not matter if the invoices are addressed to the employees.

Input tax can similarly be allowed for sole proprietors, partners and directors provided that the move has a business purpose rather than a personal one.

(C & E Manual V1-13, Chapter 2A para 18.5).

(17) **Sporting, recreational and sponsorship activities.** There can be considerable difficulties in establishing to what extent, if any, there is entitlement to deduct input tax in respect of sporting, recreational and sponsorship activities. C & E's policy in this area is to ensure that the legitimate costs of a taxable person in promoting his business or providing facilities to his staff are allowed, whilst not providing, in effect, a tax subsidy to persons who control businesses in respect of their own favoured sporting or recreational activities.

    (*a*) *Provisions for staff.* Where sports and recreational facilities are available to all employees, whether or not for a charge, any VAT incurred can be treated as input tax. This equally applies where smaller businesses are unable to provide suitable facilities within their own organisation and provide membership for their employees at external establishments.

    Where such facilities (e.g. membership of a golf or health club etc.) are provided as a 'perk' to specific employees, the provisions relating to private use of services in 47.5 OUTPUT TAX may apply.

    (*b*) *Provisions for sole proprietors, partners and company directors.* Where the sporting or recreational facilities provided (e.g. membership of a golf or country club) are available only to the proprietor, partners, or directors of a company (and the relatives and friends of these persons), it is unlikely that this expenditure can be treated as being for the purpose of the business and the VAT incurred does not therefore qualify as input tax. Even if membership does result in business contacts, following the decision in *C & E Commrs v Rosner QB 1993, [1994] STC 228*, the expenditure is probably not sufficiently connected to the purpose of the business.

    (*c*) *Sponsorship, advertising and business promotion.* In certain cases, there is undoubtedly widespread exposure gained by the sponsoring business (e.g. 'Dunhill' golf masters, FA 'Carling' Premiership, etc.) so that no difficult arises in allowing input tax deduction. In the case of sponsorship of sporting events by smaller businesses, there is however more likelihood that the 'sponsorship' is actually conducted for a private purpose (e.g. a trader may 'sponsor' a local amateur football because of a personal connection with the team).

    Similarly, participation in various sporting or recreational events may be claimed to be for business purposes in the form of advertising or promotion.

    C & E approach such cases by applying the 'business purpose' test in 35.6 above. If, at the time the VAT is incurred, the business purpose tests are met, the VAT is input tax. It is irrelevant whether the business's intentions are misconceived or that the envisaged benefits do not materialise, and the fact that the participant enjoys the activity is not sufficient reason in itself to deny input tax.

    C & E officers may consider the following questions in reaching any decision as to the deductibility of VAT incurred as input tax.

    1.   Does the sole proprietor, partner or director actively participate in the sport?

    2.   If the trader cannot take part because of injury, business commitments, etc. is another (independent) person employed to drive, etc.?

    3.   Does a member of the trader's family actively take part in the sport?

    4.   Is there a connection between the sport and the business?

    5.   Where does the sporting activity take place?

6. Is there supplementary advertising at the racing venue or in programmes?

7. Is there related advertising or promotional material?

8. Does the business name appear on the sporting vehicle, transporter, clothing, etc.?

9. For companies and partnerships is there a record of a decision to use sporting facilities for advertising?

10. Can the business produce any evidence of research into the benefits to be obtained by the advertising?

11. Are the benefits of the advertising monitored?

12. Is the car, boat, etc. an asset of the business?

13. What other forms of advertising are there?

14. Has the Inland Revenue given a ruling?

15. If the intention of the alleged advertising or promotion is the expansion of trade, could the business cope with an expansion of trade?

(C & E Manual V1-13, Chapter 2A paras 16.1-16.4, Table 11).

(18) **Subsistence expenses.** Where an employee is paid a flat rate for subsistence expenses, no VAT can be claimed as input tax. If the business pays the actual cost of the supplies, input tax incurred can be reclaimed as below. If the business pays a proportion of the actual costs, it can reclaim as input tax the VAT fraction (see 47.2 OUTPUT TAX) of the amount it pays.

Meals. If the business provides canteen facilities, all input tax incurred in providing these facilities can be recovered subject to the normal rules (even on meals for a sole proprietor, partner or director). Any VAT incurred on meals for employees can be treated as input tax. In the case of a sole proprietor, partner or director, the VAT must be incurred on meals taken away from the normal place of work on a business trip.

Hotel accommodation. All VAT incurred on accommodation for employers and employees when away from the normal place of work on business trips can be treated as input tax. See, however, *Co-operative Insurance Society Ltd, [1997] VATDR 65 (14862)* where input tax was disallowed on hotel accommodation reserved by employees and only deductible if reserved by the company.

Where, occasionally, an employee uses overnight accommodation near the normal work place, VAT incurred is input tax and deductible if the employer requires the employee to stay in the accommodation and the expense is fully borne by the business and recorded as such in the accounting records. For other persons, whether VAT is deductible on such accommodation depends on the facts of the particular case. For example, if a partner stays at an hotel near to the normal work-place because there is a rail strike which will make it difficult to get to work and the business bears the cost, this is accepted as being for the purpose of the business.

(C & E Notice 700, para 4.7; C & E Manual V1-13, Chapter 2A para 18.1).

See also *British Broadcasting Corporation [1974] VATTR 100 (73)* and *Ledamaster Ltd (344)*. See 9 BUSINESS ENTERTAINMENT where accommodation, meals etc. are provided for persons other than employees.

(19) **Viability studies by accountants.** See 36.11 INSOLVENCY.

36 Insolvency

Cross-references. See 5.6 APPEALS by persons becoming insolvent; 6.9 ASSESSMENTS for assessments on persons representing insolvent persons.

36.1 EFFECT OF INSOLVENCY

Person carrying on the business. If a taxable person becomes 'bankrupt or incapacitated', C & E may treat any person carrying on the business as a taxable person from the date of the bankruptcy or incapacity until either some other person is registered in respect of the taxable supplies made (or intended to be made) by that taxable person or the incapacity ceases. Any person carrying on the business must notify C & E in writing within 21 days of

- the nature of any incapacity and the date on which it began; and

- the date of any bankruptcy order.

The VAT provisions apply to any person treated as carrying on the business as though he were a registered person.

[VATA 1994, s 46(4); SI 1995/2518, Reg 9; SI 1996/1250, Reg 5].

Where any person becomes bankrupt or incapacitated and control of his assets passes to another person, that other person must, if C & E require and so long as he has control, comply with the general accounting, record and payment requirements of VAT. However, any requirement to pay VAT only applies to the extent of the assets of the incapacitated person over which he has control so that he is treated to that extent as if he were the incapacitated person himself. *[SI 1995/2518, Reg 30].*

If no person carries on the business (i.e. taxable supplies cease to be made) the normal procedures for cancellation of registration apply (see 59.26 REGISTRATION).

Companies in receivership and liquidation. In relation to a company which is a taxable person, the references above to a taxable person becoming 'bankrupt or incapacitated' are to be construed as references to its going into liquidation or receivership or to an administration order being made in relation to it. *[SI 1995/2518, Reg 9].* See *Sargent v C & E Commrs CA, [1995] STC 398* where it was held that the appointment of a receiver by a mortgagee under *Law of Property Act 1925* did not entitle C & E to treat the receiver as a taxable person. 'Incapacitated' must be construed as 'incapable of carrying on business'. This would only result from administrative receivership, liquidation or administration and not from the partial incapacity resulting from the appointment of a receiver of specific properties. However, such a receiver is still obliged to account to C & E for VAT on rents from properties which the company has opted to tax.

36.2 NOTIFICATION OF INSOLVENCY

Official receivers and insolvency practitioners appointed as the person in charge over the affairs of an insolvent VAT-registered person must notify C & E of their appointment. This must be done on Form VAT 769 obtainable from any VAT office. The completed form should be sent, within 21 days of appointment, to the VAT office which controls the area of the principal place of business of the insolvent registered person. Form VAT 769 should not be used in the following circumstances and notification should simply be given in writing to that VAT office.

- Notification of a proposed creditors meeting for either voluntary arrangements or creditors voluntary liquidations.

- The appointment of a receiver under *Law of Property Act*.

- The appointment of a receiver or manager under a fixed charge only.

- The appointment of a receiver under the *Agricultural Credits Act 1928* over assets of a farm estate.

- The appointment of a provisional liquidator (as such a person has no status with regard to the trader's VAT registration).

Where a liquidator is appointed after the appointment of an administrative receiver, it is not necessary to complete a second Form VAT 769. C & E will however need extra information (e.g. who is in control of the assets and who will be responsible for completing VAT returns). This information, together with the name, address and date of appointment of the liquidator, should be sent to HM Customs and Excise, Insolvency operations, Queens Dock, Liverpool L74 4AA.

Where a liquidator or trustee is appointed after the administration of an official receiver, C & E should be advised of the appointment using Form VAT 769. Where the liquidator or trustee has difficulty in obtaining the necessary information within the 21 days notification period, C & E will only expect notification to be made within 21 days of that person becoming aware of the information.

(C & E Notice 700/56/94, para 5).

36.3 **CLAIMS BY C & E**

On notification of an insolvency, C & E will calculate its claim based on the amount outstanding at the 'relevant date'.

'Relevant date' is

- in relation to a company which is being wound up

    (i) where the company is being wound up by a court and the winding-up order was made immediately upon the discharge of an administration order, the date of the making of the administration order;

    (ii) in a case not within (i) above where the company is being wound up by the court and had not commenced to be wound up voluntarily before the date of the making of the winding-up order, the date of appointment (or first appointment) of a provisional liquidator or, if no such appointment has been made, the date of the making of the winding-up order; and

    (iii) in any other case not within (i) or (ii) above, the date of the passing of the resolution for the winding up of the company;

- in relation to a company in receivership, the date of appointment of the receiver; and

- in relation to a bankrupt

    (i) where at the time the bankruptcy order was made there was an interim receiver of the debtor's estate appointed under *Insolvency Act 1986, s 286*, the date on which the interim receiver was first appointed after the presentation of the bankruptcy petition; and

    (ii) in any other case, the date of making the bankruptcy order.

[*Insolvency Act 1986, 6 Sch*].

The person in charge of the insolvency has the responsibility for the VAT affairs of the trader from the relevant date, with the exception of *Law of Property Act* receiverships, fixed charge receiverships, voluntary arrangements, deeds of arrangement and County Court administration orders where the individual/business continues to trade. (C & E Notice 700/56/94, para 6).

The claim notified to the person in charge of the insolvency will show the aggregated totals of the preferential and non-preferential debts due to C & E. A breakdown of the claim details is available on request.

De Voil Indirect Tax Service. See V5.187.

36.4   **Preferential claim**

Any VAT which is referable to the period of six months next before the relevant date is a preferential debt in the insolvency.

Where the whole of a prescribed accounting period falls within the six-month period, the whole of the VAT for that period is referable to the relevant period. In any other case, the VAT liability for the accounting period is apportioned between the non-preferential claim and the preferential claim according to the number of days within the accounting period. (The normal prescribed accounting period in which the relevant date occurs is in any case divided into two periods, see 2.2(*e*) ACCOUNTING PERIODS AND RETURNS.)

[*IA 1986, 6 Sch*]. (C & E Notice 700/56/94, paras 7, 9).

36.5   **Non-preferential claim**

The non-preferential claim comprises the following.

• Any amount of outstanding VAT incurred in the period prior to the six month preferential period.

• The amount of any penalty, default surcharge or default interest assessed under *VATA 1994, s 76* in respect of any period before the relevant date i.e. even if relating to the six months before the relevant date. This is because the penalty etc. is recoverable 'as if it were' VAT and is not VAT as such.

• Import duties, including import VAT.

(C & E Notice 700/56/94, paras 8, 12).

36.6   **Assessments**

Where a return has not been submitted for any prescribed accounting period prior to the relevant date, C & E will raise an assessment and initially base their claim upon the amount so assessed. Where the person in charge of the insolvency submits an acceptable VAT return for the period in question, the assessment will be withdrawn.

Where an assessment is raised following a VAT inspection or voluntary disclosure before the relevant date, any additional VAT due is related directly to the original accounting period in determining whether it is preferential or non-preferential.

(C & E Notice 700/56/94, paras 10, 11).

36.7   **Set-off of credits**

As a general rule, under *VATA 1994, s 81(3)(3A)* any amount due from C & E to any person ('the credit') must be set against any sum due from that person by way of VAT, penalty, interest or surcharge ('the debit') and to the extent of the set-off, the obligations of both C & E and that person are discharged. See 51.9 PAYMENT OF VAT for full details.

However this general rule does not apply where

(*a*) an 'insolvency procedure' has been applied to the person entitled to the credit;

(*b*) the credit became due after that procedure was so applied; and

(*c*) the liability to pay the debit either

    (i) arose before that procedure was so applied; or

    (ii) (having arisen afterwards) relates to, or to matters occurring in the course of, the carrying on of any business at times before the procedure was so applied.

For these purposes, the time when an '*insolvency procedure*' is to be taken to be applied to any person is when

  (i) a bankruptcy order is made in relation to that person (unless any of (vi)–(viii) below already applies to that person);

  (ii) a winding up order is made in relation to that person (unless any of (iii)–(viii) already applies to that person);

  (iii) an administration order is made in relation to that person (unless any of (iv) or (vi)–(viii) already applies to that person);

  (iv) that person is put into administrative receivership;

  (v) that person, being a corporation, passes a resolution for voluntary winding up;

  (vi) any approved voluntary arrangement comes into force in relation to that person;

  (vii) a registered deed of arrangement takes effect in relation to that person; or

  (viii) that person's estate becomes vested in any other person as that person's trustee under a trust deed.

[*VATA 1994, s 81(4)(5), 13 Sch 21; FA 1995, s 27; SI 1994/1253*].

De Voil Indirect Tax Service. See V5.172.

36.8 **Crown set-off**

C & E can offer credits arising from insolvent traders VAT repayment claims accruing before the relevant date to other government departments. [*IA 1986, s 323; SI 1986/1925, Rule 4.90*]. See also *Re Cushla v C & E Commrs CD, [1979] STC 615* and *Re DH Curtis (Builders) Ltd, [1978] 2 All ER 183*.

C & E currently only operate the Crown set-off procedure for repayments which exceed £500 (£5,000 before 13 April 1998). Any VAT repayments due falling below the limit are automatically repaid to the person in charge of the insolvency (or to the trader in the case of administration, voluntary arrangements, deeds of arrangement and County Court administration orders).

If a secured creditor has a valid registered debenture agreement containing a fixed charge on book debts, C & E will repay VAT credits to the person in charge of the insolvency without set-off provided they are satisfied that there will be a shortfall to the debenture holder.

(C & E Notice 700/56/94, paras 39–42).

36.9   **Dividends**

If the person in charge of the insolvency declares a dividend, cheques due to C & E should be made payable to 'Customs and Excise' and sent to Insolvency Operations Branch, Liverpool. The receipts and payments accounts should also be sent. Dividends for businesses in administration, voluntary arrangements, deeds of arrangement or County Court administration orders should be sent to the appropriate VAT office. (C & E Notice 700/56/94, para 28).

36.10   **RETURNS**

All returns completed by the person in charge of the insolvency must be submitted to VAT Central Unit in Southend.

Pre-insolvency returns. The insolvent trader is responsible for submitting pre-insolvency returns. However, unsigned VAT returns completed by the person in charge of the insolvency are acceptable carrying the legend 'completed from the books and records of the company/trader'.

Split period return covering the relevant date. Where the relevant date (see 36.3 above) falls within a prescribed accounting period, that period is divided into two periods. The first period ends on the day prior to the relevant date. The return for that period is issued directly to the person in charge of the insolvency and must be submitted by the last day of the following month. Default surcharge is not applicable to this return. The second period begins on the relevant date and ends (and all subsequent periods end) on the normal last day for the prescribed accounting periods of the insolvent trader. [*SI 1995/2518, Reg 25(3)*].

Post-insolvency returns are the responsibility of the person in charge of the insolvency (except for *Law of Property Act* receiverships, fixed charge receiverships, voluntary arrangements and County Court administration orders where the individual/business continues to trade). Returns are issued automatically to the person in charge by C & E until deregistration is agreed. The returns must be submitted, and any VAT paid, by the normal due date (see 51.1 PAYMENT OF VAT).

Repayments due are repaid direct to the person in charge of the insolvency in the name of the insolvent business c/o the person in charge except that

• repayments for traders in voluntary arrangements, deeds of arrangement or County Court administration orders are sent to the address of the registered business (unless the trader has given written permission for repayments to be sent to the person in charge); and

• repayments for traders in administration are sent to the business address (although, on application by the administrator, repayments can be sent c/o the administrator).

Repayment supplement will be added if the normal conditions are satisfied.

Penalties, default surcharge and interest. Currently, these are not applied to post-insolvency returns except in the case of administration orders, deeds of arrangement, County Court administration orders and voluntary arrangements.

Compliance. C & E reserve the right to check the accuracy of returns submitted and to require the books and records to be available for inspection.

(C & E Notice 700/56/94, paras 15–21).

36.11   **MISCELLANEOUS VAT PROCEDURES**

Bad debt relief. BAD DEBT RELIEF (7) can be claimed in insolvencies subject to the normal rules. Claims can be made on the normal VAT return where the VAT registration remains open and on Form VAT 426 where registration has been cancelled. A letter scheduling the claim, together with copies of the relevant invoices, must be submitted to Insolvency Operations for approval. C & E need to establish in which periods the supplies subject to the claim were made, whether returns have been submitted for those periods and whether the VAT due for each period has been paid. (C & E Notice 700/56/94, paras 29–31). See also 7.9 BAD DEBT RELIEF for a concession concerning the repayment of input tax where an insolvency practitioner receives notice of a claim for bad debt relief on a pre-insolvency transaction.

Cash accounting scheme (see 63.2 SPECIAL SCHEMES). C & E do not allow the cash accounting scheme to be applied during an insolvency by the person in charge and the normal VAT accounting rules must be followed. VAT on all supplies made and received in the six months before the relevant date, but not previously accounted for, must be entered on the VAT return for the period immediately preceding the relevant date. Such VAT is treated as a liability arising prior to insolvency. Traders in administration, voluntary arrangements, deeds of arrangement or County Court administration orders can continue to use cash accounting. (C & E Notice 700/56/94, paras 33, 34).

Credit notes. Where the person in charge of the insolvency issues or receives a credit note for supplies made in a pre-insolvency VAT period, the adjustment of VAT is related back to the earlier period and C & E's claim in the insolvency will be reduced or increased as the case may be. To enable C & E to make the necessary adjustments in their claim, the person in charge must forward a schedule of the credit notes in question detailing VAT elements and dates of original supply.

Where the person in charge issues or receives a credit note relating to post relevant date supplies, the VAT liability can be adjusted on the next available return.

(C & E Notice 700/56/94, para 35–38).

Partial exemption. The provisions relating to PARTIAL EXEMPTION (49) apply to all VAT-registered businesses including those which are insolvent. The person in charge must comply with these requirements in respect of returns completed for pre and post relevant date VAT periods. An insolvent business can apply to change the method of calculating entitlement to input tax recovery if there has been a substantial change in circumstances although such changes cannot be applied retrospectively.

Where a business is already partly exempt, the annual adjustment should be made at the end of the business's partial exemption year. Approval may be sought from the VAT office to allow the annual adjustment to be made in the VAT period which ends with the relevant date.

(C & E Notice 700/56/94, paras 49, 50).

VAT on insolvency practitioners' fees. As the practitioner's services do not relate to any specific supply, fees are a general overhead of the business concerned.

(a)   *Insolvent businesses which continue to trade.*

- Where the business remains fully taxable it can deduct input tax on the practitioner's fees. If the business sells assets and incurs exempt input tax, it will have to apply a partial exemption method in the normal way.

- Where the business remains partly exempt, deduction of input tax is subject to restriction in accordance with the partial exemption method in place.

(b)   *Insolvent businesses which cease to trade but which remain registered.* The principal activity will be the sale of assets. As anything done in connection with the termination or intended termination of a business is done in the course or furtherance of that business, input tax incurred on the practitioner's fees should be considered in the light of the taxable status of the business prior to the insolvency. Where the business was previously fully taxable, the input tax on these fees is fully deductible. Where the business was previously partially exempt, the business should continue to use the method in place in the normal way.

A change of partial exemption method should be requested from the VAT office if, in the light of changing circumstances, the method in place no longer produces a fair and reasonable attribution of input tax to taxable supplies. Any change of method cannot be applied retrospectively.

Where the practitioner's fees include costs charged by third parties, these should be separately identified and deducted to the extent that they are used to make taxable supplies.

(C & E Manual V1-15, Chapter 3 para 1.16).

Distress. See 17.3 CUSTOMS AND EXCISE: POWERS for C & E's right to levy distress. Once a bankruptcy order or compulsory winding up order has been made, any distress action not yet completed (i.e. where the goods distrained have not yet been sold) is abandoned. However, where a levy for distress or walking possession agreement (see 52.13 PENALTIES) is in place before the appointment of a liquidator in a voluntary winding up or an administrative receiver, the distress remains valid and will be carried out.

Where a floating charge crystallises into a fixed charge on insolvency, C & E recognise that this charge takes priority over any levy they may have in place.

Any money received by C & E for the sale of distrained goods is set off against the earliest pre-insolvency liability.

(C & E Notice 700/56/94, paras 43–47).

Records. The person in charge may destroy the books, papers and records, including VAT records, of an insolvent company after one year from the date of dissolution. [*SI 1986/1994, Rule 32*]. C & E have agreed to this in principle despite the normal requirements to retain VAT records for six years. (C & E Notice 700/56/94, para 60).

Viability studies by accountants. Accountants engaged to conduct viability studies are treated as making supplies of their services to the person who has commissioned the work, instructed them and who receives the end product. The effect of this is as follows.

* Where either the company or the bank commission the work, the accountants should issue any invoices to the company or bank (as the case may be). The supply is then received for business purposes and input tax is deductible subject to the normal rules. The supply is not necessarily made to the person paying for the services. The fact that the other party, or a third party, receives a copy of the report is not relevant.

* Where the bank receives one report and the company another, the accountant is making two separate supplies and should issue separate invoices to allow recovery of input tax subject to the normal rules.

* Where the company and bank issue joint instructions and receive copies of the same report, the accountant should issue invoices for 50% of the cost to each party.

* Where the company commissions the work but does not receive a copy of the report, the accountant's supply is to the company but is not used for business purposes. Therefore neither the company nor the bank can recover any input tax.

(C & E Business Brief 6/95, 28 March 1995).

36.12 DEREGISTRATION

Deregistration should be applied for as soon as trading has ceased and VAT on remaining taxable stocks and assets is £250 or less.

C & E issue Form VAT 167 (a deregistration questionnaire) at the same time as lodging their claim. The deregistration process then depends on the type of insolvency.

• In an administrative receivership, deregistration is not effected until confirmation that it is appropriate has been agreed with the receiver.

• In a bankruptcy or compulsory or voluntary winding up, Form VAT 168 is automatically issued five weeks after Form VAT 167 warning that, unless a reply is received within seven days, deregistration will be automatically effected on the eighth day without notification. If at any time after the issue of Form VAT 167 and within seven days of issue of Form VAT 168, the person in charge of the insolvency contacts C & E to say that deregistration is not appropriate, the deregistration process will be deferred.

In either case, once deregistration has been agreed, a final VAT return (Form VAT 193) is issued for completion.

(C & E Notice 700/56/94, paras 22–25).

36.13 POST-DEREGISTRATION

Output tax. Any output tax arising after the date of deregistration can be accounted for on Form VAT 833. The form is available from Insolvency Operations and must be returned there with full payment of any VAT due.

Input tax. Post-deregistration input tax claims should be made on Form VAT 426 (available from the VAT office) which is specially designed for 'insolvency practitioners'. Subject to the normal rules, the form can be used to claim

• VAT on services supplied after deregistration but which relates to business carried on before deregistration;

• VAT on goods and services supplied and invoiced before deregistration that has not already been claimed on a VAT return;

• VAT on the services of agents (e.g. solicitors, estate agents, stockbrokers) unless relating to exempt supplies; and

• VAT on realisation fees.

VAT relating to a petitioning creditor's costs cannot be claimed.

No invoices need to be submitted with the claim which should be sent to VAT 426 Claims Section, Insolvency Operations, HM Customs and Excise, Queens Dock, Liverpool L74 4AA. The claim should be processed and paid within 15 working days.

C & E will randomly select some claims for verification by VAT officers who will make arrangements to visit within 30 working days of receipt of the claim. In most cases, claims will be paid before the visit.

An '*insolvency practitioner*' is a trustee in bankruptcy; a trustee in sequestration (Scotland); an official receiver; an official assignee (NI); a liquidator or an administrative receiver. The scheme is *not* available for use by solvent registered traders, office holders in informal insolvencies and other incapacitated traders. These categories include supervisors in voluntary arrangements, administrators in administration orders; a trustee appointed under a trust deed (Scotland); a receiver appointed under the *Law of*

Property Act 1925 ; a receiver appointed in a partnership dispute; a receiver appointed in a court; and a receiver appointed under the *Agricultural Credits Act 1928*.

(C & E Notice 700/56/94, paras 26, 27).

36.14   **GROUPS**

In a VAT group of companies, the claim for preferential debts extends to a non-representative member because under *VATA 1994, s 43(1)* such a member is jointly and severally liable for VAT due from the representative member (*Re Nadler Enterprises Ltd CD, [1980] STC 457*). See 31 GROUPS OF COMPANIES.

Where the representative member of a group becomes insolvent, C & E regard the group treatment as ceasing to have effect from the relevant date. All the members of the group are automatically deregistered and each solvent member which continues to trade is automatically re-registered. Any insolvent member can also apply to be re-registered provided the company continues to trade. Continuation of group treatment may be allowed on request, however, but this will require prompt action to avoid automatic deregistration.

If the representative member of a group remains solvent but another group member becomes insolvent, C & E will not automatically exclude that member from the group.

37 Insurance

De Voil Indirect Tax Service. See V6.159–162B.

The contents of this chapter are as follows.

37.1 INTRODUCTION

Output tax. The VAT liability of insurance services depends upon whether the supply is treated as taking place in, or outside, the UK. If it is treated as taking place in the UK, the supply is normally exempt. However, supplies of insurance services by UK suppliers to certain overseas persons are treated as taking place outside the UK and are consequently outside the scope of UK VAT. See 37.2 below for the place of supply of insurance services.

Supplies by insurers and reinsurers are considered in 37.4 to 37.8 below and supplies by insurance brokers, agents and intermediaries are considered in 37.9 to 37.13 below.

Input tax. Under the normal rules, input tax relating to taxable supplies of services can be recovered in full but input tax relating to exempt supplies is not recoverable. Special rules, however, apply to insurance (and financial) services which, in certain circumstances, allow input tax to be recovered where it relates to exempt supplies or supplies which would be exempt if treated as taking place in the UK. See 37.3 below.

37.2 PLACE OF SUPPLY OF INSURANCE SERVICES

Special place of supply rules apply to services falling within *VATA 1994, 5 Sch 1–8*. These include insurance services (*5 Sch 5*) and services rendered by one person to another in procuring such services for the other (*5 Sch 8*).

The place of supply of such services is treated as being

(*a*) where the *recipient* belongs if the recipient

- belongs in a country, other than the Isle of Man, which is not an EC country; or

- belongs in an EC country other than that of the supplier and the insurance services are supplied to the recipient for business purposes; and

(*b*) where the *supplier* belongs in all other cases, i.e. where the recipient

- belongs in the UK or Isle of Man; or

- belongs in an EC country but not in the same country as the supplier and receives the supply other than for business purposes.

[*VATA 1994, s 7(10)(11); SI 1992/3121, Art 16*].

See 64.19 SUPPLY for the place of belonging. For the countries comprising the EC, see 21.2 EUROPEAN COMMUNITY: GENERAL.

37.3   **INPUT TAX RECOVERY IN RESPECT OF INSURANCE SERVICES**

Subject to the normal rules, input tax may be recovered which relates to

(*a*)   taxable supplies of insurance services (i.e. supplies with a place of supply in the UK other than exempt supplies);

(*b*)   supplies of insurance services with a place of supply outside the UK which would be taxable if made in the UK; and

(*c*)   supplies of insurance services which

   (i)   are supplied to a person who belongs outside the EC; or

   (ii)   are directly linked to the export of goods to a place outside the EC; or

   (iii)   consist of making the arrangements for a supply of services within (i) or (ii) above

where that supply is exempt or would have been exempt if made in the UK.

To satisfy C & E that the recipient of a supply belongs outside the EC, the appropriate documentation (e.g. policy documents, cover notes, credit/debit notes, broker's slips and any relevant correspondence) must be produced. (C & E Notice 701/36/97, para 6.2).

Apart from the special cases in (*c*) above, input tax which relates to exempt supplies of insurance services cannot be recovered.

[*VATA 1994, s 26(1)(2); SI 1992/3123*].

37.4   **SUPPLIES BY INSURERS AND REINSURERS WITH EFFECT FROM 19 MARCH 1997**

EC legislation. See 22.18(*a*) EUROPEAN COMMUNITY LEGISLATION.

The provision of insurance or reinsurance in the UK is exempt from VAT where made by any of the following persons ('*permitted persons*').

(*a*)   A person who provides it in the course of any insurance business which he is authorised to carry on under *Insurance Companies Act 1982, ss 3, 4.*

Authorisation is granted by the Secretary of State for Trade and Industry who specifies the classes of insurance which may be underwritten in each case.

(*b*)   A person who provides it in the course of any business in respect of which he is exempt under *Insurance Companies Act 1982, s 2* from the requirement to be so authorised.

Authorisation is not required by

- a member of Lloyd's;

- a Friendly Society (see 37.14 below);

- a trade union or employers' association where the insurance business is limited to the provision for its members of provident benefits or strike benefits; and

- an insurance company only providing benefits in kind insurance.

(c) An insurer or reinsurer who belongs outside the UK where the insurance or reinsurance relates to any of the risks or other things described in *Insurance Companies Act 1982, 1, 2 Sch.*

(d) The Export Credits Guarantee Department.

[*VATA 1994, 9 Sch Group 2, Items 1–3; FA 1997, s 38*].

As a consequence of the above, the place of supply rules in 37.2 above, and the input tax recovery rules in 37.3 above, the VAT position of insurance and reinsurance in the UK can be summarised as follows.

	Insured belonging in			
	UK	*EC (non-business)*	*EC (business)*	*Non-EC*
Supplies by permitted persons				
Insurance directly related to the export of goods to a place outside the EC	E(R)	E(R)	OS(R)	OS(R)
All other classes of insurance	E	E	OS	OS(R)
Supplies by non-permitted persons				
All classes of insurance	S	S	OS(R)	OS(R)

Key

E	=	Exempt (no input tax recovery)
E(R)	=	Exempt but with refund of related input tax
OS	=	Outside the scope of UK VAT with no refund of related input tax
OS(R)	=	Outside the scope of UK VAT with refund of related input tax
S	=	Standard rated (with input tax recovery)

To qualify as insurance directly related to the export of goods to a place outside the EC, the insurance must cover the risks of the person who owns the goods or is responsible for their export.

(C & E Notice 701/36/97, paras 2.1–2.4).

In *Winterthur Life UK Ltd (14935)* the operation of personal pension schemes by a group of companies was held to be an exempt supply of services within *VATA 1994, 9 Sch Group 2, Item 1*. On the facts, the services were not simply trust administration but embodied insurance contracts and were 'part and parcel' of the provision of insurance.

37.5   **Marine, aviation and transport ('MAT') insurance**

MAT insurance includes insurance for the actual fabric of aircraft and ships as well as freight in transit but not

- motor and land vehicles;

- oil and gas rigs to be permanently fixed to the sea bed;

- specific policies for ships laid up, aircraft grounded, and ships and aircraft under repair; and

- port and airport owners' and operators' liability and manufacturers' product liability.

The supply of insurance and reinsurance in respect of any MAT risk by a permitted person follows the same liability as in 37.4 above. No unusual problems arise where the place of supply is in the UK, but the treatment of MAT insurance supplied as an international service may present difficulties as a result of the way in which the insurance industry operates. The following guidelines have been agreed between C & E and the Association of British Insurers, Lloyd's of London, the Institute of London Underwriters and the British Insurance and Investment Association.

The place of belonging of the insured is to be determined using the following rules.

(*a*) *Where the insurer's address is shown on the broker's slip* (or equivalent document) or where it can be determined by the broker or other intermediary, this address is to be taken as the place of belonging of the insured.

(*b*) *Where the insured has more than one address*, the one on the slip or equivalent document should be used unless it is clear that this is simply an administrative address for payment or other purposes.

(*c*) *Where business is written in conjunction with an overseas agent* and it is not possible to identify the address of each insured dealing with the agent, the agent's address may be taken as the place of belonging of the insured persons.

(*d*) *Where the place of belonging of the insured cannot otherwise be determined*, then it should be decided by reference to the country of origin of the business, the address of the originating broker/cover holder or any additional information on the slip. In the case of conflict between indicators, best judgement should be used.

Insurers and brokers should code transactions as either

Z (indicating an entitlement to input tax recovery) if the insurance is provided to a person belonging outside the EC or if the insurance is directly linked to goods being exported outside the EC;

X (indicating no entitlement to input tax recovery) if the insurance is provided to a person belonging in the EC and is not directly linked to goods being exported outside the EC; or

M (where it is not possible to determine the place of belonging of the assured under the above guide-lines) with 50% of the attributable input tax being recoverable and 50% irrecoverable. Use of the M code should be regarded as a last resort which is rarely required.

Multiple insured. Certain insurances (e.g. hull) often have multiple insured identified on the slip including the owner, managers, operators, time charterers and mortgagors. Where possible, the principal insured should be identified and their place of belonging used to decide the VAT code. The principal insured may be the only named insured (as distinct from others shown as additional insured) or may be the first-named on the policy. Where the principal insured cannot be identified, the places of belonging of all the insured should be ascertained (if practicable) and the business coded X if all belong inside the EC, Z if all belong outside the EC, and M if some but not all belong outside the EC.

(C & E Notice 701/36/97, para 2.5).

Also see C & E Notice 700/57/95 for details of an arrangement allowed to MAT insurance underwriters who are members of a particular trade association in respect of claims-related input tax and associated imported services.

37.6   Engineering insurance

Engineering insurance is concerned with the provision of insurance on plant, machinery and structures on land. It may comprise

(*a*)   an insurance only policy;

(*b*)   an inspection only contract; or

(*c*)   a combined inspection and insurance policy.

A contract falling within (*b*) above is a contract for taxable inspection services and a contract under (*c*) above is a mixed supply of inspection and insurance services. Normal VAT rules must be applied to determine the liability of such supplies. See 47.3 OUTPUT TAX for suggested methods of calculating VAT on mixed supplies.

Before 1 April 1997, contracts within (*c*) above could be treated as relating entirely to exempt insurance where the contract contained an endorsement worded as follows (see C & E Notice 700/57/95).

'The company shall have the right to inspect the insured plant at all reasonable times during the Period of Insurance and the Company will make periodical inspections of the plant including inspections required by any statutory provisions indicated in this Policy and the Insured agrees to properly prepare and make available the plant at no expense to the Company to enable the Company to carry out such inspections and report thereon'.

This special treatment, which had been agreed between C & E and the Association of British Insurers, was withdrawn with effect from 1 April 1997.

(C & E Notice 701/36/97, para 2.6).

37.7   Insurance claims

Payment of claims. The payment of money by way of financial restitution to the insured in respect of an insurance claim is not the consideration for a supply and is not in itself a supply for VAT purposes. (C & E Notice 701/36/97, para 2.7).

Costs relating to insurance claims. Services and goods in relation to a claim are normally supplied to the policyholder, not the insurer. As such, the insurer cannot treat the VAT on the supply as input tax. This normally applies to

• repairs,

• replacement of goods,

• legal costs in relation to a claim,

• supplies where the insurer exercises his right to pursue or defend a claim in the name of the policyholder (i.e. in a subrogated claim), and

• services of loss assessors

and for these purposes it is immaterial whether the supply is commissioned by the policyholder or by the insurer on his behalf.

Policyholders who are registered for VAT can deduct as input tax any VAT on such supplies of goods or services received where the insurance claim relates to their business.

Where, however, an insurer obtains services for his own purposes, the services are supplied to the insurer and any input tax is deductible subject to the insurer's partial exemption method. This includes

• legal services relating to advice on the drafting or interpretation of a policy;

- legal services in the context of a dispute with a policyholder; and

- services of loss adjusters and similar experts (who assess the value of any loss of an insurance claim).

See also 37.15 below where legal and other services are supplied from overseas.

Where an insurer has goods supplied to him for transfer to the policyholder in settlement of a claim, the insurer may treat the VAT incurred as input tax but, if so, must also account for output tax on the cost price of the goods when handed over. Alternatively, the insurer can refrain from claiming input tax on the supply to him in which case no output tax is due on the supply to the policyholder.

(C & E Notice 701/36/97, paras 2.7, 5.4).

Attribution of VAT on claims costs. From 1 May 1995, for partial exemption purposes VAT incurred by insurers on the costs of settling insurance claims is directly attributable to the supply of insurance which gives rise to the claim (and therefore either wholly recoverable or wholly restricted according to the principles for recovering input tax in 37.3 above). This follows the decision in *C & E Commrs v Deutsche Ruck UK Reinsurance Co Ltd QB 1994, [1995] STC 495.* Previously, C & E had regarded such costs as general overheads and the VAT on them as non-attributable input tax to be apportioned under the insurer's partial exemption method. Businesses must apply direct attribution from 1 May 1995 but may make a retrospective claim back to 12 August 1993, the date of the original tribunal decision, provided they have the necessary records to support the claim.

(C & E Notice 701/36/97, paras 2.7, 2.8).

37.8   **Surrender of goods following an insurance claim**

The disposal of

- works of art, antiques and collectors' items, and

- second-hand goods (i.e. tangible moveable property that is suitable for further use either as it is or after repair)

by an insurer who has taken possession of them in settlement of a claim under an insurance policy (e.g. salvaged goods damaged by fire or water or stolen goods recovered after a claim has been paid) is outside the scope of VAT provided the following conditions are met.

(*a*) The goods are in the same condition at the time of disposal as when they were taken into the insurer's possession.

(*b*) For goods other than motor cars

  (i) if the goods had been supplied in the UK by the policyholder, that supply would not have been chargeable with VAT or would have been chargeable on less than full value;

  (ii) if the goods have been imported into the UK, they must have borne VAT which has neither been reclaimed nor refunded; and

  (iii) the goods must not have been reimported having previously been exported from the UK free of VAT by reason of zero-rating.

(*c*) In the case of motor cars, the VAT on any previous supply, acquisition or importation must have been wholly excluded from credit.

37.9 Insurance

[*SI 1992/3122, Art 4; SI 1995/1268, Art 4; SI 1995/1269; SI 1995/1385; SI 1995/1667*].

Where the above conditions are not satisfied, VAT is chargeable on the full amount realised on the sale (not the original cost of the asset, see *Darlington Finance Ltd, [1982] VATTR 233 (1337)*). The insurer will therefore need to know the VAT status of the policyholder and be able to cross reference this information to the disposal of each item in order to decide whether VAT must be accounted for.

Motor vehicles received by an insurer as scrap metal are treated as tangible moveable property rather than motor cars. Insurers are not required to account for VAT on the disposal of the scrap unless the policyholder would have charged VAT.

(C & E Notice 701/36/97, para 2.9).

37.9 **SUPPLIES BY INSURANCE BROKERS, AGENTS AND OTHER INTERMEDIARIES WITH EFFECT FROM 19 MARCH 1997**

Subject to the exceptions in 37.10 below, the provision by an insurance broker or an insurance agent of any of the 'services of an insurance intermediary' is exempt from VAT where those services are

(*a*) related to the provision of exempt insurance or reinsurance within 37.4 above (whether or not a contract of insurance or reinsurance is finally concluded); and

(*b*) provided by the broker or agent in the course of acting in an '*intermediary capacity*' i.e. acting as an intermediary (or one of the intermediaries) between a person providing exempt insurance under 37.4 above and a person who is seeking insurance or reinsurance or is an insured person.

'*Services of an insurance intermediary*' consist of any of the following.

(i) Bringing together, with a view to the insurance or reinsurance of risks, of persons seeking and persons providing insurance and reinsurance.

It is sometime difficult to distinguish between exempt introductory services under this heading and advertising services which are excluded from exemption (see 37.10(*a*) below). C & E accept that there is a single exempt supply of insurance-related introductory services where

• the intermediary is targeting its own customer base;

• the intermediary is paid per successful take-up of an insurance policy; and

• the product or the insurer is endorsed by the intermediary.

(C & E Notice 701/36/97, para 3.5).

(ii) Carrying out work preparatory to the conclusion of a contract of insurance or reinsurance.

(iii) Assistance in the administration and performance of such contracts, including claims handling (see 37.13 below).

(iv) The collection of premiums.

[*VATA 1994, 9 Sch Group 2, Item 4, Notes (1)(2); FA 1997, s 38*].

Value of services. The consideration for the provision of insurance-related services in an intermediary capacity is the gross commission (i.e. before deduction of any commission allowable in turn to other intermediaries), flat-rate fee or recharge of costs incurred, whichever method applies to the particular transaction. (C & E Notice 701/36/97, para 3.10).

37.10   **Supplies not regarded as services of an insurance intermediary**

Supplies of the following services are specifically excluded from exemption under 37.9 above.

(*a*)   Market research, product design, advertising, promotional or similar services (or the collection, collation and provision of information for use in connection with such activities).

(*b*)   Valuation or inspection services.

(*c*)   Services by loss adjusters, average adjusters, motor assessors, surveyors or other experts unless

(i)   the services consist of claims handling under a contract of insurance or reinsurance; and

(ii)   the person handling the claim is authorised to act on behalf of the insurer or reinsurer and has written authority to accept or reject the claim, and to settle any amount agreed to be paid.

See 37.13 below.

(*d*)   Services supplied in pursuance of a contract of insurance or reinsurance (or any arrangements in connection with such a contract) either instead of any financial indemnity which the insurer is contractually obliged to provide or for the purpose of satisfying any claim under that contract (in whole or part). This applies, for example, where a plumber's services are supplied free of charge to the insured to mend a burst pipe and the insurer meets the plumber's fee. (C & E Notice 701/36/97, para 4.6).

[*VATA 1994, 9 Sch Group 2, Notes (7)-(10); FA 1997, s 38*].

Where one of the above excluded supplies is provided as a minor and ancillary part of a single composite supply of exempt insurance-related services provided in an intermediary capacity, the entire supply is treated as exempt. (C & E Notice 701/36/97, para 3.12).

37.11   **Insurance supplied with other goods and services**

Insurance is frequently supplied as part of a package with other goods or services, with the supplier of the goods also arranging insurance. Examples include mechanical breakdown insurance (MBI) supplied with cars and domestic appliances, insurance with car hire, travel insurance, removal insurance, and property and liability insurance for tenants.

Where insurance is arranged for a customer in connection with the supply of any goods or services, the supply of arranging the insurance may be treated as an exempt supply under 37.9 above if the following conditions are met.

(*a*)   The insurance is supplied by a permitted person and qualifies for exemption under 37.4 above.

(*b*)   It is the customer's own risk which is being insured, i.e. the individual customer's risk is referred to in the policy. It is not necessary for the customer to be specifically named. Where both the supplier of taxable goods and services and the customer are the insured, it is sufficient for the policy to refer to, for example, 'J Smith and customers'.

(*c*)   Where

(i)   the goods or services are liable to VAT (and not zero-rated), and

(ii) the insurance-related services are provided by the supplier of those goods or services (or a person 'connected' with that person who deals directly with the customer in connection with the insurance)

the amount of the premium under the contract of insurance, and any other amounts which the customer is required to pay in connection with the insurance transaction; must be set out in a document disclosed to the customer at or before the time when the insurance transaction is entered into.

See 69.3 VALUATION for when a person is '*connected*' with another.

C & E may set out requirements in a C & E Notice as to preparation and form of the document, manner of disclosing its contents to the customer and delivery of a copy of the document to the customer. Where a person supplies SECOND-HAND GOODS (61) under one of the margin schemes, the relevant document for disclosure of the information is the VAT invoice issued under the scheme.

[*VATA 1994, 9 Sch Group 2, Notes (3)-(6); FA 1997, s 38*].

The disclosure conditions under (*c*) above may create a problem where transactions take place over the telephone, or by some other form of electronic communication, and the customer and supplier are not physically in the same place at the same time. Under powers given to them in *SI 1995/2518, Reg 31(2)*, C & E have indicated that, to fall within the exemption, a person selling insurance with taxable goods and services by means of electronic communication must

- make full disclosure of the premium at the time of the transaction (e.g. a trader selling holidays over the telephone must orally inform the customer of the amount of the premium and any fee charged over and above the premium in relation to the insurance);

- prepare, and issue to the customer, a document with the information required as above; and

- have in place a system whereby the sales staff must annotate a document (even if this only involves ticking a box) at the time they make the oral disclosure to customers to indicate that they have done so. Traders must retain a copy of these records as they would their normal VAT records.

Block policies. A block policy is sometimes taken out by a supplier of goods and services to cover a number of small transactions requiring insurance cover over a set period (e.g. by removal companies). Where cover relates to both the risk of the supplier's goods and services and to the customers' risks, any insurance commission retained is consideration for an exempt supply provided the above conditions are satisfied.

(C & E Notice 701/36/97, paras 3.6-3.8, Appendix B).

MBI sold with second-hand cars. See 61.31 SECOND-HAND GOODS.

De Voil Indirect Tax Service. See V4.121.

37.12 **Supplies of international services by insurance intermediaries**

The liability of a supply of insurance-related intermediary services is determined, as for supplies by insurers and reinsurers, by the place of belonging of the person to whom the supply is made (see 37.2 above). The following table summarises the position with regard to UK VAT liability and recovery of related input tax.

Underlying insurance to person belonging in

	UK	EC *(non-business)*	EC *(business)*	Non-EC
Intermediary services directly related to the export of goods to a place outside the EC	E(R)	E(R)	OS(R)	OS(R)
Intermediary services of all other classes of insurance	E	E	OS	OS(R)

Key

E   = Exempt (no input tax recovery)
E(R) = Exempt but with refund of related input tax
OS   = Outside the scope of UK VAT with no refund of related input tax
OS(R) = Outside the scope of UK VAT with refund of related input tax

Notes

(1)   The above table assumes that the intermediary services are supplied to the insured. The same rules apply if the services are supplied to an insurance company except that it is the place of belonging of the insurance company which is relevant.

(2)   The special rules in 37.5 above for MAT insurance (but not MAT reinsurance) also apply to intermediaries' services.

(3)   A supply of making arrangements for the provision of reinsurance is assumed to be made to the ceding insurer and it is the place of belonging of that insurer which is relevant.

(C & E Notice 701/36/97, paras 3.13–3.16).

37.13   **Claims handling**

The supply of claims handling services by insurance intermediaries is exempt from VAT (see 37.9(iii) above). Claims handling is not specifically defined in the legislation but may include

- checking that documents are correctly completed;

- ensuring that the claim falls within the terms of the policy;

- processing the claim;

- ensuring that insurers are advised of their exposure;

- agreeing the validity and/or quantum of the claim; and

- arranging for settlement to be made.

Claims handling may also include a number of elements of an advisory, investigative or administrative nature which are subject to VAT. However, if these elements form only a minor and ancillary part of a single composite supply of claims handling, the entire supply can be treated as exempt.

Loss adjusters, motor assessors, etc. Services of loss adjusters, average adjusters, motor assessors, surveyors and other experts are excluded from exemption where in connection with the *assessment* of a claim but are exempt where (*a*) the services consist in the handling of a claim under a contract of insurance or reinsurance;

(*b*) the person handling the claim is authorised when doing so to act on behalf of the insurer or reinsurer; and

(*c*) that person's authority so to act includes written authority to determine whether to accept or reject the claim and, where accepting it in whole or in part, to settle the amount to be paid on the claim.

[*VATA 1994, 9 Sch Group 2, Note (9); FA 1997, s 38*].

The written delegated authority under (*c*) above must be given before the loss adjuster, etc. commences action in respect of a claim. It should allow the loss adjuster, etc. to investigate claims, perform any service necessary for the claim to be settled and agree the amount of a claim or cost of repair or replacement without reference to the insurer. It can also include avoiding or repudiating claims. It must bind the insurance company to pay the amount of the claim or meet the costs of repair or replacement as determined by the agent.

Where claims handling is undertaken and the conditions in (*a*)–(*c*) above are satisfied, any consideration received for a mixed supply of claims handling and assessment services are regarded as consideration for an exempt supply. Where the conditions are not satisfied (e.g. because the loss adjusters, etc. only have authority to accept claims up to a determined monetary limit or only in respect of specific types of claim) the services are standard-rated if supplied in the UK.

If an insurer gives written authority to a person (e.g. a broker) who in turn given written authority to a loss adjuster, the loss adjuster's services are exempt provided the original authority to the broker made it clear that the broker had the power to delegate the authority.

Determination of liability for claims handling services. C & E give the following table summarising the liability of a claims handling service.

Customer belongs in	*Claims handling services exempt in the UK supplied to an insurer belonging in*		
	UK	*Other EC*	*Non-EC*
UK	E	OS	OS(R)
Other EC	E	OS	OS(R)
Non-EC	E(R)	OS(R)	OS(R)

Key

E	=	Exempt (no input tax recovery)
E(R)	=	Exempt with input tax recovery
OS	=	Outside the scope with no input tax recovery
OS(R)	=	Outside the scope with input tax recovery

If a supply of claims handling services does not qualify for exemption, it is a taxable supply if made in the UK and outside the scope of UK VAT if the place of supply is outside the UK. Input tax recovery is available in respect of all such supplies, irrespective of the place of belonging of the insurer or the insured person.

(C & E Notice 701/36/97, paras 4.1–4.5).

37.14 **MISCELLANEOUS INSURANCE MATTERS**

Protection and Indemnity (P & I) Clubs. A P & I Club is normally a mutual association of ship owners established to insure its members and specialising mainly in third party liability cover and insurance of the balance of collision risks not covered by the company or London market. The club is deemed to be making a supply of insurance, the liabilities of which are determined as in the table in 37.4 above.

P & I Club managers are required to be separately VAT-registered from the one or more clubs they manage. The usual functions of the managers are dealing with the day-to-day running of the club, employing staff, assessing the level and weighting of contributions. If P & I Club managers are empowered to accept risks on behalf of the club, then they are deemed to be making arrangements for the provision of insurance and the liability of their supplies is determined as in the table in 37.9 above. The partial exemption recovery rate of the managers should follow that of the P & I Club(s) they manage unless the managers make other supplies.

(C & E Notice 701/36/97, paras 5.1-5.3).

Subscriptions to friendly societies. The insurance capital of friendly societies is provided by subscriptions from members and is deemed to be exempt under 37.4(*b*) above. If the subscription also covers other goods and services, only the part relating to insurance is exempt unless those other goods and services are also exempt under another provision (e.g. *VATA 1994, 9 Sch Group 7* provides exemption for certain supplies relating to health and welfare). (C & E Notice 701/36/97, para 5.5).

Medical and welfare funds. Subscriptions to such funds which, although not friendly societies, provide *specified* benefits in the event of illness, accident etc., are exempt provided the fund is a person permitted to carry on insurance business.

Where the benefits are *not specified* and the amounts paid out are at the discretion of persons controlling the fund, it may be possible to establish with the VAT office that the income received should be treated as donations and therefore outside the scope of VAT. Ordinarily the subscriber gets no benefit for the money paid other than a right to receive a copy of the annual report and accounts and the right to vote at general meetings. If a subscription obtains any other benefit for the member, it is standard-rated.

(C & E Notice 701/36/97, para 5.6).

Broker-managed funds offered by life assurance companies. Life assurance backed broker-managed funds are provided under contracts between the life company which operates the fund, the policyholder and the broker who arranges the policy (usually referred to as the 'Broker Fund Adviser'). The Broker Fund Adviser, with authorisation from the policy holder/investor, provides investment advice to the life assurance company, recommending the switching of money invested between the various funds operated by the assurance company or, where permitted, directly into other forms of investment (e.g. shares or gilts).

Commission paid to the Broker Fund Adviser for arranging the life insurance policy is exempt under 37.9 above. Any other fees for services (including investment advisory services and any 'performance fee' based on the increased value of investments) provided by the Broker Fund Adviser who arranged the life assurance policy are standard-rated. Where the investment advisory services are provided by a third party (whether by another Broker Fund Adviser or a sub-contractor) fees for such services are also standard-rated.

(C & E Notice 701/36/97, para 5.7).

Premiums collected by deduction from pay. A charge for collecting premiums is only exempt if made by the person who made the arrangements for the provision or renewal of the insurance (or his successor in business). Otherwise, the service is standard-rated (e.g. where collected by a debt-collector).

However, where an employer who has agreed with an insurer to use the existing payroll system to collect premiums from employees by deduction from pay, any consideration received by the employer from the insurer is exempt under *VATA 1994, 9 Sch Group 5, Item 5* (see 27.3 FINANCE).

(C & E Notice 701/36/97, para 5.8).

Contact and representative offices of overseas insurers/reinsurers. Such offices are established for public relations purposes generally. They are not permitted to accept insurance business in the UK and do not normally make supplies in the UK.

A contact office can apply for voluntary registration in the UK if it incurs input tax in connection with supplies of insurance made outside the EC by the overseas insurer. Input tax reclaimed should be based on the proportion of supplies made (as a result of contacts made by the contact office) by the overseas head office/branch which would attract input tax if they had been supplied in the UK. Where the overseas head office/branch is unable to provide a breakdown of its supplies for this purpose, the notional liability of its supplies can be determined as follows.

- If the head office/branch is inside the EC, it is treated as if it makes supplies which are outside the scope of UK VAT, with no entitlement to recovery of related input tax.

- If the head office/branch is outside the EC, it is treated as if it makes supplies which are outside the scope of UK VAT, with entitlement to recovery of input tax.

- If some branches to which the contact office supplies services are inside, and some outside, the EC, the proportion of its input tax which may be reclaimed can be arrived at using the ratio of the number of non-EC branches to the total number of EC and non-EC branches. Alternatively, the contact office may apply for an alternative method. See C & E Notice 700/57/95 for details of an agreement negotiated with the Association of British Insurers about recovery of input tax incurred in the UK in connection with supplies by branches outside the EC.

(C & E Notice 701/36/97, para 5.9).

Run-off services. Where an insurer has ceased to underwrite insurance (or a particular class) but a liability remains to deal with claims under contracts already underwritten, such contracts are said to be 'running-off'. Any addition premiums receivable under existing contracts follow the liability of the original supply of insurance.

An insurer using a partial exemption method based on the ratio of supplies which attract input tax recovery to total supplies should, to prevent distortion, exclude return premiums from the calculations of run off business only. Alternatively, to avoid complex calculations, the insurer may apply for a flat rate recovery percentage to be applied to gross input tax based on the premium income for the last three years of active underwriting.

(C & E Notice 701/36/97, para 5.10).

Disbursements. Where an individual customer's or tenant's own risks are insured under the terms of the policy, and the premium to the insurer is recovered from the customer/tenant by the supplier/landlord, the insurance premium may be treated as a disbursement provided

- the customer/tenant has specifically requested the supplier/landlord to obtain the insurance cover on their behalf;

- the customer's/tenant's own risks are insured under the policy;

- the supplier/landlord recovers the exact premium from the customer/tenant;

- the amount paid by the customer/tenant is in respect of cover for him alone; and

- the exact amount of the insurance charge is separately itemised on the invoice.

Any commission which the supplier/landlord receives from the insurance company for arranging the supply is exempt under 37.9 above provided the normal conditions are met. (C & E Notice 701/36/97, para 5.11).

Groups of companies. Where a holding company arranges insurance cover for the group, any amount charged to each company for procuring insurance can be treated as exempt under *VATA 1994, 9 Sch Group 2, Item 4* (see 37.9 above) but only where each company's risks are insured under the policy and the conditions in 37.11 above are met. Where the exact insurance premium is charged to an associated or subsidiary company, this may be treated as a disbursement if the conditions under the heading *Disbursements* above are satisfied.

Where the subsidiary company and the company which arranges the insurance are part of the same VAT group (see 31 GROUPS OF COMPANIES) then any amounts charged for insurance are outside the scope of VAT.

(C & E Notice 701/36/97, para 5.12).

Guarantees and warranties for goods. There is no separate supply of insurance if

(*a*)   domestic electrical goods are sold with the benefit of a free 'warranty', or

(*b*)   any charge is made for an 'extended warranty' covering a longer period

where the warranty represents nothing more than the retailer's or manufacturer's obligation to put right certain defects or offer a replacement if the goods prove faulty. In the case of (*b*) above, the charge is standard-rated.

Where, however, an extended warranty is an insurance policy supplied by a permitted insurer, then charges made to the customer by the retailer or manufacturer must be dealt with, as the case may be, in accordance with 37.11 above for insurance supplied with goods and services or under the heading *Disbursements* above.

Certain businesses charge customers an amount described as a 'warranty' which is paid into a fund that is used to meet the cost of any repairs necessary under the terms of the warranty. The business independently takes out an insurance policy to protect itself against the risk of having to pay claims should there be a shortfall in the fund. As there is no contract between the insurer and the customer, the charge for the warranty is standard-rated.

(C & E Notice 701/36/97, para 5.13).

Add-ons. Add-ons are services provided as part of a package with the main supply of insurance and may be supplied in the following ways.

- To the policyholder and under the contract of insurance provided by the insurer underwriting the main supply of insurance. If the add-on itself constitutes insurance (e.g. a contract for legal expenses insurance is added to a contract for public liability cover) the entire supply to the policyholder is exempt.

- To the policyholder as an insurance provided by an insurer who has not underwritten the main supply of insurance. The entire supply is exempt. Each insurer is treated as making an exempt supply equivalent to the part of the premium they have underwritten.

- Under a contract of insurance or reinsurance provided by an insurer (the 'add-on' insurer) to another insurer (the 'direct' insurer) who has a contract with a non-insurer policyholder. The premium received by the add-on insurer from the direct insurer is exempt from VAT.

- Under a contract for non-insurance services provided by a person (including an insurer) to the insurer underwriting the contract of insurance, for integration into that supply. There may be a liability to VAT on this supply. The insurer making the supply of insurance to the policyholder may not dissect the premium charged to the policyholder and levy VAT on the element attributable to the cost of the services.

- Under a contract for non-insurance services provided by a person (including an insurer) to the policyholder. There may be a liability to VAT on the supply of the non-insurance services to the policyholder.

(C & E Notice 701/36/97, para 5.15).

37.15   ACCOUNTING FOR VAT

Tax points.

(*a*) *Insurers/reinsurers.* Although, as a general rule, supplies of insurance are exempt, the time of supply may be important for partial exemption purposes, e.g. to determine the recoverable proportion of non-attributable output tax where an outputs-based method is used.

The *basic* tax point occurs on completion of the cover, i.e. when the insurance contract is finalised and signed.

The *actual* tax point should occur when the underwriter accepts a proportion of the risk by signing the broker's slip (generally known as 'line slip' or 'risk slip'). However, as underwriters do not always know the value of the supply until notification is received from the broker in the form of a 'closing slip' listing the underwriter's share of the risk and the premium receivable, C & E have accepted that insurers may apply to use the date of the closing slip as an accommodation tax point.

(*b*) *Brokers and intermediaries.* The normal time of supply rules apply. See 64.49 SUPPLY. The actual tax point occurs when a debit note is issued to the insured to collect the premium or the date on which payment is received, whichever happens first.

(C & E Notice 701/36/97, para 6.1).

Recovery of input tax. See 37.3 above.

Reverse charge on certain imported services. If a person belonging in the UK *receives* supplies of certain services, including insurance services, for business purposes from outside the UK, he must account for VAT on them as if *he* had supplied them in the UK, provided the services would have been standard-rated if supplied to a UK customer. For full details of these provisions, see 39.4 INTERNATIONAL SERVICES. The reverse charge does not apply to services received from an overseas establishment within the same legal entity since this is not a supply for VAT purposes.

Businesses with more than one establishment. Where an insurance business has establishments, including branches or agencies, both inside and outside the UK, and services are received from outside the UK within these provisions, it is necessary to determine which establishment most directly uses or benefits from the services. If this is an overseas branch or agency, the supply is outside the scope of UK VAT but if a UK establishment, the reverse charge rules may apply. Which establishment actually pays for the services does not affect the VAT liability.

(C & E Notice 701/36/97, paras 6.3–6.6).

37.16 EXEMPT SUPPLIES OF INSURANCE BEFORE 19 MARCH 1997

The following supplies were exempt from VAT unless, as a result of the place of supply rules in 37.2 above, the supply was outside the scope of UK VAT.

(*a*) **The provision of insurance and reinsurance** by

- a person permitted to carry out insurance business under *Insurance Companies Act 1982, s 2* ;

- an insurer who belonged outside the UK against any risks or other things described in *Insurance Companies Act 1982, 1, 2 Sch* ; and

- the Export Credits Guarantee Department.

(*b*) **The making of arrangements for the provision of an insurance or reinsurance in (*a*) above.** This exempted the services of insurance broking and insurance agent's services, including the supply of services of renewing insurance. *Not included* were services which did not constitute the making of arrangements for insurance.

The consideration was the gross commission (i.e. before any commission allowable in turn to other intermediaries), flat-rate fee or recharge of costs incurred.

Tribunal cases. In *Barclays Bank plc, [1991] VATTR 466 (6469)* an insurance broker identified insurance products which it could recommend to customers of an associated company; negotiated the terms, conditions and premiums for these products; arranged for the associated company to mail shot its customers and provided a help-line for those who required further information or assistance. It was held that exemption extended to these services which, although not insurance broking transactions, were services of a kind normally performed by such persons and were related to, or carried out as part of, the insurance broking business.

In *Countrywide Insurance Marketing Ltd, [1993] VATTR 277 (11443)* a number of insurance brokers established a limited company which arranged for insurers to underwrite new insurance products. The company negotiated policy details, premium levels and rates of commission. The products were then sold via the brokers with the company receiving a share of the commission. The company also handled proposal forms and negotiated with insurers on behalf of brokers and clients in cases of difficulty. The tribunal held that the company's commission income was exempt as the legislation did not restrict exemption to cases where the taxpayer negotiated a specific insurance contract with the person insured.

In *Curtis Eddington & Say (11699)* the company developed an insurance policy for travellers, negotiated the scope of the cover offered and premium rates with an insurer and then allowed ferry operators to market the insurance to its customers. The tribunal held that the commission income received from insurers was exempt.

Initially, C & E lodged appeals against the above decisions but subsequently accepted, as an interim measure pending a review of the scope of exemption for certain insurance services, that such services were exempt. (C & E News Release 52/94, 15 December 1994).

'Insurance' supplied with goods or other services. Where goods or services were supplied and a charge was also made for 'insurance', such supplies were not exempt unless the insurance was provided by a person permitted to carry out insurance *and* it was the customer's own risk which was insured, i.e. the individual customer's risk was specifically referred to in the policy. Even if the amount was separately itemised on the invoice, there was no exempt supply where the supplier was simply passing on the cost of insuring his own liability, for example, in the event of loss, theft or

injury to third parties. A car hire company was held not to be entitled to treat any part of its receipts as consideration for the making of arrangements for the provision of insurance (*CJ Kiff Ltd, [1981] VATTR 88 (1084)*).

See also *Ford (t/a Donald Ford Financial Services, [1987] VATTR 130) (2432)*.

(c) **The handling of claims by insurance brokers and agents and authorised insurers as in (*a*) above**. Specifically excluded from exemption were

- supplies by loss adjusters, motor assessors, surveyors and other experts (but see below), and

- legal services

in connection with the assessment of any claim.

The term 'handling' included any service (e.g. claims checking) which was necessary to enable a final settlement of a claim to be made.

The excluded services were normally restricted to valuing insurance claims and advising the insurer of the amount that should be paid. C & E regarded supplies made by loss adjusters, motor assessors and similar experts as exempt from VAT where the service was provided under a written delegated authority from the insurer which bound the insurer to the settlement figure notified by the loss adjuster, etc. The authority had to be given before the loss adjuster, etc. commenced action in respect of any claim. If an insurer gave a written authority to another person (e.g. a broker) who in turn issued its own written authority to the loss adjuster, the loss adjuster's services were exempt provided the original authority given by the insurer made it clear that the recipient had power to delegate its own authority in this way. Any services which were merely advisory in nature, with no authority to settle, were liable to VAT at the standard rate. (C & E Business Brief 9/94, 30 March 1994).

For fuller details, see Tolley's Value Added Tax 1997/98 and earlier editions.

38   Interaction with Other Taxes

38.1   DIRECT TAXES

Direct taxes which are likely to interact with VAT are income tax, corporation tax and capital gains tax. In general such taxes are imposed on profits or gains or some other measure of monies receivable less monies payable. VAT as an indirect tax is charged on the *supply* of goods and services in the course or furtherance of a business [*VATA 1994, s 4*], so it is immaterial for the charging of VAT whether there is any money payment and whether any profit is made on the supply. For information regarding direct taxes see Tolley's Income Tax, Tolley's Corporation Tax and Tolley's Capital Gains Tax.

38.2   Business profits

Taxable persons making wholly taxable supplies. In general, a taxable person making wholly taxable supplies should treat the receipt for income tax or corporation tax purposes as being exclusive of any VAT charged. Similarly expenditure for income tax, etc. purposes (including capital items) should be treated as being exclusive of VAT if input VAT is able to be reclaimed on the related supply. If credit for input tax is specifically denied (e.g. most supplies of motor cars and business entertainment) the expenditure inclusive of VAT should be taken into account for income tax purposes. Any allowance made for bad debts for income tax purposes is inclusive of the VAT which has been accounted for on the related supply. (VAT on bad debts may be reclaimed from C & E in certain circumstances, see 7 BAD DEBT RELIEF. It follows that if VAT is recoverable from C & E it cannot be claimed for income tax purposes or alternatively a recovery of VAT should be treated as a taxable income receipt if a VAT-inclusive bad debt has previously been allowed.)

Taxable persons making both exempt and taxable supplies. A taxable person who makes both exempt and taxable supplies should treat income tax receipts as above. However, as under the partial exemption rules such a person will only be able to obtain credit for part of the input VAT applicable to expense etc. payments made, it is necessary to allocate the VAT ultimately suffered to the various expense payments made. Inspectors of taxes are prepared to consider any reasonable arrangements made to carry out this apportionment. Where credit for VAT input is specifically denied, the related expenditure is VAT-inclusive for income tax purposes as explained above.

Non-taxable persons. A person who is *not* a taxable person (e.g. making wholly exempt supplies or below the registration limit) should treat all expenses, etc. as being VAT-inclusive for income tax, etc. purposes (including capital allowances).

(Inland Revenue Statement of Practice SP B1 7 May 1973).

38.3   Stock

Individuals, partnerships and companies, who are taxable persons for VAT should treat the cost of purchases, and hence the value of stock, as being VAT-exclusive. A taxable person who makes both taxable and exempt supplies is unable to obtain credit for input tax attributable to exempt supplies and accordingly the cost of purchases and value of trading stock should be inclusive of the VAT unable to be credited. (Inland Revenue Statement of Practice SP B2 3 December 1974).

38.4   Schedule E income tax

Returns of expenses incurred by employees etc. and subsequently reimbursed by the employer (Forms P9D and P11D) should include any amounts of VAT suffered in connection with the expenses, whether or not the employer may subsequently obtain credit for the relevant input tax. Similar observations apply to returns of employee pecuniary liabilities met by the employer and to expenditure incurred by the employer in providing a benefit (including the use of an asset) for an employee. (Inland Revenue Statements of Practice SP A6 29 March 1973 and SP A7 17 July 1974).

Entertainers' expenses. Where agents' fees paid by actors, musicians, etc. are deductible for Schedule E purposes, any additional VAT payable is also deductible. [*ICTA 1988, s 201A; FA 1990, s 77*].

38.5   Subcontractors in the construction industry

A subcontractor who is a taxable person for VAT should account for VAT on the total consideration which he charges for his services. Where the appropriate valid tax exemption certificate is not held or not presented, the person paying the consideration is obliged to make a deduction at a specified rate from the part of the payment representing labour and profit on materials. VAT and cost of materials are excluded. [*ICTA 1988, s 559(4)*]. (Inland Revenue Pamphlet IR 14/15).

38.6   Capital gains tax

If VAT is payable in respect of the acquisition of an asset but is available for credit by a taxable person, then the cost of the asset for capital gains tax purposes is the cost exclusive of VAT. Where no VAT credit is available the cost is inclusive of VAT ultimately suffered.

Where an asset is disposed of, any VAT on the supply of the asset is disregarded in computing the disposal consideration for capital gains tax purposes. It appears that a taxable person making both taxable and exempt supplies should treat as part of the capital gains tax cost of an asset the input VAT that was not available for credit in respect of the acquisition (see under 38.2 above). (Inland Revenue Statement of Practice SP D7 7 June 1973).

38.7   Capital allowances

Where the CAPITAL GOODS SCHEME (10) applies adjustments to the original input tax reclaimed may be necessary for a period of up to 10 years. Any additional VAT liability under the scheme is to be treated as extra qualifying capital expenditure incurred at the time when the VAT is paid. Similarly, any additional VAT rebate is to be taken into account in the capital allowances computation for the period in which it is repaid by C & E. Earlier capital allowances computations are not disturbed. [*FA 1991, s 59, 14 Sch*].

38.8   VAT penalties, surcharge and interest

No deduction is allowed in computing any income, profit or loss for tax purposes in respect of

- default surcharge under *VATA 1994, s 59* (see 52.15 PENALTIES);

- a penalty under *VATA 1994, ss 60–70* (see 52.9–52.14, 52.17–52.19 PENALTIES); or

- interest under *VATA 1994, s 74* (see 51.5 PAYMENT OF VAT).

Repayment supplement for VAT under *VATA 1994, s 79* is disregarded for income tax and corporation tax purposes.

[*ICTA 1988, s 827; F(No 2)A 1992, 3 Sch 95*].

38.9   **INDIRECT TAXES**

In valuing imported goods for VAT purposes, indirect taxes (e.g. customs duty) levied (whether abroad or in the UK) are specifically taken into account if not already included in a price in money. See 69.7 VALUATION.

38.10   **Stamp duty**

(a)   **New non-domestic buildings.** The amount or value of the consideration for the sale is the gross amount inclusive of VAT. Stamp duty is therefore calculated on the VAT-inclusive price.

(b)   **Other transactions in non-domestic property** not falling within (a) above are exempt from VAT. The vendor or lessor may however elect to waive exemption. Where the election has already been exercised at the time of the transaction, stamp duty is chargeable on the purchase price, premium or rent including VAT. Where the election has not been exercised at that time, VAT should similarly be included in any payments to which an election *could* still apply (which will depend on the facts of each case).

Neither a formal notice of election made to C & E, nor any notification to the purchaser or lessee that such an election has been made, attracts stamp duty.

(c)   **Rent.** Where VAT is charged on the rent under a lease, and is itself treated as rent under the lease, stamp duty is charged on the VAT-inclusive figure. If the lease provides for payment of VAT on the rent otherwise than as rent, stamp duty is charged on the VAT element as consideration payable periodically under *Stamp Act 1891, s 56*. In either case the rate of VAT in force at the date of execution of the lease is to be used in the calculation.

In the case of a formal deed of variation or similar document varying the terms of the original lease so as to provide for payment of VAT by way of additional rent, further stamp duty may be payable under *Stamp Act 1891, s 77(5)*.

(d)   **Agreements for leases.** The provisions of (b) and (c) above also apply to such agreements if they are stamped. [*Stamp Act 1891, s 75*].

Stamp duty itself does not attract a charge to VAT.

(Inland Revenue Statement of Practice SP 11/91).

See also *Glenrothes Development Corp v IRC CS, [1993] STC 74* confirming that consideration for stamp duty purposes under the heading 'Conveyance or Transfer on Sale' in *Stamp Act 1891, 1 Sch* should include VAT where chargeable.

39 International Services

Cross-references. See 37.4, 37.12 and 37.13 INSURANCE for the supply of international insurance services; 41 ISLE OF MAN; 68 TRANSPORT AND FREIGHT for certain international movements of passengers and freight.

De Voil Indirect Tax Service. See V4.246.

39.1 **INTRODUCTION**

Certain services *received by* UK persons from outside the UK are deemed to be *supplied by* those persons who must account for VAT on them if required to be registered. See 39.4 below.

In addition, certain supplies of international services *made by* UK taxable persons are zero-rated or outside the scope of UK VAT. See 39.5 *et seq.* below.

39.2 **TERRITORIAL EXTENT**

The UK consists of Great Britain, Northern Ireland and the territorial sea of the UK (i.e. waters within 12 nautical miles of the coast line). [*VATA 1994, s 96(11)*].

For VAT purposes the Isle of Man is treated as part of the UK and VAT is chargeable there under Manx law which generally parallels UK legislation. See 41 ISLE OF MAN. *References in this chapter to the UK apply also to the Isle of Man unless otherwise indicated.*

39.3 **PLACE OF SUPPLY OF SERVICES**

See 64.18 *et seq.* SUPPLY for a detailed consideration of the place of supply of services.

39.4 **REVERSE CHARGE ON SERVICES RECEIVED FROM ABROAD**

Normally, the supplier of a service is the person who must account to the tax authorities for any VAT due on the supply. However, in certain situations, the position is reversed and it is the customer who must account for any VAT due. This is known as the '*reverse charge*' procedure.

Situations in which the reverse charge procedure applies in the UK. There are three different situations in which the procedures can apply.

(*a*) *Services within VATA 1994, 5 Sch 1–8.* The reverse charge procedure applies where a person who belongs outside the UK supplies '*relevant services*' (i.e. services within *VATA 1994, 5 Sch 1–8*, see 64.27 SUPPLY) to a *person* who belongs in the UK for the purposes of any business carried on by him and the place of supply of those services is in the UK. [*VATA 1994, s 8(1)*].

See 64.19 SUPPLY for the place of belonging.

The consequence of the provisions applying to a *person* rather than a *taxable person* is that anyone carrying on a business in the UK will become liable to be registered for VAT if the total value reverse charge services within these provisions and turnover from any taxable business supplies made in the UK exceed the registration limit. (C & E Notice 741, paras 14.13).

Where services within *VATA 1994, 5 Sch 1–8* (except exempt services) are purchased by an overseas member of a UK VAT group and provided to a UK member of that VAT group, its representative member is required to account for any UK VAT due under the intra-group reverse charge provisions. See 31.6 GROUPS OF COMPANIES.

(b) *Services with an EC simplification.* The place of supply of certain services made in the EC can be further adjusted if the customer gives a VAT registration number from a different EC country. As a result, the reverse charge provisions apply to the following services where a UK recipient receives a supply for business purposes from a supplier belonging outside the UK and gives the supplier his UK VAT registration number.

- Valuation of, or work carried out on, any goods. See 64.25 SUPPLY.

- Intra-EC freight transport services and related ancillary services. See 64.29 SUPPLY and 68.26 and 68.28 TRANSPORT AND FRIEGHT.

- Arranging intra-EC freight transport services and related ancillary services. See 64.29 SUPPLY and 68.30 TRANSPORT AND FREIGHT.

- Most intermediary services supplied in the EC. See 64.31 SUPPLY.

The reverse charge cannot apply to these services if the recipient is not already VAT-registered in the UK. Such supplies do not count as taxable supplies for the purposes of determining liability to registration.

Where the conditions are not met (e.g. because the supplies are used for non-business purposes or the UK recipient is not VAT-registered) the supplier must account for the VAT due in the appropriate EC country.

(C & E Notice 741, paras 14.16, 14.17, 14.22).

(c) *Extension to other services supplied within the UK.* The reverse charge procedure applies to all services not falling within (a) above where the place of supply is the UK, the supplier belongs outside the UK and the recipient is a UK VAT-registered person who uses the services for business purposes. [*VATA 1994, 5 Sch 9; SI 1997/1523, Reg 3*].

This covers the following services.

- Services relating to land. See 64.21 SUPPLY.

- Services supplied where physically carried out. See 64.22–64.25 SUPPLY.

- Passenger transport services. See 64.29 SUPPLY.

- Freight transport services not covered by (b) above. See 64.29 SUPPLY.

- Hire of means of transport. See 64.30 SUPPLY.

The reverse charge cannot apply to these services if the recipient is not already VAT-registered in the UK. Such supplies do not count as taxable supplies for the purposes of determining liability to registration.

Where the conditions are not met (e.g. because the supplies are used for non-business purposes or the UK recipient is not VAT-registered or does not provide a VAT registration number) the supplier must account for the VAT due. If not already registered in the UK, the supplier may be liable to register (subject to the registration limit).

The existence of the reverse charge procedure for these services does not prevent overseas suppliers from registering for VAT in the UK under the normal rules. If they do register, they must invoice UK VAT in the normal way and the recipient is not then required to account for VAT under the reverse charge procedure.

(C & E Notice 741, paras 14.23, 14.27–14.30).

The reverse charge procedure does not apply to

● services where the supplier belongs in the UK;

● services which, under the place of supply rules, are supplied in another country which, by definition, are outside the scope of UK VAT and are subject to VAT, if any, in that other country; or

● services provided by an overseas establishment within the same legal entity since this is not a supply for VAT purposes.

(C & E Notice 741, paras 14.8, 14.9).

Accounting for VAT and recovery of input tax. Where the reverse charge procedure applies, the recipient of the services must act as both the supplier and the recipient of the services. On the same VAT return, the recipient must

● account for output tax, calculated on the full value of the supply received, in Box 1;

● (subject to the normal rules) include the VAT as input tax in Box 4; and

● include the full value of the supply in both Boxes 6 and 7.

Exempt and zero-rated supplies. The reverse charge does not apply to exempt services. [*VATA 1994, s 8(2)*]. In the case of zero-rated services, although there is no output tax due and no input tax to recover, Boxes 6 and 7 of the VAT return should be completed.

Partial exemption rules. Supplies which are treated as made by the recipient under these rules are not to be taken into account as output for the purpose of calculating entitlement to input tax deduction under the PARTIAL EXEMPTION (49) rules. [*VATA 1994, s 8(3)*].

The effect of the provisions is that the reverse charge has no net cost to the recipient if he can attribute the input tax to taxable supplies and can therefore reclaim it in full. If he cannot, the effect is to put him in the same position as if had received the supply from a UK supplier rather than from one outside the UK.

UK VAT incurred by the overseas supplier. The overseas supplier whose customer accounts for VAT under the reverse charge procedure may be able to reclaim VAT incurred in the UK on supplies made to it through the mechanism of the *8th* or *13th Directive.* See 21.21 EUROPEAN COMMUNITY: GENERAL and 48.5 OVERSEAS TRADERS for applications to the UK for refunds of VAT by persons established in other EC countries and outside the EC respectively.

(C & E Notice 741, paras 14.4, 14.5, 14.10, 14.12, 14.18, 14.26).

Value of supply. The value of the deemed supply is to be taken to be the consideration in money for which the services were in fact supplied or, where the consideration did not consist or not wholly consist of money, such amount in money as is equivalent to that consideration. [*VATA 1994, 6 Sch 8*]. The consideration payable to the overseas supplier for the services excludes UK VAT but includes any taxes levied abroad. (C & E Notice 741, para 14.6).

Time of supply. The time of supply of such services is the date the supplies are paid for or, if the consideration is not in money, the last day of the prescribed accounting period in which the services are performed. [*VATA 1994, s 8(4); SI 1995/2518, Reg 82*].

De Voil Indirect Tax Service. See V3.231.

39.5   VAT LIABILITY OF INTERNATIONAL SERVICES

The liability of a supply of international services depends on the rules for the place of supply of services. These are considered in detail in 64.18 *et seq.* SUPPLY. Where the place of supply is deemed to be outside the UK, the services are outside the scope of UK VAT. Where the place of supply is deemed to be in the UK, the services are subject to the normal UK provisions. Apart from the specific categories of zero-rating for international services in 39.6–39.8 below, international services deemed to be supplied in the UK are therefore standard-rated unless they can be treated as ZERO-RATED SUPPLIES (72) or EXEMPT SUPPLIES (24) under the general rules.

See 35.3 INPUT TAX for the position regarding the right to deduct input tax in respect of most (but not all) international services deemed to be made outside the UK.

39.6   Training supplied to overseas Governments

By concession, zero-rating applies to training services (other than exempt training within 20.4 EDUCATION) supplied in the UK to overseas Governments for the purpose of their sovereign activities (and not their business activities). The supplier must retain a statement in writing from the Government concerned (or its accredited representative) certifying that the trainees are employed in the furtherance of its sovereign activities. *Included* is the training of Government officials, public servants and members of organisations such as the armed forces, police, emergency services and similar bodies answerable to the Government concerned. *Excluded* is training of personnel from Government-owned businesses or sponsored commercial organisations such as state airlines or nationalised industries. Relief does not extend to any associated services supplied *separately* (e.g. accommodation or transport). (C & E Notice 48, ESC 2.21; C & E Notice 744D, paras 4.1-4.4).

39.7   Work on goods obtained, acquired or temporarily imported for that purpose and subsequent export

EC legislation. See 22.21(*b*) EUROPEAN COMMUNITY LEGISLATION.

The supply of services of work carried out on goods which, for that purpose, have been obtained or acquired in, or imported into, any EC country is zero-rated provided the goods are intended to be (and are) subsequently exported to a place outside the EC. The goods must be exported by (or on behalf of) the supplier or, where the recipient of the services belongs outside the EC, by (or on behalf of) the recipient. *Excluded* are any services of a description falling within *VATA 1994, 9 Sch Group 2* (insurance) or *Group 5* (finance). [*VATA 1994, 8 Sch Group 7, Item 1*].

See 64.19 SUPPLY for the concept of belonging. The goods must be exported within a reasonable time after the work on them has been carried out. The goods must not be used in the UK between the time of leaving the supplier's premises and exportation. Normal rules apply for proof of export of the goods (see 25.24 EXPORTS). If, in anticipation of export, the supply is zero-rated but, in the event, the goods are either used before export or export does not take place, it will be necessary to reconsider both the place of supply of the services and, if it is in the UK, the appropriate VAT rate.

Any goods used in conjunction with the work performed (e.g. spare parts, paint, etc.) should be treated as part of the supply of services.

Included are

● alterations and repairs, calibrations, cleaning, insulating, lacquering, painting, polishing, resetting (jewellery), cutting (of precious stones), sharpening, varnishing and waterproofing;

● the repair of freight containers;

- services directly related to the 'covering' of a mare provided the mare is exported before the birth of the foal;

- the gelding and/or breaking in of a young horse (e.g. training yearling racehorses to the stage where they can be ridden safely in races) but note that actual racing is not accepted as training and if any horse is acquired or temporarily imported with the intention of racing it in the EC before re-export, zero-rating under this provision will not be allowed; and

- the restoration of classic cars.

Not included is

- work which is not physical work carried out on the goods themselves (e.g. mere inspection or testing and analysis);

- repair or other work which becomes necessary after acquisition or importation of goods (e.g. incidental running repairs while the goods are being used); and

- valuation services.

(C & E Notice 744D, paras 2.1–2.4).

De Voil Indirect Tax Service. See V4.246.

39.8 **Services of intermediaries**

There are special place of supply rules for services of intermediaries, the place of supply depending upon both the nature of the main goods or services whose supply is being arranged and the location of the customer. See 64.31 SUPPLY. Where the supply of an intermediary's services is within the scope of UK VAT, it is zero-rated if consisting of the making of arrangements for

- the export of any goods to a place outside the EC;

- a supply of services of the description specified in *VATA 1994, 8 Sch Group 7, Item 1* (see 39.7 above); or

- any supply of services which is made outside the EC.

Excluded are any services of a description falling within *VATA 1994, 9 Sch Group 2* (insurance) or *Group 5* (finance).

[*VATA 1994, 8 Sch Group 7, Item 2*].

The intermediary's services can be supplied to the supplier (in finding a customer) or the customer (in finding a supplier) or even to both.

(C & E Notice 744D, paras 3.1–3.3).

39.9 **TELECOMMUNICATION SERVICES**

Before 1 July 1997, telecommunication services were supplied where the provider belonged and thus UK providers had to account for UK VAT on services supplied to all their customers. Similarly, providers in other EC countries had to account for VAT locally. However, non-EC providers were not required to account for EC VAT on supplies to EC customers and this created distortion of competition between EC and non-EC providers.

As a result, with effect from 1 July 1997, there are special rules for relevant telecommunications services. See 64.27(*h*) SUPPLY for the definition of telecommunication services.

Place of supply rules and summary of UK VAT position. See 64.26–64.28 SUPPLY.

Reverse charge on services received from abroad. Where the reverse charge procedure on services received from abroad applies to relevant telecommunication services, the normal value and time of supply rules are applied (see 39.4 above) but only to the extent that the services are

- performed on or after 1 July 1997; and

- not chargeable to VAT in another EC country.

There are special transitional provisions where services are performed on or after 1 July 1997 but the period over which they were performed commenced before that date.

[*SI 1997/1523, Regs 4, 7, 10*].

Continuous supplies of telecommunications services. Special time of supply rules apply to continuous supplies of any services. See 64.50 SUPPLY. Special transitional provisions modify the rules as follows for telecommunications services.

- The continuous supply rules do not treat relevant telecommunications services as supplied after 30 June 1997 where the period to which the payment for those services relates ended before 1 July 1997.

- Relevant telecommunications services are treated as supplied on 1 July 1997 where payment was made before that date in respect of a period which ends after 30 June 1997.

- Where relevant telecommunications services are treated as supplied after 30 June, the supply is treated as taking place only to the extent covered by the payment or, if lower, such part of the payment as is properly attributable to such part of the period covered by the payment as falls after 30 June 1997.

[*SI 1995/2518, Regs 90(4)(5), 90A, 90B; SI 1997/1525; SI 1998/765*].

Rights to relevant telecommunications services. A 'right' to relevant telecommunications services is treated as supplied in the same place as the supply of the services to which the right relates (whether or not the right is exercised).

A 'right' includes any right, option or priority with respect to the supply of services and the supply of an interest deriving from any right or services.

[*SI 1992/3121, Art 21; SI 1997/1524, Art 5*].

There are complex transitional provisions where a supply of relevant telecommunications services takes place on or after 1 July 1997, but by virtue of the exercise of a right granted before that date, and the consideration for those services is less than the open market value on the basis that they had not been supplied by virtue of the right. [*SI 1997/1523, Arts 5, 6, 8*].

40 Invoices

Cross-references. See 52.12 PENALTIES for improper use of invoices; 57.3 and 57.10 RECORDS for obligations to retain invoices and adjustments of errors in invoices; 63.20 SPECIAL SCHEMES for invoices raised by flat-rate farmers; 69.5 VALUATION for discounts on invoices.

De Voil Indirect Tax Service. See V3.511–529.

The contents of this chapter are as follows.

40.1 OBLIGATION TO PROVIDE A VAT INVOICE

With certain exceptions or unless C & E allow otherwise, a registered person *must* provide the customer with an invoice showing specified particulars including VAT (a '*VAT invoice*') in the following circumstances.

(*a*) He makes a supply of goods or services in the UK (other than an exempt supply) to a taxable person.

(*b*) He makes a supply of goods or services (other than an exempt supply) to a person in another EC country. This covers

(i) standard-rated supplies to a person registered in another EC country;

(ii) zero-rated supplies for acquisition by a person registered in another EC country; and

(iii) standard-rated supplies to a non-taxable person (e.g. a public body, charity or an unregistered business) in another EC country;

(iv) distance sales of goods (e.g. by mail order) to unregistered persons in other EC countries; and

(v) the supply of a new means of transport (see 23.31 EUROPEAN COMMUNITY: SINGLE MARKET) to a person in another EC country.

(*c*) He receives a payment on account from a person in another EC country in respect of a supply he has made or intends to make.

A VAT invoice is important as it is normally essential evidence to support a customer's claim for deduction of input tax. The supplier must keep the copy and the original should be retained by the recipient.

[*VATA 1994, 11 Sch 2(1); SI 1995/2518, Reg 13(1)*].

Exceptions. The above provisions do not apply to the following supplies.

● Exempt supplies.

● Zero-rated supplies (other than supplies for acquisition by a person registered in another EC country, see (*b*)(ii) above). [*SI 1995/2518, Reg 20(a)*].

- Supplies where the VAT charged is excluded from credit under *VATA 1994, s 25(7)* (e.g. business entertaining and certain motor cars) [*SI 1995/2518, Reg 20(b)*] although a VAT invoice may be issued in such cases.

- Supplies on which VAT is charged but which are not made for a consideration. [*SI 1995/2518, Reg 20(c)*]. This includes gifts and private use of goods. See, however, 40.2 below under the heading *Business gifts* for 'tax certificates' issued in connection with business gifts to support a deduction of input tax.

- Sales of second-hand goods under one of the special schemes. [*SI 1995/2518, Reg 20(d)*]. Invoices for such sales must not show any VAT. See 61.11 and 61.45 SECOND-HAND GOODS for the special invoices required.

- Supplies that fall within the TOUR OPERATORS' MARGIN SCHEME (66). VAT invoices must not be issued for such supplies.

- Supplies where the customer operates an approved self-billing arrangement. See 40.2 below.

- Supplies by retailers unless the customer requests a VAT invoice.

- Supplies by one member to another in the same VAT group.

- Transactions between one division and another of a company registered in the names of its divisions. See 59.30 REGISTRATION.

- Supplies where the taxable person is entitled to issue, and does issue, invoices relating to services performed in fiscal and other warehousing regimes. [*SI 1995/2518, Reg 13(1); SI 1996/1250, Reg 6*]. See 70.19 WAREHOUSED GOODS AND FREE ZONES.

De Voil Indirect Tax Service. See V3.513.

40.2   **DOCUMENTS TREATED AS VAT INVOICES**

Self-billing. Where a registered taxable person (the 'customer') provides a document to himself in respect of a supply of goods or services to him by another taxable person registered in the UK (the 'supplier'), that document may be treated as a VAT invoice with the approval of C & E. [*SI 1995/2518, Reg 13(3)*]. Registered persons wishing to use such a system should write to their VAT office explaining the need for such a system. To be approved, it must be shown that the supplier agrees to self-billing and will not issue VAT invoices for the relevant transactions. (C & E Notice 700, para 6.9).

Customers using self-billing arrangements must

- not issue self-billing documents which claim to be VAT invoices on behalf of unregistered suppliers (if such documents are issued, any amount claimed as input tax will be disallowed, see *MJ Gleeson Group plc (13332)*);

- keep an up-to-date list showing names, addresses and VAT registration numbers of all suppliers;

- send a copy of that list to the VAT office when acknowledging acceptance of the conditions (and thereafter on request);

- complete the self-billing documents showing the supplier's name, address and VAT registration number, together with all other details required for a full VAT invoice (see 40.4 below);

- clearly mark each self-billing document with the statement

  'The VAT shown is your output tax due to Customs and Excise'; and

- advise all suppliers concerned under the arrangements of C & E's approval and conditions and require immediate notification of any changes in the VAT registration position.

Tax points. See 64.35 SUPPLY.

(C & E Manual V1-24, section 4.31).

If the document prepared by the recipient understates the VAT chargeable on the supply, C & E may, by notice served on the recipient and the supplier, elect that the amount of VAT understated by the document is VAT due from the recipient and not the supplier. [*VATA 1994, s 29*].

Copy purchase invoices used as sales invoices. A business may use photocopies of purchase invoices to serve as sales invoices (e.g. for onward supplies to associated companies at cost) provided the photocopy is adapted to meet the full requirements of a VAT invoice (see 40.4 below). In particular the adapted invoice must show

- the new supplier's name and address;
- the new customer's name and address;
- the new date of supply (if applicable); and
- a unique reference number.

(C & E Manual V1-24, section 2.27).

Sales by auctioneer, bailiff etc. Where goods (including land) forming part of the assets of a business carried on by a taxable person are, under any power exercisable by another person, sold by that person in or towards satisfaction of a debt owed by the taxable person, the goods are deemed to be supplied by the taxable person in the course or furtherance of his business.

The particulars of the VAT chargeable on the supply must be provided on a sale by auction by the auctioneer and where the sale is otherwise than by auction by the person selling the goods. The document issued to the buyer is treated as a VAT invoice. [*VATA 1994, 4 Sch 7, 9; SI 1995/2518, Reg 13(2)*]. See 2.18 ACCOUNTING PERIODS AND RETURNS.

Authenticated receipts in the construction industry. See 42.45 LAND AND BUILDINGS.

Business gifts. Where a business makes a gift of goods on which VAT is due (see 47.4 OUTPUT TAX), and the recipient uses the goods for business purposes, that person can recover the VAT as input tax (subject to the normal rules). The donor cannot issue a VAT invoice (because there is no consideration) but instead may provide the recipient with a 'tax certificate' which can be used as evidence to support a deduction of input tax. The tax certificate may be on normal invoicing documentation overwritten with the statement

'*Tax certificate*

No payment is necessary for these goods. Output tax has been accounted for on the supply.'

Full details of the goods must be shown on the documentation and the amount of VAT shown must be the amount of output tax accounted for to C & E.

(C & E Notice 700/35/97, para 1.4).

The following are not to be regarded as VAT invoices.

- Any **consignment or delivery note** or similar document or any copy thereof issued by the supplier where goods are removed before it is known whether a supply will take place (e.g. goods on approval or sale or return) or where the tax point is treated as taking place at the time an invoice is issued under the 14 day rule (see 64.39 SUPPLY). [*SI 1995/2518, Reg 14(3)*].

- **Pro forma invoices** used to offer goods or services to potential customers even if showing all the details required for a tax invoice. Such an invoice must be clearly marked 'This is not a VAT invoice'. (C & E Notice 700, para 6.8).

De Voil Indirect Tax Service. See V3.522–524; V3.528; V3.529.

40.3   **PARTICULARS REQUIRED ON VAT INVOICES**

A VAT invoice must contain certain basic information. See 40.4 below. Special rules apply to

- VAT invoices issued to person in other EC countries (see 40.5 below);
- invoices where the person supplied accounts for the VAT (see 40.6 below);
- retailers' invoices (see 40.7 below);
- invoices issued by cash and carry wholesaler (see 40.8 below);
- arrangements for particular businesses (see 40.9 below); and
- invoices using corporate purchasing cards (see 40.10 below).

40.4   **VAT invoices generally**

Unless C & E allow otherwise, VAT invoices must show the following.

(*a*)   Identifying number.

(*b*)   Time of the supply, i.e. tax point.

Where it is a trader's practice to show only the tax point date on a VAT invoice and no other date appears, this date need not be identified as the tax point. Where more than one date appears, the tax point must be separately identified. (C & E Manual V1-24, section 2.7).

(*c*)   Date of issue of the document.

(*d*)   Name, address and registration number of the supplier.

(*e*)   Name and address of the person to whom the goods or services are supplied.

(*f*)   Type of supply by reference to the following categories:

- by sale,
- on hire purchase or any similar transaction,
- by loan,
- by way of exchange,
- on hire, lease or rental,
- of goods made from customer's materials,
- by sale on commission,

- on sale or return or similar terms, or

- any other type of supply which C & E may at any time by notice specify;

(*g*) A description sufficient to identify the goods or services supplied.

Where services are supplied, a description of the services may be taken as sufficient to describe also the type of supply under (*f*) above and their extent under (*h*) below. For professional services, a description such as 'professional services rendered' is acceptable.

See 40.8 below for use of coded descriptions by cash and carry wholesalers. Coded descriptions may also be accepted in other circumstances (e.g. builders' merchants) where businesses whose trade is restricted to a large number of specialised parts or fittings issue illustrated catalogues to customers.

(C & E Manual V1-24, sections 2.7, 2.8).

(*h*) For each description, the quantity of the goods or extent of the services, the rate of VAT and amount payable, excluding VAT, expressed in sterling.

(*i*) Gross amount payable, excluding VAT, expressed in sterling.

(*j*) Rate of any cash discount offered.

(*k*) Each rate of VAT chargeable and the amount of VAT chargeable, expressed in sterling, at each rate.

(*l*) Total amount of VAT chargeable.

Exempt or zero-rated supplies. Where an invoice contains particulars of goods or services which are exempt or zero-rated in addition to taxable supplies, those goods or services must be distinguished on the invoice and must be totalled separately.

Leasing of motor cars. Where an invoice relates wholly or partly to the letting on hire of a motor car other than for self-drive, the invoice must state whether the car is a qualifying vehicle (see 45.11 MOTOR CARS).

[*VATA 1994, 11 Sch 2(2A); FA 1996, s 38; SI 1995/2518, Reg 14(1)(4)(5); SI 1995/3147; SI 1996/1250, Reg 7*].

Foreign currency invoices. If a VAT invoice is issued in a foreign currency, all values required to be entered for VAT purposes under (*h*)-(*l*) above must be converted into sterling. See 69.6 VALUATION. (C & E Notice 700, para 6.3). Where, however, the invoice is in euros, it is not necessary to make line by line conversions as under (*h*) above. (C & E News Release 23 December 1998).

De Voil Indirect Tax Service. See V3.514.

40.5   **VAT invoices to persons in other EC countries**

Unless C & E allow otherwise, where a registered person provides a VAT invoice to a person in another EC country, it must show

- the information specified in 40.4(*a*)–(*g*) and (*j*) above;

- the letters 'GB' as a prefix to his registration number;

- the registration number, if any, of the recipient if the supply of goods or services containing the alphabetical code of the EC country in which the recipient is registered, namely

Austria — AT
Belgium — BE
Denmark — DK
Finland — FI
France — FR
Germany — DE
Greece — EL
Ireland — IE
Italy — IT
Luxembourg — LU
Netherlands — NL
Portugal — PT
Spain — ES
Sweden — SE

- the gross amount payable, excluding VAT;

- where the supply is of a new means of transport (see 23.31 EUROPEAN COMMUNITY: SINGLE MARKET) a description sufficient to identify it as such;

- for each description, the quantity of the goods or the extent of the services, and where a positive rate of VAT is chargeable, the rate of VAT and the amount payable, excluding VAT, expressed in sterling; and

- where the supply of goods is a taxable supply, the information specified in 40.4(*k*) and (*l*) above.

[*VATA 1994, 11 Sch 2(2A); FA 1996, s 38; SI 1995/2518, Regs 2, 14(2); SI 1996/1250, Reg 7*].

Note that there is no requirement for the gross amount payable (excluding VAT) to be in sterling. Where, therefore, a VAT invoice is issued in respect of a zero-rated supply for acquisition by a customer registered in another EC country and their registration number is quoted on the invoice, the invoice may be in any currency. Where UK VAT is chargeable (e.g. on distance sales) this must always be expressed in sterling.

De Voil Indirect Tax Service. See V3.515.

40.6   **VAT invoices where person supplied accounts for the VAT**

Any supply in respect of which the person supplied must account for and pay the output tax on behalf of the supplier, that fact, and the amount of VAT to be accounted for and paid, must be shown on the VAT invoice. [*SI 1995/2518, Reg 14(5)*].

40.7   **Retailers' invoices**

Where the registered taxable person is a retailer, he is not required to provide a VAT invoice unless a customer requests it. Where an invoice is requested, one of the following options may be available.

(*a*)   **Less detailed VAT invoices.** Provided the consideration does not exceed £100 and provided the supply is not to a person in another EC country, the VAT invoice need only contain particulars of

- the name, address and registration number of the retailer;

- the time of supply;

- a description sufficient to identify the goods or services supplied;

- the total amount payable including VAT; and
- for each rate of VAT chargeable, the gross amount payable including VAT, and the VAT rate applicable.

The effect of the above is that where an EC customer requests an invoice a full VAT invoice must be issued.

The invoice must not contain any reference to any exempt supply.

[*SI 1995/2518, Reg 16*].

See 40.9 below for VAT invoices for petrol and derv.

Where *credit cards* are accepted, the sales voucher given to the cardholder at the time of sale may be adapted to serve as a less detailed VAT invoice by including all the above information. Where an invoice is issued as well as the credit card voucher, only one of the documents must be in the form of a VAT invoice.

To calculate the amount of VAT in a VAT-inclusive price, the VAT fraction (currently 7/47) must be applied to the total invoice amount.

(*b*)   **Modified VAT invoices.** Provided the customer agrees an invoice can be issued showing the *VAT-inclusive* value of each standard-rated supply (instead of the VAT-exclusive value — see 40.4(*h*) above). At the foot of the invoice, there must be shown separately

- the total VAT-inclusive value of standard-rated supplies;
- the total VAT payable on those supplies;
- the total value, excluding VAT, of those supplies;
- the total value of any zero-rated supplies included on the invoice; and
- the total value of any exempt supplies included on the invoice.

In all other respects the invoice should show the details required for a full VAT invoice (see 40.4 above).

Where options (*a*) or (*b*) are not available, a full VAT invoice under 40.4 above must be supplied. (C & E Notice 700, para 6.5).

Petrol and diesel oil (derv). Where the VAT-inclusive amount is £100 or less, a less detailed VAT invoice may be issued (see (*a*) above). Where the VAT-inclusive amount is more than £100, the particulars required on a full VAT invoice are modified so that the vehicle registration number and not the customer's name and address is shown on the VAT invoice. The type of supply and the number of gallons/litres need not be shown. (C & E Notice 700, para 6.6).

Foreign currency invoices. If a VAT invoice is issued in a foreign currency, all values required to be entered for VAT purposes under (*a*) and (*b*) above must be converted into sterling. See 69.6 VALUATION.

De Voil Indirect Tax Service. See V3.555.

40.8   **Cash and carry wholesalers**

Cash and carry wholesalers pose special problems because, although in many respects they resemble normal retailers, they sell mainly to registered customers and have to provide VAT invoices. Under the special arrangements detailed below, they may adapt their till rolls to meet the VAT invoice requirements. Official approval is not required to operate the arrangements but all the conditions must be fully complied with. If not, C & E may require normal VAT invoices to be issued.

The essential features of the arrangements are as follows.

(a) The arrangements can only be used for sales of goods and not for services.

(b) A product code is used which identifies the different classes of goods sold. The coding system should be devised by the wholesaler using a number of at least two digits and probably three or more digits where the range of products sold is wide. As far as possible, codes should identify classes of goods to limit the use for re-coding in the event of a change of rate affecting part of a group. Groups of products under the same code number should be of a similar type, but goods subject to different rates of VAT must not be described under the same code number. Codes should not normally be allocated to groups which cover individual products that have widely differing mark-ups (e.g. a single code should not be allocated to beers, wine and spirits).

(c) Product code lists are prepared and provided to all VAT-registered customers who must retain them for VAT inspection. Suppliers must issue new code lists, showing the operative date, whenever the coding is changed. These should preferably be sent to all VAT-registered customers but it is essential that all VAT-registered customers have up-to-date code lists.

(d) The till roll must provide all the following details to satisfy VAT invoice requirements.

- *Identifying number and date.*

- *Time of supply* (if earlier than invoice date).

- *Supplier's name, address and registration number.*

- *Customer's name (or trading name) and address.* This may be indicated by a reference number allocated by the wholesaler provided the wholesaler keeps a record of numbers allocated and advises customers of their number in writing. If the wholesaler issues 'buying cards' to customers, the card number may be used but C & E prefer the number to be the customer's VAT registration number where possible.

- *Type of supply.* As the majority of supplies are by 'sale' it is not necessary for the description 'sale' or 'cash sale' to appear on the till roll.

- *Description sufficient to identify the goods.* See (b) and (c) above for use of product codes and product code lists.

- *Quantity and price for each line.* Each entry must represent a single item or single unit pack unless there is a specific indication to the contrary.

- *Rates and amount of VAT charged.* Where, for technical reasons, the rate cannot be shown as a percentage, a code may be used but if so it must be explained in the product code list (see (c) above). If invoices contain a mixture of positive-rated and zero-rated goods, each line must be marked with the appropriate rate indicator.

- *Total of VAT and goods at each positive rate of VAT.*

- *Total amount of VAT charged.*

(e) Copy till rolls and product code lists must be kept for six years or such shorter period as C & E may allow.

Credits to customer. Where credits are returned to customers through the cash register, the item must be marked as a credit. If there are sales items as well as credits on the same invoice, the total of goods and VAT may be shown net of credits. The wholesaler must ensure that the deduction is made within the correct VAT category.

(C & E Notice 700, para 6.7; C & E Manual V1-24, sections 4.8-4.15).

40.9   Arrangements for particular businesses

(*a*) **Authenticated receipts in the construction industry**. See 42.45 LAND AND BUILDINGS.

(*b*) **Banks**. It has been agreed with the British Bankers' Association that a bank may modify the details required on a full VAT invoice in the following ways.

- The customer's account number may be used instead of the address on VAT invoices for services provided by the bank.

- Identifying numbers may be omitted from such invoices.

- The bank branch or department issuing invoices may use their sorting code number in place of the bank address.

(C & E Manual V1-24, section 4.7).

(*c*) **Cash and carry wholesalers**. See 40.8 above.

(*d*) **Retailers**. See 40.7 above.

(*e*) **Solicitors**. For reasons of confidentiality, many solicitors invoice clients with a two-part document, usually consisting of

- a bill section in the upper part showing separate charges for professional services and expenses; and

- a tear-off VAT invoice in the lower part for production to C & E.

The bill section must not be capable of being mistaken for a VAT invoice. In particular it should not show the supplier's VAT registration number and should preferably contain a statement such as 'This is not a VAT invoice'. If VAT is shown as a separate amount, the rate should not be specified and a clear reference to the accompanying VAT invoice should be made.

The VAT invoice section should contain a description of the supply sufficient to identify it as solicitor's professional services.

(C & E Manual V1-24, section 4.41).

(*f*) **Stockbrokers**. Contract notes are frequently the only transaction records issued by stockbrokers who adapt them for use as VAT invoices. As contract notes often show only an abbreviated address for the client (or show no address at all), C & E have agreed with the Stock Exchange Council that computerised unique code reference numbers will be accepted in lieu of addresses on contract notes used as VAT invoices provided

- clients are formally advised of their code reference numbers and asked to retain the advice for production to C & E when required; and

- the record of code reference numbers is available for similar inspection at the offices of the stockbroker.

C & E reserve the right to insist on full addresses being shown if considered necessary in any particular case.

(C & E Manual V1-24, section 4.42).

40.10   **Corporate purchasing (procurement) cards**

Such cards are designed to eliminate much of the paperwork in the purchasing process. Where a purchase is made, the supplier normally transmits the invoice information to the appropriate card company or bank (the 'transmission date'). At agreed intervals, the purchaser receives a VAT invoice report from the card company or bank. Some purchasing cards offer two levels of invoice detail, the level of detail received by the cardholder being dependent upon the capability of the supplier's accounting system. The provisions in both (*a*) and (*b*) below have the force of law under *VATA 1994, 11 Sch 2; SI 1995/2518, Regs 13, 14*.

(*a*)   *Line Item Detail (LID) invoices*. These provide detailed, itemised information on a line-by-line basis. C & E have agreed to waive the requirement to show the date of issue of the document under 40.4(*c*) above. The invoice report issued to the purchaser will show the transmission date for each transaction and is acceptable as evidence for input tax recovery (subject to the normal rules) from that date.

(*b*)   *Summary VAT invoices*. Where a supplier's system cannot transmit LID invoices, C & E generally do not require a supplier to issue an invoice to the customer. Instead they accept a Summary VAT invoice report issued by the card company or bank in support of an input tax claim provided no single transaction has a value of more than £5,000 and the report contains the following information.

• Value of the supply.

• VAT amount charged.

• VAT rate.

• Time of supply.

• Description of the goods.

• Supplier's name, address and VAT registration number.

• Customer's name and address.

A supplier must issue a VAT invoice if the value of a 'single transaction' exceeds £5,000 or if specifically requested by the customer. In the latter case, the invoice must be clearly endorsed 'Paid by Purchasing Card – Supplementary VAT invoice'. A '*single transaction*' is the total value of purchases made using a card at any one time, e.g. one 'swipe' of the card.

In all cases, the supplier must continue to generate contemporaneous VAT invoices for output tax accounting purposes for all purchasing card transactions.

(C & E Notice 701/48/97, paras 3-6).

40.11   **CALCULATION OF VAT ON INVOICES**

The total VAT payable on all goods and services on an invoice may be rounded down to the nearest penny.

Calculations of VAT based on lines of goods or services included with other goods or services in the same invoice must either be made by (i) rounding down to the nearest 0.1p *or* (ii) rounding to the nearest 1p or 0.5p.

For example, 86.76p and 86.74p would both be rounded down to 86.7p under (i) but rounded up to 87p and down to 86.50p respectively under method (ii). Whichever method is used must be adopted consistently.

Calculations of VAT based on VAT per unit or per article, e.g. for price lists or machine accounting, calculations must be either (i) to four decimal places and then rounded down to three places (e.g. £0.0024 rounded down to £0.002 (0.2p)); *or* (ii) to the nearest 1p or 0.5p (but not to 'nil' i.e. a minimum of 0.5p per article or unit).

(C & E Notice 700, para 6.10).

A taxpayer is not entitled to 'round-up' or 'round-down' fractions of a penny in respect of the VAT chargeable on individual items included in an invoice, but only on the total amount of VAT included in the invoice (*Catchlord, [1985] VATTR 238 (1966)*).

40.12   TIME LIMITS

A VAT invoice or a document treated as VAT invoice under 40.2 above must be provided within 30 days after the time when the supply is treated as taking place (see 64.32 *et seq.* SUPPLY) or within such longer period after that time as C & E allow in general or special directions. [*VATA 1994, 11 Sch 2(2); SI 1995/2518, Reg 13(5)*]. Extension of this time limit is permitted *without application* where

- an extension has been allowed for tax point purposes under the 14 day rule (see 64.39 and 64.49 SUPPLY);

- special accounting arrangements have been approved; or

- where a newly registered business has not been notified of its VAT registration number (in which case the VAT invoice must be issued within 30 days from the date of advice of that number).

In all other cases, application must be made, in writing, to the VAT office for an extension of the time limit.

(C & E Notice 700, para 6.1(c)).

De Voil Indirect Tax Service. See V3.517.

40.13   COMPUTER INVOICING

Computers may be used to

- provide customers with VAT invoices on magnetic tape or disc, etc.;

- transmit VAT invoice details by electronic means direct to customers' computers;

- receive VAT invoices on magnetic tape or disc, etc. from suppliers; and

- receive VAT invoice details by electronic means for suppliers direct on to a computer.

In such circumstances, the provisions relating to VAT invoices are only treated as complied with if the person producing or transmitting the information and the person receiving it have given C & E at least one month's notice in writing of their intention to do so, and comply with any requirements C & E may impose. [*VATA 1994, 11 Sch 3*].

An invoice produced by a computer, either on paper, magnetic media or for direct transmission, must include all the information required for a normal VAT invoice (see 40.3 *et seq.* above).

(C & E Notice 700, para 6.11).

For powers of C & E to inspect the computer and associated apparatus see 17.10 CUSTOMS AND EXCISE: POWERS.

De Voil Indirect Tax Service. See V3.516.

40.14   **TRANSMISSION OF INVOICES**

As an alternative to sending VAT invoices by post, they may be sent to customers by fax or e-mail. The normal rules regarding VAT invoices apply. Invoices received in either of these ways are acceptable as evidence for input tax deduction (subject to the normal rules). However, the following should be borne in mind.

- *Transmission by fax.* If the customer has a thermal-paper fax machine, the invoice may not be permanent and the customer may not be able to fulfil the obligation to preserve the invoice for six years. It is suggested that the supplier warns the customer of this possibility, preferably on the VAT invoice itself.

- *Transmission by e-mail.* C & E must be notified if this method is to be used to send invoices under the self-billing scheme (see 40.2 above) as there is a danger that the e-mail message can be corrupted during transmission. Suppliers using this method of transmission should advise clients, preferably on the VAT invoice, to contact them if any invoice received is not satisfactory.

(C & E Notice 700, para 6.12).

40.15   **CREDIT NOTES**

Where credit or contingent discount (e.g. discount on condition that the customer buys more goods at a later date) is allowed to a customer who can reclaim all the VAT on the supply as input tax, there is no obligation to adjust the original VAT charge provided both parties agree not to do so although records of outputs and inputs will still need to be adjusted. Otherwise an adjustment should be made to the original VAT charge in the appropriate period. See 57.6 RECORDS. A credit note should be issued to the customer and a copy retained. Alternatively, if both parties agree, the customer can issue a VAT debit note. A valid debit note places the same legal obligations on both parties as a valid credit note and must fulfil the same conditions.

To be valid for VAT purposes, a credit or debit note must reflect a genuine mistake or overcharge or an agreed reduction in the value of the supply and be issued within one month of this being discovered or agreed. It must give value to the customer, i.e. represent a genuine entitlement or claim on the part of the customer for the amount overcharged to be either refunded or offset against the value of future supplies. It should be headed 'credit note' or 'debit note' as appropriate and show

(*a*)   identifying number and date of issue;

(*b*)   supplier's and customer's name and address;

(*c*)   supplier's registration number;

(*d*)   description identifying goods or services for which credit is given;

(*e*)   quantity and amount credited for each description and reason for credit, e.g. 'returned goods';

(*f*)   total amount credited excluding VAT;

(*g*)   rate and amount of VAT credited;

(*h*)   number and date of the original VAT invoice. If not possible, C & E will need to be satisfied that VAT has been accounted for on the original supply.

Where a credit note includes credits for zero-rated or exempt supplies, each must be totalled separately and the credit note must show clearly that no credit for VAT has been given for them.

Credit notes issued without VAT adjustment should state 'This is not a credit note for VAT'. It will still be necessary to adjust records of outputs and inputs in order to complete the VAT returns.

Accounting for credit or debit notes. If an adjustment has to be made, the records of taxable supplies and output tax must be adjusted for credits allowed. Any VAT adjustment arising from the issue or receipt of a credit or debit note must be made in the VAT account for the period in which the adjustment is made in the business accounts. With effect from 1 May 1997, no VAT adjustment must be made more than three years after the end of the prescribed accounting period in which the original supply took place (unless the adjustment occurred in a prescribed accounting period beginning before 1 May 1997 and the return for the period in which effect was given to it in the business records had not been made, and was not required to have been made, before that date). [*SI 1995/2518, Reg 38, SI 1997/1086, Reg 6*].

If the VAT credits allowed to customers exceed the VAT charged on sales in any prescribed accounting period, a minus figure must be entered in Box 1 of the VAT return.

Bankruptcy, insolvent liquidation and administrative receivership. The tax point for credit or debit notes issued by or on behalf of insolvent traders is the date on which the supply was originally made or received.

Cancelled registrations. The tax point for any credit or debit note issued or received after the date of cancellation of registration is the date of the original supply. If this happens after the final VAT return has been submitted, the VAT office should be contacted.

VAT rate. The rate of VAT to be used for a credit or debit note is the one in force at the tax point of the original supply.

Returned or replaced goods. Where such goods are replaced with similar goods, the original VAT charge may stand or be cancelled (by issuing a credit note if a VAT invoice has previously been issued) and VAT charged on the replacement. If the original VAT charge is allowed to stand, VAT need not be accounted for on the replacement goods provided they are supplied free of charge. If supplied at a *lower* price, the VAT charged may be reduced by a credit note. If supplied at a *higher* price, additional VAT must be accounted for.

(C & E Notice 700, paras 7.1, 7.2).

Bad debt relief. Output tax paid on an invoice which proves to be a bad debt cannot subsequently be reclaimed by issuing a credit note for the unpaid amount. See 7 BAD DEBT RELIEF.

De Voil Indirect Tax Service. See V3.519; V3.520.

40.16   **Correction of VAT invoices following a change in the VAT rate**

Under *VATA 1994, s 88*, a trader may elect to override certain of the normal tax point rules which determine whether a particular supply is taxable at the old or new rate when there is a change in the rate of VAT or in the descriptions of exempt or zero–rated supplies. The trader is allowed to account for VAT at the old rates on supplies actually 'made' before the date of change but for which the invoice and payment tax points would have occurred later. See 56.6 RATES OF VAT for full details.

Where under the above circumstances a VAT invoice is issued before the election, the supplier must within 14 days provide the customer with a credit note headed 'Credit note – change of VAT rate' showing the information required in 40.15 (*a*)–(*d*), (*g*) and (*h*) above. [*SI 1995/2518, Reg 15*]. See 57.6 and 57.9 RECORDS for the recording of credit notes.

41 Isle of Man

De Voil Indirect Tax Service. See V1.202; V1.208; V1.222.

41.1 ADMINISTRATION

The Isle of Man (IOM) is not part of the UK and the common tax area between the two countries results from an administrative agreement between the UK and the IOM governments contained in the *Customs and Excise Agreement 1979* (as amended). In the UK, the agreement was implemented by the *Isle of Man Act 1979*. Section 6 of that Act relates to VAT.

VAT is administered and collected in the IOM by the Manx Customs and Excise Service under the *Value Added Tax Act 1996* (of Tynwald).

The spirit of the agreement between the UK and IOM is that IOM legislation parallels UK legislation and procedures, with certain exceptions, but so that VAT is not charged twice on the same transaction. [*IMA 1979, s 6; SI 1982/1067; SI 1982/1068*]. Differences include

- legislation relating to VAT on gaming machines under *VATA 1994, s 23* (see 58.3 RECREATION AND SPORT) does not have an equivalent in the IOM [*IMA 1979, s 1(d)*];

- legislation relating to refund of VAT on the construction of new homes by do–it–yourself housebuilders under *VATA 1994, s 35* (see 42.52 LAND AND BUILDINGS) does not have an equivalent in the IOM [*SI 1982/1067, Art 9*]; and

- the rate of VAT on accommodation in hotels and similar establishments in the IOM, including the provision of holiday accommodation and the letting of camp sites, is 5%.

41.2 REGISTRATION

Separate VAT registers are maintained in the IOM and the UK. There are special provisions for determining, or enabling C & E to determine, where a person is to be registered who would otherwise be liable to be registered in both places.

A person who is *liable to be registered* in the UK under *VATA 1994, 1 Sch 1* (see 59.3 REGISTRATION) and who

(*a*) has 'an establishment' both in the UK and the IOM, or

(*b*) does not have an establishment in either country

will be registered in the UK or IOM as C & E determine; but unless or until they determine that he should be registered in the IOM, he is required to be registered in the UK. C & E may, however, at any time determine that a person within (*a*) or (*b*) above

- who is registered in the UK, is instead to be registered in the IOM, in which case he ceases to be, or required to be, registered in the UK from such date as they determine (although still remaining liable for payment of VAT on business assets held on the last day of registration, see 59.27 REGISTRATION); and

- who is registered in the IOM, is instead to be registered in the UK from such date as they determine, in which case any amount of VAT required to be paid in the IOM is deemed to have been an amount of VAT due in the UK.

Where a person is registered, or required to be registered, in the IOM, the provisions of *VATA 1994, 1 Sch 5* (notification of liability for, and date of registration in, the UK, see 59.4 REGISTRATION) and *VATA 1994, 1 Sch 9* (entitlement to be registered, see 59.2 REGISTRATION) do not apply to that person. C & E may, however, determine that any person to whom those provisions do apply shall be registered in the IOM.

A person registered in the UK who has no establishment in the IOM, or is the representative member of a VAT group (see 31.2 GROUPS OF COMPANIES) no member of which has an establishment there, must notify C & E if such an establishment is subsequently acquired. Such notification may be treated as an event requiring the cancellation of the person's, or that group's, registration.

'An establishment' in a country is where there is a place from which a person carries on a business in that country or carries on business through a branch or agent in that country. For this purpose an agent is a person who has the authority or capacity to create legal relations between his principal and a third party. [*SI 1982/1067, Arts 11, 12*].

De Voil Indirect Tax Service. See V2.140; V2.156.

41.3   **Imports, exports and removals**

Within the common tax area of the UK and the IOM, a registered business accounts for VAT in the country in which it is registered. For example, an IOM business, making taxable supplies in the UK accounts for the VAT in the IOM. If the business imports goods into the common tax area, the import VAT can be paid (or deferred) and reclaimed as input tax in the IOM subject to the normal rules for input tax deduction.

Movements of goods from the UK to the IOM and vice versa are not normally treated as exports or imports provided that, for goods removed from the IOM to the UK

• any VAT due has been accounted for in the IOM, or

• if the goods are relieved of VAT in the IOM, the conditions of that relief have not been broken.

42 Land and Buildings

Cross-references. See 7.10 BAD DEBT RELIEF for sales of repossessed properties by lenders; CAPITAL GOODS SCHEME (10) for the deduction, and adjustment of deduction, of input tax on certain land and buildings by partly exempt businesses; 64.21 SUPPLY for the place of supply of services relating to land outside the UK and the Isle of Man.

De Voil Indirect Tax Service. See V6.117–120A; V6.175–180A.

The contents of this chapter are as follows.

PART I GENERAL

42.1 DEFINITIONS AND MEANINGS OF TERMS

The following general definitions and terms apply for the purposes of this chapter.

'Approved alteration'

An approved alteration means any of the following.

(a) In the case of a *'protected building'* (see below) which is an ecclesiastical building excluded from the planning consent requirements by *Planning (Listed Buildings and Conservation Areas) Act 1990, s 60*, any works of alteration. A building used or available for use by a minister of religion wholly or mainly as a residence from which to perform the duties of his office is not to be treated as an ecclesiastical building for these purposes.

In England and Wales, the religious denominations which have been granted exclusion are the Church of England, the Church in Wales, the Roman Catholic Church, the Methodist Church, the Baptist Union of Great Britain and the Baptist

Union of Wales, and the United Reformed Church. These bodies have agreed to guidelines imposed by the Department of National Heritage.

In Scotland and Northern Ireland, all listed churches (or their equivalent in Northern Ireland) are excluded from planning consent requirements for the purposes of VAT relief on alterations. Subject to the normal rules, any alteration is zero-rated provided the church is currently used for religious purposes. (*Note.* Consideration is being given to restricting the scope of ecclesiastical exemption.) (C & E Notice 708, para 8.5).

Alterations to ecclesiastical buildings which require planning consent fall within (*c*) below.

(*b*) In the case of a '*protected building*' (see below) which is a scheduled monument within *Historic Monuments Act (Northern Ireland) 1971* and in respect of which a protection order under that *Act* is in force, any work of alteration for which consent has been given under *Section 10* of that *Act*.

Where a building is both a scheduled monument and a listed building within (*c*) below, only scheduled monument procedures apply for VAT purposes. (C & E Notice 708, para 8.7).

(*c*) In any other case, works of alteration which cannot be carried out unless authorised under *Planning (Listed Buildings and Conservation Areas) Act 1990, Planning (Listed Buildings and Conservation Areas) (Scotland) Act 1997, Planning (Northern Ireland) Order 1972* or *Ancient Monuments and Archaeological Areas Act 1979* and for which consent has been obtained under the appropriate legislation.

Such consent is usually referred to as 'listed building consent' which is not the same as planning permission. Generally, listed building consent is needed for work on a listed building which would affect its character as a building of special architectural or historic interest. The construction of an extension or alterations following partial demolition would certainly require consent but it is difficult to generalise about less radical work, e.g. internal alterations. Listed building consent is, however, sometimes given for the partial or total demolition of unlisted buildings in conservation areas and it is essential to ensure that a building is on the statutory lists and not assume that it is because listed building consent has been given. (C & E Notice 708, para 8.4).

For alterations to buildings on Crown or Duchy land, listed building consent may not be needed even though it would be needed for similar alterations to listed buildings elsewhere. In such cases, approved alterations are those for which consent would otherwise have been required.

Approved alterations do *not* include the following.

• Any works of repair or maintenance (even if included in the listed building consent).

• Any incidental alteration to the 'fabric' of a building which results from the carrying out of repairs or maintenance work (e.g. alteration in appearance due to use of modern materials/techniques for repair or maintenance work). '*Fabric*' means the basic structure of the building and includes walls, roofs, internal surfaces, floors, stairs, landings and all doors and windows. (C & E Notice 708, para 8.1).

• The alteration of a building within the '*curtilage*' (see below) of a listed dwelling to create a new dwelling such as a 'granny annex' where the separate use or disposal of the annex is prevented by any planning consent or similar provision;

• The construction of a building 'separate' from, but in the curtilage (see below) of, a protected building (which is standard-rated even if the work has listed building or scheduled monument consent). The only exceptions are (i) the construction of a completely new self-contained dwelling (including a garage built at the same time for use with it) where there are no restrictions on disposal; and (ii) a completely new self-contained building for use solely for a '*relevant residential purpose*' or a '*relevant charitable purpose*' (see below).

See *C & E Commrs v Arbib QB, [1995] STC 490* for a consideration of the meaning of 'separate'. In that case, a swimming pool connected to a listed farmhouse by a covered walkway and a brick wall was held not to be a separate building so that the building work on it fell to be zero-rated.

[*VATA 1994, 8 Sch Group 6, Item 2 and Notes (6)-(8), (10); SI 1995/283*]. (C & E Notice 708, paras 8.10, 8.12)

'Construction of a building'

Construction of a building does not include

- converting, reconstructing or altering an existing building;

- enlarging or extending an existing building except to the extent that this creates an additional dwelling or dwellings; or

- constructing an annexe to an existing building unless

  (i) the annexe is intended solely for use for a '*relevant charitable purpose*' (see below);

  (ii) it is capable of functioning independently from the existing building; and

  (iii) the only access (or main access where more than one) to the annexe is *not* via the existing building and *vice versa*.

For these purposes, a building only ceases to be an existing building when

- it is demolished completely to 'ground level' (for this purpose ground level may include the 'slab' of the ground floor of the former building); or

- the part remaining above ground level consists of no more than a single façade (double façade where a corner site), the retention of which is a condition or requirement of statutory planning consent or similar permission.

[*VATA 1994, 8 Sch Group 5, Notes (16)-(18); SI 1995/280*].

C & E also regard the following as the construction of new buildings.

- The building on to an existing house of another house to form two semi-detached houses without internal access to the existing building, provided planning permission, etc. does not prevent its separate use or disposal.

- The building of a new house within an existing terrace of houses on the site of a house that has been totally demolished ('infilling') (or totally demolished except for the front façade where that façade has been retained because of the conditions of the planning consent).

- The construction of a new, self-contained flat which enlarges or extends an existing building and there is no prohibition on the separate use or disposal of the flat under the terms of the statutory planning consent or similar provision. This does not include the extension or enlargement of an existing dwelling, or part of a dwelling, even if the result of the work is an additional dwelling.

(C & E Notice 708, para 6.1).

'Curtilage'

A reasonable amount of land surrounding the building. This may include other buildings. What constitutes a reasonable amount of land will depend on the type of building and its setting. (C & E Notice 708, Glossary).

'Dwelling'

For the purposes of zero-rating, a building is designed as a dwelling or number of dwellings where the following conditions are satisfied in relation to each dwelling.

- The dwelling consists of self-contained living accommodation.

- There is no provision for direct internal access from the dwelling to any other dwelling or part of a dwelling.

- The separate use, letting or disposal of the dwelling is not prohibited by the terms of any covenant, statutory planning consent or similar provision.

- Statutory planning consent has been granted in respect of that dwelling and its construction or conversion has been carried out in accordance with that consent.

[*VATA 1994, 8 Sch Group 5, Note (2); SI 1995/280*].

'Grant'

Grant includes assignment or surrender. [*VATA 1994, 8 Sch Group 5, Note 2; SI 1995/280*].

A *grant* is a sale, leasing or letting of land. An *assignment* is the transfer of the unexpired portion of a lease by the existing tenant to a new tenant. A *surrender* is the giving up of an '*interest in or right over*' or '*licence to occupy*' land (see below) to the grantor. (C & E Notice 742, para 2.5).

The grant of any interest frequently gives rise to a number of further supplies at later times. For example, a supply is made each time that a payment is received for rent. In such cases, the liability of each subsequent supply is determined at the time when that supply is made rather than by reference to the time of the original grant. [*VATA 1994, s 96(10A); FA 1997, s 35(1)*].

'In the course of construction'

It is a matter of fact when a building has been completed. It is normally when the building has been finished according to the original plans but, in cases of doubt, a building can be regarded as still under construction up to the date of the certificate of completion or when contracts have been completed and all building regulations complied with. The date when a building is first occupied (or ready to be occupied) may also be an indication if any of the above indicators cannot be relied upon. Where a new dwelling has been completed, any further work to the building (e.g. the addition of a conservatory) is standard-rated.

Where a new building is occupied in stages, 'first occupation' applies to the occupation of any part of it. However, occupation of the ground floor of a block of flats or qualifying building shortly before the upper floors are fitted out does not prevent the work on the upper floors from being zero-rated.

Snagging. Where a contract provides for snagging work to be carried out 'free of charge' for a limited period, then the work is treated as further work for the original contract payment. Snagging work may also be carried out to fulfil obligations under a retention clause.

(C & E Notice 708, paras 7.1-7.3).

42.1 Land and Buildings

A building has been held to be in the course of construction until the main structure is completed, the windows glazed and all essential services and fittings, such as plumbing and electricity, have been installed. Thereafter the building ceases to be in course of construction and the phase of fitting out and furnishing is ready to begin (*University of Hull (180)*). Tree planting, etc. in an estate development, even if a prerequisite to the construction of buildings under the terms of the planning permission, is not 'in the course of construction' (*Tilbury (1102)*).

'Interest in or right over'

An interest in land can be

- a *legal interest*, i.e. the formal ownership of the freehold or leasehold of a property which belongs to the person registered at the Land Registry, and certain rights over someone else's land; or

- a *beneficial (or equitable) interest*, i.e. the right to receive the benefit of supplies of it (e.g. the sales proceeds or rental income).

A beneficial interest may be held and transferred separately from the legal interest.

Rights over land include

- *'profits à prendre'*, i.e. rights granted to specific people to take mineral or natural produce from another person's land;

- *easements* or *wayleaves* (in Scotland, *servitudes*) which grant to the owner of neighbouring land the right of way, light or water, etc. so as to make his property better and more convenient; and

- *rights of entry* which allow someone to come onto land to perform a specific function, e.g. the right to lay water pipes.

(C & E Notice 742, para 2.6).

'Licence to occupy'

A licence to occupy land arises where the owner allows someone to occupy land, in writing or orally, but under terms which fall short of a formal tenancy. C & E's interpretation of the law has been that the grant must amount to the occupation of the land (rather than the right to use the facilities it may offer) and the occupier must have a clearly defined area or site to the exclusion of other people. (C & E Notice 742, para 2.7). However, following the decision in *Abbotsley Golf and Squash Club Ltd (15042)* where, applying dicta of Lord Templeman in *Street v Mountford, HL [1985] 1 AC 809*, the tribunal held that exclusivity of occupation was an essential condition of a tenancy but not of a licence to occupy, C & E have been advised that, although exclusivity can be an appropriate test in may cases, it is not so in every situation.

C & E are reviewing the definition of the term 'licence to occupy'. Without prejudice to the outcome of the review, while it is in progress businesses should use the following criteria to determine whether a supply amounts to a 'licence to occupy land' as opposed to a lesser right to come onto land.

(a) C & E will normally continue to accept that a 'licence to occupy land' exists where there is a licence in relation to a clearly defined area or piece of land, which in substance and reality permits the licensee an exclusive right of occupation during the times prescribed in the licence. It is possible to have exclusive occupation of land even though the licensor can at any time come onto the land, and even though the period granted under the licence is not continuous (e.g. every Tuesday and Thursday afternoon).

(*b*) In addition, following *Abbotsley Golf and Squash Club Ltd* above, C & E accept that there can be a 'licence to occupy land' where the land in question is not occupied exclusively by the licensee provided

- the licence is in relation to a clearly defined area or piece of land;

- the licence in substance and reality allows the licensee to physically occupy the land; and

- the rights granted are in relation to the occupation of the land thereby providing for the licensee's physical enjoyment or exploitation of the land.

Examples of when there is likely to be a licence to occupy land.

- Granting a person a pitch in a market or at a car boot sale (even if only for one day, see *Tameside Metropolitan Borough Council, [1979] VATTR 93 (733)*).

- Hiring out a hall to a person, e.g. for a conference or a reception.

- Granting a concession to operate a shop within a shop where the concessionaire is granted an area from which to sell their goods or services.

- The provision of a stand or similar space to a person at an exhibition. See, however, *International Trade and Exhibitions J/V Ltd (14212)* where the tribunal held that supplies relating to exhibitions went far beyond licences to occupy land and the exhibitors obtained a supply of advertising services.

- The provision to the owner of coin-operated machines of sites on which to locate the machines. See *C & E Commrs v Sinclair Collis Ltd, QB [1998] STC 841* (overruling the earlier tribunal decision in *Wolverhampton and Dudley Breweries plc, [1990] VATTR 131 (5351)*).

Examples of when there is unlikely to be a licence to occupy land

- Ambulatory concessions (e.g. ice-cream vans on the beach).

- Allowing the general public admission to premises, etc. (see 58.6 RECREATION AND SPORT but note that admission to certain one-off fund-raising events by charities may be exempt).

- Hairdressers' chairs in open-plan salons. See *Price (1443); Field & Field (t/a Paul Field Hair and Beauty Salon (2047); Genc [1988] VATTR 16 (2595)* and *Winder (t/a Anthony and Patricia) (11784)* although in other cases the tribunal has held that a licence to occupy land existed (see *Quaife (1394)* and *Daniels & Daniels (t/a Group Montage) (12014)*). Subsequent, however, to these decisions, in *Simon Harris Hair Design Ltd (13939)* the tribunal held that there was a single standard-rated supply by the owner to the stylists even though each stylist had (and was separately charged for) an allocated space within the salon. A licence to occupy that space was economically useless without the right to use other facilities such as junior staff, basins and dryers. As a result of this decision, C & E officers have been advised to assess VAT where it is clear that the stylists are working in an open plan salon and use the facilities of the premises as a whole. (C & E Business Brief 13/96, 1 July 1996).

(C & E Business Brief 22/98, 3 November 1998).

See also *Altman Blane & Co (12381)* where payments for non-exclusive use of a room were held to be exempt.

'Major interest'

A major interest in relation to land means the fee simple (freehold) or a tenancy (lease) for a term certain exceeding 21 years. In Scotland, it means (*a*)   the estate or interest of the proprietor of the *dominium utile* or,

(*b*)   in the case of land not held under feudal tenure, the estate or interest of the owner, or the lessee's interest under a lease for a period of not less than 20 years.

[*VATA 1994, s 96(1); FA 1998, s 24*].

Before 31 July 1998, the legislation in (*b*) above referred to a period exceeding 21 years although in practice C & E treated Scottish leases of 20 years as the grant of a major interest. The reason for the change is that the practical effect of Scottish land law is to prohibit leases of over 20 years in domestic property.

'Non-residential'

Non-residential in relation to a building or part of a building means

*   neither designed nor adapted for use as a '*dwelling*' (see above), number of dwellings or for a '*relevant residential purpose*' (see below), or

*   if so designed or adapted, constructed before 1 April 1973 and not used for such purposes at any time since that date.

References to a non-residential building or a non-residential part of a building do not include a reference to a garage occupied together with a dwelling.

[*VATA 1994, 8 Sch Group 5, Notes (7) and (8); SI 1995/280*].

'Person constructing a building'

This means either

*   a speculative builder constructing a building on his own land; or

*   someone who commissions the construction of a building on his own land, where

    (i)   supplies of construction services are made to him,

    (ii) he exercises some measure of control over the construction of the building (e.g. control over design and planning); and

    (iii) he sells the freehold or grants a long lease in all or part of the building.

(C & E Notice 708, para 15.2).

In *C & E Commrs v Link Housing Association Ltd CS, [1992] STC 718*, the court held that the phrase 'a person constructing' should be read as meaning 'a person who has constructed' and the original builder is therefore entitled to zero-rate his supply of a dwelling, however long after construction that might be. (In the case of *Link* the houses had been constructed before the introduction of VAT in 1973.) It held that the phrase is purely descriptive and designed only to ensure that it was the person who was constructing or had constructed the building who was entitled to zero-rating. C & E have taken the narrow view that the decision applies only in relation to input tax on disposal costs. (C & E Business Brief 15/92, 5 October 1992).

'Protected building'

A protected building means any building which is

*   a listed building (within the meaning of *Planning (Listed Buildings and Conservation Areas) Act 1990* or *Planning (Listed Buildings and Conservation Areas) (Scotland) Act 1997* or *Planning (Northern Ireland) Order 1991)*, or

*   a scheduled monument (within the meaning of *Ancient Monuments and Archaeological Areas Act 1979* or *Historic Monuments Act (Northern Ireland) 1971)*

and which satisfies one of the following conditions.

(*a*) It is designed to remain as or become a dwelling or number of dwellings. This condition is satisfied where, in relation to each dwelling

- the dwelling consists of self-contained living accommodation; and

- there is no provision for direct internal access from the dwelling to any other dwelling or part of a dwelling; and

- the separate use or disposal of the dwelling is not prohibited by the terms of any covenant, statutory planning consent or similar provision.

Included is a garage (occupied together with the dwelling) either constructed at the same time as the building or, where the building has been substantially reconstructed, at the same time as that reconstruction.

(*b*) It is intended for use solely for a '*relevant residential purpose*' or a '*relevant charitable purpose*' (see below) after the reconstruction or alteration.

[*VATA 1994, 8 Sch Group 6, Notes (1) and (2); SI 1995/283*].

A protected building also includes an object or structure within the curtilage of a listed building, which although not fixed to the building, forms part of the land and has done so since before 1 July 1948 (the date listed building control began in its present form).

Unlisted buildings in conservation areas and buildings included in a local authority's non-statutory list of buildings of local interest (which used to be known as 'Grade III' buildings) are not protected buildings for the purposes of VAT relief.

(C & E Notice 708, para 8.3).

'Relevant charitable purpose'

This means use by a charity in either or both of the following ways.

(*a*) *Otherwise than in the course or furtherance of a business*. It is essential that all or part of the building is used for non-business purposes. The term 'business' is a widely drawn concept. See 12.4 CHARITIES and more generally 8 BUSINESS. See also *Newtownbutler Playgroup Ltd (13741)*. Where the building is used for business and non-business purposes, business use can be ignored if

- the building will be used solely for non-business purposes for more than 90% of the total time it is available for use; or

- in the case of non-business charitable educational establishments (e.g. a grant maintained sixth form college) the number of fee paying students is less than 10% of the total students calculated on a full-time equivalent basis.

The construction of a garage, within the curtilage of a church building, for cars used for pastoral work has been held be for a relevant charitable purpose, any private use being *de minimis* and disregarded (*St Dunstans's Roman Catholic Church Southborough, [1997] VATDR 17 (15472)*).

(*b*) *As a village hall or similarly in providing social or recreational facilities for a local community*. In the opinion of C & E, in order to qualify, the building must be owned, organised and administered by the local community for the benefit of the community. This contention was accepted by the tribunal in *Ormiston Charitable Trust (13187)* but was rejected in *Jubilee Hall Recreation Centre Ltd v C & E Commrs QB, [1997] STC 414* by Lightman J who also stated that the words 'local community' were not restricted to those residing in a particular community and include those working in the locality. The facilities on offer should be multi-purpose, be available for use by the local community at large (rather than just a particular section of it) and be used for a variety of public and private purposes.

C & E have appealed against this decision. See also *St Dunstan's Educational Foundation (14901)* where the hall was for use by an independent fee-paying school (a charity) and the community at specific times. *Included* are such buildings as sports pavilions constructed and used similarly to a village hall. *Excluded* are civil engineering works such as tennis courts, bowling greens or running tracks; buildings such as swimming pools or cinemas (which are not used in the same way as village halls); and leisure and sports centres run by charities on commercial lines.

[*VATA 1994, 8 Sch Group 5, Note 6; SI 1995/280*]. (C & E Notice 708, paras 2.7, 3.2).

'Relevant housing association'

A relevant housing association is

- in England and Wales, a registered social landlord within the meaning of *Housing Act 1996, Part I* (before 1 March 1997 a registered housing association within the meaning of *Housing Associations Act 1985*);

- in Scotland, a Scottish registered housing association within the meaning of *Housing Associations Act 1985*; and

- in Northern Ireland, a Northern Irish registered housing association within the meaning of *Housing (Northern Ireland) Order 1992 (SI 1992/1725), Part II.*

[*VATA 1994, 8 Sch Group 5, Note (21), 10 Sch 3(8); SI 1997/50; SI 1997/51*].

'Relevant residential purpose'

A building is used for relevant residential purposes where some of the facilities (e.g. kitchens, dining rooms and bathrooms) are shared. Specifically, use for a relevant residential purpose means use as

- a home or other institution providing residential accommodation either for children or with personal care for persons in need of such care by reason of old age, disablement, past or present dependence on alcohol or drugs or past or present mental disorder;

- a hospice;

- residential accommodation for students or school pupils or members of any of the armed forces;

- a monastery, nunnery or similar establishment; or

- an institution which is the sole or main residence of at least 90% of its residents.

Excluded is the use as a hospital, prison or similar institution or an hotel or inn or similar establishment.

Where a number of buildings are constructed at the same time and on the same site and are intended to be used together as a unit solely for a relevant residential purpose, each of those buildings (to the extent that they would not otherwise be so regarded) are to be treated as intended for use solely for a relevant residential purpose.

[*VATA 1994, 8 Sch Group 5, Notes (4) and (5); SI 1995/280*].

For example, a separate laundry or dining block can be zero-rated if built at the same time as a new residential home for the elderly provided a single application for planning permission has been submitted and approved for that construction. Where a new facility is built at a later date it is standard-rated (unless qualifying for relevant residential purposes in its own right. (C & E Notice 708, para 6.2).

'Residential accommodation' for students, etc. merely signifies lodging, sleeping or overnight accommodation and does not suggest the need for such accommodation to be for any fixed or minimum period (*Urdd Gobaith Cymru, [1997] VATDR 273 (14881)*). C & E have accepted this decision with regard to residential accommodation generally and changed their policy (previously having required a 'substantial degree of permanence' criteria). As a result

- adjustments can be made (subject to the three year cap and unjust enrichment rules) where VAT has been charged purely by a failure to meet the previous length of stay criteria; and

- zero-rating under 42.33 below (conversion services supplied to a housing association) or 42.48(*c*) below (grant of a major interest in a converted building) and refunds under 42.52 below (conversion by a DIY housebuilder) are no longer available where the original building is residential under the new interpretation. By concession, where a written legally binding obligation to make the supply in question was in force before 10 June 1998 or where the work of conversion commenced before that date, zero-rating or a DIY refund will be allowed for the conversion (subject to the normal rules).

(C & E Business Briefs 6/98, 11 February 1998 and 13/98, 9 June 1998).

'Site'

Zero-rating applies to the grant of a major interest in the land on which a qualifying building stands, together with a reasonable plot of land surrounding it. What is a reasonable plot depends on the size, nature and situation of the building and the nature of the surrounding land. The site of a house should be regarded as the plot for that house and not the border of any estate or group of houses being constructed. The site of a block of flats, or a building for use for a '*relevant residential purpose*' or '*relevant charitable purpose*' (see above) includes any communal areas.

The supply of land by a speculative builder is not regarded as the supply of a site unless a building is clearly under construction on it (i.e. it has progressed beyond foundation stage). The grant of a major interest in a site on which no construction work beyond foundation stage has been undertaken is exempt under 42.2 below (subject to the exercise of the option to tax under 42.20 below where possible). (C & E Notice 708, para 15.4).

De Voil Indirect Tax Service. See V4.232.

PART II LAND AND PROPERTY TRANSACTIONS

42.2   EXEMPT SUPPLIES

See 22.18(*b*) and (*l*) EUROPEAN COMMUNITY LEGISLATION for the provisions of the *EC Sixth Directive*.

The 'grant' of any

- 'interest in or right over' land,

- 'licence to occupy' land, or

- in relation to Scotland, any 'personal right' to call for or be granted any such interest or right (see below)

is, subject to certain exceptions, an exempt supply. [*VATA 1994, 9 Sch Group 1*].

See 42.1 above for the meaning of '*grant*', '*interest in or right over*' and '*licence to occupy*'.

'*Land*' includes buildings, walls, trees, plants and other structures and natural objects in, under or over it as long as they remain attached to it. (C & E Notice 742, para 2.4). Where fixtures are included with a building or land, they are not treated as supplies for VAT purposes and their liability is the same as that for the land or buildings with which they are being supplied. (C & E Notice 742, para 7.9).

A '*personal right*' in Scotland is a contractual right, as opposed to a legal right, over the property itself. Such personal rights are exempt in the rest of the UK as equitable interests in land. (C & E Notice 742, para 2.6).

Under *EC Sixth Directive, Art 13B(h)* countries must exempt the supply of land which has not been built upon other than '*building land*' i.e. any unimproved or improved land defined as such by the individual country. In *Norbury Developments Ltd, [1996] VATDR 531 (14482)* the tribunal held that building land should therefore be taxable rather than exempt unless the exemption was authorised by *Art 28(3)(b)* (which allows countries to continue to exempt certain supplies, including building land, for a transitional period). The tribunal referred the case to the CJEC for a ruling on the interpretation of *Art 28(3)(b)*.

Exceptions include

● the first grant of a major interest in a 'qualifying building' i.e.

 (i) a dwelling or building intended for use for a relevant residential or charitable purpose,

 (ii) a dwelling converted from a non-residential building, or

 (iii) a substantially reconstructed protected building

 by the person constructing, converting or, as the case may be, reconstructing it (which is zero-rated, see 42.48 and 42.49 below);

● the sale of the freehold interest in a new or uncompleted non-qualifying building or civil engineering work (which is standard-rated, see 42.4 below);

● supplies falling within one of the categories in 42.5 to 42.14 below which are specifically excluded from exemption and standard-rated;

● any supply which would otherwise be exempt but in respect of which an election to waive exemption ('option to tax') has been exercised (see 42.20 below);

● a supply subject to a developmental tenancy, lease or licence (which is standard-rated, see 42.28 below); and

● certain supplies which form part of the transfer of a business as a going concern (which are outside the scope of VAT, see 8.10 *et seq.* BUSINESS).

Options to purchase/sell or lease land. A person granted an option to purchase property (a 'call option') acquires the right to buy it at a future date for a specified price. That right is an interest in land and therefore the grant of the option is exempt if the purchase of the property would be exempt at the time of the grant. If the purchase would be taxable at that time, the grant of the option is taxable (see 42.14 below). The same principles apply to option to acquire leases or rights over or licences to occupy land.

A person granted an option to sell land at a fixed price at a future date (a 'put' option) does not receive an interest in land and the grant of such an option is always standard-rated.

(C & E Notice 742, para 3.5).

De Voil Indirect Tax Service. See V4.111; V4.112.

42.3   STANDARD-RATED SUPPLIES

The supplies of land within 42.4 to 42.14 below are excluded from the general exemption for land under 42.2 above and are standard-rated.

42.4   New and uncompleted non-qualifying/commercial buildings and civil engineering works

The 'grant' or assignment of the fee simple (freehold interest) in

(a)   a building which has not been 'completed' and which is not a '*qualifying building*' (i.e. is neither designed as a 'dwelling' or number of dwellings nor intended for use for solely a 'relevant residential purpose' or a 'relevant charitable purpose'),

(b)   a 'new' building which is not to be used as a qualifying building after the grant,

(c)   a civil engineering work which has not been completed, or

(d)   a new civil engineering work

is standard-rated. (Supplies of qualifying buildings are exempt unless zero-rated under the provisions in 42.48 or 42.49 below.)

A building/civil engineering work is to be taken as '*completed*' when an architect/ engineer issues a certificate of practical completion in relation to it or it is fully occupied/used, whichever happens first. It is to be taken as '*new*' if it was completed less than three years before the grant.

See 42.1 above for the meaning of '*grant*', '*relevant residential purpose*' and '*relevant charitable purpose*'.

Issue of certificates. A grant or assignment cannot be taken as relating to a building (or part) intended for use solely for a relevant residential or charitable purpose as above unless

(i)   it is made to a person who intends to use the building (or part) for such a purpose; and

(ii)   before it is made, that person has given the grantor a certificate stating that the grant relates to such a building.

See 42.51 below for further details on issue and form of certificates.

Part-qualifying buildings. Where part of a building is designed as a dwelling or number of dwellings or intended for relevant use as above and part is not (e.g. shop premises with a flat over them) an apportionment is necessary if the grant does not relate exclusively to one part or the other.

[*VATA 1994, 9 Sch Group 1, Item 1(a) and Notes 1 to 6*].

Options, etc. to purchase. See 42.14 below.

Mixed supplies of land and civil engineering work. Unless the option to tax has been exercised (see 42.20 below) the sale of freehold land containing new civil engineering works, without constituting such work in its entirety (e.g. building land on which roads have been built and pipes laid for connection to mains services), is a mixed supply. A suitable apportionment must be made on any objective basis which gives a fair and reasonable result. If on the basis of cost, the cost of the civil engineering work must reflect the cost of the land covered by the work (usually nil if the work is underground, e.g. drains and sewers) and the cost of installing or constructing the work itself. Where any bare land is ancillary to a civil engineering work (e.g. an airfield, docks or oil refinery) the land can be treated as part of the civil engineering work and the freehold sale of a civil engineering work and its site gives rise to a single standard-rated supply if it is new. (C & E Notice 742, para 3.2, 3.3).

De Voil Indirect Tax Service. See V4.113.

42.5 **Gaming and fishing rights**

The 'grant' of any interest, right or licence to take game or fish is standard-rated unless, at the time of the grant, the grantor grants to the grantee the fee simple of the land over which the right to take game or fish is exercisable. Where a grant of an interest in or right over land or a licence to occupy land includes a valuable right to take game or fish, an apportionment must be made to determine the exempt and standard-rated parts. [*VATA 1994, 9 Sch Group 1, Item 1(c) and Note 8*].

See 58.14 RECREATION AND SPORT for further details.

Options, etc. to purchase. See 42.14 below.

42.6 **Hotel accommodation**

The provision in an hotel, inn, boarding house or 'similar establishment' of sleeping accommodation or of accommodation in rooms which are provided in conjunction with sleeping accommodation or for the purposes of a supply of catering is standard-rated. '*Similar establishment*' includes premises in which there is provided furnished sleeping accommodation, whether with or without the provision of board or facilities for the preparation of food, which are used by, or held out as being suitable for use by, visitors or travellers. [*VATA 1994, 9 Sch Group 1, Item 1(d) and Note 9*].

Where guests stay for a continuous period of four weeks or more, VAT is chargeable on a reduced value from the 29th day.

See 33.1 to 33.4 HOTELS AND HOLIDAY ACCOMMODATION for further details.

Options, etc. to purchase. See 42.14 below.

42.7 **Holiday accommodation**

The grant of any interest in or right over or licence to occupy holiday accommodation (including any accommodation in a building, hut, chalet, caravan, houseboat (see 42.56 below) or tent which is advertised or held out as holiday accommodation or as suitable for holiday or leisure use) is standard-rated. *Excluded* is the grant of the fee simple, or a lease, etc. for a premium, in a building which is not a 'new building'.

[*VATA 1994, 9 Sch Group 1, Item 1(e) and Notes 12 and 13*].

See 33.5 to 33.9 HOTELS AND HOLIDAY ACCOMMODATION for further details.

Options, etc. to purchase. See 42.14 below.

42.8 **Caravan and tent pitches and camping facilities**

The provision of 'seasonal pitches' for caravans, and the grant or assignment of facilities at caravan parks to persons for whom such pitches are provided, are standard-rated. The provision of pitches for tents or of camping facilities is also standard-rated.

A '*seasonal pitch*' is

(*a*)   any pitch which is provided for a period of less than a year; and (*b*) a pitch provided for a year or more but which the person to whom it is provided is prevented by the terms of any covenant, statutory planning consent or similar permission from occupying by living in a caravan at all times throughout the period for which the pitch is provided.

[*VATA 1994, 9 Sch Group 1, Items 1(f)(g) and Note 14*].

Following the tribunal decision in *Ashworth (Mrs B), [1194] VATTR 275 (12924)*, C & E accept that a pitch will only be regarded as seasonal under (*b*) above if it is on a site, or part of a site, which is advertised or held out for holiday use. (C & E Leaflet 701/20/96, para 3).

The effect of the above is that the provision of pitches at permanent residential caravan parks and sites for gypsies ('travellers') are exempt. Also exempt are pitches on seasonal sites which are not advertised or held out for holiday use where, although the caravan cannot be occupied throughout the year due to a time-related restriction on occupancy, it can nevertheless be used as a person's principal private residence. (C & E Leaflet 701/20/96, para 3).

The supply of rented accommodation in any caravan or mobile home is exempt unless the accommodation is holiday accommodation which is always standard-rated under 42.7 above.

See also 42.55 below for caravans generally.

Options, etc. to purchase. See 42.14 below.

De Voil Indirect Tax Service. See V4.113.

42.9 **Parking facilities**

The grant or assignment of facilities for parking a vehicle is standard-rated. [*VATA 1994, 9 Sch Group 1, Item 1(h)*].

There is normally a standard-rated supply of parking facilities if a specific and distinguishable grant or assignment is made and the facilities are designed for, or provided specifically for the purpose of, parking vehicles.

Standard-rated supplies include the following.

(*a*) The letting or licensing of garages (even if used for other purposes, e.g. storage of goods) or designated parking bays or spaces. See *C & E Commrs v Trinity Factoring Services Ltd CS, [1994] STC 504* where the court held that the lease of a lock-up garage was standard-rated even though the lessor and lessee had agreed in advance that the garage would be used for the storage of goods. *Prima facie* facilities had been granted for parking a vehicle and the terms of the lease did not preclude such usage.

(*b*) The provision of rights to park vehicles (and accompanying trailers) in, for example, car parks and commercial garages.

(*c*) The letting or licensing of land specifically for the construction of a garage or for use solely for the parking of a vehicle.

(*d*) The letting or licensing of a purpose-built car park (e.g. to a car park operator).

(*e*) The letting of taxi ranks.

(*f*) The provision of bicycle storage.

(*g*) The freehold sale of a 'new' or partly completed garage, car park or car parking facilities other than in conjunction with the sale of a new dwelling. A garage, etc. or dwelling is taken to be *'new'* if it was completed less than three years before the grant. See 42.4 above. (The sale of a garage or parking space together with a new dwelling by the person constructing it is normally zero-rated under 42.48 below unless the dwelling is standard-rated holiday accommodation under 42.7 above.)

Exempt supplies. The following supplies are not regarded by C & E as supplies of parking facilities and are therefore exempt under the general provisions in 42.2 above (subject to the exercise of an option to tax under 42.20 below).

  (i) The letting of land or buildings (other than garages) where the conveyance or contract makes no specific reference to use for parking facilities.

 (ii) The letting of land or buildings where any reference to parking a vehicle is incidental to the main use (but see (viii) below).

(iii) The letting of land or buildings to a motor dealer for storing stock-in-trade.

(iv) The letting of land or buildings to a vehicle transportation firm, a vehicle distributor or a vehicle auctioneer for business use.

 (v) The letting of land (including land used at other times as a car park) for purposes such as a market or car boot sale.

(vi) The letting of land for the exhibition of vehicles.

The letting of land to a travelling fair or circus (and the incidental parking of vehicles).

(viii) The letting of a garage or parking space in conjunction with the *letting* of a dwelling for permanent residential use provided it is reasonably near to the dwelling and the letting is by the same landlord to the same tenant (whether under a single or separate agreement). See also *Skatteministeriet v Henriksen, CJEC 1989, [1990] STC 768.* (If the dwelling is owned freehold, the letting is standard-rated under (*a*) above.)

(ix) The freehold sale of garages, car parks or parking facilities which are not 'new' (whether for subsequent letting or the purchaser's own use). See (*g*) above for the meaning of '*new*'.

The supply of garage or other parking facilities provided in conjunction with the letting of *commercial* premises is treated as a single supply provided both lettings are by the same landlord to the same tenant and *either* the facilities are on or reasonably near the property *or* the facilities are with a complex. The supply may therefore be exempt or, where the option to tax under 42.20 below has been exercised, standard-rated. In any other circumstances, the provision of parking facilities with commercial property is standard-rated. See also *Skatteministeriet v Henriksen, CJEC 1989, [1990] STC 768.*

Local authority parking meters. Parking at meter bays operated by local authorities on public roads is not provided by way of business and is outside the scope of VAT.

(C & E Leaflet 701/24/92).

Caravans and houseboats. See 42.55 and 42.56 below for parking facilities for caravans and houseboats.

Options, etc. to purchase. See 42.14 below.

De Voil Indirect Tax Service. See V4.113.

42.10 **Timber rights**

The grant or assignment of any right to fell and remove standing timber is standard-rated. [*VATA 1994, 9 Sch Group 1, Item 1(j)*].

The grant must be separate and specific. If land is sold which happens to contain standing timber which the buyer will be able to fell, the whole supply is exempt with the option to tax under 42.20 below. (C & E Notice 742, para 2.8).

Options, etc. to purchase. See 42.14 below.

42.11   **Storage and mooring of aircraft, ships, etc.**

The grant or assignment of facilities for housing, or storage of, an aircraft or for 'mooring', or storage of, a ship, boat or other vessel is standard-rated. '*Mooring*' includes anchoring or berthing.

[*VATA 1994, 9 Sch Group 1, Item 1(k) and Note 15*].

Even if a person is merely granted permission to lay down his own mooring and owns the ground tackle, the grant is considered to be excluded from exemption and taxable at the standard rate whether or not there is a formal lease or licence. (C & E Press Notice 355, 25 June 1975). See also *J W Fisher (179)* and *Strand Ship Building Co Ltd (1651)*.

See however 68.9 TRANSPORT AND FREIGHT for facilities zero-rated when supplied in ports or customs airports and 42.56 below for special rules which apply to the mooring of some houseboats.

Options, etc. to purchase. See 42.14 below.

42.12   **Boxes, seats, etc.**

The grant or assignment of any right to occupy a box, seat or other accommodation at a sports ground, theatre, concert hall or other place of entertainment is standard-rated. [*VATA 1994, 9 Sch Group 1, Item 1(l)*]. Included is any kind of accommodation which is intended for use by individuals or groups for viewing a match, race, show or other form of entertainment, regardless of whether the entertainment is actually in progress when the accommodation is used. (C & E Notice 742, para 2.8).

Options, etc. to purchase. See 42.14 below.

42.13   **Sports facilities**

The grant or assignment of facilities for playing any sport or participating in any physical recreation is standard-rated. [*VATA 1994, 9 Sch Group 1, Item 1(m)*].

Exemption is, however, retained where the facilities are to be used for more than 24 hours or, provided certain conditions are met, a series of at least ten shorter periods. See 58.8 RECREATION AND SPORT. See also 58.9 for certain sporting services provided by non-profit making bodies.

42.14   **Options, etc. to purchase interests or rights within 42.4 to 42.13 above**

The grant of any right, including

- an equitable right,

- a right under an option or right of pre-emption, or

- in relation to land in Scotland, a 'personal right',

to call for or to be granted an interest or right which would fall to be standard-rated under 42.4 to 42.13 above is also standard-rated.

42.15 Land and Buildings

A *'personal right'* in Scotland is a contractual right, as opposed to a legal right, over the property itself. (C & E Notice 742, para 2.6).

[*VATA 1994, 9 Sch Group 1, Item 1(n)*].

42.15 SUPPLIES BETWEEN LANDLORDS AND TENANTS

Grant of a lease. The grant of a lease is, subject to certain exceptions, exempt from VAT. See 42.2 above.

Subsequent supplies under a lease. The granting of a lease usually gives rise to a number of further supplies at later times. For example, a supply is made each time that a payment is received for rent or the lease is surrendered or assigned. In such cases, the liability of each subsequent supply is determined at the time when that supply is made rather than by reference to the time of the original grant. [*VATA 1994, s 96(10A); FA 1997, s 35(1)*].

Inducements (reverse premiums). C & E regard an inducement paid by

* a landlord to a prospective tenant for the latter to enter into a lease, or

* a tenant to a third party to accept the assignment of a lease or the grant of a sub-lease

as consideration for a standard-rated supply of services on the basis that, when the supply takes place, the tenant/assignee is not in a position to make any supply of an interest in property to the landlord/assignor which could be exempt from VAT. C & E also regard this as applying where a landlord makes a payment to a tenant for carrying out building or refurbishment works. The input tax incurred by the landlord on the payment to the tenant is attributable to the leasing of the property and is normally only recoverable if the landlord has opted to tax. (C & E Notice 742, para 4.2).

See, however, *Mirror Group plc (15443)* where the tribunal held that, following the decision in *Lubbock Fine & Co v C & E Commrs CJEC 1993, [1994] STC 101*, a supply could qualify for exemption even where it was made by the tenant rather than by the landlord and that there was no sound reason for excluding from exemption 'a transaction by which a lease is created, where that transaction differs from the grant of a lease in return for a premium payable by the tenant, essentially because the tenant pays no premium while the landlord provides him with an inducement to secure his entry into the lease and his consequential compliance with the tenant's covenants'. Similarly, in *Cantor Fitzgerald International, [1997] VATDR 233 (15070)* the tribunal, also following the decision in *Lubbock Fine & Co* above, held that the fact that the monetary consideration for the assignment of an underlease moved from assignor to assignee rather than vice versa was immaterial. The payment was for the variation of the contractual relationship established by the original underlease, and was exempt from VAT. C & E have appealed against the tribunal decision in *Mirror Group plc* to the High Court and, in *Cantor Fitzgerald International*, the High Court, on appeal, have referred the case to the CJEC for clarification. Pending the final outcome of these cases, businesses receiving payments in identical circumstances may choose not to account for VAT on the transaction in which case C & E may issue a protective assessment. If the final decision is in C & E's favour, businesses will be required to pay the VAT and interest in all cases. Alternatively, businesses may continue to account for VAT on such payments and submit claims for repayment and statutory interest if the final decision goes against C & E (subject to the three-year capping limit). (C & E Business Brief 28/97, 12 December 1997; C & E Business Brief 17/98, 10 August 1998).

Rents. Rental income is generally exempt from VAT although the landlord may opt to tax rents from non-domestic property (see 42.20 below).

- *Rental guarantees.* Where the purchaser of a lease or freehold of commercial property is given a guarantee by the seller that the seller will pay the open market rent of the property if tenants cannot be found, any payment under the guarantee generally falls outside the scope of VAT. (An exception would be where the documents clearly show that the payments under the guarantees are in consideration of the purchaser taking the property.) The payment is not to be regarded as a reduction in the value of the original lease or freehold sale unless the documentation shows that both parties agree to this. There *is* a supply for VAT purposes where the purchaser formally lets the property back to the seller. (C & E Notice 742, para 4.3).

- *Rent adjustments when buildings are sold or leases assigned.* Rent adjustments between landlords on the sale of tenanted property and between tenants on the assignment of a lease are outside the scope of VAT. Where a building in respect of which the option to tax has been exercised is sold and an adjustment made on the completion statement for rent received in advance to be paid over to the incoming landlord, a credit note must not be issued to the occupational tenants for any VAT charged on this portion of the rent. For VAT purposes the consideration for the sale of the building or the assignment of the lease is the full value of the supply before any rent adjustment is made. (C & E Notice 742, para 4.11).

- *Recovery of rent from third parties.* Where a tenant assigns a lease to a new tenant, the new tenant becomes liable for the rent to the landlord. If the new tenant defaults, under the law of privity of contract, the landlord can invoke the original covenant made by the old tenant and require him to pay the rent instead. This has no effect on the supply position for VAT purposes. The supply of property is still from the landlord to the new tenant and, if the landlord has opted to tax, any VAT invoice should be issued to the new tenant who alone has the right to recover the VAT charged as input tax.

  Similarly where a tenant sublets a property and the tenant is in default, the landlord can serve notice under *Law of Distress Amendment Act 1908, s 6* on the sub-tenant and collect arrears of rent from him. The sub-tenant can, in turn, reduce the rent payable to the defaulting tenant under the sub-lease by the amounts paid to the landlord. However, such actions have no effect on the nature of supplies for VAT purposes. The landlord continues to make supplies to the tenant who makes supplies to the sub-tenant. Where the landlord has opted to tax the rents, any VAT invoice should be addressed to the tenant who alone has the right to recover the VAT charged as input tax.

  Sureties and guarantors. Any rents paid by a surety or guarantor follow the liability of the original rent.

  (C & E Notice 742, para 7.5).

- *Rent-free periods.* The grant by a landlord of a rent-free period is not a supply for VAT purposes except where the rent-free period is given in exchange for something which the tenant agrees to do (e.g. carry out works for the benefit of the landlord). In the latter case, VAT is due on the amount of the rent foregone. (C & E Notice 742, para 4.2).

- *Rent paid while premises unoccupied.* In *Harper Collins Publishers Ltd (12040)*, the company, following reorganisation, moved out of two floors of its leased business premises but was unable to sublet immediately. The landlords in the meantime exercised the option to tax (see 42.20 below). The tribunal held that, although unoccupied, the two floors were still retained by the company for business purposes, the original purpose in taking the leases not having changed. Input tax suffered on the rents paid could be recovered (in this instance in part only by inclusion in the residual input tax on general overheads under the company's partial exemption computations).

Mortgage capping payments (i.e. where the developer or other seller of a leasehold or freehold in property agrees to pay the additional expense to the purchaser of a rise in the mortgage rate over a specified percentage) are treated as for *Rental guarantees* above. (C & E Notice 742, para 4.4).

Surrender of lease. The grant of an 'interest in or right over' land or a 'licence to occupy' land includes a surrender of that interest, etc. [*VATA 1994, 9 Sch Group 1 and Note (1); SI 1995/282*].

The general provisions relating to grants in 42.2 above therefore also apply to surrenders, i.e. they are exempt subject to certain exceptions. Similarly the assignment of any interest, etc. back to the lessor or licensor, by the lessee or licensee, is generally exempt. However, a surrender of an interest falling within the exclusions from exemption in 42.4 to 42.14 above remains standard-rated and where a tenant has, prior to the surrender, opted to tax the property in question under 42.20 below, the surrender is covered by the election and therefore taxable. (C & E Notice 742, para 4.5).

Variations of leases. Sometimes a lease is varied either to alter its terms (e.g. so that it can be used for different purposes), to extend the length of the tenancy or to alter the demised premises (e.g. by renting additional floor space). Under English land law, the effect of such a variation is that the old lease is deemed to be surrendered (see above) and a new lease granted in its place. Where there is no consideration, no supply is seen as taking place. (C & E Notice 742, para 4.7).

Reverse surrenders and assignments. Normally, when a lease is surrendered, consideration is paid by the landlord to the tenant. A *'reverse surrender'* occurs where a tenant surrenders an onerous lease to the landlord before the term of the lease has expired and pays the landlord to accept the surrender.

The grant of an interest in or right over land, or of any licence to occupy land, includes the supply made by the person to whom an interest is surrendered when there is a reverse surrender. [*VATA 1994, 9 Sch Group 1 and Notes (1) and (1A)*]. The general provisions relating to grants in 42.2 above therefore also apply to reverse surrenders, i.e. they are exempt subject to certain exceptions. Where the person making the supply (i.e. the landlord) has opted to tax the property, the supply is standard-rated. (C & E Notice 742, para 4.6).

Lifting of restricted covenants. Restrictive covenants are placed on land to control the use of the land. The lifting of a restricted covenant on land (e.g. to permit development which was previously forbidden) is exempt from VAT (unless the person receiving the payment has opted to tax). (C & E Notice 742, para 4.8).

Statutory compensation paid by a landlord to a tenant under the terms of the *Landlord and Tenant Act 1954* or the *Agricultural Tenancies Act 1995* is outside the scope of VAT. This applies even if, for example, an agricultural tenant has issued a 'notice to quit' having decided to retire from farming. Examples of items for which statutory compensation is given on a tenant quitting property are milk quotas left behind, manurial values and standing crops.

Where the landlord and tenant agree that the tenant will leave in return for additional payments, these payments are consideration for the tenant surrendering the lease and are exempt unless the tenant has opted to tax.

(C & E Notice 742, para 4.9).

Indemnity payments under lease agreements. In general any payment made by a prospective tenant to obtain the grant of a lease or licence, including any disbursement or indemnification of the costs incurred by the landlord, is part of the consideration for that grant.

Many leases provide that an existing tenant reimburses the landlord for legal or other advisory costs incurred by the landlord as a result of the tenant exercising rights already granted under the lease. For example, the tenant may be able to assign the lease, sublet or make alterations provided the tenant first obtains the landlord's consent (which can only be refused on reasonable grounds). Such reimbursements by the tenant to the landlord are consideration for the principal supply of the lease.

Any VAT charged by the landlord's advisers is related to their supply of services to the landlord. The tenant cannot deduct it as input tax even though bearing the cost. If the landlord has opted to tax the property, the landlord must charge the tenant VAT which is recoverable where the tenant is using the property to make taxable supplies. (C & E Notice 742, para 4.10).

If a tenant makes a payment to the landlord to obtain an *additional* right, it is consideration for the variation of the lease (see above).

Dilapidation payments. A lease may provide for the landlord to recover from a tenant, at or near the end of the lease, an amount to cover the cost of restoring the property to its original condition. Such dilapidation payments represent a claim for damages by the landlord against the tenant. The payment is not consideration for a supply for VAT purposes and is outside the scope of VAT. (C & E Notice 742, para 4.12).

Developmental leases. See 42.28 below.

Mesne profits. These are damages for the profits lost by a landlord by reason of wrongful occupation of his property and can only be recovered in respect of continued occupation of property after that right of occupation has expired. As such, an award of mesne profits is not consideration for a supply and is outside the scope of VAT. Where a landlord on the cash accounting system has opted to tax and, in addition to a claim for mesne profits, arrears of rent accrue, payment received following litigation should be treated firstly as relating to rent arrears and only then as relating to mesne profits to the extent that the total received exceeds the outstanding rents. (If the landlord is not on the cash accounting basis, the tax points for the periods in respect of which he is claiming rent arrears will have already been determined under the normal rules.) (Law Society's Gazette, 14 October 1992, p 16).

De Voil Indirect Tax Service. See V4.111.

42.16   SERVICE CHARGES, ETC.

The VAT treatment of service charges and other payments relating to premises depends upon the nature of the property and the terms of the arrangements.

(*a*)   **General services for tenants of leasehold non-domestic property provided by the landlord**. Leases often stipulate that the landlord will provide, and the tenants pay for, the services required for the upkeep of the building as a whole. The lease may provide for an inclusive rental or it may require the tenants to contribute by means of an additional charge to the basic rent, generally referred to as a service or maintenance charge. This service charge assumes the same VAT liability as the premium or rent payable under the lease or licence provided

(i) it is connected with the external fabric or the common parts of the building, etc. as opposed to the demised areas of the property of the individual occupants; and

(ii) it is paid for by all the occupants though a common service charge.

The service charge is therefore generally exempt unless the landlord has opted to tax the property (see 42.20 below) or the underlying lease is standard-rated e.g. holiday or time share accommodation (see 33.5 HOTELS AND HOLIDAY ACCOMMODATION).

(C & E Notice 742, paras 5.2, 5.3, 5.5).

(*b*)   **Specific services for tenants of leasehold non-domestic property provided by the landlord.** A payment made by a tenant to the landlord may be

● for the supply of the property and therefore exempt or, if the option to tax has been exercised, standard-rated,

● for supplies other than of the property and separately taxable, or

● disbursements and therefore outside the scope of VAT (see 4.7 AGENTS).

The following are typical examples.

(i) *Insurance and rates.* If the landlord is the policyholder or rateable person, any payment for insurance or rates from the tenant is part payment for the main supply. If the tenants are the policyholders or rateable persons, any payments on their behalf by the landlord should be treated as disbursements. See 37.14 INSURANCE. See also 37.11 INSURANCE for insurance supplied with other goods and services.

(ii) *Telephones.* If the telephone account is in the name of the landlord, any charge to the tenants (including calls, installation and rental) is standard-rated. If the account is in the name of the tenant but the landlord pays the bill, any recovery from the tenant is a disbursement.

(iii) *Reception and switchboard.* A charge by the landlord under the terms of the lease for use of such facilities which form a common part of the premises is further consideration for the main supply.

(iv) *Office services.* A separate charge for such services (e.g. typing and photocopying) is a separate standard-rated supply. If, however, under the terms of the lease, one inclusive charge is made for office services and accommodation, and the tenant is expected to pay for the services whether used or not, the liability for the services follows that of the main supply.

(v) *Fixtures and fittings.* These are regarded as part of the overall supply of the property and any charges for them are normally included in the rent. Where a separate charge is made by the landlord, the supply is standard-rated.

(vi) *Electricity, light and heat.* Where the tenants have secondary credit meters or coin operated meters or are allowed to receive an identifiable supply of fuel and power for which a separate charge is made, the charge by the landlord is for a separate supply of fuel and power. For unmetered supplies, C & E's policy is that where the supply of heat, etc. forms an integral part of the supply of accommodation, there is a single composite supply which is exempt from VAT. Where a tenant has the option of taking any services as additional services for an identifiable consideration, these form a separate single supply which takes its own VAT liability. See, however, *Suffolk Heritage Housing Association Ltd (13713)* where the tribunal held that the association's long standing practice of recovering heating costs as a separate charge from the rent should be treated as a separate supply for VAT purposes. C & E have appealed against this decision to the High Court.

(vii) *Management charges.* Charges by landlords for managing a development as a whole and administering the collection of service charges is additional consideration for the main supply.

(viii) *Recreational facilities.* The supply of such facilities (e.g. swimming pool or gymnasium) to tenants at no separate extra charge follows the liability of the main supply.

(C & E Notice 742, paras 5.6, 5.7; C & E Business Brief 2/96, 9 February 1996).

(c) **Services for occupants of leasehold non-domestic property provided by third parties.** Where a person is responsible for providing services to occupants of property but has no interest in that property (e.g. a managing agent) the supply of services is standard-rated as they are not part of the supply of the accommodation itself. (C & E Notice 742, para 5.4).

(d) **Services supplied to freehold occupants of non-domestic property.** Service charges raised where the property has been sold freehold are a separate standard-rated supply as there is no continuing supply of accommodation to the occupant by the provider of the services. (C & E Notice 742, para 5.3).

(e) **Occupation of premises as joint tenants.** Where the premises are occupied as joint tenants or licensees, each party has, either separately or together, entered into an agreement with the landlord. Any sums collected by one of the tenants from the other occupants for their share of the rent, rates, etc. and passed on to the landlord should be treated as disbursements. See 4.7 AGENTS. (C & E Notice 742, para 5.8).

(f) **Shared premises.** Where the owner or tenant of premises does not grant other occupants an exempt licence to occupy, any service charge must be standard-rated. This applies even if the owner/tenant is simply passing on appropriate shares of costs (e.g. electricity, gas, telephone and staff wages). The only exception is where a bill is paid which is entirely the liability of another occupant (e.g. a telephone bill or insurance premium in the other occupant's name) which can be treated as a disbursement. (C & E Notice 742, para 5.9).

(g) **Service charges on domestic accommodation.** Services charges relating to the upkeep of the common areas of

- an estate of dwellings, or
- a domestic dwelling if it is multi-occupied

are exempt from VAT under the general exemption for land in 42.2 above if paid

- *by* leasehold owners under the terms of the lease, or
- by persons renting property *to* the lessor or ground landlord.

Services charges paid by freehold owners of domestic property and by anyone for services not supplied by or under the direction of the lessor or ground landlord are standard-rated (because they cannot be consideration for any supply of land)

However, by concession, all *mandatory* service charges paid by the occupants of residential property (but not holiday accommodation) towards

(i) the upkeep of the common areas of the estate (paths, driveways and landscaped general areas) or the common areas of the block of flats (e.g. general corridors and stairwells), and

(ii) the general maintenance of the exterior of the block of flats or individual dwellings (e.g. painting and window cleaning) if the residents cannot refuse this, and

(iii) the provision of a warden, superintendent, caretaker, etc.

are exempt from VAT. Optional services supplied personally to a resident (e.g. carpet cleaning, shopping) are normally standard-rated. (C & E Notice 48, ESC 2.22).

Other services supplied. The provisions of (*b*)(vi)–(viii) above also apply to tenants of domestic accommodation.

Managing agents. Where a ground landlord is legally responsible for the provisions of services but contracts with a managing agent to supply the services on his behalf, the supply by the managing agent is to the landlord and is standard-rated.

(C & E Notice 742, paras 5.7, 5.10, 5.11).

42.17 JOINT OWNERSHIP OF LAND AND BENEFICIAL INTERESTS

Joint owners. Where more than one person owns land or receives the benefit of the consideration from the grant of an interest in land, (e.g. tenants in common), those persons are treated as a single person. If they are required to register for VAT purposes, they must register as if they were a partnership even if no legal partnership exists. (C & E Notice 742, para 7.2).

Beneficial interests. Where the benefit of the consideration for a grant, etc. accrues to the beneficial owner but that person is not the person making the grant (the legal owner) the beneficial owner is deemed to be the legal owner for VAT purposes and any input tax entitlement attributable to the grant is also transferred to the beneficial owner. [*VATA 1994, 10 Sch 8(1)*]. For example, where property is held on bare trusts, although the trustees are the legal owners, if the benefit of the income accruing from the property passes to beneficiaries it is they who are treated as the person making the grant and who can, subject to the normal rules, claim any input tax arising. (C & E Notice 742, para 7.1).

Benefit accruing to trustees. Where the benefit of the consideration for a grant, etc. accrues directly to trustees, it is the trustees who should, if required, register for VAT.

This position could be changed by provisions in *FA 1995, s 26*. C & E recognise, however, that there would be problems in implementing the revised provisions, particularly because of the requirement for joint and several liability and have issued a discussion paper entitled 'VAT Registration of Businesses Carried on by Trusts'. It is likely that the outcome of their proposals in that paper could make the revised provisions redundant.

Subject to this reservation, *with effect from a date to be appointed*, where the grant, assignment or surrender of any interest in, right over or licence to occupy land (including, in relation to Scotland, any personal right to call for or be granted such an interest, etc.), is made by more than one person (the 'grantors'), the grantors would be treated in relation to that supply (and any other supply with respect to which the grantors are the same) as a single person ('the property-owner'). The property-owner would be distinct from each of the individual grantors (who might be, for example a builder, site owner and financier or the joint beneficiaries under a bare trust) and would therefore be liable to registration (in the name of the grantors acting together) subject to the normal rules. This would apply even if any of the grantors were already registered and ensures that the individual activities of any grantor do not fall within the scope of the provisions. The grantors would be jointly and severally liable in respect of the property-owner's obligations. Any notice addressed to a registered property-owner and served on any of the grantors would be treated as served on the property-owner and therefore would apply to all the grantors.

On any change in some (but not all) of the persons treated as the grantors in relation to a supply,

- that change would be disregarded for these purposes in relation to any accounting period beginning before the change was notified to C & E; and

- any notice (including an assessment) relating to such a period served after the change is notified would apply to all those who were grantors in the period or periods to which the notice referred.

Where the legal and beneficial ownership of the land were not vested in the same person, the person owning the legal interest would be taken to be the person to whom the benefit of the consideration for the grant, etc. accrued and thus the person by whom the grant was treated as being made. However, on a joint application by the legal and beneficial owners, C & E could direct that the beneficial owners were to be so treated.

[*VATA 1994, s 51A, 10 Sch 8(2)(3); FA 1995, s 26*].

42.18   **MORTGAGES**

The mortgaging of a property, as security for borrowing money, is not regarded as a supply of the property for VAT purposes.

Sales of repossessed property.

(*a*)   *Sales under a power of sale.* Where a financial institution or any other lender sells land or buildings under a power of sale in satisfaction of a debt owed to it, there is a supply of the property by the *borrower*. If VAT is due on that supply, (e.g. because the borrower is the freehold owner of a partly constructed or new non-qualifying building or civil engineering work within 42.4 above or because the borrower has opted to tax the property), the *lender* or other person selling the property is responsible for accounting for that VAT using the procedure set out in 2.18 ACCOUNTING PERIODS AND RETURNS. The seller cannot opt to tax the property unless it has been agreed in the mortgage deed that the seller has the power to opt to tax on the borrower's behalf.

(*b*)   *Foreclosures.* If, instead of selling property under a power of sale, a lender obtains a Court Order and forecloses on land or buildings belonging to the borrower, there is a supply by the borrower to the lender of the land or building unless it is treated as an asset of a business transferred as a going concern (see 8.10 BUSINESS). If the land or building is subsequently sold, this is a supply by the lender foreclosing, who may, if he wishes, opt to tax the property.

Renting out of repossessed property. If a lender

- repossesses land or buildings, or

- appoints a *Law of Property Act* receiver without foreclosing

and rents the property out to tenants, a supply by the borrower takes place if the rental income received by the lender is used to reduce the debt owed or to service interest payments due in respect of that debt. If the supply is a taxable supply, the lender may account for VAT using the procedure set out in 2.18 ACCOUNTING PERIODS AND RETURNS.

(C & E Notice 742, paras 6.1–6.3)

See also 7.10 BAD DEBT RELIEF for recovery of VAT on costs incurred by mortgage lenders.

42.19   OTHER LAND TRANSACTIONS

Compulsory purchase. The disposal of land under a compulsory purchase order is an exempt supply unless standard-rated because it is a new building or civil engineering work within 42.4 above, holiday accommodation less than three years old (see 42.7 above) or the option to tax has been exercised (see 42.20 below). If the full amount of compensation is not known at what would otherwise be the time of supply under the normal rules, there is a tax point each time any compensation payment is received. (*SI 1995/2518, Reg 84(1)* ; C & E Notice 742, para 7.4). See, however, *L Landau (13644)* where the tribunal chairman gave the opinion that VAT generally became chargeable on the transfer of the right to dispose of the land and the taxable amount included consideration to be obtained later. Where consideration was not quantified, there was no reason why VAT should not be accounted for on an estimated amount.

Dedications of roads and sewers, transactions under planning agreements, etc. If a developer

(*a*) dedicates, for no monetary consideration, a new road to a local authority (under *Highways Act 1980* or *Roads (Scotland) Act 1984*) or a new sewer or ancillary works to a sewerage undertaker (under *Water Industries Act 1991* or *Sewerage (Scotland) Act 1968*), or

(*b*) provides goods or services free, or at a purely nominal charge, to a local or other authority (under *Town and Country Planning Acts* or other similar agreements which may loosely be described as 'planning gain agreements'), or

(*c*) transfers (usually for a nominal consideration) the *basic* amenities of estate roads, footpaths, communal parking and open space of a private housing or industrial estate to a management company which maintains them,

this does not constitute a taxable supply by the developer and no VAT is chargeable.

Included under (*b*) are buildings such as community centres or schools, amenity land or civil engineering works or an agreement to construct something on land already owned by a local authority or third party.

Any input tax incurred on such work is, however, attributable to the supply (or self-supply) of the main development (i.e. houses, shops, community centre, factory units, etc.) and recoverable or not depending upon whether that supply is taxable or exempt.

Any sums of money which have to be paid by the developer to the local authority, etc. (e.g. for the future maintenance of the building or land or as a contribution towards improvement of the infrastructure) are not consideration for a taxable supply to the developer by the local authority, etc.

(C & E Notice 742, paras 7.11–7.14).

Free supplies of land and property. The normal rules for business gifts and private use of property apply (see 47.4 and 47.5 OUTPUT TAX) where

• land is disposed of, or made available to someone for private or non-business use, free of charge, and

• the supply is standard-rated either in its own right or because the option to tax has been exercised on the property.

Transfer of a business as a going concern. See 8.10 *et seq.* BUSINESS.

Cancelling registration. VAT may be due on land and property forming part of the business assets at the close of business or on the last day of registration as if it were a business supply on that date. See 59.27 REGISTRATION.

42.20   ELECTION TO WAIVE EXEMPTION (OPTION TO TAX)

The 'election to waive exemption' provisions (more frequently known as the 'option to tax' provisions) allow supplies of certain property, which would otherwise be exempt under *VATA 1994, 9 Sch Group 1* (see 42.2 above) to be standard-rated. [*VATA 1994, 10 Sch 2(1); SI 1994/3013*]. The purpose of the option is to allow the recovery of input tax which would otherwise be lost under the partial exemption rules. The option to tax does not have effect in relation to certain supplies of property (see 42.22 below).

42.21   Effect of opting to tax

Once a person has opted to tax any property, he must charge VAT on *all* future supplies made in relation to that property which would otherwise be exempt (normal tax point rules applying) unless

*   the supply falls within 42.22 below, or

*   the option has been revoked (see below).

It is not possible, for example, to opt to tax rents but then not tax a subsequent sale of the property. The option remains effective even if the property is sold and re-acquired. It also remains effective if the person exercising the option ceases to be registered for VAT. It may, therefore, be necessary to re-register if sales proceeds would cause the registration threshold to be exceeded.

(C & E Notice 742, para 8.2).

Revoking the option to tax. Once made, the option to tax can only be revoked in the following limited circumstances.

(*a*)   It can be revoked with effect from the date on which it has effect provided that

*   written consent of C & E is obtained within three months from that date;

*   no VAT has become chargeable and no credit for input tax has been claimed by virtue of the election; and

*   the property has not been sold together with a business (or part of a business) which has been treated as neither a supply of goods nor services under the rules relating to the transfer of a business as a going concern (see 8.10 *et seq.* BUSINESS).

(*b*)   The option to tax may be revoked where more than 20 years have elapsed since the date on which it had effect. Revocation takes effect from the date on which written consent is given by C & E or such later date as they specify in their written consent.

[*VATA 1994, 10 Sch 3(4)(5); SI 1995/279*].

Effect on existing leases. Unless the lease specifically provides otherwise, the lessor or licensor has a right to add VAT to the rent agreed under the lease following an option to tax. [*VATA 1994, s 89*].

If an election has been made but, under the terms of the lease, VAT cannot be added, any rent received should be treated as VAT-inclusive and the VAT element calculated by multiplying the rent received the appropriate VAT fraction (currently 7/47). (C & E Notice 742, para 8.6).

Groups of companies. Where a company is a member of a VAT group (see 31.2 GROUPS OF COMPANIES), the supply of any property it makes must be standard-rated if any member of the group has opted to tax the property, whether before or after joining the group. If a company leaves a group but retains an interest in a property on which the group would have charged VAT, the company must standard-rate any supplies of that property which it subsequently makes. [*VATA 1994, 10 Sch 2(1), 3(7)*]. (C & E Notice 742, para 8.3).

De Voil Indirect Tax Service. See V4.115.

42.22   **Supplies not affected by an option**

There are some supplies which an option to tax does not affect and which remain exempt even though the option has been exercised on the property in question. These are as follows.

(*a*)   **Dwellings, etc.** Any supply in relation to a building (or part of a building) intended for use as a 'dwelling' or a number of dwellings or solely for a 'relevant residential purpose'. See 42.1 above for the meaning of '*dwelling*' and '*relevant residential purpose*'.

However, for supplies made on or after 19 March 1997 (and previously by concession for supplies from 12 February 1996 onwards, see C & E News Release 9/96, 13 February 1996 and C & E Notice 48, ESC 2.16), this restriction does not apply and an option to tax can still be applied where

- the person making the grant and the person to whom it is made agree in writing, at or before the time of the grant, that the option to tax is to apply; and

- at the time the supply is made, the person purchasing the property intends to convert it from a non-residential building to residential use for the purpose of making a supply which is zero-rated under 42.48(*c*) below.

A supply of a building (or part of a building) cannot be taken as intended for use for a relevant residential purpose unless, before it is made, the person to whom the supply is made gives the supplier a certificate to that effect. See 42.51 below.

(*b*)   **Charitable use.** A supply in relation to a building (or part of a building) intended for use solely for a '*relevant charitable purpose*' (see 42.1 above) other than as an office. Use of part of the building as an office may be ignored if merely incidental. (C & E Notice 742, para 8.4). A supply of a building (or part of a building) cannot be taken as intended for use for a relevant charitable purpose unless, before it is made, the person to whom the supply is made gives the supplier a certificate to that effect. See 42.51 below.

(*c*)   **Residential caravans.** A supply of a pitch for a residential caravan. For this purpose, a caravan is not a residential caravan if residence in it throughout the year is prevented by the terms of a covenant, statutory planning consent or similar permission (i.e. the caravan cannot lawfully be occupied as a permanent residence).

(*d*)   **Residential houseboats.** A supply of facilities for the mooring (including anchoring or berthing) of a residential houseboat. For this purpose, a houseboat is a boat or other floating structure designed or adapted for use solely as a place of permanent habitation and not having means of, or capable of being readily adapted for, self-propulsion. A houseboat is not a residential houseboat if residence in it throughout the year is prevented by the terms of a covenant, statutory planning consent or similar permission (i.e. the houseboat cannot lawfully be occupied as a permanent residence).

(*e*) **Housing associations.** A supply to a 'relevant housing association' which has given the supplier a certificate stating that the land is to be used (after any necessary demolition work) for the construction of a building or buildings for use as a 'dwelling' or a number of dwellings or solely for a 'relevant residential purpose'. See 42.1 above for the meaning of '*relevant housing association*', '*dwelling*' and '*relevant residential purpose*'.

(*f*) **DIY builders.** A supply of land to an individual where the land is to be used for the construction, otherwise than in the course or furtherance of a business carried on by him, of a building intended for use by him as a dwelling.

(*g*) **Certain supplies used other than for taxable business supplies.** In relation to a supply made on or after 19 March 1997 (other than a supply arising from a 'relevant pre-commencement grant', see below), where

(i) the supply arises from a grant made by a person (the '*grantor*') who was a developer of the land; and

(ii) the grant is made in relation to land, a building or part of a building which is treated as a capital item owned by the grantor for the purposes of the capital goods scheme (see 10.2 CAPITAL GOODS SCHEME);

(iii) the grant is made during the period of adjustment of input tax for the capital item under the capital goods scheme (see 10.3 CAPITAL GOODS SCHEME); and

(iv) at the time of the grant, the grantor or a 'person responsible for financing the grantor's development' intended or expected that the property would, at any time during that period of adjustment, be occupied, or continue to be occupied, other than wholly or mainly for 'eligible purposes' by

- the grantor;

- a person responsible for financing the grantor's development; or

- a person connected with either such person under *ICTA 1988, s 839*, see 69.3 VALUATION.

Occupation for '*eligible purposes*' means

- occupation by a taxable person for the purpose of making supplies which are in the course or furtherance of a business and of such a description that he is entitled to credit for any wholly attributable input tax;

- occupation by a statutory body within *VATA 1994, s 33* (see 43.2 LOCAL AUTHORITIES AND STATUTORY BODIES) to the extent that the body occupies the land for non-business purposes; or

- occupation by a government department.

For these purposes, where occupation is by a person who is not a taxable person but whose supplies are treated for the purposes of *VATA 1994* as made by another person who is a taxable person, those two persons are to be regarded as a single taxable person.

A '*person responsible for financing the grantor's development*' is a person who has

- provided finance for the grantor's development of the land; or

- entered into any agreement, arrangement or understanding (whether or not legally enforceable) to provide finance for the grantor's development of the land.

Providing funds is widely defined. It includes directly or indirectly providing funds *either* to meet the whole (or part) of the cost of acquisition, construction or reconstruction, etc. of the land or building in question *or* to discharge the whole (or part) of any liability incurred in raising funds to meet that cost. It also includes directly or indirectly procuring the provision of funds by another person for either of those purposes. The funds may be provided by way of loan, guarantee or other security, consideration for a share issue used to raise the funds or any other transfer of assets or value as a consequence of which the funds are made available.

Any contribution to the cost of the development is likely to be considered to be financing it. The purpose of this restriction on the option to tax is to deal with the situation where a person funds the purchase or construction of a building with a view to occupying it for VAT-exempt or non-business purposes. It is not intended to disturb ordinary arms-length commercial leasing arrangements and genuine speculative property development. In these circumstances a tenant simply paying rent is not providing finance for the landlord's development. (C & E Notice 742, para 8.4). See also *Winterthur Life UK Ltd (No 2) (15785)*.

A *'relevant pre-commencement grant'* is a grant made

• before 26 November 1996; or

• after 25 November 1996 and before 30 November 1999 whose terms were the subject of a written agreement entered into before 26 November 1996.

(*h*) **Supplies between connected persons.** After 29 November 1994 and before 27 November 1996, a grant where

(i) the grantor and grantee were connected persons under the provisions of *ICTA 1988, s 839* (see 69.3 VALUATION); and

(ii) either of them was not a fully taxable person at the end of the prescribed accounting period in which the grant was made, i.e. not entitled to credit for input tax on all supplies, acquisitions and importations in that period (apart from input tax which is normally excluded from credit).

By concession, with retrospective effect from 30 November 1994, C & E could treat as a fully taxable person for these purposes any person who was able to recover 80% or more of input tax incurred in the VAT period in which the grant was made or would have been able to if it were not for exempt supplies of property. (C & E Notice 48, ESC 2.19). Additionally, where a small self-administered pension scheme owned trading premises which were occupied by an associated trading company, the pension scheme could be treated as a fully taxable person. In such a case, the disapplication of the option to tax only applied if the associated trading company was not fully taxable (applying the 80% concession if necessary). C & E would also consider individual cases where businesses were not able to take advantage of the concession but where the grant had a clearly demonstrable ordinary commercial motivation and justification and was not motivated by tax avoidance. (C & E Notice 48, ESC 2.20; C & E News Release 62/95, 21 December 1995).

(*i*) **Transfers of going concerns.** In certain circumstances, a supply of property can be treated as part of the transfer of a business as a going concern, in which case it will not be a supply for VAT purposes and is not affected by the option. See 8.12 BUSINESS.

Where a grant within (*a*) to (*f*) above gives rise to supplies at different times after the making of the grant (e.g. rent), the liability of each of those supplies is determined at the time when the supply is made rather than by reference to the time of the original grant.

Supplies partially affected by an option. Where an option to tax a property has been exercised and the option cannot have effect in relation to part of that property (e.g. a shop with a flat to be used as a dwelling over it), the consideration for any supply must be apportioned between the standard-rated element and the exempt or zero-rated part. [*VATA 1994, 8 Sch Group 5, Note 10, 10 Sch 9; SI 1995/279; SI 1995/280*]. The apportionment must be made on an objective basis which gives a fair and reasonable result. It need not be approved by C & E in advance but will be subject to inspection and approval during the normal control visit. (C & E Notice 742, para 8.4).

[*VATA 1994, s 96(10A), 10 Sch 2(2)(2A)(2B)(3)(3AA)(3A), 3(3A)(7A)(8)(8A), 9; FA 1997, ss 35–37; SI 1994/3013; SI 1995/279; SI 1997/51*].

42.23   **Scope of the option**

Land. An option to tax land has effect in relation to any land specified, or of a description specified, in the election. [*VATA 1994, 10 Sch 3(2)*]. It does not affect any adjoining land (but see below for special provisions relating to agricultural land before 1 March 1995) or any building later constructed on the land. Land includes civil engineering works which are part of the land. Land within the curtilage of a building is treated as part of the building (see below). (C & E Notice 742, para 8.5).

Buildings. Where an election is made in relation to, or to part of, a building (or planned building) it has effect in relation to the whole of the building and the land within its curtilage. For these purposes, the following are taken to be a single building.

(*a*)   Buildings linked internally or by a covered walkway.

(*b*)   Complexes consisting of a number of units grouped around a fully enclosed concourse.

[*VATA 1994, 10 Sch 3(3); SI 1995/279*].

Land within the curtilage of a building is that lying immediately around it and which forms the grounds of the building. This may include forecourts, yards, parking bays and landscaped areas.

When a building is destroyed or demolished, the option ceases to apply to the land on which it stands. There is no obligation to opt to tax a new building constructed on the site.

(C & E Notice 742, para 8.5).

Agricultural land and buildings. It is possible to opt to tax discrete parcels of agricultural land without this having any effect on adjoining agricultural land. When notifying an option to tax a discrete area of land, a map or plan detailing the land should be enclosed. (C & E Notice 742, para 8.5).

42.24   **How to opt**

Prior permission where previous exempt supply. Where, after 31 July 1989 and before the date the option is to take effect (see below), an exempt supply of a property has (or will be) made, a person cannot opt to tax that property unless either of the following applies.

(*a*)   He has obtained prior written permission to opt from C & E. The letter to C & E seeking permission should give details of

•   the date from which the election is to have effect;

•   the use which has, and will be, made of the property; and

•   a suggested attribution of the input tax incurred since 31 July 1989 between the exempt use of the property and the intended taxable use.

If C & E are satisfied that the proposed attribution is fair and reasonable, they will give *permission* to opt to tax on the date stated. The written notification procedure below must then be followed. Permission from C & E must not be treated as having exercised the option to tax. (C & E Notice 742, para 8.8).

(*b*) Any of the following conditions for automatic permission specified in C & E Notice 742, para 8.6 (which have the force of law) are met.

- It is a mixed development and the only exempt supplies (sales, leasing or lettings) have been in relation to the dwellings.

- Where the person seeking to opt does not wish to recover any input tax on goods, services or acquisitions received before the option to tax has effect; *and*

  (i) the consideration for exempt supplies up to the date the option to tax is to take effect has been solely by way of rent; and

  (ii) the only input tax sought to be recovered after the option to tax takes effect is on day-to-day overheads.

- Where the person seeking to opt does wish to recover input tax incurred before the option to tax takes effect but

  (i) this input tax relates solely to tax charged by a tenant or tenants on the surrender of a lease;

  (ii) the building or relevant part has since been unoccupied; and

  (iii) there will be no further exempt supplies of the property.

- The exempt supplies have been incidental to the main use of the property, for example the siting of an advertising hoarding within the curtilage of a building.

[*VATA 1994, 10 Sch 3(9)*].

Written notification. Whether or not prior permission is required as above, to have legal effect, written notification of the option to tax must be given to C & E, together with such other information as they require, within 30 days of the date of election (or such longer period as C & E allow). (Note that where an election made before 1 March 1995 did not require to be notified to C & E because the total value for all supplies of the property covered by the election were expected to be less than £20,000 in the following twelve months, such an election remains valid after 1 March 1995 and does not require written notification after that date.) [*VATA 1994, 10 Sch 3(6); SI 1995/279*].

The written notification must state unambiguously what property is covered by the option to tax and the date from which the option has effect. The notification should either be in the following format or contain all the same information.

Notification of election to waive exemption (option to tax)

1. Registration details

Trading name

VAT registration number

Address

2. Election details

Date of election

Property/properties covered by the election

(Give full postal address (including postcodes), building names and supply highlighted plans/map where appropriate)

I hereby confirm that I have read the relevant Chapter in Public Notice 742 and that the information provided is correct.

I have the authority to sign this form on behalf of the above registration.

Signature

Name

Position   Date

(C & E Notice 742, para 8.6, Appendix H).

Effective date of option to tax. An option to tax has effect from the date on which it is made (or such later date specified in the election). Where the election was made before 1 November 1989, it had effect from 1 August 1989 (or such later date specified in the election). [*VATA 1994, 10 Sch 3(1)*].

42.25   Recovery of input tax

Input tax incurred from the date of the option to tax. Once the option to tax has been made, the supplier (i.e. the landlord or vendor) can recover input tax on any related expenditure subject to the normal rules.

Input tax incurred before the date of the option to tax. Recovery of input tax depends upon whether or not there have been any exempt supplies in relation to the property after 31 July 1989 and before the date of the option to tax.

- Where there have been no such exempt supplies, input tax incurred in relation to the property after 31 July 1989 can be recovered, subject to the normal rules.

- Where any such exempt supply has been made (or is intended to be made before the proposed date for option to have effect), written permission must be obtained from C & E before the option to tax is exercised unless the conditions for automatic permission apply (see 42.24 above). If permission is received and the option exercised, application can be made to C & E to recover a fair and reasonable proportion of the VAT incurred in the period from 1 August 1989 to the date the option has effect, taking into account the exempt use of the property and the intended taxable use. (In practice, where written permission is required from C & E, the application should include a suggested attribution of input tax between exempt and taxable use, see 42.24 above.)

[*VATA 1994, 10 Sch 2(4)–(9); SI 1995/279*].

Repayment of input tax. Where input tax has been reclaimed in relation to the option to tax but the option cannot have effect under 42.22 above (e.g. because the property is sold to a housing association), any input tax claimed in relation to the option is repayable. (C & E Notice 742, para 8.4).

Connected persons. Where the option to tax could not be applied to certain transactions between connected persons after 29 November 1994 and before 27 November 1996 (see 42.22(*h*) above),

- input tax incurred before 30 November 1994 but after the date of the option to tax was deductible (even if the ultimate supply was exempt because the option to tax was disapplied) although adjustments may have been required under the CAPITAL GOODS SCHEME (10);

- input tax incurred after 29 November 1994 was irrecoverable (subject to the partial exemption *de minimis* rules) where it was known at the time of incurring the input tax that the option would not apply (the input tax being attributed to the future exempt supply); and

- input tax incurred after 29 November 1994 was deductible where, at the time of incurring the input tax, it was intended to make a taxable supply by virtue of the option. However, where the option could not subsequently apply at the time of the grant, any input tax which had been claimed was repayable. (C & E Notice 742, para 8.4).

Brewers' tenanted properties. Agreement has been reached between C & E and the Brewers' Society on the deduction of input tax in respect of tied tenanted licensed houses containing a residential element where the brewer has elected to waive exemption on the rents from all its tenanted properties. See C & E Notice 700/57/94 for full details.

De Voil Indirect Tax Service. See V3.453.

42.26   **RESIDENTIAL AND CHARITABLE BUILDINGS: CHANGE OF USE**

Disposal, part disposal or letting. Where, after 31 March 1989,

(*a*)   a person receives a zero-rated grant or other supply of a building (or part) intended solely for use for a 'relevant residential purpose' or a 'relevant charitable purpose' (see 42.1 above), and

(*b*)   within the period of ten years beginning with the day on which the building was completed that person grants an 'interest in or right over' or 'licence to occupy' the building (or part) so that it is no longer intended for such a relevant purpose,

the grant is treated as a business supply taxable at the standard rate. An apportionment can be made where as a result of the grant, only part of the building originally zero-rated ceases to be used for a relevant purpose.

A building is to be taken as '*completed*' when an architect issues a certificate of practical completion in relation to it or it is fully occupied, whichever happens first.

Change of use without disposal. Where, after 31 March 1989, (*a*) above applies and, within the period of ten years beginning with the day on which the building is 'completed' the person uses the building (or part) for a non-relevant purpose, he is treated as having made, at that time, a standard-rated self-supply in the course or furtherance of a business. The deemed value of the supply is such that the VAT chargeable on it is equal to the amount of VAT that would have been chargeable on the relevant zero-rated supply if the building (or part) no longer used for a qualifying purpose had not been zero-rated at that earlier time (i.e. the value of the supply is not adjusted to current market value and changes in VAT rates are ignored).

A building is to be taken as '*completed*' when an architect issues a certificate of practical completion in relation to it or it is fully occupied, whichever happens first.

[*VATA 1994, 10 Sch 1*].

See 42.1 above for '*relevant residential purpose*', '*relevant charitable purpose*', and '*interest in or right over*' and '*licence to occupy*' a building.

De Voil Indirect Tax Service. See V3.248.

42.27   **THE DEVELOPER'S SELF-SUPPLY CHARGE**

FA 1989 introduced a self-supply charge where non-domestic buildings and civil engineering works were put to an exempt use within ten years of completion. The charge was abolished for all developments commencing on or after 1 March 1995 and phased out for earlier developments over the period to 1 March 1997, on which date there was an automatic self-supply on certain buildings.

Scope of the provisions. Subject to below, the self-supply provisions applied to

(i) any building neither designed as a 'dwelling' or number of dwellings nor intended solely for use for a 'relevant residential purpose' or a 'relevant charitable purpose' (see 42.1 above for definitions);

(ii) any civil engineering work other than a work necessary for the development of a permanent park for residential caravans; and

(iii) certain reconstructions, enlargements and extensions of existing buildings or works within (i) or (ii) above (see 42.29 below).

The provisions did not apply

(*a*) to a building within (i) above or work within (ii) above, construction of which commenced before 1 August 1989 or after 28 February 1995;

(*b*) in relation to the person who constructed a building if, before 21 June 1988, he incurred a legally binding obligation to make a grant or assignment of a major interest in the building (or part of it) or its site;

(*c*) in relation to the person who constructed a building if, before 21 June 1988, he incurred a legally binding obligation to construct the building (or any development of which it formed part) provided planning permission for the construction was granted before that date and the person made a grant or assignment of a major interest in the building or its site before 21 June 1993;

(*d*) in relation to a building or work if, before 21 June 1988, a legally binding obligation was incurred to make supplies in relation to it under what is now *VATA 1994, 8 Sch Group 5, Item 2* (see 42.31 below);

(*e*) to a reconstruction, etc. within (iii) above which was commenced before 1 January 1992;

(*f*) where, after completion and before what would otherwise have been the occasion of charge under the self-supply provisions, there had already been a standard-rated grant of the fee simple (freehold interest) in the building or work which fell within 42.4(*b*) or (*d*) above;

(*g*) if construction of a building or work within (i) or (ii) above commenced before 1 March 1995 but had not been completed by that date and the developer

(i) made no claim after that date for credit for input tax, entitlement to which was dependent upon his being treated in due course as having made a self-supply within these provisions (i.e. input tax was only recovered under the agreed partial exemption method); and

(ii) either had made no such claim prior to 1 March 1995 or repaid to C & E any input tax so claimed. (Any repayment had to be made on the VAT return for the quarter ending 31 May, 30 June or 31 July 1995 as appropriate.)

[*VATA 1994, 10 Sch 5(2)(3)(3A), 13 Sch 10; SI 1995/279*]. (C & E Business Brief 7/95, 4 April 1995).

For the above purposes, C & E accepted that construction work commenced when a meaningful start was made followed by significant on-going work. The granting of planning permission, the exchange of contracts, and payments to contractors were among the matters to be taken into account. Demolition and site clearance were not themselves considered to be the start of work, but pile driving and other foundation work was. (C & E Notice 742, paras 9.6, 9.8).

When the charge arose. A self-supply charge arose on the earlier of the following dates.

(A) On the *first* occasion after 31 July 1989 on which the 'developer'

    (i) granted or assigned an 'interest in or right over' or a 'licence to occupy' the building or work (or any part of it) which was an exempt supply (even if following initial taxable use); or

    (ii) occupied the building or used the work in connection with an exempt business activity when not a 'fully taxable person' (or, if he was a member of a VAT group, when the representative member of that group was not a fully taxable person).

(B) 1 March 1997.

[*VATA 1994, 10 Sch 5(1); SI 1995/279*].

See 42.1 above for the meaning of '*interest in or right over*' and '*licence to occupy*'.

By concession, no charge arose under (B) above on 1 March 1997 where

- construction of the building or civil engineering work was still in progress on that date and the value of the self-supply (see 42.28 below) including all construction costs incurred before and after that date were less than £100,000; or

- a building or civil engineering work was completed before 1 March 1995 and was fully occupied or used by a government department, health authority, local authority or similar body for non-business purposes;

- a building or civil engineering work was completed before 1 March 1995 and was fully occupied or used before 1 March 1997;

- a building or civil engineering work was completed before 1 March 1995, was the subject of an option to tax, and input tax was provisionally recovered in anticipation of granting a taxable interest.

(C & E Notice 48, ESC 2.23; C & E Notice 742, para 9.19B, Appendix J).

'*Developer*' in relation to a building or work meant the person who constructed it, ordered it to be constructed or financed the construction, in either case with a view to granting an interest in or right over or licence to occupy it (or any part of it) or occupying or using it (or any part of it) for his own purposes. Where the developer was a member of a VAT group (see 31.2 GROUPS OF COMPANIES) and granted an interest in or right over or licence to occupy the building or work to another member of the group, any member of the group was treated as the developer of that building or work. [*VATA 1994, 10 Sch 5(5)–(7)*].

'*Fully taxable person*'. A person was a fully taxable person throughout a prescribed accounting period in relation to any building or work if, at the end of that period, he was entitled to credit for input tax on all supplies to, and acquisition and importations by, him in the period (other than any input tax specifically excluded from credit under the normal provisions). Alternatively, he was treated as fully taxable if the building or work was not used by him at any time during the period in, or in connection with, making an exempt supply of goods or services. [*VATA 1994, 10 Sch 5(4); SI 1995/279*].

For a consideration of the application of the self-supply provisions, see *C & E Commrs v Robert Gordon's College HL, [1995] STC 1093*.

Part qualifying buildings. Where part of a building fell within these provisions and part did not (e.g. a shop with a flat over it) the supply had to be apportioned. [*VATA 1994, 8 Sch Group 5, Note 10, 10 Sch 9; SI 1995/279; SI 1995/280*].

De Voil Indirect Tax Service. See V3.251–254.

42.28   **The VAT treatment**

Input tax on the construction. Subject to the normal rules, where a VAT-registered person realised that, even though he was not going to make a taxable supply of the property or use it for a taxable purpose, he was going to make a self-supply, he could deduct input tax incurred in the construction of the building or work in full (subject to the normal rules). This included any VAT charged on the grant of the land to him, VAT charged on goods and services supplied to him for the purposes of construction and any VAT accounted for on a self-supply of construction services (see 42.43 below). (C & E Notice 742, para 9.25).

Charge to VAT on the self-supply. Where a charge arose under the provisions in 42.27 above, the interest in or right over or licence to occupy the building or work held by the developer was treated as supplied *to* him for his business purposes and supplied *by* him at the standard rate in the course or furtherance of that business. This supply was treated as taking place on 1 March 1997 where 42.27(B) above applied. Otherwise where 42.27(A) above applied it was treated as taking place on the last day of the prescribed accounting period during which the chargeable occasion occurred or, if later, on the last day of the prescribed accounting period during which the building or work became substantially ready for occupation or use. [*VATA 1994, 10 Sch 6(1)(9); SI 1995/279*].

Value of self-supply. The supply was taken to be a taxable supply, the value of which was the aggregate of the following.

(*a*)   The value of grants, relating to the land on which the building or work was constructed, made to the developer. This was normally the amounts paid, or due to be paid, for the interest in the land, excluding VAT, stamp duty and Land Registry costs. (C & E Notice 742, para 9.21). The following were specifically excluded.

•   Where construction of the building or work commenced before 1 January 1992, any rents the amount of which could not be ascertained by the developer at the time of the self-supply (e.g. where the rent payable to the freeholder was expressed as a percentage of the rents the developer might receive in the future).

•   In relation to developments commencing after 31 December 1991, any rent due after the time of the self-supply, and any rent already paid attributable to a building on the land which had subsequently been demolished.

•   In relation to developments commencing after 31 December 1991, the value of any grants made pursuant to a developmental tenancy, lease or licence (which after that date were standard-rated, see below).

(*b*)   The value of all taxable supplies of goods and services, other than any that were zero-rated, made for or in connection with the construction of the building or work. When calculating a self-supply charge automatically triggered at 1 March 1997, only costs incurred to that date had to be taken into account.

Included were builders' and contractors' services (whether VAT-registered or not), materials used in the construction and fitting out, professional and management fees, demolition and site clearance, site security, equipment hire and landscaping. Also included was the value of any self-supply of construction services (see 42.43 below) and the standard-rated cost of implementing any planning gain agreement (see 42.19 above). By concession, after 30 September 1992, only the value of supplies made to the developer had to be included in the calculation (e.g. fitting out work supplied to the prospective tenant under a separate contract was ignored).

In the case of a fixed price contract, the full price had to be included, even if there were retentions. If the price of the contract was subsequently varied, VAT was adjusted on the return for the later period in which the adjustment became known.

Where the value of the self-supply would, as calculated, be less than £100,000, no supply was treated as having been made under these provisions.

[*VATA 1994, 10 Sch 6(2)(5)(6); SI 1995/279*]. (C & E Notice 742, para 9.20; C & E Notice 748, ESC 22 now withdrawn).

Change in the rate of VAT. Where there was an *increase* in the rate of VAT during the period of construction, VAT due under (*b*) above at the time of the self-supply had to be accounted for at the old (lower) rate on the supply of goods actually delivered, or services actually performed, before the date of change. VAT had to be accounted for on the remaining goods and services within (*b*) and the cost of the land under (*a*) above at the new (higher) rate. [*VATA 1994, 10 Sch 6(3)(4)*].

Input tax deduction on the self-supply. The VAT accounted for on the self-supply could be treated as input tax. It could not, however, be attributed to the self-supply. Instead it was recoverable to the extent that the building or work was used for making taxable supplies. If, therefore, a building was only used to make exempt supplies, none of the VAT was recoverable. Any of this VAT recovered is also subject to adjustment in later years under the provisions of the CAPITAL GOODS SCHEME (10) where the extent to which the building is used for making taxable supplies changes. (C & E Notice 742, para 9.7).

Developmental tenancies, leases and licences. In relation to constructions beginning after 31 December 1991, where a developer was a tenant, lessee or licencee:

- If he became liable to a self-supply under 42.27(A) above, he immediately had to notify his landlord, lessor or licensor of

  (i) the date on which he had accounted for VAT on the self-supply; and

  (ii) in a case falling within 42.29(*b*) below, the 'appropriate fraction' as there shown.

  From that date, the tenancy, lease or licence is treated as being a developmental tenancy, lease or licence and any supply pursuant to it (e.g. future rent payable to the landlord, lessor or licensor) is standard-rated in full or, where (ii) applied, to the extent of the appropriate fraction.

  If the developer assigns his lease, etc. to a third party, the landlord's supplies to the new tenant will also be standard-rated because they are under the same lease. The grant of a new lease by the landlord or the sale of his interest in the property is not affected by the provisions.

- If he became liable to a self-supply under 42.27(B) above on 1 March 1997, rents due under the tenancy, etc. are exempt (unless the landlord has opted to tax).

[*VATA 1994, 9 Sch Group 1, Item 1(b), Note 7, 10 Sch 7; SI 1995/279*]. (C & E Notice 742, para 9.16).

42.29   **Reconstructions, extensions and enlargements**

The provisions in 42.27 and 42.28 above applied in relation to the following reconstructions, enlargements and extensions as if

- references to the building or work were references to the reconstructed, enlarged or extended building or work, and

- reference to construction were references to reconstruction, enlargement or extension.

There was, however, no similar relief to that for new buildings where there had been a standard-rated supply of the fee simple of a redeveloped building before the developer's supply was triggered (see 42.27(*f*) above).

(*a*) A reconstruction, enlargement or 'extension' of an existing building which was commenced after 31 December 1991 and before 1 March 1995 and which was carried out wholly or partly on land ('new building land') adjoining the curtilage of the existing building.

This did *not* apply if the developer had held an interest in at least 75% of all the land (new and existing) throughout the ten years ending with the last day of the prescribed accounting period during which the reconstructed, enlarged or extended building became substantially ready for occupation.

Where the reconstruction, etc. fell within this provision but did not also fall within (*c*) below, the reference in 42.28(*a*) above to the value of grants relating to land on which the building was constructed was taken as a reference to the value of grants relating to the new business land (i.e. the self-supply charge was based on the cost of works and the new land).

The full cost of the new building land had to be brought into charge, not just that part on which the extension, etc. was built. See *Shutes, Robinson & Ling (Doctors), [1993] VATTR 459 (11552)* where, in addition to the extension, part of the land was used as a car park and the remainder was landscaped.

(*b*) A reconstruction, enlargement or extension of an existing building which was commenced after 31 December 1991 and before 1 March 1995 as a result of which the gross external floor area of the reconstructed, enlarged or extended building (excluding any floor area on new building land) exceeded the gross external floor area of the existing building by not less than 20% of the gross external floor area of the existing building.

This did *not* apply if the developer had

- held an interest in at least 75% of the land throughout the ten years ending with the last day of the prescribed accounting period during which the reconstructed, enlarged or extended building became substantially ready for occupation; or

- previously accounted for VAT on the existing building under a self-supply charge.

Where the reconstruction, etc. fell within this provision but did not also fall within (*c*) below, for the purposes of calculating the value of the grants of land under 42.28(*a*) above, any rent paid by the developer before the commencement of reconstruction, etc. could be deducted from the cost of the land. The net figure was then multiplied by the 'appropriate fraction' i.e.

$$\frac{A}{B}$$

where

A = the additional gross external floor area resulting from the reconstruction, etc. (excluding any floor area on new building land under (*a*) above)

B = the gross external floor area of the building as reconstructed, etc. (excluding any floor area on new building land)

The gross external floor area was measured by taking the area of the building, including internal and external walls, less any parts of the building such as lift shafts and tanks which could not be inhabited. It was not the 'footprint' of the building (i.e. the ground floor alone). (C & E Notice 742, para 9.17).

(*c*)   A reconstruction of an existing building which was commenced after 31 December 1991 and before 1 March 1995 and in the course of which at least 80% of the area of the floor structures of the existing building were removed.

This does *not* apply if the developer had previously accounted for VAT on the building under a self-supply charge.

For the purposes of calculating the value of the grants of land under 42.28(*a*) above, any rent paid by the developer before the commencement of reconstruction could be deducted from the cost of the land.

(*d*)   A reconstruction, enlargement or extension of a civil engineering work which was commenced after 31 December 1991 and before 1 March 1995 and which was carried out wholly or partly on land ('new land') adjoining the land on, or in, which the existing work was situated.

This did *not* apply if the developer had held an interest in at least 75% of the land on which the work stood or was constructed throughout the ten years ending with the last day of the prescribed accounting period during which the reconstructed, enlarged or extended work became substantially ready for use.

Where the reconstruction, etc. fell within this provision, the reference in 42.28(*a*) above to the value of grants relating to land on which the work was constructed was to be taken as a reference to the value of grants relating to the new land (i.e. the self-supply charge was based on the cost of works and the new land).

'*Extension*' included an annex having external access to the existing building.

[*VATA 1994, 10 Sch 5(2)(8)–(10), 6(6)–(8); SI 1995/279*].

Partnerships. Where, under (*a*), (*b*) or (*d*) above, the developer was a partnership, the provisions did not apply if the partnership had held a 75% interest throughout the relevant ten-year period even though individual partners may have changed. (C & E Notice 742, para 9.3).

PART III BUILDING AND CONSTRUCTION

42.30   SUPPLIES OF GOODS AND SERVICES IN THE CONSTRUCTION INDUSTRY

Zero-rating normally applies to the following.

(*a*)   Services supplied in the course of construction of new dwellings, certain other relevant residential and charitable buildings. See 42.31 below.

(*b*)   Services supplied in the course of construction of civil engineering work for the development of a new permanent residential caravan park. See 42.32 below.

(*c*)   Services supplied to a relevant housing association in the course of converting non-residential buildings into residential buildings. See 42.33 below.

(*d*)   Approved alterations to protected buildings. See 42.34 below.

(*e*)   Certain building materials and other goods incorporated into a building by a builder who is also supplying zero-rated services within (*a*)-(*d*) above. See 42.37 and 42.38 below.

All work that is not specifically zero-rated is standard-rated. This includes

- the construction of a new building not within (a)-(d) above;

- repair and maintenance work; and

- (with certain exceptions) work done to an existing building, including any alteration, extension, reconstruction, enlargement or annexation.

(C & E Notice 708, paras 2.1, 2.2).

De Voil Indirect Tax Service. See V4.237–V4.242.

42.31   **Services supplied in the course of zero-rated construction of dwellings and relevant residential and charitable buildings**

Services supplied 'in the course of construction' of a building

(a)   designed as a 'dwelling' or number of dwellings, or

(b)   intended for use solely for a 'relevant residential purpose' or 'relevant charitable purpose'

and which relate to the construction, are zero-rated. Specifically excluded (and therefore standard-rated) are

- the services of an architect, surveyor or any person acting as a consultant or in a supervisory capacity; and

- the hire of goods and the private use of goods.

See 42.1 above for definitions of '*in the course of construction*', '*dwelling*', '*relevant residential purpose*', and '*relevant charitable purpose*'.

With certain exceptions, '*constructing a building*' specifically excludes converting, reconstructing, altering, enlarging and extending an existing building or constructing an annexe to an existing building. See 42.1 above for full details.

[*VATA 1994, 8 Sch Group 5, Item 2(a) and Note (20); SI 1995/280*].

See 42.35 below for examples of services zero-rated under these provisions and 42.36 below for services not regarded as within these provisions and therefore standard-rated.

Annexes. Given the definitions of 'dwelling' and 'constructing a building' (see 42.1 above), most small additional accommodation built on to, or in the grounds of, an existing house (commonly known as 'granny annexes') is standard-rated even where the new structure is entirely separate from the original building. (C & E Notice 708, para 2.5).

The definition of 'constructing a building' specifically includes, however, the addition of an annex to an existing building for use for relevant charitable purposes provided certain conditions are met (see 42.1 above). Such annexes may be zero-rated. The intention of this relief is to treat a charity annex connected by a door or corridor to another building in the same way as a fully independent structure separate from an existing building. As a guide, the new annex should be capable of fulfilling the function for which it was designed if the connection or corridor were to be closed. The provision does not zero-rate an enlargement or extension to an existing charity building. (C & E Notice 708, para 2.8).

Garages. The construction of a building designed as a dwelling or number of dwellings includes the construction of a garage. The dwelling and the garage must be constructed at the same time and the garage must be intended for occupation with the dwelling or one of the dwellings. [*VATA 1994, 8 Sch Group 5, Note (3); SI 1995/280*].

Civil engineering work. The supply of civil engineering work in the course of construction of a new dwelling or other qualifying building under these provisions can be zero-rated if within the 'curtilage' (see 42.1 above) of the dwelling or on the site of the development. This covers the construction of new roads and the provision of mains water, sewerage, gas and electricity up to the nearest point of connection. (Where a mains connection point for electricity, gas or water is beyond the perimeter, zero-rating can be extended to the work required to make the connection to the nearest existing supply.) (C & E Notice 708, paras 2.3, 11.7). The civil engineering work should be carried out contemporaneously or consecutively in relation to the new building and have a substantial connection with it (*C & E Commrs v Rannoch School Ltd CS, [1993] STC 389*). The fact that a dwelling has not been sold does not prevent the work from qualifying for zero-rating (*Lamberts Construction Ltd (8882)*).

Part qualifying buildings and services. Where part of a building qualifies under the above provisions and part does not (e.g. shop premises with a flat over them), a supply of services relating only to the qualifying part of the building is zero-rated and, similarly, a supply of services relating only to the non-qualifying part is standard-rated. In the case of any other supply, an apportionment must be made to determine the extent to which the supply is zero-rated.

Similarly, where a service falling within the above provisions is supplied in part in relation to the construction of a building and in part for other purposes (e.g. a mixed site development including new dwellings and shops), an apportionment may be made to determine the extent to which the supply is to be treated as falling within the above provisions.

[*VATA 1994, 8 Sch Group 5, Notes (10) and (11); SI 1995/280*].

Recipient of services. Where all or part of a building is intended for use solely for a relevant residential purpose or a relevant charitable purpose, no supply of services relating to the building (or part of it) can be taken for the above purposes as relating to a building intended for such use unless it is made to a person who intends to use the building (or part) for such a purpose. [*VATA 1994, 8 Sch Group 5, Note (12); SI 1995/280*]. The main effect of this is that, although the main contractor can zero-rate the construction of such a building, a subcontractor must standard-rate all supplies to the main contractor on such building projects. See also 42.40 below.

Issue of certificates. Where all or part of a building is intended for use solely for a relevant residential or charitable purpose, a supplier of services within these provisions cannot zero-rate the supply until the customer has given him a certificate to that effect. See 42.51 below.

42.32 **Services supplied in the course of construction of civil engineering work for new permanent residential caravan parks**

Services supplied 'in the course of construction' of any civil engineering work necessary for the development of a permanent park for 'residential caravans', and which relate to the construction, are zero-rated. Specifically excluded (and therefore standard-rated) are

- the services of an architect, surveyor or any person acting as a consultant or in a supervisory capacity; and

- the hire of goods and the private use of goods.

See 42.1 above for the meaning of '*in the course of construction*'. The construction of a civil engineering work does not include the conversion, reconstruction, alteration or enlargement of a work.

'*Residential caravan*'. A caravan is not a residential caravan if residence in it throughout the year is prevented by the terms of a covenant, statutory planning consent or similar permission.

[*VATA 1994, 8 Sch Group 5, Item 2(b) and Notes (15), (19) and (20); SI 1995/280*].

The construction of any recreational facilities and non-residential buildings (e.g. social centres, shops, fitness clubs, doctor's surgeries) at a residential caravan park is standard-rated. The construction of a manager's house or flat can be zero-rated under the rules in 42.31 above.

Examples of zero-rated civil engineering work

- Laying new roads, drives, parking bays and paths.

- Laying new pitches or bases for the homes.

- Installing water, electricity and gas supplies.

- Groundworks (drainage and sewerage), septic tanks and other sewage treatment plant.

Examples of standard-rated civil engineering work

- Tennis courts, swimming pools and similar work.

(C & E Notice 708, paras 5.1, 5.2).

42.33 **Services supplied to a relevant housing association in the course of converting non-residential buildings into residential buildings**

Services supplied to a 'relevant housing association' in the course of conversion of

(*a*) a 'non-residential' building, or

(*b*) a non-residential part of a building

into a building (or part of a building)

(i) designed as a 'dwelling' or number of dwellings, or

(ii) intended solely for use for a 'relevant residential purpose'

and which relate to the conversion, are zero-rated.

Specifically excluded (and therefore standard-rated) are

- the services of an architect, surveyor or any person acting as a consultant or in a supervisory capacity; and

- the hire of goods and the private use of goods.

Where (*b*) above applies and the building already contains a residential part, then for zero-rating to apply, the conversion must either be to a building for use for a relevant residential purpose or must create an additional dwelling or dwellings.

See 42.1 above for definitions of '*relevant housing association*', '*non-residential*', '*dwelling*', and '*relevant residential purpose*'.

[*VATA 1994, 8 Sch Group 5, Item 3 and Notes (9), (20) and (21); SI 1995/280; SI 1997/50*].

See 42.35 below for examples of services zero-rated under these provisions and 42.36 below for services not regarded as within these provisions and therefore standard-rated.

Garages. The conversion of a non-residential building to a building designed as a dwelling or number of dwellings includes the conversion of a non-residential building to a garage. The dwelling and the garage must be converted at the same time and the garage must be intended for occupation with the dwelling or one of the dwellings. [*VATA 1994, 8 Sch Group 5, Note (3); SI 1995/280*].

Part qualifying buildings and services. Where part of a building qualifies under the above provisions and part does not (e.g. shop premises with a flat over them), a supply of services relating only to the qualifying part of the building is zero-rated and, similarly, a supply of services relating only to the non-qualifying part is standard-rated. In the case of any other supply, an apportionment must be made to determine the extent to which the supply is zero-rated.

Similarly, where a service falling within the above provisions is supplied in part in relation to the conversion of a building and in part for other purposes (e.g. a mixed site development including new dwellings and shops), an apportionment may be made to determine the extent to which the supply is to be treated as falling within the above provisions.

[*VATA 1994, 8 Sch Group 5, Notes (10) and (11); SI 1995/280*].

Issue of certificates. Before *any* conversion work supplied to a relevant housing association can be zero-rated, the housing association must complete a certificate in the following format.

1. Name and address of organisation
    Registration number
2. I confirm that this organisation is a: (tick one)
    Registered Social Landlord within the meaning of Part I of the
    Housing Act 1996 ❐
    Registered Housing Association within the meaning of the
    Housing Associations Act 1985 (Scottish registered housing
    associations) or within the meaning of Part II of the Housing
    (Northern Ireland) Order 1992 (Northern Irish registered
    housing association. ❐
3. Address of the building being converted/land being purchased:
4. I confirm that the above building is being converted to[1]:
    I confirm that the above land will be used solely for the
    construction of[1]: (tick one)
    A dwelling ❐
    A number of dwellings ❐
    A relevant residential building ❐
    [1]*delete as appropriate*
5. Name (print): Position held:
    Signed: Date:
6. Name, address and VAT registration number of the building
    contractor/vendor

In addition, where, after conversion, all or part of a building is intended for use solely for a relevant residential purpose, a supplier of services within these provisions cannot zero-rate the supply until the housing association has given him a certificate to that effect. See 42.51 below.

Concession for charities. Where a charity is in business but is not a relevant housing association, C & E will consider making refunds of VAT to the charity if it wishes to convert one of its buildings into residential accommodation but is prevented by legal constraints from granting a 'major interest' (see 42.1 above) in that accommodation. Further information is available from the VAT office. *Note* that the supplier of the conversion work must still charge VAT in these cases and the charity must claim a refund. It is not possible to zero-rate the supply. (C & E Notice 708, para 4.4).

42.34 Approved alterations to protected buildings

The supply of services in the course of an 'approved alteration' of a 'protected building' is zero-rated. Specifically excluded (and therefore standard-rated) are

- the services of an architect, surveyor or any person acting as a consultant or in a supervisory capacity; and

- the hire of goods and the private use of goods.

See 42.1 above for the definitions of *'approved alteration'* and *'protected building'*.

[*VATA 1994, 8 Sch Group 6, Item 2 and Note (11) ; SI 1995/283*].

Provided the necessary conditions are satisfied, this provision can be used to zero-rate services supplied in carrying out an approved alteration to

- a protected building which is a dwelling, relevant residential building or relevant charitable building; and

- any other protected building in order to convert it into a dwelling, relevant residential building or relevant charitable building.

See 42.35 below for examples of services zero-rated under these provisions and 42.36 below for services not regarded as within these provisions and therefore standard-rated.

Zero-rating may include work which in other circumstances would be standard-rated as work of repair and maintenance (e.g. replastering to make good the immediate area following the removal of a dividing wall). However, where any further work is carried out at the same time which is not in the course of the approved alteration (e.g. patching up existing plastering in other areas of the building) this is repair and maintenance. In cases where a service is supplied partly in relation to an approved alteration and partly for other purposes (e.g. repairs and maintenance), an apportionment must be made to determine the part zero-rated. [*VATA 1994, 8 Sch Group 6, Note (9); SI 1995/283*]. (C & E Notice 708, paras 8.8, 8.11).

Issue of certificate by recipient of services. Where all or part of a protected building is intended for use solely for a relevant residential or charitable purpose, a supplier of approved alterations to the building within these provisions cannot zero-rate the supply until the customer has given him a certificate to that effect. See 42.51 below.

42.35 Examples of zero-rated services

Zero-rating only applies to services supplied

- in the course of construction of a building or civil engineering work within 42.31 or 42.32 above respectively;

- in the course of conversion of a building by a housing association within 42.33 above; or

- in the course of an approved alteration to a protected building within 42.34 above.

Included where appropriate are those services which are directly relevant to the beginning or ending of the construction work, etc. and in general are carried out prior to completion and first occupation. The services which can be zero-rated include the following.

- Demolition work carried out as part of a single project for the construction of dwellings or qualifying buildings (see 42.41 below).

- Site clearance.

- Earth moving.

- Necessary civil engineering work in the course of the construction of dwellings or qualifying buildings (but not tennis courts, swimming pools and similar works).

- Laying of foundations.

- Bricklaying, plastering, carpentry, roofing and plumbing services.

- Mechanical and electrical services (including central heating).

- Plant hire provided with an operator or driver.

- Scaffolding/formwork/falsework erection and dismantling (but not hire, and not erection and hire when supplied together and not separately itemised).

- Incorporation of builders' materials (see 42.37 below).

- Fitting of kitchen units and worktops, and domestic appliances (but not the appliances themselves which are standard-rated — see 42.39 below — except for those listed in 42.38 below).

- Fitting of carpets (but not the carpets themselves, see 42.39 below).

- Internal and external cleaning ('builders' cleans').

- First time decoration.

- Office partitioning (for non-business charity use).

- Construction of vehicle crossings.

- Remedial and repair work carried out while a dwelling or other qualifying building is under construction.

- Site restoration including the clearance and removal of rubble (if supplied with other construction services), levelling and drainage of land, application of top soil, laying of grass and the construction of simple paths and patios.

- Walls and fences.

(C & E Notice 708, paras 9.1, 11.1-11.6).

42.36   Examples of standard-rated services

The following services are always standard-rated.

- Site investigations (before the letting of any building contract).

- Temporary fencing around a site.

- Concrete testing.

- Site security.

- Catering.

- Cleaning of site offices, huts etc.

- Temporary lighting.

- Transport and haulage to and from site.

- Plant hire without operator.

- Professional services of architects, engineers, surveyors, solicitors, estate agents, valuers, consultants, and other persons supplying supervisory services.

- Construction management services.

- Landscaping including planting of trees, flowers, etc. and the construction of fish ponds and rockeries or other ornamental works, etc.

- Transport of rubble, etc. where supplied as a separate service.

- Hire of scaffolding, formwork or falsework.

(C & E Notice 708, paras 9.2, 11.3-11.5).

42.37 **Zero-rated building materials**

Subject to the exceptions in 42.39 below, a person supplying zero-rated construction services within 42.31 to 42.34 above can also zero-rate the supply of 'building materials' which he incorporates into the building (or its site) in question.

'*Building materials*' in relation to a particular building, mean goods 'ordinarily' incorporated or installed as fittings by builders in a building of that description (or its site) but do not include any of the supplies within 42.39(*a*)-(*c*) below.

[*VATA 1994, 8 Sch Group 5, Item 4 and Notes (22) and (23), Group 6, Item 3 and Note (3); SI 1995/280; SI 1995/283*].

'*Ordinarily*' implies incorporation in all sections of the market e.g. not just expensive homes (*Creighton Griffiths (Investments) Ltd, [1982] VATTR 175 (1442)*) although goods which need to be installed in defined areas of the country (e.g. sound-proofing near airports) can still qualify (*British Airports Authority (No 5) (477)*).

Building materials include normal builders' hardware and sanitary ware in addition to the following.

Examples of items zero-rated when installed in new dwellings and other qualifying buildings

- Window frames and glazing.

- Doors.

- Letter boxes.

- Fireplaces and surrounds.

- Guttering.

- Power points (including combination shaver points/lights but not light bulbs or tubes).

- Outside lights (provided they are standard fittings but not light bulbs or tubes).

- Immersion heaters, boilers, hot and cold water tanks.

- Radiators and central heating.

- Built-in heating appliances.

- Fire and burglar alarms and smoke detectors.

- Air conditioning equipment.

- Equipment to provide ventilation.

- Dust extractors.

- Lifts and hoists.

- 'Communal' TV aerials in blocks of flats, etc.

- Warden call systems.

- Work surfaces or fitted cupboards in kitchens (including those fitted in utility rooms).

- Kitchen sinks.

- Baths, basins and bidets.

- Lavatory bowls and cisterns.

- Shower units.

- Fixed towel rails, toilet roll holders, soap dishes, etc.

- Airing cupboards, under-stair storage cupboards, cloaks/vestibule cupboards, larders, closets and other similar basic storage facilities which are formed by becoming part of the fabric of the building.

- Items which provide storage capacity as an incidental result of their primary function. Such items include:

    (a)   Shelves formed as a result of constructing simple box work over pipes.

    (b)   *Vanity units.* Following the decision in *Edmond Homes Ltd (11567),* C & E accept that zero-rating applies where wash hand basins installed in bathrooms and cloakrooms are supported by base units rather than pedestals. The unit will typically be a box like structure entirely below the line of the top of the basin and contain a shelf and a covering door or doors, the only storage space being directly beneath the basin itself. More extensive vanity units are regarded as standard-rated (see 42.39 below).

- Simple bedroom wardrobes. Following the decisions in *C & E Commrs v McLean Homes Midland Ltd QB, [1993] STC 335* and *SH Wade (13164),* C & E accept simple bedroom wardrobes *installed on their own* as zero-rated. A simple bedroom wardrobe is one enclosing a space bordered by the walls, ceiling and floor. The sides and back would be formed by using three walls of the room (or two walls and a stub wall) so that, on opening, the building walls (normally bare or painted plaster) can be seen. The wardrobe should feature no more than a single shelf running the full length of the wardrobe, a rail for hanging clothes and a closing door or doors. The wardrobe could be fitted across the whole of the end of a room.

    Other wardrobes, however fitted, are regarded as furniture and standard-rated (see 42.39 below).

Examples of items zero-rated when installed in new relevant charitable buildings (other than dwellings or relevant residential buildings)

General: lighting systems (excluding non-fixed bulbs and tubes); smoke detectors; blinds and shutters; mirrors.

Schools: blackboards fixed to or forming part of the walls; gymnasium wall bars; name boards; notice and display boards; mirrors and barres (in ballet schools).

Churches: altars; church bells; organs; fonts; lecterns; pulpits; amplification equipment; humidifying plant.

(C & E Notice 708, para 9.3, Appendices D and E).

42.38   **Zero-rated electrical goods**

Electrical goods are normally standard-rated (see 42.39 below). The following goods can, however, be zero-rated when supplied with zero-rated construction services within 42.31 to 42.34 above.

● An appliance designed to heat space or water (or both) or designed to provide ventilation, air cooling, air purification or dust extraction.

● A door-entry system, waste disposal unit or machine for compacting waste but only if in each case it is intended for use in a building designed as a number of dwellings, e.g. a block of flats.

● A burglar alarm, fire alarm or fire safety equipment designed solely for the purpose of enabling aid to be summoned in an emergency.

● A lift or hoist.

[*VATA 1994, 8 Sch Group 5, Note (22), Group 6, Note (3); SI 1995/280; SI 1995/283*].

Fixed amplification equipment in churches may also be zero-rated. (C & E Notice 708, para 9.4).

42.39   **Standard-rated goods**

Zero-rating of goods can only apply where the conditions in 42.37 or 42.38 above are met. Standard-rating applies where

● goods are incorporated into a building but are supplied with standard-rated construction services;

● the goods are not of a kind ordinarily incorporated or installed by builders in the type of building being constructed (e.g. trees, shrubs and flowers, see *McLean Homes East Anglia Ltd, [1992] VATTR 460 (7748)*, and curtains);

● the goods are not incorporated in the building or its structure (e.g. free-standing items); or

● the goods are supplied without construction services (e.g. a builders' merchant providing delivered goods).

In addition to this, the following goods are specifically excluded from the definition of building materials and their supply is always standard-rated.

(*a*)   Finished or prefabricated 'furniture' (other than furniture designed to be fitted in kitchens) and materials for the construction of 'fitted furniture' (other than kitchen furniture).

'*Furniture*' is not defined in law. Tribunals and the courts have indicated that whether an item is furniture is very much a matter of impression, but have indicated that the function of furniture includes 'convenient places to hang things or to store things; as decoration for a house; and to provide areas for the preparation of food, or for work of various kinds associated with domestic, social or working life'. This is not an exhaustive list.

Example of furniture which is standard-rated

Domestic: beds, bedside cabinets, bookcases, chairs, chests of drawers, cupboards, dining tables, dressing tables, linen chests, sideboards, wall units such as bathroom cabinets, etc.

Commercial: desks, tables, chairs and other seating.

Scientific/medical: laboratory benches, dental cabinetry.

Schools: (as for *Commercial* and *Scientific*).

Churches: pews, choir stalls, clergy stalls.

'*Fitted furniture*' is taken by C & E to mean units of furniture as commonly supplied by specialist retailers/manufacturers or constructed/assembled on site from component parts which are designed to be (and actually are) fixed to the wall of the room.

'*Bedroom wardrobes*'. Certain simple bedroom wardrobes can be zero-rated (see 42.37 above) but C & E regard as standard-rated furniture

- more elaborate wardrobes (however fitted);

- simple bedroom wardrobes installed as part of a larger installation of furniture in the room (typically as part of a matching range);

- the installation of a cupboard in the corner of a room where one side is a closing end panel;

- units whose design includes, for example, an element to bridge over a bed or create a dressing table;

- wardrobes which contain internal panelling, typically as part of a modular or carcass system; and

- wardrobes with internal divisions, drawers, shoe racks or other features.

Vanity units. Basin supports which contain a simple cupboard beneath can be zero-rated (see 42.37 above). More elaborate vanity units, typically with other storage space constructed on either or both sides of the basin, are standard-rated furniture.

(C & E Business Brief 12/97, 5 June 1997).

(*b*) Electrical or gas appliances except for those specifically zero-rated (see 42.38 above). Standard-rated items include refrigerators; cookers (including split-level cookers); washing and dish-washing machines; tumble dryers; and waste disposal units and entry phone systems (except in buildings designed as a number of dwellings, e.g. blocks of flats, see 42.38 above).

(*c*) Carpets or carpeting material.

[*VATA 1994, 8 Sch Group 5, Note (22), Group 6, Note (3); SI 1995/280; SI 1995/283*]. (C & E Notice 708, para 9.5, Appendices B and C).

42.40 Subcontractors

A subcontractor (i.e. a building contractor who does not work directly for the customer) must charge VAT unless working on

- the construction of a new dwelling (see 42.31); or

- an approved alteration to a protected building which is designed as or will become a dwelling (see 42.34 above).

Work on any other buildings (including all commercial buildings, relevant residential buildings and relevant charitable buildings) and conversions to dwellings must be standard-rated.

(C & E Notice 708, para 11.1).

42.41   **Demolition services**

The demolition of a building or civil engineering work is zero-rated if undertaken as part of a single project for the construction of a new dwelling or other qualifying building or work.

Demolition contracts generally involve both

- the demolition of the property by the contractor, and

- the granting by the site owner to the contractor of the right to remove materials.

If the agreement specifies charges or values for each part, there are two separate supplies and the right to remove materials is standard-rated. Where only one charge or amount is specified, there is a single supply (either of demolition services or the right to remove, depending on which of these the charge or amount relates to).

(C & E Notice 708, para 11.9).

42.42   **Building contracts**

The total process of procuring a building project (design, construction and project management) can be achieved in a number of ways. Normally, an architect or professional agent is appointed for design and cost control services who in turn engages a contractor to carry out the building work.

Design and build contracts. Where the design, workmanship and materials are supplied by a contractor under a 'design and build' lump sum contract, the VAT liability of the design element follows that of the building work. This also applies where the part of the lump sum for the design element is shown separately for internal analysis purposes only by the two contracting parties. If there is a separate supply of design or similar professional services to the client, this is always standard-rated.

Management contracts. Under such contracts, the client normally first appoints a professional design team and engages a management contractor to advise them. If the project goes ahead, the management contractor's fee is based on the likely total cost of the project. The managing contractor does not carry out any of the building work but directly engages 'works contractors' to do it. The management contractor's fee and the proper cost of all the works contracts are paid to the management contractor by the client and this amount represents the consideration for the contract. It is zero or standard-rated depending on the liability of the building construction work carried out. If the project does not go ahead, the preliminary advisory services of the management contractor are always standard-rated.

Project/construction management contracts. Under such contracts, the client normally engages a construction company to be responsible for planning, managing and co-ordinating the whole project and for establishing competitive bids for all elements of the work. The actual orders for the building work are placed by the client with works contractors employed directly by him. The management fee paid to the project manager is standard-rated. Any construction site services provided by the project manager and works, etc. supplied to the client by the works contractors are standard-rated, unless they are supplied in the course of construction of dwellings or qualifying buildings and are related to their construction.

(C & E Notice 708, paras 10.1–10.3).

42.43 Self-supply of construction services

Where a person, in the course or furtherance of a business carried on by him and for the purpose of that business and otherwise than for a consideration,

(a) constructs a building;

(b) extends, alters, or constructs an annex to, any building such that additional floor area of not less than 10% of the floor area of the original building is created;

(c) constructs any civil engineering work; or

(d) carries out any demolition work at the same time as, or in preparation for, any of the work in (a) to (c) above,

then, unless the open market value of the services performed is less than £100,000, the services are treated as both supplied to him for the purpose of that business and supplied by him in the course or furtherance of it, i.e. self-supplied.

The value of any services which would be zero-rated if supplied in the course or furtherance of a business by a taxable person should be ignored.

VAT must be accounted for to C & E on the open market value of the services performed (subject to the *de minimis* limit of £100,000). This output tax on the self-supply can be recovered as input tax in the same period to the extent that it is attributable to taxable supplies under the normal rules i.e. to the extent that the building in question is used or to be used for making taxable supplies. Therefore

- where the building or work is occupied or used for a taxable business activity, or is sold or let after the exercise of an option to tax, the self-supply VAT should be fully recoverable;

- where the building or work is used wholly for exempt purposes or let without the option to tax being exercised, the self-supply VAT is not recoverable; and

- where the building or work is used partly for exempt and partly for taxable business purposes, VAT on the self supply charge is recoverable according to the partial exemption method used.

Note also that where the value of the self-supply exceeds £250,000, adjustments may be required in future years under the CAPITAL GOODS SCHEME (10).

Input tax on purchases of goods and services for such building works are treated as relating to the taxable self-supply, Input tax may therefore be claimed in full (subject to the normal rules).

In relation to GROUPS OF COMPANIES (31), for these purposes all companies within the group are treated as one person but anything done which would fall to be treated under these provisions as services supplied to and by that person are to be treated as supplied to and by the representative member (see 31.4 GROUPS OF COMPANIES).

[*SI 1989/472*]. (C & E Notice 708, paras 12.1, 12.2).

De Voil Indirect Tax Service. See V3.244.

42.44 Time of supply

(A) **Stage or interim payment contracts.** Where services, or services together with goods, are supplied in the course of the construction, alteration, demolition, repair or maintenance of a building or of any civil engineering work under a contract which provides for payment for such supplies to be made periodically or from time to time (often referred to as 'stage' or 'interim' payment contracts), those services (or goods and services) are treated as separately and successively supplied at the earliest of the following times.

   (i) Each time a payment is received by the supplier (before 1 January 1998 where the consideration for the contract was wholly in money).

   (ii) Each time the supplier issues a VAT invoice.

   (iii) For services performed after 8 December 1997, to the extent that services have not already been treated as supplied under (i) or (ii) above, 18 months after the date on which those services were 'performed'.

[*SI 1995 No 2518, Reg 93; SI 1997/2887, Reg 5*].

Included are supplies made by architects, surveyors, consultants and those acting in a supervisory capacity. (C & E Notice 708, para 13.1).

There is no basic tax point when the work is completed. This is to reflect the fact that delay often arises in agreeing the value of work performed and in particular the amount of the final instalment under the contract. However, this has been used as a basis for tax avoidance schemes and the additional tax point in (iii) above was introduced to block such schemes. It applies to any VAT not already accounted for, including any VAT on outstanding retention payments and on amounts in dispute. In the latter case, VAT should be based on the amount the supplier considers is due, any under or overpayments being adjusted by means of a further invoice or credit note as appropriate.

For the purposes of (iii) above, C & E regard construction services as '*performed*' when all the work has been completed apart from invoicing. In the case of a main contractor, this will be when the building or civil engineering work is completed. Unless there is undue delay, C & E normally accept this as the date of the architect's certificate of completion. Subcontractors' services may be performed before the building is completed and basic principles must be applied to determine when their work is completed.

Where work ceases before the contract is completed (e.g. because of a dispute between the parties to the contract or the liquidation of one of them) services are regarded as having been performed at the time the work ceases.

Where construction contracts have a 'snagging' period (i.e. a period during which the contractor must rectify any defects becoming apparent), this period by definition begins after the construction services have been completed.

(C & E Business Brief 1/98, 7 January 1998).

(B) **Single payment contracts.** The rules in (A) above do not apply where the work is carried out under a single payment contract, even if payment of part of the price is to be delayed under a retention clause (see below). Single payment contracts are subject to the normal tax point rules (see 64.49 SUPPLY) including the creation of a basic tax point when the work has been completed. The retention element is subject to the special rules below. (C & E Notice 708, para 13.1).

(C) **Retention payments.** Building contracts frequently include retention clauses which allow customers to hold back a proportion of the contract price on completion of the work pending full and satisfactory performance of the contract and rectification of any immediate faults that are found.

For single payment contracts under (B) above, VAT would fall due on the retained element at the basic tax point (i.e. on completion of the work). However, in such instances, the tax point for the retained element is the earlier of

   • the time when a payment in respect of the retention is received, or

- the date the supplier issues a VAT invoice relating to the retention.

For stage or interim payment contracts under (A) above, similar rules applied before 1 January 1998. However, with effect from that date, such contracts are specifically excluded from these provisions.

[*SI 1995/2518, Reg 89; SI 1997/2887, Reg 3*].

(D) **Goods supplied without services.** Where materials, etc. are not supplied in connection with the supply of services (e.g. a supply by a builders' merchant to a builder), the time of supply is that under the normal rules for supplies of goods (see 64.39 SUPPLY).

42.45 Authenticated receipts for stage payments

The authenticated receipt procedure allows a supplier to issue an authenticated receipt for payment instead of a normal VAT invoice provided that it contains all the particulars required on a VAT invoice (see 40.2 and 40.3 INVOICES) and that no VAT invoice or similar document is issued. Use of the procedure should be mutually agreed between the customer and the supplier.

The procedure only operates when

- services (or services together with goods) are supplied in the course of the construction, alteration, demolition, repair or maintenance of a building or any civil engineering work; and

- the contract provides for the payment for such services to be made periodically or from time to time.

The procedure (which is not to be confused with self-billing, for which see 40.2 INVOICES) is operated by the customer preparing a receipt for supplies received and forwarding it to the supplier with payment. The receipt is not valid for VAT purposes until it has been authenticated by the supplier. An authenticated receipt is not a VAT invoice and does not create a tax point. The tax point for the supply is therefore solely determined by the receipt of payment by the supplier.

The customer can claim input tax relief in the VAT period in which the supplier receives the stage payment, without waiting for an authenticated receipt although he must obtain and keep a copy of the authenticated receipt as acceptable evidence for input tax purposes. Suppliers cannot issue authenticated receipts until payment have been received.

SI 1995/2518, Reg 13(4)]. (C & E Notice 708, para 13.2).

42.46 Deductions for income tax and CITB levy

Income tax. Where a contractor is required to make a deduction on account of income tax from a payment to a sub-contractor who is not exempt from such deduction, the value of the sub-contractor's services for VAT purposes is the gross amount charged by him, before deduction is made.

CITB levy. Any deduction in respect of the Construction Industry Training Board levy, which has been agreed by the sub-contractor, can be deducted from the gross amount for the purposes of calculating VAT due, and the value of the supply is treated as reduced by any such levy.

(C & E Notice 708, para 14.3).

42.47   **DEVELOPERS CONSTRUCTING DWELLINGS AND OTHER QUALIFYING BUILDINGS**

EC legislation. See 22.18(*k*) EUROPEAN COMMUNITY LEGISLATION.

Provided various conditions are met, zero-rating applies to the first sale of, or grant of a long lease in, a building or its site by

- a person constructing a dwelling or dwellings or a building to be used for a relevant residential or charitable purpose (see 42.48 below);

- a person converting a non-residential building into a dwelling or dwellings or a building to be used for a relevant residential purpose (see 42.48 below); and

- a person substantially reconstructing a protected building for use as a dwelling or dwellings or for use for a relevant residential or charitable purpose (see 42.49 below).

42.48   **Supplies of qualifying buildings**

Zero-rating applies to the first 'grant' of a 'major interest' in, or in any part of, the building, dwelling or its 'site' by the following.

(*a*)   A person 'constructing' a building designed as a 'dwelling' or number of dwellings unless either

    (i)   the interest granted is such that the grantee is not entitled to reside in the building, or part, throughout the year (e.g. a time share); or

    (ii)   residence there throughout the year or the use of the building or part as the grantee's principal private residence, is prevented by the terms of a covenant, statutory planning consent or similar permission (i.e. accommodation which cannot lawfully be occupied as a permanent residence).

(*b*)   A person 'constructing' a building intended for use solely for a 'relevant residential purpose' or a 'relevant charitable purpose'.

(*c*)   A person converting

    (i)   a 'non-residential' building, or

    (ii)   a non-residential part of a building

into a building designed as a 'dwelling' or number of dwellings or a building intended for use solely for a 'relevant residential purpose'.

Where (ii) applies and the building already contains a residential part, then for zero-rating to apply, the conversion must either be to a building for use for a relevant residential purpose or must create an additional dwelling or dwellings. For example, relief applies where a building comprises a public house and flat and the public house is converted to create a flat or flats or a residential home in addition to the existing flat. Conversely, the relief would not apply if the existing flat was extended to incorporate what was the public house into one large dwelling as no additional dwelling has been created. (C & E Notice 708, para 16.2).

[*VATA 1994, 8 Sch Group 5, Item 1 and Notes (9) and (13); SI 1995/280*].

See 42.1 above for definitions of '*grant*', '*major interest*', '*site*', '*constructing*', '*dwelling*', '*relevant residential purpose*', '*relevant charitable purpose*' and '*non-residential*'.

Garages. The construction of, or the conversion of a non-residential building to, a building designed as a dwelling or number of dwellings includes the construction of, or conversion of a non-residential building to, a garage. The dwelling and the garage must be constructed or converted at the same time and the garage must be intended for occupation with the dwelling or one of the dwellings. [*VATA 1994, 8 Sch Group 5, Note (3); SI 1995/280*].

Tenancies and leases. Where the major interest is a tenancy or lease, zero-rating only applies to the premium payable on the grant or, if no premium is payable, the first payment of rent due under the tenancy or lease. [*VATA 1994, 8 Sch Group 5, Note (14); SI 1995/280*]. (The effect of this is that zero-rating only covers the sum payable when the lease is granted and subsequent payments such as ground rent or service charges cannot be zero-rated.)

The first grant of a major interest by the person constructing following a period of short-term lets is zero-rated. (C & E Notice 708, para 15.6).

Part-qualifying buildings. Where part of a building qualifies for zero-rating under (*a*)–(*c*) above and part does not (e.g. shop premises with a flat over them), a grant or supply relating only to the part within those provisions is to be treated as relating to a zero-rated building and, similarly, a grant or supply relating only to the part outside those provisions is not to be so treated. In the case of any other grant or supply, an apportionment must be made to determine the extent to which it is to be so treated. [*VATA 1994, 8 Sch Group 5, Note (10); SI 1995/280*].

Issue of certificates. Where all or any part of a building is intended for use solely for a relevant residential or charitable purpose, the grant of a major interest cannot be zero-rated under these provisions unless, before the grant is made, the grantee has given the grantor a certificate to that effect. See 42.51 below.

Change of use of relevant residential or charitable buildings. Where the grant of a major interest in a building is zero-rated under these provisions because the grantee certifies that the building will be used for a relevant residential or charitable purpose, the grantee will be treated as making a standard-rated supply of the property if, within ten years of its completion, he either sells, lets or uses the building for any other purpose. See 42.26 for full details.

Partly-constructed buildings. The grant of a major interest in a qualifying building which is only partly completed (e.g. which has progressed beyond foundation stage but is not structurally complete) is zero-rated. If the person to whom the grant is made continues the construction, he may also zero rate the first supply of a major interest in it (provided that supply also meets the conditions for zero-rating). (C & E Notice 708, para 15.5).

Joint ownership and beneficial interests. See 42.17 above.

De Voil Indirect Tax Service. See V4.233; V4.234.

42.49   Protected buildings

The first 'grant' by a person 'substantially reconstructing' a 'protected building' of a 'major interest' in, or in any part of, the building or its site is zero-rated. [*VATA 1994, 8 Sch Group 6, Item 1; SI 1995/283*].

See 42.1 above for the definitions of '*grant*', '*protected building*' and '*major interest*'.

The grant of an interest in a building designed as a 'dwelling' (see 42.1 above) or number of dwellings (the site of such a building) is *not* zero-rated under these provisions if either

   (i) the interest granted is such that the grantee is not entitled to reside in the building throughout the year (e.g. a time share); or

(ii) residence there throughout the year, or use of the building as the grantee's principal private residence, is prevented by the terms of a covenant, statutory planning consent or similar permission (i.e. accommodation which cannot lawfully be occupied as a permanent residence).

[*VATA 1994, 8 Sch Group 5, Note (13), Group 6, Note (3); SI 1995/283*].

'Substantially reconstructing'. A protected building is not to be regarded as substantially reconstructed unless one or both of the following conditions are fulfilled when the reconstruction is completed.

- At least 60% of the cost of the reconstruction work would, if supplied by a taxable person, qualify for zero-rating as the supply of services in the course of approved alterations under 42.34 above or building materials and other items to carry out those works under 42.37 or 42.38 above.

- The reconstructed building incorporates no more of the original building before reconstruction began than the external walls, together with other external features of architectural or historic interest.

[*VATA 1994, 8 Sch Group 6, Note (4); SI 1995/283*].

Garages. Where a grant of a major interest in a substantially reconstructed dwelling is zero-rated under these provisions, zero-rating extends to a garage within the 'curtilage' (see 42.1 above) of the protected building. (C & E Notice 708, para 19.3).

Extensions. The grant of a major interest in a protected building is not zero-rated as a 'substantial reconstruction' where the only major alteration is the addition of an extension. However, as the extension to a protected building is an 'approved alteration', provided other major works are carried out to reconstruct the building, it can be included in the 60% substantial reconstruction calculations (see above). (C & E Notice 708, para 19.5).

Tenancies and leases. Where the major interest is a tenancy or lease, zero-rating only applies to the premium payable on the grant or, if no premium is payable, the first payment of rent due under the tenancy or lease. [*VATA 1994, 8 Sch Group 5, Note (14); Group 6, Note (3); SI 1995/283*]. (The effect of this is that zero-rating only covers the sum payable when the lease is granted and subsequent payments such as ground rent or service charges cannot be zero-rated.)

The first grant of a major interest by the person constructing following a period of short-term lets is zero-rated. (C & E Notice 708, para 15.6).

Part-qualifying buildings. Where *part only* of a protected building which is substantially reconstructed is designed to remain as or become a dwelling or number of dwellings or is intended for use solely for a relevant residential or relevant charitable purpose (e.g. shop premises with a flat over them)

- a grant relating only to the part so designed or intended for such use (or its site) is to be treated as relating to a building so designed or intended for such use;

- a grant relating only to the part neither so designed nor intended for such use (or its site) is not to be so treated; and

- in the case of any other grant relating to, or to any part of, the building (or its site), an apportionment must be made to determine the extent to which it is to be so treated.

[*VATA 1994, 8 Sch Group 6, Note (5); SI 1995/283*].

Issue of certificates. Where all or any part of the substantially reconstructed building is intended for use solely for a relevant residential or charitable purpose, the grant of a major interest cannot be zero-rated under these provisions unless, before the grant is made, the grantee has given the grantor a certificate to that effect. See 42.51 below.

Joint owners and beneficial interests. See 42.17 above.

Evidence for zero-rating. For zero-rating to apply, the VAT office must be satisfied that a substantial reconstruction has been carried out. The following evidence must be obtained (and kept for inspection).

●

Evidence that the building is listed.

● Copies of the application for, and grant of, listed building consent, together with any associated schedules, plans, drawings and correspondence.

● Plans, drawings, descriptions and photographs before and after the work was carried out, to show that the work amounted to a substantial reconstruction.

● An analysis of the work done to the building distinguishing which work was approved alterations and which was repair or maintenance, together with a breakdown of the costs of such work (including any demolition work preceding reconstruction, but excluding professional fees). Any own labour costs should be included.

(C & E Notice 708, para 19.7).

Exempt supplies. Other supplies of protected buildings not within the above provisions are normally exempt, e.g. where

● the building has not been substantially reconstructed;

● the interest granted is not a major interest;

● a major interest is granted by a person other than the person who owns the building and carries out, or commissions a builder to carry out, the substantial reconstruction; or

● the building is not used as a dwelling or for a qualifying purpose.

(C & E Notice 708, para 19.10).

See, however, 42.20 above for the option to tax under certain circumstances.

Buildings subject to immunity certificates. An immunity certificate is a certificate issued by the Secretary of State to the effect that a building cannot be listed for a period of five years. It gives the owner an opportunity to work on the building without the additional burden of supplementary planning controls which apply to listed buildings. It is possible, however, that the advantageous treatment afforded to the reconstruction of a listed building was not appreciated when application for immunity from listing was made. By concession, therefore, a building which, following its substantial reconstruction, is intended to be used solely for a relevant charitable purpose, may be treated as a listed building if, at the time of the grant of a major interest, there is in force an immunity certificate issued before 1 March 1996. (C & E News Release 25/96, 16 April 1996).

De Voil Indirect Tax Service. See V4.235.

42.50   Deduction of input tax by developers

Goods incorporated into the building or its site. Where a taxable person constructing a building or effecting any works to a building, in either case for the purpose of granting a major interest in the building (or any part of it) or its 'site' (see 42.1

above), incorporates goods other than building materials in any part of the building or its site, input tax on the supply, acquisition or importation of the goods is excluded from credit. [*SI 1992/3222, Art 6; SI 1995/281*].

See 42.37 and 42.38 above for examples of zero-rated building materials and zero-rated electrical goods and 42.39 above for a list of standard-rated goods on which VAT is not recoverable under these provisions.

Input tax on related services of installing the goods can be reclaimed provided the services are separately identified and VAT is correctly charged by the person supplying them.

Goods not incorporated into the building. Input tax can be recovered on goods which are not incorporated into the building or its site (e.g. free-standing items). A separate supply takes place when these goods are sold with the building on which output tax must be accounted for.

Goods incorporated outside the site. Input tax on goods incorporated outside the site of the building (e.g. roads for a housing estate dedicated to a local authority or transferred to a management company) can be recovered subject to limitations. See 42.19 above.

(C & E Notice 708, para 18.1).

Showhouses. VAT cannot be reclaimed on standard-rated goods within 42.39 above incorporated into a showhouse if they are to be included in the sale of the house. No output tax is due when these goods are sold with the house.

Input tax can be recovered on those goods which are not incorporated into the showhouse (e.g. free-standing items) but are used for display purposes. Output tax must be accounted for when these goods are sold. (C & E Notice 708, para 18.3).

De Voil Indirect Tax Service. See V3.444.

42.51   **CERTIFICATES WHERE BUILDING INTENDED FOR USE FOR A RELEVANT RESIDENTIAL OR RELEVANT CHARITABLE PURPOSE**

Where all or part of a building is intended for use solely for a 'relevant residential purpose' or a 'relevant charitable purpose' (see 42.1 above),

(*a*)   a supply relating to the building (or any part of it) cannot be taken as relating to a building intended for such use unless it is made to a person who intends to use the building (or part) for such purposes (the 'customer'); and

(*b*)   a grant or other supply relating to the building (or any part of it) cannot be taken as relating to a building intended for such use unless, before it is made, the customer has given to the grantor or supplier a certificate, in such form as is prescribed by C & E, stating that the grant or other supply so relates.

[*VATA 1994, 8 Sch Group 5, Note (12), Group 6, Note (3); SI 1995/280*].

The effect of the above is that, before a developer or builder can zero rate certain grants and other supplies, he must obtain a certificate from the customer showing how much of the building is to be used for relevant residential or charitable purposes. A certificate must be used for any of the following supplies.

(1)   The first grant of a major interest in a building (or part of a building) for use solely for a relevant residential purpose or a relevant charitable purpose (see 42.48 above).

(2)   The first grant of a major interest in a building (or part of a building) for use solely for a relevant residential purpose by the person who has converted it (see 42.48 above).

(3)   The supply of goods and services in the course of construction of a new building intended solely for a relevant residential purpose or a relevant charitable purpose (see 42.31 above).

(4)   The supply of goods and services in the course of construction of a connected annex intended solely for a relevant charitable purpose (see 42.31 above).

(5)   The supply of goods and services in the course of an approved alteration to a protected building intended solely for use for a relevant residential purpose or a relevant charitable purpose (see 42.34 above).

(6)   The supply to a relevant housing association of goods and services in the course of conversion of a non-residential building (or a non-residential part of a building) into a building (or part of a building) intended for use solely for a relevant residential purpose (see 42.33 above).

The builder should receive two copies of the certificate from the customer (one for own records and one to be made available to C & E), together with any supporting plans and documents. The responsibility for zero-rating, however, remains with the builder who must take all reasonable steps to check the validity of the certificate (including correspondence with the customer) and should consult the VAT office if in doubt. Where, however, despite taking all reasonable steps to check the validity of the declaration, nonetheless the builder fails to identify the inaccuracy and in good faith makes the supplies concerned at the zero rate, C & E will not seek to recover the VAT due from the builder.

Form of certificate. The form of certificate prescribed by C & E (which has the force of law) is as follows.

Certificate for developers and building contractors in respect of relevant residential and relevant charitable buildings

1.   Name and address of business(es)/charity(ies) using the building:
VAT Registration number (if applicable):

2.   Address of qualifying premises (if different from above):

3.   Date (or estimated date) of completion of building:
Estimated value of supply £

4.   I/We certify that I/We have read the current edition of VAT Notice 708 *Buildings and construction*. This certificate is being issued in respect of the supply described in that Notice at paragraph 3.3, sub-paragraph:

(1) the first grant of a major interest in a relevant residential building	yes/no
(2) the first grant of a major interest in a relevant charitable building	yes/no
(3) the first grant of a major interest in a building converted into a relevant residential building	yes/no
(4) the construction of a relevant residential building	yes/no
(5) the construction of a relevant charitable building	yes/no
(6) the construction of an annex to a relevant charitable building	yes/no
(7) an approved alteration to a relevant residential building	yes/no
(8) an approved alteration to a relevant charitable building	yes/no

(9) the conversion, for a relevant housing association, of a
building into a relevant residential building   yes/no

5. I/We certify that the information given above is correct and
    complete. I am/We are aware of the law as contained in Group 5
    or Group 6 of Schedule 8 to the VAT Act 1994 and claim relief
    accordingly. I/We also certify that this organisation (in
    conjunction with any other organisations where applicable) is to
    use this building or identified parts of this building solely for a
    qualifying purpose. I/We understand that if the building or zero-
    rated part of it is disposed of, let or otherwise used for a non-
    qualifying purpose within the period of ten years from the date of
    its completion, a taxable supply will have been made, and this
    organisation (and any other organisations where applicable) will
    account for tax at the standard rate.

    Name (print): . . . . Position held: . . . .

    Signed: . . . . Date: . . . .

6. Name, address and VAT registration number of developer or
    building contractor:

7. Date certificate received by developer or builder:

8. Date certificate received by VAT office:

Apportionment. Where only part of a new building is to be used for a qualifying
purpose, supplies can be apportioned (the qualifying part being zero-rated and the
non-qualifying part being standard-rated) provided

*   the builder is given a certificate identifying the building to be used for a qualifying
    purpose; and

*   the certificate is supported by plans and written descriptions of the qualifying part.

If the customer cannot show which parts of the building will be qualifying and which will
not, (or if the same part of the building is to be used for qualifying and non-qualifying
purposes at different times) then all the construction services must be standard-rated.
However, by concession, the non-qualifying use can be ignored if

*   the building will be used solely for qualifying purposes for more than 90% of the
    total time it is available for use; or

*   in the case of non-business charitable educational establishments (e.g. a grant-
    maintained sixth form college) the number of fee paying students is less than 10%
    of the total students calculated on a full-time equivalent basis.

Limitation on issue of certificates. Certificates under (3) to (6) above can only be
issued to main contractors (other than architects, surveyors and persons acting as
consultants or in a supervisory capacity) who are directly employed by the person
eligible to issue the certificate. Certificates cannot be passed from main contractors to
sub-contractors. Sub-contractors must therefore charge VAT at the tandard rate on
their services. See also 42.40 above.

(C & E Notice 708, paras 3.1–3.4, Appendix A; C & E Notice 48, ESC 2.11).

42.52   **DO-IT-YOURSELF HOUSEBUILDERS**

C & E must refund any VAT chargeable on the supply, acquisition or importation of any
goods used in connection with construction or conversion work where the following
conditions are satisfied.

(*a*) The work must comprise

    (i) the 'construction of a building' designed as a 'dwelling' or number of dwellings;

    (ii) the constructing of a building for use solely for a 'relevant residential purpose' or for a 'relevant charitable purpose'; or

    (iii) a *'residential conversion'*, i.e. the conversion of a 'non-residential' building or the non-residential part of a building into *either* a building designed as a dwelling or number of dwellings *or* a building intended solely for a relevant residential purpose *or* anything which would fall into either of those categories if different parts of a building were treated as separate buildings.

(*b*) The work is carried out lawfully and otherwise than in the course or furtherance of any business.

(*c*) The goods are building materials which, in the course of the works, are incorporated in the building in question or its site. See 42.37 and 42.38 above. Refunds can be claimed on the building materials which would be zero-rated when supplied with the zero-rated work but *not* on those which would be standard-rated.

(*d*) The claim is made within such time and in such form and manner, contains such information, and is accompanied by such documents as C & E require. See 42.53 below.

See 42.1 above for the definitions of *'construction of a building'*, *'dwelling'*, *'relevant residential purpose'*, *'relevant charitable purpose'* and *'non-residential'*.

Refund also covers VAT chargeable on a supply of any goods under the law of another EC country.

Conversions using contractors, etc. Where a person carries out a residential conversion and arranges for the work to be done by someone else ('a contractor'), then provided

    (i) the condition in (*b*) above is satisfied, and

    (ii) the contractor is not acting as an architect, surveyor or consultant or in a supervisory capacity,

C & E must, on a claim, refund any VAT chargeable on any services consisting of work done by the contractor.

Garages. The construction of, or the conversion of a non-residential building to, a building designed as a dwelling or number of dwellings includes the construction of, or conversion to, a garage. The dwelling and the garage must be constructed or converted at the same time and the garage must be intended for occupation with the dwelling or one of the dwellings.

[*VATA 1994, s 35; FA 1995, s 33; FA 1996, s 30*].

Who can use the scheme. Refunds may be claimed by private owner-occupiers provided the property is not being built or converted with the intention to sell or let or for some other business purposes (in which case condition (*b*) is not satisfied). This does not affect the right of a private owner-occupier to make a claim even though they run a business from home or decide to sell the property at a later date.

Charities may also claim refunds in this way (although note that conversion work within (*a*)(iii) above only qualifies if resulting in residential accommodation and not a building intended for a relevant charitable purpose).

Sports clubs, etc. and associations which charge subscriptions for membership (or fees to non-members) and Housing Associations are regarded as being in business and cannot use the scheme.

Specialist help may be employed and it is not necessary for claimants to do any of the work themselves except as the organiser of the construction or conversion work. The key condition is that the work must not be carried out for a business reason.

Other work. Provided they are built at the same time as the main work, claims can be made for the construction of a conservatory attached to the dwelling, a driveway and main paths on the site, boundary and retaining walls and boundary fences. Refunds cannot be claimed for ornamental garden features, landscaping and planting, greenhouses or garden sheds. Adding features to an already completed building (e.g. a conservatory, patio, double-glazed windows, central heating or a garage) is not eligible for a refund. A building is normally complete when it has been finished according to the original plans or in accordance with Building Regulations. In cases of doubt, a building can be regarded as still under construction up until the date when a certificate of completion is issued by the local planning authority and all Building Regulations are complied with.

Goods and services not covered. Refunds cannot be claimed on building materials which would be standard-rated even when supplied with zero-rated building work. See 42.39 above. In addition VAT cannot be reclaimed on

- professional and supervisory services, including fees of architects and surveyors, and any other fees for management, consultancy, design and planning;

- purchase or hire of tools and equipment;

- consumables which are not incorporated in the building (e.g. cleaning materials);

- transport and haulage charges;

- temporary fencing; and

- skip hire.

(C & E Notice 719, paras 2.2, 3.5, 3.7–3.9, 4.5).

De Voil Indirect Tax Service. See V5.164.

42.53   **Making the claim**

Claim forms are available from C & E and are contained in the Claim Pack (VAT 431) which gives full details of how to complete the forms. Only one claim can be made for each building. The completed claim form and supporting evidence (see below) must be sent to the VAT office no later than three months after the completion of the construction or conversion. If this is not possible for any reason, C & E should be informed. The claim will be acknowledged within ten working days and, if there are no further enquiries, refunds will normally be made within 30 working days.

Unless C & E agree otherwise, the following documentation must be sent with the return.

- A certificate of completion from the local authority, for Building Regulation purposes or otherwise, or such other evidence of completion as is satisfactory to C & E. C & E have indicated that they will also accept

  (i) a habitation certificate or letter from the local authority (or, in Scotland, a temporary certificate of habitation);

  (ii) a valuation rating or council tax assessment; and

  (iii) a certificate from a bank or building society stating 'This is to certify that the .... Bank/Society* released on .... (insert date) the last instalment of its loan secured on the dwelling/building* at .... (insert address) because it then regarded that building as complete.'

    * Delete as applicable

- Invoices for all eligible goods (and, for conversion, any services) supplied to the claimant for which a claim is being made. The invoices must show

  (i) the supplier's VAT registration number;

  (ii) quantity and description of the goods and/or services;

  (iii) the price of each item; and

  (iv) if the value of the goods is over £100 (including VAT) the name and address of the claimant.

  Any adjustments made by a supplier for returned goods, credits or discounts must be reflected in the claim.

  For conversions only, where a single all inclusive invoice is received from a contractor, a detailed estimate or specification of the work carried out must be submitted with the claim. This is important as any goods and services on which VAT cannot be reclaimed must be separately identified and excluded from the claim.

- In respect of eligible goods imported from outside the EC, proof of importation (e.g. originals of any shipping or transit documents) and evidence of the VAT paid.

- In respect of acquisitions from other EC countries, invoices for the goods with amounts converted to sterling on the VAT claim. The rate of VAT may be different from the standard rate in the UK.

- Documentary evidence that planning permission for the building has been granted. The plans should also be included.

- A certificate signed by a quantity surveyor or architect that the goods shown in the claim were or, in his judgment, were likely to have been, incorporated in the building or its site.

(*SI 1995/2518, Regs 200, 201*). (C & E Notice 719, paras 5.1–5.7).

Appeals. If a claim for a refund is refused or C & E disagree with the amount of the refund, an appeal may be made to a VAT tribunal. See 5.3(*g*) APPEALS.

PART IV CARAVANS AND HOUSEBOATS

42.54 ZERO-RATED SUPPLIES OF CARAVANS AND HOUSEBOATS

Supplies of the following are zero-rated.

(*a*) **Caravans** exceeding the limits of size currently in force for trailers which may be towed on roads by a motor vehicle having an unladen weight of less than 2,030 kilogrammes. *Excluded* are certain removable contents, see 42.55 below. [*VATA 1994, 8 Sch Group 9, Item 1 and Note (a)*].

The term 'caravan' is not defined for VAT purposes. Its ordinary use covers mobile homes, statics, residentials, park homes, caravan holiday homes and tourers.

At present the limits apply to any caravan either more than 7 metres (22.9 feet) long or more than 2.3 metres (7.5 feet) wide (excluding towing bars and similar apparatus used solely for the purpose of attaching the caravan to a vehicle). The supply of a caravan below these limits is standard-rated. (C & E Notice 701/20/96, para 1).

(*b*) **Houseboats** i.e. boats or other floating decked structures designed or adapted for use solely as places of permanent habitation and not having means of, or capable of being readily adapted for, self-propulsion. *Excluded* are certain removable contents. [*VATA 1994, 8 Sch Group 9, Item 2 and Note (a)*].

(c) **Caravans or houseboats** qualifying under (a) or (b) above which are let or loaned or, if business assets, are put to any private use or are used, or made available to any person for use, for non-business purposes, subject to the overriding exception for accommodation below. [*VATA 1994, 8 Sch Group 9, Item 3*]. Yachts and barges are unlikely to be houseboats for VAT purposes because they are either capable of self-propulsion or can be easily adapted.

The supply of *accommodation* is excluded. [*VATA 1994, 8 Sch Group 9, Note (b)*].

De Voil Indirect Tax Service. See V4.275.

42.55 **CARAVANS**

Fixtures, fittings and removable contents. If the supply of a caravan is zero-rated, then zero-rating also includes any goods which a builder would ordinarily incorporate into a new house e.g. sinks, baths, WCs, fixed partitions and water heaters. See 42.37 and 42.38 above for further details. Other fixtures, and any removable contents supplied with the caravan (e.g. tables, chairs, mattresses, seat cushions, etc.), are standard-rated. Methods for arriving at the value of removable contents in new and used caravans are described below. Those methods do not have to be used but any different method must give a fair and reasonable result.

New caravans. Standard-rated removable contents included in the price of a new caravan can be calculated by reference to the costs incurred.

Example

A caravan is purchased from a manufacturer for resale. Its cost is £20,000 plus £150 VAT giving a total cost of £20,150. It is sold for £30,000 including VAT.

The VAT on sale must be the same proportion of the sale price as it was of the total cost.

$$\text{VAT due} = \text{sale price} \times \frac{\text{VAT on purchase}}{\text{total cost}}$$

$$£30,000 \times \frac{150}{£20,150} = £223.32$$

If further removable contents are added to those provided by the manufacturer (or some provided are taken out) before sale, these costs must be added/subtracted as appropriate before making the above calculations.

If a caravan and its removable contents are advertised at separate prices and the customer is entirely free to purchase the caravan at the lower price without the removable contents, then the charges for the removable contents may be treated as a separate taxable supply.

Used caravans. Standard-rated removable contents included in the price of used caravans can be calculated using either of the following methods.

• Calculate a precise value for each of the standard-rated removable contents. Adequate documentary evidence must be produced to support each valuation if required, e.g. values realised at public auction.

• Take the value of standard-rated removable contents to be 10% of the VAT-exclusive selling price of the complete caravan. This is a standard method of apportionment that has been agreed with the National Caravan Council Ltd and the British Holiday and Home Parks Association Ltd. If the caravan is sold at a VAT-inclusive price, the VAT element in that price is currently 7/407ths. If the margin scheme is used for sale of the caravan, then the 10% apportionment is applied to the margin rather than the full selling price. Charges for delivery, unloading and positioning and connections to mains are regarded as part of a single supply of the caravan (see below) and therefore form part of the price for the purposes of this calculation.

Whichever method is adopted, it must be applied consistently to all supplies.

Pitches. See 42.8 above.

Accommodation. The supply of holiday accommodation in a caravan already sited is standard-rated. See 33.9 HOTELS AND HOLIDAY ACCOMMODATION. Other supplies of accommodation in caravans (e.g. in caravans set aside for permanent residential use) are exempt.

Electricity and gas. Supplies of electricity and gas to a caravan are liable at the lower rate provided the users actual consumption can be identified (i.e. it is metered). Otherwise, the liability of the supply follows that of the main supply of the pitch rental. *For touring caravans*, where there is an optional hook-up charge and the caravan owner chooses to have electricity supplied to the pitch, the supply is subject to VAT at the lower rate. Any non-optional charge forms part of the overall pitch fee which is standard-rated.

Water and sewerage charges. Charges by park owners to individual caravan owners for such utilities may be zero-rated to the extent that the charges cover onward supplies to their caravans. The total supplies made to the park owner must be apportioned and consumption by the communal buildings, other common parts of the park and caravans owned by the park owner must be excluded before the zero-rated charges to individual caravan owners are arrived at. Apportionment on the basis of rateable value would normally be acceptable. *For touring caravans*, optional hook-up charges to water and sewerage services are zero-rated. Any non-optional charge forms part of the overall pitch fee which is standard-rated.

Local authority charges. *For seasonal or holiday parks*, the park owner must pay non-domestic rates on the whole site. If the park owner attributes a proportion of the rates to individual caravan owners using the official apportionment made by the local valuation officer, any charge is outside the scope of VAT. Any onward charge for the remainder of the rates element for the communal buildings, general facilities, etc. is part of the pitch fee rental and standard-rated. *For permanent caravan parks*, caravans not owned by the site owner attract non-domestic rates and are subject to council tax for which the resident or owner is liable.

Service charges. Service charges for general upkeep and maintenance of the park follow the liability of the pitch fee or rent. Individual services to particular residents are normally standard-rated (see under *Other charges* below).

Car parking charges are normally standard-rated. However, the supply of a garage or parking space in conjunction with the supply of a permanent residential caravan pitch is exempt provided

- the landlord retains ownership of the land on which the garage or parking space is sited; and

- the garage or parking space is reasonably close to the caravan pitch i.e. within the site complex.

Storage of touring caravans is standard-rated.

Insurance. Insurance supplied to a park owner to cover general liability or 'risks' which is separately recharged to caravan owners follows the liability of the pitch fee or rent. Where a park owner is asked by a caravan owner to arrange insurance cover for the caravan owner's risks, any charge made for arranging the insurance is exempt provided the caravan owner is the recipient of the supply of insurance made by the insurer. If not, any charge made is standard-rated. Similarly, any commission received for arranging the insurance on the caravan owner's behalf is exempt.

Any payments received in relation to the renewal of existing insurance policies follow the liability of the original supplies as above.

Delivery, unloading and positioning charges made by the supplier of the caravan at the same time as that supply follow the liability of the caravan. At other times, such charges are standard-rated.

Connection to mains services. Charges by park owners to caravan owners for connecting mains services (gas, electricity, water and sewerage) directly *from* the pitch *to* their caravans form part of the consideration for the supply of the caravan. This is restricted to the one-off connection fee and does not include general maintenance or the provision of infrastructure which provides the utilities to the pitch itself.

Park owners' commission on sales of second-hand sited caravans. The 'commission' which a park owner is entitled to receive under the Mobile Homes Acts and/or Code of Practice when a caravan owner sells a caravan 'on site' at his park follows the liability of the pitch fee or rent. Any additional charge to the seller, e.g. for agency services, is standard-rated.

Reservation fees or premiums charged by the park owner follow the liability of the pitch fee or rent.

Fees received by park owners from third parties. Any commission from a caravan manufacturer/dealer for the sale of a caravan is standard-rated. A premium payment received to reserve a pitch on behalf of a purchaser of a caravan follows the liability of the pitch fee.

Brick skirtings and pitches. Any one-off charge directly related to the obligations under the pitch agreement (e.g. the construction of pitches, bases and the park infrastructure) generally follow the liability of the supply of the pitch. The provision of brick skirting is generally integral to the agreement to supply the caravan and follows the liability of that supply.

Other charges made to individual caravan owners by the park owner (e.g. holiday booking services, off-season storage and security, club membership, repair and maintenance of caravans and drainage of water-systems) are standard-rated.

(C & E Notice 701/20/96, paras 2–18, Annex C; C & E Notice 700/57/95).

For a general consideration of the recovery of input tax in relation to caravan parks, see *Stonecliff Caravan Park, [1993] VATTR 464 (11097)* and *Harpcombe Ltd QB, [1996] STC 726.*

42.56   **HOUSEBOATS**

Fixtures, fittings and removable contents, Accommodation, Delivery, etc. and Connection to mains services. The same provisions apply as for caravans in 42.55 above.

Mooring rights for a houseboat are exempt. See 42.11 above for moorings generally.

Garages and parking spaces supplied to the owners of houseboats are exempt provided the garage or parking space is

- supplied by the person who is supplying the mooring; and

- reasonably close to the mooring.

(C & E Notice 701/20/96, paras 19–24).

43   Local Authorities and Statutory Bodies

Cross-references. See 8.1 BUSINESS for the meaning of business; 20.12 EDUCATION; 51.10 PAYMENT OF VAT for repayment supplement; 52.10 and 52.11 PENALTIES for serious misdeclaration or neglect resulting in understatements or overclaims; 53.4 PENSION FUNDS.

De Voil Indirect Tax Service. See V6.153–156.

43.1   BODIES GOVERNED BY PUBLIC LAW

Under *EC 6th Directive, Art 4.5*, any state, regional and local government authority or other 'body governed by public law' is not considered to be a taxable person in respect of any activity or transaction where the following conditions are met.

(*a*)   *The body is engaged in the activity or transaction as a public authority.* It is irrelevant whether the body collects dues, fees, contributions or payments in connection with the activity or transaction.

There is nothing in EC legislation specifying those activities in which bodies engage as public authorities and it does not follow that just because a body is a public authority that all activities it undertakes are non-taxable activities (or 'non-business' as such activities are more commonly referred to in the UK).

Apart from the special categories of activities within (*c*) below which are always regarded as business, activities which can be, or are, provided in competition with the private sector are generally considered to be business activities. On the other hand, activities engaged in as public authorities are those which are covered by the special legal regime applicable to the particular body and which are not carried out in competition with the private sector. See *Comune di Carpaneto Piacentino and Others v Ufficio Provinciale Imposta sul Valore Aggiunto di Piacenza CJEC, [1990] 3 CMLR 153; Norwich City Council (11822)* and *Metropolitan Borough of Wirral (14674).*

See the Appendix to this chapter for the VAT status of the most common activities of local authorities.

(*b*)   *Treatment as a non-taxable person does not lead to a significant distortion of competition.* There is no definition in UK law to quantify the term 'significant' in relation to distortion of competition. In *Comune di Carpaneto Piacentino* above the CJEC considered the matter but did no more than decide that individual countries should determine whether distortion of competition was significant and that they were not required to lay down precise quantitative limits. C & E have always taken the view that distortion of competition will only be considered 'significant' where its distortive effect is potentially so great that it could be felt nationally rather than only locally.

Many of the activities of local authorities are subject to competitive tendering. Services provided under a statutory obligation to a third party using an outside body acting as agent (e.g. domestic refuse collection) are non-business provided there is no competition between the local authority and others to supply the services to the third party.

(*c*)   *Unless carried out on such a scale as to be negligible, the activity does not relate to*

- telecommunications;

- the supply of water, gas, electricity and steam;

- the transport of goods;

- port and airport services;

- passenger transport;

- supply of new goods manufactured for sale;

- the transactions of agricultural intervention agencies in respect of agricultural products carried out pursuant to Regulations on the common organisation of the market in these products;

- the running of trade fairs and exhibitions;

- warehousing;

- the activities of commercial publicity bodies;

- the activities of travel agencies;

- the running of staff shops, co-operatives and industrial canteens and similar institutions; and

- transactions of radio and television bodies of a commercial nature.

'*Body governed by public law*' is not defined in the *EC 6th Directive* but in *EC Council Directive 93/36* it is interpreted as any body

- established for the specific purpose of meeting needs in the general interest, not having an industrial or commercial character;

- having legal personality; and

- financed, for the most part, by the State, or regional or local authorities, or other bodies governed by public law, or subject to management supervision by those bodies, or having an administrative, managerial or supervisory board, more than half of whose members are appointed by the State, regional or local authorities or by other bodies governed by public law.

(C & E Notice 749, para 3.2; C & E Manual V1-14, Chapter 1 para 1.2, Chapter 2 paras 2.3, 2.7, 2.8).

See also *Arts Council of Great Britain (11991)* and *Royal Academy of Music (11871)*.

De Voil Indirect Tax Service. See V2.108.

43.2   **Statutory bodies**

Certain bodies governed by public law within 43.1 above are given special treatment for UK VAT purposes. The specified bodies are as follows.

(*a*) A '*local authority*', i.e. the council of a county, district, London borough, parish or group of parishes (or, in Wales, community or group of communities), the Common Council of the City of London, the Council of the Isles of Scilly, and any joint committee or joint board established by two or more of the foregoing and, in relation to Scotland, a regional, islands or district council within the meaning of the *Local Government (Scotland) Act 1973*, any combination and any joint committee or joint board established by two or more of the foregoing, and any joint board to which *section 226* of that Act applies. [*VATA 1994, s 96(4)*].

There are many bodies closely associated with local authorities, receiving funding from them or having local authority members on their boards, which are not themselves a local authority for these purposes. Local authorities may discharge certain of their functions through committees and they have an interest in other committees (e.g. those responsible for the day-to-day management of community centres, youth clubs and sports halls). Only those committees which are discharging a local authority function may be treated as a local authority and it is therefore necessary to determine whether a particular committee is in fact doing so. For a committee to be considered as discharging a local authority function it must

(i) be established by a local authority, or two or more authorities, under *Local Government Act 1972, s 101(2)* or be preserved under *Local Government Act 1972, s 101(9)* (or be a sub-committee of any such committee); and

(ii) have voting rights restricted to local authority members, unless exception to this requirement is provided by *SI 1990/1553, Regs 4 or 5*.

C & E do not consider the following bodies to be local authorities.

- Joint boards/committees established by persons other than local authorities, even where they include local authorities as members or participants, e.g. boards established by order of a Minister of the Crown.

- Bodies where voting rights are not restricted to local authority members unless the exceptions in *SI 1990/1553* apply.

- Bodies which merely receive financial assistance from local authorities.

- Committees set up under *Local Government Act 1972, s 102(4)*. These are committees whose role is advisory only.

- Community Councils in Scotland and England.

- Community Associations.

- Parish meetings.

(C & E Manual V1-14, Chapter 2 para 3.4).

(*b*) A river purification board established under *Local Government (Scotland) Act 1973, s 135* and a water development board within the meaning of the *Water (Scotland) Act 1980, s 109*.

(*c*) An internal drainage board.

(*d*) A passenger transport authority or executive established under *Part II* of the *Transport Act 1968*.

(*e*) A port health authority within the meaning of *Public Health (Control of Disease) Act 1984*, and a port local authority and joint port local authority constituted under *Part X* of the *Public Health (Scotland) Act 1897*.

(*f*) A police authority and the Receiver for the Metropolitan Police District.

(*g*) A development corporation within the *New Towns Act 1981* or the *New Towns (Scotland) Act 1968*; a new town commission within the *New Towns Act (Northern Ireland) 1965* and the Commission for the New Towns.

(*h*) A general lighthouse authority within the meaning of *Part VIII* of the *Merchant Shipping Act 1995* (except that no VAT refund is made which C & E consider is attributable to activities other than the provision, maintenance or management of lights or other navigational aids).

(*i*) The British Broadcasting Corporation.

(*j*) A nominated news provider as defined in *Broadcasting Act 1990, s 31(3)* (except that no VAT refund is made which C & E consider is attributable to activities other than the provision of news programmes for broadcasting by holders of regional Channel 3 licences within the meaning of *Part 1* of that Act).

(k) Any body specified by an order made by the Treasury. Currently, these comprise

- Welsh National Water Development Authority [*SI 1973/2121*];

- the Commissions for Local Administration in England, Wales, and Scotland; and the Commission for Local Authority Accounts in Scotland [*SI 1976/2028*];

- the Inner London Education Authority, the Inner London Interim Education Authority; The Northumbria Interim Police Authority; the London Fire and Civil Defence Authority; the London Residuary Body; a metropolitan county Police Authority, Fire and Civil Defence Authority, Passenger Transport Authority or Residuary Body [*SI 1985/1101*];

- a probation committee constituted by the *Powers of Criminal Courts Act 1973, s 47, 3 Sch 2* ; a magistrates' courts committee established under *Justice of the Peace Act 1979, s 19* ; and the charter trustees constituted by *Local Government Act 1972, s 246(4) or (5)* [*SI 1986/336*];

- authorities established under *Local Government Act 1985, s 10* [*SI 1986/532*];

- National Rivers Authority [*SI 1989/1217*];

- the Environment Agency [*SI 1995/1978*];

- a National Park authority (within the meaning of *Environment Act 1995, s 63*) [*SI 1995/2999*];

- a fire authority constituted by a combination scheme made under *Fire Service Act 1947, s 6* [*SI 1995/2999*]; and

- charter trustees established under *Local Government Act 1992, s 17* or any other statutory instrument made under *Part II* of that Act.

[*VATA 1994, s 33(3)–(5); Merchant Shipping Act 1995, 13 Sch; SI 1997/2558*].

The above authorities are subject to VAT on their business activities in the ordinary way. On their non-business activities, although they must not normally charge output tax (see 43.4 below), they can recover input tax they suffered under a special refund scheme (see 43.5 below).

43.3   REGISTRATION

Every local authority which makes any taxable supplies in the course or furtherance of its business is required to be registered whatever the value of its supplies. [*VATA 1994, s 42*]. Other public bodies, including those listed in 43.2 above, are required to be registered only if their taxable supplies exceed the limit for REGISTRATION (59). They may apply for voluntary registration. Separate registration is normally required for

(a) any committee or body which has close links with a local authority but is legally separate from it (e.g. housing trusts and enterprise agencies); and

(b) local authority joint committees

although application may be made to waive the requirement for separate registration under (b) above if it is preferred to account for VAT under the registration of the parent or member authority. (C & E Notice 749, para 3.1).

Even if a local authority or other statutory body is not required to register under the general requirements based on taxable supplies in the UK, it may be liable to register for VAT where it makes certain acquisitions of goods from other EC countries in excess of an annual threshold. See 59.18 REGISTRATION.

43.4 **CHARGING VAT**

A body within 43.1 above (which includes any body within 43.2 above) that is registered, or liable to be registered, for VAT must charge and account for VAT on all its taxable supplies. This applies whether the customer is a private individual, trader, government department or another public body or local authority. It must not however charge VAT on non-business supplies (although see below for certain supplies between local authorities). The VAT status of the most common activities of local authorities are listed in the Appendix to this chapter.

Supplies of goods between local authorities. VAT must be charged on goods sold by the Local Authority Purchasing Consortia to other local authorities and on goods sold between local authorities (C & E Notice 749, Appendix B; C & E Business Brief 10/93, 26 March 1993; C & E Business Brief 7/94, 7 March 1994).

Supplies of services between local authorities. Such supplies should be treated as follows.

- Supplies of services made under a statutory obligation

    (i) should be treated as non-business if not in competition with the private sector; and

    (ii) should be treated as business and subject to the appropriate rate of VAT if in competition with the private sector.

- Supplies of services not made under a statutory obligation

    (i) should be treated as non-business if not in competition with the private sector but may be taxed if both parties agree; and

    (ii) should be treated as business and subject to the appropriate rate of VAT if in competition with the private sector.

- Supplies of services that include any supply of goods should be treated as business and are subject to VAT at the appropriate rate.

(C & E Business Brief 9/95, 18 May 1995).

See also VAT Information Sheet 5/98, June 1998 for transitional arrangements up to 31 March 1999 for supplies to new unitary authorities under local government reorganisation with effect from 1 April 1998.

43.5 **RECLAIMING VAT**

Refund scheme for non-business activities. Generally, there is no entitlement to recovery of VAT incurred for the purposes of non-business activities. However, a special refund scheme permits a body within 43.2 above to reclaim the VAT chargeable on supplies of goods or services, acquisitions of goods from another EC country and imports of goods from outside the EC where the supply, acquisition or importation is not for the purposes of a business activity carried on by the body concerned. A claim is required in such form as C & E determine. [*VATA 1994, s 33(1)*]. A body does not have to be registered for VAT to claim the refund but if it is not registered, it cannot reclaim the VAT charged at source on acquisitions from other EC countries.

The purpose of this provision is to prevent VAT being a burden on local authority funding. The arrangement relates only to goods and services supplied *direct* to a body. This condition is met if the body

- places the order;

- receives the supply;

- makes payment from its own funds or certain trust funds or donated funds (see below); and

- receives a VAT invoice addressed to it. In the case of local authorities invoices are sometimes made out in the name of a particular local authority institution (e.g. a school) or even an employee (e.g. a head teacher). Provided that the purchase meets all the other conditions for inclusion in the scheme then the VAT on such invoices may be recovered. (C & E Manual V1-14, Chapter 2 para 3.6).

See VAT Information Sheet 4/98 for the treatment of community projects with voluntary groups.

The scheme extends to

- purchases made from funds of a trust but only if

    (i) the claim relates to the non-business activities of the trust;

    (ii) the local authority acts as sole trustee without payment; and

    (iii) the purposes of the trust relate so closely to the municipal activities of the authority that they cannot be reasonably distinguished (e.g. the upkeep of a village hall); and

- purchases made from funds given to a local authority for specified purposes provided the local authority

    (i) makes the purchase itself (i.e. places the order, receives the supply and a VAT invoice addressed to it and makes payment);

    (ii) retains ownership of the purchase and uses it for its own non-business purposes; and

    (iii) keeps sufficient records of the purchase and the purpose for which it is made.

(C & E Notice 749, paras 4.1–4.3).

Where such non-business supplies, acquisitions or importations cannot be conveniently distinguished from business supplies, etc, the refund is the amount remaining after deducting from the whole of the VAT chargeable such proportion as C & E consider to be attributable to business purposes. [*VATA 1994, s 33(2)*].

Non-recoverable VAT. VAT which is specifically excluded from credit by the Treasury under *VATA 1994, s 25(7)* in relation to business activities is also excluded from credit by bodies in respect of their non-business activities. [*VATA 1994, s 33(6)*]. See, for example, 9 BUSINESS ENTERTAINMENT and 45.3 MOTOR CARS. Bodies can reclaim VAT under the scheme on motor cars used *exclusively* for their non-business activity although where any car is made available for private use, the restriction on input tax recovery applies (C & E Notice 700/64/96, para 39).

Claiming the refund. Bodies registered for VAT make the claim by including the amount refundable in Box 4 on the VAT return.

Unregistered bodies must apply in writing for a refund. The claim must relate to a period of at least one month and, if for under £100, must cover a period of at least twelve months. The period chosen should always end on the last day of a calendar month. The claim should be set out as follows:

VCU/VOPS GD
HM Customs and Excise
2nd Floor
Alexander House
21 Victoria Street
Southend-on-Sea
SS99 1AU

I am claiming a refund of £   for the period   to   to cover VAT charged on goods and services bought for [insert name of authority] non-business activities. *The tax claimed includes VAT incurred for exempt business activities which can be reclaimed under paragraph 4.4 of Notice 749.

Signed

For [insert name of authority]
Address

Contact name
Contact telephone number

* Delete as appropriate

(C & E Notice 749, para 4.7, Appendix D).

Input tax attributable to taxable business activities. VAT incurred on goods or services used, or to be used, for business purposes can be treated as input tax and is deductible subject to the normal rules.

Input tax attributable to exempt business activities. Input tax attributable to exempt business activities is normally not recoverable (subject to the partial exemption *de minimis* provisions). However, local authorities and similar bodies within 43.2 above are not covered by the normal partial exemption regulations and are allowed to recover input tax relating to exempt supplies where C & E consider it to be an 'insignificant' proportion of the total VAT incurred. [*VATA 1994, s 33(2)*]. '*Insignificant*' means

- not more than £625 per month on average; or

- less than 5% of the total VAT incurred on all purchases in a year, including those from business and non-business activities.

Where the input tax attributable to exempt supplies exceeds both of the above limits, then none of it may be recovered.

In calculating the input tax attributable to exempt business activities, an appropriate proportion of the input tax incurred on general expenditure, including overheads, must be included.

When applying the above limits, VAT can be ignored on those exempt supplies listed in 49.3 PARTIAL EXEMPTION which partly exempt businesses outside the financial sector can ignore. See also 53.4 PENSION FUNDS for concessional treatment for certain local authority pension funds.

A calculation must be carried out at the end of each financial year and any necessary adjustment should be included in the VAT return for the next period. Where a local authority does not close down accounts at the financial year end and, for a limited time, continues to process 'old year' transactions, it may apply to the VAT office for approval to make any adjustment on a later return.

Special partial exemption method. C & E have developed the following partial exemption method which bodies may use. If a body wishes to adopt that method (or another method other than the normal standard partial exemption method, see 49.6 PARTIAL EXEMPTION) it must obtain written agreement from the VAT office prior to the start of the financial year in which it is to be used.

Step 1   *Identification of exempt activity.* List, within committee, all budget headings/ cost centres that contain any element of exempt activity.

Step 2   *Identifying taxable expenditure.* Within each budget heading/cost centre identified above, record all expenditure (net of VAT) for both capital and revenue that would normally carry VAT.

Step 3   *Recharges.* Recharges to budget heads/cost centres that contain any element of exempt activity may be treated as a fully standard-rated expenditure item. Alternatively a full analysis of recharges may be carried out as follows.

1.   Identify each main budget heading that makes any recharges.

For each budget heading:

2.   Calculate percentage of taxable expenditure.

3.   Calculate a weighting figure:

$$\frac{\text{total expenditure}}{\text{total expenditure} + \text{recharges in}}$$

4.   Multiply recharges out by weighting figure.

5.   Multiply result of 4 by result of 2.

Using total figures for all budget headings:

6.   Divide 4 by recharges out. (*Average factor*)

7.   Divide 5 by 6. (*Taxable value of recharges*)

8.   Divide 7 by recharges out to give weighted taxable %. (*Average taxable %*)

9.   The average taxable percentage should be applied to determine the taxable element of all recharges impacting on exempt activities.

Step 4   *Calculate percentage of exempt related input tax.* Add up the standard-rated expenditure identified in Steps 2 and 3 and calculate the VAT thereon by multiplying by 17.5%.

If the total at Step 4 is insignificant (see above) then no further calculations are required. Otherwise, a progressively detailed analysis must be made of the amount of expenditure which is put to exempt use. If, at any stage, the total is insignificant, no further action is required. There is no set method of allocation or apportionment. A body may adopt a different method for each particular area or activity based on the information available (e.g. number of staff, amount of income, floor area used, number of sessions, etc.) provided it can demonstrate that any method used is fair and equitable. Where, despite detailed analysis of the amount of expenditure put to exempt use, the above limits are still exceeded, none of the VAT relating to exempt supplies is recoverable.

Change of intention. With effect from 1 April 1998, where the local authority incurs VAT and intends to use that VAT in making taxable supplies or exempt supplies or in carrying on a non-business activity, but changes that intention before it actually makes those supplies or undertakes that activity, it must review the original attribution and make any appropriate adjustment.

● Change from taxable or non-business to exempt use

(1)   VAT is provisionally treated as recoverable in full in the year in which it is incurred.

(2)   If in a subsequent year the authority actually uses it, or forms an intention to use it, in making an exempt supply, that amount of VAT should be identified.

(3)   The VAT identified under (2) must be added to the total exempt input tax determined by the refund calculation for the year in which that VAT was originally incurred, and the revised result using the same method should be noted.

(4)   The combined effect of all changes required to the calculation at (3) above should be compared to the *de minimis* limit for the year in which the VAT was originally incurred. If the revised result remains below the *de minimis* limit for that year, no further action should be taken. If the revised result calculated exceeds, or still exceeds, the *de minimis* limit for that year, then the VAT identified under (2) above must be repaid to C & E on the next VAT return.

(5)   It is only that VAT in respect of which there has been a change that needs to be repaid. No adjustment is required in respect of any other VAT included in the original refund calculation.

- Changes from exempt to taxable or non-business use

(1)   The VAT is treated as exempt input tax in the year in which it is incurred.

(2)   If in a subsequent year the authority uses it, or forms the intention to use it, in making a taxable supply or carrying out a non-business activity, that amount of VAT should be identified.

(3)   If, in the year in which the VAT was originally incurred, the authority was within its *de minimis* limit such that the VAT identified under (2) above was recovered in full, no further adjustment should be made. If, however, the authority exceeded the *de minimis* limit for that year so that the VAT identified under (2) above was originally restricted and repaid to C & E, that amount may be reclaimed on the next VAT return.

(4)   It is only that VAT identified under (2) above that may be reclaimed from C & E. No adjustment must be made in respect of any other VAT included in the original refund calculation.

Error in attribution. With effect from 1 April 1998, if, in a subsequent year, it transpires that the original attribution of VAT incurred to taxable or exempt supplies or non-business activities was incorrect, the authority must rework the refund calculation for the earlier year in which the VAT was originally attributed and amend its calculation as follows.

- If the authority was within the *de minimis* limit for the earlier year but, as a result of the amended calculation, exempt input tax is increased so that the *de minimis* limit is exceeded, the authority must repay all the exempt input tax.

- If the authority had already exceeded the *de minimis* limit for the earlier year but, as a result of the amended calculation, the amount of exempt input tax increases, the authority should repay that additional exempt input tax.

- If the authority had exceeded its *de minimis* limit for the earlier year but, as a result of the amended calculation, the amount of exempt input tax decreases so that the authority is now within its *de minimis* limit, the authority can reclaim all the exempt input tax it repaid to C & E on account of previously exceeding its *de minimis* limit in the earlier year.

- If the authority had exceeded its *de minimis* limit for the earlier year and as a result of the amended calculation, the amount of exempt input tax decreases but still exceeds its *de minimis* limit, the authority can reclaim the amount by which its exempt input tax has been reduced.

All adjustments should be made in accordance with the provisions for voluntary disclosure of errors in 57.11 RECORDS.

Capital goods scheme items. With effect from 1 April 1998, where a local authority has an asset within the capital goods scheme and the extent to which that asset is used in making exempt supplies changes, it must carry out an adjustment to the amount of VAT reclaimed on the initial acquisition (see 10 CAPITAL GOODS SCHEME). For the purpose of the special partial exemption method for local authorities, a change in the exempt use includes both a change from taxable to exempt use and from non-business to exempt use (and vice versa).

- Change from taxable or non-business use to exempt use.

  (1) The adjustment as calculated should not be treated as exempt input tax for the purposes of the refund calculation for the year in question, and does not count towards the authority's *de minimis* limit.

  (2) If, at the end of the year, the authority remains within its *de minimis* limit, no further action need be taken in respect of the adjustment. However, If the authority exceeds its *de minimis* limit and becomes partly exempt, the adjustment must be repaid to C & E at the same time as the exempt input tax is repaid.

- Change from exempt to taxable or non-business use

  (1) The adjustment as calculated should not be treated as input tax for the purposes of the refund calculation for the year in question, and does not count towards the authority's *de minimis* limit.

  (2) If the VAT incurred on the initial acquisition of the asset was recovered in full because, in that year, the authority remained below its *de minimis* limit, no further action is required in respect of the adjustment as the VAT was not originally restricted. However, if some or all of the VAT on the initial acquisition of the item was restricted because the authority exceeded its *de minimis* limit in that year, the amount of the adjustment can be reclaimed in line with other adjustments following the refund calculation.

Authorities should keep a record of relevant capital assets and the amount of VAT initially incurred and claimed as, although they may originally be *de minimis*, an adjustment may be required several years later when the *de minimis* limit is exceeded.

Change in VAT liability. With effect from 1 April 1998, where a local authority attributes any VAT incurred

- to an intended taxable or non-business supply but, before that supply or activity takes place, there is a change in the VAT liability of the supply or activity so that it becomes exempt, or

- to an intended exempt supply but, before that supply takes place, there is a change in the VAT liability of that supply such that it becomes taxable or non-business,

there is no requirement to change retrospectively the original attribution of the VAT.

(C & E Notice 749, para 4.4, 4.5, Appendices E and F; C & E Manual V1-14, Chapter 2 para 3.8; VAT Information Sheet 7/98, June 1998).

See also *Mayor and Burgesses of London Borough of Haringey v C & E Commrs QB, [1995] STC 830* and C & E Business Brief 11/95, 2 June 1995.

Estimated returns by local authorities. A local authority, because of the wide range of its activities, is not always able to process all its purchase invoices in time to include them on the appropriate VAT return. It may therefore apply to C & E for permission to estimate input tax and *Sec 33* refunds due. If approved, the local authority must calculate the average time lag for the processing of invoices, i.e. the time from receipt of an invoice to the date of payment. Although any appropriate method may be used, C & E suggest the following method.

- Carry out a sampling exercise on a fully representative basis in each spending department so as to produce information on the typical time lag experienced. Samples should exclude any transactions not involving VAT.

- Calculate the overall time lag for all departments using a weighting to take into account the relative amounts spent by the various departments.

The estimate for any return period is then calculated using the formula

$$I \times \frac{P}{C}$$

where

I = Input tax and *Sec 33* refunds on payments made during the period

P = Number of weeks taken to process invoices

C = Number of weeks covered by the claim

The estimate is then added to the normal claim on payments made in the period. In the following and successive VAT periods, the estimate added in the previous month is deducted and the new estimate based on the current period included.

To take account of any changes in the time lag, a similar sampling exercise should be undertaken every two years and also when there is a fundamental change to the accounting system or payment policy.

(C & E Manual V1-24, section 5.8 and Appendix D).

De Voil Indirect Tax Service. See V5.162.

43.6 **GOVERNMENT DEPARTMENTS**

The Crown is not excluded from VAT and any taxable supplies made by or to it are treated in the same way as taxable supplies by taxable persons.

Where a 'Government department' supplies goods or services which do not amount to the carrying on of a business but it appears to the Treasury that similar supplies are or might be supplied by taxable persons, then the Treasury may direct that the supplies by the department are treated as supplies in the course or furtherance of a business.

Where VAT is chargeable on the supply of goods or services to a Government department, on the acquisition of goods by a Government department from another EC country or on the importation of any goods by a Government department from outside the EC and the supply, acquisition or importation is not for the purpose of any business carried on by the department (or treated as such under the above provisions) then, on a claim, the VAT may still be refunded if the Treasury so directs. The claim must be in such form and manner as C & E determine and any refund is conditional on the department complying with requirements as to the keeping, preservation and production of records relating to the supply.

The Treasury may similarly so direct where one Government department supplies another department or the supplies are to or from the Crown Estate Commissioners.

'*Government department*' includes the National Assembly for Wales, a NI department, a Northern Ireland health and social services body, any body of persons exercising functions on behalf of a Minister of the Crown (including a health service body and a National Health Service trust) and any part of such a department designated for these purposes by the Treasury.

[*VATA 1994, s 41*].

In practice, the Treasury periodically issues a direction with a list of eligible government departments and a list of eligible goods and services on which VAT will be refunded provided the supply of those goods and services is not for the purposes of either any business carried on by the department or any supply by the department treated as a supply in the course or furtherance of a business. The latest such direction was reproduced in The London Gazette on 24 July 1998. The Treasury also issues a direction listing, for each government department, those supplies which are treated as supplied in the course or furtherance of a business when supplied by that department. The latest such direction was dated 3 March 1993 and has been subsequently amended by directions on 3 March 1994, 9 March 1995, 6 March 1996, 3 March 1997 and 16 March 1998.

For supplies by government departments of welfare services otherwise than for a profit, see 43.7 below.

De Voil Indirect Tax Service. See V5.161

43.7   **WELFARE SERVICES**

EC legislation. See 22.17(*g*) EUROPEAN COMMUNITY LEGISLATION.

The supply, 'otherwise than for a profit', by a 'public body' of 'welfare services' and of goods supplied in connection therewith is exempt.

'*Public body*' means a government department (see 43.6 above), local authority (see 43.1 above) and any other body which acts under any enactment or instrument for public purposes and not for its own profit and which performs functions similar to those of a government department or local authority.

'*Welfare services*' means services directly connected with

- the provision of 'care', treatment or instruction designed to promote the physical or mental welfare of elderly, sick, distressed or disabled persons;

- the 'protection of children and young persons'; or

- the provision of 'spiritual welfare' by a religious institution as part of a course of instruction or a retreat, not being a course or retreat designed primarily to provide recreation or a holiday.

Excluded is the supply of accommodation or catering unless ancillary to the provision of care, treatment or instruction.

[*VATA 1994, 9 Sch Group 7, Item 9*].

The identical provisions apply to such supplies made by charities. See 12.9 CHARITIES for C & E's interpretation of '*otherwise than for a profit*' (substituting 'public body' for 'charity'), '*welfare*', '*care*', '*protection of children and young persons*' and '*spiritual welfare*'.

Transport services. The supply of transport services for sick or injured persons in vehicles specially designed for that purpose is exempt. [*VATA 1994, 9 Sch Group 7, Item 11*].

43.8   **BUILDING REGULATION FEES**

In England and Wales, from 13 January 1997 competition exists across the whole range of building control work and local authorities should charge VAT at the standard rate on all building regulation fees. From 1 January 1996 to 12 January 1997, local authorities did not have to charge VAT on building regulation fees which were outside the current approval of NHBC (Building Control Services) Ltd under *Building (Approved Inspector) Regulations 1985*. Fees charged where there was private competition had to be standard-rated.

Any VAT charged on building regulation services between 11 November 1985 and 31 December 1995 where there was no competition may be reclaimed by the person who paid it to the local authority, provided that it has not already been recovered as input tax. The three year time limit for claims does not apply to such repayments. Most local authorities have authorised C & E to act as their agent in which case, until 30 June 1998, the claimant should send the original invoice or other evidence of payment together with a claim form VAT 72 to

Building Regulations VAT Claims Office
Chaucers Walk
Furthergate Industrial Estate
Blackburn
BB1 3AF

Authorities which have elected to make refunds themselves directly to claimants will issue a credit note for the VAT refunded. After 30 June 1998, any outstanding claims must be made directly to the local authority.

Claim forms are obtainable from local authorities, VAT Advice Centres or the VAT claims office above.

In Scotland and Northern Ireland, the supply of building control services is the monopoly of local authorities and classed as non-business for VAT purposes.

(C & E Business Brief 26/95, 11 December 1995; C & E News Release 10/96,16 February 1996; C & E Business Brief 5/97, 5 March 1997; C & E Business Brief 27/97, 21 November 1997).

43.9   **ADMISSION CHARGES**

Subject to certain restrictions, admission charges by public bodies to

- a museum, gallery, art exhibition or zoo, or

- a theatrical, musical or choreographic performance of a cultural nature

are exempt. See 58.6 RECREATION AND SPORT for full details.

43.10   **STATUTORY WORK IN DEFAULT**

Local authorities are empowered, by specific legislative provisions, to issue notices requiring that works are carried out in a number of situations.

- Where the recipient of the notice agrees to the work being carried out and arranges the work with either a contractor or with the local authority, the supply of the contractor's services is to the recipient of the notice. If the local authority arranges the contractor's supplies on the recipient's behalf they may treat these supplies as being to the authority and by the authority under VATA 1994, s 47(3). The VAT incurred by the local authority is recoverable as input tax under *VATA 1994, s 25*.

- Where the recipient of the notice refuses to comply, the local authority may exercise its statutory powers, have the work carried out and recover the cost of the works from the recipient. In these circumstances the authority is not making a supply for VAT purposes. The VAT incurred by the local authority can be recovered under *VATA 1994, s 33*. See also *Glasgow City Council (15491)* where the tribunal held that works in default and the subsequent recovery of costs under *Housing (Scotland) Act 1987, ss 108, 109* were not supplies for VAT purposes.

(C & E Business Brief 19/98, 15 September 1998).

APPENDIX: VAT STATUS OF ACTIVITIES OF LOCAL AUTHORITIES, ETC.

1. EDUCATION

(a) Education

Supply of primary and secondary education including the recovery of costs from other local authorities for education of their pupils	Non-business
School visits supplied to its own pupils as part of the curriculum	Non-business
Provision of pre-school education (without charge)	Non-business
Adult education	Business
Training, retraining or research not provided under a statutory obligation	Business
Government funded training schemes	Business
Careers services provided under *Employment Rights Act 1993*	Non-business where provided under a direction from the Secretary of State, otherwise business

(b) Supplies provided in connection with education, etc.

Sale of goods closely related to the provision of education forming part of the curriculum, other than clothing or sports equipment	Non-business where sold to its own pupils in class, at or below cost and for regular classroom use, otherwise business
Sale of clothing or sports equipment	Business
Meals supplied to own pupils in schools	Non-business
Sales of food and drink to own pupils e.g. from vending machines	Non-business where sold in a school catering outlet and sales of catering predominate, otherwise business
Sales of food and drink supplied otherwise than in school catering outlets	Business
Sales of meals, etc. to staff and visitors where separately identified	Business
Supplies of goods and services, e.g. catering, to grant-maintained schools	Business
Supplies of goods and services in connection with non-statutory education, etc.	Business
Sale of classwork to pupils as part of statutory education	Non-business
Sale of classwork in all other circumstances	Business
Boarding and transportation provided for a charge as part of non-business education	Non-business

Local Authorities and Statutory Bodies

The provision of facilities to youth club members in return for their subscriptions or for additional payment where the facilities are directly related to the club's ordinary activities	Business
Supply of teachers	Business unless supplied under a statutory obligation or separately identified below
Supply of staff to Compact initiatives	Non-business
Release of teachers to examination boards	Non-business
Supply of teachers under a mentorship scheme	Non-business
(c) **Administration of education**	
Examination and enrolment fees	Follows the liability of the education
Administration of admissions policy for non-LEA maintained schools	Business
Preparation of statements for special needs pupils	Non-business
Provision of information. Assessment and administration of complaints relating to the National Curriculum	Non-business
Provision of examination services to non-LEA maintained schools	Business
School inspections	Business
(d) **Miscellaneous**	
Student awards, scholarships, bursaries etc.	Outside the scope of VAT
Internal repairs, etc. to voluntary aided schools for which the local authority is responsible under the *Education Act 1944*	Non-business
Provision of information on schools, e.g. to parents, under the *Education Act 1944*	Non-business

2. ENTERTAINMENT, CULTURE AND RECREATION

(a) **Library services**

Loan of books and talking books, including reservation fees and fees for late returns	Non-business
Temporary readers' deposits and library membership fees	Non-business
Prison and hospital library services	Non-business
Loans of pictures, cassettes, videos, computer games, vinyl and compact disks; associated fees, subscriptions and charges for late returns	Business
Charges for loss or damage of loan items	Outside the scope
Supply of library services to grant-maintained schools, etc.	Business

(b) Holidays and related supplies

Supply of holidays other than	Business
School trips	see section 1 above
Statutory care	see section 4 below
Letting of accommodation for holiday purposes and provision of camping facilities	Business
Letting of pitches for beach huts and holiday caravans	Business
Mooring rights for houseboats	Business
Hire of deck chairs	Business

(c) Provision of facilities and admissions

Hunting, shooting and fishing rights	Business
Letting of halls or rooms	Business
Letting of circus or fair sites	Business
Letting of facilities for playing sport or participating in any physical recreation	Business
Separately identifiable supplies made in conjunction with the letting of rooms or hire or sports facilities, e.g. catering or cloakroom facilities	Business
Grant of trading concessions, e.g. catering	Business
Facilities for betting and gaming	Business
Admissions to entertainments including sporting events, concerts and theatres	Business
Admission charges to parks, museums and art galleries	Business
Admissions to swimming pools and leisure centres	Business

(d) Miscellaneous

Gaming and amusement machines	Business
Lotteries	Business
Competition entry fees	Business
Sponsorship of events	Business
Sales of programmes which do not secure admission to performances	Business
Club subscriptions	Business

3. ENVIRONMENTAL HEALTH AND PROTECTION

(a) Sampling, testing and inspections

Adjusting, stamping, testing and verification services under *Weights and Measures Act 1985*	Non-business
EC evaluation and surveillance of non-automatic weighing instruments (under *Non-Automatic Weighing Instruments (EEC Requirements) Regulations 1992*)	Business

Local Authorities and Statutory Bodies

EC verification of non-automatic weighing instruments (under *Non-Automatic Weighing Instruments (EEC Requirements) Regulations 1992*)	Non-business
Sample and analysis of private water supplies under *Private Water Supplies Regulations 1991*	Non-business
Inspection of imported food under *Imported Food Regulations 1984*	Non-business
Emergency investigation and enforcement functions under *Food Environment Protection Act 1985* and *Food Safety Act 1990*	Non-business
Roadworthiness tests of buses, cars, light goods vehicles and motorcycles under *Road Traffic Act 1988*	Business

(*b*) Waste control and pollution

Provision of radioactive waste tips	Non-business
Charges for special precautions taken for disposal of radioactive waste under *Radioactive Substances Act 1960*	Non-business
Supply of information relating to the keeping and use of radioactive substances	Non-business
Arrangements for and the collection of domestic refuse under *Environmental Protection Act 1990* and *Controlled Waste Regulations 1992*	Non-business
Collection of commercial and industrial refuse	Non-business where no specific charge is made, otherwise business
Sale of refuse	Business
Provision of receptacles for holding refuse	Non-business where no specific charge is made, otherwise business
Recycling credits paid under *Environmental Protection Act 1990, s 52*	Non-business
Arrangements for the disposal of controlled waste and provision of civic amenity sites	Non-business
Charges for waste management licences under *Environmental Protection Act 1990, s 41*	Non-business
Charges for licences for the treatment, keeping or disposal of waste on land or the disposal of waste by means of a mobile plant	Non-business
Charges for applications and registrations of controlled waste carriers under *Control of Pollution (Amendment) Act 1989*	Non-business
Charges for applications and registrations of waste brokers under *Waste Management Licensing Regulations 1994*	Non-business
Charges for copies of entries into register of controlled waste carriers	First copy of each entry non-business, subsequent copies business
Authorisation for the operation of prescribed industrial processes relating to air pollution control	Non-business
Register of controlled processes	Non-business
Removal of litter under *Environmental Protection Act 1990, s 89*	Non-business

(c) Cleansing and sanitation

Admission to public conveniences	Non-business
Admission to baths and wash houses	Business
Supply of cleaning and laundry services	Business
Sale of sanitary protection products and condoms	Business
Cleansing of private streets	Non-business where no specific charge is made, otherwise business
Emptying of privies	Non-business where no specific charge is made, otherwise business
Emptying of cesspools	Business
Emptying of industrial waste tanks	Business
Rodent control and disinfection	Non-business where no specific charge is made, otherwise business
Unblocking, cleaning, etc. of drains	Non-business where no specific charge is made, otherwise business

(d) Animals and livestock

Fees for the maintenance and release of dogs under *Environmental Protection Act 1990*	Non-business
Accommodation of animals in quarantine stations, including the provision of ancillary services	Business
Licence of red meat slaughterhouses and knackers yards under *Slaughterhouses Act 1974*	Non-business
Slaughterhouse services	Business
Stallage, standings or pennage	Business
Cold storage	Business
Sale of condemned meat or offal	Business
Sale of kitchen waste for animal feeding purposes (e.g. as pig food)	Business
Pest control	Non-business where no specific charge is made, otherwise business

(e) Miscellaneous

Burials under *Public Health (Control of Disease Act) 1984*	Non-business
Operation of mortuaries under the *Public Health Act 1936*	Non-business where directed by the Secretary of State, otherwise business
Operation of cemeteries and crematoria	Business

Local Authorities and Statutory Bodies

4. HEALTH AND SOCIAL SERVICES

(a) Care of the elderly

Provision of residential accommodation under *National Assistance Act 1948, Health Service Act 1977* or *Mental Health (Scotland) Act 1984* to a local authority's own clients	Non-business
Domiciliary laundry services when supplied to residents	Non-business
Welfare services including meals on wheels and home helps e.g. under *National Assistance Act 1948, Health Services, Public Health Act 1968* or *Social Work (Scotland) Act 1968*	Non-business
Supply of distress alarms	Business
Rentals of telephone, television or radio (under *Chronically Sick and Disabled Persons Act 1970*)	Non-business
Administration fees for care and repair schemes under *Local Government and Housing Act 1989*	Business
Recreational holidays for elderly people	Business
Holidays and outings provided as part of statutory care	Non-business

(b) Care and maintenance of children

Crèche facilities and playgroups	Business
Maintenance of children on remand	Non-business
Guardian ad litem (probation) fees	Non-business
Provision of accommodation and maintenance of children taken into care by a care order made under *Children Act 1989* or *Social Work (Scotland) Act 1968*	Non-business
Inspection of private children's homes under *Children Act 1989* and *Children's Homes Regulations 1991* or *Social Work (Residential Establishments – Child Care) Regulations 1987*	Non-business
Counselling and assessment services under *Adoption Act 1976* or *Adoption (Scotland) Act 1978* and provision of temporary board and lodgings to prospective parents and children	Non-business

(c) Activities relating to people with disabilities

Car badges for disabled persons	Non-business
Adaptation of local authority owned property for people with disabilities	Non-business
Adaptation work to privately owned property supplied to people with disabilities	Business
Sheltered employment under *Disabled Persons (Employment Act) 1958* as amended by *Local Government Act 1972*	Business
Sale of work from sheltered workshops	Business

(d) Miscellaneous

Meals provided as part of care in social service establishments	Non-business

Meals provided other than as part of care in social service establishments	Business
Accommodation supplied to staff in local authority residential establishments	Non-business
Accommodation supplied to guests and visitors in local authority residential accommodation	Business
Sale of occupational therapy products	Non-business where retained by the patient, otherwise business
Issue of vouchers on welfare grounds e.g. for purchase of school uniforms	Non-business
Provision of care, other than to own clients	Business
Funding from health authorities which does not constitute the consideration for a supply	Outside the scope of VAT
Supply of social workers	Non-business where supplied under a statutory obligation or monopoly, otherwise business
Social work including social therapy clubs	Non-business
Sale of food to voluntary organisations for onward supply to the elderly	Business

5. LAND AND PROPERTY

(a) Domestic accommodation and related activities

Provision of housing under *Housing Act 1985*	Non-business
Provision of bed and breakfast accommodation to the homeless under *Housing (Homeless Persons) Act 1977* and *Housing Act 1985*	Non-business
Sale of domestic accommodation under the 'right to buy' (*Housing Act 1985*)	Non-business
Incentives paid to tenants to move out under *Housing Act 1988*	Non-business
Sales of leases under *Leasehold Reform Act 1967*	Non-business
Construction of domestic accommodation for sale	Business
Residents' parking permits	Non-business
Provision of allotments under *Allotments Acts 1908-1950* and *Allotment (Scotland) Acts 1922-1950*	Non-business
Supply of central heating, double glazing, repairs and maintenance etc.	Non-business where tenant has no option or where supplied as part of a single supply of accommodation. Business where optional or at the request of the tenant

Local Authorities and Statutory Bodies

Service charges on local authority houses and flats sold leasehold	Non-business
Service charges on local authority houses sold freehold and, in Scotland, flats or houses held on feudal tenure	Business
Provision of sites for gypsy encampments	Business
Repairs and maintenance carried out in connection with a control order issued under *Housing Act 1985*	Non-business
Compensation	Non-business but see 42.1 and 42.13 LAND AND BUILDINGS for compulsory purchase and statutory compensation respectively

(b) Commercial land and property transactions

Commercial property lease, sale, repair and maintenance	Business
Sale or lease of land or property as a result of development funded by city challenge, safer city, derelict land grants etc.	Business
Grant of a licence to occupy land	Business
Letting of sites and pitches for market stalls etc.	Business
Letting of leisure centres, halls, rooms, pavilions etc.	Business
Admissions to premises	Business
Grant of mineral rights	Business
Letting of cattle markets and small holdings	Business
Rent of sites for kiosks, cafés, etc. e.g. at bus stations	Business
Supply of the right for an independent operator to use a municipal bus station	Business
Management of property	Business
Caretaking services	Business
Installation of fixtures and fittings in buildings	Business

(c) Planning

Planning application fees	Non-business
Building Regulation fees	Non-business where local authorities retain a statutory monopoly, otherwise business
Regularisation fees	Non-business
Listed building consent under *Planning (Listed Buildings and Conservation Areas) Act 1990*	Non-business
Provision of information on unused and under-used land	Non-business

(d) Miscellaneous

Default and emergency works carried out under specific legal provisions	Non-business
Renovation and other home improvement grants	Outside the scope of VAT
Recovery of costs from landlords for restoring disconnected utility supplies under *Local Government (Miscellaneous Provisions) Act 1976*	Business
Contributions made by occupants towards exterior works of group repair schemes under *Local Government and Housing Act 1989, s 27*	Outside the scope of VAT
Recovery of cost of acquisition and works to unoccupied listed buildings	Non-business
Charges made to third parties to recover the cost of repairing damage to local authority property	Non-business
Maintenance of closed churchyards in connection with an order served under *Local Government Act 1972*	Non-business
Archaeological investigations carried out under *Ancient Monuments and Archaeological Areas Act 1979*	Non-business

6. ROADS AND SEWERS

(a) Highways

Highway works for the Department of Transport under *Highways Act 1980, s 6* or *Roads (Scotland) Act 1984, s 4* including reimbursement of audit fees	Non-business
Reimbursement of cost of maintenance works to highways carried out under *Local Government Act 1972, s 187*	Non-business
Private street works, alterations, repairs and maintenance	Business
Contributions received by a local authority towards highway works under *New Roads and Street Works Act 1991, s 23*	Non-business
Dedication of roads, and the provision of goods, services or cash contributions e.g. under *Town and Country Planning Act 1990* or similar planning gain agreements	Outside the scope of VAT
Road, bridge and tunnel tolls	Non-business
Erection of directional signs	Non-business
Traffic census provided to the Department of Transport	Business
Construction of vehicle or garage crossings (dropped kerb access)	Non-business
Reinstatement work to highways carried out for public utility companies under *New Roads and Street Works Act 1991, s 70 (s 129* in Scotland)	Business
Investigation, inspection, emergency and remedial works under *New Roads and Street Works Act 1991, ss 72-75 (ss 131-135* in Scotland) relating to reinstatement of highways	Non-business
Street management, e.g. the naming of streets	Non-business

Local Authorities and Statutory Bodies

Stopping up of highways, footpaths and bridleways under *Town and Country Planning Act 1990* or *Highways Act 1980* e.g. in connection with the construction of a new or special road	Non-business
Recovery of costs *under New Roads and Street Works Act 1991, s 76* in connection with temporary traffic orders	Non-business

(b) Parking and traffic regulations

Parking meter charges, including excess parking, *under Road Traffic Regulation Act 1984* (highways only)	Non-business
Off street parking, including excess parking, in garages, buildings and open spaces etc. (other than in conjunction with local authority domestic accommodation)	Business
Payments received in respect of Penalty Charge Notices (PCNs) issued under *Road Traffic Act 1991*	Outside the scope of VAT
Contributions towards the promotion of road safety under *Road Traffic Act 1988*	Outside the scope of VAT
Weighbridge charges	Business
Park and ride schemes	Business

(c) Sewers

Sewer connections, repairs and improvement work	Non-business where no specific charge is made, otherwise business
Cleaning, maintenance, unblocking etc. of sewers	Non-business where no specific charge is made, otherwise business
Supervision fees for the inspection of sewers under *Water Industry Act 1991, s 104*	Non-business for sewers which the local authority has agreed to adopt, otherwise business
Default work to sewers e.g. under *Building Act 1984, s 59, Local Government (Miscellaneous Provisions) Act 1976, s 35* or *Public Health Act 1961, s 17(1)*	Non-business

7. STATUTORY LICENCES AND FEES

(a) Licensing and approvals

Approval of premises for civil marriages under *Marriage Act 1994*	Non-business
Issue of site licences for caravans under *Caravan Sites Control and Development Act 1960*	Non-business
Licence of public charitable collections under *Charities Act 1992*	Non-business
Licences issued under *Betting, Gaming and Lotteries Act 1963, Gaming Act 1968* and *Lotteries and Amusements Act 1976*	Non-business
Authorisation of performances under the *Hypnotism Act 1952*	Non-business

Licence of premises used for public performances of plays under *Theatre Act 1968* and of places of entertainment under *Local Government (Miscellaneous Provisions) Act 1982*	Non-business
Cinema licences under *Cinemas Act 1985*	Non-business
Licence of premises open for refreshment and entertainment under *Late Night Refreshment Houses Act 1969, London Local Authorities Act 1990* and *Civic Government (Scotland) Act 1982, s 42*	Non-business
Licence of sex shops under *Local Government (Miscellaneous Provisions) Act 1982* and *Civic Government (Scotland) Act 1982, s 45*	Non-business
Licence and inspection of pet shops, animal boarding and riding establishments	Non-business
Licence for petrol sites under *Petroleum (Consolidation) Act 1928*	Non-business
Licence of taxis and private hire vehicles and certificates of compliance under *Transport Act 1985* and *Motor Vehicles (Tests) Regulations 1981* and *Civic Government (Scotland) Act 1982, ss 10–23*	Non-business
Licences and registration of firearms	Non-business
Street trader licences	Non-business
Pleasure boat licences	Non-business

(*b*) Registration and certification

Registration fees for pleasure boats on rivers	Non-business
Registration of childminders, and day-care providers under *Children Act 1989*	Non-business
Registration and inspection of private and voluntary residential care homes	Non-business
Registration of war charities	Non-business
Registration of births, marriages and deaths including provision of documentary evidence	Non-business
Cremation certificates	Non-business
Registration of persons engaging in acupuncture, tattooing, ear piercing and electrolysis under *Local Government (Miscellaneous Provisions) Act 1982*	Non-business
Register of common land and related searches under *Commons Registration Act 1965*	Non-business
Register of local land charges under *Local Land Charges Act 1975*	Non-business
Issue of safety certificates under *Safety of Sports Grounds Act 1975* (as amended by *Fire Safety and Safety of Places of Sport Act 1987*)	Non-business
Registration of premises under *Explosives Act 1875*	Non-business

(*c*) Provision of information

Supply of information under *Local Government (Access to Information) Act 1985* including the first copy of a document or replacement document	Non-business

Local Authorities and Statutory Bodies

Access to information under *Data Protection Act 1984*	Non-business
Register of parliamentary and local government electors under *Representation of the People Act 1983*	Non-business
Index of local charities under *Charities Act 1960*	Non-business

(d) Miscellaneous

Sale of depositions	Non-business
Administration of elections	Non-business
Civil marriage ceremonies	Non-business
Definitive maps of public rights of way under *Wildlife and Countryside Act 1981*	Non-business
Publication of designated conservation areas under *Planning (Listed Buildings and Conservation Areas) Act 1990*	Non-business
Collection of fines and recovery of expenses under *District Courts (Scotland) Act 1975*	Non-business
Granting of consent to display outside advertisements under *Town and Country Planning (Control of Advertisements) Regulations 1992*	Non-business

8. POLICE, FIRE AND CIVIL DEFENCE

(a) Police

Attendance at incidents	Non-business
Attendance at sporting events, etc.	Non-business where supplied under the conditions of a safety certificate
Provision of additional officers	Non-business where at the instigation of the Police, otherwise business
Police officers assisting other forces under *Police Act 1964, s 14*	Non-business
Transport of prisoners and transport of deportees for the Home Office	Non-business where carried out under a statutory monopoly, otherwise business
Information and photographs about road accidents	Non-business
Police photographs supplied for prosecution or official purposes	Non-business
Removal and storage of abandoned vehicles	Non-business
Disposal of abandoned vehicles and unclaimed property	Business
False alarm penalties	Non-business
Accommodation supplied to police officers or cadets in section houses	Non-business
Accommodation of prisoners for the Home Office under *Imprisonment (Temporary Prisons) Act 1980*	Non-business

Supply of staff to the police federation	Non-business

(b) Fire service

Fees for interviews and fire reports (including photographs)	Non-business
Special services of fire brigade, e.g. for filming, house testing etc.	Business
Fire prevention advice	Business
Fire fighting training to private employers	Business
Inspection of premises and processing of applications for fire certificates under *Fire Precautions Act 1971*	Non-business
Supply of fire detection and other equipment	Business
Sale of cap badges and uniforms, etc.	Business

(c) Miscellaneous

Recovery of costs of emergency plans made under *Control of Industrial Major Accident Hazards Regulations 1984*	Non-business
Secondment of probation officers to prison departments	Non-business where supplied under a statutory obligation, otherwise business
Funding from Home Office towards local authorities expenses in running attendance centres	Non-business
Secondment of police and fire service staff including to government departments and common police services	Non-business where supplied under a statutory obligation, otherwise business
Advertising (e.g. on vehicles)	Business

9. MISCELLANEOUS

Charges for private telephone calls including any administration fees	Business
Administration of pension funds other than of own employees	Business
Administration of pension funds for own employees under *Superannuation Regulations 1986*	Non-business
Advertising	Business
Appointment and financing of coroners	Non-business
Burials, cremations and related supplies (other than ministers' services and cremation certificates)	Business
Car leasing to employees	Business
Compensation	Outside the scope of VAT except where it is consideration for a supply (see also under 5. above)
Supply of computer services under *Local Government (Miscellaneous Provisions) Act 1976* etc.	Business

Local Authorities and Statutory Bodies

Copies of documents not supplied under a statutory obligation	Business
Duty free or bonded storage	Business
Finance and insurance	Business
Supply of food and drink to employees	Business
Supplies of fuel and power	Business
Business gifts and entertainment	Business
Non-business gifts, entertainment and long service awards	Non-business
Lost property charges	Business
Sale of lost, abandoned, salvaged forfeit or recycled goods etc.	Business
Sale of works of art, antiques etc.	Business
Passenger transport	Business
Payphones and phone cards	Business
Sale of petrol	Business
Use of photocopier	Business
Port harbour dues	Business
Sale of postage stamps	Business
Supply of printing and stationery	Business
Recoupment, reimbursement, contributions to costs which do not constitute consideration for any supply	Non-business
Secondment of staff	Non-business where supplied under a statutory obligation or monopoly, otherwise business
Sponsorship	Business
Supply of trees, shrubs, plants, etc.	Business
Sale of vehicles, equipment, materials, scrap, etc.	Business

(C & E Notice 749A).

Local authorities and NHS joint stores depots. See VAT Information Sheet 3/98, June 1998.

Community projects with voluntary groups, etc. See VAT Information Sheet 4/98, June 1998.

44   Management Services and Supplies of Staff

44.1   MANAGEMENT SERVICES

Management services commonly arise where several traders who are separately registered for VAT, but are associated in some way, decide that one of them should purchase overhead items required by the various businesses, pay all the bills, and then recover an agreed proportion of the costs from the other traders participating in the scheme. Such an arrangement is common where the same office facilities and/or staff are shared. The 'management charges' or 'service charges' normally contain elements of staff salaries, office equipment, rent, rates, heating and lighting, stationery, telephone and postage, etc. Although such arrangements are 'domestic' and may not involve any element of profit, there may nevertheless be a taxable supply for VAT purposes, as under *VATA 1994, s 5(2)(b)* anything which is not a supply of goods but is done for a consideration is a supply of services. However there is no taxable supply if the persons involved are part of the same legal entity or if facilities are provided between businesses covered by a single VAT registration, e.g. businesses run by the same legal partnership or business included in a VAT group registration (see 31 GROUPS OF COMPANIES).

See *Smith & Williamson; Smith & Williamson Securities, [1976] VATTR 215 (281)* and *C & E Commrs v Tilling Management Services Ltd* at 44.3 below. For decisions as to whether such supplies are made in the course or furtherance of a business or are domestic arrangements not in the course of any business, see *Cumbrae Properties (1963) Ltd QB, [1981] STC 799, Durham Aged Mineworkers' Homes Association v C & E Commrs QB, [1994] STC 553* and *Processed Vegetable Growers Association Ltd, [1973] VATTR 87 (25)*. For the position where charges are raised between companies for use of capital, see *Laurence Scott Ltd, [1986] VATTR 1 (2004)*.

44.2   Sharing of premises

The VAT treatment of any costs recovered relating to premises shared with other persons depends upon the precise terms of the arrangements. See 42.16 LAND AND BUILDINGS for a general consideration of service charges and joint occupation of premises.

44.3   Management services and group relief

C & E have expressed the following views.

(a) If Company A incurs a tax loss and surrenders it to Company B under *ICTA 1988, s 402* without any payment, C & E do not see any taxable supply of goods or services for VAT purposes.

(b) If Company A incurs a tax loss and surrenders it to Company B under *ICTA 1988, s 402* with a payment or credit to current account for the surrender of the tax loss, again C & E do not see any taxable supply of goods or services.

(c) It is possible in cases (a) and (b) above, that Company A might render management services to Company B without a separate charge being made for those services. The position here depends on whether there is any arrangement linking the provision of management services to, say, the procurement or making of group relief payments. If there is, then C & E would see a non-monetary consideration for the management services which would have to be valued to determine the amount of VAT due. If there is no such arrangement, then if the management services are provided free of charge there is no taxable supply.

(*d*) Again, Company A may render management services to Company B and make a charge for those services, at the same time surrendering group relief, with or without payment. In such a case there is clearly a taxable supply of management services, but what has to be determined is whether the money charge is the full consideration for the supply. If there is an arrangement linking the supply of management services to the procurement or making of group relief payments, then once again there would be a non-monetary consideration which would have to be valued. In such circumstances VAT would be due on the full consideration, i.e. on the sum of the monetary and non-monetary considerations. However, if there is no link between the management services and the group relief payments, then VAT will be due only on the charge actually made for the management services.

C & E have also confirmed that where services are rendered between companies within the same VAT group registration then no liability to VAT arises.

(CCAB Statement TR344 June 1979).

See also *C & E v Tilling Management Services Ltd QB 1978, [1979] STC 365*.

44.4   SUPPLIES OF STAFF

Definition. A supply of staff (which includes directors and other office holders) is made for VAT purposes if the use of an individual who is contractually employed by the supplier is provided to another person for consideration. This applies whether the terms of the individual's employment are set out in a formal contract or letter of appointment, or are on a less formal basis. The determining factor is that the staff are not contractually employed by the recipient but come under its direction. Where staff are supplied to another person but continue to operate under the direction of the supplier, this is not a supply of staff, but is a supply of those services. (The distinction is significant where the services may be zero–rated or exempt, or when determining whether or not the supply is made in the UK.)

Liability. A supply of staff is normally regarded as being made in the course or furtherance of a business and VAT must be accounted for at the standard rate. This is subject to the following exceptions

* Certain supplies of staff are not always made in the course or furtherance of business and thus may be outside the scope of VAT. These include

  (i) secondments between and by government departments,

  (ii) secondments between National Health bodies, and

  (iii) some secondments between local authorities and by local authorities where they have a statutory obligation or monopoly.

* The supply of staff to a person who belongs outside the EC or a business belonging in another EC country is outside the scope of UK VAT.

Where supplies of staff are received from a person who belongs outside the UK, VAT must be accounted for on those supplies at the standard rate under the 'reverse charge' procedure (see 39.4 INTERNATIONAL SERVICES).

Value of supply. VAT must be charged on the full amount of the consideration for the supply of staff (whether full-time or part-time). As well as any fee, this includes recovery of staff costs from the recipient, e.g. salary, NICs and pension contribution. Even if the arrangements do not involve the recipient paying these staff costs to the supplier (e.g. because the salary is paid directly to the individual or the NICs directly to the DSS) these amounts are still part of the consideration for the taxable supply of staff. See below for limited concessions in certain cases where the recipient of the staff pays their salaries directly to the employees and/or meets the employer's obligations for PAYE, NICs, pension contributions, etc. Even where a concession applies, VAT must still be accounted for on any payments that the recipient makes direct to the employer.

Similar rules apply to the value of supplies received from outside the UK under the reverse charge procedure.

(C & E Leaflet 700/34/94, paras 1-4).

Concession for hire of staff by employment businesses. From 1 April 1997 where an employment business within the meaning of the *Employment Agencies Act 1973* supplies a member of its staff (the employee) to another business which

• is responsible for paying the employee's remuneration directly to the employee, and/or

• discharges the obligations of the employment business to pay to any third party PAYE, NICs, pension contributions and similar payments relating to the employee,

then, to the extent that any such payments form the consideration (or part) for the supply of the employee to the other business, they are disregarded in determining the value of the supply of the employee.

This concession was due to expire on 31 December 1998. However, following the government announcement on 25 September 1998 of new rules governing the conduct of employment bureaux, the concession has been extended until the new rules and the VAT arrangements for temporary workers supplied by employment bureaux (see 4.13 AGENTS) are in place.

Concession for secondment of staff by businesses other than employment businesses. From 1 April 1997, where an employer (other than an employment business within the meaning of the *Employment Agencies Act 1973*) seconds a member of its staff (the employee) to another business which

(*a*) exercises exclusive control over the allocation and performance of the employee's duties during the period of secondment; and

(*b*) is responsible for paying the employee's remuneration directly to the employee and/or discharges the employer's obligations to pay to any third party PAYE, NICs, pension contributions and similar payments relating to the employee,

then, to the extent that any payments within (*b*) above form the consideration (or part) for the secondment of the employee to the other business, they are disregarded in determining the value of seconding the employee. For these purposes, an employer is not to be treated as seconding an employee to another business if the placing of the employee with that other business is done with a view to the employer (or any person associated with him) deriving any financial gain from

• the placing of the employee with the other business, or

• any other arrangements or understandings (whether or not contractually binding and whether or not for any consideration) between the employer (or any person associated with him) and the other business (or any person associated with it) with which the employee is placed.

Concession for placement of disabled workers under the Sheltered Placement Scheme (or any similar scheme). From 1 April 1997 where the sponsor of a disabled worker places the worker with a host company under the Sheltered Placement Scheme (or any similar scheme) and the host company

• is responsible for paying the worker's remuneration directly to the worker; and/or

- discharges the sponsor's obligations to pay to any third party PAYE, NICs, pension contributions and similar payments relating to the worker,

then, to the extent that any such payments form the consideration (or part) for the placing of the worker with the host company, they are disregarded in determining the value of placing the worker with the host company.

(C & E Leaflet 700/34/94, Appendix; C & E Business Brief 7/97, 23 March 1997; C & E Business Brief 20./98, 28 September 1998).

Staff hire concession applying before 1 April 1997. By concession, businesses hiring out staff were not required to charge VAT on the salary costs of the staff concerned where the client business paid the staff direct or met the employer's obligation to make payments to third parties (e.g. PAYE, NICs or pension contributions). The concession was withdrawn from general use with effect from 1 April 1997 because, contrary to the original intention, services contractors (e.g. security and cleaning companies) had been attempting to use it to cover the provision of *services* to partially exempt clients, thereby avoiding VAT. (C & E Business Brief 4/97, 25 February 1997).

Employment agencies and bureaux. See 4.13 AGENTS.

Charities. See 12.4 CHARITIES.

44.5   **Temporary suspension of an employment contract**

Where an employee takes up a temporary post with another employer, there is no supply of staff provided that

(*a*)   the temporary post is organised on the employee's own initiative; and

(*b*)   the second employer issues the employee with a new contract or letter of appointment, temporarily suspending the employee's contract with the first employer.

To avoid doubt, a temporary suspension should normally be supported by evidence that

- there is an agreement with the first employer that the employee is to be transferred for a fixed or open-ended period, often with an entitlement to return;
- there are new conditions of employment with the second employer;
- the second employer has control over the terms and conditions of employment; or
- the second employer fixes the salary.

(C & E Leaflet 700/34/94, para 5).

44.6   **Joint employment**

In cases of joint employment, there is no supply of staff for VAT purposes between the joint employers.

Staff are regarded as jointly employed if their contracts of employment or letters of appointment make it clear that they have more than one employer. The contract must specify who the employers are (e.g. 'Company A, Company B and Company C' or 'Company A and its subsidiaries').

Staff are not regarded as jointly employed (and the provisions of 44.4 above apply) if their contract is with a single company or person, even if it

- lays down that the employee's duties include assisting other companies;
- lays down that the employee will work full-time for another company; or

- shows by the job title that the employee works for a group of associated companies (e.g. group accountant).

(C & E Leaflet 700/34/94, para 6).

44.7   Paymaster services for associated companies

Paymaster services commonly arise in two situations.

- Where staff are jointly employed, one of the joint employers may undertake to pay all salaries, National Insurance and pension contributions which are then recovered from the other employers.

- Where a number of associated companies each employs its own staff, one company may pay all salaries, etc. on behalf of the others, each associate then paying its share of the costs to the paymaster.

In either case, the recovery of monies paid out by the paymaster is not subject to VAT and is treated as a disbursement (see 4.7 AGENTS).

VAT must be accounted for on any charge made for paymaster services over and above the reimbursement of the costs paid out unless

(*a*)   the recipient belongs outside the EC or is a business which belongs in another EC country (in which case the supply is outside the scope of UK VAT); or

(*b*)   the supply is between companies within the same VAT group registration (in which case it is disregarded).

(C & E Leaflet 700/34/94, para 7).

44.8   Appointments to directorships and other offices

The appointments of an individual as a director or other paid office holder (e.g. secretary, treasurer) can give rise to a VAT liability as a supply of staff in the following ways.

- **Employees and directors.** If a company allows an employee or director to serve as a director of a second company, following an approach from that company, it must account for VAT on any payment it receives for agreeing to the appointment. This does not apply where

    (i)   an individual director or employee personally arranges to be appointed to the directorship of a second company and receives payment from that company in return, in which case the company is not required to account for VAT on any payments to the appointee. The appointment must be a purely personal one and not a means for the first company to deliver its service (e.g. consultancy services);

    (ii)   a company is exercising a legal or contractual right to appoint one of its directors or employees to a directorship of another company (e.g. in a subsidiary or investee company), in which case there is no supply for VAT purposes; or

    (iii)   in the case of a bank or similar institution it appoints a director to the board of a UK investee company as the condition of a loan, in which case any charges for the director's services are part of the consideration for the loan and treated as an exempt supply. (Hansard 3 February 1993, Cols 185, 186).

- **Sole proprietors and partnerships providing professional services.** A sole proprietor providing professional services (e.g. a solicitor or accountant) or a

611

partner in a firm providing such services who takes up a professional appointment as a director, etc. must account for VAT on any payment received if

(i) the appointment results from the professional expertise exercised in the business or partnership business,

(ii) the duties as a director, etc. involve, at least in part, the use of that expertise, and

(iii) in the case of a partnership, the payments received accrue to the partnership and are not retained by the partner personally.

Where, however, under the terms of an appointment as an office holder, the person concerned is treated as an employee, any fees or payments made to the sole proprietor or partner personally are outside the scope of VAT.

(C & E Leaflet 700/34/94, paras 8–11).

45   Motor Cars

Cross-references. See 23.34 EUROPEAN COMMUNITY: SINGLE MARKET for the refund of VAT on the supply of a new motor car by a non-taxable person to another EC country; 23.35 EUROPEAN COMMUNITY: SINGLE MARKET for the acquisition of a new motor car from another EC country by a non-taxable person; 25.16 EXPORTS for sale of vehicles outside the EC; 34.22 IMPORTS; 61 SECOND-HAND GOODS for the second-hand scheme for motor cars and 62 SELF-SUPPLY for explanation of such deemed supplies.

De Voil Indirect Tax Service. See V6.165–168B.

The contents of this chapter are as follows.

45.1   DEFINITION OF A MOTOR CAR

For VAT purposes a motor car is any motor vehicle of a kind normally used on public roads which has three or more wheels and either

(*a*) is constructed or adapted solely or mainly for the carriage of passengers; or

(*b*) has to the rear of the driver's seat roofed accommodation which is fitted with side windows or which is constructed or adapted for the fitting of side windows.

It does not include

(i) vehicles capable of accommodating only one person or suitable for carrying twelve or more persons;

(ii) vehicles of not less than three tonnes unladen weight;

(iii) caravans, ambulances and prison vans;

(iv) vehicles of a type approved by the Assistant Commissioner of Police of the Metropolis as conforming to the conditions of fitness for the time being laid down by him for the purposes of the *London Cab Order 1934* [*SRO 1934/1346*]; or

(v) vehicles constructed for a special purpose other than the carriage of persons and having no other accommodation for carrying persons than such as is incidental to that purpose.

[*SI 1992/3122, Art 2*].

In a case concerning provisions in *Car Tax Act 1983* similar to *SI 1992/3122, Art 2*, it was held that in (*b*) above 'accommodation' means only accommodation for passengers and, if the space is unsuitable for this purpose, the vehicle is not within the definition even if there are side windows (*R v C & E Commrs (ex p Nissan UK Ltd) CA, [1988] BTC 8003*).

Vehicles regarded as motor cars

- *Imported versions of saloon cars* even where they are 'normally used on public roads' which are outside the UK (*Withers of Winsford Ltd v C & E Commrs QB, [1988] STC 431*).

- Double cab pick ups, i.e. light pick-up vehicles which incorporate two rows of seats with additional windows at the side and to the rear of the driver (even though such vehicles are taxed as commercial vehicles for duty purposes). (C & E Manual V1-13, Chapter 2A section 11.4). See, however, *W Hamilton & Son (14812)* where a converted Toyota Hilux double cab was held not to be a motor car as it was suitable for carrying twelve persons.

- An *estate car* with the rear seat removed (*County Telecommunications Systems Ltd (10224)*); used for business purposes by a builder (*Gardner (MC) (588)*); and licensed as a goods vehicle and used by a garage and grocery store (*Howarth (632)*).

- A Chevrolet K10 Blazer (*Yarlett (1490)*).

- A Citroen van modified by fitting windows behind the driver's seat (*Browsers Bookshop (2837)*).

- A Daihatsu Fourtrak Estate (*Specialised Cars Ltd (11123)*).

- A Datsun pick-up truck, modified by the addition of a detachable hard top superstructure with two side windows and a hatchback to the rear of the driver's seat but no seating accommodation (*HKS Coachworks Ltd (1124)* but see *R v C & E Commrs (ex p Nissan UK Ltd)* above).

- A Ford Escort, the rear seats of which could be folded away (*RC Lucia (5776)*).

- An Isuzu pick-up (*BC Kunz (t/a Wharfdale Finance Co) (13514)*).

- A Land Rover converted into a 'motor car' by being fitted with a hard top body with side windows and upholstered seats (*Chartcliff Ltd (262)*); or by being modified by the addition of a metal canopy with side windows (*Wigley (7300)*).

- A Range Rover even though first registered, and taxed, as a heavy goods vehicle and not used for domestic purposes (*C & E Commrs v Jeynes t/a Midland International (Hire) Caterers QB 1983, [1984] STC 30*).

- A Suzuki jeep modified by the fitting of a rear seat although it had no rear windows (*S Compton (t/a Stan Compton Electrical Engineers & Contractors) (10259)*); and a Suzuki Vitara Sport (*W McAdam (13286)*).

- A Toyota Hiace van fitted with side windows (*Knapp (778)*); a Toyota Previa with the middle and rear rows of seats removed for delivery purposes (*Gorringe Pine (14036)*); and a Toyota Spacecruiser with the rear seats removed and a hanging rail for transporting clothes installed (*Mr & Mrs M Gohil (t/a Gohil Fashions) (15435)*).

- A Volkswagen tipping truck with, in addition to the driver's cab with room for one other passenger, a second roofed cab behind the driver's cab with room for three more passengers (*Weatherproof Flat Roofing (Plymouth) Ltd (1240)*); a Volkswagen pick-up truck with roofed accommodation fitted with side windows to the rear of the driver's seat (*Readings & Headley (1535)*); and a Volkswagen Caravelle with removable rear seats (*Intercraft UK Romania (13707)*).

Vehicles not regarded as motor cars

- Ice cream vans, mobile shops and offices, hearses (see also *KP Davies (831)*) and bullion vans (which are all regarded as falling under (v) above). (C & E Notice 700/64/96, Appendix A).

- Vehicles originally suitable for carrying twelve or more persons but with seating capacity reduced below twelve because of the provision of wheelchair space for disabled passengers. (C & E Notice 48, ESC 2.12). To benefit from this concession, the owner must make a written request to his VAT office giving details of the vehicle and with a declaration that it conforms with recognised standards of construction and is equipped with approved fittings and means of access for disabled travellers. (HC Official Report, 21 March 1991, vol 188 cols 506, 507).

- London type taxis (FX 4 models) which are used outside the London area (which are regarded by C & E as falling within (iv) above). (VAT Notes (No 1) 1986/87).

- Motor caravans provided they conform with criteria agreed with the Society of Motor Manufacturers and Traders (SMMT). The agreement specifies that, to be treated as a motor caravan, the vehicle must incorporate a permanently installed sink and cooking facilities; seating arrangements to enable diners to sit at the meal table; at least one bed with a minimum length of 1.82 metres; and a permanently installed fresh water tank with a minimum capacity of 10 litres. (C & E Manual V1-13, Chapter 2A para 11.5).

- A pick-up truck with an attached, removable canopy (*K M Batty (2199)*).

- A Daihatsu Fourtrak Commercial Hard Top with two folding rear seats (*AL Yeoman Ltd (4470)*).

- A Ford van fitted with wooden benches but no side windows (*Chartcliff Ltd (262)*); and a Ford Transit van adapted by inserting rear seats of heavy duty plastic but with no rear windows, handrails or seat belts (*Chichester Plant Contractors Ltd (6575)*).

- A Land Rover with two folding seats in the rear (*Bolinge Hill Farm (4217)*); a 12-seat Land Rover with the rear bench seats removed (*P Oddonetto (5208)*); and a Land Rover modified by a half-sized window in the nearside rear panel (*TH Sheppard (13815)*).

- A Peugot van modified by adding a window on each side behind the driver's seat for safety reasons (*John Beharrell Ltd, [1991] VATTR 497 (6530)*).

De Voil Indirect Tax Service. See V1.281.

45.2   **TRANSACTIONS INVOLVING MOTOR CARS**

The Treasury may, by order, provide that VAT charged on specified supplies, acquisitions and importations is excluded from credit for input tax against output tax. [*VATA 1994,s 25(7)*]. Provisions relating to motor cars have been made under *The Value Added Tax (Cars) Order 1992* (*SI 1992/3122*) and the *Value Added Tax (Input Tax) Order 1992* (*SI 1992/3222*) as amended. With certain exceptions, a taxable person cannot reclaim input tax on the purchase of a car (see 45.3 below) and no VAT is chargeable when the car is sold unless the selling price exceeds the purchase price (see 45.4 below). Certain transactions are not treated as taxable supplies (see 45.5 below) and special rules apply to self-supplies (see 45.6 below). For the position of car dealers see 45.7 below.

The validity of the UK input tax blocking order was upheld in *Royscot Leasing Ltd v C & E Commrs ; Royscot Industrial Leasing Ltd v C & E Commrs ; Allied Domecq plc v C & E Commrs ;* and *TC Harrison Group Ltd v C & E Commrs QB [1996] STC 898.* On appeal, the Court of Appeal directed that the case should be referred to the CJEC for a ruling on whether the UK legislation was valid under European law. In the related case of *EC Commission v French Republic, CJEC [1998] STC 805,* the court held that there was nothing in European law to prevent EC countries continuing to apply provisions to limit the deduction of input tax.

Fleet buyer bonuses and dealer demonstration bonuses. A fleet buyer bonus is given by a manufacturer or sole concessionaire to a customer who makes a bulk purchase of vehicles. A dealer demonstrator bonus is a payment made, or credit allowed, by a manufacturer or sole concessionaire to a dealer who agrees to adopt a car as a demonstration vehicle. C & E now accept that such bonuses are normally to be treated as discounts by the manufacturer or sole concessionaires which reduce the value of their supplies. (C & E Business Brief 16/97, 21 July 1997).

Fleet leasing bonuses. A fleet leasing bonus is given by a car manufacturer or dealer to a business which has leased a number of vehicles previously sold by the manufacturer or dealer to intermediaries. C & E now accept that such bonuses are normally to be treated as discounts by the manufacturer or dealer which reduce the value of their supplies (rather than consideration for a supply of services by the customer). (C & E Business Brief 1/98, 7 January 1998).

45.3   Purchase of a car

Apart from the special cases listed below, VAT cannot be reclaimed on the purchase (including acquisition or importation) of a motor car as defined in 45.1 above. Purchase means not only outright purchase but also any purchase under a hire purchase agreement or any other agreement whereby property in the car eventually passes e.g. a lease–purchase agreement. See 45.11 below for input tax on cars leased or hired.

VAT on supplies integral with the supply of a motor car is only deductible where input tax on the motor car is deductible. This includes manufacturer's warranty (although VAT on the purchase of an extension of the period of warranty is deductible). It has been held to include manufacturer's delivery charges passed on by dealers to customers (*Wimpey Construction UK Ltd, [1979] VATTR 174 (808)*). However, in *C & E Commrs v British Telecommunications plc CA, [1998] STC 544* where BT purchased cars directly from the manufacturers, the court ruled that BT was entitled to reclaim input tax. Although delivery by the manufacturer was a term of the contract, BT need not have entered into a contract requiring delivery to be made to them and the contractual arrangements created a separate supply of cars and delivery. C & E have applied for leave to appeal against this decision to the House of Lords. Businesses which consider that the decision applies to their circumstances may claim a refund of overpaid VAT in periods before 18 March 1998, subject to the three year cap and possible unjust enrichment. (C & E Business Brief 12/98, 21 May 1998).

See 45.13 below for fitted optional extras and accessories.

(C & E Notice 700/64/96, paras 33, 34).

Special cases. VAT may be reclaimed on the purchase, acquisition or importation of a motor car in the following special circumstances.

(*a*) **Exclusive business use.** The motor car is a 'qualifying' motor car supplied to, or acquired or imported by, a taxable person who intends to use the motor car exclusively for business purposes. This condition is not satisfied if the taxable person intends to

   (i) let it on hire to any person either for no consideration or consideration less than would be payable in an arm's length commercial transaction; or

   (ii) make it available, otherwise than by letting on hire, to any person (including, where the taxable person is an individual, himself or, where the taxable person is a partnership, a partner) for private use (whether or not for a consideration).

The main beneficiaries of this provision are likely to be leasing companies because there is self-evidently no private use of the car within (ii) above. However, cars that *may* also qualify include genuine pool cars, some demonstration cars and service rental ('courtesy') cars. The test is that they are not available for private use, are not allocated to a single individual and are never left overnight at home. (For this purpose, a motor trade garage with attached residential accommodation is treated as business premises.) Research and development cars used by manufacturers and other companies engaged in research and development (e.g. component manufacturers) also qualify for input tax recovery.

A car cannot be treated as used for wholly business purposes simply because a charge is made to an employee for its use. This will only apply if the car is made available on the same basis as an arm's length commercial leasing under (i) above which does not apply where a charge is made for private motoring based upon the proportion of private use.

To claim input tax for exclusive business use, there must be a genuine intention not to make the car available for private use at the time the VAT is incurred. In *Lowe (15124)* the tribunal accepted that a large four-wheel drive vehicle had been purchased exclusively for business use as the trader already owned two other vehicles, including a saloon car used for private journeys. Similarly in *Thompson (14777)* the appellant successfully contended that four cars which he purchased were used exclusively for business purposes as he had insured them for business use only so that they would be uninsured if used for any private purpose. However, there have been a significant number of cases where the appellant was unsuccessful. See, for example, *GDG Jones (14535)* and *PC & AM Wood (14804)*. In the latter case, the tribunal observed, applying *dicta* of the Advocate-General in *Enkler v Finanzamt Homburg, CJEC [1996] STC 1316*, that 'the important point is that the consumer always has the opportunity to use the asset whenever he finds it necessary or desirable to do so'. If circumstances change and the car is subsequently made available for private use, output tax must be accounted for at the time of change on the full current value of the car. C & E have indicated that they will look closely at all cases of purported change of intention and, in the case of incorrect claims, will charge interest and penalties where appropriate.

(C & E Notice 700/64/96, paras 16–18; VAT Information Sheet 12/95, 1 June 1995; C & E Business Brief 15/95, 31 July 1995).

(*b*) **Mini-cabs, self drive hire, driving instruction.** The motor car is a 'qualifying' motor car supplied to, or acquired or imported by, a taxable person who intends to use the motor car primarily

    (i) to provide it on hire with the services of a driver for the purposes of carrying passengers;

    (ii) to provide it for 'self-drive hire'; or

    (iii) as a vehicle in which instruction in driving of a motor car is to be given by him.

'*Self-drive hire*' means hire where the hirer is the person normally expected to drive the motor car and the period of hire to each hirer (together with the period of hire of any other motor car expected to be hired to him by the taxable person) will normally be less than both 30 consecutive days and 90 days in any twelve month period.

(*c*) **Motability Scheme.** The motor car is unused and is supplied to a taxable person whose only taxable supplies are concerned with the letting of motor cars on hire to another taxable person whose business consists predominantly of making supplies within *VATA 1994, 8 Sch Group 12, item 14* (see 32.17(*k*) HEALTH AND WATER UTILITIES).

A '*qualifying*' motor car for the purposes of (*a*) and (*b*) above is generally one which has never been supplied, acquired or imported in circumstances where VAT was wholly excluded from credit as input tax. Under normal circumstances, therefore, a qualifying car will be a new car or a used car where the previous owners were able to recover VAT on their purchase in full (e.g. cars disposed of by a leasing company with a registration letter of 'N' or later are likely to be qualifying cars).

This is subject to two qualifications.

(1) Specifically excluded from qualifying is a motor car which is supplied, etc. to a taxable person on or after 1 August 1995 and which has been supplied on a letting

on hire by him before that date. However C & E are, by concession, prepared to accept a car as 'qualifying' (despite any prepayment of leasing charges made before 1 August 1995) provided the car is first registered and the lease is first invoiced on or after 1 August 1995; the invoice identifies the car as 'qualifying'; and both the lessor and lessee follow the tax rules applying to qualifying vehicles (which includes applying the 50% block to the lessee's deduction of VAT on the prepayment, see 45.11 below). (C & E Business Brief 21/95, 8 October 1995).

(2)   As a transitional measure, a taxable person may elect to treat a motor car as a qualifying motor car if it was supplied, etc. to him before 1 August 1995 in circumstances where VAT was wholly excluded from credit as input tax; it is first registered on or after 1 August 1995; and it was not supplied on a letting on hire by him before that date. Where such an election is made and the motor car meets all the necessary conditions for 100% input tax relief, input tax may be recovered in the first VAT period commencing on or after 1 August 1995.

[*SI 1992/3222, Art 7; SI 1995/281; SI 1995/1666*].

Fleet buyer bonuses. See 45.2 above.

De Voil Indirect Tax Service. See V3.443.

45.4   **Disposal of a motor car used in a business**

Where input tax was wholly excluded from credit on the purchase of the car. Following the decision in *EC Commission v Italian Republic, CJEC [1997] STC 1062*, the onward sale of a motor car on which input tax was blocked on purchase should be treated as exempt, regardless of whether it is sold at a profit or loss. C & E are considering changes which may be necessary to UK legislation to implement this decision.

In the meantime, businesses may chose either to exempt the supply or continue to apply the existing legislation outlined below which taxes any profit margin. Treating the supply as exempt may affect any partial exemption computation. A business choosing to use the exemption option pending legislation changes must apply it to all disposals of input tax blocked cars, not just those sold at a profit. A VAT group must apply the option to all group members. Claims for refund of overpaid VAT (subject to the three year cap) can be submitted where input tax blocked cars have been sold at a profit. Such claims must take into account any partial exemption implications of treating the sale of cars as exempt.

Before the decision in EC Commission v Italian Republic, under existing UK legislation where a car is sold at a profit, VAT is chargeable as if the supply were for a consideration equal to the excess of

*   the consideration for which the motor car is supplied, over

*   the consideration for which it was obtained i.e. its purchase price or, in the case of an acquisition from another EC country or importation from outside the EC, its value for the purposes of that acquisition or importation plus any VAT chargeable.

Where the car has previously been treated as self-supplied by the taxable person to himself under 45.6 below, the value of that self-supply plus the VAT chargeable thereon is substituted for the purchase price. [*SI 1992/3222, Art 7; SI 1995/1666*].

The excess is regarded as being VAT inclusive i.e. VAT is calculated by applying the VAT fraction (see 47.2 OUTPUT TAX) to the excess. A VAT invoice must *not* be issued and VAT must not be shown separately but documentary evidence of the purchase and sale must be retained. The car can be sold under the margin scheme for SECOND–HAND GOODS (61). (C & E Notice 700/64/96, para 10).

If a car is sold at a loss, the supply is treated as outside the scope of VAT.

Where any input tax was deductible on the purchase of the car, output tax must be accounted for on the full selling price. A VAT invoice must be issued to a VAT-registered buyer who requests one. Such a car cannot be sold under the margin scheme for SECOND-HAND GOODS (61). (C & E Notice 700/64/96, para 10).

45.5   **Transactions not treated as taxable supplies**

The following transactions relating to motor cars have been designated as outside the scope of VAT so as to be neither a supply of goods nor a supply of services.

(*a*)   The disposal by a person who repossessed it under the terms of a 'finance agreement' of a used motor car in the same condition as it was when it was so repossessed. This does not apply unless the VAT on any previous supply, acquisition or importation was wholly excluded from credit under 45.3 above.

'*Finance agreement*' means any agreement for the sale of goods whereby the property in those goods is not to be transferred until the whole of the price has been paid and the seller retains the right to repossess the goods.

As a finance company that repossesses a motor car may have some practical difficulty in establishing whether or not input tax has previously been blocked, C & E have agreed with the trade that where

• an 'N' or later registration prefix car has been supplied under the terms of a finance agreement to a leasing company or car dealer, or

• a 'K' or later registration prefix car has been similarly supplied to a taxi, driving school or daily rental business

the finance company should treat the repossessed car as input tax relieved by the purchaser (unless it has evidence to the contrary) and therefore account for VAT on its sale. (C & E Manual V1-9, Chapter 2A para 11.27).

(*b*)   The disposal of a used motor car by an 'insurer' who has taken it in settlement of a claim under a policy of insurance where the car is disposed of in the same condition as it was when it was so acquired. This does not apply unless the VAT on any previous supply, acquisition or importation was wholly excluded from credit under 45.3 above.

'*Insurer*' means a person permitted under *Insurance Companies Act 1982, s 2* to effect and carry out contracts of insurance against risks of loss or damage to motor vehicles.

(*c*)   The disposal of a motor car for no consideration (e.g. scrap). This does not apply unless the VAT on any previous supply, acquisition or importation was wholly excluded from credit under 45.3 above.

(*d*)   Services in connection with a supply of a used motor car provided by an agent acting in his own name to the purchaser of the motor car, the consideration for which is taken into account in calculating the price at which the agent sold the car. See 61.26 SECOND-HAND GOODS.

(*e*)   Services in connection with the sale of a used motor car provided by an auctioneer acting in his own name to the vendor or purchaser of the motor car, the consideration for which is taken into account in calculating the price at which the agent obtained (or, as the case may be, sold) the car. See 61.53 SECOND-HAND GOODS.

(*f*)   Where a taxable person has purchased or has let on hire a motor car

(i) the letting on hire of that motor car by the taxable person to any person for no consideration or consideration less than would be payable in an arm's length commercial transaction, or

(ii) the making available of that motor car (otherwise than by letting on hire) by the taxable person to any person for private use (whether or not for a consideration)

provided that VAT on any previous supply, acquisition, importation or letting on hire of the motor car was wholly excluded from credit under 45.3 above or partly excluded from credit under 45.11 below.

Where the taxable person is an individual or partnership, included under (ii) above is the making available of the motor car to the individual himself or a partner.

The effect of this is that most charges to employees for the private use of a car are not taxable. See 45.18 below.

[VATA 1994, s 5(3); SI 1992/3122, Arts 2, 4; SI 1995/1269; SI 1995/1667].

45.6   Self-supply

A motor car is treated as self-supplied by a taxable person in the following circumstances.

(*a*) Where a motor car not falling within (*b*) below is

(i) produced by a taxable person otherwise than by conversion of a vehicle obtained by him, or

(ii) produced by a taxable person by the conversion of another vehicle (whether a motor car or not) and VAT on the supply to, or acquisition or importation by, the taxable person of that vehicle was not wholly excluded from credit, or

(iii) supplied to, or acquired or imported by, a taxable person and input tax on that supply, acquisition or importation was not wholly excluded from credit,

and that motor car has not been supplied by him in the course or furtherance of any business carried on by him but is used by him otherwise than exclusively for business purposes.

(*b*) Where a motor car has been supplied to, or acquired or imported by, a taxable person primarily for the purpose of

(i) being provided by him for hire with the services of a driver for the purposes of carrying passengers, or

(ii) being provided by him for self-drive hire, or

(iii) being used as a vehicle in which driving instruction is being given by him,

and the motor car is neither supplied nor converted into another vehicle (whether or not a motor car) by the taxable person in the course or furtherance of his business but is used primarily for a purpose not falling within (i)-(iii) above other than some other exclusively business purpose. See 45.3 above for the interpretation of exclusive business use.

Where a group registration is in operation, self-supplies by group members are deemed to be made by the representative members.

[VATA 1994, ss 5(5), 43(2); SI 1992/3122, Arts 5–7; SI 1995/1269; SI 1995/1667].

Value of self-supply. *If the car is new*, the value of the self-supply by a UK manufacturer is the full cost of manufacturing the vehicle including related production overheads. For volume manufacturers, this can be taken to be 2/3rds of the current retail list price. Non-volume manufacturers may also use this approximation with the agreement of C & E. For non-manufacturing traders, the self-supply cost should include the purchase price plus any cost of incorporated parts of UK manufacture and delivery charge. Discounts received after the time of supply should be disregarded unless contractually agreed before that time. Where delivery charges cannot be determined, a fixed charge of £50 per vehicle may be used. (C & E Notice 700/57/95).

If the car is used, the value of the self-supply is the current purchase price of a vehicle *identical* in every respect (including age and condition and, where appropriate, any accessories fitted) to the car concerned or, if that is not available, the price for the purchase of a *similar* car. Failing this, it is the current production cost [*VATA 1994, 6 Sch 6; SI 1992/1867*] or 2/3rds of the current list price approximation of a new vehicle. (C & E Notice 700/57/95).

Time of self-supply. The time of supply is treated as taking place when the motor car is appropriated to the use giving rise to the self-supply. [*VATA 1994, s 6(11)*].

Appropriation for this purpose cannot normally be said to have taken place until at least the occurrence of some overt, unconditional event that can be said to show appropriation to the use that gives rise to the supply, e.g. use of the vehicle in the business as a demonstration model. The tax point is then the date when, by any positive and recorded action, the car is transferred from new car sales stock. A mere intention to appropriate the motor car is not normally sufficient to create a tax point in these circumstances. (C & E Notice 700, para 5.4(b); C & E Manual V1-11, Chapter 3 para 8.50).

See 45.8 below if the vehicle has been converted and then applied for business use.

See also *A & B Motors (Newton-le-Willows) Ltd, [1981] VATTR 29 (1024)*.

De Voil Indirect Tax Service. See V3.242.

45.7   **Car dealers**

A car dealer (i.e. a person whose business is the buying and selling of cars) can reclaim as input tax VAT charged on used and unused cars purchased or imported for sale. If the car is bought for use for a purpose which does not qualify for input tax recovery (e.g. as a demonstrator that will be taken home at night) VAT must not be reclaimed.

On sale of a car on which input tax was recovered, VAT must be charged on the full selling price. See also 45.6 above for self-supply e.g. where an unused car on which VAT has been reclaimed is transferred from sales stock to use in the business that would not qualify for input tax recovery.

(C & E Notice 700/64/96, para 35).

Premium, 'nearly new' and 'personal import' cars. Franchised dealers are not permitted by the terms of their franchise to sell a new car to another dealer. Therefore non-franchised dealers must secure regular supplies by other means, e.g. by employing an agent to purchase a car from a franchised dealer. Similarly, 'personal import' cars are sometimes acquired by VAT-registered dealers from private importers immediately following their importation.

With effect from 1 April 1998, the normal rules for supplying goods through buying agents apply (see 4.6 AGENTS). Non-franchised dealers are only able to recover input tax on the purchase of a motor car if it is purchased

- directly from a manufacturer or another dealer;

- through an agent acting in the name of the non-franchised dealer; or

- through an 'undisclosed agent' acting in his own name if the agent is registered for VAT and has issued a proper VAT invoice. However, to be registered, such an agent must be in business for VAT purposes and, given the nature of the tests which must be applied to establish this (see 8.2 BUSINESS), it is unlikely that C & E will regard the intention to sell a single car as constituting 'business'. Even if registered, an undisclosed agent will suffer a block on input tax recovery on the purchase of a car if it is made available for private use. This may apply if there is a gap between the purchase of the car and the supply to the non-franchised dealer.

(C & E Business Brief 4/98, 9 February 1998).

Before 1 April 1998, by administrative concession,

- if an agent (including an employee or director) of a non-franchised dealer acquired a car on the dealer's behalf, output tax was due on the full selling-price of the car when re-sold but the VAT charged by the franchised dealer on the original sale to the agent could be counted as input tax by the non-franchised dealer provided he held the franchised dealer's VAT invoice. In the case of 'personal imports' the dealer could count the VAT paid at importation as input tax provided he held evidence of the payment; and

- in all other cases where a car was acquired by a non-franchised dealer from a person with whom he had no direct association, it was accepted that the car was used and thus eligible for the second-hand car scheme relief when re-sold.

(C & E Press Notice 748, 25 June 1982).

Damaged or stolen cars. The following rules apply.

- *Insurance compensation.* All compensation payments received from insurers are outside the scope of VAT.

- *Damage to unused cars in transit.* Where a car is damaged whilst in transit to dealer's premises, the carriers may only recover VAT paid on car repairs if the supply of repairs is to them. If manufacturers or dealers arrange for the repairs, the VAT is their input tax (even if the carrier is liable for the cost of the repair).

- *Damage to unused cars at dealer's premises.* If an unused car is held on sale or return and is damaged beyond repair, the dealer may adopt the car in order to sell it as a write-off. VAT incurred on the supply of damaged cars to the dealer is deductible but the dealer must account for output tax on the price at which the car is sold.

  If a damaged car is adopted for use in the dealer's business, the input tax is not deductible.

  Any VAT incurred by the dealer in carrying out repairs is input tax, whether the damaged car is to be sold or used in the business.

- *Cars stolen in transit.* A car stolen from the carriers in transit has not been supplied and therefore no output tax is due from the manufacturer, dealer or carrier.

- *Unadopted cars stolen from dealers.* If a dealer has not adopted a car that is held on sale or return and it is stolen, there is no supply and no output tax due.

- *Adopted cars stolen from dealers.* If a car has been adopted by a dealer for resale and it is stolen, the dealer can recover input tax on the purchase of the car but does not have to account for output tax unless the car had been supplied to a customer.

(C & E Manual V1-13, Chapter 2A para 11.22).

Dealer demonstration bonuses. See 45.2 above.

45.8   Conversion of a vehicle into a motor car and vice versa

Where a vehicle on which VAT has been reclaimed is converted into a car which is retained for use,

- if that use would not qualify for input tax recovery under 45.3 above, VAT must be accounted for at the time of the conversion on the current value of the vehicle including the cost of conversion. VAT can be reclaimed on any parts bought for the conversion provided the car is used for business purposes; and

- if that use would qualify for input tax relief under 45.3 above, no VAT is due at the time of conversion but if the car is subsequently put to a non-qualifying use, VAT must be accounted for at that later time.

Where a vehicle is converted into a car for resale, VAT must be accounted for in the normal way on the full selling price.

Examples of the conversion of a vehicle into a motor car are:

- The fitting of a side window or windows into a van to the rear of the driver's seat.

- The fitting of a rear seat or seats to a van, even without the insertion of side windows.

- The removal of seats from a twelve-seater vehicle.

(C & E Notice 700/64/96, para 12).

See, however, *Bolinge Hill Farm (4217); P Oddonetto (5208); John Beharrell Ltd, [1991] VATTR 497 (6530)* and *Chichester Plant Contractors Ltd (6575)*.

Where a car is purchased for the purpose of converting it into a vehicle other than a car, VAT incurred on the purchase can be deducted and, if the vehicle is subsequently sold, VAT must be accounted for in the normal way on the full selling price. Where a car is purchased and *subsequently* converted into another vehicle, there is no entitlement to retrospective recovery of any blocked input tax but on any later sale, following the decision in *EC Commission v Italian Republic, CJEC [1997] STC 1062*, advantage may be taken of the exemption under 45.4 above. (C & E Manual V1-13, Chapter 2A para 11.8).

45.9   Car kits

Where a car is made from a kit or separately purchased parts, any VAT charged as input tax may be reclaimed subject to the normal rules. If the finished car is used in the business for a purpose that would not qualify for input tax recovery, VAT must be accounted for under the self-supply rules (see 45.6 above). The tax value must be based on the VAT-exclusive cost of the parts and the cost of construction. The VAT cannot be reclaimed. If the finished car is sold, VAT must be accounted for in the normal way. (C & E Notice 700/64/96, para 38).

45.10   MOTOR EXPENSES

Provided the vehicle is used in the business, VAT on leasing or hiring a vehicle, road fuel (whether bought by the business or reimbursed to employees), repair and maintenance charges and vehicle accessories can be treated as input tax. This applies even if the vehicle is used partly for private motoring. Private usage may, however, create a liability to output tax.

The provisions are considered in more detail in 45.11 to 45.19 below. For these purposes it is important to understand the difference between 'business' and 'private' motoring.

A *'business'* journey is one made by an employer or employee for the purpose of the business.

A '*private*' journey is any journey not for the purpose of the business.

Travel between a person's home and normal workplace is private motoring. Travel from home to any other place for business purposes is a business journey.

(C & E Notice 700/64/96, para 2).

45.11   Leasing or hiring a motor car

The following provisions apply to motor cars which are hired or leased for business purposes. They do not apply to hire purchase or lease-purchase agreements, for which see 45.3 above.

If a motor car as defined in 45.1 above is leased or hired, only 50% of the input VAT on the rental charges is available for the credit except in the following circumstances when 100% relief is available.

(*a*)   The motor car is a 'qualifying' motor car let on hire to a taxable person who intends to use the motor car exclusively for business purposes. This condition is *not* satisfied if the taxable person intends to

- let it on hire to any person either for no consideration or consideration less than would be payable in an arm's length commercial transaction; or

- make it available, otherwise than by letting on hire, to any person (including, where the taxable person is an individual, himself or, where the taxable person is a partnership, a partner) for private use (whether or not for a consideration).

(*b*)   The motor car is a 'qualifying' motor car let on hire to a taxable person who intends to use the motor car primarily

- to provide it on hire with the services of a driver for the purposes of carrying passengers;

- to provide it for 'self-drive hire'; or

- as a vehicle in which instruction in driving of a motor car is to be given by him.

'*Self-drive hire*' means hire where the hirer is the person normally expected to drive the motor car and the period of hire to each hirer (together with the period of hire of any other motor car expected to be hired to him by the taxable person) will normally be less than both 30 consecutive days and 90 days in any twelve month period.

(*c*)   The motor car is not a 'qualifying' motor car. However, following the decision in *C & E Commrs v BRS Automotive Ltd, CA [1998] STC 1210* (where a tax avoidance scheme was used to exploit the change to the VAT treatment of business cars which took effect from 1 August 1995) this does not apply to leasing charges after 12 November 1998 to a lessee if the only reason that the motor car is not a qualifying motor car is that it was let on hire to that same lessee before 1 August 1995. For further details of the effect of the anti-avoidance provisions, see C & E Business Brief 25/98, 16 December 1998.

(*d*)   The motor car is unused and is let on hire to a taxable person whose business consists predominantly of making supplies within *VATA 1994, 8 Sch Group 12, item 14* (see 32.17(*k*) HEALTH AND WATER UTILITIES) by a taxable person whose only taxable supplies are concerned with the letting on hire of motor cars to such taxable persons.

See 45.3 above for the definition of a '*qualifying*' motor car.

[*SI 1992/3222, Art 7; SI 1995/281; SI 1995/1666; SI 1998/2767*].

Identifying qualifying cars on leasing invoices. C & E have agreed with a main leasing trade organisation a recommended form of invoice for leasing companies to adopt for lettings. The invoice must clearly identify whether or not the car is a qualifying car (a legal requirement, see 40.4 INVOICES) and, if it is, the amount of VAT which is potentially subject to the 50% input tax restriction (depending upon the customer's use). Where the leasing company has not indicated whether the car is a qualifying car or not, the lessee can assume that a car with an 'M' registration or earlier prefix is non-qualifying and recover VAT in full subject to the normal rules. A car with an 'N' or later registration prefix should normally be treated as a qualifying car and the 50% restriction applied (unless the usage qualifies for 100% deduction under (*a*) or (*b*) above). Full input tax relief may however be claimed on rental charges on 'N' registration cars if the hirer incurred any VAT on rental on it before 1 August 1995.

The requirement to identify whether or not a car is a qualifying car does not apply to self-drive hire cars (see below). Unless there is evidence to the contrary, any self-drive hire car should be treated as a qualifying car if it has a 'K' registration or later prefix.

Charges subject to the 50% restriction. There are frequently two distinct elements of the rental: basic rental for the provision of the car (including depreciation, funding cost, VED and a proportion of overheads/profit) and an optional additional charge (covering repairs, maintenance and roadside assistance and a proportion of overheads/profit). Provided the additional charges are separately described in the contract hire agreement and periodic invoices and are genuinely optional, VAT on the basic rental is subject to the 50% restriction but VAT on the optional charge is recoverable in full subject to the normal rules. VAT on an excess mileage charge should similarly be separated into two distinct elements on a basis identical to the split of the rental. For full details, see the agreement between the British Vehicle Rental and Leasing Association and C & E reproduced in C & E Notice 700/57/95.

Rental rebates. Where a lessor sells a car at the end of a lease and uses the proceeds to rebate the monthly rental payments made to the lessee, a lessee who incurred a 50% input tax restriction on the rental charges on the car need only adjust for 50% of the VAT on the credit note issued by the lessor for rebate of rentals.

Early lease termination. Where a lease is terminated early, the leasing company may treat both the termination payment and any rental rebate as taxable or treat both as outside the scope. If it chooses to tax, it will normally set off the termination payment against any rebate and issue a VAT invoice for the difference.

- Where the termination payment exceeds the rebate, any VAT is not subject to the 50% restriction.

- Where any rebate exceeds the termination payment, the leasing company must issue a credit note. A lessee who incurred a 50% input tax restriction on the rental charges need only adjust for 50% of the VAT on the credit note.

Self-drive hire (daily rental). The 50% restriction applies to self-drive hire as well as leasing on a longer-term basis. However, by concession, C & E are currently prepared to accept that it does not apply if a car is used for five days or less for use in the business. If a car is hired for more than five days the restriction applies if the car is to replace a car normally available for private use. It also applies to other hirings of more than five days unless sufficient records are kept to demonstrate that the car was hired and used for business purposes.

Interaction with other apportionments. Where the 50% input tax restriction applies and there are both business and non-business activities and/or exempt supplies, the order for carrying out the various apportionments is

- VAT incurred between business and non-business activities (see 35.7 INPUT TAX)

- 50% input tax restriction on the VAT amount which relates to business activities

- any necessary PARTIAL EXEMPTION (49) calculation.

(C & E Notice 700/64/96, paras 21-27; VAT Information Sheet 12/95; C & E Business Brief 15/95, 31 July 1995).

Fleet leasing bonuses. See 45.2 above. Receipt of such a bonus reduces the VAT recoverable by the customer (if any) on the lease payments. For example, where 50% of the VAT incurred on lease payments can be recovered, VAT due on the bonus payment is

$7/47 \times 50\% \times$ gross bonus payment

(C & E Business Brief 1/98, 7 January 1998).

45.12 Repairs and maintenance

If a vehicle is used for business purposes, VAT on repairs and maintenance can be treated as input tax provided the work done is paid for by the business. This applies even if the vehicle is used for private motoring and even if no VAT is reclaimed on any road fuel in order to avoid use of the scale charges, see 45.16 below. VAT on repairs etc. covered by a mileage allowance or relating to a vehicle used by a sole trader or partner for private motoring only cannot be treated as input tax. (C & E Notice 700/64/96, para 28).

If an employer agrees to pay the full cost of repair and maintenance of employees' private cars, the VAT incurred may be treated as input tax provided the costs are recorded in the trader's accounts. (C & E Manual V1-13, Chapter 2A para 11.60).

45.13 Accessories

VAT charged on accessories fitted to a car when purchased cannot be reclaimed even if optional and separately itemised on the sales invoice. See *Turmeau (1135)*.

VAT on accessories subsequently purchased can only be treated as input tax if

- the vehicle is owned by the business or used in the business but not owned by it (e.g. an employee's or director's own car); and

- the accessory has a business use (e.g. a radio telephone).

(C & E Notice 700/64/96, para 29).

Input tax on personalised number plates has been disallowed in a considerable number of cases including *Ava Knit Ltd (1461)* and *E N Jones (5023)* but allowed in *MW Alexander (7208); Sunner & Sons (8857)* and *Hamlet's (Radio & TV) Ltd (12716)*. See Tolley's VAT Cases.

45.14 Fuel bought by the business

VAT on all fuel purchased by the business can be reclaimed subject to the normal rules. This applies even if it is used for private motoring (but see 45.16 below for accounting for VAT by means of a scale charge for fuel for private motoring. If the business makes supplies of fuel where the scale charge does not apply, VAT on all purchases can be treated as input tax but output tax must be accounted for on any private use of fuel. (C & E Notice 700/64/96, para 30).

Partly exempt traders. A partly exempt trader can reclaim input tax on fuel used for private motoring and must account for output tax on private motoring using the scale charge in the normal way.

Input tax in respect of business motoring is recoverable to the extent that the vehicle is used to make taxable supplies, i.e. VAT on fuel for business motoring must be included in the partial exemption calculation.

Where business and private motoring cannot be separated, all input tax on fuel must be included in the partial exemption calculations. In such a case, the scale charge can be reduced to equal the percentage of input tax recovered under the partial exemption method. See 45.16 below.

(C & E Notice 700/64/96, para 36).

Non-business activities. VAT on non-business journeys (e.g. journeys in connection with charitable activities of charities) is not reclaimable. Where fuel is used for both business and non-business activities, the total cost should be apportioned. (C & E Notice 700/64/96, para 37).

45.15   Fuel bought by employees

Road fuel bought by an employee (or any other non-taxable person) is treated as having been supplied to a business for business purposes provided one of the following methods of reimbursement is adopted.

(*a*)   The employee is reimbursed for the actual cost of the fuel.

(*b*)   The employee is paid an amount determined by reference to the total distance travelled by the vehicle (whether or not including private or non-business mileage) and the cylinder capacity of the vehicle.

Normally this will take the form of a mileage allowance which may also cover reimbursement of other costs. If so, input tax on road fuel is calculated by multiplying the fuel element of the mileage allowance by the VAT fraction.

C & E require the business to keep a record for each employee showing

• mileage travelled

• whether journeys are both business and private

• the cylinder capacity of the vehicle

• the rate of the mileage allowance

• the amount of input tax claimed.

C & E do not require the business to keep the invoices for the fuel bought by the employee. In most cases the expense claim will give enough information for the basic record.

Reimbursement by either method can also cover fuel bought for private use although in such a case the business must then account for output tax on the private use using the scale charges (see 45.16 and 45.17 below).

[*SI 1991/2306*]. (C & E Notice 700/64/96, para 31).

De Voil Indirect Tax Service. See V3.436.

45.16   Fuel for private motoring

Where in any prescribed accounting period a taxable person supplies 'fuel for private motoring' to an individual, VAT must be accounted for using the scale charges in 45.17 below which represent the VAT-inclusive value of the fuel in respect of any one vehicle.

'Fuel for private motoring' is fuel which is (or has previously been) supplied to, acquired from another EC country by, imported from outside the EC by, or manufactured by, a taxable person in the course of his business and which is

- provided or to be provided by the taxable person to an individual by reason of his employment or office for private use in his 'own vehicle' or a vehicle allocated to him;

- where the taxable person is an individual, appropriated or to be appropriated by him for private use in his own vehicle; or

- where the taxable person is a partnership, provided or to be provided to any of the individual partners for private use in his own vehicle.

Fuel is not regarded as provided to any person for his private use if it is supplied at a price not less than that at which it was supplied to or imported by the taxable person, or in the case of manufactured fuel, at a price not less than the aggregate of costs of raw materials and of manufacturing together with any excise duty thereon. See below for the VAT treatment where fuel is charged at such a price.

'Business travel' is that which an individual is necessarily obliged to do in the performance of the duties of his employment, the partnership, or in the case of the taxable person himself, his business.

'Own vehicle' includes any vehicle of which for the time being the individual has the use (other than a vehicle 'allocated to' him).

'Vehicle' means any mechanically propelled road vehicle other than a motor cycle or an invalid carriage. C & E have, however, confirmed that the scale rate charges will apply only to cars (see below).

A vehicle is at any time *'allocated to'* an individual if at that time it is made available (without any transfer of property in it) either to the individual himself or to any other person, and is so made available by reason of the individual's employment and for private use. However, a vehicle is not regarded as allocated to an individual by reason of his employment if, in any prescribed accounting period, it is a pooled car i.e.

- it was made available to, and actually used by, more than one of the employees or one or more (of the) employers and, in the case of each of them, it was made available to him by reason of his employment but was not in the period ordinarily used by any one of them to the exclusion of the others;

- in the case of each of the employees, any private use of the vehicle made by him was merely incidental to his other use of it in that period; and

- it was not normally kept overnight on or in the vicinity of any residential premises where any of the employees was residing, except while being kept overnight on premises occupied by the person making the vehicle available to them.

The provision of fuel is treated as a supply in the course or furtherance of a business by the taxable person at the time when fuel for private use is put into the fuel tank of the individual's own vehicle or a vehicle allocated to him. An appropriation by a taxable person to his own private use is treated as a supply to himself in his private capacity. A provision of fuel by a member of a group within *VATA 1994, s 43* (see 31 GROUPS OF COMPANIES) is treated as provision by the representative member.

Input tax. VAT on the supply, acquisition or importation of fuel for private use is to be treated as input tax subject to the normal rules notwithstanding that the fuel is not used or to be used for business purposes.

Changing vehicles. Where an individual is supplied with fuel for private use for one vehicle in respect of part of a prescribed accounting period and another vehicle for another part of the same period, then, provided that at the end of the period one of the vehicles neither belongs to him nor is allocated to him, supplies made to the individual are treated as made in respect of one vehicle only. Where each vehicle falls within the same category in the above tables, the table is applied as if fuel had been supplied for one vehicle only throughout the period. Otherwise the figures are rateably apportioned depending on the period for which fuel for private use was supplied for each vehicle. [*VATA 1994, ss 56, 57*].

Records. Where scale charges apply, records must be kept showing the number of vehicles for which free or below cost fuel is supplied; the cylinder capacity of each vehicle; and the name of the person using each vehicle. If a vehicle is changed, the date of change and the engine capacity of the replacement vehicle must also be shown.

Concession not to pay scale charges. If fuel is supplied for private motoring free or for less than the amount paid for it, the only way to avoid accounting for VAT using the scale charge is by not reclaiming input tax on *any* fuel purchased whether used for business or private motoring in cars or commercial vehicles. (C & E Notice 748, ESC 7). If this method is adopted, the VAT office must be advised before the start of the period in which it is to take effect. The VAT office will then treat the decision as remaining in force until told otherwise.

If fuel is supplied for private motoring for a charge which equals or exceeds the amount paid for it, output tax is calculated by multiplying the amount charged for the petrol by the VAT fraction (see 47.2 OUTPUT TAX). In this case there is no requirement to use the scale charge.

No private motoring paid for by the business. In such a case the scale charge does not apply but the taxable person must be able to show this from his business records. This is not possible for many businesses at the time of purchase. Claims that the cost of private mileage has not been included in the business accounts or that input tax relates only to the cost of business mileage have to be supported by detailed records including the business and total mileage and the cost of all fuel bought. See *Timewade Ltd (12786)*. (C & E Notice 700/64/96, paras 3, 5, 13).

Road fuel used for private motoring in vehicles other than cars. Where road fuel is used in other vehicles, e.g. vans, the normal VAT rules apply. VAT on fuel supplied to a registered person for use by employees, or VAT on fuel used by sole proprietors or partners, can be treated as input tax and VAT must be accounted for on private use. If preferred, input tax can be apportioned. (C & E Notice 700/64/96, para 4).

Partly exempt traders. Where a partly exempt business is unable to separate business and private motoring, all input tax on fuel (including that for private motoring) must be apportioned in the partial exemption calculations. To compensate for this, the scale charge for private motoring may be reduced to equal the percentage of input tax recovered under the partial exemption method. For example, if only 80% of the input tax is recovered, only 80% of the appropriate scale charge is to be paid. Where an annual adjustment is carried out, the scale charge must also be adjusted. (C & E Manual V1-15, Chapter 3 para 1.15).

Accounting for VAT. The output tax per the scale charge table in 45.17 below should be included in the total output tax figure on the return. The scale charge for the fuel should be included in the total value of outputs on the return.

Example

L Ltd provides its employees with cars and pays all day-to-day running expenses, including the cost of any petrol used for private motoring. Each employee submits a monthly return showing opening and closing mileage, together with fuel and servicing receipts for the period.

T, the sales director, has a 2,000cc car and puts in a monthly claim for July 1998. He supports this with petrol bills totalling £97.80 and a service invoice for £94.00 (£80.00 plus VAT £14.00). The company prepares monthly VAT returns.

The company should code the expenses claim as follows.

		£
Debit		
Servicing		80.00
Fuel £97.80 × $^{40}/_{47}$	83.23	
Scale charge — see 45.17 below	13.25	
		96.48
Input VAT — on service	14.00	
— on petrol £97.80 × $^{7}/_{47}$	14.57	
		28.57
		£205.05

Credit		
Expenses reimbursed to T		
£97.80 + £94.00		191.80
Output VAT		13.25
		£205.05

De Voil Indirect Tax Service. See V3.266.

45.17 **Fuel for private motoring — scale charges**

Prescribed accounting periods beginning after 5.4.98

Cylinder capacity	*Annual VAT returns*		*Quarterly VAT returns*		*Monthly VAT returns*	
	Scale charge	VAT due per vehicle	Scale charge	VAT due per vehicle	Scale charge	VAT due per vehicle
	£	£	£	£	£	£
Diesel engine						
2,000 or less	785	116.91	196	29.19	65	9.68
More than 2,000	995	148.19	248	36.93	82	12.21
Other engines						
1,400 or less	850	126.59	212	31.57	70	10.42
1,401 to 2,000	1,075	160.10	268	39.91	89	13.25
More than 2,000	1,585	236.06	396	58.97	132	19.65

[*SI 1998/788*].

Prescribed accounting periods beginning after 5.4.97 and before 6.4.98

Cylinder capacity	Annual VAT returns		Quarterly VAT returns		Monthly VAT returns	
	Scale charge	VAT due per vehicle	Scale charge	VAT due per vehicle	Scale charge	VAT due per vehicle
	£	£	£	£	£	£
Diesel engine						
2,000 or less	740	110.21	185	27.55	61	9.08
More than 2,000	940	140.00	235	35.00	78	11.61
Other engines						
1,400 or less	800	119.14	200	29.78	66	9.82
1,401 to 2,000	1,010	150.42	252	37.53	84	12.51
More than 2,000	1,490	221.91	372	55.40	124	18.46

[SI 1996/2948].

Prescribed accounting periods beginning after 5.4.96 and before 6.4.97

Cylinder capacity	Annual VAT returns		Quarterly VAT returns		Monthly VAT returns	
	Scale charge	VAT due per vehicle	Scale charge	VAT due per vehicle	Scale charge	VAT due per vehicle
	£	£	£	£	£	£
Diesel engine						
2,000 or less	640	95.31	160	23.82	53	7.89
More than 2,000	820	122.12	205	30.53	68	10.12
Other engines						
1,400 or less	710	105.74	177	26.36	59	8.78
1,401 to 2,000	890	132.55	222	33.06	74	11.02
More than 2,000	1,320	196.59	330	49.14	110	16.38

[SI 1995/3040].

Prescribed accounting periods beginning after 5.4.95 and before 6.4.96

Cylinder capacity	Annual VAT returns		Quarterly VAT returns		Monthly VAT returns	
	Scale charge	VAT due per vehicle	Scale charge	VAT due per vehicle	Scale charge	VAT due per vehicle
	£	£	£	£	£	£
Diesel engine						
2,000 or less	605	90.10	151	22.48	50	7.44
More than 2,000	780	116.17	195	29.04	65	9.68
Other engines						
1,400 or less	670	99.78	167	24.87	55	8.19
1,401 to 2,000	850	126.59	212	31.57	70	10.42
More than 2,000	1,260	187.65	315	46.91	105	15.63

[FA 1995, s 30].

45.18   Motor Cars

45.18   Private motoring – charge for use of a vehicle

A charge is made for the use of a motor car or any other vehicle if

- any employee, director or partner pays in cash or by deduction from salary or wages (including 'top-up' charges where by the employee pays for use of a more expensive car than their normal requirement); or

- any other person pays consideration of any kind.

Charge for use. Certain charges for the private use of a motor car are treated as neither a supply of goods or services. See 45.5(*f*) above. The effect of this is that a taxable person must account for VAT on any charge for the use of a vehicle unless, *in the case of a motor car*,

(i)   the car is owned by the taxable person and input VAT on it was wholly excluded from credit on the supply to, or acquisition or importation by, that taxable person (see 45.3 above); or

(ii)   the car is leased by the taxable person and the 50% input tax restriction applies to the leasing charges incurred (see 45.11 above); or

(iii)   the car is leased by the taxable person and input VAT on the car was wholly excluded from credit on the supply to, or acquisition or importation by, the leasing company. Leasing companies should identify these cars on their invoices as 'non-qualifying' cars. In practice, any car leased with an 'M' or earlier registration prefix falls into this category.

Health authorities. By a Treasury direction under *VATA 1994, s 41*, health authorities which lease cars after 1 August 1995 are not subject to the 50% block on VAT incurred. This means that any charges made to an employee are subject to VAT unless the health authority gives the employee a choice between

- a particular rate of wages, salary or employment, and

- a lower rate and, in addition, the right to the private use of the car

in which case the salary sacrifice element of any charge is excluded from VAT. Contributions for cars leased prior to 1 August 95 are not subject to VAT. [*SI 1992/630*]. (C & E Manual V1-13, Chapter 2A para 11.35).

Charge for running costs, etc. The charges which are excluded from VAT above are those which represent consideration for use, i.e. the provision of a car. Output tax must be accounted for on any *separate* charge made to cover running costs, maintenance, repairs, etc. even if the vehicle is a car on which charges for use are not taxable. In practice, businesses often make a single charge for use of a vehicle, running costs and fuel. In such cases, the total charge should be apportioned. VAT on the fuel must be accounted for on the basis of the scale charge (see 45.16 and 45.17 above) and the charge for use (if any) and running costs calculated separately. For simplification, where

- a single charge is made based on the capital cost of the car (e.g. using the AA rate)

- the car falls within (i)-(iii) above so that it is one upon which charges for use are not taxable

the whole of the charge can be treated as non-taxable, even if there is an element of running costs. VAT must still be accounted for on fuel separately.

(C & E Notice 700/64/96, paras 6-8).

45.19   Private motoring — vehicle used for no payment

VAT is not normally due if a car which has been purchased or leased for the purposes of the business is used for private motoring free of charge. VAT must, however, be accounted for on any free private use of

- a car on which input tax was claimed because it was primarily for taxi hire, self-drive hire or driving instruction; and

- a vehicle other than a car.

The tax value of the supply is the cost of making the vehicle available. Over any period of time, this includes depreciation, repairs and other running costs (excluding any VAT recovered as input tax) but excludes fuel costs (VAT on which must be accounted for separately, see 45.16 above) and costs which were not subject to VAT (e.g. road tax and insurance). The costs incurred should be multiplied by the proportion that private mileage bears to total mileage.

(C & E Notice 700/64/96, para 9).

45.20   **SECOND-HAND SCHEME FOR MOTOR CARS**

In general, VAT is charged on the full value of any goods, including second-hand motor cars, sold by a taxable person. The Treasury may however, by order, provide for a taxable person to opt to charge VAT on the profit margin (instead of full value). [*VATA 1994, ss 32, 50A: FA 1995, s 24*]. An order under these provisions has been made by *SI 1995/1268* which covers all second-hand goods. It replaces previous provisions made by *The Value Added Tax (Cars) Order 1992 (SI 1992/3122)* (which itself replaced an earlier similar order (*SI 1980/442*)). The effect of the provisions is that, provided all the conditions are met, the margin scheme may be used to account for VAT only on the amount by which the selling price exceeds the purchase price. The gross margin includes the VAT to be accounted for.

For full details of the margin scheme, see 61 SECOND-HAND GOODS.

46 Northern Ireland

46.1   The provisions of the *VATA 1994* apply to Northern Ireland [*VATA 1994, s 101(3)*] but not the Republic of Ireland.

Refund of VAT to Government of Northern Ireland. C & E must refund to the NI Government any VAT charged on

- the supply of goods or services to that Government,

- the acquisition of goods by that Government from another EC country, or

- the importation of any goods by that Government from a place outside the EC

after deducting an amount (agreed between C & E and the Department of Finance and Personnel for NI) attributable to supplies, acquisitions and importations for the purposes of a business carried on by that Government.

[*VATA 1994, s 99*].

See also 43.6 LOCAL AUTHORITIES AND STATUTORY BODIES for supplies by 'government departments', including those in NI.

47 Output Tax

Cross-references. See 2.18 ACCOUNTING PERIODS AND RETURNS for goods sold in satisfaction of a debt by a person selling under a power of sale; 7 BAD DEBT RELIEF ; 24 EXEMPT SUPPLIES; 27.19 FINANCE for output tax under hire purchase, conditional sale and credit sale agreements; 56.3–56.17 RATES OF VAT for changes in the rate of tax; 59.27 REGISTRATION for output tax on the deemed supply of business assets when a trader is deregistered; 60 RETAIL SCHEMES for special schemes for retailers; 61 SECOND-HAND GOODS for special schemes in operation for such goods; 62.2 SELF-SUPPLY for output tax on stationery produced and used by partly exempt traders; 69.5 VALUATION for calculation of output tax where discounts are allowed; 72 ZERO-RATED SUPPLIES.

De Voil Indirect Tax Service. See V3.5.

47.1 GENERAL

Output tax in relation to a 'taxable person' means VAT on

- supplies which he makes; and

- acquisitions of goods by him from another EC country (including VAT which is also counted as input tax under 35.1(*b*) INPUT TAX).

A '*taxable person*' is a person who is, or is required to be, registered under *VATA 1994*.

[*VATA 1994, ss 3(1), 24(2)*].

Output tax on supplies. A taxable person must charge VAT on any taxable supply of goods or services made in the UK in the course or furtherance of any business carried on by him.

A '*taxable supply*' is a supply of goods or services made in the UK other than an exempt supply. [*VATA 1994, s 4*]. See 8.1 BUSINESS for the meaning of 'business'. For VAT purposes the UK includes the territorial sea of the UK (i.e. waters within twelve nautical miles of the coast-line).

The output tax is normally the liability of the person making the supply. [*VATA 1994, s 1(2)*]. As a general rule, the determination of the liability of VAT is the responsibility of the supplier. In certain special cases, a supply can be zero-rated where a customer gives the supplier a declaration claiming eligibility for such treatment. Under these circumstances, if the supplier, despite having taken all reasonable steps to check the validity of the declaration, fails to identify any inaccuracy and, in good faith, makes the supply at the zero rate, C & E will not seek to recover the VAT due from the supplier. (C & E Notice 748, ESC A16).

The VAT becomes due at the time of supply [*VATA 1994, s 1(2)*] but in practice is accounted for and paid by reference to tax returns completed for prescribed accounting periods. See 2 ACCOUNTING PERIODS AND RETURNS and 51 PAYMENT OF TAX.

Certain small businesses are allowed to account for VAT on the basis of cash received and/or by means of only one VAT return a year. See 63 SPECIAL SCHEMES.

Output tax on acquisitions. See 23.3 EUROPEAN COMMUNITY: SINGLE MARKET for tax on acquisitions from other EC countries.

Rates of output tax. There are currently two main rates of output tax, standard rate (17.5%) and zero rate (nil). See 72 ZERO-RATED SUPPLIES for the effects of zero-rating and the categories of goods and services to which it applies. A lower rate applies to certain supplies of FUEL AND POWER (29).

Misunderstanding. VAT undercharged by a registered trader on account of a *bona fide* misunderstanding may be remitted provided all the following conditions are fulfilled.

(*a*)   There is no reason to believe that the VAT has been knowingly evaded.

(*b*)   There is no evidence of negligence.

(*c*)   The misunderstanding does not concern an aspect of VAT clearly covered in general guidance published by C & E or in specific instructions to the trader concerned.

(*d*)   The VAT due was not charged, could not now reasonably be expected to be charged to customers, and will not be charged.

Where at the time the misunderstanding comes to light there are unfulfilled firm orders from customers, for which the price quoted has been based mistakenly on the assumption that no VAT, or less VAT than properly due, would be chargeable, VAT undercharged may be remitted in respect of such orders provided the conditions above are met. (C & E Notice 48, ESC 2.4).

De Voil Indirect Tax Service. See V3.501; V3.502.

47.2   VAT FRACTION

Normally, VAT is calculated at the appropriate percentage of a price which has first been decided without VAT and the VAT invoice shows these separate amounts. Sometimes, however, VAT has to be calculated from a price in which it is already included (e.g. in a less detailed tax invoice). To do this, the VAT fraction is req

$$\text{VAT fraction} = \frac{\text{rate of tax}}{100 + \text{rate of tax}}$$

Rate of VAT	*VAT fraction*
17½%	7/47
8%	2/27
5%	1/21

Example

M refills his car with petrol and receives a less detailed invoice totalling £36.78.

The VAT included is £36.78 × 7/47 = £5.48.

47.3   OUTPUT TAX ON MULTIPLE SUPPLIES

In addition to straightforward transactions, a particular supply may be complicated by being either a single (composite) supply or a multiple (mixed) supply (see 64.6 SUPPLY). There is a multiple supply where a single inclusive price is charged for a number of separate supplies of goods or services. Where all supplies are liable to VAT at the same rate, output tax due is calculated in the normal way. Otherwise the tax value of each supply must be calculated in order to arrive at the total output tax due. Any calculation of the apportionment of the total price must be fair and justifiable.

Example 1   Apportionment based on cost of both supplies: VAT-inclusive price

A VAT-inclusive price of £140 is charged for a supply of zero-rated goods which cost £23 and standard-rated goods which cost £40 (excluding VAT).

Proportion of the total cost represented by standard-rated goods	$\dfrac{(40 + \text{VAT})}{(40 + \text{VAT}) + 23} = \dfrac{47}{70}$
VAT-inclusive price of standard-rated goods	$\dfrac{47}{70} \times £140 =$ £94
VAT included $=£94 \times$ VAT fraction	$£94 \times \dfrac{7}{47} =$ £14
Tax value of zero-rated supply	$£140 - £94 =$ £46

Total price is therefore apportioned
Value of standard-rated supply	80
VAT on standard-rated supply	14
Value of zero-rated supply	46
	£140

Example 2   Apportionment based on cost of both supplies: VAT-exclusive price

A VAT-exclusive price of £126 is charged for a supply of zero-rated goods which cost £23 and standard-rated goods which cost £40 (excluding VAT).

Proportion of the total cost represented by standard-rated goods	$\dfrac{40}{63}$
VAT-exclusive value of standard-rated goods	$\dfrac{40}{63} \times £126 =$ £80
VAT on standard-rated goods	$£80 \times 17.5\% =$ £14
Tax value of zero-rated supplies	$£126 - £80 =$ £46

Total price is therefore
Value of standard-rated supply	80
Value of zero-rated supply	46
	126
VAT on £80 at 17.5%	14
	£140

Example 3   Apportionment based on the cost of one supply only

A VAT-inclusive price of £142 is charged for a supply of zero-rated goods which cost £26 and standard-rated services, the cost of which cannot be identified. A fair and reasonable uplift on the zero-rated goods, consistent with actual profit margins of the business, is 50%.

Value of zero-rated supplies	$£26 + 50\% =$ £39
VAT-inclusive price of the standard-rated goods	$£142 - £39 =$ £103
VAT on standard-rated goods $=£103 \times$ VAT fraction	$£103 \times \dfrac{7}{47} =$ £15.34

The total price is therefore apportioned
Value of zero-rated supply	39.00
Value of standard-rated supply	87.66
	126.66
VAT on £87.66 at 17.5%	15.34
	£142.00

Example 4.   Apportionment based on market values: VAT-inclusive price

A VAT-inclusive price of £200 is charged for a zero-rated supply (which would separately be charged at £50) and a standard-rated supply (which would separately be charged at £200 including VAT).

Proportion of the total normal price represented by standard-rated goods	$\dfrac{200}{200+50} = \dfrac{4}{5}$	
VAT-inclusive price of standard-rated goods	$\dfrac{4}{5} \times £200 =$	£160
VAT included = £160 × VAT fraction	$£160 \times \dfrac{7}{47} =$	£23.83
Tax value of zero-rated supply	$£200 - £160 =$	£40

The total price is therefore apportioned

Value of standard-rated supply (£160 – £23.83)	136.17
VAT on standard-rated supply	23.83
Value of zero-rated supply	40.00
	£200.00

Apportionment is only necessary where the price charged is the only consideration for the supplies. If the consideration is not wholly in money, VAT must be accounted for as explained in 69.2(*b*) VALUATION.

Apportionment must not be used if the goods and services supplied together make up a *composite* supply (e.g. a launderette cannot be treated as supplying separate supplies of water, heat, use of machines, etc., only the single service of washing or drying clothes taxable at the standard rate).

(C & E Notice 700, para 3.2, Appendix E).

47.4   **BUSINESS GIFTS**

For VAT purposes, an article is a gift where the donor is not obliged to give it and the recipient is not obliged to do or give anything in return. (C & E Notice 700, para 3.10). Business gifts cover a wide range of items including

- brochures, posters and advertising matter;

- 'executive presents';

- long service awards (see *RHM Bakeries (Northern) Ltd v C & E Commrs QB 1978, [1979] STC 72*);

- retirement gifts;

- goods supplied to employees under attendance or safety at work schemes;

- items distributed to trade customers;

- prizes dispensed from amusement and gaming machines (see 58.3 RECREATION AND SPORT); and

- prizes of goods in betting and gaming and free lotteries (see 58.1 RECREATION AND SPORT).

(C & E Notice 700/35/97, para 1.1).

Gifts of goods. A gift of business assets (including land) is a supply of goods [*VATA 1994, 4 Sch 5(1), 9*] and is taxable as such subject to certain exceptions and special rules, including the following.

(*a*) There is no supply (and no VAT liability arises) unless the donor (or, after 16 March 1998, any of his 'predecessors') has or will become entitled to credit for any input tax on the supply, acquisition or importation of the goods.

For this purpose, a person is the '*predecessor*' of the donor where the donor acquired the goods from him under a transaction relating to the transfer of a business as a going concern which was treated as neither a supply of goods nor a supply or services (see 8.10 *et seq* BUSINESS). The donor's predecessors include the predecessors of his predecessor through any number of transactions. The effect of this is that, for no VAT liability to arise, no entitlement to input tax on the goods must have arisen through any number of such going concern transactions.

[*VATA 1994, 4 Sch 5(5)(5A); FA 1998, s 21*].

(*b*) There is no supply (and no VAT liability arises) on a gift of goods for business purposes, not forming part of a series or succession of gifts to the same person, where the 'cost to the donor of acquiring or producing the goods' was £15 or less (excluding VAT).

After 16 March 1998, in determining the '*cost to the donor of acquiring or producing the goods*', where the donor acquired the goods under a transaction relating to the transfer of a business as a going concern which was treated as neither a supply of goods nor a supply or services (see 8.10 *et seq* BUSINESS), the donor and his 'predecessors' are treated as if they were the same person. For this purpose, a '*predecessor*' is the transferor under such a transaction and a person's predecessors include the predecessors of his predecessor through any number of transactions. The effect of this is that the cost of the goods gifted remains unchanged by the transfer of a business as a going concern through any number of such transfers.

[*VATA 1994, 4 Sch 5(2)(2A); FA 1996, s 33; FA 1998, s 21*].

Where gifts are made to the same person on more than one occasion, this is a series or succession of gifts and VAT is due on all the goods regardless of cost. However, if it is simply by chance that the same person receives a gift more than once, then C & E do not regard this as a series or succession of gifts, i.e. it is the intention of the donor that is important. Examples of gifts which may not form part of a series or succession include

● annual gifts (such as at Christmas);

● gifts distributed on a random basis, e.g. where a salesman gives small personal items to trade contacts;

● small items given away to trade customers, e.g. ashtrays and beer mats given away by brewers; and

● advertising posters handed out for display at the premises of trade customers.

(C & E Notice 700/35/97, para 1.3).

(*c*) Samples (see 47.9 below).

(*d*) No VAT is due on free meals or drinks to employees by way of catering (see 11.4 CATERING) or the provision of accommodation for employees in a hotel, etc. (see 33.3 HOTELS AND HOLIDAY ACCOMMODATION). [*VATA 1994, 6 Sch 10*].

(*e*) No further VAT may be due where additional goods or services are offered with normal taxable supplies as part of a business promotion (see 67 TRADING STAMP AND PROMOTION SCHEMES).

(*f*) Prizes donated for competitions in newspapers and magazines (for which special rules apply, see 58.18 RECREATION AND SPORT).

(*g*) Free fuel to employees for private motoring (for which special rules apply, see 45.16 MOTOR CARS).

(*h*) Free meals or drinks to non-employees is not normally a supply and no VAT is due (but see 9 BUSINESS ENTERTAINMENT for non-deductible input tax).

(*i*) A gift of goods to a charity for sale or export by it (or to a taxable person, such as a charity's trading subsidiary, covenanting all the profits of sale to a charity) is zero-rated. [*VATA 1994, 8 Sch Group 15, Item 2*].

(*j*) Where a business consist of promoting a sporting, entertainment or similar activity and

- the business does no more than organise an event at which trophies are given away,

- there is no other associated competition/event, and

- a charge is made for admission to see the presentation

part of the admission charge is regarded as being payment for the trophies and no further VAT is due on the 'gift' of the trophies.

(C & E Notice 700/35/97, para 1.1).

Input tax on goods purchased for business gifts is deductible. If the recipient of the goods also uses them for business purposes, that person can recover any VAT charged on the gift as input tax (subject to the normal rules). The donor cannot issue a VAT invoice (because there is no consideration) but see 40.2 INVOICES for the form of a VAT certificate which can be issued instead.

Value of the supply. Where a gift of goods is a taxable supply, the value of the goods on which VAT must be accounted for is the price the person would have to pay (excluding VAT), at the time of the supply, to purchase goods *identical* in every respect (including age and condition) to the goods concerned. Where that value cannot be ascertained, the price for the purchase of goods *similar* to, and of the same age and condition as, the goods concerned must be used. If that value is also not possible to ascertain, the cost of producing the goods concerned at that time is to be used. [*VATA 1994, 6 Sch 6*].

A gift of services where the recipient is not required to do or give anything in return is generally not a taxable supply. See, however, 47.5 below where bought-in services are used by any person outside the business free of charge.

Inducements, etc. Goods or services supplied on condition that a purchase is made or some action is performed of benefit are not 'gifts'. Neither are articles supplied under 'self-introduction' or 'introduce-a-friend' schemes by retail mail order companies where the introducer has a contractual right to receive the chosen articles. See *GUS Merchandise Corporation Ltd v C & E Commrs CA, [1981] STC 569* and *Empire Stores Ltd v C & E Commrs CJEC, [1994] STC 623*. In the latter case, the Court held that the consideration for the supply of the introductory goods consisted of a supply of services (the introduction of potential customers), the value of which was the expense which the recipient was prepared to incur in order to obtain those services, i.e. the price paid for the goods (and not their estimated retail catalogue price). See also *C & E Commrs v Westmorland Motorway Services Ltd CA, [1998] STC 431* where free meals given to coach drivers as an inducement to stop at a motorway service station were held to be valued at the normal retail price of the meals.

47.5   PRIVATE OR NON-BUSINESS USE OF GOODS AND SERVICES

Goods. Where goods (including land) belonging to a business are put to private use or are used or made available to any person (e.g. employees, family and friends) outside the business, a taxable supply takes place.

There is no supply (and no VAT liability arises) unless the person carrying on the business (or, after 16 March 1998, any of his 'predecessors') has or will become entitled to credit for any input tax on the supply, acquisition or importation of the goods.

For this purpose, a person is a *'predecessor'* of the person carrying on the business where that person acquired the goods from the predecessor under a transaction relating to the transfer of a business as a going concern which was treated as neither a supply of goods nor a supply or services (see 8.10 *et seq.* BUSINESS). A person's predecessors include the predecessors of his predecessor through any number of transactions. The effect of this is that, for no VAT liability to arise, no entitlement to input tax on the goods must have arisen through any number of such going concern transactions.

If the private use is permanent, the supply is one of goods and where no consideration is given, the provisions in 47.4 above apply.

If the private use is only temporary, the supply is one of services and where no consideration is given, output tax is due on the cost to the taxable person of providing the services. Over a period of time, this is the amount of depreciation of the goods (plus any other costs related to the goods) multiplied by the proportion which the private use forms to the total use. (C & E Notice 700, para 3.13). See *C & E Commrs v Teknequip Ltd QB, [1987] STC 664* where a company yacht was used by employees and for entertaining customers. In *Julius Fillibeck Söhne GmbH & Co KG v Finanzamt Neustadt, CJEC 1997, [1998] STC 513*, the CJEC held that, in principle, the provision of free transport by an employer to its employees was use outside the business. However, this did not apply when, having regard to special circumstances such as changes in the place of work and difficulty in finding other means of transport, the requirements of the business made it necessary for the employer to provide transport for employees. In such cases the supply was not effected for purposes other than those of the business.

[*VATA 1994, 4 Sch 5(1)(4)(5)(5A), 9, 6 Sch 7; FA 1995, s 33(3); FA 1998, s 21*].

Special rules apply to private use of road fuel and motor cars. See 45.16 and 45.18 MOTOR CARS respectively.

See 64.54 SUPPLY for the time of supply of the private use of goods.

Services. Where a person carrying on a business puts services which have been supplied to him to any private use, a taxable supply takes place. Private use includes use outside the business by any person and own personal use where a business is carried on by an individual. The provisions do not apply, however,

- where the services are used, or made available for use, for a consideration;

- where no input tax has been deducted or will become deductible on the supply to him;

- where any part of the input tax on the supply to him was not counted as input tax because of an apportionment under *VATA 1994, s 24(5)*, see 35.7 INPUT TAX (i.e. the provisions do not apply where an apportionment has been made between business and non-business use at the time of supply);

- where the services supplied consist of

  (i) the provision in the course of catering of food or beverages to employees; or

  (ii) the provision of accommodation for employees in a hotel, inn, boarding house or similar establishment; or

- where the services supplied consist of the letting on hire of a motor car and 50% of the input tax has already been excluded from credit (see 45.11 MOTOR CARS).

The value of the supply is that part of the value of the supply of services to him as fairly and reasonably represents the cost to him of providing the services. The total VAT charged (cumulative where the services are supplied on more than one occasion) cannot exceed the amount of input tax which has been deducted or will become deductible.

Anti-avoidance re business transfers. After 17 March 1998, where the transfer of the assets of a business as a going concern is treated as neither a supply of goods nor a supply of services (see 8.10 *et seq.* BUSINESS) the liability of the transferee to tax under these provisions is determined as if the transferor and the transferee were the same person. Where the business has been transferred VAT-free as a going concern more than once, the transferee is treated as if he and all the previous transferors were the same person.

[*SI 1993/1507; SI 1995/1668; SI 1998/762*].

The above provisions relating to private use of services are concerned with major changes of use which continue over time or are permanent. Minor or occasional private or non-business use will be treated as *de minimis* and will not give rise to a liability to VAT. The type of services affected include computer software, building construction and refurbishment, particularly to domestic premises, and sporting rights.

Calculating the VAT due. There are no set rules for calculating the VAT due. If use of services permanently changes from business to non-business use, the accounting convention normally adopted for depreciating business assets may be used to calculate the VAT due, i.e. the value on which VAT is due is

$$\text{Cost of services} \times \frac{\text{Projected period of non-business use}}{\text{Period over which comparable assets are depreciated}}$$

Alternatively, any other fair and reasonable basis can be used. VAT should not be accounted for beyond the point at which

- the asset is fully depreciated, or

- the accumulated VAT accounted for equals the amount of input tax on the service which has proved to be not attributable to business use,

whichever is the earlier.

(C & E Business Brief 17/94, 12 September 1994).

Employee benefits and perks. The provisions apply where services are made available to employees in the form of a bonus, reward or perk (e.g. membership of a club, hotel accommodation or a holiday) analogous to a business gift of goods. However, VAT incurred on perks can only be deducted as input tax if the services are supplied to the employer (see 35.5 INPUT TAX) which will not be the case with most perks. Where the services are supplied to the employee, the employer cannot deduct input tax and therefore the above provisions do not apply.

C & E do not in any case apply the provisions to services obtained by a business for what may be termed genuine business purposes. These include

- retraining prior to redundancy;

- subsistence;

- relocation expenses;

- information technology supplied for working at home;

- domestic accommodation;

- out-placement;

- sports and recreational facilities available to staff in general (see 35.13 INPUT TAX); and

- mobile telephones (although an apportionment under 35.7 INPUT TAX may be appropriate).

(C & E Manual V1-13, Chapter 2 para 5.16).

De Voil Indirect Tax Service. See V3.212; V3.216.

47.6   PACKAGING

Normal and necessary packaging, including ordinary tins, bottles and jars, is treated as part of the goods which it contains so that if the goods are zero-rated, zero-rating also applies to the packaging. However

- where the packaging is more than normal or necessary, there is a mixed supply (see 47.3 above) and VAT is due on the packaging. This applies to storage containers and other types of packaging which could be sold separately;

- where an additional charge is made with a supply of goods for their container to ensure that it is safely returned and the additional charge is to be refunded on its safe return, this additional charge is not subject to VAT; and

- where an additional charge is raised to cover the loan, hire or use of a container, then the charge is standard-rated.

(C & E Notice 700, para 3.3).

47.7   Food packaging

Where the purpose of the packaging is simply to contain, protect and promote the food it contains, C & E consider it as part of the supply of the food inside, rather than a supply in its own right, and it takes the same liability as its contents. This is so even if the packaging is more than the minimum strictly necessary. This follows the decision in *United Biscuits (UK) Ltd t/a Simmers CS, [1992] STC 325* where it was held that decorative biscuit tins amounting to 55% of the total production cost (as opposed to 28% for ordinary cardboard packaging) were normal packaging for biscuits. The court held that the tin was integral to the biscuits, not merely in the sense that it was the container in which they were packaged, but further in that it prolonged their shelf-life and kept the biscuits in better condition once consumption had begun.

Where packaging is clearly designed to be 'extra' to the food, there is a mixed supply of food and packaging and normally the total price must be apportioned in order to arrive at the output tax due (see 47.3 above). Subject to the linked goods concession below, this applies to the following types of containers.

- Any container specifically advertised or held out for sale as having a value in its own right (e.g. by advertising the product as 'with a free storage tin').

- Any container with a clear and obviously intended after-use (e.g. tumblers containing coffee, honey or preserves in ceramic serving bowls).

- Storage jars obviously intended for use in storing future supplies of the product.

- Biscuit tins containing built-in hydroscopic crystals.

- Tea caddies (but not simple tins bearing the supplier's name and details of the weight and variety of tea where it is the supplier's practice to sell tea in this way).

- Ceramic pâté pots and other ceramic containers which are clearly suitable for future decorative use. See, however, *Paterson Arran Ltd (15041)* where, following *United Biscuits Ltd* above, zero-rating was applied to the sale of quality biscuits in a ceramic jar aimed at the Christmas market, even though the jar represented 70% of the total cost.

- Hampers and picnic baskets (other than simple cardboard cartons).

Outer cases and boxes, etc. and seasonal packaging (although frequently more elaborate than supplied during the rest of the year) are not normally considered separate supplies unless falling within one of the above categories.

Linked goods concession. Where, however, standard-rated packaging is supplied with zero-rated food, the supply can be treated as a single supply of zero-rated food provided the packaging

- is not charged at a separate price;

- costs no more than 20% of the total cost of the supply; and

- costs no more than £1 (excluding VAT).

(C & E Notice 701/14/97, paras 4.1, 4.3).

47.8   **POSTAGE AND DELIVERY CHARGES**

Delivered goods. These are supplied if, in order to fulfil a contract for the sale of the goods, they must be delivered to an address nominated by the customer and the supplier remains responsible for the goods until they have been delivered. The address need not be that of the customer himself, e.g. delivery may be to a third party such as his own customer. The important tests are whether delivery is included in the contract, rather than an optional extra, and whether the supplier is responsible for safe delivery.

In the opinion of C & E, if the contract with the customer is for a supply of delivered goods (or no separate charge for delivery is made) there is only a single supply, the VAT liability of which depends on the nature of the goods supplied. It does not matter whether the charge for delivery is separately itemised or invoiced. Examples of supplies of delivered goods are mail order sales and doorstep deliveries of milk or newspapers.

See also *C & E Commrs v Plantiflor Ltd, QB [1998] STI 1567* where the court, reversing the decision of the tribunal, held that the company was not acting as an agent of its customers in arranging an exempt supply of delivery services by the Post Office. The amounts charged to customers for delivery were part of the consideration received by the company. The court did, however, confirm that, contrary to C & E's view, the delivery charges could be treated as consideration for a separate supply of services.

Delivery services. Unless the contract with the customer is for the supply of delivered goods as above, there is a separate supply of delivery services which is normally standard-rated (even if the charges are equal to the exempt supply made by the Post Office). Special rules, however, apply if the delivery forms part of the movement of goods to or from a place outside the UK, see 68.24 TRANSPORT AND FREIGHT.

Where a charge is made for handling goods which are being sold by another person (e.g. a charge for distributing a publisher's newspaper), the supply is standard-rated (but see *Direct mailing services* below).

Retail schemes. For supplies of *delivered goods,*

- under the Point of Sale scheme, include the full amount charged in daily gross takings;

- under Apportionment Scheme 1, include the full amount charged in daily gross takings and do not adjust the record of purchases;

- under Apportionment Scheme 2 and the Direct Calculation schemes, include the full amount charged in daily gross takings and also allow for the delivery charge element in the calculation of expected selling prices; and

- under the old retail schemes, the full amount charged was included in daily gross takings whichever scheme was used.

If delivery services are provided for an extra charge,

- under the Point of Sale scheme and the Apportionment schemes, account for VAT due on the delivery services outside the scheme used;

- under the Direct Calculation schemes,

   (i) where minority goods are zero-rated, include delivery charges in daily gross takings; and

   (ii) where minority goods are standard-rated, the delivery charges will not be included in the expected selling prices calculation but can be added back as part of the standard-rated sales figure. Otherwise, account for VAT due on delivery services outside the scheme; and

- under the old retail schemes, delivery charges could be included in daily gross takings under Schemes A, B, B1, B2 and F but under the other schemes VAT had to be accounted for outside the scheme used.

(C & E Notice 727/3/97, para 3.10; C & E Notice 727/4/97, para 3.11; C & E Notice 727/5/97, para 3.10).

Direct mailing services. Where a supplier provides the service of posting client's mail (e.g. publicity or advertising material), the supplier may treat the postal charges as a disbursement for VAT purposes provided

(*a*) the general conditions for treatment as a disbursement are satisfied (see 4.7 AGENTS);

(*b*) the client specifies the recipients or has access to their names and addresses prior to despatch; and

(*c*) the supplier passes any Post Office discount or rebate to the client in full. Where a discount or rebate is obtained by posting mail for various clients at the same time, a fair apportionment must be made.

If conditions (*a*) to (*c*) are not met, the full amount of postal charges must be included in the value of the direct mailing service. This is normally standard-rated if the mail is sent to addresses in the UK. Special rules, however, apply if the delivery is, or forms part of, the movement of goods to or from a place outside the UK, see 68.24 TRANSPORT AND FREIGHT.

Packing services. A separate supply of packing services will normally be standard-rated. Special rules, however, apply if the delivery forms part of the movement of goods to or from a place outside the UK, see 68.24 TRANSPORT AND FREIGHT.

(C & E Notice 700, para 3.4; C & E Notice 700/24/94).

47.9   **SAMPLES**

A gift to any person of a sample of any goods is not a taxable supply except that, where a number of identical samples (or samples not differing in any material respect) are given to the same person (whether on one or different occasions), only one of those samples is deemed not to be a supply.

[*VATA 1994, 4 Sch 5(2)(3)*].

Samples for testing. No VAT is due on samples given free of charge to someone for testing. The limit of one sample per person (see above) may be exceeded if it can be shown that the items are given for quality assurance testing either on behalf of the supplier or a potential customer.

Samples given to the general public via an intermediary (e.g. samples supplied by a manufacturer to a retailer for giving away as samples to the retailer's customers). No VAT is due provided the following conditions are met.

- Neither the supplier nor the intermediary charge for the goods.

- The samples are supplied for genuine business purposes and are given as an illustrative example of the product.

- The samples remain the property of the supplier until they are given to the final customer.

- Any samples not used are returned to the supplier or destroyed.

Sale of samples. If a person sells goods given to him as samples, VAT is due on the sale.

(C & E Notice 700/35/97, paras 3.1-3.4).

47.10 **LOST, STOLEN OR DESTROYED GOODS**

C & E may require a taxable person from time to time to account for goods supplied to, or acquired or imported by, him in the course or furtherance of his business (including any goods transferred from another EC country). If such goods have been lost or destroyed, C & E may assess him on the VAT which would have been chargeable in respect of the supply of the goods if he is unable to prove such loss or destruction. [*VATA 1994, s 73(7)*].

Where, therefore, a taxable person can prove that his goods have been lost, stolen or destroyed, output tax is only chargeable if the goods have been supplied. Where goods are *lost, etc. in transit* to the customer, then

- if, under the contract, the customer is responsible for any loss before delivery, output tax is due; and

- if, under the contract, the supplier is responsible for any such loss, output tax is due where a VAT invoice has been issued. If a VAT invoice has not been issued, no output tax is due because there has not been a supply.

Goods obtained by fraud. A registered trader who has been defrauded of goods may, in certain circumstances, be able to recover the VAT which has been accounted for as output tax to C & E. Provided the fraud has been reported to the police, application for recovery should be made in writing to the VAT office, together with evidence of the complaint to the police and a verifiable description of the goods in question. (C & E Business Brief 19/96, 16 September 1996). This is a relaxation of the earlier requirement that a conviction for the fraud had to also be obtained (see C & E Press Notice, 20 September 1982).

Insurance claims. If damaged goods are surrendered to an insurer under the terms of an insurance policy, output tax is not due.

(C & E Notice 700, para 3.14).

See also 23.19 EUROPEAN COMMUNITY: SINGLE MARKET for goods lost, etc. in transit to other EC countries.

De Voil Indirect Tax Service. See V5.158.

47.11   **VIDEO CASSETTE FILMS: RENTAL AND PART-EXCHANGE**

Rental of a video cassette, where the customer must normally return it by a given date and the film remains the property of the supplier, is a supply of services. The value for tax purposes is the amount paid for the use of the film over the rental period.

In a **part-exchange transaction**, the customer's film is accepted as payment (or part payment) for another film which then becomes the customer's property. Part-exchange is a supply of goods the value of which is the amount the customer would have had to pay for the film if there were no part-exchange.

Output tax using one of the special RETAIL SCHEMES **(60)**.

Rental. All rental payments and membership fees (see below) can be included in gross takings under

• the Point of Sale scheme;

• Direct Calculation Schemes 1 and 2 (provided the minority goods under the scheme are zero and/or lower-rated); and

• under old Schemes A, B and F.

Under any other scheme, such receipts must be excluded from gross takings and dealt with outside the scheme. If films are also sold or part-exchanged, such sales can be dealt with under the scheme as below but only films which the supplier expects to sell or part-exchange can be included in the scheme calculations as 'goods received for resale'.

Part-exchange. Whichever scheme is used, the full normal retail selling price, including VAT, must be included in gross takings without deduction for the value of films taken in part-exchange. A separate record must be kept of all part-exchange transactions showing the amount included in gross takings. Where a cassette is taken in part-exchange, it must be included in the record of 'goods received for resale'. On resale, the payment received must be included in gross takings.

Output tax where a retail scheme is not used.

Rental. VAT must be accounted for in the normal way on all payments received for the use of films.

Part-exchange. VAT must be accounted for on the amount the customer would have had to pay if there had been no part-exchange.

Other charges.

Membership fees are taxable on the full amount charged even if refunded when the customer gives up membership.

Deposits. A refundable deposit for the safe return of a rental film is not taxable even if retained because the film is lost or damaged.

Overdue films. A charge for an overdue film is further payment for the use of the film and liable to VAT.

(C & E Leaflet 700/14/93).

47.12   PAYPHONES

Telephones. Where a payphone is rented from British Telecom or another supplier, the person renting the machine makes the supplies to the users and VAT is due on these supplies. Output tax is calculated by applying the VAT fraction to the money removed.

With some installations it is possible to switch from payphone mode to domestic mode and make calls without inserting money. If the domestic mode is used to make non-business calls, all VAT charged by British Telecom cannot be treated as input tax.

Phonecards. See 60.9(3) RETAIL SCHEMES.

(C & E Notice 700, para 3.16).

47.13   MOTOR VEHICLE TESTS

MOT tests. C & E have introduced simplified arrangements on the VAT treatment of Ministry of Transport (MOT) tests.

From 1 November 1996, the charge for an MOT test provided direct by a test centre to its customers is outside the scope of VAT, provided it does not exceed the statutory maximum. Any discount given by a test centre to an unapproved garage is treated as a normal trade discount and will no longer be seen as consideration for a taxable supply by the unapproved garage to the test centre.

Where an unapproved garage shows the exact amount charged by the test centre separately on the invoice to its customer, and meets the other conditions for disbursements in C & E Notice 700, para 10.8 (see 4.7 AGENTS), it may treat this element as a disbursement and also outside the scope of VAT.

Any amount charged over and above the amount charged by the test centre is consideration for its own service of arranging the test on behalf of its customer and is taxable at the standard rate. If the unapproved garage chooses not to treat the amount charged by the test centre as a disbursement, or otherwise does not satisfy all the conditions for disbursements, it must account for VAT on the full invoiced amount.

(C & E Notice 700, para 10.10; C & E Business Brief 21/96, 17 October 1996).

Driving tests. Fees charged by the Department of Transport (and training bodies appointed by them) for Part 1 of the *motorcycle driving test* are liable to VAT at the standard rate. The Department of Transport supplies Part 2 of the test and *other motor vehicle driving tests* as part of its statutory obligation and the fees involved remain outside the scope of VAT. (C & E Press Notice 909, 27 April 1984).

47.14   ROYALTY AND LICENCE FEES

Where a customer is recharged with payments made for royalty or licence fees incurred in making the supply to him, these charges are not disbursements for VAT purposes. The recharge is part of the consideration for the supply to the customer and VAT must be accounted for on the full value including the recharge. (VAT Notes (No 2) 1985/86).

47.15   VENDING MACHINES

Where customers are provided with 'free' use of vending or similar machines then, provided the customer pays the same price for the products dispensed (coffee, tea, etc.) as other customers who simply buy the product, no VAT is due on the hire of the machines. If, however, a higher amount is charged, VAT must be accounted for at the standard rate on the price difference. (C & E Notice 700/7/94, para 23). For supplies in the course of catering, see 11.1 CATERING.

47.16   **SUPPLIES BY PAWNBROKERS**

Redeemed pledges. There is no supply for VAT purposes if a person redeems a pledge within the agreed redemption period.

Unredeemed pledges. The following rules apply. The relevant law is in *Consumer Credit Act 1974, ss 120, 121.*

(a)   *Loans not exceeding £25 with a six month redemption period.* Ownership of the pledge passes to the pawnbroker if the goods are not redeemed within the six months statutory redemption period. A disposal of the goods to a third party after that time is a taxable supply.

Where, however, the goods are restored by the pawnbroker to their original owner within three months following the end of the redemption period, the transaction is treated as a redeemed pledge and there is no supply for VAT purposes. [*SI 1986/896*]. The pawnbroker must record the redemption in his pledge stock records and stamp the 'Credit Agreement and Pawn Receipt' with the date of redemption and keep it for inspection by C & E. If the pawnbroker and pledgor have agreed to extend the original agreement by one or more further six month periods, the three month 'grace period' starts when the extension expires.

The restoration of an unredeemed pledge more than three months after the redemption period is a taxable supply.

(b)   *Other loans.* For loans over £25 or where the redemption period has been agreed for a period other than six months, ownership of the pledge does not pass to the pawnbroker at the end of the redemption period. The onward supply to a third party is not, therefore, a taxable supply by the pawnbroker. It is, however, a taxable supply by the pledgor if he is a taxable person and the pledge is something he has acquired in the course of his business. The pawnbroker (or auctioneer if the goods are sold by auction) must follow the procedure in 2.18 ACCOUNTING PERIODS AND RETURNS.

Other charges.

- *Interest payments* received under credit agreements are exempt from VAT. See 27.8 FINANCE.

- *Valuation fees* relating to the pledged goods are regarded as part of the charge for the loan and are exempt.

- *Charges for selling unredeemed pledges*, provision for which is made in the loan contract, are exempt as a further charge for the granting of credit. Included is an element for cleaning and repairing the goods before they are put on display.

(C & E Leaflet 700/31/94).

Second-hand goods scheme. Pawnbrokers may use the scheme for SECOND-HAND GOODS (61) for sales of unredeemed pawns within (a) above provided the normal scheme conditions are met. The purchase price is the amount of the loan plus the initial six months interest payable, less any payment received. The interest relating to the three month period of grace and other items such as cleaning, repair charges, storage and overhead expenses must not be added to the purchase price. (C & E Notice 718, para 11B).

Pawnbrokers selling at auction. A pawnbroker may use the auctioneers' scheme for the sale of eligible second-hand goods (see 61.61 SECOND-HAND GOODS) provided the pawn value is greater than £25 and the pledgor is not VAT-registered. If the pledgor is VAT-registered, VAT must be accounted for on the full selling price. (C & E Notice 718, para 51A).

47.17 COMPENSATION PAYMENTS

Out of court settlements. Where payments are made under out-of-court settlements of disputes after proceedings have been commenced, C & E take the view that

- if payments are in essence compensatory and do not relate directly to the supply of goods or services, they are outside the scope of VAT (even if the settlement is expressed in terms that the payment is consideration for the plaintiff's agreement to abandon his rights to bring legal action); and

- if payments are consideration for the specific taxable supply of goods by the plaintiff (e.g. where the dispute concerns the payment for an earlier taxable supply) the payments are taxable.

(C & E News Release 82/87, 19 November 1987).

See also *Leslie Reich (9548)* and *Whites Metal Co (2400)*.

Surrender of firearms. Compensation payments made by the Home Office to VAT-registered firearms dealers required to surrender certain calibre handguns are taxable supplies under *EC Sixth Directive, Art 5(4)(a)* (see 22.7(*a*) EUROPEAN COMMUNITY LEGISLATION) where the surrendered firearms were business stock. The compensation payments therefore include a VAT element. Under powers contained in *SI 1995/2518, Reg 25(5)*, C & E are prepared to allow any VAT due to be accounted for on the VAT return for the period in which the payment of compensation is received. (C & E Business Brief, 27/97, 21 November 1997).

Compensation payments generally. For cases concerning whether compensation was in respect of a taxable supply or outside the scope of VAT, see *Hurley Robinson Partnership (750)* (compensation payment following a disputed bill); *Cooper Chasney Ltd (4898)* (payment for surrender of rights to product name); *F Penny (t/a FMS Management Services (10398)* (compensation payment for loss of consultancy); *Holiday Inns (UK) Ltd, [1993] VATTR 321 (10609)* (compensation payment for loss of future fees—although this decision was disapproved of in *Croydon Hotel & Leisure Co Ltd, [1997] VATDR 254 (14920)*); *Galaxy Equipment (Europe) Ltd (11415)* (compensation for faulty goods); *Hometex Trading Ltd (13012)* (compensation payments made by order of court); and *Financial & General Print Ltd (13795)* (compensation for payments to lessor under a finance lease).

Compensation under *EC Council Regulation 1336/86* for discontinuing milk production is not subject to VAT (*Mohr v Finanzamt Bad Segeberg, CJEC [1996] STC 328*).

47.18 AGRICULTURAL GRANT SCHEMES

For the time being, VAT is not to be applied to payments under the following grant schemes.

Ministry of Agriculture, Fisheries and Food

Farm Woodland Scheme
Set Aside Scheme
Agricultural Act 1986, s 18 (Environmentally Sensitive Areas)
Outgoers under the *Milk (Cessation of Production) Act 1985*

Department of the Environment

Nature Conservancy Council management agreements
Countryside Premium Scheme for Set Aside Land
Countryside Commission Community Forests Scheme

Forestry Commission

Woodland Grant Scheme

Farm Woodland Scheme

(C & E Press Release 58/89, 9 August 1989).

47.19 MILK QUOTAS

The VAT liability of the supply or transfer of a milk quota depends upon whether it is supplied with or without land.

- Where the supply or transfer of a milk quota is linked with the supply of land under one agreement, there is a single supply and VAT liability follows that of the land. This applies whether the land is sold freehold or leasehold and even if separate identifiable sums are shown on the invoice and paid for the land and quota.

- The supply or transfer of a milk quota without land is a standard-rated supply of services.

- Where a milk quota is transferred with a grazing licence, there are two separate supplies, a zero-rated supply of animal feeding stuffs through the grazing licence and a standard-rated supply of the milk quota.

(C & E Business Brief 17/94, 12 September 1994).

For further information, see C & E VAT Manual Part 7, Chapter 1 Part G.

47.20 SOLICITORS' OATH FEES

Under *Solicitors Act 1974, s 81* every solicitor holding a practising certificate may exercise the powers of a commissioner for oaths. Oath fees are regarded as deriving from the personal qualification of a solicitor, such that the solicitor who administers oaths receives the fees in a personal capacity. Whether or not VAT is due will depend upon the circumstances of the individual solicitor concerned.

(*a*) *Sole practitioners and partners.* Fees received in respect of oaths administered by a solicitor in sole practice or a partner in a firm of solicitors are regarded as consideration for services supplied in the course of the business. If the practice/partnership is registered for VAT, VAT is due. Fees received in a prescribed accounting period should be treated as VAT-inclusive.

(*b*) *Assistant solicitors.* VAT treatment depends upon whether or not the assistant solicitor accounts to the firm for oath fees received.

- Where fees are accounted for to the firm, they are part of the firm's business receipts and VAT must be accounted for as under (*a*) above.

- Where the firm allows the assistant solicitor to retain fees personally, the fees will not be subject to VAT unless the assistant solicitor is individually registered for VAT by virtue of other activities (or required to be registered taking into account the level of oath fees received).

(*c*) *Solicitors employed otherwise than in practice or retired solicitors.* Any fees received will not be subject to VAT unless the individual is registered for VAT by virtue of other activities (or required to be registered taking into account the level of oath fees received).

(Law Society's Gazette, 8 June 1994).

48 Overseas Traders

Cross-references. See 4.8 AGENTS for tax representatives and agents employed by overseas traders; 39 INTERNATIONAL SERVICES for services generally made to or by overseas traders.

48.1 **REGISTRATION**

An overseas trader *must* register for VAT in the UK if

- he makes taxable supplies of goods and services in the UK in the course of furtherance of his business (see 47.1 OUTPUT TAX) and the total value of those supplies exceeds the VAT registration threshold (see 59.3 REGISTRATION);

- the business is registered for VAT in another EC country, he sells and delivers goods in the UK to customers who are not VAT-registered ('distance sales') and the value of those distance sales exceeds the relevant threshold (see 59.12 REGISTRATION); or

- he acquires goods in the UK directly from a VAT-registered supplier in EC country (see 23.3 EUROPEAN COMMUNITY: SINGLE MARKET) and the total value of the acquisitions exceeds the acquisitions threshold (see 59.19 REGISTRATION).

For VAT purposes, the UK includes the territorial sea of the UK (i.e. waters within twelve nautical miles of the coastline).

There is no need to register if the only UK supplies are supplies of services on which the customer is liable to account for any VAT due under the 'reverse charge' procedure. See 39.4 INTERNATIONAL SERVICES.

An overseas trader *may* also be registered if

- he has started in business but is not yet making taxable supplies, provided he can show the intention of making taxable supplies in the future as part of his business; or

- his turnover is below the threshold, provided he can prove to C & E that he is carrying on a business for VAT purposes and making taxable supplies.

See also 48.4 below for entitlement to be registered in the UK in certain circumstances where no taxable supplies are made in the UK.

Consequences of registration. An overseas trader who is registered or required to be registered for VAT in the UK must account for VAT in respect of those supplies and acquisitions. He is also liable to VAT on importations of any goods into the UK (see 34 IMPORTS) and on the acquisition in the UK of exciseable goods or of new means of transport from another EC country whether or not he is required to be registered (see 23.9 and 23.35 EUROPEAN COMMUNITY: SINGLE MARKET respectively).

[*VATA 1994, ss 1, 3, 4, 10, 96(11)*]. (C & E Notice 700/4/97, paras 2.1–2.4).

See 64.8 SUPPLY for the place of supply of goods and 64.18 SUPPLY for the place of supply of services.

48.2 **Registration procedure**

To apply for registration, an overseas trader must complete a VAT registration application form. This will be

- Form VAT 1 if in respect of taxable supplies;

- Form VAT 1A if in respect of distance sales; or

- Form VAT 1B if in respect of acquisitions.

Overseas trader with a business establishment in the UK. Registration will be effected at the principal UK place of business. VAT records and accounts should be kept at this address and produced there for inspection by C & E when required. A person at that address must be responsible for the VAT affairs. If that person is an employee, written authority to act should normally be given. A suggested letter of authority approved by C & E is:

'. . . (Name of principal) of . . . (Address of principal) hereby appoints . . . (Name of UK agent or employee) of . . . (Address of UK agent or employee) to act as agent for the purpose of dealing with all their legal obligations in respect of Value Added Tax. This letter authorises the above-named agent to sign VAT return forms 100 and any other document needed for the purpose of enabling the agent or employee to comply with the VAT obligations of the principal.

Signed . . . (Signature of principal)
Date

If the named person has been notified to the Registrar of Companies as a UK resident authorised to accept service of process on behalf of the company, a separate authority is not required. Neither is a separate authority required where the person concerned is a partner registered in the UK.

(C&E Notice 700/4/97, para 3.2).

Overseas trader with no business establishment in the UK. In such circumstances the overseas trader has three options.

1.   He may appoint a VAT representative who will be jointly and severally liable for any VAT debts. The overseas trader must still complete a VAT registration form. In addition to this, both the overseas trader and the VAT representative must complete a Form VAT 1TR. See 4.8 AGENTS for further details on VAT representatives.

2.   He may appoint an agent to deal with the VAT affairs. The agent cannot be held responsible to C&E for any VAT debts and C&E reserve the right not to deal with any particular agent and may insist on a VAT representative being appointed. The overseas trader must still complete a VAT registration form. In addition, C&E will need a letter of authority as above.

3.   He may deal with all the VAT obligations (including registration, returns and record-keeping) personally. To register, the overseas trader should contact the Aberdeen VAT office at 28 Guild Street, Aberdeen AB9 2DY (Tel. 01224 844653/4/5).

(C & E Notice 700/4/97, paras, 3.3, 5.1–5.6).

A '*business establishment*' is usually premises from which trading activities directly related to the business are carried out. Where a business provides book-keeping, accountancy or invoicing services at its premises for a 'non-established taxable person' who does not actually make supplies in the UK, C&E do not consider the premises to be a business establishment.

A '*non-established taxable person*' is any person who

- is not normally resident in the UK,

- does not have a business establishment in the UK, and

- if a company, is not incorporated in the UK.

(C & E Notice 700/4/97, paras 1.2, 3.1).

48.3 Overseas Traders

48.3 Alternatives to registration

Accounting for VAT through customers. *VATA 1994, s 14* implements the VAT simplification procedures for triangular trade between EC countries and the UK. The provisions allow UK customers to be designated as liable to account for the VAT that would otherwise be due to be accounted for by intermediate suppliers in other EC countries. See 23.22 EUROPEAN COMMUNITY: SINGLE MARKET for fuller details.

Import agents. An overseas trader not registered for VAT in the UK who

- imports goods for onward supply in the UK, and

- does not supply any other goods or services within the UK to a total value exceeding the current registration limit,

can arrange for a UK-resident agent registered for VAT to import and supply the goods on his behalf. The agent is treated as importing and supplying the goods as principal. He must make any necessary Customs entries as the importer, pay or defer the VAT and take delivery of the goods. He can reclaim any import VAT as input tax (subject to the normal rules) but must issue proper VAT invoices for the supplies of the goods and charge and account for VAT on the onward sale in the normal way. The agent's supply of services to the overseas principal is standard-rated. (C & E Notice 702, para 2.7).

48.4 Registration where no taxable supplies made in the UK

Entitlement to be registered. Where a person who is not liable to be registered under *VATA 1994* and is not already so registered satisfies C & E that

(*a*) he has a business establishment (including a branch or agency) in the UK or his 'usual place of residence' is in the UK,

(*b*) he does not make and does not intend to make taxable supplies, and

(*c*) he makes (or is carrying on a business and intends to make in the course or furtherance of that business) supplies within 35.3(*b*) or (*c*) INPUT TAX,

C & E must, on request, register that person from the day on which the request is made or from such earlier date as is mutually agreed. The inclusion of supplies within 35.3(*c*) INPUT TAX was made statutory with effect from 19 March 1997 but had previously been applied by concession.

The '*usual place of residence*' of a company means the place where it is legally constituted. [*VATA 1994, 1 Sch 10; FA 1997, s 32*]. (C & E News Release No 14, 26 November 1996).

Application for registration must be made in such form and containing such particulars as C & E prescribe by regulations. Application must currently be made on Form VAT 1 and must include a signed declaration that all the information entered on it, or accompanying it, is true and complete. A partnership applying for registration must also complete Form VAT 2. [*VATA 1994, 1 Sch 17; SI 1995/2518 Reg 5(1)*].

Notification of end of entitlement to be registered. A person registered under the above provisions who ceases to satisfy the conditions in (*b*) or (*c*) above must notify C & E of that fact within 30 days of the day on which he does so unless he would, when he so ceases, be otherwise liable or entitled to be registered. [*VATA 1994, 1 Sch 12*].

The notification must be in writing and state the date on which the registered person formed the intention of making taxable supplies or, as the case may be, ceased to make, or have the intention of making, supplies within (*c*) above. [*SI 1995/2518, Reg 5(3)*].

De Voil Indirect Tax Service. See V2.146.

48.5   **APPLICATIONS TO THE UK FOR REFUNDS OF VAT BY PERSONS ESTABLISHED OUTSIDE THE EC**

Subject to the conditions below, a trader carrying on a business established in a '*third country*' (i.e. a country outside the EC) is entitled to be repaid VAT charged on goods imported by him into the UK in respect of which no other relief is available or on supplies made to him in the UK if that VAT would be input tax were he a taxable person in the UK provided that in the period of claim

(*a*)   he was not registered or liable or eligible to be registered for VAT in the UK;

(*b*)   he was not established in any EC country; or

(*c*)   he made no supplies of goods and services in the UK other than

> (i)   transport of freight outside the UK or to or from a place outside the UK (and ancillary services);

> (ii)   services where the VAT on the supply is payable solely by the person to whom they are supplied under the reverse charge provisions (see 39.4 INTERNATIONAL SERVICES); or

> (iii)   goods where the VAT on the supply is payable solely by the person to whom they are supplied.

Unless C & E allow otherwise, repayments will not be made to traders established in a third country having a comparable system of turnover taxes unless that country provides reciprocal arrangements for refunds to be made to taxable persons established in the UK.

For these purposes a person is treated as established in a country if he has a business establishment there or he has no business establishment anywhere and his usual place of residence is there. The usual place of residence of a company is where it is legally constituted. A person carrying on business through a branch or agency in any country is treated as having a business establishment there.

Method of claiming. Claim forms are obtainable from any VAT office or the '*appropriate authority*', i.e.

HM Customs and Excise
VAT Overseas Repayments
8th/13th Directive
Custom House
PO Box 34
Londonderry
BT48 7AE
Northern Ireland

Forms must be completed in English and must be sent to the above address, together with the supporting documentation and a certificate of status issued by the official authority of the third country in which the trader is established unless C & E are already in possession of such a certificate issued not more than twelve months before the date of the claim. C & E will refuse to accept any supporting documentation if it already bears an official stamp indicating that it has been furnished in support of an earlier claim.

Non-refundable VAT. Refunds cannot be claimed on VAT incurred on

● a supply which is not used for the purpose of the business;

● the part of a supply which is not used for the purpose of the business where it is used partly for business and partly for other purposes;

- any supply or importation which the trader has used or intends to use for the purpose of any supply by him in the UK;

- any supply or importation which has been exported or is intended for exportation from the UK by or on behalf of the trader;

- VAT charged on a supply which if made to a taxable person would be excluded from credit (see 35.8 INPUT TAX); and

- VAT charged on a supply to a travel agent which is for the direct benefit of a traveller other than the travel agent or his employee.

Minimum claim and time limit. The claim must be made not later than six months after the end of the 'prescribed year' in which the VAT is incurred. The *'prescribed year'* is the year ended 30 June. Any claim must be for a period of not less than three months (unless less than three months of the prescribed year remains) and not more than one year.

If the claim is for less than one year, it must be for at least £130 unless it is for the final part of the prescribed year. No claim can be for less than £16.

Method of repayment. The refund will be made within six months of receiving a satisfactory claim and will normally be made by payable order issued directly to the claimant or his appointed agent. Payments can only be made directly into a UK bank account.

[*VATA 1994, s 39; SI 1995/2518, Regs 185–197*]. (C & E Notice 723, paras 2.1–2.11).

De Voil Indirect Tax Service. See V5.152.

49 Partial Exemption

Cross-references. See 10 CAPITAL GOODS SCHEME for deduction, and adjustment of deduction, of input tax on capital items by partly exempt businesses; 31.10 GROUPS OF COMPANIES for input tax incurred by holding companies; 22.23, 22.24 EUROPEAN COMMUNITY LEGISLATION; 24 EXEMPT SUPPLIES.

De Voil Indirect Tax Service. See V3.461–470.

49.1 INTRODUCTION

A registered business which makes both taxable and exempt supplies cannot charge VAT on the exempt supplies and equally cannot normally reclaim the VAT incurred on the purchases used to make those supplies. Where input tax cannot be claimed because it relates to an exempt supply, it is known as *exempt input tax* and the registered business is known as *partly exempt*. See 24 EXEMPT SUPPLIES and supporting chapters for details of goods and services the supplies of which are exempt.

A partly exempt business will normally have to use an approved partial exemption method (see 49.5–49.7 below) to work out how much of its input tax can be reclaimed. This would usually be the standard method (see 49.6 below) unless it feels that this would not give a fair or reasonable result, in which case it can apply to the local VAT office for a special method (see 49.7 below). All methods should provide for direct attribution and apportionment of the input tax incurred. Direct attribution involves identifying VAT on goods and services which are used exclusively to make taxable supplies or exempt supplies: the former is deductible, the latter is not. Apportionment is required for the remaining input tax (e.g. on overheads) which cannot be directly attributed.

Where a partly exempt business prepares VAT returns and deducts input tax on a quarterly or monthly basis, the input tax deduction is provisional. The business also has a longer period at the end of which it is required to review the extent of its allowable input tax and revise its deduction accordingly. In general, the longer period ends on the last day of the quarter ending March, April or May and the adjustment is known as the annual adjustment. Newly registered traders have a longer period known as a registration period. See 49.9 below.

There are rules to allow a business which only incurs minor amounts of exempt input tax to treat that exempt input tax as if it were allowable input tax. These rules should be considered each quarter and again at the time of the annual adjustment. See 49.3 and 49.4 below.

Where a business has deducted VAT based on its intention to use the relevant goods and services to make taxable supplies and at any time within six years, not having made the intended supply, it changes its mind and uses, or forms the intention to use, the goods and services to make an exempt supply, it must adjust its original claim. Conversely, rules permit a claim where VAT was restricted because the business's original intention was to make exempt supplies but in the event a taxable supply is either subsequently intended or made. See 49.10 below.

Capital goods scheme. The capital goods scheme covers input tax incurred in respect of land and property or computers above certain values. Under the scheme, the owner of the capital item must review the extent to which the item is used to make taxable supplies over a period of time (five or ten years) and make an adjustment where appropriate. See 10 CAPITAL GOODS SCHEME.

Non-business activities. Any VAT incurred relating to non-business activities is not input tax for these purposes. Where a partly exempt person also carries on non-business activities, he must first determine the proportion of VAT incurred relating to those activities and disregard any such VAT before applying the rules in this chapter. See 35.7 INPUT TAX for the calculation of VAT of non-business activities.

49.2   GENERAL PROVISIONS RELATING TO ALLOWABLE INPUT TAX

The amount of allowable input tax for which a taxable person is entitled to credit at the end of any period is so much of the input tax on supplies, acquisitions and importations in the period as is allowable as being attributable to the following supplies made, or to be made, by the taxable person in the course or furtherance of his business.

(*a*)   '*Taxable supplies*', i.e. supplies of goods and services made in the UK other than exempt supplies.

(*b*)   Supplies outside the UK which would be taxable supplies if made in the UK.

(*c*)   Supplies of services which

(i)   are supplied to a person who belongs outside the EC, or

(ii) are directly linked to the export of goods to a place outside the EC, or

(iii) consist of the making of arrangements for a supply of services within (i) or (ii) above

provided that the supply is exempt (or would have been exempt if made in the UK) by virtue of *VATA 1994, 9 Sch Group 2* (insurance) or *VATA 1994, 9 Sch Group 5, Items 1–8* (finance).

C & E must make regulations for securing a fair and reasonable attribution of input tax to the supplies within (*a*) to (*c*) above.

[*VATA 1994, ss 4(2), 26; SI 1992/3123*].

Regulations made are considered in 49.3 to 49.10 below. In those paragraphs

● '*exempt input tax*' means input tax, or a proportion of input tax, which is attributable to

(i)   exempt supplies; and

(ii) supplies outside the UK which would be exempt if made in the UK (other than those supplies falling within (*c*) above); and

● nothing is to be construed as allowing a taxable person to deduct the whole or any part of the VAT on the importation or acquisition by him of goods or the supply to him of goods or services where those goods or services are not used or to be used by him in making supplies in the course or furtherance of a business carried on by him.

[*SI 1995/2518, Regs 99(1)(a), 100*].

49.3   TREATMENT OF INPUT TAX ATTRIBUTABLE TO EXEMPT SUPPLIES AS BEING ATTRIBUTABLE TO TAXABLE SUPPLIES

Subject to below, any exempt input tax attributable to the following 'supplies' is treated as attributable to taxable supplies.

(*a*)   Any deposit of money.

(*b*)   Any services of making arrangements for the provision of insurance or reinsurance within *VATA 1994, 9 Sch Group 2, Item 3* (see 37.9 INSURANCE).

(*c*) Any services of arranging mortgages or hire purchase, credit sale or conditional sale transactions.

(*d*) The assignment of any debt due to the assignor in respect of a supply of goods or services by him.

(*e*) The granting of any lease or tenancy of or any licence to occupy any land where in any longer period (see 49.9 below)

  (i) the input tax attributable to *all* such supplies by the grantor is less than £1,000; and

  (ii) no exempt input tax is incurred by the grantor in respect of any exempt supply other than a supply within (*a*) to (*d*) above.

The above does not apply in the following circumstances.

(i) Where the supply is made by a taxable person in the course of carrying on a business of, or similar to, a bank, accepting house, insurance company, insurance agent or broker, investment trust, unit trust, investment company, Stock Exchange broker or dealer, share dealing company, trustee of a pension fund, unit trust management company, building society, discount house, finance house, friendly society, money lender, money broker, mortgage broker, pawnbroker, debt factor, or credit or charge card company. But a person who carries on one or more of these businesses is not treated as having made the supply in the course of carrying on such a business if he made the supply exclusively in the course of carrying on a business which is not in the list.

For these purposes, a business is any economic activity carried on by a legal entity. If a legal entity carries on more than one business, each business is looked at separately when determining whether exempt output tax can be ignored under these provisions. (C & E Notice 706, para 16).

(ii) Where the exempt input tax of the taxable person, excluding any attributable to supplies within (*a*) to (*e*) above, cannot be treated as *de minimis* under 49.4 below.

'*Supplies*' for the above purposes (except in the expression 'taxable supplies') is to be construed as including supplies made outside the UK which would be exempt if made in the UK (other than those supplies falling within 49.2(*c*) above).

[*SI 1995/2518, Reg 105*].

The effect of the above is that a business must apply the following tests at the end of each VAT period and for each longer period (see 49.9 below).

● Where all exempt input tax relates to supplies within (*a*) to (*e*) (and the business does not fall within (i) above), there is no need to use a partial exemption method and the taxable person is treated as fully taxable.

● Where all exempt input tax does not relate to supplies within (*a*) to (*e*) above (and the business does not fall within (i) above), exempt input tax related to such supplies can still be ignored provided exempt input tax related to other supplies does not exceed the *de minimis* limit in 49.4 below. However, in such a case, a method will still be required to work out whether exempt input tax related to other supplies exceeds the *de minimis* limit.

● Where exempt input tax related to supplies not falling within (*a*) to (*e*) above exceeds the *de minimis* limit in 49.4 below or where the business falls within (i) above, all exempt input tax must be taken into account when applying the *de minimis* rules.

49.4   Partial Exemption

Where exempt input tax is regularly incurred relating to supplies within (*b*) or (*c*) above on a large scale, it may be that the making of such supplies constitutes, in effect, a separate business in its own right similar to one of those listed above. If so all exempt input tax incurred by that business must be included when applying the *de minimis* rules in 49.4 below.

(C & E Notice 706, para 15).

49.4   De minimis limit

Where in any prescribed accounting period or longer period the exempt input tax of a taxable person

(*a*)   does not amount to more than £625 per month on average; and

(*b*)   does not exceed more than one half of all his input tax for the period concerned

all such input tax in that period is treated as attributable to taxable supplies (and therefore recoverable in full subject to the normal rules). [*SI 1995/2518, Reg 106(1)*].

When applying these provisions to a longer period

- any treatment of exempt input tax as attributable to taxable supplies in any prescribed accounting period is disregarded; and

- no account is to be taken of any amounts which may be deductible or payable under the CAPITAL GOODS SCHEME (10).

[*SI 1995/2518, Reg 106(2)*].

'*On average*' means the average over the relevant prescribed accounting period or, as the case may be, longer period. For group registrations, the rules apply to the group as a whole. (C & E Notice 706, para 17).

Exempt input tax is not only that directly related to exempt activities. It also includes the exempt proportion of input tax related to both taxable and exempt activities (e.g. that on overhead expenses). It may therefore be necessary to apply a partial exemption method in order to determine whether exempt input tax exceeds the *de minimis* limit.

In applying the *de minimis* limits to exempt input tax, input tax claimed is to be counted as input tax of the period in which the supply is made — not, where different, the period in which the claim is made (*Trevor Toys Ltd (7805)*). For example, VAT incurred on goods and services before the date of registration, and which at the time of purchase were used to make exempt supplies, cannot be recovered because the partial exemption *de minimis* limit is not applicable to this VAT.

De Voil Indirect Tax Service. See V3.465.

49.5   METHODS OF CALCULATION

If a taxable person cannot be treated as fully taxable under the rules in 49.3 and 49.4 above, he cannot recover all his input tax. He should normally use the standard method in 49.6 below to calculate provisionally how much input tax can be reclaimed but in certain circumstances it may be possible to apply a special method, subject to prior approval of C & E. See 49.7 below. The provisional attribution may then need to be adjusted at the end of a 'longer period', normally twelve months. See 49.9 below. Both the provisional attribution and the annual adjustment must be made on the basis of facts as they existed at the time when the input tax was incurred, not on the changed facts as they existed at the time the claim was made. See *C & E Commrs v University of Wales*

College of Cardiff QB, [1995] STC 611 where apportionment was based on income received in the relevant periods rather than subsequent use.

49.6   **The standard method**

Subject to 49.7 below, the amount of input tax which a taxable person is entitled to deduct provisionally is the amount attributable to taxable supplies in accordance with the following rules.

(i) Identify goods imported or acquired by, and goods or services supplied to, the taxable person in the period.

(ii) Input tax on such of those goods and services as are used, or are to be used, by him *exclusively* in making taxable supplies is attributed to taxable supplies.

The exclusive rule cannot be side-stepped by splitting a supply and saying that a part of it has been exclusively used. It is the whole of the supply received that must be considered.

Example

B rents out domestic property (exempt) and is also constructing a new house for immediate sale (zero-rated). B receives a single supply of 1000 bricks and decides that 700 bricks will be used for the new house and 300 for repairing a wall at a rented property.

B cannot directly attribute 70% of the input tax on the bricks. He has received only one supply of 1000 bricks and cannot claim that that supply has been exclusively used to make either a taxable or an exempt supply. The input tax on the bricks must be included in (iv) below and apportioned.

(C & E Manual V1-15, Chapter 2 para 3.3).

(iii) No part of the input tax on such of those goods or services as are used, or to be used, by him in making exempt supplies, or in carrying on any activity other than the making of taxable supplies (but see below), must be attributed to taxable supplies.

(iv) A proportion of the remaining input tax on such of those goods and services as are used, or to be used, by him in making both taxable and exempt supplies is to be attributable to taxable supplies calculated as follows.

$$\text{Remaining input tax} \times \frac{\text{value of taxable supplies}}{\text{value of all supplies}}$$

The ratio of the value of taxable supplies to the value of all supplies is to be expressed as a percentage and, if not a whole number, it is to be rounded *up* to the next whole number.

In calculating the proportion under (iv) above, the following must be excluded.

(*a*) Any sum receivable by the taxable person in respect of any supply of capital goods used for the purposes of his business.

(*b*) Any sum receivable by the taxable person in respect of any of the following descriptions of supplies made by him where such supplies are incidental to one or more of his business activities.

- Any supply falling within *VATA 1994, 8 Sch Group 5, Item 1* or *Group 6, Item 1* (see 42.48 and 42.49 LAND AND BUILDINGS).

- Any exempt grant which falls within *VATA 1994, 9 Sch Group 1, Item 1* (see 42.2 LAND AND BUILDINGS).

- Any standard-rated grant which falls within *VATA 1994, 9 Sch Group 1, Item 1(a)* (see 42.4 LAND AND BUILDINGS).

- Any grant which would fall within (iii) above but for an election having been made to opt to tax under *VATA 1994, 10 Sch 2* (see 42.20 LAND AND BUILDINGS).

- Any supply which falls within *VATA 1994, 9 Sch Group 5* (finance).

What constitutes an 'incidental' supply can be viewed in two ways. First, it can be a one-off situation (e.g. the sale of a factory by a fully taxable manufacturing company) where there is activity but not sufficient to be regarded as a business. Secondly, it could be regular income (e.g. interest from bank deposits which are received passively, incurring no related input tax) where in reality, there is no activity at all. In *C H Beazer (Holdings) plc (3283)* the tribunal considered incidental to mean 'occurring or liable to occur in fortuitous or subordinate conjunction with'. C & E's policy is to identify all the business activities and then consider whether the supply in question is incidental to *any* of these business activities (not just the *main* activities). It is possible that a supply might be distortive but not incidental. In such a case, it is open to the trader to apply for, or C & E to direct, a special method. C & E Manual V1-15, Chapter 2 para 6.5).

(*c*) That part of the value of any supply of goods on which output tax is not chargeable by virtue of a Treasury order under *VATA 1994, s 25(7)* unless the taxable person has imported, acquired or been supplied with the goods for the purpose of selling them (e.g. the selling price of a motor car used in the business — unless sold for a profit, in which case the difference between buying and selling price (excluding VAT) must be excluded).

(*d*) The value of any supply which, under or by virtue of any provision of *VATA 1994*, the taxable person makes to himself.

[*SI 1995/2518, Reg 101*].

(*e*) The value of any goods or services not supplied in the course of business.

(*f*) The value of any goods or services provided as a business transaction which is neither a taxable nor an exempt supply (e.g. the transfer of a business as a going concern).

(*g*) The value of certain imported services specified in *VATA 1994, 5 Sch* subject to the reverse charge under *VATA 1994, s 8(1)* (see 39.4 INTERNATIONAL SERVICES).

(C & E Notice 706, para 20).

In principle, input tax cannot be reclaimed on goods and services used in any activity other than the making of taxable supplies (see (iii) above). However, in certain circumstances (e.g. input tax on research and development costs, abortive supplies or transferring a business as a going concern) C & E may accept that this input tax is wholly or partly claimable. Advice should be sought from C & E. (C & E Notice 706, para 19).

Outside the scope activities. With effect from 1 January 1993, because of a change in the place of supply of services rules, some supplies which were previously zero-rated are outside the scope of UK VAT. Partly exempt businesses which had been using the standard method for calculating deductible input tax and including zero-rated values in the proportional calculations may include outside the scope values from that date. The value of outside the scope supplies with a right to deduct input tax are to be treated as 'taxable' supplies and the values of outside the scope supplies with no such right are to be treated as 'exempt' supplies. The method used, however, becomes a special method subject to approval by C & E. Businesses are required to exclude any distortive or incidental outside the scope values from calculations to the extent that zero-rated supplies would previously have been excluded. (C & E Notice 725, para 12.2).

In *C & E Commrs v Liverpool School of Performing Arts QB, [1998] STC 274*, C & E issued a ruling that outside the scope supplies were not to be treated as taxable supplies for the purposes of the partial exemption provisions, but should be apportioned in accordance with *SI 1995/2518, Reg 103* (see 49.8 below). The court held that *Reg 103* was ancillary to *Reg 101* above and simply designed to ensure that outside the scope supplies were treated in the same way as taxable supplies. Where, under *EC Sixth Directive, Art 17(3)(a)*, a taxable person was entitled to recover input tax on supplies outside the UK which would have been taxable supplies if made in the UK, such supplies should be treated as taxable supplies in determining the proportion of residual input tax attributable to taxable supplies under *Reg 101(2)(d)* (see (iv) above). C & E have lodged an appeal against this decision.

Example

In its tax year beginning on 1 April 1998, X Ltd makes the following supplies

	Total (excl VAT)	Standard rated (excl VAT)	Exempt
First quarter	442,004	392,286	49,718
Second quarter	310,929	266,712	44,217
Third quarter	505,867	493,614	12,253
Fourth quarter	897,135	876,387	20,748
	£2,155,935	£2,028,999	£126,936

Input tax for the year is analysed as follows

	Attributable to taxable supplies £	Attributable to exempt supplies £	Remaining input tax £	Total input tax £
First quarter	36,409	4,847	11,751	53,007
Second quarter	20,245	311	5,212	25,768
Third quarter	34,698	1,195	10,963	46,856
Fourth quarter	69,707	5,975	9,357	85,039
	£161,059	£12,328	£37,283	£210,670

First quarter

	£	£
Input tax attributable to taxable supplies	36,409	

$$\frac{392,286}{442,004} = 88.75\%$$

	£	£
£11,751 × 89% =	10,458	
		46,867

Second quarter

	£	£
Input tax attributable to taxable supplies	20,245	
	c/f 20,245	46,867

| | b/f 20,245 | 46,867 |

Proportion of remaining input tax deductible

$$\frac{266,712}{310,929} = 88.75\%$$

| £5,212 × 86% = | 4,482 |
| | £24,727 |

The value of exempt input tax is

£1,041 (311 + [5,212 – 4,482]). As this is not more than £625 per month on average, all input tax in the quarter is recoverable.

| Deductible input tax | 25,768 |
| | £72,635 |

Third quarter

| Input tax attributable to taxable supplies | 34,698 |

Proportion of remaining input tax deductible

$$\frac{493,614}{505,867} = 97.58\%$$

| £10,963 × 98% = | 10,744 |
| | £45,442 |

The value of exempt input tax is

£1,414 (1,195 + [10,963 – 10,744]). As this is not more than £625 per month on average, all input tax in the quarter is recoverable.

| Deductible input tax | 46,856 |

Fourth quarter

| Input tax attributable to taxable supplies | 69,707 |

Proportion of remaining input tax deductible

$$\frac{876,387}{897,135} = 97.69\%$$

£9,357 × 98% =	9,170
	78,877
	£198,368

For the annual adjustment required, see Example 1 in 49.9 below.

De Voil Indirect Tax Service. See V3.461.

49.7   Special methods

C & E may approve or direct the use by a taxable person of another method other than that specified in 49.6 above except that

(*a*) there must not be included in the calculation (if the method would otherwise allow it)

(i) the value of any supply which, under or by virtue of any provision of *VATA 1994*, the taxable person makes to himself; and

(ii) the input tax on such a supply; and

(*b*) despite any provision to the contrary effect in the method approved, in calculating the proportion of any input tax on goods or services used or to be used by the taxable person in making both taxable and exempt supplies which is to be treated as attributable to taxable supplies, the value of any supply within 49.6(*a*)–(*d*) above must be excluded (i.e. those supplies which must be excluded from the standard method of calculation must also be excluded from any special method).

A taxable person using a special method approved or directed by C & E must continue to use it until C & E approve or direct the termination of its use. Any direction for the use, or termination of use, of a scheme takes effect from the date of the direction or such later date as C & E specify. Retrospective changes of method are not allowed. However, C & E may approve a change of method with effect from the start of the tax year in which the written application is received (although there is no statutory basis for this). This policy is being reviewed because it has been applied inappropriately in some instances but no decision on any change has been made.

[*SI 1995/2518, Reg 102*]. (C & E Manual V1-15, Chapter 2 para 7.6).

There is no legal requirement that application for, or approval of, a special method must be in writing although this will be the normal practice. Either C & E or the taxable person may wish to argue that a special method has been given *de facto* approval. In *Wellington Private Hospital [1993] VATTR 86 (10627)* the tribunal found that the criteria to be met for *de facto* approval were that the taxpayer must have knowingly adopted or sought to adopt a special method and C & E must have been aware of what the taxpayer was doing or seeking to do. In that case, although permission had not been given to adopt a special method, a visiting officer had not questioned the method used when inspecting the records, thereby giving *de facto* approval. The hospital was bound by that approval. However, the *de facto* approval could not have been given until the visiting officer saw the method in use at the first visit following its application. Accordingly, there was no agreement to the use of the special method for earlier periods and the hospital was entitled to recalculate its liability for those periods using the standard method.

A special method can be any method agreed by C & E and devised to suit the needs of the particular business, e.g. one based on any of the following ratios.

- Taxable input tax divided by total input tax.

- Taxable input tax divided by taxable input tax plus exempt input tax.

- Taxable inputs (net of VAT) divided by all inputs (net of VAT).

- Taxable inputs (net of VAT) divided by taxable inputs plus exempt inputs (both net of VAT).

- The number of taxable transactions made divided by all transactions (taxable and exempt) carried out.

- The floor space occupied by staff involved exclusively in taxable activity divided by total floor space.

- Time spent exclusively on taxable activity divided by all time spent.

The ratio should be expressed as a percentage to two or more decimal places. It should not be rounded up as with the standard method. The only exception is where a special method is employed using output values to apportion a single residual amount.

A special method may also be based on separate calculations for different sectors of the business or, in the case of a group registration, different businesses or groups of businesses within the VAT group.

49.7 Partial Exemption

C & E may approve a provisional claim in each quarter based on the claimable proportion for the previous tax year (after annual adjustment).

C & E should be informed of any change in the business which has a substantial effect on the amount of input tax claimable. The special method will then be reviewed by C & E and if no longer suitable, a direction to stop using the method will be issued. The taxable person must then either use the standard method or propose an alternative special method.

(C & E Notice 706, para 21; C & E Manual V1-15, Chapter 2 paras 7.13, 7.16).

Agreements with trade bodies. C & E have agreed special methods with the Building Societies Association, the Association of British Factors and Discounters, the Finance Houses Association Ltd, the Association of British Insurers and the Association of Investment Trust Companies. See C & E Notice 700/57/94 for full details.

Outside the scope activities. With effect from 1 January 1993, because of a change in the place of supply of services rules, some supplies which were previously zero-rated are outside the scope of UK VAT. Partly exempt businesses which have been using a special method which used the values of supplies for calculating deductible input tax may continue to use those values which have become outside the scope subject to approval by C & E. Businesses are required to exclude any distortive or incidental outside the scope values from calculations to the extent that zero-rated supplies would previously have been excluded. (C & E Notice 725, para 12.2).

Example

The facts are the same as in the example in 49.6 above except that C & E allow X Ltd to use a special method and calculate the proportion of remaining input tax attributable to taxable supplies by the formula

$$\text{Remaining input tax} \times \frac{\text{Input tax attributable to taxable supplies}}{\text{Total input tax}}$$

	£	£
First quarter		
Input tax attributable to taxable supplies	36,409	
Proportion of remaining input tax deductible		
$£11,751 \times \dfrac{36,409}{53,007} =$	8,071	
		44,480
Second quarter		
Input tax attributable to taxable supplies	20,245	
Proportion of remaining input tax deductible		
$£5,212 \times \dfrac{20,245}{25,768} =$	4,095	
		£24,340

The value of exempt input tax is
£1,428 (311 + [5,212 – 4,095]). As this is not more than £625
per month on average, all input tax in the quarter is
recoverable.

c/f 44,480

b/f 44,480

Deductible input tax		25,768

Third quarter

Input tax attributable to taxable supplies   34,698

Proportion of remaining input tax deductible

$$£10,963 \times \frac{34,698}{46,856} =$$ 8,118

42,816

Fourth quarter

Input tax attributable to taxable supplies   69,707

Proportion of remaining input tax deductible

$$£9,357 \times \frac{69,707}{85,039} =$$ 7,670

77,377

£190,441

For the annual adjustment required at the end of the tax year, see Example 2 in 49.9 below.

De Voil Indirect Tax Service. See V3.462.

49.8   **ATTRIBUTION OF INPUT TAX**

Foreign supplies. Input tax incurred by a taxable person in any prescribed accounting period on goods imported or acquired by, or goods or services supplied to, him which are used (or to be used) by him in whole or in part in making supplies within 49.2 (*b*) or (*c*) above *must* be attributed to taxable supplies to the extent that the goods or services are so used (or to be used). The attribution must be expressed as a proportion of the whole use (or intended use).

Where the supplies in question comprise

- financial services within *VATA 1994, 9 Sch Group 5, Items 1 or 6* (see 27.3(*a*) and 27.11(*a*) FINANCE) which are incidental to one or more of the taxable person's main business activities; and

- any other supply

input tax must be attributed as above despite any provision to the contrary effect in any method required or approved by C & E. This is designed to block VAT avoidance schemes on share issues incidental to the main core business.

[*SI 1995/2518, Reg 103*].

As a consequence of the above, where a company issues its own shares, input tax incurred on related costs is deductible according to the liability of the issue. If the issue is a wholly exempt supply, the input tax is not recoverable (subject to the *de minimis* limits). If all the shares are sold to persons outside the EC, the input tax is claimable in full. Otherwise, if some of the shares are sold to persons outside the EC, whether or not there is an existing partial exemption method in place, input tax on the share costs must be separately identified and only the proportion attributable to that part of the issue sold outside the EC is claimable. In most cases, this can be most accurately done by using the ratio.

Number of shares sold outside the EC

   Total number of shares sold

but if this method of calculation does not provide a fair and reasonable result, an alternative method of calculation may be used.

(C & E Notice 706, para 12A).

Self-supplies. Where under or by virtue of any provision of *VATA 1983* a person makes a supply to himself, the input tax on that supply must not be allowable as attributable to that supply. [*SI 1995/2518, Reg 104*].

VAT groups. When considering attribution of input tax incurred by a VAT group, the use of the goods or services by the group as a whole must be considered. If they are used to make an internal supply (which is not a supply for VAT purposes) and that internal supply is then used to make an exempt supply outside the group, then the input tax incurred on the original supply received by the group is exempt input tax. (C & E Notice 706, para 5; C & E Manual V1-15, Chapter 2 para 3.5).

Ultimate purpose of transactions. It is not possible to deduct input tax used for making an exempt supply even if the ultimate purpose of the transaction is the carrying out of a taxable transaction (*BLP Group plc v C & E Commrs, CJEC [1995] STC 424*). In that case, the company incurred input tax on professional fees in connection with the disposal of shares in a subsidiary company in order to pay debts. The court held that the input tax was not recoverable as it related to the exempt sales of shares, even though the ultimate purpose of this exempt supply was to enable the business to continue to make taxable supplies.

Acquiring a business as a going concern. Following the decision in *C & E v UBAF Bank Ltd CA, [1996] STC 372*, C & E have confirmed that, with effect from 1 June 1996, where a business acquires assets by way of the transfer of a going concern, and the assets are used exclusively to make taxable supplies, the VAT incurred on the cost of acquiring those assets should be attributed to those taxable supplies and can be recovered in full. Conversely if the assets of the acquired business are to be used exclusively to make exempt supplies, none of the input tax on the cost of acquiring those assets can be recovered. However if the assets are to be used in making both taxable and exempt supplies, any input tax incurred is non-attributable and must be apportioned in accordance with the agreed VAT partial exemption method. In *UBAF Bank Ltd* the court held that input tax on professional fees incurred in connection with the acquisition of shares was on supplies wholly used, or to be used, by the bank in making taxable supplies of equipment leasing and recoverable in full. Before that decision, C & E had treated such costs as general business overhead costs. (C & E Business Brief 7/96, 3 May 1996).

De Voil Indirect Tax Service. See V3.464.

49.9   **ANNUAL ADJUSTMENTS**

The deductions of input tax for each prescribed accounting period are provisional whichever method is adopted. This is because the amount deductible in some such periods may be unfairly affected e.g. by seasonal variations. It is normally necessary, therefore, to recalculate the amount of input tax reclaimable over a 'longer period'. If a special method is used, the letter of approval will state whether an annual adjustment is required.

Where a taxable person incurs exempt input tax during any 'tax year', his '*longer period*' corresponds with that tax year unless he did not incur exempt input tax during his immediately preceding tax year or 'registration period' in which case his longer period begins on the first day of the first prescribed accounting period in which he incurs exempt input tax and ends on the last day of that tax year. Where, however, his only exempt input tax is incurred in the last accounting period of his tax year, no longer accounting period is applied in respect of that tax year.

Where a taxable person incurs exempt input tax during his registration period, his longer period begins on the first day on which he incurs exempt input tax and ends on the day before the commencement of his first tax year.

In the case of a person ceasing to be taxable during a longer period, that period ends on the day he ceases to be taxable.

C & E may approve a longer period which does not correspond with a tax year (e.g. if a business changes methods during a tax year, C & E can agree to a mid-year adjustment).

'*Tax year*' is the twelve months ending on 31 March, 30 April or 31 May according to the prescribed accounting periods allocated. C & E may approve or direct that a tax year be for a period other than twelve months. These powers are mostly exercised where businesses ask to change their VAT return dates (in order to bring their tax year end into line with the end of their financial year) or change their tax year to end with a different existing return date (e.g. from 31 March to 31 December to coincide with its financial year end).

The '*registration period*' of a taxable person means the period commencing on his effective date of registration and ending on the day before the commencement of his first tax year.

[*SI 1995/2518, Reg 99*]. (C & E Manual V1-15, Chapter 2 paras 8.3–8.5).

Calculation of annual adjustments. Where all the exempt input tax in the longer period cannot be treated as attributable to taxable supplies under the rules in 49.3 and 49.4 above, then, unless C & E dispense with the requirements, a taxable person must calculate the reclaimable proportion of any remaining input tax not directly attributed on the same basis as in each of the prescribed accounting periods but using the figures for the longer period. Any difference between the amount of reclaimable input tax recalculated at the end of the longer period and the total amount provisionally deducted during the prescribed accounting periods is an over or under declaration of VAT and must be entered on the VAT return for the first tax period after the end of the longer period (unless C & E allow otherwise).

If the recalculation shows that the exempt input tax is below the limits in 49.4 above, any input tax not already reclaimed is an under deduction of VAT and should be entered on the next VAT return.

[*SI 1995/2518, Reg 107*].

Example 1

At the end of the tax year, X Ltd in the example in 49.6 above must carry out the following annual adjustment.

	£
Input tax attributable to taxable supplies	161,059
Proportion of remaining input tax deductible	
$\dfrac{2,028,999}{2,155,935} = 94.11\%$	
£37,283 × 95% =	35,419
Deductible input tax for year	c/f 196,478

49.10 Partial Exemption

	b/f 196,478
Deducted over the four quarters	198,368
Under declaration to be paid to C & E	£1,890

Example 2

At the end of the tax year, X Ltd in the example in 49.7 above must carry out the following annual adjustment.

	£
Input tax attributable to taxable supplies	161,059
Proportion of remaining input tax deductible	
$£37,283 \times \dfrac{161,059}{210,670} =$	28,503
Deductible input tax for year	189,562
Deducted over the four quarters	190,441
Under declaration to be paid to C & E	£879

De Voil Indirect Tax Service. See V3.466.

49.10 **ADJUSTMENTS FOR CHANGE IN USE OF GOODS AND SERVICES**

Adjustments must be made under the following circumstances.

(*a*) Where a taxable person has deducted an amount of input tax which has been attributed to taxable supplies because he intended to use the goods or services in making either

   (i) 'taxable supplies', or

   (ii) both taxable and 'exempt supplies',

and during a period of six years commencing on the first day of the prescribed accounting period in which the attribution was determined and before that intention is fulfilled, he uses or forms an intention to use the goods or services in making exempt supplies (or where (i) above applies, in making both taxable and exempt supplies).

Subject to below, under such circumstances, unless C & E allow otherwise, the taxable person must account for an amount equal to the input tax which has ceased to be attributable to taxable supplies in accordance with the method he was required to use when the input tax was first attributed. This should be done on the return for the prescribed accounting period in which the use occurs or the intention is formed.

In *Belgium v Ghent Coal Terminal NV, CJEC [1998] STC 260*, a company purchased some land, had work carried out on it and reclaimed the input tax on these supplies. Subsequently the local council required the company to exchange the land before it had been used for any taxable purpose. The CJEC held that the right to deduction was exercisable immediately the inputs were incurred and, once it had arisen, remained acquired even if, by reason of circumstances beyond its control, the taxable person never used the goods or services in question for the purposes of taxable transactions. This would not apply in cases of fraud or abuse and such a supply might give rise to a subsequent adjustment under the CAPITAL GOODS SCHEME (10).

In *C & E Commrs v Briararch Ltd; C & E Commrs v Curtis Henderson Ltd QB, [1992] STC 732* the court held that apportionment of input tax applied under this provision where a property is, or is intended to be, the subject of sequential supplies at different VAT liabilities. In the cases involved, the companies had reclaimed input tax in full on the basis that the properties concerned would be the subject of taxable supplies but, when the building work was completed, they were obliged to obtain temporary rental income on short leases which was an exempt supply. See also *Cooper and Chapman (Builders) Ltd v C & E Commrs QB, [1993] STC 1* where a building was converted into flats with the intention that they would all be let as holiday accommodation (standard-rated) but, after some flats had been so let, the company granted a one-year lease of the whole building (an exempt supply).

(*b*) Where a taxable person has incurred input tax which has not been attributed to taxable supplies because he intended to use the goods or services in making either

  (i) 'exempt supplies', or

  (ii) both 'taxable' and exempt supplies

and during a period of six years commencing on the first day of the prescribed accounting period in which the attribution was determined and before that intention is fulfilled, he uses or forms an intention to use the goods or services in making taxable supplies (or where (i) above applies, in making both taxable and exempt supplies).

Subject to below, under such circumstances, C & E must, on application by the taxable person in such form as C & E require, repay to him an amount equal to the input tax which has become attributable to taxable supplies in accordance with the method he was required to use when the input tax was first attributed.

In practice, the taxable person should write to his VAT office and, as soon as C & E have confirmed the amount to be repaid, enter the amount due in the VAT account as an underclaim and include it in the next VAT return. (C & E Notice 706, para 7).

Any question as to the nature of a supply under (*a*) or (*b*) above is to be determined in accordance with the legislation and rules in force at the time when the input tax was first attributed. Thus if a taxable person recovers input tax based upon an intention to make taxable supplies but, before those supplies are made, the liability changes and those intended supplies become exempt, no clawback is due under (*a*) above. In the reverse situation where liability changes from exempt to taxable, no payback can be claimed under (*b*) above. (C & E Manual V1-15, Chapter 2 para 10.2).

Where (*a*) or (*b*) above applies, subject to the provisions relating to foreign supplies in 49.8 above, if

• the use to which the goods or services are put (or to which they are intended to be put) includes the making of supplies outside the UK, and

• at the time when the taxable person was first required to attribute the input tax he was not required to use a method approved or directed under 49.7 above (or he was required to use such a method but that method did not expressly provide for the attribution of input tax attributable to supplies outside the UK)

then the relevant amount under (*a*) or (*b*) above is to be calculated by reference to the extent to which the goods or services concerned are used (or intended to be used) in making taxable supplies, expressed as a proportion of the whole use (or intended use).

'*Taxable supplies*' includes supplies within 49.2(*b*) or (*c*) above.

'*Exempt supplies*' includes supplies outside the UK which would be exempt supplies if made in the UK (other than those supplies falling within 49.2(*c*) above).

[*SI 1995/2518, Regs 108–110*].

De Voil Indirect Tax Service. See V3.467.

49.11   TREATMENT IN SPECIAL CIRCUMSTANCES

(1) **Abortive supplies.** There may be occasions where a business incurs VAT in connection with intended supplies that are never actually made. If the goods or services are used to make an alternative supply of a different liability, then the adjustment provisions in 49.10 above apply. However, where the initial intention is frustrated and the goods or services are not used to make any supply (e.g. architect's fees on an aborted building project) C & E's policy is to treat such abortive supplies as part of the general overhead costs of the business. In effect, the input tax forms part of the residual non-attributable input tax. If an intention to make supplies is formed and frustrated in the same return period, any related input tax should be treated as residual input tax in that quarter's return. Otherwise an adjustment is subsequently required when the original intention is frustrated. (C & E Manual V1-15, Chapter 3 para 1.1).

(2) **Holding companies.** See 31.9 GROUPS OF COMPANIES.

(3) **Costs incurred on the acquisitions of shares.** Where a business acquires shares, it is not making any supply and therefore in principle input tax on the costs of acquiring the shares is not deductible. However, C & E's policy is to allow such costs to be treated as a general business expense and the input tax is treated as non-attributable. It is a requirement that the costs are separately identified before being allowed to be so treated. (C & E Manual V1-15, Chapter 3 para 1.3).

(4) **Advice on raising capital.** Where a business seeks general advice on how to raise capital prior to a final decision on how that capital is to be raised, the cost can be treated as general business expenditure provided that it can be separately identified. As general business expenditure, any input tax is treated as non-attributable. (C & E Manual V1-15, Chapter 3 para 1.4).

(5) **Share issues.** See 49.8 above.

(6) **Transfers of going concerns** (TOGCs). For the position of the transferee acquiring the business, see 49.8 above.

   In the case of the transferor, since the sale of the business as a going concern is not a supply, input tax incurred on the costs of selling the business cannot be attributed to a supply by the transferor. These costs are therefore treated as a general business expense and the input tax is residual input tax. (C & E Manual V1-15, Chapter 3 para 1.6).

(7) **Research and development.** Input tax on research and development work is normally not attributable to any supply by the business. Input tax recovery is, therefore, determined by the liability of the activities which the research and development supports. Where research and development work is of a more general nature which cannot be said to lead directly to identifiable supplies, provided that it does not relate to any non-business activities, the input tax can be treated as part of the business's non-attributable input tax. (C & E Manual V1-15, Chapter 3 para 1.7).

(8) **Free supplies of catering for employees.** Where employees are provided with food or drink free of charge, the employer is making a taxable supply, albeit for a nil consideration. See 11.4 CATERING. Any input tax attributable to the supply is fully recoverable. (C & E Manual V1-15, Chapter 3 para 1.9).

(9) **Dilapidations.** Where a business occupies leased premises, the terms of the lease may require it to repair any damage to the property and to replace any defective fixtures and fittings. Any input tax incurred in carrying out this work is incurred in pursuance of an obligation placed it by the lease and can be recovered to the extent

that the premises have been used in making taxable supplies. This contrasts with the treatment of input tax incurred by a freeholder in making premises ready for letting. In this case, the input tax is directly attributable to the lease granted to the future tenant and its recoverability depends on whether the lease is taxable or exempt. (C & E Manual V1-15, Chapter 3 para 1.11).

(10) **Costs of settling insurance claims.** See 37.7 INSURANCE.

(11) **Credit notes.** For credit notes generally, see 40.15 INVOICES. The following rules apply to the partial exemption calculations.

Credit notes received.

● If received in the same VAT period as the original supply, the VAT return should be prepared on the basis of the adjusted input tax taking into account both the credit note and the original invoice.

● If received in a subsequent VAT period but in the same tax year, no adjustment is due in the subsequent VAT period. The amended input tax value should be substituted for the original input tax value in the annual adjustment and the adjustment calculated in the normal way.

● If received in a subsequent VAT period not in the same tax year, the annual adjustment covering the original VAT period should be reconsidered to see what effect the revised value has on that annual adjustment. Any resulting amendment should be included in the VAT period covering the date of the credit note and is an adjustment outside the partial exemption calculations of that VAT period.

Credit notes issued.

● If issued in the same VAT period as the original supply, the amended value should be used in any proportional calculation used to determine the recoverable proportion of non-attributable input tax.

● If issued in a subsequent VAT period but in the same tax year, no adjustment is necessary in the subsequent VAT period. The amended value should be used in any proportional calculation under the annual adjustment.

● If issued in a subsequent VAT period but not in the same tax year, the annual adjustment covering the original output should be reconsidered. Any resulting amendment should be included in the VAT period covering the date of the credit note and is an adjustment outside the partial exemption calculations of that VAT period.

(C & E Manual V1-15, Chapter 3 para 1.14).

(12) **Petrol scale charges.** See 45.16 MOTOR CARS.

(13) **VAT on insolvency practitioners' fees.** See 36.11 INSOLVENCY.

(14) **MOT testing.** VAT incurred by an approved garage in relation to the annual testing of motor vehicles on behalf of the Department of Transport is for the purpose of its business and can be claimed in full. Where the business is partly exempt, the business should isolate any VAT incurred in respect of MOT testing and recover this in full. Any remaining input tax should be recovered according to the normal partial exemption rules. (C & E Manual V1-15, Chapter 3 para 1.17).

(15) **Reverse charge on services from abroad.** VAT must be accounted for on certain services received from abroad. See 39.4 INTERNATIONAL SERVICES. The VAT can also be treated as input tax. However, for partial exemption purposes these services are not regarded as supplies and input tax on these imported services

can only be claimed in full if the services are used wholly for the making of taxable supplies. If used partly for taxable supplies, the input tax must be included in the non-attributable input tax and apportioned according to the partial exemption method used. Where the standard method is used, the value of imported services must not be included in the calculation.

Input tax on imported services must be included when applying the rules in 49.4 above.

(C & E Notice 706, para 18).

(16) **Self-supplies.** Where a business cannot be treated as fully taxable under 49.3 and 49.4 above and produces *stationery or similar material* for its own use to a value above the VAT registration limit, it must account for VAT on those self-supplies. See 62.2 SELF-SUPPLIES for VAT treatment generally including the deduction of related input tax.

In certain circumstances a business may similarly be required to account for VAT on self-supplies of construction services. See 42.43 LAND AND BUILDINGS. See also 42.27 LAND AND BUILDINGS for the treatment of input tax in connection with the developer's self-supply charge which ceased to apply from 1 March 1997.

(17) **Belated claims for input tax.** Where a partly exempt business makes a belated claim for input tax, it can only recover input tax to the extent that it would have been recoverable had it been claimed in the VAT period in which it was charged. The business must therefore work out its recoverable input tax using the rules in force when it was charged. It must also consider what effect such a claim has on other input tax deducted in that period and the relevant longer period calculation. For example, if a business is using a method based upon input tax, then a revision to either its taxable or total input tax values alters the amount of residual input tax deductible. The business must also reconsider its *de minimis* position for the initial VAT period and longer period in the light of the revised values for exempt input tax following the amended calculation.

Any resulting claim due is proper to the VAT period covering the time that the claim is made even though the amount allowed is dependant upon the VAT period covering the tax point of the claim. Any such claim is outside the calculations and *de minimis* measurement for the VAT period when the claim is actually made.

(C & E Manual V1-15, Chapter 3 para 1.19).

(18) **Divisional registration.** A corporate body may apply to be registered in the names of its separate divisions. See 59.30 REGISTRATION. Such an application cannot be accepted if the exempt input tax of the corporate body as a whole exceeds the limits in 49.4 above. When calculating whether these limits are exceeded, input tax relating to supplies within 49.3(a)–(e) above can be ignored, subject to the conditions mentioned in that paragraph. (C & E Notice 706, para 6).

(19) **Group registration.** The normal rules for group registration apply (see 31 GROUPS OF COMPANIES). Input tax recovery by a VAT group must be considered in terms of the use by the VAT group as a whole of the goods and services received by each individual member. All intra-group supplies are disregarded. Thus input tax on advice received by company A used to provide advice intra-group to company B is exempt input tax if company B uses the advice it receives to make supplies with no right to deduct. Company A may therefore incurs exempt input tax on behalf of the VAT group even if it only makes taxable supplies itself.

A VAT group can only have one partial exemption method as there is only one taxable person and the *de minimis limit* must also be applied to the group as a whole.

However, when applying the rules in 49.3 above and when determining whether financial or real estate transactions are incidental for the purposes of the special method in 49.7 above, the businesses carried on by the members of a VAT group are treated separately.

(C & E Notice 706, para 5; C & E Manual V1-15, Chapter 3 para 1.21).

(20) **Local authorities.** See 43.5 LOCAL AUTHORITIES AND STATUTORY BODIES.

(21) **Margin schemes – values of outputs.** Where a partly exempt business uses the TOUR OPERATORS' MARGIN SCHEME (66) and is using a method based on output values, it should use the value of the margin within the calculation since, in law, that is the value of the supplies made. In all other margin schemes, the total value of the supply is the value to be used in the calculation. (C & E Manual V1-15, Chapter 3 para 1.24).

(22) **Land and property.**

(a) *Input tax and the option to tax.* See 42.25 LAND AND BUILDINGS.

(b) *Part-exchange houses.* Where a builder takes a customer's existing house in part-exchange for the new home, C & E generally accept that input tax incurred on legal fees, valuation and structural reports, and sundry costs (e.g. checking and closing down the gas, electricity or water systems) is used in making both the zero-rated supply of the new house and the ultimate exempt sale of the part-exchange house. As a result, the input tax incurred on these items can properly be treated as residual input tax to be apportioned by means of the builder's agreed partial exemption method. On the other hand, they regard any input tax on estate agents fees and remedial costs (i.e. repair or maintenance costs) known about at the time of purchase to be attributable exclusively to the intended exempt sale and therefore restricted in full, subject to the *de minimis* limit.

Where the builder is using the standard method for partial exemption under 49.6 above, whether the proceeds for the exempt sale of the part exchange house can be considered an 'incidental' supply depends on the facts of each individual case. In the view of C & E, if the builder advertises that it will take existing houses in part-exchange for new houses, this would suggest that the sales of the existing houses are either part of the trader's main house building business or else a separate business of selling used houses. They would not then be incidental real estate transactions. Conversely, where a builder does not normally accept existing houses in part-exchange but does so exceptionally in order to dispose of a new house that has proved hard to sell, the sale of the existing house would be incidental to its main business.

Where a builder uses a special partial exemption method, the 'incidental' criterion may not arise, but the method should fairly apportioned non-attributable input tax to reflect the use of the builder's general overheads in dealing with the sale of part-exchange houses. On some occasions the supply of part-exchange houses may well be distortive even if they are not incidental.

(C & E Manual V1-15, Chapter 3 paras 3.4, 3.5).

49.12 RECORDS AND ACCOUNTS

See RECORDS (57) for records and accounts which every registered person is required by law to keep. In addition, a partly exempt business must also keep records that show

- how taxable and exempt input tax has been calculated in each return period and longer period;

49.12 Partial Exemption

- how the simplification rules in 49.3 above or *de minimis* rules in 49.4 above have been applied; and

- any further information that C & E have stipulated in a partial exemption special method approval letter.

(C & E Notice 706, para 13; C & E Manual V1-15, Chapter 1 para 1.6).

50   Partnerships

Cross-references. See 8.5 BUSINESS for deemed partnerships.

De Voil Indirect Tax Service. See V2.110.

50.1   PARTNERSHIPS FOR VAT PURPOSES

In English law a partnership, or firm, is not a legal entity but is defined as 'the relation which subsists between persons carrying on business in common with a view to profit' [*Partnership Act 1890, s 1(1)*].

In Scottish law a partnership is a legal person distinct from the partners who compose it.

Despite this, in general VAT legislation applies similarly under English and Scottish law so that the partnership itself is treated as a taxable person.

Whether a partnership exists and, if so, from what date is a question of fact. The stated intentions of the parties concerned are not necessarily conclusive. See *Leighton-Jones and Craig (t/a Saddletramps) (597)* approving *dicta* in *Weiner v Harris [1910] 1 KB 285.*

For alleged husband and wife partnerships see *Cooper (1218)*, *Jackson (RD & Mrs SL) (1959)* and *Britton (VJ) [1986] VATTR 209 (2173)* and for an alleged partnership with infant children see *Bridgeman (1206).*

For whether joint venture agreements amount to a partnership, see *Strathearn Gordon Associates Ltd [1985] VATTR 79 (1884)*, *Keydon Estates Ltd (4471)* and *Fivegrange Ltd (5338).*

50.2   REGISTRATION

VAT registration of persons carrying on business in partnership, or carrying on in partnership any other activities in the course or furtherance of which they acquire goods from another EC country, may be in the name of the firm. In such a case, no account is to be taken of any change in the partnership in determining for the purposes of *VATA 1994* whether goods or services are supplied to or by such persons or are acquired by such persons from another EC country. [*VATA 1994, s 45(1)*].

Where separate businesses are carried on by the same individuals in partnership only one registration applies (*C & E Commrs v Glassborow and Another QB, [1974] STC 142*). Where two separate businesses are carried on, each by an individual who forms a partnership with the other as a limited partner, separate registration applies (*Saunders and Sorrell [1980] VATTR 53 (913)*).

In practice an application to be registered (Form VAT 1) for a partnership must also be accompanied by Form VAT 2. [*SI 1995/2518, Reg 5(1)*].

50.3   CEASING TO BE A PARTNER

A person who ceases to be a partner will continue to be regarded as a partner for VAT purposes until the date on which the change is notified to C & E. This is without prejudice to *Partnership Act 1890, s 36* which provides, *inter alia*, that a person who deals with a firm after a change in its constitution is entitled to treat all apparent members of the old firm as still being members of the firm until he has notice of the change. A former partner is deemed to be served with any notice, whether of assessment or otherwise, which is served on the partnership and relates to any matter which occurred during, or before, the prescribed accounting period in which C & E were notified that he ceased to be a partner. [*VATA 1994, s 45(2)(3)*].

50.4 LIABILITY FOR VAT

The provisions in 50.2 and 50.3 above do not affect the extent to which a partner is liable for VAT owed by the partnership. This liability is determined by *Partnership Act 1890, s 9* which provides that

(*a*) every partner is liable jointly with the other partners for all debts and obligations of the firm incurred while he is a partner; and

(*b*) after death, a partner's estate is severally liable for such debts so far as they remain unsatisfied but subject to the prior payment of his separate debts.

However, where a person is a partner during part only of a prescribed accounting period his liability for VAT on the supply of goods or services during the accounting period, or on the acquisition during that period of any goods from another EC country, is limited to such proportion of the firm's liability as may be just.

[*VATA 1994, s 45(5)*].

50.5 NOTICES TO AND BY PARTNERSHIPS

Notices to partnerships. Any notice (whether an assessment or otherwise) addressed to the partnership by the name in which it is registered and validly served under *VATA 1994* will be regarded as served on the partnership (including any former partners as in 50.3 above). This is without prejudice to *Partnership Act 1890, s 16* which provides that notice to any partner who habitually acts in the partnership business operates as notice to the firm generally, except in cases of fraud involving that particular partner. [*VATA 1994, s 45(4)*].

Notices by partnerships. Where any notice is required to be given for VAT purposes, it is the joint and several liability of all the partners to give it, but it is sufficient if it is given by one partner. *In Scotland*, any authorised person, whether a partner or not, may give the required notice as specified by *Partnership Act 1890, s 6*. [*VATA 1994, 11 Sch 7; SI 1995/2518, Reg 7*]. Notice of appeal may be made in the partnership name (see 5.6 APPEALS).

50.6 PARTNERS HOLDING OFFICES

Where a person (including partners of a firm), in the course or furtherance of a trade, profession or vocation, accepts any office, services supplied by him as the holder of that office are treated as supplied in the course or furtherance of the trade etc. [*VATA 1994, s 94(4)*]. This point will obviously be of importance if the recipient of a supply suffers restriction of input tax or, as regards the supplier, the consideration for the supply was fixed with no contemplation that VAT was applicable. See *Lean & Rose, [1974] VATTR 7 (54)* where, on the facts, a solicitor who was a partner in a private practice was held to have a personal contract as a part-time salaried solicitor of a borough council and, accordingly, was not making taxable supplies.

See also 44.8 MANAGEMENT SERVICES AND SUPPLIES OF STAFF.

51   Payment of VAT

Cross-references. See 2.18 ACCOUNTING PERIODS AND RETURNS for payments by persons selling under a power of sale; 5.4 APPEALS for payment of VAT as a condition of appeal; 6.1 ASSESSMENTS for repayments of VAT made in error; 17.1-17.4 CUSTOMS AND EXCISE POWERS for power to require security or production of evidence before making repayments, power to recover VAT and power to distraint for payment and diligence (Scotland); 34 IMPORTS for VAT payable on importation; and 36.3 INSOLVENCY for priority of payment in insolvency.

The contents of this chapter are as follows.

51.1   PAYMENT OF VAT

Subject to the provisions in 51.3 and 51.4 below, VAT due for a prescribed accounting period is payable to the Controller at VAT Central Unit, Southend-on-Sea not later than the last day on which the return for that period must be submitted i.e.

- for Form VAT 100 (the normal return) not later than one month after the end of the prescribed accounting period; and

- for Form VAT 193 (final return) not later than one month after the effective date for cancellation of registration (or, in the case of a taxable person not registered, one month after the date when liability to be registered ceases).

[*SI 1995/2518, Regs 25(1)(4),40(2); SI 1996/1250, Reg 9*].

Where the amount of VAT due to C & E is under £1, no payment need be made. [*VATA 1994, 11 Sch 2(13)*]. Such amount should not be carried forward to the next return. (C & E Notice 700, para 9.7(c)).

De Voil Indirect Tax Service. See V5.109.

51.2   Method of payment

VAT can be paid by

- cheque/postal order crossed 'A/c payee' and made payable to 'HM Customs and Excise' and with a line through any spaces on the 'pay' line; or

- electronic means such as Bank Giro transfer, Bankers Automated Clearing Systems (BACS) or Clearing House Automated Payment System (CHAPS). If paying by BACS or CHAPS the payer's bank must quote the VAT registration number as the payer's reference and make the payment to

Bank of England
Threadneedle Street
London EC1V 1PA

Sort Code 10 00 00
Account No 52055000

(C & E Notice 700, para 9.7).

51.3 Payment of VAT

Payments in euro. From 1 January 1999, UK businesses can pay VAT (and other duties) in euro, although banks are not making BACS euro direct debit available. All declarations must continue to be made in sterling. Exchange rate are likely to fluctuate between the time payment is initiated and the time the payment is cleared. Businesses will be credited with the sterling value received by C & E and any over/under payments will be dealt with using existing debt management practices. Costs incurred by C & E in converting euro payments into sterling will not be passed on to businesses and will be borne by C & E. (C & E News Release 23 December 1998).

Non-payment. If the taxpayer is unable to pay all the VAT due, he should still send in the VAT return by the due date and write to the VAT office explaining why he cannot pay. C & E may be able to help businesses experiencing short-term difficulty by agreeing a brief period in which to pay a VAT debt. Post-dated cheques should *not* be sent. If sent and dated after the due date for payment, the taxpayer will automatically be in default under 52.15 PENALTIES below. Where a compromise solution cannot be agreed or no response is received to a request for payment, C & E may take action to recover the VAT due. This may include the issue of a distress warrant (diligence warrant in Scotland) under which assets may be removed and sold (see 17.3 and 17.4 CUSTOMS AND EXCISE: POWERS) or requesting the court to make a bankruptcy or winding up order (see 36 INSOLVENCY). (C & E Leaflet 700/12/95; C & E Notice 700/54/94).

Unpaid cheques. Due to the cost involved, C & E do not re-present cheques to banks which have previously been returned unpaid through lack of funds. The onus is on the taxpayer to cancel and replace any such cheques. (VAT Notes No 4 1996).

51.3 Extending the due date

C & E have indicated that, subject to the prior approval of VAT Central Unit, payment using the credit transfer system effectively extends the due date for payment of VAT by seven days although payment must still be initiated a few days before the extended due date to ensure that it reaches the C & E account on time. See *Barney and Freeman, [1990] VATTR 119 (4849)* and *Matilot Ltd (4847)*.

However a payment is made, C & E expect it to be in their hands on the due date. If this falls on a weekend or a bank holiday, payment must be initiated to reach C & E on the last working day beforehand. Application for the extended due date can be made to the VAT office or Credit Transfer Section (VCU 4A), VAT Central Unit, HM Customs & Excise, Alexander House, 21 Victoria Street, Southend-on-Sea SS99 1AA. If National Giro transfer is not to be used, the application must specify the method. Central Unit will insist that all returns and payments are made on time and all payments are made by credit transfer before agreeing to the extension. Taxable persons with a history of late payments may be refused the extension.

51.4 Payments on account

The Treasury may, if they consider it is desirable to do so in the interests of national economy, provide by SI that certain taxable persons must make payments on account of their VAT liability for a prescribed accounting period. [*VATA 1994, s 28; FA 1996, s 34; FA 1997, s 43*]. Under these provisions, every VAT registered business with an annual VAT liability of more than £2 million is required to be in the Payments on Account (POA) scheme. Once in the scheme each business must make interim payments at the end of the second and third months of each VAT quarter as POAs of the quarterly VAT liability. A balancing payment for the quarter is then made with the VAT return. All POAs and balancing payments must be made by electronic transfer. The detailed provisions of the POA scheme are set out below.

When the scheme must be used. POAs are required to be made, in respect of each prescribed accounting period exceeding one month beginning after 31 March each year, by

(*a*)   a taxable person whose total liability for VAT for the prescribed accounting periods ending in the period of one year up to the last day of his prescribed accounting period ending next before the previous 1 December (i.e. normally the year ending the previous 30 September, 31 October or 30 November) exceeded £2 million; and

(*b*)   a taxable person whose total liability for VAT did not exceed £2 million in the period specified in (a) above but did exceed that amount in the prescribed accounting periods ending in any subsequent period of one year.

The period of one year referred to under (*a*) or (*b*) above is known as the '*basis period*'.

VAT liability is calculated by adding together the VAT due to be declared on returns (including assessments or voluntary disclosures) and, if applicable, the VAT due on imports and goods ex warehouse. If liability exceeds £2 million, C & E will notify the business that it is in the scheme.

Timing of payments. POAs must be sent so as to clear Customs' account not later than the last working day of the second and third months of every VAT quarterly period (with the exception of the first period in the scheme when only one payment is required at the end of the third month). Quarterly balancing payments must also be cleared by the last working day of the month following the return period. Where non-standard period end dates have been agreed with C & E, payments must be cleared to Customs' account by the due date for those returns (or the last working date before the due date if that date is not a working date).

Set POAs. Unless one of the alternatives below is used, set POAs must be made.

The initial level of POAs are determined by the VAT liability in the period in which the £2 million threshold was exceeded under (*a*) or (*b*) above. The amount of each POA is one twenty-fourth of the total amount of VAT (excluding VAT on imports from outside the EC and goods ex warehouse) for that period. If the business has been in operation for less than twelve months, the payments will be calculated on a proportionate basis.

C & E must notify the business of the amounts it is required to pay and how these amounts have been calculated.

From the beginning of the next annual cycle for POAs, the amount of the POAs is one twenty-fourth of the total amount of VAT (excluding VAT on imports from outside the EC and goods ex warehouse) which the business was liable to pay in its reference year determined as follows.

VAT return periods: quarters ending	*Reference year*	*Annual cycle begins*
30 Mar, 30 Jun, 30 Sept, 31 Dec	Y/ended 30 Sept	1 Apr
30 Apr, 31 July, 31 Oct, 31 Jan	Y/ended 31 Oct	1 May
31 May, 31 Aug, 30 Nov, 28/29 Feb	Y/ended 30 Nov	1 June

Alternatives to set POAs. The following alternatives are available to set POAs.

• *Monthly VAT returns*. The business can change to monthly VAT returns by contacting the VAT office. It will be expected to continue making such returns for a reasonable period, normally at least twelve months. If monthly returns are prepared and payment made by electronic means (see below) or credit transfer, a further seven days beyond the due date may be allowed to render returns and make payments. This is the only circumstance in which a business liable to be in the POA scheme may be granted such an extension.

- *Payments based on actual liabilities.* A business may elect to pay its actual VAT liability for the preceding month instead of the set POAs but without rendering a monthly VAT return. Such an election must be made in writing to C & E stating the date on which it is to take effect (which must not be less than 30 days after the date of notification). Such an election then continues to have effect until a date notified in writing to C & E. An election cannot be withdrawn earlier than the first anniversary of the date on which it took effect and, where an election is withdrawn, a further election cannot be made within twelve months of the date of withdrawal. C & E may at any time give written notice that an election is to cease with effect from a specified date where they are not satisfied that the correct amounts are being paid. An appeal may be made against any such notice.

Payments based on actual liabilities may be beneficial where there are seasonal variations in the VAT liability. However, where the business is in credit in any month, no immediate repayment is made. Neither can a credit in respect of the first month of an accounting period be netted off against a liability for the second month to reduce the POA for that month. The business must wait to bring the credit forward to the VAT return as normal. Where immediate repayments are required, the business should consider changing to monthly returns.

Although this option was not available before 1 June 1996, see *Balocchi v Ministero delle Finanze dello Stato, CJEC 1993, [1997] STC 640* where the CJEC ruled that if national provisions are such that payments on account are transformed into payments in advance because of the seasonal nature of the trade, such provisions are contrary to the *EC 6th Directive.*

Method of payment. Payment must be made by electronic transfer direct to C & E's account. The VAT registration number should be quoted as a reference when making payments. Acceptable methods of payment are

- Clearing House Automated Payment System (CHAPS);

- Bankers Automated Clearing System (BACS);

- bank giro credit using official C & E bank giro slips (available by contacting ASD 2C, Alexander House, 21 Victoria Avenue, Southend on Sea, Essex, SS99 1AA; tel 01702 366376);

- (exceptionally) bank giro credit using non-official slips; and

- standing order.

In all cases the business must make the necessary arrangements to ensure the payment is received on time. The seven days period of grace previously allowed for payment by credit transfer (see 51.3 above) has been withdrawn for payments under the POA scheme. Whichever payment method is used, the same method must also be used to make any balancing payments due in respect of VAT returns.

C & E's bank details for making the payments are

Bank	Bank of England
Bank Account Number	52055000
Sort Code	
CHAPs, BACS, SO	10-00-00
official giro credits	10-70-90
non-official giro credits	10-70-50

Failure to pay. Where a business fails to make a POA by the due date, the payment is recoverable as if it were VAT due. For prescribed accounting periods ending after 1 June 1996, the business is also liable to the default surcharge. See 52.15 PENALTIES.

Completion of VAT return. VAT returns should be completed and submitted in the normal way. The figures must not be adjusted to take account of POAs made. The amount to be paid is the net liability shown on the return less any payments on account already made in respect of that period.

Overpayments. Where the payments made on account for a prescribed accounting period exceed the total due in that period, the excess must be repaid by C & E (if not liable to set-off under *VATA 1994, s 81*, see 51.9 below). If the return is a repayment return, the repayment will be made in the normal way and the POAs made in the quarter will also be repaid.

Removal from scheme. Where VAT liability in a reference year (see above) falls below £2 million, a business will be removed from the POA scheme six months later. For example, if the liability in the year to 30 September 1997 is below £2 million, the last payment on account will be due in March 1998. C & E will notify the business of its withdrawal from the scheme and the effective date of withdrawal.

If the total VAT liability in any completed year ending after a reference year is less than £1.6 million, written application may be made to C & E to cease making POAs. The requirement to make such payments then ceases with effect from the date of written approval by C & E.

Reduction in payments on account. If

- the total VAT liability (excluding VAT on imports from outside the EC and goods ex warehouse) in any completed year ending after the year on which current payments are based is less than 80% of the liability for that year, or

- C & E are satisfied that the total VAT liability (excluding VAT on imports from outside the EC and goods ex warehouse) in any year which has commenced but not yet ended will be less than 80% of that liability

written application can be made to have the POAs reduce to reflect the current liability. Further payments on account will then be based on one twenty-fourth of the reduced amount with effect from the date of written approval by C & E.

Increase in payments on account. C & E may increase the POAs due where the total VAT liability (excluding VAT on imports from outside the EC and goods ex warehouse) in any year ending after the year on which current POAs are based exceeds by 20% or more the total liability for that year. Where they do so, further payments on account will be based on one twenty-fourth of the increased amount. There are similar provisions as above to reduce the payments on account where VAT liability in any subsequent year falls below 80% of the increased amount.

Businesses carried on in divisions. Where a company is registered for VAT in the names of divisions, each division is regarded as a separate business for the POA scheme, i.e. the £2 million test is applied to each division (and not the company as a whole). Any overpayment by a division is not liable to set-off against a liability of the company or another division.

Groups of companies. The POA scheme applies to a VAT group as if all the companies in the group were one taxable person. The representative member is responsible for the POA but, in default, all members are jointly and severally liable.

[*SI 1993/2001; SI 1995/291; SI 1995 No 2518, Reg 40A, 44-48; SI 1996 No 1196; SI 1996 No 1198; SI 1997/2542*]. (C & E Notice 700/60/96).

De Voil Indirect Tax Service. See V5.110.

51.5 **INTEREST PAYABLE ON VAT (DEFAULT INTEREST)**

Circumstances in which interest may be charged. A taxable person may be charged interest in the following circumstances.

(*a*) Where C & E raise an assessment for a prescribed accounting period to recover any VAT which has been underdeclared or overclaimed on a VAT return.

(*b*) Where C & E raise an assessment for a prescribed accounting period in respect of which an earlier assessment has already been notified (i.e. where C & E issue an assessment following the failure to submit a VAT return but a further assessment is necessary as the original assessment is later found to be too low).

(*c*) Where C & E raise an assessment relating to a prescribed accounting period which exceeds three months and begins on the date with effect from which the person concerned was, or was required to be, registered.

(*d*) Where C & E raise an assessment relating to a prescribed accounting period at the beginning of which the person concerned was, but should no longer have been, exempted from registration under *VATA 1994, 1 Sch 14(1)* (see 59.6 REGISTRATION) or *VATA 1994, 3 Sch 8* (see 59.22 REGISTRATION).

(*e*) Where, before an assessment is made under (*a*)-(*d*) above, the VAT due or other amount concerned is paid by voluntary disclosure (so that no assessment is necessary). Interest is only charged on voluntary disclosures where the net value of errors exceeds £2,000 (i.e. it will not be charged where the taxable person could have adjusted the errors in his current VAT return but chose instead to make voluntary disclosure direct to C & E).

[*VATA 1994, s 74(1)(2); FA 1996, s 197*].

In general interest will only be charged where it represents '*commercial restitution*', i.e. compensation required where C & E have been deprived of VAT for a period of time because of

• the failure to submit a VAT return and the acceptance of an assessment that is too low; or

• an underdeclaration of the amount of VAT due on a return where that VAT is not recoverable by a third party as if it were input tax.

In exceptional circumstances, interest may be charged as a compliance measure (e.g. where, despite warnings, a taxpayer fails persistently to account for VAT at the right time).

(C & E Notice 700/43/96, paras 2, 3, Annexes A and B).

Circumstances in which interest will not be charged. C & E will not charge interest if the net value of errors discovered on previous VAT returns is £2,000 or less (see (*e*) above). In addition, interest will not be charged on the following.

• VAT declared on returns but unpaid.

• Assessments raised because a VAT return has not been rendered on time (but see (*b*) above for follow-up assessments).

• Penalties and interest.

• Amendments made to VAT returns before they are fully processed.

(C & E Notice 700/43/96, para 4).

Calculation of interest. Interest runs on the amount assessed or paid from the 'reckonable date' (even if not a business day) until the date of payment. In practice, however, interest runs to the date shown on the Notice of Assessment (Form VAT 655) or the Notice of Voluntary Disclosure (Form VAT 657). If any interest-bearing VAT shown on the Notice is not paid within 30 days, a further liability to interest arises. Interest will continue to be charged on a monthly basis and notified on Form VAT 658 or VAT 659 until all the interest-bearing VAT charged on the original assessment or voluntary disclosure is paid. However, interest is limited to a maximum of three years prior to the date of calculation shown on the Notice of Assessment or Notice of Voluntary Disclosure.

The *'reckonable date'* is the latest date on which a return is required for the prescribed accounting period to which the amount assessed or paid relates (i.e. one month after the end of the period) except that

- where the amount assessed or paid is an incorrect repayment of VAT or a payment in respect of excess credits, the reckonable date is the seventh day after C & E authorised the repayment; and

- where an assessment is made under *VATA 1994, s 73(7)* in respect of goods which cannot be accounted for (see 6.1(*e*) ASSESSMENTS), the sum assessed is to be taken to relate to the period for which the assessment was made.

[*VATA 1994, ss 74(1)-(3)(5), 76(1)(7)(8), 13 Sch 18*]. (C & E Notice 700/43/96, paras 5, 6, 8).

Rate of interest. With effect from 6 July 1998, the rate of interest is adjusted automatically from the 6th of each month by reference to changes in the average of base lending rates of certain clearing banks. Rates of interest are:

6 October 1991 – 5 November 1992	9.25%	[*SI 1991/2195*]
6 November 1992 – 5 December 1992	7.75%	[*SI 1992/2745*]
6 December 1992 – 5 March 1993	7%	[*SI 1992/3015*]
6 March 1993 – 5 January 1994	6.25%	[*SI 1993/421*]
6 January 1994 – 5 October 1994	5.5%	[*SI 1993/3168*]
6 October 1994 – 5 March 1995	6.25%	[*SI 1994/2542*]
6 March 1995 – 5 February 1996	7%	[*SI 1995/521*]
6 February 1996 – 5 July 1998	6.25%	[*SI 1996/165*]
6 July 1998 – 5 January 1998	9.5%	[*SI 1998/1461*]
6 January 1999 –	8.5%	

Invoices issued by unauthorised persons. Where an 'unauthorised person' issues an invoice showing an amount as being or including VAT, interest runs on the appropriate amount from the date of the invoice to the date of payment.

'*Unauthorised person*' means anyone other than

- a person registered for VAT; or

- a body corporate within a group registration; or

- a person treated as carrying on the business of a taxable person who has died or become bankrupt or incapacitated; or

- a person selling business assets of a taxable person towards satisfaction of a debt owed by that taxable person (e.g. sale of assets seized by a bailiff); or

- a person acting on behalf of the Crown.

[*VATA 1994, s 74(4)*].

Appeals, etc. If a taxpayer disagrees with the imposition of interest or with the amount of interest charged, he may ask C & E to reconsider the matter. This will be done by an officer not involved in the original decision.

If still not satisfied with the amount of the interest charged, the taxpayer may appeal to a VAT tribunal (see 5.3(*q*) APPEALS). There is no right of appeal against the rate of, or liability to, interest. A tribunal can only vary the amount of interest assessed insofar as it is necessary to reduce it to an amount which is appropriate under the above provisions. [*VATA 1994, s 84(6)*].

De Voil Indirect Tax Service. See V5.361–365.

51.6   REPAYMENT OF VAT

If at the end of a prescribed accounting period allowable credits exceed any output tax due, the appropriate repayment will be made by C & E except that where the amount of VAT due from C & E is under £1, no repayment will be made. If the taxpayer has failed to submit any return for an earlier period, C & E may withhold payment until he has complied with those requirements. [*VATA 1994, s 25(3)(5), 11 Sch 2(13)*]. See also the right of set-off under 51.9 below.

Method of repayment. C & E will make repayments by the Bankers Automated Clearing System (BACS). In order to receive repayment by this method, the VAT office must be advised of the bank account details in writing. (This is a requirement on the application for VAT registration.) In exceptional circumstances when bank account details are not known, C & E will make repayment by payable order. If repayment is not received within three weeks, the VAT office should be contacted. (C & E Notice 700, para 9.7; C & E Notice 700/12/95).

51.7   Recovery of overpaid VAT

Where a person has paid an amount to C & E by way of VAT which was not VAT due to them, C & E are liable to repay that VAT [*VATA 1994, s 80(1)*] provided the following conditions are satisfied.

(1) **A claim is made in writing.**

The claim must state the amount of the claim and the method by which it was calculated on the basis of the documentary evidence in the claimant's possession. [*VATA 1994, s 80(2)(6); SI 1995/2518, Reg 37*].

(2) **The repayment does not unjustly enrich the claimant.**

C & E can refuse to make the repayment where the claimant would be unjustly enriched. [*VATA 1994, s 80(3)*]. The legislation does not define 'unjust enrichment'. For a general consideration of the principle, see *Société Comateb v Directeur Général de Douanes et Droites Indirects, CJEC [1997] STC 1006, Marks and Spencer plc, [1997] VATDR 85 (14692, 14693)* and *Creative Facility Ltd; Oblique Press Ltd (10891)*.

Loss or damage to the claimant. For the purposes of making any repayments on or after 19 March 1997, where, for all practical purposes, the customer bears the VAT, any loss or damage (e.g. lost turnover or lower profits) alleged by the claimant must be disregarded (except to the extent shown otherwise by the claimant) when considering whether a VAT refund would amount to unjust enrichment. [*VATA 1994, s 80(3A)-(3C); FA 1997, s 46(1)(4)*].

Arrangements for reimbursing customers. With effect from 11 February 1998, where a claimant accepts that, by receiving a refund of overpaid VAT, it would be unjustly enriched, C & E will only make the refund if, on or before the time of making the claim, the claimant gives the following written undertakings.

(a) At the date of the undertakings he is able to identify the names and addresses of the customers he has reimbursed or intends to reimburse.

(b) The reimbursements will be completed by no later than 90 days after the repayment by C & E.

(c) No deduction will be made from the 'relevant amount' by way of fee or charge (however expressed or effected).

(d) Reimbursement will be made only in cash or by cheque.

(e) Any part of the relevant amount that is not reimbursed within the time limit in (b) above will be repaid to C & E.

(f) Any interest paid by C & E on the relevant amount will be treated in the same way as the relevant amount falls to be treated under (b) and (c).

(g) The claimant will keep records of the names and addresses of those customers whom he has reimbursed or intends to reimburse; the total amount reimbursed to each such customer; the total amount of interest included in each total amount reimbursed to each customer; and the date that each reimbursement is made.

(h) The records in (g) above will be produced to C & E on receipt of written notice to that effect from a C & E officer. The notice must state the place and time at which the records are to be produced and may be given before or after C & E have made the repayment to the claimant.

The 'relevant amount' means that part (which may be the whole) of the claim which the claimant has reimbursed or intends to reimburse to customers.

The claimant must, without prior demand, make any repayments due to C & E under (e) or (f) above within 14 days of the end of the 90 day period referred to in (b) above.

[VATA 1994, s 80A; FA 1997, s 46(2); SI 1995/2518, Regs 37A-37H; SI 1998/59].

Where C & E accept that a claimant has not been unjustly enriched, the reimbursement arrangements do not apply and no undertaking will be required. (C & E Business Brief 4/98, 9 February 1998).

(3) **The claim is made within the appropriate time limit**.

With effect from 18 July 1996, subject to below, C & E are not liable to repay any amount paid to them more than three years before the making of the claim. This applies to claims made before and after 18 July 1996, including those relating to overpayments made before 18 July 1996 except that where

• court or tribunal proceedings questioning any decision of C & E were started before 18 July 1996;

• those proceedings determine that C & E's decision was wrong or should be put aside;

• the claim for repayment is made after the proceedings started; and

• the claim relates *either* to VAT paid on the basis of the disputed decision *or* VAT paid before the date of the determination (or, if earlier, 18 July 1996) on grounds corresponding to those on which the disputed decision was made,

the three-year time limit works backwards from the date the proceedings began (and not the date any claim is subsequently lodged).

[VATA 1994, s 80(4); FA 1997, s 47(1)-(5)(11)].

It should be noted that *VATA 1994, s 80* only applies where a business has 'paid' an amount by way of VAT to C & E, i.e. it relates to claims for refunds by payment traders. The three-year cap on other claims for refund was not introduced until 1 May 1997 (see 51.8 below). C & E originally took the view that payment traders were those who, over a period of time, had paid more VAT to C & E than they had received by way of credits. They now, however, accept that it is necessary to look at each individual VAT return and that, consequently, the three-year cap introduced with effect from 18 July 1996 only applies where money was actually paid to C & E for a particular VAT accounting period. In all other cases, the three-year cap runs from 1 May 1997 under 51.8 below. If affected by this change of policy, businesses which submitted refund claims between 18 July 1996 and 1 May 1997 should contact their VAT office to request reconsideration of their claims. See C & E Business Brief 2/98, 27 January 1998.

Before 18 July 1996, a claim had to be made within six years from the date on which the amount was paid or, where it was paid to C & E by reason of a mistake, within six years from the date on which the claimant discovered the mistake or could with reasonable diligence have discovered it.

Assessment of overpaid repayment. See 6.5 ASSESSMENTS for C & E's power to assess for recovery of repayments made under the above provisions in excess of the repayment liability.

51.8   Claims for refunds other than amounts overpaid as VAT

The three-year time limit introduced with effect from 18 July 1996 under 51.7 above relates only to the recovery of overpaid VAT, i.e. it relates to claims for refunds by payment traders. No similar provisions were introduced at that time for capping other claims, including those by repayments traders, and there remained a number of methods for reclaiming VAT which were not subject to the three-year cap. This anomaly was corrected by *VAT (Amendment) Regulations 1997*.

Subject to the exceptions below, the three-year time limit is extended to the following with effect from 1 May 1997.

(*a*)   **Late claims for input tax.** Input tax should normally be claimed on the VAT return for the period in which the VAT becomes chargeable although it may be claimed in a later period. From 1 May 1997, input tax cannot be claimed more than three years after the date by which the return for the period during which the VAT was chargeable is required to be made. [*SI 1995/2518, Reg 29(1A); SI 1997/1086, Reg 4*].

(*b*)   **Correction of errors.** Where the net errors discovered in a prescribed accounting period do not exceed £2,000, the VAT account for that period can be adjusted. With effect from 1 May 1997, errors cannot be corrected using this method more than three years after the prescribed accounting period in which they arose. The three-year time limit does not apply where errors are discovered in a prescribed accounting period beginning before 1 May 1997 and the return for that period was not made, and was not required to be made, before that date. [*SI 1985/2518, Reg 34; SI 1997/1086, Reg 5*].

(*c*)   **Adjustments to take account of increases and decreases in consideration** (e.g. following issue of credit/debit notes). With effect from 1 May 1997, no VAT adjustment must be made for any increase/decrease in the taxable consideration due on a supply made or received more than three years after the end of the prescribed accounting period in which the original supply took place (unless the VAT adjustment occurred in a prescribed accounting period beginning before 1 May 1997 and the return for the period in which effect was given to it in the business records had not been made, and was not required to have been made, before that date). [*SI 1995/2518, Reg 38, SI 1997/1086, Reg 6*].

(d) **Pre-registration expenses.** With effect from 1 May 1997, VAT on goods (or services performed on those goods) cannot be reclaimed if the goods were supplied to, or acquired or imported by, the business more than three years before the date it was, or was required to be, registered. This does not apply where the business was registered before 1 May 1997 and did not make any returns before that date. [*SI 1995/2518, Reg 111(1)-(4), SI 1997/1086, Reg 7*].

(e) **Post-deregistration expenses.** With effect from 1 May 1997, no claim for refunds of VAT on post-registration services can be made more than three years after the date on which the supply of services was made (unless the person ceased to be registered, or ceased to be required to be registered, before 1 May 1997 and the supply was made before that date). [*SI 1995/2518, Reg 111(5)-(7); SI 1997/1086, Reg 7*].

(f) **Adjustments under the capital goods scheme.** With effect from 1 May 1997, adjustments to input tax incurred on capital items can only be made on a return for a prescribed accounting period commencing within three years of the end of the period when the adjustment should have been made. [*SI 1995/2518, Reg 115(6)-(8); SI 1997/1086, Reg 8*].

(g) **Claims for bad debt relief.** With effect from 1 May 1997, a claim for bad debt relief must be made within three years and six months from the later of

   (i) the date on which the consideration for the supply became due; and

   (ii) the date of supply

unless the later of those dates fell before 1 May 1997. [*SI 1995/2518, Reg 165A; SI 1997/1086, Reg 10*].

The three-year time limit does not apply to the following

• Claims or adjustments made under any agreement reached before 1 May 1997 with trade bodies or individual businesses where the agreement specified the period of the claim and that a claim could be made later than 1 May 1997 without the three year limit applying.

• Claims submitted after 1 May 1997 but where negotiations were taking place and the quantum agreed in writing before that date.

• Claims or adjustments which cover VAT appearing on both sides of a VAT return and therefore cancel each other out (e.g. those in respect of acquisition VAT or the reverse charge).

• Correction of tax point errors.

• Simple duplications of output tax.

• Returns following *compulsory* backdated registration for VAT. Where a business is registered for VAT with retrospective effect, it can claim input tax on its first return even if the VAT was incurred more than three years previously.

• Claims by DIY housebuilders.

• Claims by bodies such as local authorities under *VATA 1994, s 33* in relation to VAT incurred on non-business activities.

• Penalties paid which are subsequently shown not to be due.

• Claims for input tax which could not have been made earlier because the supplier failed to issue a VAT invoice.

(C & E News Release No 10, 26 November 1996; C & E Business Brief 9/97, 27 March 1997).

51.9   Payment of VAT

Legal proceedings commencing before 1 May 1997. Where legal proceedings began before 1 May 1997, the three-year limit on any subsequent claim or adjustment by the appellant dates from the day legal proceedings began or the date a claim was submitted, whichever is the earlier.

51.9   RIGHT OF SET-OFF

Subject to special provisions for insolvent traders (see 36.7 INSOLVENCY)

(*a*)   any amount is due from C & E to any person under *VATA 1994* ; and

(*b*)   that person is liable to pay any sum by way of VAT, penalty, interest or surcharge,

the amount in (*a*) must be set against the sum in (*b*) and, to the extent of the set-off, the obligations of C & E and the person concerned are discharged.

In respect of payments and repayments by C & E on or after 18 July 1996 (including those relating to liabilities arising before that date), where C & E are liable to pay or repay any VAT to the taxpayer because of a mistake previously made about the VAT due, they may set off against their payment any sum which is due from the taxpayer (including VAT, penalties, interest or surcharges) which arises because of that mistake. The normal time limits for enabling recovery (e.g. by assessment) do not apply.

[*VATA 1994, s 81(3)(3A); FA 1997, s 48*].

These provisions permit C & E to adopt commercial practice and strike a balance between all types of debits and credits within a taxpayer's account. The effect of the change from 18 July 1996 is that where a taxpayer has overpaid VAT (e.g. because exempt supplies have been treated as taxable) but as a consequence has overclaimed input tax, C & E can reduce the repayment to take account of the overclaimed input tax even if they are out of time to issue an assessment for that input tax (e.g. because of lengthy litigation).

51.10   REPAYMENT SUPPLEMENT

Where a person is entitled to a repayment of VAT credits under *VATA 1994, s 25(3)* or where a registered statutory body is entitled to a refund under *VATA 1994, s 33* (see 43.5 LOCAL AUTHORITIES AND STATUTORY BODIES) the payment due is increased by a supplement of 5% of that amount or £50, whichever is the greater, provided

(*a*)   the return or claim is received by C & E not later than the last day on which it is required to be made;

(*b*)   C & E do not issue a written instruction directing the making of the payment or refund due within 30 days of the date of the receipt of the return or claim; and

(*c*)   the amount shown as due on the return or claim does not exceed the amount in fact due by more than 5% of that amount or £250, whichever is the greater.

Any supplement paid is treated (except for the purposes of determining the amount of the supplement) as an amount due by way of credit under *VATA 1994, s 25(3)* or an amount due by way of refund under *VATA 1994, s 33*. Where the repayment, therefore, is not due in whole or in part and is recoverable by assessment, interest may be due on the repayment supplement as well as the VAT. See 51.5 above.

In calculating the period of 30 days in (*b*) above periods relating to the following are left out of account.

*   The raising and answering of any reasonable inquiry relating to the return or claim in question. Following the decision in *C & E Commrs v L Rowland & Co (Retail)*

Ltd QB, [1992] STC 647, this period begins with the date on which C & E first consider it necessary to make such an inquiry and ends with the date on which C & E either satisfy themselves that they have received a complete answer to their inquiry or determine not to make the inquiry or, if they have already made it, not to pursue it further. In the *Rowland* case, the court held that only the time between C & E raising enquiries with the registered person or his representative and their replying to these enquiries could be left out of account. (C & E News Release 39/92, 6 August 1992).

- The correction by C & E of any errors or omissions in the return or claim. The period begins on the date when the error or omission first came to their notice and ends on the date when it is corrected by them.

- In a case where a person is entitled to a repayment of VAT credits, the continuing failure to submit returns in respect of an earlier prescribed accounting period. The period is determined in accordance with a certificate of C & E issued to that effect under *VATA 1994, 11 Sch 14(1)(b)*.

- In a case where a person is entitled to a repayment of VAT credits, failure to produce documents or give security as a condition of repayment of VAT under *VATA 1994, 11 Sch 4(1)*. The period begins on the date of the service of the written notice of C & E requiring the production of documents or giving of security and ends on the date when they received the required documents or the required security.

[*VATA 1994, s 79; SI 1995/2518, Regs 198, 199*].

For a general consideration of how VAT repayment claims are received and internally processed by C & E and the their code of practice for dealing with repayment returns, see C & E Notice 700/58/98 *Treatment of VAT repayment returns and VAT repayment supplement.*

Repayment supplement will not be paid on

- bad debt relief claims;

- refunds paid to EC traders;

- refunds to do-it-yourself housebuilders;

- claims relating to services received after deregistration;

- amounts notified by C & E as overdeclared (including those resulting from voluntary disclosures made in writing to the VAT office); or

- claims for interest as a result of official error.

(C & E Notice 700, para 9.8).

De Voil Indirect Tax Service. See V5.191; V5.192.

51.11   **INTEREST PAYABLE BY C & E IN CASES OF OFFICIAL ERROR**

Where, due to an error by C & E, a person has

(a)   accounted to C & E for output tax which was not due to them and which in consequence they are liable to repay, or

(b)   failed to claim credit for input tax to which he was entitled and which C & E are in consequence liable to pay to him, or

(c)   otherwise than under (a) or (b) paid to C & E any VAT not due and which they are in consequence liable to repay, or (*d*) suffered delay in receiving payment of an amount due from C & E in connection with VAT (but not any amount of interest due under these provisions),

then, if they would not otherwise by liable to do so, C & E must pay interest to him for the 'applicable period' at the following rates. With effect from 6 July 1998, the rate of interest is adjusted automatically from the 6th of each month by reference to changes in the average of base lending rates of certain clearing banks.

16.10.91–5.2.93	10.25%	[*SI 1991/2282*]
6.2.93–31.3.97	8%	[*SI 1993/192*]
1.4.97–5.1.99	6%	[*SI 1997/1016; SI 1998/1461*]
6.1.99	5%	

These provisions do not require C & E to pay interest on any amount on which repayment supplement is due under 51.10 above, or on the amount of that repayment supplement. Additionally, where a claim for any payment or repayment has to be made, interest is only due on the amount of the claim which C & E are required to satisfy or have satisfied (i.e. interest is limited to the period for which VAT is refundable under *VATA 1994, s 80*).

Claims. Interest is only due if a claim is made in writing for that purpose. Any claim made after 17 July 1996 must be made within three years after the end of the applicable period to which it relates. For claims made before 18 July 1996, the time limit was six years from the date on which the claimant discovered, or with reasonable diligence could have discovered, the error.

Period of interest. The '*applicable period*' is the period beginning with the date that C & E

- under (*a*) or (*b*) above received payment, or as the case may be authorised a repayment or set off, for the return period to which the output tax or input tax related;

- under (*c*) above, received the payment; or

- under (*d*) above, might reasonably have been expected to authorise the payment or set off in question

and ending with the date on which C & E authorised payment of the amount on which the interest is payable. References to C & E 'authorising' a payment of any amount include references to their discharging liability to pay that amount by way of set-off against VAT due to them. Broadly, statutory interest is therefore payable on the net amount repayable by C & E at any particular time.

In calculating the applicable period, the following periods are to be left out of account.

(i) *In relation to any period beginning on or after 19 March 1997*, any period by which C & E's authorisation of the payment of interest is delayed by the claimant's conduct. This includes, in particular, any period referable to

- unreasonable delay in making the claim for interest or the claim for payment or repayment of the amount on which interest is claimed;

- a failure by the claimant or his representative to provide C & E with all the information they require to determine the amount of the payment or repayment due and the interest thereon (whether at or before the time of making the claim or subsequently in response to a request by C & E); and

- the making of a claim (as part of or in association with the claim for payment or repayment or interest) to anything to which the claimant was not entitled.

For these purposes, there is to be taken as referable to a person's failure to provide information in response to a request by C & E any period beginning with the date on which C & E reasonably require the person to provide it and ending with the earliest date they could reasonably conclude that the information required has been supplied or is no longer necessary.

(ii) In relation to any period beginning before 19 March 1996, any period referable to the raising and answering of any reasonable inquiry to entitlement to interest. There is to be taken as so referable any period beginning with the date on which C & E first consider it necessary to make such an enquiry and ending with the date on which C & E are satisfied that they have received a complete answer to their inquiry or determine not to make the inquiry or, if they have already made it, not to pursue it further.

Appeals. An appeal may be made to a VAT tribunal against a decision of C & E not to pay interest under these provisions (see 5.3 APPEALS).

[*VATA 1994, s 78; FA 1996, s 197; FA 1997, s 44*].

A claim for interest was upheld where C & E incorrectly advised that input tax had to be apportioned because some of the company's income was outside the scope of VAT. This ruling (although pre-dating it) was inconsistent with the decision in *Lennartz v Finanzamt Munchen III* (see 35.7 INPUT TAX) and led to the company failing to claim credit for input tax to which it was entitled (*North East Media Development Trust Ltd (13104)*. Following the decision, the company claimed interest on the whole of the input tax which C & E had wrongly refused to repay. However, the tribunal upheld C & E's contention that interest should be computed upon an amount equal to the net overpayment of VAT (*North East Media Development Trust Ltd (13425)*).

A claim for interest was also upheld where the organisation contended that a C & E leaflet had not been updated and that it had been misled by a VAT officer (*Wydale Hall (14273)*).

Assessment of overpaid interest. See 6.5 ASSESSMENTS for C & E's power to assess for interest that has been overpaid to a claimant under the above provisions.

De Voil Indirect Tax Service. See V5.196.

51.12   INTEREST PAYABLE BY C & E: GENERAL TREATMENT

Any interest payable to a person by C & E on a sum due to him under or by virtue of any provision of *VATA 1994*, is treated (except for the purposes of determining entitlement to, or the amount of, that interest) as an amount due by way of credit under *VATA 1994, s 25(3)*. [*VATA 1994, s 81(1)(2)*]. It may therefore be set off against any output tax due or payment may be withheld where outstanding returns are due for earlier periods. Also where the sum is not due in whole or in part and is recovered by assessment, interest may be due to C & E on the interest paid as well as the VAT.

51.13   AWARD OF INTEREST BY TRIBUNAL

Where a tribunal decides that any 'VAT paid or deposited' should be repaid to the appellant or any amount of input tax should be paid to him, it may direct that the amount is repaid with interest at such rate as it may specify. Similarly where an appeal has been entertained despite the fact that VAT determined by C & E has not been paid or deposited (see 5.21 APPEALS) and it is found on the appeal that the amount is due, such amount must be paid with interest at such rate as the tribunal may specify. [*VATA 1994, s 84(8)*].

'*Tax paid or deposited*' includes paying VAT charged on a supply 'without prejudice' should the VAT be found not to be payable (*WJM Mahoney, [1976] VATTR 241 (258)*).

Although the award of interest is mandatory the rate has been subject to a variety of treatments by tribunals.

52 Penalties

Cross-references. See 5.2 APPEALS for penalty for failure to comply with a direction of a tribunal.

De Voil Indirect Tax Service. See V5.3.

The contents of this chapter are as follows.

52.1 CRIMINAL OFFENCES AND PENALTIES

Criminal proceedings may be brought under the offences in 52.2 to 52.7 below. Most VAT defaults are, however, dealt with by civil penalties and only serious cases of fraudulent VAT evasion are investigated as criminal matters. The proceedings may only be instituted by C & E or a law officer of the Crown.

Except as otherwise provided in the C & E *Acts,*

- proceedings for an indictable offence must be commenced within 20 years of the date when the offence was committed; and

- proceedings for a summary offence must be commenced within three years of that date but, subject to that, may be commenced at any time within six months from the date on which sufficient evidence to warrant the proceedings came to the knowledge of the prosecuting authority. For these purposes, a certificate of the prosecuting authority as to the date on which the evidence came to its knowledge is conclusive evidence of the fact.

There are further detailed provisions relating to service of process, place of trial, non-payment of penalties, application of penalties, proof of certain documents and other procedural matters. [*CEMA 1979, ss 145–151, 153–155; VATA 1994, s 72(12)*].

False statements to the prejudice of the Crown and public revenue are indictable as a criminal offence (*R v Hudson CCA 1956, 36 TC 561*). False statements may also involve liability to imprisonment for up to two years, under the *Perjury Act 1911, s 5*, for 'knowingly and wilfully' making materially false statements etc. for VAT purposes.

Mitigation. C & E may, as they see fit, stay or compound any proceedings (except those on indictment in Scotland) or, after judgment, mitigate or remit any pecuniary penalty, or order any person who has been imprisoned to be discharged before the end of his term of imprisonment. [*CEMA 1979, s 152; VATA 1994, s 72(12)*].

De Voil Indirect Tax Service. See V5.301–308.

52.2   **Fraudulent evasion of VAT**

A person who is knowingly concerned in, or in taking steps with a view to, the fraudulent 'evasion of VAT' by him or any other person, is liable

- on summary conviction, to a penalty of the 'statutory maximum' or three times the 'amount of VAT', whichever is the greater, *or* imprisonment for a term not exceeding six months *or* to both; or

- on conviction on indictment, to a penalty of any amount *or* to imprisonment for a term not exceeding seven years *or* to both.

'*Evasion of VAT*' includes obtaining

(i) a payment of a VAT credit;

(ii) a refund under *VATA 1994, s 35* (do-it-yourself housebuilders), *VATA 1994, s 36* or *VATA 1983, s 22* (bad debts) or *VATA 1994, s 40* (new means of transport supplied to another EC country by a non-taxable person);

(iii) a refund under regulations made by virtue of *VATA 1994, s 13(5)* (VAT paid in the UK on an acquisition from another EC country where VAT has already been paid in that other country); or

(iv) a repayment under *VATA 1994, s 39* (repayment of VAT to those in business overseas).

'*Amount of VAT*' in relation to a payment within (i) above is the aggregate of the amount (if any) falsely claimed as input tax and the amount (if any) by which output tax was falsely understated. In relation to a refund or repayment within (ii) to (iv) above, it is the amount falsely claimed.

A person acting under the authority of C & E may arrest anyone whom he has reasonable grounds for suspecting to be guilty of an offence.

[*VATA 1994, s 72(1)(2)(9)*].

'*Statutory maximum*' is currently £5,000.

Nothing in the above denies the right for an assessment to be made in respect of the VAT actually evaded.

'Evasion' includes deliberate non–payment of VAT and it is not necessary to show any permanent intention to deprive (*R v Dealy CA Criminal Division 1994, [1995] STC 217*).

'*Taking of steps*' to evade VAT need not necessarily be confined to the taking of positive steps (*R v McCarthy CA Criminal Division, [1981] STC 298*).

The existence of the above provisions does not rule out the possibility of conviction under the common law offence of cheating the public revenue. This offence is preserved by the *Theft Act 1968, s 32(1)* and can include any form of fraudulent conduct which results in diverting money from the public revenue and in depriving the public revenue of money to which it is entitled. In practice, the common law charge is reserved for serious cases and the penalties, including imprisonment, are unlimited. No positive act of deception is required. An omission to do an act is sufficient. See *R v Mavji CA, [1986] STC 508* and *R v Redford CA, [1988] STC 845*.

52.3 Penalties

Most cases of VAT evasion are dealt with under the civil provisions (see 52.9 below) but, for aggravated or serious offences, the matter may be investigated for criminal proceedings. In general, cases are dealt with under criminal proceedings where one or more of the following applies.

- The VAT evaded is at least £75,000 in total over the last three years.

- The offence is committed by lawyers, accountants or others who advise businesses in respect of financial matters.

- There is a conspiracy to evade VAT by people not within the same legal entity.

- The evasion involves a business registered for VAT whose activities are undertaken primarily to obtain a payment through false returns or to provide false invoices or false evidence of export for fraudulent purposes.

- There has been a previous VAT or C & E offence resulting in the imposition of a penalty, the compounding of proceedings (see below) or a criminal conviction.

- There is an element of novelty or ingenuity in the offence capable of adoption by others.

- The evader occupies a prominent position in the field of law or government.

- The evasion is executed in conjunction with other criminal activities.

- There is, during the course of investigation of a civil offence, a deliberate intent to deceive.

- There is justification, because of the gravity of the offence, for a search warrant to be used.

- The evader is an undischarged bankrupt.

- Taxable supplies take place without security being provided when such security has been required under *VATA 1994, 11 Sch 4(2)*.

Compounding. As an alternative to criminal proceedings, under *CEMA 1979, s 152* C & E may accept a financial settlement in lieu of proceedings. This is referred to as compounding. The decision whether to prosecute or compound proceedings is taken on the merits of each case.

(C & E Notice 700, para 12.3).

De Voil Indirect Tax Service. See V5.311.

52.3   False documents and statements

Any person who

(*a*)   produces, furnishes, sends or otherwise makes use of, for the purposes of VAT, any document which is false in a material particular with the intent to deceive or secure that a machine will respond to the document as if it were a true document; or

(*b*)   causes a document to be produced etc. as in (*a*) above; or

(*c*)   makes any statement in furnishing information for the purposes of VAT which he knows to be false in a material particular *or* who recklessly makes a statement which is false in a material particular,

is liable

- on summary conviction, to a penalty of the 'statutory maximum' (see 52.2 above) *or* to imprisonment for a term not exceeding six months *or* to both. Where the document referred to is a return *or* a refund or repayment under 52.2(ii)–(iv) above *or* the information under (*c*) above is contained in or relevant to such a document, an alternative penalty of three times the amount falsely claimed is, if greater, substituted for the statutory maximum; or

- on conviction on indictment, to a penalty of any amount *or* to imprisonment for a term not exceeding seven years *or* to both.

A person acting under the authority of C & E may arrest anyone whom he has reasonable grounds for suspecting to be guilty of an offence.

[*VATA 1994, s 72(3)–(7)(9)*].

De Voil Indirect Tax Service. See V5.312; V5.313.

52.4 Conduct which must have involved an offence

Where a person's conduct during any specified period must have involved the commission by him of one or more offences under 52.2 or 52.3 above, then, whether or not the particulars of the offence are known, he is guilty of an offence and liable

- on summary conviction, to a penalty of the greater of the 'statutory maximum' (see 52.2 above) and three times the amount of any VAT that was, or was intended to be, evaded by his conduct *or* to imprisonment for a term not exceeding six months *or* to both; or

- on conviction on indictment, to a penalty of any amount *or* to imprisonment for a term not exceeding seven years *or* to both.

See 52.2 above for 'evasion of VAT'.

A person acting under the authority of C & E may arrest anyone whom he has reasonable grounds for suspecting to be guilty of an offence.

[*VATA 1994, s 72(8)(9)*].

De Voil Indirect Tax Service. See V5.314.

52.5 Knowledge that evasion intended

A person who acquires possession of, or deals with, any goods or accepts the supply of services, having reason to believe that VAT on the supply, acquisition or importation has been or will be evaded, is liable to a penalty on summary conviction of the greater of level 5 on the 'standard scale' or three times the amount of the VAT evaded. [*VATA 1994, s 72(10)*].

'*Standard scale*' can be altered by statutory instrument and level 5 is currently £5,000.

De Voil Indirect Tax Service. See V5.316.

52.6 Failure to provide security

A person who is required, under *VATA 1994, 11 Sch 4(2)*, to give security for the future payment of VAT as a condition of making taxable supplies (see 17.1 CUSTOMS AND EXCISE: POWERS) and who makes such supplies without providing that security is liable on summary conviction to a penalty of level 5 on the standard scale (see 52.5 above). [*VATA 1994, s 72(11)*].

De Voil Indirect Tax Service. See V5.317.

52.7 Penalties

52.7 Bribery and obstruction of officers

Any person who offers or gives a bribe to a C & E officer, and any such officer who accepts such a bribe, is liable to a penalty on summary conviction of £5,000 and may be arrested. Any person who obstructs, hinders, molests, or assaults an officer or does anything which is likely to impede any search or production of evidence is liable

- on summary conviction to a prescribed penalty (currently £2,500) *or* imprisonment for a term not exceeding three months *or* to both; or

- on conviction on indictment, to a penalty of any amount *or* to imprisonment for a term not exceeding two years *or* to both.

[*CEMA 1979, ss 15, 16*].

52.8 CIVIL PENALTIES

In addition to the criminal penalties under 52.1 to 52.7 above, there are also civil penalties and surcharges. These are detailed in 52.9 to 52.19 below.

Reasonable excuse for conduct. No penalty or surcharge arises under 52.10 to 52.15 and 52.17 to 52.19 below if the person concerned can satisfy C & E, or on appeal a tribunal, that there is a reasonable excuse for his conduct. Although 'reasonable excuse' is not defined (and, therefore, to be determined by C & E or tribunal) the following are not to be taken as a reasonable excuse.

- An insufficiency of funds to pay any VAT due.

- Where reliance is placed on 'any other person' to perform any task, the fact of that reliance or any other dilatoriness or inaccuracy on the part of the person relied upon. See *C & E Commrs v Harris and Another QB, [1989] STC 907*. '*Any other person*' is not restricted to outside advisers and includes a company's accountant (*Profile Security Services (South) Ltd v C & E Commrs QB, [1996] STC 808*).

[*VATA 1994, s 71(1)*].

It is necessary to distinguish between the reason and the excuse. Although insufficiency of funds by itself is not a reasonable excuse, where the shortfall is totally unforeseen and not due to the normal hazards of trade (e.g. the dishonesty of a former employee) the defence of reasonable excuse may possibly be invoked (*C & E Commrs v Salevon Ltd QB, [1989] STC 907*). See also *C & E Commrs v Steptoe CA, [1992] STC 757* where it was held that there was reasonable excuse where the taxpayer was unable to pay the VAT due because the customer for whom he worked almost exclusively was persistently late in paying invoices. The correct test is whether, given the exercise of reasonable foresight, due diligence and a proper regard for the fact that the VAT will become due on a particular date, the lack of funds which led to the default was reasonably avoidable.

C & E have indicated the following *guidelines* on the interpretation of 'reasonable excuse' although any decision will be judged by C & E or a VAT tribunal on the circumstances of the individual case.

(*a*) **Reasonable excuse for late registration**

- *Compassionate circumstances* where an individual is totally responsible for running a small business and he, or a member of his immediate family, was seriously ill or recovering from such an illness at the time notification was required.

- *Transfer of a business as a going concern* where such a business is taken over with little or no break in the trading and returns have been submitted and VAT paid on time under the registration number of the previous owner.

- *Doubt about liabilities of supplies* where there is written evidence of an enquiry to C & E about the liability of supplies and liability has remained in doubt.

- *Uncertainty about employment status* where there are genuine doubts as to whether a person is employed or self-employed or where correspondence with the Inland Revenue can be produced about these doubts.

(C & E Notice 700/41/95, para 7).

(b) **Reasonable excuse for not sending in return or paying VAT on time**

- *Computer breakdown* where the essential records are held on computer and it breaks down either just before or during the preparation of the return. Reasonable steps to correct the fault must be taken.

- *Illness* of the person normally responsible for preparing the return provided it can be shown that no-one else was capable of completing the return. If the illness is prolonged, reasonable steps to get someone else to complete the return must be taken.

- *Loss of key personnel* responsible for preparing the return at short notice where there is no-one else to complete it on time.

- *Unexpected cash crisis* where funds are unavailable to pay VAT because of the sudden reduction or withdrawal of overdraft facilities, sudden non-payment by a normally reliable customer, insolvency of a large customer, fraud, burglary or act of God such as fire.

- *Loss of records.* The excuse only applies if records for the current VAT period are stolen or destroyed. If records relating to a future VAT return are lost, C & E must be notified immediately. If the records are elsewhere (e.g. with accountants or the Inland Revenue) it is the taxpayer's responsibility to get them, or copies of them, back.

C & E will take into account whether the circumstances could have been foreseen and, if so, what steps were taken to make alternative arrangements; whether the VAT office was contacted for help or advice; whether sufficient priority was given to completing the VAT return; and whether the VAT (or a reasonable estimate) was paid by the due date.

(C & E Notice 700/50/97, para 3.3).

There have been numerous tribunal decisions as to whether, on the facts of a particular case, there is a reasonable excuse against the assessment of a penalty. For a summary of these see the chapters DEFAULT SURCHARGE, PENALTIES: FAILURE TO NOTIFY, ETC, PENALTIES: MISDECLARATION and PENALTIES: REGULATORY PROVISIONS in Tolley's VAT Cases.

Mitigation. See 52.20 below.

Right of set-off. See 51.9 PAYMENT OF VAT.

De Voil Indirect Tax Service. See V5.335.

52.9   **VAT evasion: conduct involving dishonesty**

Most cases of VAT evasion are dealt with under the following civil provisions but, for aggravated or serious offences, the matter may be investigated for criminal proceedings. See 52.2 above for criminal proceedings and an indication of where cases are likely to be dealt with as such.

52.9 Penalties

Where

(a) for the purpose of 'evading VAT', a person does any act or omits to take any action; and

(b) his conduct involves dishonesty (whether or not it is such as to give rise to criminal liability),

he is liable to a penalty equal to 'the amount of the VAT evaded' (or sought to be evaded). However, where he is convicted of a criminal offence by reason of conduct within (a) and (b) above, he is not also liable to a penalty under these provisions.

'*Evading VAT*' includes dishonestly obtaining a VAT credit; a refund under *VATA 1994, s 35* (do-it-yourself builders), *VATA 1994, s 36* or *VATA 1983, s 22* (bad debts) or *VATA 1994, s 40* (new means of transport supplied to another EC country by a non-taxable person); a refund under regulations made by virtue of *VATA 1994, s 13(5)* (VAT paid in the UK on an acquisition from another EC country where VAT has already been paid in that other country on the acquisition); and a repayment under *VATA 1994, s 39* (repayment of VAT to those in business overseas).

'*The amount of VAT evaded*' is the amount falsely claimed by way of credit for input tax (including any amount claimed as a deduction from VAT due) or the amount by which output tax is falsely understated *or* the amount falsely claimed by way of refund or repayment.

In any criminal proceedings against the person concerned in respect of any offence in connection with VAT or in any proceedings against him for recovery of any sum due, statements made or documents produced on his behalf are not inadmissible on the grounds that he was (or may have been) induced to make or produce them after it had been brought to his attention that

(i) C & E might assess a civil penalty rather than bring criminal proceedings against him if he made a full confession of any dishonest conduct and gave full facilities for investigation; or

(ii) the penalties might be mitigated.

[*VATA 1994, ss 60, 71(2)*].

The penalty can be applied in cases of non-registration and is not restricted to cases where there has been a fraudulent understatement of output tax or overstatement of input tax (*CS Stevenson v C & E Commrs CA, [1996] STC 1096*).

Mitigation. See 52.20 below for mitigation generally. The penalty for VAT evasion can be significantly reduced by the C & E investigating officer. Reductions from the 100% penalty figure will normally be made for three reasons, to the maximum percentages specified, as follows.

- An early and truthful explanation as to why the arrears arose and the extent of them — up to 40%.

- Co-operation in establishing the true amount of arrears — up to 25%.

- Attending interviews and producing records and information as required — up to 10%.

The maximum reduction obtainable is normally therefore 75% of the VAT undeclared although in exceptional cases (e.g. where a full and unprompted voluntary disclosure has been made) consideration will be given to a further reduction.

(C & E Notice 730).

For a consideration of the test of 'dishonesty' see *K S Nandera (7880)*.

Liability of directors etc. Where the conduct of a body corporate gives rise to a penalty under the above provisions and it appears to C & E that that conduct, in whole or part, is attributable to the dishonesty of a person who is (or at the material time was) a director or 'managing officer' (the named officer) of the body corporate, C & E may serve a notice on the named officer proposing to recover all or part of the penalty from him. The portion specified is then assessable and recoverable as if the named officer were personally liable to that part of the penalty. The body corporate is then only assessed on the balance, if any, and is discharged from liability on the amount assessed on the named officer.

The body corporate may appeal against C & E's decision as to its liability to the penalty and against the amount of the full penalty as if it were specified in an assessment. The named officer may appeal against the decision that the conduct of the body corporate is, in whole or part, attributable to his dishonesty and against the portion of the penalty which C & E propose to recover from him. Otherwise, there are no grounds for appeal.

'*Managing officer*' means any manager, secretary or other similar officer of the body corporate and any person purporting to act in any such capacity or as a director. Where the affairs of a body corporate are managed by its members, the provisions apply in relation to the conduct of a member in connection with his functions of management as if he were a director of the body corporate.

[*VATA 1994, s 61*].

The notification of liability to a director, etc. must show both the amount of the basic penalty and the portion of it which C & E propose to recover from that director (*MK & ME Nazif (13616)*). See *C & E Commrs v Bassimeh CA, [1997] STC 33* for apportionment of penalties where there is more than one culpable director.

De Voil Indirect Tax Service. See V5.341.

52.10   **Misdeclaration or neglect resulting in VAT loss**

Subject to below, a person is liable to a penalty where

(*a*)   a return is made understating liability to VAT or overstating entitlement to a repayment of VAT credits, or

(*b*)   an assessment is made understating liability to VAT and, within 30 days from the date of the assessment, the taxpayer has not taken all such steps as are reasonable to draw the understatement to the attention of C & E

and the 'VAT which would have been lost' for the period concerned if the inaccuracy had not been discovered equals or exceeds the lesser of

● where (*a*) above applies, £1 million and 30% of the 'gross amount of VAT'; and

● where (*b*) above applies, £1 million and 30% of the 'true amount of VAT for the period'.

The penalty is 15% of the VAT which would have been lost.

Where supplementary assessments are raised, any penalty is calculated at the percentage rate in force at the time of the original assessment. A penalty is assessed on the date of the decision to make the assessment and the calculation of the amount due, not the date of the notice of assessment if different (*Dart (9066)*).

'*VAT which would have been lost*'. This is the amount of the understatement of liability or, as the case may be, overstatement of entitlement to repayment for the prescribed accounting period in question.

52.10 Penalties

'*Gross amount of VAT*' is the total of the amount of input tax and output tax which should have been stated in the return for that period. Input tax for this purpose includes any refunds or repayments due in the period which may be aggregated with input tax on the return.

'*True amount of VAT*' means the VAT due from the person concerned or, as the case may be, the amount of the payment to which he is entitled in the period.

For the purposes of ascertaining the '*VAT which would have been lost*', the '*gross amount of VAT*' and the '*true amount of VAT*' where any under or over statement is correspondingly adjusted in a subsequent return, each of those returns is assumed to be a correct statement (so far as not inaccurate in any other respect) for the prescribed accounting period to which it relates.

A person is not liable to a penalty under these provisions

(A) if he is convicted of a criminal offence or assessed to a penalty under 52.9 above by reason of conduct within (*a*) or (*b*) above; or

(B) where he satisfies C & E, or on appeal a tribunal, that there is 'reasonable excuse' for the conduct (see 52.8 above); or

(C) if, at a time when he had no reason to believe that C & E were enquiring into his affairs, he furnished them with full information with respect to the inaccuracy concerned.

Additionally, C & E have announced that such a penalty *will not normally be imposed*

(D) unless the net VAT underdeclared or overclaimed exceeds £2,000 in a prescribed accounting period;

(E) during a 'period of grace' from the end of the prescribed accounting period in which the misdeclaration is made to the date for furnishing the VAT return for the following accounting period;

(F) when a misdeclaration has been corrected by a compensating misdeclaration in respect of the same transaction for the following accounting period with no overall loss of VAT; or

(G) where the misdeclaration has been disclosed

- *before C & E begin to make enquiries* (i.e. normally when an appointment is made to visit and inspect the records); or

- *after a visit has been arranged* (unless C & E believe that the errors were discovered earlier and only disclosed because of the proposed visit); or

- *during or after a visit* (unless they believe the disclosure was prompted by an enquiry into the trader's affairs).

In such cases, the disclosure will be treated as a voluntary disclosure, see 57.11 RECORDS. (C & E Leaflet 700/45/93, para 2).

See 52.20 below for mitigation of penalties.

Local authorities and similar bodies. The provisions above and in 52.11 below apply to LOCAL AUTHORITIES AND STATUTORY BODIES (43). Any reference to VAT credit is to be taken to include a reference to a refund under *VATA 1994, s 33* and any reference to a credit for input tax to include a reference to VAT chargeable on supplies, acquisitions from other EC countries or importations which were not for the purpose of any business carried on by the body.

[*VATA 1994, ss 63, 71(2), 13 Sch 15*]. See also C & E Leaflet 700/42/93.

De Voil Indirect Tax Service. See V5.343; V5.345.

52.11   Repeated misdeclarations

A person is liable to a repeated misdeclaration penalty where the following circumstances apply.

(i) He makes a 'material inaccuracy' in respect of any prescribed accounting period. Subject to below, a 'material inaccuracy' arises where a return is made which understates liability to VAT or overstates entitlement to a repayment of VAT credits and the 'VAT which would have been lost' for that period if the inaccuracy had not been discovered equals or exceeds whichever is the lesser of £500,000 and 10% of the 'gross amount of VAT' for that period. See 52.10 above for the meaning of 'VAT which would have been lost' and 'gross amount of VAT'.

(ii) C & E serve a penalty liability notice on the person concerned before the end of the five consecutive prescribed accounting periods beginning with the period in respect of which there was the material inaccuracy.

(iii) The penalty liability notice specifies a penalty period of eight consecutive prescribed accounting periods beginning with the period in which the date of the notice falls.

(iv) He makes at least two further material inaccuracies in prescribed accounting periods within the penalty period.

No liability arises in respect of the first further material inaccuracy under (iv) above but for the second and any subsequent material inaccuracy the person concerned is liable to a penalty of 15% of the VAT which would have been lost for that prescribed accounting period if the inaccuracy had not been discovered.

The penalty is not imposed where the misdeclaration has been voluntarily disclosed as under 52.10(G) above.

An inaccuracy is not regarded as material in the following circumstances.

(*a*) The person concerned satisfies C & E, or on appeal a tribunal, that there is a reasonable excuse for the inaccuracy (see 52.8 above).

(*b*) At a time when he had no reason to believe that C & E were enquiring into his affairs, he furnished them with full information with respect to the inaccuracy.

(*c*) By reason of conduct falling within (i) above, the person is convicted of an offence or assessed to a penalty under 52.9 or 52.10 above in respect of that inaccuracy. With effect from 29 April 1996, this, however, does not prevent an inaccuracy resulting in the assessment of a penalty under 52.10 above from being regarded as

- a material inaccuracy in respect of which C & E may serve a penalty liability notice under (ii) above; or

- the first further material inaccuracy under (iv) above.

Where under (*a*)–(*c*) above an inaccuracy is not regarded as material for the purposes of serving a penalty liability notice, any such notice served in respect of that inaccuracy is deemed not to have been served.

[*VATA 1994, s 64, 13 Sch 16; FA 1996, s 36*].

See also 52.20 below for mitigation of civil penalties.

De Voil Indirect Tax Service. See V5.344.

52.12   Failures to notify and unauthorised issue of invoices

Failure to notify. Where a person fails to comply with

52.12 Penalties

(a) *VATA 1994, 1 Sch 5* (duty to notify liability for registration on the basis of supplies in the previous year under 59.3(*a*) REGISTRATION) or *VATA 1994, 1 Sch 6* (duty to notify liability for registration on the basis of supplies in the next 30 days under 59.3(*b*) REGISTRATION),

(b) *VATA 1994, 1 Sch 7* (duty to notify liability for registration on the transfer of a going concern under 59.3(*c*) REGISTRATION),

(c) *VATA 1994, 1 Sch 14(2)(3)* (change in nature of suppliers etc. by a person exempted from registration, see 59.6 REGISTRATION),

(d) *VATA 1994, 2 Sch 3* (duty to notify liability for registration in respect of supplies from other EC countries, see 59.13 REGISTRATION),

(e) *VATA 1994, 3 Sch 3* (duty to notify liability for registration in respect of acquisitions from other EC countries, see 59.20 REGISTRATION),

(f) *VATA 1994, 3 Sch 8(2)* (duty to notify change in nature of supplies by a person exempt from registration in respect of acquisitions from other EC countries, see 59.22 REGISTRATION), or

(g) regulations under *VATA 1994, 11 Sch 2(4)* (notification of acquisition of excise duty goods or new means of transport, see 23.9 and 23.35 EUROPEAN COMMUNITY: SINGLE MARKET respectively)

he is, subject to below, liable to a penalty of the greater of £50 and

- 5% of the 'relevant VAT' where C & E are notified or become aware of the failure no more than nine months late (three months late where (*g*) above applies);

- 10% of the relevant VAT where notification etc. is over nine months late but not more than 18 months late (over three months but no more than six months where (*g*) above applies); and

- 15% of the relevant VAT in any other case.

Where supplementary assessments are raised, any penalty is calculated at the percentage rate in force at the time of the original assessment (if different).

'*Relevant VAT*' is

(i) subject to below, where (*a*), (*d*) or (*e*) above applies, the VAT for which the person would be liable for the period beginning on the date he was required to be registered and ending on the date on which C & E received notification, or otherwise became fully aware, of his liability to be registered;

(ii) subject to below, where (*b*) above applies, the VAT for which the person would be liable for the period beginning on the date he was required to be registered (or, if later 1 January 1996) and ending on the date on which C & E received notification, or otherwise became fully aware, of his liability to be registered;

(iii) where (*c*) or (*f*) above applies, the VAT for which the person would be liable for the period beginning on the date on which the change in the nature of the supplies, etc. occurred and ending on the date on which C & E received notification, or otherwise became fully aware, of that change; and

(iv) where (*g*) above applies, the VAT on the acquisition to which the failure relates.

Where the relevant VAT under (i) or (ii) above includes VAT on the acquisition of goods from another EC country and C & E are satisfied that VAT has been paid under the law of another EC country on the supply in question (either to a supplier or directly to the fiscal authority), an allowance is to be made for the VAT so paid (not exceeding the amount of the VAT due).

A person is not liable to a penalty under these provisions where by reason of conduct falling within (*a*)–(*g*) above, he is convicted of an offence or assessed to a penalty under 52.9 above. Conduct falling within the provisions does not give rise to a penalty if the person concerned satisfies C & E, or on appeal a tribunal, that there is a 'reasonable excuse' for his conduct. See 52.8 above for '*reasonable excuse*'. See also 52.20 for mitigation.

Unauthorised issue of invoices. Where an 'unauthorised person' issues one or more invoices showing an amount as being, or including, VAT he is, subject to below, liable to a penalty of the greater of £50 and a percentage of the 'relevant VAT' as follows.

Penalty assessed	*% of relevant VAT*
Before 1.1.95	30%
1.1.95 onwards	15%

Where supplementary assessments are raised, any penalty is calculated at the percentage rate in force at the time of the original assessment.

'*Relevant VAT*' is the amount which is, or is the aggregate of, the amounts which are

- shown on the invoice or invoices as VAT; or

- to be taken as representing VAT.

'*Unauthorised person*' means anyone other than

- a person registered for VAT; or

- a body corporate within a group registration; or

- a person treated as carrying on the business of a taxable person who has died or become bankrupt or incapacitated; or

- a person selling business assets of a taxable person towards satisfaction of a debt owed by that taxable person (e.g. sale of assets seized by a bailiff); or

- a person acting on behalf of the Crown.

It also includes any person who issues an invoice showing a fixed flat rate compensation percentage under the special scheme for farmers when not authorised to do so (see 63.15 SPECIAL SCHEMES).

A person is not liable to a penalty under these provisions where by reason of his conduct, he is convicted of an offence or assessed to a penalty under 52.9 above. Conduct falling within the provisions does not give rise to a penalty if the person concerned satisfies C & E, or on appeal a tribunal, that there is a 'reasonable excuse' for his conduct. See 52.8 above for '*reasonable excuse*'. See also 52.20 below for mitigation.

[*VATA 1994, s 67; FA 1995, s 32; FA 1996, s 37*].

C & E will notify liability to a penalty under these provisions on Form VAT 291. (C & E Notice 700/41/95, para 9).

De Voil Indirect Tax Service. See V5.347–350.

52.13   **Breaches of walking possession agreements**

The following provisions apply where distress is authorised to be levied on the goods and chattels of a person in default who has refused or neglected to pay any VAT due (or any amount recoverable as if it were VAT due) and the person levying the distress and the person in default have entered into a 'walking possession agreement'. See 17.3 CUSTOMS AND EXCISE: POWERS for levying of distress.

52.14 Penalties

If the person in default breaches the undertakings contained in that agreement, he is liable to a penalty equal to half of the VAT due or amount recoverable unless he satisfies C & E, or on appeal a tribunal, that there is a 'reasonable excuse' for the breach in question. See 52.8 above for *'reasonable excuse'*.

'Walking possession agreement' is an agreement under which the property distrained is allowed to remain in the possession of the person in default and its sale delayed in return for

- an acknowledgement that the property is under distraint, and

- an undertaking not to remove or allow removal of the property from the premises named in the agreement without the consent of C & E and subject to such conditions as they impose.

These provisions do not apply in Scotland.

[*VATA 1994, s 68; FA 1997, s 53(7)*].

De Voil Indirect Tax Service. See V5.351.

52.14 **Breaches of regulatory provisions**

Penalties are payable under the circumstances in (*a*) and (*b*) below but if the person in default is, by reason of his conduct within those circumstances, convicted of an offence or assessed for a penalty under 52.9 or 52.10 above or a surcharge under 52.15 or 52.16 below, he is not also liable to a penalty under these provisions. Additionally, no liability to a penalty arises under the following provisions if the person concerned satisfies C & E, or on appeal a tribunal, that there is a 'reasonable excuse' for the failure. See 52.8 above for *'reasonable excuse'*.

(*a*) If any person fails to comply with a requirement to preserve records under *VATA 1994, 11 Sch 6(3)* (see 57.3 RECORDS) he is liable to a penalty of £500.

(*b*) A person is liable to a penalty where he fails to comply with any requirement imposed under

- (i) *VATA 1994, 1 Sch 11* or *12* (notification of end of liability or entitlement to be registered, see 59.9 REGISTRATION);

- (ii) *VATA 1994, 2 Sch 5* (notification of matters affecting the continuation of registration in respect of supplies from other EC countries, see 59.16 REGISTRATION);

- (iii) *VATA 1994, 3 Sch 5* (notification of matters affecting the continuation of registration in respect of acquisitions from other EC countries, see 59.24 REGISTRATION);

- (iv) any regulations made under *VATA 1994, s 48* requiring a VAT representative, for the purposes of registration, to notify C & E that his appointment has taken effect or ceased to have effect, see 4.11 AGENTS ;

- (v) *VATA 1994, 11 Sch 6(1)* (duty to keep records, see 57.1 RECORDS);

- (vi) *VATA 1994, 11 Sch 7* (furnishing of information and production of documents, see 17.5 CUSTOMS AND EXCISE: POWERS);

- (vii) any regulations or rules made under that *Act* (other than procedural rules for tribunals);

- (viii) any Treasury order made under that *Act* ;

(ix) any regulations made under the *European Communities Act 1972* and relating to VAT; or

(x) *VATA 1994, s 18A* (conditions imposed by C & E in connection with fiscal warehousing, see 70.12 WAREHOUSED GOODS AND FREE ZONES).

No penalty can be assessed under (v) to (ix) above unless, within the two years preceding the assessment, C & E have issued a written warning of the consequences of a continuing failure to comply with the requirements.

The daily rate of penalty is £5 if there has been no previous occasion in the two-year period preceding the beginning of the failure in question on which the person concerned has failed to comply with that requirement. If there has been one such occasion in that period, the daily rate is £10 and in any other case, the daily rate is £15. The maximum penalty payable is 100 days at the appropriate rate and the minimum penalty is £50.

Where a person's failure to comply with any VAT regulation consists of not paying VAT or failing to make a return in the required time, for the daily penalties above, there is substituted, if greater, a daily penalty of 1/6th, 1/3rd or 1/2 of one per cent of the 'VAT due' in respect of that period. '*VAT due*' is, if a return has been furnished, the amount shown on the return; otherwise, it is the amount assessed by C & E.

For the purposes of calculating the penalty

• a failure is disregarded if, as a result, the person becomes liable to a surcharge under 52.15 or 52.16 below;

• a continuing failure is regarded as one occasion of failure occurring on the date on which it began;

• if the same omission gives rise to a failure to comply with more than one such requirement, it is regarded as the occasion of only one failure;

• if the failure is to comply with the requirements concerning furnishing of returns or payment of VAT, a previous failure to comply with either requirement is regarded as a failure to comply with the requirement in question; and

• any earlier failure is disregarded where C & E, or on appeal a tribunal, have been satisfied that there is a 'reasonable excuse' for the failure. See 52.8 above for '*reasonable excuse*'.

Where C & E issue a notice of assessment specifying a date (not later than the date of the notice) to which the penalty is calculated, if the person liable pays the penalty within the period notified by C & E in the assessment, then the penalty is treated as paid on the specified date (and no further penalty accrues after that date). If the penalty is not paid within the notified period, a further assessment may be made to recover additional penalties.

The Treasury may, by statutory instrument, adjust any of the monetary sums above but not so as to apply to a failure which began before the date on which the order comes into force.

[*VATA 1994, ss 69, 76(2)(7)(8); FA 1996, s 35(6), 3 Sch 9*].

De Voil Indirect Tax Service. See V5.352–354.

52.15   **Default surcharge**

Unless the provisions in 52.16 below apply, if, by the last day on which a taxable person is required to 'furnish' a return for a prescribed accounting period, C & E have not 'received' that return (or have received the return but not the amount of VAT shown on the return as payable) the taxable person is in default for the purposes of these provisions. See below for the interpretation of *'furnish'* and *'received'*.

Subject to below, a taxable person is liable to a surcharge under these provisions where

(*a*) he is in default in respect of a prescribed accounting period;

(*b*) C & E serve on him either

- a *surcharge liability notice* specifying a surcharge period from the date of the notice to the first anniversary of the last day of the prescribed accounting period under (*a*) above; or

- where that last day occurs during an existing surcharge period, a *surcharge liability notice extension* extending the existing surcharge period to the first anniversary of the last day of the prescribed accounting period under (*a*) above;

(*c*) he is again in default in respect of another prescribed accounting period which ends within the surcharge period specified in (or extended by) that notice; and

(*d*) he has 'outstanding VAT' for the prescribed accounting period in (*c*). (There is, therefore, no *liability* to surcharge if a nil or repayment return is submitted late or the VAT due is paid on time but the return is submitted late. C & E will, however, record the default and issue a surcharge liability extension notice.)

The surcharge is the greater of £30 and the 'specified percentage' of his outstanding VAT for the prescribed accounting period under (*d*) above.

The 'specified percentage' is determined by reference to the number of prescribed accounting periods in respect of which he is in default in the surcharge period and for which he has outstanding VAT.

	Specified percentage
In relation to the first such period	2%
In relation to the second such period	5%
In relation to the third such period	10%
In relation to each such period after the third	15%

A person has *'outstanding VAT'* for a prescribed accounting period if some or all of the VAT due for that period has not been paid by the last day on which he is required to make a return for that period.

Where a liability to surcharge is established, C & E will not issue a surcharge assessment at the 2% or 5% rates for an amount of less than £200. In these circumstances a default will be recorded, a surcharge liability extension notice will be issued, and the rate of surcharge will increase if there are any further defaults in the surcharge period. (C & E Notice 700, para 9.6(c)).

A person is not liable to a surcharge and not to be treated as having been in default in respect of the prescribed accounting period in question if he satisfies C & E, or on appeal a tribunal, that in the case of a default which is 'material to the surcharge' either of the following applies.

(i) The return or, as the case may be, the VAT shown on it, was despatched at such time and in such manner that it was reasonable to expect that it would be received by C & E within the appropriate time limit. The despatch of a cheque within reasonable time cannot be equated with the despatch of the VAT where the cheque proves to be worthless (*C & E Commrs v Palco Industry Co Ltd QB, [1990] STC 594*). See also below under the heading *Meaning of 'furnish' and 'received'*.

(ii) There is a 'reasonable excuse' for the return or VAT not having been despatched. See 52.8 above for '*reasonable excuse*'.

A default is '*material to the surcharge*' if it is *either* the default which gave rise to the surcharge *or* is a default taken into account in the service of the surcharge liability notice upon which the surcharge depends and the person concerned has not been previously liable to a surcharge in respect of a prescribed accounting period ending within the surcharge period specified in, or extended by, the notice.

Where a person is treated as not having been in default under (i) or (ii) above, any surcharge liability notice the service of which depended on that default is deemed not to have been served.

A default is also to be left out of account for the above purposes if the conduct giving rise to the default falls within 52.14(*b*) above and the person is assessed to a penalty under those provisions.

[*VATA 1994, s 59, 13 Sch 14; FA 1996, s 35(4)*].

Surcharge liability notices. For non-receipt of a surcharge liability notice, see *C & E Commrs v Medway Draughting & Technical Services Ltd; C & E Commrs v Adplates Offset Ltd QB, [1989] STC 346*. Where a surcharge liability notice has not been received, subsequent extension notices are not effective as valid surcharge liability notices as they only specify the end of the surcharge period and not the date on which it began; any surcharge assessments must therefore be discharged (*Dow Engineering (5771)*). A surcharge liability notice which incorrectly stated that a return had not been received (when it had been received late) has been held to be invalid (*Coleman Machines Ltd (3196)*).

Appeals. A person who thinks he has grounds for appeal against a default surcharge should write to his VAT office within 30 days of the date of issue of the *surcharge liability notice extension* and ask them to reconsider the case. The VAT office will either confirm the original decision and give 21 days in which to lodge an appeal with a VAT tribunal or send a revised decision and give 30 days in which to lodge such an appeal. Alternatively a person can appeal directly to a VAT tribunal without contacting the VAT office in which case he must do so within 30 days of the issue of the *surcharge liability notice extension*. A VAT tribunal cannot hear an appeal until a surcharge liability notice extension has been issued (see *Expert Systems Design Ltd (7974)*). At this stage an appeal can be made against any or all of the defaults which led to the person becoming liable to the surcharge. This is the only time that the VAT tribunal can be asked to hear an appeal against these defaults. If the person later becomes liable to a further surcharge because he has defaulted again, he will be outside the time limit for appealing against the earlier defaults. It is not necessary to pay the surcharge before appealing to a VAT tribunal but all outstanding returns and VAT must be paid.

Meaning of 'furnish' and 'received'. 'Furnish' means putting the return into the possession of C & E. The current VAT return states 'You could be liable to a financial penalty if your completed return and all the VAT payable are not received by the due date'. Given this, and the use of the word 'received', a clear distinction should be drawn for those purposes between 'received' and 'despatched'. 'Received' should be taken to mean actual receipt by C & E. Earlier decisions (see *Aikman v White CS 1985, [1986] STC 1* and *Hayman v Griffiths and Another; Walker v Hanby QB, [1987] STC 649*), that C & E adopted the Post Office as their agents by requesting the use of prepaid envelopes and that a return is furnished when complete and posted, should no longer therefore be relied upon for these purposes (*C & E Commrs v W Timms & Son (Builders) Ltd QB, [1992] STC 374*). C & E have indicated that a return will be accepted as posted on time if posted at least one working day before the due date (assuming it has been sent in the official envelope or by first class post). (STI 1991, p 389). Despite this apparent assurance, tribunals have continued to uphold default surcharge assessments in such circumstances. C & E have also indicated that where the due date falls on a weekend or bank holiday, the return and the VAT due will be accepted as received in time if received on the next following working day. See, however, *La Reine (Limoges Porcelain) Ltd (10468)* where the tribunal held that a return due on a Sunday and posted at 7 p.m. on the previous Friday had not been posted early enough that it was reasonable to expect that it would be received by C & E on or before the Sunday. This decision was not followed, and was implicitly disapproved of, in *Halstead Motor Company, [1995] VATDR 201 (13373)*.

De Voil Indirect Tax Service. See V5.371–380.

52.16   *Default surcharge: payments on account*

The following provisions apply in relation to prescribed accounting periods ending on or after 1 June 1996 but disregarding any payments on account due before that date.

A taxable person is in default in respect of any prescribed accounting period for which he is required to make payments on account (see 51.4 PAYMENT OF VAT) IF

(i) C & E have not received in full any payment on account by the due date; or

(ii) he would be in default in respect of that period under 52.15 above (but for the fact that periods in respect of which payments on account are required are specifically excluded from those provisions).

Subject to below, a taxable person is liable to a surcharge under these provisions where

(a) he is in default in respect of a prescribed accounting period;

(b) C & E serve on him either

- a *surcharge liability notice* specifying a surcharge period from the date of the notice to the first anniversary of the last day of the prescribed accounting period under *(a)* above; or

- where that last day occurs during an existing surcharge period, a *surcharge liability notice extension* extending the existing surcharge period to the first anniversary of the last day of the prescribed accounting period under *(a)* above;

(c) he is again in default in respect of another prescribed accounting period which ends within the surcharge period specified in (or extended by) that notice; and

(d) the 'aggregate value of defaults' for that prescribed accounting period is more than nil. The *'aggregate value of defaults'* is the total value of

- any payment or payments on account (or part payment or payments) not received by C & E by the due date for such payments; and

- any outstanding VAT due for the period not paid by the last day on which he is required to make a return for that period (less the amount of unpaid payments on account).

The surcharge is the greater of £30 and the 'specified percentage' of the aggregate value of defaults for the prescribed accounting period under *(d)* above.

The *'specified percentage'* is determined by reference to the number of prescribed accounting periods in respect of which he is in default in the surcharge period and for which the value of his defaults is more than nil.

	Specified percentage
In relation to the first such period	2%
In relation to the second such period	5%
In relation to the third such period	10%
In relation to each such period after the third	15%

A person is not liable to a surcharge and not to be treated as having been in default in respect of the prescribed accounting period in question if he satisfies C & E, or on appeal a tribunal, that in the case of a default which is 'material to the surcharge' either of the following applies.

(A)   The payment on account (where (i) above applies) or the return or VAT shown on it (where (ii) above applies) was despatched at such time and in such manner that it was reasonable to expect that it would be received by C & E by the due date.

A payment on account is not to be taken as received by the due date unless, by the last day for payment, all the transactions can be completed that need to be completed before the whole of the payment becomes available to C & E.

The despatch of a cheque within reasonable time cannot be equated with the despatch of the VAT where the cheque proves to be worthless (*C & E Commrs v Palco Industry Co Ltd QB, [1990] STC 594*). See also 52.15 above under the heading *Meaning of 'furnish' and 'received'*.

(B)   There is a 'reasonable excuse' for the payment on account (where (i) above applies) or the return or VAT (where (ii) above applies) not having been despatched. See 52.8 above for '*reasonable excuse*'.

A default is '*material to the surcharge*' if it is either the default which gave rise to the surcharge or is a default taken into account in the service of the surcharge liability notice upon which the surcharge depends and the person concerned has not been previously liable to a surcharge in respect of a prescribed accounting period ending within the surcharge period specified in, or extended by, the notice.

Where a person is treated as not having been in default under (A) or (B) above, any surcharge liability notice the service of which depended on that default is deemed not to have been served.

A default is also to be left out of account for the above purposes if the conduct giving rise to the default falls within 52.14(*b*) above and the person is assessed to a penalty under those provisions.

[*VATA 1994, s 59A; FA 1996, s 35(2)*].

See *VATA 1994, s 59B* for deeming provisions where a prescribed accounting period in respect of which payments on account are required ends within a surcharge period begun or extended by the service of a surcharge liability notice under 52.15 above; and a prescribed accounting period for which payments on account are not required ends within a surcharge period begun or extended by the service of a surcharge liability notice under the above provisions.

See also 52.15 above under the headings *Surcharge liability notices* and *Appeals*, which provisions also apply to default surcharges in relation to payments on account.

52.17   **Incorrect certificates as to zero-rating**

Where a person

(*a*)   gives a supplier a certificate that the supply or supplies fall, or will fall, wholly or partly within *VATA 1994, 8 Sch Group 5 or 6* or *VATA 1994, 9 Sch Group 1* (see 42.51 LAND AND BUILDINGS), (*b*)   gives a supplier a certificate mentioned in *FA 1989, 3 Sch 13* that the supply or supplies falls within the transitional rules relating to land and buildings at 1 April 1989, or

(*c*)   prepares or gives a certificate in connection with fiscal warehousing as required by *VATA 1994, s 18B* or *s 18C* (see 70.15 and 70.19 WAREHOUSED GOODS AND FREE ZONES respectively)

and the certificate is incorrect, the person giving or preparing the certificate is liable to a penalty equal to the difference between the VAT which should have been charged and the VAT actually charged.

A person is not liable to a penalty under these provisions if

(i)   he satisfies C & E or, on appeal, a VAT tribunal, that there is reasonable excuse for his having given or prepared the certificate; or

(ii)   by reason of his having given or prepared it, he is convicted of an offence.

[*VATA 1994, s 62; FA 1996, 3 Sch 8*].

De Voil Indirect Tax Service. See V5.342.

52.18   Inaccuracies in EC sales lists (ESLs)

Where

(*a*)   a person has submitted an ESL (see 2.19 ACCOUNTING PERIODS AND RETURNS) containing a 'material inaccuracy' to C & E;

(*b*)   within six months of discovering that inaccuracy, C & E have issued him with a written warning identifying the statement and stating that future inaccuracies might result in the service of a notice under these provisions;

(*c*)   the person submits a second ESL containing a material inaccuracy to C & E and the 'submission date' is within the period of two years beginning with the day after the warning was issued;

(*d*)   C & E have, within six months of discovering the second inaccuracy served on him a notice identifying the ESL and stating that future inaccuracies will attract a penalty under these provisions; and

(*e*)   the person submits yet another ESL containing a material inaccuracy to C & E the submission date of which is not more than two years after

•   he service of the notice under (*d*) above; or

•   the date on which any previous ESL attracting a penalty was submitted,

that person is liable to a penalty of £100 in respect of the statement under (*e*) above.

An ESL contains a '*material inaccuracy*' if, having regard to the matters to be included, the inclusion or omission of any information is misleading in any material respect.

'*Submission date*' means the last date for submission of the ESL or the day on which it was actually submitted, whichever is the earlier.

An inaccuracy is not regarded as material for these purposes if

(i)   the person submitting the ESL satisfies C & E, or on appeal a VAT tribunal, that there is a 'reasonable excuse' for the inaccuracy (see 52.8 above);

(ii)   at a time when he had no reason to believe that C & E were enquiring into his affairs, he furnished them with full information with respect to the inaccuracy; or

(iii)   he is convicted of an offence by reason of the submission of the ESL containing the material inaccuracy.

Where the only ESL identified in a warning under (*b*) above or a notice under (*d*) above is one which is regarded as containing no material inaccuracies (whether by virtue of (i) to (iii) above or otherwise) that warning or notice is deemed not to have been issued or served.

[*VATA 1994, s 65*].

De Voil Indirect Tax Service. See V5.346.

52.19   **Failure to submit EC sales lists (ESLs)**

If by the last day on which a person is required to submit an ESL (see 2.19 ACCOUNTING PERIODS AND RETURNS) for any period, C & E has not received the statement, that person is regarded for the purposes of these provisions as being in default in relation to that statement until such time as it is delivered.

Where any person is in default in respect of any ESL, C & E may serve a notice on him stating that he is in default but that no action will be taken if the default is remedied within 14 days of the notice, otherwise he will become liable to a penalty as calculated below. The notice may also state that the person will become liable, without further notice, to penalties if he commits any more defaults before a period of twelve months has elapsed without his being in default.

Where such a notice is served, the person will become liable

(*a*)   in respect of the ESL to which the notice relates to a penalty of the greater of £50 *or* £5 for each day the default continues after the 14 day period (up to a maximum of 100 days); and

(*b*)   in respect of any other ESL in relation to which he is in default, the last day for submission of which is after the service and before the expiry of the notice, to a penalty of the greater of £50 *or*, as the case may be, £5, £10 or £15 for each day the default continues up to a maximum of 100 days. The daily fine is £5, £10 or £15 depending upon whether the ESL in question is the first, second, or third or subsequent ESL (including, where applicable, the ESL within (*a*) above) in respect of which the person has become liable to a penalty while the notice is in force.

For the purposes of (*b*) above, the notice continues in force for twelve months from the date of service but, where at any time in that twelve month period the person defaults in submitting an ESL other than one in relation to which he was in default when the notice was served, the notice continues until a period of twelve months has elapsed without that person becoming liable to a penalty under these provisions in respect of any ESL.

A person is not treated as being in default in relation to an ESL under these provisions if he satisfies C & E, or on appeal a tribunal, that

●   the ESL has been submitted at such time and in such manner that it was reasonable to expect that it would be received by C & E within the appropriate time limit; or

●   there is a 'reasonable excuse' for the ESL not having been dispatched (see 52.8 above).

In such a case, he is not liable to a penalty in respect of that ESL and any notice served on him exclusively in relation to the failure to submit that ESL has no effect for the purposes of these provisions.

[*VATA 1994, s 66*].

De Voil Indirect Tax Service. See V5.355.

52.20 Penalties

MITIGATION OF CIVIL PENALTIES

Mitigation by C & E. In relation to penalties assessed under 52.9 to 52.12 above, C & E may reduce the penalty to such amount (including nil) as they think proper but, in doing so, must not take into account

- insufficiency of funds available to any person to pay VAT due or the penalty;

- the fact that there has been no significant loss of VAT; or

- the fact that the person liable to the penalty or a person acting on his behalf has acted in good faith.

C & E have no powers to mitigate a penalty under 52.13 to 52.19 above.

See 52.9 above for C & E's policy with regard to mitigation of VAT evasion penalties.

Mitigation by a tribunal. An appeal may be made to a tribunal against any liability to a penalty or surcharge under 52.9 to 52.19 above or the amount of any such penalty or surcharge in an assessment. See 5.3(*n*)(*q*) APPEALS. The tribunal has similar powers of mitigation as C & E above. In addition, where a penalty has been mitigated by C & E, a VAT tribunal may, on an appeal relating to the penalty, cancel the reduction in whole or in part.

Subject to the above, a tribunal may not vary the amount assessed by way of penalty or surcharge other than to reduce it to the amount which is appropriate under the relevant provisions.

[VATA 1994, ss 70, 84(6), 13 Sch 17].

De Voil Indirect Tax Service. See V5.334.

53   Pension Schemes

De Voil Indirect Tax Service. See V6.169–172A.

53.1   FUNDED PENSION SCHEMES

A funded pension scheme is a pension scheme in which the employers' and employees' contributions are vested in separate trustees, who may be individuals or corporate bodies. The pension scheme is separate and distinct from the employer's business. The VAT provisions in 53.2 and 53.3 below apply to such schemes but not to

(*a*)   schemes where the employer makes provision for the payment of pensions by a segregated reserve fund in the balance sheet, represented by specific assets;

(*b*)   unfunded pension schemes where the employer simply promises to pay the employee a pension at a certain age but does not set aside funds for this purpose; or

(*c*)   insurance-based schemes where premiums are paid to an insurer to provide a retirement benefit for one or more named employees by way of insurance policies.

The normal VAT rules apply to schemes within (*a*)-(*c*) above.

(C & E Notice 700/17/96, para 2).

53.2   Employers

Input tax deductible. The *management* of a pension fund for own employees (but not normally the business activities of the pension fund) is part of an employer's business. A VAT-registered employer can therefore deduct input tax incurred in setting up the fund and on its day-to-day management. This applies even where the responsibility for the general management of the scheme rests with the trustees or the trustees pay for the services provided. C & E give the following examples of expenses on which input tax may be reclaimed.

- Making of arrangements for setting up the pension fund

- Management of the scheme (i.e. collection of contributions and payment of pensions)

- Advice on a review of the scheme and implementing any changes

- Accountancy and audit services relating to the management of the scheme (e.g. preparation of annual accounts)

- Actuarial valuations of the assets of the fund

- Actuarial advice in connection with the fund's administration

- Providing general statistics in connection with the performance of the fund's investments, properties, etc.

- Legal instructions and general legal advice including drafting of Trust deeds insofar as they relate to the management of the scheme

To claim input tax, the employer must hold a VAT invoice made out in his name. Where the supplies are paid for by the trustees on behalf of the employer, the employer should arrange for the invoice to be issued in his name.

Input tax not deductible. Except where the employer is the sole trustee of his pension scheme (see below), the pension fund itself is not part of the employer's business. Any VAT incurred on supplies relating to the *business* activities carried on by the trustees (e.g. making investments, acquiring property and collecting rents) is not input tax of the employer even if he pays for such expenses. C & E give the following examples of services on which employers cannot claim input tax.

- Advice in connection with making investments

- Brokerage charges

- Rent and service charge collection for property holdings

- Producing records and accounts in connection with property purchases, lettings and disposals, investments, etc.

- Trustees services (i.e. services of a profession trustee in managing the assets of the fund)

- Legal fees paid on behalf of representative beneficiaries in connection with changes in pension fund arrangements

- Custodian charges

For cases concerning the recoverability of input tax by employers, see *Linotype & Machinery Ltd, [1978] VATTR 123 (594), Manchester Ship Canal Co v C & E Commrs QB, [1982] STC 351* and *Ultimate Advisory Services Ltd (9523)*.

Sole trustees. Where an employer is the sole trustee of a pension fund for his own employees, the business and trustees activities are indivisible for VAT purposes. The employer is entitled to treat all input tax incurred on supplies received in connection with the fund as input tax. See *C & E Commrs v British Railways Board (No 1) CA, [1976] STC 359*. However, if either the business or the pension fund makes exempt supplies, the amount of input tax deductible may be restricted. See 49 PARTIAL EXEMPTION.

Management of the pension scheme.

(a) *Services performed by the employer*. Where an employer uses own staff to manage the pension fund and these services are provided free of charge, there is no supply for VAT purposes. See *National Coal Board v C & E Commrs QB, [1982] STC 863*. The employer's entitlement to claim input tax on office overhead expenses is not affected.

If an employer is reimbursed by the trustees (or specifically charges them) for costs incurred in managing the pension scheme and the services fall within those on which input tax is deductible (see above), there is no need to account for output tax on the supply to the trustees. However, if such arrangements apply to services for investment advice or other services connected with the pension fund's own business activities, the employer is making a taxable supply to the trustees and must account for output tax.

(b) *Services performed by third parties*. Where a third party (e.g. a fund manager, property manager or professional trustee) is used to manage a pension scheme and their charges cover both general management (input tax deductible) and investment services (input tax non-deductible) the input tax must be apportioned. Normally this apportionment will be made by the supplier. If, however, the supplier only issues one invoice for a composite supply, 30% of the input tax shown may be treated as deductible unless the employer provides a detailed breakdown to support a different figure.

Pensions provided for employees of more than one company. Where a pension fund covers pension arrangements for employees of several companies which are not in the same VAT group registration, each employer may treat as input tax only that proportion of VAT incurred on the management of the fund that is attributable to his own business. Where the person supplying the services to the fund issues a single invoice, one of the participating employers (or, in the case of entirely separate employers, the trustees) may act in the capacity of paymaster and claim all the VAT incurred for the eligible services, issuing a VAT invoice to each of the other employers for their share of the costs and VAT thereon. The other employers can then treat that VAT as their input tax.

Cessation of business by employer. If an employer ceases business, the trustees of any continuing pension scheme who are VAT-registered may treat VAT incurred on services connected with the management of the scheme as their input tax (subject to the normal rules). If this situation arises, the trustees should inform their VAT office.

(C & E Notice 700/17/96, paras 5–11).

53.3   **Trustees**

Where the trustees of a pension fund make taxable supplies, they may be required to register for VAT. See 59 REGISTRATION for details. If registered, the trustees can treat VAT on goods and services used for the purposes of their business activities as input tax. However, except where the employer has ceased to be in business (see 53.2 above) VAT on supplies for the purposes of the management of the pension scheme is not input tax since these supplies are regarded as the responsibility of the employer. Recovery of input tax may also be restricted under the PARTIAL EXEMPTION (49) rules.

Corporate trustee in a VAT group registration. Where the sole trustee of a pension fund is a corporate body, it may be possible for that trustee to form part of a VAT group registration with the employer. See 31.2 and 31.3 GROUPS OF COMPANIES for eligibility and application for group treatment. If a corporate trustee becomes such a member, the representative member of the group is entitled to treat the VAT incurred on supplies to the trustee as input tax. Subject to the normal rules, this means that the representative member can deduct as input tax VAT incurred on both the *management* and *business* activities of the pension fund. See *BOC International Ltd, [1982] VATTR 84 (1248).*

Where the fund provides pensions for employees of companies outside the VAT group registration, any VAT incurred in respect of the *management* of the scheme for those companies is not for the purposes of the representative member's business and not allowable. VAT must therefore be apportioned between that attributable to employees within the VAT group (allowable) and outside the group (non-allowable). Alternatively, the representative member may elect to use the paymaster arrangements. See 53.2 above under *Pensions provided for employees of more than one company.*

All members of a group registration are jointly and severally liable for VAT due from the representative member and in the event of that member being unable to meet the VAT debt of the group, as a general rule each member will be liable for the amount of the debt arising during the period that it was a member of the group. However, where corporate trustees are included in a group registration, C & E have been advised that this liability does not extend to the assets of any trust (e.g. a pension fund) of which the corporate trustee is the trustee, except to the extent that the group VAT debt is attributable in whole or part to the administration of the trust.

Any supplies made by the corporate trustee in a VAT group (including dealing in the assets of the fund) are treated as made by the representative member. Therefore any exempt supplies made must be taken into account in the partial exemption position of the VAT group.

Fund managers, property managers, professional trustees, etc. may provide

- supplies to the employer in connection with the management of the scheme;
- supplies to the pension fund in connection with its business activities; and
- supplies in a fiduciary capacity (e.g. disposing of the fund's assets).

It is important to distinguish between the various kinds of services supplied so that separate VAT invoices can be issued to the employer and the trustees for input tax recovery purposes. If services cannot be segregated, C & E are prepared to allow the total value of services to be divided in the ratio of 30% to the employer and 70% to the trustees. Any other apportionment will only be agreed to by C & E if detailed information in support of the split is provided.

(C & E Notice 700/77/96, paras 12-17).

53.4   LOCAL AUTHORITY PENSION FUNDS

Unlike other employers, local authorities may be prevented by legislation from setting up a separate Trust to administer their pension fund. Local authority pension funds are usually therefore similar to sole trustee schemes (see 53.2 above). The assets of the fund are vested in the authority and the funds' activities cannot be separated from the other activities of the authority. Consequently any exempt input tax incurred, such as that relating to investments, would normally have to be included when the authority calculates whether it has exceeded the 5% *de minimis* limit above which it loses all its exempt input tax. See 43.5 LOCAL AUTHORITIES AND STATUTORY BODIES.

Administration expenses. Recovery of these expenses by local authorities should be broadly in line with that of other pension scheme providers.

- If the authority administers the scheme free of charge, then this is a non-business activity of the authority and it may recover the *VATA 1994, s 33*.

- If the scheme includes employees of other local authorities (scheduled bodies) who are obliged to remain within the scheme, any charge for the administration to those other authorities is a non-business activity of the authority. The VAT incurred is recoverable under *VATA 1994, s 33*.

- If the scheme includes employees of non-authority bodies (admitted bodies) for whom it is not obliged to provide a pension scheme, any charge for the administration of the scheme is a business activity of the authority and is standard-rated. If no charge is made but the level of contribution is adjusted to reflect a charge, this is viewed as consideration for the supply of administration services.

Investment expenses. C & E's general view is that the investment activities undertaken by pension funds are carried out in the course or furtherance of a business (although they will consider representations from any local authority which believes that it can demonstrate that it has some non-business investment activities). Most of the VAT incurred on these investment activities is exempt input tax. If the authority remains within its *de minimis* limit it can recover this VAT. However, if the level of exempt input tax incurred pushes the authority over its *de minimis* limit it loses *all* its exempt input tax.

Administrative concession. By concession, with effect from the year commencing 1 April 1998 (C & E will consider requests for the concession to be applied for the year commencing 1 April 1997) when the percentage of exempt input tax is calculated for the purposes of the *VATA 1994, s 33* recovery method, the expenses relating to employees for whom the authority is obliged by law to provide a pension scheme may be excluded from the calculation (from both the numerator and denominator). The following conditions must be satisfied.

(*a*) The local authority must be prevented by legislation from setting up separate trustees for its pension fund.

(*b*) When VAT relating to the expenses of the pension fund is incurred, it must be reclaimed in accordance with the guidance set out above for administration and investment expenses.

(*c*) Prior written agreement must be obtained from the VAT office. The concession will form part of the authority's *Sec 33* recovery method and should be agreed at the same time as the method.

(*d*) VAT relating to those persons for whom the authority is not obliged to provide a pension fund, such as admitted bodies, must be included in the *Sec 33* calculation.

(*e*) All VAT relating to those persons for whom the authority is obliged to provide pensions must be excluded from the *Sec 33* calculation. This includes the VAT incurred in respect of the non-business and taxable activities, whether administration or investment activities.

(*f*) Sufficient records must be kept to enable the pension fund expenses to be easily identified.

(*g*) The concession must operate for at least one year and coincide with a complete tax year.

Any abuse or misapplication of its provisions may result in the withdrawal of the concession in particular cases.

If, having excluded the pension fund expenses under the concession, the authority remains *de minimis*, it will be entitled to recover all its VAT including that relating to the exempt pension fund activities. If, however, the authority exceeds the *de minimis* limit even with these pension fund activities excluded, it will not be entitled to recover the VAT incurred on any of its exempt activities, including that relating to the pension fund. If exempt input tax has been recovered prior to the authority exceeding its *de minimis* levels, the authority will be required to repay this VAT to C & E.

(VAT Information Sheet 6/98, June 1998).

54   Printed Matter, Etc.

Cross-references. See 4.14 AGENTS for printed matter distributed by estate agents.

De Voil Indirect Tax Service. See V4.273.

The contents of this chapter are as follows.

54.1   INTRODUCTION

To determine the liability for any supply involving printed or similar matter, it is helpful to consider the following questions.

(*a*)   *Is a complete item of printed or similar matter being supplied?* If not (or if unsure), consider 54.2 to 54.8 below for guidance on the processes leading to the production of printed matter.

(*b*)   *Is the printed matter being supplied in its own right?* If not (or if unsure), see 54.9 to 54.15 below for printed matter supplied with other services and 54.16 below for printed matter supplied with other goods.

If satisfied that the answers to both of the above questions (*a*) and (*b*) are 'yes', then see 54.17 to 54.28 below for categories of printed matter which can be zero-rated. Other items are normally standard-rated (see 54.29 below).

Certain printed matter can also be imported free of VAT. See 54.30 below.

54.2   PRODUCTION PROCESS OF PRINTED MATTER

Any article of printed matter goes through a production process, beginning with the original idea and ending with a complete article of printed matter. For the purposes of VAT liability, this process may be divided into five stages.

- Preliminary services (see 54.3 below).

- Preparatory work (see 54.4 below).

- The production of goods (see 54.5 below).

- Post-production services (see 54.6 below).

- Alterations (see 54.7 below).

See also 54.8 below where subcontractors are used.

(C & E Manual V1-7, Chapter 3 section 2.2).

54.3   Preliminary services

This stage covers the drawing together of the basic contents of a work which will later become an article of printed matter.

Preliminary services may be supplied in two ways.

- A business may supply an article while it is still at the preliminary service stage (e.g. an author writing and supplying a manuscript or the copy for a pamphlet or leaflet). This supply is always standard-rated. The customer is paying for the thoughts of the author to which any printed matter is incidental.

- A business may be contracted to provide a continuous process, starting with preliminary services and culminating in the issue, on a wide scale, of an article of printed matter (e.g. a contract to research the information for a catalogue, and then arrange the production and printing). In such a case, provided there is no separate supply of the preliminary services, they can be treated as an integral part of the supply of the printed matter.

(C & E Manual V1-7, Chapter 3 section 2.3).

54.4   Preparatory work

Preparatory work includes graphic design, typesetting, printing of large sheets containing several individual pages or leaflets, and cutting, folding and collating such sheets.

Preparatory work may be supplied in two ways.

- If the business has a contract to supply printed matter, preparatory work may be treated as part of the same supply.

- If the business does not supply printed matter, any supply of preparatory work must be standard-rated.

See *AP Carpenter (15253)* (whether a graphic designer was responsible for the production of a brochure) and 54.5 below to establish whether the business has supplied zero-rated goods.

Abortive fees. If work is aborted before printed matter is produced, any 'abortive work fee' charged is standard-rated, as the preparatory work did not result in the production of printed matter.

(C & E Manual V1-7, Chapter 3 section 2.4).

54.5   Production of goods

At some stage in the production process, goods are given the essential characteristics of a zero-rated article of printed matter. This stage will vary according to the article concerned. C & E give the following examples although emphasising that a flexible approach should be adopted.

(a) *Book production* – when sheets are bound into a cover. See also *GUS Catalogue Order Ltd (2958)* where catalogues covered with a temporary cardboard cover were held to be recognisable as books and the remaining work of permanently covering was post-production services (see 54.6 below).

(*b*)   *Loose-leaf book* – when complete set of sheets are hole-punched.

(*c*)   *Pamphlets* – when pages are stapled together or saddle-stitched.

(*d*)   *Leaflets* – when large sheets are cut into single sheets of leaflets.

It is important to identify the stage at which zero-rated goods are produced for the following reasons.

- If a business undertakes this stage of the production process, it may always zero-rate its supply. For example, a business which binds the pages of a book into a cover (even if the pages have been printed, cut and collated elsewhere) has produced a book and may zero-rate its supply.

- If a business has a contract to supply zero-rated printed matter, C & E regard both the preparatory work (see 54.4 above) and any post-production services (see 54.6 below) as part of that supply. Those stages may thus also be zero-rated.

Amendments and self-contained instalments. Both amendments to complete ring-bound books and self-contained instalments of books are normally zero-rated (see 54.18 below). A business responsible for the production stage at which the zero-rated goods are produced can zero-rate its supply.

Part works. The production of 'part works' which do not form a self-contained instalment (see 54.18 below) is treated fundamentally differently. By concession, C & E allow such part works to be zero-rated provided the completed work would itself be zero-rated as a book. However, this concession applies only to retail or mail order sales. A business which produces these part works has not produced goods which are eligible for relief according to a strict interpretation of the law and cannot therefore zero-rate its supply to the retailer or mail order house.

(C & E Manual V1-7, Chapter 3 section 2.5).

Incomplete publications. Component parts of books, journals (e.g. covers, unbound pages, illustrations) in the course of production are standard-rated as they have not been assembled into completed books (*Butler & Tanner Ltd [1974] VATTR 72 (68)*). (C & E Leaflet 701/10/85, para 11).

54.6   Post-production services

Even when goods are already recognisable as zero-rated books, booklets, leaflets, etc, further service may be required (e.g. packing books for delivery, packaging and wrapping loose-leafs for delivery, inserting pamphlets in envelopes, folding and trimming leaflets).

If a business has supplied zero-rated printed matter (see 54.5 above), post-production services may be zero-rated as part of the same supply. Otherwise, any supply of post-production services must be standard-rated.

(C & E Manual V1-7, Chapter 3 section 2.6).

54.7   Alterations

If an article of zero-rated printed matter is produced and then altered at a later stage, such alterations are always standard-rated as they do not produce new zero-rated goods. However, if the goods which result from the alteration are then sold on to a third party, that sale can be zero-rated.

(C & E Manual V1-7, Chapter 3 section 2.8).

54.8   **Use of sub-contractors and general example**

A printer with a contract to the final customer to supply zero-rated printed matter may zero-rate any preparatory work (see 54.4 above) or post-production services (see 54.6 above) charged to the customer, even if sub-contractors have been employed to perform some parts of the production process.

However, a sub-contractor can only zero-rate preparatory or post-production work when these services are supplied in conjunction with zero-rated printed matter.

Example

An author produces a manuscript for a booklet and sells it to a publisher. The publisher agrees to supply 10,000 copies of the booklet to a retailer and employs three separate sub-contractors who

(1)   type-set the manuscript;

(2)   print, cut, collate and stitch together the booklets; and

(3)   package and deliver the booklets.

The supply by the author to the publisher is a standard-rated supply of preliminary services. The services of sub-contractor (1) are standard-rated as preparatory work. The stitching carried out by sub-contractor (2) is a zero-rated supply because it produces zero-rated goods. The printing, cutting and collating can also therefore be zero-rated as they are supplied in conjunction with zero-rated printed matter. The services of sub-contractor (3) are standard-rated as the supply of post-production services in isolation. The whole charge by the publishing house to the retailer can be zero-rated as a supply of booklets.

(C & E Manual V1-7, Chapter 3 section 2.7 and section 5 Table B).

54.9   **PRINTED MATTER SUPPLIED WITH OTHER SERVICES**

Sometimes printed matter may be supplied in conjunction with other services. If so, it is purchased, at least in part, for its value as a service and not for its value as printed matter. If this is the case, zero-rating under 54.17 *et seq.* below may not be available. The following are common situations where printed matter is supplied with other services.

● Individually commissioned items. See 54.10 below.

● Printed matter used to supply discount facilities. See 54.11 below.

● Printed matter supplied in conjunction with correspondence courses. See 54.12 below.

● Printed matter supplied in return for a subscription. See 54.13 below.

● Programmes supplied as part of an admission fee. See 54.14 below.

● Subsidy or vanity publishing. See 54.15 below.

54.10   **Individually commissioned items**

Zero-rating does not apply where the printed matter is made to the order of a particular individual and is no value to anyone else (e.g. charts produced to give astrological information about a specific individual, born on a particular day and year). The fundamental characteristic of an individually commissioned item is that the customer instigates and controls its production. Indicators of this are that the item is not made freely available, or that the copyright is passed over to the customer on completion. The value of the supply lies in the research services rather than the printed matter.

54.11 Printed Matter, Etc.

Where extra copies are printed of a publication which was originally individually commissioned, the value normally lies in the printed matter rather than the research services. The extra copies may be zero-rated provided

(*a*) they would qualify under the normal zero-rating rules; and

(*b*) they are priced only to cover the extra production costs and a reasonable profit margin.

(C & E Manual V1-7, Chapter 3 section 2.10).

54.11 Printed matter used to supply discount facilities

Where a publication contains a number of discount vouchers and details of establishments where the vouchers may be used, the important point to establish is where the value of the publication lies. If it has some value as printed matter in its own right, some allowance must be made for this element which may be zero-rated under the normal requirements in 54.17 *et seq.* below. However, if a person would only really buy the publication for the discounts which it contains, there is one standard-rated supply of discount services to which the printed matter is incidental.

C & E consider the following in reaching a decision in any particular case.

- Is it possible to physically separate the vouchers from the guide, and if so, are the two parts ever offered for sale separately?

- How is the guide promoted – is the 'discount' aspect stressed?

- Does the price increase if more vouchers are supplied?

- What is the historical background – has the guide ever been supplied independently with no vouchers or is this an entirely new venture?

(C & E Manual V1-7, Chapter 3 section 2.11).

See also *Status Cards Ltd (128)*, *Graham Leisure Ltd (1304)* and *Interleisure Club Ltd (7458)*.

54.12 Printed matter supplied with correspondence courses

Correspondence courses often involve a mixture of tuition in class and home study through course manuals or booklets.

If the printed matter has value in its own right, then if it qualifies for zero-rating under the normal rules in 54.17 *et seq.* below, the course fees can be apportioned to allow for a reasonable zero-rated element.

If the printed matter is an integral part of the course and is meaningless without the tuition, there is one supply of tuition which is normally standard-rated. C & E regard this as occurring where

(*a*) the printed matter is not generally sold separately from the course itself;

(*b*) the printed matter could not function on its own without attendance at classes etc; and

(*c*) it would not be possible to complete home study by using the supplied printed matter without assistance from the course in other ways.

(C & E Manual V1-7, Chapter 3 section 2.12).

Fees for correspondence and residential courses have been held to be apportionable between the supply of books (zero-rated) and tuition (standard-rated) in *The Rapid*

Results College Ltd, [1973] VATTR 197 (48), LSA (Full Time Courses) Ltd, [1983] VATTR 256 (1507) and *Force One Training Ltd (13619).* Compare, however, *EW (Computer Training) Ltd (5453)* where manuals were held to form part of a single supply of standard-rated tuition and *International News Syndicate Ltd (14425)* where the small element of external tuition was held to be incidental and the whole supply treated as zero-rated.

54.13   **Printed matter supplied in return for a subscription**

Membership subscriptions. Many subscription fees to organisations entitle the members to printed matter such as books or magazines. Where the book or magazine is given free to members and

- is not available to anyone else, or

- is obtainable by non-members at a price

the membership fee may be apportioned to reflect a reasonable zero-rated element relating to the printed matter provided it is eligible for zero-rating under the normal rules in 54.17 *et seq.* below.

An apportionment of the membership fee is not necessary where

- members are able to purchase printed matter more cheaply than non-members (a standard-rated supply of the right to obtain a discount);

- printed matter is given away free to both members and non-members (no membership benefit); and

- printed matter is supplied to both members and non-members for the same price (no membership benefit although there is a separate taxable supply of printed matter which may be zero-rated subject to the normal rules in 54.17 *et seq.* below).

Magazine subscriptions. Where magazines are supplied on an annual subscription basis, the whole supply may be zero-rated provided only the magazine is being supplied. However, where the subscription confers other rights (e.g. the right to buy goods at discounted rates or the right to participate in selling schemes and thereby earn commission) the subscription should be apportioned to reflect the zero-rated element relating to the magazine.

(C & E Manual V1-7, Chapter 3 section 2.13).

54.14   **Programmes supplied as part of an admission fee**

It is common practice for admission to events to include the provision of a programme. C & E accept that in these situations the admission fee should be apportioned to allow for a reasonable element in respect of the programme. This element may be zero-rated if the programme qualifies under the normal rules in 54.17 *et seq.* below.

(C & E Manual V1-7, Chapter 3 section 2.14).

See also *Jarmain, [1979] VATTR 41 (723)* and 58.6 RECREATION AND SPORT.

54.15   **Subsidy or vanity publishing**

An author who is unable to have a work published through the usual commercial channels may sometimes pay for it to be published. This is known as either 'subsidy' publishing or 'vanity' publishing.

Where the publisher, in return for a payment from the author, produces a quantity of books which are *all* delivered to the author, the payment by the author to the publisher is a consideration for a supply of books and is zero-rated.

More usually, however, the author is supplied only with a small number of copies of the book. The publisher retains the bulk of the print run, selling the books in the normal manner and paying the author a royalty on copies sold. In such cases, payment by the author to the publisher is partly the consideration for the zero-rated supply of books to the author and partly consideration for standard-rated publishing services (e.g. marketing the remaining books, providing statutory copies to the British Library, etc. and arranging for details to be included in directories such as 'Books in Print'). The following simplified method of calculation of the zero-rated and standard-rated supplies has been agreed between C & E and the British Printing Industries Federation.

Step A   Calculate non-variable costs of initial print run.

Step B   Calculate variable costs of initial print run.

Step C   Divide total at Step B by number of copies in initial print run and multiply by number of copies issued to author.

Step D   Add totals at Step A and Step C to calculate cost of the zero-rated element of the supply.

Step E   Total costs of initial print run and run on charges to establish full cost of supply.

Step F   Divide total at Step D by total at Step E to calculate zero-rated percentage of cost of supply.

Step G   Apply percentage in Step F to the net sales charge to establish the zero-rated element of the supply made.

A business which does not wish to calculate an apportionment for each individual supply may calculate an apportionment on the basis of an average resulting from the application of the above to a number of representative supplies made. The method is subject to review by C & E to ensure it produces a fair result and should also be regularly reviewed by the business to take account of changing circumstances.

(C & E Manual V1-7, Chapter 3 section 2.15; C & E Notice 700/57/95).

54.16   PRINTED MATTER SUPPLIED WITH OTHER GOODS

Goods which would normally be zero-rated as printed matter may be supplied in conjunction with other goods which are not printed matter. (Where a package consists entirely of articles of printed matter, some zero-rated and some standard-rated, see 54.27 below.)

The four possible liability situations are as follows.

(*a*)   **Where a standard-rated article is an integral part of the zero-rated printed matter.** In such a case, the whole supply is zero-rated. In practice, relief for most of these supplies is covered by *VATA 1994, 8 Sch Group 3, Item 6* which zero-rates covers, cases, and other similar articles supplied with zero-rated printed matter and not separately accounted for (see 54.26 below).

(*b*)   **Where the zero-rated printed matter is an integral part of a standard-rated supply.** In such a case, the whole supply is standard-rated (e.g. where a washing machine manufacturer issues an instruction booklet with each new machine sold).

(*c*) **'Multiple' or 'mixed' supplies where two or more articles have value in their own right**. If the articles are sold for a single price, apportionment will be necessary (e.g. books issued with films or tapes, and children's colouring books issued with felt-tip pens).

Cover-mounted items (e.g. a sachet of perfume or a CD) linked to a magazine fall into this category in principle and the selling price must be apportioned. However, by concession, the cover-mounted item can be zero-rated provided

    (i) no separate charge is made;

    (ii) the issue is sold at the same price as other issues without a cover-mounted item; and

    (iii) the cost of the items included with any individual issue does not exceed 20% of the total cost of the combined supply or £1 (excluding VAT).

This concession applies whether the linking is done by the publisher, distributor or retailer provided the conditions are satisfied at the point of linkage.

(*d*) **'Single' or 'composite' supplies.** This is where two or more articles are identifiable and separable but are meaningless in isolation and thus have to be taxed at one rate. Where a composite supply includes printed matter, almost inevitably the whole supply will be standard-rated. This is because the zero-rating provisions for printed matter are drafted on the basis of physical entities and the whole composite supply could not be described as a 'book', 'booklet' etc.

(C & E Manual V1-7, Chapter 3 section 2.16–2.18; C & E Leaflet 701/10/85, para 23).

For further consideration of mixed and composite supplies, see 64.6 SUPPLY.

54.17   **ZERO-RATED PRINTED MATTER**

Supplies of the following are zero-rated.

- Books and booklets (see 54.18 below).
- Brochures and pamphlets (see 54.19 below).
- Leaflets (see 54.20 below).
- Newspapers (see 54.21 below).
- Journals and periodicals (see 54.22 below).
- Children's picture books and painting books (see 54.23 below).
- Music (printed, duplicated or manuscript) (see 54.24 below).
- Maps, charts and topographical plans (see 54.25 below).
- Covers, cases and other articles supplied with any of the above items and not separately accounted for (see 54.26 below).

Included is the letting on hire or loan of, or the supply of a part interest in, any of the above items. The most common example of this is the hire of collections of books (particularly technical manuals) to educational institutions by wholesalers or publishers.

Not included are plans or drawings for industrial, architectural, engineering, commercial or similar purposes.

[*VATA 1994, 8 Sch Group 3*].

The legislation does not define any of the above articles. In the absence of any legal definition, C & E rely on the concept of the 'ordinary and everyday' meaning of the

54.18 Printed Matter, Etc.

words. When judging whether an article meets this meaning, the primary consideration is its physical characteristics. The function of an article is a secondary question and is only important if it is so far removed from the normal function of an article as to prevent that article qualifying as a 'book', 'leaflet' etc. in the ordinary meaning of those words. Similarly, it is the article itself which is to be judged, not the method of production. C & E, for example, consider that, in addition to books, etc. printed in the traditional way, hand-written documents, photocopies, and even faxes may still qualify.

Examples of zero-rated items. Apart from items specifically mentioned 54.18 to 54.26 below, C & E would normally expect the following items to be zero-rated although liability should not be determined from the list alone and reference should be made to the appropriate paragraph of the text.

Accounts (fully printed)
Advertising leaflets
Agendas (fully printed)
Almanacs
Amendments (loose leaf)
Annuals
Antique books and maps
Articles of association (complete in booklet form)
Astronomical charts
Atlases
Autograph books (completed)
Bibliographies
Bulletins
Catalogues
Circulars
Company reports
Comics
Crossword books
Diaries (completed)
Handbills
Holiday and tourist guides
Knitting patterns (not if single/double sheeted)
Mail order catalogues
Manuals
Memorandum of association (complete in booklet form)
Monographs
Orders of service whether printed on paper or card (from 20 December 1996)
Programmes (see 54.14 above)
Recipe books
Road maps
Scrap books (completed)
Staff journals
Timetables (in book or leaflet form)
Travel brochures

(C & E Manual V1-7, Chapter 3 section 1.6; C & E Leaflet 701/10/85, paras 1, 4a, Annex B).

54.18   Books and booklets

To qualify for zero-rating as a complete book or booklet, C & E usually require an article to satisfy the following physical characteristics.

(*a*)   It must have several pages.

(*b*)   It must have a cover that is stiffer than the pages. (Articles which fail this test may still be eligible for zero-rating under 54.19 below.)

(*c*)   It must either be bound or adapted for inclusion in a ring-binder.

C & E consider that it is the act of binding that makes a collection of papers into a complete book. This can take place either by traditional book-binding or by the issue of a ring-bound book. They therefore allow zero-rating for

• complete sets of loose leaves, adapted for inclusion in a binder of the customer's choice;

• a binder (titled or untitled) which is supplied in conjunction with the complete loose leaf pages of a book; and

• a binder bearing the exact title of the book it is intended to contain but supplied independently of the book itself. In such a case the book must be complete when the binder is issued, loose-leaved, and incapable of existence without its binder. See *A E Walker Ltd, [1973] VATTR 8 (3)* and *Marshall Cavendish Ltd, [1973] VATTR 65 (16)*.

A book or booklet may be printed in any language or characters (e.g. Braille or shorthand), photocopied, typed or hand-written, provided it is bound in book or booklet form or adapted for inclusion in a ring-binder. Zero-rated items include literary works, reference books, directories and antique books.

Loose-leaf books published in self-contained instalments. Unless a loose-leaf work, when viewed independently, is a book at the time of supply, it is not strictly entitled to zero-rating. By concession, if at that time an instalment is part of a larger finite work which itself would fall to be zero-rated as a book, then the component parts may also be zero-rated where they are supplied either direct by the publisher or through a distribution chain to the final consumer. (C & E Notice 48, ESC 2.17). However, as each instalment may be used on its own, C & E do not consider the binder to be essential until the completed book is assembled and do not allow zero-rating if the binder is issued prior to that stage.

Part works. These are publications that are designed to build up into a loose-leaf book. They usually cover a special interest or hobby such as wildlife, cookery etc, and are distributed either by mail order or through newsagents. Part works are issued in either magazine format with the pages stapled together or as a collection of loose pages which may be wrapped in clear plastic or lightly gummed together. The pages are often not consecutive and are designed to be separated and placed in the appropriate section of a binder.

If the completed work would itself be zero-rated as a book, then each part work may also be zero-rated. With part works, C & E also consider the binder to be an essential part of the book, and it may thus be zero-rated when issued with any part work.

Once a complete ring-bound book has been supplied, any amendments to it may be zero-rated.

The function test. Articles which have the physical characteristics of books may nevertheless be standard-rated if their main function is not that of a book. These fall into two main categories.

(i)   *Articles which do not convey information by means of text.* Since children's picture books are specifically zero-rated (see 54.23 below), C & E take the view that adults' picture books would have also been specifically relieved if that was the intention of the law. They therefore expect items that are intended for adults to convey information by means of text in order to be eligible for zero-rating. This text may be in any language, or in Braille. Articles which ordinarily fail this test (and are standard-rated) include

- albums containing collections of picture cards or stamps, where 25% or more of the album is set aside for the mounting of cards or stamps;

- photograph collections such as wedding albums;

- books of postcards;

- books of posters or frameable prints; and

- books giving samples of types of carpet, paint, paper, etc.

Such articles may still qualify for zero-rating if containing text with value in its own right rather than being merely incidental to the pictures, stamps, samples, etc.

Books of plans or drawings for industrial, architectural, engineering, commercial or similar purposes are specifically excluded from zero-rating by *VATA 1994, 8 Sch Group 3.*

(ii) *Articles whose main significance lies in parts to be completed or detached.*

- Accounts books and exercise books are standard-rated.

- Diaries and address books. C & E regard address books and unused diaries as standard-rated and completed diaries as zero-rated. This view was upheld in *C & E Commrs v Colour Offset Ltd QB 1994, [1995] STC 85* which confirmed that 'book' should be given its ordinary meaning i.e. as having the minimum characteristics of something to be read or looked at. A filled-in diary of historic or literary interest might be a book but a blank diary was not a book in the ordinary sense. Neither was an address book simply because its name included the word 'book'. Compare, however, *Scholastic Publications Ltd (14213)* where a children's publication containing a year planner and address section was held to be zero-rated as the remaining pages (more than 50% overall) were quizzes and jokes 'designed to be read as entertainment'.

- School work books, etc. Where these are in question and answer format, C & E policy is that the spaces provided for the insertion of answers are purely incidental to the essential character of the publication. They may thus qualify for zero-rating if they have the physical characteristics of books or booklets. This policy extends to examination papers in question and answer format (e.g. multiple choice). However, where the main value of a school work book, etc. is in the parts to be completed, that article is standard-rated.

See also *WF Graham (Northampton) Ltd (908)* and C & E Manual V1-7, Chapter 3 Table F for examples of rulings given by C & E on articles which have parts to be completed or detached.

(C & E Manual V1-7, Chapter 3 section 3.3–3.6; C & E Leaflet 701/10/85, para 2).

54.19   **Brochures and pamphlets.** To qualify for zero-rating as a brochure or pamphlet, C & E usually require the article to satisfy the following physical characteristics.

(*a*)   It must consist of either several pages fastened together or a single folded sheet.

(*b*)   It must be designed to be held in the hand and read.

The function test. Articles which have the physical characteristics of brochures and pamphlets may nevertheless be standard-rated if their main function is not that of such articles. These fall into two main categories.

- *Articles whose main significance lies in parts to be completed or detached.* C & E take the view that brochures or pamphlets with more than 25% of their total area for completion or detachment should be standard-rated. However, there is no basis in law for this and the '25% test' is no more than a rule of thumb.

  See also *Full Force Marketing Ltd; Framesouth Ltd (15270)* where the sale of an A4 document incorporating a 'discount card' entitling the holder to obtain free meals was essentially a supply of standard-rated services rather than a zero-rated brochure.

- *Articles which do not convey information by means of text.* As a brochure is normally an advertising vehicle, it will often contain numerous illustrations. However, there must be some thematic text to link these illustrations in order for zero-rating to be accepted.

Some brochures contain several sheets of text but also have a fixed flap or pocket into which leaflets or business cards may be inserted. These may be zero-rated as C & E accept that the fixed flap or pocket does not alter the primary function of the brochure i.e. which is to convey information.

However, if a single sheet, 'wallet' type brochure contains a fixed flap or pocket, C & E regard its main purpose as the carrying of other papers regardless of the amounts of text. Such articles are therefore standard-rated.

A wallet containing zero-rated reading material does not become a brochure with the folder acting as an outer cover. In these circumstances, C & E view the wallet as a means of creating a package of printed matter. See 54.27 below.

(C & E Manual V1-7, Chapter 3 section 3.7–3.10; C & E Leaflet 701/10/85, para 3).

54.20   **Leaflets**

There is no definition of a 'leaflet' and whether a particular product qualifies for zero-rating as a leaflet is a matter of fact and impression.

C & E look for certain physical characteristics if an article is to qualify as a leaflet. They consider (*a*) and (*b*) below to be the mandatory features of a zero-rated leaflet and (*c*)-(*f*) below as other indicating factors.

(*a*)   It must be limp i.e. not printed on stiff paper, laminated paper, or card. In *Panini Publishing Ltd (3876)* the tribunal held that a leaflet must be limp and generally, if not inevitably, on unlaminated paper. However, in *Multiform Printing Ltd, [1996] VATDR 580 (13931)* it was held that there is no need for a leaflet to be flimsy. Following the decision in the latter case, from 14 February 1996, C & E are prepared to accept as leaflets articles printed on material of a kind normally sold as 'paper'. However, if the 'paper' exceeds 180 gsm, a written ruling should be obtained from the VAT office before zero-rating the article as a leaflet.

(*b*)   It must be designed to be held in the hand for reading by individuals rather than for general display e.g. car stickers. See *Arbroath Herald Ltd (182)*.

(*c*)   It should consist of a single sheet of paper not greater than A4 size (although larger publications up to A2 size can be zero-rated provided they are printed on both sides, folded down to A4 or smaller, and meet other conditions). See *Cronsvale Ltd [1983] VATTR 313 (1552)* where the tribunal held a leaflet to mean a small-sized leaf of paper or a sheet folded into leaves (but not stitched) and containing printed matter, chiefly for gratuitous distribution.

(*d*)   It should be complete in itself (and not part of a larger work).

(*e*)   It should be widely distributed (i.e. intended to reach an audience of at least 50) either free or for a nominal consideration. This rules out

- very small productions; and

- letters with an individual's name or address added (which thereby restrict the letter to an audience of one). The supply of uncompleted 'stock' or basic letters is zero-rated if the portion for completion consists of no more than the recipient's name and address, a reference number and a signature.

(*f*)   It should convey information by means of text. Articles that are principally photographs with no significant or thematic text to support those photographs cannot be zero-rated.

The function test. Articles which have the physical characteristics of leaflets may nevertheless be standard-rated if their main function is not that of a leaflet. These fall into two main categories.

(i)   *Articles whose main function is not to convey information.* (e.g. all types of tickets, coupons, vouchers and labels and fragrance samples).

(ii)   *Articles primarily intended for completion or detachment.* C & E take the view that leaflets with more than 25% of their total area for completion or detachment should be standard-rated. However, there is no basis in law for this and the '25% test' is no more than a rule of thumb.

(C & E Manual V1-7, Chapter 3 section 3.11–3.15; C & E Leaflet 701/10/85, paras 4, 4b).

54.21   Newspapers

To qualify for zero-rating as a newspaper, C & E usually require an article to satisfy the following conditions.

(*a*)   It should consist of several sheets, which are either folded or bound together.

(*b*)   It must be published at regular intervals (usually daily or at least weekly) in a continuous series under the same title, each issue being dated and/or serially numbered. The intervals between publication should be determined by the wishes of the publisher, not prompted by some external event.

Included are 'souvenir' issues of established newspapers (e.g. those commemorating a royal marriage or the results of a general election). *Not included* are theatre or sporting programmes even if issued in the format of a newspaper.

The function test. To qualify as a newspaper, a publication must be predominantly devoted to the dissemination of 'news' in the broad sense of the word – i.e. information about recent or imminent events. 'Non-news' articles (e.g. crossword puzzles) should be an incidental feature.

For a general consideration of the requirements of a newspaper, see *Evans and Marland Ltd (t/a Greyform Publications), [1988] VATTR 115 (3138).*

Delivery and handling charges. Charges for delivered newspapers are normally zero-rated (see 47.8 OUTPUT TAX). This should be distinguished from handling charges which a publisher pays a newspaper proprietor for agreeing to distribute a free magazine in conjunction with a newspaper and which the newspaper will, in turn, pay its newsagents for its insertion and delivery to householders. C & E view both payments as standard-rated, regardless of the liability of the printed matter involved.

(C & E Manual V1-7, Chapter 3 section 3.16–3.19; C & E Leaflet 701/10/85, para 5).

54.22   **Journals and periodicals**

To qualify for zero-rating as a journal or periodical, C & E usually require an article to satisfy the following conditions.

(*a*)   It should consist of several sheets, which are either folded or bound together.

(*b*)   It must be published in a series at regular intervals (more frequently than once a year). The intervals between publication should be determined by the wishes of the publisher, not prompted by some external event.

The function test. To qualify as a journal or periodical, an article must fulfil the following functional requirements.

 (i)   It must be designed for reading and not be primarily a collection of stationery items (e.g. forms for completion or spaces for note taking) packaged in journal or periodical format.

(ii)   It must convey information primarily by means of text. C & E do not regard magazines which are almost entirely collections of posters or prints as journals or periodicals although poster magazines, which have text on one side and a related picture which is capable of use as a poster on the other, are eligible for zero-rating. See, however, *EMAP Consumer Magazines Ltd (13322)* where a magazine consisting mainly of posters was held to be a periodical even though some could not be fully viewed without removing the staples.

(iii)   Its main purpose must be to convey information, not to act as a vehicle for self-promotion. Journals or periodicals may contain a wide variety of information. They may be of interest to a particular specialist group or profession (e.g. lawyers, publicans or pharmacists) or appeal to a wide section of the population (e.g. popular fiction magazines). They may also consist almost entirely of advertisements providing that these originate from a number of sources. However publications which serve primarily to promote the proprietor's own business, either by way of written articles or advertisements, do not qualify as periodicals.

See also *Snushall (a firm) v C & E Commrs, QB [1992] STC 537* where the tribunal held that a monthly property guide, consisting almost entirely of advertisements for houses but with one or two articles on the housing market, could not be regarded as a journal as it contained no news and could not be regarded as a periodical as it was not sold to the public.

(C & E Manual V1-7, Chapter 3 section 3.20–3.22; C & E Leaflet 701/10/85, para 6).

54.23   **Children's picture books and painting books**

To qualify for zero-rating under this heading, C & E usually require an article to satisfy the following physical characteristics.

(*a*)   It must have several pages.

(*b*)   It must be either bound, fastened, or folded in a 'concertina' fashion.

(*c*)   It must be printed on paper, cardboard, textiles (e.g. rag books) or waterproof plastic (in the case of 'bath-time books').

The function test. Many children's picture or painting books also involve other elements more akin to toys or stationery. It is therefore necessary to establish the main function of article. Zero-rating will only apply if it is that of a picture or painting book.

Children's picture books. Included are books where the reader is invited first to read and then to cut out an item from the story. *Not included* are books where the reader is mainly directed towards cutting out parts after which there is little left that can be considered to be a book and 'pop-up' books where the 'pop-up' images are not related to a printed narrative text. The value of such articles is as toys and they should therefore be standard-rated.

C & E suggest that books with at least 25% text (other than assembly instructions) may be zero-rated. However, there is no basis in law for this and the '25% test' is no more than a rule of thumb.

For a general consideration of children's reading books and picture books, see *W F Graham (Northampton) Ltd (908)*.

Children's painting books. C & E interpret 'painting books' as including most types of books which are designed to exercise a child's mind other than by way of a traditional 'story'. *Included* are books in which the outlines of pictures are copied or coloured in, puzzle books, 'dot-to-dot' books and books which feature pictures onto which stickers are stuck or transfers are superimposed. Also included are books with 'invisible' outlines and those in which small amounts of water colour for colouring are contained in the book. *Not included* are articles which include puzzles, pictures for colouring, etc, but which are primarily cut-out toys or board games and articles which are primarily stationery for children to write in.

(C & E Manual V1-7, Chapter 3 section 3.23–3.25; C & E Leaflet 701/10/85, paras 7, 8).

54.24   Music

Any complete music which is presented on paper is zero-rated whether instrumental or vocal, printed or manuscript, bound or loose, illustrated or not and in any system of notation. *Not included* are

- music rolls;

- manuscript paper; and

- articles which are primarily educational aids for the teaching of music (e.g. pictures of how to play chords on the guitar) although these articles may qualify for relief as a book or booklet under 54.18 above depending upon their physical characteristics. See also *Flip Cards (Marine) Ltd (14483)* where 'music' was defined as 'the written or printed score or set of parts of a musical composition' and held not to include cards containing questions and answers about music.

(C & E Manual V1-7, Chapter 3 section 3.26; C & E Leaflet 701/10/85, para 9).

54.25   Maps, charts and topographical plans

To qualify for zero-rating as a map, chart or topographical plan, C & E require an article to satisfy the following physical characteristics.

(*a*) It must be two-dimensional. This excludes globes and other three-dimensional articles and 'novelty maps' printed onto items such as mugs.

(*b*) It must provide a geographical representation of an area of land, sea or the heavens (e.g. national or county boundaries may be marked or natural features such as rivers or mountain ranges named). Although it must be more than an aerial photograph, the representation need not be strictly accurate or to scale. It may cover only a minor area of the printed matter, the remainder of which is devoted to supporting pictures or text. C & E have, for example, accepted the following as having the physical characteristics of maps.

- A recipe map of Ireland devoted 80% to text and illustrations of recipes, the map only featuring numbered counties.

- An angling map of the British Isles devoted mainly to pictures of fish, the only detail on the map being the naming of prominent rivers.

- A 'Clan Map of Scotland' devoted 80% to text and pictures of tartans and clan badges, the map only showing rivers, main towns, and clan locations.

The restriction of relief for charts to geographical representations is supported by the decision in *Brooks Histograph Ltd, [1984] VATTR 46 (1570)* where the tribunal held that the word 'chart' must be construed in the context in which it appears. Since it appears between the words 'maps' and 'topographical plans' it refers to an area of land, sea or the skies and not to an historical chart.

The maps, etc. may be printed on paper or other material and in the form of a single or folded sheets or a collection of such sheets bound together in book form e.g. atlases.

The function test. To qualify for zero-rating under this heading, the primary function of the article must be for use as a map, chart, or topographical plan. C & E do not regard the following as satisfying the test.

- Decorative textile articles (e.g. scarves, tea towels or tapestries) which bear a map.

- Framed maps which are primarily decorative articles. Zero-rating can be applied where a map remains functional rather than decorative even after framing (e.g. where laminated and mounted onto wood or soft board to allow the use of marker pens and/or to enable pins to be inserted).

Plans or drawings for industrial, architectural, engineering, commercial or similar purposes are excluded from zero-rating by *VATA 1994, 8 Sch Group 3*.

(C & E Manual V1-7, Chapter 3 section 3.27, 3.28; C & E Leaflet 701/10/85, para 10).

54.26   **Covers, cases and other articles**

Zero-rating also applies to covers, cases and other articles supplied with items within 54.18 to 54.25 above and not separately accounted for. *Included* are dust covers, clasps, book marks, or presentation cases.

Certain booksellers specialise in providing public libraries with books fitted with plastic dust-jackets, ticket-pockets and similar accessories. In these limited circumstances, the fact that invoices normally show separate charges for books and for the fitting of the jackets, etc. does not preclude zero-rating simply because these articles are 'separately accounted for'.

C & E do not accept that zero-rating under this heading applies to

- covers which are a means of packaging a multiplicity of articles (e.g. plastic envelopes enclosing direct mail packs or children's activity packs), and

- printed folders into which other printed matter articles are inserted

for which see 54.27 below.

Binders. For the treatment of loose-leaf binders, see 54.18 above.

(C & E Manual V1-7, Chapter 3 section 3.29, 3.30; C & E Leaflet 701/10/85, para 17).

54.27   **Packages of printed matter**

Packages on zero-rated and standard-rated printed matter. By concession to the printing trade, where standard and zero-rated printed matter are supplied together as a 'package' for a single price, the liability of a package may be calculated according to the liability of the articles which predominate within it. This can be determined in one of two ways.

(*a*)   Where a package contains a number of items of similar significance (e.g. three forms, two letters and a leaflet) the liability of the whole package should be determined by deciding which liability applies to the majority of the contents (ignoring the outer envelope). If the numbers are equal, the package should be judged upon the basis of which items cost the most to produce.

(*b*)   Where a package consists of several items but one item has far more significance than the others (e.g. a package consisting of a zero-rated 50-page booklet and eight standard-rated forms for completion) the most significant article dictates the liability of the package as a whole.

For these purposes, C & E regard a '*package*' as a collection of printed matter enclosed in some sort of wrapper. The most common examples are

- packages contained in an outer polythene or paper envelope (e.g. a package sent to a shareholder which includes company reports, circulars, a proxy voting form and a reply-paid envelope); and

- cardboard folders with pockets into which are inserted a variety of forms, leaflets, etc.

(C & E Manual V1-7, Chapter 3 section 4.1–4.5).

Packages of printed and non-printed matter. See 54.16 above.

Charity direct mail packs. See 54.28 below.

54.28   **Supplies of printed advertising to charities**

Supplies of advertising within (*a*) or (*b*) below are zero-rated if made to a charity for either of the following purposes.

(i)   Raising money for the charity. This includes

- asking for donations, legacies, etc.

- advertising fund-raising events, e.g. jumble sales, fêtes, etc.

- advertising goods for sale where all the proceeds go to the charity

(ii)   Making known the objects, or reason for the objects, of the charity. This includes

- telling of the good work carried on by the charity

- explaining the need for the charity to exist

- offering help (e.g. by drawing services provided to the attention of the public)

- describing the activities of the charity (this would include the general trading activities for charities such as museums)

- giving the time of church services

- asking for volunteers (see under the heading *Job recruitment advertisements* below)

- asking for aid goods to enable the charity to carry out its objects (e.g. disaster relief)

- announcing a forthcoming open day (although this should be more than the name, venue and time of opening)

- listing courses provided

- seeking to recruit pupils by describing the types of courses/facilities available and specifying the particular age range of the pupils

- offering bursaries

- advertising a special conference connected with the furtherance of the charity's objectives (this does not include AGMs and regular meetings)

The charity must provide the supplier with a declaration that the advertisement is for a qualifying purpose.

(C & E Manual V1-9, Chapter 2 para 10.7; C & E Notice 701/1/95, para 16). See Annex H of that Notice for the suggested form of the declaration required.

(*a*) The publication of an advertisement in any newspaper, journal, poster, programme, annual, leaflet, brochure, pamphlet, periodical or similar publication. [*VATA 1994, 8 Sch Group 15, Item 8(b)*]. This wording implies that the service of publication must be supplied by a third party and not by the charity itself (*Royal Society for the Encouragement of the Arts, Manufacture and Commerce QB 1996, [1997] STC 437*).

In *Royal Society for the Encouragement of the Arts, Manufacture and Commerce* the tribunal chairman gave the opinion that, for an advertisement to come within the scope of these provisions, its *principal* purposes must be for one of the purposes listed above. He also commented that C & E Notice 701/1/95, para 16 went further than the statute by including supplies of stationery and certain other items within the zero-rating provisions. Although the tribunal's decision was reversed on appeal (on another point), as a result of these comments C & E have changed their view on what is eligible for zero-rating.

With effect from 27 August 1996, C & E continue to allow zero-rating of

- pre-printed paperboard collecting boxes;

- pre-printed collecting envelopes;

- pre-printed letters appealing solely for money for the charity;

- envelopes used in conjunction with appeal letters and for forwarding donations provided they are over-printed with an appeal request related to that contained in the letter; and

- lapel stickers

but have concluded that zero-rating can no longer be applied (as previously) to advertisements on draw tickets and note-paper and general use envelopes.

(C & E Business Brief 18/96, 27 August 1996).

C & E have never accepted zero-rating as applying to advertising on clothing of any material, mugs and similar commemorative items, Christmas cards and calendars. (C & E Notice 701/1/95, para 16).

(*b*) Any goods or services in connection with the preparation of an advertisement within (*a*) above (e.g. design, artwork, typesetting and printing). [*VATA 1994, 8 Sch Group 15, Item 8(c)*]. The services must, however, be provided by the same third-party supplier that supplies the publication within (*a*) above (*Royal Society for the Encouragement of the Arts, Manufacture and Commerce QB 1996, [1997] STC 437*).

Job recruitment advertisements. *With effect from 1 June 1996*, following the chairman's comments in *The Royal Society for the Encouragement of Arts, Manufacture &*

Commerce, C & E no longer accept that recruitment advertising for paid staff by a charity is eligible for zero-rating even if containing a 'qualifying' message. Advertisements for volunteers (including advertisements for people to work overseas at local rates of pay plus travelling expenses) continue to qualify for zero-rating. (C & E Business Brief 9/96, 24 May 1996). See also *RNIB Properties Ltd (15748)*.

From 5 November 1992 to 31 May 1996, C & E regarded job recruitment advertising as eligible for zero-rating provided the advertisement included a qualifying advertisement within the above provisions. (C & E Business Brief 1/95, 11 January 1995).

Liability of charity direct mail packs. Charity direct mail packs are packages of material sent to existing or prospective supporters of a charity. They typically comprise a number of articles within an outer envelope (e.g. letters requesting support, annual reports, leaflets, donation forms, collectors envelopes and window stickers). The following procedure should be used to determine the liability of such direct mail packs.

1.   Determine those articles which qualify for zero-rating under *VATA 1994, 8 Sch Group 15* (see (*a*) above).

2.   Determine whether any articles individually qualify for zero-rating under *VATA 1994, 8 Sch Group 3* (see 54.18 to 54.26 above).

3.   Consider the liability for the whole package under 54.27 above.

4.   If the package as a whole is zero-rated under 54.27, zero-rating can also be applied to preparatory work under (*b*) above on any items which qualify for zero-rating under (*a*) above.

If the package as a whole is standard-rated under 54.27 above, zero-rating applies only to those articles which are eligible for zero-rating under (*a*) above. If any preparatory work has been supplied in connection with these articles, this may also be zero-rated under (*b*) above.

Example

A charity pack contains the following.

	Zero-rated under *Group 15*	Zero-rated under *Group 3*
1. A letter requesting support, addressed 'Dear Supporter'.	Yes	Yes
2. A 60-page Annual Report.	No	Yes
3. A booklet containing an order of service for the Christmas carol concert.	No	Yes
4. A newspaper.	No	Yes
5. A Christmas card.	No	No
6. A collector's envelope bearing a qualifying advertisement.	Yes	No
7. A vinyl car sticker.	No	No

Only articles 1 and 6 qualify for relief as printed advertising matter supplied to charities under (*a*) above. However, using either of the tests under 54.27 above, the package as a whole may be zero-rated as printed matter under *VATA 1994, 8 Sch Group 3*. In addition, any preparatory work supplied in connection with articles 1 and 6 may also be zero-rated under (*b*) above if the customer has completed the necessary declaration.

(C & E Manual V1-7, Chapter 3 section 5, Table E).

54.29   **STANDARD-RATED PRINTED MATTER**

In addition to the items specifically mentioned as standard-rated in 54.17 to 54.28 above, C & E also regard the following as standard-rated.

Acceptance cards
Account books
Address books
Albums
Amendment slips
Announcement cards
Appointment cards
Autograph albums
Badges
Ballot papers
Bingo cards
Biorhythm charts
Book tokens
Bookmakers' tickets
Business cards
Calendars
Cassette inlay cards
Certificates
Cheque books
Cigarette cards
Cloakroom tickets
Colour cards
Compliment slips
Cookery cards
Copy books
Coupons
Credit cards
Delivery notes
Diaries (unused)
Dividend warrants
Draft forms
Dressmaking patterns
Engineers' plans
Envelopes
Exercise books
Fashion drawings
Folders
Forms
Football pool coupons
Games
Greetings cards
Index cards
Invitation cards
Invoices
Knitting patterns (single/double sheeted)
Labels
Letter heading
Log books
Lottery tickets
Manuscript paper

Medical records
Memo pads
Menu cards
Microfiche
Microfilm
Note books
Order books
Photograph albums
Playing cards
Postcards
Printed pictures
Questionnaires
Receipt books
Record books and labels
Registers
Rent books
Reply-paid coupons
Scrap books (blank)
Seals
Stickers
Tags
Tickets
Transcripts
Visiting cards
Vouchers
Wastepaper
Wills

(C & E Leaflet 701/10/85, Annex B).

Photocopies. Photocopies of zero-rated items are standard-rated unless

- the copies are complete in themselves and have the characteristics of a zero-rated item; or

- form a single sheet and meet all the criteria for being treated as a leaflet.

Posters. Sheets intended for public display are standard-rated but see 54.22 above for 'poster-magazines'.

Letters. Individual manuscript or typed letters are standard-rated as are collections of such letters which are unbound or loosely bound. Permanently bound collections are zero-rated. See 54.20 above for printed stocks of standard letters.

Book tokens. Printing of book tokens is standard-rated. On the sale of a book token to the general public for its face value or less, no VAT is due. Otherwise VAT must be accounted for on the difference between the selling price and its face value.

C & E Leaflet 701/10/85, paras 11, 13, 15, 22).

54.30 **IMPORTED PRINTED MATTER**

The following printed matter may be imported free of VAT from a country outside the EC.

- Documents sent free of charge to public services in the EC.

- Publications of foreign governments or official international organisations for free distribution.

- Ballot papers for elections organised by bodies outside the EC.

- Specimen signatures and circulars concerning signatures forming part of exchanges of information between banks and public services.

- Official printed matter sent to a Central Bank in the EC.

- Documents from a company incorporated outside the EC to holders of its issued securities.

- Files and other documents for use at international meetings etc. and reports of such gatherings.

- Plans, drawings etc. sent by any person for participating in a competition in the EC or to obtain or fulfil an order executed outside the EC.

- Documents to be used in examinations held in the EC on behalf of institutions established outside the EC.

- Printed forms to be used as official documents in international trade.

- Printed forms, labels, tickets etc. sent to travel agents in the EC by transport and tourist undertakings outside the EC.

- Used commercial documents.

- Official printed forms from national or international authorities.

- Printed matter sent from associations outside the EC for distribution by corresponding associations in the EC.

- Documents for free distribution to encourage persons to visit countries outside the EC, particularly for cultural, tourist, sporting, religious, trade or professional meetings or events (provided the goods do not contain more than 25% of private commercial advertising).

- Free distribution copies of hotel lists and yearbooks published for official tourist agencies of countries outside the EC, and timetables for transport services in such countries (provided the goods do not contain more than 25% of private commercial advertising).

- Yearbooks, lists of telephone and telex numbers, hotel lists, catalogues for fairs, specimens of craft goods of negligible value and literature on museums, universities etc. supplied as reference material to accredited representatives etc. appointed by official national tourist agencies and not intended for distribution.

- Official publications issued under the authority of the country of exportation, international institutions, regional or local authorities and bodies governed by public law established in the country of exportation (provided VAT or any other tax has been paid on the publication or printed matter in the third country from which it has been exported and the publication etc. has not benefited from any relief from payment by virtue of exportation).

- Printed matter distributed by political organisations, officially recognised in the UK, established in countries outside the EC on the occasion of European Parliament or national elections in the country in which the printed matter originates (provided VAT or any other tax has been paid on the publication or printed matter in the third country from which it has been exported and the publication etc. has not benefited from any relief from payment by virtue of exportation).

[*SI 1984/746, Art 2(5), 2 Sch Group 7; SI 1992/3120*].

See also 34.23 IMPORTS.

55 Purchase Tax

55.1   Purchase tax ceased to apply with effect from the introduction of VAT on 1 April 1973.

Where a vehicle on which purchase tax was remitted under *Purchase Tax Act 1963, s 23* (vehicles for use outside the UK) is brought back into the UK, the vehicle is not then to be treated for VAT purposes as being acquired from another EC country or, as the case may be, imported from a place outside the EC. [*VATA 1994, 13 Sch 3*].

56   Rates of VAT

Cross-references. See 22.15 EUROPEAN COMMUNITY: LEGISLATION for rates allowed under the *EC Sixth Directive*; 64.32–64.58 SUPPLY for the rules relating to the tax point of supply.

56.1   VAT is levied on the supply of goods and services, the acquisition of goods from another EC country and the importation of goods from a place outside the EC. The Treasury may, by Order, vary the rate of VAT for the time being in force by a percentage of the current rate not exceeding 25% but any Order ceases to have effect one year from the date on which it takes effect unless continued by a further Order. [*VATA 1994, s 2*].

56.2   **RATES**

Subject to certain EXEMPT SUPPLIES (24) and ZERO-RATED SUPPLIES (72), the standard rate has been

1.4.73–28.7.74	10%	[*FA 1972, s 9(1)*]
29.7.74–17.6.79	8%	[*SI 1974/1224*]
18.6.79–31.3.91	15%	[*F(No 2)A 1979, s 1*]
1.4.91–	17½%	[*FA 1991, s 13*]

See also 29.2 FUEL AND POWER for a lower rate applying to fuel supplied for domestic use.

56.3   **CHANGE IN VAT RATES**

The provisions in 56.4 to 56.17 below apply when there is a change in the VAT rate (i.e. the standard rate is changed or a new rate is introduced) or where there is a change in the VAT liability of particular supplies (e.g. a supply previously standard-rated becomes zero-rated through a change in the law or its interpretation). Any such change is effective from a specific date and VAT is due at the new rate on supplies made on or after that date. The date on which supplies of goods and services are treated as taking place for the purposes of charging VAT is governed by the tax point rules (see 64.32–64.58 SUPPLY). Normally no change of rate can apply to any supply with a tax point before the effective date of change (but see 56.6 below and the special rules for warehoused goods in 56.17 below). See 60.7 RETAIL SCHEMES for the effects of a change in VAT rates or VAT liabilities where one or more of the special retail schemes are in operation but see also 56.6 below. (C & E Notice 700, Appendix C, paras 1–3).

56.4   **VAT returns**

VAT returns should be completed according to the normal rules (see 2 ACCOUNTING PERIODS AND RETURNS). VAT due at the old and new rates should not be shown separately. (C & E Notice 700, Appendix C, para 6).

56.5   **Reclaiming input tax**

Input tax following a change in VAT rate or VAT liability must be reclaimed at the rate charged by the supplier. Where the amount of VAT is not separately shown (e.g. on a less detailed VAT invoice — see 40.7 INVOICES), VAT is calculated by applying the VAT fraction which was appropriate at the tax point (see 64.32–64.58 SUPPLY). See also 56.9 below for continuous supplies of services invoiced ahead of the supply. (C & E Notice 700, Appendix C, para 5).

56.6   **Output tax – general principles**

When there is a change in the VAT rate or a VAT liability, VAT is chargeable according to the normal tax point rules (see 64.32–64.58 SUPPLY) unless the taxpayer elects for the special change of rate provisions below. It is not possible to avoid the consequences of an announced increase in VAT by preparing invoices which, although agreed by the customer, are not issued (i.e. physically sent or given to him) before the date of change. See *C & E Commrs v Woolfold Motor Co Ltd QB, [1983] STC 715*. In any case, an invoice issued for a zero-rated supply does not create a tax point.

Special change of rate provisions.

(*a*) On an election, *the rate at which VAT is chargeable on a supply, or any question whether the supply is zero-rated or exempt*, is determined by the *basic tax point* only i.e. the date on which goods are removed or made available or on which services are performed. Election may be made for all affected supplies or only some of them but an election may not be made where VAT invoices are issued under a self-billing arrangement (see 40.2 INVOICES) or when goods are sold from the assets of a business in satisfaction of a debt. [*VATA 1994, s 88(2)(6)*]. The effect of the election is that, where the VAT rate increases, VAT may be charged at the old rate on goods removed or services performed before the date of change even though the tax point would normally be established by the issue of a VAT invoice after the change. Similarly, where the VAT rate goes down, VAT may be charged at the new rate on goods removed or services performed after the date of change, even though payment has been received or a VAT invoice issued before that date.

(C & E Notice 700, Appendix C, para 7).

(*b*) On an election, *the rate at which VAT is chargeable on an acquisition of goods from another EC country, or any question as to whether it is zero-rated or exempt*, is determined by reference to the time of the first removal of the goods involved in the transaction (or, in the case of goods on sale or return, such later time when it becomes certain that they have been acquired). [*VATA 1994, s 88(4)(7)*].

56.7   Credit notes

Where an invoice has already been issued showing VAT at the old rate, it must be corrected with a credit note issued within 14 days of the change. See 40.16 INVOICES for details. (C & E Notice 700, Appendix C, para 7).

56.8   Supplies of services

Output tax may be charged at the old rate on the part completed before the date of a change in the VAT rate and at the new rate on the part completed on or after that date provided the supply can be apportioned on a basis of measurable work or in accordance with a supplier's normal costing or pricing system. Where VAT is reduced in this way and a VAT invoice was issued or payment was received before the date of VAT change, a credit note must be provided (see above). (C & E Notice 700, Appendix C, para 8).

56.9   Continuous supplies of goods and services

Where there is a continuous supply of goods or services (including hire, lease and rental of goods) VAT is normally chargeable at the rate applying at each tax point. See 64.50 SUPPLY for services and 64.46 SUPPLY for a continuous supply of goods in the form of water, gas and electricity. Any VAT invoice issued up to one year ahead, giving the amounts and dates when payments are due, is invalid in respect of payments due after the change (and not received before it). [*SI 1995/2518, Reg 90(3)*]. A new invoice, referring to and cancelling the superseded part of the original invoice, must be issued. The customer cannot use the original invoice to support a claim for input tax after the change and must make the necessary adjustments on receipt of the new invoice.

Where a continuous supply spans a change in the VAT rate, VAT may be accounted for at the *old* rate on that part of the supply made before the change even though the normal tax point would occur after the change (e.g. where a payment is received in arrears of the supply). Conversely, VAT may be accounted for at the *new* rate on that part of the supply made after the change even though the normal tax point occurred before the change (e.g. where a payment is received in advance of the supply). In each case, VAT should be accounted for on the basis of the value of goods actually supplied or services actually performed before or after the change as appropriate. Where VAT liability is reduced on a supply for which a VAT invoice has been issued at a higher rate, a credit note must be issued (see above). (C & E Notice 700, Appendix C, para 9).

56.10   Facilities provided by clubs, associations, etc.

Clubs, associations, etc. supplying facilities in return for a member's subscription must normally account for VAT at the rate applying when the subscription is received or a VAT invoice is issued, whichever happens first. Where payment is made by instalments or separate invoices are issued, the procedure for continuous supply of services should be followed (see above). (C & E Notice 700, Appendix C, para 10).

56.11   Hire purchase, conditional and credit sales

Under any of these agreements, there is a single supply of goods and the normal tax point is the earliest of

(*a*)   the date of removal of the goods;

(*b*)   the date of issue of the agreement (provided the agreement is in the form of a VAT invoice); and

(*c*)   the date of the issue of a separate VAT invoice.

See 64.42 SUPPLY.

The signing of an agreement, or its date, does not constitute a tax point. Where there is a change in the VAT rate, the tax point will be whichever of (*a*) to (*c*) above results in the lower rate of VAT being charged. (C & E Notice 700, Appendix C, para 11).

56.12   Deposits and payments in advance of the basic tax point

Where full or part payment is made, or a VAT invoice issued, before the basic tax point (see above), VAT will normally be due on the amount paid or invoiced at the rate in force at that date. Where full payment is made in advance but the money is loaned back to the customer on the understanding that it will be repaid as the work proceeds, the transaction has been held to be genuine and not to fall foul of the decision in *W T Ramsay Ltd v IRC* even if the scheme is designed purely to save VAT. A similar decision has been reached where monies are paid into deposit accounts of the builders but only released against architects' certificates (*C & E Commrs v Faith Construction Ltd and related appeals CA, [1989] STC 539*). If there is a change in the VAT rate before the supply is actually made, the earlier tax point may be disregarded if more VAT would be payable. Instead, VAT may be charged at the rate applicable when the supply is made and a credit note issued (see above) to amend the VAT invoice. These provisions do not apply to deposits taken as security (e.g. to ensure safe return of goods hired out) which are refundable or subject to forfeiture *or* if the deposit does not relate to a particular supply or contract (e.g. money paid into a client's account). (C & E Notice 700, Appendix C, para 12).

56.13   Credit and contingent discounts

Where a credit note (not arising from the change in rate) is issued to adjust an original invoice, VAT should be credited at the rate in force at the tax point of the original supply. Where contingent discount is allowed and the original VAT charge is adjusted, VAT should be credited at the rate in force at the time of each supply qualifying for the discount. (C & E Notice 700, Appendix C, para 13).

56.14   Price escalation clauses and other adjustments

Where an additional payment is required after a change in the VAT rate and after the tax point for the original supply determined under the normal rules, VAT is chargeable on the further payment at the old rate. Where VAT was not determined under the normal rules on the original supply, the tax point for the additional payment is the earlier of the date of receipt of a further payment or the issue of a VAT invoice and VAT is chargeable at the rate then in force. (C & E Notice 700, Appendix C, para 14).

56.15   Existing contracts

Where, after the making of a contract for the supply of goods or services and before those goods or services are supplied, there is a change in the VAT charged, then, unless the contract provides otherwise, the consideration for the supply is increased or decreased by an amount equal to the change. These provisions apply in relation to a tenancy or lease as they apply in relation to a contract.

A landlord is able to add VAT to the rent where

- he makes an election to charge VAT on rents at the standard rate under the option to tax provisions (see 42.20 LAND AND BUILDINGS); or

- there is an increase in the rate of VAT

unless the terms of the lease specifically prevent him from passing on VAT to his tenants. [*VATA 1994, s 89*].

C & E do not advise on contracts. (C & E Notice 700, Appendix C, para 15).

56.16   Second-hand goods

VAT chargeable on the sale of a second-hand article under the Margin Scheme for SECOND-HAND GOODS (61) is calculated by applying the appropriate VAT fraction at the tax point to the VAT-inclusive amount. The tax point is the earlier of the date of removal of the goods and the receipt of payment. If there is a change in the VAT rate before the goods are removed, VAT may be accounted for at the rate in force when the goods are removed even if payment has already been received. (*Note.* A VAT invoice must not be issued for goods supplied under a second-hand scheme). (C & E Notice 700, Appendix C, para 16).

56.17   Warehoused goods

Imported goods. When imported goods are removed from bonded warehouse for home use, the rate of VAT chargeable is that in force at the time of removal.

Home-produced goods subject to excise duty which have been supplied whilst in warehouse. The rate of VAT chargeable is that in force when the excise duty is paid. For goods relieved of excise duty, the rate of VAT chargeable is that applicable at the time of their removal from warehouse.

(C & E Notice 700, Appendix C, para 17).

56.18   ENERGY SAVING MATERIALS

With effect from 1 July 1998, a supply to a 'qualifying person' of

(*a*)   any services of 'installing' 'energy-saving materials' in that person's sole or main 'residence', and

(*b*)   the energy savings materials themselves by the person installing those materials

is subject to VAT at the reduced rate of 5% to the extent that the consideration for the supply is funded by a grant made under a 'relevant scheme'. A '*relevant scheme*' is a scheme which has as one of its objects the funding of energy-saving materials in the homes of qualifying persons and which disburses grants (in whole or part) out of funds made available to it for that objective by a government department, the EC, a local authority or an arrangement approved by the electricity or gas regulators (OFFER or OFGAS).

[VATA 1994, A1 Sch 1, 1A, 5; SI 1998/1375].

'**Qualifying persons**'. A '*qualifying person*' is a person who, at the time of the supply, is aged 60 or over or is in receipt of one or more of the following benefits.

- Council tax benefit

- Disability living allowance

- Disability working allowance

- Family credit

- Housing benefit

- An income-based jobseeker's allowance

- Income support

- Industrial injuries disablement pension payable at the increased rate to include constant attendance allowance

- War disablement pension payable at the increased rate to include constant attendance allowance or mobility supplement

[VATA 1994, A1 Sch 5; SI 1998/1375].

Where there are qualifying and non-qualifying persons living in the same dwelling, relief applies if the supply is to a qualifying person. In practice, for a supply to be to a qualifying person, that person must be responsible for ordering the work to be done. (VAT Information Sheet 9/98, June 1998).

'**Installing**'. The relief is only available where the energy-saving materials are installed by the person providing the material. This would normally be a builder, specialist installer, local authority or a utility company but any business can install and qualify for relief provided all the conditions are met. Installation may involve a process by which the materials are permanently fixed in place although some products may simply need to be unrolled (e.g. loft insulation). Where an installer has to undertake minor building work as part of the fitting (e.g. planing doors or windows, enlarging loft hatches) or painting/plastering to make good after installation, such work is also eligible for the reduced rate provided other conditions for the relief are met. Such work done by a separate builder does not qualify. (VAT Information Sheet 9/98, June 1998).

'**Energy-saving materials**' means the following.

- Insulation for walls, floors, ceilings, roofs or lofts or for water tanks, pipes or other plumbing fittings. It includes materials which are designed, and held out for sale, as having insulating qualities but does not include essentially decorative products or treatments (e.g. curtains, carpets, decorative stone cladding).

- Draught stripping for windows and doors. These are typically plastic or foam strips held out for use by fixing around interior and exterior doors, windows and loft hatches.

- Central heating and hot water system controls. Included are manual or electronic timers, thermostats, and mechanical or electronic valves including thermostatic radiator valves.

Where qualifying energy-saving materials as above are installed in a package with other incidental supplies designed to promote energy efficiency (e.g. compact fluorescent light-bulbs and energy-efficient advice), the reduced rate can be applied to the whole package provided, as a rule of thumb, value of the qualifying materials are more than 50% of the total value. Otherwise an apportionment must be made (see below).

Relief does not apply to the installation of double glazing and similar products (e.g. low-emissivity glass) or the supply of energy-efficient domestic appliances.

[*VATA 1994, A1 Sch 5; SI 1998/1375*]. (VAT Information Sheet 9/98, June 1998).

'**Residence**' means any sort of home, including houses, flats, residential caravans and houseboats. (VAT Information Sheet 9/98, June 1998).

Apportionment. Where a grant is made to fund supplies within (*a*) or (*b*) above (relevant supplies) and other supplies (non-relevant supplies), the proportion of the grant attributed to the relevant supplies is

$$G \times \frac{A}{B}$$

where

G = the full grant received
A = the consideration reasonably attributable to the relevant supplies (excluding VAT)
B = the total consideration for relevant and non-relevant supplies (excluding VAT)

[*VATA 1994, A1 Sch 1B, 5; SI 1998/1375*].

Example

A builder installs energy-saving materials to a value of £300 and carries out other building work to a value of £700 (both excluding VAT) for C in his main residence. £200 of the work is funded by a qualifying grant.

Where grant-awarding body allocates the grant to installation of energy-saving materials

	£	£
Value of grant-funded work (excluding VAT)	200.00	
VAT thereon (5%)	10.00	
		210.00
Value of other non-funded work (excluding VAT)	800.00	
VAT thereon (17.5%)	140.00	
		940.00
Total cost including VAT		1,150.00
Grant received		200.00
Contribution from C		£950.00

Where grant-awarding body does not specify the allocation of the grant

Proportion of total grant allocated to energy-saving materials

$$200 \times \frac{300}{1000} = £60$$

	£	£
Value of grant-funded work (excluding VAT)	60.00	
VAT thereon (5%)	3.00	
		63.00
Value of other non-funded work (excluding VAT)	940.00	
VAT thereon (17.5%)	164.50	
		1,104.00
Total cost including VAT		1,167.50
Grant received		200.00
Contribution from C		£967.50

57 Records

Cross-references. See 17.5 CUSTOMS AND EXCISE POWERS for the production of documents; 40 INVOICES for details to be recorded on sales invoices; 63.5 SPECIAL SCHEMES for records under the cash accounting scheme; 63.19 and 63.20 SPECIAL SCHEMES for records and invoices under the flat-rate scheme for farmers.

The contents of this chapter are as follows.

57.1 GENERAL REQUIREMENTS FOR RECORDS BY TAXABLE PERSONS

Every taxable person must keep such records as C & E may require. [*VATA 1994, 11 Sch 6(1)*].

Specifically, every taxable person must, for the purposes of accounting for VAT, keep the following records.

- His business and accounting records.

- His VAT account.

- Copies of all VAT invoices issued by him.

- VAT invoices received by him.

- Certificates issued under provisions relating to fiscal or other warehouse regimes.

- Documentation received by him relating to acquisitions of any goods from other EC countries.

- Copy documentation issued by him, and documentation received by him, relating to the transfer, dispatch or transportation of goods by him to other EC countries.

- Documentation relating to importations and exportations by him.

- All credit notes, debit notes and other documents which evidence an increase or decrease in consideration that are received, and copies of all such documents that are issued by him.

[*SI 1995/2518, Reg 31; SI 1996/1250, Reg 8*].

Additionally, C & E may supplement the above provisions by a Notice published by them for that purpose. [*SI 1995/2518, Reg 31*]. These requirements, which are contained in C & E Notice 700, Section 8, are considered below in this chapter. They supplement the statutory requirements and *have legal force*.

Business records include, in addition to specific items listed above, orders and delivery notes, relevant business correspondence, appointment and job books, purchases and sales books, cash books and other account books, records of daily takings such as till rolls, annual accounts, including trading and profit and loss accounts and bank statements and paying-in slips.

Unless the business mainly involves the supply of goods and services direct to the public and less detailed VAT invoices are issued (see 40.7 INVOICES) all VAT invoices must also be retained. *Cash and carry wholesalers* must keep all till rolls and product code lists.

Records must be kept of all taxable goods and services received or supplied in the course of business (standard and zero-rated), together with any exempt supplies, gifts or loans of goods, taxable self-supplies and any goods acquired or produced in the course of business which are put to private or other non-business use.

All records must be kept up to date and be in sufficient detail to allow calculation of VAT. They do not have to be kept in any set way but must be in a form which will enable C & E officers to check easily the figures on the VAT return. Records must be readily available to C & E officers on request. If a taxable person has more than one place of business, a list of all branches must be kept at the principal place of business.

(C & E Notice 700, paras 8.1, 8.3).

Special records. In addition to the above general requirements, special records are necessary where the taxable person is operating the cash accounting scheme (see 63.5 SPECIAL SCHEMES), the flat-rate scheme for farmers (see 63.19 SPECIAL SCHEMES), one of the RETAIL SCHEMES (60) or one of the schemes for SECOND-HAND GOODS (61). These requirements are dealt with in the appropriate chapter. See also 23.27 EUROPEAN COMMUNITY: SINGLE MARKET for the requirement to keep a register of temporary movement of goods to and from other EC countries.

Penalties are payable for failure to keep and preserve records. See 52.14 PENALTIES.

De Voil Indirect Tax Service. See V5.201.

57.2   **RECORDS BY NON-TAXABLE PERSONS**

Non-taxable persons are generally outside the scope of VAT and are not therefore required to keep any records for VAT purposes. However, any person who, at a time when he is not a taxable person, acquires in the UK from another EC country any goods which are subject to excise duty or which consist of a new means of transport must keep such records of the acquisition as C & E specify in any Notice published by them. [*SI 1995/2518, Reg 31*]. See 23.9 and 23.35 EUROPEAN COMMUNITY: SINGLE MARKET.

57.3   **PRESERVATION OF RECORDS**

Every taxable person must keep and preserve such records as are required for a period of six years or such lessor period as C & E allow. [*VATA 1994, 11 Sch 6(3)*]. If this causes storage problems or involves undue expense, the VAT office should be consulted. They will be able to advise whether some records can be retained for a shorter period. Agreement of C & E must be obtained before any business records are destroyed within six years. (C & E Notice 700, para 8.1).

C & E are unlikely to agree to a shorter retention period than

- one year for production records, stock records (other than for second-hand schemes), job cards, appointment books, diaries, business letters and import/export documentation;

- three years for day books, ledgers, cash books, second-hand scheme stock books, purchase invoices, copy sales invoices, credit notes, debit notes and authenticated receipts;

- four years for daily gross takings records, records relating to retail scheme calculations and catering estimates; and

- five years for bank statements and paying-in books, management accounts and annual accounts.

Any records containing the VAT account must always be kept for the full six years.

(C & E Manual V1-24, section 1.11).

De Voil Indirect Tax Service. See V5.202.

57.4   **Forms in which records may be preserved**

The duty to preserve records may be discharged by the preservation of the information contained in them by such means as C & E may approve. [*VATA 1994, 11 Sch 6(4)*]. In addition to the preservation of the full original records, C & E have approved the use of the following.

- **Microfilm and microfiche** provided that the copies can readily be produced and that there are adequate facilities for C & E to view when required. Clearance must be obtained in advance from the VAT office before any transfer to microfilm or microfiche. C & E may require the old and new systems to be operated side by side for a limited time.

- **Computer records** provided the storage media e.g. magnetic tape, disc etc. can readily be converted into a legible form on request by C & E. Where records are kept on a computer, C & E can have access to it and can check its operation and the information stored. They can also ask for help from anyone concerned with the operation of the computer or its software. See 17.10 CUSTOMS AND EXCISE: POWERS. Where the records are kept by a computer bureau, the taxable person is responsible for arranging for the bureau to make the records available to C & E when required. Normally this will be at the principal place of business. Where a taxable person decides to use a computer or the services of a bureau for VAT accounting after registration, the VAT office should be notified (at the systems design stage or earlier for in-house computers).

(C & E Notice 700, para 8.1(d)(e)).

As a condition of approval C & E may impose such reasonable requirements as appear to them necessary for securing that the information will be readily available to them as if the original records had been kept. [*VATA 1994, 11 Sch 6(5)*]. C & E may refuse or withdraw approval for the use of microfilm etc. or computer media in any individual case if their requirements cannot be met.

De Voil Indirect Tax Service. See V5.206; V5.207.

57.5   **RECORDS OF OUTPUT TAX**

Note. The following does not apply to supplies dealt with under one of the special schemes for retailers. For records required in these cases, see 60 RETAIL SCHEMES.

Records must be kept of all supplies made in the course of business including goods sent out on sale or return, approval or similar terms. Information recorded must contain all the information required on VAT invoices. See 40.3 INVOICES. Where fully detailed invoices are issued and filed so as to be readily available, the record required is a summary (in the same order as copy invoices) enabling separate totals to be produced for each VAT period of

57.6 Records

(a) the amount of VAT chargeable on supplies and acquisitions. The VAT on adjustment for credits allowed (see 57.6 below) should be deducted from the amount of VAT payable in the VAT account (see 57.12 below);

(b) the VAT-exclusive value of standard-rated and zero-rated supplies and acquisitions;

(c) the value of any exempt supplies and acquisitions; and

(d) the amount of VAT due on goods imported by post (other than Datapost) with a value not exceeding £2,000 (see 34.3 IMPORTS) and on certain services received from abroad (see 39.4 INTERNATIONAL SERVICES). These amounts should also be carried to the VAT payable portion of the VAT account (see 57.12 below).

Under (b) and (c) above, no deduction should be made for *cash* discounts allowed but any credits allowed (see 57.6 below) should be deducted.

Goods given away or put to private or other non-business use. If acquired or produced in the course of business, VAT is due and a record must be kept showing date of transaction, description and quantity of the goods, VAT-exclusive cost and rate and amount of VAT chargeable. See 47.4 and 47.5 OUTPUT TAX for the value of the supply.

Self-supplies. See 45.6 MOTOR CARS for motor cars used by motor manufacturers or dealers who have produced or acquired them in the course of business. Records must show the tax point, value on which VAT is chargeable and the rate and amount of VAT. See 62.2 SELF-SUPPLY for records to be kept by a partly exempt trader who self-supplies certain printed matter.

(C & E Notice 700, para 8.4).

57.6   RECORDS OF CREDITS ALLOWED TO CUSTOMERS

Note. Where a RETAIL SCHEME (60) is used, the following only applies where the credit involves a VAT invoice.

Records must be kept of all credits allowed for taxable (including zero-rated) and exempt supplies and acquisitions. A record of a credit relating to

- **a VAT invoice** must contain the information required on VAT invoices (see 40.3 INVOICES) or indicate (e.g. by cross-reference to filed copies of credit notes) where the details can be found; and

- **zero-rated or exempt supplies** must show the date and amount of the credit and indicate whether an export is a zero-rated supply in the UK or an exempt supply.

For VAT purposes where filed copies of credit notes are complete and accessible no separate record need be kept.

VAT adjustments. If it is necessary to make a VAT adjustment for a credit allowed (see 40.15 INVOICES), the VAT should be deducted from the amount of VAT payable in the VAT account (see 57.12 below). Records of taxable supplies and output tax for credits allowed may be adjusted in the most convenient way provided the nature and reason are clear from the accounts or supporting documents. Where a credit note is entered in the business accounts in a period later than that in which the original supply was made, the VAT payable portion of the VAT account should be adjusted in that later period. See 57.12 below.

(C & E Notice 700, para 8.5).

57.7   RECORDS OF INPUT TAX

EC legislation. See 22.26 EUROPEAN COMMUNITY LEGISLATION.

UK legislation. Records must be kept of all taxable (including zero-rated) supplies received and acquisitions made in the course of business in such a way that the details of each transaction and evidence of the VAT charged are entered fully or can easily be found. Unless C & E otherwise allow, the following must be held to support a claim to input tax.

(*a*) **Suppliers' invoices.** Where the supply is from another taxable person, the claimant must hold a VAT invoice or a document treated as such (see 40.1 and 40.2 INVOICES). See also 63.20 SPECIAL SCHEMES for invoices from flat-rate farmers. An invoice marked 'pro forma' or 'this is not a VAT invoice' is not acceptable for the purposes of reclaiming VAT.

Exception. No VAT invoice is required where total expenditure, including VAT, is £25 or less and relates to telephone calls from public or private telephones, purchases through coin-operated machines or car park charges (except for on-street parking meters which are statutory fees levied by local authorities and not subject to VAT).

Incomplete invoices. Normally the invoice or other document should contain the full particulars required for a valid VAT invoice. See 40.3 *et seq.* INVOICES. However, C & E may accept as satisfactory evidence an invoice complete except for

- an identifying number;

- the customer's name and address; and

- the tax point (provided there is a date which can be taken to be the tax point)

provided the supplies in question are clearly for business purposes.

Originals normally required. VAT invoices held to substantiate claims to input tax should be originals. Copies are not normally accepted.

Where, however, the accounting arrangements require the original VAT invoice to be sent to a destination within the business which is different from the registered address for VAT (e.g. a branch), C & E may accept a photocopy of the original as evidence in support of input tax claims provided

- each photocopy is certified by a responsible officer as being a true copy of the original; and

- the original invoice is produced for inspection by C & E on formal request.

All requirements of a VAT invoice apply to the photocopy. C & E will notify the business in writing of the conditions and the business must give a written acceptance.

Invoices sent by fax or E-mail. C & E now accept that, as an alternative to sending VAT invoices by post, they may be sent to customers by fax or E-mail. See 40.14 INVOICES. If the invoice is received via fax and the recipient has a thermal-paper fax machine, the invoice may not be permanent and the recipient may not be able to fulfil the obligation to preserve the invoice for six years.

Cash and carry wholesalers' invoices. If the invoice is only in the form of a till roll with goods represented by product code numbers, an up-to-date copy of the wholesaler's product code list must be kept with the till rolls.

Invoices in name of employees. Certain invoices made out in the name of employees can be accepted as evidence for input tax purposes. See 35.5 INPUT TAX.

Court and tribunal decisions. A claim for input tax has been allowed where invoices were destroyed accidentally (*JJ Newman (781,903)*) and where invoices were lost on a change of residence but had previously been checked by the firm's accountants (*Read and Smith, [1982] VATTR 12 (1188)*). See *Chavda (t/a Hare Wines) (9895)* where the tribunal held that C & E had not acted reasonably by refusing to exercise their discretion to accept other documentary evidence (delivery notes) of the input tax incurred by the appellant. However, in the vast majority of tribunal and court decisions, claims for input tax without supporting invoices have been rejected and it has been ruled that *EC 6th Directive, Art 22(3)* confers on countries the power to require production of original invoices (*Reisdorf v Finanzamt Köln-West, CJEC [1997] STC 180*). Where C & E refuse to use their discretion to allow credit, tribunals only have a supervisory jurisdiction, the burden of proof being on the appellant to show that C & E acted unreasonably. See *Kohanzad v C & E Commrs QB, [1994] STC 967* and the Invoices and Credit Notes chapter in Tolley's VAT Cases.

(*b*) **Evidence of VAT on goods imported or removed from bonded warehouse.** On importation of goods, the claimant must hold a document showing him as importer, consignee or owner and showing an amount of VAT charged on the goods and authenticated or issued by the proper officer. For goods which have been removed from warehouse, the claimant must hold a document authenticated or issued by the proper officer showing the claimant's particulars and the amount of the VAT charged on the goods. See 34.11 IMPORTS for the official evidence (or other acceptable evidence) required which serves the same purpose as a VAT invoice from a registered UK supplier.

(*c*) **Evidence of VAT on goods acquired from another EC country.** On the acquisition of goods from another EC country, the claimant must hold a document required to be issued by the authority in that other country showing the claimant's VAT registration number (including the prefix 'GB'), the registration number of the supplier (including alphabetical code), the consideration for the supply exclusive of VAT, the date of issue of the document and a description of the goods supplied sufficient to identify them. Where the goods are a new means of transport (see 23.31 EUROPEAN COMMUNITY: SINGLE MARKET) the description must be sufficient to identify the acquisition as a new means of transport.

(*d*) **Evidence of services received from abroad.** Where any of the services listed in *VATA 1994, 5 Sch* are received from abroad (see 39.4 INTERNATIONAL SERVICES) the relevant invoice from the person supplying the services should be held.

[*SI 1995/2518, Reg 29(2)*]. (C & E Notice 700, para 8.6; C & E Manual V1-13, Chapter 2, paras 8.7, 8.8).

Non-deductible items. VAT is not reclaimable on certain supplies received for the business e.g. motor cars and entertainment expenses (see 35.8 INPUT TAX for details). However, a record must be kept of such supplies received even though the VAT charged is not to be included in the total carried to the VAT account.

De Voil Indirect Tax Service. See V3.421; V3.425–427.

57.8 **Form of records**

Where fully detailed invoices are received and filed so as to be readily available, the record required is a summary (in the same order as the invoices are filed) enabling a separate total to be produced for each VAT period of

(*a*) the amount of VAT charged on goods and services received including any VAT paid at import or on removal from bonded warehouse. Where adjustment is required for credit received from suppliers in the period (see 57.9 below) this should be deducted;

(*b*) the amount of VAT due on any goods imported by post (other than Datapost) with a value of £2,000 or less and on certain services received from abroad (see 39.4 INTERNATIONAL SERVICES);

(*c*) the VAT-exclusive value of all supplies received, including all such goods and services within (*b*) above.

Subject to the normal rules, the total amount of deductible input tax ((*a*) plus (*b*)) should be carried to the VAT allowable portion of the VAT account (see 57.12 below).

Under (*c*) above no deduction for *cash* discounts should be made but all credits received from suppliers should be deducted.

An add-list is an acceptable summary if it shows VAT and values separately itemised in the order in which the VAT invoices are batched or filed. Alternatively **cashbook accounting for inputs** may be used where it is the normal accounting practice to claim input tax when suppliers are paid. In practice the cash book payments record is adapted to serve as a record of inputs. On a change in basis of accounting to this method, VAT already claimed on a previous return should be excluded. See also 63.2 SPECIAL SCHEMES.

Note. If any of the RETAIL SCHEMES (60) is used, the cash book can also be used to work out the value of goods received for resale provided amounts owed to suppliers at the beginning of the period are subtracted and amounts owed at the end of the period are added.

(C & E Notice 700, para 8.7).

57.9 **RECORDS OF CREDITS RECEIVED FROM SUPPLIERS**

Records must be kept of all credits received for taxable (including zero-rated) inputs. A record of a credit relating to

* **a VAT invoice** must contain the information listed in 40.3 *et seq.* INVOICES, or indicate (e.g. by cross-reference to filed credit notes) where the details can be found; and

* **zero-rated supplies** need only indicate the date and amount of the credit.

For VAT purposes, where filed credit notes are complete and easily accessible, no separate record need be kept.

VAT adjustments. Where a credit is received relating to deductible input tax (see 40.15 INVOICES) and a VAT adjustment has to be made, records of supplies received and input tax must be adjusted. Whatever method is used to do this, the nature of the adjustment and reason for it must be clear from the accounts and supporting documents. At the end of each VAT period the deductible input tax entered in the VAT account and the VAT return entries must be the net amount, i.e. after deducting any VAT credits received in the period. If VAT credits received from suppliers exceed VAT charged on purchases in any VAT period, a minus figure (shown in brackets) should be entered in the input tax box on the VAT return. Where debit notes are issued to suppliers from whom credit is due and the commercial records are then adjusted, the VAT record may also be adjusted at that time. If later credit notes are received from suppliers, any errors should be corrected but the debit and credit notes should not be both used as accounting documents.

Provided both parties to the transaction agree, the *original* VAT charged need not be adjusted on a debit note issued by a fully taxable person.

(C & E Notice 700, para 8.8).

57.10   Records

57.10   **ADJUSTMENT OF ERRORS IN VAT INVOICES**

If VAT calculated on an invoice is *higher* than the amount properly due, the higher amount must be accounted for unless the error is corrected by issuing a credit note to the customer.

If VAT calculated is *lower* than the amount properly due, the full correct amount must be accounted for, whether or not the error is corrected with the customer (e.g. by means of a supplementary invoice). If the VAT shown on the invoice is too low and the supplier is unwilling or unable to recover the whole of the balance due from the customer, a VAT adjustment, calculated from the total VAT-inclusive amount actually charged, must be made.

Example

	£
Value of goods on VAT invoice	500
VAT at 17.5% but incorrectly stated as	55
	£555
Actual VAT due	£87.50
Adjusted VAT due	
£555 × 7/47 (VAT fraction)	82.66
Deduct VAT charged	55.00
Balance payable	£27.66

See 47.2 OUTPUT TAX for calculation of the VAT fraction.

If an error is corrected with the customer, output tax due should be adjusted at the end of the VAT period in which the error is corrected. The credit note or supplementary invoice must refer to the number and date of the original invoice and show the correct and incorrect amounts of VAT.

See 40.15 INVOICES for details required on the credit note.

Time limit. With effect from 1 May 1997, any adjustment to take account of an increase or decrease in consideration cannot be made more than three years after the end of the prescribed accounting period in which the original supply took place. See 51.8 PAYMENT OF VAT.

(C & E Notice 700, para 8.9).

De Voil Indirect Tax Service. See V3.518; V3.519.

57.11   **VOLUNTARY DISCLOSURE OF ERRORS IN PREVIOUS VAT RETURNS**

Errors on returns discovered by C & E may give rise to a misdeclaration penalty (see 52.10 PENALTIES). To avoid this, any errors discovered should be voluntarily disclosed before C & E begin to make enquiries (i.e. normally before an appointment is made to visit and inspect the records). In addition, a misdeclaration penalty will not normally be imposed where voluntary disclosure is made

- after a visit has been arranged (unless C & E believe that the errors were discovered earlier and only disclosed because of the proposed visit) or

- during or after a visit (unless C & E believe that disclosure was prompted by the enquiry).

Each error should be recorded as soon as it is discovered showing the period in which it occurred, whether it was output or input tax-related and where the supporting documentation can be found.

Method of disclosure. Depending upon the net value of all errors discovered during a prescribed accounting period (found by working out the total amounts due to, and repayable by, C & E and subtracting the smaller from the larger), there are two methods of disclosing errors made on VAT returns already submitted.

(a) *Where the net value of errors discovered does not exceed £2,000*, the VAT account for the period can be adjusted (see 57.12 below) and the value of that adjustment included in the current VAT return. Where errors are adjusted in this way, no default interest will be charged and the correction becomes part of the VAT for the period in which it is made.

(b) *Where the net value of errors discovered exceeds £2,000 or where it does not but the taxpayer so chooses*, the VAT office must be informed.

Disclosure can be made on a special form (Form VAT 652 obtainable from the VAT office) or by letter. Details must be given of the period in which the errors occurred; whether the errors were input or output tax errors; whether the individual error amounts were due to, or repayable by, C & E; and the total amount payable or repayable.

Interest *may* be charged on disclosures made this way but only where the net value of the errors exceeds £2,000. In such cases, to stop any interest accumulating, full payment should be sent with the disclosure to the VAT office.

The VAT office will pass on the details to VAT Central Unit who will amend their records and issue a 'Notice of Voluntary Disclosure' and a 'Statement of Account' showing the current balance and any interest.

Time limit for corrections. With effect from 1 May 1997, errors cannot be corrected using the method in (a) above more than three years after the prescribed accounting period in which they arose, except that there is no time limit for correcting

● errors arising from simple duplication of output tax; or

● tax point errors where an amount of VAT has been declared on the return which immediately precedes or follows the return for which the amount was due.

As a transitional provision, the three-year time limit does not apply where errors are discovered in a prescribed accounting period beginning before 1 May 1997 and the return for that period was not made, and was not required to be made, before that date.

Voluntary disclosures are not required for adjustments made as a result of

● issuing or receiving credit and debit notes (see 40.15 INVOICES);

● partial exemption annual adjustments;

● where a retail scheme is used, recalculations required under Apportionment Scheme 1 and Direct Calculation Scheme 2 (or under old Schemes B1, D, G and J);

● ceasing to use old retail scheme E;

● use of an approved estimation procedure;

● claims for bad debt relief;

● the capital goods scheme; or

● certain exports (see 25.28 EXPORTS).

[*SI 1995/2518, Reg 34; SI 1997/1086, Reg 5*]. (C & E Leaflet 700/45/93).

De Voil Indirect Tax Service. See V3.419; V3.506; V5.144.

57.12 VAT ACCOUNT

Every taxable person must keep and maintain an account to be known as the VAT account. It must be divided into separate parts relating to the prescribed accounting periods of the taxable person and each part must be divided into two portions known as 'the VAT payable portion' and 'the VAT allowable portion'.

The **VAT payable portion** comprises the following.

- Output tax due from the taxable person for that prescribed accounting period.

- Output tax due on acquisitions from other EC countries by the taxable person for that prescribed accounting period.

- Corrections to the VAT payable portion of a previous return which may be corrected on the current return (see 57.11 above).

- Subject to the time limit below, a positive/negative entry where there is an increase/decrease in the taxable consideration due on a supply *made* in a previous accounting period. The entry must be made in the return for the period in which the adjustment is given effect in the business accounts (unless the taxable person is insolvent in which case the entry must be made in the return for the period in which the supply was made).

  With effect from 1 May 1997, no adjustment must be made where that increase/decrease occurs more than three years after the end of the prescribed accounting period in which the original supply took place (unless the increase/decrease occurs in a prescribed accounting period beginning before 1 May 1997 and the return for the period in which effect is given to it in the business records has not been made, and was not required to have been made, before that date).

  It is essential that a credit note or debit note is prepared to support the adjustment (see 40.15 INVOICES). It is not possible to adjust the consideration on the original invoice without such a document (*British Telecommunications plc (14669)*).

- Adjustments to the amount of VAT payable by the taxable person for that prescribed accounting period which is required, or allowed, by or under any VAT *Regulations*.

The **VAT allowable portion** comprises the following.

- Input tax allowable to the taxable person for that prescribed accounting period.

- Input tax allowable in respect of acquisitions from other EC countries by the taxable person for that prescribed accounting period.

- Corrections of the VAT allowable portion of a previous return which may be corrected on the current return (see 57.11 above).

- Subject to the time limit below, a positive/negative entry where there is an increase/decrease in the taxable consideration due on a supply *received* in a previous accounting period. The entry must be made in the return for the period in which the adjustment is given effect in the business accounts (unless the taxable person is insolvent in which case the entry must be made in the return for the period in which the supply was received).

  With effect from 1 May 1997, no adjustment must be made where that increase/decrease occurs more than three years after the end of the prescribed accounting period in which the original supply took place (unless the increase/decrease occurs in a prescribed accounting period beginning before 1 May 1997 and the return for the period in which effect is given to it in the business records has not been made, and was not required to have been made, before that date).

It is essential that a credit note or debit note is prepared to support the adjustment (see 40.15 INVOICES).

- Adjustments to the amount of input tax allowable to the taxable person for that prescribed accounting period which is required, or allowed, by or under any VAT *Regulations*.

[*SI 1995/2518, Regs 32, 38;SI 1997/1086, Reg 6*].

De Voil Indirect Tax Service. See V5.211.

57.13 AUDIT OF VAT RECORDS

Where a business is subject to an independent audit, the audit will normally cover the VAT account and other records relating to VAT. However, as an auditor's responsibilities normally arise under statute, this does not mean that the auditor must make a specific reference to the VAT records in his report. (C & E Notice 700, para 8.1(f)).

De Voil Indirect Tax Service. See V5.203.

58   Recreation and Sport

Cross-references. See 22.17(*m*) and (*o*) EUROPEAN COMMUNITY LEGISLATION for exemption of certain sporting services supplied by non-profit-making organisations.

The contents of this chapter are as follows.

58.1   BETTING AND GAMING

EC legislation. See 22.18(*j*) EUROPEAN COMMUNITY LEGISLATION.

UK legislation. The provision of any facilities for the placing of bets or the playing of any 'game of chance' is exempt. Not included are

(*a*)   admission to any premises; or

(*b*)   the granting of a right to take part in a game in respect of which a charge may be made by virtue of regulations under the *Gaming Act 1968, s 14* or the *Betting, Gaming, Lotteries and Amusements (NI) Order 1985* (i.e. session and participation charges levied at premises which are licensed, or by clubs which are registered, under *Gaming Act 1968, Part II*); or

(*c*)   club subscription (including those to gaming, bingo and bridge clubs, etc.); or

(*d*)   the provision of a gaming machine (see 58.3 below).

[*VATA 1994, 9 Sch Group 4, Item 1 and Note (1)*].

'*Game of chance*' has the same meaning as in the *Gaming Act 1968, s 52(1)* (or the NI equivalent, see (*b*) above). Basically, it is either a game of pure chance (e.g. dice or roulette) where the result cannot be influenced by the player or a game of chance and skill combined (e.g. whist or rubber bridge) where the player either cannot eliminate chance or can only do so by exercising superlative skill. Pool betting is included as is bingo (see 58.2 below for special provisions). See also *W & D Grantham (853)*.

Many other games, including any athletic game or sport, are not included. The supply of the right to play games of skill (e.g. 'spot the ball' and similar newspaper competitions, duplicate bridge and chess) is standard-rated.

Value of the exempt supply. The value of the exempt output is the full amount of stakes or takings less only any money paid out as winnings or, if prizes are goods, their cost (including VAT) to the supplier. Betting or gaming duty is not deductible.

Session or participating charges (i.e. charges made to play, normally separate from the stakes risked by players in the game) are standard-rated if falling within (*b*) above but otherwise are exempt.

Small scale gaming. *Gaming Act 1968, s 40* allows small scale gaming at certain clubs and institutes. The maximum participation charge is laid down. Such charges are exempt unless made by a club registered or licensed under *Gaming Act 1968, Part II* when standard-rated (see (*b*) above).

Gaming for fund-raising purposes. *Gaming Act 1968, s 41* allows small scale gaming (including bingo, bridge and whist) other than on licensed or registered premises within (*b*) above, but only for fund-raising purposes. The maximum payment to play and the maximum prize money are specified. Any charge to take part in such a game is exempt (apart from admission charges which are always standard-rated).

Agents. Pools agents and collectors are not required to account for VAT on commission received. The services of bookmakers who act as agents for other bookmakers or the Tote in accepting bets, and the services of bookmakers' agents, are also exempt.

Prizes. The following treatment applies.

• Cash prizes are outside the scope of VAT.

• Prizes of goods in free lotteries and as bonus prizes in cash bingo are gifts and VAT is due if the current purchase price exceeds £15. Prizes of services are outside the scope of VAT. See 47.4 OUTPUT TAX.

• Prizes of goods or services in exempt betting and gaming should be treated as part of the exempt supply. Output tax is not due but the input tax on purchase is not deductible (subject to the partial exemption *de minimis* limits).

• Where prizes of goods or services are given in taxable competitions (e.g. spot the ball) no further VAT is due.

Betting and gaming duties. For information, see the following C & E Notices available from Excise offices: pool betting duty (147); general betting duty (off course) (451); gaming licence duty (453); general betting duty (on course) (455).

(C & E Leaflet 701/26/95).

De Voil Indirect Tax Service. See V4.131; V6.130C.

58.2   **Bingo**

Definitions. '*Session and participating charges*' are charges for the right to take part in the game. They are levied in addition to, and often separate from, the stakes which are risked in the game or any admission charge.

'*Stake money*' is the amount of money paid by each of the players (excluding admission and participating charges) which they risk in the game and which is returned as winnings to the winning player(s).

Prize bingo. This is a game were the prizes are not in cash and is normally played as a main activity in shopping centres and seaside arcades under conditions imposed by *Lotteries and Amusements Act 1976, s 16.*

Session and participating charges are exempt. [*VATA 1994, 9 Sch Group 4, Item 1*]. This applies even if the charges exceed the maximum permitted under law.

Prizes given are not a separate supply for VAT purposes and are part of the exempt supply. VAT need not be accounted for on goods given as prizes (even if costing more than £15).

Value of exempt supply. The value of the exempt supply is the total amount charged to play bingo less the VAT-inclusive cost of the goods given as prizes.

58.2 Recreation and Sport

For each VAT period

Step 1   Add up gross session and participation charges including any prize vouchers used to pay for further games of bingo. Do not deduct any bingo duty payable   A

Step 2   Calculate

The VAT-inclusive cost of goods and value of vouchers given as prizes. Where vouchers are given as prizes and redeemed for goods, include only the VAT-inclusive cost of the goods, not the face value of the vouchers   B

Any cash prizes given. Do not include any participation charges used as additional prize money   C

Payments made to retailers who redeem prize vouchers for goods   D

Exempt output = A- (B + C + D)

Admission charges are standard-rated. See 58.6 below.

Cash bingo.

Session and participating charges. The VAT liability depends on the premises.

(*a*)   Where cash bingo is played on premises licensed or registered under *Gaming Act 1968, Part II* (or *Betting, Gaming, Lotteries and Amusements (Northern Ireland) Order 1985, Chapter III*), charges may be made by virtue of regulations under *section 14* of that Act (or, as the case may be, *Art 76* of that Order). Any such charges are excluded from exemption by *VATA 1994, 9 Sch Group 4, Note (1)* and are standard-rated. This applies to licensed bingo clubs.

It is important not to confuse licensing or registration under *Gaming Act, Part II* with registration under *Part III* of the Act which applies to gaming machines. If registered under *Part III* alone, bingo session and participating charges can be exempt under (*b*) below.

(*b*)   Where cash bingo is promoted at other premises or clubs, the session and participating charges are exempt within the following limits.

- Small scale bingo played at a club or miners' welfare institute under the provisions of *Gaming Act 1968, s 40* (or *Betting, Gaming, Lotteries and Amusements (Northern Ireland) Order 1985, Art 128*). The club must have at least 25 members, not be of a temporary character, and have other activities in addition to gaming. There is a maximum 50p participation charge by the club which is intended to do no more than cover the cost of facilities provided. There is no limit on the stakes provided all money is returned to the players as prizes. Gaming must be confined to members of the club or their *bona fide* guests and may not be advertised.

- Fund-raising bingo played at a function (e.g. fête, dance, etc.) under *Gaming Act 1968, s 41* (or *Betting, Gaming, Lotteries and Amusements (Northern Ireland) Order 1985, Art 126*). Only one payment, not exceeding £3, can be made whether by way of entrance fee or stake or otherwise. The total value of all prizes must generally not exceed £300 per day. All proceeds, after deduction of prize money and expenses, must be devoted to purposes other than private gain. The activity can be advertised and can be open to the public.

Value of exempt supply. Where session and participating charges are exempt, the value of the exempt output is the total amount charged to play bingo less the stake money.

For each VAT period

Step 1   Add up gross session and participation charges. Do not deduct
any bingo duty   A

Step 2   Add up the stake money given back to players as prizes. Do not
include any participation charges used as additional prize money   B

Exempt output = A - B

Stake money is outside the scope of VAT.

Admission charges are standard-rated. See 58.6 below.

Composite bingo charges. Where a single payment is made covering stake money,
participation fee and possibly admission fee, the total charge must be apportioned and
the correct VAT liability applied to each part.

Bonus prizes in games of cash bingo are gifts and VAT must be accounted for on the
current purchase price where this is more than £15 (excluding VAT).

'*Linked*' *cash bingo* is where two or more clubs join together in a telephone link to play a
single simultaneous game. Each club must account for VAT on admission and
participation charges at its own premises. The central organiser is responsible for
accounting for any administrative charges.

'*Multiple*' *cash bingo* (the national game) is where the same game of bingo is played
separately in each of a group of clubs. Each club must account for VAT on admission and
participation charges at its own premises. The amount remitted by each of the premises
to the organiser for use as prize money is outside the scope of VAT.

'*Instant*', '*parti*' and '*mechanised*' *bingo*. These may be played as an interval game and
become operative when a coin is inserted. The club normally retains part of the charge as
a participation charge and returns the balance, less bingo duty, as prizes in the game. The
participation fee is standard-rated.

(C & E Leaflet 701/27/97).

Bingo duty. For details, see C & E Notice 457 available from Excise offices.

De Voil Indirect Tax Service. See V6.130A.

58.3   **Gaming and amusement machines**

The provision of a 'gaming machine' is specifically excluded from the general exemption
from VAT applying to betting and the playing of games of chance (see 58.1 above). The
takings from gaming machines (and 'amusement machines' generally) are therefore
standard-rated. Note that the provisions of *VATA 1994, s 23* below do not apply to the
Isle of Man. [*IMA 1979, s 1(d)*].

'*Gaming machine*' means a machine constructed or adapted for playing a game of chance
on which a player pays to play (except where he has an opportunity to play payment-free
as the result of having previously played successfully) either by inserting a coin or token
into the machine or in some other way. The element of chance must be provided by
means of the machine. [*VATA 1994, s 23(4), 9 Sch Group 4, Note (3)*]. This definition
includes 'amusement with prizes' machines, jackpot machines, crane grab machines and
pin tables. A machine which involves the playing of a game of chance may fall within the
definition of a gaming machine even though no prize can be won.

An '*amusement machine*' is one on which there is no prize in any circumstances or where
the prize depends on the skill or knowledge of the player and is not dependent on chance,
e.g. video games (not video poker machines) and juke boxes.

Hiring of machines and site rentals. Hire charges, whether for a fixed rental or a share of the profits, are standard-rated. Charges for siting machines are exempt under *VATA 1994, 9 Sch Group 1* as a supply of a licence to occupy land (see 42.2 LAND AND BUILDINGS) although the supplier can opt to tax the supply (see 42.20 LAND AND BUILDINGS). See, however, *The Wolverhampton and Dudley Breweries plc, [1990] VATTR 131 (5351)* where it was held that the real subject of an agreement for the siting of amusement machines in public houses were the machines themselves and not the use or enjoyment of the land on which they stood. Consequently the agreements did not amount to licences to occupy land and were standard-rated.

Accounting for VAT on machine takings. VAT on the takings must be accounted for by the person who supplies the use of the machine to the public.

In respect of gaming machines, this is the occupier of the premises where the machine is situated. For licensed commercial gaming premises it is the holder of the licence or that person's employee. For registered clubs or miners' institutes it is any officer or member of the club or any person employed by them. For travelling pleasure fairs, it is the showman who owns or operates the fair. For any other premises (e.g. public houses, amusement arcades, etc.) it is the person named on the permit issued under *Gaming Act 1968, Part III*. For an unlicensed gaming machine, it is normally the person who controls its operation, but the supply will depend on the particular arrangements in each case. See also *R v Ryan & Others CA, [1994] STC 446* where, in a criminal prosecution, the machine owners were held to be liable to account for VAT on the unlawful operation of unlawful credit gaming machines.

In respect of amusement machines, the person who supplies the use of the machine to the public is either the site operator (if the machine is purchased, hired or rented by the occupier of the premises on which it is sited) or the owner of the machine (where the owner pays a rent to the occupier of the premises on which the machine is sited). If the machine is operated on a profit-sharing basis, the supplier of its use to the public will be the person who controls its operation.

Calculation of VAT due. The tax point for supplies made from coin-operated machines is the date the machine is used. However, as an administrative convenience, operators may delay accounting for VAT until the takings are removed from the machine. (C & E Notice 48, ESC 2.6). For all other purposes, the normal tax point rules apply. Therefore in the event of a theft of takings from a machine, VAT must still be accounted for in full on any supplies that have been made from the machine.

Taxable take. Whenever cash or tokens are removed from the machine, the 'taxable take' must be calculated and recorded. '*Taxable take*' is the amount paid by persons to play the game less the amount (if any) received by persons playing successfully (other than the person making the supply and persons acting on his behalf). [*VATA 1994, s 23(1)(2)*]. Included is any money in the 'tubes' in excess of the float. Any foreign coins, fakes or facsimiles inserted may be disregarded. In practice, when the machine is opened, the float should be restored to its original level with cash and tokens taken from the machine. The balance of coins and tokens remaining in the machine is then the taxable take upon which VAT is due. VAT is calculated by applying the VAT fraction (currently 7/47) to this amount. No deduction must be made for hire or rental charges to the machine owner; any share of profits or other charge due to another person; any payments made out of the takings such as those under maintenance contracts; or gaming machine licence duty. See also *Glawe Spiel-und Unterhaltungsgeräte Aufstellungsgesellschaft mbH & Co KG v Finanzamt Hamburg-Barmbek-Uhlenhorst, CJEC [1994] STC 543* where it was held that the taxable amount did not include the prescribed proportion of the coins inserted which had, by statute, to be paid out as winnings.

Usually the taxable take should be calculated for each individual machine. However, in the case of an amusement arcade with large numbers of machines, C & E may give approval to the calculation on a site-wide basis.

Tokens. The insertion of a token into a machine should be treated as the payment of an amount equal to that for which the token can be obtained. [*VATA 1994, s 23(3)*].

Replayable tokens. The receipt of a replayable token (i.e. those that can be used to play the machine) by a person playing successfully is treated as the receipt of an amount equal to its cash value. [*VATA 1994, s 23(3)*]. Any such tokens previously returned to the machine through the 'no play' token return slot by the site occupier or gaming machine owner are outside the scope of VAT.

Non-replayable tokens. The receipt of a non-replayable token which can be exchanged for money by a successful player is treated as the receipt of an amount equal to its exchange value. [*VATA 1994, s 23(3)*]. Non-replayable tokens which are exchangeable for cash or goods sold by the person accounting for VAT should therefore be treated in the same way as replayable tokens. Where non-replayable tokens have no recognised cash value and are exchangeable for goods not sold by the person accounting for VAT, the full amount of cash removed from the machine must be recorded, after any necessary adjustment to the cash float. No deduction should be made for tokens won or put into the float or for prizes given in exchange for these tokens.

See also *Feehan v C & E Commrs QB 1994, [1995] STC 75.* The wording of the legislation contemplates payment for playing by insertion of a token 'into the machine' but there is no such restriction on the receipt of winning being 'from a machine'. In that case, the court therefore upheld the tribunal's decision that the value of the supply was the net amount of receipts after deducting winnings paid to players by the publican.

Retail schemes. Treatment of gaming and amusement machine takings depends on the scheme used.

- Under a point of sale scheme, taxable take of the machine should be added to standard-rated daily gross takings on the day the cash and/or tokens are removed. (C & E Notice 727/3/97, para 3.2).

- Under an apportionment scheme, takings should be excluded from daily gross takings and VAT calculated outside the scheme. (C & E Notice 727/4/97, para 3.2).

- Under a direct calculation scheme,

  (i) where minority goods are zero-rated or lower-rated, taxable take of the machine should be added to daily gross takings on the day the cash and/or tokens are removed; and

  (ii) where minority goods are standard-rated or lower-rated, takings should be excluded from daily gross takings and VAT calculated outside the scheme.

  (C & E Notice 727/5/97, para 3.2)

- Under earlier schemes, where retail scheme A, B, B1, B2 or F was used, taxable takings were added to daily gross takings. Where any other scheme was used (or where one of those schemes was used but a separate record of takings was kept) takings were excluded from the retail scheme calculations and calculated separately.

Prizes. Machine prizes (e.g. from a crane grab machine) are treated as business gifts and VAT need not be accounted for on the value if costing less than £15. See 47.4 OUTPUT TAX. VAT on prize goods exchanged for tokens with a recognised cash value is calculated on the normal retail selling price of the goods or, where such goods are not sold by the supplier to the general public, the equivalent cash value of the tokens accepted in exchange. Input tax incurred on the purchase of the prize goods can be reclaimed in the normal way.

Gaming machine licence duty. This is outside the scope of VAT if either the licence is obtained by the occupier of the premises where the machine is sited or the machine owner obtains the licence on behalf of the site occupier and itemises its cost separately on the invoice for the machine. However if the gaming machine supplier charges for the supply of a licensed machine, the cost of obtaining the licence is part of a single supply of a gaming machine, and the whole amount is standard-rated.

(C & E Leaflet 701/13/95).

For details of gaming machine licence duty, see C & E Notice 454 available from Excise offices.

De Voil Indirect Tax Service. See V4.131; V6.130.

58.4   **LOTTERIES**

Under the *EC 6th Directive*, lotteries are exempt from VAT subject to conditions and limitations laid down by each country (see 22.18(*j*) EUROPEAN COMMUNITY LEGISLATION). Under UK law, the granting of a right to take part in a lottery is exempt under *VATA 1994, 9 Sch Group 4, Item 2*.

There is no statutory definition of 'lottery'. From case law, it is taken to mean the distribution of prizes by chance where the persons taking part in the operation, or a substantial number of them, make a payment or consideration in return for obtaining their chance of a prize. Where any merit or skill plays a part in determining the outcome, the event is not a lottery but a competition.

Exemption covers the sale of the lottery tickets to the public. The value of the exempt supply is the gross proceeds from ticket sales *less* the cash and goods (inclusive of VAT) given as prizes. See below for free lotteries.

Under *Lotteries and Amusement Act 1976*, lotteries may be run by or on behalf of societies which are established for

• charitable purposes;

• participation in sports or cultural activities; or

• other purposes which are neither commercial nor for private gain.

The society must nominate and authorise in writing an individual member to be the promoter of the lottery (although the exempt supply is still treated as having been made by the society). If the society sets up a separate development association or other organisation to promote its lottery, it is that association which makes the exempt supply. The payment of the net proceeds of the lottery by that association to the society is outside the scope of VAT.

Local authorities may also promote lotteries under *Lotteries Regulations 1977*.

Lottery management companies. A '*lottery management company*' is an individual, partnership or limited company that supplies lottery management services to a society, development association or local authority. This service is usually comprehensive and may include arranging for printing of tickets, organising publicity, arranging ticket sales and paying out prizes. A lottery management company cannot promote a lottery.

The supply of lottery management services is standard-rated and VAT must be accounted for on

• any fee or commission paid by the lottery promoter; *plus*

- any additional amounts retained from gross ticket sales to cover the cost of running the lottery (including commission received and retained by selling agents used by the lottery management company)

less the amount paid out in cash prizes and the VAT-inclusive cost of goods given as prizes.

However, if a lottery management company also sells tickets itself using its own outlets and employees (rather than merely arranging for their sale by independent sellers), it can exempt this direct selling service like any other ticket seller (see below). If the company does not specify a separate charge for its own selling service, it must apportion its global charge to the promoter between exempt and standard-rated supplies. The exempt element must be shown separately on the VAT invoice. See 47.3 OUTPUT TAX for methods of apportionment.

Lottery ticket sellers. The service of selling lottery tickets is an exempt supply but it is important to know in what capacity a person is selling the tickets to establish who is to be attributed with the receipt of the income from the ticket sales.

- *If the seller is an employee of a lottery management company,* that company is supplying the exempt service and can apportion its charges to the promoter (see above).

- *If the seller is an independent selling agent,* the seller's exempt output is the fee or commission the seller receives plus any other amounts which the seller is entitled to deduct.

- *If the seller is acting as a principal* (having bought the tickets from the lottery management company or promoter for sale to the public), the ticket seller's exempt income is the money retained from sales of tickets.

If a ticket seller is a retailer using one of the retail schemes, the exempt outputs and any money taken from ticket sales must be excluded from the scheme calculations.

Treatment of prizes. If prizes are given as an integral part of the supply of the right to participate in a lottery, they may be treated as part of the right to enter it and no output VAT is due on the award. See below, however, for free lotteries. Any VAT incurred on purchasing prizes can be deducted as input tax subject to the normal partial exemption rules.

No VAT is due on prizes of services.

Free lotteries. If a lottery is free to enter, there is no exempt supply. Any goods given as prizes should be treated as business gifts and VAT must be accounted for on the VAT-exclusive cost if the prize exceeds £15. Input tax is then deductible in the normal manner. However, there are two special exemptions to the normal rule.

- When cars are given as prizes, no output tax is due because VAT cannot be deducted when they are purchased to be given away.

- VAT incurred on holidays provided as prizes cannot be reclaimed under the business entertainment provisions.

(C & E Leaflet 701/28/97).

De Voil Indirect Tax Service. See V4.131; V6.130.

58.5 **SPORTS AND PHYSICAL RECREATION COMPETITIONS — ENTRY FEES**

An entry fee for the right to enter a 'competition' is normally standard-rated. However the grant of a right to enter a competition in 'sport or physical recreation' is exempt if

58.6 Recreation and Sport

(*a*) the entry fee is allocated wholly towards the provision of a prize or prizes awarded in that competition; or

(*b*) the grant is made by a 'non-profit making body' established for the purposes of sport or physical recreation *except* where, before 1 April 1994, the entry fee consists wholly or partly of a charge which the body ordinarily makes for the use of its facilities or the admission to its premises.

[*VATA 1994, 9 Sch Group 10, Items 1 and 2*].

The exception under (*b*) above does not apply if the body is running the competition at a ground belonging to another organisation which ordinarily makes charges for facilities, etc.

'*Competition*' means a structured and organised contest, tournament or race where prizes or titles are awarded. Prizes may consist of money, goods or cups, etc.

'*Sports or physical recreation*' covers sports such as cricket, football, athletics, etc.; racing (including horse, greyhound and pigeon racing); motor sports and other physical recreation, e.g. darts, snooker, angling, archery, dancing and clay pigeon shooting. *Not included* are chess, card games, animal showing and newspaper competitions.

See 58.9 below for the interpretation of '*non-profit making body*'.

Value of the exempt supply. This is normally the full amount of entry fees (without deduction for prizes). Special rules apply as follows.

• Where non-essential standard-rated goods or services (e.g. catering) which are not sold to other people are supplied to competitors, the entry fee must be apportioned. No apportionment is required if essential standard-rated goods, etc. (e.g. hire of equipment) are supplied under these circumstances.

• Where the entry fee covers the supply of standard-rated goods or services normally sold to people not taking part in a competition, VAT must be accounted for on the whole entry fee.

• Where the entry fee covers the supply of zero-rated goods or services, the entry fee may be apportioned provided the zero-rated items are available to non-competitors.

Prizes. No VAT is due on prizes of goods costing £15 or less, services or the loan of challenge cups, shields and other perpetual trophies which remain the property of the organisation or club mounting the competition. Cash prizes are outside the scope of VAT. Prizes of goods costing over £15 are regarded as gifts. VAT must be accounted for on the cost of the goods (and input tax incurred on the purchase can be deducted).

(C & E Leaflet 701/34/89).

De Voil Indirect Tax Service. See V4.161.

58.6 **ADMISSION CHARGES TO ENTERTAINMENT, CULTURAL ACTIVITIES, SPORT, ETC.**

Standard-rated admission charges. Normally the full amount of any admission charges are standard-rated (but see below for certain admissions which may be exempt). *Included* are admissions to cinemas, theatres, swimming pools, amusement arcades and fun fairs, dances, sports events, museums and galleries, parks and gardens, historic houses, an area of the countryside for general recreational purposes, zoos and safari parks and air shows.

Exempt admission charges. With effect from 1 June 1996, the following admission charges are exempt.

(*a*)   Admission charges by a 'public body' to

   (i)   a 'museum, gallery, art exhibition or zoo', or

   (ii)   a theatrical, musical or choreographic performance of a cultural nature

unless the exemption would be likely to create 'distortions of competition' such as to place a commercial enterprise carried on by a taxable person at a disadvantage.

The performance under (ii) above must be provided exclusively by one or more public bodies, one or more 'eligible bodies' (see (*b*) below) or any combination of public bodies and eligible bodies. (Exemption does not apply where, for example, a local authority acts as ticket broker for a commercial promoter with whom it has a profit-sharing arrangement.)

A '*public body*' means

● a local authority;

● a government department within the meaning of *VATA 1994, s 41(6)* (see 43.6 LOCAL AUTHORITIES AND STATUTORY BODIES); or

● a non-departmental public body which is listed in the 1995 edition of the publication prepared by the Office of Public Service and known as 'Public Bodies'. (Copies of this document may be obtained from HMSO.)

'*Distortions of competition*'. The public body must take steps to notify all identifiable commercial suppliers of 'related' facilities or performances (e.g. if it wishes to exempt charges to a museum, it must notify all commercial undertakings in its area falling within (i) above but not those falling within (ii) above). Notice must be in writing but can be by individual letter or public notice in the local press for its geographical area. The notice must specify a date by which objections to exemption must be lodged. If no objections are received, the body can then start to exempt supplies but must retain copies of relevant correspondence and advertisements for future examination. If any objection is received, the VAT office should be asked for a ruling and in the meantime supplies should not be exempt. Once exemption is in place, it is not necessary to check on competition for each performance under (i) above or to make periodic checks for a new commercial supplier. It is for that supplier to approach the VAT office. (C & E Notice 701/47/96, paras 3.6–3.11).

In cases where exemption would be financially disadvantageous to a public body (e.g. by restricting the recovery of input tax on building, refurbishment and other capital projects) and the body wishes to continue to tax admission charges, C & E's current policy is not to compel the body to exempt although this will remain subject to review. (C & E Notice 701/47/96, para 3.5).

(*b*)   Admission charges by an 'eligible body' to

   (i)   a 'museum, gallery, art exhibition or zoo', or

   (ii)   a theatrical, musical or choreographic performance of a cultural nature.

An '*eligible body*' means any body (other than a public body, see (*a*) above) which

● is precluded from distributing, and does not distribute, any profit it makes;

● applies any profits made from admission charges exempt under this provision to the continuance or improvement of the facilities made available by means of the supplies; and

● is managed and administered on a voluntary basis by persons who have no direct or indirect financial interest in its activities. If the body makes any payment for managerial or administration services it is not eligible for exemption. Reimbursement of expenses, audit charges, honoraria and payments of a similar nature will not necessarily disqualify a body from exemption; neither will the employment of staff or payments for guides, zoo keepers, producers or choreographers etc. provided such persons are not involved in the management or administration of the organisation (C & E Notice 701/47/96, paras 4.3-4.6). See also *Glastonbury Abbey, [1996] VATDR 307 (14579)*.

[VATA 1994, 9 Sch Group 13; SI 1996/1256].

What qualifies as a '*museum, gallery, art exhibition or zoo*' under (*a*)(i) and (*b*)(i) above has to be judged by reference to the normal everyday meaning of the words and taking into account evidence such as the nature of the exhibits and whether, for example, a museum belongs to a representative body for museums. '*Performance*' under (*a*)(ii) and (*b*)(ii) above also has to be judged on its individual merits but C & E accept that any form of stage play, opera, musical comedy, classical music, jazz, ballet or dance is cultural for these purposes. (C & E Notice 701/47/96, paras 2.3, 2.4).

Fund-raising events by charities and other non-profit-making bodies. The supply of goods and services in connection with certain special one-off fund-raising events may also be exempt. See 12.9 CHARITIES and 14.11 CLUBS AND ASSOCIATIONS.

Donations in lieu of admission. True donations are outside the scope of VAT. To be accepted as a donation for VAT purposes, it must be clear to the donor that admission can be gained whether or not a payment is given and the size of the payment is entirely up to him, e.g. a 'free-will' collection in the hall or sports ground or a collection box placed near the entrance. Where a person has to pay to get in, or is made to think that he has to do so, the payment is a standard-rated admission charge (unless otherwise exempt). For donations in addition to charging admission at charitable functions see 12.10 CHARITIES.

Admission by programme only. A programme which contains a substantial amount of reading matter or information may qualify for zero-rating. See 54.14 PRINTED MATTER, ETC. However, a programme does not qualify for zero-rating if it is no more than an elaborate ticket which has to be bought to get into the event, etc. Payment for such a programme is the consideration for admission even if payment cannot be legally enforced. Otherwise, where a programme does qualify for zero-rating but the price charged also includes an element of admission charge, an apportionment can be made. The zero-rated part should be based on the unit cost of the programme plus a reasonable mark-up.

Accounting for VAT. The 'promoter' must account for the VAT. This is the person with administrative or financial control over the event, e.g. the person hiring the stadium, paying the performers or organising publicity. For sports matches the promoter is normally the home club or association. Where the game is not played on the home team's ground, the promoter is still the team which would have been the home team if it had a suitable ground. If a game is required to be played on a neutral ground, the promoter is usually the body running the competition concerned, e.g. a governing body of the sport. The promoter of a benefit or testimonial match may be the player himself, his club or a special benefit committee.

Recovery of input tax. Admission for a charge is always a business activity for VAT purposes and related input tax incurred will normally be deductible unless the admission charges are exempt (see above) in which case the partial exemption rules may apply.

If the public is admitted free of charge to any premises there is no business activity and VAT incurred is not input tax. If the premises are also used for business purposes, input tax may be apportioned, see 35.7 INPUT TAX.

(C & E Leaflet 700/22/89).

Boxes, seats, etc. See 42.12 LAND AND BUILDINGS.

58.7   **SPORT AND PHYSICAL RECREATION FACILITIES**

Subject to the exemptions in 58.8 and 58.9–58.13 below, the granting of facilities for playing any sport or participating in any physical recreation is standard-rated. The grant of any right to call for or be granted facilities which would be standard-rated under this provision is also standard-rated. Included is an equitable right, a right under an option or right to pre-emption and, in relation to Scotland, a personal right.

[*VATA 1994, 9 Sch Group 1, Item 1(m)(n)*].

Standard-rating has been applied to the supply of a football ground for international matches, the presence of ticket-paying spectators not preventing the facilities granted being those for playing sport rather than a licence to occupy land (*Queens Park Football Club Ltd, (1988) VATTR 76 (2776)*). C & E accept that this decision applies to supplies by other sporting stadia, both indoors and outdoors. (C & E News Release 72/88, 20 September 1988). Standard-rating has also been applied to the use of a practice range at a golf club (*L H Johnson (14955)*).

De Voil Indirect Tax Service. See V6.131.

58.8   **Letting of facilities**

The letting of facilities designed or adapted for playing any sport or taking part in physical recreation is normally standard-rated. However, the letting of such facilities may be exempt if the letting is for over 24 hours or there is a series of lettings to the same person over a period of time. Exemption will also apply if certain general purpose facilities are hired for sporting use or if sports facilities are hired out for non-sporting purposes. See below for further details.

24 hour rule. Where the facilities are provided for a continuous period of use exceeding 24 hours, the grant is exempt.

Series of lets. Also exempt is the granting of such facilities for a series of ten or more periods (whether or not exceeding 24 hours) to a school, club, association or an organisation representing affiliated clubs or constituent associations where

(i) each period is in respect of the same activity carried on at the same place;

(ii) the interval between each period is not less than one day and not more than fourteen days;

(iii) consideration is payable by reference to the whole series and is evidenced by written agreement; and

(iv) the grantee has exclusive use of the facilities.

[*VATA 1994, 9 Sch Group 1 Note 16*].

Under (i) above, a different pitch, court or lane at the same sports ground or premises would count as the same place.

Under (iii) above, a formal agreement, an exchange of letters or an invoice issued in advance of the series requiring payment for the whole of the series would be acceptable as evidence. This condition would not be breached if a refund is given because a facility is not available for use on a booked date because of an unforeseen non-availability but a refund in any other circumstances would breach the requirements.

Sports facilities include stadia, swimming pools, tennis and squash courts, gymnasia, dance studios, golf courses, skating rinks, cricket and football pitches and other specially designed, adapted or equipped land or premises. Where there is a group of adjacent courts, lanes or pitches, each can be regarded as a separate facility. Premises count as sports facilities if they are designed or adapted for playing any sport or taking part in physical recreation. For example, the presence of fixed basketball nets in halls or mirrors and bars in dance studios normally mean that those premises are sports facilities.

Other exempt supplies. The hire of the following facilities are regarded as exempt supplies.

- General purpose halls, including village and church halls, which contain no sports facilities or equipment beyond floor markings for, say badminton, even if the purpose of those wanting to use the hall on a particular occasion happens to be to play badminton.

- Sports facilities hired for non-sporting purposes, e.g. football pitches for fêtes or sports halls for political meetings.

(C & E Leaflet 742/1/90, paras 2, 4, 5).

Services supplied with the hire of sports facilities. Changing room facilities, floodlighting, etc. are incidental to the main supply and have the same VAT liability even if the invoice itemises them separately. The provision of optional extra equipment or services (e.g. supplies of staff) constitutes a separate supply and are subject to VAT according to their normal liability. (C & E Leaflet 742/1/90, para 6).

Option to tax. A supplier may be able to choose to standard-rate some of the above supplies which would otherwise be exempt. See 42.20 LAND AND BUILDINGS.

58.9 Sporting services provided by non-profit making bodies

Exemption applies to the supply of services closely linked with and essential to sport or physical recreation supplied to 'individuals' 'taking part in' the activity where the supplies are made by

- a 'non-profit making body' having members to those of its members who are granted membership for a period of three months or more; and

- a 'non-profit making body' which does not run a membership scheme (e.g. a charity).

Specifically excluded are

- the supply of any services of residential accommodation, catering or transport; and

- supplies by local authorities, government departments and non-departmental public bodies such as Sports Councils. Any exemption for supplies made by such bodies was initially postponed for further consideration on the impact of input tax recovery, sports building projects, etc. Following a review, C & E has decided not to extend the exemption. (C & E Business Brief 9/95, 18 May 1995).

[*VATA 1994, 9 Sch Group 10, Item 3 and Notes 1–3*].

'*Individuals*' should be interpreted as including families. (C & E Notice 701/45/94, para 10).

'*Taking part in*' includes playing, competing, refereeing, umpiring, judging, coaching and training but not watching or being involved in administration. (C & E Notice 701/45/94, para 12).

'*Non-profit making body*'. A body whose constitution or articles of association preclude it from distributing surpluses of income over expenditure to its members, shareholders or any other party (other than in the event of a liquidation or cessation of activities) will normally be accepted as non-profit making for these purposes. However, the lack of any provision precluding distribution will not necessarily be the sole factor in determining whether an organisation is non-profit making. The term will be given its natural meaning applying the principles in *C & E Commrs v Bell Concord Educational Trust Ltd CA 1988, [1989] STC 264*. For example, in view of the ruling in that case that 'the words "otherwise than for profit" refer to the objects for which the organisation is established and not the budget policy being pursued', sporting services will not be excluded from exemption simply because profits on certain activities are used to subsidise other activities (e.g. profits on the bar are used to subsidise subscriptions). (C & E Notice 701/45/94, paras 6–8).

De Voil Indirect Tax Service. See V4.161.

58.10   *Individuals qualifying as members of a membership body*

Where a body has a membership scheme, exemption applies to services supplied to *playing* members granted membership for a period of three months or more (including life membership subscriptions). There must be written evidence to that effect. A formal agreement, exchange of letters, an invoice issued in advance for at least three months' membership, or the actual receipt for the subscription is sufficient evidence. Provision for a refund in the event of the unforeseen non-availability of the membership facilities would not breach the three-months' membership requirement, but provision for a refund in other circumstances (such as premature resignation) would.

Admission to membership for less than three months at the end of a membership year with continuation of membership for the succeeding year will qualify playing membership services for exemption.

Exemption does not apply to

- corporate membership;

- members' guests (whoever pays the guest's fee);

- temporary members (i.e. under three months' membership);

- visitors of any kind to members' organisations; or

- social and non-playing members.

(C & E Notice 701/45/94, paras 13–17).

'Privilege cards', issued in conjunction with a monthly or three-monthly season ticket and entitling cardholders to free admission to a sports centre run by a non-profit making body, do not make the holders 'members' thereby resulting in the standard-rating of facilities used by other 'non-members' (*Basingstoke and District Sports Trust Ltd, [1995] VATDR 405 (13347)*).

Following this decision, C & E issued the following clarification.

(i) Where a body does not operate a full membership scheme (e.g. where members do not have voting rights or any form of control over the management of the centre), sporting and physical education services provided are exempt from VAT subject to the normal conditions. This applies irrespective of whether users are called 'members' for the purpose of obtaining discount on use of the facilities.

(ii) Where a body operates a full membership scheme but limits its application to selected activities or locations, exemption of qualifying services is limited to supplies to members even if other activities are not within the membership scheme. For example, where a body provides a swimming pool and squash courts and the membership scheme is only for squash players, supplies to all users of the pool, other than squash members, is standard-rated even though there is no membership scheme for the swimming pool.

(C & E Business Brief 3/96, 16 February 1996).

58.11   Recreation and Sport

58.11   *Sports qualifying for exemption*

Activities which are purely recreational in nature or entail no significant element of physical activity designed to improve physical fitness do not qualify for exemption (e.g. chess, dominoes, darts, unmanned racing or showing of animals or birds).

The following sports, etc. qualify for exemption as being those sports officially recognised by the Sports Councils.

Aikido	American football	Angling
Archery	Arm wrestling	Association football
Athletics	Badminton	Ballooning
Baseball	Basketball	Baton twirling
Biathlon	Bicycle polo	Billiards
Bobsleigh	Boccia	Bowls
Boxing	Camogie	Canoeing
Caving	Chinese martial arts	Cricket
Croquet	Crossbow	Curling
Cycling	Dragon boat racing	Equestrian
Exercise and fitness	Fencing	Field sports
Fives	Flying*	Gaelic football
Gliding	Golf	Gymnastics
Handball	Hang/paragliding	Highland games
Hockey	Horse racing	Hovering
Hurling	Ice hockey	Ice skating
Jet skiing	Ju jitsu	Judo
Kabaddi	Karate	Kendo
Korfball	Lacrosse	Lawn tennis
Life saving	Luge	Modern pentathlon
Motor cycling	Motor sports	Mountaineering
Movement and dance	Netball	Octopush
Orienteering	Parachuting	Petanque
Polo	Pony Trekking	Pool
Quoits	Racketball	Rackets
Racquetball	Rambling	Real tennis
Roller hockey	Roller skating	Rounders
Rowing	Rugby league	Rugby union
Sailing/yachting**	Sand and land yachting**	Shinty
Shooting	Skateboarding	Skiing
Skipping	Skittles	Snooker
Snowboarding	Softball	Sombo wrestling
Squash	Street hockey	Sub-aqua
Surf life saving	Surfing	Swimming
Table tennis	Taekwondo	Tang soo do
Tenpin bowling	Trampolining	Triathlon
Tug of war	Unihoc	Volleyball
Water skiing	Weightlifting	Wrestling
Yoga		

* Includes those model flying activities, success in which is dependent on physical skill or fitness.

** Includes canal cruising from 6 October 1997.

Application may be made to C & E to include other activities. C & E will then consult with the Department of National Heritage, the Sports Councils and other representative bodies and give a decision in writing. If exemption is refused, an appeal can be made to a VAT tribunal.

(C & E Notice 701/45/94, paras 19–21, Annex D).

Pigeon racing does not qualify for exemption (*Royal Pigeon Racing Association (14006)*).

58.12   *Services qualifying for exemption*

Services qualifying for exemption where supplied by a non-profit making membership body to its qualifying members or, where applicable, by a non-profit making non-membership body to individuals include the following.

*   Use of changing rooms, showers and playing equipment including trolley and locker hire.

*   Provision of playing area (e.g. court, pitch or green fees).

*   Use of multi-sport playing facilities.

*   Refereeing, umpiring and judging services.

*   Coaching, training and physical education services.

*   Membership subscriptions and joining fees covering active participation in sport. Where subscriptions cover a mixture of exempt, zero-rated and/or standard-rated supplies, it is not normally necessary to apportion playing subscriptions unless the taxable elements (e.g. non-playing benefits) are significant. For example, it is not necessary to split the playing subscription where the supply of the right to use the club bar is an integral part of the supply of playing services. Where however a club wishes to apportion other elements of the subscription (such as zero-rated printed matter) or other types of subscription (such as social membership), it must apportion all types and elements of subscriptions.

*   Fee for remaining on the waiting list for membership but only if

    (i)   it is deducted from the new member's first subscription or entrance fee and this itself qualifies for exemption; and

    (ii) it is refundable in the event that the candidate fails to become a member for any reason including voluntary withdrawal.

    Otherwise the fee is standard-rated.

*   Match fees for the use of playing facilities. Match fees covering the cost of catering and transport are standard-rated except to the extent that the fee included a supply of transport which qualifies for zero-rating. Match fees covering a mixture of exempt and standard-rated/zero-rated elements can be apportioned. See 47.3 OUTPUT TAX.

*   Mooring, hangarage, use of workshops and storage of equipment essential to the sporting activity.

Services not qualifying for exemption include

*   social and non-playing membership subscriptions;

*   admission charges for spectators;

*   use of residential accommodation;

*   use of transport; and

*   catering, bars, gaming machines and social functions.

(C & E Notice 701/45/94, paras 18, 24).

58.13 Recreation and Sport

See *Royal Thames Yacht Club (14046)* where the subscriptions of ordinary members was apportioned between exempt sporting facilities and standard-rated clubhouse facilities which were capable of being enjoyed to the exclusion of the sporting facilities.

58.13   *Subscriptions to sports governing bodies*

Such subscriptions are exempt insofar as they can be attributed to 'services closely linked and essential to sport' which are supplied to individuals either direct or via sports clubs. Where affiliation to a governing body is restricted to groups of individuals such as members' clubs, the governing body may still exempt the supply of playing services to clubs provided the affiliation fee is calculated on a basis which can be related to an individual (e.g. per person or directly linked to the number of club members) and the services are closely linked to active participation in the sport. Services giving priority purchase rights for international match or tournament admission tickets continue to be standard-rated.

(C & E Notice 701/45/94, para 22).

58.14   **SPORTING RIGHTS**

The grant of any interest, right or licence to take game or fish is standard-rated subject to the exceptions in 58.15 to 58.17 below where sporting rights and land are sold or leased together. The grant of any right to call for or be granted an interest or right which would be standard-rated under this provision is also standard-rated. Included is an equitable right, a right under an option or right to pre-emption and, in relation to Scotland, a personal right. [*VATA 1994, 9 Sch Group 1, Item 1(c)(n)*].

De Voil Indirect Tax Service. See V4.113.

58.15   **Sporting rights and land**

Where, at the time of the grant of the rights

- the grantor grants the grantee the fee simple (broadly freehold in England and Wales and *dominium directum* or *dominium utile* in Scotland) of the land over which the right to take game or fish is exercisable, or

- the sporting rights are leased together with that land and the sporting rights represent no more than 10% of the value of the whole supply,

the total consideration is taken to be for the supply of the land alone and is exempt (unless the grantor has opted to tax the supply, see 42.20 LAND AND BUILDINGS, in which case the whole of the supply is standard-rated).

Where the sporting rights are leased with the land and represent more than 10% of the value of the whole supply, an apportionment must be made between the standard-rated rights and the exempt supply of land (unless the option to tax has been exercised).

[*VATA 1994, 9 Sch Group 1, Item 1(c)*]. (C & E Leaflet 742/2/92, paras 2, 10).

58.16   **Shooting rights only**

Standard-rating applies to a grant over land owned by the grantor or over which he has the shooting rights. The provisions cover both freehold sales of rights and leasing or letting for any length of time.

Shooting in hand. If a landowner keeps control of the shooting over his land ('shooting in hand') and invites others to join him in shooting, there is no business activity (and no input tax can therefore be recovered) if the individuals are asked to contribute towards the costs of maintaining the shoot provided

(*a*)   only friends and relatives are permitted to shoot;

(*b*)   the availability of the shoot is not advertised to the public;

(*c*)   taking one year with another, the shooting accounts show a loss equivalent to, at least, the usual contribution made by one of the individuals who take part; and

(*d*)   the loss is borne by the landowner personally rather than by the estate or farm business.

Syndicates. A group of individuals set up solely to share the expenses of a shoot is not normally in business and therefore not regarded as making supplies to the individual members. However, if the syndicate regularly supplies shooting facilities to non-members, or makes taxable supplies of other goods or services, it is regarded as being in business and all its activities, including the supply of shooting facilities to its members, are business activities.

(C & E Leaflet 742/2/92, paras 4–6).

See also *C & E Commrs v Lord Fisher QB, [1981] STC 238* where, on the facts, shooting was not held to constitute a business and *J O Williams (14240)* where a farmer was treated as carrying on a business for VAT purposes even though the Inland Revenue treated the shooting as 'hobby farming' giving rise to neither a profit or a loss.

58.17   **Fishing only**

Standard-rating applies to the grant of rights to take fish either from the grantor's own waters or from waters over which he has fishing rights. The provisions apply to both freehold sales of the rights and letting or leasing for any length of time.

Still-water fisheries. Any charges made to fishermen are standard-rated even if both fishing rights and fish are supplied. However, if the grantor allows a person freely to choose whether to take away fish caught or to throw them back, and makes a separate charge solely for those fish taken away, that charge is accepted to be the consideration for the zero-rated supply of fish (provided they are edible).

Rod licences which themselves do not give specific right to fish, issued by the National Rivers Authority or similar bodies, are outside the scope of VAT.

Time-shares in fishing rights are standard-rated.

(C & E Leaflet 742/2/92, paras 7–12).

58.18   **SPONSORSHIP INCOME**

Sponsorship is the term commonly used for financial or other support in the form of goods and services given by businesses or members of the public to sports, arts, education, charities, etc. C & E take the view that where there is a written or oral agreement or understanding that the sponsor will receive some form of benefit (e.g. advertising, free or reduced price ticket, hospitality, etc.) the recipient of the sponsorship makes supplies for VAT purposes. See, however, *EMAP MacLaren* below. Where, on the other hand, the sponsor's support is freely given and secures nothing in return, the recipient does not make a taxable supply and the sponsorship (whether in the form of money, goods or services) can be treated as a donation outside the scope of VAT. A taxable supply will not be created by the simple acknowledgement of support such as giving a flag or sticker, inclusion of a list of supporters in a programme or on a notice, naming a building or university chair after the donor, or putting the donor's name on the back of a seat in a theatre.

Example of taxable supplies

- Naming an event after the sponsor.

- Display of the sponsor's company logo or trading name on shirts worn by a team.

- Display of the sponsor's logo in programmes or at the venue.

- Free or reduced price admission tickets.

- Access to special events such as premieres or gala evenings.

- Entertainment or hospitality facilities.

- Exclusive or priority booking rights.

In *C & E Commrs v Tron Theatre Ltd CS 1993, [1994] STC 177* sponsors were entitled, amongst other things, to priority bookings. It was held that the theatre would not have provided the goods and services it did for less than the consideration which the sponsors paid. As a result, the whole of the sponsorship received was consideration in money within *VATA 1994, s 19(2)* and subject to VAT.

However, in *C & E Commrs v EMAP MacLaren Ltd QB, [1997] STC 490* a company published a scientific periodical and organised cash awards to scientists. The costs of the awards was met by sponsors who received publicity in the periodical and tickets to attend the annual award. It was held that the sponsorship payments were not consideration obtained in return for the supply of benefits to sponsors.

Accounting for VAT. VAT must normally be accounted for on everything received under the sponsorship agreement, including anything distributed as prizes or paid over as expenses to third parties. A VAT invoice must be issued to any VAT-registered sponsor. The sponsor can then reclaim the VAT as input tax subject to the normal rules. Where the amount of the sponsorship was agreed without reference to VAT, it must be treated as VAT-inclusive.

Sponsorship for non-business activities. Where a person is sponsored for something which is not in the course or furtherance of a business (e.g. a hobby), any services supplied to the sponsor are outside the scope of VAT unless such services are on such a scale as to be considered a business in their own right.

(C & E Leaflet 701/41/95).

See *Bird Racing (Management) Ltd (11630)* where a company incorporated with the aim of attracting sponsorship for a motor racing driver was held, on the facts, to be predominantly concerned with the making of taxable supplies to sponsors for a consideration and therefore carrying on a business and entitled to be registered for VAT.

58.19   **POSTAGE STAMPS AND PHILATELIC SUPPLIES**

Unused current or valid UK or Isle of Man postage stamps. The sale of unused UK or Isle of Man stamps which are valid for postage, i.e. stamps on which the value is

- in decimal currency,

- currently valid for 1st or 2nd class postage, or

- £1, or a multiple of £1, of the present monarch's reign

is not chargeable to VAT if sold at or below face value. If supplied over face value, VAT must be accounted for at the standard rate on the amount by which the consideration exceeds face value. Similarly, on the sale of philatelic items which consist of, or contain, unused and valid UK or Isle of Man stamps, VAT must be accounted for on the full amount charged less the face value of the valid stamps.

All other stamps. All other stamps, including

- all used stamps,

- all foreign stamps, and

- unused UK and Isle of Man stamps of earlier reigns or of the current reign but with a face value in pre-decimal currency

are standard-rated although they may fall to be treated as collector's items and eligible for sale under the margin scheme for SECOND-HAND GOODS (61).

First day covers. First day covers (i.e. envelopes bearing postage stamps which have been postmarked by the postal authorities on the first day of issue) are standard-rated on full selling price without allowance for the face value of the stamp if the envelope with the new stamps is posted to the customer on the first day of issue. However, if an envelope and unfranked stamps (whether fixed or not) are sold for the customer to post himself, the face value of the unused stamps is disregarded.

Stamped stationery. Stamped stationery which is unused and valid for postage in the UK is standard-rated on the amount charged less the face value of the stamps. This applies whether the stamps are printed on the stationery or are ordinary postage stamps to be affixed.

Postage and packing. Any such charges for postage and packing of stamps or philatelic supplies are standard-rated (even if no VAT is due on the stamps themselves). For postage charges generally, see 47.8 OUTPUT TAX.

(C & E Notice 701/8/97).

59 Registration

Cross-references. See 8.5 BUSINESS for anti-avoidance measures to combat business splitting and the conditions for the separation of a previously single business into independent parts for registration purposes; 8.10 BUSINESS for sale or transfer of a business as a going concern; 31 GROUPS OF COMPANIES for group registration; 35.10 INPUT TAX for VAT paid on goods and services obtained before registration; 36 INSOLVENCY for the effect of individuals becoming bankrupt or companies entering receivership or liquidation; 41 ISLE OF MAN; 48.1–48.4 OVERSEAS TRADERS where registration is required by an overseas trader making supplies in the UK and not making supplies in the UK respectively; 50.2 PARTNERSHIPS for partnership registration.

De Voil Indirect Tax Service. See V2.1.

The contents of this chapter are as follows.

59.1 REGISTRATION IN RESPECT OF UK SUPPLIES

A 'person' making or intending to make 'taxable supplies' of goods or services in the course or furtherance of a business is required to be registered if taxable turnover, or prospective turnover, exceeds, or is expected to exceed, certain prescribed limits.

'*Taxable supplies*' are the supplies of goods or services made in the UK other than EXEMPT SUPPLIES (24). [*VATA 1994, s 4(2)*].

'*Person*' includes a sole proprietor, partnership, limited company, club, association or charity.

It is the person who is required to register, not the business or businesses carried on. Thus where a person is operating more than one business, even though they are dissimilar, *all* the person's business activities must be covered by one registration (*C & E Commrs v Glassborow and Another QB, [1974] STC 142*). This applies even if one or more of the businesses would be under the registration limit if carried out alone.

There are anti-avoidance provisions to prevent loss of VAT through disaggregation i.e. the artificial splitting of a single business to avoid registration and VAT. See 8.5 BUSINESS.

De Voil Indirect Tax Service. See V2.101–103.

59.2   **Entitlement to be registered**

Where a person who is not liable to be registered under *VATA 1994* and is not already so registered satisfies C & E that he

(*a*)   makes taxable supplies; or

(*b*)   is carrying on a business and intends to make such supplies in the course or furtherance of that business,

C & E must, if he so requests, register him from the day on which the request is made or from such earlier date as is mutually agreed. [*VATA 1994, 1 Sch 9*]. With effect from 1 April 1997, retrospective registration is restricted to a date no earlier than three years before the date of application. (C & E Notice 700/1/97, para 1.13).

Evidence to satisfy C & E that there is a firm intention to make taxable supplies can include details of arrangements made to date, proposed contracts, planning permission, details of purchases or patents applied for. (C & E Notice 700/1/97, para 1.15).

In respect of property owners and developers, applicants are required to state the nature of their intended supplies in order that the VAT office can confirm the liability of such supplies (this may involve notification of election to opt to tax otherwise exempt supplies); confirm that they have commenced preparatory activities; and indicate the amounts of input tax they have incurred to date. The minimum evidence that C & E require of preparatory activity is that an applicant has commissioned a feasibility study for which a consideration has, or will be, charged. Other types of acceptable evidence include that the applicant

- holds title to land or buildings, or is currently negotiating to purchase, or holds an option to purchase;

- holds full or outline planning permission or is shortly to apply for it;

- has commissioned architect's services with a view to applying for planning permission or legal or other professional services in connection with the intended sale or letting of the property; or

- where appropriate has obtained from his customers the certification required for zero-rating of old people's homes, non-business charity buildings etc. or listed building consent for the conversion of substantially reconstructed protected buildings to residential use.

(C & E News Release 65/90, 25 September 1990).

See also 48.4 OVERSEAS TRADERS for entitlement to registration for certain overseas traders not making taxable supplies in the UK but with business establishments in the UK.

Businesses only making exempt supplies. A business which only makes exempt supplies is not normally entitled to be registered for VAT. However, where a business does not make or intend to make taxable supplies but makes

(i) supplies outside the UK which would be taxable supplies if made in the UK, or

(ii) with effect from 19 March 1997, supplies falling within 35.3(*c*) INPUT TAX,

it may choose to register in order to recover the input tax on those supplies. [*VATA 1994, 1 Sch 10; FA 1997, s 32*]. From 1 January 1993 to 18 March 1997, voluntary registration was allowed by concession where (ii) above applied. (C & E Notice 748, ESC 25, now withdrawn).

De Voil Indirect Tax Service. See V2.120; V2.121; V2.144; V2.145.

59.3   **Compulsory registration**

A person who makes taxable supplies but is not registered under *VATA 1994* becomes liable to be registered under these provisions as follows.

(*a*)   At the end of any month if the value of his taxable supplies in the period of one year then ending has exceeded the limit in Table A below. (If taxable supplies have been made for a period of less than 12 months, the value of all taxable supplies to the end of the month in question must be compared to the limit in Table A below, see *Mr & Mrs Norton (151)*.)

(*b*)   At any time, if there are reasonable grounds for believing that the value of his taxable supplies in the period of 30 days then beginning will exceed the limit in Table A below.

(*c*)   Where a business carried on by a taxable person is transferred to another person as a going concern and the transferee is not registered under *VATA 1994* at the time of the transfer, the transferee becomes liable to be registered under these provisions at that time if

(i) the value of his taxable supplies in the period of one year ending at the time of the transfer has exceeded the limit in Table A below; or

(ii) there are reasonable grounds for believing that the value of his taxable supplies in the period of 30 days beginning at the time of the transfer will exceed the limit in Table A below.

For these purposes, the transferee is treated as having carried on the business before as well as after the transfer, i.e. under (i) above the transferor's taxable supplies in the one year to the date of transfer must also be taken into account.

Table A
Effective date

1.4.98–	£50,000
1.12.97–31.3.98	£49,000
27.11.96–30.11.97	£48,000
29.11.95–26.11.96	£47,000
30.11.94–28.11.95	£46,000
1.12.93–29.11.94	£45,000

A person does not become liable to be registered under (*a*) or (*c*)(i) above if C & E are satisfied that the value of his taxable supplies in the period of one year beginning at the time at which he would become liable to be registered will not exceed the limit in Table B below. See, however, dicta of Lord Granchester in *WF Shephard (2232)*. Where a trader has not applied to C & E at the right time to consider the relevant circumstances, this exception can only be relied upon by a trader if he establishes that, at the right time, C & E could not reasonably have come to any conclusion other than that taxable supplies in the year would not exceed the relevant amount. This *dicta* was followed in *RJ & J Nash (14944)* where, although it was accepted that turnover had fallen below the registration limit following a transfer of a going concern, there were no grounds on which C & E could have been expected, at the date of the transfer, to have believed that this would be the case.

Table B
Effective date
1.4.98–	£48,000
1.12.97–31.3.98	£47,000
27.11.96–30.11.97	£46,000
29.11.95–26.11.96	£45,000
30.11.94–28.11.95	£44,000
1.12.93–29.11.94	£43,000

[*VATA 1994, s 49(1)(a), 1 Sch 1(1)–(3); SI 1993/2953; SI 1994/2905; SI 1995/3037; SI 1996/2950; SI 1997/1628; SI 1998/761*].

A person is treated as having become liable to be registered at any time when he would have become so liable under the above provisions but for any registration which is subsequently cancelled under 59.10(*d*), 59.17(*b*) or 59.25(*c*) below. [*VATA 1994, 1 Sch 1(5)*].

Taxable supplies. The following supplies are disregarded in determining whether the registration limits above have been exceeded.

- *Capital assets.* Supplies of goods or services that are 'capital assets' of the business in the course or furtherance of which they are supplied. However, this is not to include the taxable supply of an interest in, right over or licence to occupy any land which is not zero-rated. [*VATA 1994, 1 Sch 1(7)(8)*]. 'Capital assets' include plant, machinery, office machinery (including computers), office furniture, used company cars and patent rights which have been exploited and which are being sold. The definition covers goods and rights which have been used in the business as 'equipment'. (VAT Notes (No 2) 1982/83, para 10).

- *Overseas traders.* Any supplies which are taxable supplies only because an overseas trader making distance sales in the UK is required to register under *VATA 1994, 2 Sch* (see 59.11 *et seq.* below). [*VATA 1994, 1 Sch 1(7)*].

- *Previous registration.* For the purposes of (*a*) and (*c*)(i) above, supplies made at a time when the person was previously registered under *VATA 1994* if his registration was cancelled otherwise than under 59.10(*d*), 59.17(*b*) or 59.25(*c*) below and C & E are satisfied that before his registration was cancelled he had given them all the information they needed in order to determine whether to cancel his registration. [*VATA 1994, 1 Sch 1(4)*].

- *Fiscal warehousing.* Supplies to which *VATA 1994, s 18B(4)* (last acquisition or supply before removal from fiscal warehousing) applies and supplies treated as made under *VATA 1994, s 18C(3)* (self-supply of services on removal of goods from warehousing). See 70.17 and 70.20 WAREHOUSED GOODS AND FREE ZONES respectively. [*VATA 1994, 1 Sch 1(9); FA 1996, 3 Sch 13*].

Otherwise, all taxable supplies (but not exempt supplies) made in the UK (and Isle of Man) must be taken into account.

Exempt supplies. A person making only exempt supplies cannot normally be required to register for VAT. See, however, 39.4(*a*) INTERNATIONAL SERVICES for the possible requirement to register where a person making exempt supplies only receives imported services subject to the reverse charge in excess of the current VAT registration limit. See also 62.2 SELF-SUPPLY where own business stationery is produced to a value in excess of the current VAT registration limit.

De Voil Indirect Tax Service. See V2.135–137.

59.4   **Notification and date of registration**

Where a person becomes liable to be registered by virtue of

(a)   59.3(a) above, he must notify C & E of the liability within 30 days of the end of the relevant month. C & E must then register him (whether or not he so notifies them) with effect from the end of the month following the relevant month or from such earlier date as is mutually agreed;

(b)   59.3(b) above, he must notify C & E of the liability before the end of the period by reference to which the liability arises. C & E must then register him (whether or not he so notifies them) with effect from the beginning of that period;

(c)   59.3(c) above, he must notify C & E of the liability within 30 days of the time when the business is transferred. C & E must then register any such person (whether or not he so notifies them) with effect from the time when the business is transferred; and

(d)   59.3(a) above *and* 59.3(b) or 59.3(c) above at the same time, C & E must register him under (b) or (c) above, as the case may be, rather than under (a) above.

[*VATA 1994, 1 Sch 5–8*].

Failure to notify. Failure to notify a liability to register may incur a penalty. See 52.12 PENALTIES. Late notification of a liability to register will result in the backdating of the registration, C & E having no discretion in the matter (*SJ Whitehead, [1975] VATTR 152 (202)*) and VAT must be accounted for from the correct date whether or not it has been charged (*JR Atkinson (309)*).

De Voil Indirect Tax Service. See V2.128.

59.5   **Application for registration**

Application for registration under 59.2 and 59.3 above must be made in such form and containing such particulars as C & E may by regulation prescribe. Application must currently be made on Form VAT 1 or Form VAT 20 (Welsh version) and must include a signed declaration that all information entered in it, or accompanying it, is true and complete. C & E Notice 700/1 *Should I be Registered for VAT?* has extensive notes on how to complete the form. A partnership applying for registration must also complete Form VAT 2. [*VATA 1994, 1 Sch 17; SI 1995/2518, Reg 5(1)*]. See also 50.2 PARTNERSHIPS.

When submitting the above VAT application form, details to support an application for VAT periods to correspond with the financial year of the business (see 2.2(d) ACCOUNTING PERIODS AND RETURNS) should be sent if appropriate.

The completed application forms, with any extra information requested by C & E, should be sent to the appropriate VAT Registration Office. When C & E have checked the details on the application form, they send a certificate of registration (Form VAT 4) showing the effective date of registration, the registration number, the date on which the first prescribed accounting period ends and the length of future prescribed accounting periods (i.e. three-monthly or monthly). If a reply is not received from C & E within three weeks of submitting Form VAT 1, it is advisable to contact them to make sure that the application was received. (C & E Notice 700/1/97, para 1.17).

C & E may amend a certificate of registration issued with the wrong date and issue assessments for any earlier periods then coming within the scope of VAT (*Maidstone Sailing Club (per DG Oliver) (511)*). The certificate is no more than a notification of the registration date and number. Other matters shown on the certificate, including the dates on which returns are to be made, are entered as matters of administrative convenience and therefore are not appealable matters within *VATA 1994, s 83(a)* (*Punchwell Ltd, [1981] VATTR 93 (1085)*). Further, the allocation of registration numbers is within the administrative discretion of C & E (see *L Reich & Sons Ltd (97)* where C & E refused to reallocate the registration number of a company to a newly formed subsidiary which took over the trade previously carried on by the parent company).

If a person is liable for VAT registration (see 59.3 above) VAT records must be kept and VAT charged to customers from the date that person is required to be registered (see 59.4 above). This is not necessarily the date liability to register was notified to C & E or the date the certificate of registration is received.

If a person is not liable for registration but is requesting registration (see 59.2 above) and this is granted, VAT records must be kept and VAT charged to customers from the date of registration i.e. normally the date requested on the application form. This is not necessarily the date the certificate of registration is received.

In either case, VAT can be charged before the actual date of registration but VAT must not be shown as a separate item on any invoice sent out before the registration number is known. Prices can be adjusted to include VAT and a proper VAT invoice should then be issued within 30 days of receiving the VAT registration number.

(C & E Notice 700/1/97, para 1.19).

De Voil Indirect Tax Service. See V2.126.

59.6   **Exemption from registration**

Where a person who makes or intends to make taxable supplies satisfies C & E that 'any such supply' is zero-rated (or would be so if he were a taxable person) they may, if he so requests and they think fit, grant exemption from registration under the above provisions. On a material change in the nature of the supplies made, the person exempted must notify C & E of the change within 30 days of the end of the day on which it occurred or, if no particular day is so identifiable, within 30 days of the end of the particular quarter in which it occurred. On a material alteration in any quarter in the proportion of taxable supplies of such a person that are zero-rated, he must notify C & E of the alteration within 30 days of the end of that quarter. Exemption applies until it appears to C & E that the request should no longer be acted upon or the request is withdrawn by the trader. [*VATA 1994, 1 Sch 14*].

'*Any such supply*' has its ordinary meaning and C & E therefore have discretion in applying the provisions where not all of the supplies are zero-rated (*Fong, [1978] VATTR 75 (590)*). C & E will therefore exempt a person from registration if only a small proportion of his taxable supplies is standard-rated provided that, if registered, input tax would normally exceed output tax. Even if a person applies for exemption, it is still necessary to complete Form VAT 1. (C & E Notice 700/1/97, para 1.12).

A material alteration affecting exemption from registration would arise where, if the person was registered, output tax would exceed input tax in any twelve month period. (C & E Notice 700, para 11.9).

Exemption saves a person the trouble and expense of having to keep proper records and accounts for VAT purposes and rendering returns but it does mean that input tax paid on purchases of goods or services for the business is not reclaimable.

De Voil Indirect Tax Service. See V2.124.

59.7   Changes in circumstances

Except where other time limits are specified, a registered person must notify C & E, within 30 days and with full written particulars of any change in the name, constitution or ownership of the business or any other event which may necessitate the variation of the register or cancellation of registration. [*SI 1995/2518, Reg 5(2)*].

The VAT office (*not* VAT Central Unit) should be advised of the changes. Some changes require registration to be cancelled (see 59.10(*a*)(ii) below). Registration details must be amended where there is a change in the

- name or trading name of the business or the name and/or address of any partner in the business;

- composition of a partnership but one or more of the former partners remains in the partnership;

- name and/or address of the UK agent for VAT purposes appointed by an overseas company or resident;

- address of the principal place at which the business is carried on;

- trade classification of the business;

- status from limited liability to unlimited liability, or vice versa, under *Companies Act 1985, ss 49–52* ; or

- bank or National Giro account number or bank sorting code. If the annual accounting scheme is used, the registered person must notify the bank and VAT Central Unit Annual Accounting Section immediately.

(C & E Notice 700, para 11.2).

Registration number and date of change must be given in any correspondence with the VAT office.

See also 31.3 GROUPS OF COMPANIES for changes affecting the composition of a VAT group; 19.1 DEATH for persons carrying on a business from the date of death of a taxable person; and 36.1 INSOLVENCY where a taxable person becomes bankrupt or a liquidator or receiver is appointed.

59.8   Cessation of liability to be registered

A person who has become liable to be registered under 59.3 above only ceases to be liable to be registered in the following circumstances.

- At any time if C & E are satisfied that

    (i) he has ceased to make taxable supplies; or

    (ii) he is not at that time a person in relation to whom any of the conditions in 59.3(*a*)–(*c*) above is satisfied.

- If C & E are satisfied that the value of his taxable supplies in the period of one year then beginning will not exceed the following specified limits.

Effective date

1 April 1998	£48,000
1 December 1997	£47,000
27 November 1996	£46,000
29 November 1995	£45,000
30 November 1994	£44,000
1 December 1993	£43,000

However that person does not cease to be liable to be registered under these provisions if C & E are satisfied that the reason the value of his taxable supplies will not exceed the above limit is that in the period in question he will cease making taxable supplies or will suspend making them for a period of 30 days or more.

Taxable supplies. In determining the value of a person's supplies for the above purposes, supplies of goods or services that are 'capital assets' of the business in the course or furtherance of which they are supplied are disregarded. However this is not to include the taxable supply of an interest in, right over or licence to occupy any land which is not zero-rated. See 59.3 above for the definition of '*capital assets*'.

Any supplies which are taxable supplies only because an overseas trader making distance sales in the UK is required to register under *VATA 1994, 2 Sch* (see 59.11 *et seq.* below) can also be disregarded in determining the value of his supplies for the above purposes.

Taxable supplies for the above purposes are determined on the basis that no VAT is chargeable on the supply (i.e. VAT-exclusive).

[*VATA 1994, 1 Sch 3, 4, 15, 16; SI 1993/2953; SI 1994/2905; SI 1995/3037; SI 1996/2950; SI 1997/1628; SI 1998/761*].

59.9   **Notification of end of liability or entitlement to registration**

A person registered under 59.2 or 59.3 above who ceases to make or have the intention of making taxable supplies must notify C & E of that fact within 30 days of the date on which he does so unless he would, when he so ceases, be otherwise liable or entitled to be registered under 59.11 *et seq.* or 59.18 *et seq.* below. [*VATA 1994, 1 Sch 11*]. The notification must be in writing and state the date on which the registered person ceased to make or have the intention of making taxable supplies. [*SI 1995/2518, Reg 5(3)*]. See 52.14 PENALTIES for failure to notify within 30 days.

See 48.4 OVERSEAS TRADERS for similar provisions applying to overseas traders not making taxable supplies in the UK but with a business establishment in the UK.

59.10   **Cancellation of registration**

The registration of a registered person can or, as the case may be, must be cancelled in the following circumstances, whenever the person concerned was registered.

(*a*)   A registered person *must* notify C & E in writing within 30 days and request cancellation of his registration if

(i)   he ceases to make taxable supplies (see 59.9 above) whether the cessation is due to closing down or selling the business or any other reason (unless he is liable, or entitled to be, registered in respect of acquisitions from another EC country, see 59.18 below);

(ii)   if there is a change in his legal status (e.g. a sole proprietor takes in one or more partners, a partnership is dissolved and the business run by a sole proprietor, a company is incorporated to take over the business previously carried on by a sole proprietor or partnership, or a company is wound up and replaced by a sole proprietor or partnership);

(iii)   he was allowed registration on the basis that he intended to make taxable supplies and ceases to have that intention (see 59.9 above); or

(iv)   he is an overseas trader who was allowed registration on the basis that he made, or intended to make, supplies outside the UK which would have been taxable supplies if they had been made in the UK and he has stopped making, or intending to make, those supplies (see 48.4 OVERSEAS TRADERS).

(*b*)   A registered person *may* request C & E to cancel his registration if

(i)   he ceases to be liable to be registered under 59.8 above. If C & E are satisfied that he is not so liable (and that he would not at that time be liable to registration under 59.11 *et seq.* or 59.18 *et seq.* below if his registration under these provisions was disregarded) they *must* cancel his registration with effect from the day on which the request is made or such later date as is mutually agreed; or

(ii)   his turnover exceeds the registration limits but he satisfies the conditions for exemption under 59.6 above.

(*c*)   Where C & E are satisfied that a registered person has ceased to be 'registrable', they may cancel his registration with effect from the day on which he so ceased or from such later date as is mutually agreed. '*Registrable*' means liable to be registered or entitled to be registered. See 59.3 and 59.2 above respectively. However, C & E must not at any time cancel the person's registration unless they are satisfied that he would not at that time be liable to registration under 59.11 *et seq.* or 59.18 *et seq.* below if his registration under these provisions was disregarded.

(*d*)   Where C & E are satisfied that on the day on which a registered person was registered he was not registrable, they may cancel his registration with effect from that day.

[*VATA 1994, 1 Sch 13, 18*]. (C & E Notice 700, para 11.1; C & E Notice 700/11/98, paras 1, 2).

De Voil Indirect Tax Service. See V2.151–153.

59.11   REGISTRATION IN RESPECT OF SUPPLIES FROM ANOTHER EC COUNTRY ('DISTANCE SELLING')

Additional registration requirements may apply in respect of 'distance selling'. This occurs when a supplier in one EC country supplies goods, and is responsible for their delivery, to any person in another EC country who is not registered for VAT. This may include supplies not only to private individuals but to public bodies, charities and businesses too small to register or with activities that are entirely exempt. The most obvious example of this type of supply is mail order. VAT on sales to non-VAT registered customers in another EC country are in principle charged and accounted for by the supplier in the country from which the goods are dispatched. However, once the value of distance sales to any particular EC country has exceeded an annual threshold, further sales are subject to VAT in the EC country of destination and the supplier is liable to register for VAT in that country or appoint a VAT representative (see 4.8 AGENTS) who will be responsible for accounting for VAT there on his behalf.

The provisions outlined in 59.12 to 59.17 below relate to the registration of suppliers from other EC countries not already registered for VAT in the UK.

Registration by UK suppliers in other EC countries. See 23.18 EUROPEAN COMMUNITY: SINGLE MARKET.

De Voil Indirect Tax Service. See V2.171–177.

59.12 **Liability to be registered**

A 'person' who is not registered under *VATA 1994*, and is not liable to be registered under 59.3 above, becomes liable to be registered under these provisions on any day if, in the period beginning with 1 January in that year, he has made 'relevant supplies' whose value exceeds £70,000.

In addition, a person who is not registered or liable to be registered as above becomes liable to be registered under these provisions (whatever the value of supplies) in the following circumstances.

(*a*) He has exercised an option, under the laws of another EC country where he is taxable, to treat relevant supplies made by him as taking place outside that country and

- the supplies to which the option relates involve the removal of the goods from that country;

- if the option had not been exercised, under the law of that country the supplies would have been treated as taking place in that country; and

- he makes any relevant supply in the UK at a time when the option is in force.

(*b*) He makes a supply of goods subject to duty of excise where

- the supply involves the removal of the goods to the UK by, or under the directions of, the person making the supply;

- the supply is a transaction under which goods are acquired in the UK from another EC country by a person who is not a taxable person;

- the supply is made in the course or furtherance of a business carried on by the supplier and is not treated as a supply only by virtue of *VATA 1994, 4 Sch 5(1)* or *(6)* (transfers of goods forming part of the assets of the business).

VAT registration may not be necessary, however, if the consignment of excise goods is supplied to the UK via a Registered Excise Dealer and Shipper (REDS). See C & E Notice 725 for further details.

'*Person*' includes a sole proprietor, partnership, limited company, club, association or charity. It is the person who is required to register, not the business or businesses carried on. The registration covers all the businesses of the registered person in the UK.

A supply of goods is a '*relevant supply*' where

(i) the supply involves the removal of the goods to the UK by, or under the directions of, the person making the supply;

(ii) the supply does not involve the installation or assembly of goods at a place in the UK;

(iii) the supply is a transaction under which goods are acquired in the UK from another EC country by a person who is not a taxable person; and

(iv) the supply is made in the course or furtherance of a business carried on by the supplier and is not

- an exempt supply;

- a supply of goods subject to a duty of excise;

- a new means of transport (see 23.31 EUROPEAN COMMUNITY: SINGLE MARKET); or

- treated as a supply only by virtue of *VATA 1994, 4 Sch 5(1)* or *(6)* (transfers of goods forming part of the assets of the business).

A person is treated as having become liable to be registered under the above provisions at any time when he would have become so liable but for any registration which is subsequently cancelled under 59.10(*d*) above or 59.17(*b*) or 59.25(*c*) below.

In determining the value of relevant supplies for the above purposes, any part of the consideration representing a VAT liability of the supplier under the law of another EC country is disregarded. Also disregarded are supplies to which *VATA 1994, s 18B(4)* (last acquisition or supply of goods before removal from fiscal warehousing) applies. See 70.17 WAREHOUSED GOODS AND FREE ZONES.

[*VATA 1994, 2 Sch 1, 10; FA 1996, 3 Sch 14*].

Persons already registered in the UK. If a person making relevant supplies of distance sales is already registered for VAT in the UK under 59.3 above in respect of taxable supplies, he does not need also to register under these provisions and need not account for VAT in the UK on distance sales until the threshold above is reached. (C & E Leaflet 700/1A/97, para 2.2).

59.13   Notification of liability and registration

A person who becomes liable to registration under 59.12 above must notify C & E of the fact within 30 days after that day.

C & E must then register him (whether or not he so notifies them) with effect from the day on which the liability to register arose or from such earlier time as is agreed between them.

[*VATA 1994, 2 Sch 3, 9*].

Notification must be in such form and contain such particulars as C & E prescribe. Application must currently be made on Form VAT 1A which includes a signed declaration that all the information entered on the form, and accompanying it, is correct and complete. [*SI 1995/2518, Reg 5(1)*].

Where the person being registered is a partnership, Form VAT 2 must also be completed.

See 48.2 OVERSEAS TRADERS for the registration procedure for overseas traders generally, including those with no business establishment in the UK.

59.14   Request to be registered

A person who is not liable to be registered under *VATA 1994* and is not already so registered may request to be registered under these provisions. Provided he can satisfy C & E that he intends

(*a*) to exercise an option referred to in 59.12(*a*) above and, from a specified date, to make relevant supplies to which the option relates, or

(*b*) from a specified date to make relevant supplies in relation to any such option which has already been exercised, or

(*c*) from a specified date to make supplies satisfying the conditions in 59.12(*b*) above,

C & E may then, subject to such conditions as they think fit, register him from such date as is agreed between them. Any person who decides to opt to tax under this provision before reaching the threshold must notify C & E at least 30 days before the date of the first supply to which the option is intended to apply. Application should be made using

Form VAT 1A (and also Form VAT 1TR if a VAT representative is being appointed). Written evidence should be enclosed showing that firm arrangements have been made to make distance sales.

Where a person who requests registration under the above provisions is also entitled to be registered under 59.2 above or, as the case may be, 48.4 OVERSEAS TRADERS, he must be registered under those provisions.

[*VATA 1994, 2 Sch 4*].

59.15   **Cessation of liability**

A person who has become liable to be registered under 59.12 above ceases to be liable if at any time

(*a*)   his relevant supplies in the year ended 31 December last before that time did not exceed £70,000 and did not include any dutiable supply falling within 59.12 above;

(*b*)   C & E are satisfied that the value of his relevant supplies in the year immediately following that year will not exceed £70,000 and will not include any such dutiable supply; and

(*c*)   no such option as is mentioned in 59.12(*a*) above is in force in relation to him.

[*VATA 1994, 2 Sch 2*].

59.16   **Notification of matters affecting registration**

A person must notify the following matters to C & E in writing within 30 days.

(*a*)   Where he is registered under these provisions and 'ceases to be registrable under *VATA 1994*'. Notification must state the date on which he ceased to make, or have the intention of making, taxable supplies.

(*b*)   Where he is registered under 59.14 above, the exercise of any option or, as the case may be, the first occasion after registration when he makes a supply.

(*c*)   Where he has exercised an option under 59.12(*a*) above, and the option ceases to have effect (as a consequence of its revocation or otherwise) in relation to any relevant supplies by him.

A person '*ceases to be registrable under VATA 1994*' where

●   he ceases to be a person who would be liable or entitled to be registered under that *Act* if his registration were disregarded; or

●   he has been registered under 59.14 above and ceases to have any intention to exercise an option or make supplies as there mentioned.

Notification must be in such form and contain such particulars as C & E prescribe.

[*VATA 1994, 2 Sch 5, 9; SI 1995/2518, Reg 5(3)*].

Changes in circumstances. A person registered under these provisions must notify C & E, within 30 days and with full written particulars, of any change in the name, constitution or ownership of the business or any other event which may necessitate the variation of the register or cancellation of registration. [*SI 1995/2518, Reg 5(2)*].

59.17   **Cancellation of registration**

Subject to below, the registration of a person registered under these provisions must, or as the case may be, can be cancelled in the following circumstances.

(*a*) Where a person registered under these provisions satisfies C & E that he is not liable to be so registered, they *must*, on request, cancel his registration with effect from the day on which the request is made or such later date as is mutually agreed. C & E must be satisfied that, at the date of the proposed cancellation, the person would not be liable to be registered under any other provision of *VATA 1994.*

(*b*) Where C & E are satisfied that, on the day on which a person was registered under these provisions, he was not liable to be registered (or, where he was registered under 59.14 above, did not have the intention by reference to which he was registered), they may cancel his registration with effect from that day.

(*c*) Where C & E are satisfied that a person who has been registered under 59.14 above and is not for the time being liable to be registered under 59.12 above

(i) has not, by the date specified in his request to be registered, carried out the intentions by reference to which he was registered; or

(ii) has contravened any condition of his registration,

they may cancel his registration from the date so specified or, as the case may be, the date of the contravention (or such later date as may be agreed between them). C & E must be satisfied that, at the date of the proposed cancellation, the person would not be liable or entitled to be registered under any other provision of *VATA 1994.*

The registration of a person who has exercised an option with 59.12(*a*) above cannot be cancelled unless it has been in force for two complete calendar years.

[*VATA 1994, 2 Sch 6, 7*].

59.18 REGISTRATION IN RESPECT OF ACQUISITIONS FROM OTHER EC COUNTRIES

VAT on goods purchased from other EC countries is no longer paid when the goods enter the UK. Instead, for most transactions between registered persons, VAT becomes due on the acquisition of the goods by the customer and is accounted for on the normal VAT return. Where a person is not registered for VAT in the UK, any goods purchased from a registered supplier in another EC country bear VAT at origin. To avoid distortions of VAT, additional registration requirements apply in respect of certain acquisitions from other EC countries by persons who acquire goods in excess of an annual threshold but who are not registered, or required to be registered, under the provisions in 59.1 *et seq.* or 59.11 *et seq.* above. The provisions apply to any person not currently registered (including public bodies, charities and even private individuals if they are not acting in a purely personal capacity).

De Voil Indirect Tax Service. See V2.181–188.

59.19 Liability to be registered

A 'person' who is not registered under *VATA 1994*, and is not liable to be registered under 59.3 or 59.12 above, becomes liable to be registered under these provisions if

(*a*) at the end of any month, in the period beginning with 1 January in that year, he has made 'relevant acquisitions' whose value exceeds, or

(*b*) there are reasonable grounds for believing that the value of his relevant acquisitions in the period of 30 days then beginning will exceed,

the following limits.

Effective date

1.4.98–	£50,000
1.1.98–31.3.98	£49,000
1.1.97–31.12.97	£48,000
1.1.96–31.12.96	£47,000
1.1.95–31.12.95	£46,000
1.1.94–31.12.94	£45,000

'*Person*' includes a sole proprietor, partnership, limited company, club, association or charity. It is the person who is required to register, not the business or businesses carried on. The registration covers all the businesses of the registered person in the UK.

An acquisition of goods from another EC country is a '*relevant acquisition*' where

(i)   it is a 'taxable acquisition' of goods other than goods which are either subject to a duty of excise or consist of a new means of transport (see 23.9 and 23.35 EUROPEAN COMMUNITY: SINGLE MARKET respectively); and

(ii) it is treated as taking place in the UK.

An acquisition is not, however, a relevant acquisition where, although the goods are transported to the UK, they are deemed to be supplied in the UK (e.g. installed goods).

For these purposes, a '*taxable acquisition*' is one which is not an 'exempt acquisition' and under which

- the goods are acquired in the course or furtherance of

  (i)   any business carried on by any person; or

  (ii) any activities carried on otherwise than by way of business by any body corporate or by any club, association, organisation or other unincorporated body;

- it is the person who carries on that business or, as the case may be, those activities who acquires the goods; and

- the supplier is taxable in another EC country at the time of the transaction and the transaction is in the course or furtherance of his business.

An '*exempt acquisition*' is one under which the goods are acquired in pursuance of an exempt supply.

A person is treated as having become liable to be registered under the above provisions at any time when he would have become so liable but for any registration which is subsequently cancelled under 59.10(*d*) or 59.17(*b*) above or 59.25(*c*) below.

In determining the value of relevant acquisitions for the above purposes, any part of the consideration representing a VAT liability of the supplier under the law of another EC country is disregarded. Also disregarded are supplies to which *VATA 1994, s 18B(4)* (last acquisition or supply of goods before removal from fiscal warehousing) applies. See 70.17 WAREHOUSED GOODS AND FREE ZONES.

[*VATA 1994, s 31(1), 3 Sch 1, 10, 11; FA 1996, 3 Sch 15; SI 1993/2953; SI 1994/2905; SI 1995/3037; SI 1996/2950; SI 1997/1628; SI 1998/761*].

59.20   **Notification of liability and registration**

A person who becomes liable to registration under 59.19 above must notify C & E of that fact as follows.

(*a*)   Where 59.19(a) above applies, within 30 days of the end of the relevant month.

C & E must then register him (whether or not he so notifies them) with effect from the end of the month following the relevant month or from such earlier date as is agreed between them.

(*b*) Where 59.19(*b*) above applies, before the end of the period by reference to which the liability arises.

C & E must then register him (whether or not he so notifies them) with effect from the beginning of that period.

[*VATA 1994, 3 Sch 3, 10*].

Notification must be in such form and contain such particulars as C & E prescribe. Application must currently be made on Form VAT 1B which includes a signed declaration that all the information entered on the form, and accompanying it, is correct and complete. [*SI 1995/2518, Reg 5(1)*]. Once registered, in addition to accounting for VAT on acquisitions, VAT must be accounted for on any taxable supplies made.

Where the person being registered is a partnership, Form VAT 2 must also be completed.

59.21 Entitlement to be registered

Where a person who is not liable to be registered under *VATA 1994* and is not already so registered satisfies C & E that

(*a*) he makes relevant acquisitions, or

(*b*) he intends to make relevant acquisitions from a specified date,

C & E must, if he so requests, register him from the day on which the request is made or such earlier date as is mutually agreed. Any person who decides to register voluntarily under this provision before reaching the threshold must notify C & E at least 30 days before the date from which registration is to be effective. Application should be made on Form VAT 1B and where (*b*) above applies evidence should be enclosed showing that firm arrangements have been made to make acquisitions.

Where a person who requests registration under the above provisions is also entitled to be registered under 59.2 above or, as the case may be, 48.4 OVERSEAS TRADERS, he must be registered under those provisions.

[*VATA 1994, 3 Sch 4*].

59.22 Exemption from registration

Where a person who makes or intends to make relevant acquisitions satisfies C & E that any such acquisitions would be zero-rated if they were taxable supplies by a taxable person, C & E may, if the person so requests and they think fit, grant exemption from registration under these provisions.

Where a person exempted under these provisions makes a relevant acquisition which would not be zero-rated if it were a taxable supply by a taxable person, he must notify C & E within 30 days of the date of acquisition.

The exemption remains in force until it appears to C & E that the request should no longer be acted upon or until it is withdrawn.

[*VATA 1994, 3 Sch 8*].

59.23   Cessation of liability to be registered

A person who has become liable to be registered under 59.19 above ceases to be liable if at any time

(*a*)   his relevant acquisitions in the year ended 31 December last before that time did not exceed, and

(*b*)   C & E are satisfied that the value of his relevant acquisitions in the year immediately following that year will not exceed

the following limits.

Effective date
1.4.98–   £50,000
1.1.98–31.3.98   £49,000
1.1.97–31.12.97   £48,000
1.1.96–31.12.96   £47,000
1.1.95–31.12.95   £46,000
1.1.94–31.12.94   £45,000

However, that person does not cease to be liable to be registered under these provisions at any time if there are reasonable grounds for believing that the value of his relevant acquisitions in the period of 30 days then beginning will exceed that limit.

[*VATA 1994, 3 Sch 2; SI 1993/2953; SI 1994/2905; SI 1995/3037; SI 1996/2950; SI 1997/1628; SI 1998/761*].

59.24   Notification of matters affecting registration

A person must notify the following matters to C & E in writing within 30 days.

(*a*)   Where he is registered under these provisions and 'ceases to be registrable under *VATA 1994*'. Notification must state the date on which he ceased to make, or have the intention of making, a relevant acquisition.

(*b*)   Where he is registered under 59.21(*b*) above, the first occasion after registration when he makes a relevant acquisition.

A person '*ceases to be registrable under VATA 1994*' where

•   he ceases to be a person who would be liable or entitled to be registered under that *Act* if his registration were disregarded; or

•   he has been registered under 59.21(*b*) above and ceases to have any intention of making relevant acquisitions.

[*VATA 1994, 3 Sch 5, 10; SI 1995/2518, Reg 5(3)*].

Changes in circumstances. A person registered under these provisions must notify C & E, within 30 days and with full written particulars, of any change in the name, constitution or ownership of the business or any other event which may necessitate the variation of the register or cancellation of registration. [*SI 1995/2518, Reg 5(2)*].

59.25   Cancellation of registration

The registration of a person registered under these provisions must, or as the case may be, can be cancelled in the following circumstances.

(*a*)   Subject to below, where a person registered under these provisions satisfies C & E that he is not liable to be so registered, they *must*, on request, cancel his registration with effect from the day on which the request is made or such later date as is mutually agreed. C & E must be satisfied that, at the date of the proposed cancellation, the person would not be liable to be registered under any other provision of *VATA 1994*.

(*b*) Subject to below, where C & E are satisfied that a person registered under these provisions has, since his registration, ceased to be 'registrable' under these provisions, they may cancel his registration with effect from the day on which he so ceased or such later day as is mutually agreed. C & E must also be satisfied that, at the date of the proposed cancellation, the person would not be liable or entitled to be registered under any other provision of *VATA 1994*.

(*c*) Where C & E are satisfied that, on the day on which a person was registered under these provisions

   (i) he was not registrable under these provisions, or

   (ii) where he was registered under 59.21(*b*) above, he did not have the intention by reference to which he was registered,

   they may cancel his registration with effect from that day.

(*d*) Where C & E are satisfied that a person who has been registered under 59.21(*b*) above and is not for the time being liable to be registered under 59.19 above

   (i) has not, by the date specified in his request to be registered, begun to make relevant supplies, or

   (ii) has contravened any condition of his registration,

   they may cancel his registration from the date so specified or, as the case may be, the date of the contravention (or such later date as may be mutually agreed). C & E must also be satisfied that, at the date of the proposed cancellation, the person would not be liable or entitled to be registered under any other provision of *VATA 1994*.

A person is '*registrable*' under these provisions at any time when he is liable to be registered under these provisions or makes relevant acquisitions.

The registration of a person

•   who is registered under 59.21 above, or

•   who would not be liable or entitled to be registered under any provision of *VATA 1994* except 59.21 above if he were not registered,

cannot be cancelled under (*a*) or (*b*) above unless it has been in force for two complete calendar years.

[*VATA 1994, 3 Sch 6, 7*].

59.26 CONSEQUENCES OF DEREGISTRATION

Notice of cancellation and final return. When the date of cancellation of registration has been arranged, either a formal notice of cancellation (Form VAT 35) or a formal notice of exemption from registration (Form VAT 8) is sent. Unless the registration number has been re-allocated to a person who is taking over the business as a going concern (see 8.10 BUSINESS), a final return Form VAT 193 or VAT 197 (Welsh version) is issued. See 2.2 and 2.3 ACCOUNTING PERIODS AND RETURNS. (C & E Notice 700/11/98, para 18).

VAT invoices must not normally be issued or VAT charged as from the date of cancellation (although where a deregistered person has undercharged VAT on a supply made before deregistration, C & E may agree to a VAT invoice being raised to the customer concerned so that the trader does not have to account for any additional VAT due from his own resources). The previous VAT registration number must not be shown on any invoices issued. The VAT office should be consulted before using an existing stock of invoices and crossing out the registration number. If a self-billing arrangement or the authenticated receipt procedure for the construction industry are in operation (see 40.2 INVOICES) customers must be notified immediately of the deregistration and informed that VAT must not be charged. (C & E Notice 700/11/98, para 8; C & E Manual V1-24, section 2.15).

Input tax cannot be claimed on purchases made from the date of deregistration except for VAT on the supply of certain services after deregistration made for the purposes of the business carried on before that time. See 35.11 INPUT TAX.

Partial exemption. Where partial exemption applies to the business, a final adjustment in accordance with the normal partial exemption method must be made on the final return. The period for the final adjustment normally runs from the beginning of the tax year to the date of registration. However, where no exempt input tax was incurred in the previous tax year or, as the case may be, the registration period (see 49.9 PARTIAL EXEMPTION for definitions) the period for final adjustment runs from the first day of the prescribed accounting period in the final tax year in which exempt input tax is incurred and ends on the date of deregistration. (C & E Notice 700/11/98, para 13).

Capital goods scheme. A final adjustment may be required in respect of items still within the adjustment period. See 10.9 CAPITAL GOODS SCHEME.

Records. All VAT records including a list of all business assets on hand, together with their values, should be kept *whether or not they are liable to VAT*. (C & E Notice 700/11/98, para 17). See also 57.1 RECORDS for preservation of records generally.

59.27 **Payment of VAT on business assets**

VAT must be accounted for on the final return of any 'goods' forming part of the business assets which are on hand at the close of business or on the last day of registration as if they were supplied in the course or furtherance of the business unless

(*a*) the business is transferred as a going concern to another taxable person (see 8.10 BUSINESS);

(*b*) the taxable person has died, become bankrupt or incapacitated and the business is carried on by another person who under *VATA 1994, s 46(4)* is treated as a taxable person (see 19.1 DEATH and 36.1 INSOLVENCY); or

(*c*) the VAT on the deemed supply would not be more than £250.

'*Goods*' for these purposes means tangible goods (e.g. unsold stock, plant, furniture, commercial vehicles, computer, etc.) and intangible goods such as patents, copyrights and goodwill can be disregarded. (C& E Notice 700/11/98, para 11). Land forming part of the business assets is treated as if it were goods. [*VATA 1994, 4 Sch 9*].

The provisions do not apply to any goods where the taxable person can show to the satisfaction of C & E that

(i) no credit for input tax has been allowed to him in respect of the supply of goods, their acquisition from another EC country or their importation from a place outside the EC; and

(ii) the goods did not become his as part of the assets of a business transferred as a going concern from another taxable person (see 8.10 BUSINESS); and

(iii) he has not obtained rebate of purchase tax or revenue duty under *FA 1973, s 4* which was allowed when VAT was introduced.

The provisions also do not apply where a person ceased to be a taxable person in consequence of being certified to join the flat rate scheme for farmers (see 63.15 SPECIAL SCHEMES).

[*VATA 1994, 4 Sch 8*].

Included under (i) above are goods bought from unregistered businesses; motor cars (except qualifying cars on which input tax has been claimed); goods bought under the provisions of one of the second-hand schemes; goods used wholly for business entertainment; goods that have been directly attributed to an exempt business activity (unless the input tax was reclaimable through the partial exemption rules); goods not bought for business purposes; and land or buildings which were obtained free of VAT even though they have been used to make standard-rated supplies (such as holiday accommodation or because an option to tax has been exercised). (C & E Notice 700/11/98, para 11).

Value of the supply. The value of the goods on which VAT must be accounted for is the price the person would have to pay (excluding VAT), at the time of the supply, to purchase goods *identical* in every respect (including age and condition) to the goods concerned. Where that value cannot be ascertained, the price for the purchase of goods *similar* to, and of the same age and condition as, the goods concerned must be used. If that value is also not possible to ascertain, the cost of producing the goods concerned at that time is to be used. [*VATA 1994, 6 Sch 6*]. See, however, *A McCormick, [1991] VATTR 1996 (5724)* where the tribunal held that stock should be valued at the time of deregistration and if it was unsaleable and of no value, no VAT was due.

De Voil Indirect Tax Service. See V3.261.

59.28   Retail schemes

Whichever retail scheme is used, the provisions under 59.27 above apply.

Where a retail business is sold as a going concern, any retail schemes previously operated must be wound up at the date of deregistration and cannot be transferred to the buyer. But if the transfer of the business is the result of a simple change in legal entity (e.g. if a sole proprietor takes one or more persons into partnership) and trade continues as before without a break, then the trader must continue to use the same scheme as before. (C & E Notice 700/11/98, para 15). See also 60.6 RETAIL SCHEMES for rules to be followed when ceasing to use a retail scheme.

Before 1 March 1997, where the standard method of calculating gross takings was used and self-financed credit supplies were made, VAT normally had to be paid on any amounts due from customers when registration was cancelled. See, however, *R v C & E Commrs (ex p Littlewoods Home Shopping Group Ltd) CA, [1998] STC 445* where the court held that this practice was unlawful and contrary to EC law.

59.29   TRANSFER OF REGISTRATION

Where a business is transferred as a going concern (see 8.10 BUSINESS) then provided

(*a*) the transferor's registration under *VATA 1994, 1 Sch* has not already been cancelled; and

(*b*) on the transfer of the business the registration of the transferor is to be cancelled *and* the transferee either becomes liable or entitled to be registered under that *Schedule*,

C & E may, under powers given to them in *VATA 1994, s 49*, cancel the transferor's registration and, from the date of the transfer, register the transferee with the registration number previously allocated to the transferor. An application must be made on Form VAT 68 by, or on behalf of, both parties. The application constitutes notice by the transferor of end of liability or entitlement to registration (see 59.9 above) but must be submitted within 30 days of the transfer to avoid any penalty for late notification. [*SI 1995/2518, Reg 6(1)(2)*].

Where a registration number has been re-allocated as above then both the previous and new owners must agree to the following consequences.

- Any liability of the transferor at the transfer date to submit a return or to account for or pay VAT becomes the liability of the transferee (see *WH & AJ Ponsonby v C & E Commrs QB 1987, [1988] STC 28* and *Bjelica (t/a Eddy's Domestic Appliance) v C & E Commrs CA, [1995] STC 329* where the previous firm should have registered twelve years before it actually did and the new firm was held liable for the VAT).

- Any right of the transferor, whether or not existing at the date of the transfer, to credit for or to repayment of input tax becomes the right of the transferee (e.g. VAT recoverable on any services supplied to the previous owner for his business before the transfer but which are invoiced afterwards).

- Any right of either the transferor, whether or not existing at the date of transfer, or the transferee to payment by C & E for recoverable input tax under *VATA 1994, s 25(3)* is satisfied by payment to either of them.

- From 1 May 1997, any right of the transferor, whether or not existing at the date of the transfer, to a claim for bad debt relief becomes the right of the transferee but, equally, any liability of the transferor to make repayments of input tax where bad debt relief has been claimed and the transferor was the debtor also becomes the liability of the transferee. See 7.2 and 7.9 BAD DEBT RELIEF.

- Where the transferee has been registered with the registration number of the transferor during a prescribed accounting period subsequent to that in which the transfer of the business took place but with effect from the date of the transfer of the business, any return made, VAT accounted for or paid or right to credit for input tax claimed, is treated as having been done by the transferee (whether in fact done by, or in the name of, the transferee or transferor).

[*SI 1995/2518, Reg 6(3)(4); SI 1997/1086, Reg 3*].

Full details of the re-allocation of a VAT registration number are given on Form VAT 68 obtainable from a VAT office.

Any special arrangements relating to the previous owner's registration (e.g. self-billing) will normally cease from the date of transfer. The previous owner must still follow the procedure for cancelling registration. (C & E Notice 700/9/96, para 3.2).

De Voil Indirect Tax Service. See V2.131.

59.30   **CORPORATE BODIES ORGANISED IN DIVISIONS**

A 'body corporate' carrying on its 'business' in several divisions may, if it requests and C & E see fit, register in the names of those divisions. For these purposes, 'business' includes any other activities in the course or furtherance of which the body corporate acquires goods from another EC country. [*VATA 1994, s 46(1)(6)*]. See 31.2 GROUPS OF COMPANIES for the meaning of '*body corporate*'.

Divisional registration is a facility which allows a corporate body carrying on business through a number of self-accounting units to register each of those units or divisions separately for VAT. Each division is given a separate VAT registration number and makes its own VAT return but does not become a separate taxable person. The corporate body as a whole is the taxable person and remains liable for all the VAT debts and obligations of all of the divisions.

Conditions for divisional registration. The conditions imposed by C & E are as follows.

(*a*) It must be satisfied that real difficulties would be experienced in submitting a single VAT return for the corporate body as a whole within 30 days of the end of the tax period.

(*b*) All the activities of the corporate body must be registered, including those divisions whose turnover is under the registration limits (see 59.3 above).

(*c*) All divisions must be independent units with their own accounting systems and must be

- operating from different geographical locations;

- supplying different commodities; or

- carrying out different functions (e.g. manufacture, wholesale, retail, export, etc.).

(*d*) The corporate body as a whole must be, or be treated as being, fully taxable, i.e. where any exempt supplies are made, input tax attributable to these exempt supplies ('exempt input tax') must be less than the *de minimis* limits in 49.4 PARTIAL EXEMPTION. The *de minimis* limits apply to the whole corporate body (not to each division or just those divisions making exempt supplies).

(*e*) VAT returns must be made by all divisions for the same VAT periods, which will be allocated by C & E unless an application for non-standard VAT periods is approved. Where the corporate body as a whole expects to receive regular repayments of VAT, monthly returns may be allowed but, in such a case, all of the divisions must make monthly returns.

(*f*) VAT invoices must not be issued for transactions between divisions of the same corporate body as they are not supplies for VAT purposes.

If, once registered in divisions, a body corporate ceases to satisfy any of the above conditions, it must notify C & E in writing within 30 days. C & E will then decide whether to allow the divisional registration to continue.

Applications must be made by letter explaining the reasons for the application and the difficulties in rendering a single consolidated VAT return for the whole body corporate. A Form VAT 1 must also be completed for each division with the full name of the body corporate entered in Box 1 and Box 2 completed with the name of the division followed by the name of the corporate body (e.g. Textile/North West division of ABC Ltd). The letter, Form VAT 1 and a copy of the certificate of incorporation (or other proof of incorporation) should normally be sent to the VAT office for the existing registration or the Regional Registration Unit for that VAT office.

Changes in divisions. Applications should be made by letter, and on Form VAT 1, to the VAT office to add further divisions. The VAT office must be informed in writing if an existing division is sold off or closed down.

Divisional registration and group treatment under 31.1 GROUPS OF COMPANIES are mutually exclusive. Where a company which is a member of a VAT group wishes to register some of its divisions separately, it must first apply to leave the VAT group. Similarly, a body corporate with divisional registration which wishes to form or join a VAT group must first apply to cancel the registration of all of its divisions.

Overseas bodies. A body corporate constituted outside the UK may apply for divisional registration provided it has at least two self-accounting units in the UK and is prepared to comply with the above conditions. One of the UK divisions is deemed to cover the activities of those divisions or sites which are outside the UK so that, if any of those overseas divisions, etc. starts to make taxable supplies in the UK, VAT is accounted for on those supplies by the UK-based division covering for them.

(C & E Leaflet 700/3/98).

De Voil Indirect Tax Service. See V2.149.

60 Retail Schemes

Cross-references. See 11.3 CATERING for accounting for supplies of catering when take-away food is also sold; 47.11 OUTPUT TAX for video cassettes; 57 RECORDS; 63.13 SPECIAL SCHEMES for the annual accounting scheme; and 67 TRADING STAMP AND PROMOTION SCHEMES where such schemes are operated under a retail scheme.

De Voil Indirect Tax Service. See V3.551–585; V6.183–185.

The contents of this chapter are as follows.

60.1 INTRODUCTION

VAT retail schemes were introduced at the start of VAT in 1973 because it was recognised that many businesses dealing directly with the public (primarily shopkeepers) and making supplies at different rates of VAT would be unable to keep records of every sale in order to calculate the VAT due in the normal way. The retail schemes are therefore methods for arriving at the value of taxable retail supplies and determining what proportion of those sales are taxable at different rates of VAT.

C & E's powers. Under *VATA 1994, 11 Sch 2(6)* and *SI 1995 No 2518, Regs 67, 68*, C & E are empowered to permit the value of supplies by a retailer which are taxable at other than the zero rate to be determined by a method

- described in a notice published by them, or

- agreed with the retailer.

They may refuse to permit a retailer to use a particular scheme in the following circumstances.

(*a*)   If the use of any particular scheme does not produce a fair and reasonable valuation during any period.

(*b*)   It is necessary to do so for the protection of the revenue.

(*c*)   The retailer could reasonably be expected to account for VAT in the normal way.

Since the introduction of VAT, there has been a revolution in information technology available to, and used by, retailers (e.g. use of bar codes and sophisticated till technology). C & E consider that these changes mean that the original need for retail schemes, which only provide an approximation of the VAT due, is greatly diminished. They are, therefore, examining every retailer's need to continue using a retail scheme and will only permit the use of a scheme where the retailer cannot reasonably be expected to account for VAT in the normal way, i.e. by identifying each individual supply, its value and the rate of VAT. (VAT Information Sheet 7/96, December 1996).

Where both retail and non-retail sales are made, a retail scheme can only be used for the retail sales and VAT on the non-retail sales must be accounted for outside the scheme in the normal way. See *The Oxford, Swindon and Gloucester Co-operative Society v C & E Commrs QB, [1995] STC 583*.

Sales to other VAT-registered businesses. These must normally not be included in a retail scheme. However, by exception, *occasional* cash sales (e.g. a garage supplying petrol to a VAT-registered customer or a retail DIY store supplying building materials to a VAT-registered builder) may be included within a retail scheme.

60.2   **SUMMARY OF SCHEMES**

A retail business with an annual VAT-exclusive turnover over £10 million and which needs to use a retail scheme is only eligible to do so if it agrees a bespoke scheme with C & E. See 60.13 below.

Apart from such bespoke schemes, there are five published standard schemes.

(*a*)   **Point of Sale scheme**. VAT due is calculated by identifying the correct VAT liability of supplies at the time of sale, e.g. by using electronic tills. See 60.14 below.

(*b*)   **Apportionment Scheme 1**. This is the simpler apportionment scheme designed for smaller businesses with an annual VAT-exclusive turnover under £1 million. Each VAT period, the retailer must work out the value of purchases for resale at different rates of VAT and apply the proportions of those purchase values to sales. For example, if 82% of the value of goods purchased for retail sale are standard-rated, it is assumed that 82% of takings are from standard-rated sales. Once a year, a similar calculation is made based on purchases for the year and any over or under payment adjusted. See 60.15 below.

(*c*) **Apportionment Scheme 2**. Under this scheme, a retailer must calculate the expected selling prices (ESPs) of standard-rated and lower-rated goods received for retail sale. He must then work out the ratio of these to the expected selling prices of all goods received for retail sale and apply this ratio to takings. For example, if 82% of the ESPs of goods received for retail sale are standard-rated and 18% are zero-rated, then 82% of takings are treated as standard-rated and 18% zero-rated. See 60.16 below.

(*d*) **Direct Calculation Scheme 1**. This is available to businesses with an annual VAT-exclusive turnover not exceeding £1 million. It works by calculating expected selling prices (ESPs) of goods for retail sale at one or more rates of VAT so that the proportion of takings on which VAT is due can be calculated. ESPs are always calculated for minority goods, i.e. those goods at the rate of VAT which forms the smallest proportion of retail supplies. For example, if 82% of sales are standard-rated and 18% are zero-rated, the minority goods are zero-rated. Expected selling prices of the zero-rated goods received, made or grown for retail sale are calculated and deducted from takings to arrive at a figure for standard-rated takings. See 60.17 below.

(*e*) **Direct Calculation Scheme 2**. This scheme works in exactly the same way as Direct Calculation Scheme 1 but requires an annual stock-take adjustment. See 60.18 below.

(C & E Notice 727, paras 7-9).

60.3   **CHOOSING A SCHEME**

A retailer can chose to use any of the published schemes provided

- he meets the conditions for use of the scheme in question; and

- C & E have not refused to let him use the scheme (see 60.1 above).

The following general comparisons can be made of the different schemes.

Point of Sale scheme

- Only available scheme if all supplies are standard-rated or all supplies are lower-rated.

- Can be used for services, catering supplies, self-made and self-grown goods.

- Does not involve stock-taking or working out expected selling prices.

- No annual adjustment required.

- The scheme is potentially both the simplest and most accurate but electronic tills are expensive and staff must be able to operate the system correctly at all times.

Apportionment Scheme 1

- Cannot be used for services, catering supplies, self-made or self-grown goods.

- Turnover limit of £1 million.

- Does not involve stock-taking or working out expected selling prices.

- Annual adjustment required.

- The scheme is relatively simple. However, if on average a higher mark-up is achieved for zero-rated goods than standard-rated or lower-rated goods, more VAT could be payable under this scheme than another available alternative scheme.

Apportionment Scheme 2

- Cannot be used for services or catering supplies but can be used for self-made or self-grown goods.

- Stock-taking required at the start of using the scheme, but not thereafter.

- Expected selling prices must be worked out.

- No annual adjustment required but a rolling calculation used.

- The scheme can be complex to operate but if worked properly it will provide a more accurate valuation of supplies over a period of time.

Direct Calculation Scheme 1

- Services can only be included if they are liable at a different rate from the minority goods.

- Cannot be used for catering supplies but can be used for self-made or self-grown goods.

- Turnover limit of £1 million.

- Expected selling prices must be worked out. The scheme can produce inaccuracies if expected selling prices are not calculated accurately. In addition, where expected selling prices are set for standard-rated goods and stock of these goods has a slow turnover, the scheme may not be the most appropriate as VAT is paid in the period in which the goods are received and not necessarily when they are sold.

- Does not involve stock-taking.

- No annual adjustment required.

- The scheme can be relatively simple where goods are sold at two rates of VAT and there is a small proportion of supplies at one of those rates.

- The scheme can be complex to work where goods are sold at three rates of VAT although it may be possible to account for a small number of goods at a third rate outside the scheme.

Direct Calculation Scheme 2

- Services can only be included if they are liable at a different rate from the minority goods.

- Cannot be used for catering supplies but can be used for self-made or self-grown goods.

- Expected selling prices must be worked out. The scheme can produce inaccuracies if expected selling prices are not calculated accurately. In addition, where expected selling prices are set for standard-rated goods and stock of these goods has a slow turnover, the scheme may not be the most appropriate as VAT is paid in the period in which the goods are received and not necessarily when they are sold.

- Stock-taking required at the start of using the scheme and annually thereafter.

- Annual adjustment required.

(C & E Notice 727, paras 7-9, Appendix B).

60.4 **MIXTURE OF SCHEMES AND SEPARATE ACCOUNTING BY DIFFERENT PARTS OF THE BUSINESS**

A retailer cannot use more than one scheme at any one time except as indicated in any notice published by C & E or as specifically allowed by them. [*SI 1995 No 2518, Reg 69*].

Currently C & E allow the following mixtures of schemes. (Note that it is always possible to use the normal method of accounting with any scheme or any allowable mixture of schemes.)

Mixtures of schemes. It may be necessary to use different schemes in different parts of the business. Provided the retailer is eligible to use the relevant schemes, the Point of Sale scheme can be mixed with either Direct Calculation Scheme 1 or 2 or Apportionment Scheme 1 or 2. It is not possible to mix

- Apportionment Scheme 1 and 2;

- Direct Calculation Scheme 1 and 2; or

- Apportionment Scheme 1 or 2 with Direct Calculation Scheme 1 or 2.

(C & E Notice 727, para 10).

Old scheme calculations. Provided all the relevant conditions were satisfied, Schemes A and F could be used in any combination in different parts of the business together with, if required, either

- any *one* of the other schemes for the remainder of the business; or

- Schemes E and H in the remaining parts of the business.

If the business had separate accounting units retailing different goods and services, other mixtures of schemes were possible provided agreement was first obtained from the VAT office.

Note that the annual turnover limits that applied to Schemes B2, C, D and D1 applied to the whole retail business, not just the part of the business in which that scheme was used.

Using the same scheme in different parts of a business. The same scheme can be used separately at a number of distinct business locations. If so, under any scheme other than the Point of Sale scheme, it may be necessary to make adjustments to account for transfers between the different parts of the business. Details of such adjustments must be agreed with the VAT office. (C & E Notice 727, para 10).

Old scheme calculations. Provided all the relevant conditions were satisfied, Schemes A, B, B1, B2, C, E, E1 and F could be applied, with separate VAT calculations, in different parts of a business. To use Scheme B in this way, each part of the business had to satisfy the 50% zero-rated turnover rule. Such an arrangement could not normally be applied using Schemes D, D1, H or J but where a business had always been divided into separate accounting units, the VAT office could give approval. Note that the annual turnover limits that applied to Schemes B2, C, D and D1 applied to the whole retail business, not just the part of the business in which that scheme was used.

60.5   CHANGING SCHEMES

Compulsory change of scheme. A retailer must cease to use a particular scheme if he becomes ineligible to use it. From the start of the next VAT accounting period, he must then change to another scheme (or a mixture of schemes if permitted, see 60.4 above) or to the normal method of accounting.

Voluntary change of scheme. A scheme can be changed for any reason from the end of a complete year reckoned from the beginning of the VAT period in which the scheme was first adopted. [*SI 1995 No 2518, Reg 71*]. If, for exceptional reasons, a change is required at any other time, written agreement from the VAT office is required.

Where the annual accounting scheme is used, a retail scheme can only be changed at the end of the annual accounting year.

Retrospective changes. Retrospective changes to a retail scheme are not normally allowed. See *Summerfield (108)* and *RJ Vulgar, [1976] VATTR 197 (304)* where C & E's decision not to exercise discretion to allow retrospective changes in the scheme was upheld by the tribunal. In *A & C Wadlewski (13340)* the tribunal held that C & E's refusal was unreasonable because of the high proportion of additional VAT payable but this decision was not followed in *L & J Lewis, [1996] VATDR 541 (14085)* or *L & P Fryer (14265)*.

C & E may, in exceptional cases, allow retrospective change. Application should be made in writing to the VAT office giving as much detail as possible. The maximum period of recalculation is three years. The retailer must have been eligible to use the new scheme during the full period of recalculation.

(C & E Notice 727, para 11; C & E Notice 727/3/97, para 2.5; C & E Notice 727/4/97, para 2.7; C & E Notice 727/5/97, para 2.7).

60.6 CEASING TO USE A SCHEME

A retailer must notify C & E before ceasing to account for VAT under a retail scheme. He may then be required to pay VAT on such proportion as C & E consider fair and reasonable of any sums due to him at the end of the prescribed accounting period in which he last used the scheme. [*SI 1995 No 2518, Reg 72*].

See under the individual scheme rules for adjustments which may be necessary on ceasing to use a particular scheme. Apart from these special rules, C & E may require additional adjustments where unusual patterns of trade prevent the chosen scheme from producing a fair and reasonable result.

The following points should also be noted.

- Only goods sold by retail can be included in the retail scheme. If a retailer ceases to use a scheme because he sells all or part of his business as a going concern, the value of stock transferred must be excluded from the retail scheme.

- On ceasing to trade, VAT may become due on the value of stocks and assets. See 59.27 REGISTRATION.

(C & E Notice 727, para 12).

60.7 CHANGE IN VAT RATE AND VAT LIABILITIES

A change in the VAT rate means that a rate of VAT has been changed or a new rate has been introduced. A change in VAT liability occurs when a supply which is either exempt or zero-rated becomes taxable at a positive rate or vice versa. Either change may affect the particular scheme used and a retailer must then take the necessary steps relating to his chosen scheme as directed in C & E Notices or as agreed with C & E. [*SI 1995 No 2518, Reg 75*].

If the change of rate falls halfway through a VAT period, the retailer must make two calculations: one using the old VAT rate and one using the new rate. This will reflect supplies made before and after the rate change. These amounts must then be added together to give the VAT liability for the period.

(C & E Notice 727, Appendix A).

Effect on gross takings. Any change in the rate of VAT or liability is effective from a specified date. VAT is due at the new rate on all amounts charged for supplies made on or after the date of change, with the following provisos.

60.8 Retail Schemes

(*a*) The special provisions in 56.3 *et seq*. RATES OF VAT can be applied to individual transactions provided they are dealt with outside the retail scheme.

(*b*) *Before 1 March 1997*, where the standard method of calculating gross takings was used (see 60.8 below), VAT was normally due at the new rate on payments received on or after the date of change. Following the decisions in *C & E Commrs v Next plc; C & E Commrs v Grattan plc QB, [1995] STC 651*, C & E accepted that where supplies were made on credit before a change in rate but payment was received after the change, VAT was due at the old rate applying at the time of supply and not the new rate applying at the time of payment. As a result, C & E repaid VAT to businesses where, following the change in the standard rate of VAT in 1991, they had indicated the contrary view that VAT was due at the new rate applying at the time of payment. However, in *R v C & E Commrs (ex p Littlewoods Home Shopping Group Ltd) CA, [1998] STC 445* the Court stated that the cases of *Next* and *Grattan* were 'wrongly decided and should be overruled'. C & E will not require repayment of refunds made in such circumstances before 18 July 1996 but intend to review subsequent refunds and determine whether assessments for repayments under *VATA 1994, s 80(4A)* are appropriate. (C & E Business Brief 11/98, 1 May 1998; C & E Business Brief 22/98, 3 November 1998).

60.8 GROSS TAKINGS

All retail schemes work by applying the appropriate VAT fraction(s) to positive-rated daily gross takings in order to establish the amount of VAT due. It is therefore necessary to keep a record of daily gross takings. This will normally be a till roll or copies of sales vouchers.

Inclusions in daily gross takings. The following must be included in daily gross takings, *the provisions having the force of law*.

- All payments as they are received from cash customers. This includes payment by notes and coins, cheques, debit or credit card vouchers, Switch, Delta or similar electronic transactions, and electronic cash.

- The full value, including VAT, of credit sales (excluding any disclosed exempt charge for credit) on the day the supply is made.

- The value of any goods taken out of the business for own use. See also 60.9(24) below.

- The cash value of any payment in kind for retail sales.

- The face value of gift, book and record vouchers, etc. taken in place of cash (but see also 60.9(18) below).

- Any other payments for retail sales.

Adjustments to daily gross takings. The till roll or other record of sales, together with the additions listed above, constitutes daily gross takings and it is this figure (not simply the cash in the till) which must be used when calculating output tax due under the scheme. See *Courage Ltd (8808)*. Daily gross takings must not, therefore, be reduced by losses from the till caused by theft or the cashier giving too much change or accepting too little in payment. However, daily gross takings may be reduced for the following.

- Receipts recorded for exempt supplies.

- Receipts for goods or services which are to be accounted for outside the scheme.

- Refunds given to customers in respect of taxable supplies to cover accidental overcharges or where goods are unsuitable or faulty.

- Instalments in respect of credit sales.

- Void transactions (where an incorrect transaction has not been voided at the time of the error).

- Illegible credit card transactions (where a customer's account details are not legible on the credit card voucher and therefore cannot be presented at the bank).

- Unsigned or dishonoured cheques from cash customers (but not from credit customers).

- Counterfeit notes.

- Where a cheque guarantee card is incorrectly accepted as a credit card.

- Acceptance of out-of-date coupons which have previously been included in daily gross takings but which are not honoured by the promoters.

- Supervisor's float discrepancies.

- Till breakdowns (where incorrect till readings are recorded due to mechanical faults, e.g. till programming error, false reading and till reset by an engineer).

- Use of training tills (where the till used by staff for training has been returned to the sales floor without the zeroing of figures).

- Customer overspends using Shopacheck.

- Inadvertent acceptance of foreign currency (where discovered at a later time, e.g. when cashing up).

A record of any adjustments to the daily gross taking should always be kept.

If any adjustment is made for which a payment is subsequently received, the amount received must be included in daily gross takings.

See also 60.9 below generally for special transactions which may require adjustments to be made to figures for daily gross takings.

(C & E Notice 727, Appendix F; C & E Notice 727/3/97, para 2.1, Appendix B; C & E Notice 727/4/97, para 2.2, Appendix B; C & E Notice 727/5/97, para 2.2, Appendix B).

Old scheme calculations. Before 1 March 1997, in addition to the method detailed above, an alternative method (the 'standard method') for calculating daily gross takings was available. Under that method, self-financed credit sales were not included until payment was received (so that no VAT was payable on bad debts).

The retailer could choose which method to adopt (see *C & E Commrs v J Boardmans (1980) Ltd QB, [1986] STC 10*) but whichever method was used, it could only be changed in exceptional circumstances and with the written approval of C & E.

On withdrawal of the standard method on 28 February 1997, C & E initially took the view that all retailers using it should account for VAT on their self-financed debtors on that date. In most cases the VAT was required either in full on the VAT return which included 28 February 1997 or by adding 10% of the value of the self-financed debtors (making any fair and reasonable adjustment for exempt supplies and potential bad debts) to daily gross takings for each month from March to December 1997 inclusive. However, following the decision in *R v C & E Commrs (ex p Littlewoods Home Shopping Group Ltd) CA, [1998] STC 445*, C & E accept that self-financed debtors at 28 February 1997 should not be subject to VAT and the VAT collected in 1997 should be repaid.

See also *C & E Commrs v Kingfisher plc QB 1993, [1994] STC 63* for the treatment of self-financed credit sales where a company T within a group registration issued credit cards for use by customers of retail companies within the group. As the group was a single corporate body, VAT only had to be accounted for at the time payment was received from customers of T.

(VAT Information Sheet 7/96, December 1996; C & E Business Briefs 2/97, 7 February 1997, 10/97, 30 April 1997 and 11/98, 1 May 1998).

De Voil Indirect Tax Service. See V3.556-558.

60.9 **SPECIAL TRANSACTIONS**

The following is a list of the more common transactions which might have to be taken into account in using a retail scheme and/or calculating gross takings.

(1) **Acquisitions from other EC countries.** Suppliers from elsewhere in the EC do not charge VAT on their sales and the retailer must account for VAT at the rate applicable to the goods in the UK. See 23.3 *et seq.* EUROPEAN COMMUNITY: SINGLE MARKET for further details.

For retail scheme purposes, references to zero-rated goods apply only to goods which are zero-rated in the UK. Goods which are zero-rated on acquisition from other EC countries, but standard-rated in the UK, must be treated as standard-rated goods in the retail scheme calculations.

See (23) below for goods imported from outside the EC.

(2) **Amusement and gaming machine takings.** See 58.3 RECREATION AND SPORT.

(3) **BT phonecards.** From 1 June 1996, BT phonecards have their monetary value displayed on them and their sale is outside the scope of VAT (provided they are not sold for more than face value). Sales should be excluded from daily gross takings. VAT on commission received from BT must be accounted for outside the retail scheme. Any residual sales of pre-June 1996 BT phonecards are standard-rated.

Old scheme calculations. From 1 June 1996, sales had to be excluded from the schemes as above. Under Schemes E, E1, H and J the value of the BT phonecards received for resale had to be excluded from expected selling price totals used in the scheme calculations. (VAT Notes No 2 1996). Before 1 June 1996 (and for sales of old-style cards after that date) a retailer acting as agent in the sale of BT phonecards was making a standard-rated supply.

• Under Schemes A, B, B1, B2 and F, the total amount received from customers was included in daily gross takings.

• Under Schemes C, D and D1, sales of phonecards were accounted for outside the scheme.

• Under Schemes E, E1, H and J, the face value of the phonecards received for resale was included in the expected selling price totals used in the scheme calculations. The total amount received from customers was included in daily gross takings.

(4) **Business entertainment/gifts.** *If goods are purchased specifically to be consumed in the course of business entertainment or to supply as gifts,*

• under the Point of Sale scheme, any VAT due must be accounted for by adding the value of the goods to daily gross takings at the relevant time; and

• under the Apportionment Schemes 1 and 2 and Direct Calculation Schemes 1 and 2, any VAT due on the supply must be accounted for outside the scheme.

See 47.4 OUTPUT TAX for VAT due on gifts.

If goods from normal stock are used for business entertainment or supplied as gifts,

- under the Point of Sale scheme, any VAT due must be accounted for by adding the value of the goods to daily gross takings at the relevant time;

- under Apportionment Scheme 1, the full value of the goods should be included in daily gross takings;

- under Apportionment Scheme 2, the full value of the goods should be included in daily gross takings and the necessary adjustment should be made to expected selling prices;

- under Direct Calculation Schemes 1 and 2, VAT can be accounted for under the scheme as follows:

  (i) if the goods are lower-rated or standard-rated and the minority goods are zero-rated, by adding the value of the supply to daily gross takings; and

  (ii) if the minority goods are lower-rated or standard-rated, no addition to the daily gross takings is necessary but the expected selling prices must be adjusted to reflect the value to be accounted for.

Old scheme calculations.

- Where goods were purchased specifically to be consumed in the course of business entertainment or to supply as gifts, the goods were excluded from the records of goods received for resale and any VAT due on the supply of the gift was accounted for outside the retail scheme.

- Where goods from normal stock were used for business entertaining or supplied as gifts, the full cost was included in gross takings under all schemes. In addition the scheme records had to be adjusted

  (i) under Schemes B, B1 and B2 if the goods were zero-rated; and

  (ii) under Schemes C, E and E1 so that VAT was chargeable only on the cost of the goods.

(5) **Business overheads.** Any purchases of goods and services which are not for resale should be excluded from the scheme calculations.

(6) **Business promotion schemes.** See 67 TRADING STAMP AND PROMOTION SCHEMES.

(7) **Cash discounts.** If goods are offered on cash discount or early settlement terms, the discounted value should be included in daily gross takings at the time of supply.

Old scheme calculations. The full amount payable had to be included in daily gross takings at the time of supply, discounts only being deductible when actually taken up by the customer. Before 1 March 1997, where the standard method of calculating gross takings was used (see 60.8 above) the actual amount paid by customers had to be included in daily gross takings.

(8) **Catering supplies.** Apportionment Schemes 1 and 2 and Direct Calculation Schemes 1 and 2 all assume that goods bought at one rate of VAT will be sold at the same rate. Food bought at the zero-rate often becomes standard-rated when supplied in the course of catering and therefore the Point of Sale scheme must normally be used for such supplies. See, however, 11.3 CATERING for a catering adaptation which may be used.

Old scheme calculations. Catering supplies could be dealt with either

- under Scheme A or F;

- under the normal method of accounting; or

- under a special scheme described in 11.3 CATERING.

If non-catering retail supplies were also made, Scheme A or F could be used for the whole business. Alternatively, non-catering supplies could be dealt with under any eligible scheme provided completely separate records were kept.

(9) **Credit card transactions.** Retailers are allowed to charge different prices to customers using a credit card. The different prices charged may either take the form of discounts to cash customers (see (7) above) or a surcharge being made to those paying by credit card. With effect from 10 August 1998,

- if the charge for payment by credit card is made by the supplier of the goods/services being bought, C & E regard this as a further payment for the purchase, VAT being payable at the same rate as on the goods/services; and

- if the charge is made by an agent acting for the supplier of the goods/services (e.g. a travel agent acting on behalf of a tour operator) C & E consider that the charge is for a separate supply of exempt services (i.e. accepting payment in the form of a credit card).

(10) **Credit transactions.** The full value of the goods must be included in daily gross takings at the time of supply. Do not wait until payment is received and do not include instalments as they are received. Additional rules apply depending upon the way credit sales are financed.

(a) Where *credit for customers is arranged through a finance house, etc.* which takes ownership of the goods, C & E take the view that, in most cases, the transaction should be treated as a cash sale to the finance house and the full amount payable by the customer should by included in daily gross takings at the time of supply. In some circumstances, however, VAT may only be due on the amount received from the finance company. In *Primback Ltd v C & E Commrs CA, [1996] STC 757* the Court of Appeal, reversing the decision in the High Court, held by a majority decision that, where a discount on the full price is allowed to a finance house to compensate for interest-free credit to customers, VAT need only be accounted for on the payments received by the retailer from the finance company. C & E have lodged an appeal to the House of Lords which has referred the case to the CJEC. For action to be taken by retailers pending the outcome of that appeal, see C & E Business Brief 15/96, 22 July 1996.

(b) Where *credit transactions are financed from own resources*, any separate credit charge (additional to the cash price) is exempt from VAT provided that it is disclosed to the customer (see 27.9 FINANCE). If so, it should be excluded from daily gross takings.

Old scheme calculations. Similar provisions applied to self-financed credit sales except that, before 1 March 1997, in cases where the standard method of calculating daily gross takings was used, the full amount paid by the customer, including VAT and service charge, had to be included in gross takings. Under Schemes A, B, B1, B2, D, D1, F, H and J, the credit charges had to be deducted from gross takings before making the scheme calculations using a method agreed in writing with the VAT office. The credit charge had to be apportioned to VAT periods on the basis of payments received. It was not permissible to deduct the total charge in the period of the transaction. Under Schemes C, E and E1, no adjustment was required for credit charges as the method used to calculate output tax was not based on daily gross takings.

(11) **Delivery charges.** See 47.8 OUTPUT TAX.

(12) **Deposits**. Deposits which are advance payments must be included in daily gross takings. Other deposits (e.g. those taken as security for the safe return of goods hired out) must be excluded (regardless of whether the deposit is eventually refunded or forfeited for loss or damage).

(13) **Dishonoured cheques and counterfeit bank notes**. Unsigned or dishonoured cheques from cash customers (but not credit customers) and counterfeit notes received may be deducted from daily gross takings.

Old scheme calculations. Similar provisions applied except that, before 1 March 1997, in cases where the standard method of calculating gross takings was used,

- under Schemes A, B, B1, D, D1, F, H and J, dishonoured cheques, etc. could be deducted from daily gross takings whether from cash or credit customers;

- under Schemes B2 and C, dishonoured cheques, etc. could not be deducted from daily gross takings (because these schemes used a notional figure for such takings); and

- under Schemes E and E1, if the dishonoured cheque, etc. was for a standard-rated cash sale, it could be deducted from daily gross takings but no deduction could be made in respect of dishonoured cheques, etc. received from credit customers.

(14) **Disposal of business assets**. VAT must be accounted for outside the retail scheme.

Old scheme calculations.

- Under Schemes A, B, B1 and B2, if the supply was standard-rated, it could be included in the scheme calculations. If zero-rated, it had to be dealt with outside the scheme.

- Under Schemes C, D, D1, E, E1, H and J, the disposal had to be dealt with outside the scheme.

- Under Scheme F, VAT could be accounted for in the scheme calculations.

(15) **Exempt supplies**. These must always be dealt with outside the scheme, whichever scheme is used.

(16) **Exports (to countries outside the EC)**.

Retail exports. Where goods are supplied for retail export under the retail export scheme, including supplies to entitled EC residents and ships' crews going abroad (see 25.11 to 25.15 EXPORTS) the supplies must be allowed for in the scheme calculations as follows.

(*a*)   Under the Point of Sale scheme, Apportionment Schemes 1 and 2 and, if the minority goods are zero-rated, Direct Calculation Schemes 1 and 2, follow the normal scheme rules but

   (i) include all takings, including VAT, for goods sold for retail export in daily gross takings. (Do not deduct the refunds which are expected to be made to the customer);

   (ii) at the end of each period, add up the takings for standard-rated goods actually exported. (This is the total of amounts shown on the officially certified forms returned during the period);

   (iii) calculate notional VAT on the takings at (ii) above, using the VAT fraction that applied at the time the sale was included in gross takings; and

   (iv) subtract the notional VAT at (iii) from the scheme output tax.

(*b*)   Under Direct Calculation Schemes 1 and 2 where the minority goods are standard-rated, follow the normal scheme rules but at the end of each VAT period

(i)   add up the original expected selling prices, including VAT, of the standard-rated goods which have actually been exported. (These will be the goods shown on the officially certified forms returned during the period);

(ii)   calculate notional VAT on the total at (i) above using the VAT fraction that applied when the amounts were included in the scheme calculations; and

(iii)   subtract the notional VAT at (ii) from the scheme output tax.

Old scheme calculations.

- Under Schemes A, B, B1, B2, D, D1, F, H and J, similar procedure as in (*a*) above applied;

- Under Scheme C, the normal scheme rules set out in 60.27 below applied but at the end of each VAT period, it was necessary to

(i)   calculate the cost, including VAT, of the standard-rated goods actually exported. (These were the goods shown on the officially certified forms returned during the period); and

(ii)   subtract the amount in (i) above from the total at Step 1 in 60.27 below and then follow Steps 2 to 4 in the normal way.

- Under Schemes E and E1, similar procedure as in (*b*) above applied.

Direct and indirect exports. Where goods are directly exported or supplied in the UK to an overseas trader for subsequent export,

- under the Point of Sale scheme, the supplies must be dealt with outside the scheme;

- under Apportionment Schemes 1 and 2 and, if the minority goods are zero-rated, Direct Calculation Schemes 1 and 2, the procedure is similar to that for retail exports in (*a*) above except that the calculations relate to goods sent for export and the comments in brackets do not apply. If proof of export is not received within three months of the date of supply, the notional VAT calculated under (*a*)(iii) above must be included as an addition on the VAT payable side of the VAT account for the current VAT period; and

- under Direct Calculation Schemes 1 and 2 where the minority goods are standard-rated, the procedure is similar to that for retail exports in (*b*) above except that the calculations relate to goods sent for export and the comment in brackets does not apply. If proof of export is not received within three months of the date of supply, the notional VAT calculated under (*b*)(ii) above must be included as an addition on the VAT payable side of the VAT account for the current VAT period.

Old scheme calculations. Supplies had to be allowed for in the scheme calculations. The procedure was similar to that for retail exports above except that the calculations related to goods sent for export and the comments in brackets did not apply. If proof of export was not received within three months of the date of supply, the notional VAT calculated had to be included as an addition on the VAT payable side of the VAT account for the current VAT period. Under Scheme C, the cost of the goods, including VAT, had to be added to the total in Step 1 at 60.27 below in the scheme calculation for that VAT period.

See (28) below for retail sales to persons from other EC countries.

(17) **Florists.** See 60.20 below.

(18) **Gift, book, and record vouchers.** *On sale*, such vouchers should not be included in daily gross takings. If sold for above face value, the excess is consideration for a supply of services and VAT must be accounted for outside the retail scheme.

On redemption, vouchers must be included in daily gross takings at face value *unless* the retailer has evidence to prove that a particular voucher was originally sold at below face value, in which case the discounted amount can be included in daily gross takings.

Vouchers sold with other products for a single charge. This is a multiple supply and VAT is only due on the portion of the payment that relates to the goods (e.g. where a gift voucher is issued with a 'greetings' card).

Free vouchers. If vouchers are issued free of charge, no VAT is due on issue. On redemption for goods, no VAT is due unless the cost of the goods exceeds £15 in which case VAT is due on the full amount. However, if similar vouchers are also sold and the two types cannot be identified at the time of redemption, then, at redemption, all vouchers must be included in daily gross takings at face value.

VAT invoices. If, when vouchers are redeemed, a VAT invoice is issued, the sale must be dealt with outside the retail scheme.

Old scheme calculations. On sale, such vouchers were not to be included in daily gross takings. If sold for above face value, under Schemes C, E and E1, the additional charge had to be dealt with outside the scheme. Under all other schemes, the excess was included in daily gross takings. *On redemption*, vouchers had to be included in daily gross takings at face value.

(19) **Goods bought at one rate and sold at another.** For some goods, the rate of VAT depends upon how they are held out for sale, e.g. meat held out for sale for human consumption is zero-rated but the same meat held out for sale for pet food is standard-rated.

For the provisions applying to chemists, see 60.19 below and for a special scheme for take-away food, see 11.3 CATERING.

All other goods bought at one rate and sold at another must be treated as follows.

Point of Sale scheme. No action is required because takings are separated into each rate of VAT at the point of sale.

Apportionment Schemes 1 and 2 and Direct Calculation Schemes 1 and 2.

- Where separate stocks are kept of goods that are held out for sale at the different VAT rates, on receipt such goods must be entered in the records of goods for resale at the VAT rate that will apply when they are sold.

- Where common stocks are kept of those goods that are drawn on to sell at different VAT rates, such goods must initially be entered in the scheme records at cost or expected selling price (depending on the scheme used) at the rate of VAT that applied when the goods were received. But when the goods are put up or held out for sale at the other VAT rate, it is necessary to deduct the appropriate amounts from the scheme records at the VAT rate that applied when the goods were received and enter the corresponding amounts in the scheme records at the VAT rate that applies when the goods are sold.

Old scheme calculations. Under Scheme B2 or C, such goods had to be dealt with separately outside the scheme. Under Schemes B, B1, D, D1, E, E1, H and J, similar provisions applied as for Apportionment and Direct Calculation schemes above. Under Scheme F, no action was required because takings were separated at each rate of VAT at the point of sale. Scheme A could not be used for zero-rated sales.

(20) **Goods bought from unregistered suppliers.** Where goods for retail sale are bought from unregistered suppliers,

- under Apportionment Schemes 1 and 2, such goods must be included in the retail scheme calculation at the appropriate rate; and

- under Direct Calculation Schemes 1 and 2, only such goods which are taxable at the minority rate must be included in expected selling price calculations.

(21) **Goods sold on sale or return or similar terms.** A separate record must be kept of goods supplied on a sale or return basis. Such goods should only be included in daily gross takings when the customer adopts the goods. See (12) above if the customer pays a deposit.

(22) **Imports (from countries outside the EC).** The normal scheme rules apply, as for other purchases, under all schemes.

See (1) above for goods acquired from other EC countries.

Old scheme provisions. For the purposes of Schemes B2, C, D and D1, the cost of any goods imported or removed from warehouse was the duty paid, delivered price, including any VAT.

(23) **Part-exchange.** Where goods or services are accepted in part exchange, the full retail selling price, including VAT, of the goods supplied must be included in daily gross takings.

Where any goods taken in part-exchange are subsequently resold, it may be possible to sell them under the margin scheme for SECOND-HAND GOODS (61). If not, they can be included in the retail scheme calculations.

(24) **Private or personal use of goods.** VAT is normally due on any goods purchased for resale that are taken out of the business for personal or private use. See 47.5 OUTPUT TAX.

- Under the Point of Sale scheme, the value of any positive-rated goods taken for private or personal use must be included in daily gross takings.

- Under Apportionment Scheme 1, the value of such goods must be included in daily gross takings.

- Under Apportionment Scheme 2, the value of such goods must be included in daily gross takings and the necessary adjustments must be made to expected selling prices.

- Under the Direct Calculation Schemes 1 and 2,

  (i) if the minority goods are zero-rated, the value of any positive-rated goods taken for private or personal use must be included in daily gross takings; and

  (ii) if minority goods are lower-rated or standard-rated, the value of any positive-rated goods taken for private or personal use should be added to expected selling prices and daily gross takings.

Old scheme calculations. Where VAT was due on private or personal use of goods, the cost of the goods had to be included in daily gross takings. In addition the scheme records had to be adjusted

- under Schemes B, B1 and B2 if the goods were zero-rated; and

- under Schemes C, E and E1 so that VAT was chargeable only on the cost of the goods.

(25) **Recall of goods by manufacturers.** If a manufacturer recalls contaminated or otherwise faulty goods,

- under Apportionment Scheme 1, purchase records must be adjusted;

- under Apportionment Scheme 2 and Direct Calculation Schemes 1 and 2, expected selling price records must be adjusted.

(26) **Refunds to customers.** Amounts refunded or credited to customers can be deducted from daily gross takings to a maximum of the amount originally charged.

(27) **Rented payphones.** If a payphone is rented from British Telecom or another supplier, the retailer makes a supply of services to the user of the telephone. VAT is due on the money removed from the payphone which should be dealt with as follows.

- Under the Point of Sale scheme, include the money in standard-rated daily gross takings.

- Under Apportionment Schemes 1 and 2, deal with the supply outside the scheme.

- Under Direct Calculation schemes 1 and 2

  (i) where minority goods are zero-rated or lower-rated, include the money in daily gross takings; and

  (ii) where the minority goods are standard-rated, deal with the supply outside the scheme.

Old scheme calculations. Under Schemes A, B, B1, B2, and F, the money removed from the payphone was included in daily gross takings. Under Schemes C, D, D1, E, E1, H and J, the money removed had to be dealt with outside the scheme.

See also 47.12 OUTPUT TAX.

(28) **Retail sales to persons from other EC countries.** Any retail sale made in the UK to a person from another member state should be accounted for as a normal domestic retail sale. Special arrangements apply to distance selling, i.e. where goods are sold to persons in other EC countries who are not registered for VAT and the supplier is responsible for delivery to the customer. See 23.18 EUROPEAN COMMUNITY: SINGLE MARKET.

See (16) above for exports to countries outside the EC.

(29) **Road fuel.** If road fuel is used for private motoring, VAT due must be accounted for outside the scheme. See 45.16 MOTOR CARS.

(30) **Sale of discount vouchers (or discount cards).** The VAT consequences of selling vouchers or cards entitling the holder to discounts on purchases depend upon where the vouchers or cards can be used.

  (*a*) If vouchers or cards can only be used for purchases from the retailer selling them, he should include the payment received in daily gross takings. Under the Point of Sale scheme, if, for example, the card can only be used for purchases of zero-rated goods, the amount charged for the card should be added to zero-rated takings.

    (*b*)   If vouchers or cards can be used at several traders, this is a standard-rated supply of services. See *C & E Commrs v Granton Marketing Ltd; C & E Commrs v Wentwalk Ltd CA, [1996] STC 1049.*

- Under the Point of Sale scheme, payments received should be added to standard-rated daily gross takings.

- Under Apportionment Schemes 1 and 2 and Direct Calculation Schemes 1 and 2, payments received must be dealt with outside the scheme used.

(31) **Sale or assignment of debts.** Where debts due from customers are sold or assigned, no further action is required as the correct amount will have already been included in daily gross takings at the time of supply.

Old scheme calculations. Similar rules applied except that, before 1 March 1997 in cases where the standard method of calculating gross takings was used, the full value of the debt outstanding, including VAT (not just the amount for which it was assigned) had to be included in daily gross takings at the time the debt was sold or assigned. Amounts subsequently received for the sale or assignment could be excluded.

(32) **Saving stamps, travel cards and pools coupons.** If a retailer

- buys and sells travel cards and/or savings stamps for gas, electricity, television licences, etc, or

- receives commission from distributing and collecting pools coupons

these must be dealt with outside the retail scheme and not be included in daily gross takings. This follows the decision in *TE, M & IJ Parr, [1985] VATTR 250 (1967).*

(33) **Second-hand goods.** VAT on second-hand goods sold, may be accounted for

- within the retail scheme in the same way as new goods; or

- under the margin scheme for SECOND-HAND GOODS (61).

(C & E Notice 727/3/97, paras 3.1–3.30; C & E Notice 727/4/97, paras 3.1–3.33; C & E Notice 727/5/97, paras 3.1–3.32).

60.10   EXPECTED SELLING PRICES ('ESPs')

Under certain of the retail schemes, a retailer must

- calculate ESPs; and

- make adjustments to those ESPs to reflect factors which prevent him from achieving them.

ESPs are used to calculate the expected value of retail sales at different rates. The way ESPs are calculated has, therefore, a direct effect on the VAT paid and must be done as accurately as possible. For this reason, calculations should never include

- goods sold by wholesale;

- goods bought for private use; or

- disposals of stocks resulting from a sale of all or part of the business.

(C & E Notice 727/4/97, para 2.3; C & E Notice 727/5/97, para 2.3).

60.11   Calculating ESPs

ESPs can be calculated in any way which produces a fair and reasonable result. The same method must always be used and, whatever method is used, the adjustments described below must also be made. The most common methods of calculation are as follows.

(a) *Mark up each line of goods* (the most accurate).

(b) *Mark up classes of goods* (e.g. vegetables or confectionery). This method can only be used if

- it is not possible to mark up each line (as in (a) above);

- the variation in mark up within the group is no more than 10% (20% under the old scheme calculations);

- the mark up is reviewed each quarter; and

- the class of goods has a commercial basis and is not constructed artificially.

(c) *Use recommended retail prices.* This method can only be used if

- recommended retail prices can be recorded on receipt of the goods; and

- purchases invoices or other supplier documentation (i) shows the VAT-inclusive recommended retail price of each separate line of goods; (ii) distinguishes standard-rated, lower-rated and zero-rated items; and (iii) totals goods at each rate of VAT.

(C & E Notice 727/4/97, para 2.3; C & E Notice 727/5/97, para 2.3).

Example

In a particular class of zero-rated goods, a retailer purchases the following lines at the actual mark-ups shown.

Line of goods	Purchase price £	Actual mark-up	Expected selling price £
A	150	7%	160.50
B	70	5%	73.50
C	50	16%	58.00
D	30	19%	35.70
E	70	10%	77.00
F	30	6%	31.80
	£400		£436.50

Using the actual mark-up for each line of goods, expected selling prices are £436.50.

If, however, it was not possible to break down the total purchase price of £400 between the various lines, the average mark-up basis could be used.

$$\text{Average mark-up} = \frac{(7 + 5 + 16 + 19 + 10 + 6)}{6} = 10.5\%$$

Expected selling prices are £442 (£400 × 1.105).

Old scheme calculations. Under Schemes B, B1, E, H and J, ESPs could be worked out using any of the above methods or any other method agreed in writing with the VAT office.

Under Scheme E1, expected selling prices had to be calculated on a line-by-line basis and the guidance in 60.31 below followed.

60.12   **Adjustment to ESPs**

As ESPs will rarely be fully achieved, adjustments must be made at the end of each VAT period to take account of factors which affect the selling price. These include (i.e. the list is not exhaustive)

- price changes (increases and decreases), e.g. sell by date reductions;

- special offers and promotion schemes;

- wastage;

- freezer breakdowns;

- breakages;

- shrinkage (i.e. pilferage and loss of stock); and

- bad debts that have been written off in the period.

How such adjustments are made is up to the individual retailer but a consistent method must be used (both within each period and from one period to the next). Records of adjustments and working papers must be kept with the retail scheme calculations.

If it proves difficult to make such adjustments, it may be more appropriate to use another scheme. Alternatively, the VAT office may agree to a method of sampling where reductions cannot be established accurately or the omission of certain adjustments where the effect does not distort the retail scheme.

(C & E Notice 727/4/97, para 2.3; C & E Notice 727/5/97, para 2.3).

Old scheme calculations. Under Schemes B, B1 and E, adjustments had to be made on the above lines at the end of each VAT period. Under Schemes H and J, the retailer had to follow the guidance in 60.36 or 60.39 below respectively, as the case may be.

60.13   **BESPOKE RETAIL SCHEMES**

If VAT-exclusive taxable retail supplies in the previous twelve months have exceeded £10 million, a retailer cannot continue to use a published retail scheme and must then do one of the following.

(*a*)   **Account for VAT in the normal way.** This does not require the issue of a VAT invoice to unregistered customers. However, it does require the VAT-exclusive value and VAT to be identified for each supply and periodic total of those amounts to be produced.

(*b*)   **Agree a bespoke scheme with C & E.** C & E will only agree to a bespoke scheme if

- the retailer cannot be expected to account for VAT normally under (*a*) above;

- the method produces a fair and reasonable result;

- the method reflects commercial reality and does not unnecessarily complicate the accounting system of the business or C & E's ability to audit the VAT declarations; and

- they do not consider it necessary to withhold agreement for the protection of the revenue.

A bespoke scheme must be used for all periods during which the business is ineligible to use a published scheme. Retailers with annual turnover approaching £10 million are therefore advised to contact the VAT office well in advance so that the details and conditions of any bespoke scheme can be agreed.

A bespoke scheme will normally be based on a published scheme (or a mixture of published schemes) but it can be based on any method which meets the conditions set by C & E under (*b*) above. C & E are unlikely to agree a bespoke scheme based on a scheme with a threshold cap of £1 million (i.e. currently Apportionment Scheme 1 or Direct Calculation Scheme 1).

Key elements of a bespoke scheme. Any bespoke scheme will be agreed in writing and include the following provisions.

- The start date and review date of the agreement.

- Details of which supplies will be accounted for within the scheme and which, if any, will be accounted for in the normal way.

- Full details of the method of valuing retail supplies.

  Under a scheme based on the Point of Sale scheme, this should cover product VAT coding (including adjustments for errors and mixed-rate products), unscanned products, non-EPOS departments and tills, till breakdowns, refunds, special offers, vouchers, multisaves, staff discount, etc.

  Under a scheme based on expected selling prices (ESPs), it should cover the basis of setting and adjusting ESPs, product VAT coding (including adjustments for errors and mixed-rate products), direct deliveries to customers, treatment of services, trading patterns, the level of calculation (business, store, department), etc.

  See C & E Notice 727/2/97, Appendices B and C for further details but even these checklists are only a guide and any special circumstances should also be covered.

- Full details of the method of valuing daily gross takings including use of tills, till breakdowns, deliveries direct to customers, adjustments for special transactions (see 60.9 above), etc. See C & E Notice 727/2/97, Appendix A further details but even this checklist is only a guide and any special transactions should also be covered.

- Name, status and signature of a C & E officer and an authorised signatory of the retailer.

The agreement is based on full disclosure of the current business structure and trading patterns. If these change to such an extent that the agreed method ceases to produce a fair and reasonable result, the VAT office must be informed immediately in writing.

Any changes to the scheme will normally be made with mutual consent although C & E may withdraw their agreement and refuse the use of the scheme if it ceases to meet any of the conditions under (*b*) above.

Retrospective changes may be appropriate where there is a fundamental flaw in the scheme.

(C & E Notice 727/2/97, paras 2–5).

60.14   **POINT OF SALE SCHEME**

The Point of Sale scheme can be used if

- taxable turnover does not exceed £10 million (if so a bespoke scheme must be agreed, see 60.13 above); and

- either

  (i) all supplies are made at one positive rate (i.e. all lower-rated or all standard-rated) — if so the Point of Sale scheme is the *only* retail scheme which can be used; or

  (ii) supplies are made at two or more rates and the correct liability of supplies can be identified at the time of sale. This usually means using a till system capable of distinguishing between goods sold at different rates. Alternatively, separate tills can be used for different rates.

How to calculate output tax. For each VAT period (quarterly or monthly)

Step 1	Add up daily gross takings from standard-rated supplies =	A
Step 2	Add up daily gross takings from lower-rated supplies =	B
Step 3	To calculate output tax, add the total at Step 1 multiplied by the VAT fraction for standard-rated goods to the total at Step 2 multiplied by the VAT fraction for lower-rated goods	

In algebraic form output tax is

Sales after 31.8.97 (VAT at 5% on lower-rated goods)

$(A \times 7/47) + (B \times 1/21)$

Sales before 1.9.97 (VAT at 8% on lower-rated goods)

$(A \times 7/47) + (B \times 2/27)$

Gross takings. See 60.8 and 60.9 above for gross takings together with adjustments and special transactions which have to be taken into account.

Records. In addition to the normal records required, a record of daily gross takings must be kept.

Annual accounting scheme. If this scheme is also used, see 63.13 SPECIAL SCHEMES.

Change in VAT rate. See 60.7 above.

Cancellation of registration. VAT is due on business assets, including stock in hand. See 59.27 and 59.28 REGISTRATION.

(C & E Notice 727/3/97, para 1.5, Appendix A).

Example

N Ltd is a garden centre selling plants and gardening equipment. It also sells gardening books and magazines and barbecue supplies. Due to the product mix, the company splits takings at the time of sale using multi-button tills. At the end of its VAT period, standard-rate takings totalled £125,639.34, zero-rated sales of books, etc. totalled £1,549.28 and lower-rated sales of barbecue fuels totalled £194.32.

Output tax for the period is

$$(£125,639.34 \times \frac{7}{47}) + (£194.32 \times \frac{1}{21}) = £18,712.24 + £9.25 = £18,721.49$$

60.15   **APPORTIONMENT SCHEME 1**

In order to use the scheme

- supplies must be made at two different rates of VAT;

- total VAT-exclusive retail sales must be less than £1 million per year. The limit applies to the whole business, e.g. the scheme cannot be applied to one shop if total turnover of two or more shops owned exceeds the limit; and

- any supplies of services, grown or self-made goods or supplies of catering must be dealt with outside the scheme.

How to calculate output tax. For each VAT period (whether quarterly or monthly)

Step 1	Add up daily gross takings =	A
Step 2	Add up the cost, including VAT, of all goods received for resale at the standard rate =	B
Step 3	Add up the cost, including VAT, of all goods received for resale at the lower rate =	C
Step 4	Add up the cost, including VAT, of all goods received for resale at standard, lower and zero rates =	D
Step 5	Calculate the proportion of daily gross takings from sales at the standard rate by dividing the total at Step 2 by the total at Step 4 and multiplying by the total in Step 1	
Step 6	Calculate the proportion of daily gross takings from sales at the lower rate by dividing the total at Step 3 by the total at Step 4 and multiplying by the total in Step 1	
Step 7	To calculate output tax, add the total at Step 5 multiplied by the VAT fraction for standard-rated goods to the total at Step 6 multiplied by the VAT fraction for lower-rated goods	

In algebraic form output tax is

Sales after 31.8.97 (VAT at 5% on lower-rated goods)

$$\left(\frac{B}{D} \times A \times 7/47\right) + \left(\frac{C}{D} \times A \times 1/21\right)$$

Sales before 1.9.97 (VAT at 8% on lower-rated goods)

$$\left(\frac{B}{D} \times A \times 7/47\right) + \left(\frac{C}{D} \times A \times 2/27\right)$$

Annual adjustment. An annual adjustment has to be made to cover any under or overpayment of VAT. The adjustment must be made on

- 31 March — for retailers with three-monthly VAT periods ending on 30 June, 30 September, 31 December and 31 March and all retailers with monthly VAT periods;

- 30 April — for retailers with three-monthly VAT periods ending on 31 July, 31 October, 31 January and 30 April; and

- 31 May — for retailers with three-monthly VAT periods ending on 31 August, 30 November, 28/29 February and 31 May.

If, at the first appropriate date for the annual adjustment, the scheme has been operated for one VAT period or less, no adjustment is required until the following year. The first adjustment must include all VAT periods from first use of the scheme. For all later adjustments, only VAT periods since the previous adjustment are included. The adjustment is calculated as follows.

Step A	Calculate the VAT due by following the procedure as in Steps 1 to 7 above but using takings and cost figures for the period since the last adjustments (or, as the case may be, from the start of using the scheme) =	D

Step B   Add together the output tax already accounted for
                  under the scheme in the year =   E

If D is less than E, too much VAT has been paid and the difference should be included
in the VAT deductible side of the VAT return for the period covering the adjustment. If
D is greater than E, too little VAT has been paid and the difference must be included in
the VAT payable side of the VAT return for that period.

Gross takings. See 60.8 and 60.9 above for gross takings together with adjustments and
special transactions which must be taken into account.

Imports and acquisitions. The cost of goods received for resale under Steps 2 to 4
above include

• any imports from outside the EC at the full price paid (including customs duty and
  VAT), and

• any goods acquired from another EC country at the full price paid (including excise
  duty and with the addition of VAT at the appropriate UK rate).

Opening stock. Goods in stock when the scheme is started are not normally treated as
goods received in the period. However, if there are any stock items which are to be sold
but not replenished, these may be included in the calculations unless already allowed for
in a previous scheme.

Records. In addition to the normal records required, records must be kept of daily gross
takings.

Annual accounting scheme. If this scheme is also used, see 63.13 SPECIAL SCHEMES.

Ceasing to use the scheme. The annual adjustment as explained above must be
carried out for the period from the last adjustment to the date of ceasing to use the
scheme. This applies even if leaving the scheme before the anniversary of starting to use
the scheme.

Cancellation of registration. VAT is due on business assets, including stock in hand.
See 59.27 and 59.28 REGISTRATION.

(C & E Notice 727/4/97, paras 1.5, 2.1, 2.8 Appendix A1).

Example

B Ltd has figures for the four quarterly periods in a VAT year as follows.

Example

B Ltd has figures for the four quarterly periods in a VAT year as follows.

	Cost of standard-rated goods for resale (incl VAT)	Cost of lower-rated goods for resale (incl VAT)	Total cost of goods for resale (incl VAT)	Gross takings
	£	£	£	£
First quarter	9,429	78	15,701	21,714.55
Second quarter	10,418	124	17,840	24,316.51
Third quarter	9,972	312	15,919	21,899.29
Fourth quarter	7,076	25	11,293	16,149.61
	£36,895	£539	£60,753	£84,079.96

First quarter

Standard-rated sales are

$$\frac{9,429}{15,701} \times \pounds21,714.55 = \pounds13,040.35$$

Lower-rated sales are

$$\frac{78}{15,701} \times \pounds21,714.55 = \pounds107.87$$

Output tax = $(\pounds13,040.35 \times \frac{7}{47}) + (\pounds107.87 \times \frac{1}{21}) =$ 1,947.32

By similar calculations output tax in the remaining quarters is

Second quarter	2,122.96
Third quarter	2,063.57
Fourth quarter	1,508.80
	£7,642.65

Annual adjustment

Standard-rated sales for the year are

$$\frac{36,895}{60,753} \times \pounds84,079.96 = \pounds51,061.35$$

Lower-rated sales for the year are

$$\frac{539}{60,753} \times \pounds84,079.96 = \pounds745.96$$

Output tax = $(\pounds51,061.35 \times \frac{7}{47}) + (\pounds745.96 \times \frac{1}{21}) =$ £7,640.40

£2.25 must be included in the VAT deductible side of the VAT return.

60.16   **APPORTIONMENT SCHEME 2**

In order to use the scheme

- taxable turnover must be less than £10 million (if above a bespoke scheme must be used, see 60.13 above);

- supplies must be made at two different rates of VAT;

- it must be possible to calculate expected selling prices of goods in stock when the scheme is started; and

- any supplies of services or catering must be dealt with outside the scheme.

How to calculate output tax.

(a) *For the first three quarterly VAT periods or the first eleven monthly VAT periods*

Step 1	Calculate the expected selling price, including VAT, of standard-rated goods for retail sale in stock at the commencement of using the scheme =	A
Step 2	Calculate the expected selling price, including VAT, of lower-rated goods in stock for retail sale at the commencement of using the scheme =	B

Step 3   Calculate the expected selling price, including VAT, of *all* goods in stock for retail sale at the commencement of using the scheme =   C

Step 4   Add up daily gross takings for the VAT period =   D

Step 5   Add up expected selling prices, including VAT, of standard-rated goods
● received, made or grown for retail sale since starting to use the scheme; and
● acquired from other EC countries since starting to use the scheme =   E

Step 6   Add the total in Step 5 to the total in Step 1

Step 7   Add up expected selling prices, including VAT, of lower-rated goods
● received, made or grown for retail sale since starting to use the scheme; and

● acquired from other EC countries since starting to use the scheme =   F

Step 8   Add the total in Step 7 to the total in Step 2

Step 9   Add up expected selling prices, including VAT, of *all* goods (standard, lower and zero-rated)
● received, made or grown for retail sale since starting to use the scheme; and
● acquired from other EC countries since starting to use the scheme =   G

Step 10   Add the total in Step 9 to the total in Step 3

Step 11   Calculate the proportion of gross takings from sales at the standard rate by dividing the total at Step 6 by the total at Step 10 and multiplying by the total at Step 4

Step 12   Calculate the proportion of gross takings from sales at the lower rate by dividing the total at Step 8 by the total at Step 10 and multiplying by the total at Step 4

Step 13   To calculate output tax, add the total at Step 11 multiplied by the VAT fraction for standard-rated goods to the total at Step 12 multiplied by the VAT fraction for lower-rated goods

In algebraic form, output tax is

Sales after 31.8.97 (VAT at 5% on lower-rated goods)

$$\left(\frac{A + E}{C + G} \times D \times 7/47\right) + \left(\frac{B + F}{C + G} \times D \times 1/21\right)$$

Sales before 1.9.87 (VAT at 8% on lower-rated goods)

$$\left(\frac{A + E}{C + G} \times D \times 7/47\right) + \left(\frac{B + F}{C + G} \times D \times 2/27\right)$$

(*b*) *For the fourth and all later quarterly VAT periods or the twelfth and all later monthly VAT periods*

Step A   Add up daily gross takings for the VAT period =   H

Step B   Add up expected selling prices, including VAT, of standard-rated goods
- received, made or grown for retail sale; and
- acquired from other EC countries

in the current VAT period and the previous three quarterly (or eleven monthly) VAT periods =   J

Step C   Add up expected selling prices, including VAT, of lower-rated goods
- received, made or grown for retail sale; and
- acquired from other EC countries

in the current VAT period and the previous three quarterly (or eleven monthly) VAT periods =   K

Step D   Add up expected selling prices, including VAT, of *all* goods (standard, lower and zero-rated)
- received, made or grown for retail sale; and
- acquired from other EC countries

in the current VAT period and the previous three quarterly (or eleven monthly) VAT periods =   L

Step E   Calculate the proportion of gross takings from sales at the standard rate by dividing the total at Step B by the total at Step D and multiplying by the total in Step A

Step F   Calculate the proportion of gross takings from sales at the lower rate by dividing the total at Step C by the total at Step D and multiplying by the total at Step A

Step G   To calculate output tax, add the total at Step E multiplied by the VAT fraction for standard-rated goods to the total at Step F multiplied by the VAT fraction for lower-rated goods

In algebraic form output tax is

Sales after 31.8.97 (VAT at 5% on lower-rated goods)

$$\left(\frac{J}{L} \times H \times 7/47\right) + \left(\frac{K}{L} \times H \times 1/21\right)$$

Sales before 1.9.87 (VAT at 8% on lower-rated goods)

$$\left(\frac{J}{L} \times H \times 7/47\right) + \left(\frac{K}{L} \times H \times 2/27\right)$$

Opening stock. If it is not possible to perform a physical stock take on the date of starting to use the scheme, the ESP values of goods received for resale in the previous three months may be used.

Gross takings. See 60.8 and 60.9 above for gross takings together with adjustments and special transactions which must be taken into account.

Expected selling prices. See 60.10 to 60.12 above for calculation of expected selling prices.

Records. In addition to the normal records required, records must be kept of daily gross takings and expected selling prices.

60.16 Retail Schemes

Annual accounting scheme. If this scheme is also used, see 63.13 SPECIAL SCHEMES.

Ceasing to use the scheme. No adjustment is normally necessary unless ceasing to use the scheme in part only of the business. In such a case, the rolling calculation for that part still using the scheme must not include stock and expected selling prices of the part no longer using the scheme.

Cancellation of registration. VAT is due on business assets, including stock in hand. See 59.27 and 59.28 REGISTRATION.

(C & E Notice 727/4/97, para 1.5, 2.1, 2.8, Appendix A2).

Example

Z Ltd owns a store and can analyse all purchases of stock for resale. It decides to use Apportionment Scheme 2 and calculates that the expected selling price, including VAT, of stock for retail sale at the commencement of using the scheme is £818,703, of which £331,379 represents standard-rated lines. Trading figures for the first four quarters under the scheme are

	ESP of standard-rated goods received for resale (incl VAT) £	Total ESP of goods received for resale (incl VAT) £	Gross takings £
First quarter	393,741	1,009,199	835,265
Second quarter	400,829	891,685	829,524
Third quarter	314,227	905,859	1,018,784
Fourth quarter	493,207	1,235,087	1,486,381

Output tax is calculated as follows

First quarter

Opening stock	331,379	818,703
First quarter	393,741	1,009,199
	£725,120	£1,827,902

$$\text{Standard-rated sales} = \frac{725,120}{1,827,902} \times £835,265 = £331,345$$

$$\text{Output tax} = £331,435 \times \frac{7}{47} \qquad\qquad \underline{£49,349.25}$$

Second quarter

Opening stock	331,379	818,703
First quarter	393,741	1,009,199
Second quarter	400,829	891,685
	£1,125,949	£2,719,587

$$\text{Standard-rated sales} = \frac{1,125,949}{2,719,587} \times £829,524 = £343,435$$

$$\text{Output tax} = £343,435 \times \frac{7}{47} \qquad\qquad \underline{£51,149.89}$$

828

Third quarter

Opening stock	331,379	818,703
First quarter	393,741	1,009,199
Second quarter	400,829	891,685
Third quarter	314,227	905,859
	£1,440,176	£3,625,446

$$\text{Standard-rated sales} = \frac{1,440,176}{3,625,446} \times £1,018,784 = £404,702$$

Output tax = $£404,702 \times \dfrac{7}{47}$ £60,274.76

Fourth quarter

First quarter	393,741	1,009,199
Second quarter	400,829	891,685
Third quarter	314,227	905,859
Fourth quarter	493,207	1,235,087
	£1,602,004	£4,041,830

$$\text{Standard-rated sales} = \frac{1,602,004}{4,041,830} \times £1,486,381 = £589,136$$

Output tax = $£589,136 \times \dfrac{7}{47}$ £87,743.66

60.17   DIRECT CALCULATION SCHEME 1

In order to use the scheme

- total VAT-exclusive retails sales must be less than £1 million per year. The limit applies to the whole business, e.g. the scheme cannot be applied to one shop if total turnover of two or more shops owned exceeds the limit;

- any supplies of services with the same VAT liability as the minority goods must be dealt with outside the scheme; and

- any supplies of catering must be dealt with outside the scheme.

The scheme works by calculating expected selling prices (ESPs) of goods for retail sale. ESPs are only calculated for minority goods, i.e. those goods at the rate of VAT which

- where goods are supplied at two rates of VAT, forms the smallest proportion of retail supplies; or

- where goods are supplied at three rates of VAT, forms the two smaller proportions of retail supplies.

How to calculate output tax. For each VAT period (quarterly or monthly)

(a) *Where the minority goods are zero-rated and/or lower-rated (i.e. main goods are standard-rated).*

Step 1	Add up daily gross takings	A
Step 2	Add up ESPs of zero-rated goods received, made or grown for retail sale	B

Step 3	Add up ESPs of lower-rated goods received, made or grown for retail sale	C

Step 4   Calculate the standard-rated element of takings by deducting the totals at Step 2 and Step 3 from the total at Step 1

Step 5   To calculate output tax, add the total in Step 4 multiplied by the VAT fraction for standard-rated goods to the total in Step 3 multiplied by the VAT fraction for lower-rated goods

In algebraic form, output tax is

Sales after 31.8.97 (VAT at 5% on lower-rated goods)

$((A - B - C) \times 7/47) + (C \times 1/21)$

Sales before 1.9.98 (VAT at 8% on lower-rated goods)

$((A - B - C) \times 7/47) + (C \times 2/27)$

(*b*)   *Where the minority goods are standard-rated and/or lower-rated (i.e. main goods are zero-rated).*

Step 1   Add up daily gross takings. (Although this figure is not used in the calculation, it is still a requirement of operating the scheme and is also used in completing the VAT return.)

Step 2	Add up ESPs of standard-rated goods received, made or grown for retail sale	D
Step 3	Add up ESPs of lower-rated goods received, made or grown for retail sale	E

Step 4   To calculate output tax, add the total in Step 2 multiplied by the VAT fraction for standard-rated goods to the total in Step 3 multiplied by the VAT fraction for lower-rated goods

In algebraic form, output tax is

Sales after 31.8.97 (VAT at 5% on lower-rated goods)

$(D \times 7/47) + (E \times 1/21)$

Sales before 1.9.98 (VAT at 8% on lower-rated goods)

$(D \times 7/47) + (E \times 2/27)$

Gross takings. See 60.8 and 60.9 above for gross takings together with adjustments and special transactions which must be taken into account.

Expected selling prices. See 60.10 to 60.12 above for calculation of expected selling prices.

Opening stock. Goods in stock when the scheme is started are not normally treated as goods received in the period. However, if there are any stock items which are to be sold but not replenished, these may be included in the calculations unless already allowed for in a previous scheme.

Records. In addition to the normal records required, records must be kept of daily gross takings and expected selling prices.

Annual accounting scheme. If this scheme is also used, see 63.13 SPECIAL SCHEMES.

Cancellation of registration. VAT is due on business assets, including stock in hand. See 59.27 and 59.28 REGISTRATION.

(C & E Notice 727/5/97, paras 1.4, 2.1, Appendix A1).

Example

K runs a newsagent's shop. In addition to sales of newspapers and magazines (zero-rated), he also sells confectionery and tobacco (standard-rated), a limited range of food items (zero-rated) and barbecue fuels (lower-rated). At the end of a VAT period, gross takings are £18,714.55. The expected selling prices of purchases in the period are £11,236.19 for standard-rated goods, £8,154.27 for zero-rated goods and £157.93 for lower-rated goods.

The minority goods are zero-rated and lower-rated. Output tax is calculated as follows.

	£	£
Gross takings		18,714.55
Expected selling prices of zero-rated goods	8,154.27	
Expected selling prices of lower-rated goods	157.93	
		8,312.20
Standard-rated element of takings		£10,402.35

Output tax $= (£10,402.35 \times \frac{7}{47}) + (£157.93 \times \frac{1}{21}) =$ £1,556.81

60.18   DIRECT CALCULATION SCHEME 2

In order to use the scheme

- taxable turnover must be less than £10 million (if above a bespoke scheme must be used, see 60.13 above);

- it must be possible to calculate expected selling prices of minority goods in stock when the scheme is started and annually thereafter;

- any supplies of services with the same VAT liability as the minority goods must be dealt with outside the scheme; and

- any supplies of catering must be dealt with outside the scheme.

The scheme works by calculating expected selling prices (ESPs) of goods for retail sale. ESPs are only calculated for '*minority goods*', i.e. those goods at the rate of VAT which

- where goods are supplied at two rates of VAT, forms the smallest proportion of retail supplies; or

- where goods are supplied at three rates of VAT, forms the two smaller proportions of retail supplies.

How to calculate output tax. For each VAT period, the same rules apply as for Direct Calculation Scheme 1, see 60.17 above.

Annual adjustment. This scheme is based on retail trade over a full year which runs from the beginning of the first VAT period in which the scheme was used. An annual adjustment is required after making the output tax calculation for the fourth quarter (twelfth month) and any difference is accounted for on the return for that period. The adjustment must take into account any disposals since the last adjustment which were not by way of retail sale. This is done by excluding, from the figures used in the calculation, the value of any goods which were previously part of the scheme calculation (or included in the opening stock figure) but have not been sold by way of retail sale.

60.18   Retail Schemes

(a)   *Where the minority goods are zero-rated and/or lower-rated (i.e. main goods are standard-rated).*

| Step 1 | Add up daily gross takings for the year | A |

Step 2   For zero-rated goods for retail sale calculate:
- ESPs of such goods in stock at the beginning of the year

plus
- ESPs of such goods received, made or grown for retail in the year

less
- ESPs of such goods in stock at the end of the year   B

Step 3   For lower-rated goods for retail sale calculate:
- ESPs of such goods in stock at the beginning of the year

plus
- ESPs of such goods received, made or grown for retail in the year

less
- ESPs of such goods in stock at the end of the year   C

Step 4   Calculate the standard-rated element of takings for the year by deducting the totals at Step 2 and Step 3 from the total at Step 1

Step 5   To calculate output tax, add the total in Step 4 multiplied by the VAT fraction for standard-rated goods to the total in Step 3 multiplied by the VAT fraction for lower-rated goods

In algebraic form, output tax is

Sales after 31.8.97 (VAT at 5% on lower-rated goods)

$$((A - B - C) \times 7/47) + (C \times 1/21)$$

Sales before 1.9.98 (VAT at 8% on lower-rated goods)

$$((A - B - C) \times 7/47) + (C \times 2/27)$$

This gives the correct total for output tax due for the year. If the total is less than that calculated under the scheme in the four quarters (twelve months), the difference should be included in the VAT deductible side of the VAT account for the fourth quarter (twelfth month). Similarly, if the total is more, the difference should be included in the VAT payable side of the VAT account for that period.

(b)   *Where the minority goods are standard-rated and/or lower-rated (i.e. main goods are zero-rated).*

Step 1   For standard-rated goods for retail sale calculate:
- ESPs of such goods in stock at the beginning of the year

plus
- ESPs of such goods received, made or grown for retail in the year

less
- ESPs of such goods in stock at the end of the year   D

Step 2   For lower-rated goods for retail sale calculate:
- ESPs of such goods in stock at the beginning of the year

plus
- ESPs of such goods received, made or grown for retail in the year

less
- ESPs of such goods in stock at the end of the year   E

Step 3   To calculate output tax, add the total at Step 1 multiplied by the VAT fraction for standard-rated goods to the total at Step 2 multiplied by the VAT fraction for lower-rated goods

In algebraic form, output tax is

Sales after 31.8.97 (VAT at 5% on lower-rated goods)

$(D \times 7/47) + (E \times 1/21)$

Sales before 1.9.98 (VAT at 8% on lower-rated goods)

$(D \times 7/47) + (E \times 2/27)$

This gives the correct total for output tax due for the year. If the total is less than that calculated under the scheme in the four quarters (twelve months), the difference should be included in the VAT deductible side of the VAT account for the fourth quarter (twelfth month). Similarly, if the total is more, the difference should be included in the VAT payable side of the VAT account for that period.

Gross takings. See 60.8 and 60.9 above for gross takings together with adjustments and special transactions which must be taken into account.

Expected selling prices. See 60.10 to 60.12 above for calculation of expected selling prices.

Opening stock. Goods in stock when the scheme is started are not normally treated as goods received in the period. However, if there are any stock items which are to be sold but not replenished, these may be included in the calculations unless already allowed for in a previous scheme.

Records. In addition to the normal records required, records must be kept of daily gross takings and expected selling prices.

Annual accounting scheme. If this scheme is also used, see 63.13 SPECIAL SCHEMES.

Ceasing to use the scheme. The annual adjustment as explained above must be carried out for the period from the last adjustment to the date of ceasing to use the scheme. This applies even if leaving the scheme before the anniversary of starting to use the scheme.

Cancellation of registration. VAT is due on business assets, including stock in hand. See 59.27 and 59.28 REGISTRATION.

(C & E Notice 727/5/97, paras 1.4, 2.1, 2.8, Appendix A1, A2).

Example

K decides to use Direct Calculation Scheme 2. When he starts to use the scheme, his opening stock, valued at expected selling prices, is

	£
Standard-rated goods	3,145.91
Zero-rated goods	2,250.34
Lower-rated goods	142.51

For the first four quarters, his relevant details are

	ESP of standard-rated goods purchased	ESP of zero-rated goods purchased	ESP of lower-rated goods purchased	Gross takings
	£	£	£	£
First quarter	11,236.19	8,154.27	157.93	18,714.55
Second quarter	9,075.02	11,667.67	259.32	20,726.40
Third quarter	9,872.90	10,124.75	137.54	20,855.88
Fourth quarter	11,431.39	11,008.62	21.43	22,649.04
	£41,615.50	£40,955.31	£576.22	£82,945.87

At the end of the fourth quarter, his closing stock, valued at expected selling prices, is

	£
Standard-rated goods	4,217.22
Zero-rated goods	3,151.44
Lower-rated goods	119.19

First quarter

The minority goods are zero-rated and lower-rated. Output tax is calculated as follows.

	£	£
Gross takings		18,714.55
ESP of zero-rated goods	8,154.27	
ESP of lower-rated goods	157.93	
		8,312.20
Standard-rated element of takings		£10,402.35

Output tax = $(£10,402.35 \times \frac{7}{47}) + (£157.93 \times \frac{1}{21})$ = £1,556.81

Second quarter

The minority goods are standard-rated and lower-rated. Output tax is calculated as follows.

Output tax = $(£9,075.02 \times \frac{7}{47}) + (£259.32 \times \frac{1}{21})$ = £1,363.95

Third quarter

The minority goods are standard-rated and lower-rated. Output tax is calculated as follows.

Output tax = $(£9,872.90 \times \frac{7}{47}) + (£137.54 \times \frac{1}{21})$ = £1,476.98

Fourth quarter

The minority goods are zero-rated and lower-rated. Output tax is calculated as follows.

	£	£
Gross takings		22,649.04
ESP of zero-rated goods	11,008.62	
ESP of lower-rated goods	21.43	
		11,030.05
Standard-rated element of takings		£11,618.99

Output tax = $(£11,618.99 \times \frac{7}{47}) + (£21.43 \times \frac{1}{21}) =$ £1,731.51

The annual adjustment is as follows

The minority goods are zero-rated and lower-rated. Output tax is calculated as follows

	£	£
Gross takings		82,945.87
Less zero-rated goods		
opening stock:	2,250.34	
ESP of goods purchased	40,955.31	
	43,205.65	
closing stock	3,151.44	
	40,054.21	
	42,891.66	
Less lower-rated goods		
opening stock:	142.51	
ESP of goods purchased	576.22	
	718.73	
closing stock	119.19	
		599.54
Standard-rated element of takings		£42,292.12

Output tax = $(£42,292.12 \times \frac{7}{47}) + (£599.54 \times \frac{1}{21}) =$ 6,327.38

Output tax already calculated
£1,556.81 + £1,363.95 + £1476.98 + £1,731.51   6,129.25

Additional VAT payable with return for fourth quarter   £198.13

60.19   **RETAIL CHEMISTS**

Many of the goods that a retail chemist buys at the standard rate may subsequently be either sold over the counter (at the standard rate) or dispensed on prescription (normally at the zero rate but, with effect from 1 January 1998, at the standard rate where dispensed for a patient being cared for in a nursing home or hospital). See 42.14 and 32.17 HEALTH AND WATER UTILITIES. There is thus no direct relationship between the proportions of goods bought and sold at the different rates of VAT.

C & E Notice 727, Appendix D gives the following guidance on how the standard schemes need to be adjusted to take account of this fact. *At the time of writing, this advice has not been amended to reflect the change in liability of prescriptions for patients being cared for in hospitals and nursing homes (see above).*

Point of Sale scheme. Under this scheme the correct rate of VAT is identified at the time of supply and no adjustment is therefore necessary.

60.19 Retail Schemes

Apportionment Scheme 1 and Direct Calculation Schemes 1 and 2. The following adjustments are required at the end of each VAT period.

Step 1	Calculate output tax under the normal scheme rules — daily gross takings to include the total amount from prescription charges and NHS cheque (less the value of any exempt supplies such as rota payments)	A
Step 2	Add up payments *received* in the period for all *Group 12* goods, even if not supplied in the period. (Any exempt or standard-rated supplies in the NHS cheque must be excluded.)	B
Step 3	Estimate the value of goods included in Step 2 that were zero-rated on receipt. (This must be based on a sample of actual purchases for a representative period, taking account of seasonal fluctuations, etc. A new estimation must be made each VAT period.) =	C
Step 4	Subtract the total at Step 3 from the total at Step 2	
Step 5	Work out the VAT included in Step 1 from *Group 12* goods by multiplying the total at Step 4 by the VAT fraction	
Step 6	Calculate output tax by deducting the total at Step 5 from the total at Step 1	

In algebraic form, output tax is

$$A - ((B - C) \times 7/47)$$

Where a Direct Calculation scheme is used, a retail chemist must normally calculate expected selling prices for minority goods (see 60.17 and 60.18 above). If the minority goods are standard-rated when sold but the minority of purchases are zero-rated, the chemist may calculate expected selling prices on the basis of the zero-rated goods received for resale.

(C & E Notice 727, Appendix D).

Old scheme calculations. *Under Schemes A and F*, the rate of VAT on supplies was identified at the point of sale and no adjustment was therefore necessary.

Schemes B, C, D, D1, E, H and J. The following calculation was necessary at the end of each VAT period.

Step 1	Calculate scheme output tax under the normal scheme rules (including prescription charges and NHS cheques less the value of any exempt supplies e.g. rota payments, rural dispensing payments) =	A
Step 2	Total the payments *received* in the period for *Group 12* goods whenever supplied. (Any exempt or standard-rated supplies in the NHS cheque had to be excluded).	B
Step 3	Estimate, on the pattern of supplies of such goods over the previous six months, how much of the total in Step 2 related to goods which were standard-rated on receipt =	C

Step 4   Work out the VAT included in Step 1 from *Group 12*
                goods by multiplying the total at Step 3 by the VAT
                fraction

Step 5   Calculate output tax by deducting the total at Step 4
                from the total at Step 1

In algebraic form output tax was

$A - (C \times 7/47)$

Scheme G. The computation proceeded as in Steps 1 to 3 above. To find the output tax, the total at Step 3 was multiplied by the VAT fraction and then one-eighth was added to the total before subtracting the result from the total in Step 1. In algebraic form output tax was

$A - \frac{9}{8}(C \times 7/47)$

(C & E Notice 727 (1993 edition), Appendix B — now withdrawn).

60.20   **RETAIL FLORISTS**

The following provisions apply to florists and other retailers who are members of organisations such as Interflora, Teleflorist and Flowergram which facilitate the purchase and delivery of flowers. The provisions have the force of law under *SI 1995/2518, Reg 67.*

The adjustments to be made depend upon the retail scheme used and whether the florist is the '*sending member*' (i.e. the member receiving payment direct from the customer) or the '*executing member*' (i.e. the member delivering the flowers and receiving payment from the organisation).

Point of Sale scheme.

- *Sending member.* No adjustment is required by a sending member. Payments received should be included in daily gross takings at the time of the order. Documentation from the agency should be ignored for VAT purposes.

- *Executing member.* Do not include payments received from the agency in daily gross takings and account for any VAT due outside the retail scheme.

Apportionment schemes.

- *Sending member.* Identify from agency documentation the value of supplies made as a sending member and account for any VAT due outside the retail scheme. Do not include payments for those supplies in daily gross takings under the retail scheme calculations.

- *Executing member.* Do not include payments received from the agency in daily gross takings and account for any VAT due outside the retail scheme on the basis of agency documentation.

    If Apportionment Scheme 1 is used, exclude the value of flowers sent as an executing member from purchase records.

    If Apportionment Scheme 2 is used, adjust expected selling prices for the value of flowers sent as an executing member and accounted for outside the retail scheme.

Direct calculation schemes.

- *Sending member.* Identify from agency documentation the value of supplies made as a sending member and account for any VAT due outside the retail scheme. Do not include payments for those supplies in daily gross takings under the retail scheme calculations.

- *Executing member.* Do not include payments received from the agency in daily gross takings and account for any VAT due outside the retail scheme on the basis of agency documentation. Adjust expected selling prices for the value of flowers sent as an executing member and accounted for outside the retail scheme.

(C & E Notice 727, Appendix E).

Old scheme calculations. In addition to the normal rules for the schemes, the following also had to be included in gross takings.

(*a*) *Teleflorist transactions.* Under Schemes A, B, B1, B2 and F

- service and communication charges;

- the total gross values and total delivery charges as shown on the monthly summaries of orders passed to the trader for delivery, via Teleflorist, from overseas; and

- if the delivery was to be made in the UK by a member registered for VAT, the value of the goods and delivery charges.

After calculating the VAT due under the scheme, the VAT shown on the self-billed invoice portion of the monthly Teleflorist statement had to be added.

(*b*) *Interflora transactions.* Under Schemes A, B, B1, B2 and F

- all payments received from customers for both inland and overseas Interflora orders; and

- totals shown in the column headed 'Incl Outputs' on the monthly Interflora statements received during the period.

Cash balances shown on Teleflorist and Interflora statements were not to be included in gross takings or purchase records.

(C & E Leaflet 727/1/87 now withdrawn).

60.21 TAX FREE SHOPS, AIRLINES AND FERRY OPERATORS ('VENDOR CONTROL' SCHEME)

The scheme applies only to intra-EC transactions. The scheme can be used if

(*a*) either

- duty and/or tax free goods are supplied within an airport, port or Channel Tunnel terminal in a shop which is approved by C & E for those purposes; or

- 'Value Allowance' goods are supplied on intra-EC journeys by an airline or ferry operator;

(*b*) both standard-rated and zero-rated supplies are made;

(*c*) takings at each rate of VAT can be accurately separated at the time of each sale; and

(*d*) any supplies of other goods are dealt with outside the scheme.

The *'Value Allowance'* is the allowance limit for goods, other than tobacco products, alcoholic beverages and perfumes, set under *VATA 1994, 8 Sch Group 14.* See 23.20 EUROPEAN COMMUNITY: SINGLE MARKET.

Most sales within (*a*) above are zero-rated under *VATA 1994, 8 Sch Group 14* but where a traveller (or group of travellers) makes purchases which exceed the Value Allowance, VAT is due. Where only one item is purchased and it exceeds the Value Allowance, if that item would normally be standard-rated in the UK, the full value is standard-rated, without any duty/tax free allowance. Where several items are purchased which in total exceed the Value Allowance, the total value of the spanning item, if normally standard-rated in the UK, becomes liable to VAT at the standard rate.

How to calculate output tax. For each VAT period for intra-EC transactions

Step 1	Add up daily gross takings including zero-rated goods =	A
Step 2	Add up zero-rated sales =	B
Step 3	Add up individual 'gift' items over the Value Allowance =	C
Step 4	Add up gross takings relating to excise goods =	D
Step 5	Add up gross takings for perfumes and toilet waters =	E
Step 6	A – (B + C + D + E) =	F
Step 7	Number of transactions in the period (note (1)) =	G
Step 8	Group size factor (note (2)) =	H
Step 9	G × H × Value Allowance × 1.175 =	J
Step 10	F – J =	K

To find output tax

  (i) for 'basket' items, if positive, multiply K by the VAT fraction and

  (ii) for individual items over the Value Allowance, multiply C by the VAT fraction (note (3)).

Notes

(1) A transaction is the total bill of each customer purchase from duty free shop, etc., excluding third country sales, individual items over the Value Allowance and single transactions of excisable goods, perfumes or toilet waters.

Where difficulty is encountered in arriving at a method of identifying the total number of transactions (G) in Step 7 above, a *pro rata* method can be used to determine G as follows.

$$G = \frac{F \times T}{A}$$

where

F = Total value in Step 6 above

A = Total value in Step 1 above

T = Total number of transactions in Step 1 above

(2) The average group size factor is currently set at 2. This will be reviewed every two years.

(3) Where individual gift items are held out for sale in the price range between the Value Allowance and the Value Allowance plus VAT at the standard rate (e.g. if the

Value Allowance is £75, for individual gift items in the price range £75.01 to £88.13), VAT due on such individual items can be calculated separately as follows.

Value Allowance × number of individual sales items in price range =   R

Total value of goods sold in the price range =   S

To find output tax on goods in the price range, multiply (S – R) by the VAT fraction.

This output tax must be added to the remaining output tax calculated under (i) and (ii) above. Note that if this method is used, Steps 3 and 7 should exclude the value and number of transactions of individual gift items in the price range.

Gross takings. See 60.8 and 60.9 above for gross takings together with adjustments and special transactions which must be taken into account.

Records. In addition to the normal records required, records must be kept of daily gross takings from standard-rated sales.

Change in the rate of VAT. See 60.7 above.

(VAT Information Sheet 1/94 and memorandum thereto dated 1 November 1994).

60.22   OLD SCHEME RULES

Following a review undertaken in 1995 and 1996, the 15 existing retail schemes have been replaced by the Point of Sale scheme, Apportionment Schemes 1 and 2 and Direction Calculation Schemes 1 and 2 described in detail above. The key changes are

- Schemes A and F continue in revised form as the Point of Sale Scheme;

- Scheme D continues in revised form as Apportionment Scheme 1;

- Scheme H continues in revised form as Apportionment Scheme 2;

- Schemes B and E continue in revised form as the Direct Calculation Scheme 1;

- Schemes B1 and E1 continue in revised form as the Direct Calculation Scheme 2; and

- Schemes B2, C, D1, G, J, J1 and J2 have been withdrawn for supplies made after 31 March 1998.

Where one of the old schemes continues in revised form, it must be operated in accordance with the revised provisions by 31 March 1998 at the latest.

After 1 August 1997, it is not possible to start to use, or to change to, any of the old schemes.

Details of the operation of the old schemes are considered in 60.23 to 60.43 below.

60.23   Scheme A

This was the only scheme which could be used if all sales were positive-rated. It could not be used for zero-rated sales.

How to calculate output tax. For each VAT period (whether quarterly or monthly)

Step 1	Add up daily gross takings from standard-rated supplies =	A
Step 2	Add up daily gross takings from lower-rated supplies =	B

Step 3   To calculate output tax, add the total at Step 1 multiplied by the VAT fraction for standard-rated supplies to the total at Step 2 multiplied by the VAT fraction for lower-rated goods

In algebraic form output tax is:

Sales before 1.9.97 (VAT at 8% on lower-rated goods)

$(A \times 7/47) + (B \times 2/27)$

Sales after 1.9.97 (VAT at 5% on lower-rated goods)

$(A \times 7/47) + (B \times 1/21)$

Gross takings. See 60.8 and 60.9 above for gross takings together with adjustments and special transactions which had to be taken into account.

Records. In addition to the normal records required, a record of daily gross takings had to be kept.

Annual accounting scheme. If this scheme was also used, see 63.13 SPECIAL SCHEMES.

Change in VAT rate. See 60.7 above.

Change in VAT liability of goods or services. If the VAT liability of any goods or services supplied changed from standard-rated to zero-rated, either VAT on those goods or services had subsequently to be accounted for outside the scheme or another scheme had to be adopted.

Cancellation of registration. VAT was due on business assets, including stock in hand. See 59.27 and 59.28 REGISTRATION.

(C & E Notice 727 (1993 edition), para 88, Appendix C, paras 6, 7; C & E Leaflet 727/7/93 — both now withdrawn).

60.24   **Scheme B**

In order to use this scheme,

(*a*)   supplies had to be made at two rates of VAT, i.e. at either

- standard and zero rate;

- standard and lower rate; or

- lower and zero rate;

(*b*)   any services supplied within the scheme had to be standard-rated and any zero-rated services had to be dealt with separately outside the scheme;

(*c*)   takings from zero-rated sales could not be more than 50% of the total value, including VAT, of all standard-rated and zero-rated supplies dealt with under the scheme in a year; and

(*d*)   with effect from 27 November 1996, taxable retail turnover had to be less than £1 million. From that date,

- retailers with turnover over £1 million could not start using the scheme (existing users could continue to use the scheme up to 31 March 1997 but thereafter had to use an alternative accounting method); and

- retailers with turnover below £1 million could continue to use the scheme but had to monitor turnover regularly and, as soon as it is clear that the limit had been or would be exceeded, had to cease using the scheme at the end of the next VAT period.

Scheme B could not be used for supplies of catering.

How to calculate output tax. For each VAT period (quarterly or monthly)

Where zero-rated supplies were made

Step 1	Add up daily gross takings =	A
Step 2	Add up expected selling prices of zero-rated goods received, made or grown for resale (where goods are bought from non-registered suppliers, include only those goods which are zero-rated) =	B
Step 3	Calculate positive-rated takings by deducting the total in Step 2 from the total in Step 1	
Step 4	To calculate output tax , multiply the total in Step 3 by the appropriate VAT fraction	

In algebraic form output tax is

For supplies at the standard rate (17.5%)

$(A - B) \times 7/47$

For supplies made at the lower rate

$(A - B) \times 2/27$ (VAT at 8% on supplies before 1.9.97)

$(A - B) \times 1/21$ (VAT at 5% on supplies after 31.8.97)

Where standard-rated and lower-rated supplies were made

Step 1	Add up daily gross takings =	A
Step 2	Add up expected selling prices of lower-rated goods received, made or grown for resale =	B
Step 3	Calculate standard-rated takings by deducting the total in Step 2 from the total in Step 1	
Step 4	To calculate output tax, add the total at Step 2 multiplied by the VAT fraction for lower-rated goods to the total at Step 3 multiplied by the VAT fraction for standard-rated goods	

In algebraic form output tax is

$(B \times 2/27) + ((A - B) \times 7/47)$ for supplies before 1.9.97

$(B \times 1/21) + ((A - B) \times 7/47)$ for supplies made after 31.8.97

Gross takings. See 60.8 and 60.9 above for gross takings together with adjustments and special transactions which had to be taken into account.

Expected selling prices. See 60.10 to 60.12 above for the calculation of expected selling prices.

Negative output tax. An unusually large purchase of zero-rated goods in a particular quarter could give rise to a 'negative' output tax figure. Where this occurred, the figure had to be entered in Box 1 of the VAT return in the normal way and enclosed in brackets.

Opening stock. Goods in stock when the scheme was started were not normally treated as goods received for resale. However, if there were any lines in that stock which were to be sold but not replenished, these could be treated as goods received for resale. Stock acquired on the transfer of a business as a going concern by a business already using Scheme B constituted goods received for resale rather than opening stock (*Co-operative Wholesale Society Ltd QB, [1995] STC 983*).

Records. In addition to the normal records required, records of daily gross takings and total expected selling prices for zero-rated goods had to be kept.

Annual accounting scheme. If this scheme was also used, see 63.13 SPECIAL SCHEMES.

Change in VAT rate. See 60.7 above.

Change in VAT liability of goods or services. If any *services* supplied changed from standard-rated to zero-rated, either

• such services had to be accounted for outside the scheme; or

• another scheme had be adopted.

If the VAT liability on *goods* changed, Scheme B could still be used provided the conditions in (*a*) to (*d*) above applied after the change.

From the day of change, values of B (see Step 2 above) had to include expected selling prices of goods which had become zero-rated and exclude expected selling prices of goods which had become standard-rated.

Cancellation of registration. VAT was due on business assets, including stock in hand. See 59.27 and 59.28 REGISTRATION.

(C & E Notice 727 (1993 edition), para 88, Appendix C, paras 8, 9; C & E Leaflet 727/8/93 — both now withdrawn).

60.25   **Scheme B1**

This scheme worked in the same way as Scheme B above except that there was no 50% turnover limit for zero-rated goods and users had to make an annual stock adjustment.

In order to use the scheme,

(*a*)   supplies had to be made at two rates of VAT, i.e. at either

• standard and zero rate;

• standard and lower rate; or

• lower and zero rate;

(*b*)   any services supplied within the scheme had to be standard-rated;

(*c*)   it had to be possible to calculate

• zero-rated stock on hand (where supplies were made at the zero rate and a positive rate), or

• lower-rated stock on hand (where supplies were made at a combination of two positive rates)

both when the scheme was started and at the end of each scheme year; and

(*d*)   any supplies of catering had to be dealt with outside the scheme.

How to calculate output tax. For each VAT period, the same rules applied as for Scheme B, see 60.24 above.

60.25 Retail Schemes

Annual adjustment. Where quarterly returns were prepared, before making the return for the fourth VAT period the following procedure had to be carried out.

Where zero-rated supplies were made

Step 1	Add up the expected selling prices of zero-rated goods in stock at the beginning of the year =	A
Step 2	Add up daily gross takings for the last four periods =	B
Step 3	Add up the expected selling prices of zero-rated goods received, made or grown for resale in the last four VAT periods =	C
Step 4	Add up the expected selling prices of zero-rated goods in stock at the end of the fourth VAT period =	D
Step 5	To work out the expected selling prices of zero-rated goods sold in the four VAT periods, add the total in Step 1 to the total in Step 3 and deduct the total in Step 4	
Step 6	To work out the positive-rated takings for the last four periods, deduct the total at Step 5 from the total at Step 2	
Step 7	To calculate output tax, multiply the total at Step 6 by the appropriate VAT fraction	

In algebraic form, output tax is

For supplies at the standard rate (17.5%)

$(B - A - C + D) \times 7/47$

For supplies made at the lower rate

$(B - A - C + D) \times 2/27$ (VAT at 8% for supplies before 1.9.97)

$(B - A - C + D) \times 1/21$ (VAT at 5% for supplies after 31.8.97)

Where standard-rated and lower-rated supplies were made

Step 1	Add up the expected selling prices of lower-rated goods in stock at the beginning of the year =	A
Step 2	Add up daily gross takings for the year =	B
Step 3	Add up expected selling prices of lower-rated goods received, made or grown for resale in the last four VAT periods =	C
Step 4	Add up expected selling prices of lower-rated goods in stock at the end of the fourth VAT period =	D
Step 5	To work out the expected selling prices of lower-rated goods sold in the four VAT periods, add the total in Step 1 to the total in Step 3 and deduct the total in Step 4	
Step 6	To work out the standard-rated takings for the last four periods, deduct the total at Step 5 from the total at Step 2	
Step 7	To calculate output tax, add the total at Step 5 multiplied by the VAT fraction for lower-rated goods to the total at Step 6 multiplied by the VAT fraction for standard-rated goods	

In algebraic form output tax is

$$((A + C - D) \times 2/27) + ((B - A - C + D) \times 7/47)$$

This gave the correct total for output tax due for the year. If the total was less than that calculated under the scheme in the four VAT periods, the difference had to be included in the VAT deductible side of the VAT account for the fourth VAT period. Similarly if the total was more, the difference had to be included in the VAT payable side of the VAT account for that period.

Where monthly returns were prepared the same principles applied except that calculations were made in the twelfth VAT period and were based on the last twelve VAT periods.

Gross takings. See 60.8 and 60.9 above for gross takings together with adjustments and special transactions which had to be taken into account.

Expected selling prices. See 60.10 to 60.12 above for the calculation of expected selling prices.

Negative output tax. An unusually large purchase of zero-rated goods in a particular period could give rise to a 'negative' output tax figure. Where this occurred, the figure had to be entered in Box 1 of the VAT return in the normal way and enclosed in brackets.

Records. In addition to the normal records required, records of daily gross takings and total expected selling prices for each class of zero-rated goods had to be kept.

Annual accounting scheme. If this scheme was also used, see 63.13 SPECIAL SCHEMES.

Change in VAT rate. See 60.7 above. In addition, on a change in the VAT rate, it was necessary to make an adjustment as for the annual adjustment above but covering the period from the last adjustment (or, if no previous adjustment had been made, from the date the scheme was first used) until the close of business on the day before the rate change. But if this period only amounted to one VAT period or less, there was no need to make the adjustment until the following year.

Change in VAT liability. If any *services* supplied changed from standard rate to zero rate, either

- such services had to be accounted for outside the scheme; or

- another scheme had to be adopted.

If the VAT liability on goods changed, from the day of the change, values of expected selling prices of zero-rated goods received, made or grown for resale (see Step 3 above) had to include goods which had become taxable at the zero rate and exclude goods which had become taxable at the standard rate.

Ceasing to use the scheme. The annual adjustment as explained above had to be carried out for the period from the last annual adjustment to the date of ceasing to use the scheme.

Cancellation of registration. VAT was due on business assets, including stock in hand. See 59.27 and 59.28 REGISTRATION.

(C & E Notice 727 (1993 edition), paras 83, 88, Appendix C, paras 10, 11; C & E Leaflet 727/8A/93 — both now withdrawn).

60.26   **Scheme B2**

In order to use the scheme,

- positive-rated and zero-rated supplies had to be made (i.e. either standard-rated and zero-rated sales or lower-rated and zero-rated sales);

- any services supplied within the scheme had to be standard-rated and any zero-rated services had to be dealt with separately outside the scheme;

- any supplies of zero-rated self-made or grown goods or supplies of catering had to be dealt with outside the scheme; and

- total taxable retail sales (including VAT) had to be £750,000 a year or less. The limit applied to the whole business, e.g. the scheme could not be applied to one shop if the total turnover of two or more shops owned exceeds the limit. There was a 25% tolerance built into the scheme which meant that it could still be used where taxable turnover grew because of inflation or expansion, provided it did not exceed £937,500. If this limit was exceeded, a new scheme had to be used. It was also possible to start using the scheme if turnover was more than £750,000 (but less than £937,500) provided turnover was expected to fall below £750,000 during the next twelve months.

How to calculate output tax. For each VAT period whether quarterly or monthly

Step 1	Add up daily gross takings =	A
Step 2	Add up the cost of each type of zero-rated goods received for resale (where goods are bought from non-registered suppliers, include only those goods which are zero-rated) =	B
Step 3	Ascertain the fixed mark-up percentage for each type of zero-rated goods (see below) =	C
Step 4	Calculate the total mark-up for each type of zero-rated goods by multiplying the total in Step 2 by the percentage in Step 3	
Step 5	Calculate the selling price of each type of zero-rated goods by adding the total at Step 2 to the total at Step 4	
Step 6	Calculate the proportion of gross takings from positive-rated sales by deducting the total at Step 5 from the total at Step 1	
Step 7	To calculate output tax, multiply the total in Step 6 by the appropriate VAT fraction	

In algebraic form, output tax is

For supplies at the standard rate (17.5%)

$(A - B(1 + C)) \times 7/47$

For supplies at the lower rate

$(A - B(1 + C)) \times 2/27$ (VAT at 8% for supplies before 1.9.97)

$(A - B(1 + C)) \times 1/21$ (VAT at 5% for supplies after 31.8.97)

Fixed mark-ups were as follows.

Type of goods	Fixed mark-up
Food	20%
Children's clothing and footwear	35%
Books, booklets, maps, etc.	40%
Newspapers, magazines, periodicals, etc.	33%
Goods not specified elsewhere	15%

Gross takings. See 60.8 and 60.9 above for gross takings together with adjustments and special transactions which had to be taken into account.

Expected selling prices. See 60.10 to 60.12 above for the calculation of expected selling prices.

Imports and acquisitions. The cost of zero–rated goods received for resale under Step 2 above included

- any imports from outside the EC at the full price paid (including customs duty), and

- any goods acquired from another EC country which were eligible for zero–rating when supplied in the UK at the full price paid (including any VAT or excise duty).

Opening stock. Goods in stock when the scheme was started were not normally treated as goods for resale. However, if there were any lines in that stock which were to be sold but not replenished, these could be treated as goods received for resale.

Negative output tax. An unusually large purchase of zero–rated goods in a particular period could give rise to a 'negative' output tax figure. Where this occurred, the figure had to be entered in Box 1 of the VAT return in the normal way and enclosed in brackets.

Records. In addition to the normal records required, records of daily gross takings and cost of zero–rated goods received for resale for each type of goods had be kept.

General note. Scheme B2 used fixed mark–ups for each type of zero–rated goods. If the average mark–up on zero–rated goods in a particular business was higher than the fixed mark–up, more VAT could be payable under this scheme than under another available alternative scheme.

Annual accounting scheme. If this scheme was also used, see 63.13 SPECIAL SCHEMES.

Change in VAT rate. See 60.7 above.

Changes in VAT liability. From the day of change, the record of zero–rated goods received for resale had to

- include goods which had become taxable at the zero rate; and

- exclude goods which had become taxable at the standard rate.

Cancellation of registration. VAT was due on business assets, including stock in hand. See 59.27 and 59.28 REGISTRATION.

(C & E Notice 727 (1993 edition), para 88, Appendix C, paras 12, 13; C & E Leaflet 727/8B/93 — both now withdrawn).

60.27   **Scheme C**

In order to use this scheme

- goods could be supplied at any rate of VAT although some of the zero–rated goods had to be supplied in the UK;

- total taxable retail sales (including VAT) had to be £125,000 or less per year. The limit applied to the whole business, e.g. the scheme could not be applied to one shop if total turnover of two or more shops owned exceeded the limit. There was a 25% tolerance built into the scheme which meant that it could still be used where taxable turnover grew because of inflation or expansion, provided it did not exceed £156,250. If this limit was exceeded, a new scheme had to be used. It was also possible to start using the scheme if turnover was more than £125,000 (but less than

£156,250) provided turnover was expected to fall below £125,000 during the next twelve months;

- the trade classification shown on the VAT registration certificate had to be from 8201 to 8239 (see below); and

- any supplies of services, grown or self-made goods or catering had to be dealt with outside the scheme.

How to calculate output tax. For each VAT period (whether quarterly or monthly)

Step 1	Add up the total cost, including VAT, of standard-rated goods received for resale in the VAT period (where goods are received from non-registered suppliers, include those goods which are standard-rated) =	A
Step 2	Ascertain the fixed mark-up fraction for the particular trade (see below) =	B
Step 3	Calculate the total mark-up on the goods by multiplying the total in Step 1 by the fraction in Step 2	
Step 4	Calculate the selling price of the goods by adding the totals in Steps 1 and 3	
Step 5	To calculate output tax, multiply the total in Step 4 by the VAT fraction	

In algebraic form output tax is

$A(1 + B) \times 7/47$

Fixed mark-ups were set by trade classification as follows and had to be used irrespective of actual mark-up in a particular business.

Band	Trade classification/type of business		Fixed mark-up
1	8207	Off-licences	15½%
	8214	Confectioners, tobacconists and newsagents	
2	8201	Grocers	20%
	8202	Dairymen	
	8203	Butchers	
	8204	Fishmongers and poulterers	
	8206	Bakers (selling wholly or mainly bought-in goods)	
3	8205	Greengrocers and fruiterers	40%
	8222	Radio and electrical goods (excluding radio and TV rental and relay shops)	
	8225	Cycle and perambulator shops	
	8227	Chemists and photographic shops	
4	8211	Department stores	50%
	8212	Variety and other general stores	
	8216	Men's and boys' wear shops	
	8217	Women's and girls' wear, household textiles and general clothing shops	
	8219	Domestic furniture shops, floor coverings shops, furniture and upholstery repairers	

Band	Trade classification/type of business		Fixed mark-up
	8221	Antique dealers, second-hand furniture shops, art dealers, picture framers and dealers in stamps and coins	
	8223	Radio and TV rental shops	
	8224	Hardware, china, wallpaper and paint shops	
	8226	Bookshops and stationers	
	8228	Opticians	
	8231	Leather goods, sports goods, toys and fancy goods shops	
	8232	Music shops (including records)	
	8234	Pet and pet food shops	
	8239	Other non-food shops	
5	8215	Footwear shops	60%
	8218	Retail furriers	
	8233	Florists, nursery and garden shops	
6	8213	General mail order houses	70%
7	8229	Jewellery, watch and clock retailers and repairers	75%
8*		Specified businesses – health food and wholefood shops	50%

*If the business was in Band 8, that mark-up had to be used and not one of those for Bands 1 to 7.

Gross takings. See 60.8 and 60.9 above for gross takings together with adjustments and special transactions which had to be taken into account.

Imports and acquisitions. The cost of standard-rated goods received for resale under Step 1 above included

- any imports from outside the EC at the full price paid (including VAT and customs duty); and

- any goods acquired from another EC country at the full price paid (including any excise duty and with the addition of VAT at the appropriate rate).

Opening stock. Goods in stock when the scheme was started were not normally treated as goods for resale. However, if there were any lines in that stock which were to be sold but not replenished, these could be treated as goods received for resale.

Ceasing to use the scheme. No adjustment could be made to scheme calculations for closing stocks.

Records. In addition to the normal records required, records had to be kept of the cost, including VAT, of standard-rated goods received for resale and daily gross takings (for completion of the VAT return).

General note. Scheme C involved little paperwork but as a fixed mark-up had to be adopted, if the average mark-up on standard-rated goods in a particular business was less than the fixed mark-up for the business, more VAT could be payable under this scheme than under an available alternative scheme.

Annual accounting scheme. If this scheme was also used, see 63.13 SPECIAL SCHEMES.

Change in VAT rate. See 60.7 above.

60.28 Retail Schemes

Change in VAT liability of goods or services. From the day of the change, the record of standard-rated goods received for resale had to include goods which had become standard-rated and/or exclude goods which had become zero-rated.

Cancellation of registration. VAT was due on business assets, including stock in hand. See 59.27 and 59.28 REGISTRATION.

(C & E Notice (1993 edition) 727, para 88, Appendix C, paras 14, 15; C & E Leaflet 727/9/93 — both now withdrawn).

60.28 Scheme D

In order to use this scheme

- positive and zero-rated supplies had to be made;

- total taxable retail sales (including VAT) had to be £1 million or less per year. The limit applied to the whole business, e.g. the scheme could not be applied to one shop if total turnover of two or more shops owned exceeded the limit. There was a 25% tolerance built into the scheme which meant that it could still be used where taxable turnover grew because of inflation or expansion, provided it did not exceed £1,250,000. If this limit was exceeded, a new scheme had to be used. It was also possible to start using the scheme if turnover was more than £1 million (but less than £1,250,000) provided turnover was expected to fall below £1 million during the next twelve months; and

- any supplies of services, grown or self-made goods or supplies of catering had to be dealt with outside the scheme.

How to calculate output tax. For each VAT period (whether quarterly or monthly)

Step 1	Add up daily gross takings =	A
Step 2	Add up the cost, including VAT, of all goods for resale at the lower rate =	B
Step 3	Add up the cost, including VAT, of all goods for resale at the standard rate =	C
Step 4	Add up the cost, including VAT, of all goods for resale at all rates (i.e. zero, lower and standard rate) =	D
Step 5	Calculate the proportion of daily takings from sales at the lower rate by dividing the total at Step 2 by the total at Step 4 and multiplying by the total in Step 1	
Step 6	Calculate the proportion of daily takings from sales at the standard rate by dividing the total at Step 3 by the total at Step 4 and multiplying by the total in Step 1	
Step 7	To calculate output tax, add the total at Step 5 multiplied by the VAT fraction for lower-rated goods to the total at Step 6 multiplied by the VAT fraction for standard-rated goods	

In algebraic form, output tax is

Sales before 1.9.97 (VAT at 8% on lower-rated goods)

$$\left(\frac{B}{D} \times A \times 2/27\right) + \left(\frac{C}{D} \times A \times 7/47\right)$$

Sales after 31.8.97 (VAT at 5% on lower-rated goods)

$$\left(\frac{B}{D} \times A \times 1/21\right) + \left(\frac{C}{D} \times A \times 7/47\right)$$

Annual adjustment. An annual adjustment had to be made to cover any under or overpayment of VAT. The adjustment was made on

- 31 March – for retailers with three-monthly VAT periods ending on 30 June, 30 September, 31 December and 31 March and all retailers with monthly VAT periods;

- 30 April – for retailers with three-monthly VAT periods ending on 31 July, 31 October, 31 January and 30 April; and

- 31 May – for retailers with three-monthly VAT periods ending on 31 August, 30 November, 28/29 February and 31 May.

If, at the first appropriate date for the annual adjustment, the scheme had been operated for one VAT period or less, no adjustment was required until the following year. Otherwise, in the first year of use, the adjustment was made in the ordinary way but calculations related to the period from first use of the scheme. The adjustment was calculated as follows. ows.

Step A	Calculate the VAT due by following the procedure as in Steps 1 to 7 above but using takings and cost figures for the year to date rather than the VAT period =	D
Step B	Add together the output tax already accounted for under the scheme in the year =	E

If D was less than E, too much VAT had been paid and the difference had to be included in the VAT deductible side of the VAT return for the period covering the adjustment. If D was greater than E, too little VAT had been paid and the difference had to be included in the VAT payable side of the VAT return for that period.

For all adjustments as above (other than the first) only VAT periods since the previous adjustment were included. This would cover a period of one year unless there had been a change in the VAT rate in that year. On such an event, a scheme adjustment was also required (see below) and the following 'annual' adjustment had only to cover the period from the date of change to the normal date.

Gross takings. See 60.8 and 60.9 above for gross takings together with adjustments and special transactions which had to be taken into account.

Imports and acquisitions. The cost of goods received for resale under Steps 2 to 4 above included

- any imports from outside the EC at the full price paid (including customs duty and VAT), and

- any goods acquired from another EC country at the full price paid (including excise duty and with the addition of VAT at the appropriate UK rate).

Opening stock. Goods in stock when the scheme was started were not normally treated as goods for resale. However, if there were any lines in that stock which were to be sold but not replenished, these could be treated as goods received for resale.

Records. In addition to the normal records required, records had to be kept of daily gross takings and the cost, including VAT, of all goods received for resale.

General note. If, on average, a retailer used a higher mark-up for zero-rated goods than standard-rated goods, the VAT liability could be higher under Scheme D than under an available alternative scheme.

Annual accounting scheme. If this scheme was also used, see 63.13 SPECIAL SCHEMES.

Change in VAT rate. See 60.7 above.

Scheme adjustment. In addition, when there was a change in the VAT rate, an adjustment had be made as described in Steps A and B for the annual adjustment above but covering the period from the last adjustment (or, if no previous adjustments had been made, from the date the scheme was first operated) until the close of business on the day before the rate change. However, if this period only amounted to one VAT period or less, no adjustment had to be made until the following year.

Change in VAT liability of goods or services. From the day of change, the record of goods received for resale had to include all goods affected by the change at their new rate of VAT.

Ceasing to use the scheme. The annual adjustment as explained above had to be carried out for the period from the last adjustment to the date of ceasing to use the scheme.

Cancellation of registration. VAT was due on business assets, including stock in hand. See 59.27 and 59.28 REGISTRATION.

(C & E Notice 727 (1993 edition), paras 83, 88, Appendix C, paras 16, 17; C & E Leaflet 727/10/93 — both now withdrawn).

60.29   **Scheme D1**

In order to use the scheme

- standard-rated and zero-rated supplies of goods had to be made;

- total taxable retail sales (including VAT) had to be £1 million or less per year. The limit applied to the whole business, e.g. the scheme could not be applied to one shop if total turnover of two or more shops owned exceeded the limit. There was a 25% tolerance built into the scheme which meant that it could still be used where taxable turnover grew because of inflation or expansion, provided it did not exceed £1,250,000. If this limit was exceeded, a new scheme had to be used. It was also possible to start using the scheme if turnover was more than £1 million (but less than £1,250,000) provided turnover was expected to fall below £1 million during the next twelve months;

- the value of purchases from unregistered suppliers and from suppliers who offered prompt payment discounts *which were not taken up* could not exceed 25% of total purchases of goods for resale; and

- any supplies of services, grown or self-made goods or supplies of catering had to be dealt with outside the scheme.

How to calculate output tax. For each VAT period (whether monthly or quarterly)

Step 1   Add up daily gross takings =   A

Step 2   Add up the VAT charged on all goods received for
                resale in the VAT period =   B

Step 3   Add up cost, including VAT, of standard and zero-
              rated goods received for resale in the tax period =   C

Step 4   To calculate output tax, divide the total in Step 2 by the
              total in Step 3 and multiply by the total in Step 1

In algebraic form, output tax is

$$\frac{B}{C} \times A$$

Annual adjustment. An annual adjustment had to be made to cover any under or overpayments of VAT. The adjustment was made on

- 31 March – for retailers with three-monthly VAT periods ending on 30 June, 30 September, 31 December and 31 March and all retailers with monthly VAT periods;

- 30 April – for retailers with three-monthly VAT periods ending on 31 July, 31 October, 31 January and 30 April; and

- 31 May – for retailers with three-monthly VAT periods ending on 31 August, 30 November, 28/29 February and 31 May.

If, at the appropriate date for the annual adjustment, the scheme had been operated for one VAT period or less, no adjustment was required until the following year. Otherwise, in the first year of the scheme, the adjustment was made in the ordinary way but calculations related to a period from first use of the scheme. The adjustment was calculated as follows.

Step A   Calculate output tax for the year by following the
              procedure as in Steps 1 to 4 above but using takings and
              cost figures for the year to date rather than the VAT
              period =   D

Step B   Add together the output tax already calculated under
              the scheme in the year (four three-monthly or twelve
              monthly periods) =   E

If D was less than E, too much VAT had been paid and the difference had to be included in the VAT deductible side of the VAT return for the period covering the adjustment. If D was greater than E, too little VAT had been paid and the difference had to be included in the VAT payable side of the VAT return for that period.

Purchases from unregistered suppliers and suppliers who offered prompt payment discounts ('distortion purchases'). At the same time as making the annual adjustment above, the following comparison had to be made.

(1)   Add up the cost of goods received for resale from
              unregistered suppliers in the year =   F

(2)   Add up the cost, including VAT, of goods received for
              resale from suppliers who offered prompt payment
              discounts *which were not taken up* =   G

(3)   Add up the cost, including VAT, of standard and
              zero-rated goods received for resale during the year =   H

(4)   Calculate the percentage of distortion purchases from
              supplier within (1) and (2), i.e.

$$\frac{F + G}{H} \times 100 = P\%$$

If P% was less than 10%, no further action was required.

If P% was more than 10% but less than 25%, an additional annual adjustment had to be made (see below).

If P% was more than 25%, as well as making the additional annual adjustment (see below), the VAT office had to be notified and the retailer had to change to another scheme.

Additional annual adjustment.

(1)	Calculate how much of gross takings relates to distortion purchases by multiplying the total gross takings for the year by the percentage P above =	J
(2)	Calculate the notional amount of VAT on purchases from unregistered suppliers by adding up the cost of *standard-rated* goods received for resale from unregistered suppliers in the year and multiplying the total by the VAT fraction =	K
(3)	Calculate the shortfall in VAT caused by prompt payment discounts by • adding up the VAT-exclusive value of standard-rated goods received for resale in the year from suppliers who offer prompt payment discounts which were not taken up and multiplying the total by the VAT fraction and deducting from this total • the VAT charged on goods received for resale in the year from suppliers who offered prompt payment discounts *which were not taken up* =	L
(4)	Calculate the total notional VAT by adding the total in (2) to the total in (3)	
(5)	Calculate the total VAT-inclusive value of the distortion purchases in the year by adding up • the cost of standard and zero-rated goods received for resale in the year from unregistered suppliers; and • the cost, including VAT, of standard and zero-rated goods received for resale from suppliers who offered prompt payment discounts which were not taken up =	M
(6)	Calculate how much additional VAT is due by dividing the total at (4) by the total at (5) and multiplying by the total at (1)	

In algebraic form, the additional VAT is

$$\frac{K + L}{M} \times J$$

The additional VAT had to be included in the VAT payable side of the VAT account for the period covering the adjustment.

Gross takings. See 60.8 and 60.9 above for gross takings together with adjustments and special transactions which had to be taken into account.

Imports and acquisitions. The cost of goods received for resale included

- any imports from outside the EC at the full price paid (including VAT and customs duty); and

- any goods acquired from another EC country at the full price paid (including any excise duty and with the addition of VAT at the appropriate UK rate).

Opening stock. Goods in stock when the scheme was started were not normally treated as goods for resale. However, if there were any lines in that stock which were to be sold but not replenished, these could be treated as goods received for resale.

Records. In addition to the normal records required, records had to be kept of

- daily gross takings;

- the cost, including VAT, of all goods received for resale; and

- the cost of all goods received for resale from unregistered suppliers and from suppliers who offer prompt payment discounts (which were not taken up).

General note. If, on average, a retailer used a higher mark-up for zero-rated goods than for standard-rated goods, the VAT liability could be higher under Scheme D1 than under an available alternative scheme.

Annual accounting scheme. If this scheme is also used, see 63.13 SPECIAL SCHEMES.

Change in VAT rate. Because the VAT fraction was not used in the calculation of output tax, a change in the VAT rate did not affect the scheme calculations.

Change in VAT liability. From the day of change, the record of goods received for resale had to include all goods affected by the change at their new rate of VAT.

Ceasing to use the scheme. The annual adjustment as explained above had to be carried out for the period from the last adjustment to the date of ceasing to use the scheme.

Cancellation of registration. VAT was due on business assets, including stock in hand. See 59.27 and 59.28 REGISTRATION.

(C & E Notice 727 (1993 edition), paras 83, 88, Appendix C, paras 18, 19; C & E Leaflet 727/10A/93 — both now withdrawn).

60.30   **Scheme E**

This scheme was based on projecting standard-rated purchases to their expected selling prices to arrive at standard-rated takings. In order to use this scheme

- supplies of goods had to be made at more than one rate of VAT;

- it had to be possible to calculate positive-rated stock on hand when the scheme was started. Physical stock-taking had to be carried out if possible. Otherwise, the value of goods received for resale in the three months before using the scheme could be used; and

- any supplies of standard-rated services or catering had to be dealt with outside the scheme.

How to calculate output tax

For the first VAT period (whether quarterly or monthly)

Step 1	Add up the expected selling prices, including VAT, of the standard-rated goods in stock for resale at the commencement of using the scheme =	A
Step 2	Add up the expected selling prices, including VAT, of the standard-rated goods received, made or grown for resale in the VAT period (where goods are bought from non-registered suppliers, include those goods which would be standard-rated) =	B
Step 3	Calculate the total of Steps 1 and 2	
Step 4	Add up the expected selling prices, including VAT, of lower-rated goods in stock for resale at the commencement of using the scheme =	C
Step 5	Add up the expected selling prices, including VAT, of the lower-rated goods received, made or grown for resale in the VAT period (where goods are bought from non-registered suppliers, include those goods which would be lower-rated) =	D
Step 6	Calculate the total of Steps 4 and 5	
Step 7	To calculate output tax, add the total in Step 3 multiplied by the VAT fraction for standard-rated goods to the total at Step 6 multiplied by the VAT fraction for lower-rated goods	

In algebraic form, output tax is

Sales before 1.9.97 (VAT at 8% on lower-rated goods)

$$((A + B) \times 7/47) + ((C + D) \times 2/27)$$

Sales after 31.8.97 (VAT at 5% on lower-rated goods)

$$((A + B) \times 7/47) + ((C + D) \times 1/21)$$

Second and subsequent VAT periods

To find the output tax, add the total in Step 2 multiplied by the VAT fraction for standard-rated goods to the total in Step 5 multiplied by the VAT fraction for lower-rated goods.

In algebraic form output tax is

Sales before 1.9.97 (VAT at 8% on lower-rated goods)

$$(B \times 7/47) + (D \times 2/27)$$

Sales after 31.8.97 (VAT at 5% on lower-rated goods)

$$(B \times 7/47) + (D \times 1/21)$$

Gross takings. See 60.8 and 60.9 above for gross takings together with adjustments and special transactions which had to be taken into account.

Expected selling prices. See 60.10 to 60.12 above for the calculation of expected selling prices.

Records. In addition to normal records required, records must be kept of

- expected selling prices, including VAT, for each class of standard-rated goods received, made or grown for resale; and

- daily gross takings (for completion of the VAT return).

Annual accounting scheme. If this scheme was also used, see 63.13 SPECIAL SCHEMES.

Change in VAT rate.

- *If the change occurred at the beginning of the VAT period,* output tax for the period was calculated by following Steps 1 to 7 above as if the period in question were the first VAT period but including VAT at the new rate and apply the new VAT fraction. As VAT had already been paid on the opening stock in a previous VAT period, a VAT credit was due. This was calculated by applying the old VAT fraction to the expected selling prices, including VAT at the old rate, of all the standard-rated goods in stock at the close of business on the day before the change. The amount of tax credit had to be entered in Box 4 on the VAT return.

- *If the change occurred during a VAT period,* output tax was calculated for that period in two separate parts as if each were a whole VAT period. The first period ran from the beginning of the VAT period to the close of business on the day before the change. Output tax was calculated using the method applicable to second and subsequent VAT periods above and applying the old VAT rate and fraction (unless this was also the first VAT period of using the scheme when output tax was calculated by following Steps 1 to 7 above).

  The second period ran from the day of change to the end of the VAT period. Output tax was calculated by following Steps 1 to 7 above as if the period in question were the first VAT period but including VAT at the new rate and applying the new VAT fraction. A VAT credit was due on the stock held at the close of business on the day before the change, calculated by applying the old VAT fraction to the expected selling prices, including VAT at the old rate, of all the standard-rated goods in stock at that time. The amount of credit had to be entered in Box 4 on the VAT return.

Change in VAT liability of goods. Whether the change took place at the beginning of, or during, the VAT period, the calculation was as for a change in the VAT rate above except that the values of the VAT fraction did not change. C & E confirmed that where the VAT liability changed on selected goods, stocks of which could be identified, it was only necessary to calculate the expected selling prices, including VAT at the old and new rates, on those particular items in stock and not on *all* stocks.

From the day of the change, the record of standard-rated goods received, made or grown for resale had to include goods which had become standard-rated and/or exclude goods which had become zero-rated.

Ceasing to use the scheme. Credit could be taken for any VAT paid on standard-rated goods in stock at the time of ceasing to use the scheme (including on the forced change to one of the new schemes). The amount had to be shown in Box 4 on the next VAT return.

Cancellation of registration. No VAT was due on stocks held but VAT was due on business equipment. See 59.27 and 59.28 REGISTRATION for payment of VAT on business assets generally.

General note. As VAT was paid on stock before it was sold, the scheme was best suited to a business with a fast turnover of standard-rated goods.

60.31 Retail Schemes

(C & E Notice 727 (1993 edition), paras 83, 88, Appendix C, paras 20, 21; C & E Leaflet 727/11/93 — both now withdrawn).

60.31 Scheme E1

In order to use the scheme

- positive and zero-rated supplies of goods had to be made;
- detailed stock records were required; and
- any supplies of standard-rated services or supplies of catering had to be dealt with outside the scheme.

How to calculate tax. For each VAT period (whether quarterly or monthly returns) and for each line of positive-rated goods

Step 1	Record the unit selling price, including VAT, of the line =	A
Step 2	Record the quantity of stock on hand at the beginning of the VAT period plus the quantity received, made or grown for resale during the VAT period =	B
Step 3	Record the quantity of stock on hand at the end of the VAT period =	C
Step 4	Calculate actual sales by deducting the total at Step 3 from the total at Step 2	
Step 5	Calculate takings for the supply of these goods by multiplying the unit selling price in Step 1 by the total at Step 4	
Step 6	To calculate output tax, repeat Steps 1-5 for each line to find total takings and multiply this figure by the relevant VAT fraction	

In algebraic form output tax is

For each line of supplies at the standard rate

$A(B - C) \times 7/47$

For each line of supplies at the lower rate

$A(B - C) \times 2/27$ (VAT at 8% for supplies before 1.9.97)

$A(B - C) \times 1/21$ (VAT at 5% for supplies after 31.8.97)

Records. In addition to the normal records required, records had to be kept of

- daily gross takings (to complete the VAT return); and,
- for each standard-rated line of goods, the quantity of stock on hand at the beginning of each VAT period, the quantity of goods received, made or grown for resale during each VAT period, and the unit selling price (including VAT).

Gross takings. See 60.8 and 60.9 above for gross takings together with adjustments and special transactions which had to be taken into account.

General note. Under this scheme output tax for each period was exactly equal to the amount charged to customers but it was one of the more complicated schemes involving much paperwork.

Annual accounting scheme. If this scheme was also used, see 63.13 SPECIAL SCHEMES.

Change in VAT rate. See 60.7 above.

Change in VAT liability. If the change was at the beginning of the VAT period, the scheme was operated in the normal way. If the change was during a VAT period, the procedure for a change in the VAT rate had to be followed (i.e. the VAT period was split into two periods) but with no change in the VAT fraction. From the day of change, the record of standard-rated goods received, made or grown for resale had to

- include goods which had become taxable at the standard rate; and

- exclude goods which had become taxable at the zero rate.

(C & E Notice 727 (1993 edition), para 88, Appendix C, paras 22, 23; C & E Leaflet 727/11A/93 — both now withdrawn).

60.32   **Scheme F**

Under this scheme takings had to be separated at the point of sale (e.g. by using separate or multi-total tills) into standard-rated, lower-rated and zero-rated supplies. The scheme was then simple to operate.

How to calculate output tax. For each VAT period (whether quarterly or monthly)

Step 1	Add up daily gross takings from standard-rated sales =	A
Step 2	Add up daily gross takings from lower-rated sales =	B
Step 3	To calculate output tax, add the total in Step 1 multiplied by the VAT fraction for standard-rated goods to the total in Step 2 multiplied by the VAT fraction for lower-rated goods	

In algebraic form output tax is

Sales before 1.9.97 (VAT at 8% on lower-rated goods)

$(A \times 7/47) + (B \times 2/27)$

Sales after 31.8.97 (VAT at 5% on lower-rated goods)

$(A \times 7/47) + (B \times 1/21)$

Gross takings. See 60.8 and 60.9 above for gross takings together with adjustments and special transactions which had to be taken into account.

Records. In addition to the normal records required, a record of daily gross takings had to be kept.

Annual accounting scheme. If this scheme was also used, see 63.13 SPECIAL SCHEMES.

Change in VAT rate. See 60.7 above.

Change in VAT liability of goods or services. The scheme had to be operated in the normal way but from the day of change, the record of daily gross takings from standard-rated sales had to include takings from supplies which had become standard-rated and/or exclude takings from supplies which had become zero-rated.

Cancellation of registration. VAT was due on business assets, including stock in hand. See 59.27 and 59.28 REGISTRATION.

60.33   Retail Schemes

(C & E Notice 727 (1993 edition), para 88, Appendix C, paras 24, 25; C & E Leaflet 727/12/93 — both now withdrawn).

60.33   **Scheme G**

Entry to this scheme was closed on 1 October 1991. The scheme was based on apportioning gross takings on the basis of positive-rated and zero-rated purchases of goods for resale. In order to use the scheme

- positive-rated and zero-rated supplies had to be made;

- it had to be possible to calculate stock on hand for each positive-rated item when the scheme was started; and

- any supplies of services, grown or self-made goods or supplies of catering had to be dealt with outside the scheme.

How to calculate output tax. For the first three quarterly VAT periods or the first eleven monthly VAT periods

Step 1	Calculate the amount paid, including VAT, for standard-rated goods in stock for resale at the commencement of using the scheme =	A
Step 2	Calculate the amount paid, including VAT, for lower-rated goods in stock for resale at the commencement of using the scheme =	B
Step 3	Calculate the amount paid, including VAT, for zero, lower and standard-rated goods in stock for resale at the commencement of using the scheme =	C
Step 4	Add up daily gross takings for the VAT period =	D
Step 5	Add up the cost, including VAT, of standard-rated goods received for resale since starting to use the scheme =	E
Step 6	Add the total in Step 5 to the total in Step 1	
Step 7	Add up the cost, including VAT, of lower-rated goods received for resale since starting to use the scheme =	F
Step 8	Add the total in Step 7 to the total in Step 2	
Step 9	Add up the cost, including VAT, of all goods received for resale since starting to use the scheme =	G
Step 10	Add the total in Step 9 to the total in Step 3	
Step 11	Calculate the proportion of gross takings from sales at the standard rate by dividing the total at Step 6 by the total at Step 10 and multiplying by the total at Step 4	
Step 12	Calculate the proportion of gross takings from sales at the lower rate by dividing the total at Step 8 by the total at Step 10 and multiplying by the total at Step 4	
Step 13	To calculate output tax, add the total at Step 11 multiplied by the VAT fraction for standard-rated goods to the total at Step 12 multiplied by the VAT fraction for lower-rated goods, and then add one-eighth to the total	

In algebraic form, output tax is

Sales before 1.9.97 (VAT at 8% on lower-rated goods)

$$\frac{9}{8}\left[\left(\frac{A+E}{C+G}\times D\times 7/47\right)+\left(\frac{B+F}{C+G}\times D\times 2/27\right)\right]$$

Sales after 31.8.97 (VAT at 5% on lower-rated goods)

$$\frac{9}{8}\left[\left(\frac{A+E}{C+G}\times D\times 7/47\right)+\left(\frac{B+F}{C+G}\times D\times 1/21\right)\right]$$

For the fourth and all later quarterly VAT periods or the twelfth and all later monthly VAT periods

Step A	Add up daily gross takings for the VAT period =	H
Step B	Add up the cost, including VAT, of standard-rated goods received for resale in the current VAT period and the previous three quarterly or eleven monthly VAT periods =	J
Step C	Add up the cost, including VAT, of lower-rated goods received for resale in the current VAT period and the previous three quarterly or eleven monthly VAT periods =	K
Step D	Add up the cost, including VAT, of all goods received for resale in the current VAT period and the previous three quarterly or eleven monthly VAT periods =	L
Step E	Calculate the proportion of gross takings from sales at the standard rate by dividing the total at Step B by the total at Step D and multiplying by the total at Step A	
Step F	Calculate the proportion of gross takings from sales at the lower rate by dividing the total at Step C by the total at Step D and multiplying by the total at Step A	
Step G	To calculate output tax, add the total at Step E multiplied by the VAT fraction for standard-rated goods to the total at Step F multiplied by the VAT fraction for lower-rated goods, and then add one-eighth to the total	

In algebraic form, output tax is

Sales before 1.9.97 (VAT at 8% on lower-rated goods)

$$\frac{9}{8}\left[\left(\frac{J}{L}\times H\times 7/47\right)+\left(\frac{K}{L}\times H\times 2/27\right)\right]$$

Sales after 31.8.97 (VAT at 5% on lower-rated goods)

$$\frac{9}{8}\left[\left(\frac{J}{L}\times H\times 7/47\right)+\left(\frac{K}{L}\times H\times 1/21\right)\right]$$

Gross takings. See 60.8 and 60.9 above for gross takings together with adjustments and special transactions which had to be taken into account.

Imports and acquisitions. The cost of goods received for resale included

- any imports from outside the EC at the full price paid (including customs duty and VAT); and

- any goods acquired from another EC country at the full price paid (including excise duty and with the addition of VAT at the appropriate UK rate).

Records. In addition to the normal records required, records had to be kept of daily gross takings and the cost, including VAT, of goods received for resale.

Annual accounting scheme. If this scheme was also used, see 63.13 SPECIAL SCHEMES.

Cancellation of registration. VAT was due on business assets, including stock in hand. See 59.27 and 59.28 REGISTRATION.

General note. If, on average, a retailer used a higher mark-up for zero-rated goods than standard-rated goods, he paid more VAT under Scheme G than under another scheme. This was partly because the scheme was based on purchase prices rather than selling prices, but also because an additional one-eighth adjustment was made in arriving at output tax. If turnover was below £1 million, less VAT would have been paid (with a similar method of calculation) under Scheme D.

(C & E Notice 727 (1987 edition) paras 22, 24, 25; C & E Leaflet 727/13/87 — both now withdrawn).

60.34   *Scheme G — change in VAT rate*

If the change occurred at the beginning of a VAT period, the scheme had to be operated as before but applying the new VAT fraction after the change.

If the change occurred during a VAT period, output tax had to be calculated for that VAT period in two separate parts as if each were a whole VAT period.

The first period ran from the beginning of the VAT period to the close of business on the day before the change. Depending upon how long the scheme had been in operation, Steps 1–13 or Steps A–G in 60.33 above had to be carried out as if for the whole of the current VAT period but only including gross takings for the first part of that period as above. (The cost figures of goods received for resale used to calculate the proportion of gross takings from standard-rated sales therefore included goods received for resale in the whole of the current VAT period.) The old VAT fraction had to be used in the computation.

The second period ran from the day of change to the end of the current VAT period. The calculation followed the same format but including only gross takings of the second period and using the new VAT fraction.

(C & E Notice 727 (1987 edition), Appendix C, para 20).

60.35   *Scheme G — change in VAT liability of goods*

Minor changes. Where a change did not affect more than 5% of annual taxable turnover within the scheme, a retailer could, if he wished, from the day of change, record the cost of any goods affected at the new rate and make no other adjustments. If one minor change was treated in this way, any later such change had also to be so treated.

Where any change affected more than 5% of scheme turnover (or where a retailer chose not to use the special rule above) the appropriate procedure set out below had to be followed.

Change in VAT liability of goods supplied at the beginning of the VAT period. One of two methods could be adopted.

(1)   *Method A.* The scheme was used from the day of change as if it were being used for the first time. See under 60.33 above for how to calculate VAT in the opening three quarterly or eleven monthly periods. A retailer could however, if he wished, exclude goods in stock from the calculation. Gross takings had to include all amounts payable for goods supplied after the change even if the goods formed part of stock before the change.

(2)   *Method B.* The scheme was operated as normally from the date of change but figures for cost of goods received for resale in the relevant previous periods were adjusted as follows.

Step 1	Add up separately the total cost, including VAT, of standard-rated goods received for resale in each of the previous three quarterly or eleven monthly VAT periods
Step 2	Add to each of the totals in Step 1, the cost of any goods received in those periods which, because of the change, have become taxable at the standard rate and subtract any which have become taxable at the zero rate
Step 3	Calculate corresponding totals and adjustments as in Steps 1 and 2 above for zero-rated goods received for resale

Change in VAT liability of goods supplied during a VAT period. Output tax had to be calculated for the VAT period in two separate parts as if each were a whole VAT period. The *first period* ran from the beginning of the VAT period to the close of business on the day before the change. Normal scheme calculations were made using gross takings from the part-period only. The *second period* ran from the day of change to the end of the VAT period. Whether Method A or Method B was adopted, only gross takings and goods received for resale in the part-period had to be used. Under Method B, the new totals for the three quarterly (or eleven monthly) VAT periods before the change also had to be used.

Change in VAT liability at the same time as a change in VAT rate. The rules on a change in VAT liability took precedence but the new VAT fraction had to be used where appropriate.

(C & E Notice 727 (1987 edition), Appendix C, para 21 now withdrawn).

60.36   **Scheme H**

This scheme was based on apportioning gross takings on the basis of expected selling prices of zero-rated and standard-rated goods received, made or grown for resale. In order to use this scheme

● positive and zero-rated supplies had to be made;

● it had to be possible to calculate stock on hand when the scheme was started. Physical stock-taking had to be carried out if possible. Otherwise the value of goods received for resale in the three months before using the scheme could be used; and

● any supplies of services or catering had to be dealt with outside the scheme.

How to calculate output tax. *For the first three quarterly VAT periods or the first eleven monthly VAT periods*

Step 1	Calculate the expected selling price, including VAT, of standard-rated goods in stock at the commencement of using the scheme =	A

Step 2	Calculate the expected selling price, including VAT, of lower-rated goods in stock at the commencement of using the scheme =	B
Step 3	Calculate the expected selling price, including VAT, of all goods in stock at the commencement of using the scheme =	C
Step 4	Add up daily gross takings for the VAT period =	D
Step 5	Add up expected selling prices, including VAT, of standard-rated goods received, made or grown for resale since starting to use the scheme =	E
Step 6	Add the total in Step 5 to the total in Step 1	
Step 7	Add up expected selling prices, including VAT, of lower-rated goods received, made or grown for resale since starting to use the scheme =	F
Step 8	Add the total in Step 7 to the total in Step 2	
Step 9	Add up expected selling prices, including VAT, of all goods received, made or grown for resale since starting to use the scheme =	G
Step 10	Add the total in Step 9 to the total in Step 3	
Step 11	Calculate the proportion of gross takings from sales at the standard rate by dividing the total at Step 6 by the total at Step 10 and multiplying by the total at Step 4	
Step 12	Calculate the proportion of gross takings from sales at the lower rate by dividing the total at Step 8 by the total at Step 10 and multiplying by the total at Step 4	
Step 13	To calculate output tax, add the total at Step 11 multiplied by the VAT fraction for standard-rated goods to the total at Step 12 multiplied by the VAT fraction for lower-rated goods	

In algebraic form, output tax is

Sales before 1.9.87 (VAT at 8% on lower-rated goods)

$$\left(\frac{A+E}{C+G} \times D \times 7/47\right) + \left(\frac{B+F}{C+G} \times D \times 2/27\right)$$

Sales after 31.8.97 (VAT at 5% on lower-rated goods)

$$\left(\frac{A+E}{C+G} \times D \times 7/47\right) + \left(\frac{B+F}{C+G} \times D \times 1/21\right)$$

For the fourth and all later quarterly VAT periods or the twelfth and all later monthly VAT periods

Step A	Add up daily gross takings for the VAT period =	H
Step B	Add up expected selling prices, including VAT, of standard-rated goods received, made or grown for resale in the current VAT period and the previous three quarterly or eleven monthly VAT periods =	J

Step C	Add up expected selling prices, including VAT, of lower-rated goods received, made or grown for resale in the current VAT period and the previous three quarterly or eleven monthly VAT periods =

K

Step D	Add up expected selling prices, including VAT, of all goods received, made or grown for resale in the current VAT period and the previous three quarterly or eleven monthly VAT periods =

L

Step E   Calculate the proportion of gross takings from sales at the standard rate by dividing the total at Step B by the total at Step D and multiplying by the total in Step A

Step F   Calculate the proportion of gross takings from sales at the lower rate by dividing the total at Step C by the total at Step D and multiplying by the total at Step A

Step G   To calculate output tax, add the total at Step E multiplied by the VAT fraction for standard-rated goods to the total at Step F multiplied by the VAT fraction for lower-rated goods

In algebraic form output tax is

Sales before 1.9.87 (VAT at 8% on lower-rated goods)

$$\left(\frac{J}{L} \times H \times 7/47\right) + \left(\frac{K}{L} \times H \times 2/27\right)$$

Sales after 31.8.97 (VAT at 5% on lower-rated goods)

$$\left(\frac{J}{L} \times H \times 7/47\right) + \left(\frac{K}{L} \times H \times 1/21\right)$$

Gross takings. See 60.8 and 60.9 above for gross takings together with adjustments and special transactions which had to be taken into account.

Expected selling prices. See 60.10 to 60.12 above for the calculation of expected selling prices. Whichever method was adopted, the retailer had regularly to review the mark-ups used in the scheme calculations and make adjustments to expected selling prices either by prospective adjustment or retrospective adjustment. Retrospective adjustments could only be made with the written agreement of the VAT office and the retailer had to show that he could make all the retrospective adjustments accurately and consistently.

- *Prospective adjustments.* When working out expected selling prices, all factors known at that time had to be taken into account. This meant adjusting for expected wastage, breakage, pilferage, sell-by date reductions and any other anticipated price changes. This had to be done as accurately as possible because, once the expected selling prices were set, no further adjustment could be made.

- *Retrospective adjustments.* At the end of each VAT period, adjustments had to be made for any sales where the expected selling price had not been received, e.g. due to price changes, special offers, wholesale sales and bad debts that had been written off.

Records. In addition to the normal records required, records had to be kept of daily gross takings and expected selling prices.

Annual accounting scheme. If this scheme was also used, see 63.13 SPECIAL SCHEMES.

60.37 Retail Schemes

Cancellation of registration. VAT was due on business assets, including stock in hand. See 59.27 and 59.28 REGISTRATION.

(C & E Notice 727 (1993 edition), para 88; C & E Leaflet 727/14/93 — both now withdrawn).

60.37 *Scheme H — change in VAT rate*

If the change occurred at the beginning of the VAT period, the scheme had to be operated as before but applying the new VAT fraction after the change.

If the change occurred during a VAT period, output tax had to be calculated for that VAT period in two separate parts as if each were a whole VAT period.

The first period ran from the beginning of the VAT period to the close of business on the day before the change. Depending upon how long the scheme had been in operation, Steps 1-13 or Steps A-G in 60.36 above had to be carried out as if for the whole of the current VAT period but only including gross takings for the first part of that period as above. (The expected selling prices of goods received, made or grown for resale used to calculate the proportion of gross takings from standard-rated sales therefore included goods received, made or grown for resale in the whole of the current VAT period.) The old VAT fraction was used in the computation.

The second period ran from the day of change to the end of the current VAT period. The calculation followed the same format but including only gross takings of the second period and using the new VAT fraction.

(C & E Notice 727 (1993 edition), Appendix C, para 26).

60.38 *Scheme H — change in VAT liability of goods*

Minor changes. Where a change did not affect more than 5% of annual taxable turnover within the scheme, a retailer could, if he wished, from the day of change, record the expected selling prices of any goods affected at the new rate and make no other adjustments. If one minor change was treated in this way, any later such change also had to be so treated.

Where any change affected more than 5% of scheme turnover (or where a retailer chose not to use the special rule above) the appropriate procedure set out below had to be followed.

Change in VAT liability of goods supplied at the beginning of the VAT period. One of two methods could be adopted.

(1) *Method A.* The scheme was used from the day of change as if it were being used for the first time. See under 60.36 above for how to calculate VAT in the opening three quarterly or eleven monthly periods. A retailer could however, if he wished, exclude goods in stock from the calculation. Gross takings had to include all amounts payable for goods supplied after the change even if the goods formed part of stock before the change.

(2) *Method B.* The scheme was operated as normally from the date of change but figures for expected selling prices in the relevant previous periods were adjusted as follows.

Step 1   Add up separately the expected selling prices, including VAT, of goods received, made or grown for resale in each of the previous three quarterly or eleven monthly VAT periods

Step 2   Add to each of the totals in Step 1, the expected selling prices of goods received, made or grown for resale in those periods which, because of the change, have become taxable at the standard rate and subtract any which become taxable at the zero rate

Step 3   Calculate corresponding totals and adjustments as in Steps 1 and 2 above for expected selling prices of zero-rated goods received, made or grown for resale

Change in VAT liability of goods supplied during a VAT period. Output tax had to be calculated for the VAT period in two separate parts as if each were a whole VAT period. The *first period* ran from the beginning of the VAT period to the close of business on the day before the change. Normal scheme calculations were made using gross takings from the part-period only. The *second period* ran from the day of change to the end of the VAT period. Whether Method A or Method B was adopted, only gross takings and goods received, made or grown for resale in the part-period had to be used. Under Method B, the new totals for the three quarterly (or eleven monthly) VAT periods before the change also had to be used.

Change in VAT liability at the same time as a change in VAT rate. The rules on a change in VAT liability took precedence but the new VAT fraction had to be used where appropriate.

(C & E Notice 727 (1993 edition), Appendix C, para 27).

60.39   Scheme J

Under the scheme, gross takings were apportioned on the basis of expected selling prices of zero-rated and standard-rated goods received, made or grown for resale. The scheme was based on a retailer's trade for a full year which ran from the beginning of the first VAT period in which the scheme was used. At the end of each year, an annual adjustment was made to correct for any over-payments or under-payments. At the beginning of each year, the whole method of calculating VAT was started again. In order to use this scheme

- positive-rated and zero-rated supplies had to be made;

- detailed stock records at each positive rate were required; and

- any supplies of services and catering had to be dealt with outside the scheme.

How to calculate output VAT. For each VAT period

Step 1	Calculate the expected selling prices, including VAT, of standard-rated goods in stock at the beginning of the year =	A
Step 2	Calculate the expected selling price, including VAT, of lower-rated goods in stock at the beginning of the year =	B
Step 3	Calculate the expected selling price, including VAT, of all goods in stock at the beginning of the year =	C
Step 4	Add up daily gross takings for the VAT period =	D
Step 5	Add up expected selling prices, including VAT, of standard-rated goods received, made or grown for resale since the beginning of the year =	E

Step 6	Add the total in Step 5 to the total in Step 1
Step 7	Add up expected selling prices, including VAT, of lower-rated goods received, made or grown for resale since the beginning of the year =
Step 8	Add the total in Step 7 to the total in Step 2
Step 9	Add up expected selling prices, including VAT, of all goods received, made or grown for resale since the beginning of the year =
Step 10	Add the total in Step 9 to the total in Step 3
Step 11	Calculate the proportion of gross takings from sales at the standard rate by dividing the total at Step 6 by the total at Step 10 and multiplying by the total at Step 4
Step 12	Calculate the proportion of gross takings from sales at the lower rate by dividing the total at Step 8 by the total at Step 10 and multiplying by the total at Step 4
Step 13	To calculate output tax, add the total at Step 11 multiplied by the VAT fraction for standard-rated goods to the total at Step 12 multiplied by the VAT fraction for lower-rated goods

In Step 7: F
In Step 9: G

In algebraic form output tax is

Sales before 1.9.97 (VAT at 8% on lower-rated goods)

$$\left(\frac{A+E}{C+G} \times D \times 7/47\right) + \left(\frac{B+F}{C+G} \times D \times 2/27\right)$$

Sales after 31.8.97 (VAT at 5% on lower-rated goods)

$$\left(\frac{A+E}{C+G} \times D \times 7/47\right) + \left(\frac{B+F}{C+G} \times D \times 1/21\right)$$

Annual adjustment. At the end of each year, the following adjustments had to be made.

Step A	Calculate expected selling prices, including VAT, of standard-rated goods in stock at the beginning of the year =
Step B	Calculate the expected selling price, including VAT, of lower-rated goods in stock at the beginning of the year =
Step C	Calculate the expected selling price, including VAT, of all goods in stock at the beginning of the year =
Step D	Add up daily gross takings for the last four quarterly or twelve monthly VAT periods =
Step E	Add up expected selling prices, including VAT, of standard-rated goods received, made or grown for resale in the last four quarterly or twelve monthly VAT periods =

In Step A: M
In Step B: N
In Step C: O
In Step D: P
In Step E: Q

Step F	Add up expected selling prices, including VAT, of lower-rated goods received, made or grown for resale in the last four quarterly or twelve monthly VAT periods =	R
Step G	Add up expected selling prices, including VAT, of all goods received, made or grown for resale in the last four quarterly or twelve monthly VAT periods =	S
Step H	Calculate expected selling prices, including VAT, of standard-rated goods in stock at the end of the fourth quarterly or twelfth monthly VAT period =	T
Step J	Calculate the expected selling price, including VAT, of lower-rated goods in stock at the end of the fourth quarterly or twelfth monthly VAT period =	U
Step K	Calculate the expected selling price, including VAT, of all goods in stock at the end of the fourth quarterly or twelfth monthly VAT period =	V
Step L	To work out the expected selling prices, including VAT, of all standard-rated goods sold in the four quarterly or twelve monthly periods, add the total in Step A to the total in Step E and deduct total in Step H	
Step M	To work out the expected selling prices, including VAT, of all lower-rated goods sold in the four quarterly or twelve monthly periods, add the total in Step B to the total in Step F and deduct total in Step J	
Step N	To work out the expected selling prices, including VAT, of all goods sold in the four quarterly or twelve monthly periods, add the total in Step C to the total in Step G and deduct total in Step K	
Step O	Calculate the proportion of daily gross takings from sales at the standard rate by dividing the total at Step L by the total at Step N and multiplying by the total at Step D	
Step P	Calculate the proportion of daily gross takings from sales at the lower rate by dividing the total at Step M by the total at Step N and multiplying by the total at Step D	
Step Q	To calculate output tax, add the total at Step O multiplied by the VAT fraction for standard-rated goods to the total at Step P multiplied by the VAT fraction for lower-rated goods	

In algebraic form output tax is

Sales before 1.9.97 (VAT at 8% on lower-rated goods)

$$\left(\frac{M + Q - T}{O + S - V} \times P \times 7/47\right) + \left(\frac{N + R - S}{O + S - V} \times P \times 2/27\right)$$

Sales after 31.8.97 (VAT at 5% on lower-rated goods)

$$\left(\frac{M + Q - T}{O + S - V} \times P \times 7/47\right) + \left(\frac{N + R - S}{O + S - V} \times P \times 1/21\right)$$

This gave the correct total for output tax due for the year. If the total output tax on the four quarterly or twelve monthly returns was greater, too much VAT had been paid and the difference had to be included in the VAT deductible side of the VAT account for the fourth quarter or twelfth month. Similarly if the total output tax on these returns was less, too little VAT had been paid and the difference had to be included in the VAT payable side of the VAT account for that period.

Gross takings. See 60.8 and 60.9 above for gross takings together with adjustments and special transactions which had to be taken into account.

Expected selling prices. See 60.10–60.12 above for the calculation of expected selling prices. Whichever method was adopted, the retailer had regularly to review the mark-ups used in the scheme calculations and make adjustments to expected selling prices either by prospective adjustment or retrospective adjustment. Retrospective adjustments could only be made with the written agreement of the VAT office and the retailer had to show that he could make all the retrospective adjustments accurately and consistently.

- *Prospective adjustments.* When working out expected selling prices, all factors known at that time had to be taken into account. This meant adjusting for expected wastage, breakage, pilferage, sell-by date reductions and any other anticipated price changes. This had to be done as accurately as possible because, once the expected selling prices were set, no further adjustment could be made.

- *Retrospective adjustments.* At the end of each VAT period, adjustments had to be made for any sales where the expected selling price had not been received, e.g. due to price changes, special offers, wholesale sales and bad debts that had been written off.

Records. In addition to the normal records required, records had to be kept of daily gross takings and expected selling prices.

Annual accounting scheme. If this scheme was also used, see 63.13 SPECIAL SCHEMES.

Ceasing to use the scheme. The annual adjustment as explained above had to be carried out.

Cancellation of registration. VAT was due on business assets, including stock in hand. See 59.27 and 59.28 REGISTRATION.

General notes. Scheme J was one of the more accurate schemes but was complicated and required a lot of paperwork. Where zero-rated goods had a short shelf life, and so only formed a small part of stock at any one time, VAT could be overpaid until the annual adjustment was made.

(C & E Notice 727 (1993 edition), paras 83, 88; C & E Leaflet 727/15/93 — both now withdrawn).

60.40   *Scheme J — change in VAT rate*

Whenever there was a change in the standard rate of VAT, it was necessary to calculate the total expected selling prices of stock items at the close of business on the day before the change as follows

- standard-rated stock including VAT at the old rate;

- standard-rated stock including VAT at the new rate;

- all stock including VAT at the old rate; and

- all stock including VAT at the new rate.

Change in VAT rate during a VAT period. Output tax had to be calculated for the VAT period in two separate parts as if each were a whole VAT period. The first period ran from the beginning of the VAT period to the close of business on the day before the change. Output tax was calculated in the normal way (see Steps 1–13 in 60.39 above) but using the old VAT fraction. The second period ran from the day of change to the end of the VAT period. Output tax was calculated in the normal way (see Steps 1–13 in 60.39 above) using the new VAT fraction but

- (i) in Steps 1 to 3 using stock figures at the beginning of the second period and with VAT included at the new rate;
- (ii) in Step 4 including daily gross takings for the second period only; and
- (iii) in Steps 5, 7 and 9 including expected selling prices of goods received, made or grown for resale in the second period only.

Later VAT periods in the same year as the change in VAT rate. The normal procedure (see Steps 1–13 at 60.39 above) had to be applied, using the new VAT fraction, but as modified by (i)–(iii) above.

Annual adjustment at the end of the year. The annual adjustment also had to be calculated separately for the period from the beginning of the year to the day before the change ('period one') and from the day of change to the end of the year ('period two'). The normal procedure (see Steps A–Q for the annual adjustment at 60.39 above) had to be applied with the following modifications.

- Period one (old VAT fraction)
  - (i) In Steps D to G, only gross takings and goods received, etc. in period one were included.
  - (ii) In Steps H to K the figures for stock at the end of the first period were substituted (including VAT at the old rate).
- Period two (new VAT fraction)
  - (i) In Steps A to C the figures for stock at the end of period one (beginning of period two) were substituted (including VAT at the new rate).
  - (ii) In Steps D to G, only gross takings and goods received, etc. in period two were included.

Change in VAT rate at the beginning of a VAT period (but not at the beginning of the year). In the period of change and any later periods in the same year, the same procedure was used as for later VAT periods following a change in VAT rate during a VAT period (see above). The method of calculating the annual adjustment at the end of the year was also the same whether the change took place during a VAT period or at the beginning of a VAT period other than the beginning of the year.

Change in rates at the end of the year. The annual adjustment was calculated in the normal way (see Steps A to Q under annual adjustment at 60.39 above). Closing stocks at Steps H to K included VAT at the old rate. The usual scheme calculations were made for the next year starting on the day of change (see Steps 1–13 in 60.39 above). Opening stock at Steps 1 to 3 included VAT at the new rate.

(C & E Notice 727 (1993 edition), Appendix C, paras 28, 29).

60.41   *Scheme J — change in VAT liability of goods*

Minor changes. Where a change did not affect more than 5% of annual taxable turnover within the scheme, a retailer could, if he wished, from the day of change, record the expected selling prices of any goods affected at the new rate and make no other adjustments. If one minor change was treated in this way, any later such change also had to be so treated.

Where any change affected more than 5% of the scheme turnover (or where the retailer chose not to use the special rule above), the rules as for a change in VAT rate (see 60.40 above) had to be adopted remembering that

- the VAT fraction had not changed; and

- from the day of change, goods received, made or grown for resale that were affected by the change had to be recorded at their new rate of VAT.

(C & E Notice 727 (1993 edition), Appendix C, para 30).

60.42   **Scheme J Adaptation 1: three-monthly stock evaluations**

Under this adaptation, each VAT period stood on its own and no annual adjustment was required but expected selling prices, including VAT, of both standard-rated and zero-rated goods in stock had to be calculated every three months. Output tax was calculated in the normal way for the annual adjustment (see Steps A–Q at 60.39 above) except that all references to stocks were to those held at the beginning or end of the three-monthly period and all references to gross takings and goods received, etc. for resale were to figures for that three-monthly period.

Change in VAT rate. Whenever there was a change in VAT rate, it was necessary to calculate the total expected selling prices of stock items at the close of business on the day before the date of change as follows.

(*a*)   Standard-rated stock including VAT at the old rate.

(*b*)   Standard-rated stock including VAT at the new rate.

(*c*)   Standard-rated and zero-rated stock including VAT at the old rate.

(*d*)   Standard-rated and zero-rated stock including VAT at the new rate.

Change in VAT rate at the beginning of the VAT period. The scheme had to be operated as before but using the new VAT fraction to work out output tax. In Steps 1 to 3 at 60.39 above, the expected selling prices of goods in stock at the beginning of the period were those at the new rate, i.e. (*b*) and (*d*) above.

Change in VAT rate during a VAT period. Output tax for the period had to be calculated in two separate parts as if each were a whole VAT period. The first period ran from the beginning of the VAT period to the close of business on the day before the change. Output tax was calculated in the normal way using the old VAT fraction. Expected selling prices of goods in stock at the end of the period were those under (*a*) and (*c*) above. The second period ran from the day of change to the end of the VAT period. Output tax was calculated in the normal way using the new VAT fraction. Expected selling prices of goods in stock at the beginning of the period were those under (*b*) and (*d*) above.

Changes in VAT liabilities. The same provisions applied as for Scheme J, see 60.41 above.

(C & E Notice 727 (1993 edition), Appendix C, paras 31, 32; C & E Leaflet 727/15/93 — both now withdrawn).

60.43   **Scheme J Adaptation 2: temporary omission of opening stock**

Under this adaptation, figures for opening stocks were ignored in the first three quarterly VAT periods of the year (i.e. following the procedure in Steps 1–13 at 60.39

above but assuming values of A to C in Steps 1 to 3 were all nil). In the fourth VAT period of the year, the annual adjustment had be calculated exactly in the normal way (see Steps A to Q at 60.39 above). Output tax for that period was the total arrived at under the annual adjustment less output tax calculated for the first three periods.

Change in VAT rate. The same provisions applied as for Scheme J (see 60.40 above) except that stock figures continued to be left out of account in the first three quarterly VAT periods. The annual adjustment was calculated exactly as under Scheme J.

Change in VAT liabilities. The same provisions applied as for Scheme J (see 60.41 above).

(C & E Notice 727 (1993 edition), Appendix C, paras 34-36; C & E Leaflet 727/15/93 — both now withdrawn).

61   Second-Hand Goods

Cross-references. See 7.7 BAD DEBT RELIEF ; 34.30 IMPORTS for the sale of temporarily imported second-hand goods by auction; 37.11 INSURANCE for insurance supplied in a package with second-hand goods; 47.16 OUTPUT TAX for sales by pawnbrokers; 56.16 RATES OF VAT for the effect of a change in the rate of VAT between payment and removal of goods.

De Voil Indirect Tax Service. See V3.531–548.

The contents of this chapter are as follows.

61.1   INTRODUCTION

In general, VAT is charged on the full value of any goods, including second-hand goods, sold by a taxable person. The Treasury may, however, by statutory instrument, provide for a taxable person to opt to charge VAT on the profit margin (instead of their value) on supplies of

- works of art, antiques or collectors' items;

- motor vehicles;

- second-hand goods; and

- goods through a person who acts as an agent, but in his own name, in relation to the supply.

The purpose of this is to avoid double taxation on goods which have previously borne VAT when sold as new. [*VATA 1994, s 50A; FA 1995, s 24*].

The Margin Scheme covers virtually all second-hand goods. See 61.2 to 61.38 below for details. A similar scheme is available throughout the EC and goods sold under the scheme anywhere in the EC are taxable in the country of origin rather than that of destination. They are not therefore subject to the normal distance selling rules and are not subject to acquisition VAT when taken into another EC country.

There is also a Global Accounting Scheme in the UK because of the low value, bulk volume goods some dealers handle and the impracticality of keeping detailed records of purchases and sales. Under the scheme, VAT is accounted for on the difference between the total purchases and sales of eligible goods in each VAT period rather than on an item by item basis. See 61.39 to 61.52 below for full details.

De Voil Indirect Tax Service. See V3.531; V3.532.

61.2   THE MARGIN SCHEME

Dealers. The margin scheme may be operated by a dealer who is registered for VAT provided all the conditions in 61.4 below are met. Subject to those conditions being satisfied, VAT is chargeable only on the seller's 'profit margin' i.e. the difference between the price at which the goods were obtained and the price at which they are supplied. [*VATA 1994, s 50A(4); FA 1995, s 24*]. Although VAT is charged on the profit margin only, taxable turnover for the purposes of registration includes the total value (exclusive of VAT) of the goods. The seller's margin is not revealed to the buyer.

The margin scheme is, however, optional and dealers may still sell eligible goods outside the scheme in the normal way, even if bought under the scheme. In this case, there is no input tax to deduct on the purchase and VAT must be charged on the full selling price. Goods which do not fulfil all the conditions of the margin scheme must be sold outside the scheme under the normal arrangements.

Non-dealers. The scheme may also be used by any other taxable person who is not a dealer but who sells an eligible article in the course of business. In this case, it is not necessary to comply with the full record-keeping requirements provided the other conditions are met and evidence of the purchase and selling price is kept. (C & E Notice 718, para 5).

Disallowance of input tax. Any input tax charged on the supply to, or acquisition or importation by, a taxable person of eligible goods is excluded from credit where

(*a*)   VAT on the supply was chargeable on the profit margin under the UK margin scheme or corresponding provision of the law of another EC country;

(*b*)   in the case of a motor car, VAT was charged on the margin because of an earlier input tax restriction; or

(*c*)   the goods are

(i)   a work of art, antique or collector's item within 61.3(*b*)–(*d*) below and the taxable person imported the goods himself, or

(ii)   a work of art within 61.3(*b*) below and were supplied to the taxable person by, or acquired from another EC country by him from, its creator or his successor in title

and the taxable person has opted to account for VAT chargeable on his supplies of such goods on the profit margin and not elected to account for VAT by reference to value.

[*SI 1992/3222, Art 4; SI 1995/1267; SI 1995/1666*].

61.3   Eligible goods

The following goods are eligible for the margin scheme.

(*a*)   **Second-hand goods** i.e. tangible moveable property that is suitable for further use (as it is or after repair) other than the following.

   (i)   Items within (*b*) below.

   (ii)   Goods (including coins) consisting of or containing precious metals where the VAT-exclusive consideration for the supply is, or is equivalent to, an amount which does not exceed the open market value of the metal contained in the goods. (For gold coins sold at or below the open market value, the special accounting and payment scheme for gold applies, see 30.4 GOLD AND PRECIOUS METALS.)

   (iii)   Precious stones i.e. stones of any age which are not mounted, set or strung.

(*b*)   **Works of art** comprising the following goods.

   (i)   Pictures, collages and similar decorative plaques, paintings and drawings, executed entirely by hand by the artist, other than plans and drawings for architectural, engineering, industrial, commercial, topographical or similar purpose, hand-decorated manufactured articles, theatrical scenery, studio back cloths or the like of painted canvas.

   (ii)   Original engravings, prints and lithographs, being impressions produced in limited numbers directly in black and white or in colour of one or of several plates executed entirely by hand by the artists, irrespective of the process or of the material employed by him, but not including any mechanical or photomechanical process.

   (iii)   Original sculptures and statuary, in any material, provided that they are executed entirely by the artist; sculpture casts the production of which is limited to eight copies (or in relation to statuary casts produced before 1 January 1989, such greater number as C & E allow) and supervised by the artist or his successors in title.

   (iv)   Tapestries and wall textiles made by hand from original designs provided by artists, provided that there are not more than eight copies of each.

   (v)   Individual pieces of ceramics executed entirely by the artist and signed by him.

   (vi)   Enamels on copper, executed entirely by hand, limited to eight numbered copies bearing the signature of the artist or the studio, excluding articles of jewellery and goldsmiths' and silversmiths' wares.

   (vii)   Photographs taken by the artist, printed by him or under his supervision, signed and numbered and limited to 30 copies, all sizes and mounts included.

(*c*)   **Collectors' items** comprising the following goods.

   (i)   Postage or revenue stamps, postmarks, first-day covers, pre-stamped stationery and the like, franked or if unfranked not being of legal tender and not intended for use as legal tender.

(ii) Collections and collectors' pieces of zoological, botanical, mineralogical, anatomical, historical, archaeological, palaeontological, ethnographic or numismatic interest.

(*d*)   **Antiques** i.e. objects not falling within (*b*) or (*c*) above which are more than 100 years old.

[*SI 1995/1268, Art 2*].

Goods on hand at 1 January 1995 (when the current provisions were introduced), which were not eligible for the scheme when purchased, can be sold under the scheme provided they qualify as eligible goods with effect from that date; the conditions of the margin scheme are met; and evidence of the purchase price is held. (C & E Notice 718, para 4).

61.4   **Conditions of the scheme**

A taxable person may opt to use the margin scheme and account for VAT on the profit margin provided the following conditions are met.

(*a*)   He took possession of the goods by any of the following means.

(i) On a supply on which no VAT was chargeable. This includes a zero-rated supply (*Peugeot Motor Co plc, [1998] VATDR 1 (15314)*).

(ii) On a supply on which VAT was chargeable on the profit margin under the UK margin scheme or under the corresponding provisions in the Isle of Man or another EC country.

(iii) Under a transaction treated as neither a supply of goods nor a supply of services (see 64.5 SUPPLY). With effect from 2 July 1997, this does not automatically apply where the transaction in question was the transfer of the assets of a business as a going concern. In such a case, to qualify as eligible goods for the second-hand scheme, the goods taken over must have been eligible goods in the hands of the previous owner (unless eligible only by a previous transfer of a going concern).

(iv) If the goods are a work of art, on a supply, or acquisition from another EC country, from the creator or his successor in title (whether or not the purchase invoice shows VAT separately).

(v) If the goods are a work of art, collectors' item or antique, by importing the goods himself.

(vi) If the goods are a motor car, on a supply on which VAT was charged on the margin because of an earlier input tax restriction.

(*b*)   The supply by the taxable person is not a letting on hire.

(*c*)   The goods are not sold by the taxable person on a VAT invoice or similar document showing an amount as being VAT or as being attributable to VAT.

(*d*)   If the supply is of an airgun, the taxable person is registered for the purposes of the *Firearms Act 1968*.

(*e*)   If the supply by the taxable person is the sale of repossessed assets within 27.22 FINANCE, the supply satisfies the conditions for treatment as outside the scope of VAT as there stated.

(*f*)   If the supply by the taxable person is a motor car which he produced himself, the car has previously been supplied by him in the course or furtherance of his business or treated as self-supplied under 45.6 MOTOR CARS.

(*g*) The taxable person keeps such records and accounts as C & E specify.

Works of art, etc. A taxable person may opt to use the margin scheme for eligible goods which he took possession of under (*a*)(iv) above but only if, at the same time, he exercises the option in relation to any eligible goods taken possession of under (*a*)(v) above (and vice versa). Where he does exercise the option, it must be notified to C & E in writing and takes effect from the date of notification or such later date as is specified in the notice. The option then applies to all supplies of such goods made by the taxable person in the period ending two years after the date on which it first had effect or until the date on which written notification of its revocation is given to C & E, whichever is the later. This does not affect his right to account for VAT on any particular supply on its full value but, in such a case, input tax on the supply, acquisition or importation cannot be recovered until the period in which VAT is accounted for on the sale. (VAT Information Sheet 11/95, 1 June 1995).

[*SI 1992/3122, Art 8(1)-(3); SI 1995/1268, Art 12(1)-(4)(8); SI 1995/1269; SI 1997/1615; SI 1997/1616*].

61.5 Reclaiming VAT on expenses

Subject to the normal rules, a taxable person may reclaim VAT charged on business overheads, repairs, parts and accessories etc. but must not add these costs to the purchase price of the goods sold under the scheme.

There is no input tax to reclaim on items purchased for resale under the scheme.

(C & E Notice 718, para 6).

61.6 Purchases

The following provisions have the force of law.

On a purchase from a private person, a trader must check that the goods are eligible for the scheme and, if so, make out a purchase invoice showing

- seller's name and address;
- own name and address;
- stock book number (in numerical order) and day book number or similar reference to the accounting records;
- invoice number;
- date of transaction;
- description of the goods including any unique identification (e.g. registration number, make/model, hallmark, type, class, chassis number, etc.); and
- total price.

The buyer must get the seller to sign and date the invoice, certifying that he/she is the seller of the goods at the stated price. The certificate can be given on a separate document, such as a letter, provided that it is cross-referenced to the invoice. Details of the purchase must be entered in the stock book (see 61.23 below).

On purchase from another dealer, the same procedure applies as above except that the invoice will be made out by the other dealer who must also certify on the invoice that 'Input tax deduction has not been and will not be claimed in respect of the goods on this invoice'.

(C & E Notice 718, paras 14, 15).

61.7   *Purchases from other EC countries*

The margin scheme is available throughout the EC. Eligible goods sold under the scheme in any EC countru are taxable in the country of origin rather than of destination and are not subject to the normal distance selling rules.

- *Goods bought from a registered business in another EC country under the margin scheme.* Eligible goods are subject to VAT in the other EC country. The removal of the goods to the UK is not to be treated as an acquisition [*SI 1995/1268, Art 7*] and there is consequently no liability to acquisition VAT on entry into the UK. The invoice will not show VAT as a separate item. The goods may therefore be sold under the margin scheme.

- *Goods bought from a registered business in another EC country on a VAT invoice.* The goods will be liable to VAT on acquisition in the UK. This may be reclaimed subject to the normal rules and, if so, the goods cannot be resold under the margin scheme. See 61.28 below for acquisitions of second-hand cars.

- *Goods bought from a private individual in another EC country.* No VAT is due when the goods are brought into the UK and the goods can therefore be sold under the scheme.

(C & E Notice 718, para 52).

61.8   *Imports from outside the EC*

VAT is normally due on importation of second-hand goods and the margin scheme cannot be used to sell the goods. On sale, VAT must be charged on the full selling price, the VAT paid at importation being deductible subject to the normal rules. This general rule is subject to the following exceptions.

- Certain works of art, antiques, collections and collectors' pieces are entitled to a reduced valuation at importation (see 71.3 WORKS OF ART, ETC.). Where any of the works of art, etc. listed in 61.3 above are imported, the purchaser may either use the margin scheme or import and resell the goods under the normal VAT rules.

- Importation of second-hand cars on which input tax is irrecoverable may be sold under the margin scheme. See 61.29 below.

(C & E Notice 718, paras 57–59).

61.9   *Bulk purchases*

Where a number of eligible goods are bought at an inclusive price with the intention of reselling them separately, the price paid must be apportioned. There is no set way of doing this but the method used must be fair and reasonable and the price allocated to each must be as accurate as possible. The separate figures must be shown in the stock book (see 61.23 below). (C & E Notice 718, para 7).

Alternatively, the global accounting scheme may be used for low-value bulk purchases. See 61.39 to 61.52 below.

61.10   *Purchases of repossessed goods from insurance companies or finance houses*

Sales of eligible goods by an insurance company which has taken possession of them in settlement of an insurance claim or by a finance company which has repossessed them are outside the scope of VAT provided certain conditions are met. See 27.22 FINANCE. As no VAT is charged on the supply of the goods, they can be purchased for sale under the margin scheme provided the necessary scheme conditions in 61.4 are satisfied. (C & E Notice 718, para 8).

61.11 **Sales**

Note. The following provisions have the force of law.

On the sale of eligible goods, the trader must check that the rules in 61.6 above were applied on purchase and, if so, make out a sales invoice showing

- own name and address and VAT registration number;

- buyer's name and address;

- stock book number and day book number or similar reference in the accounts;

- invoice number;

- date of sale;

- particulars of the goods including any unique reference number (e.g. registration number, make/model, hallmark, type, class, chassis number, etc.); and

- total price, including VAT. Where more than one item is sold on the same invoice, a separate price must be shown for each item.

The invoice must not show VAT as a separate item.

If any insurance product is being sold with the goods, the full price of this must be disclosed separately on the invoice, plus any fees charged for the product outside the contract of insurance. See 37.11 INSURANCE.

The seller must sign and date the invoice, certifying on it that 'input tax deduction has not been and will not be claimed by me in respect of goods sold on this invoice'. The customer must also sign and date the invoice, stating that he is the buyer of the goods at the price shown.

The seller must then give the invoice to his customer, keep a copy for his own records and enter details of the sale in the stock book (see 61.23 below).

(C & E Notice 718, paras 7, 16, 17).

61.12 *Sales to other EC countries*

The margin scheme is available throughout the EC. Eligible goods sold under the scheme in any EC country are taxable in the country of origin rather than of destination and are not subject to the normal distance selling rules.

- *Sales by UK dealers to dealers in other EC countries.*

  Sales made under the margin scheme are taxable in the same way as sales within the UK. No further VAT is due from the buyer when the goods are taken into the other EC country. Alternatively, the goods can be sold outside the margin scheme in which case the sale can be zero-rated subject to the normal conditions for supplies of goods to VAT-registered customers in other EC countries (see 23.11 EUROPEAN COMMUNITY: SINGLE MARKET). The buyer must then account for VAT in his own country and cannot sell the goods under the margin scheme.

- *Sales by UK dealers to private individuals in other EC countries.* Such sales are taxable in the UK on the margin.

(C & E Notice 718, para 53).

61.13   *Exports outside the EC*

Where eligible goods are sold for direct export, the sale is zero-rated provided appropriate evidence of exportation is held. See 25.24 EXPORTS. The retail export scheme can also be used to zero-rate the indirect export of certain second-hand goods. See 25.13 EXPORTS.

Where a vehicle is supplied to an overseas person for export, the transaction may be zero-rated provided the vehicle is only used in the UK for the trip to the place of departure from the EC. See 25.17 EXPORTS.

See also 25.19 EXPORTS for special provisions relating to sailaway boats.

(C & E Notice 718, paras 62, 72).

61.14   *Transfers of own goods to another EC country*

The transfer of goods within the same legal entity from one EC country to another is deemed to be a supply for VAT purposes. See 23.23 EUROPEAN COMMUNITY: SINGLE MARKET. Where goods are transferred under the margin scheme from the UK to another EC country (e.g. for sale, or use in the business, in that member state) there is no liability to UK VAT on the goods provided that they are transferred from the UK at the price for which they were obtained. There should be no liability to account for acquisition VAT in the other EC country. (C & E Notice 718, para 54).

61.15   *Part exchange*

If a dealer sells eligible goods and takes other goods in part exchange, his selling price includes the amount allowed for the other goods as well as the amount received in cash from the buyer.

Example

A car is sold for £2,000 cash plus a car for which £1,000 is allowed in part exchange.

A selling price of £3,000 must be entered in the stock book. As the article taken in exchange is an eligible article which is to be resold under the scheme, the rules in 61.6 must be followed. The amount allowed in part exchange (£1,000) is the purchase price. The purchase must also be recorded in the stock book (see 61.23 above).

(C & E Notice 718, para 22).

61.16   *Hire purchase sales*

Note. The following provisions have the force of law.

Eligible goods sold under a hire purchase agreement are sold to the finance company which in turn sells them to the customer. The sale should be treated as a cash sale and the cash price of the goods (as shown on the HP agreement) should be entered in the stock book as the selling price. No VAT is charged on the finance charges if itemised separately.

A copy of the HP agreement can be treated as the sales invoice provided

- it shows all the identifying details required; and
- the cash price is shown as the gross price payable i.e. the amount borrowed plus cash paid, plus any amount allowed for part exchange (see 61.15 above).

VAT must not be shown separately on the HP agreement or any invoice.

(C & E Notice 718, para 21).

If a taxable person sells an article received as a gift, he must charge VAT on its full selling price.

No VAT is chargeable on eligible goods which could have been sold under the scheme but which are given away.

(C & E Notice 718, para 9).

61.18   *Private sales*

The private sale of goods which are not assets of the business is usually outside the scope of VAT.

Where a sole proprietor transfers eligible goods from a private holding to the business, VAT may be accounted for under the margin scheme provided evidence can be produced of the purchase price when originally bought for private use. If not, VAT must be accounted for on the full selling price.

(C & E Notice 718, para 10).

61.19   *Sales from stately homes*

If owners of stately homes admit members of the public for a charge, any works of art, etc. owned and displayed to the public are treated as business assets and their disposal is normally subject to VAT. There is, however, special VAT relief in certain cases. See 71.6 WORKS OF ART, ETC.

See also 71.1 WORKS OF ART, ETC. for exemption from VAT on certain disposals to approved bodies, and property accepted in satisfaction of inheritance tax, under the 'douceur' arrangement.

61.20   *Shares in eligible goods*

If a share in an eligible article held in stock is sold, no output tax is due on the sale of the share and a VAT invoice must not be issued to the purchaser.

When an item in which other people own shares is sold under the margin scheme, the full amount of VAT due must be accounted for (not just VAT on the taxable person's share of the proceeds). The purchase price is the full purchase price and statements must be issued to the other shareholders showing their share of the sale proceeds, excluding VAT. See also 61.21 below.

(C & E Notice 718, para 23).

61.21   **Joint purchases and sales**

The following procedure (which has the force of law) should be used where dealers jointly buy an eligible article for resale.

(*a*) **On purchase**, one of the joint buyers (JB1) must keep the purchase invoice with the details set out under 61.6 above and must invoice the other joint buyer(s) for the agreed contribution towards the cost, excluding VAT. Each invoice must be endorsed 'This payment is your contribution towards the purchase of the above article. I shall be accounting for the full amount of VAT due under the scheme when it is sold.' Copies of the invoice(s) must be retained.

JB1 must record the full purchase details in his stock book, together with details of the sales invoices to the other joint buyer(s).

(*b*)   **On resale by the original buyer,** JB1 must enter the sales and accounting details in his stock book. The selling price is the full joint selling price (not just JB1's share of the proceeds). If more convenient, JB1 can make a new entry in his stock book for the whole transaction, treating the purchase and sale as being made by him and closing the original entry by cross-reference to the new entry.

JB1 must then issue a statement to the other joint buyer(s) showing their share of the proceeds of sale, excluding VAT. The statement must be endorsed 'This payment is your share of the proceeds of sale of [insert details]. I am accounting for the full amount of VAT due on the sale under the scheme.'

(*c*)   **On resale by another joint buyer (JB2),** he must obtain the original purchase invoice from JB1 and complete his stock book treating the purchase and sale as being made entirely by him. The purchase price is the full joint purchase price and the selling price is the full joint selling price.

JB2 must then issue a statement to the other joint buyer(s) as in (*b*) above.

JB1, the original buyer, must close the entry in his stock book stating that VAT has been accounted for by JB2 and cross-refer to the statement received from JB2.

(C & E Notice 718, para 24).

61.22   Records and accounts

The following requirements as to records and accounts have the force of law. [*SI 1992/3122, Art 8(1); SI 1995/1268, Art 12(1); SI 1995/1269*]. They are in addition to the records generally required of all taxable persons. See RECORDS (57).

A taxable person selling goods under the scheme must keep the purchase invoice (see 61.6 above) and a copy of the sales invoice (see 61.11 above), together with a stock book or similar records (see 61.23 below). All records must be kept for six years. Failure to comply with any of the requirements renders the taxable person liable for VAT on the full value of his sales. (C & E Notice 718, para 12). See *C & E Commrs v JH Corbitt (Numismatists) Ltd HL, [1980] STC 231.* The requirements as to the records to be kept do not impose an obligation on the trader to verify the identity of purchasers (*Bord (9824)*).

See, however, 61.39 *et seq.* below for a simplified method of operating the margin scheme (global accounting).

Motor cars. There is an alternative special method of calculating VAT for second-hand cars where the dealer has the required information on the purchase or sale of the car but not both. See 61.35 below.

Horses and ponies. Special records are required. See 61.37 below.

61.23   *Stock book*

A stock book or similar record must be kept with separate headings for each of the following.

Purchase details
Stock number in numerical sequence
Date of purchase
Purchase invoice number
Name of seller

Any unique identification number (e.g. car registration)
Description of the goods (e.g. type, make or model)

Sales details
Date of sale
Sales invoice number
Name of buyer

Accounting details
Purchase price
Selling price or other method of disposal
Margin on sale
VAT due

The purchase price must be the price on the invoice which has been agreed between the buyer and seller and must not be altered. Separate entries must be made where purchases bought in bulk are to be sold separately (see 61.9 above).

Other information can also be included but the above details must always be shown and the stock book must be kept up-to-date.

(C & E Notice 718, para 13, 14).

61.24 **Calculation of VAT**

If eligible goods are sold for the same as, or less than, the price paid, no VAT is due. The loss cannot be set against profit made on other transactions.

If eligible goods are sold for more than the price paid, VAT is chargeable on the profit margin i.e. the amount by which the consideration for the goods are sold exceeds the purchase price. The profit margin is regarded as being VAT-inclusive i.e. the VAT included is

VAT-inclusive margin × VAT fraction (currently 7/47)

Profit margin. The following rules apply for the purpose of determining the profit margin.

(*a*) The price at which the goods were obtained is calculated

- where the taxable person took possession of the goods by a supply, in the same way as the consideration for the supply would normally be calculated (see 69.2 *et seq.* VALUATION);

- where the taxable person is a sole proprietor and the goods were supplied to him in a private capacity, in the same way as the consideration for the supply to him as a private individual would be calculated;

- where the goods are a work of art which was acquired by the taxable person from the creator or his successor in title in another EC country, in the same way as the value of the acquisition would be calculated for VAT purposes (see 69.8 VALUATION) plus the VAT chargeable on the acquisition;

- where the goods are a work of art, antique or collector's item which the taxable person has imported himself, in the same way as the value would be calculated for the purposes of importation (see 69.7 VALUATION) plus any VAT chargeable on their importation; and

- with effect from 18 March 1998, where the taxable person took possession of the goods under a transaction relating to the transfer of the assets of a business as a going concern (TOGC) which was treated as neither a supply of goods nor a supply of services (see 8.10 *et seq.* BUSINESS), as the price at which the earliest of his 'predecessors' obtained the goods. For this purpose a '*predecessor*' is a transferor under a TOGC and a person's predecessors include the predecessors of his predecessors through any number of TOGCs. The effect of this is that the purchase price of the eligible goods is the price paid by the last person to acquire the goods, other than by way of a TOGC. Where, therefore, a business is bought as a going concern, the purchaser will always require the original purchase invoice to calculate the margin on the goods (the transferor can retain a copy for his records). If the transferor retains his stock records, the purchaser can enter the goods obtained under the TOGC in his own stock records. (C & E Notice 718, para 11E).

(*b*) The price at which the goods are sold is calculated in the same way as the consideration for the supply would be calculated for VAT purposes (see 69.2 *et seq.* VALUATION).

[*SI 1992/3122, Art 8(5); SI 1995/1268, Art 12(5); SI 1995/1269; SI 1998/759; SI 1998/760*].

The margin cannot be reduced by deducting expenses e.g. repairs, spares, overheads, cleaning, etc.

Motor cars. There is an alternative special method of calculating VAT for second-hand cars where the dealer has the required information on the purchase or sale of the car but not both. See 61.35 below.

61.25 Completion of VAT return

See 2.5 *et seq.* ACCOUNTING PERIODS AND RETURNS for notes on the completion of Form VAT 100. The following special rules apply to eligible goods bought and sold under the margin scheme.

Box 1   Include the output tax on all eligible goods sold in the period covered by the return.

Box 6   Include the full selling price of all eligible goods sold during the period, less any VAT.

Box 7   Include the purchase price (inclusive of VAT) of eligible goods bought in the period.

(C & E Notice 718, para 19).

61.26 Agents

Agents who act in their own name in relation to a supply of goods are, for VAT purposes, regarding as making a supply of those goods and may therefore be required to account for VAT. See 4.4 AGENTS.

Agents acting in this way in relation to eligible goods, may use the margin scheme provided the conditions of the scheme are met. The price at which the goods were obtained is calculated in the normal way (see 61.24 above) and is the gross amount passed on to the seller of the goods. The selling price calculated in the normal way is increased by the amount of the consideration payable to the agent in respect of his services to the buyer in connection with the supply of goods (i.e. any incidental expenses and commission charged to the buyer). [*SI 1992/3122, Art 8(6); SI 1995/1268, Art 12(6); SI 1995/1269*].

61.27   Second-Hand Goods

The following should be dealt with outside the margin scheme under the normal VAT rules.

- Other optional charges to the buyer not directly linked to the goods such as packing, transport and insurance costs.

- Any commission or other services supplied to the seller.

- Any services to the buyer which are exempt from VAT (e.g. insurance as a permitted insurer or the making of arrangements for insurance by a permitted insurer provided the disclosure provisions are complied with, see 37.11 INSURANCE).

(C & E Notice 718, para 20).

61.27   Second-hand cars — special provisions

Note. The provisions of this paragraph and 61.28-61.35 below have the force of law.

Motor cars are defined in 45.1 MOTOR CARS. Only second-hand cars can be sold under the margin scheme. To be eligible, the car must have been driven on the road for business or pleasure purposes or have been appropriated by a dealer for use in the business before being sold. Neither the registration of the car for road use nor the delivery mileage incurred transporting a vehicle to a dealer turn a car into a used car for the purposes of the margin scheme. See also *Lincoln Street Motors (Birmingham) Ltd, [1981] VATTR 120 (1100).*

(C & E Notice 718, para 63).

The margin scheme cannot be used for any vehicle on which input tax was claimed on purchase. See 45.4 MOTOR CARS for sales of such cars.

61.28   *Purchases from other EC countries*

Where a second-hand car is bought from a private individual, or from a registered dealer under the margin scheme, in another EC country, no VAT is due when the car is brought into the UK and the margin scheme can be used for the onward sale.

Where a second-hand car is bought outside the margin scheme from a registered dealer in another EC country, acquisition VAT is due when the car is brought into the UK. This VAT on acquisition can only be recovered in restricted circumstances (see 45.3 MOTOR CARS). Where it cannot be reclaimed, on sale VAT can be accounted for on the profit margin rather than the full selling price. The purchase price of the car is its value for VAT at acquisition plus the VAT due. This should be entered in the stock book.

(C & E Notice 718, para 70).

61.29   *Imports*

VAT is due at the standard rate on the importation of a second-hand car unless it meets the criteria for returned goods relief (see 34.24 IMPORTS) or it can be classified as a collector's piece. The VAT can only be claimed as input tax in restricted circumstances (see 45.3 MOTOR CARS). Where it cannot be reclaimed, on sale VAT can be accounted for on the profit margin rather than full selling price (see 45.4 MOTOR CARS). The purchase price of the car is its value for importation purposes plus the VAT itself. A copy of the import entry or certificate of VAT due must be retained.

Personal imports. If a dealer buys a car from an unconnected person who has personally imported it, the car may be sold under the margin scheme. Where, however, the car is imported by an employee, agent or other person connected with the trader for sale in the dealer's business, the margin scheme cannot be used for the subsequent sale as the vehicle is not second-hand.

(C & E Notice 718, paras 63, 70).

61.30   *Road fund licences (vehicle excise duty) and MOTs*

Where a car is purchased with an unexpired licence which is surrendered. Refunds of road fund licences are treated as being outside the scope of VAT. The price of the car should not be adjusted to reflect the refund.

Where a car is sold with a valid road fund licence or a licence is offered with the car as part of the agreed sale price, there is a single supply and the selling price entered in the stock book must include the value of the licence.

Where a licence is obtained after the negotiation for the sale of a car, the licence may be treated as a separate supply provided the conditions for treatment as a disbursement are met. See 4.7 AGENTS. If those conditions cannot be met, the car and the licence are treated as a single supply and VAT must be accounted for on the margin of the total value.

Where a car is sold with an MOT, this is a single supply and the full selling price, without deduction of any value for the MOT, must be recorded in the stock book and used to calculate the margin.

(C & E Notice 718, paras 65, 65A).

61.31   *Mechanical breakdown insurance and warranties*

A *'warranty'* is an undertaking or guarantee by a dealer that, if a vehicle proves to be faulty within a specified time limit or mileage, the dealer will bear the cost of repair or replacement parts.

'Mechanical breakdown insurance' (MBI) is a contract of insurance, supplied by someone other than the dealer, providing cover against the risk of the vehicle proving faulty within a specified time limit or mileage.

(*a*)   *Free warranties or MBI.* The selling price of the car includes the cost of providing the warranty or MBI. The price of the car on the invoice must be entered in the stock book. Any mention of the warranty or MBI on the invoice must show that no separate charge is being made.

(*b*)   *Warranties or MBI for which a separate charge is made.* The VAT treatment depends upon who provides the warranty or MBI and whether the risk covered is the dealer's or the customer's.

   (i)   MBI provided by a 'permitted insurer' is exempt. However, the charge made by a dealer to a customer can only be exempt if it is clear that coverage is restricted to the customer's risk, the contract of insurance is between the insurer and the customer, and the insurance-related charge is disclosed to the customer and evidenced at the time of sale. (Where the contract is between the insurer and the dealer and it is the dealer's risk of having to repair defective cars that is being covered, any charge made by the dealer to the customer is standard-rated.)

   If the dealer *advertises* the vehicle and the MBI at separate prices and gives the customer the option of taking up the MBI, the amount charged for the MBI can be treated as exempt. Where a reduced price is subsequently negotiated for

887

the car including MBI, the price originally advertised for the MBI should be treated as the value of the exempt supply of MBI. Where negotiations result in the supply of upgraded MBI, the separately advertised price of the upgraded MBI may be used as the value of the exempt supply of MBI.

If the dealer *advertises* the car and the MBI premium at a single price, any commission income received in relation to the insurance is standard-rated (although the net value of the insurance paid to and retained by the insurer remains exempt). In order to exempt any commission, the dealer must disclose the premium to the buyer. If a dealer also charges the customer a fee in addition to the premium, this must also be disclosed separately; otherwise this fee *and any commission* are standard-rated.

(ii) Warranties and MBI provided by a person other than a 'permitted insurer' (including the dealer) are standard-rated.

(c) *Other situations.* The supply of a warranty or MBI under any other type of scheme is standard-rated. This applies, for example, to 'stop loss' arrangements under which the dealer or insurance broker sets up a fund into which amounts charged to customers for warranties or MBI are paid and from which repair claims are met. Insurance cover is then obtained from a permitted insurer against any deficiency in the fund.

Any standard-rated commission or fees under (*b*) above or, if not charged separately, standard-rated warranty charges under (*c*) above must be deducted from the vehicle's selling price before the gross margin is calculated.

(C & E Notice 718, para 73).

61.32   *Demonstration cars*

Where a dealer sells new cars and adopts one for a demonstration use that includes making the cars available for private use, one of the following arrangements apply.

● *New cars on which VAT has not been reclaimed.* If stock is held on a sale or return basis when the car is adopted for demonstration purposes, input tax cannot be deducted on its purchase. On sale, the provisions in 45.4 MOTOR CARS apply. The purchase price is that invoiced by the manufacturer, including VAT, when the car is adopted. Any accessories subsequently fitted are not included.

● *New cars on which VAT has been or may be reclaimed.* VAT must be accounted for at the time of adoption of the car. The value for VAT purposes is what the car would cost to purchase at that time, inclusive of any accessories fitted before the car is adopted. On sale, the provisions in 45.4 MOTOR CARS apply. The value of any accessories fitted after adoption will be reflected in the selling price.

(C & E Notice 718, para 66).

61.33   *Rebuilt motor cars*

If a motor car is rebuilt from one or more used cars and the Driver and Vehicle Licensing Authority (DVLA) do not require it to be re-registered, it can be sold under the margin scheme. The purchase price to be entered in the stock book is the price paid for the car for which the registration number is carried forward. If, however, the DVLA give the car a new registration number, the scheme cannot be used and VAT must be accounted for on the full selling price. (C & E Notice 718, para 67).

61.34   *Auctions*

See 61.53 *et seq.* below for the general provisions relating to auctions.

Purchase of car at auction on which input tax has previously been reclaimed. If a second-hand car is bought at auction the buyer may reclaim the VAT charged provided

- the car is purchased for a qualifying purpose allowing VAT to be recovered (see 45.3 MOTOR CARS);

- the car is bought from another qualifying trader who recovered VAT on the previous purchase of the car; and

- a VAT invoice is received.

Selling a car at auction on which input tax has previously been reclaimed. The auctioneer must be advised if input tax has been recovered on the purchase so that a correct invoice can be drawn up.

(C & E Notice 718, para 69).

61.35 *Calculation of VAT due*

Where all required records are held, the normal rules in 61.24 above apply.

Where records in respect of either the purchase or the sale are available (but not both), the VAT office should be contacted. Where they consider that the mark-up achieved on the supply does not exceed 100%, C & E may allow VAT to be accounted for on either

- the price paid for the car (where the necessary purchase records have been kept); or

- half the selling price (where the necessary sales records have been kept).

Otherwise the sale must be dealt with outside the scheme, accounting for VAT on the full selling price.

(C & E Notice 718, para 64; C & E Notice 48, ESC 2.8).

61.36 Second-hand motor-cycles — special provisions

Converted 'off-road' motor-cycles. If an 'off-road' motor-cycle on which VAT has been reclaimed is converted for road use, it cannot be sold under the scheme.

Road fund licences, Mechanical breakdown insurance and warranties and *Rebuilt motor-cycles.* The provisions applying to motor cars apply equally to motor-cycles. See 61.30, 61.31 and 61.33 above respectively.

61.37 Second-hand horses and ponies — special provisions

Note. The provisions of this paragraph have the force of law.

The general rules and conditions of the margin scheme also apply to the sale of second-hand horses and ponies. The following rules, relating specifically to second-hand horses and ponies, are published by C & E in their Notice 718 and have the force of law.

Horses which the trader has bred and is selling for the first time are not second-hand.

Records and accounts. To sell horses and ponies under the margin scheme, special three-part forms (produced in numbered sets) with a VAT summary sheet at the back must be used. These are sold by

The British Equestrian Trade Association,
Wothersome Grange,
Bramham,
Wetherby,
West Yorkshire LS23 6LY

The three parts of the form are

Part A   Seller's stock record
Part B   Seller's copy sales invoice
Part C   Customer's purchase invoice

These forms are the basis of stock and sales records. No other records are required to operate the scheme. It is not necessary to keep a stock book or invoices. A separate form must be properly completed for each horse etc. or VAT becomes due on the full selling price i.e. the records are mandatory.

(a) *Purchase of a horse or pony from a private person.* After ensuring that the horse or pony is eligible for the margin scheme, the 'description' and 'written description' sections of Parts A, B and C must be completed in accordance with the standard laid down by the Royal College of Veterinary Surgeons in their booklet 'Colour and Markings of Horses' (obtainable from the Royal College of Veterinary Surgeons, 32 Belgrave Square, London SW1). If the animal is not registered with a recognised Breed Society, Stud Book or Register, the buyer and a vet must sign Parts A, B and C to certify that the animal is the one described on the form. If the animal is registered, the signatures are not necessary. The buyer must then give the form a stock number in numerical sequence and complete the Purchase Record section on the reverse of Part A. The seller must sign the reverse of Part A stating that he is the seller at the price shown. The buyer must retain all parts of the form which will be needed on a subsequent sale.

(b) *Purchase of a horse or pony from someone selling under the scheme.* Similar rules apply as in (a) above but the seller must give the buyer Part C of the form to be kept with the partially completed form. The seller does not have to sign the declaration on the reverse of Part A. If the animal is unregistered, the Part C from the seller should have already been signed by a vet confirming the description. The details of the vet's name, practice etc. can be copied by the buyer on to his form. There is no need for a vet to sign.

(c) *Sale of a horse or pony.* Check that the correct procedure was followed under (a) or (b) above on purchase. If not, the margin scheme cannot be used. If the correct procedure was followed, on sale the sales record sections on the reverse of Parts A, B and C must be completed. The buyer must sign the reverse of Parts B and C certifying that he is the buyer at the stated price and the seller must sign the non-deduction of input tax clause on the reverse of Part B. The seller then retains Parts A and B and gives Part C to the buyer.

The VAT record on the reverse of Part A must be completed.

(d) *Purchases at auction.* The normal rules for purchases under (a) or (b) above apply. If the animal is being sold under the margin scheme, the auctioneer will pass the seller's completed Part C to the buyer. The buyer must keep this with his own partially completed form. If the animal is being sold by a private person, the buyer must get the auctioneer to complete and sign the certificate on the reverse of Part A of his form.

(e) *Sales at auction.* The auctioneer must be told that the animal is being sold under the margin scheme and be given Parts B and C of the seller's form which must already be completed as regards his purchase. After the sale, the auctioneer must complete the sales details on the reverse of Parts B and C, adding his name, address and signature. He then returns Part C to the buyer and Part B to the seller. The seller must then complete the sales and VAT record on the reverse of Part A and sign the non-deduction of input tax clause on the reverse of Part B.

(C & E Notice 718, paras 74–79).

61.38   **Other second-hand goods — special provisions**

- **Caravans and motor caravans.** The provisions on *Road fund licences* and *Mechanical breakdown insurance and warranties* applying to motor cars apply equally to caravans. See 61.30 and 61.31 above respectively.

- **Boats and outboard motors.** If a zero-rated boat is converted into a standard-rated one (e.g. by putting an engine into a houseboat) it cannot be sold under the scheme and VAT must be charged on the full selling price.

- **Firearms.** To qualify under the scheme, an air gun must be sold by a person registered as a firearms dealer under *Firearms Act 1968*.

61.39   **GLOBAL ACCOUNTING SCHEME**

The global accounting scheme is a simplified system of accounting for VAT on low value, bulk volume, margin scheme goods where it may be impractical to keep detailed records required under the normal scheme. Dealers using the global accounting scheme account for VAT on the difference between the total purchases and total sales of eligible goods in each prescribed accounting period (rather than on an item by item basis). The scheme automatically allows for a loss on one transaction to be set against the profit from others.

The provisions of the scheme as set out in 61.40–61.52 below have the force of law.

De Voil Indirect Tax Service. See V3.535.

61.40   **Eligible goods**

The global accounting scheme can be used for any of the eligible goods within 61.3 above other than

(*a*)   motor vehicles including motor cycles (except those broken up for scrap, see below);

(*b*)   aircraft;

(*c*)   boats and outboard motors;

(*d*)   caravans and motor caravans;

(*e*)   horses and ponies.

[*SI 1995 / 1268, Art 13*].

Dealers in goods within (*a*)–(*e*) above are able to keep records on an item by item basis and can therefore use the normal margin scheme of accounting. (In any case, the cost of the majority of such goods purchased are likely to exceed £500 and would therefore be excluded from the global accounting scheme, see 61.41 below.)

Salvage companies. Motor vehicles cannot normally be sold under the global accounting scheme. However, provided the vehicle is otherwise eligible for the margin scheme, it may be included in the global accounting scheme when broken up by a salvage company for onward sale as scrap. The normal commercial documents must be kept to show that the vehicle no longer exists in order to demonstrate that it is eligible for global accounting.

61.41   **Conditions for using the scheme**

A person who is registered for VAT may use the scheme provided the following conditions are met.

(*a*)   The goods were not purchased on an invoice on which VAT was shown separately.

(*b*)   Every individual item for which the scheme is used must have been obtained for a price of £500 or less. See 61.24 above for the calculation of price. See 61.44 below for bulk purchases and collections.

(*c*)   The goods are not sold on a VAT invoice or similar document showing an amount as being VAT or as being attributable to VAT.

(*d*)   Such records and accounts are kept as specified by C & E.

[*SI 1995/1268, Art 13*]. (C & E Notice 718, paras 25, 26).

61.42   Reclaiming VAT on expenses

Subject to the normal rules, a taxable person may reclaim any VAT he is charged on business overheads, restoration, repairs, spares, etc. but must not add these costs to the purchase price of the goods for the purposes of the scheme. (C & E Notice 718, para 39).

61.43   Purchases

On a purchase from a private person or a dealer who is not VAT-registered, a dealer must check that the goods are eligible for the global accounting scheme and, if so, make out a purchase invoice showing

● own name and address;

● invoice number;

● date of transaction;

● description of the goods; and

● total price.

● An endorsement stating 'Global accounting scheme'.

Details of the purchase must be entered in the purchase record or summary (see 61.49 below).

On purchase from a VAT-registered dealer, the same procedure applies as above except that the invoice will be made out by the other dealer. The VAT included in the total price must not be shown separately.

(C & E Notice 718, paras 29, 30).

61.44   *Bulk purchases and collections*

Bulk purchases. The scheme may be used for bulk purchases with a combined price in excess of £500 but if any individual item included has a purchase price of more than £500, it must be deducted from the total purchase price and excluded from the scheme. There is no set way to apportion total price between individual items but C & E must be satisfied that it is fair and reasonable. Any item costing over £500 can then be sold under either the margin scheme (if eligible) or the normal VAT rules.

Collections. Collections (e.g. of stamps) purchased can be split and sold separately or formed into other collections for sale under the scheme. Two or more items purchased separately can also be combined to produce one item for resale (e.g. by using one item as a spare part for another).

(C & E Notice 718, para 27).

61.45   **Sales**

On the sale of eligible goods, the dealer must check that the rules in 61.43 above where applied on purchase.

For sales to other dealers, a dealer must issue (and keep a copy of) a sales invoice showing

- own name and address and VAT registration number;
- invoice number;
- date of sale;
- description of the goods;
- total price, including VAT; and
- an endorsement stating 'Global accounting scheme'.

The VAT included in the total price must not be shown separately.

All other sales should be recorded in the normal way (e.g. by using a cash register).

Details of the daily gross takings and/or totals of copy invoices must be entered in the sales record or summary (see 61.49 below). It is therefore essential to be able to distinguish between sales under the global accounting scheme and other types of transactions at the point of sale.

(C & E Notice 718, paras 31, 32).

61.46   **Transactions with overseas persons**

Acquisitions by UK dealers from dealers in other EC countries. Eligible goods are subject to VAT in the other EC country with no liability to acquisition VAT on entry into the UK. The invoice will not show VAT as a separate item. The goods may therefore be sold under the scheme.

Acquisition by UK dealers from private individuals in other EC countries. No VAT is due when the goods are brought into the UK and the goods can therefore be sold under the scheme.

Imports by UK dealers from outside the EC. VAT is due on importation of the goods in the normal way and the global accounting scheme cannot be used to sell imported goods. VAT must be charged on such goods at the full selling price. The VAT paid at importation is deductible subject to the normal rules.

Sales by UK dealers to dealers/private individuals in other EC countries. Such sales are taxable in the UK with no further liability to pay VAT when they are removed to another EC country. Eligible goods can be included under the scheme.

Exports by UK dealers outside the EC. Where eligible goods are sold for export, the sale is zero-rated provided appropriate evidence of exportation is held. See 25.24 EXPORTS. Such sales should therefore be dealt with outside the scheme.

61.47   **Records and accounts**

Global accounting scheme records do not have to be kept in any set way but must be complete, up-to-date and clearly distinguishable from any other records. Records must be kept of purchases and sales (see 61.49 below) and workings used to calculate the VAT due. All scheme records must be preserved for six years.

The global accounting scheme records are in addition to those generally required of all taxable persons. See RECORDS (57).

Failure to comply with any of the requirements as to records renders the taxable person liable for VAT on the full value of his sales.

(C & E Notice 718, para 28).

61.48   *Stock*

Stock on hand when starting to use the global accounting scheme. Any such eligible stock can treated in either of the following ways.

- Taken into the scheme and included in the calculations for the first accounting period. Some form of stock take or valuation will be required. Where possible, stock should be identified separately and its purchase price established from invoices. Where stock cannot be related to original purchase invoices, the purchase value must be determined in some other way. There is no set way of doing this but C & E must be satisfied that the method used is fair and reasonable. Any documents used to establish the stock valuation must be kept for six years.

- Not taken into the scheme. If the goods are then sold under the global accounting scheme, there is no 'purchase credit' to set against the sale and VAT will be accounted for on the full selling price rather than the profit margin.

Eligible stock already included in stock records under the margin scheme can either be sold under the margin scheme or transferred to the global accounting scheme. In the latter case, the stock must be deleted from the margin scheme stock book and cross referred to and included in the global accounting scheme records.

(C & E Notice 718, paras 36–38).

61.49   *Purchases and sales summaries*

Summary records must be kept of purchases and sales for each accounting period. These do not have to be kept in any particular way but they must include the following details taken from any sales invoices issued.

- Invoice number.

- Date of sale.

- Description of goods.

- Total price.

(C & E Notice 718, para 33).

61.50   Calculation of VAT due

VAT is chargeable on the 'total profit margin' on goods supplied during a prescribed accounting period. '*Total profit margin*' is the amount (if any) by which the total sales exceed total purchases in the VAT period. See 61.24(*a*) and (*b*) above for the rules for determining the price at which goods are purchased and sold.

The excess is the VAT-inclusive margin i.e. the VAT included is

VAT-inclusive margin × VAT fraction (currently 7/47)

Negative margin. If there is a negative margin (because total purchases exceed total sales), no VAT is due and the negative margin is carried forward to the following prescribed accounting period for inclusion in the calculation of the total purchases of that period. A negative margin cannot be set off against other VAT due in the same VAT period on transactions outside the global accounting scheme.

Copies of all calculations must be kept as part of the records.

[*SI 1995/1268, Art 13*]. (C & E Notice 718, para 34).

61.51   Adjustments

Removing goods from the scheme. Where purchases are initially included in the global accounting scheme purchase records but it is subsequently decided to sell the goods outside the scheme (e.g. because they are zero-rated on sale for export outside the EC) the scheme records must be adjusted. In the period in which the goods are removed from the scheme, total purchases should be reduced by an amount equal to the purchase value of the excluded goods. There is no set way to apportion values to individual items but it must be fair and reasonable and it must be possible to demonstrate to C & E how the value was determined.

Goods stolen or destroyed. Any loss of goods by breakage, theft or destruction must be adjusted by the deduction of their purchase price in the global accounting scheme purchase records.

(C & E Notice 718, paras 35, 40).

61.52   Completion of VAT return

See 2.5 *et seq*. ACCOUNTING PERIODS AND RETURNS for notes on the completion of Form VAT 100. The following special rules apply to eligible goods bought and sold under the global accounting scheme.

Box 1   Where there is a positive margin, include the output tax calculated by reference to the difference between total purchases and total sales of eligible goods in the period covered by the return.

Box 6   Include the full selling price of all eligible goods sold under the scheme during the period, less any VAT included in that price.

Box 7   Include the purchase price (inclusive of VAT) of eligible goods bought in the period.

Any negative margins should not be included on the VAT return.

61.53   THE AUCTIONEERS' SCHEME

Agents who act in their own name in relation to a supply of goods are, for VAT purposes, regarding as making a supply of those goods and may therefore be required to account for VAT. See 4.4 AGENTS. Auctioneers acting in this way in relation to eligible goods, may use the margin scheme provided the conditions of the scheme are met. See 61.2 to 61.38 above and in particular 61.26 above which deals with agents.

Alternatively, auctioneers may use a special margin scheme devised particularly for them. The auctioneers' scheme allows an auctioneer who invoices in his own name to sell qualifying goods on behalf of a third party vendor without charging VAT separately on commission charged to the vendor or buyer's premium charged to the buyer, such services being taken into account in determining the margin on the supply of goods. The provisions of the scheme as set out in 61.54–61.61 below have the force of law. The scheme is optional and the auctioneer, in conjunction with his client, may decide whether or not to use the scheme for any particular transaction. If the auctioneer is not eligible to use the scheme, or decides not to use it, the normal VAT rules for agents apply. See 4 AGENTS.

Tax point. Where goods are treated as supplied both to and by the auctioneer, there is a common tax point for both supplies which will normally be the earlier of

- the handing over of the goods by the auctioneer to the buyer; or

- the receipt of payment by the auctioneer.

Sales under the auctioneers' scheme to other EC countries are treated in the same way as sales within the UK. The sales are liable to VAT in the UK and no further VAT is due in the country of destination.

(C & E Notice 718, paras 41, 48).

De Voil Indirect Tax Service. See V3.533.

61.54 **Conditions of the scheme**

The auctioneer's scheme can be used for sales of the following goods.

(*a*) Eligible goods (see 61.3 above) provided the following conditions are met.

   (i) The seller is

- not registered for VAT;

- a VAT-registered person supplying goods under the margin scheme (see 61.2 to 61.38 above) or the global accounting scheme (see 61.39 to 61.52 above);

- an insurance company selling eligible goods which they have acquired as a result of an insurance claim provided that the goods are sold at auction in the same state; or

- a finance company selling eligible goods which they have repossessed provided that they are sold at auction in the same state.

   (ii) The auctioneer follows the record-keeping requirements of the margin scheme relating to purchases (see 61.6 above), sales (see 61.11 above) and stock book (see 61.23 above) and complies with the other conditions outlined in the following paragraphs.

It is important that the auctioneer checks with the vendor before the sale whether the goods are eligible for inclusion in the auctioneers' scheme.

(C & E Notice 718, para 42).

(*b*) With effect from 1 January 1998 by extra-statutory concession, all goods grown, made or produced (including bloodstock or livestock reared from birth) by unregistered (non-taxable) persons.

As a condition of the relief, the auctioneer must obtain a signed certificate from the vendor giving

- the vendor's name and address;

- a description of the goods; and

- confirmation that he/she is not registered, nor required to be registered, for VAT.

The auctioneer must retain the certificate with his VAT records.

(C & E Business Brief 23/98, 18 November 1998).

Works of art, etc. As with the margin scheme, auctioneers acting in their own names may opt to use the auctioneers' scheme for works of art, collectors' items and antiques which they have imported themselves for onward sale and works of art obtained from the creator or his successor in title for onward sale, despite the fact that VAT has been charged on the acquisition, supply or importation. See 61.4 above under the heading *Works of art, etc.* for the conditions to be met.

61.55   **Charges to be included/excluded under the scheme**

Any commission or other charges made by the auctioneer to the vendor or buyer which are dependent on the sale of the goods must be included in the auctioneers' scheme calculation as set out in 61.59 below. Treatment of other charges are as follows.

- **Incidental expenses**. Any incidental expenses incurred and charged onward to the client must be included in the scheme calculations.

- **Disbursements for VAT purposes**. Any costs passed on to the client which meet all the conditions regarding disbursements under 4.7 AGENTS can be excluded from the auctioneers' scheme.

- **Exempt supplies**. Any services supplied to the buyer or seller which are exempt (e.g. making arrangements for the provision of insurance by a permitted insurer provided the disclosure requirements are complied with, see 37.11 INSURANCE) should be excluded from the scheme calculations.

- **Services to an overseas seller**. See 64.18 to 64.31 SUPPLY for the rules relating to the place of supply of services. Where the place of supply is in the UK, any services to an overseas supplier must be included in the auctioneers' scheme calculations. Where, however, the supply is treated as taking place outside the UK (e.g. supplies of certain services where the recipient belongs outside the EC or is in business in another EC country, see 64.26 SUPPLY) the supply is outside the scope of UK VAT and should be excluded from the auctioneers' scheme calculations.

- **Other charges**. Charges for other supplies which are optional and not directly related to the hammer price (e.g. delivery of goods after sale) may be excluded from the auctioneers' scheme calculations.

(C & E Notice 718, para 46).

61.56   **Zero-rated sales**

Where the auctioneers' scheme is used for the sale of zero-rated goods (e.g. exports), the auctioneers' margin is also zero-rated. Any charges made outside the scheme are liable to VAT in the normal way. The normal conditions for zero-rating apply. See 25.1 EXPORTS. (C & E Notice 718, paras 47, 49).

61.57   **Invoicing**

Auctioneers using the scheme must not itemise VAT separately on any statement or invoice issued to the seller or buyer except where goods or services are provided in addition to, but separately from, the purchase or sale. Such non-scheme items should be invoiced under the normal VAT rules.

Purchase invoices. The auctioneer should issue to the seller of the goods a statement or other document satisfying the conditions of a purchase invoice under 61.6 above and showing

- the hammer price of the goods;

- the amount of commission due from the seller; and

- the net amount due from the seller.

This statement serves as an invoice to the auctioneer from the seller of the goods.

Sales invoices. The auctioneer should issue to the buyer of the goods an invoice or other document satisfying the conditions in 61.11 above (including the certificate regarding input tax deduction) and showing

- the hammer price of the goods;

- any other charges made; and

- the amount due from the buyer.

Invoices generally. If more convenient, descriptions of the goods may be omitted from purchases and sales invoices provided the invoices are clearly cross-referred to another document which describes the goods. For example the invoices may show the lot number in an auction sale catalogue but in such a case the seller/buyer must keep a copy of the catalogue.

If both scheme and non-scheme supplies are made to the same customer, either separate invoices can be issued or all supplies can be included on the same invoice. In the latter case, the invoice must clearly distinguish between the two types of supply and comply with all the relevant provisions for both. In the case of a sales invoice, it must also show clearly the amount of the selling price which will form the basis of the purchase price for the buyer's margin scheme or global accounting scheme records.

VAT-inclusive charges. Under the auctioneers' scheme, the auctioneer must not show the *amount* of VAT which is included in the commission charge or buyer's premium. Instead, where, for example, net commission is £100 he should do one of the following.

- Show a VAT-inclusive rate of commission/premium and state that it includes VAT, e.g.

  'VAT-inclusive commission at 11.75%...........£117.50'

- Show a VAT-exclusive rate of commission and state that it is plus VAT at the current rate, e.g.

  'Commission at 10% plus VAT at 17.5%...........£117.50'

- Make no reference to VAT in connection with the commission charges and add a statement regarding VAT on the invoice, e.g.

  'Commission...........£117.50

  This amount includes VAT which must not be shown separately or reclaimed as input tax.'

(C & E Notice 718, para 44).

61.58 **Re-invoicing**

If goods have been sold under the auctioneers' scheme but the buyer subsequently decides that he wishes to treat the transaction outside the scheme (paying VAT separately on the hammer price and the other charges), the auctioneer may re-invoice for the transaction under the normal VAT rules provided

(*a*) the auctioneer can comply with all the relevant VAT regulations of the substitute transaction;

(*b*) at the time of the amendment, the auctioneer and buyer hold all the original evidence relating to the transaction;

(*c*) the auctioneer cancels the first entry in his records and cross-refers to the amended transaction; and

(*d*) any substitute document (e.g. a VAT invoice) issued to the buyer clearly refers to the original transaction and states that it is cancelled and that the buyer should amend his VAT records accordingly.

(C & E Notice 718, para 45).

61.59   Calculation of VAT

The purchase price, selling price, margin and VAT due are calculated from the successful bid price (hammer price) and commission and other charges.

'*Purchase price*' is the hammer price less commission and any other charges made to the seller for services supplied in connection with the sale of the goods (see 61.55 above).

'*Selling price*' is the hammer price plus the buyer's premium and any other charges made to the buyer for services supplied in connection with the sale of the goods (see 61.55 above).

The margin is the difference between the purchase price and the selling price. The margin is regarded as being VAT-inclusive i.e. the VAT included is

VAT-inclusive margin × VAT fraction (currently 7/47)

Example

Goods are sold at auction for £1,000 (the hammer price). Commission is charged to the seller at 10% net of VAT and a buyer's premium is charged of 15% net of VAT.

Commission = (£1,000 × 10%) + 17.5% VAT =	£117.50
Purchase price = £1,000 – £117.50 =	£882.50
Buyer's premium = (£1,000 × 15%) + 17.5% VAT =	£176.25
Selling price = £1,000 + £176.25 =	£1,176.25
Margin = £1,176.25 – £882.50 =	£293.75
Output tax = £293.75 × 7/47 =	£43.75

[*SI 1992/3122, Art 8(7); SI 1995/1268, Art 12(7); SI 1995/1269*]. (C & E Notice 718, para 43, Annex 3).

61.60   Dealers buying at auction

Where a taxable dealer buys goods at an auction and wishes to use either the margin scheme or the global accounting scheme for the onward sale of the goods, he should

● check that the goods will be eligible for onward sale under the chosen scheme (e.g. if VAT is charged separately on the hammer price, the goods will not qualify for either scheme);

● after the sale, tell the auctioneer that he wishes to use the margin scheme or the global accounting scheme for the onward sale so that the correct documentation is obtained; and

● follow the record-keeping requirements under the chosen scheme.

61.61   Second-Hand Goods

Any buyer's premium or other charges integral to the supply of the goods on which the auctioneer does not charge VAT separately form part of the purchase price. The figure entered in the stock records is the total price shown on the invoice for goods and services supplied under the auctioneers' scheme.

The auctioneer may also charge separately for other items outside the auctioneers' scheme. These may or may not be on the same invoice as the auctioneers' scheme items. In either case, they cannot be treated as part of the purchase price but any VAT charged on them can be reclaimed subject to the normal rules.

(C & E Notice 718, para 50).

61.61   **Dealers selling at auction under the margin scheme or global accounting scheme**

A taxable dealer selling at auction under the margin scheme or global accounting scheme must inform the auctioneer accordingly. After the sale

- the auctioneer will give the seller an account showing the hammer price of the goods, less any commission charged and the net amount payable;

- the seller must

   (i)   sign and date the account, certifying on it that 'Input tax deduction has not been and will not be claimed by me in respect of the goods sold on this invoice'; and

   (ii) follow the record-keeping requirements for the margin scheme or global accounting scheme, as the case may be.

Any commission or other charges on which, under the auctioneers' scheme, VAT is not charged separately are deducted from the hammer price to establish the selling price. This net price, which should be clearly shown on the account received from the auctioneer, is the sales figure to be entered in the stock book.

If the auctioneer separately charges for other items outside the auctioneers' scheme, these cannot be deducted from the selling price for the margin scheme or global accounting scheme calculations but any VAT charged on them may be reclaimed subject to the normal VAT rules.

(C & E Notice 718, para 51).

62   Self-Supply

Cross-references. See 42.26 LAND AND BUILDINGS for change of use of residential and charitable buildings; 42.27 LAND AND BUILDINGS for developers of certain non-residential buildings; 42.43 LAND AND BUILDINGS for self-supply of certain construction services; 45.6 MOTOR CARS for self-supply of motor cars; 64.45 SUPPLY for the time of self-supply.

De Voil Indirect Tax Service. See V3.241.

62.1   SCOPE OF SELF-SUPPLY

The Treasury may, by order, provide that where specified goods are taken possession of or produced by a person (not necessarily a *taxable* person) in the course or furtherance of a business carried on by him *and*

(*a*)   are neither supplied to another person nor incorporated in other goods produced in the course or furtherance of that business; *but*

(*b*)   are used by him for the purpose of a business carried on by him,

the goods are treated for VAT purposes as being both supplied to him for the purpose of that business and supplied by him in the course or furtherance of it. [*VATA 1994, s 5(5)(7)*].

Such a power is aimed to prevent an advantage being gained by a person who produces for himself goods on which, if supplied externally, either input tax would be specifically denied, or on which input tax would be denied or restricted because of exempt output supplies being made by the person concerned. Specific orders have been made as regards motor cars (see 45.6 MOTOR CARS) and stationery (see 62.2 below).

Similar powers to the above as regards goods are also applied to services. [*VATA 1994, s 5(6)*]. See 42.43 LAND AND BUILDINGS for self-supply of certain construction services.

62.2   STATIONERY

PRINTED MATTER (54) (whether zero-rated or not) has been designated under the order-making powers in 62.1 above. The powers do *not* apply if

(*a*)   the person is a fully taxable person (i.e. the only input tax to which he is not entitled to credit in any prescribed accounting period or longer period is input tax which is specifically excluded from credit, see 35.8 INPUT TAX);

(*b*)   the value of the stationery supplies which would fall to be treated as self-supplied would not make that person liable to be registered (see 59 REGISTRATION) if those supplies were the only ones made by that person; or

(*c*)   the C & E are satisfied that the VAT (if any) which would fall to be accounted for, less corresponding input tax, is negligible and have given a direction that the order is not to apply. C & E may, on application, agree that the self-supply provisions need not be applied where net VAT accruing from the application of the provisions (i.e. output tax due from standard-rated self-supplies of stationery less any deductible input tax arising from the self-supply) would not exceed £100 in a tax year. Approval will be given in writing and will normally include a requirement that the business notifies the VAT office in writing if the pattern or volume of in-house production changes. (C & E Manual V1-15, Chapter 3 para 1.23).

The representative member of a group of companies is deemed to be subject to the self-supply provisions for all the group members' self-supplies.

[*SI 1995/1268, Art 11*].

The effect of the above is that the self-supply provisions apply where a person cannot be treated as fully taxable under the partial exemption rules and the value of self-supplies alone exceed the VAT registration limits. The provisions apply to stationery or other printed matter consisting completely or partly of paper, paperboard or similar material. *Excluded* are such items which are supplied to third parties, either alone or incorporated with other goods, or manufactured by third parties from the person's own materials. Stationery produced by typewriting, duplicating and photocopying is also excluded.

Value of the self-supply. The value of the stationery on which VAT must be accounted for is the price the person would have to pay (excluding VAT), at the time of the supply, to purchase stationery *identical* in every respect to the stationery concerned. Where that value cannot be ascertained, the price for the purchase of stationery *similar* to the stationery concerned must be used. If that value is also not possible to ascertain, the cost of producing the stationery concerned at that time is to be used. [*VATA 1994, 6 Sch 6*].

Time of self supply. The time of supply is treated as taking place when the stationery is appropriated for business use. [*VATA 1994, s 6(11)*].

Appropriation for this purpose cannot normally be said to have taken place until at least the occurrence of some overt, unconditional event that can be said to show appropriation to business use. The tax point is then the date when, by any positive and recorded action, the supplier indicates his intention to use the stationery for business purposes. A mere intention to appropriate the stationery is not normally sufficient to create a tax point in these circumstances. (C & E Notice 700, para 5.4(b); C & E Manual V1-11, Chapter 3 para 8.50).

Records of stationery produced (a statutory requirement) must include quantity and description; tax point (described as the time when any positive or recorded action indicates an intention to use the stationery for business purposes); value for VAT purposes; and the rate and amount of VAT due.

Partial exemption calculation. If the provisions apply, a partial exemption calculation for the amount of input tax able to be reclaimed will be required. All input tax incurred on goods and services used to manufacture the self-supplied stationery (e.g. paper, ink, machinery and its repair) is reclaimable.

Self-supplies of stationery are treated both as outputs and inputs of the business. How much of the self-charged input tax can be claimed is determined by the partial exemption method used.

- Where all self-supplied stationery is used wholly in making taxable supplies, all of the input tax is deductible.

- Where it is all used in making exempt supplies or carrying out activities other than the making of taxable supplies, none of the input tax is deductible.

- Where it is used for both purposes, the input tax must be added to the rest of the non-attributable input tax of the business and apportioned according to the partial exemption method used.

If non-attributable input tax is apportioned using the standard method which includes a calculation based on the ratio of taxable supplies to all supplies, the value of the self-supplies must be excluded from the calculation.

Example

	£
Value of standard-rated self-supplies of stationery (excluding VAT)	19,000.00
Value of zero-rated self-supplies of stationery	1,000.00
Value of taxable outputs (excluding self-supplies of stationery)	100,000.00

Value of exempt outputs	900,000.00
Other non-attributable input tax (e.g. on general overheads)	20,000.00

Assume that all self-supplied stationery is used partly for taxable supplies and partly for exempt supplies (i.e. it is all non-attributable)

Value of total outputs (excluding self-supplies)	1,000,000.00
Percentage of taxable supplies	10%
Non-attributable input tax on self-supplies (equal to output tax on standard-rated self-supplies) 17.5% × £19,000	3,325.00
Other non-attributable input tax	20,000.00
Total non-attributable input tax	£23,325.00
Claimable portion £23,325 × 10%	£2,332.50

The full input tax claim would therefore be for £2,332.50 *plus* all input tax on goods and services for use in the manufacture of self-supplied stationery *plus* all other input tax on supplies and imports used wholly for the making of taxable supplies.

Output tax on self-supplies must be included on returns even if full credit for input tax is obtained for a particular accounting period because of the application of the partial exemption rules. In such circumstances an amount of input tax equal to the output tax should be provisionally deducted from the output tax accountable on the self-supplies. The value of self-supplies must be included in the total value of taxable outputs, whether fully taxable or not.

The self-supply provisions can only cease to be applied, on application, if the value of such supplies falls below the registration threshold limits *and* the value of other taxable supplies does not exceed the limits set for cancellation of registration.

(C & E Leaflet 706/1/92).

De Voil Indirect Tax Service. See V3.243.

63 Special Schemes

63.1 INTRODUCTION

The following special schemes are available to VAT-registered persons.

- **Cash accounting scheme.** Subject to conditions, including an annual turnover limit, this scheme can be used by any taxable person. See 63.2 to 63.8 below.

- **Annual accounting scheme.** Subject to meeting certain conditions, including an annual turnover limit, a taxable person can apply to C & E to prepare an annual VAT return and make payments on account during the year. See 63.9 to 63.14 below.

- **Retail schemes.** There are a number of different retail schemes designed to suit different types of retail business. See 60 RETAIL SCHEMES.

- **Second-hand schemes.** In general, VAT is charged on the full value of any goods, including second-hand goods, sold by a taxable person. However, provided certain conditions are met, VAT can be charged on the profit margin (instead of value) on supplies of second-hand goods; works of art, antiques and collectors' items; and goods sold through an agent acting in his own name in relation to the supply. See 61 SECOND-HAND GOODS for details.

- **Tour operators' margin scheme.** All UK businesses that buy travel, hotel and holiday services, etc. from third parties and resell these supplies as principals *must* use a special scheme under which VAT has to be accounted for on the difference between the VAT-inclusive purchase price and selling price. See 66 TOUR OPERATORS' MARGIN SCHEME.

- **Flat-rate scheme for farmers.** A flat-rate scheme is available to farmers as an option to registering for VAT. Once in the scheme, VAT is not accounted for on sales of goods and services within certain designated activities and input tax is not recoverable on purchases. To compensate for this the farmer charges, and retains, a fixed flat-rate addition on sales, within those activities, to VAT-registered persons. See 63.15 to 63.20 below.

- **Racehorse owners.** A special arrangement has been made between C & E and the thoroughbred horseracing and breeding industry. See 63.21 to 63.23 below.

63.2 CASH ACCOUNTING SCHEME

A taxable person may, subject to conditions, account for and pay VAT on the basis of cash or other consideration paid and received. The conditions are as laid down in *Regulations* and as described in C & E Notice 731 *which in this respect has the force of law*. C & E may vary the terms of the scheme by publishing a fresh Notice or a Notice which amends an existing Notice but without prejudicing the right of a person to withdraw from the scheme. [*SI 1995/2518, Regs 57, 59; SI 1997/1614, Reg 4*].

The main advantages of the scheme are automatic bad debt relief and the deferral of the time for payment of VAT where extended credit is given. The scheme will probably not be beneficial for net repayment businesses or where most sales are for cash. (C & E Notice 731, para 4).

De Voil Indirect Tax Service. See V2.166.

63.3   Joining the scheme

A taxable person may begin to operate the scheme from the beginning of any prescribed accounting period, and without applying to C & E for permission, if he meets the following conditions.

(*a*)   He has reasonable grounds for believing that the value of his taxable supplies (excluding VAT) in the period of one year then beginning will not exceed £350,000. All standard and zero-rated supplies should be included except supplies of capital assets previously used within the business. Exempt supplies should be excluded.

(*b*)   He has made all the VAT returns which he is required to make and either

- paid over all VAT due to C & E (including penalties and interest); or

- agreed an arrangement with C & E for such amount as is outstanding to be paid in instalments over a specified period.

Where a person has appealed to a VAT tribunal on a matter affecting his eligibility to use the scheme (e.g. payment of a penalty for VAT evasion involving dishonest conduct, withdrawal of continued use of the scheme, refusal of access to the scheme, or the amount of VAT due on a return because C & E claim the person is ineligible to use the scheme) he must not use the scheme until the appeal is resolved.

(*c*)   He has not in the previous year

- been convicted of any offences in connection with VAT;

- accepted an offer to compound proceedings in connection with a VAT offence;

- been assessed to a penalty for VAT evasion involving dishonest conduct (see 52.9 PENALTIES); or

- previously been in the cash accounting scheme but ceased to be entitled to continue to operate it.

A person cannot begin to operate the scheme if C & E consider that, for the protection of the revenue, he should not be able to do so.

[*SI 1995/2518, Reg 58(1)(4); SI 1997/1614, Reg 3*]. (C & E Notice 731, paras 3, 7).

63.4   Supplies to be dealt with outside the scheme

The following transactions must be dealt with outside the cash accounting scheme in the normal way.

- Hire purchase agreements.

- Conditional sale agreements.

- Credit sale agreements.

- Lease purchase agreements.

- Supplies where a VAT invoice is issued and full payment of the amount shown on the invoice is not due for a period in excess of six months (twelve months before 3 July 1997) from the date of issue of the invoice.

- After 2 July 1997, supplies in respect of which a VAT invoice is issued in advance of the delivery or making available of the goods or the performance of the services, as the case may be. This does not apply where goods have been delivered or made available in part (or, as the case may be, services have been performed in part) and the VAT invoice in question relates solely to that part.

- The importation of goods, the acquisition of goods from another EC country or the removal of goods from a warehouse or free zone. The scheme can be used to account for VAT on the onward supply of these goods in the UK.

[*SI 1995/2518, Regs 58(2)(3); SI 1997/1614, Reg 3*]. (C & E Notice 731, paras 11, 12).

63.5 Records

All the normal requirements regarding copies of VAT invoices and evidence of input tax apply. In addition, it is necessary to keep either a cash book summarising all payments made and received with a separate column for VAT or some other records that will satisfy C & E that payments made and received can be easily linked to records of the transaction.

Receipted VAT invoices. Any payment made in money (i.e. banknotes or coin) to another taxable person must generally be supported by a receipted and dated invoice (the other taxable person must on request provide such an invoice). The VAT invoice does not have to be separately receipted if the accompanying till or similar receipt states 'cash sale' or clearly indicates that cash has been given (e.g. through an analysis of change given). C & E will only question non-receipted cash purchase invoices where there is clearly no evidence of cash payment. If payment is made by cheque, the VAT invoice does not have to be receipted.

Where payment is received in cash, a receipted and dated VAT invoice must be issued if requested and a copy retained.

Such receipted invoices form part of the VAT records and must be retained for six years or lesser period as C & E allow.

[*SI 1995/2518, Reg 65*]. (C & E Notice 731, para 8; C & E Manual V1-23, Chapter 4 para 5.1).

63.6 Accounting for VAT

Output tax must be accounted for in the return for the VAT period in which payment or other consideration is received. For this purpose payment by

- *cash* is received on the date the money is received;
- *cheque* is received on the date the cheque is received or, if later, the date on the cheque. If the cheque is not honoured, no VAT is due and an adjustment can be made if VAT has already been accounted for;
- *credit card* is received on the date the sales voucher is made out (*not* the date when payment is received from the card company); and
- *giros, standing orders and direct debits* are received on the day the account is credited.

Where the scheme is used from the date of registration, VAT must not be accounted for on any payments received for supplies made before that date. Similarly, where an existing VAT-registered business starts to use the scheme, it should separate in its records any payments received for transactions already accounted for under the normal method of accounting.

Deposits. VAT on deposits must normally be accounted for when received unless the deposit is not payment for supplies (e.g. deposits taken as security which are either returned or forfeited) in which case there is no requirement to account for VAT.

Factored debts. With effect from 22 September 1997:

(a) Where factored debts are sold or formally assigned to a factor (so that they become the debts of the factor), output tax must be accounted for on their full value in the period in which they are sold or assigned. If, at a later date, the factored debts are formally assigned back in full or in part, to the business, it may claim BAD DEBT RELIEF (7) on any unpaid element subject to the normal rules.

(b) Where a business merely uses a factor or invoice discounter as a debt collector and retains legal title to the debt, the initial advance made by the factor to the business is not a payment for the purposes of the cash accounting scheme, it is simply a loan. The business should account for output tax at the point at which the customer pays the factor. This will be evident on statements issued by the factor to the business. If the payment received is less than the full value of the supply (because a commission or other charge is payable to the factor) VAT is still due on the full value of the supply.

Before 22 September 1997, (b) above applied whether or not the debts were sold or formally assigned to the factor.

(C & E Notice 731, para 12A; C & E Business Brief 26/97, 12 November 1997).

Input tax can be reclaimed in the return for the VAT period in which payment is made or other consideration is given *provided* a proper VAT invoice is held. For this purpose payment by

- *cash* is made on the date a receipted VAT invoice is received;

- *cheque* is made on the date the cheque is sent to the supplier or, if later, the date on the cheque. If the cheque is not honoured, no VAT is reclaimable;

- *credit card* is made when the supplier makes out the sales voucher (*not* the date when payment is made to the card company); and

- *giros, standing orders and direct debits* are made on the day the account is debited.

If advance payment is made by way of deposit, VAT can be reclaimed when the payment is made. But if the deposit is given as security (see above) VAT cannot be reclaimed.

Part payment. Where a payment is made or received which covers more than one invoice or represents part payment of an invoice and/or the payment relates to both standard and zero-rated supplies, a fair and reasonable apportionment must be applied. Normally invoices should be dealt with in the order in which they are received or issued.

Prompt payment discount. Where this is offered, VAT is chargeable on the discounted VAT-exclusive invoice price even if the customer does not take up the offer. Where an eligible business using cash accounting offers such a discount, the VAT to be accounted for is that charged on the invoice and not the VAT fraction of the payment reflecting the invoice total (otherwise too much VAT will be accounted for). Similarly, where a business using the cash accounting scheme receives such a discount, input tax reclaimable is limited to the VAT charged on the invoice.

Exports. The scheme can be used to account for VAT which becomes due on goods exported or despatched to another EC country where satisfactory evidence of export or despatch has not been received within the time limit. VAT must be accounted for when the time limit expires on all payments already received.

[*SI 1995/2518, Regs 57, 65*]. (C & E Notice 731, paras 9–11, 14; C & E Manual V1-23, Chapter 4 paras 5.1–5.3).

63.7   **Leaving the scheme**

(a) **Turnover exceeding the limit.** Unless C & E allow or direct otherwise, a person must withdraw from the cash accounting scheme immediately at the end of a prescribed accounting period if the value of his taxable supplies in the year then ending has exceeded £437,500. Exceptionally, C & E may allow a person to remain in the scheme where he can demonstrate that

- this limit was exceeded because of a large 'one-off' sale which has not occurred before and is not expected to recur;

- the sale arose from genuine commercial activity and does not give an undue advantage over competitors; and

- there are reasonable grounds for believing that turnover in the next twelve months will be below £350,000.

Application must be made in writing to, and will be confirmed in writing by, the VAT office.

Before 3 July 1997, a person had to withdraw from the scheme if

- the value of his taxable supplies in any year ending at the end of a prescribed accounting period exceeded £437,500; and

- the value of his taxable supplies in the next year exceeded £350,000,

withdrawal applying from the end of that second year.

(*b*) **Voluntary withdrawal.** A person may withdraw from the scheme at the end of a prescribed accounting period.

Before 3 July 1997, it was necessary to show that either no benefit was derived from remaining in the scheme or it was not possible, by reason of the accounting system, to comply with the requirements of the scheme. Otherwise, a person normally had to stay in the scheme for at least two years and could then return to the normal method of accounting on the anniversary of starting to use the scheme.

(*c*) **Expulsion from the scheme.** A person is not entitled to continue to operate the scheme in the following circumstances.

- He has, while operating the scheme,

    (i) been convicted of an offence in connection with VAT;

    (ii) made a payment to compound such proceedings; or

    (iii) been assessed to a penalty under *VATA 1994, s 60* (VAT evasion involving dishonesty)

    C & E will automatically withdraw the business from the scheme.

    Before 3 July 1997, in addition to the above, a person had to withdraw from the scheme if he was assessed to a penalty under *VATA 1994, s 67* (failure to notify and unauthorised issue of invoices). C & E could also expel a person from the scheme if, while operating it, he had been assessed to a penalty under *VATA 1994, s 63* (misdeclaration or neglect resulting in VAT loss) or *VATA 1994, s 69* (breach of regulatory provisions) or to a default surcharge under *VATA 1994, s 59*.

- He has failed to leave the scheme as provided for in (*a*) above.

- Before 3 July 1997, he claimed input tax as though he had not been operating the scheme.

- C & E consider it necessary for the protection of the revenue that he is not so entitled.

Any termination of authorisation is appealable.

Subsequent accounting for VAT. A person who ceases to operate the cash accounting scheme because of (*a*) or (*b*) above or ceases to be entitled to use the scheme under (*c*) above must, on the return for the prescribed accounting period of cessation, account for

- all the VAT which he would have been required to pay to C&E during the time the scheme was operated if he had not been operating the scheme, less

- all VAT accounted for and paid to C & E in accordance with the scheme,

subject to any adjustment for credit for input tax. Where, however, this would require the person to account for VAT on bad debts, in cases where (*a*) or (*b*) above applies C & E are prepared to allow the outstanding VAT to be paid and the bad debt claim to be made on the same return. All the conditions for claiming BAD DEBT RELIEF (7) must be complied with (except the condition that the person must have already accounted for and paid the VAT on the supply).

Before 3 July 1997, a person who ceased to operate the cash accounting scheme because of (*a*) or (*b*) above could continue to use it for supplies made and received while the scheme was in operation but otherwise had to return to the normal method of accounting. C & E could, however, require the procedure detailed above to be followed.

[*SI 1995/2518, Regs 60, 61, 64; SI 1997/1614, Regs 5, 6, 9*]. (C & E Notice 731, paras 17–19A; C & E Manual V1-23, Chapter 4 para 7.2).

63.8   **Cessation of business**

Where a person operating the cash accounting scheme ceases business or ceases to be registered, he must, within two months or such longer period as C & E allow, account for and pay VAT due on all supplies made and received up to the date of cessation which has not otherwise been accounted for, subject to any adjustment for credit for input tax.

Insolvency. Where a person operating the cash accounting scheme becomes insolvent, he must, within two months of the date of insolvency, account for VAT due on all supplies made and received up to the date of insolvency which has not otherwise been accounted for, subject to any credit for input tax.

Transfer of a business as a going concern. Where a business or part of a business carried on by a person operating the cash accounting scheme is transferred as a going concern

- if the transferee does not take over the registration number of the business, the transferor must, within two months or such longer period as C & E allow, account for and pay VAT due on all supplies made and received which has not otherwise been accounted for, subject to any adjustment for credit for input tax; and

- if the transferor does take over the VAT registration number of the business, the transferee must continue to account for and pay VAT as if he were a person operating the scheme on supplies made and received by the transferor before the date of the transfer.

[*SI 1995/2518, Regs 62, 63; SI 1997/1614, Regs 7,8*].

63.9   **ANNUAL ACCOUNTING SCHEME**

Under *VATA 1994, s 25(1)* regulations may be made allowing a taxable person to account for and pay VAT for prescribed accounting periods of other than three months. The annual accounting scheme allows taxable persons to complete one VAT return each year. Depending upon the level of turnover, quarterly or monthly interim payments on account are required (based on an estimate of the amount of VAT due) although some smaller businesses are exempt from this requirement. The annual VAT return must be completed and sent to C & E, with any balancing payment, within two months of the end of the annual VAT accounting period.

The main advantages of the scheme are

- a reduction in the number of VAT returns required;

- an extra month to complete the annual return and account for any balance of VAT due;

- no requirement to make any interim payments if turnover is below £100,000 and the amount of VAT paid to C & E in the previous year was less than £2,000;

- no requirement to make quarterly calculations or annual adjustments where a retail scheme is used or partial exemption applies; and

- being able to align the VAT accounting period with the financial year end.

(C & E Notice 732, para 3).

De Voil Indirect Tax Service. See V2.167.

63.10   Admission to the scheme

Conditions for admission. A taxable person is eligible to apply to join the scheme if he meets all the following conditions.

(*a*)   He has been registered for at least twelve months at the date of his application for authorisation.

(*b*)   He has reasonable grounds for believing that the value of his taxable supplies in the period of twelve months beginning at the date of his application will not exceed £300,000. For this purpose, all standard and zero-rated supplies should be included except supplies of capital assets previously used in the business. Exempt supplies should be excluded. (C & E Notice 732, para 2).

(*c*)   Registration is not in the name of a group (see 31 GROUPS OF COMPANIES) or a division (see 59.30 REGISTRATION).

(*d*)   He has not ceased to operate the scheme for any reason under 63.14 below in the twelve months preceding the date of application.

C & E may refuse to permit a person to use the scheme where they consider it necessary to do so for the protection of the revenue.

[*SI 1995/2518, Reg 52; SI 1996/542*].

A taxable person will not be allowed to join the scheme if he has a rising VAT debt. However, entry will not necessarily be refused if there is a small debt. In such a case, the debt will be pursued through the normal procedures and payment of it will not be spread over the annual accounting period. (C & E Notice 732, para 2).

Application procedure. Applications to use the scheme must be made on the Form VAT 600 at the end of C & E Notice 732 and sent to the VAT Office. Notes on the completion of the form are included in the Notice.

If the application to join the scheme is accepted and the VAT return for the period immediately preceding the date of application has been submitted, C & E will notify the applicant of the amount and timing of any interim payments to be made, the method of payment chosen (with bank mandate forms if appropriate) and the due date for submission of the annual return and balancing payment. (C & E Notice 732, para 28).

Annual accounting year and **transitional accounting period**. A taxable person applying to join the scheme must indicate on the application form the month to the end of which he wishes his annual accounting year to run. He may however apply to join the scheme at any time. If accepted, the first accounting period under the scheme will run from the first day of the accounting period in which the application is made until the chosen year end. This period is called the '*transitional accounting period*'. Subsequent periods of twelve months are '*annual accounting years*'.

Example

C Ltd, currently preparing VAT returns for calendar quarters and statutory accounts to 30 June each year, applies to join the annual accounting scheme on 28 November 1997. It chooses 30 June as the end of its annual accounting year to tie in with the financial accounts.

If accepted, C Ltd will join the scheme with effect from 1 October 1997 and have a transitional accounting period from 1 October 1997 to 30 June 1998. Thereafter, it will have annual accounting years ending on 30 June each year.

[*SI 1995/2518, Reg 49; SI 1996/542*].

The annual accounting year can be changed after joining the scheme (e.g. to tie in with a change in financial year end) but no annual accounting period can be longer than twelve months. This may mean that one or two short period returns are received. (C & E Notice 732, para 15).

63.11   **Conditions for using the scheme**

To remain within the scheme, a person must comply with the following conditions.

(*a*)   Make any interim payments on account required by the notified due date. See 63.12 below.

(*b*)   Submit a VAT return, together with any balancing payment of VAT due to C & E declared on that return

- in respect of a transitional accounting period of four months or more or an annual accounting year (see 63.10 above) by the end of the second month following that period or year; and

- in respect of a transitional accounting period of less than four months by the end of the first month following that period.

[*SI 1995/2518, Regs 50(2)(b), 51(a)(iii)(b); SI 1996/542*].

(*c*)   Tell the VAT office immediately if there is any significant change in the business after starting to use the scheme (e.g. a change in the VAT liability of goods supplied, the opening of a new outlet or a downturn in business). (C & E Notice 732, para 22).

63.12   **Payments on account**

Provisions applying with effect from 1 April 1996 or, for persons already in the annual accounting scheme on that date, the start of their next annual accounting year. A taxable person authorised to use the annual accounting scheme must make interim payments on account as follows.

For the transitional period (see 63.10 above)

(*a*)   Where the transitional period is less than four months, no interim payments are required.

(*b*) Where the transitional period is four months or more and taxable supplies in the twelve months to the start of the transitional period did not exceed £100,000, then if the amount of VAT due to C & E in respect of that twelve-month period was

- more than £2,000, 20% of the VAT due for that previous twelve-month period is due as an interim payment no later than the last 'working day' of the 4th, and where the period has such months, 7th and 10th months of the transitional accounting period; and

- £2,000 or less, no quarterly payments need be made.

(*c*) Where the transitional period is four months or more and taxable supplies in the twelve months to the start of the transitional period exceeded £100,000, monthly interim payments are due, commencing on the last working day of the 4th month of the transitional period, each equal to 10% of the VAT due for that twelve-month period.

For subsequent annual accounting periods

(*a*) Where taxable supplies in the twelve months to the start of the current annual accounting period did not exceed £100,000 (£110,000 where quarterly interim payments were made in that year), then if the amount of VAT due to C & E in respect of that twelve-month period was

- more than £2,000, three quarterly interim payments are due. These amounts will each be equal to 20% of the VAT due for that previous twelve-month period and are payable no later than the last 'working day' of the 4th, 7th and 10th months of the annual accounting year; and

- £2,000 or less, no quarterly payments need be made.

(*b*) In all other cases where (*a*) above does not apply, nine monthly interim payments are due, commencing on the last working day of the 4th month of the annual accounting year, each equal to 10% of the VAT due for the twelve months to the start of the current annual accounting year.

'*Working day*' means any day of the week other than Saturday, Sunday, a bank holiday or a public holiday.

[*SI 1995/2518, Regs 49, 50(2)(3), 51; SI 1996/542*].

Interim payments are normally calculated on the previous year's liability but where there is a change to the VAT liability, the level of interim payments may be revised.

Additional voluntary payments can be made at any time. All interim payments, including voluntary payments, are rounded to the nearest £5. (C & E Notice 732, paras 6, 7).

Method of payment. All interim payments, whether monthly or quarterly, must be made by electronic means (direct debit, standing order, bank giro credit, Bankers Automated Clearing Service (BACS) or the Clearing House Automated Payment System (CHAPS)). Final payment can be made by cheque, bank giro credit, BACS or CHAPS. (C & E Notice 732, paras 9, 10).

Missing a payment. C & E will send a reminder if an interim payment on account is not received. Payment will have to be made by bank giro credit (a transfer slip will be enclosed with the reminder) or by BACS. (C & E Notice 732, para 11).

For annual accounting periods commencing before 1 April 1996, a taxable person authorised to use the scheme had to pay, by direct debit, nine monthly interim payments, commencing on the last working day of the 4th month of the annual accounting year. Each payment was equal to 10% of the VAT due for the twelve months to the start of the current annual accounting year.

63.13 Accounting for VAT

Retail schemes. Where a retail scheme is used, it is only necessary to do the scheme calculation once a year to coincide with the end of the annual accounting period.

- Under the Point of Sale scheme and Direct Calculation Scheme 1 (and under the old Schemes A, B, B2, C, E, E1, F) the usual method should be adopted but using the figures for the full year.

- Under Apportionment Scheme 1 and Direct Calculation Scheme 2 (and under old Schemes B1, D, D1 and J), output tax is calculated using the figures and scheme method for the period covered by the annual VAT return. The retail scheme adjustment must coincide with the end of the annual accounting period. If the transitional period (see 63.10 above) is for part of a year, the retail scheme calculation must be made at the end of that period.

- Under Apportionment Scheme 2 (and under old Schemes G and H), the method of calculation for the fourth and later quarterly VAT periods must be followed but using the figures for the VAT year in each step.

See 60 RETAIL SCHEMES for detailed calculations under each scheme.

Partial exemption. Partly-exempt traders who have to make annual adjustments must have an annual accounting year which coincides with the date of the annual adjustment. This means that it is not necessary to do the partial exemption calculation for each quarter, just the annual adjustment for the whole VAT year.

Significant changes in the business should be notified to the VAT office immediately (see 63.11(*c*) above). C & E will take any necessary action to amend the level of interim payments.

Annual VAT return. The annual return is completed in the same way as a normal VAT return. It is important that the figure for the value of outputs in Box 6 is accurate as this will be used as a basis for allowing continued use of the scheme.

The figure shown in Box 5 of the return is the amount of VAT due for the year. The amount payable with the VAT return is the figure in Box 5 less the total of interim payments made during the year (if any). C & E will send details of any interim payments received in time to prepare the return. Final payment can be made by cheque, bank giro credit, BACS or CHAPS. If the total amount paid by interim payments is more than the net VAT payable, C & E will refund the difference automatically.

Subsequent annual accounting years. Provided the person is still authorised to use the scheme, he must continue to use it in the next annual accounting year. [*SI 1995/2518, Reg 53(1); SI 1996/542*]. Following submission of an annual return, C & E will notify the interim payments for the next accounting year. If interim payments are made by direct debit, no action is required. In any other case, arrangements must be made with the bank to ensure that the required updated interim payments are made.

(C & E Notice 732, paras 16–23).

63.14 Leaving the scheme

A person ceases to be authorised to use the annual accounting scheme in the following circumstances.

(*a*)   **Turnover exceeding the limit.**

- After the end of any transitional accounting period (see 63.10 above) if the value of taxable supplies in that period has exceeded £375,000.

- After the end of any annual accounting year if the value of taxable supplies in that year has exceeded £375,000.

(*b*)   **Expulsion by C & E.** C & E *may* terminate an authorisation to use the scheme from any date where

- a false statement has been made by or on behalf of a person in relation to the application to use the scheme;

- a person fails to make any VAT return under the scheme by the due date;

- a person fails to make any payment due under the scheme;

- a person notifies C & E that he has reason to believe that the value of taxable supplies in the current transitional accounting period (see 63.10 above) or annual accounting year will exceed £375,000 (which he is obliged to do in writing within 30 days);

- they have reason to believe that the value of taxable supplies made by a person using the scheme will exceed £375,000 in the current transitional accounting period (see 63.10 above) or annual accounting year;

- it is necessary to do so for the protection of the revenue; or

- a person using the scheme has not paid over to C & E all VAT shown as due on any return made before authorisation and all VAT shown as due on any assessment made (including interest and penalties). See, however, 63.10 above for C & E policy where there is a small amount of VAT outstanding at the time of application to join the scheme.

(*c*)   **Cessation of business.** Where a person authorised to use the scheme

- becomes insolvent and ceases to trade (other than for the purposes of disposing of stocks and assets),

- ceases business or ceases to be registered, or

- dies or becomes bankrupt or incapacitated

authorisation to use the scheme terminates on the date on which any such event occurs.

(*d*)   **Voluntary withdrawal.** A person authorised to use the scheme may cease to operate it of his own volition at any time. Authorisation to use the scheme terminates from the date C & E are notified in writing.

[*SI 1995/2518, Regs 53(2), 54, 55(1); SI 1996/542*].

Consequences of leaving the scheme. Where a person leaves the annual accounting scheme, he (or, as the case may be, his representative) must make a final return under the scheme and pay any outstanding tax due under it within two months of the date on which his authorisation is terminated. From the day following termination, he must account for and pay VAT in the normal way and cannot rejoin the scheme for 12 months (three years before 1 April 1996).

[*SI 1995/2518, Reg 55(2); SI 1996/542*].

63.15   FLAT-RATE SCHEME FOR FARMERS

There is an optional flat-rate scheme for farmers. Farmers already registered for VAT may either remain registered or de-register and join the flat-rate scheme. Farmers whose turnover is below the registration limit may also use the scheme if they would otherwise qualify for voluntary registration.

A farmer has to apply to C & E to join the scheme. C & E may then certify him for the purposes of these provisions where satisfied that

- he is carrying on a business involving one or more designated activities (see 63.16 below); and

- he has complied with the necessary conditions for admission to the scheme (see 63.17 below).

[*VATA 1994, s 54*].

Certification. If the application is accepted, the farmer is issued with a certificate (showing a unique reference number) which is proof that he qualifies for the scheme. If application is refused, an appeal may be made to a VAT tribunal.

Where a person is so certified, goods and services supplied as part of those designated activities are disregarded in determining whether he is, has become or has ceased to become liable or entitled to be registered for VAT under *VATA 1994, 1 Sch*.

[*SI 1995/2518, Reg 203*].

The flat-rate addition. Farmers who are certified (and therefore not registered for VAT) do not have to account for VAT on sales of goods and services within the designated activities but are not able to recover input tax incurred on purchases.

To compensate for this, on sales of designated goods and services to VAT-registered persons, farmers *may* charge a fixed flat-rate addition of 4% on top of the sales price. This applies even if some of the goods would otherwise be zero-rated. The farmer retains this addition and the registered person is able to recover it as if it were VAT (subject to the normal rules). [*VATA 1994, s 54(3)(4); SI 1992/3221; SI 1995/2518, Reg 209*].

The flat-rate addition must not be charged on supplies of goods and services which are not designated (e.g. sales of machinery) or on supplies to non-registered persons (e.g. the public or other flat-rate farmers).

Sales through farmers' groups and co-operatives. Where a farmer sells produce in this way, the goods are combined with the produce of other farmers and the buyer has no way of knowing whether any of his suppliers are flat-rate farmers. In such cases, the buyer should pay the farmer's group only the price agreed for the produce *without the flat rate addition*. The group should pay the flat rate addition to those farmers who have a certificate when the proceeds of sale are shared out. The farmer's group can reclaim this addition on its own VAT return as though it were input tax.

Auctioneers of agricultural produce.

- *Where the auctioneer acts as agent for the flat-rate farmer*, the produce remains the property of the farmer until it is sold. The farmer cannot charge the flat-rate addition to the auctioneer (as he does not take title to the goods) but can charge it to the eventual buyer if the buyer is VAT-registered.

- *Where a VAT-registered auctioneer acts as principal* (buying and selling the produce) the farmer can charge the flat rate addition to the auctioneer who can reclaim it as input tax. When the auctioneer sells the goods, VAT must be charged on the sale under the normal rules.

Sales to other EC countries. A flat rate farmer can charge the flat rate addition on designated sales to VAT-registered persons in other EC countries (even though no VAT would have been due on the sale). The customer in the other country can reclaim the flat rate addition charged provided he receives a flat rate invoice.

Buying from other EC countries. Where a VAT-registered person in the UK acquires goods or services from a farmer in another EC country who charges the flat-rate addition, this can be reclaimed but from the VAT authority in the supplier's country (and not from C & E). The VAT office can give details of the procedure to be followed.

If a flat-rate farmer acquires goods from another EC country in excess of an annual threshold, he may have to register for VAT and lose the flat-rate status. See 59.18 REGISTRATION.

Sales made outside the EC. A flat-rate farmer can charge the addition on designated goods and services to purchasers outside the EC provided the goods are used for the business purposes of the purchaser.

Non-farming activities. If the taxable turnover of non-farming activities (e.g. bed and breakfast) is less than the VAT registration threshold, a farmer can still be a flat-rate farmer. He must not charge VAT or the flat-rate addition on the non-farming activities.

If his turnover of non-farming activities is above the VAT threshold, a farmer must remain registered for VAT (or, if already in the flat-rate scheme, have his certificate cancelled and register for VAT). The farmer will not be eligible to join the flat-rate scheme unless

- the non-farming activities are zero-rated, in which case the farmer may ask for exemption from registration (see 59.6 REGISTRATION) and join the scheme; or

- the non-farming business is run as a separate business by a different legal entity (e.g. a farmer could run his farming activities as a sole proprietor and a bed and breakfast business in partnership with another person).

(C & E Leaflet 700/46/93, paras 3, 15–20).

Deregistration. Farmers who deregister to join the flat-rate scheme do not have to account for VAT on their stocks and assets on hand, even where they have claimed input tax when purchasing them. [*VATA 1994, 4 Sch 8(3)*].

De Voil Indirect Tax Service. See V2.191–198; V6.143–146A.

63.16 Designated activities

For the purposes of the scheme, a farmer is someone who engages in any of the following activities.

(*a*) **Crop production** comprising any of the following.

- *General agriculture including viticulture.* Included is turf and reeds grown as a crop (e.g. thatching) but not peat and top soil. Also included is the growing of grape vines and the production by vineyards of their own wine up to and including the sale of the wine.

- *Growing of fruit, vegetables, flowers and ornamental plants (in the open and under glass).* Included are bulbs, tubers, cut flowers, branches and foliage and plants initially seeded elsewhere but subsequently bought by flat rate farmers to grow into mature plants for sale.

- *Production of mushrooms, spices, seeds and propagating materials.*

- *Nursery production* i.e. the rearing of young plants, including vegetables, fruit, trees and shrubs, for sale. Also included is the sale of these products by farmers (i) who allow members of the public to come onto their farms to pick produce to buy (pick-your-own) and (ii) in their own farm shop provided the produce has undergone no further process than being harvested, cut and put into containers on the premises (although in such cases the flat-rate addition can only be charged when the produce is sold to a VAT-registered person).

(*b*)   **Stock farming** comprising any of the following.

- *General stock farming.* Included is the breeding, rearing and care of animals which are either: eaten by humans; not eaten by humans but which produce food which is eaten by humans; not eaten by humans but eaten by other animals; not eaten by humans or animals but which are farmed for their skin, fur or wool; or fall into none of these categories but are specifically used in connection with agricultural production activities, e.g. sheepdogs. Included are animals ranging from the normal farm animals to mink, game birds (unless raised specifically for shooting), pigeons, deer and ostriches where they are raised for food and solely for the sale of their feathers. Excluded are animals raised as pets and butterflies. The preparation of animals for showing at agricultural shows and the showing of animals themselves will fall within the scheme. Training as a specialist activity is a non-agricultural supply and falls outside the scheme. Horses which leave breeders to be trained by a specialist trainer will be considered to have left the flat-rate scheme when they enter the trainer's yard. Where horses are bred, reared and trained for racing on the same premises (permit holders), once the horses are put into training, the training activity falls outside the flat-rate scheme.

- *Poultry and rabbit farming.* Included is the breeding and rearing of chicken, ducks, geese, turkeys, pigeons and game birds (unless raised specifically for shooting) which are generally eaten by humans and/or animals.

- *Bee-keeping and silkworm farming* up to and including the sale of the bees or silkworm cocoons.

- *Snail farming* comprising the breeding and rearing of edible snails and their farming for any other purpose.

(*c*)   **Forestry.** This covers the growing and sale of all kinds of trees within the farmer's own woodlands and activities carried out within that area by the farmer and his employees using the farmer's machinery. Included is the growing and selling of trees (either standing or felled) and the conversion of felled timber into sawlogs, fencing materials and firewood, etc. Excluded is any processing beyond this stage.

(*d*)   **Fisheries** comprising fresh-water fishing; fish farming (any fish); breeding of mussels, oysters and other molluscs and crustaceans; and frog farming.

(*e*)   **Processing** by a farmer of products derived from his own activities within (*a*)–(*d*) above using only such means as are normally employed in the course of such activities. Included is the gutting of fish; drying of hops; slaughter and preparation of animals raised by the farmer for sale at the farm gate; and the picking and packaging of fruit for sale on the farm.

(*f*)   **Supplies of agricultural services,** by a person who also carries out one or more other designated activities falling within (*a*)–(*e*) above, comprising

- field work, reaping and mowing, threshing, bailing, collecting, harvesting, sowing and planting;

- packing and preparation of agricultural products for market (including drying, cleaning, grinding, disinfecting and ensilaging);

- storage of agricultural products;

- stock minding, rearing and fattening of animals within (*b*) above or fish within (*d*) above;

- hiring out of equipment for use in any designated activity;

- technical assistance in relation to any designated activity (including thatching if the flat rate farmer has grown the reeds, deer management (e.g. culling and preventing deer going on to forestry land), vermin control and agricultural pest control);

- destruction of weeds and pests, dusting and spraying of crops and land;

- operation of irrigation and drainage equipment; and

- lopping, tree felling and other forestry services (including clearing undergrowth, spraying trees, marking trees for felling, making inventories of trees suitable for felling, and creating firebreaks.

The services must be performed by the farmer himself or his employees. Any equipment he uses in carrying out the services, or any equipment he hires to another person, must be equipment which he also uses for carrying out his other designated activities.

Not included within the scheme are persons whose primary activity is to buy and sell animals (dealers) or who engage in an activity once removed from farming (e.g. dairy co-operatives and sawmills). The sale or leasing of milk quotas (whether or not they are sold with land) is not a designated activity.

[*SI 1992/3220*]. (C & E Leaflet 700/46/93, para 2, Annexes A and B; C & E Manual V1-23, Chapter 2 Appendix A).

63.17 **Admission to the scheme and changes in circumstances**

C & E must certify a person for the purposes of the flat-rate scheme if the following conditions are satisfied.

(*a*) He satisfies C & E that he is carrying on one or more designated activities within 63.16 above.

(*b*) If he is currently registered for VAT, that registration is cancelled. See 63.15 above for the position where non-farming activities are also carried on.

(*c*) He has not, in the three years before the date of application for certification,

- been convicted of any offences in connection with VAT;

- accepted an offer to compound proceedings in connection with a VAT offence; or

- been assessed to a penalty for VAT evasion involving dishonest conduct (see 52.9 PENALTIES).

(*d*) He makes an application for certification on the correct form (Form VAT 98).

(*e*) He satisfies C & E that, in the year following the date of his certification, the amounts of the flat-rate additions which he charges will not exceed the amount of input tax to which he would otherwise be entitled to credit by £3,000 or more. This will always be satisfied where the estimated value of agricultural supplies (shown in Box 4 of Form VAT 98) is £75,000 or less. If that figure is greater than £75,000, C & E will calculate 4% of the figure in Box 4 and deduct input tax claimed in the last twelve months. They will allow certification if the net figure is less than £3,000 (provided the other conditions are met). If the net figure is more than £3,000 they will normally refuse certification although where the net figure is less than £3,500 they may allow certification if satisfied that the figures used are insufficiently accurate to be successfully defended on an appeal to a VAT tribunal. (C & E Manual V1-23, Chapter 2 Table 3).

[*SI 1995/2518, Reg 204*].

Date of admission. The certificate issued by C & E is effective from the date on which application is received by C & E or, if the applicant so requests, from a date 30 days or less after that date. Alternatively it may be such earlier date as C & E agree to. No certificate can, however, be effective before 1 January 1993 or before any existing VAT registration is cancelled. [*SI 1995/2518, Reg 205*].

Further certification. Where a person who has been certified under the scheme, and is no longer so certified, makes a further application, he cannot be certified for a period of three years from the date of cancellation of the previous certificate except as follows.

(i) Where he has not been registered, or required to be registered, for VAT at any time since the cancellation of his previous certificate, C & E may certify him from the date of his further application.

(ii) Where he has been registered for VAT during that time but no VAT was due on his business assets on hand at the date of deregistration under *VATA 1983, 2 Sch 7* because the VAT would not have been more than £250, C & E may certify him on a date after the expiry of one year from the date of cancellation of his previous certificate.

[*SI 1995/2518, Reg 208*].

Changes in circumstances. The certificate issued by C & E shows the full name of the business if the owner is a sole proprietor or company and the address of the business. In the case of a partnership, it shows the trading name of the partnership or, if it does not have one, the names of at least two partners (although, in such a case, the certificate still covers all the partners listed in the application form). C & E must be informed of any change of name or address, any changes in the members of a partnership and if a sole proprietor takes a partner. (C & E Leaflet 700/46/93, para 13). A new certificate will then be issued.

63.18 **Cancellation of certificates**

C & E may or, as the case may be, must cancel a person's certificate in any of the following circumstances and from the date stated.

(*a*) Where a statement false in a material particular was made by him or on his behalf in connection with his application. Cancellation is from the date C & E discover that such a statement has been made.

(*b*) He has been convicted of, or has accepted an offer to compound proceedings in connection with, a VAT offence or has been assessed to a VAT penalty. Cancellation is from the date of conviction, date of payment of the sum to compound proceedings or 30 days after the date the assessment is notified.

(*c*) He ceases to be involved in designated activities. Cancellation is from the date of cessation.

(*d*) He dies or becomes bankrupt or incapacitated. Cancellation is from the date of death, etc. C & E may, however, in such cases, until such time as some other person is certified in respect of those activities, treat as a certified person any person carrying on those designated activities. That person must inform C & E in writing within 30 days of the fact that he is carrying on the activities and the date of death, bankruptcy or incapacity.

Where the certified person is a company, the reference to bankruptcy is to be construed as a reference to liquidation, receivership or administration as the case may be.

(e) He is liable to be registered for VAT. Cancellation is from the effective date of registration.

(f) He makes an application in writing for cancellation. Cancellation is from a date not less than one year after the effective date of his certificate or such earlier date as C & E agree to.

(g) He makes an application in writing for voluntary VAT registration (which application is deemed to be an application for cancellation of his certificate). Cancellation is from a date not less than one year after the effective date of his certificate or such earlier date as C & E agree to.

(h) C & E consider it is necessary to do so for the protection of the revenue (e.g. because the farmer is found to be recovering substantially more as a flat-rate farmer than he would if registered for VAT in the normal way). Cancellation is from the date on which C & E consider a risk to the revenue arises.

(i) C & E are not satisfied that any of the grounds for cancellation of a certificate within (a)–(g) above do not apply. Cancellation is from the date in (a)–(g) as appropriate.

[*SI 1995/2518, Regs 206, 207*].

A flat-rate farmer who leaves the scheme to register for VAT is not entitled to claim relief for any VAT incurred on purchases whilst he was a member of the scheme. (C & E Manual V1-23, Chapter 2 para 4.5).

63.19 Records

Every certified person must comply with such requirements relating to keeping, preserving and producing records as C & E notify to him. In particular every certified person must

(a) keep and preserve business and accounting records and copies of all invoices showing flat-rate additions (see 63.20 below) for six years (or such lesser period as C & E allow); and

(b) upon demand by a person acting under the authority of C & E (an '*authorised person*') produce, or cause to be produced, for inspection by that person any document within (a) above. The document must be produced at the principal place of business (or at such other place as may be reasonably required) at such time as may reasonably be required. The authorised person may take copies or make extracts of any document and may, at a reasonable time and for a reasonable period, remove any document. Where any document removed is reasonably required for the proper conduct of the business, a copy must be provided free of charge as soon as practicable. If any documents removed are lost or damaged, reasonable compensation must be paid.

[*SI 1995/2518, Regs 210, 211*].

63.20 Invoices

In order that a registered person in receipt of a supply of designated goods and services may treat the flat-rate addition as if it were input tax for VAT purposes, the farmer must issue an invoice containing the following particulars.

- An identifying invoice number.

- His name, address and certificate number.

- The name and address of the person to whom the goods or services are supplied.

- The time of the supply.

- A description of the goods or services supplied.

- The consideration of the supply excluding the flat-rate addition.

- An amount entitled 'Flat-rate Addition' or 'FRA'.

[*SI 1995/2518, Reg 209*].

See 52.12 PENALTIES for the penalty for unauthorised issue of flat-rate farming invoices.

63.21   **VAT REGISTRATION SCHEME FOR RACEHORSE OWNERS**

The VAT registration scheme (the 'scheme') for racehorse owners was introduced on 16 March 1993 with the agreement of the thoroughbred horseracing and breeding industry. From that date, subject to conditions, owners are accepted as carrying on a business and can register for VAT.

Conditions for registration. *With effect from 1 January 1998*, an owner of racehorses can apply for VAT registration under the Scheme if

(*a*) the horses are covered by a sponsorship agreement registered at Weatherbys or by a trainer's sponsorship agreement registered at Weatherbys; or

(*b*) the owner can show that he has received business income from horseracing activities (e.g. appearance money or sponsored number cloths) and will continue to do so.

Normal procedure applies on application for registration (see 59.5 REGISTRATION) with the additional requirement that Form D1 (owners not in partnership) or D2 (partnerships), certified as correct by Weatherbys, must be sent to C & E with the VAT registration form(s). Forms D1 and D2 are obtained from, and must be sent for certification to, VAT Declarations, Weatherbys, Sanders Road, Wellingborough, Northants, NN8 4BX.

Where a part share only in a racehorse is owned, the part owner can register in his own name if owning at least 50% of the horse. Otherwise, he must register in partnership with the other joint owners. (Similarly, an owner already registered before 1 January 1998 can treat a part share bought on or after 1 January 1998 within the existing registration only if at least 50% of the horse is acquired; otherwise he must register as a partner with the other part owners.)

After registration

- if sponsorship is lost, the owner can only remain registered if actively seeking new sponsorship; and

- any horses owned which are not covered by a sponsorship agreement can only be treated as part of the business if the owner can show that he is actively seeking sponsorship for them.

(C & E Notice 700/67/97, paras 1.1–1.7).

Input tax. Once registered under the Scheme, input tax can be deducted subject to the normal rules.

Output tax. Output tax must be accounted for on sponsorship income, prize money and appearance money. Weatherbys operate a self-billing system for prize money and appearance money on behalf of the British Horseracing Board, issuing owners with monthly statements ('transaction analysis summaries') showing the VAT payable to C & E on prize and appearance money. They also show certain expenditure (e.g. jockey's services) on which input tax can be reclaimed.

Sales of whole horses are supplies of goods.

- If the horse is in the UK at the time of sale, the place of supply is the UK and VAT is due at the standard rate unless

  (i) the horse is exported outside the EC (zero-rated); or

  (ii) the horse is sold to a person registered for VAT in another EC country and is removed to that country (zero-rated in the UK with the buyer accounting for acquisition VAT in his own country).

- If the horse is in another EC country at the time of sale, VAT is, in principle, due in that country subject to the VAT rules applying there.

Sales of part shares of horses are supplies of services. If the seller belongs in the UK (see 64.19 SUPPLY) the supply of a part share is subject to UK VAT wherever the buyer belongs. If the seller belongs in another EC country, there is a supply in that country.

Gifts, etc. VAT is due on racehorses given away or put to non-business use, based on their open market value at the time.

Margin scheme. Where no VAT was charged on the purchase, the margin scheme for second-hand goods can be used and VAT accounted for on the profit margin. See 61 SECOND-HAND GOODS generally and, in particular, 61.37 for special provisions applying to horses.

(C & E Notice 700/67/97, paras 2.1-2.7).

Owners who may be registered for VAT outside the scheme. See 8.4(*a*) BUSINESS for owners whose business activities are connected with bloodstock.

If an owner's normal business activities are not connected with bloodstock, C & E normally only accept that a racehorse forms part of that business if the owner can show there are sound reasons for the purchase (e.g. to advertise the business).

(C & E Notice 700/67/97, para 1.8).

63.22   Special arrangements for point-to-point horses

From 1 January 1998, an owner of a 'qualifying horse' (i.e. a horse with a sponsorship agreement which is entered in a hunter chase) can register for VAT under the scheme for the hunter chasing season only (January to June). Registration procedure is as in 63.21 above. If already registered for VAT (under these arrangements, under the scheme or because of other business activities) there is no requirements to apply for separate registration but Form D1 or D2 as appropriate must still be completed. After the end of the hunter chasing season, VAT registration can be retained provided

- the owner can show the intention to enter the horse in hunter chases in the following season; and

- the existing sponsorship agreement is to continue or the owner intends to obtain sponsorship before the horse competes in the first race in the new season.

If these conditions cannot be met, either registration will be cancelled or, if it is continuing for other reasons, no further input tax can be recovered in respect of the horse.

(C & E Notice 700/67/97, paras 3.1, 3.2).

Output tax. Output tax must be accounted for on sponsorship income, prize money and appearance money received on qualifying horses. VAT is normally due on the sale of a qualifying horse (including a horse which the owner bred and on which he recovered VAT on the 'cost of production'). Where no VAT was charged on the purchase, the margin scheme for second-hand goods can be used and VAT accounted for on the profit margin. See 61 SECOND-HAND GOODS generally and, in particular 61.37 for special provisions applying to horses. VAT is also due if a horse ceases to be a qualifying horse (e.g. by being put to permanent non-business use). In such a case, output tax must be accounted for on 50% of the open market value at the time. (C & E Notice 700/67/97, para 3.3).

Input tax. Once a horse becomes a qualifying horse, 50% of the VAT incurred on its purchase can be recovered provided incurred no more than three years before the date of registration. (The 50% restriction is a rule of thumb apportionment to recognise that the horse is used for business and private purposes.) All VAT incurred on training, keep and other costs of a qualifying horse can be recovered with effect from the date of registration, plus 50% of such costs incurred in the six months prior to registration or the date it runs in a hunter chase.

VAT incurred on the purchase or construction of fixed assets (e.g. a stable block or horse transporter) can be recovered in full if used solely for qualifying horses. Where the asset is used for qualifying and non-qualifying horses, the VAT must be apportioned. This applies to VAT incurred post-registration and pre-registration (subject to the three-year time limit).

(C & E Notice 700/67/97, para 3.4).

63.23   **VAT treatment of racing clubs, etc.**

Racing clubs may take a number of forms.

(*a*) **Investment companies selling shares**. A limited company sells its shares (an exempt supply) and uses the funds to buy racehorses in the company name. Profits may be distributed to shareholders as dividends.

Unless the company has other business activities involving the making of taxable supplies, it can only register for VAT if it meets the conditions of the Scheme in 63.21 above. Any benefits available to shareholders (e.g. visits to trainers, free badges, etc.) are disregarded for VAT purposes.

(*b*) **Racing partnerships selling shares**. A limited company or partnership sets up a racing partnership offering for sale a specific number of shares in racehorses. Proceeds from prize money, sale of racehorses, etc. are distributed to the owners on termination of the partnership.

The sale of shares is outside the scope of VAT. Any benefits the owners of the shares receive (e.g. visits to trainers, free badges, etc.) are disregarded for VAT purposes. Unless the partnership has other business activities involving the making of taxable supplies, it can only register for VAT if it meets the conditions of the scheme in 63.21 above.

(*c*) **Members racing club raising subscriptions**. A limited company, partnership or sole proprietor calling itself a 'racing club' (or having the characteristics of a club) invites persons to become members on payment of subscriptions. The subscriptions are used to buy racehorses, etc. and at the end of the year surplus income is distributed to members.

- *If members receive benefits* (e.g. newsletters, visits to trainers, tipping service), the club is carrying on a business. [*VATA 1994, s 94(2)*]. See 14.1 CLUBS AND ASSOCIATIONS. The subscription income is taxable and the club must register for VAT if above the registration threshold. The scheme under 63.21 above does not apply.

- *If members receive no benefits*, the club is not in business and the subscriptions are outside the scope of VAT. The club can only register for VAT if it meets the conditions of the scheme in 63.21 above.

(C & E Notice 700/67/97, paras 4.1-4.5).

64   Supply

The contents of this chapter are as follows.

64.1   INTRODUCTION

A transaction is within the scope of UK VAT if the following four conditions are satisfied.

- It is a supply of goods or services.

- It takes place in the UK.

- It is made by a taxable person.

- It is made in the course or furtherance of any business carried on by that person.

[*VATA 1994, s 4(1)*].

The first two conditions are considered in this chapter.

Supplies for VAT purposes. Even before deciding whether goods or services are being supplied, it is necessary to determine whether a transaction is in fact a supply for VAT purposes by considering the following questions.

(*a*)   **Is there any consideration?** Under both EC and UK law, a supply takes place for VAT purposes when something is provided or done for a consideration. [*VATA 1994, s 5(2)*]. A supply can be made in many ways, the most common being the transfer of ownership or the transfer of possession of goods, or the provision of a services by one person to another. See 64.2 below for further coverage of the meaning of supply.

Consideration for VAT purposes has a wide meaning and covers anything which might be done, given or made in exchange for something else. It does not refer only to money. It includes something exchanged in a barter transaction, such as in a part exchange, or a service performed in return for another service, or it may simply be a condition imposed upon the making of the supply. Provided there is a direct link between the supply made and the consideration given, and the consideration is capable of being expressed in money, there is a supply for VAT purposes. See 69.2 VALUATION for further coverage of the meaning of consideration.

(*b*)   **If there is no consideration, is the transaction one which is deemed to be a supply for VAT purposes?** Even if there is no consideration, certain transactions made for no consideration (i.e. free) are deemed to be supplies of goods or services for VAT purposes. These are the

- permanent transfer/disposal of business assets (*VATA 1994, 4 Sch 5(1)*), see 47.4 OUTPUT TAX;

- temporary use of business assets for non-business purposes (*VATA 1994, 4 Sch 5(4)*), see 47.5 OUTPUT TAX;

- retention of certain business assets on deregistration (*VATA 1994, 4 Sch 8*), see 59.27 REGISTRATION;

- self-supply of goods or services (by statutory instruments made under *VATA 1994, s 5(5)(6)*), see 62 SELF-SUPPLY; and

- private or other non-business use of services supplied to the business (*SI 1993/1507*), see 47.5 OUTPUT TAX.

(*c*) **Does the transaction fail to be a supply or is it a supply which is disregarded for VAT purposes?** A transaction is not a supply for VAT purposes if

- there is no consideration for the supply and it is not a deemed supply under (*b*) above;

- the transaction is within the same legal entity;

- there is a specific exclusion in VAT legislation, i.e.

    (i) a business gift costing the donor £15 or less, unless forming part of a series or succession made to the same person (*VATA 1994, 4 Sch 5*), see 47.4 OUTPUT TAX ;

    (ii) an industrial sample (*VATA 1994, 4 Sch 5*), see 47.4 OUTPUT TAX ; or

    (iii) the transaction is deemed to be 'neither a supply of goods nor services', see 64.5 below.

Supplies of goods and services. Once it has been established that a transaction is a supply, it is then necessary to determine whether it is a supply of goods (see 64.3 below) or a supply of services (see 64.4 below). Certain transactions, although supplies, are regarded as supplies of neither goods nor services and are outside the scope of VAT (see 64.5 below).

The distinction as to whether a supply is one of goods or services is important as different rules apply to the place and time of supply. Also the treatment of the international supply of goods and services is different.

VAT invoices. A VAT invoice never creates a supply or alters the nature of the supply. It is the nature of the underlying transaction which determines the supply position.

(C & E Manual V1-3, Chapter 1).

64.2   **MEANING OF SUPPLY**

The legislation does not define the term 'supply'. Subject to express provisions to the contrary, supply includes all forms of supply, but not anything done otherwise than for consideration. Anything which is not a supply of goods but is done for a consideration (including, if so done, the granting, assignment or surrender of any right) is a supply of services. [*VATA 1994, s 5(2)*].

In *C & E Commrs v Oliver QB 1979, [1980] STC 73*, it was held that supply of goods has a wide interpretation. It is the passing of possession in goods pursuant to an agreement whereunder the supplier agrees to part and the recipient agrees to take possession. By 'possession' is meant in this context control over the goods, in the sense of having immediate facility for their use. This may or may not involve the physical removal of the goods. See also *Carlton Lodge Club v C & E Commrs QB, [1974] STC 507*.

In *Tolsma v Inspecteur der Omzetbelasting Leeuwarden, CJEC [1994] STC 509* an individual who played a barrel organ on the public highway, and invited donations from the public, was held not to be supplying services for a consideration. There was no agreement between the parties and also 'no necessary link between the musical service and the payment to which it gave rise'.

Illegal supplies. The principle of fiscal neutrality requires that all supplies of goods for a consideration are subject to VAT unless the goods are subject to a total prohibition on circulation because they are intrinsically harmful or because all competition between a lawful economic sector and an unlawful sector is precluded. In *Witzemann v Hauptzollamt Munchen-Mitte, CJEC 1990, [1993] STC 108*, the Advocate-General stated that 'illegality manifests itself in many forms and there are many products that either cannot be lawfully traded or trade in which is subject to certain restrictions: drugs, counterfeit money, weapons, pornography, the pelts of certain animals, stolen goods and so forth. Not every transaction tainted with illegality will be exempt from taxation. A line must be drawn between, on the one hand, transactions that lie so clearly outside the sphere of legitimate economic activity that, instead of being taxed, they can only be the subject of criminal prosecution and, on the other hand, transactions which, though unlawful, must none the less be taxed, if only for the sake of ensuring, in the name of fiscal neutrality, that the criminal is not treated more favourably than the legitimate trader'.

Thus the illegal sale of drugs is not a supply for VAT purposes (*Mol v Inspecteur der Invoerrechten Accijnzen, CJEC 1988, [1989] BVC 205*) but the supply of counterfeit perfume is. See *R v Goodwin and Unstead CA, [1997] STC 22, CJEC [1998] STC 699.* The prohibition on such products stems from the fact that they infringe intellectual property rights and is conditional not absolute (as in the case of drugs and counterfeit money). There is scope for competition between counterfeit perfumes and perfumes which are traded lawfully and although supply of the former is unlawful, such perfume is not liable to seizure in the hands of the final customer. The unlawful operation of a form of roulette was similarly held to be a supply for VAT purposes in *Fischer v Finanzamt Donaueschingen, CJEC [1998] STC 708.* However, although the unlawful playing of a game of chance is a supply, it is not taxable where the corresponding activity is exempt when carried on lawfully by a licensed casino.

De Voil Indirect Tax Service. See V3.102-104.

64.3   SUPPLIES OF GOODS

EC legislation. See 22.7 EUROPEAN COMMUNITY LEGISLATION.

UK legislation. The Treasury may, by Order, deem any transaction to be a supply of services and not a supply of goods (or vice versa). [*VATA 1994, s 5(3)*]. Subject to this, the following supplies are to be treated as supplies of goods.

(*a*)   **Any transfer of the whole property in goods.** [*VATA 1994, 4 Sch 1(1)*]. This means the transfer of ownership of the goods. Where there are doubts about whether title has been transferred, it is important to ascertain the intention of the parties by looking at the wording of any agreement/contract, the conduct of the parties and the particular circumstances. It also usually means the transfer of both title and possession of, or control over, the goods.

If possession is transferred but title is retained (e.g. where goods are let out on hire) this is a supply of services (see 64.4 below). However, if possession is transferred in circumstances where title would normally pass but does not because the holder of the goods did not have good title (e.g. the sale of stolen goods) this is a supply of goods as if title had passed. See *C & E Commrs v Oliver QB 1979, [1980] STC 73.*

(C & E Manual V1-3, Chapter 2A paras 1.4, 2.2).

The transfer of an undivided share of property is a supply of services (see 64.4 below). For the distinction, see *Sir John Astor, [1981] VATTR 1974 (1030)*.

(*b*) **The transfer of possession of goods** under an agreement for the sale of the goods or under agreements which expressly contemplate that the property also will pass at some time in the future (determined by, or ascertainable from, the agreements but in any case not later than when the goods are fully paid for). [*VATA 1994, 4 Sch 1(2)*]. Where the conditions for future transfer are not satisfied, the supply is a supply of services (see 64.4 below).

Supplies under hire purchase contracts, conditional sale agreements and reservation of title agreements are thus supplies of goods. The simple hire or lease of goods, on the other hand, does not envisage the future transfer of title and is a supply of services. However, there a many other types of agreement where the distinction is not clear cut. In cases of doubt it is necessary to look at both the written agreement and the intention of any overall scheme operated. *EC 6th Directive, Art 5(4)* provides that there is a supply of goods where 'in the normal course of events' ownership will pass at the latest upon payment of the final instalment. Some final payments are referred to as 'option payments' where the customer has an option whether to purchase or not. Where these payments are very small, it is very unlikely that the customer would not take up the option and 'in the normal course of events' title will pass. An agreement with such an option is likely to be a single supply of goods at the outset.

(C & E Manual V1-3, Chapter 2A paras 1.4, 2.6).

(*c*) **The supply of any form of power, heat, refrigeration or ventilation.** [*VATA 1994, 4 Sch 3*].

(*d*) **The grant, assignment or surrender of a 'major interest' in land.** [*VATA 1994, 4 Sch 4*]. See 42.1 LAND AND BUILDINGS for the definition of '*major interest*'.

(*e*) **Disposal of business assets.** There is a supply of goods where goods forming part of the assets of a business are transferred or disposed of, by or under the directions of the person carrying on the business, so as no longer to form part of those assets (whether or not for consideration). [*VATA 1994, 4 Sch 5(1)*]. This includes

- the sale of assets (e.g. fixed assets);

- assets permanently taken into private use; and

- assets given away.

Business gifts and industrial samples are excluded provided certain conditions are met. [*VATA 1994, 4 Sch 5(2)(3); FA 1996, s 33; FA 1998, s 21*]. See 47.4 OUTPUT TAX for business gifts, 47.5 OUTPUT TAX for private use of business assets and 47.9 OUTPUT TAX for samples.

Land. Where the business assets include land,

- the grant or assignment of a major interest in the land, or

- the grant or assignment of any interest in, right over or licence to occupy the land concerned otherwise than for a consideration

is a supply of goods. Any other supply of the land is a supply of services.

[*VATA 1994, 4 Sch 9*].

De Voil Indirect Tax Service. See V3.211.

(*f*) **Transfers of own goods between EC countries.** There is a supply of goods where, in a case not falling within (*e*) above, goods forming part of the assets of any business are removed in the course of that business from one EC country by or under the directions of the person carrying on the business and taken to another EC country. This applies whether or not the removal is, or is connected with, a transaction for a consideration. [*VATA 1994, 4 Sch 6*]. There are, however, a number of exceptions and special rules. See 23.23 EUROPEAN COMMUNITY: SINGLE MARKET for full details.

(*g*) **Sales in satisfaction of a debt.** Where in the case of a business carried on by a taxable person, goods forming part of the assets of the business are, under any power exercisable by another person, sold by the other person in or towards satisfaction of a debt owed by the taxable person, they are deemed to be supplied by the taxable person in the course or furtherance of his business. [*VATA 1994, 4 Sch 7*]. Land forming part of the assets of the business is treated as if it were goods and any sale includes a reference to a grant or assignment of any interest in, right over or licence to occupy the land concerned. [*VATA 1994, 4 Sch 9*].

The above provisions only apply if the creditor has the power in law to sell the goods. It does not apply, for example, where the seller has illegally repossessed (i.e. stolen) the goods. (C & E Manual V1-3, Chapter 2A para 4.8).

See 2.18 ACCOUNTING PERIODS AND RETURNS for the statement to be furnished to C & E by the person exercising the power.

(*h*) **Deemed supplies on ceasing to be a taxable person.** Where a person ceases to be a taxable person, any goods then forming part of the assets of a business carried on by him are (subject to certain exceptions) deemed to be supplied by him in the course of furtherance of his business immediately before he ceases to be a taxable person. [*VATA 1994, 4 Sch 8*]. See 59.27 REGISTRATION for further details.

(*i*) **Self-supplies.** Where specific goods taken possession of or produced by a person in the course or furtherance of his business are neither supplied to another person nor incorporated in other goods produced in the course or furtherance of that business but are used by him for the purpose of the business, the Treasury have power, by Order, to provide that the goods are deemed to be supplied *to* him for the purpose of the business and *by* him in the course or furtherance of it. [*VATA 1994, s 5(5), 6(11)*]. Orders have been made in respect of printed matter (see 62.2 SELF-SUPPLY) motor cars (see 45.6 MOTOR CARS) and certain construction services (see 42.43 LAND AND BUILDINGS).

(*j*) **Water.** The supply of water insofar as it is not otherwise a supply of goods is to be treated as a supply of goods (and not services). [*SI 1989/1114*].

Returned goods and repossessions. If goods supplied are later returned to the supplier for any reason, the VAT treatment of the act of returning the goods depends on whether title to the goods has passed or not.

• *If goods are returned because they are faulty or not in accordance with the sales contract*, the original transaction may be voided. The transfer of title is cancelled and neither the original sale of the faulty or unsatisfactory goods nor their return is a supply. If the goods are replaced without further charge, this is strictly speaking a new supply although it is common practice, usually accepted by C & E, for the original invoice to remain unaltered.

If the faulty or unsatisfactory goods are repaired or improved for the customer and this work is performed in order to meet the original contract, the work is part of that original supply.

• *If goods are returned where title has passed* and the transfer is not cancelled as above, title passes back to the supplier and a second supply is made.

- *If an agreement within (b) above is terminated prematurely and the goods are repossessed*, such a later event cannot change the nature of a transaction. The agreement was a supply of goods for VAT purposes at the outset and this does not change. However, the repossession of the goods is neither a supply of goods (as title has not yet passed) nor a supply of services (as there is no consideration).

(C & E Manual V1-3, Chapter 2A paras 2.3, 2.7).

De Voil Indirect Tax Service. See V3.112.

64.4 **SUPPLIES OF SERVICES**

EC legislation. See 22.8 EUROPEAN COMMUNITY LEGISLATION.

UK legislation. Anything which is not a supply of goods but is done for a consideration (including, if so done, the granting, assignment or surrender of any right) is a supply of services. The Treasury may however, by Order, deem any transaction to be treated as a supply of goods and not a supply of services (or vice versa). [*VATA 1994, s 5(2)(b)(3)*]. Subject to this, the following supplies are to be treated as supplies of services.

(*a*) **The transfer of any undivided share of the property in goods.** [*VATA 1994, 4 Sch 1(1)*]. This refers to goods that can be owned equally by more than one person, i.e. where the title to the goods is shared. If all the shares in equally-owned goods are simultaneously sold to one person, there is a supply of goods, but if only one of the part shares is sold, title to the goods does not pass to the new owner of the part-share. As title does not pass, this supply is not of goods but of services. The most common example of an undivided share in property is a part-share ('nomination') in a racehorse. (C & E Manual V1-3, Chapter 2A para 2.4).

Unascertained (unallocated) goods. Unallocated goods are goods which remain an unidentifiable part of a larger stock of goods held by a supplier as opposed to 'allocated' goods which are set apart and earmarked as belonging to, or reserved for, a specific customer. Where goods are sold but are never allocated, title in the goods does not pass so the supply is one of services and not of goods. (C & E Manual V1-3, Chapter 2A para 2.11).

Fiscal warehousing. As an exception to this general rule, the transfer of any undivided share of property in eligible goods where the supply is relieved from VAT under the fiscal warehousing regime is treated as a supply of goods and not a supply of services. See 70.15 and 70.16 WAREHOUSED GOODS AND FREE ZONES.

(*b*) **The transfer of possession of goods** where the conditions in 64.3(*b*) above are not satisfied. [*VATA 1994, 4 Sch 1(1)*]. Included is the hire, lease, rental or loan of goods.

(*c*) **Work done on another person's goods.** With effect from 1 January 1996, any work done on another person's goods is a supply of services. (Previously, where the treatment or process changed the character of the goods resulting in new or different goods, the person performing the process made a supply of goods.) Where the work produces goods, the services can be zero-rated if the goods produced are zero-rated goods. See 72.3 ZERO-RATED SUPPLIES.

(*d*) **Non-business use of goods and services.** Where, by or under the direction of a person carrying on a business, goods held or used for the purposes of the business are put to private or non-business use, whether or not for a consideration, that is a supply of services. [*VATA 1994, 4 Sch 5(4)*]. Similarly, where a person carrying on a business puts services supplied to the business to any private or non-business use for no consideration, that is a supply of services. [*SI 1993/1507*].

See 47.5 OUTPUT TAX for further details.

(e) **Exchange units**. The exchange of a reconditioned article for an unserviceable article of a similar kind by a person who regularly offers, in the course or furtherance of his business, to provide a reconditioning facility by that means. [*SI 1995/1268, Art 6*]. VAT must be accounted for on the full amount charged for the exchange unit. If the charge to the customer is reduced by giving a refund when the unserviceable article is handed in, the procedure in 40.15 INVOICES should be adopted.

If the exchange is not part of the person's normal business practice (e.g. where, on a 'one-off' basis, a serviceable article is exchanged for an unserviceable one) or if goods are exchanged for other goods at a reduced price in any other circumstances, the transaction is a supply of goods and should be treated as a part-exchange. (C & E Notice 700, para 3.7).

(f) **Services received from abroad**. Where a person who belongs abroad supplies certain services to a person who belongs in the UK for the purposes of any business carried on by him and the place of supply of those services is in the UK, the same consequences apply as if the taxable person had himself supplied the services in the UK in the course or furtherance of his business and that supply were a taxable supply. See 39.4 INTERNATIONAL SERVICES.

De Voil Indirect Tax Service. See V3.113.

64.5 **SUPPLIES OF NEITHER GOODS NOR SERVICES**

The following transactions are treated as neither a supply of goods nor a supply of services.

(a) **Transfer of a business as a going concern**. The supply by a person of the assets of his business to another person to whom he transfers his business (or part thereof) as a going concern (provided certain conditions are satisfied). See 8.10 *et seq.* BUSINESS.

(b) **The assignment of rights under a HP or conditional sales agreement**, and the goods comprised therein, by the owner to a bank or other financial institution. See 27.20 FINANCE.

(c) **Repossession of goods**. The sale of certain goods by a person, including a finance company, who has repossessed them under the terms of a finance agreement or by an insured in settlement of a claim under an insurance policy (provided certain conditions are met). See 27.22 FINANCE.

(d) **Groups of companies**. Where a group registration is in force, most supplies of goods or services by a member of the group to another member of the group are disregarded for VAT purposes. See 31.4 GROUPS OF COMPANIES.

(e) **Supplies of dutiable goods in warehouse**. Where imported goods subject to duty are supplied while warehoused in bond, the supply is disregarded for VAT purposes if the goods are supplied before payment of the duty to which they are subject. See 70.4 WAREHOUSED GOODS AND FREE ZONES.

(f) **Motor cars**. In addition to the sale of motor cars within (c) above,

- the disposal of a motor car for no consideration (e.g. as scrap) where, on any previous supply or importation, input tax on the motor car in question has been excluded from credit; and

- the letting on hire of a motor vehicle for less than full consideration or the making available of a motor car (otherwise than by letting) to any person for private use.

See 45.5 MOTOR CARS.

(g) **Companies organised in divisions.** Transactions between divisions of the same corporate body are not supplies for VAT purposes. See 59.30 REGISTRATION.

(h) **Supplies by pawnbrokers.** The supply by a taxable person of goods the property in which passed to him as pawnee by virtue of *Consumer Credit Act 1974, s 120(1)(a)* where the supply is to a person who was the pawnor of those goods and the supply is made not later than three months after the taxable person acquired the property in the goods. [*SI 1986/896*]. See 47.16 OUTPUT TAX for supplies generally by pawnbrokers.

(i) **Temporary importations.** Sales of temporarily imported goods provided the goods remain eligible for temporary importation arrangements and the supply is to a person established outside the EC. [*SI 1992/3130*].

Additionally, the sale *by auction* of

(i) second-hand goods temporarily imported with a view to sale by auction, and

(ii) works of art temporarily imported for exhibition with a view to possible sale by auction

is treated as outside the scope of VAT. [*SI 1995/958*]. See 34.30 IMPORTS.

(j) **Second-hand goods scheme.** The removal of goods to the UK under a supply to a person in the UK made by a person in another EC country who accounts for VAT there on the profit margin under the laws of that country similar to the margin scheme in the UK. [*SI 1995/1268, Art 8*]. No VAT is chargeable on such a supply in the UK and the goods may be sold under the margin scheme. See 61.7 SECOND–HAND GOODS.

(o) **Agents acting in their own name in relation to second-hand goods.** Services provided by an agent acting in his own name to the purchaser of second-hand goods where the consideration for the services is taken into account in calculating the price at which the agent obtained the goods. [*SI 1995/1268, Art 9*]. See 61.26 SECOND–HAND GOODS.

(p) **Auctioneers in relation to second-hand goods.** Services provided by an auctioneer acting in his own name to the vendor or purchaser of second-hand goods where the consideration for the services is taken into account in calculating the price at which the auctioneer obtained, or as the case may be, sold the goods. [*SI 1995/1268, Art 10*]. See 61.59 SECOND–HAND GOODS.

De Voil Indirect Tax Service. See V3.114.

64.6 **SINGLE AND MULTIPLE SUPPLIES**

A particular transaction may consists of a number of elements which may or may not be separate supplies. It may be a combination of two or more goods (e.g. food in luxury packaging), two or more services (e.g. washing and drying facilities provided in a launderette) or goods and services (e.g. the sale of a programme including admission to an event).

For such transactions, it is therefore necessary to distinguish between

• a 'single' (or 'composite') supply, i.e. where there is one overall type of supply (either goods or services) and one VAT liability; and

• a 'multiple' (or 'mixed') supply, i.e. where the two or more components are separate supplies, each of which is either a supply of goods or services and each of which has its own VAT liability.

In *British United Provident Association Ltd v C & E Commrs (and cross-appeal); Wellington Private Hospital Ltd v C & E Commrs CA, [1997] STC 445* Millett LJ held that the proper question to ask is whether one element of the transaction is so dominated by another element of the transaction as to lose any separate identity as a supply for fiscal purposes, leaving the latter, the dominant element of the transaction, as the only supply. If the elements of the transaction were not in this relationship with each other, each remained as a supply in its own right with its separate fiscal consequences. In determining whether what would otherwise be two supplies should be regarded as a single supply, consideration should be given to whether one element was an 'integral' part of the other or was 'ancillary' or 'incidental' to the other. Millett LJ also held that, for VAT purposes, C & E could treat as separate transactions what the contracting parties had treated as a single composite supply but could not join together what the contracting parties had treated as separate.

C & E regard an '*integral*' component as one which is intrinsic, i.e. a part of the whole which is being supplied. Therefore, this includes anything which is essential or necessary (e.g. the engine in a car) or incidental, but goes further to include non-essential elements which are integral to the actual supply being made. An '*incidental*' element of a supply is one which naturally accompanies the main supply, and generally is not a significant part of it. Examples of incidental elements are the instruction booklet accompanying new equipment, e.g. a video recorder, the services of packing/transport and packaging materials. An incidental element is an integral part of the single, overall supply. (C & E Manual V1-3, Chapter 2A para 5.2).

Single supply. Where this is established, no apportionment must be made and the supply as a whole must be considered to determine the VAT liability, if any.

Single supplies have been held to include

- services of a launderette (which cannot be treated as separate supplies of water heat, use of machine, etc., only the single service of washing or drying clothes) (*Mander Laundries Ltd, [1973] VATTR 136 (31)*);

- air travel and any catering supplied during the flight (a single supply of zero-rated transport) (*British Airways plc v C & E Commrs, CA [1990] STC 632*);

- services of a stud farm providing the supply of the keep of a mare with everything that is involved in maintaining her in reasonable condition and safety (a single standard-rated supply so that the supply of animal feeding stuffs included cannot be zero-rated) (*C & E Commrs v DD Scott QB 1977, [1978] STC 191*); and

- a course in dress designing and pattern construction consisting of a folder containing an instruction booklet and instruction sheets, a teaching strip of fabric, some miniature patterns and a fabric requirement planner (although having some unusual features, nevertheless a zero-rated brochure) (*Betty Foster (Fashion Sewing) Ltd, [1976] VATTR 229 (299)*).

For the treatment of delivery charges, see 47.8 OUTPUT TAX.

Two-part tariff. This occurs where there are two or more payments for a single supply. This concept was introduced in *British Railways Board v C & E Commrs CA, [1977] STC 221*) where there were two payments, one for a student card allowing students to buy cut-price travel tickets, and the other which the student made when obtaining the actual ticket. The court held that the two payments were both for the supply of discounted travel paid at different stages, rather than for two separate supplies (of the right to a discount and then discounted travel).

The secondary supply has to be part of the composite supply, not an optional extra or subject to availability, and both payments have to be made to the same entity for the concept of 'two-part tariff' to be valid. (C & E Manual V1-3, Chapter 2A para 5.3).

Multiple supply. In a multiple supply, even though the supplies are often paid for together, the individual components are not integral to each other and are separate supplies. Common examples of situations where multiple supplies might occur are

- annual subscriptions to the AA (apportionable between the benefits – a magazine, booklet, maps and information, pick-up services, repairs, etc – to which members are entitled (*C & E Commrs v The Automobile Assn QB, [1974] STC 192*);

- fees for correspondence and residential courses (apportionable between the supply of books (zero-rated) and tuition (standard-rated))(*The Rapid Results College Ltd, [1973] VATTR 197 (48), LSA (Full Time Courses) Ltd, [1983] VATTR 256 (1507)* and *Force One Training Ltd (13619)*). Compare, however, *EW (Computer Training) Ltd (5453)* where manuals were held to form part of a single supply of standard-rated tuition and *International News Syndicate Ltd (14425)* where the small element of external tuition was held to be incidental and the whole supply treated as zero-rated;

- children's colouring books issued with felt tip pens, where the pens are not restricted in use to the book they are sold with;

- a book with an accompanying audio or video tape, each of which may be used independently of the book, and which require particular equipment for their use;

- consideration under contracts providing for both the hire of a television set from a rental company and the insurance of the set by an insurance company within the same VAT group (*Thorn EMI plc; Granada plc, [1993] VATTR 94 (9782)*); and

- payment for programmes sold to persons attending stamp fairs, etc. for which no admission charges as such are made (*Jarmain, [1979] VATTR 41 (723)*).

Where all the supplies are liable to VAT at the same rate, there is no problem and output tax due is calculated in the normal way. Where, however, there are a mixture of zero-rated, standard-rated and/or exempt supplies, the value of each supply for VAT purposes must be calculated in order to arrive at the total output tax due. Any calculation of the apportionment of the total price must be fair and justifiable. See 47.3 OUTPUT TAX for alternative computations acceptable to C & E.

De Voil Indirect Tax Service. See V3.105–107.

64.7   **PLACE OF SUPPLY: GENERAL PROVISIONS**

Having determined that a supply of goods or services has taken place, the second conditions to be satisfied if the transaction is to fall within the scope of UK VAT is that the supply takes place within the UK (see 64.1 above). The place of supply rules are different for goods and for services. See 64.3-64.5 above for a consideration of what constitutes a supply of goods and a supply of services (or neither).

EC law relating to the place of supply of goods is contained in *EC 6th Directive, Arts 8, 28b(B)* (see 22.9 and 22.36 EUROPEAN COMMUNITY LEGISLATION). EC law relating to the place of supply of services is contained in *EC 6th Directive, Arts 9, 28b(C)-(F)* (see 22.10 and 22.37-22.39 EUROPEAN COMMUNITY LEGISLATION).

UK law relating to the place of supply is contained in *VATA 1994, ss 7, 9*. The Treasury are empowered to vary the normal rules by statutory instrument [*VATA 1994, s 7(11)*] and to date three main Orders have been made.

- *VAT (Tour Operators) Order 1987 (SI 1987/1806)* which relates to supplies of designated travel services by tour operators and other persons who buy in and resell travel facilities (see 66.5 TOUR OPERATORS' MARGIN SCHEME);

- *VAT (Place of Supply of Services) Order 1992 (SI 1992/3121)* which has a general impact on the place of supply of services (see 64.18 *et seq.* below); and

- *VAT (Place of Supply of Goods) Order 1992 (SI 1992/3283)* which relates to supplies of goods on board ships, aircraft and trains involved in intra-EC transport (see 64.16 below).

Registration of UK suppliers in other EC countries. Where the place of supply of goods or services is outside the UK, there is no UK VAT liability. However, a UK supplier who makes supplies in another EC country may be liable to register there, subject to the registration rules applicable in that country. If they do not have an establishment there, they may have to appoint a local tax representative to account for VAT on their behalf. UK suppliers must make their own enquiries about registration in other EC countries with the authorities of the country concerned: C & E cannot advise on the rules applicable in other countries. See 21 EUROPEAN COMMUNITY: GENERAL for the addresses of VAT authorities in other EC countries.

Registration of traders who have no place of business in the UK. Similarly, a trader belonging outside the UK with no place of business here may be liable to UK VAT registration where the place of supply of those goods or services is in the UK. See 48 OVERSEAS TRADERS for further details.

Territory of the UK and EC. The UK comprises Great Britain, Northern Ireland and the waters within twelve nautical miles of their coastlines. For VAT purposes it includes the Isle of Man but not the Channel Islands or Gibraltar. See 21.2 EUROPEAN COMMUNITY: GENERAL for the VAT territory of the EC.

64.8   **PLACE OF SUPPLY OF GOODS**

Subject to certain simplification procedures (see 64.17 below) and special provisions relating to warehoused goods (see 70.2 to 70.11 WAREHOUSED GOODS AND FREE ZONES), the provisions relating to the place of supply of goods are to be found in *VATA 1994, s 7* (see 64.9-64.14 below) and *The VAT (Place of Supply of Goods) Order 1992, SI 1992/3283* (see 64.15 below). It should be noted that *Sec 7* has a hierarchical structure. The place of supply of any goods may be determined by working through the rules in 64.9-64.14 below in order until one applicable to the particular supply in question is reached. [*VATA 1994, s 7(1); FA 1996, 3 Sch 2*].

When trying to determine the place of supply of goods, the following points should be borne in mind.

- The place of supply rules can only apply if there has been a supply or a deemed supply of goods. This is particularly important when considering some intra-EC movements which are not regarded as supplies (see, for example, 23.24 EUROPEAN COMMUNITY: SINGLE MARKET for temporary movements of own goods to other EC countries).

- When applying the place of supply of goods rules, other data (e.g. the time of supply, invoicing routes, payment arrangements and where the parties involved belong) should be ignored.

- Different rules apply for supplies of services (see 64.18 *et seq.* below).

- Where there are a number of supplies but only one movement of goods, the removal of the goods can only relate to one supply.

- EC countries have introduced simplification procedures for certain situations involving triangular trade or installed and assembled goods. These adapt the normal rules to avoid unnecessary registrations whilst achieving the desired result. See 64.17 below.

The terms 'removed' and 'removal' are used in the UK place of supply rules. They are not legally defined and should be treated as having their ordinary and everyday meaning, i.e. the goods are physically moved from one location to another.

(C & E Manual V1-4, Chapter 2A paras 2.2, 2.11).

De Voil Indirect Tax Service. See V3.171–177.

64.9   Goods which do not leave or enter the UK

Where the supply of any goods does not involve their removal from or to the UK, they are treated as supplied

- in the UK if they are in the UK; and

- otherwise as supplied outside the UK.

[*VATA 1994, s 7(2)*].

The first situation covers the vast majority of transactions subject to VAT. The second situation includes sales on the high seas where the goods do not come to the UK and supplies sourced from outside the UK and delivered to a country other than the UK. In these cases it is important to disregard extraneous facts such as where the order was placed, the invoice route or how and where payment was made. (C & E Manual V1-4, Chapter 2A para 2.3).

64.10   Installed or assembled goods

Goods whose place of supply is not determined under 64.9 above are treated as supplied

- in the UK where their supply involves their installation or assembly at a place in the UK to which they are removed; and

- outside the UK where their supply involves their installation or assembly at a place outside the UK to which they are removed.

[*VATA 1994, s 7(3)*].

By concession, where a *one-off* supply of installed or assembled goods would be treated as made in the UK, it is treated as made outside the UK if

- the supplier is not registered for VAT in the UK;

- no further UK business is anticipated;

- the goods are imported from outside the EC; and

- the customer acts as importer and shows the full value of the goods, including installation and assembly costs on the import entry.

(C & E Business Brief 1/98, 7 January 1998).

The terms 'installation' and 'assembly' should be given their ordinary and everyday meaning. Typically, the supply will involve complex machinery or equipment requiring the expertise of the manufacturer to make it operational. However, the terms can cover a wide variety of situations, including those where the installation element by the manufacturer is minimal. It depends entirely on whether the contract between supplier and customer requires any element of installation or assembly of the goods by the supplier. Where there are separate contracts with the same supplier to supply the goods and to perform the installation or assembly, C & E will normally treat them as being for a single supply of installed or assembled goods.

If the main supplier sub-contracts the work of installation or assembly to a third party, the place of supply for the main supplier is where the goods are installed or assembled by the sub-contractor.

(C & E Manual V1-4, Chapter 2A para 2.4).

See 64.17 below for details of a simplified procedure which eligible EC traders can use to avoid the need to register for VAT in the UK.

64.11   Distance sales to the UK

Goods whose place of supply is not determined under 64.9 or 64.10 above are treated as supplied in the UK where

(*a*)   the supply involves the removal of the goods to the UK by or under the direction of the supplier;

(*b*)   the supply is a transaction under which the goods are acquired in the UK from another EC country by a person who is not registered or required to be registered under *VATA 1994* ;

(*c*)   the supplier is, or is liable to be, registered under *VATA 1994, 2 Sch* by virtue of his distance sales in the UK, see 59.11 REGISTRATION (or would be so liable if he were not registrable under *VATA 1994, 1 Sch* in respect of UK supplies, see 59.1 REGISTRATION); and

(*d*)   the supply is neither

- a supply of goods consisting of a new means of transport (see 23.31 EUROPEAN COMMUNITY: SINGLE MARKET); nor

- anything which is treated as a supply by virtue only of *VATA 1994, 4 Sch 5(1)* (disposal of business assets, see 64.3(*e*) above or *VATA 1994, 4 Sch 6* (transfer of own goods between EC countries, see 23.23 EUROPEAN COMMUNITY: SINGLE MARKET).

[*VATA 1994, s 7(4)*].

The provisions in (*c*) above apply where

- the supplier has exceeded the threshold for supplies within (*a*) and (*b*) above to customers in the UK (currently £70,000) and becomes liable to register; or

- the supplier has distance sales below the threshold but has opted to become registered in the UK; or

- the goods are subject to excise duty in which case the threshold does not apply.

(C & E Manual V1-4, Chapter 2A para 2.5).

64.12   Distance sales from the UK

Goods whose place of supply is not determined under 64.9-64.11 above and which do not consist of a new means of transport (see 23.31 EUROPEAN COMMUNITY: SINGLE MARKET) are treated as supplied outside the UK where

(*a*)   the supply involves the removal of the goods to another EC country by or under the direction of the supplier;

(*b*)   the person who makes the supply is taxable in another EC country;

(*c*) the provisions of the law of that other EC country corresponding to the provisions under 64.11(*c*) above make the supplier liable to be registered and account for VAT in that country.

This does not, however, apply where the liability under (*c*) above depends on the exercise by any person of an option in the UK corresponding to such an option made by an overseas trader under 59.12(*a*) REGISTRATION unless that person has given (and not withdrawn) a notification to C & E that his supplies are to be treated as taking place outside the UK.

[*VATA 1994, s 7(5)*].

The provisions in (*c*) above apply where

- the supplier has exceeded the threshold for supplies within (*a*) and (*b*) above to customers in the other EC country (currently either 35,000 ECU (£24,000) or 100,000 ECU (£70,000) depending on the EC country concerned) and becomes liable to register in that country; or

- the supplier has distance sales below that threshold but has opted to become registered in that country; or

- the goods are subject to excise duty in that country in which case the threshold does not apply.

(C & E Manual V1-4, Chapter 2A para 2.5).

64.13   **Imported goods**

Goods whose place of supply is not determined under 64.9-64.12 above are treated as supplied in the UK where

(*a*) their supply involves their being imported from a place outside the EC; and

(*b*) the supplier is the person by whom, or under whose direction, they are so imported.

[*VATA 1994, s 7(6)*].

The place of supply of imported goods is therefore determined by reference to the importer.

- Where the supplier imports the goods, the place of supply is the UK (under the above rules).

- Where the customer imports the goods, the place of supply is outside the UK (under 64.14(*b*) below).

Chain supplies. For a chain of supplies, it is necessary to determine who was responsible for importation of the goods.

Example

A supplies goods to B who re-supplies the goods to C who, in turn, re-supplies the goods to D. The goods are imported into the UK from a third country and remain in the UK.

- If A is the importer, all three supplies are in the UK.

- If B is the importer, the supply from A to B is outside the UK and the supplies from B to C and C to D are in the UK.

- If C is the importer, the supplies from A to B and B to C are outside the UK and the supply from C to D is in the UK.

- If D is the importer, all three supplies are outside the UK.

It is irrelevant where, or to whom, the goods were delivered in the UK after importation, where the goods were at the time of any of the supplies, and what were the invoice and payment dates.

(C & E Manual V1-4, Chapter 2A para 2.6).

64.14 **Other goods which leave or enter the UK**

Goods whose place of supply is not determined under 64.9–64.13 above but whose supply involves their removal to or from the UK are treated

(*a*) as supplied in the UK where their supply involves their removal from the UK without also involving their previous removal to the UK; and

(*b*) as supplied outside the UK in any other case.

[*VATA 1994, s 7(7)*].

These provisions cover

- under (*a*) above,

   (i) the removal of goods from the UK to another EC country (other than distance sales within 64.12 above); and

   (ii) the export of goods from the UK; and

- under (*b*) above,

   (i) the removal of goods to the UK from another EC country (other than distance sales within 64.11 above); and

   (ii) the importation of goods from outside the EC where the UK customer is the person responsible for the importation (see 64.13 above).

Intra-EC chain supplies. Where a number of supplies are linked, it is necessary to determine which supply involved the removal of the goods from one EC country to another. Only one supply can relate to the removal and if there is doubt it should be resolved by reference to the terms of the contract.

Example

French company A supplies goods located in France to another French company B which re-supplies the goods to a UK company C which, in turn, re-supplies the goods to another UK company D. The goods physically pass direct from A in France to D in the UK.

Subject to below

- if the contract between A and B required delivery of the goods to D in the UK then

   (i) the supply from A to B is outside the UK under (*b*) above (because it involves removal of the goods to the UK); and

   (ii) the supplies from B to C and from C to D are in the UK under 64.9 above; and

- if the contract between B and C required B to transport the goods to the UK then

   (i) the supply from A to B would be outside the UK under 64.9 above;

   (ii) the supply from B to C would be outside the UK under (*b*) above; and

   (iii) the supply from C to D would be in the UK under 64.9 above.

The time of supply, invoicing arrangements and payment, etc. are not relevant when determining the place of supply.

Note, however, that the above analysis gives the strict interpretation of the law. In such intra-EC situations, the C & E adopt a pragmatic approach if it gives a reasonable result. In the above scenario, if A and B are only registered in France and C and D are only registered in the UK, then they are content for the supply between B and C to be treated as the intra-EC supply whichever party was contractually bound to transport the goods to the UK. Most EC countries adopt a similarly pragmatic approach but, unlike the simplification procedures in 64.17 below, it has no statutory basis.

(C & E Manual V1-4, Chapter 2A paras 2.7, 2.8).

64.15 Goods temporarily leaving the UK in the course of a removal to another place in the UK

For the purposes of 64.9-64.14 above, where, in the course of their removal from a place in the UK to another place in the UK, goods leave and re-enter the UK, the removal is not treated as a removal from or to the UK. [*VATA 1994, s 7(8)*]. This would occur, for example, where goods moved from Northern Ireland to England passed through the Irish Republic.

64.16 Goods supplied on board intra-EC transport

Except for goods supplied as part of a 'pleasure cruise', goods which are supplied on board a ship, aircraft or train in the course of 'community transport' are treated as supplied at the 'point of departure' except that goods supplied for consumption on board are treated as supplied outside the EC.

'*Pleasure cruise*' includes a cruise wholly or partly for the purposes of education or training.

'*Community transport*' means transportation of passengers between a point of departure and a point of arrival in the course of which there is a stop in an EC country other than that of the point of departure and there is no stop in a country which is not an EC country.

[*SI 1992/3283*].

64.17 Simplification procedures

The measures outlined below may, in certain circumstances, be legitimately used to avoid unnecessary VAT registration in the UK. They do not alter the basic place of supply rules but are mechanisms to vary the normal requirements so as to achieve the desired result.

(*a*) **Import agents acting for an overseas supplier who has no place of business in the UK.** An overseas trader who imports goods into the UK for onward sale is making supplies in the UK (see 64.13 above). Where the overseas trader is not liable to register for VAT in the UK he may, as an alternative to registration, appoint a UK-resident agent who is registered for VAT to act on his behalf. See 48.3 OVERSEAS TRADERS for further details.

(*b*) **Installed or assembled goods.** The place of supply for installed or assembled goods is the place where installation or assembly takes place (see 64.10 above). To avoid an overseas person making such a supply in the UK having to register for VAT in the UK, the UK customer can account for the VAT as acquisition VAT if the following conditions are satisfied.

- The goods must be sourced from outside the UK.

- The overseas supplier must be registered for VAT in another EC country and must not be registered, or required to be registered, for VAT in the UK because of other supplies made here.

- The customer must be registered for VAT in the UK.

See 23.28 EUROPEAN COMMUNITY: SINGLE MARKET for full details including notification procedures and invoice and record requirements.

The above only applies to supplies in the UK. Traders making such supplies in other EC countries should contact the appropriate authority in that country.

(*c*) **Triangular EC trade.** In a typical triangular situation, a supplier A in one EC country supplies goods to, and invoices, an intermediary supplier B in another EC country who in turn supplies the goods to, and invoices, a customer C in a third EC country. The goods, however, pass directly from A to C. To avoid having to register for VAT in the country of destination of the goods, B can opt for C to account for the VAT due there provided

- B is not registered, or liable to be registered, in the EC country of destination of the goods but is registered in another EC country; and

- C is registered for VAT in the country of destination.

See 23.22 EUROPEAN COMMUNITY: SINGLE MARKET for full details.

(C & E Manual V1-4, Chapter 2A paras 3.1-3.4).

64.18   **PLACE OF SUPPLY OF SERVICES**

Significance of place of supply. For VAT purposes, the place where a supply is deemed to be made is called the *place of supply*. This is the only place where the supply can be liable to VAT. Thus, where the place of supply of any services is in an EC country, that supply is liable to VAT (if any) in that country and in no other country. If that country is not the UK, the supply is outside the scope of UK VAT. Where the place of supply of any services is outside the EC, that supply is not liable to VAT in any EC country (although local taxes may apply). The significance for a UK business is as follows.

- **If a UK business supplies services and the place of supply is the UK**, subject to the VAT registration limits the supply is standard-rated, zero-rated or exempt (as the case may be) and any VAT due must be accounted for to C & E. This applies regardless of where the customer belongs.

- **If a UK business supplies services and the place of supply is in another EC country**, subject to the registration limits in that country either the UK supplier or the customer is liable to account for any VAT due to the VAT authorities in that country.

(C & E Notice 741, paras 1.4, 1.5).

Place of supply rules. The rules in 64.20-64.31 below must be used to determine the place of supply of services. The basic rule is that services are made where the supplier belongs (see 64.20 below) but this is subject to a number of special rules for

- services relating to land (see 64.21 below);

- certain services which are supplied where physically carried out (see 64.22-64.25 below);

- services falling within *VATA 1994, 5 Sch 1-8* (see 64.26-64.28 below);

- transport services (see 64.29 below);

- the hiring of means of transport (see 64.30 below); and

- certain services of intermediaries (see 64.31 below).

In addition to these rules, special place of supply rules apply

- where travel, hotel, holiday and certain other supplies of a kind enjoyed by travellers are bought in from third parties and resold as principal under the tour operators' margin scheme (see 66.5 TOUR OPERATORS' MARGIN SCHEME); and

- in relation to sales of securities, and brokers' services in connection therewith, where the identity of the purchaser (and hence the place of belonging) is not known (see 27.1 FINANCE).

Rights to services. In relation to any services performed after 30 June 1997, the place of supply of a 'right to services' is the same as the place of supply of the services to which the right relates. This applies whether or not the right is exercised. A *'right to services'* includes any right, option or priority with respect to the supply of services and the supply of an interest deriving from any right to services. [*SI 1992/3121, Art 21; SI 1997/1524, Art 5*].

Anti-avoidance provisions. Where any statutory instrument made after 16 March 1998 changes the place of supply of any services to the UK with effect from a specified commencement date,

- invoices and other documents issued before the commencement date are disregarded in determining the time of supply of any services which, by virtue of the statutory instrument, would be treated as supplied in the UK if their time of supply occurred on or after the commencement date;

- any payment received by the supplier before the commencement date which relates to services performed on or after the commencement date is treated as if it were received on the commencement date;

- any payment received by the supplier on or after the commencement date which relates to services performed before the commencement date is treated as if it were received before that date; and

- a payment in respect of any services is to be taken as relating to the period of time during which those services are performed. Where a payment is received in respect of a period spanning the commencement date, an apportionment must be made on a just and reasonable basis and the payment is taken as relating to a time before that date to the extent that it is attributable to services performed before that date. The remainder of the payment (if any) is taken as relating to times on or after the commencement date.

[*VATA 1994, s 97A; FA 1998, s 22*].

Input tax recovery. Input tax attributable to certain supplies of services may be recoverable even though, under the place of supply rules, the supply is deemed to take place outside the UK and is outside the scope of UK VAT. See 35.3 INPUT TAX.

De Voil Indirect Tax Service. See V3.181–195.

64.19   Place of belonging

Services which fall under the basic place of supply rule (see 64.20 below) are supplied where the supplier belongs and services falling within *VATA 1994, 5 Sch 1–8* (see 64.26 below) are, in certain cases, supplied where the recipient belongs. It is therefore necessary to have rules defining the place of belonging of both the supplier and the recipient of a service.

Place of belonging of a supplier/recipient of services. If a supply of services is made to an *individual* and received by him *otherwise than for the purpose of any business carried on by him*, he is treated as belonging in whatever country he has his 'usual place of residence'.

Subject to this special rule for the recipient of services, the supplier/recipient of services is treated as belonging in a country if

(*a*) he has a 'business establishment' or some other 'fixed establishment' in that country and no such establishment elsewhere; or

(*b*) he has no such establishment (there or elsewhere) but his 'usual place of residence' is in that country; or

(*c*) he has such establishments both in that country and elsewhere and the establishment of his

   (i) in the case of a supplier of services, which is most directly concerned with the supply, or

   (ii) in the case of a recipient of services, at which, or for the purposes of which, the services are most directly used or to be used

  is in that country.

A supplier/recipient of services carrying on a business through a branch or agency in any country is treated as having a business establishment there.

[*VATA 1994, s 9*].

Business establishment is not defined in the legislation but is taken by C & E to mean the principal place of business. It is usually the head office, headquarters or 'seat' from which the business is run. There can only be one such place and it may take the form of an office, showroom or factory. Following the tribunal decision in *DFDS A/S (12588)* which related to similar legal provisions under the Tour Operators' Margin Scheme, C & E accept that where a trader has a headquarters in one country and other premises located in different countries, the headquarters is the 'business establishment' for the purposes of the place of supply rules, and the premises in other countries are 'other fixed establishments'. (The case was subsequently referred to the CJEC but this aspect was not disputed.)

Examples

• A business has its headquarters in the UK and branches in France, Italy and Germany. Its business establishment is in the UK.

• A company is incorporated in the UK but trades entirely from its head office in Bermuda. Its business establishment is in Bermuda.

(C & E Notice 741, paras 2.3, 2.4; C & E Manual V1-4, Chapter 2B para 5.5).

Fixed establishment is not defined in the legislation but is taken by C & E to mean an establishment (other than the business establishment) which has both the technical and human resources necessary for providing and receiving services on a permanent basis. A business may therefore have several fixed establishments, including a branch of the business. An agency may also be a fixed establishment but a trader is not regarded as carrying on business through an agency if *either* acts merely as an intermediary in bringing together customer and provider but is not directly involved in the supply chain *or* supplies only incidental elements such as clerical and typing services.

Examples

- An overseas business sets up a branch comprising staff and offices in the UK to provide services. The UK branch is a fixed establishment.

- An overseas television company sends staff and equipment to the UK to film for a week. The temporary presence of human and technical resources does not create a fixed establishment in the UK.

- A company with a business establishment overseas owns a property in the UK which it leases to tenants. The property does not in itself create a fixed establishment. However, if the company has UK offices and staff or appoints a UK agency to carry on its business by managing the property, this creates a fixed establishment in the UK.

- An overseas business contracts with UK customers to provide services. It has no human or technical resources in the UK and therefore sets up a UK subsidiary to act in its name to provide those services. The overseas business has a fixed establishment in the UK created by the agency of the subsidiary.

- A company is incorporated in the UK but trades entirely overseas from its head office in the USA, which is its business establishment. The UK registered office is a fixed establishment. See *Binder Hamlyn, [1983] VATTR 171 (1439)*.

- A UK company acts as the operating member of a consortium for offshore exploitation of oil or gas using a fixed production platform. The rig is a fixed establishment of the operating member.

(C & E Notice 741, paras 2.5, 2.6).

Usual place of residence. A *body corporate* has its usual place of residence where it is legally constituted. [*VATA 1994, s 9(5)(b)*]. C & E interpret this as the country in which its registered office is situated. (C & E Manual V1-4, Chapter 2B para 5.7). The usual place of residence of an *individual* is not defined in the legislation. C & E interpret the phrase according to the ordinary usage of the words, i.e. normally the country where the individual has set up home with his/her family and is in full-time employment. An individual is not resident in a country if only visiting as a tourist.

Examples

- A person lives in the UK, but commutes to France daily for work. He belongs in the UK.

- Overseas forces personnel on a tour of duty in the UK live in rented accommodation with their families. They have homes overseas to which they periodically return on leave. They belong in the UK throughout their tour of duty. See *USAA Ltd (10369)*.

(C & E Notice 741, paras 2.7, 2.8).

See also *Razzak & Mishari (15240)* where the tribunal, distinguishing *USAA Ltd* above, held that an Indian woman, who came to the UK in 1992 and remained here until October 1996 during the course of legal proceedings against a former employer, had her usual place of residence in India throughout that period. C & E disagree with this decision but did not appeal because of the unusual facts and the small amount of VAT involved. (C & E Manual V1-4, Chapter 2B para 5.7).

More than one establishment. For the purposes of (*c*) above, where the supplier/recipient has establishments in more than one country, the supplies made from/received at each establishment must be considered separately. For each supply of services, the establishment which is actually providing/receiving the services is normally the one most directly connected with the supply but all facts should be considered including

- for suppliers, from which establishment the services are actually provided;

- for recipients, at which establishment the services are actually consumed, effectively used or enjoyed;

- which establishment appears on the contracts, correspondence and invoices;

- where directors or others who entered into the contract are permanently based; and

- at which establishment decisions are taken and controls are exercised over the performance of the contract.

However, where an establishment is actually providing/receiving the supply of services, it is normally that establishment which is most directly connected with the supply, even if the contractual position is different.

Where the services are not supplied from/received at a particular establishment, the place of belonging is the country where the business establishment is located.

Examples

- A company whose business establishment is in France contracts with a UK bank to provide French speaking staff for the bank's international desk in London. The French supplier has a fixed establishment in the UK created by a branch, which provides staff to other customers. The French establishment deals directly with the bank without any involvement by the UK branch. The staff are supplied from the French establishment.

- An overseas business establishment contracts with private customers in the UK to provide information. The services are provided and invoiced by its UK branch. Customers' day-to-day contact is with the UK branch and they pay the UK branch. The services are actually supplied from the UK branch which is a fixed establishment.

- A UK supplier contracts to supply advertising services. Its customer has its business establishment in Austria and a fixed establishment in the UK created by its branch. Although day-to-day contact is between the supplier and the UK branch, the Austrian establishment takes all artistic and other decisions about the advertising. The supplies are received at the overseas establishment.

- A UK accountant supplies accountancy services to a UK incorporated company which has its business establishment abroad. However, the services are received in connection with the company's UK tax obligations and therefore the UK fixed establishment, created by the registered office, receives the supply.

- A UK company seconds staff to a customer which has its business establishment in the UK and a fixed establishment in the USA, created by its branch. The supplier is contracted by the UK establishment to provide staff to the USA branch. The supplier invoices the UK establishment and is paid by them. The services are most directly used by the USA branch.

(C & E Notice 741, paras 2.9, 2.10; C & E Business Brief 12/98, 21 May 1998).

Agency. The key test for agency is independence as an agency cannot operate independently of its principal. In deciding independence, what matters is the reality, function and substance, and not any mere name or legal form. Particular regard should be had to the actual arrangements which exist between the *prima facie* agency and its principal, rather than any mere wording in contracts. Where there is no independence, agencies may include a subsidiary acting for its parent principal or a company acting for its associated or unrelated principal. C & E consider that the decisions in *C & E Commrs v DFDS A/S, CJEC [1997] STC 384* and *C & E Commrs v The Chinese Channel (Hong Kong) Ltd QB, [1998] STC* 347 support their policy that a UK agency creates a fixed establishment of its overseas principal where

- it is of a certain minimum size with the permanent human and technical resources necessary for providing (or receiving) services;

- it is not, in function and substance, operating independently of the overseas business; and

- it actually supplies (or receives) the services, i.e. does more than merely bring together customer and provider or supply incidental services such as clerical or typing services.

(C & E Manual V1-4, Chapter 2B para 5.12; C & E Business Brief 12/98, 21 May 1998).

Other case law. In *Faaborg-Gelting Linien A/S v Finanzamt Flensburg, CJEC [1996] STC 774* (which related to meals provided on board Danish ferries travelling between Denmark and Germany) the court held that where, under *EC Sixth Directive, Art 9(1)*, a supply could be treated as taking place at the supplier's business establishment (offices in Denmark) or at another fixed establishment from which the services are supplied (the ferry on which the meals were being provided) then the primary point of reference had to be the former unless that did not lead to a rational result or created a conflict with another EC country. In any case, services cannot be deemed to be supplied at a fixed establishment other than the place where the supplier has established his business unless that fixed establishment is of a certain minimum size and both the human and technical resources necessary for the provision of the particular services are permanently present (*Berkholz v Finanzamt Hamburg-Mitte-Altstadt, CJEC [1985] ECR 2251; [1985] 3 CMLR 667*). See also *ARO Lease BV v Inspecteur der Belastingdienst Grote Ondernemingen Amsterdam, CJEC [1997] STC 1272.*

Securities. See 27.1 FINANCE for a special rule applying where a UK supplier cannot determine the place of belonging of a purchaser of securities.

64.20 Basic rule

Subject to the special rules in 64.21-64.31 below, a supply of services is treated as made

- in the UK if the supplier belongs in the UK; and

- in another country (and not the UK) if the supplier belongs in that other country.

[*VATA 1994, s 7(10)(11)*].

See 64.19 above for the place of belonging of the supplier.

The basic rule will therefore only apply if a supply of services does not fall under any of the special rules in 62.21-64.31 below. Before determining that a supply falls under the basic rule, the exact nature of the services must be identified and considered against those special rules.

Examples of services supplied where the supplier belongs

- Services described as management services where the actual services are not of a type covered by the special rules in 64.21-64.31 below (see, for example, 64.26 below for consultancy, accountancy, legal and financial services).

- Clerical or secretarial services or the provision of office services.

- Archiving services involving the maintenance of documents and records.

- Entertainment services not covered by the special rules in 64.21-64.31 below (see, for example, 64.23 below for live performances). This normally includes services of production assistants, hairdressers and make-up artists for films or television.

- After 31 May 1998, veterinary services (previously treated as supplied where physically carried out under 64.25 below). See C & E Business Brief 12/98, 21 May 1998.

- Broadcasting to subscribers.

(C & E Notice 741, para 3.3).

De Voil Indirect Tax Service. See V3.183.

64.21   **Services relating to land**

The following supplies of services are treated as made where the 'land' in connection with which the supply is made is situated.

(*a*)   The grant, assignment or surrender of

- an interest in or right over land;

- a personal right to call for or be granted such an interest or right; or

- a licence to occupy land or any other contractual right exerciseable over or in relation to land.

(*b*)   Any works of construction, demolition, conversion, reconstruction, alteration, enlargement, repair or maintenance of a building or civil engineering work.

(*c*)   Services such as are supplied by estate agents, auctioneers, architects, surveyors, engineers and others involved in matters relating to land.

[*SI 1992/3121, Art 5*].

'*Land*' includes all forms of land and property (growing crops, buildings, walls, fences, civil engineering works and other structures fixed permanently to the land or sea bed) and plant, machinery or equipment which is an installation or edifice in its own right (e.g. a refinery or fixed oil/gas production platform). Machinery installed in buildings other than as a fixture is normally not regarded as land but as goods. (C & E Notice 741, para 4.2). The Channel Tunnel is land within the UK as far as its mid point (C & E Manual V1-4, Chapter 2B para 7.2).

The services must relate *directly* to specific sites of land. It does not apply if there is only an indirect connection with land, or if the land-related service is only an incidental part of a more comprehensive service.

Examples of services relating to land

- The supply of hotel accommodation.

- The provision of a site for a stand at an exhibition where the exhibitor obtains the right to a defined area of the exhibition hall (see 64.24 below where sites are not defined).

- The supply of plant or machinery, together with an operator, for work on a construction site.

- Under (*c*) above, the management, conveyancing, survey or valuation of property by a solicitor, surveyor or loss adjuster.

- Services connected with oil/gas/mineral exploration or exploitation relating to specific sites of land or the seabed (see 64.23 and 64.26 below where services do not relate to specific sites).

- The surveying (such as seismic, geological or geomagnetic) of land or seabed, including associated data processing services to collate the required information.

- Legal services such as conveyancing or dealing with applications for planning permission.

- Packages of property management services which may include rent collection, arranging repairs and the maintenance of financial accounts.

Examples of services which are not land-related

- Repair and maintenance of machinery which is not installed as a fixture (which is work on goods within 64.25 below).

- The hiring out of civil engineering plant on its own (which is the hire of goods within 64.26 below).

- The secondment of staff to a building site (which is a supply of staff within 64.26 below).

- The legal administration of a deceased person's estate which happens to include property (which are legal services within 64.26 below).

- Advice or information relating to land prices or property markets as they do not relate to specific sites (see 64.26 below).

- Feasibility studies assessing the potential of particular businesses or business potential in a geographic area (which do not relate to a specific property or site and are within 64.26 below).

- Provision of a recording studio where technicians are included as part of the supply (which are engineering services within 64.26 below).

(C & E Notice 741, paras 4.4–4.6).

Overseas suppliers of services relating to UK land. Where a supplier of services relating to land in the UK belongs overseas

- if the recipient of the services is a UK VAT-registered person, the reverse charge procedure applies and the recipient is liable to account for the VAT (see 39.4 INTERNATIONAL SERVICES); and

- if the recipient of the services is not registered for UK VAT, the overseas supplier must account for any UK VAT and is liable to be registered (subject to the registration threshold).

(C & E Notice 741, paras 4.9, 4.10).

UK suppliers of services relating to land overseas. If the land is in another EC country (even if the customer belongs in the UK), the supplier may be liable to register in the country where the land is situated. See 64.7 above. If the land is outside the EC, the supply is outside the scope of UK and EC VAT (although it may be subject to the equivalent local indirect taxes).

De Voil Indirect Tax Service. See V3.188.

64.22 **Services supplied where physically carried out**

A supply of the following services is treated as made where the services are physically carried out (irrespective of where the customer belongs).

(*a*) Cultural, artistic, sporting, scientific, educational or entertainment services and any services ancillary to (including organising) any such services. See 64.23 below.

(*b*)   Services relating to exhibitions, conferences or meetings and any services ancillary to (including organising) any such services. See 64.24 below.

(*c*)   Valuation of, or work carried out on, any goods. See 64.25 below.

(*d*)   Ancillary transport services. See 64.29 below.

Tour operators. Where supplies of services within (*a*)-(*d*) above (particularly educational services and services connected with conferences and meetings) involve the onward supply as principal of bought-in supplies of accommodation, travel, etc., the provisions of the TOUR OPERATORS' MARGIN SCHEME (66) may apply.

Overseas suppliers of services physically carried out in the UK. Where a supplier of services within (*a*)-(*d*) above belongs overseas

*   if the recipient of the services is a UK VAT-registered person, the reverse charge procedure applies and the recipient is liable to account for the VAT (see 39.4 INTERNATIONAL SERVICES); and

*   if the recipient of the services is not registered for UK VAT, the overseas supplier must account for any UK VAT and is liable to be registered (subject to the registration threshold).

(C & E Notice 741, paras 5.19, 5.20).

UK suppliers of services physically carried out overseas. If the services within (a)-(d) above are physically carried out in another EC country (even if the customer belongs in the UK), the supplier may be liable to register in that country. See 64.7 above. If the services are physically carried out outside the EC, the supply is outside the scope of UK and EC VAT (although it may be subject to the equivalent local indirect taxes).

De Voil Indirect Tax Service. See V3.192.

64.23   *Cultural, artistic, sporting, scientific, educational or entertainment services*

Supplies of such services and any services ancillary to (including organising) any such services are treated as made where the services are physically carried out (irrespective of where the customer belongs). [*SI 1992/3121, Art 15(a)(c)*]. Note that the place of supply of ancillary services is where the services are themselves performed which may be different from where the main services are performed.

Examples of services included

*   Services of sportspersons appearing in exhibition matches, races or other forms of competition. Where, however, sponsorship or prize money is received, it is necessary to determine whether these monies are received as consideration for a supply (see 58.18 RECREATION AND SPORT) and if so, what is the nature of that supply. For example, sponsorship may be a payment for product endorsement or publicity appearances which may be advertising services within 64.26 below.

*   The provision of race-prepared cars. Such packages include the hire of the car and support services to ensure optimum maintenance and operation of the car throughout a series of races.

*   Scientific services of technicians carrying out tests or experiments in order to obtain data. The final compilation of the records of results, carried out in the UK, will not make the supply liable to UK VAT provided the services were otherwise performed outside the UK. However, if the services

    —   include a recommendation or conclusion based on those results, they comprise consultancy services within 64.26 below; and

- — are connected with oil, gas or mineral exploration or exploitation and relate to specific sites of land or the seabed, they fall within 64.21 above.

- Services of an actor or singer performing before a *live* audience.

- Services of an oral interpreter at an event, e.g. a meeting. Written translation services, or interpreters' services which do not take place at an event, are consultancy services within 64.26 below.

- Education and training services. Such services may be exempt if made in the UK (see 20 EDUCATION). For these purposes

  - — flying training is treated as supplied outside the UK provided the trainer aircraft leaves UK airspace, proceeds directly to a destination abroad and at least 12 hours' training is provided at that place; and

  - — sailing training is treated as supplied outside the UK provided all the training is carried out on a vessel which clears UK territorial waters for a foreign destination and remains outside those waters for the whole of the period of training (except for proceeding directly from and returning directly to the UK).

  See also 39.6 INTERNATIONAL SERVICES for an extra-statutory concession allowing zero-rating of training services supplied in the UK to overseas Governments for the purpose of their sovereign activities.

- Services of a co-ordinator in administering arrangements for a sporting event on behalf of a promoter (but not advertising services to a sponsor by the promoter which fall within 64.26 below).

- Services ancillary to a *live* performance (e.g. make-up or hairdressing services or the services of a prompter) but not services ancillary to non-live entertainment (which may be consultancy services within 64.26 below or fall within the basic rule under 64.20 above).

- Services of lighting or sound technicians at a concert (including the hire of equipment included as a part of the same supply). See also *Dudda v Finanzamt Bergisch Gladbach, CJEC [1996] STC 1290*.

(C & E Notice 741, paras 5.2, 5.4–5.7).

For a more detailed consideration of the place of supply of services provided within the entertainment industry, see the guidance notes agreed between C & E and B.E.C.T.U. reproduced in C & E Manual V1-4, Appendix J.

Accounting for VAT. See 64.22 above for accounting for VAT where overseas suppliers supply these services within the UK and UK suppliers supply these services abroad.

64.24   *Services relating to exhibitions, conferences or meetings*

Supplies of services relating to exhibitions, conferences and meetings and any services ancillary to (including organising) any such services are treated as made where the services are physically carried out (irrespective of where the customer belongs). [*SI 1992/3121, Art 15(b)(c)*]. Note that the place of supply of ancillary services is where the services are themselves performed which may be different from where the main services are performed.

Examples of services included

- The right to participate in an exhibition or the provision of an undefined site for a stand at an exhibition. The provision of a defined site for a stand at an exhibition falls within 64.21 above.

- Services of tradesmen such as carpenters and electricians erecting and fitting out stands at exhibition venues for organisers or exhibitors.

Examples of services not included

- The hiring of equipment for use at a concert without the services of technicians or operators (which falls within 64.26 below).

- Supplies of consultancy design and similar services to organisers and exhibitors (which fall within 64.26 below).

(C & E Notice 741, paras 5.2, 5.4, 5.5, 5.7; C & E Manual V1-4, Chapter 2B paras 8.12, 8.13).

Accounting for VAT. See 64.22 above for accounting for VAT where overseas suppliers supply these services within the UK and UK suppliers supply these services abroad.

64.25   *Valuation of, or work carried out on, any goods*

Subject to the exception below, services consisting of the valuation of, or work carried out on, any goods are treated as made where the services are physically carried out. [*SI 1992/3121, Art 15(d); SI 1995/3038; SI 1996/2992*]. See 64.22 above for accounting for VAT where overseas suppliers supply these services within the UK and UK suppliers supply these services abroad.

Exception. Where

(*a*)   the services are supplied to a customer registered for VAT in an EC country other than the EC country in which the services are physically carried out,

(*b*)   the customer gives a valid VAT registration number to the supplier, and

(*c*)   the goods are dispatched or transported out of the EC country where the services were physically carried out (but see below for repairs to containers)

the place of supply is the EC country where the customer is registered. (Before 1 January 1997 the requirement under (*c*) above was that the goods did not remain in the UK. The effect of the change is that, from 1 January 1997, the place of supply for such services physically carried out in another EC country for a UK registered person becomes the UK.) If the customer is registered in the same EC country as the supplier, the supplier must account for any VAT due. Otherwise, the customer must account for the VAT due.

[*SI 1992/3121, Art 14; SI 1995/3038; SI 1996/2992*].

Work carried out on 'goods' is essentially any physical service carried out on another person's goods. It includes

- processing, manufacturing or assembling;

- repairs, cleaning or restoration;

- alterations, calibrations, insulating, lacquering, painting, polishing, resetting (of jewellery), sharpening, varnishing, waterproofing, etc.; and

- nominations to stallions/covering (i.e. attempting to secure the pregnancy of mares).

'*Goods*' for this purpose include all forms of moveable tangible property, covering both finished commodities and raw materials but does not include immovable property such as permanently installed goods and fixtures (for which see 64.21 above).

Examples of services included

- Services of a sub-contractor installing machinery supplied by another person.

- Simple valuation of goods by loss adjusters, average adjusters, motor assessors, surveyors and other experts in connection with an insurance proposal or claim. The final compilation of a related report in a different country from the goods will not change the place of supply from the country where valuation work is performed. Where, however, valuation forms only a part of a supply of professional services, there is a supply of consultancy services within 64.26 below.

- Before 1 June 1998 only, veterinary services. (From that date, following the decision in *Maatschap MJM Linthorst & Others v Inspecteur der Belastingdienst/Ondernemingen Roermond, CJEC [1997] STC 1287*, veterinary services are supplied where the supplier belongs under the basic rule in 64.20 above. See C & E Business Brief 12/98, 21 May 1998.)

Examples of services not included

- Work which is not mainly physical work performed on the goods themselves, e.g. mere inspection is not 'work on goods' although it can be 'valuation' if that is the purpose of the inspection.

- Valuation of, or work carried out on, land or property (which falls within 64.21 above).

- Testing and analysis of goods. The physical work simply provides data for the required analysis (and falls within 64.26 below).

(C & E Notice 741, paras 5.11–5.14, 6.3).

Repairs to containers for EC customers. From 1 April 1998, when applying the exception above, C & E accept that containers will be leaving the UK without requiring the repairer to obtain specific evidence and will only request commercial evidence to confirm the removal where there is specific reason to do so. (Evidence of export is still required to support zero-rating where containers will be exported outside the EC.) (C & E Manual V1-4, Chapter 2B para 9.5).

64.26 **Services falling within *VATA 1994, 5 Sch 1–8***

The place of supply of any services falling within *VATA 1994, 5 Sch 1–8* (see 64.27 below) is treated as taking place

(*a*) where the recipient belongs if

    (i) the recipient belongs in a country outside the EC and the Isle of Man; or

    (ii) the recipient belongs in an EC country other than that of the supplier and the services are supplied to him for his business purposes; and

(*b*) in all other cases, where the supplier belongs under the basic rule in 64.20 above, i.e. if

    (i) the recipient belongs in the same EC country as the supplier;

    (ii) the recipient belongs in an EC country other than that of the supplier but receives the supplies in a non-business or private capacity;

    (iii) the recipient is a government body, municipal authority or similar body of another EC country (unless the services are specifically required for use in a business activity); or

(iv) the supplier is unable to determine where the recipient belongs.

[*SI 1992/3121, Art 16; SI 1995/3038*]. (C & E Notice 741, para 10.7).

See 64.19 above for the place of belonging of a supplier and 64.28 below for additional rules relating to telecommunications services and the letting on hire of goods other than means of transport. See also 27.1 FINANCE for special rules applying where a UK supplier cannot determine the place of belonging of a purchaser of securities.

Accounting for VAT

* Where a UK supplier supplies services to a recipient within (*a*)(i) above, the supply is outside the scope of UK (and EC) VAT (subject to 64.28 below).

* Where a UK supplier supplies services to a recipient within (*a*)(ii) above, the place of supply is the EC country of the recipient (subject to 64.28 below). The UK supplier does not need to account for VAT in that country and the customer must do so under the reverse charge procedure. The supplier must, however, have evidence that his customer is in business. A VAT registration number is the best evidence of this and should always be requested but alternative acceptable evidence includes a certificate from the relevant fiscal authorities, business letterheads and other commercial documents indicating the nature of the customer's business activities. Where VAT numbers are available, they should be recorded on the invoice relating to the supply. (C & E Notice 741, para 10.6).

In *Diversified Agency Services Ltd v C & E Commrs QB 1995, [1996] STC 398*, advertising services were supplied to the Spanish Tourist Board in Spain in its capacity as a state authority and not as a commercial publicity body. As there was no evidence to show that the Board was treated as liable to VAT in Spain in respect of the advertising services under the reverse charge mechanism, the services were standard-rated in the UK.

* Where a UK-registered person *receives* services within these provisions for the purposes of business from an overseas supplier, the reverse charge procedure applies. The UK recipient is liable to account for the VAT. See 39.4 INTERNATIONAL SERVICES.

Misrepresentation of status by recipient. C & E have indicated that, where the customer wrongly represents his status, they will not hold the supplier responsible for failing to charge the correct amount of VAT provided they are satisfied that the supplier acted in good faith and made the normal and prudent checks and enquiries about the status of the customer and of any documentation of certification provided by him. (Tax Faculty of the ICAEW Guidance Notes 15/94, para 46).

De Voil Indirect Tax Service. See V3.193.

64.27   *Provisions of VATA 1994, 5 Sch 1-8*

(*a*)   *Transfers and assignments of copyright, patents, licences, trademarks and similar rights.* [*VATA 1994, 5 Sch 1*].

'Similar rights' are intellectual property rights which are capable of being legally enforced. Payments for these intellectual rights (often known as 'royalties') can be made on a regular and continuing basis or take the form of a single, one-off fee. Services which do not involve intellectual property are not covered even though they may be described as a right or licence.

Examples of services included

* The assignment of rights in a cinematographic film to a distribution company.

- The assignment of rights by a performer for his/her performance to be exploited on record, film, television, etc.

- The granting of a licence to use computer software.

- The granting of a right to carry on a particular business activity within a defined territory (such as within some franchise agreements).

- The transfer of permission to use a logo.

- The granting of a right by a photographer for one of his photographs to be published in a magazine article.

Examples of services not included

- The supply of individual shares in goods (e.g. an animal or yacht) even though certain rights may be included in the supply.

- The supply of a right to obtain reduced rates for admission to conferences, meetings, etc. and similar discounts on facilities available to members of clubs, associations, societies, etc. in return for a subscription.

- The supply of the right to occupy land or property including hotel accommodation (which is a supply of services relating to land).

(C & E Notice 741, paras 11.2–11.4).

(*b*) *Advertising services. [VATA 1994, 5 Sch 2].*

This covers all services of publicising another person's name or products with a view to encouraging their sale. It includes supplies of advertising services in the established media, e.g. radio or television advertising time; of the right to place an advertisement on a hoarding; or of advertising space in any publication. It also covers promotional methods such as an entry in a telephone enquiry directory or advertising space in any electronic location.

Everything provided as part of an advertising campaign is included, even if elements of the campaign would have fallen under other place of supply rules had they been supplied in isolation.

Examples of services included

- An advertising performance or product endorsement by a personality supplied directly to the person whose products are advertised.

- The display of a sponsor's name, or product, by a sponsored person or team in return for 'sponsorship' payments (see 58.18 RECREATION AND SPORT).

- Supplies of services that are the 'means of advertising', i.e. services used in connection with specific advertising, promotion or sponsorship. For example, the supply of a master advertising film, tape, record, poster, picture or photograph, or an advertisement printing block (from which copies are made).

- The devising and undertaking of a promotional campaign by an advertising agency to launch a client's new product, even where this includes trade events or demonstrations for the public in general.

- Web site advertising.

Examples of services not included

- The provision of space or stands at a trade fair or exhibition (for the place of supply of which see 64.21 and 64.24 above).

- Organising a cocktail party for an advertising company where the event is part of a promotional campaign for the advertising company's own client.

(C & E Notice 741, paras 11.5-11.7).

(c)   *Services of consultants, engineers, consultancy bureaux, lawyers, accountants and other similar services; data processing and provision of information (but excluding from this head any services relating to land). [VATA 1994, 5 Sch 3].*

Services of consultants and consultancy bureaux. Included are

- research and development;

- market research;

- written translation services or interpreters' services which do not take place at an event (e.g. interpreting services for a telephone conference). For oral interpreting at an event, see 64.23 above;

- testing and analysis of goods (e.g. drugs, chemicals and domestic electrical appliances). The essential nature of such services is analysis by experts who use the results of the testing to reach a professional conclusion, such as whether goods meet specified standards;

- writing scientific reports;

- production of customised ('bespoke' or 'specific') computer software as well as the services of adapting existing packages (some off-the-shelf software packages are treated as supplies of goods); and

- software maintenance; involving upgrades, advice and resolving any problems. The place of performance is not relevant as solutions may be provided by telephone conversations, remote links or attending a mainframe site. However, a contract for simply maintaining computer hardware relates to work on goods (and the place of supply is covered by 64.25 above).

Not included are

- services relating to specific land or property (the place of supply of which is determined under 64.21 above);

- supplies described as management services, unless they can be shown to be essentially of consultancy services (although such services may fall elsewhere within *VATA 1994, 5 Sch 3*);

- clerical or secretarial services, the provision of office facilities and archiving services;

- services provided by a consultant which are outside the supplier's habitual area of expertise (e.g. gardening carried out by a financial adviser); and

- arbitration services (see *Von Hoffmann v Finanzamt Trier CJEC, [1997] STC 1321* where the court held that the services of a German professor acting as arbitrator for the International Chamber of Commerce based in France were not within the equivalent provisions of *EC 6th Directive, Art 9(2)(e)*).

(C & E Notice 741, paras 11.9, 11.10).

Services of engineers. The services must be of a type expected of an expert or professional. Included are

- the provision of intellectual engineering advice or design. This includes overseeing the resultant physical work, provided that any such supervision is merely to ensure that the design or other advice is properly implemented; and

- services of engineers/technicians within the entertainment industry. This covers editors and sound engineers producing an edit master from which copies can be made (films, videos, compact discs or audio tapes) as well as those who exercise a degree of artistic control or influence over material.

Not included are

- services of surveyors and consultants consisting primarily of work such as design, surveying, site supervision or valuation where these directly relate to land or property (for the place of supply of which see 64.21 above); and

- services carried out by an engineer which consist wholly or mainly of physical work on goods, including installation of goods (for the place of supply of which see 64.25 above).

(C & E Notice 741, paras 11.11, 11.12).

Services of lawyers and accountants. Included are

- legal and accountancy services in the general administration or winding up of a deceased's estate even if that estate includes land or property; and

- services described as management services, the essential nature of which comprise accountancy or legal services.

Not included are

- services consisting primarily of work which directly relates to land or property such as property management, conveyancing, or obtaining planning consent (for the place of supply of which see 64.21 above); and

- clerical or secretarial services which include the keeping of financial records.

(C & E Notice 741, paras 11.13, 11.14).

Other similar services. Included are

- services of loss adjusters and assessors in assessing the validity of claims (except where these relate to land). Such services may include examination of goods to establish a value for damage or deterioration as well as negotiating a settlement amount;

- services of surveyors providing opinions which do not relate to specific sites;

- architects' services where there is no specific site of land;

- services of fiscal agents in completing VAT returns and documentation for overseas businesses (provided that the customer does not belong in the UK for the purposes of receiving these services);

- design services;

- services of specialists or technicians which are essentially creative or artistic in nature;

- services of film directors or producers, where their services are not of rights within (*a*) above; and

- services described as management services which comprise the exercise of corporate or strategic guidance over the running of another (usually associated) company.

Not included are

- services provided by architects and surveyors which directly relate to land or property, including surveying, site supervision, conveyancing, valuation and obtaining planning consent (for the place of supply of which see 64.21 above); and

- loss adjusting services in relation to claims on land or property (for the place of supply of which see 64.21 above) and services provided by a loss adjuster which are simply the valuation of goods (for the place of supply of which see 64.25 above).

(C & E Notice 741, paras 11.15, 11.16).

Data processing is the application of programmed instructions on existing data which results in the production of required information. Not included are

- services which simply include an element of data processing;

- processing data from seismic surveys where the computer analysis relates to a specified area of land or seabed (for the place of supply of which see 64.21 above); and

- simple re-formatting where there is no change to the meaning of the content.

(C & E Notice 741, para 11.17, 11.18).

The provision of information covers the supplying of knowledge of any type and in any form. Information includes facts, data, figures and other material. Included are

- tourist information;

- weather forecasts;

- information supplied by a private enquiry agent;

- telephone helpdesk services (such as for computer software);

- satellite navigational and locational services; and

- provision of on-line information.

Not included are

- the delivery or transmission of another person's information by whatever means; and

- information relating to specific land or property (for the place of supply of which see 64.21 above).

(C & E Notice 741, paras 11.19, 11.20).

(d) *Acceptance of any obligation to refrain from pursuing or exercising, in whole or part, any business activity or any such rights as are referred to in (a) above. [VATA 1994, 5 Sch 4].*

Examples of services included

- The vendor of a business accepting an undertaking not to compete with the purchaser.

- Agreement by the owner of a trademark to refrain from using it.

(C & E Notice 741, para 11.23).

(e) *Banking, financial and insurance services (including reinsurance, but not including the provision of safe deposit facilities). [VATA 1994, 5 Sch 5].*

Examples of services included

- Granting of mortgages and loans; selling debts.

- The storage of gold bullion or gold coins by a bank or a dealer in gold who is a subsidiary of a bank.

- The sale of securities as principal.
- The sale of unallocated precious metals (gold, silver, platinum, palladium, rhodium, ruthenium, osmium and iridium) or unallocated precious metal coins.
- Debt collection services.
- Portfolio management services.
- The supply of financial futures and financial options.
- Trustees services.
- Commodity brokers' services of arranging transactions in futures and options.

Examples of services not included

- Services of physical safe custody.
- Rent collection services (for the place of supply of which see 64.21 above).

(C & E Notice 741, paras 11.25, 11.26).

(f)   *The supply of staff. [VATA 1994, 5 Sch 6].*

A supply of staff is the placing of personnel under the general control and guidance of another party as if they become employees of that other party. A clear distinction must be drawn between a supply of staff and a supply of other services by using staff. For example, the secondment, transfer or placement of a typist with a customer where the typist comes under the control and direction of that customer is the supply of staff. If typing services are supplied under a specific assignment for a customer this does not constitute the supply of staff.

Examples of services included

- The supply, secondment, loan, hire, lease or transfer as principals of personnel for a consideration by bodies such as employment or recruitment businesses or bureaux.
- The transfer for a fee by a sports club of a professional sportsman who has a contract of service with the club, e.g. a professional footballer.

Examples of services not included

- The supply by a freelance or other person of a specific service or services under a contract for services.
- Supplies by employment or recruitment businesses or agencies of making arrangements for the supply of staff between other parties (which fall within (j) below).

(C & E Notice 741, paras 11.27–11.29).

See also *American Institute of Foreign Study (UK) Ltd (13886)* where the services of travel couriers provided to associated companies were held to be supplies of staff rather than the supply of courier services.

(g)   *The letting on hire of goods other than means of transport. [VATA 1994, 5 Sch 7].*

Goods include all forms of moveable property or equipment but not land and property or equipment and machinery installed as a fixture.

Examples of services included

- The hire of mobile telephone handsets (but see (h) below if the supply is of telecommunications services).

- The hire of freight containers (but see 25.7 EXPORTS for special rules for container exports).

- The hire of computer and office equipment.

- The hire of exhibition stand furniture and equipment without any other services.

Examples of services not included

- The hire of exhibition stand space (for the place of supply of which see 64.21 and 64.24 above).

- The hire of a means of transport (for the place of supply of which see 64.21 above and 64.30 below).

- Supplies which include the services of an operator or technician (the place of supply of which depends on the nature of the services provided).

Mobile cranes are not means of transport (*BPH Equipment Ltd (13914)*).

(*h*) *After 30 June 1997, telecommunications services,* i.e. services relating to the transmission, emission or reception of signals, writing, images and sounds or information of any nature by wire, radio, optical or other electromagnetic systems, including the transfer or assignment of the right to use capacity for such transmission, emission or reception. [*VATA 1994, 5 Sch 7A; SI 1997/1523, Reg 3*].

The definition covers the sending or receiving of material by electronic or similar communications systems. This may be via cable, fibre optics, radio waves, microwaves, satellite or copper wire. It covers telephony (systems for the transmission of speech and other sound) and telegraphy (systems involving any process that provides reproduction at a distance of written, printed or pictorial matter) as well as the right to use such facilities.

Examples of services included

- telephone calls, calls delivered by cellular phones, paging, the transmission element of Electronic Data Interchange, teleconferencing and call-back services;

- switching, completion of another provider's calls, the provision of leased lines and circuits or global networks;

- telex, facsimile, multi-messaging;

- e-mail;

- basic access to the Internet and World Wide Web, the provision of e-mail addresses and chatline facilities (even if related software, some information and customer support facilities are included). If a package of Internet services is supplied where the emphasis is on content rather than communication, the supply is not of pure telecommunications services and the place of supply of the package depends on the nature of the services provided. Where services are supplied separately or services are simply delivered to a customer by electronic transmission, the place of supply depends on the nature of the services provided;

- transmission or delivery of another person's material by electronic means; and

- satellite transmission services, covering transponder rental/hire and both space segments and earth segments, which includes uplinks and downlinks via land earth stations, coastal stations, outside broadcasting units or similar.

Examples of services not included

- the supply of the 'content' of a transmission, treatment of which depends on the nature of the actual services, For example, if A contracts with B to provide general advisory services and delivers the information by fax, A is providing advisory services within *VATA 1994, 5 Sch 3* (see *(c)* above) not the transmission of a fax. The transmission of the fax is a supply of services within *VATA 1994, 5 Sch 7A* above to A by a third party;

- supplies of information ordered and delivered through the Internet;

- travel information accessed by telephone;

- granting copyright to use transmitted material;

- processing of data; and

- broadcasting to subscribers.

(C & E Notice 741, paras 11.35–11.38).

Internet services. For further details, including packages comprising a variety of internet-related elements, see C & E Manual V1-4, Chapter 2B paras 17.9–17.11 and C & E Business Brief 22/97, 10 October 1997.

See also 64.28 below and 39.9 INTERNATIONAL SERVICES.

(*j*) *The services rendered by one person to another in procuring for the other any of the services mentioned in (a)–(h) above. [VATA 1994, 5 Sch 8; SI 1997/1523, Reg 3].*

Examples of services included

- Stockbroking services.

- Insurance broking services.

- Services of patent, copyright and similar agents.

- Services of advertising agents.

Examples of services not included

- Estate agents' services in arranging supplies of land or property (for the place of supply of which see 64.21 above).

- Services of only facilitating a supply within *(a)*-*(h)* above, such as simple introduction.

(C & E Notice 741, paras 11.41, 11.42).

64.28   *Telecommunications services and the letting on hire of goods (other than means of transport)*

In relation to

- telecommunication services within *VATA 1994, 5 Sch 7A* (see 64.27(*h*) above) performed after 30 June 1997; and

- the letting on hire of goods (other than means of transport) within *VATA 1994, 5 Sch 7* (see 64.27(*g*) above) supplied after 17 March 1998

the following rules apply *in addition* to those in 64.26 above.

(*a*)   Where the supply would, under 64.26(*a*) or (*b*) above, be treated as supplied in the UK, it is not to be so treated to the extent that the 'effective use and enjoyment' takes place outside the EC. The supplier must retain evidence to substantiate such use.

(b)   Where the supply would, under 64.26(a) or (b) above, be treated as supplied outside the EC, it is to be treated as supplied in the UK to the extent that the effective use and enjoyment of the services takes place in the UK.

[SI 1992/3121, Arts 17, 18; SI 1997/1524, Art 5; SI 1998/763].

'*Effective use and enjoyment*' takes place where a recipient actually consumes the telecommunications services or uses the goods. In practice, this will be where the services are physically used or the goods are physically located, irrespective of contract, payment or beneficial interest. Where services are only partly liable to UK VAT because of the use and enjoyment provisions, there is no prescribed method of determining the extent to which services are used in the UK. Any method may be adopted which produces a fair and reasonable reflection of services. Evidence of how apportionment has been made should be retained.

Examples

- A Canadian company hires out recording equipment to a UK private individual who uses the equipment in his UK home. The place of supply is the UK. This is because the goods are used in the UK and the place of supply would otherwise have been outside the EC under 64.26(b)(ii) above.

- An Australian tourist hires a video camera from a UK provider during a visit to the UK. The place of supply is the UK. This is because the goods are used in the UK and the place of supply would otherwise have been outside the EC under 64.26(b)(ii) above.

- A UK golf shop hires out a set of golf clubs to a UK customer for use on a holiday in the USA. The place of supply is outside the EC if the customer is able to demonstrate that the golf clubs are used only in the USA. This is because the goods are used outside the EC and the place of supply would otherwise have been the UK under 64.26(b)(i) above.

- A business traveller makes a reservation at a Hong Kong hotel from his London office using a toll free number. The telecommunications services are supplied to, and used by, the Hong Kong hotel. The place of supply is outside the EC because the services are not effectively used and enjoyed in the UK.

(C & E Notice 741, paras 12.5, 12.7, 13.5, 13.6).

Summary of liabilities. The following table summarises the UK VAT position for telecommunications services. Each row must be read in its entirety to arrive at the correct position.

	UK VAT position (subject to use and enjoyment provisions)	Impact of use and enjoyment provisions
Supplier belongs in the UK		
Customer belongs		
— in the UK	Services are supplied in the UK and the supplier accounts for UK VAT[1]	Services used outside the EC are outside the scope of UK (and EC) VAT
— in another EC country and receives services for business purposes	Services are supplied in the other EC country and are outside the scope of UK VAT	Do not apply — outside UK jurisdiction

— in another EC country and receives the services for non-business purposes	Services are supplied in the UK and the supplier accounts for UK VAT [1]	Services used outside the EC are outside the scope of UK (and EC) VAT
— outside the EC	Services are supplied outside the EC and are outside the scope of UK (and EC) VAT	Services used in the UK are supplied in the UK and the supplier accounts for UK VAT[1, 2]

Supplier belongs in another EC country

Customer belongs

— in the UK and receives the services for business purposes	Services are supplied in the UK and the customer accounts for UK VAT by applying the reverse charge[1]	Services used outside the EC are outside the scope of UK (and EC) VAT
— in the UK and receives the services for non-business purposes	Services are supplied in the supplier's country and are outside the scope of UK VAT (invoices will show local VAT)	Do not apply — outside UK jurisdiction
— in another EC country	Services are supplied in another EC country and are outside the scope of UK VAT	Do not apply — outside UK jurisdiction
— outside the EC	Services are supplied outside the EC and are outside the scope of UK (and EC) VAT	Services used in the UK are supplied in the UK and the supplier accounts for UK VAT[1] unless the customer provides a UK registration number and accounts for UK VAT by applying the reverse charge[2]

Supplier belongs outside the EC

Customer belongs

— in the UK and receives the services for business purposes	Services are supplied in the UK and the customer accounts for UK VAT by applying the reverse charge[1]	Services used outside the EC are outside the scope of UK (and EC) VAT
— in the UK and receives the services for non-business purposes	Services are supplied in the supplier's country and are outside the scope of UK (and EC) VAT – use and enjoyment provisions are likely to apply	Services used in the UK are supplied in the UK and the supplier accounts for UK VAT[1]

— in another EC country and receives the services for business purposes	Services are supplied in the other EC country and are outside the scope of UK VAT	Do not apply — outside UK jurisdiction
— in another EC country and receives the services for non-business purposes	Services are supplied in the supplier's country and are outside the scope of UK (and EC) VAT	Services used in the UK are supplied in the UK and the supplier accounts for UK VAT[1]
— outside the EC	Services are supplied outside the EC and are outside the scope of UK (and EC) VAT	Services used in the UK are supplied in the UK and the supplier accounts for UK VAT[1] unless the customer provides a UK VAT registration number and accounts for UK VAT by applying the reverse charge[2]

[1]   Subject to registration threshold.

[2]   Any telecommunications services used in the UK by customers belonging outside the EC are supplied in the UK. Such services are therefore subject to UK VAT when used in the UK by non-EC visitors (e.g. public pay-phones, fax shop services and calls made from hotel rooms). As an administrative measure, the elements of telecommunications services used in the UK may be ignored if

- simply an incidental part of an established telephone contract or account held by a customer who belongs outside the EC;

- used by a temporary non-EC visitor; and

- C & E are satisfied that these conditions are not being abused.

(C & E Notice 741, para 13.7, Appendix F).

See 39.9 INTERNATIONAL SERVICES for further coverage of telecommunications services. See also 64.18 above for transitional anti-avoidance provisions in relation to the letting on hire of goods which, as a result of (b) above, are treated as supplied in the UK.

64.29   **Transport services**

Passenger transport services. Services consisting of the transport of passengers (including any accompanying luggage and/or motor vehicle) are treated as supplied in the country in which the transportation takes place (and only to the extent that it takes place in that country). [SI 1992/3121, Arts 6, 8]. For sea and air passenger transport, provided the means of transport used does not put in or land in another country on the way, any transportation as part of a journey between two points in the same country is treated as taking place wholly inside that country even where it takes place partly outside its territorial jurisdiction. This applies even if the journey is part of a longer journey involving travel to or from another country. [SI 1992/3121, Art 7].

Pleasure cruises. Any goods or services provided as part of a pleasure cruise are treated as supplied in the same place as the transportation of the passengers, and for this purpose a pleasure cruise is treated as a supply of passenger transport. [SI 1992/3121, Art 8].

See 68.15 TRANSPORT AND FREIGHT for further details and 68.14–68.23 TRANSPORT AND FREIGHT for passenger transport generally.

Overseas suppliers of passenger transport services in the UK. Where a supplier of such services belongs overseas

- if the recipient of the services is a UK VAT-registered person, the reverse charge procedure applies and the recipient is liable to account for the VAT (see 39.4 INTERNATIONAL SERVICES); and

- if the recipient of the services is not registered for UK VAT, the overseas supplier must account for any UK VAT and is liable to be registered (subject to the registration threshold).

UK suppliers of passenger transport overseas. If a UK supplier supplies passenger transport in another EC country, he may be liable to register in that country. See 64.7 above. If the services are physically carried out outside the EC, the supply is outside the scope of UK and EC VAT.

(C & E Notice 741, paras 7.7–7.9).

Freight transport and related services. Subject to special rules for intra-EC transport of goods below,

- freight transport services are treated as supplied in the country where the transportation takes place (and only to the extent that it takes place in that country); and

- ancillary freight transport services (loading, unloading, handling and similar activities) are treated as made where those services are physically performed.

For sea and air freight transport, provided the means of transport used does not put in or land in another country on the way, any transportation as part of a journey between two points in the same country is treated as taking place wholly inside that country even where it takes place partly outside its territorial jurisdiction. This applies even if the journey is part of a longer journey involving travel to or from another country.

[*SI 1992/3121, Arts 2, 6, 7, 9*].

Intra-EC freight transport and related services. There are special rules for 'intra-EC freight transport' and related services.

(*a*) Intra-EC freight transport is treated as supplied in the EC country where the transportation begins.

(*b*) Ancillary freight transport services are treated as made where they are physically performed.

(*c*) Intermediary services of arranging intra-EC freight transport (or any activity intended to facilitate the making of such a supply) are treated as supplied where the transportation begins.

(*d*) Intermediary services of arranging ancillary freight transport services in connection with intra-EC freight transport (or any activity intended to facilitate the making of such a supply) are treated as supplied in the same EC country where the ancillary transport services are physically performed.

However, where

- a service within (*a*)–(*d*) above is supplied to a customer registered for VAT in an EC country other than the EC country in which the supply would otherwise be treated as taking place, and

- the customer gives a valid VAT registration number to the supplier, the place of supply is the EC country of the customer. Where the supplier and customer belong in different EC countries, the customer must account for VAT under the reverse charge procedure.

'Intra-EC' freight transport' means transport which begins in one EC country and ends in another EC country.

[*SI 1992/3121, Arts 2, 10–12, 14*].

See 68.24–68.30 TRANSPORT AND FREIGHT for further details of freight transport services, ancillary freight transport services and services of intermediaries.

De Voil Indirect Tax Service. See V3.190.

64.30   **Hire of means of transport**

The place of supply of the letting on hire of any 'means of transport' is where the supplier belongs under the basic rule in 64.20 above *except that*

(*a*)   where the supplier belongs in the UK, to the extent that (before 1 July 1997, if) the 'effective use and enjoyment' of the letting on hire takes place outside the EC, the place of supply is outside the UK (and the EC); and

(*b*)   where the supplier belongs outside the EC, to the extent that (before 1 July 1997, if) the effective use and enjoyment of the letting on hire takes place in the UK, the place of supply is in the UK.

[*SI 1992/3121, Arts 17, 18; SI 1997/1524, Arts 3, 4; SI 1998/763*].

'*Means of transport*' includes ships, boats, yachts, hovercraft, barges or dracones (bulk liquid barges), aircraft, cars, trucks, lorries, touring caravans, trailers, motorcycles, cycles and rolling stock but does not include freight containers, static caravans, and racing cars for racing on race tracks. Mobile cranes are not means of transport (*BPH Equipment Ltd (13914)*. Provided the goods hired are a means of transport, their actual use is not important (e.g. the provisions apply to the lease of a train to a transport museum or a yacht for use in racing).

'*Effective use and enjoyment*'. C & E do not specifically give their interpretation of 'effective use and enjoyment' in the context of the hire of means of transport. See, however, 64.28 above for their interpretation of the phrase in the context of hire of other goods.

Hire of means of transport does not cover supplies which include the services of a driver, pilot operator or crew. The place of supply of such transport-related services depend on the nature of the services supplied. For example, the supply of a ship or aircraft *without crew* under a written charter party contract is the hire of a means of transport but if supplied *with crew* the place of supply is where the supplier belongs under the basic rule in 64.20 above.

(C & E Notice 741, paras 3.4–3.7, 7.4, 8.3).

Hire of means of transport in the UK from a supplier outside the EC. Where a UK-registered customer hires a means of transport in the circumstances under (*b*) above and the place of supply is in the UK, the reverse charge procedure applies. The UK recipient is required to account for the VAT. See 39.4 INTERNATIONAL SERVICES. Where the UK customer is not registered for VAT, the overseas supplier must account for any UK VAT and is liable to be registered (subject to the registration threshold).

(C & E Notice 741, paras 12.13, 12.14).

De Voil Indirect Tax Service. See V3.194.

64.31   **Services of intermediaries**

Special place of supply rules apply to

- services of estate agents in arranging supplies of land or property (see 64.21 above);

- making arrangements for a supply of intra-EC freight transport or related ancillary services (see 64.29 above); and

- making arrangements for services within *VATA 1994, 5 Sch 1-8* which are covered by the provisions in 64.26 above.

Subject to the above, the place of supply of the making of arrangements for a supply by or to another person of any goods or services (or of any other activity intended to facilitate the making of such a supply) is the same place where the supply which is being arranged is deemed to take place, *except that* where the intermediary services are supplied to a customer

- registered for VAT in an EC country other than the EC country in which the services would otherwise be treated as supplied, and

- who has given a valid VAT registration number to the supplier

the services are treated as supplied in the EC country where the customer is registered.

[*SI 1992/3121, Arts 13, 14*].

The normal rules must be followed to determine the place of supply of the supply of goods or services which is being arranged. See 64.7 *et seq.* above for the place of supply of goods and 64.18 *et seq.* above for the place of supply of services.

Accounting for VAT on intermediary services. Whether the supplier of the intermediary services or his customer has to account for VAT, if any, depends upon whether, and if so where, the customer is registered for VAT.

- Where a UK supplier arranges a supply which is made outside the EC, the supply is outside the scope of UK VAT and any other EC VAT. However, the supplier will still be able to recover any input tax incurred in making the supply.

- Where a UK supplier arranges a supply which is made within the EC to a customer who does not give a valid EC VAT number, the supplier is responsible for accounting for the VAT in the EC country where the supply is made. If not already registered there, the supplier may be required to register to account for the VAT.

- Where a UK supplier arranges a supply which is made within the EC to a customer registered for VAT in the UK for the purposes of receiving the supply, the place of supply is the UK. The supplier must charge and account for VAT to C & E in the normal way. The reverse charge procedure cannot be applied.

- Where a UK supplier arranges a supply which is made within the EC to a customer registered for VAT in another EC country for the purposes of receiving the supply, the place of supply is the customer's country and the customer must account for VAT there under the reverse charge procedure. The customer must provide the supplier with a valid VAT registration number under which the service is received and which the supplier must quote on his VAT invoice.

    Since the place of supply is outside the UK, the supply is outside the scope of UK VAT and the supplier need not charge UK VAT. However, he will still be able to recover any input tax incurred in making the supply.

Intermediary services received by UK customers from overseas suppliers. Where a supplier of intermediary services belongs overseas

- if the recipient of the services is a UK VAT-registered person, the place of supply is the UK and the reverse charge procedure applies with the recipient liable to account for the VAT (see 39.4 INTERNATIONAL SERVICES); and

- if the UK customer is not registered for UK VAT and the supply is treated as made in the UK, the overseas supplier must account for any UK VAT and is liable to be registered (subject to the registration threshold).

(C & E Notice 741, paras 9.7, 9.9, 9.13, 9.14).

Example

Intermediary A, who belongs in the UK, arranges a supply of goods between seller X and buyer Y. The goods pass directly from X to Y.

(*a*) Seller X and buyer Y are both UK VAT-registered.

The place of supply of the goods is the UK. Whether A acts for X or Y, A's services are supplied in the UK and A must account for the VAT due.

(*b*) Seller X is VAT-registered in Eire and buyer Y is VAT-registered in the UK.

The place of supply of goods is Eire.

- If A acts for X, A's services are supplied in Eire and X must account for the VAT due there under the reverse charge procedure.

- If A acts for Y, A's services are supplied in the UK (because although the underlying supply of goods is made in Eire, his customer is VAT-registered in a different EC country and therefore the place of supply is where the customer is registered). A must account for the VAT due.

(*c*) Seller X is located in Russia and buyer Y is VAT-registered in France.

The place of supply of goods is Russia. Whether A acts for X or Y, A's services are supplied outside the EC (where the underlying supply of goods is supplied). A has no UK VAT liability.

(*d*) Seller X is registered for VAT in the UK and buyer Y is located in Russia.

The place of supply of the goods is the UK. Whether A acts for X or Y, A's services are supplied in the UK (where the underlying supply of goods is supplied). A's supply is zero-rated under *VATA 1994, 8 Sch Group 7, Item 2* (see 39.8 INTERNATIONAL SERVICES).

(*e*) Seller X is registered for VAT in Denmark and buyer Y is registered for VAT in Spain.

The place of supply of the goods is Denmark.

- If A acts for X, A's services are supplied in Denmark (where the underlying supply of goods is supplied) and X must account for the VAT there under the reverse charge procedure.

- If A acts for Y, A's services are supplied in Spain (because although the underlying supply of goods is made in Denmark, his customer is VAT-registered in a different EC country and therefore the place of supply is where the customer is registered) and Y must account for the VAT there under the reverse charge procedure.

(*f*) Seller X is registered for VAT in Greece and buyer Y is an unregistered person belonging in the UK. X is not required to be registered in the UK in respect of distance sales.

The place of supply of the goods is Greece.

- If A acts for X, A's services are supplied in Greece (where the underlying supply of goods is supplied) and X must account for the VAT there under the reverse charge procedure.

- If A acts for Y, A's services are supplied in Greece (because the underlying supply of goods is made in Greece and his customer is not VAT-registered in a different EC country from that in which the underlying supply is made). A must account for the VAT due in Greece and may be liable to register for VAT there (subject to the registration limits in that country)

(C & E Manual V1-4, Chapter 3 Appendix I).

De Voil Indirect Tax Service. See V3.195.

64.32 **TIME OF SUPPLY: GENERAL PROVISIONS**

EC legislation. See 22.11 EUROPEAN COMMUNITY LEGISLATION.

VAT becomes due on a supply of goods or services at the time of supply. [*VATA 1994, s 1(2)*]. It is therefore necessary have 'time of supply' rules to determine when a supply is to be treated as taking place for VAT purposes. The resultant time is often referred to as the *tax point* (although this is not a term that is used in the legislation).

VAT must normally be accounted for on the return for the period in which the tax point occurs and at the rate of VAT in force at that time. The normal tax point rules relating to the supply of goods and services are covered in 64.39 and 64.49 below respectively. C & E have powers, at the request of a taxable person, to alter the time at which his supplies are to be treated as taking place. [*VATA 1994, s 6(10)*]. These are known as accommodation tax points. See 64.38 below.

In addition, C & E may make regulations with respect to the time at which a supply is to be treated as taking place where

(*a*) it is a supply of goods or services for a consideration the whole or part of which is determined or payable periodically, or from time to time, or at the end of any period;

(*b*) it is a supply of goods for a consideration the whole or part of which is determined at the time when the goods are appropriated for any purpose;

(*c*) there is a supply to which *VATA 1994,s 55* applies (special scheme for gold); or

(*c*) there is a supply of services under *VATA 1994, 4 Sch 5(4)* (non-business use of goods) or under a Treasury Order under *VATA 1994, s 5(4)*.

[*VATA 1994, s 6(14)*].

See 64.40–64.48 below for special provisions relating to goods and 64.50–64.58 below for special provisions relating to services.

Although the principal purpose of the time of supply rules is to fix the time for accounting for VAT, the rules have other uses including

- calculating turnover for VAT registration purposes;

- establishing the period to which supplies (including exempt supplies) are to be allocated for partial exemption purposes, and

- establishing when input tax may be deducted.

968

Exempt supplies. The time of supply for any exempt supply is determined using the normal tax point rules (see 64.39-64.58 below as appropriate) but, as an invoice issued in respect of an exempt supply is not a VAT invoice (see 64.34 below) references to the issue of a VAT invoice have no effect. Thus, for example, in the case of a single supply of exempt services, the time of supply will normally be the earlier of receipt of payment or performance of the service. (C & E Manual V1-11, Chapter 2 para 2.7).

Zero-rated supplies. The time of supply for any zero-rated supply is determined using the normal tax point rules (see 64.39-64.58 below as appropriate) but, subject to the special rules for the supply of zero-rated goods in the UK for acquisition by a registered trader in another EC country (see 23.16 EUROPEAN COMMUNITY: SINGLE MARKET), as an invoice issued in respect of a zero-rated supply is not a VAT invoice (see 64.34 below) references to the issue of a VAT invoice has no effect. Thus, for example, the tax point for a zero-rated supply of goods will normally be the earlier of receipt of payment or the removal/making available of those goods. (C & E Manual V1-11, Chapter 2 para 2.7).

Change of rate. Where there is a change in the VAT rate or a VAT liability, VAT is chargeable according to the normal tax point rules (see 64.39-64.58 below as appropriate) unless the taxpayer elects for the special change of rate provisions to apply. See 56.6 RATES OF VAT.

Retail schemes and cash accounting. In legal terms, the special RETAIL SCHEMES (60) and the cash accounting arrangements (see 63.2 SPECIAL SCHEMES) do not override the time of supply rules but amend the time at which VAT is accounted for on supplies that are eligible for inclusion within the schemes. They allow the VAT due on such supplies to be accounted for at a time different from the normal rules that require the VAT to be accounted for by reference to the tax point. Nevertheless, any questions concerning the time at which VAT should be accounted for by traders using either of these schemes should be considered in the context of the scheme rules and appropriate guidance rather than the normal time of supply rules. (C & E Manual V1-11, Chapter 1 para 3).

De Voil Indirect Tax Service. See V3.131–142.

64.33   **Identifying the correct tax point**

The following is a step-by-step guide to determine the correct tax point.

(1) Does the supply fall within the scope of an accommodation tax point granted to the person making the supply?   See 64.38

(2) Is the supply covered by an extra-statutory class concession, e.g. coins operated machines?   See 64.56

(3) If the supply is a supply of goods

    (*a*) is it the permanent diversion of goods to private or non-business use?   See 64.40

    (*b*) is it an intra-EC supply of goods eligible for zero-rating?   See 64.41

    (*c*) is it on a 'sale or return basis' or 'on approval' terms?   See 64.43

    (*d*) does it involve land in that it is   See 64.44

        (i) in connection with a compulsory purchase where the price has not been agreed?

        (ii) a further 'contingency' payment in respect of an earlier supply of the freehold?

(iii) in connection with leasehold land treated as a supply of goods?

(e) is it the self-supply of goods?   See 64.45

(f) does it involve water, gas or any form of power, heat, refrigeration or ventilation?   See 64.47

(g) does it involve the supplier's goods being held by the buyer pending agreement of the price?   See 64.47

(h) does it come within the special scheme for gold?   See 64.48

(4) If the supply is a supply of services

(a) Is it a continuous supply of services?   See 64.50

(b) does it give rise to the payment of royalties?   See 64.51

(c) does it involve construction services under a contract that provides for stage payments?   See 64.52

(d) does it involve 'reverse charge' services?   See 64.53

(e) does it involve the temporary use of business goods for private or non-business purposes?   See 64.54

(f) does it involve the free supply of services?   See 64.55

(g) does it consist of professional services made by a barrister advocate?   See 64.58 or

(5) Does the contract provide for a retention payment?   See 64.37

(6) Has an 'actual' tax point been created because

(a) the supplier received a payment or issued a VAT invoice in respect of the supply before the 'basic' tax point?   See 64.39(b)(i) for goods and 64.49(b)(i) for services

(b) the supplier has issued a VAT invoice within 14 days after the 'basic' tax point and has not previously elected to forgo the 14 day rule?   See 64.39(b)(ii) for goods and 64.49(b)(ii) for services

(c) the supplier has been granted an extension of the 14 day rule and has issued a VAT invoice within that time?   See 64.39(b)(ii) for goods and 64.49(b)(ii) for services

(7) Where none of (1)-(6) above apply, the basic tax point applies   See 64.39(a) for goods and 64.49(a) for services

(C & E Manual V1-11, Chapter 2 paras 2.3, 2.4, Appendix A).

64.34 VAT invoices and the creation of tax points

A VAT invoice can create an actual tax point under the normal rules both before and after the basic tax point occurs (see 64.39 and 64.49 below for goods and services respectively) and most of the special time of supply regulations also provide for the issue of a VAT invoice to create a tax point. In addition, in certain instances 'period' VAT invoices issued covering payments due over a period of up to one year may create tax points.

In order to establish the creation of a tax point, the following conditions must be satisfied.

(*a*) The invoice must be a proper VAT invoice which complies with the necessary requirements. See 40.3 *et seq.* INVOICES. If the invoice does not conform to the requirements, it is not a VAT invoice and cannot create a tax point. See *ABB Power Ltd, [1992] VATTR 491 (9373)* and *SR Finch (10948)*. This also means that, as a VAT invoice cannot be issued

- in respect of a zero–rated supply (except for intra–EC supplies of goods, see 64.41 below), or

- in respect of an exempt supply, or

- by a non–registered person

invoices issued in such circumstances are disregarded for time of supply purposes.

(*b*) The VAT invoice must be issued. In *C & E Commrs v Woolfold Motor Co Ltd QB, [1983] STC 715* it was held that the issue of a VAT invoice required the provision to the customer of that invoice, i.e. the customer must physically receive it. It is not sufficient for it to simply have been prepared in order to create a tax point.

Where an invoice has in fact been issued,

- it is the date of physical issue that determines the tax point. In the case of invoices issued by electronic data interchange (EDI), an invoice is issued when the data is transmitted (provided the recipient is able to receive the data); and

- where a tax point is established, it is not invalidated because the recipient has never 'processed' the invoice, e.g. by disputing it (*Hurley Robinson Partnership (750)*).

Period VAT invoices. Special time of supply rules apply to

- leasehold property (see 64.44 below),

- certain supplies of water, fuel and power (see 64.46 below), and

- continuous supplies of services (see 64.50 below)

where the supplier makes use of 'period' VAT invoices. This facility recognises that, without such arrangements, suppliers might otherwise have to issue a large volume of repetitive VAT invoices to the same customer, e.g. leased equipment subject to monthly rental payments. By adopting the period VAT invoicing arrangements, provided the invoice contains the required details in respect of two or more instalments due, the supplier can issue a single document showing all the payments due over a period of up to one year. The tax point then becomes the earlier of the receipt of the payment or the time when the payment falls due.

(C & E Manual V1-11, Chapter 2 paras 5.2-5.4).

64.35 *Self-billing*

Under an approved self-billing arrangement it is the customer who prepares the VAT invoice. See 40.2 INVOICES for further details. For time of supply purposes, not all self-billed VAT invoices can create a tax point as the law refers consistently to an invoice that has been issued by the supplier. A tax point is not normally created, therefore, where the invoice is issued by another person as in the case of a self-billing arrangement. The notable exception to this are self-billed invoices that fall within the scope of the 14 day rule where specific provision is included for self-billed invoices to be treated as if they were issued by the supplier (see 64.39 and 64.49 below for supplies of goods and services respectively). Therefore, a self-billed invoice issued within 14 days of the basic tax point has the same potential to create the tax point for the supply as if it had been issued by the supplier.

In all other circumstances (e.g. where an invoice is issued in advance of the basic tax point or is in respect of a supply covered by one of the special time of supply regulations) a tax point cannot be created by the issue of a self-billed VAT invoice.

Special arrangements for input tax deduction purposes. Because of the above, C & E have agreed special arrangements that provide the issuer of the self-billed invoice with a notional tax point *for input tax deduction purposes only.* Under this procedure,

- the person issuing the self-billed invoice must

    (*a*) show, on the original invoice, the date of despatch (but this must not be referred to as the tax point), and

    (*b*) retain a copy and show on it the day following the date of issue as the notional tax point for input tax purposes; and

- the person receiving the invoice must, *on receipt of the invoice and payment*, add the date of receipt. This becomes the tax point for output tax purposes.

(C & E Manual V1-11, Chapter 2 para 5.7; Manual V1-24, section 4.38).

64.36   *Credit notes*

The time of supply rules do not apply in any way to the issue of credit notes. Similarly, the issue of a credit note has no direct effect on a tax point once it has been established, i.e. it does not cancel or expunge an existing tax point. It normally simply permits the issuer to adjust the VAT previously accounted for in response to an earlier tax point. (C & E Manual V1-11, Chapter 2 para 5.8).

64.37   **Receipt of payment and the creation of tax points**

The receipt of a payment can create an actual tax point before the basic tax point occurs (see 64.39 and 64.49 below for goods and services respectively) and most of the special time of supply regulations also provide for the receipt of a payment to create a tax point.

Deposits. Deposits are frequently required either as an indication of good faith on the part of the customer or to put the supplier in funds to cover costs, etc. Depending on the contract, the deposit may be refundable in the event of the contract subsequently being cancelled or may be liable, either wholly or in part, to forfeiture.

Apart from security deposits (see below) a pre-payment or deposit normally creates a tax point when received where it is made in the expectation that it will eventually form part of the total payment for a supply that is contemplated by the parties to the payment. See, for example, *JD Fox Ltd (1012)* (deposits for furniture), *Bethway & Moss Ltd (2667)* (deposits for fitted kitchens) and *C & E Commrs v Richmond Theatre Management Ltd QB, [1995] STC 257* (advance payments of theatre tickets). This applies even if the deposit is refundable. See, for example, *C & E Commrs v Moonraker's Guest House Ltd, QB [1992] STC 544* (deposits for holiday accommodation) and *Clowance plc (2541)* (advance payments for time-share accommodation). For an exception to this general rule where deposits were not held to create tax points, see *Nigel Mansell Sports Co Ltd, [1991] VATTR 491 (6116)* (initial deposit from prospective customer in order to be placed on the waiting list for a sports car and paid before a firm order was placed for the car) although the facts in this case were unusual.

Security deposits. Deposits taken as security to ensure safe return of goods hired out, and which are refunded when the goods are safely returned or forfeited to compensate for loss or damage, do not normally create a tax point. A payment tax point can be created if, for example, hire charges are later offset against the refund of an amount originally received as a security deposit but only where this happens before the basic tax point, i.e. completion of the hire period. (C & E Manual V1-11, Chapter 2 paras 4.4, 4.5).

Third parties acting as stakeholders. Where a third party acts as a stakeholder (as opposed to an agent of the vendor) and receives a deposit in connection with a supply of property, a time of supply is not created until the money is released to the vendor. (C & E Notice 700, para 5.1(c)). See *Double Shield Window Co Ltd (1771).*

Payment by cheque. Under banking law, payment can only be said to have occurred when the cheque has been presented and met by the drawer's bank. In the normal course of events it takes five working days for a cheque to complete the clearance cycle. It is common banking practice for a cheque to be credited to the payee's bank account on the date it is paid in and, therefore, unless the cheque was the subject of special clearance procedures, payment for VAT purposes will not strictly occur until the fifth working day following the date of presentation. However, where a trader's normal commercial practice is to use the date a cheque is received as the date of payment for accounting purposes, and provided the cheque is subsequently presented and cleared without undue delay, that date may be used as the payment date for VAT time of supply purposes. In the event of the cheque not being honoured, however, no payment will have occurred and any VAT accounted for on this basis may be adjusted accordingly. Where presentation of a cheque is delayed for any reason, the date of clearance is to be regarded as the date of payment. (C & E Manual V1-11, Chapter 2 para 4.7).

Payment by credit card, charge card, etc. Payment is not strictly received until the sum involved is paid over to the supplier by the card company. However, a trader may be permitted to treat the date of acceptance of the card as the payment tax point where this conforms with normal commercial accounting practice of the business and provided there is no unreasonable delay in processing the transaction. C & E do not allow this in cases where the card company withholds payment pending satisfactory delivery of goods (which can occur with mail order transactions). (C & E Manual V1-11, Chapter 2 paras 4.8).

Payment by bank transfer. Whether by standing order, direct debit, home banking facilities or other forms of electronic transfer, the time of payment for VAT purposes occurs when the amount in question is actually transferred into the recipient's bank account. (C & E Manual V1-11, Chapter 2 para 4.9).

Payment by book entry. A payment tax point can be created by a book entry or an adjustment to the accounting records (e.g. supplies between group companies may be recorded by offsetting sales and purchases ledger accounts or making entries in the inter-company current accounts). The time of payment is the date on which the appropriate entries are made in the accounting records (*Pentex Oil Ltd (7989, 7991)*). In order for there to be a payment tax point by book entry, the debt must actually have been settled or expunged. Entries that simply reflect or acknowledge an outstanding debt should not be regarded as evidence of payment for tax point purposes.

Where the value of a continuous supply of services is not agreed until the annual accounts of the business are drawn up, the date the accounts are approved may be taken to represent a payment tax point where they demonstrate that the supplies have been paid for by way of adjustment to each company's accounts.

(C & E Manual V1-11, Chapter 2 para 4.10).

Retention payments. Some contracts for the supply of goods or services provide for the retention of part of the consideration pending full and satisfactory performance of the contract (or of any part of it) by the supplier. This is a common feature of construction contracts and contracts for the supply and installation of plant and machinery.

Without special provisions, under the normal rules, the VAT on the retained element of the contract price would fall due at the basic tax point (see 64.39 and 64.49 below for goods and services respectively). However, in these circumstances the tax point for the retentions is delayed until either a VAT invoice is issued, or a payment is received, in respect of the retentions (whichever is the earlier). This only applies to the retained element of the contract price and the rest of the supply is subject to the normal tax point rules. In any case, the provisions do not apply to

- a supply of goods for acquisition by a taxable person in another EC country; and

- with effect from 1 January 1998, construction services under contracts providing for stage or interim payments (see 42.44 LAND AND BUILDINGS).

[*SI 1995/2518, Reg 89; SI 1997/2887, Reg 5*].

64.38 **Accommodation tax points**

C & E may, at the request of a taxable person, alter the time at which supplies are to be treated as made by him by either advancing or delaying the tax point. [*VATA 1994, s 6(10)*]. These are often referred to as accommodation tax points, the most common of which are considered below.

- **Monthly invoicing.** Many traders invoice for their supplies periodically, typically issuing a single invoice to each customer detailing the supplies made during the preceding monthly or four/five week commercial accounting period. Provided this represents the trader's normal commercial accounting practice, C & E, on written application, may grant an accommodation tax point without the trader being required to demonstrate that the normal tax point rules cannot be complied with. Applications should state whether the accommodation tax point is to be linked to the last day of the period covered by the invoice or the date of issue of the invoice. In the latter case, this will not normally be permitted to exceed 14 days from the end of the commercial accounting period. (C & E Manual V1-11, Chapter 2 para 6.2).

- **Exempt supplies of credit.** Supplies of goods on credit can involve both a taxable supply of goods and an exempt supply of credit. There is also an exempt supply of credit when a loan is made for interest or for some other form of consideration. In either case, particularly with agreements subject to fixed rates of interest, traders can have difficulty in identifying the proportion of the periodical repayment attributable to the supply of credit and the element in respect of either the goods or repayment of the capital amount in the case of a loan of money.

  Application may be made to C & E to use a single accommodation tax point for the supply of the credit provided the time nominated as the tax point is earlier than would otherwise be the case under the normal rules. For example, for supplies of credit in conjunction with a supply of goods, the accommodation tax point might be linked to the tax point for the supply of the goods. For a loan of money, a convenient tax point might be the date of the agreement or any other date before receipt of the first instalment.

  Applications should be in writing and signed by a person eligible to sign the trader's VAT returns. In the case of group registrations, the application must be made by the representative member. A suitable form of application is set out in C & E

Manual V1-11, Appendix E. Other forms of application may be accepted provided they contain the following information.

- The identity of the supplier.
- Details sufficient to identify precisely which supplies are intended to be covered by the direction.
- The event to be treated as the tax point for the supply.

Applications involving different tax points for different categories of exempt supplies of credit are acceptable provided they can be identified without difficulty. (C & E Manual V1-11, Chapter 2 para 6.3).

- **Corporate purchasing (procurement) cards.** Such cards are intended to be used as a method of payment by corporate customers with high levels of low value expenditure (e.g. stationery, spare parts and other expenditure delegated to individual staff members). They are designed to eliminate much of the paperwork in the purchasing process. The practical arrangements are similar to the use of credit cards and charge cards. Under normal circumstances, suppliers do not issue invoices to card-holders, invoicing being carried out on the supplier's behalf by the card company or bank using transaction information transmitted through the purchasing card system. A difficulty arises with such cards as the supplier is unaware of the date on which the card company or bank actually issues the invoice to the purchaser.

  Application may be made to C & E by the supplier for an accommodation tax point. This allows the tax point for all purchase card transactions to be the time at which the supplier keys the transaction details into the purchasing card system (the 'transmission date') provided all transactions are keyed into the system no later than the basic tax point (the date the goods are sent to, or taken away by, the customer). Card issuers have made it a condition of membership that potential suppliers will apply to use the accommodation tax point. (C & E Notice 701/48/97, paras 1, 2; C & E Manual V1-11, Chapter 2 para 6.4).

- **Ministry of Defence contractors.** There can be considerable delays in agreeing contract prices in the case of supplies made by defence industry contractors to the Ministry of Defence. Where one of the centrally agreed extensions to the 14 day rule is inadequate (see 64.39 and 64.49 below for supplies of goods and services respectively) application may be made for an accommodation tax point if the difficulties are wholly as a result of delays on the part of the MoD.

  Applications should be in writing and signed by a person eligible to sign the trader's VAT returns. In the case of group registrations, the application must be made by the representative member. A suitable form of application is set out in C & E Manual V1-11, Appendix G. If C & E agree, in cases where the consideration under an MoD contract is ascertained or ascertainable at or before the time when the goods are removed or the services performed, the supply in question is treated as taking place on the date a VAT invoice is issued or a payment is received, to the extent covered by the invoice or payment, but in any case not later than six years after the goods are removed or the services performed.

  (C & E Manual V1-11, Chapter 2 para 6.5).

- **'En primeur' wine.** 'En primeur' wine is wine that is offered for sale, whilst still lying in the producer's cellars abroad, for delivery in the UK by the wine merchant at some time in the future. Trade practice is normally to require the customer to pay the net price of the wine when submitting an order. Further charges, based on the duty and VAT payable, together with the costs of transportation, etc. become due from the customer at the time of delivery.

At the time the net price is paid, it is not certain that the wine will ever actually be removed to the UK. Even if it is, the wine may be sold by the customer, before taking delivery, while it is still subject to a warehousing regime in the UK. As a result, it has been agreed that if VAT does become due, the supply may be accounted for at the time the customer is invoiced for the VAT and other charges where, in accordance with trade practice, this takes place immediately prior to delivery in the UK.

(C & E Manual V1-11, Chapter 3 para 8.59).

- **Services received by members of the Institute of London Underwriters.** All claims on members of the Institute of London Underwriters (ILU) are processed centrally by the ILU. When a claim has been finalised the ILU issues a 'claim closing slip' to the underwriters advising them of their share of the liability arising from the claim and including details of services received from abroad in respect of the claim which have already been paid for on the underwriters behalf. This can be the first notification the underwriter receives in respect of the claim.

As an accommodation tax point, all supplies relating to the provision of marine and aviation insurance which are received by member companies of the ILU from abroad and which are treated as being made by them in the UK by virtue of the reverse charge procedure may be treated as taking place at the end of the day on which the claims closing advice for the related insurance claim is issued by the ILU.

(C & E Manual V1-11, Chapter 3 para 8.31).

64.39   TIME OF SUPPLY OF GOODS

Subject to

- any accommodation tax points agreed under 64.38 above,

- the special cases in 64.40 to 64.48 below,

- any extra-statutory class concession, and

- the provisions relating to warehoused goods (see 70 WAREHOUSED GOODS AND FREE ZONES),

a supply of goods is treated as taking place at the basic or actual tax point.

(a) **Basic tax point.** The basic tax point is determined as follows.

(i) *If the goods are to be removed*, the basic tax point occurs at the time of removal.

This normally occurs when the goods are delivered by, or on behalf of, the supplier or collected by, or on behalf of, the customer. Where there is more than one supply but only one movement of the goods (e.g. where the goods are supplied via a third party such as a finance company), it is necessary to determine to which of the supplies the removal relates (the remaining supply/supplies falling within (ii) below).

Where a single supply of goods involves delivery/collection over a period of time, provided there is genuinely a single supply (and not a succession of separate supplies) the basic tax point will not occur until the time of removal of the final consignment (although actual tax points under (b) below may have been created before that time).

(ii) *If the goods are not to be removed* at the time when they are made available to the customer.

The words 'if the goods are not to be removed' must be viewed in the context of the supply itself and not the nature of the goods involved. The 'made available' basic tax point is therefore not restricted to goods that are incapable of ever being moved. Examples include

- the supply of fully-assembled and installed goods on site (delivery of the components being merely a preliminary step to enable the supplier to supply what is required under the terms of the contract); and

- in the normal case of the supply of goods via a third party finance company where the finance company does not take physical delivery of the goods, the supply of the goods to the finance company by the trader.

(*b*)   **Actual tax points**.

(i) *Advance payment or invoicing*. If, before the basic tax point, the supplier issues a VAT invoice or receives payment in respect of the supply, there is a tax point at the time the invoice is issued or payment is received, whichever occurs first, to the extent covered by the invoice or payment. (There will thus always be a further tax point where the amount invoiced or paid is less than the full value of the supply.)

(ii) *The 14 day rule*. If the supplier issues a VAT invoice (or a taxable person issues a document to himself under the self-billing arrangements, see 40.2 INVOICES) within 14 days *after* the basic tax point, then, unless he has notified C & E in writing that he does not wish the rule to applied, the tax point is the date the invoice is issued. This rule does not, however, override (*b*)(i) above.

C & E normally expect a trader to either apply the 14 day rule to all supplies or to opt out of its use altogether. However, it may be applied selectively

- by separate companies in a VAT group registration;

- for supplies subject to the self-billing arrangements and supplies subject to conventional invoicing; or

- where a trader has a genuine need to treat some supplies differently and can easily distinguish those supplies.

Extending the 14 day rule under (*b*)(ii) above. C & E may, at the request of the taxable person, extend the 14 day rule in respect of all or part of his supplies. They will not do this unless the taxable person is genuinely unable to issue an invoice within 14 days of the basic tax point, e.g. where prices cannot be determined until invoices have been received for materials or subcontractors' charges. C & E are unlikely to grant any significant period of extension as any payment received between the basic tax point and the date when the invoice is actually issued does not create a tax point. It should also be noted that the tax point is only delayed if a VAT invoice is issued within the extended period. If, for any reason, it is not, the tax point reverts to the earlier basic tax point (rather than the date of expiry of the extended period) which may have penalty implications.

The following extensions to the 14 day rule have been centrally agreed.

1.   *Members of The British Electrical and Allied Manufacturers Association, The Scientific Instruments Manufacturers Association and The Electronic Engineering Association.* If the consideration for a supply of goods made by member companies under a Government contract is not ascertained or ascertainable at or before the time when the goods are removed, the supply may be treated as taking place at the time when the member issues a VAT invoice, provided it is issued within one year of the date of removal of the goods.

2.   *Government contracts.* Where a taxable person supplies goods for an agreed price under a Government contract and the supplier's invoicing is delayed due to Government procedures (e.g. the use of Ministry of Defence Form 640) the supply may be treated as taking place at the time a VAT invoice is issued, provided it is issued within four months of the date of removal of the goods.

3.   *Local authorities.* Where a local authority supplies taxable goods in the course of business activities, the supply may be treated as taking place at the time a VAT invoice is issued, provided it is issued within two months of the date of removal of the goods.

4.   *Scrap metal.* As the consideration for a supply of 'material on valuation' in the scrap metal trade is not ascertained or ascertainable at or before the time when the goods are removed, the supply may be treated as taking place at the time a VAT invoice is issued, provided it is issued within three months of removal of the goods.

5.   *The Society of British Aerospace Companies Ltd* (SBAC). If the consideration for a supply of goods made by member companies of SBAC is not ascertained or ascertainable at or before the time when the goods are removed (because the price is subject to negotiation and agreement after the work has been completed), the supply may be treated as taking place at the time a VAT invoice is issued, provided it is issued within six months of the date of removal of the goods (one year in the case of a Government contract).

[*VATA 1994, s 6(1)(2)(4)–(6)(9)(10); FA 1996, 3 Sch 1*]. (C & E Notice 700, para 5.1(a)(b); C & E Manual V1-11, Chapter 2 paras 3.2, 3.3, 5.5, 5.6, Appendix B).

64.40   **Disposal of business assets**

Where there is a supply of goods on the transfer or disposal of business assets under *VATA 1994, 4 Sch 5(1)* (see 64.3(*e*) above), the supply is treated as taking place when the goods are transferred or disposed of. [*VATA 1994, s 6(12)*]. This includes goods transferred for no consideration (i.e. goods taken out of the business permanently for non-business use). See also 47.5 OUTPUT TAX.

64.41   **Intra-EC supplies of goods**

Supplies to VAT registered persons in other EC countries. Where a supply of goods involves

•   the removal of the goods from the UK, and

•   their acquisition in another EC country by a person who is liable for VAT on their acquisition under the provisions of that country corresponding to those in 23.3 EUROPEAN COMMUNITY: SINGLE MARKET,

the time of supply is the earlier of the 15th day of the month following that in which the goods are removed or the date of the issue of a VAT invoice (or other prescribed invoice) in respect of the supply.

[*VATA 1994, s 6(7)(8)*].

Supplies to non-VAT registered persons in other EC countries. Such supplies are subject to UK VAT and the tax point is determined under the normal rules in 64.39 above.

Acquisitions of goods by taxable persons in the UK from another EC country. The time of supply (mirroring those above for supplies from the UK to registered persons) is the earlier of the 15th day of the month following that in which the first removal of the goods occurred and the date of the issue of an invoice by the supplier under the provisions of the law in the supplier's country corresponding to those relating the VAT invoices for UK supplies. [*VATA 1994, s 12; FA 1996, 3 Sch 3; SI 1995/2518, Reg 83*].

64.42 Hire purchase, credit sales and conditional sales

The supply of the goods. If the credit is 'self-financed', there is one supply of the goods by the trader direct to the customer. If a third party finance company is involved, there will normally be two supplies (by the trader to the finance company and by the finance company to the customer). However, this should not automatically be assumed. For example, there is unlikely to be a supply of the goods to the finance company where the finance consists of an unsecured loan.

Supplies of goods on hire purchase, credit sales and conditional sales are treated in the same way as an outright sale where title passes at the outset.

- *The basic tax point* for the supply to the customer is, in most cases, the date of delivery or collection of the goods. Where there are two supplies (see above) this is the supply by the finance company. The basic tax point for the supply by the trader to the finance company normally occurs at the time the goods are made available to the finance company. Unless the agreement indicates otherwise, this may be taken to be the time when the finance agreement comes into force, possibly at the time when the last party signs up to it.

- *A VAT invoice* issued to the customer (whether it is a conventional VAT invoice or the finance agreement adapted for the purpose) creates a tax point for the supply if it is issued in advance of, or within 14 days after, the basic tax point.

- *A deposit* paid before an agreement has come into force, or before the goods have been removed, or a VAT invoice has been issued, also creates a tax point.

The supply of the credit element. The tax point for the separate supply of credit is the date of payment of the interest. Where the instalments include an element attributable to the charge for credit this will mean that a tax point occurs each time that a payment is received. See, however, 64.38 above for an accommodation tax point in these circumstances.

(C & E Manual V1-11, Chapter 3 paras 8.25–8.29).

64.43 Goods supplied on sale or return and goods on approval

The following rules apply to sale or return agreements, i.e. where goods are supplied on terms whereby the customer has a right to return the goods at any point up until the time they are adopted but, in the meantime, ownership of the goods remains with the supplier. Retail supplies on these terms are generally referred to as being 'on approval'.

If goods are sent or taken on approval or sale or return (or similar terms) so that they are removed before it is known whether a supply will take place, the basic tax point is the time when it becomes certain that the supply has taken place ('adoption') or, if sooner, twelve months after the removal. If, however, before this time a supplier issues a VAT invoice in respect of the supply, the tax point for the amount invoiced is the date the invoice is issued. [*VATA 1994, s 6(2)(c)(4)*].

'Adoption' is not defined but normally occurs when the holder of the goods does something to indicate that the option to return the goods is not going to be exercised, e.g.

- the goods become the subject of an offer for resale by the holder;

- the holder allocates the goods to a customer;
- the goods are hired out by the holder to a customer;
- the holder uses the goods otherwise than for display purposes; or
- the goods are permanently modified or adapted by the holder or to the order of the holder.

Payment received by the supplier before the basic tax point does not, of itself, create a tax point in these circumstances although it normally indicates that the goods have been adopted and thus establishes a basic tax point at that time. However, this does not apply where it is a condition of the agreement that the recipient of the goods is required to pay an amount to the supplier in order to receive the goods in the first place. Provided this does not affect the unfettered right of the recipient subsequently to return the goods, the payment in these circumstances has no time of supply significance.

(C & E Manual V1-11, Chapter 3 paras 8.45-8.47).

64.44 **Land and property**

Freehold land. The supply of freehold land is a supply of goods [*VATA 1994, 4 Sch 4*] and the normal time of supply rules apply (see 64.39 above) subject to the rules below where the total purchase price cannot be determined at the time of the transfer.

Basic tax point. As land is incapable of removal, the basic tax point is when the land is made available to the purchaser, i.e. the date of the freehold conveyance (in Scotland, the time of delivery of the disposition which is known as the settlement date). If a prospective purchaser is allowed to enter the property in advance of completion (e.g. to carry out preliminary works or testing on the site), this does not advance the basic tax point for the sale of the freehold.

Actual tax points. The basic tax point is subject to the creation of an actual tax point by the issue of a VAT invoice in advance of, or within 14 days after, the basic tax point or the receipt of a payment in advance of the basic tax point.

It is common for a contract for the sale of the freehold interest in land to require the payment of a deposit by the purchaser at the time contracts are exchanged. If this is payable either direct to the vendor or to a solicitor acting as the vendor's agent, the deposit creates a tax point to the extent of the amount received. If, on the other hand, the deposit is received by a third party (which can be the vendor's solicitor) acting in the capacity of a stakeholder holding the money on behalf of both parties pending satisfactory performance of the contract, the payment does not create a tax point until it is released by the stakeholder to the vendor.

Where the total purchase price cannot be determined at the time the grantor grants or assigns the freehold interest, the land is treated as separately and successively supplied

- in respect of that part of the consideration which was determinable at the time of the grant or assignment, under the normal tax point rules as described above and in 64.39 above; and

- in respect of any part of the consideration not so determinable, at the earlier of the times whenever any such part is received by the grantor or the grantor issues a VAT invoice in respect of it.

This would apply, for example, where the vendor is entitled to receive a further payment in the event of the purchaser later obtaining planning permission, or the final consideration is dependent on any profit from future development of the land.

[*SI 1995/2518, Reg 84(2)*]. (C & E Manual V1-11, Chapter 3 paras 8.36, 8.37, 8.41)

Long leases and tenancies. The supply of a lease or tenancy exceeding 21 years (or Scottish equivalent) is regarded as a major interest in land and is treated as a supply of goods. [*VATA 1994, 4 Sch 4*].

Subject to below, if under the grant of such a lease or tenancy the whole or part of the consideration for the grant is payable periodically or from time to time, the goods are treated as separately and successively supplied each time that a part of the consideration is received or the supplier issues a VAT invoice relating to the grant, whichever is the earlier. This applies to rent, ground rent and any premium received.

Where, however, at or about the beginning of any period not exceeding one year, the supplier issues a VAT invoice which, in addition to the normal requirements for a VAT invoice, shows

(*a*)   the dates on which any parts of the consideration are to become due for payment in the period;

(*b*)   the amount payable (excluding VAT) on each such date; and

(*c*)   the rate of VAT in force at the time of issue of the VAT invoice and the amount of VAT chargeable in accordance with that rate on each payment,

the goods are to be treated as separately and successively supplied each time that a payment in respect of the tenancy or lease becomes due or is received, whichever is the earlier. If there is a change in the rate of VAT before any of the due dates for payment under (*a*) above, the invoice ceases to be treated as a VAT invoice in respect of any supplies for which payment is due after the change (and not received before the change). [*SI 1995/2518, Reg 85*].

Short-term leases. Supplies of leases not qualifying as long term leases above are supplies of services and are normally treated as continuous supplies of services within 64.50 below.

Compulsory purchase. In most cases of compulsory purchase, the transfer does not take place until the price has been agreed and the normal time of supply rules apply (see 64.39 above and 64.49 below for supplies of goods and services respectively). However, where, by or under any enactment, an interest in or right over land is compulsorily purchased and the person from whom the land is purchased does not know the amount of the payment he is to receive at the normal time for the supply, a supply is treated as taking place each time he receives any payment for the purchase. [*SI 1995/2518, Reg 84(1)*].

64.45   **Taxable self-supplies**

Where goods are treated as self-supplied by an order made under *VATA 1994, s 5(5)*, the supply is treated as taking place when they are appropriated to the use giving rise to the self-supply. [*VATA 1994, s 6(11)*].

Orders under *VATA 1994, s 5(5)* have been made in respect of motor cars (see 45.6 MOTOR CARS) and stationery (see 62.2 SELF-SUPPLY).

64.46   **Supplies of water, gas or any form of power, heat, refrigeration or ventilation**

Subject to below, a supply of

(i)   water (other than distilled or deionised water or water of a similar purity and water comprised in any of the excepted items set out in *VATA 1994, 8 Sch Group 1*, see 28.8 FOOD),

(ii) coal gas, water gas, producer gases or similar gases,

(iii) petroleum gases, or other gaseous hydrocarbons, in a gaseous state, or

(iv) any form of power, heat, refrigeration or ventilation,

is treated as taking place whenever a payment in respect of the supply is received or a VAT invoice is issued by the supplier, whichever is the earlier.

Where the whole or part of the consideration for a supply under (i)–(iii) above or of power in the form of electricity is determined or payable periodically or from time to time, goods are treated as separately and successively supplied each time that a part of the consideration is received or the supplier issues a VAT invoice relating to the supply, whichever is the earlier. Where such separate and successive supplies are made under an agreement which provides for successive payments and the supplier, at or about the beginning of any period not exceeding one year, issues a VAT invoice which, in addition to the normal requirements for a VAT invoice, shows

(*a*)   the dates on which payments under the agreement are to become due for payment in the period;

(*b*)   the amount payable (excluding VAT) on each such date; and

(*c*)   the rate of VAT in force at the time of issue of the VAT invoice and the amount of VAT chargeable in accordance with that rate on each payment,

goods are to be treated as separately and successively supplied each time that a payment in respect of the supply becomes due or is received, whichever is the earlier. If there is a change in the rate of VAT before any of the due dates for payment under (*a*) above, the invoice ceases to be treated as a VAT invoice in respect of any supplies for which payment is due after the change (and not received before the change).

Supplies to other EC countries. Supplies within (i)–(iv) above made to a taxable person in another EC country are treated as taking place on the day of the issue of the VAT invoice in respect of the supply.

[*SI 1995/2518, Reg 86*].

64.47   **Supplier's goods in possession of buyer**

Subject to below, where goods are supplied under an agreement where

- the supplier retains the property in the goods until all or part are appropriated under the agreement by the buyer, and

- the whole or part of the consideration is determined at that time,

the tax point is the earliest of

(*a*)   the date of such appropriation by the buyer;

(*b*)   the date when a VAT invoice is issued by the supplier; or

(*c*)   the date when a payment is received by the supplier.

If, within 14 days after the appropriation under (*a*) above, the supplier issues a VAT invoice in respect of goods appropriated, then, unless he has notified C & E in writing that he does not wish the 14 day rule to apply, the tax point is the time that invoice is issued. This does not however override (*b*) or (*c*) above if earlier.

The above provisions do not apply to

- goods on sale or return (for which see 64.43 above); or

- supplier's goods in the possession of the buyer where the goods are supplied to somebody liable to account for acquisition VAT on the supply in another EC country.

[*SI 1995/2518, Reg 88*].

64.48 Gold

VATA 1994, s 55 provides a special accounting and payment system for supplies of gold. *VATA 1994, s 55(4)* disapplies all tax point rules apart from the basic tax point in 64.39 above and the sale or return provisions in 64.43 above. This means that the tax point for supplies covered by the scheme will normally be the date of removal of the goods. See 30.4 GOLD AND PRECIOUS METALS for further details of the scheme.

64.49 TIME OF SUPPLY OF SERVICES

Subject to

- any accommodation tax points agreed under 64.38 above,

- any extra-statutory class concession, and

- the special cases in 64.50 to 64.58 below,

a supply of services is treated as taking place at the basic or actual tax point.

(*a*) **Basic tax point.** The basic tax point for services is the time when the services are performed. This is normally taken as the date when all the work except any outstanding invoicing has been completed.

(*b*) **Actual tax points.**

(i) *Advance payment or invoicing.* If, before the basic tax point, the supplier issues a VAT invoice or receives payment in respect of the supply, there is tax point at the time the invoice is issued or payment is received, whichever occurs first, to the extent covered by the invoice or payment. (There will thus always be a further tax point where the amount invoiced or paid is less than the full value of the supply.)

(ii) *The 14 day rule.* If the supplier issues a VAT invoice (or a taxable person issues a document to himself under the self-billing arrangements, see 40.2 INVOICES) within 14 days *after* the basic tax point, then, unless he has notified C & E in writing that he does not wish the rule to be applied, the tax point is the date the invoice is issued. This rule does not, however, override (*b*)(i) above.

C & E normally expect a trader to either apply the 14 day rule to all supplies or to opt out of its use altogether. However, it may be applied selectively

- by separate companies in a VAT group registration;

- for supplies subject to the self-billing arrangements and supplies subject to conventional invoicing; or

- where a trader has a genuine need to treat some supplies differently and can easily distinguish those supplies.

Extending the 14 day rule under (*b*)(ii) above. C & E may, at the request of the taxable person, extend the 14 day rule in respect of all or part of his supplies. They will not do this unless the taxable person is genuinely unable to issue an invoice within 14 days of the basic tax point, e.g. where prices cannot be determined until invoices have been received. C & E are unlikely to grant any significant period of extension as any payment received between the basic tax point and the date when the invoice is actually issued does not create a tax point. It should also be noted that the tax point is only delayed if a VAT invoice is issued within the extended period. If, for any reason, it is not, the tax point reverts to the earlier basic tax point (rather than the date of expiry of the extended period) which may have penalty implications.

The following extensions to the 14 day rule have been centrally agreed.

1. *Members of The British Electrical and Allied Manufacturers Association, The Scientific Instruments Manufacturers Association and The Electronic Engineering Association.* If the consideration for a supply of services made by member companies under a Government contract is not ascertained or ascertainable at or before the time when the services are performed, the supply may be treated as taking place at the time when the member issues a VAT invoice, provided it is issued within one year of the date of performance of the services.

2. *Government contracts.* Where a taxable person supplies services for an agreed price under a Government contract and the supplier's invoicing is delayed due to Government procedures (e.g. the use of Ministry of Defence Form 640) the supply may be treated as taking place at the time a VAT invoice is issued, provided it is issued within four months of the date of performance of the services.

3. *Local authorities.* Where a local authority supplies taxable services in the course of business activities, the supply may be treated as taking place at the time a VAT invoice is issued, provided it is issued within two months of the date of performance of the services.

4. *Patent agents.* If the consideration for a supply of services by a patent agent is not ascertained or ascertainable at or before the time when the services are performed, the supply may be treated as taking place at the time a VAT invoice is issued, provided it is issued within three months of the date of performance of the service.

5. *The Society of British Aerospace Companies Ltd* (SBAC). If the consideration for a supply of services made by member companies of SBAC is not ascertained or ascertainable at or before the time when the services are performed (because the price is subject to negotiation and agreement after the work has been completed), the supply may be treated as taking place at the time a VAT invoice is issued, provided it is issued within six months of the date of performance of the services (one year in the case of a Government contract).

6. *Solicitors.* If the consideration for a supply of services by a solicitor is not ascertained or ascertainable at or before the time when the services are performed, the supply may be treated as taking place at the time a VAT invoice is issued, provided that it is issued within three months of the date of performance of the services.

[*VATA 1994, s 6(3)–(6)(9)(10)*]. (C & E Notice 700, para 5.1(a)(b); C & E Manual V1-11, Chapter 2, para 5.5, 5.6, Appendix B).

64.50   Continuous supplies of services

Subject to

*   the provisions below on advance invoicing, and

*   special provisions applying in the construction industry (see 64.52 below)

where services are supplied for any period for a consideration the whole or part of which is determined or payable periodically or from time to time, the services are treated as separately and successively supplied each time payment is received or a VAT invoice relating to the supply is issued by the supplier, whichever is the earlier. [*SI 1995/2518, Reg 90(1); SI 1997/2887, Reg 2*].

It is important to distinguish between supplies that fall within this category and work done over a period that culminates in a single supply (e.g. preparation of a client's will by a solicitor) or a series of separate supplies made over a period.

Example

A central heating engineer supplies services to a customer over a period of one year.

(1) If the engineer is simply called out to repair the customer's boiler as and when it breaks down, there is a series of separate supplies each with basic tax point based on performance.

(2) If the engineer's supplies are made under a contract to service the boiler at regular intervals and undertake repairs where necessary

- where the contract is for a fixed period at a fixed price and is not renewable (e.g. it was secured by tender), the supply represents a single supply of services performed over an extended period; and

- where the contract is open-ended or renewable and the amounts due under the contract are calculated or payable periodically or from time to time, the supply is a continuous supply of services.

The important elements are the existence of a contract (written, oral or implied) which commits the parties to doing something during the period and the on-going nature of the supply. An understanding that work will be undertaken should the need arise is not sufficient.

Examples of the type of supply that can meet the above criteria include

- the services of a trustee;

- regular or periodic maintenance work;

- services supplied by credit card companies to retailers;

- club membership;

- management services;

- agency services;

- long-term loans or secondments of staff; and

- hire, lease or rental of equipment.

(C & E Manual V1-11, Chapter 3 para 8.22).

In *B J Rice & Associates v C & E Commrs CA, [1996] STC 581* professional services were supplied and invoiced before registration but not paid for until after registration. The tribunal and High Court both held that, as an invoice raised before registration could not be a VAT invoice, the time of supply could only be the date payment was received and therefore VAT was due on the supply. The Court of Appeal, by a majority decision, reversed this decision holding that the provisions as to time of supply determine when, but not whether, VAT is to be charged. Liability is determined under *VATA 1994, s 4* which, *inter alia*, provides that VAT is charged where the supply is made by a taxable person. In this case, the supply was made at a time when the appellant was not a taxable person. See also *C & E Commrs v British Telecommunications plc CA, [1996] STC 818* for a consideration of the time of supply where customers unintentionally make overpayments. For a payment to represent consideration for a supply of services, there must be a direct link with the service provided. The inadvertent overpayment of a current debt is not a payment on account of a future liability and the recipient is under an immediate obligation to repay it.

Advance invoicing. Where separate and successive supplies of services are made under an agreement which provides for successive payments and, at or about the beginning of any period not exceeding one year, the supplier issues a VAT invoice which, in addition to the normal requirements for a VAT invoice shows

(*a*)   the dates on which payments under the agreement are to become due in the period;

(*b*)   the amount payable (excluding VAT) on each such date; and

(*c*)   the rate of VAT in force at the time of issue of the VAT invoice and the amount of VAT chargeable in accordance with that rate on each payment,

services are to be treated as separately and successively supplied each time that a payment in respect of them becomes due or is received, whichever is the earlier. If there is a change in the rate of VAT before any of the due dates for payment under (*a*) above, the invoice ceases to be treated as a VAT invoice in respect of any supplies for which payment is due after the change.

[*SI 1995/2518, Reg 90(2)(3)*].

The customer must not reclaim, as input tax, any VAT shown on the VAT invoice until the date on which the payment is due or until payment has been received by the supplier, whichever happens first. (C & E Notice 700, para 5.2). See also *The Simkins Partnership (9705)*.

Telecommunication services. Revised provisions for the place of supply of relevant telecommunications services within *VATA 1996, 5 Sch 7A* were introduced for supplies made after 30 June 1997. See 64.27(*h*) and 64.28 above. Special transitional time of supply provisions apply where such services are continuous supplies. See 39.9 INTERNATIONAL SERVICES.

64.51   Royalties and similar payments

The granting, assignment or surrender of the whole or part of any right is a supply of services. This can take various forms.

Licences. A licence is a supply of rights that specifically permits the licensee to do something in connection with a copyright or patent held by the licensor. It is may be issued for a set period (with or without option to renew) or for the life of the copyright or patent.

Where a licence is issued for a single payment, the supply is a single supply of services and the basic tax point occurs when the licence is granted. Where the licence agreement provides for payments to be made periodically, or from time to time, the service may be treated as a continuous supply within 64.50 above, VAT becoming due every time a payment is received or a VAT invoice is issued by the licensor, whichever is the earlier.

(C & E Manual V1-11, Chapter 3 paras 8.42, 8.43).

Permanent assignments. Alternatively, a supply can take the form of a permanent, outright assignment or surrender of the rights. This is normally a single supply of services to which the normal tax point rules apply. The basic tax point occurs at the time the rights are assigned.

Special provisions, however, apply if the contract provides for the assignor to receive periodic payments of royalties, repeat fees, etc. where some or all of the consideration is dependant on future events (e.g. the level of subsequent sales or repeat broadcasts).

Where the whole amount of the consideration for the supply of services was not ascertainable at the time when the services were performed and subsequently the use of the benefit of those services by a person other than the supplier gives rise to any payment of consideration for that supply which is

- in whole or in part determined or payable periodically or from time to time or at the end of any period,

- additional to the amount, if any, already payable for the supply, and

- not a payment to which the rules relating to continuous supplies of services under 64.50 above apply,

a further supply is treated as taking place each time a payment in respect of the use of the benefit of those services is received, or a VAT invoice is issued, by the supplier, whichever is the earlier.

[*SI 1995/2518, Reg 91*]. (C & E Manual V1-11, Chapter 3 paras 8.42, 8.44).

C & E take the view that *Reg 91* creates a further time of supply for the original supply. This means that the liability is determined by the VAT rate that applied to that supply at the time the rights were originally assigned. (C & E Manual V1-11, Chapter 3 para 8.44).

64.52   Supplies in the construction industry

The tax point for supplies in the construction industry depend upon the terms of payment under the contract for the supply.

(*a*)   Where the contract provides for periodic payments to the supplier (often referred to as stage payments or interim payments) a tax point arises at the earliest of

    (i)   the date a payment is received from the supplier;

    (ii)   the date the supplier issues a VAT invoice; and

    (iii)   for services performed after 8 December 1997, to the extent that the services have not already been treated as supplied under (i) or (ii) above, 18 months after the date on which the services were performed.

    [*SI 1995/2518, Reg 93; SI 1997/2887, Reg 5*].

(*b*)   Single payment contracts (even if payment of part of the price is to be delayed under a retention clause) are subject to the normal tax point rules (see 64.49 above).

See 42.44 LAND AND BUILDINGS for further details.

Retention payments. Where a contract within (*b*) above includes a retention clause, the tax point of the retained element is the earlier of the time when a payment is received in respect of the retention and the date the supplier issues an invoice relating to it. [*SI 1995/2518, Reg 89*]. Contracts within (*a*) above are specifically excluded from these provisions with effect from 1 January 1998. (Before that date, although the provisions applied to such contract, they were superfluous as the same result was achieved under *SI 1995/2518, Reg 93* above.) See 64.37 above and 42.44 LAND AND BUILDINGS for further details.

64.53   Services from outside the UK

Services which are treated as made by a person under *VATA 1994, s 8(1)* (reverse charge on services received from abroad, see 39.4 INTERNATIONAL SERVICES) are treated as being supplied when the supplies are paid for or, if the consideration is not in money, on the last day of the prescribed accounting period in which the services are performed. [*SI 1995/2518, Reg 82*].

64.54 Supply

See 64.38 above for an accommodation tax point for members of the Institute of London Underwriters.

64.54 Goods used for private or non-business use

Where business assets are put to any private use or are used (or made available to any person for use) for non-business purposes, a supply of services is treated as taking place under *VATA 1994, 4 Sch 5(4)* (see 47.5 OUTPUT TAX). The tax point for this supply of services is when the goods are appropriated to that private or non-business use [*VATA 1994, s 6(13)*]. If the services are supplied for any period, the tax point is the last day of the supplier's prescribed accounting period (or of each such accounting period) in which the goods are made available or used. [*SI 1995/2518, Reg 81(1)*].

64.55 Free supplies of services

Where services specified in any Order made by the Treasury under *VATA 1994, s 5(4)* are supplied for any period, they are to be treated as supplied on the last day of the supplier's prescribed accounting period, or of each such accounting period, in which the services are performed. [*SI 1995/2518, Reg 81(2)*].

The only order made under these provision is the *VAT (Supply of Service) Order 1993 (SI 1993/1507)*. This covers certain services, originally acquired for business purposes, which are subsequently put to private or non-business use. See 47.5 OUTPUT TAX.

64.56 Supplies through coin-operated machines

Under the normal time of supply rules, the tax point for supplies made via coin-operated machines (e.g. vending machines, amusement machines and gaming machines) is the time the machine is used (or, more strictly, the time money is inserted). However, as an accounting convenience, operators may delay accounting for VAT until the takings are removed from a machine. (C & E Notice 48, ESC 2.6).

For all other purposes, the normal tax point rules apply. Therefore in the event of

- a theft of takings from a machine, VAT must still be accounted for in full on any supplies that have been made from the machine (see *Townville (Wheldale) Miners Sports and Recreation Club and Institute (719)* where coins fraudulently extracted were subject to VAT); and

- a change in the rate of VAT, operators must revert to the normal tax point rules for the purposes of determining the VAT rates to be applied where takings removed from machines cover supplies made both before and after the rate changed (see *Glasgow Vending Services (943)*).

(C & E Manual V1-11, Chapter 3 para 8.14).

64.57 Services supplied in units at very frequent intervals

For such services (e.g. metered units) where it is not possible to work out when each unit was supplied, the tax point is taken as the date when either a VAT invoice is issued or payment is received for services performed up to a specified date (e.g. when the meter is read), whichever happens first. (C & E Notice 700, para 5.4(g)).

64.58 Barristers and advocates

Services supplied by a barrister (in Scotland, an advocate), acting in that capacity, are treated as taking place at whichever is the earliest of the following times.

(a)   When the fee in respect of those services is received.

(b)   When the barrister issues a VAT invoice in respect of them.

(c)   The day when the barrister ceases to practise as such.

[*SI 1995/2518, Reg 92*].

These special rules were introduced because a barrister cannot sue for unpaid fees and frequently can have to wait a considerable period of time before outstanding fees are received from instructing solicitors. For most supplies by practising barristers, the tax point will be the receipt of payment under (a) above as the fee notes issued to solicitors normally do not become VAT invoices until they are receipted and returned to the solicitor following payment.

C & E will, however, permit the *payment* of VAT on outstanding fees at the time of ceasing to practise to be deferred until such a time as the fees are actually received or a VAT invoice is issued, whichever is earlier, provided that the barrister asks to adopt the special procedure detailed below. The barrister may continue to issue VAT invoices after the date of cancellation of registration for fees which are outstanding provided the underlying services were performed before that date. The tax point to be shown on the invoices is the date of cessation and VAT must be charged at the rate applicable at that time.

(i)   **Barristers who make no other taxable supplies.** On ceasing to practise, the barrister must notify C & E within 30 days and state whether he intends to pay the VAT due on his outstanding fees immediately or wishes to defer payment.

If he requests deferment, C & E send, with the final VAT return, a Form VAT 811 (and return envelope) on which the barrister must itemise every standard-rated fee which is still outstanding (or give an estimate), together with the name of the matter, client and date of the first fee note. A certified copy of the completed form will be returned when deferment is approved. In the final VAT return Form 193 (or Form 197 Welsh version), the barrister must include VAT on all fees *received* between the end of his last full VAT period and the date of cancellation of registration. However, if deferment has been agreed, he will be required to pay at this time only the VAT due on fees already received or shown on a VAT invoice. A copy of Form VAT 812 is then sent quarterly on which the barrister must show VAT due on any fees received (at the rate applicable at the time of cessation) or invoiced during the period of that return. Sufficient details must be given to cross-reference to Form VAT 811. When all outstanding fees have been received and the VAT paid, the barrister must make a declaration of final payment (with any explanation for fees shown on Form VAT 811 not collected). Records must be kept for inspection for one year after the declaration of final payment.

(ii)   **Barristers who continue to make other taxable supplies.** If a barrister who ceases to practise as such continues to make other taxable supplies but can show that their value will not exceed the deregistration limit in the next twelve months (see 59.8 REGISTRATION) he may ask C & E to cancel his registration. On his final return he must include VAT on all professional fees received and other supplies made between the end of his last full VAT period and the date of cancellation of registration. If he wishes to defer payment of VAT on outstanding fees, he should adopt the procedure outlined in (i) above.

Where the barrister who ceases to practise continues to make other taxable supplies and to be registered, he must include the VAT on all fees received and other supplies made during the period which covers the date he ceased to practice on his normal VAT return for that period. If he wishes to defer payment of VAT on the outstanding fees he must apply to the VAT office as outlined under (i) above. VAT on other taxable supplies should be accounted for on subsequent VAT return Forms 100 in the normal way. VAT in respect of professional fees outstanding at the time of ceasing to practise should be shown separately.

(iii) **Practising barristers who die.** The deceased barrister's clerk should notify C & E as soon as possible and the personal representative should state not later than ten days after the grant of probate or order for administration whether he wishes to pay VAT on the barrister's outstanding professional fees forthwith or to defer payment. If he wishes to defer payment, the personal representative should follow the procedure outlined in (i) above. The personal representative will be required to give the address to which further communications should be sent and to sign a suitably adapted VAT deferment application form and periodical accounts of professional fees received.

(iv) **Barristers who are partly exempt for VAT purposes.** Where a barrister has made exempt supplies since the beginning of the VAT year in which he ceased to practise and is applying for deferment of VAT on outstanding fees, it may be necessary in due course to make a special adjustment of the input tax he has reclaimed. Advice should be obtained from the VAT office.

(C & E Leaflet 700/44/93).

De Voil Indirect Tax Service. See V5.145; V6.111; V6.112.

65 Terminal Markets

Cross-reference. See 30 GOLD AND PRECIOUS METALS.

65.1 The Treasury have been given wide powers to make provisions for the VAT treatment of dealings on terminal markets and transactions of people ordinarily engaged in such dealings. These include the right to

(a) zero-rate or exempt the supply of any goods or services;

(b) register any bodies representing persons ordinarily engaged in dealings on a terminal market;

(c) disregard such dealings *by* persons represented under (b) above in determining liability to REGISTRATION (59) for VAT purposes;

(d) disregard such dealings *between* persons represented under (b) above for all purposes; and

(e) refund input tax attributable to such dealings on a terminal market.

Different regulations may be made for different terminal markets.

[*VATA 1994, s 50*].

65.2 **QUALIFYING MARKETS AND MARKET MEMBERS**

Regulations have been made under *SI 1973/173 (as amended)* for the zero-rating of certain supplies of goods and services in the course of dealings on specified terminal markets. To qualify, transactions must involve a member of the market which includes any person ordinarily engaged in dealings on the market. The following is a list of terminal markets included in the *Order* together with persons regarded by C & E as ordinarily engaged in dealing on the markets.

Market	*Persons regarded as market members*
London Metal Exchange	Ring dealing members and other members of the London Metal Exchange.
London Rubber Market	For actuals transactions — Class P (producer members), Class A (selling agent and importer members), Class B (broker members) and Class C (dealer members) of the Rubber Trade Association of London.
	For futures transactions on the London Rubber Terminal Market — floor and associate members of the London Rubber Terminal Market Association.
London Cocoa, Coffee, Sugar, Vegetable Oil, Wool Markets and Cocoa, Coffee, Sugar, Vegetable Oil, Soya Bean Meal Futures Markets	Full and associate members of the London Cocoa, Coffee, Sugar, Vegetable Oil, Wool and GAFTA Soya Bean Meal Terminal Market Associations

International Petroleum Exchange of London	Any full or associate member.
London Potato Futures Market	Any full or associate member.
London Gold Market	Any full or associate member.
London Silver Market	Any full or associate member.
London Grain Futures Market	Any member of the Grain and Feed Trade Association.
Liverpool Barley Futures Market	Any member of the Liverpool Corn Trade Association.
London Meat Futures Market	Any full or associate member.
London Platinum and Palladium Market	Any full or associate member.
London Securities and Derivatives Exchange Ltd (OMLX) (from 1 September 1997)	Any full or associate member

[*SI 1973/173, Art 2; SI 1975/385; SI 1980/304; SI 1981/338; SI 1981/955; SI 1984/202; SI 1985/1046; SI 1987/806; SI 1997/1836*]. (C & E Leaflet 701/9/85, Annex).

65.3   **ZERO-RATED TRANSACTIONS**

The transactions which are zero-rated are

(*a*) **Actual transactions** between two market members which result in the goods being delivered provided that if the market is the

- London Metal Exchange, the transaction is between members entitled to deal in the 'ring';

- London Rubber Market, London Gold Market, London Silver Market, the transaction is between members of the respective markets;

- Liverpool Barley Futures Market, the transaction is a sale registered at the Clearing House of the Liverpool Corn Trade Association Ltd;

- London Grain Futures Market, the transaction is a sale registered at the Clearing House of the Grain and Feed Trade Association; and

- London Cocoa, Coffee, Sugar, Vegetable Oil, Wool, Soya Bean Meal Futures, Meat Futures or Potato Futures or the International Petroleum Exchange of London, the transaction is a sale registered with the International Commodities Clearing House Ltd.

(*b*) **Futures transactions** in commodities ordinarily dealt with on the relevant market between two market members *or* a market member and a person who is not a market member provided the transactions do not lead to a delivery of the goods by the seller to the buyer.

(*c*) **The grant of an option** exercisable on a future date whether between two market members or a market member and a non-member. When an option is exercised, the resulting transaction should be considered under (*a*) or (*b*) above.

'*Delivery*' is not defined but is regarded by C & E as taking place when instructions are given for the goods to be physically removed from the warehouse, vault etc. If a futures transaction leads to a delivery of the goods, VAT must be accounted for on the basis of the original contract price.

[*SI 1973/173, Art 3; SI 1975/385; SI 1981/338*]. (C & E Leaflet 701/9/85, para 1).

London Bullion Market Association. C & E have agreed with the London Bullion Market Association certain practical rules to govern the VAT treatment of supplies of bullion (gold and silver excluding coins) on the London Bullion Market. See C & E Notice 700/57/95 for full details.

De Voil Indirect Tax Service. See V4.208.

65.4 Brokers' or agents' services

Such services provided by a market maker where the transaction falls within 65.3(*a*) or (*b*) above are zero-rated. [*SI 1973/173, Art 3*]. If the transaction ceases to be eligible for zero-rating, the services also cease to be zero-rated.

Brokers' services provided by a non-member are not zero-rated even if in relation to a supply of goods zero-rated under the above provisions or under *VATA 1994, 8 Sch Group 1* (relief for food). Where a taxable person introduces business to a broker and receives from that broker a fee or share of the latter's commission or brokerage, that fee etc. is the consideration for a standard-rated supply of services, even though the broker may be a market member who zero-rates his own services under the above provisions.

International services. In the opinion of C & E, brokers' services of arranging transactions in futures and options are financial services within *VATA 1994, 5 Sch 5*. See, however, *Gardner Lohman Ltd, [1981] VATTR 76 (1081)* where the tribunal held that the grant of a purchase option to acquire cadmium through the London Metal Exchange was not a financial service within *5 Sch 5*. Subject to this, the supply of services within *5 Sch 5* is outside the scope of UK VAT where the recipient either belongs in another member state and uses the supply for business purposes or belongs outside the member states. [*SI 1992/3121, Art 16; SI 1995/3038*].

(C & E Leaflet 701/9/85, paras 2–4).

65.5 ACCOUNTING

Where a person (whether a market member or not) supplies goods or services zero-rated under the provisions in 65.3(*a*)–(*c*) above, he is not required to record such transactions for VAT purposes. If he does wish to include such items in a VAT return (e.g. to increase the proportion of input tax recoverable where exempt supplies are also made), he must record *all* of them.

Where a supply of agents' services is not zero-rated under the above provisions, VAT must be accounted for on the full amount of commission or brokerage charged before deduction of any part paid to third parties. (C & E Leaflet 701/9/85, para 5).

66 Tour Operators' Margin Scheme

Cross-references. See 33 HOTELS AND HOLIDAY ACCOMMODATION; 68 TRANSPORT AND FREIGHT.

De Voil Indirect Tax Service. See V3.591; V6.191; V6.192.

The contents of this chapter are as follows.

66.1   **INTRODUCTION**

EC legislation. See 22.29 EUROPEAN COMMUNITY LEGISLATION.

UK legislation. The tour operators' margin scheme ('TOMS') is designed to provide uniformity of VAT treatment in and between EC countries. Most businesses that, without material alteration, buy in and re-sell travel, hotel, holiday and certain other services to travellers ('margin scheme supplies') must use the TOMS to account for VAT on these supplies. In many cases, the TOMS enables VAT to be accounted for on the full value of travel supplies without the tour operator having to register and account for VAT in every EC country in which the services are enjoyed. It does, however, equally apply to tour operators that buy in and re-supply travel facilities enjoyed wholly in the UK or wholly outside the EC.

Under the scheme,

- VAT cannot be reclaimed on margin scheme supplies bought in for resale;
- VAT does not have to be accounted for on the full selling price of the margin scheme supplies, only on the difference between the VAT-inclusive purchase price and the selling price (the 'margin');
- there are special rules for determining the place, liability and time of margin scheme supplies;
- VAT invoices cannot be issued for margin scheme supplies;
- there are special rules for calculating the VAT due on the margin; and
- the value of turnover for VAT registration purposes is the margin.

The relevant law is in *VATA 1994, s 53* and the *Value Added Tax (Tour Operators) Order 1987 (SI 1987/1806)* as amended. The law gives C & E certain powers in relation to the scheme, including specifying what goods and services are covered [*SI 1987/1806, Art 3(4)*] and how to work out the value of the supplies [*SI 1987/1806, Art 7*]. **To that extent, the provisions in 66.19-66.22 below and certain other provisions as indicated in the text have the force of law.**

66.2   **WHO MUST USE THE TOMS?**

The TOMS applies in principle to anyone who buys in and resells travel facilities for the direct benefit of a traveller, and regardless of whether the facilities are used for holiday or business purposes.

There is no definition of when a taxable person is acting as a tour operator for the purposes of the TOMS. C & E regard the provisions as applying to

- a travel agent acting as principal (including those acting as undisclosed agents); or
- any person providing, for the direct benefit of a traveller, services of a kind enjoyed by travellers and commonly provided by tour operators or travel agents.

On this basis, the TOMS applies whatever the nature of the business.

(C & E Notice 709/5/98, para 2.2, Glossary).

The CJEC have confirmed that to make the application of the TOMS depend upon whether a trader was formally classified as a travel agent or tour operator would create distortion of competition. Ancillary travel services which constituted 'a small proportion of the package price compared to accommodation' would not lead to a hotelier falling within the provisions but where, in return for a package price, a hotelier habitually offered his customers travel to the hotel from distant pick-up points in addition to accommodation, such services could not be treated as purely ancillary. *TP Madgett & RM Baldwin (t/a Howden Court Hotel) v C & E Commrs, CJEC [1998] STC 1189.*

66.3   **SUPPLIES COVERED BY THE TOMS**

Subject to the exclusions in 66.9 below, the TOMS must be used for

- 'margin scheme supplies'; and

- 'margin scheme packages' i.e. single transactions which include one or more margin scheme supplies and other types of supplies (e.g. in-house supplies, see 66.10 below).

(C & E Notice 709/5/98, para 2.3).

'*Margin scheme supplies*' are those supplies which are

- bought in for the purpose of the business, and
- supplied for the benefit of a 'traveller' without material alteration or further processing

by a tour operator in an EC country in which he has established his business or has a fixed establishment.

[*SI 1987/1806, Art 3(1)*].

A '*traveller*' is a person, including a business or local authority, who receives supplies of transport and/or accommodation, other than for the purpose of re-supply.

Examples

If meeting the above conditions, the following are always treated as margin scheme supplies.

- Accommodation
- Passenger transport
- Hire of means of transport
- Use of special lounges at airports
- Trips or excursions
- Services of tour guides

Other supplies meeting the above conditions may be treated as margin scheme supplies but only if provided as part of a package with one or more of the supplies listed above. These include

- Catering
- Theatre tickets
- Sports facilities

(C & E Notice 709/5/98, Glossary).

In a Dutch case, the CJEC ruled that *EC Sixth Directive, Art 26* applies to cases where only accommodation is provided, and is not restricted to cases where transport is also provided (*Beheersmaatschappij Van Ginkel Waddinxveen BV & Others v Inspecteur de Omzetbelasting Utrecht, CJEC 1992, [1996] STC 825*). A similar decision was reached in *Hotels Abroad Ltd (13026)*. See also *Aer Lingus plc, [1992] VATTR 438 (8893)* (where vouchers for accommodation or car hire provided to executive class passengers were held not integral or incidental to the supply of air transport and therefore fell within the margin scheme) and *Virgin Atlantic Airways Ltd, [1993] VATTR 136 (11096)* (where chauffeur-driven car services provided to certain passengers on international flights were held to fall outside the scheme).

66.4   **Nature of the supply**

The sale of a package of margin scheme supplies is treated as a single supply for VAT purposes. [*SI 1987/1806, Reg 3(2)*]. The nature of the services is that of putting together the package or organising the travel services. (C & E Notice 709/5/98, para 3.5).

66.5   **Place of supply**

The application of the normal place of supply rules are varied so that margin scheme supplies are treated as supplied

- in the EC country in which the tour operator has established his business, or

- if the supply was made from a fixed establishment, in the EC country in which the fixed establishment is situated.

[*SI 1987/1806, Art 5; SI 1992/3125*].

The effect of this is as follows

(a)   Where the supplier is established in the UK only, the place of supply is the UK.

(*b*)   Where the supplier has an establishment in more than one country

- if the establishment from which the supplies are made is in the UK, the place of supply is the UK;

- if the establishment from which the supplies are made is in another EC country, the supply is outside the scope of UK VAT (but the tour operator is likely to be taxable in that other EC country and may therefore be liable to register for VAT there); and

- if the establishment from which the supplies are made is outside the EC, the supplies are not margin scheme supplies and the TOMS does not apply. The normal VAT place of supply rules apply. See 64.18 SUPPLY. [*SI 1987/1806, Art 3*].

(C & E Notice 709/5/98, para 3.6).

See 64.19 SUPPLY for a consideration of the terms 'business establishment' and 'fixed establishment'. See also *C & E Commrs v DFDS A/S CJEC, [1997] STC 384* where a UK subsidiary acted as agent for a Danish company and received commission on package tours sold on its behalf. On the facts, the subsidiary was held to be a fixed establishment.

Where margin scheme supplies are made from an establishment in another EC country, it may be necessary to register for VAT there.

66.6   **Liability of TOMS supplies**

Where margin scheme supplies are made in the UK (see 66.5 above) the whole of the margin is

- standard-rated when the supplies and enjoyed in the EC (see 21.2 EUROPEAN COMMUNITY: GENERAL for the VAT territory of the EC); and

- zero-rated when enjoyed outside the EC.

The liability of in-house supplies (see 66.10 below) is not affected by their inclusion in a margin scheme package.

Transport enjoyed inside and outside the EC. C & E have given the following guidance.

(*a*)   *Journeys without stops.* Where the journey begins or ends outside the EC, it may be treated as wholly enjoyed outside the EC. Temporary stops for 'comfort' or refuelling are not regarded as stops provided passengers cannot break their journey. Return legs should be treated in the same way as outbound journeys unless there is a material difference between the two legs (e.g. a stop).

Example

A coach journey from the UK to Switzerland via France is treated as enjoyed wholly outside the EC if there are no stops in the UK or France.

(*b*)   *Journeys with stops.*

(i) *General.* Where a journey involves travel both inside and outside the EC and a stop takes place in the EC, a fair and reasonable apportionment must be made between the EC and non-EC elements. This could be on the basis of EC/non-EC mileage or the number of nights spent inside/outside the EC.

(ii) *Cruises.* Apportionment on the basis of days in/out of the EC according to the itinerary is acceptable. For this purpose, the day on which the vessel leaves a non-EC port for an EC port may be regarded as a day outside the EC and the day on which it leaves an EC port for a non-EC port as a day in the EC. Time spent travelling between EC ports is to be regarded as inside the EC.

(iii) *Connected flights.* A second and/or subsequent flight is not regarded as a separate journey provided that the connection is made, in the case of an international connecting flight, within 24 hours of the scheduled arrival of the first flight and, in the case of a domestic connecting flight, within six hours of that time.

Examples

(1) A passenger buys a ticket for travel from London to Brazil with a change of aircraft in Paris. If the flight from Paris to Brazil is made within 24 hours of the scheduled arrival of the flight from London to Paris, the London–Paris leg is zero-rated.

(2) A passenger buys a return ticket for travel from Manchester to Brazil with a change of aircraft at London in each direction. If the outward flight from London to Brazil is made within 24 hours of the scheduled arrival of the flight from Manchester to London, the Manchester–London leg is zero-rated. On return, if the connecting flight from London to Manchester is within six hours of the scheduled arrival of the flight from Brazil to London, the Manchester–London leg is zero-rated.

[*VATA 1994, 8 Sch Group 8, Item 12*]. (C & E Notice 709/5/98, para 3.7, Appendix H).

66.7   **Time of supply**

The normal time of supply rules do not apply to TOMS supplies. Instead, one of the two methods below must be used to work out the tax point for margin scheme supplies and any in-house supplies (see 66.10 below) sold with margin scheme supplies for a single charge. Whichever method is chosen, it must be applied to all such supplies. Written permission from C & E is needed to change methods but C & E will only allow a change in exceptional circumstances and not normally during a financial year.

The two methods for working out tax points are as follows.

(*a*) The earlier of

•   the date of departure; and

•   the first date on which the traveller occupies any accommodation.

(*b*) The earlier of

•   the date of departure;

- the first date on which the traveller occupies any accommodation; and

- the date of receipt of any payment by the tour operator (or a travel agent on its behalf) which

  (i) is a single payment covering the whole selling price; or

  (ii) exceeds 20% of the selling price; or

  (iii) exceeds 20% of the selling price where added to payments received to date on which VAT has not already been accounted for.

Example

A traveller buys a package holiday to Italy commencing 15 August.

(1)   He pays a 10% deposit on 20 January and the balance on 4 July.

   The tax point is 4 July for the full selling price of the holiday. The initial deposit is less than 20% and is therefore ignored.

(2)   He pays a 25% deposit on 20 January and the balance on 4 July.

   There is a tax point for 25% of the selling price on 20 January and 75% on 4 July (each being payments exceeding 20% of the selling price).

(3)   He pays 10% per month by direct debit commencing on 20 January and ending on 20 October.

   No tax points arise on the January or February payments. There is a tax point for 30% of the selling price on 20 March (when the payments to date first exceed 20%). Again no tax points arise on the April and May payments (assuming VAT has been correctly accounted for on the March tax point). There is a second tax point for 30% of the selling price on 20 June (based on the payments for April, May and June). No tax point arises on the July payment. There is a final tax point of 40% of the selling price on 15 August (the date of departure).

Cash accounting scheme. In view of the special tax point rules above, the cash accounting scheme cannot be used for margin scheme supplies or for in-house supplies and agency supplies sold as part of a margin scheme package.

[*SI 1987/1806, Art 4*]. (C & E Notice 709/5/98, paras 3.8, 6.2).

66.8   VAT invoices

VAT invoices cannot be raised for supplies accounted for under the TOMS. This is because, at the time of supply, the true amount of VAT due is not known and can only be determined when the year-end calculation is carried out (see 66.19 and 66.20 below). (C & E Notice 709/5/98, para 3.9).

66.9   SUPPLIES OUTSIDE THE TOMS

The following supplies should be dealt with outside the UK TOMS.

- Margin scheme supplies which are not made in the UK. See 66.3 above for the place of supply provisions. Note that where the place of supply is another EC country, there may be a liability to register for VAT and apply the equivalent TOMS in that country.

- Supplies which have been arranged as an agent or intermediary provided any commission received is readily identifiable. See 66.12 below.

- In-house supplies (see 66.10 below) and agency supplies (see 66.12 below) made without margin scheme supplies.

- Supplies to business customers for subsequent resale (subject to an election to account for VAT under the TOMS) and supplies to business customers for their own consumption (where an election to exclude such supplies from the TOMS has been made). See 66.11 below.

- Educational school trips supplied to local authority which are to be enjoyed in the UK. See 66.13 below.

(C & E Notice 709/5/98, para 2.3).

Incidental supplies. The TOMS need not be used if

- no supplies of accommodation or passenger transport are bought in for resale; and

- other supplies which would normally be margin scheme supplies are bought in for resale but there are reasonable grounds for believing that the turnover from such supplies in the one year then beginning will not exceed 1% of all the supplies made in that year.

An example of such supplies might be where a hotelier buys in car hire for re-supply to hotel guests.

[*SI 1987/1806, Art 14*]. (C & E Notice 709/5/98, para 4.5).

66.10   In-house supplies

In-house supplies are supplies which are not margin scheme supplies (see 66.3 above) or agency supplies (see 66.12 below). They therefore comprise supplies which are either

- made from own resources; or

- result from purchases which the business has materially altered or further processed so that what is supplied is substantially different from what was purchased.

Where in-house supplies are sold *without* margin scheme supplies, VAT must be accounted for outside the TOMS in the normal way. In such cases, if two or more in-house supplies chargeable at different rates are sold as a package, the total consideration must be apportioned. See 47.3 OUTPUT TAX for treatment of mixed supplies.

Where in-house supplies are sold *with* margin scheme supplies as part of a package, the margin scheme calculations must be used to work out the value of all parts of the package. See 66.19 to 66.21 below.

Place of supply. The place of supply of in-house supplies, whether or not they are part of a margin scheme package, is determined using the normal VAT rules. The place of supply will therefore depend upon the nature of the services provided. See 64.18 *et seq.* SUPPLY. For example, passenger transport is supplied where it takes place (see 64.29), hotel accommodation is supplied where the accommodation is situated (see 64.21) and live entertainment is supplied where it is physically performed (see 64.23). As a result, if the place of supply is in another EC country, it may be necessary to register and account for VAT in that country.

Examples of in-house supplies. C & E give the following examples.

(*a*)   *Coach transport* where a tour operator owns or hires a coach and supplies a driver, fuel, etc.

(*b*)   *Airline charter*. Under a special scheme the supply of a charter flight by a tour operator to a customer may be treated as an in-house supply (thus retaining the zero-rating for the provision of transport) provided the tour operator meets the following conditions.

- It charters the whole aircraft and not just a block of seats.

- It enters into a contract with the airline for the provision of the aircraft and crew for an entire season (e.g. slot 1 every Wednesday from May to October). A season is defined as either a summer season (May to October), a winter sun season (November to April) or a winter sport season (December to April).

- It puts its own catering facilities on board or buys them in from a separate source. This could be a separate catering company (including one set up by the charter airline) or a specialist catering broker.

- It buys in transfer journeys from a separate source.

For further details of the scheme, including implementation and accounting implications, see VAT Information Sheet 3/96, July 1996 produced in co-operation with ABTA.

(*c*)   *Cruises* where a tour operator

- charters a vessel from another owner including deck/engine crew but employs or engages own 'hotel'/domestic/catering staff; or

- charters a vessel from another owner for a period of two years or more. The vessel need not necessarily be in service throughout the period but the owner must not have the right to use the vessel to make supplies to other customers during the period.

(*d*)   *Accommodation* where a tour operator

- owns the hotel, etc.;

- hires, leases or rents accommodation under an agreement whereby it takes responsibility for the upkeep of the property and is required to undertake any maintenance to the fabric of the building (i.e. not just general cleaning, changing bed linen, etc.); or

- rents space at a camp-site, installs its own tents or caravans, and sells accommodation in them (but not where accommodation in tents/caravans is bought in from a third party who provides both the site and tents/ accommodation or where space at a camp-site is bought in and customers provides their own tents/caravans — both of which are margin scheme supplies).

(*e*)   *Tuition* where a tour operator organises courses by putting together a number of elements such as teachers, classrooms, lecture theatres, projectors and other teaching aids, lighting, heating, etc. If a tour operator simply buys in a place on a course from a third party who has organised the course and sells this on as part of a package with transport and/or accommodation, the supply is a margin scheme supply.

(*f*)   *Conferences* where the organiser hires a room and provides necessary equipment (e.g. microphones, projectors, hand-outs), reception staff, etc. Any refreshments served at such a conference form part of the in-house supply of an organised conference, even if purchased from an outside caterer.

Where overnight accommodation and/or passenger transport for delegates is also supplied, this is not part of an organised conference and if these supplies are bought in and re-supplied without material alteration, they must be accounted for under the TOMS (but see 66.11 below where they are re-supplied to business customers). Other supplies (e.g. restaurant meals outside conference hours, theatre tickets) are also margin scheme supplies if supplied as part of a package with overnight accommodation/passenger transport.

(C & E Notice 709/5/98, para 3.6, Glossary, Appendix I).

66.11 **Supplies to business customers**
Whether supplies to business customers should be accounted for under the TOMS depends upon whether those supplies are for subsequent resale or for consumption by the business.

(*a*) **Supplies to business customers for subsequent resale (wholesale supplies)**. Subject to the trade facilitation measure below, these supplies are outside the scope of the TOMS and should be accounted for under the normal VAT rules. It is only when the transport, accommodation, etc. is provided to the traveller that the supplies are treated as margin scheme supplies and fall within the TOMS.

This allows a tour operator to set up an associated transport broking company to buy in transport from transport providers and sell it on to the tour operator outside the TOMS. This supply to the tour operator is zero-rated or outside the scope of UK VAT depending on the circumstances. See 68.14 TRANSPORT AND FREIGHT. The transport company cannot be in the same VAT group as the tour operator. For further details of the scheme, including implementation and accounting implications, see VAT Information Sheet 1/97, May 1997 produced in co-operation with ABTA.

As a trade facilitation measure, a tour operator can request permission from C & E to treat wholesale supplies as margin scheme supplies. Permission will be granted provided that

• the tour operator accounts for all its wholesale supplies under the TOMS; and

• C & E are satisfied that the tour operator can account for VAT properly and that its own officers can readily check the accuracy of the VAT returns.

Such treatment will mean that business customers cannot reclaim any VAT on margin scheme supplies received. Also, other EC countries may not recognise the concession and may require the tour operator to register and account for VAT there.

(*b*) **Supplies to business customers for their own consumption**.

With effect from 1 January 1998, subject to the trade facilitation measure below, supplies made to a business customer for use by that customer for the purposes of its business (e.g. for business travel) fall within the TOMS where they meet the definition of margin scheme supplies.

As a trade facilitation measure (which has the force of law), such supplies may be excluded from the TOMS and treated under normal VAT rules. In the case of supplies enjoyed in the UK, this enables the tour operator, with the permission of C & E, to issue VAT invoices to business customers. In the case of any supplies enjoyed in another EC country, it is a condition that VAT on those supplies has been paid to the VAT authority in that country and evidence of this is available for C & E.

Transitional arrangements at 1 January 1998. Where, before 1 January 1998, UK VAT was reclaimed on supplies (e.g. hotel accommodation) which were subsequently supplied to business customers for their own consumption on or after that date, VAT on the onward supply must be accounted for outside the TOMS. Where no VAT was reclaimed, VAT must be accounted for under the TOMS on the onward supply (subject to the facilitation measure above).

After 31 December 1995 and before 1 January 1998, the above provisions did not apply and all supplies to other businesses, whether or not for their own consumption, were treated as under (*a*) above.

[*SI 1987/1806, Art 3(3)*]. (C & E Notice 709/5/98, paras 4.1–4.3, Appendix E, TL1).

66.12 **Supplies by agents**

The TOMS does not cover

(*a*) supplies made by an agent or intermediary without margin scheme supplies; or

(*b*) supplies arranged by an agent or intermediary where the agency commission is readily identifiable. For these purposes, where a fixed amount or a fixed percentage rate of commission has been agreed this is seen as an identifiable commission. Where, on the other hand, the agent is given a net cost and allowed to set its own commission, this is an unidentified commission.

A business would normally be regarded as acting as an agent for the supplier or the customer (or both) where the following criteria are satisfied.

- There is some documentary evidence from the principal confirming that the agency exists.

- There are clear statements included in the terms and conditions of the contract with the customer that the goods or services are supplied by a named principal. An arrangement under which the principal remains undisclosed to the customer would not satisfy this condition.

- As an agent, the business would not be expected to be taking any significant commercial risk.

For the liability of arranging travel and other facilities as an agent or intermediary, see 4.17 AGENTS.

As a result of (*b*) above, a tour operator can use the 'agency option' scheme by entering into an agency arrangement, normally with a transport provider. Provided the conditions of the scheme are met, the supply of transport services is directly from the transport provider to the final customer. As the supply is not made by the tour operator, the transport services are not margin scheme supplies and fall outside the TOMS. Thus, whether supplied singly or as part of a package, the transport element and the tour operator's services of arranging the transport, are free of UK VAT (being either zero-rated or outside the scope).

Similar agency arrangements can be set up for the provision of accommodation and catering. However, as such supplies are subject to VAT at the standard-rate, the related commission will normally be standard-rated and there will be no benefit in entering into these arrangements. Additionally, in respect of accommodation, if the accommodation is in another EC country and the commission is charged to a non-VAT registered person, this could give rise to a liability for the tour operator to be VAT registered in that country. For these reasons, it is unlikely that the 'agency option' scheme should be adopted for such supplies.

66.13 Tour Operators' Margin Scheme

See 66.29 below for the accounting implications of using the 'agency option' scheme. For details of how to implement the scheme, see VAT Information Sheet 4/96, July 1996 produced in co-operation with ABTA.

(C & E Notice 709/5/98, paras 2.3, 2.4).

66.13 Supplies to LOCAL AUTHORITIES AND STATUTORY BODIES (43)

Note. The provisions of this paragraph have the force of law.

Local authority schools. The provision of an educational school trip by a local authority school to its pupils is a non-business activity for VAT purposes. The local authority is entitled to a refund of any VAT incurred under *VATA 1994, s 33* (see 43.5 LOCAL AUTHORITIES AND STATUTORY BODIES). Northern Ireland Education Boards are entitled to refunds on such supplies under *VATA 1994, s 99* (see 46.1 NORTHERN IRELAND).

A business supplying trips to such bodies which are to be enjoyed in the UK can exclude the supply from the TOMS. This means that VAT invoices can be issued to the local authority or Education Board which can recover the VAT.

The above provisions do not apply to colleges, universities and non-LEA schools because they are not entitled to such refunds. Supplies to these bodies are not, however, margin scheme supplies if the services are re-supplied by the college, etc. to its students in a business capacity. See 66.11 above.

(C & E Notice 709/5/98, para 4.4, Appendix E, TL2).

66.14 INPUT TAX

Input tax cannot be reclaimed on goods or services acquired for re-supply as margin scheme supplies. [*SI 1987/1806, Art 12*]. This applies both to VAT incurred in the UK and in other EC countries.

Input tax can be reclaimed, subject to the normal rules, on

- overheads; and

- purchases relating to in-house supplies.

VAT incurred in other EC countries on overheads and purchases relating to in-house supplies can be refunded under the procedure in 21.22 *et seq.* EUROPEAN COMMUNITY: GENERAL. Note, however, that where supplies are made in another EC country, it may be necessary to register for VAT there. If so, this refund procedure cannot be used in that country.

(C & E Notice 709/5/98, para 3.4).

66.15 REGISTRATION

For VAT registration purposes, turnover is

- the total margin on margin scheme supplies; plus

- the full value of any other taxable (including zero-rated) supplies made in the UK.

(C & E Notice 709/5/98, para 3.1).

66.16 VAT group treatment

A business making margin scheme supplies cannot belong to a VAT group (see 31 GROUPS OF COMPANIES) if any other member of the proposed or existing group

- has an overseas establishment; and

- makes supplies outside the UK which would be taxable (including zero-rated) supplies if made in the UK; and

- supplies goods or services which will become, or are intended to become, margin scheme supplies (i.e. which are for resale, whether or not by the other member concerned).

[*SI 1987/1806, Art 13*]. (C & E Notice 709/5/98, para 3.2).

66.17   CALCULATION OF MARGINS AND OUTPUT TAX

Special calculations as laid down by C & E are required under the TOMS to ensure that sales include only the margin for margin scheme supplies but the full value of any in-house supplies made. The purpose of the calculations are therefore to

- work out the total margin achieved;

- apportion the total margin between different types of supplies (e.g. margin scheme supplies (see 66.3 above) and in-house supplies (see 66.10 above));

- apportion the total margin between supplies which may have different VAT liabilities (e.g. standard-rated and zero-rated supplies);

- work out the value of in-house supplies; and

- work out the output tax on margin scheme packages.

As precise figures are not usually known at the time of preparing the VAT returns, the TOMS requires VAT to be accounted for each quarter (or month if monthly returns are made) using *provisional* figures. The final margins and output tax are based on an annual calculation and adjustment at the end of the *'financial year'*, i.e. the year for which financial accounts are made up. This final calculation determines the output tax due for the preceding financial year and provides the percentage to calculate provisional output tax in the subsequent financial year. See 66.19 to 66.22 below for the methods of calculation which *must* be used.

[*SI 1987/1806, Art 7*]. (C & E Notice 709/5/98, paras 3.3, 5.1, 5.2).

66.18   Starting to use the scheme

Where a business is newly registered or an existing business starts to use the TOMS for the first time, it must calculate a provisional margin percentage to use during the first financial year under the scheme. Depending upon the circumstances, this may be based upon

- previous trading figures;

- projected costings and margins; or

- actual quarterly figures during the first year.

Whichever method is used, the first annual adjustment (see 66.19 below) will correct any under or over payment of VAT arising in the year.

(C & E Notice 709/5/98, para 5.9).

66.19   End of year calculation (annual adjustment)

Note. The provisions of this paragraph have the force of law.

66.19 Tour Operators' Margin Scheme

The steps listed below are those needed to make the final calculations based on the actual figures for the financial year (i.e. the period for which accounts are prepared), except that

- if all supplies are liable to VAT at the same rate, the simplified calculation in 66.20 below must be used; and

- it is possible, with permission, to do a separate annual calculation for supplies enjoyed wholly outside the EC. See 66.22 below.

Any adjustment must be made on the first VAT return for a VAT period ending *after* the end of the financial year. For example, if the financial year ends on 31 March, any adjustment must be made, as the case may be, on the return to 30 April, 31 May or 30 June. It may therefore be useful to bring VAT periods in line with the financial year for accounts purposes in order to give the maximum time to calculate any adjustment. It is not necessary to wait for the production of full audited accounts before making the calculation. If the audit subsequently identifies errors or adjustments, the annual calculation should be reworked and the normal procedure for correction of errors followed. See 57.11 RECORDS.

The steps cover many combinations of supplies which means that, if not all of these different types of supplies are made, some steps can be omitted from the calculation.

The value of supplies and output tax are calculated by working out the total margin and then apportioning it between the different types and liabilities of supplies made. It is not necessary to work out a separate margin for each sale. Apportionment is based on the costs of supplies (but not indirect costs) and works on the principle that the same percentage margin is achieved on all elements of the package. For this reason, it is helpful if direct costs are recorded according to type and liability.

Total sales of margin scheme packages (see 66.24 below)

A   Add up the VAT-inclusive selling prices of margin scheme supplies and margin scheme packages supplied during the financial year

Purchase prices of margin scheme supplies (see 66.25 below)

B   Add up the VAT-inclusive purchase prices of standard-rated margin scheme supplies included in A above

C   Add up the VAT-inclusive purchase prices of zero-rated margin scheme supplies included in A above. (From 1 January 1996, the only margin scheme supplies which may be treated as zero-rated are those enjoyed outside the EC, see 66.6 above)

Direct costs of in-house supplies (see 66.26 below)

D   Add up the VAT-exclusive direct costs of standard-rated in-house supplies included in A above. Add a percentage of that amount equivalent to the standard rate of VAT

E   Add up the VAT-exclusive direct costs of zero-rated in-house supplies included in A above

F   Add up the VAT-inclusive direct costs of exempt in-house supplies included in A above. Deduct any input tax recoverable on these costs

G   Add up the direct costs of in-house supplies included in A above that are supplied outside the UK, exclusive of any VAT incurred on these costs that you are entitled to recover. Add to the total an uplift equivalent to the percentage VAT rate applicable to such supplies if VAT has been paid on these supplies to the VAT authorities in another EC country

'Costs' of agency supplies (see 66.29 below)

H	Add up the VAT-inclusive amounts paid by the business to principals in respect of the agency supplies included in A above for which the consideration received is standard-rated
I	Add up the VAT-inclusive amounts paid by the business to principals in respect of the agency supplies included in A above for which the consideration received is not standard-rated

Calculation of total margin

J	Add the total of costs at B to I above inclusive.
K	Calculate the total margin for all the supplies included in A by deducting the total at J from the total at A

Apportioning the margin

Calculate the proportion of the total margin (K) relating to each type of supply

L	Standard-rated margin scheme supplies	$\dfrac{B}{J} \times K$
M	Zero-rated margin scheme supplies	$\dfrac{C}{J} \times K$
N	Standard-rated in-house supplies	$\dfrac{D}{J} \times K$
O	Zero-rated in-house supplies	$\dfrac{E}{J} \times K$
P	Exempt in-house supplies	$\dfrac{F}{J} \times K$
Q	In-house supplies made outside the UK	$\dfrac{G}{J} \times K$
R	Standard-rated agency supplies	$\dfrac{H}{J} \times K$
S	Non-standard-rated agency supplies	$\dfrac{I}{J} \times K$

Calculation of output tax

On standard-rated margin scheme supplies	$L \times 7/47$
On standard-rated in-house supplies	$(D + N) \times 7/47$
On standard-rated agency supplies	$R \times 7/47$

Calculation of sales value

Standard-rated margin scheme supplies	$L \times 40/47$
Standard-rated in-house supplies	$(D + N) \times 40/47$
Zero-rated in-house supplies	$E + O$
Exempt in-house supplies	$F + P$
In-house supplies supplied outside the UK	$G + Q$

Annual adjustment. The difference between the provisional output tax which has been accounted for during the financial year on supplies included in A above and the total output tax due as calculated above is payable or deductible on the first VAT return for a VAT period ending *after* the end of the financial year.

(C & E Notice 709/5/98, paras 5.3, 5.5, 5.6, Appendix A, Appendix E, TL5).

66.20   Simplified calculation

Note. The provisions of this paragraph have the force of law.

If all component supplies of all margin scheme packages are liable to VAT at the same rate, the simplified method set out below must be used. It achieves the same results as the full calculation but avoids the need to work out costs of in-house supplies.

A   Add up the VAT-inclusive selling prices of margin scheme supplies and margin scheme packages supplied during the financial year

B   Add up the VAT-inclusive purchase prices of the margin scheme supplies included in A above

Output tax = $(A - B) \times 7/47$

VAT-exclusive value of margin scheme supplies and
margin scheme packages = $(A - B) \times 40/47$

Annual adjustment. The difference between the provisional output tax which has been accounted for during the financial year on supplies included in A above and the total output tax due as calculated above is payable or deductible on the first VAT return for a VAT period ending *after* the end of the financial year.

(C & E Notice 709/5/98, para 5.4, Appendix C, Appendix E, TL5).

66.21   Provisional percentages for the next financial year

Note. The provisions of this paragraph have the force of law.

When the procedure in 66.19 or 66.20 above has been completed, provisional percentages can be obtained for use in completing VAT returns for the next financial year. Revised provisional figures must be calculated each year.

Where the method in 66.19 above is used (capital letters correspond to those used in that paragraph)

1   Calculate the VAT-inclusive amount of standard-rated margin scheme supplies and margin scheme packages for the preceding financial year as a percentage of the total selling price of all margin scheme supplies and margin scheme packages in that year

$$\frac{D + L + N + R}{A} \times 100 = s\%$$

For each VAT period

2   Add up the VAT-inclusive selling prices of margin scheme supplies and margin scheme packages supplied during the VAT period = T

Provisional output tax = $T \times s\% \times 7/47$

Where the simplified calculation in 66.20 above is used (capital letters correspond to those used in that paragraph)

1   Calculate the VAT-inclusive amount of standard-rated margin scheme supplies and margin scheme packages for the preceding financial year as a percentage of the total selling price of all margin scheme supplies and margin scheme packages in that year

$$\frac{A - B}{A} \times 100 = s\%$$

For each VAT period

2   Add up the VAT-inclusive selling prices of margin scheme supplies and margin scheme packages supplied during the VAT period = T

Provisional output tax = $T \times s\% \times 7/47$

Provisional VAT-exclusive value of supplies = $(T \times s\%) \times 40/47$

(C & E Notice 709/5/98, para 5.7, Appendices B, D, Appendix E, TL5).

66.22   Separate calculation for non-EC supplies

Note. The provisions of this paragraph have the force of law.

An election can be made to make a separate calculation for supplies, or packages of supplies, provided which are enjoyed wholly outside the EC. It is only possible to change to separate calculations, or revert to a single calculation, at the start of the financial year. Written notification must be given to C & E no later than the due date for rendering the first VAT return for the financial year in which the supplies are to be made. Permission will not be granted retrospectively. C & E must be satisfied that records of costs and sales are adequate to work out accurate but separate sets of margins. See also *Aspro Travel Ltd v C & E Commrs QB 1996, [1997] STC 151.*

If separate calculations are used

- *all* margin scheme supplies and margin scheme packages enjoyed wholly outside the EC must be included in the non-EC calculation; and

- margin scheme supplies and margin scheme packages enjoyed wholly or partly within the EC (including the UK) must be included in one TOMS calculation for EC supplies.

(C & E Notice 709/5/98, para 5.8, Appendix E, TL3).

66.23   Records

Records must be kept of

- the total selling price of margin scheme packages

- the costs of each of the different types of supplies made within those margin scheme packages, such as

  (i)   standard-rated and zero-rated margin scheme supplies;

  (ii)   standard-rated, zero-rated, exempt and outside the scope in-house supplies; and

  (iii) standard-rated and other agency supplies for which commission received is not readily identifiable.

(C & E Notice 709/5/98, para 5.10).

66.24 **Working out the selling prices**

The first step in the end of year calculation (see 66.19 and 66.20 above) is to add up the selling prices of supplies with tax points during the financial year.

Include

- the total VAT-inclusive selling price of all margin scheme supplies (see 66.3 above);

- the total VAT-inclusive selling price of any in-house supplies (see 66.10 above) supplied together with margin scheme supplies;

- any Air Passenger Duty payable by the customer (see 66.31 below);

- any surcharges made;

- where sales are made through agents, the full amount paid by the customer even if a travel agent deducts commission and only passes over the balance. Where a travel agent sells a package for less than the tour operator's advertised brochure price but funds the discount itself (so that the tour operator receives the full price of the holiday but part from the traveller and part funded by the travel agent) the tour operator should still account for the full brochure price under the TOMS. (C & E Business Brief 21/98, 9 October 1998); and

- amounts received relating to any supplies, packaged with margin scheme supplies, which the business arranges as an agent and where its commission is not readily identifiable (see 66.29 below).

Reduce sales by

- any refunds made to customers for unsatisfactory service.

Do not include

- packages of supplies which do not include any margin scheme supplies (on which VAT must be accounted for under the normal rules);

- forfeited deposits and cancellation fees received from customers who cancel bookings (money paid by customers who simply fail to turn up must be included); and

- amounts collected by the business as agent if its commission is readily identifiable.

(C & E Notice 709/5/98, para 5.11).

66.25 **Purchase price of margin scheme supplies**

The second stage in the end of year calculation is to add up the total VAT-inclusive purchase prices of goods and services bought in for resale as margin scheme supplies. Only those purchases which relate to the financial year being calculated must be included, i.e. which relate to supplies included within A in 66.19 above or, as the case may be, 66.20 above.

The cost must

- take into account any discounts or price reductions received from suppliers (even if received at a later date);

- include any Air Passenger Duty payable;

- not include the cost of packages of supplies which do not include any margin scheme supplies; and

- not include indirect costs (see 66.27 below).

(C & E Notice 709/5/98, para 5.12).

Connected persons. Where goods or services are supplied to the tour operator by a connected person (see 69.3 VALUATION) and the value of the supply would otherwise be greater than its open market value, C & E may direct that the value of the supply is deemed to be its open market value for the purposes of calculating the value of margin scheme supplies. The direction must be in writing to the tour operator acquiring the supply within three years of the time of supply. It may also specify that the open market value rule is to apply to subsequent supplies acquired from the same connected person. [*SI 1987/1806, Art 8*].

66.26   **Direct costs of in-house supplies**

It is not necessary to work out the costs of in-house supplies if all supplies included in margin scheme packages are liable to VAT at the same rate. In such a case the simplified calculation under 66.20 above must be used. Otherwise, the annual calculation under 66.19 above must include the direct costs incurred in making in-house supplies which are supplied with margin scheme supplies as part of a package.

The following are examples (not exhaustive) of costs which may be included.

Direct costs of zero-rated passenger transport

- Air Passenger Duty (see 66.31 below)
- Berthing fees
- Bridge and road tolls
- Depreciation of own vehicles (calculated on the same basis as the audited accounts)
- Drivers' wages, employer's NI contributions
- Fuel, insurance and road fund licences for vehicles
- Garaging and parking
- Landing fees
- Night subsistence paid to drivers
- Rental and leasing of vehicles
- Spares, repairs and maintenance of vehicles

Only transport supplied with margin scheme supplies can be included in the TOMS calculation. If the vehicles are also used to provide transport outside the TOMS, then the annual costs must be apportioned to take account of this, normally on a mileage basis. Any other basis requires C & E approval.

Direct costs of standard-rated hotel accommodation

- Catering purchases
- Depreciation of buildings, fixtures and fittings (calculated on the same basis as the audited accounts)
- Heating and lighting
- Rates and insurance of buildings
- Rental of equipment and furniture
- Repairs, maintenance and cleaning for which the tour operator is liable

- Staff costs including wages, employer's NI contributions

Only accommodation supplied with margin scheme supplies can be included in the TOMS calculation. If premises are also used to provide accommodation outside the TOMS, then the annual costs must also be apportioned to take account of this, normally on the basis of number of guest/days booked for each type of supply.

If certain parts of the premises are not used specifically to provide accommodation (e.g. administrative offices, public bars, owner's private accommodation, etc.) costs relating to the entire premises (e.g. rates, insurance, light and heat) must be apportioned on the basis of floor area. Any other bases of apportionment require C & E approval.

See also *The Devonshire Hotel (Torquay) Ltd (14448)*.

(C & E Notice 709/5/98, para 5.13, Appendices J and K).

66.27 Indirect costs

Indirect costs must not be included in any of the calculations. Examples of indirect costs include

- brochures
- advertising the business
- office expenses (telephone, IT equipment, office stationery, rent, etc.)
- accountancy, legal and similar professional services
- hiring and employing representatives at airports and resorts (see 61.32 below)
- financial services
- market research and costs relating to research or evaluation of resorts
- commission paid to agents.

(C & E Notice 709/5/98, para 5.14).

66.28 Foreign currency purchases

Note. The provisions of this paragraph have the force of law.

If any supplies bought for resale as TOMS supplies are billed in foreign currency, these should be converted into sterling at either

(i) the rate of exchange published in the Financial Times using the Federation of Tour Operators' base date current at the time of costing the supplies;

(ii) the commercial rate of exchange current at the time that the supplies in the brochure were costed;

(iii) the rate published in the Financial Times for the date the payment is made;

(iv) the rate of exchange which was applicable to the purchase of foreign currency used to pay for the relevant supplies; or

(v) the period rate of exchange published by C & E for customs purposes at the time the date the payment is made.

Documentary evidence relating to the purchase must be kept to show which of the rates have been used. If method (i) or (ii) is used, the rate must be published in any brochure or leaflet in which the supplies are held out for sale.

Once a method has been chosen, C & E may allow a different method but only from the start of a financial year and if written notification is given to them no later than the due date for rendering the first VAT return for that financial year.

(C & E Notice 709/5/98, para 5.15, Appendix E, TL4).

66.29   **Commission received for agency supplies arranged as part of a margin scheme package**

Where any commission received for agency supplies made by the business is readily identifiable, exclude from the TOMS calculation

*   the commission received; and

*   all monies paid by the traveller for the supply arranged.

Where any commission is received which is not readily identifiable, include in the TOMS calculation

*   the gross amount paid by the traveller (in A at 66.19 above); and

*   the net amount paid to the principal (in H or I at 66.19 above).

(C & E Notice 709/5/98, para 5.16).

66.30   **Hotel and travel insurance**

The way hotel or travel insurance is treated for VAT purposes depends upon the precise contractual arrangements and whether it is the tour operator or the traveller who is the insured person.

(*a*)   Where *the insurance policy issued by the permitted insurer makes the traveller the insured person* (the normal case), there is a supply of insurance from the permitted insurer to the insured person. If the tour operator arranges for the insurance to be supplied by a named company to the traveller under such an arrangement, it is acting as an agent.

*   Where the commission received is readily identifiable, the full amount paid by the traveller for the insurance and the net premium passed on to the insurance company must be excluded from the TOMS calculations.

*   Where the commission received is not readily identifiable, values relating to the insurance must be included in the TOMS calculation (see 66.29 above).

*   Where the insurance is offered 'free' aa part of a package, the full amount paid by the traveller for the insurance must be included in the TOMS calculation. Any costs incurred in relation to such insurance must not be included in the TOMS calculation.

(*b*)   Where *the tour operator enters into an agreement with a permitted insurer under which the tour operator is the insured person*, the insurer agrees to reimburse the tour operator in respect of any claims by travellers for delay compensation, medical costs, etc. This is an indirect cost and therefore outside the TOMS. If the tour operator passes on a charge for the insurance (including any Insurance Premium Tax) to the traveller, this should be included in the selling prices in the TOMS calculation.

(C & E Notice 709/5/98, para 5.17).

66.31   **Air Passenger Duty (APD)**

Selling prices. If the cost of APD is passed on to customers (whether or not separately identified in the price) it must be included in the selling price for the purposes of the TOMS calculation.

Cost of margin scheme supplies. If air transport is bought in and resold as a margin scheme supply, any APD included in the cost (whether or not separately identified) must be included in the TOMS calculation as part of the costs of margin scheme supplies.

Cost of in-house supplies. If a tour operator makes in-house supplies of air transport as part of a margin scheme package, any APD paid by the tour operator must be included in the TOMS calculation as a direct cost of in-house supplies.

(C & E Notice 709/5/98, para 5.18).

66.32 Representatives and guides

The services of representatives at airports and resorts are not normally supplies in their own right and are therefore not regarded as in-house supplies. The costs incurred in providing these services should be treated as indirect costs for the purposes of the TOMS.

The services of a guide, however, are often supplies in their own right. If the supply is made in-house, the place of supply and the liability depends on the exact nature of the service. See 66.10 above.

(C & E Notice 709/5/98, para 5.20).

66.33 Unforeseen costs

Where it is necessary to buy in accommodation, transport, meals, etc. as a result of delays, breakdowns or other unforeseen circumstances, these costs should usually be treated as margin scheme supplies unless the cost of the additional items is

- ultimately met by someone else (e.g. an airline from whom air transport is bought in has agreed to meet any additional costs arising through flight delays) in which case the costs should be ignored in the TOMS calculation; or

- a direct cost of in-house supplies.

(C & E Notice 709/5/98, para 5.21).

66.34 Bad debt relief

See 7 BAD DEBT RELIEF generally for the rules for claiming bad debt relief and in particular paragraph 7.7 under which bad debt relief is restricted to a maximum of the VAT fraction of the profit margin.

The amount of VAT bad debt relief claimable is calculated by the formula

$$B \times s\% \times 7/47$$

where

$B =$ the amount of the bad debt

$s =$ the provisional percentage as calculated under 66.21 above for the financial year in which the supply is made

(C & E Notice 709/5/98, para 5.19).

67 Trading Stamp and Promotion Schemes

67.1 INTRODUCTION

A large number of promotional schemes exist where goods or services are given as rewards to retail customers (the public) or trade customers. These broadly fall into the following categories.

- Schemes where vouchers are issued and later redeemed for goods or services without further consideration.

- Schemes where vouchers are issued and later redeemed for cash (e.g. money-off coupons).

- Schemes where reward goods are linked with main goods either in a promotion to the public or for a trade order of a specified size.

- Discount or reward schemes.

Following the issue of a consultation paper in 1995, C & E removed the regulations on the VAT treatment of trading stamps with effect from 1 June 1996 and further reviewed the VAT treatment of all voucher schemes where the vouchers are redeemed for goods or services by the consumer without further consideration. See 67.2 below.

C & E's review of face value/gift vouchers was delayed awaiting the decisions of the CJEC in *Argos* and *Elida Gibbs* (see 67.3 below). Despite these decisions having now been promulgated for some time, C & E have still to issue a revised version of their Notice 700/7/94 *Business Promotion Schemes*. This should be borne in mind where that Notice is shown as the source of text within this chapter.

67.2 COUPONS AND VOUCHERS REDEEMED FOR GOODS AND SERVICES WITHOUT FURTHER CONSIDERATION

C & E are prepared to adopt the following policies from 1 June 1996 although they will be monitoring the revised rules closely and, if they identify any abuse, will take whatever measures are considered necessary to redress the situation. The provisions apply to a voucher (which includes a token, proof of purchase, wrapper, etc.) which is redeemed for goods or services without further payment. The voucher may be issued in a variety of ways, for example

- on the purchase of a particular item or items;

- on the purchase of goods to a specified value;

- by mailshot either generally or to selected customers or shareholders, etc; or

- as cut-out coupons in newspapers.

The provisions do not apply where

- a further payment is required on redemption (including postage and packing and/or sending unused postage stamps) or any reimbursement is received from a third party (in which case the procedure for redemption of money-off coupons in 67.4 below should be followed); or

- the vouchers bear a face/cash value (unless the vouchers can be redeemed for goods or services without further payment).

There is no longer any distinction in VAT terms between trading stamps and other forms of vouchers/coupons, etc. The general principles are as follows.

67.2 Trading Stamp and Promotion Schemes

(i) All sales of trading stamps and vouchers (with the exception of gift vouchers which bear a face value) are liable to VAT at the standard rate.

(ii) The issue of stamps by a retailer is ignored but the retailer is no longer entitled to reduce daily gross takings by the value of the stamp element.

(iii) Having taxed the sale of vouchers, C & E are prepared to accept that there has been consideration for the redemption goods included in the payment made for the stamps and/or premium goods depending on the nature of the scheme. Therefore, redemption goods are not treated as gifts.

Examples of VAT treatment of some common promotions

(a) *Manufacturers' schemes aimed at their retail/wholesale customers.*

Examples are schemes where manufacturers issue vouchers/stamps, etc. with the sale of trade goods, or use a similar 'proof of purchase' system where the redemption may be either for similar trade goods or for other goods, e.g. electrical equipment designed for the home.

C & E are prepared to treat all redemptions, in the first instance, as having been paid for by the customer when buying the 'premium' goods. The understanding is that the manufacturer in costing the promotion would have allowed for the cost of redemption goods within the normal selling price of those 'premium' goods.

However, where redemption goods are put to a non-business use by a VAT-registered customer (who would have had the benefit of input tax deduction), C & E consider the customer is then making a supply of those goods under *VATA 1994, 4 Sch 5* and VAT is due subject to the normal gift provisions. See 67.15 below and, for more detailed consideration, 47.4 OUTPUT TAX.

(b) *Retailers' schemes aimed at the public.*

For simplification purposes, C & E accept that the cost of redemption goods has been included in the consideration paid for the 'premium' goods. No further VAT is due unless (and then only to the extent that) further payment is made.

(c) *Manufacturers' schemes aimed at the public.*

Examples of such schemes are where

- the public buy from a retailer and send a proof of purchase to the manufacturer to receive something further from the manufacturer, or

- coupons are included by the manufacturer inside the product and the coupons are collected and redeemed later for goods.

C & E are prepared to accept that the manufacturer in costing the promotion has included the costs of the redemption goods within the selling price of his goods to wholesalers and retailers. Therefore they do not intend to charge further VAT on the redemption goods unless (and then only to the extent that) further payment is made.

(d) *Redemptions for services.*

Where

- a customer redeems vouchers for services which are provided by a third party, and

- that third party charges the promoter,

any VAT charged will not normally be input tax for the promoter as the services are not provided to the promoter but to the customer.

(*e*)   *Redemptions for goods provided by third parties.*

Where

● a customer redeems vouchers direct with a third party for goods, and

● that third party later charges the promoter,

depending upon the nature of the scheme such payment may be third party consideration for a supply made to the customer. Any VAT charged may not then be input tax for the promoter.

Zero-rated goods. Occasions will arise where stamps are issued with zero-rated goods but redeemed for standard-rated goods. Consequently, no VAT will be charged. At present the instances of such schemes are minimal and C & E do not propose to take any action to tax these redemptions.

(C & E Business Brief 10/96, 5 June 1996).

67.3   **COUPONS AND VOUCHERS SHOWING A FACE VALUE**

Two decisions by the CJEC have affected the VAT treatment of such vouchers.

(*a*)   *Argos Distributors Ltd CJEC, [1996] STC 1359.*

Argos operates a voucher scheme. The vouchers have a face value printed on them and customers can use the voucher to obtain goods up to the face value in Argos's showrooms. Argos sells the vouchers either at face value or at a discounted price to other traders who can either distribute them freely to members of staff or resell them to the public at up to face value. On redemption of the vouchers for goods, Argos had consistently accounted for VAT on the face value of the vouchers (as instructed by C & E) but formed the opinion that it should only have been required to account for VAT on the discounted amounts for which it had actually sold the vouchers. The CJEC found in favour of Argos. *EC Sixth Directive, Art 11(a)(1)(a)* is to be taken to mean that, where all or part of the consideration for a supply is represented by a face value voucher, the taxable amount attributable to the voucher is the money obtained by the supplier of the goods from the sale of the voucher (and not its face value). The court, however, stressed that the supplier was responsible for establishing the actual sale price of the voucher at the time of its redemption. From 1 July 1997 on redemption of vouchers by a VAT-registered customer, Argos and businesses operating similar schemes are only allowed to account for VAT on their discounted price where, at the time of redemption, it can

● identify the price at which vouchers were sold; and

● issue accurate VAT invoices.

Such sales must be accounted for outside any retail scheme being used. If a retail scheme is based on expected selling prices, these must be adjusted to reflect discounts given in respect of all redeemed vouchers sold below face value.

If a business cannot meet the above conditions on redemption of vouchers by VAT-registered businesses, VAT must be accounted for on the full face value of the vouchers.

C & E are reviewing the arrangements under which VAT is not charged on face value vouchers at the point of sale.

(C & E Business Brief 25/96, 6 December 1996).

(*b*) *Elida Gibbs Ltd, CJEC [1996] STC 1387*

Elida Gibbs manufactures toiletries and sells the products to both retailers and wholesalers. To promote retail sales, it

- issues money-off coupons which customers can present to a retailer in part payment for Elida Gibbs products and for which retailers seek reimbursement direct from the company; and

- prints cashback coupons directly onto the packaging of Elida Gibbs's products which, subject to meeting conditions, entitle any consumer to a cash refund direct from Elida Gibbs.

The company claimed a repayment of output tax which it had previously accounted for contending that the reimbursement of money-off coupons to retailers and the cashback payments to consumers constituted a retrospective discount which reduced the consideration for its supplies. The CJEC ruled in favour of the company's contentions holding that the discounts allowed by the manufacturer were deductible but credit notes should not be issued to customers. This leaves the VAT position of wholesalers and retailers unchanged and maintains the balance of VAT due from them. Retailers should account for output tax on payments received from manufacturers as well as money paid by customers. However, if a VAT-registered customer requests a VAT invoice in respect of purchases made using money-off vouchers, this should be based only on the amount paid by the customer. This achieves fiscal neutrality as required by the judgment.

Note. Because of the decision in *Elida Gibbs*, C & E have indicated that they will be reviewing the position of both manufacturers' money-off schemes and cashback schemes. The details outlined in 67.4 to 67.6 below are based on the information in the current issue of C & E Notice 700/7 *Business Promotion Schemes* which was issued in 1994 before the decisions in *Argos* and *Elida Gibbs* above. If in doubt on any particular treatment, readers are therefore strongly advised to contact their VAT office for confirmation of the current position.

67.4 **Money-off coupons**

See *Note* in 67.3 above.

Money-off coupons are coupons used to offer the public a reduction in the price of a future purchase. They can be issued in a variety of ways, for example

- on the purchase of a particular item or items;

- on the purchase of goods to a specified value;

- by mailshot either generally or to selected customers or shareholders, etc; and

- as cut-out coupons in newspapers.

They may be issued by retailers under their own schemes or by manufacturers. If such a coupon is redeemed without any additional amount being due, it should be dealt with as for a voucher exchanged for goods or services under 67.2 above.

Issue of money-off coupons. In the majority of cases, money-off coupons are regarded as issued for no consideration even if the issue is dependent upon further goods being bought. VAT is not therefore normally due on the issue of coupons in this way.

Where, however, discount coupons (or a discount card) entitling the holder to discounts on purchases are *sold*, the proceeds of sale have the same VAT liability as the goods or services purchased subsequently purchased.

- Where a retail scheme is in operation, proceeds must be included in gross takings. Unless the coupons are for a specific line of product, the VAT liability of which can be determined when the coupons are issued, retailers using the point of sale scheme may not be able, when the discount coupons are sold, to determine the liability of the goods or services against which the coupons will be redeemed. Such retailers should agree a method of how to account for VAT on such sales with C & E, possibly on the basis of the average split of zero-rated and standard-rated sales.

- Where a retail scheme is not used, and the coupon or card can be used to purchase both standard and zero-rated goods, a method of apportionment must be agreed with C & E.

The sales of discount coupons or cards which give discounts with several traders are standard-rated. See *C & E Commrs v Granton Marketing Ltd; C & E Commrs v Wentwalk Ltd CA, [1996] STC 1049* where cards which entitled the holder to a complimentary meal and wine at certain restaurants were held not to be vouchers and their supply to be standard-rated.

Redemption of money-off coupons. Following the judgment in *Boots Co plc v C & E Commrs CJEC, [1990] STC 387* C & E have accepted that money-off coupons are not to be treated as consideration when used to buy other goods but are simply evidence of entitlement to discount.

However, in *Kuwait Petroleum (GB) Ltd (14668)* where customers were given vouchers with purchases which could be redeemed for goods without further payment, the tribunal decided the case should be referred to the CJEC. The Advocate General delivered his Opinion on 9 July 1998. He upheld C & E's contention that the amount paid by the customers was entirely attributable to their original purchases, could not be treated as consideration for the redemption goods, and that there was no 'price discount' allowed to the customer. The redemption goods should therefore be treated as gifts.

See 67.8 below where a retail scheme is operated. Where no such scheme is in operation, VAT is due on the money received from the customer and the manufacturer (if any) under the normal time of supply rules.

Service charge. Any service charge made to a manufacturer for handling coupons is exempt from VAT.

(C & E Notice 700/7/94, para 14).

67.5   **Face/cash vouchers issued for a payment**

See *Note* in 67.3 above.

These vouchers, commonly called 'gift vouchers', show a cash value and are normally sold at or below face value. They can be exchanged without further payment.

(*a*)   **On sale**, no VAT is due unless sold for an amount exceeding the face value (in which case VAT is due on the excess). If a 'greetings' card is sold with the voucher, VAT is due on the price of the card.

(*b*)   **On redemption** of the gift voucher for goods or services, its face value is the consideration for payment and the value for VAT purposes (whether the gift voucher was issued below, at or above face value).

(*c*)   **If a customer making a specified purchase also receives a gift voucher**, the supply of the goods and voucher is treated as a combined or multiple supply. VAT is due only on that proportion of the payment which relates to the goods. The part of the consideration which relates to the gift voucher (usually its face value) should be omitted from daily gross takings. The face value of the voucher must be included in daily gross takings when redeemed by the customer.

(C & E Notice 700/7/94, para 16).

67.6 Face/cash vouchers issued free

See *Note* in 67.3 above.

Issue. Where a retailer issues cash vouchers entirely without payment (either monetary or non-monetary) which are to be redeemed by him, no VAT is due at the time of issue. See 67.5(*c*) above where vouchers are issued 'free' when a customer makes a specified purchase.

On redemption, if the vouchers are redeemed for goods or services

• with further payment, the procedure in 67.4 above should be applied; and

• without further payment, the procedure in 67.2 above should be applied.

Where a retailer gives away these types of vouchers but also sells them as under 67.5 above, and is unable to distinguish between those sold and those given away, on redemption VAT should be accounted for under the procedure in 67.5 above unless an alternative method is agreed with C & E.

(C & E Notice 700/7/94, para 17).

67.7 TRADING STAMPS

From 1 June 1996, the special rules that previously applied to trading stamps ceased. From that date they are treated in the same way as other vouchers.

For the provisions applying to trading stamps before 1 June 1996, see Tolley's Value Added Tax 1997/98 and earlier editions.

67.8 TREATMENT OF COUPONS AND VOUCHERS UNDER RETAIL SCHEMES

The VAT treatment under a retail scheme depends upon whether the promotion is funded solely by the retailer or by (or together with) a third party such as the manufacturer.

'Value off vouchers'. Where vouchers such as '50p off' or '10% off' are taken as part payment, only the money received from the customer should be included in daily gross takings. If the retailer subsequently receives payment for the voucher from another source, this payment must be included in daily gross takings.

With the written agreement of C & E, retailers may choose to include the manufacturer's coupons in gross takings at the time they are presented by customers. Although this means accounting for VAT at an earlier date than necessary, certain retailers may find this arrangement administratively simpler.

Any charges by the retailer to the manufacturer for handling the vouchers is payment for an exempt supply and must be excluded from daily gross takings.

Vouchers—general. The following provisions apply to vouchers issued with no value/amounts and which are redeemable for whole items.

• *Vouchers issued by the retailer to customers making a specific purchase or purchases.* No VAT is due upon issue and no further VAT is due when the voucher is used by the customer to obtain the reward goods. Under Apportionment Scheme 2 and Direct

Calculation Schemes 1 and 2, records of expected selling prices must be adjusted for the reward goods.

- *Vouchers issued freely by the retailer.* No VAT is due upon issue. When redeemed for goods, no VAT is due unless the cost of the goods is over £15 in which case VAT is due on the full value of the goods at the time they are given away. See 60.9(4) RETAIL SCHEMES for the scheme adjustments where goods from normal stock are supplied as gifts.

- *Vouchers issued by another person (e.g. a manufacturer) but redeemed by the retailer.* These are likely to be subject to the terms and conditions of that person's promotion. For example, if the retailer is given certain stocks to give away on behalf of that person, these stocks must not be included in the retail scheme calculations.

See 60.9(30) RETAIL SCHEMES for sale of discount vouchers.

If such vouchers are redeemed for cash, the cash payment is outside the scope of VAT and daily gross takings must not be altered for the cash paid.

Gift vouchers. See 60.9(18) RETAIL SCHEMES.

(C & E Notice 727/3/97, Appendix C; C & E Notice 727/4/97, Appendix C; C & E Notice 727/5/97, Appendix C).

67.9   GOODS LINKED IN A PROMOTION

Goods (or goods and services) are sometimes offered together in one promotion for a single price (e.g. coffee and chocolate biscuits or a washing machine and iron). Alternatively, a number of articles may be sold in a multibuy offer, e.g.

- 'buy two get a third free'; or

- buy a sofa and get a free foot stool.

In either case, this is a combined or multiple supply and the amount paid covers all the goods or services offered.

If the items offered are subject to VAT at different rates, apportionment is required. See 47.3 OUTPUT TAX. However, for certain small items linked with a major item which is liable to VAT at a different rate, the linked supplies concession in 67.10 below may apply.

If the offer is made to other VAT-registered traders, see also the dealer loader scheme under 67.12 below.

(C & E Notice 700/7/94, para 2).

67.10   Linked goods schemes

Theses are promotion schemes where a minor article is linked (not necessarily physically) with a main article. Where the articles are liable to VAT at different rates, the price should normally be apportioned (see 67.9 above). However, by concession, VAT can be accounted for on the minor article at the same rate as the main article (so that the selling price need not be apportioned) provided the following conditions are satisfied.

(*a*)   The minor article is not charged to the customer at a separate price.

(*b*)   The minor article costs no more than

(i)   20% of the total cost (excluding VAT) of the combined supply; and

(ii) £1 (excluding VAT) if included with goods intended for retail sale or £5 (excluding VAT) otherwise.

Where the conditions are met, the articles need not be detailed separately on the invoice.

In all other circumstances where a VAT invoice has to be issued, details of the minor article must be shown separately.

(C & E Notice 700/7/94, para 7; C & E Notice 48, ESC 2.7).

See also 28.13 FOOD for mixtures and assortments of food and 54.16 PRINTED MATTER, ETC. for promotional items in magazines.

67.11   *Accounting for linked supplies under retail schemes*

VAT must be accounted for as follows.

(*a*)   *Point of Sale scheme and Direct Calculation Schemes 1 and 2.* Treatment depends upon whether the two articles are liable to VAT at the same rate or different rates.

   (i) If both articles are liable at the same rate of VAT, there are no additional rules unless any contribution is received from a manufacturer or joint sponsor. In such a case, the contribution must be included in daily gross takings at the time of receipt.

   (ii) If the articles are liable at different rates of VAT, subject to the linked supplies concession in 67.10 above, the selling price must be apportioned either on the basis in 47.3 OUTPUT TAX or, where the goods have been linked by the manufacturer, in accordance with the information shown on the supplier's invoice.

   Where apportionment is required, the amount allocated to lower-rated or zero-rated goods must be separated from standard-rated takings before carrying out the scheme calculation.

(*b*)   *Apportionment Schemes 1 and 2.* Any contribution from the supplier or sponsor must be included in daily gross takings.

Under Apportionment Scheme 1, no adjustment to purchases is required.

Under Apportionment Scheme 2, expected selling prices (ESPs) must also be adjusted as follows.

- No adjustment is required for a full contribution. Where only partial contribution is received, ESPs for the appropriate goods must be adjusted to the extent of the amount not supported by the supplier or sponsor. Where no contribution is received, an appropriate adjustment must be made to the ESPs of the promotion goods.

- If the promotion goods are liable to VAT at different rates, the ESPs must be apportioned either on the basis in 47.3 OUTPUT TAX or, where the goods have been linked by the manufacturer, in accordance with the information shown on the supplier's invoice.

Where the linked supplies concession under 67.10 above is used, the record of purchases or ESPs of the promotion goods must be adjusted as appropriate.

(*c*)   *Old scheme calculations.*

   (i) Under Scheme A

   - For linked goods taxable at different rates, the sales had to be included in the scheme calculation. However, if the minor articles were zero-rated and did not meet the conditions for the concession in 67.10 above, the value of the minor articles had to be removed from daily gross takings.

- For linked goods taxable at the same rate, the goods had to be treated as goods received for resale within the retail scheme.

(ii) Under Schemes B, B1, D, D1, E, E1, H and J

- For linked goods taxable at different rates, the sales had to be included in the scheme calculations. If, however, the minor articles met the conditions for the linked supplies concession in 67.10 above, then the appropriate amounts had to be deducted from the scheme records at the VAT rate applying to the minor articles when they were received and the corresponding amounts had to be entered in the scheme records at the VAT rate applying to the main goods.

- For linked goods taxable at the same rate, the goods had to be treated as goods received for resale within the retail scheme.

(iii) Under Schemes B2 and C

- For linked goods taxable at different rates, VAT had to be accounted for outside the scheme.

- For linked goods taxable at the same rate, VAT on the linked goods had to be accounted for outside the scheme.

(iv) Under Scheme F

- For linked goods taxable at different rates, the sales had to be included in the scheme calculations. If, however, the minor articles did not meet the conditions for the linked supplies concession in 67.10 above, the scheme calculations had to be adjusted to take account of the minor articles.

- For linked goods taxable at the same rate, the goods had to be treated as goods received for resale within the retail scheme.

(C & E Notice 727/3/97, Appendix C; C & E Notice 727/4/97, Appendix C; C & E Notice 727/5/97, Appendix C; C & E Notice 727 (1993 edition), paras 72–74 (now withdrawn)).

67.12   **Dealer loader promotions**

These are promotional schemes where rewards are offered free of charge on condition that a *single* trade order of a specified size is made (e.g. buy ten dozen and get one dozen free). There is a combined supply of the main/qualifying items and the reward. All the supplies must be shown on the invoice but, by concession, if

(a)   the reward is of a kind to be used in the recipient's business,

(b)   the reward is not intended for the personal use of the person receiving it, and

(c)   both the main supply and reward are standard-rated,

only one price need be shown on the invoice. Otherwise, the total price must be apportioned to reflect either different rates of VAT or business/non-business supplies. In the latter case the customer cannot claim any VAT on the non-business supplies.

Supplier of the main goods different from supplier of the reward. Special rules apply where the trader supplying the reward meets the conditions in (a)–(c) above but is not directly the supplier of the main goods (e.g. where a manufacturer supplies the reward goods but the main goods are supplied via a wholesaler).

67.13 Trading Stamp and Promotion Schemes

- If the main supply and the reward are both standard-rated, no additional VAT is due on the supply of the reward goods and a VAT invoice must not be issued for them. If an invoice is issued, it must be endorsed 'No VAT charged — business promotion scheme, VAT Notice 700/7 paragraph 10 refers'. Records must be kept to allow C & E to check such supplies.

- If the main supply is zero-rated and the reward is standard-rated, VAT must be accounted for on the value of the reward and a VAT invoice can be issued.

The above would apply whether

- the manufacturer supplies the reward directly to the qualifying customer;

- a wholesaler supplies rewards to customers on the manufacturer's behalf from own stock and the manufacturer either reimburses the wholesaler or replaces the stock; or

- a wholesaler supplies the customer from 'stock' provided by the manufacturer.

(C & E Notice 700/7/94, paras 8–10).

67.13 Trade orders made over a period of time

Where a promotion scheme offers rewards on condition that trade orders are placed over a set period of time to a given value, the reward goods are being provided for no consideration. See 47.4 OUTPUT TAX for VAT on business gifts.

By concession, C & E accept that the rewards can be treated as part of a combined or multiple supply if

- the reward is of a kind to be used in the recipient's business;

- the reward is not intended for the personal use of the person receiving it, and

- the reward appears on the final qualifying invoice, i.e. at the point at which the customer qualifies for the reward.

Special rules apply as under the dealer loader scheme (see 67.12 above) where the supplier of the main goods is different from the supplier of the reward.

(C & E Notice 700/7/94, paras 11, 12).

67.14 DISCOUNT OR REWARD SCHEMES

The VAT treatment of discounts and reward goods/services depends upon whether any consideration is given by the recipient. Consideration includes not only monetary consideration but non-monetary consideration, i.e. anything agreed to be done (no matter how slight) in return for a supply of goods or services. C & E, however, accept that certain acts, including the following, are insignificant for these purposes and do not constitute non-monetary consideration.

(a) Having to buy one article either to get

- another article free; or

- a discount voucher redeemable against a further purchase; or

- a lottery ticket, etc. (see 67.18 below).

(b) Employees having to exceed certain sales levels or sell most articles in a month, etc. (see 67.19 below).

(c) The act of using an in-house credit card (see 67.18 below).

(*d*)   Entering a free prize draw.

(*e*)   Having to complete a slogan or give a recipe, etc. on entry to a competition.

(*f*)   'False value' trade-ins (see 67.18 below).

(*g*)   Agreeing to enter a contract for a pre-determined length of time.

(C & E Notice 700/7/94, paras 5, 6).

Where any non-monetary consideration is given, however small, VAT is due on that consideration. The value of the consideration is taken to be such amount in money as, with the addition of the VAT, is equivalent to the consideration, i.e. normally the price, excluding VAT, which the customer would have to pay to buy the goods or services. [*VATA 1994, s 19(3)*].

67.15   **Free gifts**

(*a*)   **Gifts of goods.** Where goods are given away without any monetary or non-monetary consideration (see 67.14 above) the VAT rules on gifts apply. If the VAT-exclusive cost of the goods is less than £15, no VAT is due. Any input tax incurred on their purchase is recoverable, subject to the normal rules (e.g. input tax on gifts of free hotel accommodation, day trips to the races, etc. would be non-deductible under the business entertainment provisions). If the VAT-exclusive cost of the goods is more than £15, output tax must be accounted for on the price the person would have to pay (excluding VAT) at the time of supply, to purchase goods identical to the goods concerned, i.e. normally their cost value. See 47.4 OUTPUT TAX for further details, including special rules applying to goods forming part of a series of gifts to the same person.

(*b*)   **If goods are lent or hired to a customer,** there is a supply of services and where no consideration is given, output tax is due on the cost of providing the services. Over a period of time, this is the amount of depreciation of the goods (plus any other costs related to the goods) multiplied by the proportion which the use outside the business forms to the total use. See 47.5 OUTPUT TAX for further details.

(c)   **The free provision of own services** (e.g. free beauty treatment) is generally not a taxable supply. There is no restriction on input tax recovery and no output tax is due. However, if the supply makes use of goods (e.g. cosmetics) which cost more than £15, output tax may be due as under (*a*) above.

(*d*)   **The free provision of bought-in services** (e.g. beauty treatment provided by another business) will give rise to a VAT liability under *SI 1993/1507*. See 47.5 OUTPUT TAX. If, however, services are merely paid for by the business but supplied directly by a third party to the customer, the business makes no supply for VAT purposes but cannot deduct any VAT charged by the provider of the services.

(C & E Notice 700/7/94, para 6).

Introductory gifts. In *Empire Stores Ltd v C & E Commrs, CJEC [1994] STC 623* a company sold goods by mail order. It offered new customers, and existing customers who introduced new customers, certain goods (such as a kettle, a toaster or an iron) free of charge as inducements. Such goods were supplied after new customers had made their first order. The company accounted for VAT on the cost of the goods, and C & E issued assessments charging tax on cost plus 50%, being their estimate of the market value of the supply. The CJEC ruled that the goods in question were supplied to the customers in consideration for a service, namely the introduction of a new customer, and not in return for the purchase by the new customer of goods from the catalogue. The value of the goods was the amount that the company was prepared to spend to get the introduction, i.e. the cost of the articles to the company. As a result of this decision, businesses should take care in drawing up promotional schemes involving incentive goods. If the scheme can be regarded as offering two items at a discounted price, VAT should only be due on the price paid by the customer. If, however, the customer is seen as giving any kind of non-monetary consideration for the incentive goods, additional VAT may be due on the cost of the incentive goods.

67.16   **Manufacturers' schemes aimed at trade customers**

Retrospective discounts. Where a discount is given on condition that the customer reaches a target purchase level within a set time, the normal procedure would be to issue a credit note for the amount of the discount. See 40.15 INVOICES. If, on the other hand, the customer is given goods to the value of the discount earned, the discount has been used to pay for the additional goods supplied. Normally, to avoid accounting for further VAT, a credit note would be issued to reflect the reduced value of the qualifying supplies and an invoice raised for the reward goods showing an equal amount of VAT. Instead, provided

(*a*)   all the goods are liable to VAT at the same rate,

(*b*)   the reward goods are supplied to the same person and for business purposes,

(*c*)   no VAT credit note is issued, and

(*d*)   records are kept to satisfy C & E of a proper audit trail,

a 'no charge' invoice can be issued without VAT for the additional goods.

(C & E Notice 700/7/94, para 20).

'Free' hire schemes for vending machines. See 47.15 OUTPUT TAX.

67.17   **Manufacturers' schemes aimed at the public**

Goods given away via a retailer. Where a manufacturer runs a promotion scheme (clearly advertised as such to the public) under which retailers are provided (for no consideration) with reward goods and give these reward goods, as agent of the manufacturer, to their customers making qualifying purchases, there is a free supply of reward goods by the manufacturer direct to the public. See 67.15(*a*) above for the output tax position. (C & E Notice 700/7/94, para 25).

Goods given as prizes for competitions in magazines, etc. If any benefit is received in exchange for the goods (e.g. a free advertisement in the magazine), there may be a barter transaction with non-monetary consideration passing both ways. See 67.14 above for the output tax position.

Where there is no exchange of benefits, there is no non-monetary consideration. See 67.15(*a*) above for the output tax position.

(C & E Notice 700/7/94, para 26).

Goods given to publishers for use as magazine inserts. There are various VAT implications depending upon the exact nature of the particular circumstances.

●   Where the goods are supplied to the publishers for a monetary consideration, VAT must be charged. When the goods are sold by the retailer with the magazine, there is a multiple supply which may have to be apportioned. See 47.3 OUTPUT TAX.

●   Where the goods are supplied to the publisher without monetary consideration but under a barter arrangement whereby non-monetary consideration is received (e.g. an advertising benefit), VAT is normally due on the non-monetary consideration.

See 67.14 above. However, where any non-monetary consideration is minimal, it may be ignored and VAT is then due as under 67.15(a) above.

- Where the goods are supplied to the publisher for no consideration (monetary or otherwise) output tax is due as under 67.15(a) above.

- Where the goods are not supplied to the publisher but both the publisher and retailer act purely as agent for the manufacturer in distributing products to retail customers, no VAT is due on free samples. See 47.9 OUTPUT TAX.

In other circumstances, the VAT office should be contacted.

(C & E Notice 700/7/94, para 30).

Cashback schemes. These are normally manufacturers' schemes aimed at the public but where goods are supplied through wholesalers and/or retailers. The cashback is a refund of money from the manufacturer directly to the final consumer if the consumer sends a proof of purchase, etc. to the manufacturer. The cashback does not affect the original VAT charged by the manufacturer and claimed (where appropriate) by the wholesaler/retailer. (C & E Notice 700/7/94, para 28).

Gas and electricity savings stamps. Some gas and electricity companies sell savings stamps to retailers for resale to members of the public who use them to pay for supplies of gas and electricity. Provided the stamps are sold for face value or less, their sale is not subject to VAT. (C & E Notice 700/7/94, para 29).

Television licence stamps are issued by the licensing authorities to enable viewers to save for the payment of a licence. The sale of these stamps is outside the scope of VAT. (C & E Notice 700/7/94, para 29).

67.18   **Retail discount schemes**

Discounts are normally treated as reductions in the consideration given so that VAT is due on the discounted price actually paid. See 69.5 VALUATION for a general consideration of discounts. The following are examples of schemes which generally fall to be treated in this way.

- **Deferred discount scheme.** This entitles a shareholder to a discount off the purchase price of goods. The discount is not deducted from the customer's payment but accumulated and paid out annually.

- **Special events.** In-store credit card holders are invited to preview sales and allowed special discounts, no payment being made by the credit company to the retailer. Alternatively, other selected groups may be offered discounts, again with no consideration being received from any other source.

- 'We will pay your VAT'.

- **Graded promotions.** Graded discount vouchers are given which offer a percentage reduction which increases with the value of the purchases made.

- **False value trade-ins.** A specific discount is given regardless of the condition of the exchange article (e.g. £50 for a customer's old cooker when buying a new model). Where the retailer varies the discount by reference to the condition of the exchange article, C & E hold that the normal part-exchange rules apply, i.e. there is a supply of goods by the customer to the retailer for a price equivalent to the discount given and a supply by the retailer to the customer at the full pre-discounted price.

Credit card discount schemes. Under such a scheme, a customer who spends a minimum amount on any one purchase using an in-house credit card is entitled to a set credit to be applied to their credit card. There is no reimbursement by the retailer to the credit card company.

Where the retailer and the credit card company are in the same VAT group, the group should only account for VAT on the discounted amount. Where they are not, the goods are sold by the retailer at their full value and VAT is due on this amount.

Lottery promotion (scratch cards). Customers who purchase certain items (at normal price) are entitled to a teaser leaflet (for no extra charge) on which certain symbols can be scratched off revealing the details of a prize. Alternatively, there may be no purchasing requirement.

- Where the prize is a free gift of goods, see 67.15(a) above.

- Where the prize is discount vouchers for use against future purchases, these are normally evidence of entitlement to a discount and VAT is due on the discounted amount only, provided there is no reimbursement from another source.

- Where the prize is gift vouchers, the voucher has not been issued for a consideration and on redemption the rules in 67.6 above apply.

(C & E Notice 700/7/94, para 6, Annex B).

67.19   **Employee awards**

If an employer wishes to reward employees exceeding sales levels, etc. by giving gifts of goods or services (e.g. free theatre tickets, restaurant meals or hotel accommodation), C & E do not regard the services provided by the employees in return as non-monetary consideration. Input tax is deductible according to the normal rules and output tax may be due under the rules for gifts in 67.15 above.

If the reward for the employee extends to non-employees (e.g. a spouse) the rules for the employee are as above but input tax in respect of non-employees may be blocked under the BUSINESS ENTERTAINMENT (9) provisions.

Goods or 'points' given by manufacturers to a customers' employees. Goods given free of charge by a manufacturer to customers' employees as a reward for promoting or selling goods are free supplies for no consideration. See 67.15(a) above for the output tax position.

Similar VAT treatment applies where customers' employees accumulate voucher 'points' for selling a manufacturer's goods and the points are redeemable for general consumer goods. Any VAT incurred by the manufacturer on the goods is deductible (subject to the normal rules).

(C & E Notice 700/7/94, paras 21, 22).

68   Transport and Freight

Cross-references. See 23.31 EUROPEAN COMMUNITY: SINGLE MARKET for new means of transport; 25.7 EXPORTS for the supply or hiring of freight containers; 45 MOTOR CARS.

De Voil Indirect Tax Service. See V4.251.

The contents of this chapter are as follows.

68.1   ZERO-RATED SUPPLIES OF SHIPS

The supply of any 'qualifying ship' is zero rated. A *'qualifying ship'* is any ship which is

(*a*)   of a gross tonnage of not less than 15 tons; and

(*b*)   neither designed nor adapted for use for recreation or pleasure.

[*VATA 1994, 8 Sch Group 8, Item 1 and Note A1; SI 1995/3039*].

'*Ship*' includes a submarine, hovercraft (see below), light vessel, fire float, dredger, barge or lighter, a mobile floating dock or crane and an offshore oil or gas installation used in the underwater exploitation or exploration of oil and gas resources, which is designed to be moved from place to place. *Not included* are

• fixed oil and gas installations (even though they might be transported to a site as a floating structure); and

• vessels which are permanently moored (e.g. as attractions) *and* not readily capable of navigation.

As a result of (*b*) above, private pleasure boats or yachts are not zero-rated even if supplied for business purposes (e.g. sail training). See also *Callison (810)* and *obiter dicta* in *Hamann v Finanzamt Hamburg-Eimsbuttel, CJEC 1989, [1991] STC 193*. Cruise ships are zero-rated provided they satisfy (*a*) above and are supplied for use in the business of providing recreational or pleasure cruises for fare-paying passengers. There is a specific zero-rating relief for houseboats without engines (see 42.54 LAND AND BUILDINGS). C & E accept that, following the decision in *DG Everett; The London Tideway Harbour Co Ltd (11736)*, houseboats with engines which are used as living accommodation are zero-rated provided they satisfy the conditions in (*a*) above. (C & E Manual V1-7, Chapter 8 Part C, section 1.10).

Gross tonnage is that ascertained under the *Merchant Shipping Acts*. If not so ascertained, it is determined, for VAT purposes only, by the formula

L × B × D × 0.235

where

L = length;
B = extreme breadth; and

D = depth measured amidships
(all measurements being in metres)

(See C & E Notice 744C, Appendix A for further details).

Hovercraft. All hovercraft are zero-rated, irrespective of gross tonnage unless designed or adapted for use for recreation or pleasure.

(C & E Notice 744C, paras 2.8, 2.9).

68.2   **ZERO-RATED SUPPLIES OF AIRCRAFT**

The supply of any 'qualifying aircraft' is zero-rated. A '*qualifying aircraft*' is any aircraft which is

- of a weight of not less than 8,000 kilogrammes; and

- neither designed nor adapted for use for recreation or pleasure.

[*VATA 1994, 8 Sch Group 8, Item 2 and Note A1; SI 1995/3039*].

'*Aircraft*' includes aeroplanes (civil and military), helicopters and airships but does not include space craft and satellites.

Weight is the authorised maximum take-off weight specified in the certificate of airworthiness or, for military aircraft, shown in the documents issued by the Ministry of Defence.

(C & E Notice 744C, paras 2.14, 2.15).

68.3   **SHIPS AND AIRCRAFT — OTHER ZERO-RATED SUPPLIES**

In addition to the supply of certain ships or aircraft (see 68.1 and 68.2 above) various other supplies and services in connection with such craft may also be zero-rated.

Parts and equipment. Zero-rating applies to

(*a*)   the supply of parts and equipment, of a kind ordinarily installed or incorporated in, and to be installed or incorporated in, the propulsion, navigation or communication systems or general structure of a qualifying ship (see 68.1 above) or a qualifying aircraft (see 68.2 above); and

(*b*)   the supply of life jackets, life rafts, smoke hoods and similar safety equipment for use in a qualifying ship or aircraft.

The letting on hire of goods within (*a*) or (*b*) above is also zero-rated.

Any supply to a Government department is excluded from zero-rating unless *either* the supply is in the course or furtherance of a business carried on by the department *or* the parts and equipment are to be installed or incorporated in ships or aircraft used for the purpose of providing rescue or assistance at sea.

[*VATA 1994, 8 Sch Group 8, Items 2A, 2B and Notes A1, 2 and 2A; SI 1995/3039*].

Parts and equipment include

- Anchors

- Catering and laundering equipment (industrial)

- Communications equipment used for the operation of the ship or aircraft

- Components to be fitted inside a ship or aircraft (e.g. electrical and navigation equipment, and video and similar entertainment equipment incorporated into airline seats)
- Cranes
- 'Expendable' parts and 'rotable' components used by the aircraft industry
- Fishing nets and equipment
- Fixed equipment to control, operate or launch weapons
- Laundering equipment (industrial)
- Lifeboats and life rafts
- Nuts, bolts, hoses, oil seals and rivets (referred to as 'consumables' by the aircraft industry)
- Propellers and rudders
- Pumps
- Radar and navigation equipment
- Safety equipment (e.g. escape chutes, life jackets, smoke hoods and oxygen masks)
- Sanitary fixtures
- Winches

Parts and equipment exclude

- Aircraft ground equipment
- Binoculars
- Bulk materials (e.g. adhesives, chemicals, fabrics, inhibitors, metals, oils, paints, solvents and thinners)
- Catering and laundering equipment (domestic)
- Crockery and cutlery
- Diving equipment
- Flight simulators or their parts
- Furniture (unfixed) and soft furnishings
- Missiles, shells, etc.
- Raw materials (e.g. fibre board, plastics, specialist metals)
- Ship's stores
- Telephones and televisions
- Tooling and equipment used for manufacturing parts or equipment
- Tools
- Underwater cameras
- Video tapes, video games and similar entertainment equipment

Evidence for zero-rating. Normal commercial documentation is sufficient provided the supplier is satisfied that the parts, etc. qualify for zero-rating. If uncertain (e.g. because the parts could be used on a qualifying or non-qualifying ship or because the customer is a government department) the supplier should obtain an undertaking from the customer that the parts etc. qualify. See Notice 744C, Appendix B for a suggested format.

(C & E Notice 744C, paras 4.3, 4.4, 4.6).

68.4   Repairs and maintenance

The repair or maintenance of a qualifying ship (see 68.1 above) or a qualifying aircraft (see 68.2 above) is zero–rated. [*VATA 1994, 8 Sch Group 8, Items 1, 2; SI 1995/3039*].

Maintenance includes testing of parts and components, cleaning, fumigation and ship's laundry (provided the articles are not personal to the crew or passengers). Parts, components and materials provided by the supplier of the repairs and maintenance are regarded as part of the zero–rated work.

Repairs and maintenance of parts and equipment can also be zero–rated provided

(*a*)   in the case of a ship

- the repair is carried out on board; or

- the part or component is removed for repair and is replaced in the same ship; and

(*b*)   in the case of an aircraft

- the repair is carried out on board; or

- the part or component is removed for repair and is replaced in the same aircraft; or

- following the repair or maintenance, the parts are returned to be held in stock for future use as spares in qualifying aircraft; or

- if they are unserviceable parts and equipment, they are exchanged for identical parts which have themselves been reconditioned, repaired or maintained.

Sub–contracted services supplied in respect of repair and maintenance of a qualifying ship or aircraft can similarly be zero–rated. The sub–contractor is advised to obtain evidence to substantiate zero–rating from the main contractor.

(C & E Notice 744C, paras 2.16, 3.1, 3.2).

68.5   Modifications and conversions

The modification or conversion of any qualifying ship (see 68.1 above) or qualifying aircraft (see 68.2 above) is zero–rated provided that, when so modified or converted, it will remain a qualifying ship or aircraft. [*VATA 1994, 8 Sch Group 8, Items 1 and 2; SI 1995/3039*]. Included are structural alterations and updating or improving serviceable equipment.

Sub–contracted services supplied in respect of modification or conversion of a qualifying ship or aircraft can similarly be zero–rated. The sub–contractor is advised to obtain evidence to substantiate zero–rating from the main contractor.

(C & E Notice 744C, paras 2.16, 3.3).

68.6   Air navigation services

The supply of 'air navigation services' are zero–rated when

- provided for qualifying aircraft (see 68.2 above); or

- supplied to a person who receives the supply for the purposes of a business carried on by him and who belongs outside the UK (whether or not provided for qualifying aircraft).

'*Air navigation services*' have the same meaning as in *Civil Aviation Act 1982, s 105(1)*, i.e. they include information, directions and other facilities furnished, issued or provided in connection with the navigation or movement of aircraft, and include the control of movement of vehicles in any part of an aerodrome used for the movement of aircraft. [*VATA 1994, 8 Sch Group 8, Items 6A, 11(b), Notes 6A and 7; SI 1995/653; SI 1995/3039*].

Air navigation services are largely provided by the Civil Aviation Authority which has been granted taxable status for its supply of these services. (C & E Business Brief 20/94, 18 November 1994).

68.7   **Charter services**

The supply of services under the charter of a qualifying ship (see 68.1 above) or a qualifying aircraft (see 68.2 above) is zero-rated unless those services consist wholly of any one or more of

- the transport of passengers,

- accommodation,

- entertainment, or

- education,

being services wholly performed in the UK. [*VATA 1994, 8 Sch Group 8, Items 1, 2 and Note 1; SI 1995/3039*].

To qualify for zero-rating under these provisions, there must be a formal written charter party contract and that contract must relate to the whole of the ship or aircraft. If only part of the cargo space or seating capacity in a ship or aircraft is supplied, the supply may qualify for relief as passenger transport (see 68.14 *et seq.* below) or freight transport (see 68.24 *et seq.* below).

Zero-rating includes services carried out under the terms of a charter for purposes other than transport (e.g. dredging and oil dispersal operations).

(C & E Notice 744C, para 2.5).

68.8   **Letting on hire**

The letting on hire of a qualifying ship (see 68.1 above) or a qualifying aircraft (see 68.2 above) is zero-rated. [*VATA 1994, 8 Sch Group 8, Items 1, 2 and Note 2; SI 1995/3039*].

Letting on hire in this context means a supply without crew or pilot in which the customer takes possession of, and has exclusive use of, the ship or aircraft to operate himself. See 64.30 SUPPLY for the place of supply of the letting on hire of transport for use outside the EC. Subject to this, any other letting or hire of a ship or aircraft is standard-rated. (C & E Notice 744C, para 2.4).

68.9   **Handling services**

Any services provided for the handling of ships or aircraft in a 'port', 'customs and excise airport' or outside the UK are zero-rated when

- provided for qualifying ships (see 68.1 above) or qualifying aircraft (see 68.2 above); or

- supplied to a person who receives the supply for the purposes of a business carried on by him and who belongs outside the UK (whether or not provided for qualifying ships and aircraft).

The letting on hire of goods is specifically excluded.

'*Port*' means any port appointed for customs purposes and includes all seaports in the UK. At a seaport the port limits include all territorial waters but do not normally extend inland beyond the waterway of the port.

'*Customs and excise airport*' means an airport designated for the landing or departure of aircraft for the purposes of the *Customs and Excise Acts* by an Order in Council made pursuant to *Civil Aviation Act 1982, s 60*. The limit of such an airport is normally the boundary of the airport itself. The designated C & E airports are Aberdeen (Dyce), Belfast (Aldergrove), Biggin Hill, Birmingham, Blackpool, Bournemouth (Hurn), Bristol, Cambridge, Cardiff, Coventry, East Midlands, Edinburgh, Exeter, Glasgow, Humberside (Hull), Leeds/Bradford, Liverpool, London City Airport, London Gatwick, London Heathrow, Luton, Lydd, Manchester International, Manston (Kent International), Newcastle, Norwich, Plymouth (Roborough), Prestwick, Shoreham, Southampton, Southend, Stansted, Sumburgh and Teeside.

[*VATA 1994, 8 Sch Group 8, Items 6(a), 11(b), Notes 5-7; SI 1995 No 3039*]. (C & E Notice 744C, Appendix C).

Ship handling includes port and harbour dues, dock and berth charges, conservancy charges (including the provision of local lights, buoys and beacons), graving dock charges, mooring charges, demurrage (where this is a charge for failure to load or discharge a ship within specified time), security and fire services, supply of crew members and the day-to-day management of a ship.

Aircraft handling includes aircraft landing, parking or housing fees, aircraft compass swinging fees, apron services, airport navigation service charges, security and fire services and the supply of crew members.

(C & E Notice 744C, paras 5.1-5.3).

68.10   Surveys and classification services

Any service supplied for, or in connection with, the surveying of any ship or aircraft or the classification of any ship or aircraft for the purposes of any register is zero-rated when

- provided in connection with any qualifying ship (see 68.1 above) or qualifying aircraft (see 68.2 above); or

- supplied to a person who receives the supply for the purposes of a business carried on by him and who belongs outside the UK (whether or not provided for qualifying ships and aircraft).

[*VATA 1994, 8 Sch Group 8, Items 9, 11(b) and Note 7; SI 1995/3039*].

Included are classification services performed by Lloyd's and other registers and survey services for aircraft in relation to the certificate of airworthiness. *Not included* are tonnage measurements or surveys of ships for registration or other purposes required by statute to be carried out by the Department of Trade (which are outside the scope of VAT) or services of arranging for the registering of ships for the purposes of the *Merchant Shipping Acts* (which are standard-rated). (C & E Notice 744C, para 7.4).

68.11   **Salvage and towage services**

Salvage and towage services supplied for shipping are zero-rated whatever the type of ship. [*VATA 1994, 8 Sch Group 8, Item 8*]. Shipping in this context includes inland waterway vessels and all floating objects. Zero-rating also covers dock gates, pier and bridge sections and buoys. It does not cover any subsequent repair work carried out (for which see 68.4 above). (C & E Notice 744C, para 7.3).

68.12   **Pilotage**

Pilotage services are zero-rated. [*VATA 1994, 8 Sch Group 8, Item 7*]. This applies to shipping only. (C & E Notice 744C, para 7.2).

68.13   **LIFEBOATS AND SLIPWAYS**

The following supplies are zero-rated.

(*a*)   The supply to, and repair or maintenance for, a charity providing rescue or assistance at sea of

- any 'lifeboat';

- carriage equipment designed solely for the launching and recovery of lifeboats;

- tractors for the sole use of the launching and recovery of lifeboats; and

- winches and hauling equipment for the sole use of the recovery of lifeboats.

(*b*)   The construction, modification, repair or maintenance for a charity providing rescue or assistance at sea of slipways used solely for the launching and recovery of lifeboats.

(*c*)   The supply of spare parts or accessories to a charity providing rescue or assistance at sea for use in or with goods under (*a*) above or slipways within (*b*) above.

Included is the letting on hire of qualifying goods.

'*Lifeboat*' means any vessel (whatever the tonnage) used or to be used solely for rescue or assistance at sea.

To qualify for zero-rating the recipient of the supply must, before the supply is made, give the supplier a certificate stating the name and address of the recipient and that the supply is of a description specified in *VATA 1994, 8 Sch Group 8, Item 3*.

[*VATA 1994, 8 Sch Group 8, Item 3 and Notes 2, 3 and 4; SI 1995/3039*].

C & E do not stipulate that a boat must possess certain features to be eligible for zero-rating but a genuine sea rescue boat would be likely to possess

- navigational equipment;

- radar;

- oxygen resuscitation equipment;

- first aid equipment;

- a prominent indication on both sides that it is a rescue boat;

- a salvage pump;

- a blue flashing beacon; and

- special tow lines and posts.

Accessories within (*c*) above include life rafts, life buoys and dinghies but not crew uniforms or life jackets.

(C & E Manual V1-9, Chapter 2 paras 8.5, 8.6).

68.14   PASSENGER TRANSPORT

De Voil Indirect Tax Service. See V3.189.

To determine the correct VAT treatment of supplies of passenger transport it is necessary to

* decide whether the supply takes place in the UK (see 68.15 below); and if so

* consider whether the supply is zero-rated (see 68.16 below) or standard-rated (see 68.18 below).

Certain supplies of passenger transport cause particular problems because they can be zero-rated or standard-rated depending upon the precise nature of the services offered. See 68.19 below for transport of vehicles on ships, 68.20 below for cruises and 68.21 below for airline passengers' perks.

See 68.23 below for taxis and hire cars.

Bought-in supplies, packages and inclusive tours. Where passenger transport is bought in and re-supplied, either on its own or as part of a package or inclusive tour, VAT must normally be accounted for under the tour operators' margin scheme. Any other travel, hotel and holiday facilities which have been bought in and re-supplied must also be accounted for using the margin scheme. An 'in-house' supply of passenger transport (e.g. the provision of a driver plus vehicle for passenger transport) does not fall within the scheme and is dealt with in the normal way *unless* it is provided together with other travel and hotel facilities which have been bought in and re-supplied, in which case the 'in-house' transport must be included in the scheme calculation. See 66 TOUR OPERATORS' MARGIN SCHEME for further details.

68.15   Place of supply

Services consisting of the transportation of passengers are treated as supplied in the country where the transportation takes place to the extent that it takes place in that country. [*SI 1992/3121, Art 6*]. As a result, subject to the special rules below, where passenger transport takes place in the UK, the UK is the place of supply. To the extent that the transport takes place outside the UK, it is outside the scope of UK VAT.

Where a business supplies passenger transport involving a journey through another EC country, it may be required to account for VAT in that country on that section of the journey (subject to the VAT registration rules applying there). In cases where cross-frontier transport is provided on an all-inclusive basis, the total consideration must be allocated on a pro-rata basis having regard to the distance covered (rather than the time spent) in each EC country (*Reisebüro Binder GmbH v Finanzamt Stuttgart-Körperschaften, CJEC 1997, [1998] STC 604*. If the business does not have an establishment in that other EC country it may need to appoint a local VAT representative to account for the VAT there on its behalf.

For sea and air passenger transport, provided the means of transport used does not put in or land in another country on the way, any transportation as part of a journey between two points in the same country is treated as taking place wholly inside that country even where it takes place partly outside its territorial jurisdiction. This applies even if the journey is part of a longer journey involving travel to or from another country. [*SI 1992/3121, Art 7*].

Example

A ferry transports passengers from Liverpool to Dublin via the Isle of Man.

The first leg (Liverpool to the Isle of Man) is treated as taking place in the UK but the remaining part of the journey (Isle of Man to Dublin) takes place outside UK territorial waters and is outside the scope of UK VAT.

Pleasure cruises. Any goods or services provided as part of a pleasure cruise are treated as supplied in the same place as the transportation of the passengers and for this purpose a pleasure cruise is treated as a supply of passenger transport. [*SI 1992/3121, Art 8*]. The place of supply of a cruise follows the general rule above i.e. it is supplied in the country in which it takes place to the extent that it takes place in that country.

Luggage and/or accompanying motor vehicles. The transportation of any luggage or motor vehicle (car, motorcycle, caravan, trailer or small commercial vehicle) accompanying in either case a passenger is treated as supplied in the same place as the passenger transport [*SI 1992/3121, Art 8*] and as a single supply with it. The transportation of an *unaccompanied* vehicle is treated as a supply of freight transport (see 68.24 below).

(C & E Notice 744A, paras 2.1–2.4).

68.16 **Zero-rating**

Subject to the standard-rated supplies in 68.18 below, the supply of passenger transport in the UK is zero-rated if falling within any of the following categories.

(*a*) **In any vehicle, ship or aircraft designed or adapted to carry twelve or more passengers.** [*VATA 1994, 8 Sch Group 8, Item 4(a)*].

For the purposes of determining the carrying capacity, the driver and crew should be treated as passengers. See also *G L Ashton (t/a Country Hotel Narrowboats)(14197)* for a consideration of whether the carrying capacity is twelve or more.

Included (subject to the seating rule) are

- cliff lifts;

- excursions by coach and train (including steam railways);

- horse drawn buses;

- mystery coach trips and boat trips;

- sight-seeing tours; and

- the transport element of 'park-and-ride' schemes designed to reduce traffic congestion in city centres.

If the carrying capacity of the vehicle, ship or aircraft is less than twelve passengers, the transport is standard-rated unless it can be zero-rated under (*b*)–(*d*) below or the special concession for disabled passengers applies (see below).

(C & E Notice 744A, para 3.2).

Aircraft. With effect from 1 May 1997, because of problems arising where smaller aircraft are adaptable to take less passengers, it has been agreed with the General Aviation and Manufacturers Association (GAMTA) that passenger transport services may be zero-rated provided

- the aircraft is designed, according to the flight manual, to carry twelve or more passengers, including crew;

- the necessary seat runners, tracks, mountings, etc. for at least twelve seats are permanently in place in the aircraft; and

- at least twelve seats, together with their safety equipment (seat belts, life jackets, oxygen masks, etc.) are maintained at all times by the operator to recognised airworthiness standards or in accordance with Ministry of Defence specifications.

Miniature and narrow-gauge railways. Passenger transport on such railways within a place of recreation or interest are standard-rated (see 68.18 below). Where they are not in such a place, or are in a place where the public have free and unrestricted access such as a public park, zero-rating is likely to depend upon factors such as

- the overall scale of the railway (distance between stations, total length of track, etc.);

- the context (whether or not one of several similar rides); and

- whether it performs a genuine passenger transport function (e.g. transports passengers around an area, up steep inclines, etc. or whether it simply takes them on a round trip).

See *Metroland Ltd (14550)* and *Narogauge Ltd (14680)*.

(C & E Manual V1-7, Chapter 8 Part A, section 1.5).

Narrowboats. In determining whether a narrowboat is designed to carry twelve or more passengers, it is the space on each boat, rather than just the number of berths, which determines the carrying capacity (*GL Ashton (t/a Country Hotel Narrowboats) (14197)*).

Cabin lifts. Each cabin in a cabin lift to a scenic headland has been held to be a separate vehicle and the transport of passengers standard-rated if the individual cabins are designed to hold less than twelve people (*Llandudno Cabinlift Co Ltd, [1973] VATTR 1 (1)*).

(b) **By the post office.** [*VATA 1994, 8 Sch Group 8, Item 4(b)*]. This applies irrespective of the type of vehicle or its carrying capacity.

(c) **On any scheduled flight.** [*VATA 1994, 8 Sch Group 8, Item 4(c)*]. This applies irrespective of the carrying capacity of the aircraft. A scheduled flight is one that is run either according to a published timetable or so regularly or frequently as to constitute a recognisable systematic series of flights. (C & E Notice 744A, para 3.4).

(d) **From a place within to a place outside the UK** (or vice versa) to the extent that those services are supplied within the UK. [*VATA 1994, 8 Sch Group 8, Item 4(d)*]. This applies irrespective of the carrying capacity of the vehicle, ship or aircraft. Zero-rating applies to single journeys, round trips and journeys to or from an oil rig situated outside UK territorial waters. It applies whether payment is received from an individual passenger or a bulk payment is received for a group, and regardless of who the customer is. (C & E Notice 744A, para 3.5).

To qualify for zero-rating as passenger transport, the vehicle, ship or aircraft must be supplied with a driver or crew. Otherwise it is the vehicle, etc. which is being supplied rather than passenger transport.

Vehicles, etc. constructed or modified to carry disabled persons. By concession, where a vehicle, etc. has

(i) a nominal carrying capacity of twelve or more persons conventionally seated,

(ii) a carrying capacity of less than twelve persons when equipped with conventional seats and/or facilities specially designed for the use of passengers with disabilities, and

(iii) the carrying capacity has not been reduced for any reason other than to provide facilities for the disabled (e.g. to carry goods) even if the vehicle is later equipped for the carriage of disabled persons

supplies of passenger transport in it may be zero-rated. If the vehicle also complies with the conditions set out in C & E Notice 744A, Appendix it will be treated as if it had, at all times, a carrying capacity of not less than twelve persons. Separate application must be made to C & E for approval of each qualifying vehicle for which the concession is sought. If a vehicle is purchased to which the concession has been previously applied, the new owner must apply for approval in his own name.

(C & E Notice 48, ESC 2.12; C & E Notice 744A, para 3.6, Appendix).

68.17   *Incidental supplies*

Where a fare is zero-rated, then whether or not a separate charge is made, zero-rating also applies to

- accompanied domestic pets;

- accompanied luggage, including cycles and prams and excess luggage;

- accompanied vehicles and trailers (including Motorail);

- airport passenger charges and passenger load supplements;

- duplicate season tickets;

- pullman supplements;

- seat reservations; and

- sleeping berths and cabins on ships (if provided in the course of ordinary transport, but see 68.21 below for cruises).

(C & E Notice 744A, paras 3.8).

Catering on aircraft is an adjunct to the supply of transport and, where no separate charge is made, the consideration for the ticket need not be apportioned (*British Airways v C & E Commrs CA, [1990] STC 643*).

Payment for an identity card enabling the holder to travel at reduced price has been held to be consideration for the provision of rail transport (*British Railways Board (No 2) v C & E Commrs CA, [1977] STC 221*).

68.18   **Standard-rated supplies**

The following are specifically excluded from zero-rating and become standard-rated.

(*a*) **Passenger transport in places of entertainment or interest**. The transport of passengers in any vehicle to, from or within

(i) a place of entertainment, recreation or amusement, or

(ii) a place of cultural, scientific, historical or similar interest

by the person who supplies a right of admission to, or use of facilities at, such a place or by a person connected with him under the provisions of *ICTA 1988, s 839* (see 69.3 VALUATION) is standard-rated. [*VATA 1994, 8 Sch Group 8, Notes (4A)(4B); SI 1994/3014*]. Such transport services are standard-rated whether included in an overall admission price or made for a separate charge.

Places affected include

- fairgrounds;

- museums;

- piers;

- safari parks;

- stately homes;

- theme parks;

- water parks; and

- zoos.

However, places where the public enjoy totally free access are not affected (e.g. national parks, seaside resorts, historic towns and villages, geographical areas such as the Norfolk Broads, or canals and lakes (unless wholly within one of the places above)).

Examples of standard-rated passenger transport services

- Transport from a car park to the entrance of a theme park or other place of entertainment or interest

- Transport within or around a theme park or other place of entertainment or interest

- Rides to or from a theme park or other place of entertainment or interest which begin or end in the vicinity of those places

The transport may be in a boat, train, tram, horse drawn or other vehicle.

The provisions do not apply to public transport to or from a place of entertainment or cultural interest when provided *independently* from an operator of such a place. Such services remain zero-rated subject to the normal conditions (e.g. a trip by coach or rail to a football ground or a coach excursion to a theme park).

Steam and other railways. Where a steam railway is one of the attractions within a place or entertainment or interest, the supply of admission to and use of the facilities is standard-rated. Other steam railway trips, without additional facilities, are normally zero-rated subject to the twelve-seat rule (see 68.16 above). For this purpose, facilities of a very minor nature at a station (e.g. a children's playground) do not count as a place of entertainment. Such zero-rating also applies even where the normal service is slightly modified for a temporary period (e.g. 'Santa Specials') where the additional facilities are incidental to, and an integral part of, the transport. However, 'Wine and Dine' and 'Steam and Cuisine' and other similar rail journeys may be mixed supplies, standard-rated or zero-rated depending upon the facts of the case; the principles outlined for cruises and other trips in 68.21 below should be followed.

(C & E Notice 744A, paras 4.3-4.7).

(*b*)   **Transport in connection with airport car parks**. The transport of passengers in any 'motor vehicle' between a car park (or land adjacent) and an airport passenger terminal (or land adjacent) by the person who supplies the parking facilities in that car park or by a person connected with him under the provisions of *ICTA 1988, s 839* (see 69.3 VALUATION) is standard-rated. '*Motor vehicle*' means any mechanically propelled vehicle intended or adapted for use on the roads. [*VATA 1994, 8 Sch Group 8, Notes (4A)-(4C); SI 1994/3014*].

The provisions apply

- even if no charge is made for the car park itself;

- even if separate charges are made for transport and parking; and

- irrespective of where the car park is in relation to the airport terminal.

Independent public passenger transport to airports by train, tube, bus or coach, the transport element of urban park-and-ride schemes and journeys from station car parks by public passenger transport are zero-rated if meeting the conditions under 68.16 above.

(C & E Notice 744A, para 4.8).

(c) **Pleasure flights.** The transport of passengers in an aircraft is standard-rated where the flight is advertised or held out to be for the purpose of

    (i) providing entertainment, recreation or amusement, or

    (ii) the experience of flying or the experience of flying in that particular aircraft

and not primarily for the purpose of transporting passengers from one place to another. [*VATA 1994, 8 Sch Group 8, Notes (4A)(4B); SI 1994/3014*].

Such flights are standard-rated even if they take off from one airport and land at another.

Standard-rated flights include

- hot air balloon rides;

- airship rides;

- 'fear of flying' flights; and

- Concorde 'flights to nowhere' and similar pleasure flights where the aircraft returns to the airport of departure or another UK airport without landing in another country.

Examples of flights which remain zero-rated are

- normal domestic and international airline passenger services (including direct flights in Concorde); and

- 'Santa' flights which land in another country.

(C & E Notice 744A, paras 4.9-4.12).

Supplies not regarded as passenger transport. The following are standard-rated because they are not regarded as the transport of passengers.

- Donkey rides and similar rides.

- Novelty rides on miniature and model railways, ghost trains, roundabouts, dippers, other fairground equipment and similar attractions (see *C & E Commrs v Blackpool Pleasure Beach Co QB, [1974] STC 138*).

- The supply of any vehicle with or without a crew for a non-passenger service (e.g. to make a film or carry goods).

(C & E Notice 744A, para 3.1).

68.19   *Ancillary supplies*

The following supplies which are often provided in connection with passenger transport are standard-rated.

- Meals, snacks, sandwiches, drinks, etc. provided in the course of catering *and supplied separately.*
- Car parking (but see 68.22 below when supplied as an airline passenger perk).
- Cycle storage.
- Left luggage and lost property.
- Platform tickets.
- Transportation of unaccompanied luggage, vehicles and trailers.

(C & E Notice 744A, para 3.10).

Club membership, entitling economy class passengers to certain facilities normally available only to first class passengers, is not an advance payment for supplies forming an integral part of passenger transport (*El Al Israel Airlines Ltd (12750)*).

68.20   Transport of vehicles on ships

The transport of vehicles on a ship (e.g. a ferry) may, depending on the circumstances, be a supply of passenger transport or freight transport. C & E's treatment is as follows.

Passenger transport

- Buses, coaches and taxis *with passengers* whether or not charged at the private car rate by the ship or ferry operator.
- Vehicles with drivers or passengers charged under the private car rate, including motorcycles, cars, caravans and trailers.
- Small commercial vehicles charged under the private car rate whether carrying passengers or freight.

Freight transport

- Unaccompanied vehicles, including buses, coaches and trailers, at whatever rate charged.
- Vehicles charged at the rate appropriate to driver-accompanied vans, lorries, buses and coaches (without passengers).
- Drivers accompanying such vehicles.

(C & E Notice 744A, para 3.11).

68.21   Cruises and other trips

This paragraph applies where a cruise operator provides cruises from own resources. It applies to all cruise operators whether supplying international and coastal holiday cruises or cruises on rivers and canals or other inland waterways, including disco, dinner, wedding reception and similar entertainment cruises. In all cases, the vessels must be designed or adapted to carry twelve or more passengers, including crew, otherwise any supplies in the UK will be automatically standard-rated. However, the provisions do not affect cruises bought in and re-supplied under the TOUR OPERATORS' MARGIN SCHEME (66).

C & E regard a business as providing a cruise from its own resources where it

- uses its own ship;
- charters a vessel from the owner for a period of two year or more whether only with deck/engine crew or with deck/engine crew and 'hotel'/domestic/catering crew.

The vessel need not necessarily be in service continuously throughout the period but the owner must not have the right to use the vessel to make supplies to other customers during the period; or

- takes a vessel including deck/engine crew but employs or engages its own 'hotel'/domestic/catering staff.

A pleasure cruise is treated as a single supply of passenger transport *for the purposes of determining the place of supply* (see 68.15 above). Once the place of supply has been established under the general rules for passenger transport in 68.15 above, for UK VAT liability purposes a cruise may be a single or multiple supply depending on the facts of the cruise.

In *The Peninsular & Oriental Steam Navigation Co QB, [1996] STC 698* a cruise sold at an inclusive price covering transport, accommodation, catering, entertainment, etc. was held to be a single supply which was zero-rated as a supply of passenger transport, the terms 'pleasure cruise' and 'passenger transport' not being necessarily mutually exclusive. Previous to this decision, it had been C & E's practice to treat such a cruise as a multiple supply. The decision in that case was, however, distinguished in *Virgin Atlantic Airways Ltd (13840)* where a company operated a river boat which it hired out with optional catering and entertainment. Invoices normally included separate charges for the different services provided. The tribunal held that the company made separate supplies of transport (the hire charge), catering and entertainment and that the supplies of transport were zero-rated.

Following the decisions in *P & O* and *Virgin Atlantic*, C & E strongly recommend that businesses consult their VAT office if in doubt about the liability of a particular cruise. The following are the main criteria they consider relevant in deciding the liability.

Single zero-rated supply of passenger transport

- The essential nature of the supply is passenger transport and the normal conditions for the relief are met;

- all elements of the cruise are integral and it would be neither practicable nor realistic to separate them; and

- the cruise is held out for sale at a single price with no specific charges or discounts for particular services taken or not taken up.

Multiple supplies

- Different elements of the cruise are the subject of separate negotiation and customer choice;

- there are separately identifiable obligations on the supplier, and separate charges;

- separate supplies are not integral to the main supply and could be omitted; and

- it must be practicable, reasonable and realistic to separate the elements of the cruise.

Where separate supplies of any of the individual elements of a cruise are made, these should be taxed according to their respective liabilities (e.g. a separate element of catering is standard-rated when supplied in the UK).

Single standard-rated supplies

- Where a cruise contains only a minor transport element which is incidental to a standard-rated supply (e.g. a wedding reception involving limited travel).

Services of intermediaries. The services of an intermediary making arrangements for the supply of a single zero-rated cruise is zero-rated to the extent that the supply takes place in the UK (see 68.30 below). Where the cruise is treated as a multiple supply, a reasonable apportionment will be accepted.

Other trips. The liability of railway and other trips provided with facilities such as catering or entertainment should be determined using the principles outlined above.

(C & E Notice 744A, paras 3.13, 3.14).

Cruises on inland waterways. The following guidance has been agreed with the British Marine Industries Federation and similar bodies. Where the cruise is held out at a single price and includes light refreshments (e.g. coffee and biscuits, tea and a sandwich), these can be regarded as integral to a zero-rated supply of passenger transport provided no discounts are given to customers who choose not to opt for such 'extras'. Cruises held out at a single price which offer more substantial catering (e.g. a three course meal) will normally be classified as a single standard-rated supply. However, where the rates for passenger transport element are clearly identified in some part of the brochure (even if a single inclusive price is shown for individual cruises in the main part of the brochure), or where transport, catering and other elements are separately itemised on bills to customers, this will be treated as a multiple supply. (C & E Manual V1-7, Chapter 8 Part A, section 1.15 and Appendix B). See, however, *A & J Hughes (t/a Pennine Boat Trips of Skipton), MAN/97/1027 (15680)* where the tribunal held that canal boat trips providing food for parties of 30 or more people were single supplies of zero-rated transport.

68.22   **Airline passenger perks**

In *Virgin Atlantic Airways Ltd v C & E Commrs; Canadian Airlines International Ltd v C & E Commrs QB, [1995] STC 341* chauffeur-driven limousine services to and from the airport, where the passenger pays one indivisible and irreducible sum for these services and the flight, were held to be part of the zero-rated supply of passenger transport. Following this decision, C & E reached agreement with the airline industry that this treatment would be extended to cover other 'passenger perks'.

To be eligible the perks must

(i) be included in the flight ticket price for the class of travel concerned, with no discount if not taken up;

(ii) form an integral part of an international flight;

(iii) not be gifts of goods (except where currently permitted, e.g. in-flight catering, toiletries); and

(iv) be restricted to one perk per customer (although the customer may be offered a number of options).

The following perks are treated as an integral part of an international flight.

● Limousine transport to and from the airport.

● Up to two days car hire for a one way ticket (four days for a return ticket).

● Car parking at the airport.

● Hotel or similar accommodation provided that it is for no more than one night's stay with breakfast and there is a direct connection with the zero-rated travel (e.g. where it is necessary to catch a connecting flight or it is required for the night prior to take-off or the night after landing).

Not included are

● restaurant meals;

- theatre trips and other entertainment provided during a trip or holiday; and

- hotel accommodation and car hire other than as specified above.

New options will not be automatically disallowed but individual prior approval must be obtained from C & E to ensure that the services are incidental to and directly connected with the air travel.

The provision of allowable perks will not, in itself, render the airline liable to use the TOUR OPERATORS' MARGIN SCHEME (66) although the provision of non-allowable perks may well do so.

(C & E Notice 744A, para 3.9).

68.23   **Taxis and hire cars**

Zero-rating of domestic passenger transport does not apply if the vehicle is designed to carry less than twelve passengers. Subject therefore to the registration limits, taxi and hire car fares are standard-rated. Most other domestic public passenger transport by road, rail, sea or air is zero-rated.

Fares. Taxi and hire-car fares, including extra charges for baggage, waiting time etc., are payments for standard-rate supplies. Tips and gratuities given voluntarily are not payments for supplies and are outside the scope of VAT. If maximum permitted fares have been set by the local authority licensing authority, these are VAT-inclusive and must be multiplied by the VAT fraction to arrive at VAT due. See 47.2 OUTPUT TAX.

Businesses engaging other drivers. Whether the staff is employed or self-employed, the business makes the supply to the customer and VAT must be accounted for on the full amount payable before deduction of drivers' wages. VAT must also be accounted for on the full fare payable where a business subcontracts work to independent businesses or to owner drivers. Self-employed drivers must register for VAT if above the registration limit.

Invoices. Registered persons must issue VAT invoices to any customer who asks for one. See 40 INVOICES.

Journeymen are self-employed drivers who do not own their own vehicles but are supplying transport to passengers on their own account. Where a proprietor supplies vehicles to journeymen and pays their NI contributions, the recovery of these amounts may be treated as disbursements subject to satisfying the necessary conditions. See 4.7 AGENTS. Supplies of fuel and rental of vehicles to journeymen are standard-rated.

Taxi associations. Independent taxi drivers may form associations which provide services (e.g. hire of radios, operation of a booking office and radio link, rest facilities) to individual members. Such services provided are standard-rated and the association must register for VAT if all charges exceed the registration limit. See also agencies below.

Taxi and hire-car agencies. Certain businesses offering taxi and hire-car services act as agents in arranging for individual self-employed drivers to make supplies of transport to customers. The agency relays bookings to the drivers for an agreed fee and may also provide other services e.g. hire of cars or radios or the collection of fares from account customers. Drivers are entitled to the full fares paid by customers although the agency's service charge may be deducted from account fares collected on their behalf. Whether the owner of a taxi business is acting as an agent in this way or has engaged the drivers to work (see above) depends upon the actual terms of any written contract or oral agreement between them.

Where an agency exists, supplies of transport are made by the drivers and VAT is only due on fares where the driver is liable to be registered for VAT. If the driver is not registered, the agency must not charge VAT or issue a VAT invoice to customers for fares.

Where the agency is liable to be registered, VAT is due at the standard rate on services supplied to the drivers and also on any services supplied to the customers in addition to the fares e.g. administration charges.

Most taxi or hire-car businesses either always act as agents or as principals engaging the drivers to work for them. Where a business wishes to operate both arrangements at the same time (e.g. an agency for cash customers but a principal-employee arrangement for account customers) it must satisfy C & E that

• the arrangement is reflected in the terms agreed with the drivers; and

• there is a genuine difference in the operation of the two sides of the business.

Where a business is operated in this way, VAT must still be accounted for on the full charge to the drivers for the rental of vehicles, radios or other services supplied.

See also *Carless v C & E Commrs QB, [1993] STC 632; Triumph & Albany Car Service (997, 1004); Mann (t/a Black & Gold Taxis) (204);* and *Hamiltax (8948)*.

Purchases of motor vehicles. VAT can be reclaimed on 'London type' taxis and any other motor car primarily used for hire with the services of a driver for the purpose of carrying passengers. See 45.1 and 45.3 MOTOR CARS.

Fuel. Input tax is reclaimable on fuel bought for use in taxis or hire-cars by the proprietor or employees and on fuel bought for supply to other drivers (e.g. journeymen) to whom a charge is made including an amount for fuel. See 45.10 to 45.19 MOTOR CARS for motor expenses generally including fuel and private motoring.

Sales of motor vehicles. If a 'London type' taxi is sold, VAT must be accounted for on the full selling price. For sales of other motor cars, see 45.4 MOTOR CARS. If a vehicle is sold with a local authority hackney carriage licence plate, there is a single supply of goods (i.e. a licensed taxi). The full selling price is the total amount charged for the vehicle and licence plate. Licence fees paid to a local authority cannot be included in the purchase price of a vehicle when working out the VAT due on the sale.

Sale of business as going concern. If the whole business is sold as a going concern, see 8.10 BUSINESS. To be treated as such a sale, the transaction must include more than just the sale of a vehicle (e.g. the rights to a radio network, goodwill, lists of customers).

(C & E Leaflet 700/25/84).

68.24 **FREIGHT TRANSPORT SERVICES**

Freight for these purposes includes

• goods/cargo;

• mail;

• documents;

• unaccompanied vehicles; and

• vehicles transported on ships which are charged at a 'driver accompanied' rate and have no passengers (for example, buses and coaches).

To determine the correct VAT treatment of supplies of freight transport or related services, it is necessary to determine

- the nature of the supply, i.e. whether it is domestic, intra-EC or international;

- whether the supply, or any part of it, takes place in the UK;

- who should account for any VAT due; and

- for UK supplies, whether the supplies are zero-rated or standard-rated.

Liability to register. If a business supplies freight transport services whose place of supply is in another EC country, the business may be liable to register for VAT in that country (subject to the VAT registration rules applying there). If it does not have an establishment there, the business may need to appoint a local VAT representative to account for the VAT on its behalf. This applies both to UK businesses making supplies in other EC countries and overseas suppliers making supplies in the UK.

(C & E Notice 744B, paras 1.3-1.5).

68.25   **Domestic freight transport**

'*Domestic freight transport*' is the transport of goods that takes place wholly within one country.

Place of supply. The place of supply of domestic freight transport is the country in which it takes place. [*SI 1992/3121, Art 6*]. For sea and air freight transport, provided the means of transport used does not put in or land in another country on the way, any transportation as part of a journey between two points in the same country is treated as taking place wholly inside that country even where it takes place partly outside its territorial jurisdiction. [*SI 1992/3121, Art 7*].

As a result of the above, where freight transport takes place wholly within the UK, the place of supply is the UK.

VAT liability. The supply of domestic freight transport in the UK is normally standard-rated except for the following exceptions.

(*a*)   The transport of goods to a place at which they are to be exported from the EC is zero-rated. [*VATA 1994, 8 Sch Group 8, Item 11*]. Any transport which is supplied in the UK may still be zero-rated even where exportation of the goods is to be from another EC country.

(*b*)   The transport of goods from a place at which they have been imported into the EC is zero-rated. [*VATA 1994, 8 Sch Group 8, Item 11*].

Zero-rating applies to any transport of goods supplied in the UK in connection with a journey from the place of importation to their 'destination' either within the UK or within another EC country. '*Destination*' for this purpose is the furthest place, in the UK or other EC country, to which the goods are consigned at importation as stated on the consignment note (or other document) by means of which the goods are imported. If that place in unknown, it is the first place to which the goods are transported after importation.

Documentary evidence must be held to show entitlement to zero-rating. The main forms of documentary evidence include consignment notes, bills of lading, certificates of shipment, airwaybills or seawaybills and Customs declaration Forms C88 (SAD). Additionally, a combination (or all) of inter-company correspondence, the customer's order document, payment details, sales invoices and advice notes may provide suitable evidence.

Where zero-rating applies, it applies whether the supplier is the main contractor or a sub-contractor, and regardless of who the customer is. Included are the services of freight forwarders who buy in and supply on freight transport as principals.

68.26   Transport and Freight

See also 68.26 below for the domestic leg of an intra-EC freight transport movement.

Accounting for the VAT. *Where the supplier belongs in the UK*, the supplier must account for the VAT due on domestic freight transport in the UK.

Where the supplier belongs overseas,

- if the customer is not UK VAT-registered, the supplier must account for any VAT due on domestic freight transport in the UK. If not already registered in the UK, the overseas supplier is liable to register (subject to the current VAT registration threshold); and

- if the customer is UK VAT-registered, the customer must account for any VAT, as the recipient of domestic freight transport services, under the reverse charge procedure (see 39.4 INTERNATIONAL SERVICES).

(C & E Notice 744B, paras 2.1, 5.2, 5.5).

68.26   Intra-EC freight transport

'*Intra-EC transport of goods*' means transportation of goods which begins in one EC country and ends in a different EC country. It includes the transport of goods

- which takes place entirely within one EC country where it is part of a single movement of goods from one EC country to another (e.g. road haulage from Dover to London for goods which are consigned from Paris to Edinburgh — see below under the heading *Domestic legs of an intra-EC freight transport movement*); and

- from one EC country to another where the journey goes through a non-EC country (e.g. transport of goods from London to Rome via Switzerland).

Place of supply. Services consisting of the intra-EC transport of goods are treated as made in the EC country in which the transportation of the goods begins. Where, however,

- the service is supplied to a customer registered for VAT in a EC country other than that in which the transportation begins, and

- the customer gives a valid VAT registration number to the supplier,

the place of supply is the EC country of the customer.

[*SI 1992/3121, Arts 10, 14*].

Accounting for the VAT. The liability to account for VAT depends upon whether, and if so where, the customer is registered for VAT.

(*a*)   Where the customer has given a valid VAT registration number

   (i) if the customer is registered in the same EC country as the supplier, the supplier must charge and account for VAT in the EC country where transportation of the goods begins; and

   (ii) if the customer is not registered in the same EC country as the supplier, the supplier does not charge VAT and the customer accounts for VAT in his own country under the reverse charge procedure (see 39.4 INTERNATIONAL SERVICES).

(*b*)   Where the customer is not registered for VAT or, if registered, fails to give a valid VAT registration number to the supplier, the supplier must account for VAT in the place were the transportation of the goods begins.

Domestic legs of an intra-EC freight transport movement. C & E treat a service consisting of a separate domestic leg of transport, which forms part of an intra-EC movement of goods, in the same way as an intra-EC movement. This means that UK suppliers of such legs need not charge UK VAT on those services supplied to a person who is registered for VAT in another EC country. Commercial evidence must be held to show that the service does form part of an intra-EC movement of goods.

(C & E Notice 744B, paras 2.3-2.5, 2.11).

68.27   **International freight transport**

'*International freight transport*' is the transport of goods between EC and non-EC countries, or wholly outside the EC.

Place of supply. The place of supply of international freight transport is the country in which the transportation takes place to the extent that it takes place in that country. [*SI 1992/3121, Art 6*].

VAT liability. The transport of 'goods' from a place within to a place outside the EC (or vice versa) is zero-rated to the extent that the supply takes place in the UK. [*VATA 1994, 8 Sch Group 8, Item 5*]. To the extent that the transport takes place outside the UK, it is outside the scope of UK VAT. (The transport of goods between two places both outside the EC is outside the scope of UK and EC VAT.) '*Goods*' includes mail and documents.

See also 68.25(*a*) and (*b*) above for zero-rating of freight transport supplied in the UK in connection with goods which are to be exported to, or have been imported from, a place outside the EC.

Zero-rating applies whether the supplier is the main contractor or a sub-contractor, and regardless of who the customer is. Included are the services of freight forwarders who buy in and supply on freight transport as principals.

(C & E Notice 744B, paras 2.2, 3.1-3.4).

68.28   **Ancillary freight transport services**

'*Ancillary transport services*' means loading, unloading, handling and similar activities. [*SI 1992/3121, Art 2*]. Included are the services of reloading, stowing, opening for inspection, cargo security services, preparing or amending bills of lading, airwaybills and certificates of shipment, packing necessary for transportation and storage.

Place of supply. Special rules apply for determining the place of supply of ancillary freight transport services.

- Ancillary transport services in connection with domestic freight transport (see 68.25 above) or international freight transport (see 68.27 above) are treated as supplied where the services are physically performed.

- Ancillary transport services in connection with the intra-EC freight transport (see 68.26 above) are treated as supplied where the services are physically performed. Where, however, the services are supplied to a customer

  (i) registered for VAT in an EC country other than that in which the services are physically performed, and

  (ii) who has given a valid VAT registration number to the supplier

  the services are treated as supplied in the customer's country.

[*SI 1992/3121, Arts 9, 14*].

VAT liability. Ancillary freight transport services supplied in the UK are normally standard-rated. However, the following services are zero-rated.

(*a*) The 'handling' or storage of goods carried in a ship or aircraft when provided in a 'port' or 'customs and excise airport' or on 'land adjacent to a port'. See 68.9 above for the meaning of '*port*' and '*customs and excise airport*'. The letting on hire of goods (including cranes and other lifting equipment) is specifically excluded.

It is not necessary for the ship or aircraft itself to qualify for zero-rating.

The UK legislation is based upon *EC 6th Directive, Art 15(8)(9)* which refers to services to meet the 'direct needs' of the ship or aircraft or its cargo. Overnight storage before loading is therefore zero-rated but not long-term storage of goods. Storage for a longer period than strictly required due to unavoidable events (e.g. industrial action) can be zero-rated. (C & E Manual V1-7, Chapter 8 Part B, section 3.7).

(*b*) The 'handling' or storage of goods at the place at which they are to be exported from the EC or have been imported into the EC.

(*c*) The 'handling' or storage of goods in connection with their transport

  (i) to a place at which they are to be exported from the EC; or

  (ii) from a place at which they have been imported into the EC to their 'destination' in the UK or within another EC country (to the extent that those services are supplied in the UK). '*Destination*' for this purpose is the furthest place, in the UK or other EC country, to which the goods are consigned at importation as stated on the consignment note (or other document) by means of which the goods are imported. If that place is unknown, it is the first place to which the goods are transported after importation.

  Documentary evidence must be held to show entitlement to zero-rating. The main forms of documentary evidence include consignment notes, bills of lading, certificates of shipment, airwaybills or seawaybills and Customs declaration Forms C88 (SAD). Additionally, a combination (or all) of inter-company correspondence, the customer's order document, payment details, sales invoices and advice notes may provide suitable evidence.

[*VATA 1994, 8 Sch Group 8, Items 6(b), 11(a) and Notes 5 and 7; SI 1995/3039*].

'*Handling*' includes cargo security services; container handling for which a box charge is made; demurrage; loading stores and discharging empties; loading, unloading, reloading, stowing, securing and shifting cargo; preparing or amending bills of lading, airwaybills and certificates of shipment; preparing or amending customs entries; presenting goods for customs examination; sorting, opening for inspection, repairing and making good, weighing and taring, taping and sealing, erasing and re-marking, labelling and re-numbering, tallying, checking, sampling, measuring or gauging of goods; stevedoring and porterage; survey of cargo (including damaged cargo); and the movement of goods to or from a ship by lighter.

'*Land adjacent to a port*' only covers the immediate quay or dock area. It does not include inland clearance depots unless physically located in the immediate quay or dock area.

Where zero-rating applies, it applies whether the supplier is the main contractor or a sub-contractor, and regardless of who the customer is. Included are the services of freight forwarders who buy in and supply on freight transport as principals.

Accounting for VAT.

(*a*) Ancillary freight transport services in connection with domestic or international freight transport. The supplier is normally responsible for any VAT due. The exception is where

- an overseas supplier supplies domestic ancillary transport services that are physically performed in the UK, and

- the customer is registered for VAT in the UK

in which case the customer accounts for VAT under the reverse charge procedure (see 39.4 INTERNATIONAL SERVICES).

(b)   *Ancillary freight transport services in connection with intra-EC freight transport.* The liability to account for VAT depends upon whether, and if so where, the customer is registered for VAT.

(i)   Where the customer has given a valid VAT registration number

- if the customer is registered in the same EC country as the supplier, the supplier must charge and account for VAT in the EC country where the ancillary services are physically performed; and

- if the customer is not registered in the same EC country as the supplier, the supplier does not charge VAT and the customer accounts for VAT in his own country under the reverse charge procedure (see 39.4 INTERNATIONAL SERVICES).

(ii)   Where the customer is not registered for VAT or, if registered, fails to give a valid VAT registration number to the supplier, the supplier must account for VAT in the place were the ancillary services are physically performed.

(C & E Notice 744B, paras 2.6-2.8, 2.11, 3.1, 4.1-4.3, 5.2, 5.5).

68.29   **The Azores and Madeira**

The supply of 'intra-Community transport services' in connection with the transport of goods

- to or from the Azores and Madeira, or

- between those places

is zero-rated to the extent that the services are treated as supplied in the United Kingdom.

'*Intra-Community transport services*' means

(a)   the 'intra-EC transport of goods' (see 68.26 above);

(b)   'ancillary transport services' (see 68.28 above) which are provided in connection with the transportation of goods within (a) above; and

(c)   the services of an intermediary in arranging for the supply by or to another person of a supply within (a) or (b) above or any other activity which is intended to facilitate the making of the supply

and for these purposes the Azores and Madeira are each to be treated as a separate EC country.

[*VATA 1994, 8 Sch Group 8, Item 13 and Note 9*].

See 68.26 above for the place of supply of intra-EC freight transport, 68.28 above for the place of supply of ancillary freight transport services and 68.30 below for the place of supply of services of intermediaries.

68.30   **INTERMEDIARY SERVICES**

Place of supply. Special rules apply for determining the place of supply of services by intermediaries making arrangements for passenger and freight transport services. Subject to below, the place of supply of making arrangements for

68.30 Transport and Freight

(*a*) a supply of

    (i) passenger transport within 68.14 above,

    (ii) domestic freight transport within 68.25 above and any related ancillary freight transport services within 68.28 above,

    (iii) international freight transport within 68.27 above and any related ancillary freight transport services within 68.28 above, and

    (iv) any activity intended to facilitate the making of a supply within (i)-(iii) above

    is the place where the supply which is being arranged is deemed to be made;

(*b*) intra-EC freight transport within 68.26 above (or any activity intended to facilitate the making of such a supply) is the place where the transportation begins; and

(*c*) ancillary freight transport services within 68.28 above relating to a supply of intra-EC freight transport within 68.26 above (or any activity intended to facilitate the making of such a supply) is the place where the ancillary transport service is physically performed.

Where, however, the intermediary services within (*a*)-(*c*) above are supplied to a customer

- registered for VAT in an EC country other than the one where the arranged supply is made, and

- who has given a valid VAT registration number to the intermediary

the intermediary's services are treated as supplied in the EC country where the customer is registered (and the customer then is responsible for accounting for any VAT due under the reverse charge procedure).

[*SI 1992/3121, Arts 11-14*].

VAT liability. If the place of supply of the intermediary services is the UK, the supply is normally standard-rated. However, zero-rating applies to the making of arrangements for

- the supply of, or space in, a qualifying ship (see 68.1 above) or qualifying aircraft (see 68.2 above);

- the supply of parts and equipment within 68.3 above;

- the supply of any *services* within 68.4 to 68.28 above (but *not* 68.29 above) which are themselves zero-rated, and

- the supply of, or space in, a ship or aircraft to a person who receives the supply for the purposes of a business carried on by him and who belongs outside the UK (whether or not the ship or aircraft is a qualifying one).

[*VATA 1994, 8 Sch Group 8, Items 10, 11(b) and Note 7; SI 1995/3039*].

Intermediary services received in the UK from overseas suppliers. Where a UK-registered person makes use of a VAT registration number for the purpose of receiving intermediary services which consist of the making of arrangements for

- domestic freight transport, or part of international transport, which takes place in the EC, or

- intra-EC freight transport and/or related freight transport services

from an intermediary who belongs in either another EC country or a country outside the EC, the place of supply is the UK and the reverse charge procedure applies. The UK recipient is required to account for the VAT. See 39.4 INTERNATIONAL SERVICES.

(C & E Notice 744B, paras 2.9, 6.1).

69 Valuation

Cross-references. See 4.20 AGENTS for valuation of supplies made by agents under 'party-plan' or 'direct' selling arrangements; 5 APPEALS for appeals regarding valuation; 47.3 OUTPUT TAX for the valuation of mixed supplies; 58.3 RECREATION AND SPORT for the valuation of supplies in respect of gaming machines; 60.8, 60.9 RETAIL SCHEMES for valuation of gross takings of retailers; 64 SUPPLY for coverage of supplies generally and the time and place of supply; 67 TRADING STAMP AND PROMOTION SCHEMES for valuation of supplies made by the promoter.

De Voil Indirect Tax Service. See V3.151–166.

69.1 INTRODUCTION

EC legislation. See 22.12–22.14 EUROPEAN COMMUNITY LEGISLATION.

UK legislation. VAT is charged on

- the supply of goods and services;

- the importation of goods; and

- the acquisition of goods from another EC country.

[*VATA 1994, s 2*].

Different valuation rules apply in each of the above cases and also depending upon whether the supply is for a consideration wholly in money or not.

69.2 SUPPLIES OF GOODS AND SERVICES

(*a*) **Consideration wholly in money.** If a supply is for a consideration in 'money', subject to 69.3–69.6 below, its value for VAT purposes is such amount as, with the addition of the VAT chargeable, is equal to the consideration. [*VATA 1994, s 19(2)*]. '*Money*' includes currencies other than sterling (see 69.6 below). [*VATA 1994, s 96(1)*]. The VAT element of a VAT-inclusive consideration is determined by multiplying that consideration by the VAT fraction (see 47.2 OUTPUT TAX).

(*b*) **Consideration not wholly in money.** If a supply is for a consideration not consisting, or not wholly consisting, of money, subject to 69.3–69.6 below its value is to be taken to be such amount in money as, with addition of the VAT chargeable, is equivalent to the consideration. [*VATA 1994, s 19(3)*]. This should normally be calculated by reference to the price, excluding VAT, which would have to be paid for the supply if money was the only consideration. (C & E Notice 700, para 3.1).

'*Consideration*' is not defined in *VATA 1994*. It has, however, been held to have its ordinary meaning in English law (*Theatres Consolidated Ltd, [1975] VATTR 13 (141)*). The word is defined in the *EC 2nd Directive, Annex A, para 13* as meaning 'everything received in return for the supply of goods or the provision of services, including incidental expenses (packing, transport, insurance, etc.) that is to say not only the cash amounts charged, but also, for example, the value of goods or services supplied by order of a public authority, the amount of compensation received.' Although the definition is not repeated in the *6th Directive*, the word 'consideration' is used in a number of places in that *Directive* and presumably it will have the same meaning. Per Lord Brightman, the meaning is close to, but not necessarily the same as, the ordinary meaning in English law (*C & E Commrs v The Apple and Pear Development Council HL, [1986] STC 192*). See also *Staatssecretaris van Financiën v Cooperatieve Vereniging Cooperatieve Aardappelenbewaarplaats GA, CJEC [1981] 3 CMLR 337*.

It is immaterial who pays for a supply and, where payment is to a third party, such payment will usually be sufficient consideration to make a supply taxable (*Lord Advocate v Largs Golf Club CS, [1985] STC 226*).

Common cases of a consideration not wholly in money are the part exchange of goods and the 'free' use of money. A 'part exchange plus cash payment' transaction involves both an output and an input supply being made. The VAT to be accounted for on the output supply of the new goods will be the amount which would have applied if there had been a purely money consideration e.g. the usual VAT-inclusive cash selling price. The VAT to be accounted for on the input supply of the part-exchanged goods will be on a similar basis, e.g. the usual VAT-inclusive selling price less the cash consideration actually passing. An example of the value of the consideration involved in the making of a 'free' use of money occurs in the practice of some members' clubs of requiring an annual cash subscription plus the grant of an interest-free loan to the club by the member. The determination by C & E that the value of the consideration attached to the interest-free loan should be computed by reference to a bank minimum lending rate was upheld (*Exeter Golf and Country Club Ltd v C & E Commrs CA, [1981] STC 211*). See also 14.5 CLUBS AND ASSOCIATIONS.

Interest charged. Where a supplier allows his customer to defer payment of the price in return for the payment of interest, in principle there is a grant of credit which is exempt. However, where, in return for an interest charge, payment is only deferred until the time of supply, such interest is not a reward for credit but part of the taxable consideration for the supply (*Muys en De Winters's Bouw-en Aannemingsbedriff BV v Staatssecretaris van Financiën, CJEC 1993, [1997] STC 665*).

De Voil Indirect Tax Service. See V3.152.

69.3 Transactions between connected persons

Where

(*a*) the value of a supply made by a taxable person for a consideration in money is less than its open market value, and

(*b*) the person making the supply and the person to whom it is made are 'connected', and

(*c*) if the supply is a taxable supply, the person to whom it is made is not entitled under *VATA 1994, ss 25, 26* to credit for all of the VAT on the supply,

C & E may direct that the value of the supply is to be taken to be its 'open market value'.

'*Open market value*' is the amount which would be taken as its value under (*a*) above assuming the supply were for such consideration in money as would be payable by a person standing in no such relationship with any person as would affect that consideration.

A direction is given by notice in writing to the person making the supply within a three year period from the time of the supply and may be varied or withdrawn by a further direction given by notice in writing. The direction may also include a direction that the value of any supply made after the date of notice and to which the above conditions apply is to be taken to be its open market value. An appeal may be made against a direction (see 5.3(*v*) APPEALS).

The above provisions do not apply to supplies made to employees in respect of catering or hotel accommodation (see 11.4 CATERING and 33.3 HOTELS AND HOLIDAY ACCOMMODATION).

[*VATA 1994, s 19(5), 6 Sch 1(1)–(3),(5),13*].

Connected persons. Persons are treated as 'connected' with another under the provisions of *ICTA 1988, s 839*. [*VATA 1994, 6 Sch 1(4)*]. These are as follows.

 (i) An individual is connected with his spouse, any 'relative' of himself or of his spouse, and with the spouse of any such relative. It appears that a widow or widower is no longer a spouse (*Vestey's (Lord) Exors and Vestey v CIR HL 1949, 31 TC 1*). Spouses divorced by decree nisi remain connected persons until the divorce is made absolute (*Aspden v Hildesley CD 1981, [1982] STC 206*).

(ii) A trustee of a settlement, in his capacity as such, is connected with

 • the settlor (if an individual); and

 • any person connected with that settlor; and

 • a 'body corporate connected with the settlement'.

(iii) Partners are connected with each other and with each other's spouses and 'relatives' except in connection with acquisitions and disposals of partnership assets made pursuant to bona fide commercial arrangements.

(iv) A 'company' is connected with another company if

 • the same person 'controls' both;

 • one is controlled by a person who has control of the other in conjunction with persons connected with him;

 • a person controls one company and persons connected with him control the other;

 • the same group of persons controls both; or

 • the companies are controlled by separate groups which can be regarded as the same by interchanging connected persons.

 (v) A company is connected with a person who (either alone or with persons connected with him) has control of it.

(vi) Persons acting together to secure or exercise control of a company are treated in relation to that company as connected with each other and with any other person acting on the direction of any of them to secure or exercise such control. Control may be 'exercised' passively. (See *Floor v Davis HL 1979, 52 TC 609*).

'*Company*' includes any body corporate, unincorporated association or unit trust scheme. It does not include a partnership.

'*Control*' is as defined in *ICTA 1988, s 416*. See Tolley's Corporation Tax for full coverage of this definition.

'*Relative*' means brother, sister, ancestor or lineal descendant.

'*Settlement*' includes any disposition, trust, covenant, agreement or arrangement. [*ICTA 1988, s 681(4)*]. It must contain an element of bounty, and does not include a transfer made for full consideration (*CIR v Plummer HL, [1979] STC 793*).

'*A body corporate connected with the settlement*' is a 'close company' (or one which would be close if resident in the UK) the 'participators' in which include the trustees of the settlement, or a company of which such a close company etc. has 'control'. '*Close company*' for this purpose is as defined by *ICTA 1988, s 414*, '*participator*' is as defined by *ICTA 1988, s 417* and 'control' in this case, is as defined by *ICTA 1988, s 840*. See Tolley's Corporation Tax for full coverage of these definitions.

'*Settlor*' is any person by whom the settlement was made or who has directly or indirectly (or by a reciprocal arrangement) provided, or undertaken to provide, funds for the settlement. [*ICTA 1988, s 681(4)*].

De Voil Indirect Tax Service. See V1.284; V3.161; V3.162.

69.4 **Supplies of goods made to non-taxable persons for retail sale**

In circumstances where

- the whole or part of a business carried on by a taxable person consists in supplying to a number of persons goods to be sold, whether by them or others, by retail, and

- those persons are not taxable persons,

C & E may direct that the value of any such supply is to be taken as its open market value. The direction is given by notice in writing to the taxable person and is effective from the date of the giving of notice or a later date as specified in the notice and may be varied or withdrawn by a further direction given by notice in writing. An appeal may be made against a direction (see 5 APPEALS).

[*VATA 1994, 6 Sch 2, 13*].

The UK government has been granted a derogation from the provisions of the *EC 6th Directive* in connection with *VATA 1994, 6 Sch 2* (see 22.30 EUROPEAN COMMUNITY LEGISLATION). See also *Direct Cosmetics Ltd v C & E Commrs, CJEC [1985] STC 479* (and the subsequent appeal by *Direct Cosmetics* and *Laughton Photographs Ltd, CJEC [1988] STC 540*) and *Gold Star Publications Ltd v C & E Commrs QB, [1992] STC 365*.

In *Fine Art Developments plc v C & E Commrs HL 1995, [1996] STC 246*, catalogues containing descriptions and pictures of goods for sale were sent to agents. Approximately 70% of the goods were sold on by the agents at catalogue price. Some goods were retained by the agents for their own use and some were sold on at less than the catalogue price. Reversing the decision of the Court of Appeal, it was held that a direction by C & E under the above provisions was valid. As VAT was a self-assessed tax, it was the duty of the company to modify its order form so as to identify the goods earmarked for onward sale. Where the company was unable to show what the actual sale price for any item was, it was open to C & E to take the catalogue price as being the true open market value.

A direction has been held to be invalid where there was no effective means of determining the open market value of the goods sold by retail (*Beckbell Ltd, [1993] VATTR 212 (9847)*).

De Voil Indirect Tax Service. See V3.161; V3.163.

69.5 **Miscellaneous aspects**

Consideration attributable to both a supply and other matters. Where a supply of any goods or services is not the only matter to which a consideration in money relates, the supply is deemed to be for such part of the consideration as is properly attributable to it. [*VATA 1994, s 19(4)*]. This provision could cover, for example, the case of a taxable person making a supply to another person but recovering at the same time a private debt made previously to that person.

Discounts offered. Where goods or services are supplied for a consideration in money and on terms allowing a discount for prompt payment, the consideration is to be taken, for the purposes of valuation, as reduced by the discount, whether or not payment is made in accordance with those terms, but this treatment does not apply where the terms include any provision for payment by instalments. [*VATA 1994, 6 Sch 4*]. The VAT invoice must show the rate of cash discount offered, the amount of the discounted consideration and VAT thereon. See also *Gold Star Publications Ltd v C & E Commrs QB, [1992] STC 365* (whether what was described as a discount for prompt payment was in fact such a discount or a commission given to demonstrators).

Unconditional discounts (e.g. because of the volume of supplies being made or the size and status of a customer) are also given similar treatment as prompt payment discounts but contingent discounts should be ignored initially for valuation purposes so that only if a customer later qualifies for the discount (e.g. purchasing further goods) can the necessary adjustment be made by issuing a credit note to adjust the tax value. (C & E Notice 700, para 3.1).

As regards prompt payment discounts, it appears that the lowest discounted tax value is to be taken.

Example

A trader supplies an article for £10,000 + VAT with payment within 60 days but offers a discount of 2% and 1% for prompt payment within 14 and 30 days respectively.

The VAT value of the supply is £10,000 less 2% i.e. £9,800. VAT, at the current rate of 17.5%, is to be accounted for on £9,800 i.e. £1,715 notwithstanding that a customer actually settles for a *total* consideration of £11,515, £11,615 or £11,715 depending on whether he actually makes payment within 14, 30 or 60 days respectively. It follows from this treatment that in the latter two cases the VAT fraction method of determining the VAT element of a VAT-inclusive consideration as explained at 69.2 above should not be used.

'Dividend' paid to members in respect of their purchases of items from the society have been held to be discount in *Co-operative Retail Services Ltd, [1992] VATTR 60 (7527)*.

Staff discounts. C & E accept that output tax is due on the discounted price under all circumstances. (C & E Business Brief 8/92, 15 June 1992).

Tokens, stamps and vouchers. See 67 TRADING STAMP AND PROMOTION SCHEMES generally.

Credit card transactions. Where a purchaser pays by credit card, the supplier's consideration is the total price charged to the customer and not the net sum received from the credit card company after deduction of commission in respect of services provided (*Chaussures Bally SA v Ministry of Finance (Belgium), CJEC 1993, [1997] STC 209*).

Self-supplies. See 45.6 MOTOR CARS and 62.2 SELF-SUPPLY for self-supply of stationery.

Business gifts. See 47.4 OUTPUT TAX.

Deregistration. See 59.27 REGISTRATION for the valuation of supplies deemed to be made on deregistration and termination of business.

Private use of goods and services. See 47.5 OUTPUT TAX.

Services received from abroad. See 39.4 INTERNATIONAL SERVICES for the valuation of certain supplies of services by persons belonging outside the UK and subject to the reverse charge.

Catering for employees etc. See 11.4 CATERING and 33.3 HOTELS and HOLIDAY ACCOMMODATION.

'Party plan' and catalogue sales. See *Naturally Yours Cosmetics Ltd v C & E Commrs, CJEC [1988] STC 879* and *C & E Commrs v Pippa-Dee Parties Ltd, QB [1991] STC 495*.

Long-term hotel accommodation. See 33.2 HOTELS AND HOLIDAY ACCOMMODATION.

69.6 **Valuation**

Money consideration for a supply paid by third parties. C & E have power to make regulations so as to require that in prescribed circumstances there is to be taken into account as constituting part of a money consideration for the purposes of VAT (as at 69.2 above) (where it would not otherwise be so taken into account) money paid in respect of the supply by persons other than those to whom the supply is made. [*VATA 1994, 6 Sch 12*]. No regulations have been made under these provisions.

Excise duty. Where

* any goods whose supply involves their removal to the UK are charged in connection with their removal with a duty of excise or car tax (or any Community customs duty or EC agricultural levy having effect for transitional provisions in connection with the accession of any state to the EC), or

* the time of supply of any dutiable goods (or goods comprising a mixture of dutiable goods and other goods) is determined under *VATA 1994, s 18(4)* (goods within the warehouse regime) to be at or after the duty point,

then the value of the supply for VAT purposes is its value apart from this provision plus the amount (so far as not already included) of any duty which has been or is to be paid in respect of the goods. [*VATA 1994, 6 Sch 3*].

See 70.8 WAREHOUSED GOODS AND FREE ZONES for the provisions of *VATA 1994, s 18(4)* and the definitions of '*dutiable goods*' and '*duty point*'.

69.6 **Currency other than sterling**

Where there is a supply of goods or services and any sum relevant for determining the value is expressed in a currency other than sterling, subject to below, that sum is to be converted into sterling at the market selling rate for that currency at the time of supply. The rates published in national newspapers are acceptable as evidence of the rates at the relevant time. The following options are, however, allowed.

* Where C & E have published a notice specifying rates of exchange, or methods of determining rates of exchange, a person may opt to use a rate so specified or determined. This alternative may be adopted for all supplies or for all supplies of a particular class or description. If adopted only for a particular class, that class and the time of adoption should be noted in the records. There is no need to notify C & E in advance that this alternative has been adopted but, once it has, it cannot be changed without first obtaining the agreement of the VAT office.

* C & E may allow a person to apply to them to use a different rate of exchange for the valuation of all or some of his supplies. Application should be made in writing to the VAT office. In considering whether to allow the application, C & E will take into account whether the proposed rate or method is determined by reference to the UK currency market, whether it is objectively verifiable and the frequency with which it is proposed to update it. Forward rates or methods deriving from forward rates are not acceptable.

* Where C & E authorised a person to use a rate before 1 January 1993 under the concessionary arrangements, that person may continue to use that rate without further notification unless the rate used wholly derives from currency markets other than in the UK. The continued use of concessionary rates is subject to review by C & E.

[*VATA 1994, 6 Sch 11*]. (C & E Notice 700, para 3.1(*f*) which has the force of law).

De Voil Indirect Tax Service. See V3.164.

69.7   IMPORTATIONS OF GOODS

The value of goods imported from a place outside the EC is, subject to below, to be determined according to the rules for Community customs duties (whether or not the goods in question are subject to such duties). These rules are set out in *Council Regulation 2913/92* and *Commission Regulation 2454/93* with effect from 1 January 1994 (previously in *Council Regulation 1224/80* and *Commission Regulations 1494/80, 1495/80* and *1496/80*). See also C & E Notice 252 (Valuation of imported goods for customs purposes, VAT and trade statistics).

The following are included in the value (so far as not already included under the above rules).

(*a*)   All taxes, duties and other charges levied outside or, by reason of importation, within the UK (but excluding VAT).

(*b*)   All incidental expenses such as commission, packing, transport and insurance costs, up to the '*first destination*' of the goods in the UK. '*First destination*' means the place mentioned on the consignment note or other importation document or, in the absence of such documentation, the place of the first transfer of cargo in the UK.

(*c*)   If at the time of importation of the goods a further destination for the goods is known, and that destination is within the UK or another EC country, all such incidental expenses resulting from the transport of the goods to that other destination.

Subject to (*a*)–(*c*) above, where the consideration is wholly or partly in money and on terms allowing a discount for prompt payment (but not payment of the price by instalments), the value of the goods is reduced by the discount if payment is made in accordance with those terms so that the discount is allowed.

[*VATA 1994, s 21(1)–(3); FA 1995, s 22; FA 1996, s 27*].

Works of art, antiques and collectors' pieces. Special valuation provisions apply for these items which have the effect of subjecting them to VAT at an effective reduced rate of 2.5%. See 71.3 WORKS OF ART ETC. for full details.

Incidental expenses. In addition to the examples given above, 'incidental expenses' also covers items such as customs clearance charges, quay rent, entry fees, demurrage, handling, loading and storage costs. Costs which are taxable under the reverse charge procedure (see 39.4 INTERNATIONAL SERVICES), e.g. royalties and licence fees, should not be included in the value for import VAT.

Buyer and seller related. Under the customs valuation rules, where the buyer and seller of the goods are related, the price paid or payable for those goods can be accepted as long as the buyer shows that the relationship has not affected the price (see C & E Notice 252, para 1.7 and 1.8 and Appendix C). The same rules apply for import VAT purposes, whether or not the goods are subject to a positive rate of customs duty.

Costs not known at time of importation. If all relevant costs cannot be established at the time the goods are entered (e.g. the cost of UK transport supplied by an independent haulier may not be known until some time later), C & E will accept estimates of incidental expenses to be included in the import VAT value, based on certain nationally agreed rates. Details of the rates are available from Entry Processing Units.

(C & E Notice 702, para 3.1).

Value declaration. If goods are liable to *ad valorem* customs duty (i.e. a duty chargeable on the basis of value), a declaration on Form C105 (Valuation Declaration) or Form C109 (General Valuation Statement), made for duty purposes, will also generally be acceptable for VAT. However, the declaration will only provide information which helps determine the customs value of the goods, and it should not be regarded as establishing their full value for VAT purposes (see above).

Where goods are not liable to ad valorem duty but are liable to VAT at the standard rate, a valuation declaration for VAT is needed only if the value exceeds £4,000 and

- the importer is not registered for VAT; or

- the importer is registered for VAT but either the goods are for non-business purposes or input tax deduction would not be allowed (e.g. on motor cars); or

- the value of the goods is not being determined under Method 1 (see Notice 252, Section I).

Whether or not a valuation declaration is required for the goods, evidence of value must be produced. Acceptable evidence is a copy of the seller's invoice or other document against which payment will be made. This will include telex or similar messages used instead of invoices.

(C & E Notice 702, para 3.3).

De Voil Indirect Tax Service. See V3.321–329.

69.8 **ACQUISITIONS FROM OTHER EC COUNTRIES**

The value of any acquisition of goods from another EC country is to be taken to be the value of the transaction in pursuance of which they are acquired as follows.

- Where the goods are acquired from another EC country by means of a taxable supply, the value of that transaction is determined under the rules in 69.2 above.

- Where the goods are acquired otherwise than in pursuance of a taxable supply, subject to 69.9–69.12 below,

 (i) if the transaction is for a consideration in money, its value is to be taken to be such amount as is equal to the consideration; and

 (ii) if the transaction is for a consideration not consisting, or not wholly consisting, of money, its value is to be taken to be such amount in money as is equivalent to the consideration.

[*VATA 1994, s 20(1)–(4); FA 1996, 3 Sch 6*].

Consideration attributable to both an acquisition and other matters. Where the transaction in pursuance of which the goods are acquired from another EC country is not the only matter to which a consideration in money relates, the transaction is deemed to be for such part of the consideration as is properly attributable to it. [*VATA 1994, s 20(5)*].

De Voil Indirect Tax Service. See V3.390.

69.9 **Transactions between connected persons**

Where in the case of any acquisition of goods from another EC country

(*a*) the value of the transaction is for a consideration in money which is less than its open market value, and

(*b*) the supplier and the person who acquires the goods are 'connected', and

(*c*) that person is not entitled under *VATA 1994, ss 25, 26* to credit for all the VAT on the acquisition,

C & E may direct that the value of the transaction is to be taken to be its 'open market value'.

'*Open market value*' is the amount which would be taken as its value assuming the transaction was for such consideration in money as would be payable by a person standing in no such relationship with any person as would affect the consideration.

A direction is given by notice in writing to the person by whom the acquisition is made within a three year period from the time of the acquisition (or, in certain cases where that person is not a taxable person and the consideration is payable periodically, from the first relevant event for the purposes of taxing the acquisition). The direction may be varied or withdrawn by a further direction given by notice in writing. The direction may also include a direction that the value of any transaction made after the date of notice and to which the above conditions apply is to be taken to be its open market value. An appeal may be made against a direction (see 5.3(*v*) APPEALS).

See 69.3 above for the meaning of '*connected persons*'.

[*VATA 1994, 7 Sch 1, 5*].

De Voil Indirect Tax Service. See V3.391.

69.10 **Goods subject to duty**

Where goods acquired in the UK from another EC country are charged in connection with their removal to the UK with a duty of excise (or any Community customs duty or EC agricultural levy having effect for transitional provisions in connection with the accession of any state to the EC), then the value of the transaction for VAT purposes is to be taken as its value apart from this provision plus the amount (if not already included) of the excise duty, Community customs duty or agricultural levy which has been or is to be paid in respect of the goods. This does not apply to any transaction relating to warehoused goods treated as taking place before the duty point (see 70.4 WAREHOUSED GOODS AND FREE ZONES).

[*VATA 1994, 7 Sch 2; SI 1995/2518, Regs 96, 97*].

69.11 **Transfers and disposals of business assets**

Where goods are acquired from another EC country under a transaction treated as a supply of goods under 64.3(*e*)(*f*) SUPPLY, the value of the relevant transaction, in a case where there is no consideration, is to be taken to be

(*a*) such consideration in money as would be payable by the supplier if he were, at the time of the acquisition, to purchase goods *identical* in every respect (including age and condition) to the goods concerned; or

(*b*) where the value in (*a*) cannot be ascertained, such consideration in money as would be payable to purchase goods *similar* to, and of the same age and condition as, the goods concerned; or

(*c*) where the value cannot be ascertained under (*a*) or (*b*), the cost of producing the goods concerned if they were produced at that time.

Any VAT included in the purchase price or production cost is to be deducted in arriving at the value to be taxed.

[*VATA 1994, 7 Sch 3*].

69.12 Valuation

69.12 Currencies other than sterling

Where goods are acquired from another EC country and any sum relevant for determining the value of the transaction is expressed in a currency other than sterling, subject to below, that sum is to be converted into sterling at the market selling rate for that currency at the time of acquisition. The rates published in national newspapers are acceptable as evidence of the rates at the relevant time. The following options are, however, allowed.

- Where C & E have published a notice specifying rates of exchange, or methods of determining rates of exchange, a person may opt to use a rate so specified or determined. This alternative may be adopted for all acquisitions or for all acquisitions of a particular class or description. If adopted only for a particular class, that class and the time of adoption should be noted in the records. There is no need to notify C & E in advance that this alternative has been adopted but, once it has, it cannot be changed without first obtaining the agreement of the VAT office.

- C & E may allow a person to apply to them to use a different rate of exchange for the valuation of all or some of his transactions. Application should be made in writing to the VAT office. In considering whether to allow the application, C & E will take into account whether the proposed rate or method is determined by reference to the UK currency market, whether it is objectively verifiable and the frequency with which it is proposed to update it. Forward rates or methods deriving from forward rates are not acceptable.

- Where C & E authorised a person to use a rate before 1 January 1993 under the concessionary arrangements applying to supplies of goods, that person may extend this to acquisitions without further notification unless the rate used wholly derives from currency markets other than in the UK. The continued use of concessionary rates is subject to review by C & E.

[*VATA 1994, 7 Sch 4*]. (C & E Notice 725, para 5.5 which has the force of law).

De Voil Indirect Tax Service. See V3.393.

70   Warehoused Goods and Free Zones

De Voil Indirect Tax Service. See V3.383; V5.141.

70.1   **INTRODUCTION**

This chapter considers the VAT treatment of goods entering, supplied within and removed from warehouses and free zones, together with the treatment of supplies of services associated with those goods.

70.2   **CUSTOMS, CUSTOMS AND EXCISE AND TAX WAREHOUSES**

When goods are warehoused for customs and/or excise purposes, payment of any VAT is suspended. Warehoused goods can be moved from one approved warehouse to another or can be exported direct from the warehouse without payment of VAT. VAT only becomes payable when the goods are removed from the warehousing regime and supplied within the UK or transferred to another customs regime which does not provide for the suspension of VAT.

A '*warehouse*' for these purposes means any warehouse where goods may be stored in any EC country without payment of any one or more of the following.

(*a*)   Community customs duty.

(*b*)   Any agricultural levy of the EC.

(*c*)   VAT on the importation of the goods into any EC country.

(*d*)   Any duty of excise or any duty which is equivalent in another EC country to a duty of excise.

[*VATA 1994, s 18(6)*].

In the UK, this comprises

•   Customs warehouses (of which there are several different types);

•   Customs and excise warehouses, i.e. authorised warehouses where goods subject to both customs duty and excise duty can be stored; and

•   Tax warehouses, i.e. authorised places where goods subject to excise duty are produced, processed, held, received or despatched under duty suspension arrangements by an authorised warehousekeeper in the course of his business. They include excise warehouses, registered premises, distilleries and refineries.

It also includes fiscal warehouses which are dealt with separately under 70.12 *et seq.* below.

Goods eligible for warehousing in the UK. The following goods are eligible for warehousing in the UK.

Customs warehouses	Third country goods of any kind except excise goods whether subject to a positive rate of duty or not
Tax warehouses (including both manufacturing premises and storage premises)	Third country goods on which customs duty has been paid
	Community goods
	UK goods comprising mineral (hydrocarbon) oils, alcohol and alcoholic beverages, manufactured tobacco

70.3 Warehoused Goods and Free Zones

Customs and excise   Third country goods warehouses

(C & E Notice 702/9/98, paras 1.3, 1.4)

70.3   Goods entering warehouses

No VAT is payable when goods are placed in a warehousing regime. VAT becomes due only when goods are removed from the warehouse to home use and is normally payable together with any suspended duty by the person who removed the goods.

Imported goods. Goods which, on arrival in the UK, are placed in a customs or customs and excise warehouse are not deemed to be imported for VAT purposes until such time as they are removed from the warehouse into home use, or any customs duties become due. The importer must make an import declaration on Form C88 (Single Administrative Document) but no import VAT is payable and no evidence for input tax is issued.

Acquisitions from other EC countries.

- '*Community goods*' are those produced or manufactured in the EC or goods received from outside the EC which have been put into free circulation in the EC. The only community goods which are in practice eligible for warehousing are those subject to excise duty (i.e. mineral oils, alcohol and alcoholic beverages and manufactured tobacco) which are received in the UK from an excise (tax) warehouse in another EC country.

  Where a UK trader acquires such goods from a registered person in another EC country and the goods are put into an approved warehouse, no import declaration (entry) is required for VAT purposes and VAT is not payable when the goods arrive in the UK.

- '*Non-community goods*' are goods received from outside the EC which have not been put into free circulation in the EC. In the context of acquisitions from other EC countries, such goods arrive in the UK from another EC country under external transit (T1) arrangements and may be warehoused in the same way as direct imports (see above).

  If a UK-registered trader acquires such goods from a EC VAT-registered trader, he does not need an import declaration (entry) solely for VAT purposes but in some circumstances may need one for customs duty purposes. In any event, VAT is not payable at this stage, and it is not necessary to account for VAT on the acquisition.

(C & E Notice 702/9/98, paras 2, 3.1; C & E Manual V1-19, Chapter 2, section 1.1).

70.4   Supplies within warehouses

Supplies of goods within warehousing regimes are usually relieved from VAT at the time they take place (see 70.5-70.7 below). VAT becomes due only when the goods are removed from the warehouse to home use and is normally payable together with any suspended duty by the person removing the goods (see 70.8 below). Similarly, certain services connected with warehoused goods are relieved when originally supplied (through the mechanism of zero-rating), but may be taxed at the standard rate when the goods to which they relate are removed from the regime. See 70.19 below. (C & E Notice 702/9/98, para 3.1; C & E Manual V1-19, Chapter 1 para 4).

70.5   *Imported goods*

Where

(a)   any goods have been removed from a place outside the EC and have entered the EC,

(b)   the 'material time' for any supply of those goods or acquisition of those goods from another EC country is while they are subject to a warehousing regime and before the 'duty point', and

(c)   such goods are not mixed with any 'dutiable goods' which were

●   produced or manufactured in the UK (in which case 70.7 below applies), or

●   acquired from another EC country (in which case 70.6 below applies),

then the supply or acquisition referred to in (b) above is treated as taking place outside the UK and is disregarded for UK VAT purposes.

The '*material time*' for a supply or acquisition is the time of removal of the goods or, in the case of a supply, if the goods are not removed, at the time they are made available to the person to whom they are supplied.

'*Dutiable goods*' means any goods which are subject to a duty of excise (or any Community customs duty or EC agricultural levy having effect for transitional purposes in connection with the accession of any country to the EC).

'*Duty point*' means the time any excise duty becomes payable or, if the goods are not subject to excise duty, the time when any Community customs debt in respect of duty on the entry of the goods into the EC would be incurred.

[*VATA 1994, s 18(1)(6)(7)*].

The effect of the above provisions is that VAT must not be charged, and a VAT invoice showing VAT must not be issued, in respect of any supplies of imported goods made within a warehousing regime.

70.6   *Acquisitions from other EC countries*

Where

●   any 'dutiable goods' are acquired from another EC country, or

●   a person makes a supply of dutiable goods which were acquired from another EC country (or a mixture of such goods and other goods)

and the 'material time' for the acquisition or supply is while the goods are subject to a warehousing regime and before the 'duty point', then where the material time for any subsequent supply of those goods is also while the goods are subject to the warehousing regime and before the duty point, the acquisition or supply is treated as taking place outside the UK (and is disregarded for UK VAT purposes).

The '*material time*' for a supply or acquisition is the time of removal of the goods or, in the case of a supply, if the goods are not removed, at the time they are made available to the person to whom they are supplied.

'*Dutiable goods*' means any goods which are subject to a duty of excise (or, any Community customs duty or EC agricultural levy having effect for transitional purposes in connection with the accession of any country to the EC).

'*Duty point*' means the time any excise duty becomes payable or, if the goods are not subject to excise duty, the time when any Community customs debt in respect of duty on the entry of the goods into the EC would be incurred.

[*VATA 1994, s 18(2)(3)(6)(7)*].

The effect of this is that any supply of such goods is disregarded for VAT purposes if the supply is followed by another supply of the goods while they are still warehoused. No VAT should be charged on such disregarded supplies. (C & E Notice 702/9/98, para 3.2).

70.7 Warehoused Goods and Free Zones

70.7   *Goods produced or manufactured in the UK subject to excise duty*

Where a person makes a supply of any 'dutiable goods' which were produced or manufactured in the UK (or a mixture of such goods and other goods) and the 'material time' for the supply is while the goods are subject to a warehousing regime and before the 'duty point', then where the material time for any subsequent supply of those goods is also while the goods are subject to the warehousing regime and before the duty point, the earlier supply is treated as taking place outside the UK (and is disregarded for UK VAT purposes).

The *'material time'* for a supply is the time of removal of the goods or, if the goods are not removed, at the time they are made available to the person to whom they are supplied.

'Dutiable goods' means any goods which are subject to a duty of excise.

'Duty point' means the time any excise duty becomes payable.

[*VATA 1994, s 18(2)(3)(6)(7); FA 1995, s 29*].

The effect of this is that any supply of such goods is disregarded for VAT purposes if the supply is followed by another supply of the goods while they are still warehoused. No VAT should be charged on such disregarded supplies. (C & E Notice 702/9/98, para 3.2).

70.8   **Removal of goods from warehouse**

VAT becomes due when goods are removed from a warehouse to home use and is normally payable by the person who removes the goods. The VAT due may be on the importation, acquisition or supply of the goods.

Imported goods. Where imported goods are removed from warehousing to home use in the UK, a removal declaration must be completed at the time the goods are removed. Any duty due must be paid and any VAT must be paid either in cash or under the duty deferment arrangements (see 34.5 IMPORTS). The value for VAT must include the duty paid. (C & E Notice 702/9/98, paras 3.3, 3.4).

Acquisitions from other EC countries. Where

- either

  (i)   'dutiable goods' are acquired from another EC country, or

  (ii)   a person makes a supply of dutiable goods which were acquired from another EC country (or a mixture of such goods and other goods),

- the 'material time' for the acquisition or supply is while the goods are subject to a warehousing regime and before the 'duty point', and

- there is no subsequent acquisition or supply of those goods whilst subject to the warehouse regime and before the duty point

the acquisition or supply is treated as taking place at the earlier of the time the goods are removed from the warehouse regime and the duty point.

The *'material time'* for a supply or acquisition is the time of removal of the goods or, in the case of a supply, if the goods are not removed, at the time they are made available to the person to whom they are supplied.

'Dutiable goods' means any goods which are subject to a duty of excise (or any Community customs duty or EC agricultural levy having effect for transitional purposes in connection with the accession of any country to the EC).

'*Duty point*' means the time any excise duty becomes payable or, if the goods are not subject to excise duty, the time when any Community customs debt in respect of duty on the entry of the goods into the EC would be incurred.

[*VATA 1994, s 18(2)–(4)(6)(7)*].

The effect of this is that the person removing the goods to home use in the UK pays any duty and must account for acquisition VAT on the VAT return for the period covering the date of removal. This VAT can be recovered as input tax on the same return, subject to the normal rules. A removal declaration must also be completed. The value for VAT purposes includes any customs and/or excise duty payable. (C & E Notice 702/9/98, paras 3.3, 3.4).

Goods produced or manufactured in the UK subject to excise duty. Where

- a person makes a supply of any 'dutiable goods' which were produced or manufactured in the UK (or a mixture of such goods and other goods),
- the 'material time' for the supply is while the goods are subject to a warehousing regime and before the 'duty point', and
- there is no subsequent supply of those goods whilst subject to the warehousing regime and before the duty point,

the supply is treated as taking place at the earlier of the time the goods are removed from the warehouse regime and the duty point.

The '*material time*' for a supply is the time of removal of the goods or, if the goods are not removed, at the time they are made available to the person to whom they are supplied.

'*Dutiable goods*' means any goods which are subject to a duty of excise.

'*Duty point*' means the time any excise duty becomes payable.

[*VATA 1994, s 18(2)(3)(6)(7); FA 1995, s 29*].

The effect of this is that the person removing the UK-produced goods from the warehouse to home use must complete a removal declaration at the time the goods are removed and pay any duty and VAT due. The value for VAT purposes includes any customs and/or excise duty payable. (C & E Notice 702/9/98, paras 3.3, 3.4).

Goods removed from warehouse to a place outside the UK. Subject to the normal rules, any supply of goods from a warehouse for export outside the EC or for supply to a taxable person in another EC country may be zero-rated. Goods removed directly to a registered warehouse in another EC country can be disregarded for UK VAT purposes.

If non-community goods (see 70.3 above) are put into free circulation in the UK before being sent to another EC country, any import VAT and customs duty must normally be paid. Similarly, if community goods (see 70.3 above) on which excise duty is payable in the UK are removed, any VAT due must be paid at the same time.

(C & E Notice 702/9/98, para 3.5).

Note that special rules apply to deliveries of goods subject to excise duty to customers in other EC countries. If the excise duty has not been paid, the goods *must* be received by a VAT-registered person in the EC country of destination. If the goods are supplied for delivery to a customer in another EC country who is not VAT-registered in that country, the supplier must use the distance selling arrangements and register for VAT there. See 23.18 EUROPEAN COMMUNITY: SINGLE MARKET.

70.9 Warehoused Goods and Free Zones

70.9 Evidence for input tax deduction

The owner of the goods will be issued with an import VAT certificate (C79) during the month after payment. This document is the official evidence needed to claim VAT paid on warehouse removals as input tax. Where an import VAT certificate is not received in time to complete the VAT return, alternative evidence of removal or payment may be used to claim input tax (in which case it is important to ensure that, when the import VAT certificate is received, it agrees with the input tax previously claimed). (C & E Notice 702/9/98, para 3.16).

70.10 Deficiency of warehoused goods

Any deficiencies of warehoused goods are deemed to be removed from the warehousing regime. Where deficiencies of imported goods are charged with duty, VAT not already paid on the imported goods is also to be charged. Similarly, any acquisition VAT on goods from another EC country which has not been accounted for should be accounted for when deficiencies occur. Deficiencies of home produced goods are not to be charged with VAT unless the goods have been supplied in warehouse before the loss. In each case, the VAT may be deducted as input tax, subject to the normal rules. (C & E Notice 702/9/98, para 3.17).

70.11 Summary tables

Receipt of goods into a UK warehouse and their removal for home use

	Duty	*VAT*
1. Goods received (a) direct from a third country; or (b) from a third country via another EC country (including goods acquired from a customs or customs and excise warehouse in another EC country) and placed in customs warehouse	Customs duty and import duty: not due on receipt into warehouse but to be paid on removal Excise duty: N/A	N/A
2. Goods received (a) direct from a third country; or (b) from a third country via another EC country (including goods acquired from a customs or customs and excise warehouse in another EC country) and placed in customs and excise warehouse	Customs duty and import duty: not due on receipt into warehouse but to be paid on removal Excise duty: duty due, but suspended whilst in warehouse	N/A

	Duty	*VAT*
3. Goods received (a) direct from a third country; or (b) from a third country via another EC country that have not been entered to free circulation on which there is a nil rate of customs duty, or the customs duty is paid on arrival in the UK. Goods then placed in a tax warehouse	Customs duty: any due is paid on arrival of the goods in the UK Excise duty: duty due, but suspended whilst in warehouse Import duty: not due on receipt into warehouse and to be paid on removal	N/A
4. Goods acquired direct from another EC country which are community goods, and are placed in an excise warehouse, including goods from tax warehouse in another EC country	Customs duty and import duty: N/A Excise duty: duty due, but suspended whilst in warehouse	VAT on acquisition suspended whilst in warehouse
(a) Goods removed from warehouse by acquirer	Customs duty and import duty: N/A Excise duty: duty due on removal	VAT accounted for in return covering the removal of the goods.
(b) Goods supplied in warehouse and removed by the customer	Customs duty and import duty: N/A Excise duty: duty due on removal	VAT due on the supply (or last supply if more than one) to be paid with the excise duty on removal. VAT on the acquisition is not accounted for
5. UK produced and/or manufactured goods in an excise warehouse or registered premises	Customs duty and import duty: N/A Excise duty: duty due on removal to home use	N/A
6. Goods (a) removed to home use by the manufacturer; or (b) supplied in warehouse and removed to home use by the customer	Customs duty and import duty: N/A Excise duty: duty due on removal to home use	VAT due on the supply (or last supply if more than one) to be paid with the excise duty on removal

70.11 Warehoused Goods and Free Zones

Receipt of goods from a UK warehouse other than to home use in the UK

	Duty	*VAT*
1. Goods for (a) direct export to a country outside the EC; or (b) export to a country outside the EC in transit through another EC country from a customs warehouse	Customs duty: not paid Excise duty: N/A	Any VAT which would be due on removal to UK home use is not payable. Supplies of goods removed from the UK may be zero-rated as exports (subject to the normal rules)
2. Goods for (a) direct export to a country outside the EC; or (b) export to a country outside the EC in transit through another EC country from a customs and excise warehouse	Customs duty: not paid Excise duty: not paid	Any VAT which would be due on removal to UK home use is not payable. Supplies of goods removed from the UK may be zero-rated as exports (subject to the normal rules)
3. Goods for (a) direct export to a country outside the EC; or (b) export to a country outside the EC in transit through another EC country from a tax warehouse	Customs duty: N/A Excise duty: not paid	Any VAT which would be due on removal to UK home use is not payable. Supplies of goods removed from the UK may be zero-rated as exports (subject to the normal rules)
4. Goods moved to another EC country under a duty suspensive regime from a customs warehouse	Customs duty: not paid Excise duty: N/A	Any VAT which would be due on removal to UK home use is not payable. Supplies direct into a customs warehouse in another EC country are outside the scope of UK VAT. Otherwise, outward movement of goods may be zero-rated (subject to the normal rules)

	Duty	*VAT*
5. Goods moved to another EC country under a duty suspensive regime from a customs and excise warehouse	Customs duty: not paid Excise duty: not paid	Any VAT which would be due on removal to UK home use is not payable. Supplies direct into a customs warehouse in another EC country are outside the scope of UK VAT. Otherwise, outward movement of goods may be zero–rated (subject to the normal rules)
6. Goods moved to another EC country on which customs duty is paid on removal from a customs warehouse	Customs duty: paid on removal from warehouse regime Excise duty: N/A	VAT is payable but may be relieved if the goods are removed in the course of an onward zero–rated supply
7. Goods moved to another EC country on which customs duty is paid on removal from a customs and excise warehouse	Customs duty: paid on removal from warehouse regime Excise duty: not paid	VAT is payable but may be relieved if the goods are removed in the course of an onward zero–rated supply
8. Goods moved to another EC country from an excise warehouse and sent under excise duty suspension to a tax warehouse	Customs duty: N/A Excise duty: not paid	Any VAT which would be due on removal to home use is not payable. Supplies direct into an excise warehouse in another EC country are outside the scope of UK VAT
9. Goods moved to another EC country from an excise warehouse and sent under excise duty suspension to a Registered Excise Dealer	Customs duty: N/A Excise duty: not paid	Any VAT which would be due on removal to home use is not payable. Outward movement of goods may be zero–rated (subject to the normal conditions)
10. Goods transferred to IPR suspension in the UK from a customs warehouse	Customs duty: to be paid on final removal from IPR regime Excise duty: N/A	Any import VAT due is to be paid with the customs duty. Supplies of goods under IPR are subject to the domestic VAT rules
11. Goods transferred to IPR drawback in the UK from a customs warehouse	Customs duty: to be paid on removal from warehouse regime Excise duty: N/A	Any import VAT due is to be paid with the customs duty. Supplies of goods under IPR are subject to the domestic VAT rules

	Duty	*VAT*
12. Goods in customs and excise warehouse. Customs duty paid while goods remain under the warehousing regime	Customs duty: paid whilst in warehouse Excise duty: to be paid when goods are removed to UK home use	Any import VAT is to be paid when goods are removed to home use

(C & E Notice 702/9/98, Appendices B, C).

70.12 FISCAL WAREHOUSING

The *EC 2nd VAT Simplification Directive* enables countries to introduce a warehousing regime to operate alongside both customs warehouses and excise warehouses. In the UK, this regime is known as fiscal warehousing.

Under the fiscal warehousing regime, certain eligible goods (see 70.14 below) can be placed in a notified warehouse and can then be traded by dealers who will not be required to be VAT-registered if that is their only business activity. Supplies of goods and certain services within a fiscal warehouse and supplies of goods intended to be placed in the regime are, subject to conditions, relieved from VAT. See 70.15 and 70.16 below.

Excise and Customs warehouses (see 70.2 *et seq.* above) may also be used for fiscal warehousing but separate authorisation is required for the fiscal warehousing regime.

Retail sales are not allowed under the conditions of a fiscal warehousing regime [*VATA 1994, s 18A(3); FA 1996, 3 Sch 5; SI 1996/1249*].

(C & E Notice 702/9/98, paras 4.1, 4.2).

70.13 Authorisation for fiscal warehousing

C & E can, on written application, approve any registered person (including any company in a group registration) as a fiscal warehousekeeper, the approval being subject to such conditions as C & E impose. [*VATA 1994, s 18A(1)(4)(7)(9); FA 1996, 3 Sch 5*].

The authorisation procedure is stringent so that C & E can rely on the operators' control procedures and records. All the following basic criteria for authorisation must be met.

• The applicant must be VAT-registered in the UK.

• All business revenue records must be of a high standard (e.g. VAT returns and payments must be up-to-date).

• If already authorised to operate any UK duty suspensive regime, the applicant must have a satisfactory proven records of operation.

• The applicant must be able to comply with the conditions of authorisation and with such regulations as may be laid down for the operation of the regime. This is important as penalties may be imposed for failure to comply.

• The administration and organisation of the business must be sound and strictly managed.

• The applicant must provide a list of the addresses of all storage sites which are to form part of the fiscal warehouse and any other premises where records are to be kept. Retail premises cannot be used as fiscal warehousing premises and all notified premises must meet health and safety legislation requirements.

- Accounts and stock control records must be capable of meeting the requirements in 70.18 below. In particular, they must be able to distinguish between fiscally warehoused goods and other stocks and be able to identify the location and quantity of any given item held within the fiscal warehousing regime at any stage.

Applications should be made to the VAT Office by completing a letter of application as described in C & E Notice 702/9/98, Appendix K. If the application is approved, authorisation will be granted in writing, conditional upon the acceptance of any conditions C & E regard as appropriate, and without time limit. [*VATA 1994, s 18A(5)(8); FA 1996, 3 Sch 5*]. See, however, under *Provisional authorisations* below.

Refusal of authorisation. C & E may refuse authorisation if the criteria are not met. The basic procedure for appeal will be set out in the letter of refusal. This allows for an initial local review by a member of staff not connected with the decision and, if necessary, an appeal to a VAT tribunal.

Provisional authorisation may be given subject to meeting outstanding criteria within a specified period of time. This may happen, for example, where the necessary premises have not been secured at the time of the application. If any outstanding condition is not met within the deadline, the application will lapse and a new application will be required.

Transferring an authorisation is not permitted, even on the sale of a business as a going concern. The new owner must apply for a fresh authorisation.

Cancelling or revoking an authorisation. Authorisation can be cancelled by giving notice in writing to C & E stating the date by which all goods will cease to be traded and removed from the warehousing regime. C & E can also revoke an authorisation at any time for any reasonable cause (e.g. non-compliance with conditions of authorisation). Except in very exceptional circumstances the warehousekeeper would be notified in advance of any intended revocation, and would always have a right to appeal. Where authorisation is withdrawn, any goods held in the fiscal warehouse regime are deemed to have been removed by the proprietor at the time of withdrawal and VAT is due. See 70.17 below.

(C & E Notice 702/9/98, paras 4.4–4.10).

70.14 **Qualifying conditions for goods**

To be eligible for the fiscal warehousing regime, goods must be

(*a*) '*eligible goods*' for fiscal warehousing purposes i.e.

- aluminium, copper, iridium, lead, nickel, palladium, platinum, rhodium, silver, tin, and zinc;
- chemicals in bulk;
- cereals;
- coffee (not roasted), tea, and cocoa beans (whole or broken, raw or roasted);
- grains and seeds (including soya beans);
- mineral oils (including propane and butane and crude petroleum oils);
- nuts;
- oil seeds and oleaginous fruit;
- olives;
- potatoes;

1073

- raw sugar;

- rubber, in primary forms or in plates, sheets or strip;

- vegetable oils and fats and their fractions (whether or not refined, but not chemically modified); and

- wool;

(*b*) in free circulation i.e. all duties, taxes and levies (including customs duty, import VAT, excise duty and any Common Agricultural Policy (CAP) duty due on the goods) must either have been paid or deferred; and

(*c*) entered in the fiscal warehousing records.

Non-eligible goods may be stored in a place which is a fiscal warehouse but cannot be subject to a fiscal warehousing regime or benefit from the conditions of fiscal warehousing.

[*VATA 1994, s 18B(6), 5A Sch; FA 1996, 3 Sch 5, 18*]. (C & E Notice 702/9/98, paras 4.3, 4.13).

70.15   **Goods entering a fiscal warehouse**

The following transactions are relieved from VAT (by being treated as taking place outside the UK) if any subsequent supply of the goods in question is made while they are subject to the fiscal warehouse regime.

(*a*) An acquisition of goods from another EC country where, after the acquisition but before any subsequent supply, the acquirer places the goods in a fiscal warehousing regime. The acquirer must, not later than the time of acquisition, prepare and keep a certificate stating that he intends to enter the goods in a fiscal warehouse.

(*b*) A supply of eligible goods (other than a retail transaction) where, after the supply in question but before any subsequent supply, the buyer places the goods in a fiscal warehousing regime. The buyer must give his supplier, not later than the time of supply, a certificate stating that he intends to enter the goods in a fiscal warehouse.

[*VATA 1994, s 18B(1)-(3); FA 1996, 3 Sch 5*].

A supply falling within (*a*) or (*b*) above is treated as a supply of goods (and not a supply of services), even if it is the transfer of an undivided share in the goods, i.e. an unidentified part of a larger stock of eligible goods. [*SI 1996/1255*]. (Normally, such a transfer of an undivided share would be treated for VAT purposes as a supply of services, see 64.4(*a*) SUPPLY.)

Certificates. The certificate required under (*a*) or (*b*) above should be in the following form.

I   (full name)
             (status in company)
of   (name and address of company)

declare that (name of company) intends to enter to the fiscal warehousing regime at the fiscal warehouse shown below on (insert date) or within (insert number) days commencing today, the goods indicated below:

- name and address of fiscal warehouse

- authorisation number of the fiscal warehousekeeper

- description of goods

- quantity of goods

* I certify that the supply of goods is eligible to be relieved from VAT under VATA 1994, sections 18B(2)(d)/18B(3) (purchases)

* I certify that the acquisition is eligible to be relieved from VAT under VATA 1994, sections 18B(1)(d)/18B(3) (acquisitions).

* Delete as appropriate

> (signature)
> (date)

Where a taxable person prepares a certificate under (*a*) above or receives one under (*b*) above, he must retain it with his VAT records. Where a non-taxable person prepares a certificate under (*a*) above, he must keep it for six years and produce it to a C & E officer on request.

[*SI 1995/2518, Regs 31(1), 145B, 1 Sch; SI 1996/1250, Regs 8, 13*]. (C & E Notice 702/9/98, Appendix I).

70.16   **Supplies within fiscal warehouses**

The following transactions are relieved from VAT (by being treated as taking place outside the UK) if any subsequent supply of the goods in question is made while they are subject to the fiscal warehouse regime.

(*a*)   An acquisition of eligible goods from another EC country where the acquisition takes place while the goods are within a fiscal warehousing regime. The acquirer must, not later than the time of acquisition, prepare and keep a certificate stating that the goods are subject to a fiscal warehousing regime.

(*b*)   A supply of eligible goods (other than a retail transaction) where the supply takes place while the goods are within a fiscal warehousing regime.

[*VATA 1994, s 18B(1)-(3); FA 1996, 3 Sch 5*].

The effect of the above is that goods acquired or supplied after being entered to the fiscal warehousing regime are treated as though they are outside the UK and not subject to the normal supply rules *unless* the supply in question is the final supply whilst the goods are warehoused.

A supply falling within (*a*) or (*b*) above is treated as a supply of goods (and not a supply of services), even if it is the transfer of an undivided share in the goods, i.e. an unidentified part of a larger stock of eligible goods. [*SI 1996/1255*]. (Normally, such a transfer of an undivided share would be treated for VAT purposes as a supply of services, see 64.4(*a*) SUPPLY.)

Registration. If transactions falling within (*a*) or (*b*) above are a trader's only UK business activities, he will not be required to register for VAT although he may apply for voluntary registration if he wishes. Liability to register for other business activities is not affected by either the value of supplies made in a fiscal warehouse or the value of deemed supplies of relieved services accounted for by the remover of the goods (see 70.20 below). [*VATA 1994, 1 Sch 1(9); FA 1996, 3 Sch 13*].

70.17   **Removal of goods from fiscal warehousing**

With certain exceptions, a charge to VAT arises when eligible goods are removed from the fiscal warehouse regime. The amount of VAT due corresponds to

- the amount which would have been due on the transaction that caused the goods to be entered to the warehouse, or

- if the goods have been supplied within the warehouse, the amount which would have been due on the last supply.

VAT will also be due on any of the relieved supplies of services relating to the goods which have been carried out after that final supply. See 70.20 below.

The VAT due on removal is the liability of the person who causes the goods to cease to be covered by the fiscal warehousing regime and is chargeable and payable at the time of removal.

- A VAT-registered trader should account for the VAT on the return covering the date of removal.

- A non-registered remover must present Form VAT 150 *Advice of removals from fiscal warehouse by persons unregistered for VAT* to the local Entry Processing Unit (EPU) even when no VAT is due on removal. Where the remover is not a taxable person but would be if such acquisitions or supplies were taken into account, although not required to register he must charge and account for VAT on any taxable transactions.

[*VATA 1994, s 18B(4)(5), 18D; FA 1996, 3 Sch 5*]. (C & E Notice 702/9/98, paras 4.14, 4.18).

Deemed removals. Where

(*a*) as a result of an operation on eligible goods in the fiscal warehousing regime, they cease to be eligible goods, or

(*b*) any person ceases to be a fiscal warehousekeeper or any premises cease to have fiscal warehouse status,

the relevant goods are treated as if they had been removed from the fiscal warehousing regime at that time by the proprietor of the goods. [*VATA 1994, s 18F(5)(6); FA 1996, 3 Sch 5*].

VAT is not due on the following removals of goods.

- Removal for use in the UK of zero-rated goods. (VAT may be due at removal based on the value of any relieved supplies of services. See 70.20 below.)

- Removal by a person for use in the UK of his own goods (either produced or purchased VAT-paid) which he entered to fiscal warehouse and which have not been sold within the fiscal warehousing regime. (VAT may be due at removal based on the value of relieved supplies of services. See 70.20 below.)

- Goods exported outside the EC. Normal conditions for zero-rating exports apply. (Any associated relieved supplies of services are also not taxable. See 70.20 below.)

- Goods removed in the course of an intra-EC supply. Normal supply/acquisition and Intrastat rules apply for VAT-registered traders. (Any associated relieved supplies of services are also not taxable. See 70.20 below.)

- Transfers to another UK fiscal warehouse.

- Transfers to a corresponding regime to fiscal warehousing in another EC country.

- Temporary removals for repair, processing, treatment or other operations. Authorisation (general or specific) must be sought from C & E and the goods must be returned to the original site or another covered by the same authorisation.

- Small quantities of negligible commercial value removed VAT-free for sampling.

[*SI 1995/2518, Reg 145H(2); SI 1996/1250, Reg 13*]. (C & E Notice 702/9/98, para 4.19).

Input tax. Any VAT paid as a result of the removal of goods from a fiscal warehouse can be reclaimed as input tax, subject to the normal rules. This will normally be on the same VAT return on which the VAT due on removal was declared as output tax. (C & E Notice 702/9/9, para 4.20).

70.18   **Duties and responsibilities of a fiscal warehousekeeper**

A fiscal warehousekeeper must record all receipts into the warehouse and keep a detailed fiscal warehousing record of stock. There are detailed provisions for recording and control over removals of goods and the transfer of goods to other UK fiscal warehouses or similar regimes in other EC countries. Records must be capable of ready use by a C & E officer and must be readily reproducible for use off the premises. All records must be kept for six years following the transfer or removal of the goods.

[*SI 1995/2518, Regs 145E–145I, 1A Sch; SI 1996/1250, Reg 13*]. (C & E Notice 702/9/98, paras 4.11, 4.21).

The procedures are stringent so that C & E can rely on the warehousekeeper's controls and records. Where goods are found to be missing or deficient, a warehousekeeper may be personally liable for the VAT which would have been chargeable on their supply. [*VATA 1994, s 18E; FA 1996, 3 Sch 5*].

70.19   **SUPPLIES OF ASSOCIATED WAREHOUSE AND FISCAL WAREHOUSE SERVICES**

From 1 June 1996, some services associated with goods held in customs, customs and excise, tax and fiscal warehouses can be relieved from VAT at the time they are supplied. In certain circumstances, VAT will become due on such services when the goods concerned are subsequently removed from the regime to home use (see 70.20 below).

Zero-rating. Where a taxable person makes a supply of 'specified services' which are performed on, or in relation to, goods subject to the warehousing regime (see 70.2–70.11 above) or the fiscal warehousing regime (see 70.12–70.18 above), the supply is zero-rated if it would otherwise be taxable.

The '*specified services*' are as follows.

(*a*)   Services of keeping the goods in question by an occupier of a warehouse or a fiscal warehousekeeper.

(*b*)   For goods subject to a warehousing regime, services of carrying out any permitted operations on the goods.

  In a customs warehouse, the services eligible for zero-rating are storage charges and the usual forms of handling which may be carried out in the warehouse These cover

  • simple operations to ensure the preservation of the goods in good condition during storage;

  • operations improving the presentation or marketability of the goods; and

  • preparing the goods for distribution or resale.

  For a detailed list, see C & E Notice 702/9/98, Appendix F.

  In a tax warehouse, services eligible are restricted to those physical services that take place in the warehouse and are directly associated with the goods held in the warehouse. These include those processes that create a new product (see C & E

Notice 702/9/98, Appendix G) and others such as storage and secondary packaging.

Not included are services such as brokerage, agents' fees and transport between warehouses but any services which would be zero-rated if supplied outside the warehouse remain zero-rated when supplied inside. (C & E Notice 702/9/98, para 3.7).

(*c*)   For goods subject to a fiscal warehousing regime, services of carrying out any non-prohibited physical operations on the goods. These are the same as those qualifying in a customs warehouse under (*b*) above and specified in C & E Notice 702/9/98, Appendix F. Written authority from C & E is required to obtain relief on supplies of services which exceed those specified operations.

Certification. No certification is required for warehousekeepers' storage charges under (*a*) above to be zero-rated. The invoice issued by the warehousekeeper to enable zero-rating should include the words 'in accordance with section 18C(1) VAT Act 1994' and no VAT should be charged. If the owner of the goods prefers the storage to be standard-rated, he should notify the warehousekeeper in writing who will then issue an invoice and include VAT at the standard rate.

For zero-rating to apply under (*b*) or (*c*) above, the recipient of the services must give the supplier a certificate declaring that the relevant goods are fiscally warehoused services and that the supply of services is eligible for zero-rating. The following is an example of the certificate although any version may be prepared provided it contains all of the information shown.

I   (full name)
            (status in company)
of   (name and address of company)

declare that the goods shown below are subject to a fiscal or other warehousing regime at the place indicated below:

*   description of goods

*   quantity of goods

*   warehouse stock number

*   name and address of fiscal or other warehouse

*   authorisation number of the relevant warehousekeeper/warehouse

and that the following services are to be performed on the goods in the fiscal or other warehouse:

(insert details of services)

I certify that the supply of services is eligible to be zero-rated for VAT purposes under section 18C(1) of the VAT Act 1994.

            (signature)
            (date)

[*VATA 1994. s 18C(1)(4); FA 1996, 3 Sch 5; SI 1995/2518, Reg 145C; SI 1996/1247; SI 1996/1250*]. (C & E Notice 702/9/98, Appendix J).

Invoicing. If the supplier of services receives a certificate as above, he must, within 30 days of the services being performed, give the recipient a VAT invoice with the following particulars (unless C & E allow otherwise).

*   An identifying number.

- The material time of the supply of the services in question.

- The date of the issue of the invoice.

- The name, address and registration number of the supplier.

- The name and an address of the person to whom the services are supplied.

- A description sufficient to identify the nature of the services supplied.

- The extent of the services and the amount payable, excluding VAT, expressed in sterling.

- The rate of any cash discount offered.

- The rate of VAT as zero per cent.

- A declaration that in respect of the supply of services in question, the requirements of *VATA 1994, s 18C(1)* (see above) will be or have been satisfied.

The supplier should retain the invoice and certificate in his records for six years (unless C & E agree otherwise) as evidence needed to support the zero-rating of the supplies.

Where no certificate is received (because the customer fails to provide it or prefers, for administrative purposes, to have the services taxed at the time of supply) the supplier should issue a VAT invoice in the usual way including VAT (as necessary) at the standard rate.

[*SI 1985/2518, Reg 145D; SI 1996/1250*]. (C & E Notice 702/9/98, para 3.8).

70.20   **Subsequent taxation of previously zero-rated services**

Subject to the exceptions below, services which, at the time of supply, are zero-rated under 70.19 above are subsequently taxed at the time the goods are removed from the warehousing or fiscal warehousing regime or, if earlier, at the duty point. At that time, a taxable (and not zero-rated) supply of services, identical to the zero-rated supply of services, is treated as being made both to the recipient of the zero-rated supply of services and by him in the course or furtherance of his business. The value of the supply is the same as for the zero-rated supply of services. VAT is chargeable on the supply even if the person treated as making it is not a taxable person.

Exceptions. The self-supply charge does not apply in the following circumstances.

- Where the services create new goods.

  If the services or processes applied to existing goods change their nature to the extent that a new product is considered to have been created (e.g. refining crude oil into motor spirit), the new product is then treated as having been produced in the UK. See C & E Notice 702/9/98, Appendix G for a list of processes undertaken in tax warehouses which are regarded as creating a new UK product. In addition, C & E also consider the mixing or blending of home produced goods with goods received from outside the EC or goods produced or manufactured in the EC as creating a new product if original goods lose their identity.

  Where such a service or process is carried out, no VAT is due in respect of that service (or the original goods) because the goods upon which the process has been carried out have ceased to exist and cannot therefore be removed from the warehouse. VAT will only be due if the new goods are subsequently supplied or further services are carried out which do not create a new UK product (e.g. secondary packaging).

- Where the goods are supplied (whilst still warehoused) after the services were provided (in which case VAT is only due on any services provided after the last supply in the warehouse).

- Where the goods are exported under duty suspension arrangements directly from the warehouse to a country outside the EC.

- Where the goods are sent under duty suspension arrangements to a customs or tax warehouse in another EC country.

[*VATA 1994, s 18C(2)(3); FA 1996, 3 Sch 5; SI 1996/1249*]. (C & E Notice 702/9/98, paras 3.10–3.12).

Accounting for VAT. It is the responsibility of the person removing the goods to ensure that the correct amount of VAT is paid at the time of entry to home use.

- For removals from customs warehouses, any VAT due in respect of previously zero-rated services is to be accounted for together with any import VAT and customs duty payable on the relevant goods, using the import entry (C88).

- For removals from tax warehouses, VAT due on the importation, or on the last supply of goods in warehouse, must be accounted for and paid (or deferred) when the goods pass the duty point or are removed to home use. VAT due on goods acquired from another EC country is accounted for on the VAT return covering the period in which they pass the duty point or are removed. Any VAT due in respect of previously zero-rated services must be accounted for together with the VAT due on the relevant goods.

- For removals from fiscal warehouses, any VAT due must be accounted for, together with the VAT due on the relieved supply of the goods.

(C & E Notice 702/9/98, paras 3.13–3.15, 4.16).

Average throughput time for accounting for previously zero-rated services. Commercial practices in certain warehousing regimes make it difficult for some traders accurately to track specific goods and associated services, and therefore they do not know for certain which goods are removed from the warehouse regime. In such circumstances, C & E can agree average throughput times for goods so that traders assume goods to have been removed from the regime by a certain date, at which time the VAT becomes due. Examples of when this arrangement may be used include

- where the services are performed on goods in bulk and the goods are then removed in smaller quantities; and

- when goods that have had a service performed on them are mixed with goods which have not.

These arrangements can apply in both customs and tax warehouses.

(C & E Manual V1-19, Chapter 2 section 2.12).

70.21   **FREE ZONES**

A free zone is a designated, secure area in which goods from both outside and within the EC (including home produced goods) can be stored without payment of certain duties and VAT. C & E may make regulations covering the control and operation of such zones and the movement of goods into and out of them and the charging of duty. [*FA 1984, s 8, 4 Sch; SI 1984/1177*]. Free zones are currently operating at West Midlands (Birmingham), Liverpool, Prestwick, Ronaldsway (Isle of Man), Southampton, Tilbury, Port of Sheerness and Humberside.

70.22   **Goods entering free zones**

Imports. VAT is not due on goods entering the UK from places outside the EC and placed in a free zone. However, customs duties may be paid on goods without import VAT having to be accounted for at the same time.

Acquisitions from other EC countries. The acquisition of goods from a registered trader in another EC country where the goods are put into a free zone is treated in the same way as the acquisition of goods in the rest of the UK, i.e. VAT must be accounted for on the acquirer's VAT return for the period covering the time of acquisition (see 23.3 *et seq.* EUROPEAN COMMUNITY: SINGLE MARKET). The value for VAT must include any duty paid.

UK-produced goods. VAT is not due on goods of UK origin which are taken into a free zone.

70.23   **Supplies within free zones**

Supplies of goods (and services) within a free zone are treated as UK supplies and are subject to the normal domestic VAT rules. This applies even if the goods were originally acquired from another the EC or, subject to the concession below, imported from outside the EC.

By concession, the supply of free zone goods which were originally imported in the UK may be zero-rated if the supplier and customer agree that the customer will clear the goods for removal from the free zone to home use and will take responsibility for the import VAT. For the purposes of this concession, removal to home use includes authorised use or consumption within the zone. (C & E Notice 48, ESC 2.15). This concession has two main benefits.

- The customer purchasing the goods would otherwise have to pay, at virtually the same time, both the VAT due on the supply (to the supplier) and the VAT due on importation (to C & E) on the removal of the goods from the free zone (see 70.24 below).

- It enables overseas traders who supply their imports in UK free zones and properly use the concession, to apply for exemption from registration in the UK.

The same goods can be the subject of a zero-rated supply only once under the concession. Supplies of free zone goods which do not meet the conditions of the concession must be treated in the same way as supplies of goods made outside free zones. (C & E Notice 702/9/98, para 5.3).

See also 70.24 below for goods supplied within a free zone for onward export to a destination outside the EC.

Supplies to non-registered persons. Where a supply is made within a free zone to a non-registered person, the amount of VAT payable on removal of the goods from the free zone is reduced by the VAT already paid on the supply. [*SI 1984/1177, Reg 27*].

70.24   **Removal of goods from free zones**

Goods removed to home use in the UK. Goods used or consumed within a free zone are considered to have been removed from the free zone and must therefore be entered to free circulation.

- If the goods are 'non-community goods' from a third country, import VAT is due on removal from the free zone to home use.

- If the goods are non-community goods from a third country via another EC country (including those from another duty suspensive regime),

    (*a*)   import VAT is due on removal from the free zone to home use; and

    (*b*)   if the goods are the subject of an acquisition on arrival in the free zone, VAT must be accounted for on the acquirer's VAT return for the period in which the acquisition tax point falls.

- If the goods are 'community goods' direct from another EC country, acquisition VAT must be accounted for on the acquirer's VAT return for the period in which the acquisition tax point occurs.

- If the goods are goods from the UK, the normal UK VAT supply rules apply.

Goods removed other than to home use.

- If the goods are exported direct to a third country, the supply can be zero-rated subject to the normal export rules (see 25.1 EXPORTS). If the goods are non-community goods, there is no requirement to pay any import VAT that may otherwise have been due on the goods.

  If goods are supplied to a customer in a free zone for onward export to a destination in a third country, the supply may be zero-rated as an export provided a copy of the Single Administrative Document (Form C88) export declaration, certified at the place of export of the goods from the EC, is obtained and retained by the trader.

- If the goods are removed direct to another EC country,

  (*a*) where the goods are non-community goods which are not put into free circulation in the UK

    (i) import VAT is not due in the UK and will be paid with the customs duty in the EC country where that duty is paid;

    (ii) if the goods are sold to a customer registered for VAT in another EC country, the supply can be zero-rated subject to the normal conditions for zero-rating an intra-EC supply (see 23.11 EUROPEAN COMMUNITY: SINGLE MARKET); and

    (iii) if the goods are sold to a customer not registered for VAT, and the goods are not for onward export from the EC, the supply of the goods is liable to VAT in the UK; and

  (*b*) where the goods are non-community goods put into free circulation on removal from the free zone,

    (i) if customs duty is paid in the UK in the course of an onward supply to an EC recipient who will account for the VAT on their acquisition, total relief from import VAT can apply. If not, import VAT is paid with the customs duty;

    (ii) if the goods are sold to a customer registered for VAT in another EC country, the supply can be zero-rated subject to the normal conditions for zero-rating an intra-EC supply (see 23.11 EUROPEAN COMMUNITY: SINGLE MARKET); and

    (iii) if the goods are sold to a customer not registered for VAT, and the goods are not for onward export from the EC, the supply of the goods is liable to VAT in the UK.

(C & E Notice 702/9/98, paras 5.4, 5.5, Appendices D and E).

See 70.3 above for the meaning of '*community goods*' and '*non-community goods*'.

70.25 Deficiency of free zone goods

Where deficiencies of imported goods are charged with duty, VAT not already paid on the imported goods is also to be charged. Similarly, any acquisition VAT on goods from another EC country which has not been accounted for should be accounted for when deficiencies occur. Deficiencies of home produced goods are not to be charged with

VAT unless the goods have been supplied in the free zone before the loss. In all cases, the VAT may be deducted as input tax, subject to the normal rules. (C & E Notice 702/9/98, para 5.7).

71 Works of Art Etc.

71.1 EXEMPTION

The disposal of certain property is exempt from VAT (in addition to inheritance tax and capital gains tax) under either of the following circumstances.

- The disposal of the 'property' is to an 'approved body' by way of gift or sale by private treaty under the 'douceur' arrangements. '*Property*' is detailed in *IHTA 1984, s 31* and includes pictures, prints, books, manuscripts, works of art, scientific collections and other such items, not yielding income, of national, scientific, historic or artistic interest.

  '*Approved bodies*' are listed in *IHTA 1984, 3 Sch* (The National Gallery, The British Museum and other similar national institutions, museums and art galleries maintained by local authorities or universities in the UK, The National Trust etc.).

- The property is accepted by the Inland Revenue in satisfaction of inheritance tax (or capital transfer tax or estate duty).

The Douceur. The price paid by a museum etc. in a private treaty sale is based on an agreed valuation of the picture or object in the open market or at auction. The amount the buyer offers to pay takes into account the exemption from capital taxes and divides the benefit of the exemption between both parties. The government has advised museums etc. that, in general, the seller should receive 25% (10% in the case of real property) of the benefit of the capital tax exemption, subject to negotiations above or below this figure where flexibility is appropriate. The final sum received by the seller will therefore be more than the net sum on an open market sale (i.e. gross value less tax) because the seller shares in the amount of tax saved. The addition is sometimes known as 'the douceur' and the arrangement is an administrative not a statutory one. Documentary evidence of the arrangement from the Capital Taxes Office will be required.

[*VATA 1994, 9 Sch Group 11; IHTA 1984, 8 Sch 24; FA 1985, 26 Sch 14*]. (C & E Notice 701/12/96, paras 2.1–2.4).

The VAT exemption applies only to disposals under private treaty sales and to acceptances in lieu. Other sales of works of art etc. by a registered person in the course or furtherance of his business remain subject to VAT. See 71.6 below for sales from stately homes.

De Voil Indirect Tax Service. See V4.166.

71.2 SECOND-HAND GOODS

Special schemes may be operated by dealers registered for VAT, or by any other taxable persons, who acquire eligible goods and sell them in the course of business. See 61 SECOND-HAND GOODS generally and in particular 61.3 for eligible works of art, etc. under the schemes.

71.3 IMPORTS

In relation to goods imported from outside the EC, the value of any of the following goods is to be taken as 14.29% of what would otherwise be their value.

(a) Any 'work of art' which was obtained by any person before 1 April 1973 otherwise than by producing it himself or by succession on the death of the person who produced it.

(*b*)   Any work of art which was previously exported from the UK

- before 1 January 1973, or

- on or after that date and before 1 January 1993 by a person who, had he supplied it in the UK at the date when it was exported, would not have had to account for VAT on the full value of the supply, or

- on or after 1 January 1993 by such a person to a place which, at the time, was outside the EC,

and which has not been imported between the time when it was exported and the importation in question.

(*c*)   Any antique more than 100 years old which is neither a work of art nor pearls or loose gem stones.

(*d*)   Any collectors' pieces of zoological, botanical, mineralogical, anatomical, historical, archaeological, palaeontological or ethnographic interest.

'*Work of art*' means any of the following.

- Paintings, drawings and pastels executed by hand but not comprised in manufactured articles that have been hand-painted or hand-decorated.

- Original engravings, lithographs and other prints.

- Original sculptures and statuary, in any material.

See 69.7 VALUATION for the valuation of imported goods and 61.3 SECOND-HAND SCHEMES for C & E's interpretation of works of art, antiques and collectors' pieces.

The effect of the above is that the goods are charged to VAT on importation at an effective reduced rate of 2.5% (14.29% of 17.5%). The Treasury may change this rate by statutory instrument. In any case, the rate of 2.5% is by way of derogation under *EC Seventh Directive* and a minimum effective rate of 5% must be applied from June 1999.

[*VATA 1994, s 21(4)–(6); FA 1995, s 22*]. (C & E News Release 20/95, 3 April 1995).

71.4   Imported goods sold by auction

Where 'works of art' are imported from outside the EC for exhibition with a view to possible sale, any sale by auction at a time when the goods are still subject to temporary importation arrangements with total exemption from import duty (see 34.30 IMPORTS) is treated as neither a supply of goods nor a supply of services. The provision of any services relating to the transfer of ownership is similarly treated.

'*Works of art*' means

- paintings, drawings and pastels executed by hand but not comprised in manufactured articles that have been hand-painted or hand-decorated; collages and similar decorative plaques;

- original engravings, lithographs and other prints; and

- original sculptures and statuary, in any material.

[*SI 1995/958*]. (C & E News Release 20/95, 5 April 1995).

71.5   Museum and gallery exhibits imported

Certain works of art imported for a purpose other than sale by approved museums, galleries or other institutions are free of VAT. The goods must be of an educational, scientific or cultural character and must be imported either free of charge, or, if for a consideration, must not be supplied to the importer in the course or furtherance of any business. [*SI 1984/746, 2 Sch Group 9; SI 1992/3120*]. The institution must be approved by the Department of Trade and Industry (DTI) and intend to exhibit the goods. The goods may be lent, hired out or transferred to other institutions which are approved under this procedure provided permission is obtained from the DTI and the VAT office informed. (C & E Notice 361 which see for details of how to claim the relief.)

71.6   **SALES FROM HISTORIC HOUSES**

If owners of historic houses admit members of the public for a charge, any objects owned and displayed in those parts of the building to which the public has access are regarded as assets of the business of opening the house. Their disposal is in the course or furtherance of the business and therefore liable to VAT. The following are cases where VAT may not be chargeable on disposal.

(*a*)   If turnover from all business activities is below the registration limit, there is no requirement to be registered even if an occasional disposal of a business asset takes the turnover over the threshold in a particular year. Continuous or regular disposals over a period, perhaps replacing some articles, may however constitute carrying on a business in their own right.

(*b*)   If owners are registered for VAT but make no charge for admission, the contents are not regarded as business assets and any disposal would be outside the scope of VAT.

(*c*)   The goods are zero-rated (e.g. books) or qualify for exemption (see 71.1 above).

(*d*)   If a gift is made from the contents which form part of the assets of the business, no output tax is due provided no input tax was claimed on the purchase of the asset. If input tax was claimed, output tax is payable on what it would have cost to purchase the goods at the time the gift is made.

(*e*)   If the owner of the business which opens the house to the public and the owner of the contents are two separate persons, a disposal by the latter would not attract VAT unless the owner had used or held them for business purposes, e.g. if he was being paid for the loan of the objects to the business of opening the house.

(*f*)   If articles are 'permanently removed' from display (e.g. for free loan, without business motive, to a public gallery or for purely personal use) VAT is chargeable on putting the articles to a non-business use if input tax was claimed on their purchase. The value for VAT is the full cost (if any) of putting the article to non-business use. Over a period of time, this is the amount of depreciation of the goods (plus any other costs related to the goods) multiplied by the proportion which the non-business use forms to the total use. C & E regard a removal from display for a year or more as a 'permanent removal'. No VAT is due on a subsequent disposal while still in non-business use.

(*g*)   If an article has been on view to the public for a very limited period or on view purely incidentally to the main business activity, it may be possible that it is not a business asset.

Where VAT incurred on the purchase, maintenance, repair or restoration of the article has been deducted as input tax, there is a strong indication that the article is a business asset.

If the proceeds from the sale of an antique etc. are used to increase the capital of a VAT-registered business or for a similar purpose (e.g. to pay off a business overdraft or purchase items for the business) the sale could be in furtherance of that business and liable to VAT. Subject to (*e*), (*f*) and *(g)* above, the disposal is taxable if the item sold has been held or used in connection with the business activities. The sale of a purely personal asset which is unconnected with the business does not attract VAT.

(C & E Notice 701/12/96, paras 1.1–1.4).

See also *RWK Stirling, [1985] VATTR 232 (1963)*.

72 Zero-Rated Supplies

De Voil Indirect Tax Service. See V4.201; V4.202.

72.1   There are currently two main rates of VAT, standard rate and zero rate. Where a taxable person supplies goods or services and the supply is zero-rated, then, *whether or not VAT would otherwise be chargeable on the supply*, no VAT is charged but the supply in all other respects is treated as a taxable supply (except that an invoice for a zero-rated supply does not constitute a VAT invoice). [*VATA 1994, s 30(1)*]. The effects of this are as follows.

- The amount of VAT on zero-rated supplies is nil but they are still taxable supplies.

- As taxable supplies, they must be taken into consideration in determining whether registration is required.

- Input tax may be reclaimed in the same way as for standard-rated supplies.

- Where a supply could be either zero-rated or exempt, zero-rating takes priority.

Zero-rating applies to a supply of goods or services and, except as otherwise provided, the acquisition of goods from another EC country or the importation of goods from a place outside the EC, falling within one of the following categories specified in *VATA 1994, 8 Sch.*

Group 1	FOOD (28).
Group 2	Sewerage services and water (see 32.20 and 32.21 HEALTH AND WATER UTILITIES).
Group 3	Books, etc. (see 54.17–54.28 PRINTED MATTER, ETC.).
Group 4	Talking books for the blind and handicapped and wireless sets for the blind (see 12.7 CHARITIES).
Group 5	Construction of buildings etc. (see 42.31–42.33, 42.37–42.39 and 42.48 LAND AND BUILDINGS).
Group 6	Protected buildings (see 42.34 and 42.49 LAND AND BUILDINGS).
Group 7	International services (see 39.7 and 39.8 INTERNATIONAL SERVICES).
Group 8	Transport (see 68 TRANSPORT AND FREIGHT).
Group 9	Caravans and houseboats (see 42.54–42.56 LAND AND BUILDINGS).
Group 10	GOLD (30).
Group 11	Bank notes (see 72.4 below).
Group 12	Dispensing of drugs, reliefs for people with disabilities etc. (see 32.14, 32.16 to 32.19 HEALTH AND WATER UTILITIES).
Group 13	Imports, exports, etc. (see 34 IMPORTS and 25.2 EXPORTS).
Group 14	Tax-free shops (see 23.20 EUROPEAN COMMUNITY: SINGLE MARKET).
Group 15	Charities, etc. (see 12.6 and 12.7 CHARITIES).
Group 16	CLOTHING AND FOOTWEAR (13).

The Treasury may vary the above Groups by adding to or deleting from them any description or by varying any description for the time being specified.

The items within the Groups are to be interpreted in accordance with the notes contained and the powers given to the Treasury to vary the Groups including powers to add to, delete or vary the notes. The descriptions of Groups (i.e. the heading shown above) are for ease of reference only and do not affect the interpretation of the description of items in the Group.

[*VATA 1994, ss 30(2)–(4),96(9)(10)*].

72.2   **EXPORTS, ETC. OF GOODS**

A supply of goods is zero-rated if C & E are satisfied that the person supplying the goods has exported them or shipped them for use as stores on a voyage or flight to an eventual destination outside the UK, or as merchandise for sale by retail to persons carried on such a voyage or flight in a ship or aircraft. [*VATA 1994, s 30(6)*]. See 25 EXPORTS for further details. Zero-rating also applies where goods are removed from the UK and acquired in another EC country by a person taxable in that country and liable for VAT on the acquisition under the law of that country. See 23.11 EUROPEAN COMMUNITY: SINGLE MARKET.

72.3   **WORK ON ANOTHER PERSON'S GOODS WHICH PRODUCES GOODS**

A supply of services which consists of applying a treatment or process to another person's goods is zero-rated if by doing so goods are produced and either

●   those goods fall within one of the zero-rating *Groups* in 72.1 above; or

●   a supply of those goods by the person applying the treatment to that other person would be zero-rated.

[*VATA 1994, s 30(2A); FA 1996, s 29(2)(5)*].

72.4   **BANK NOTES**

The issue by a bank of a note payable to bearer on demand is zero-rated. [*VATA 1994, 8 Sch Group 11*]. This applies to the Bank of England, Scottish and Northern Irish bank notes. *Issue* includes reissue.

De Voil Indirect Tax Service. See V4.279.

73 Table of Cases

Where the C & E Commissioners or the CIR are parties, the case is indexed only under the name of the taxpayer. All other cases are listed under the names of both parties.

Table of Cases

Table of Cases

Table of Cases

Table of Cases

74 Table of Statutes

References are only included where the provisions are covered in the text. Casual references to *Acts* are not included.

Table of Statutes

Table of Statutes

Table of Statutes

75   Table of Statutory Instruments

References are only included where the provisions are covered in the text. Casual references to *Statutory Instruments* are not included.

Table of Statutory Instruments

Table of Statutory Instruments

76   Table of European Community Legislation

77   Index

This index is referenced to the chapter and paragraph number.
The entries in bold capitals are main subject headings in the text.

Index

Index

Index

Index

D

E

Index

Index

Index

Index

Index

Index

Index

Index

Index

Index

Index

Index